NEGIMA! OMNIBUS 6

Ken Akamatsu

TRANSLATED BY
Toshifumi Yoshida

ADAPTED BY
Ikoi Hiroe

LETTERING AND RETOUCH BY
Steve Palmer

KC
KODANSHA
COMICS

Negima! Omnibus volume 6 is a work of fiction. Names, characters, places, and incidents are the products of the author's imagination or are used fictitiously. Any resemblance to actual events, locales, or persons, living or dead, is entirely coincidental.

A Kodansha Comics Trade Paperback Original.

Published in the United States by Kodansha Comics, an imprint of Kodansha USA Publishing, LLC, New York.

Publication rights for this English edition arranged through Kodansha Ltd., Tokyo.

First published in Japan in 2006-2007 by Kodansha Ltd., Tokyo, as *Maho sensei Negima!* volumes 16, 17 and 18.

ISBN 978-1-61262-069-5

Printed in the United States of America.

www.kodanshacomics.com

9 8 7 6 5 4 3 2

Translator: Toshifumi Yoshida
Adaptor: Ikoi Hiroe
Lettering: Steve Palmer

CONTENTS

魔法先生ネギま!

MAGISTER NEGI MAGI

16

Ken Akamatsu

赤松 健

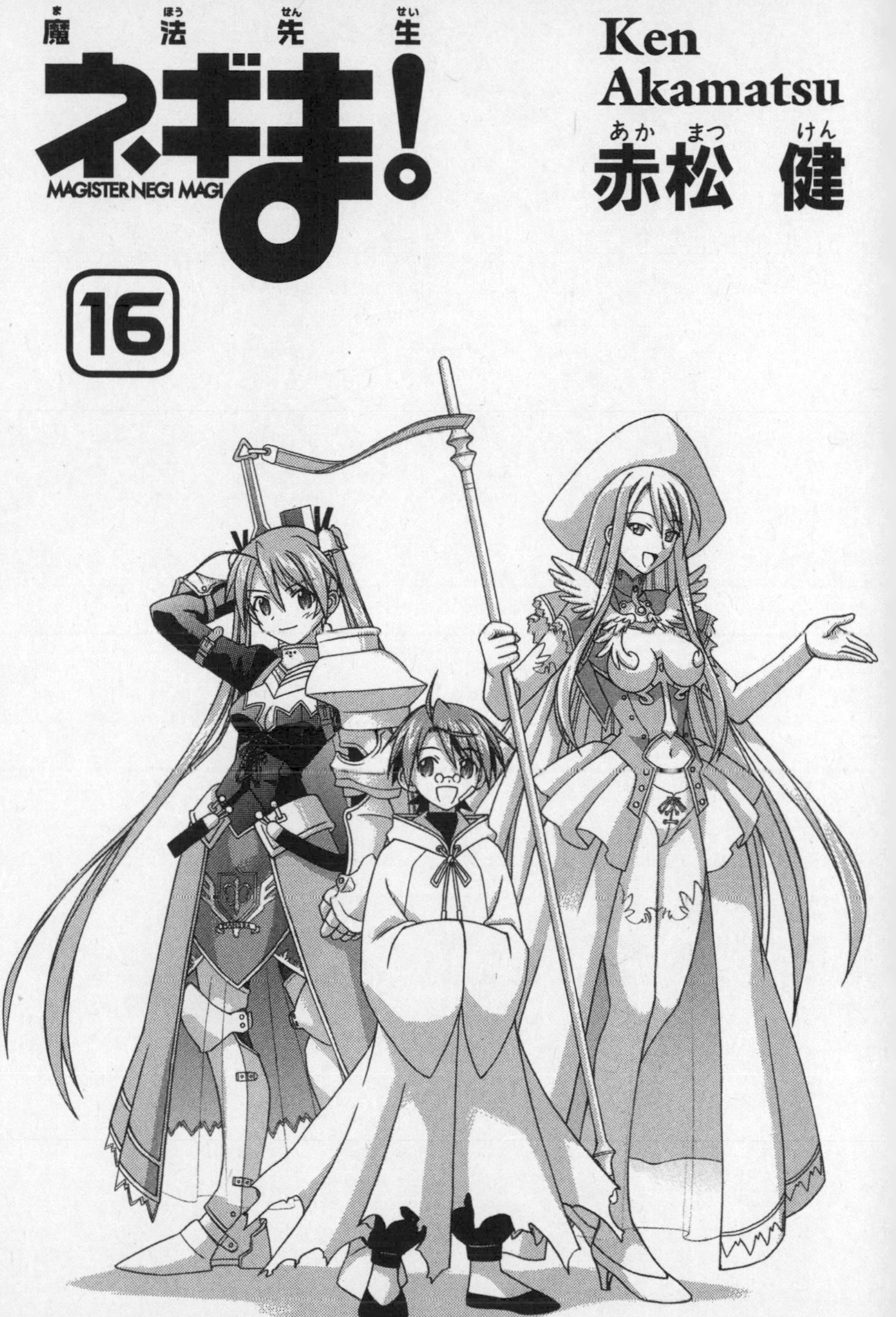

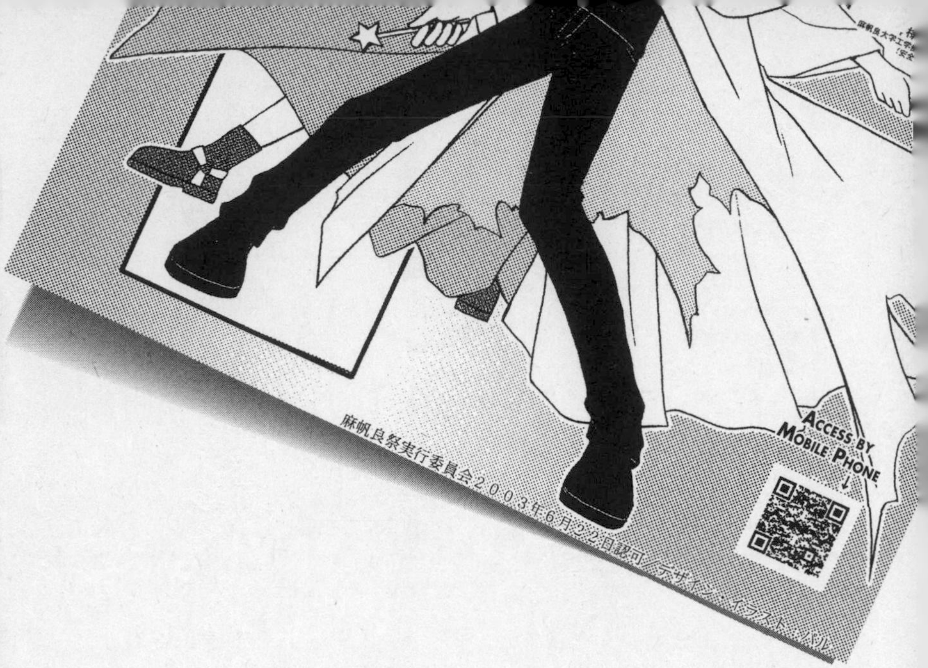
Access by Mobile Phone
麻帆良祭実行委員会2003年6月22日認可／デザイン・イラスト：パル

CONTENTS

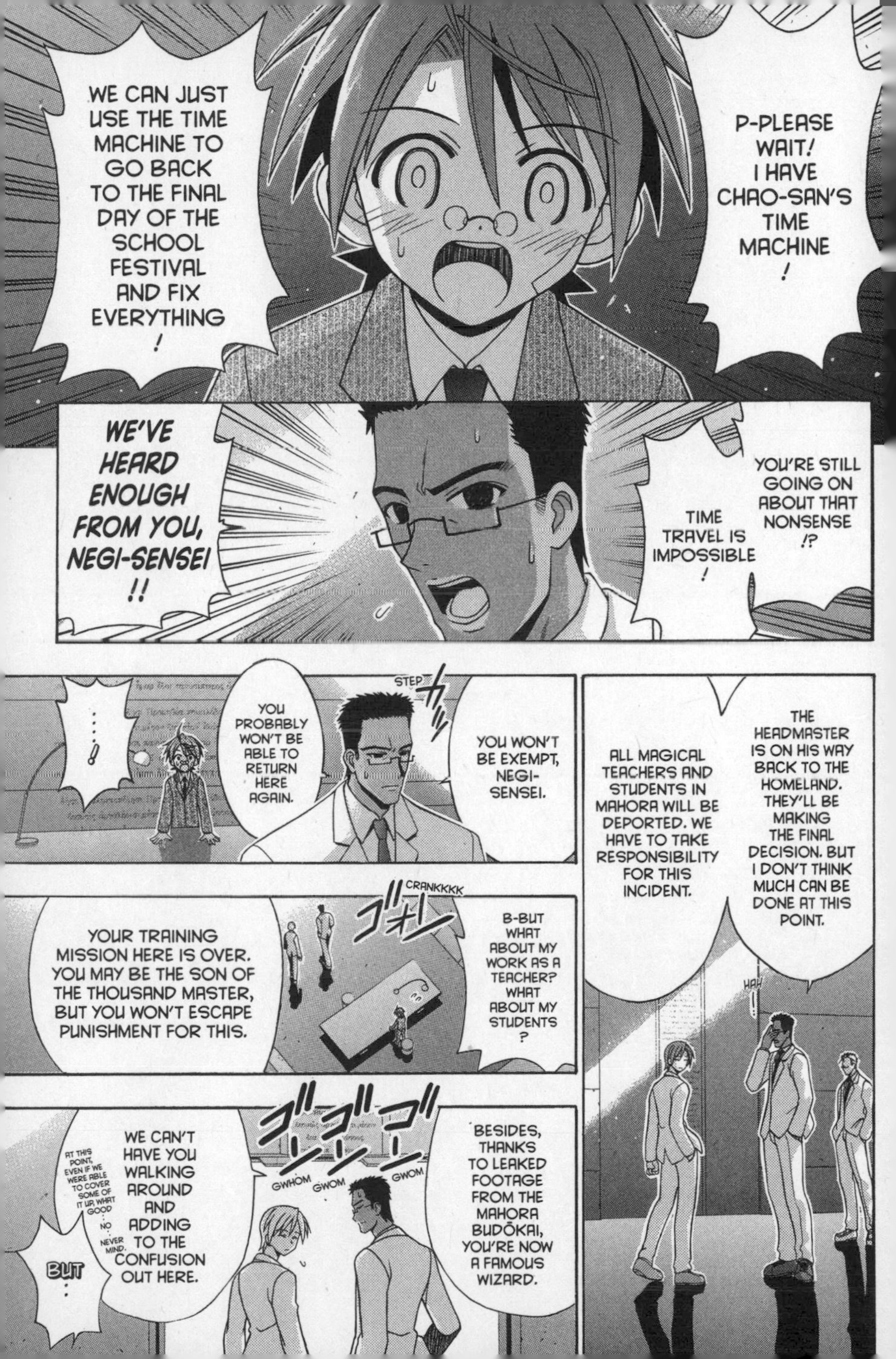
P-PLEASE WAIT! I HAVE CHAO-SAN'S TIME MACHINE!
WE CAN JUST USE THE TIME MACHINE TO GO BACK TO THE FINAL DAY OF THE SCHOOL FESTIVAL AND FIX EVERYTHING!
YOU'RE STILL GOING ON ABOUT THAT NONSENSE!?
TIME TRAVEL IS IMPOSSIBLE!
WE'VE HEARD ENOUGH FROM YOU, NEGI-SENSEI!!
THE HEADMASTER IS ON HIS WAY BACK TO THE HOMELAND. THEY'LL BE MAKING THE FINAL DECISION. BUT I DON'T THINK MUCH CAN BE DONE AT THIS POINT.
ALL MAGICAL TEACHERS AND STUDENTS IN MAHORA WILL BE DEPORTED. WE HAVE TO TAKE RESPONSIBILITY FOR THIS INCIDENT.
HAH!
STEP
YOU WON'T BE EXEMPT, NEGI-SENSEI.
YOU PROBABLY WON'T BE ABLE TO RETURN HERE AGAIN.
...!
B-BUT WHAT ABOUT MY WORK AS A TEACHER? WHAT ABOUT MY STUDENTS?
CRANKKKK
YOUR TRAINING MISSION HERE IS OVER. YOU MAY BE THE SON OF THE THOUSAND MASTER, BUT YOU WON'T ESCAPE PUNISHMENT FOR THIS.
BESIDES, THANKS TO LEAKED FOOTAGE FROM THE MAHORA BUDŌKAI, YOU'RE NOW A FAMOUS WIZARD.
GWOM
GWOM
GWHOM
WE CAN'T HAVE YOU WALKING AROUND AND ADDING TO THE CONFUSION OUT HERE.
AT THIS POINT, EVEN IF WE WERE ABLE TO COVER SOME OF IT UP, WHAT GOOD... NO... NEVER MIND.
BUT...

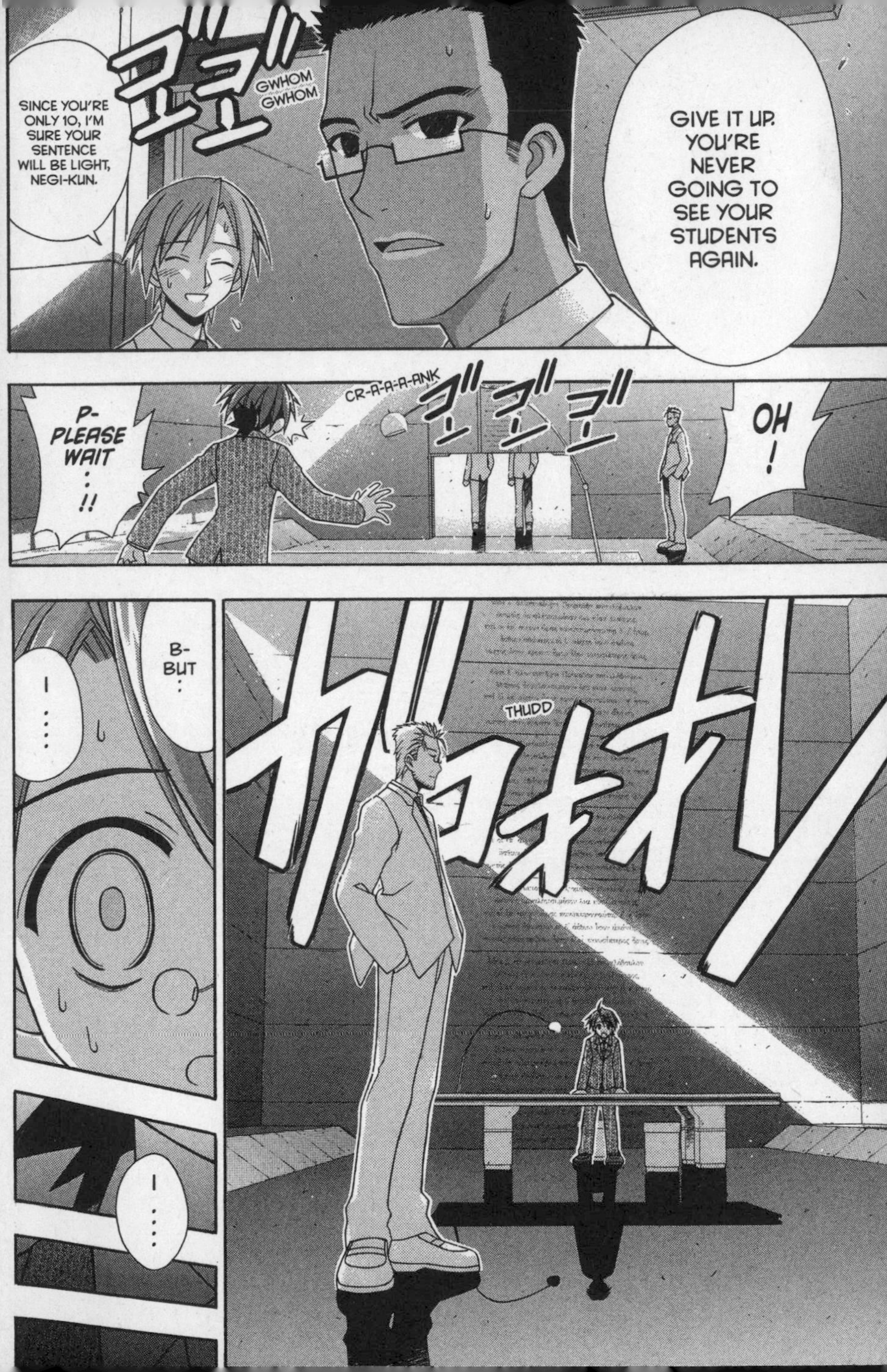
GIVE IT UP. YOU'RE NEVER GOING TO SEE YOUR STUDENTS AGAIN.
GWHOM GWHOM
SINCE YOU'RE ONLY 10, I'M SURE YOUR SENTENCE WILL BE LIGHT, NEGI-KUN.
OH!
CR-A-A-A-ANK
P-PLEASE WAIT...!!
THUDD
B-BUT...
I....
I....

BAD ENDING

SCHOOL FESTIVAL – CHAO EPISODE

ERMINE ENDING NO. 16

NEGI SPENDS THE NEXT SIX MONTHS AS AN ERMINE.
HE'LL NEVER RETURN TO MAHORA ACADEMY AGAIN.

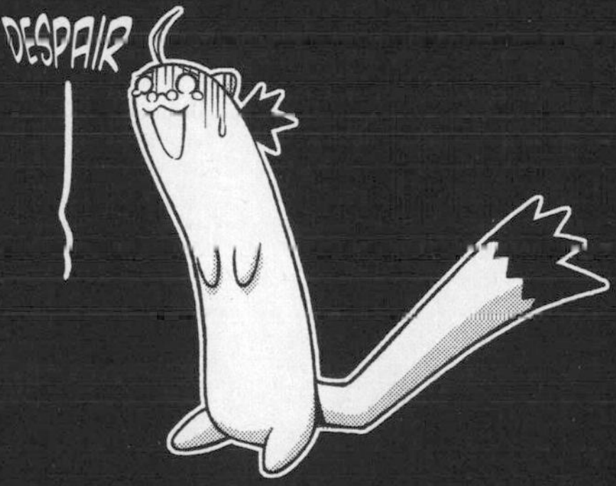
DESPAIR

TRY AGAIN ◀

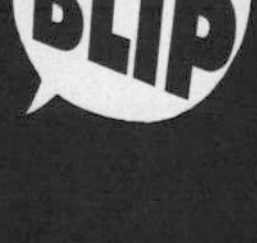
BLIP

STRATEGY TIPS: THINK ABOUT WHERE YOU MADE A MISTAKE. WAS IT A GOOD IDEA TO SPEND AN ADDITIONAL NIGHT IN EVA'S RESORT TO PLAN YOUR ATTACK? WAS IT A GOOD IDEA TO PARTICIPATE IN THE MAHORA BUDŌKAI WITHOUT TAKING PRECAUTIONS? PERHAPS ACCEPTING THE TIME MACHINE FROM CHAO IN THE FIRST PLACE WAS A BAD IDEA? RETURN TO YOUR LAST SAVE POINT AND TRY AGAIN. I'M SURE YOU'LL FIND THE ANSWER SOMEWHERE!

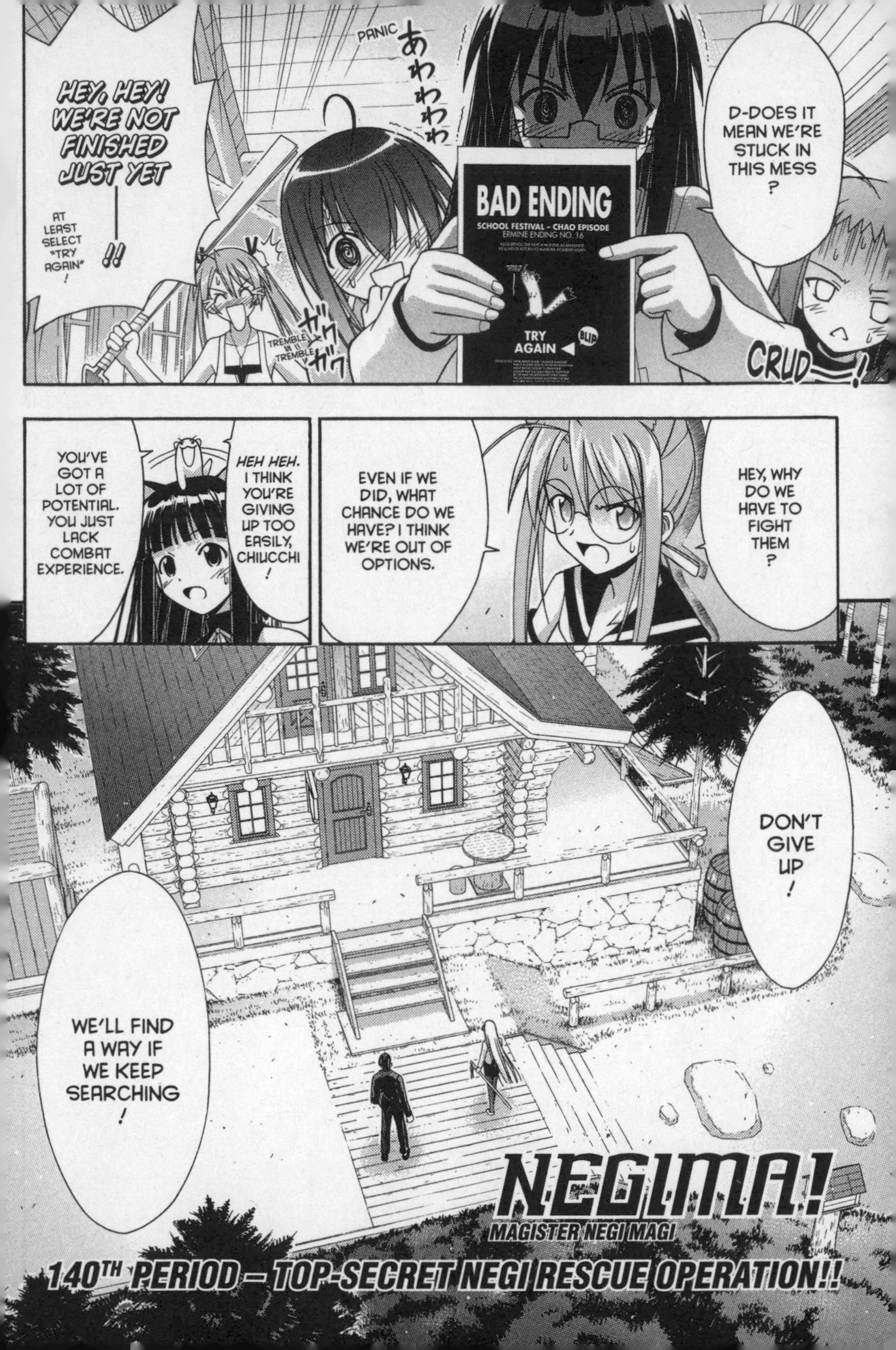

D-DOES IT MEAN WE'RE STUCK IN THIS MESS?
PANIC
あわわわわ
BAD ENDING
SCHOOL FESTIVAL – CHAO EPISODE
ERMINE ENDING NO. 16
TRY AGAIN
BLIP
CRUD—!
TREMBLE TREMBLE
HEY, HEY! WE'RE NOT FINISHED JUST YET—!!
AT LEAST SELECT "TRY AGAIN"!
HEY, WHY DO WE HAVE TO FIGHT THEM?
EVEN IF WE DID, WHAT CHANCE DO WE HAVE? I THINK WE'RE OUT OF OPTIONS.
HEH HEH. I THINK YOU'RE GIVING UP TOO EASILY, CHIUCCHI!
YOU'VE GOT A LOT OF POTENTIAL. YOU JUST LACK COMBAT EXPERIENCE.
DON'T GIVE UP!
WE'LL FIND A WAY IF WE KEEP SEARCHING!
NEGIMA!
MAGISTER NEGI MAGI
140TH PERIOD – TOP-SECRET NEGI RESCUE OPERATION!!

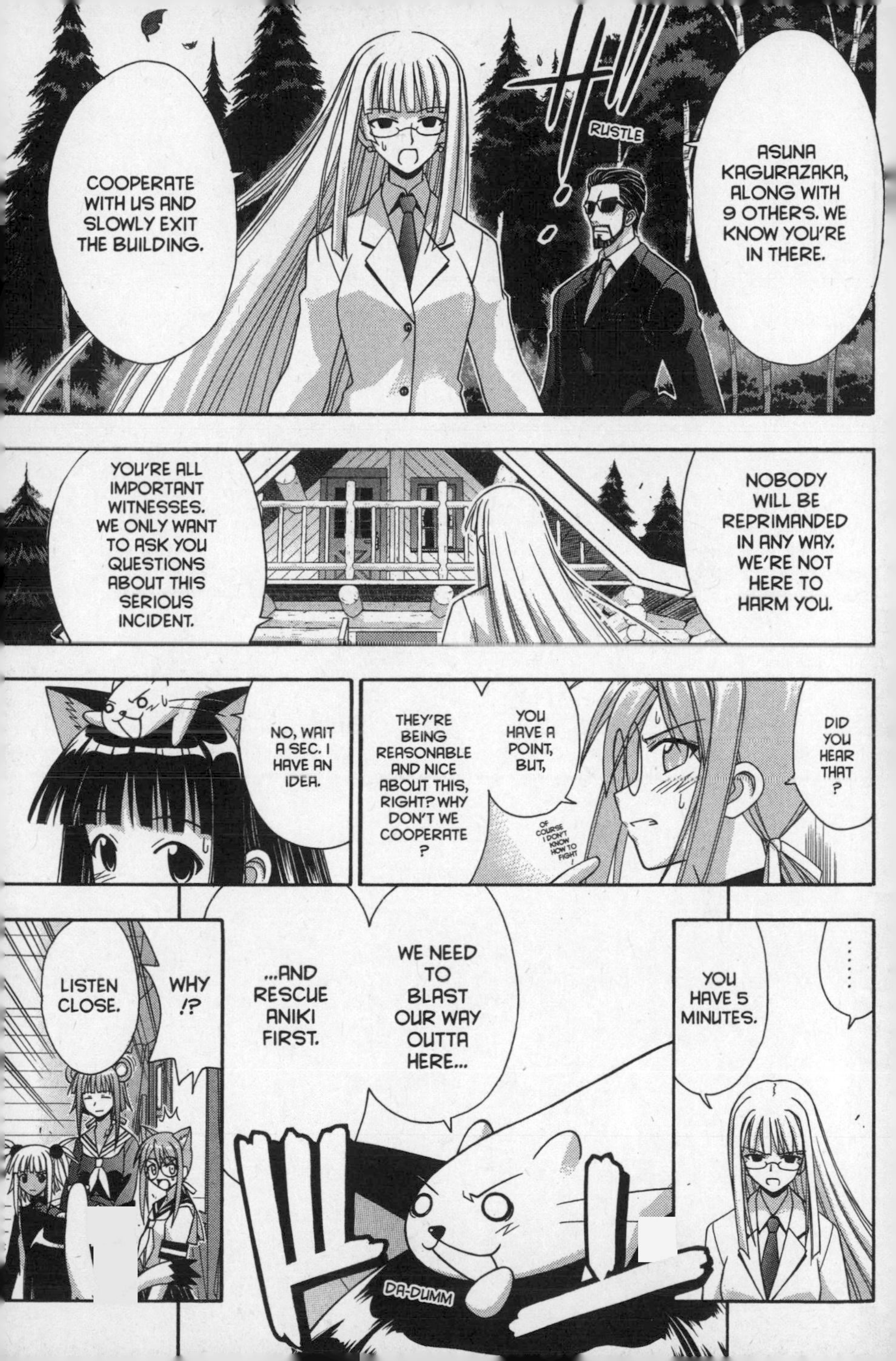
ASUNA KAGURAZAKA, ALONG WITH 9 OTHERS. WE KNOW YOU'RE IN THERE.
RUSTLE
COOPERATE WITH US AND SLOWLY EXIT THE BUILDING.
NOBODY WILL BE REPRIMANDED IN ANY WAY. WE'RE NOT HERE TO HARM YOU.
YOU'RE ALL IMPORTANT WITNESSES. WE ONLY WANT TO ASK YOU QUESTIONS ABOUT THIS SERIOUS INCIDENT.
DID YOU HEAR THAT?
YOU HAVE A POINT, BUT,
OF COURSE I DON'T KNOW HOW TO FIGHT!
THEY'RE BEING REASONABLE AND NICE ABOUT THIS, RIGHT? WHY DON'T WE COOPERATE?
NO, WAIT A SEC. I HAVE AN IDEA.
......
YOU HAVE 5 MINUTES.
WE NEED TO BLAST OUR WAY OUTTA HERE...
...AND RESCUE ANIKI FIRST.
DA-DUMM
WHY!?
LISTEN CLOSE.

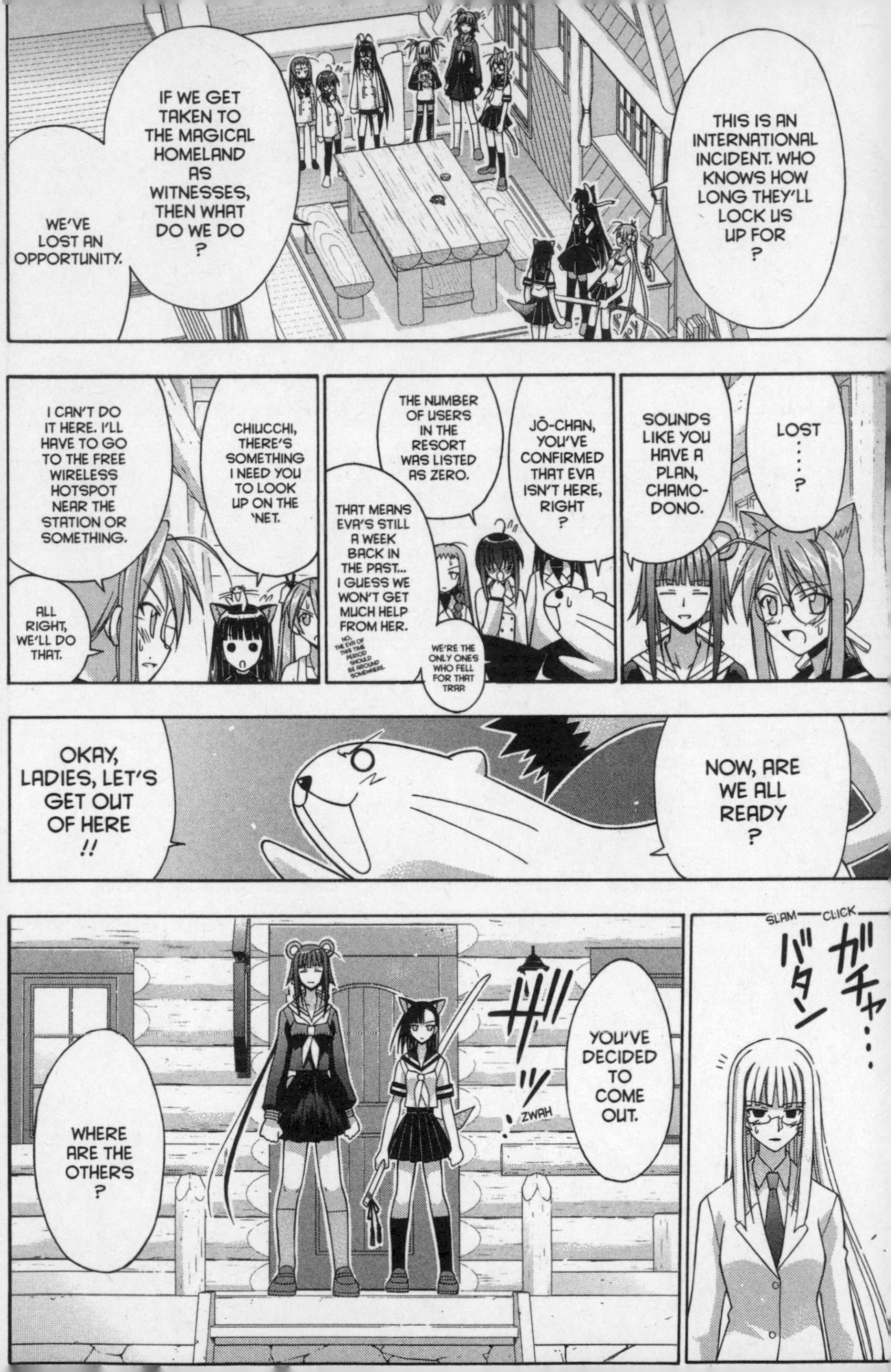
THIS IS AN INTERNATIONAL INCIDENT. WHO KNOWS HOW LONG THEY'LL LOCK US UP FOR ?
IF WE GET TAKEN TO THE MAGICAL HOMELAND AS WITNESSES, THEN WHAT DO WE DO ?
WE'VE LOST AN OPPORTUNITY.
LOST ... ?
SOUNDS LIKE YOU HAVE A PLAN, CHAMO-DONO.
JŌ-CHAN, YOU'VE CONFIRMED THAT EVA ISN'T HERE, RIGHT ?
THE NUMBER OF USERS IN THE RESORT WAS LISTED AS ZERO.
WE'RE THE ONLY ONES WHO FELL FOR THAT TRAP.
THAT MEANS EVA'S STILL A WEEK BACK IN THE PAST... I GUESS WE WON'T GET MUCH HELP FROM HER.
NO, THE EVA OF THIS TIME PERIOD SHOULD BE AROUND SOMEWHERE.
CHIUCCHI, THERE'S SOMETHING I NEED YOU TO LOOK UP ON THE 'NET.
I CAN'T DO IT HERE. I'LL HAVE TO GO TO THE FREE WIRELESS HOTSPOT NEAR THE STATION OR SOMETHING.
ALL RIGHT, WE'LL DO THAT.
NOW, ARE WE ALL READY ?
OKAY, LADIES, LET'S GET OUT OF HERE !!
ガチャ…
バタン
SLAM—CLICK
YOU'VE DECIDED TO COME OUT.
ザッ
ZWAH
WHERE ARE THE OTHERS ?

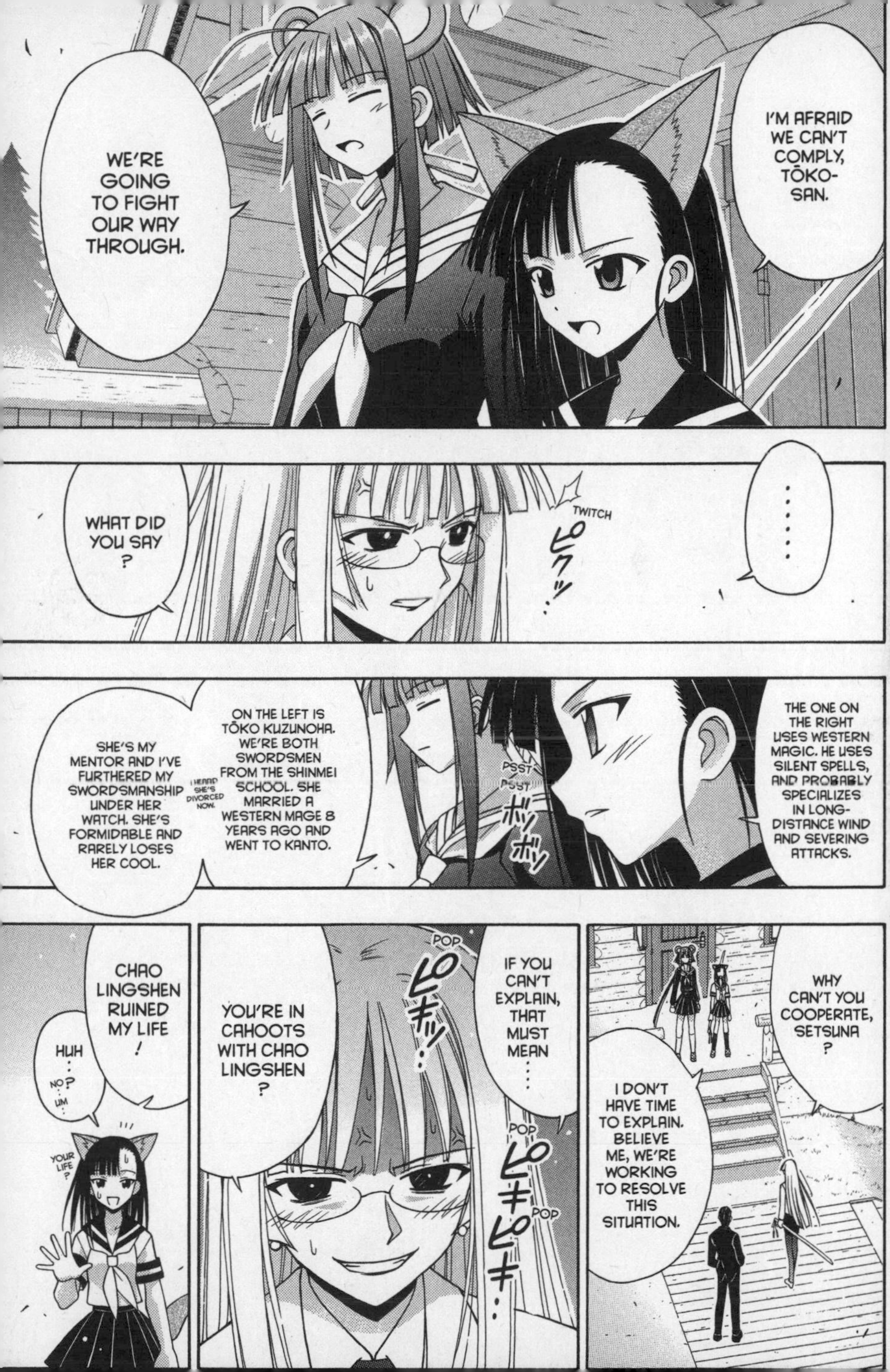
I'M AFRAID WE CAN'T COMPLY, TŌKO-SAN.
WE'RE GOING TO FIGHT OUR WAY THROUGH.
......
TWITCH
WHAT DID YOU SAY?
THE ONE ON THE RIGHT USES WESTERN MAGIC. HE USES SILENT SPELLS, AND PROBABLY SPECIALIZES IN LONG-DISTANCE WIND AND SEVERING ATTACKS.
PSST PSST
ON THE LEFT IS TŌKO KUZUNOHA. WE'RE BOTH SWORDSMEN FROM THE SHINMEI SCHOOL. SHE MARRIED A WESTERN MAGE 8 YEARS AGO AND WENT TO KANTO.
I HEARD SHE'S DIVORCED NOW.
SHE'S MY MENTOR AND I'VE FURTHERED MY SWORDSMANSHIP UNDER HER WATCH. SHE'S FORMIDABLE AND RARELY LOSES HER COOL.
WHY CAN'T YOU COOPERATE, SETSUNA?
I DON'T HAVE TIME TO EXPLAIN. BELIEVE ME, WE'RE WORKING TO RESOLVE THIS SITUATION.
POP
IF YOU CAN'T EXPLAIN, THAT MUST MEAN......
YOU'RE IN CAHOOTS WITH CHAO LINGSHEN?
POP
POP
CHAO LINGSHEN RUINED MY LIFE!
HUH... NO? UM...
YOUR LIFE?

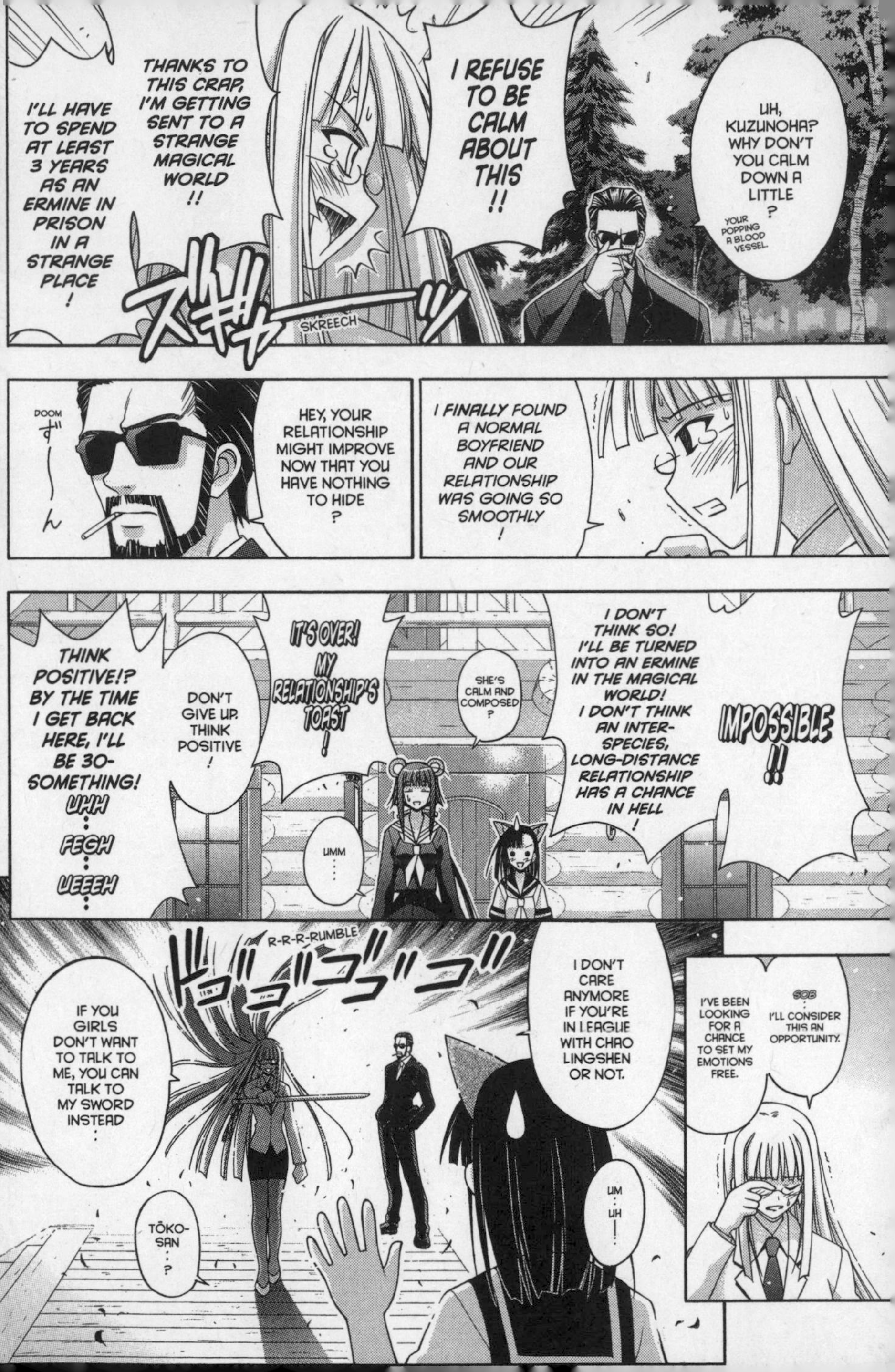
UH, KUZUNOHA? WHY DON'T YOU CALM DOWN A LITTLE?
YOUR POPPING A BLOOD VESSEL.
I REFUSE TO BE CALM ABOUT THIS!!
THANKS TO THIS CRAP, I'M GETTING SENT TO A STRANGE MAGICAL WORLD!!
I'LL HAVE TO SPEND AT LEAST 3 YEARS AS AN ERMINE IN PRISON IN A STRANGE PLACE!
SKREECH
I FINALLY FOUND A NORMAL BOYFRIEND AND OUR RELATIONSHIP WAS GOING SO SMOOTHLY!
HEY, YOUR RELATIONSHIP MIGHT IMPROVE NOW THAT YOU HAVE NOTHING TO HIDE?
DOOM
IMPOSSIBLE!!
I DON'T THINK SO! I'LL BE TURNED INTO AN ERMINE IN THE MAGICAL WORLD! I DON'T THINK AN INTER-SPECIES, LONG-DISTANCE RELATIONSHIP HAS A CHANCE IN HELL!
SHE'S CALM AND COMPOSED?
IT'S OVER! MY RELATIONSHIP'S TOAST!
DON'T GIVE UP. THINK POSITIVE!
THINK POSITIVE!? BY THE TIME I GET BACK HERE, I'LL BE 30-SOMETHING!
UHH... FEGH UEEEH...
UMM...
SOB... I'LL CONSIDER THIS AN OPPORTUNITY.
I'VE BEEN LOOKING FOR A CHANCE TO SET MY EMOTIONS FREE.
I DON'T CARE ANYMORE IF YOU'RE IN LEAGUE WITH CHAO LINGSHEN OR NOT.
R-R-R-RUMBLE
IF YOU GIRLS DON'T WANT TO TALK TO ME, YOU CAN TALK TO MY SWORD INSTEAD.
UM UH!
TŌKO-SAN..?

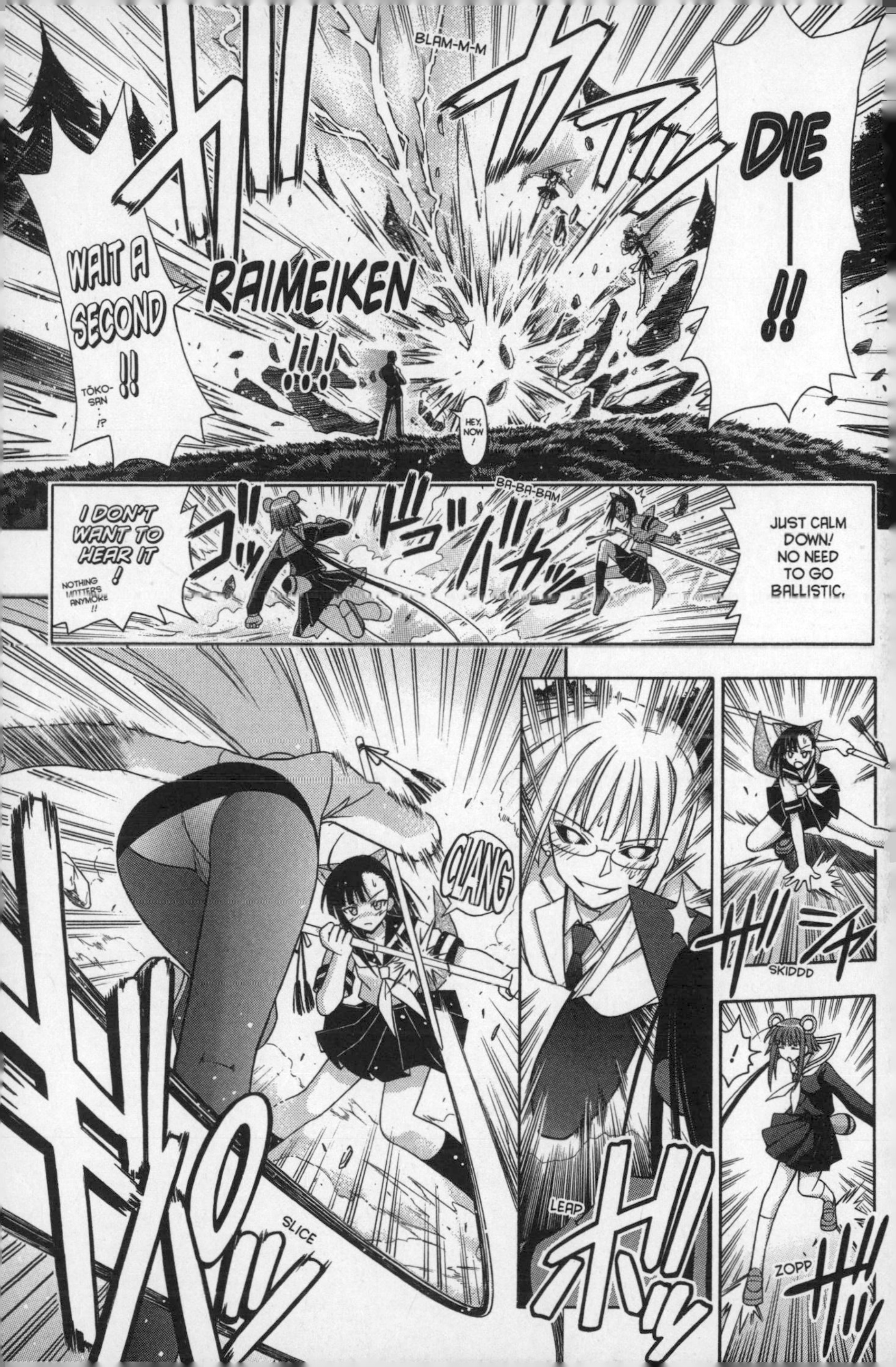
DIE—!!
BLAM-M-M
HEY, NOW!
RAIMEIKEN !!!
WAIT A SECOND !!
TŌKO-SAN...!?
JUST CALM DOWN! NO NEED TO GO BALLISTIC.
BA-BA-BAM
I DON'T WANT TO HEAR IT!
NOTHING MATTERS ANYMORE!!
SKIDDD
!
ZOPP
LEAP
CLANG
SLICE

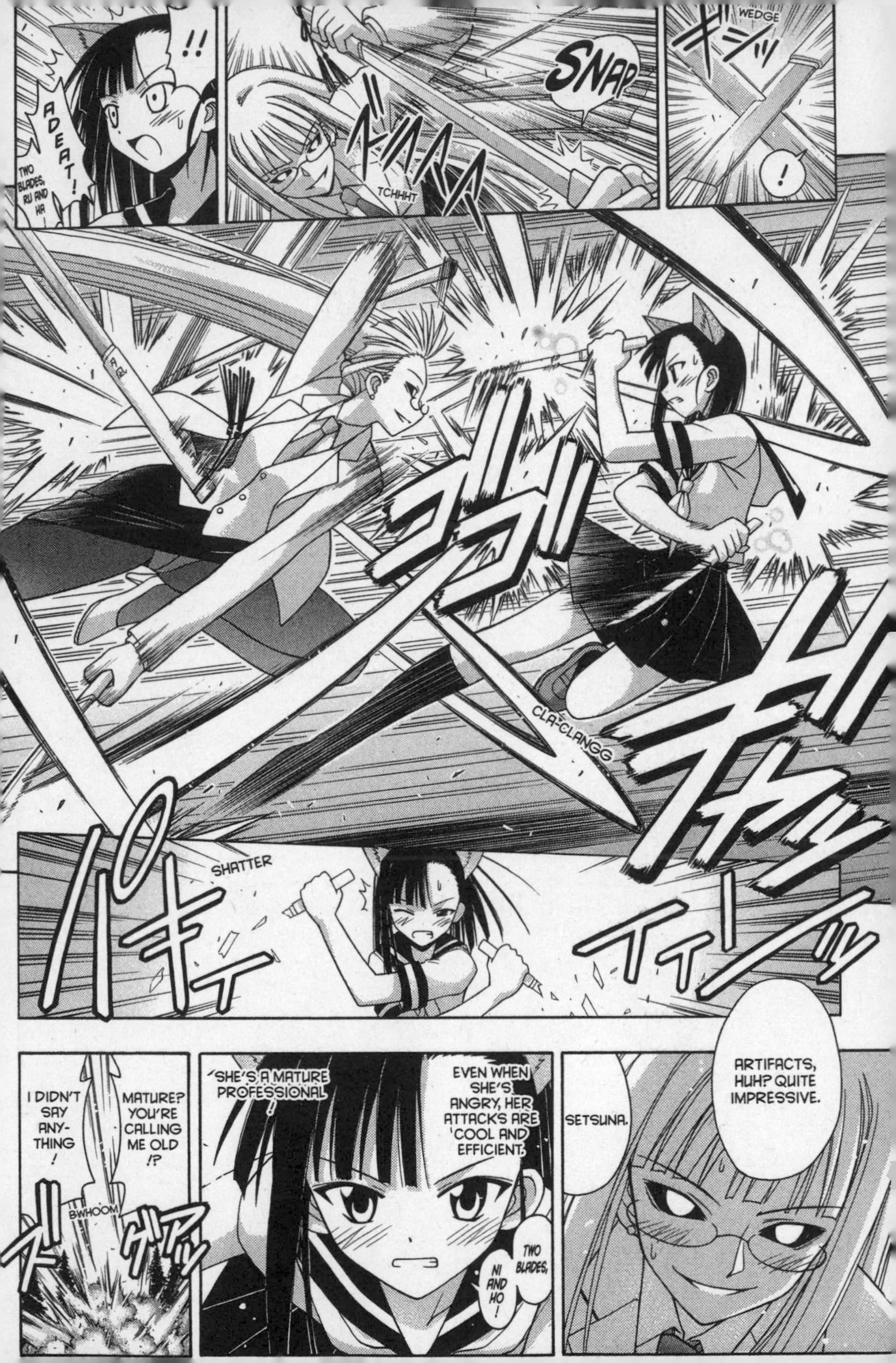
WEDGE
!
SNAP
TCHHHT
!!
ADEAT!
TWO BLADES, RU AND HA
CLA-CLANGG
SHATTER
ARTIFACTS, HUH? QUITE IMPRESSIVE.
SETSUNA.
EVEN WHEN SHE'S ANGRY, HER ATTACKS ARE COOL AND EFFICIENT.
SHE'S A MATURE PROFESSIONAL!
TWO BLADES, NI AND HO!
MATURE? YOU'RE CALLING ME OLD!?
I DIDN'T SAY ANYTHING!
BWHOOM

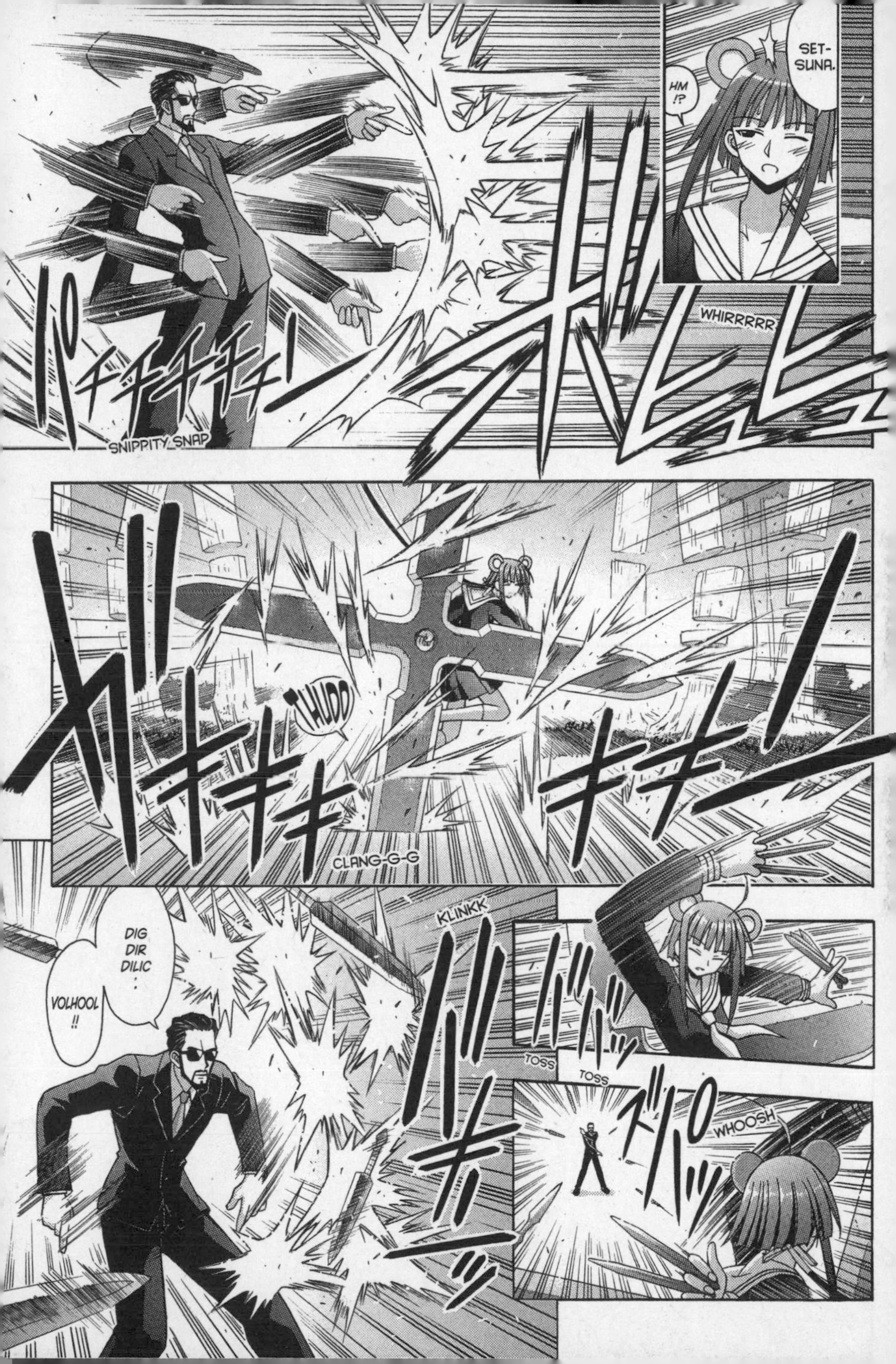
SET-SUNA.
HM !?
WHIRRRRR
SNIPPITY SNAP
THUDD
CLANG-G-G
TOSS
TOSS
WHOOSH
KLINKK
DIG DIR DILIC : VOLHOOL !!

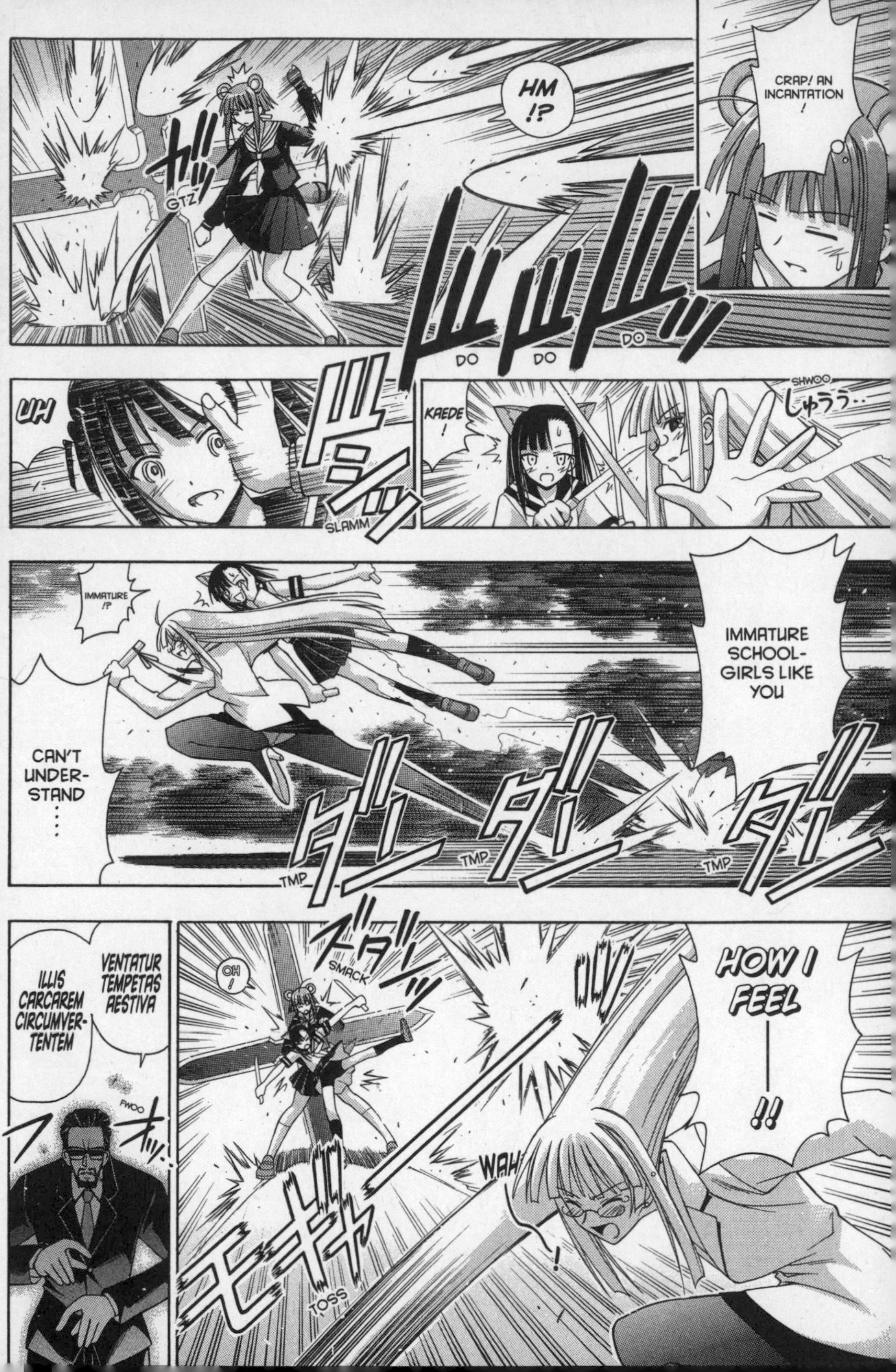

CRAP! AN INCANTATION !
HM !?
GTZ
DO
DO
DO
SHWOO
しゅうう..
KAEDE !
UH
SLAMM
IMMATURE SCHOOL-GIRLS LIKE YOU
TMP
TMP
TMP
IMMATURE !?
CAN'T UNDER-STAND ....
HOW I FEEL —— !!
!
WAH
OH !
SMACK
TOSS
VENTATUR TEMPETAS AESTIVA
ILLIS CARCAREM CIRCUMVER-TENTEM
FWOO

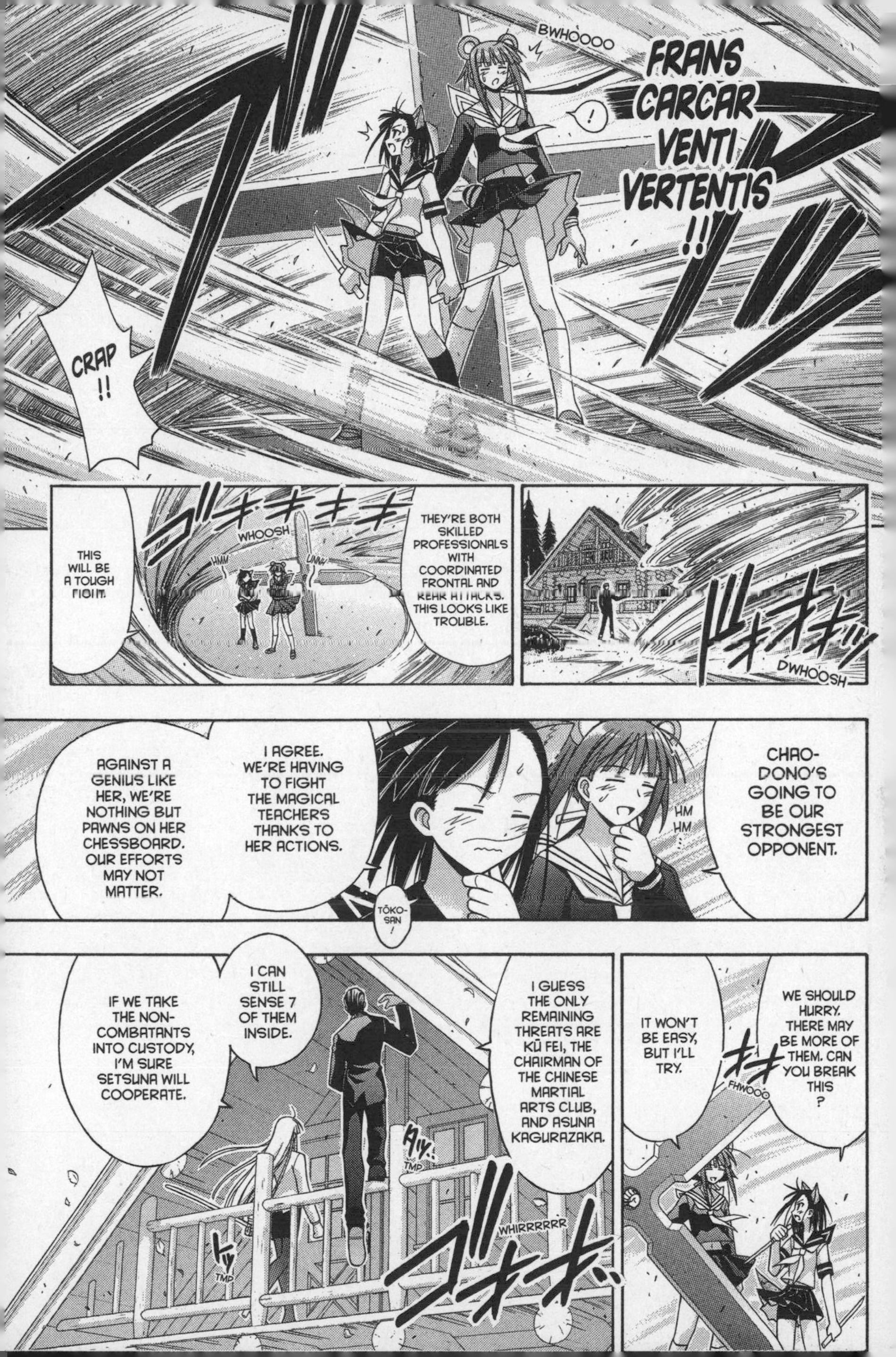
BWHOOOO
FRANS CARCAR VENTI VERTENTIS !!
!
CRAP !!
DWHOOSH
WHOOSH
THEY'RE BOTH SKILLED PROFESSIONALS WITH COORDINATED FRONTAL AND REAR ATTACKS. THIS LOOKS LIKE TROUBLE.
HMM
UNNN
THIS WILL BE A TOUGH FIGHT.
CHAO-DONO'S GOING TO BE OUR STRONGEST OPPONENT.
HM HM
I AGREE. WE'RE HAVING TO FIGHT THE MAGICAL TEACHERS THANKS TO HER ACTIONS.
TŌKO-SAN !
AGAINST A GENIUS LIKE HER, WE'RE NOTHING BUT PAWNS ON HER CHESSBOARD. OUR EFFORTS MAY NOT MATTER.
WE SHOULD HURRY. THERE MAY BE MORE OF THEM. CAN YOU BREAK THIS ?
IT WON'T BE EASY, BUT I'LL TRY.
FHWOOO
I GUESS THE ONLY REMAINING THREATS ARE KŪ FEI, THE CHAIRMAN OF THE CHINESE MARTIAL ARTS CLUB, AND ASUNA KAGURAZAKA.
I CAN STILL SENSE 7 OF THEM INSIDE.
IF WE TAKE THE NON-COMBATANTS INTO CUSTODY, I'M SURE SETSUNA WILL COOPERATE.
TMP
WHIRRRRRR
TMP

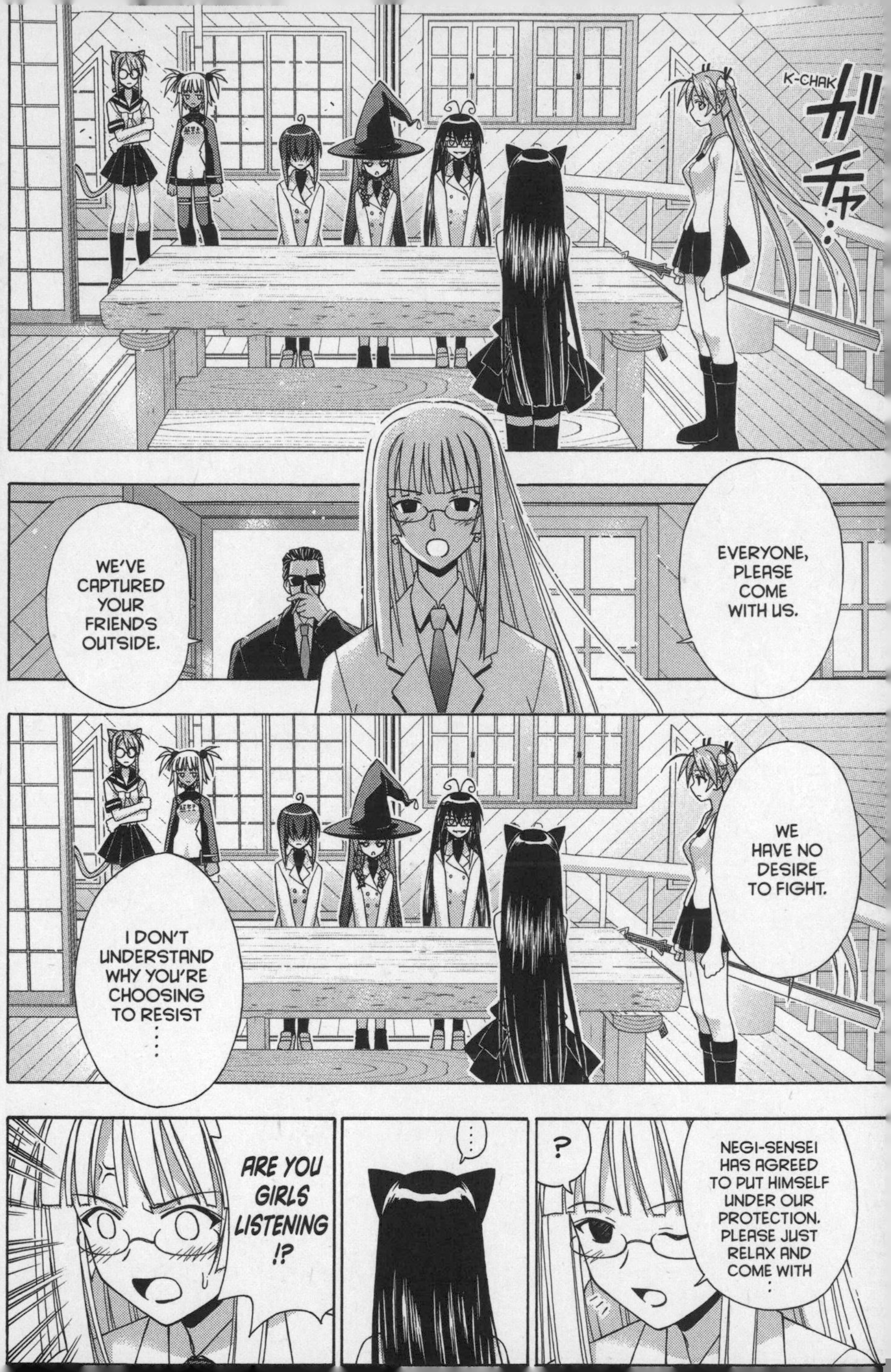
K-CHAK
ガチャ…
EVERYONE, PLEASE COME WITH US.
WE'VE CAPTURED YOUR FRIENDS OUTSIDE.
WE HAVE NO DESIRE TO FIGHT.
I DON'T UNDERSTAND WHY YOU'RE CHOOSING TO RESIST ....
?
NEGI-SENSEI HAS AGREED TO PUT HIMSELF UNDER OUR PROTECTION. PLEASE JUST RELAX AND COME WITH :
....
ARE YOU GIRLS LISTENING !?

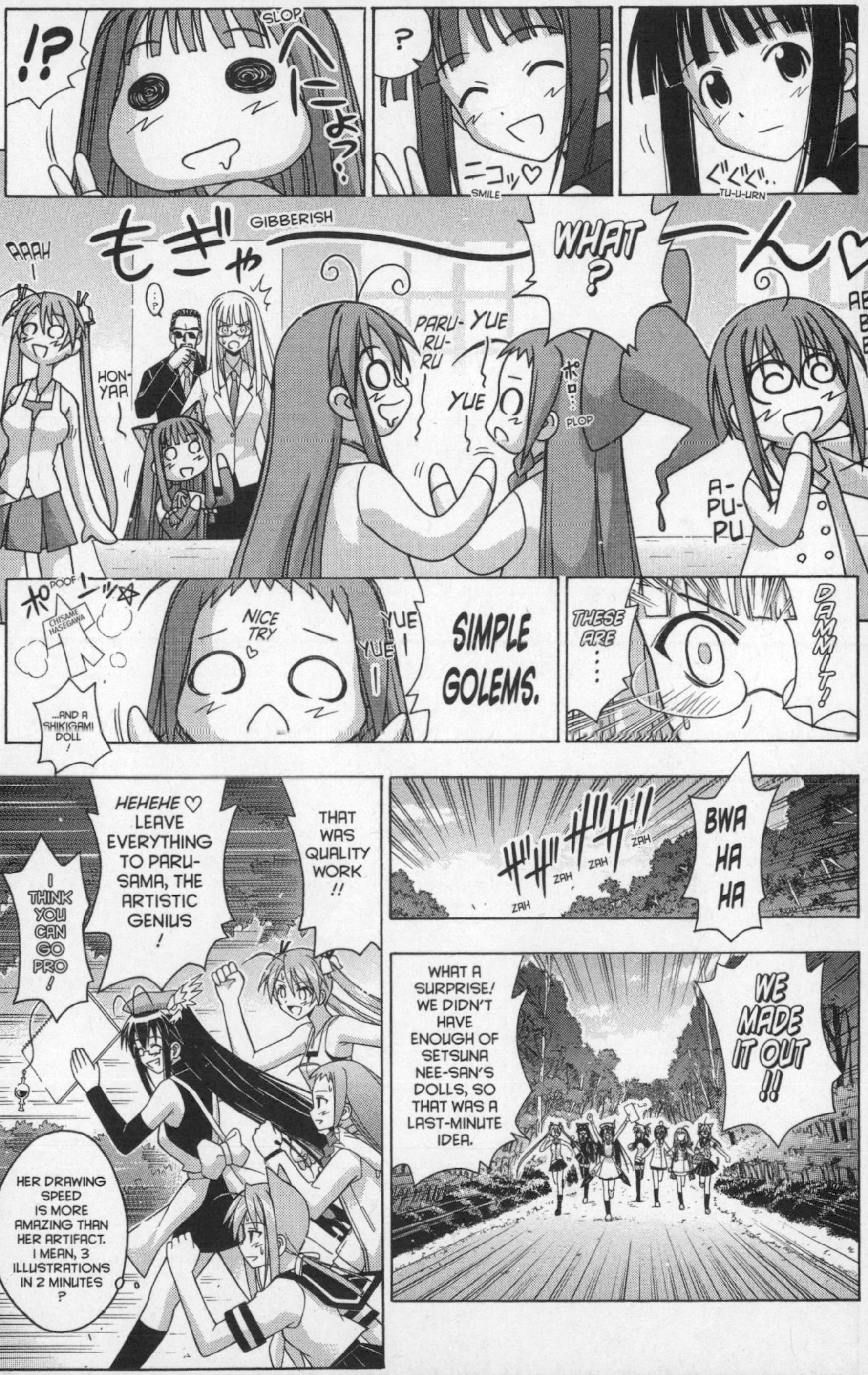

ぐぐぐ..
TU-U-URN
?
ニコッ♡
SMILE
!?
SLOP
へにょっ..
もぎゃーーーん♡
GIBBERISH
WHAT ?
A-PU-PU
YUE
YUE
PARU-RU-RU
ポロ…
PLOP
...?
HON-YAA
AAAH
BOOOING
DAMMIT!
THESE ARE ....
SIMPLE GOLEMS.
YUE YUE
NICE TRY ♡
ポーッ☆
POOF
CHISAME HASEGAWA
...AND A SHIKIGAMI DOLL!
BWA HA HA
ザザザザ
ZAH
ZAH
ZAH
ZAH
WE MADE IT OUT !!
WHAT A SURPRISE! WE DIDN'T HAVE ENOUGH OF SETSUNA NEE-SAN'S DOLLS, SO THAT WAS A LAST-MINUTE IDEA.
THAT WAS QUALITY WORK !!
HEHEHE ♡ LEAVE EVERYTHING TO PARU-SAMA, THE ARTISTIC GENIUS!
I THINK YOU CAN GO PRO!
HER DRAWING SPEED IS MORE AMAZING THAN HER ARTIFACT. I MEAN, 3 ILLUSTRATIONS IN 2 MINUTES?

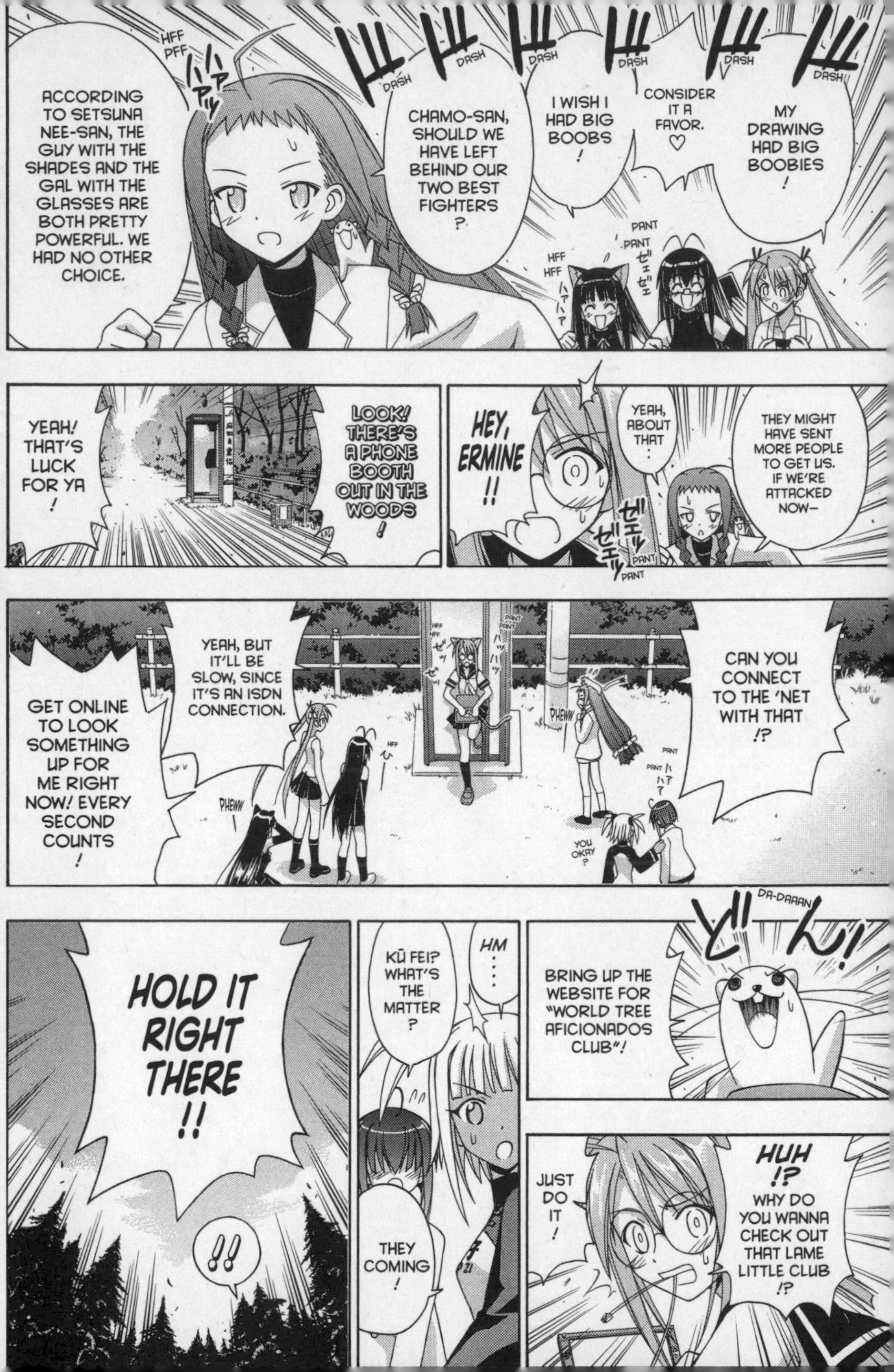
DASH DASH DASH DASH DASH DASH
MY DRAWING HAD BIG BOOBIES!
CONSIDER IT A FAVOR. ♡
I WISH I HAD BIG BOOBS!
PANT PANT
HFF HFF
CHAMO-SAN, SHOULD WE HAVE LEFT BEHIND OUR TWO BEST FIGHTERS?
HFF PFF
ACCORDING TO SETSUNA NEE-SAN, THE GUY WITH THE SHADES AND THE GAL WITH THE GLASSES ARE BOTH PRETTY POWERFUL. WE HAD NO OTHER CHOICE.
THEY MIGHT HAVE SENT MORE PEOPLE TO GET US. IF WE'RE ATTACKED NOW—
YEAH, ABOUT THAT...
HEY, ERMINE!!
PANT PANT
LOOK! THERE'S A PHONE BOOTH OUT IN THE WOODS!
YEAH! THAT'S LUCK FOR YA!
CAN YOU CONNECT TO THE 'NET WITH THAT!?
PANT PANT
YOU OKAY?
PHEW
PANT PANT
HFF HFF
YEAH, BUT IT'LL BE SLOW, SINCE IT'S AN ISDN CONNECTION.
HFF
GET ONLINE TO LOOK SOMETHING UP FOR ME RIGHT NOW! EVERY SECOND COUNTS!
PHEW
DA-DAAAN
BRING UP THE WEBSITE FOR "WORLD TREE AFICIONADOS CLUB"!
HUH!? WHY DO YOU WANNA CHECK OUT THAT LAME LITTLE CLUB!?
JUST DO IT!
HM...
KŪ FEI? WHAT'S THE MATTER?
THEY COMING!
HOLD IT RIGHT THERE!!
!!

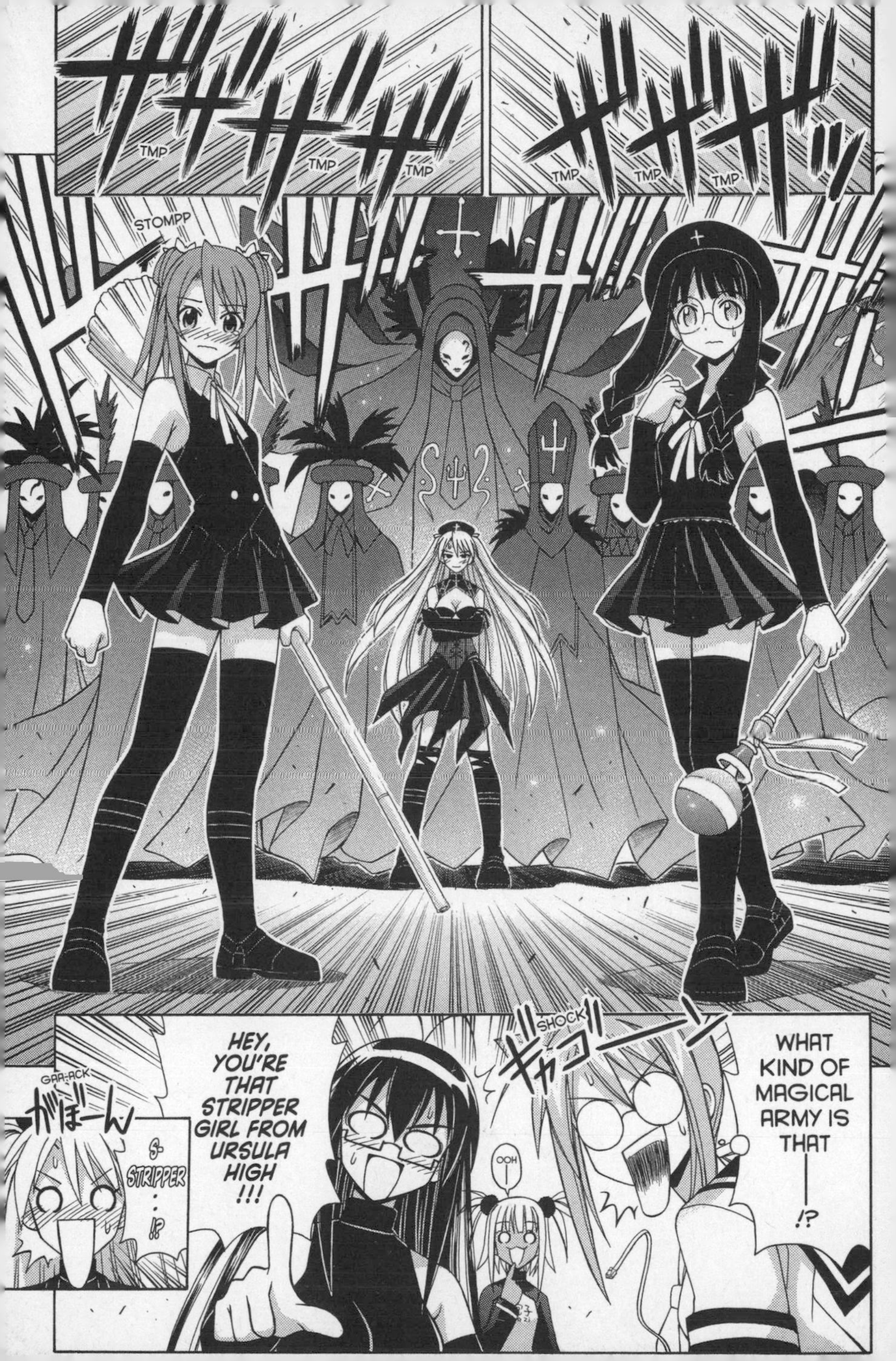

TMP
TMP
TMP
TMP
TMP
TMP
STOMPP
SHOCK
WHAT KIND OF MAGICAL ARMY IS THAT —— !?
OOH
HEY, YOU'RE THAT STRIPPER GIRL FROM URSULA HIGH !!!
GAA-ACK
S-STRIPPER . . . !?

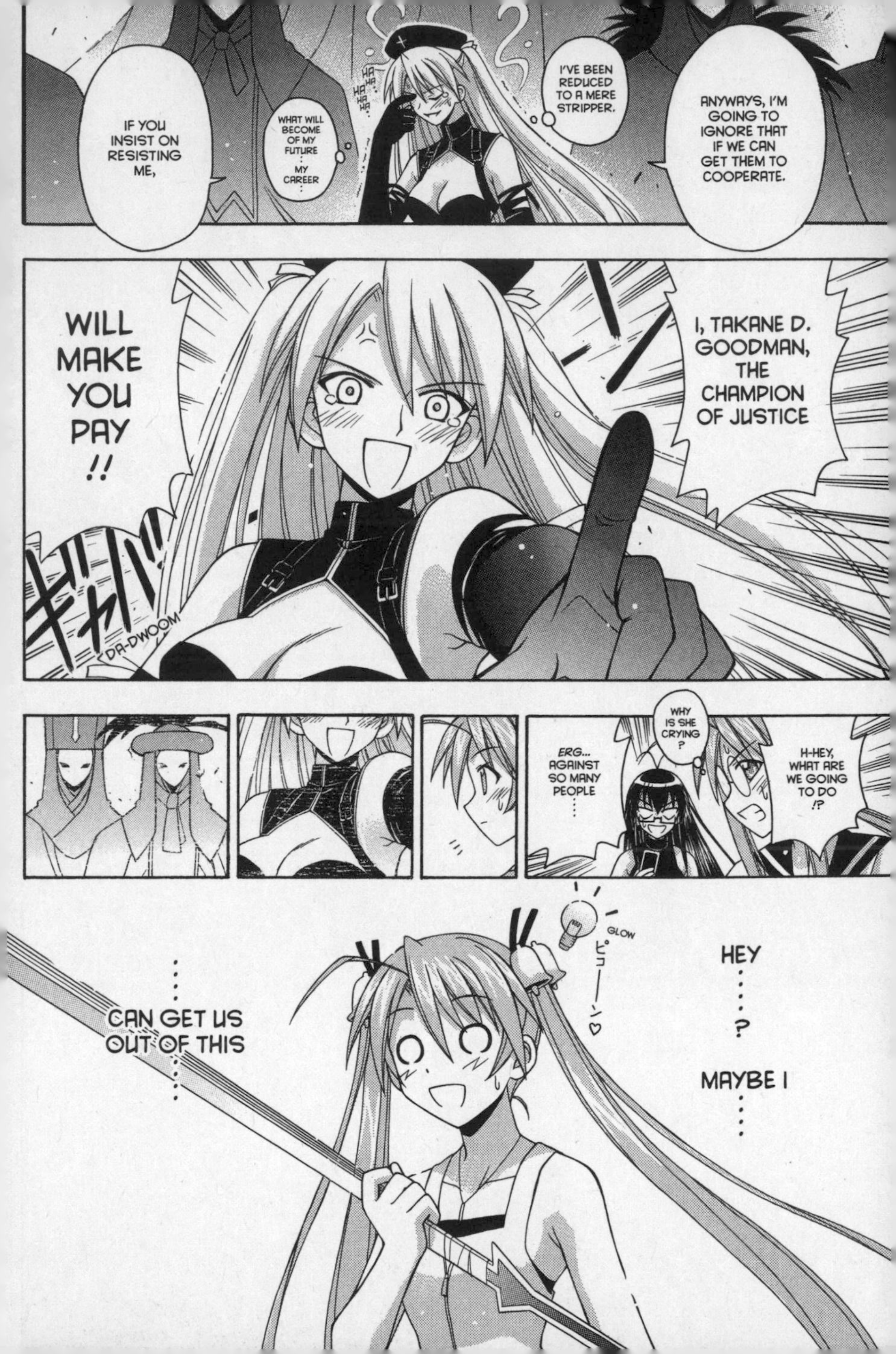
ANYWAYS, I'M GOING TO IGNORE THAT IF WE CAN GET THEM TO COOPERATE.
I'VE BEEN REDUCED TO A MERE STRIPPER.
HA HA HA HA HA
WHAT WILL BECOME OF MY FUTURE ... MY CAREER ...
IF YOU INSIST ON RESISTING ME,
I, TAKANE D. GOODMAN, THE CHAMPION OF JUSTICE
WILL MAKE YOU PAY!!
DA-DWOOM
H-HEY, WHAT ARE WE GOING TO DO!?
WHY IS SHE CRYING?
ERG... AGAINST SO MANY PEOPLE ...
GLOW
HEY ... ?
MAYBE I ...
... CAN GET US OUT OF THIS ...

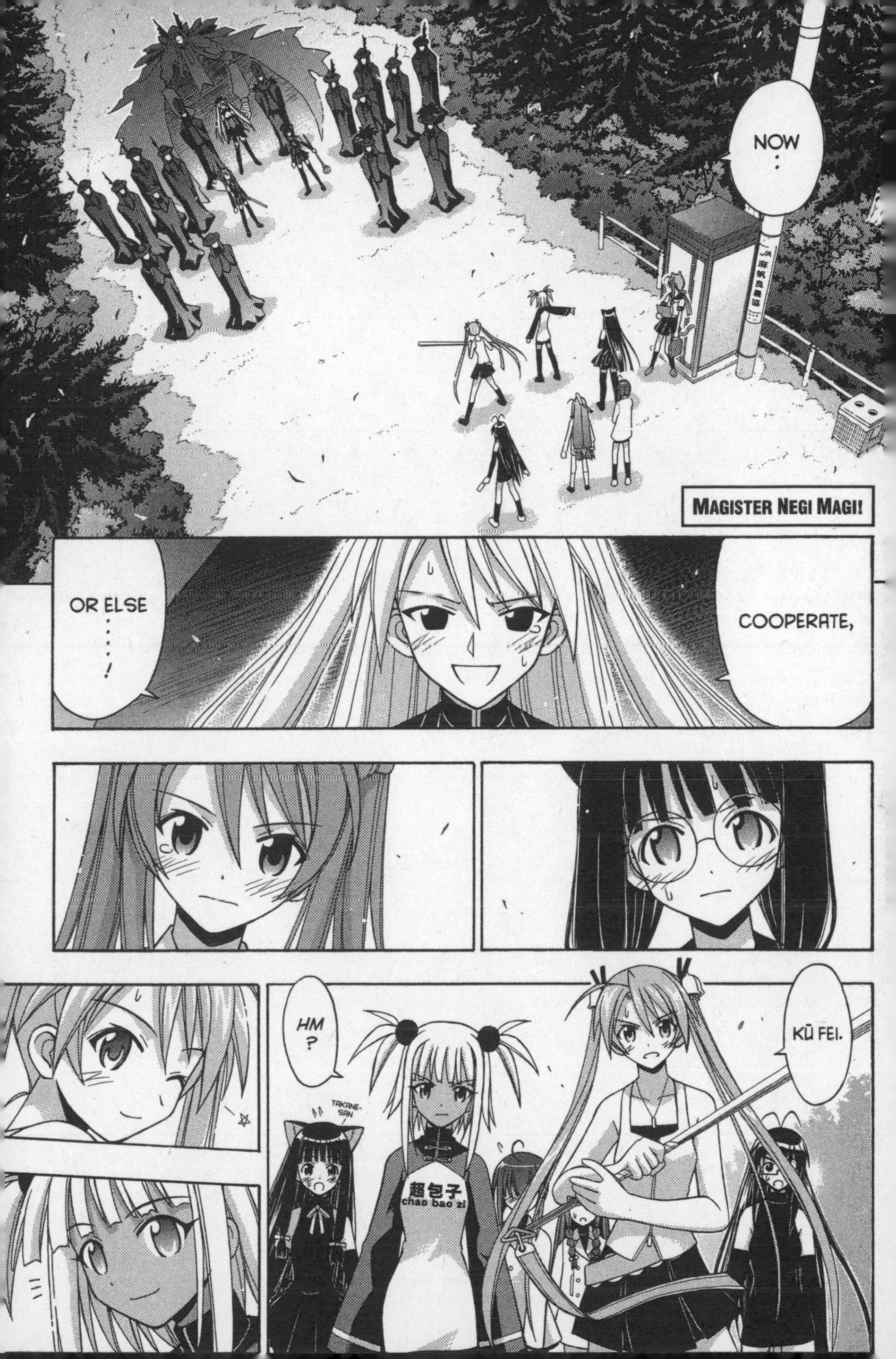
NOW...
MAGISTER NEGI MAGI!
COOPERATE,
OR ELSE.....!
KŪ FEI.
HM?
TAKANE-SAN!
超包子
chao bao zi

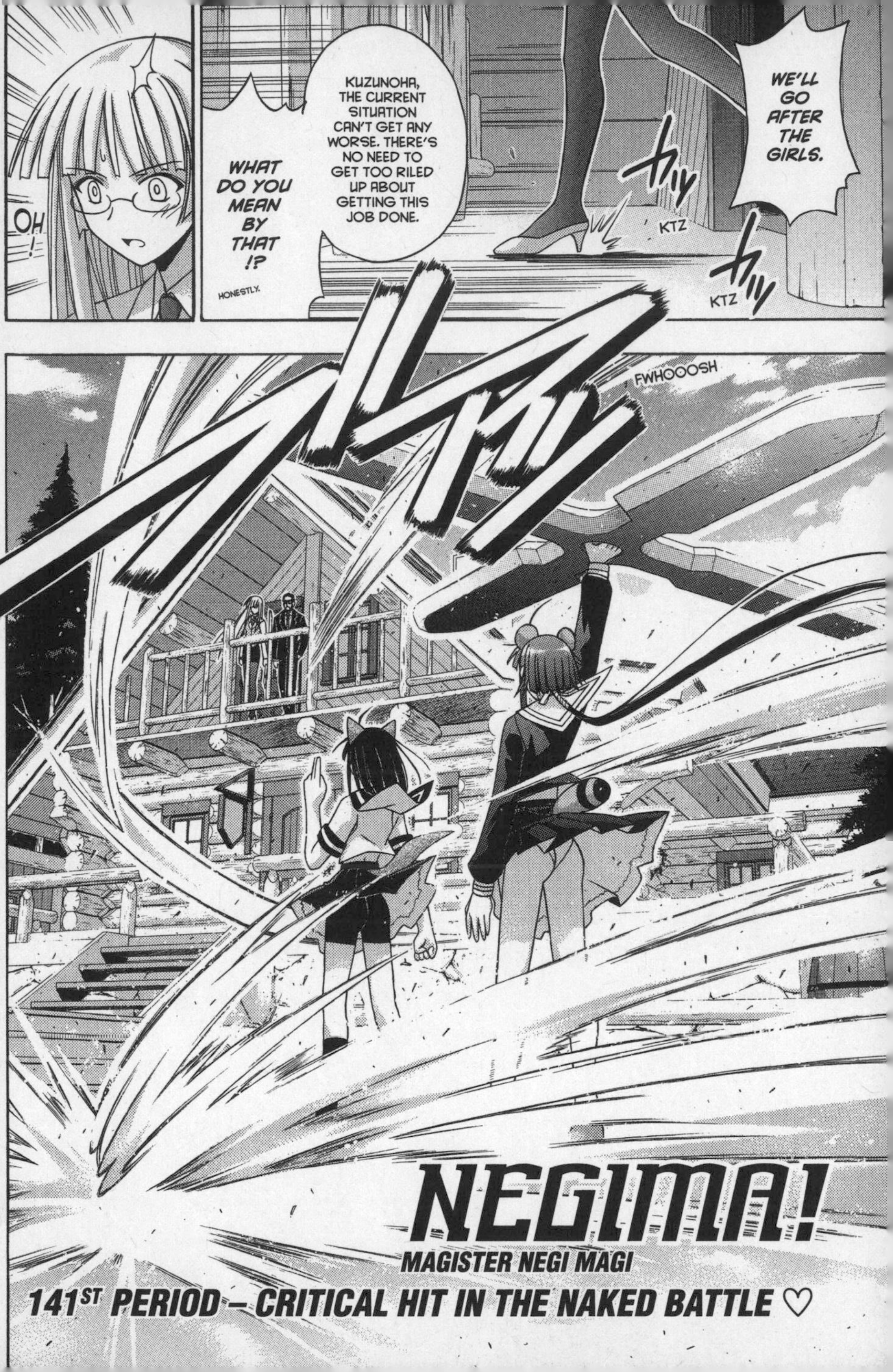
WE'LL GO AFTER THE GIRLS.
KTZ
KTZ
KUZUNOHA, THE CURRENT SITUATION CAN'T GET ANY WORSE. THERE'S NO NEED TO GET TOO RILED UP ABOUT GETTING THIS JOB DONE.
WHAT DO YOU MEAN BY THAT!?
HONESTLY.
OH!
FWHOOOSH
NEGIMA!
MAGISTER NEGI MAGI
141ST PERIOD – CRITICAL HIT IN THE NAKED BATTLE ♡

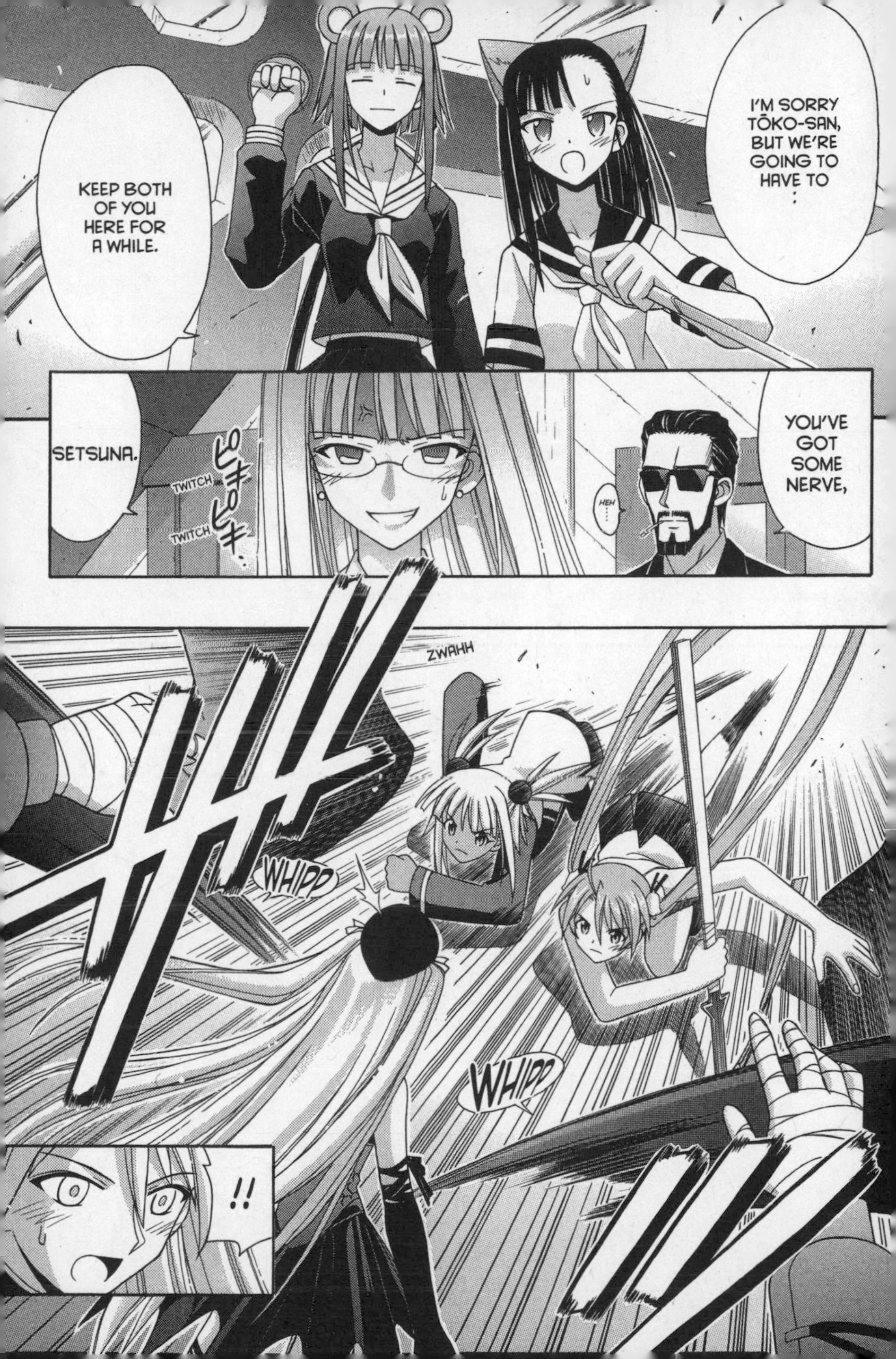

I'M SORRY TŌKO-SAN, BUT WE'RE GOING TO HAVE TO :
KEEP BOTH OF YOU HERE FOR A WHILE.
YOU'VE GOT SOME NERVE,
HEH...
TWITCH
TWITCH
SETSUNA.
ZWAHH
WHIPP
WHIPP
!!

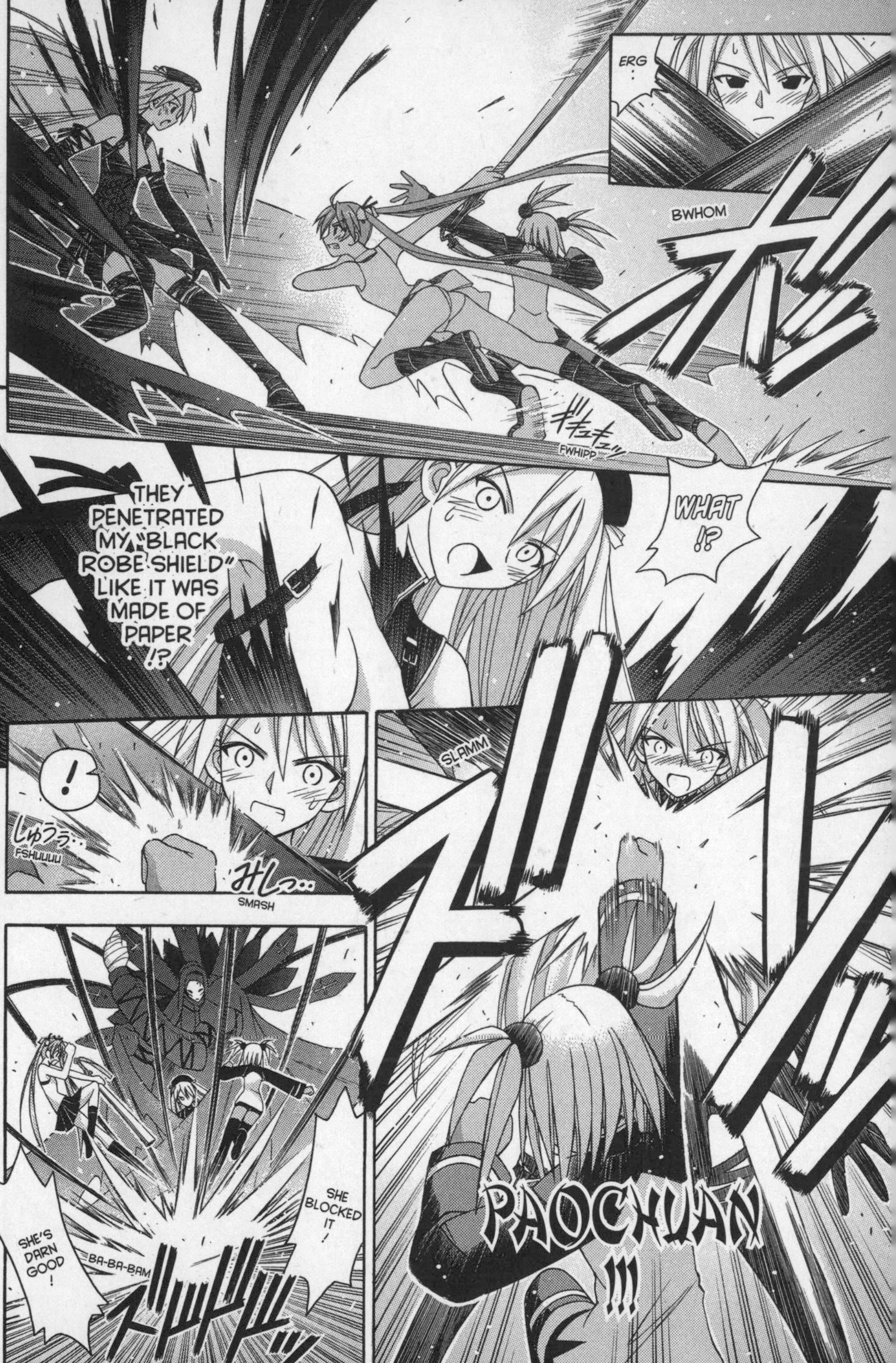
ERG...
BWHOM
FWHIPP
WHAT!?
THEY PENETRATED MY "BLACK ROBE SHIELD" LIKE IT WAS MADE OF PAPER!?
SLAMM
PAOCHUAN!!!
!
しゅうう‥
FSHUUUU
みしっ‥
SMASH
SHE BLOCKED IT!
SHE'S DARN GOOD!
BA-BA-BAM

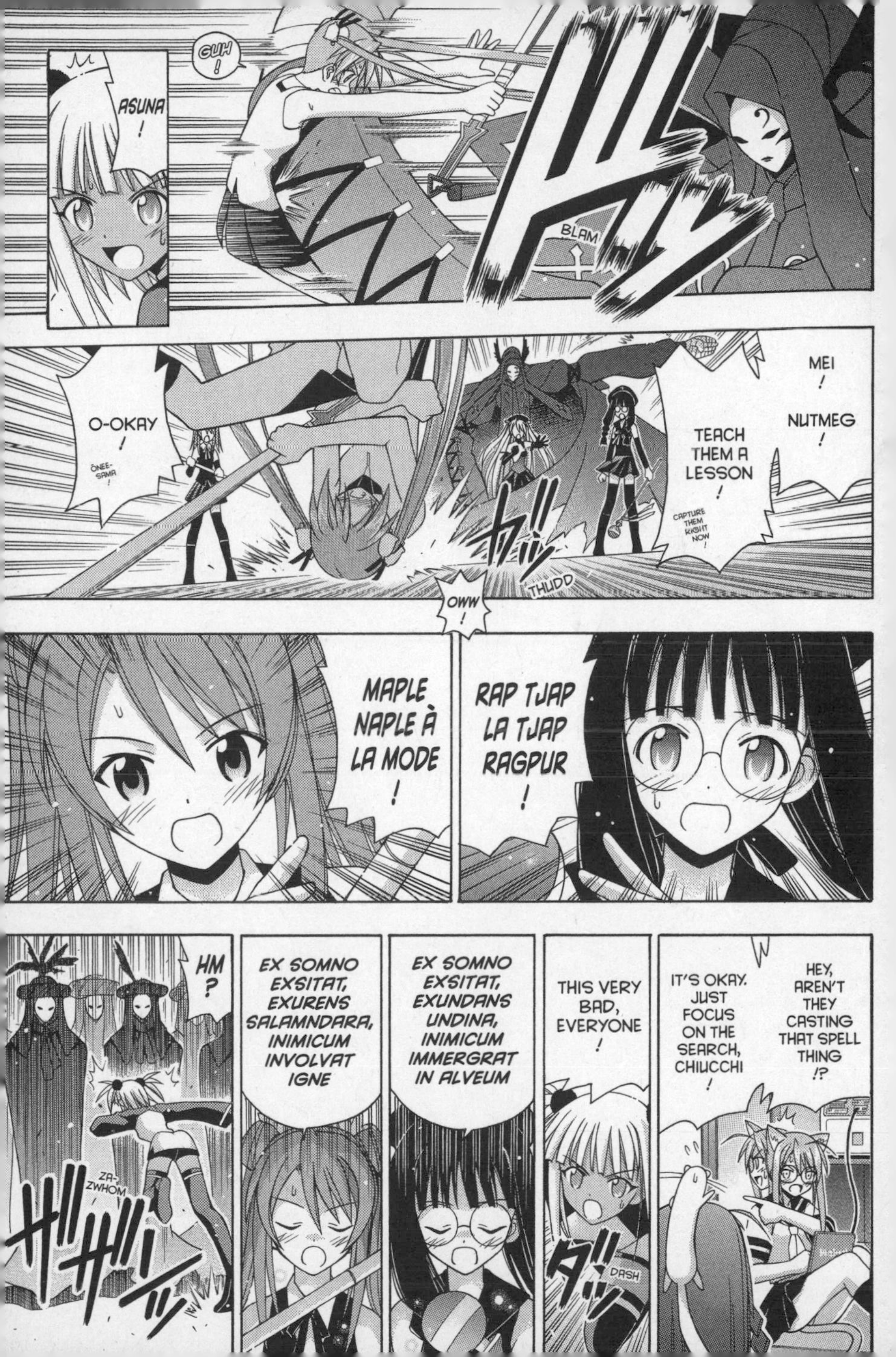
GUH!
BLAM
ASUNA!
MEI! NUTMEG!
TEACH THEM A LESSON!
CAPTURE THEM RIGHT NOW!
THUDD
O-OKAY!
ÔNEE-SAMA!
OWW!
RAP TJAP LA TJAP RAGPUR!
MAPLE NAPLE À LA MODE!
HEY, AREN'T THEY CASTING THAT SPELL THING!?
IT'S OKAY. JUST FOCUS ON THE SEARCH, CHIUCCHI!
THIS VERY BAD, EVERYONE!
DASH
EX SOMNO EXSITAT, EXUNDANS UNDINA, INIMICUM IMMERGRAT IN ALVEUM
EX SOMNO EXSITAT, EXURENS SALAMNDARA, INIMICUM INVOLVAT IGNE
HM?
ZA-ZWHOM

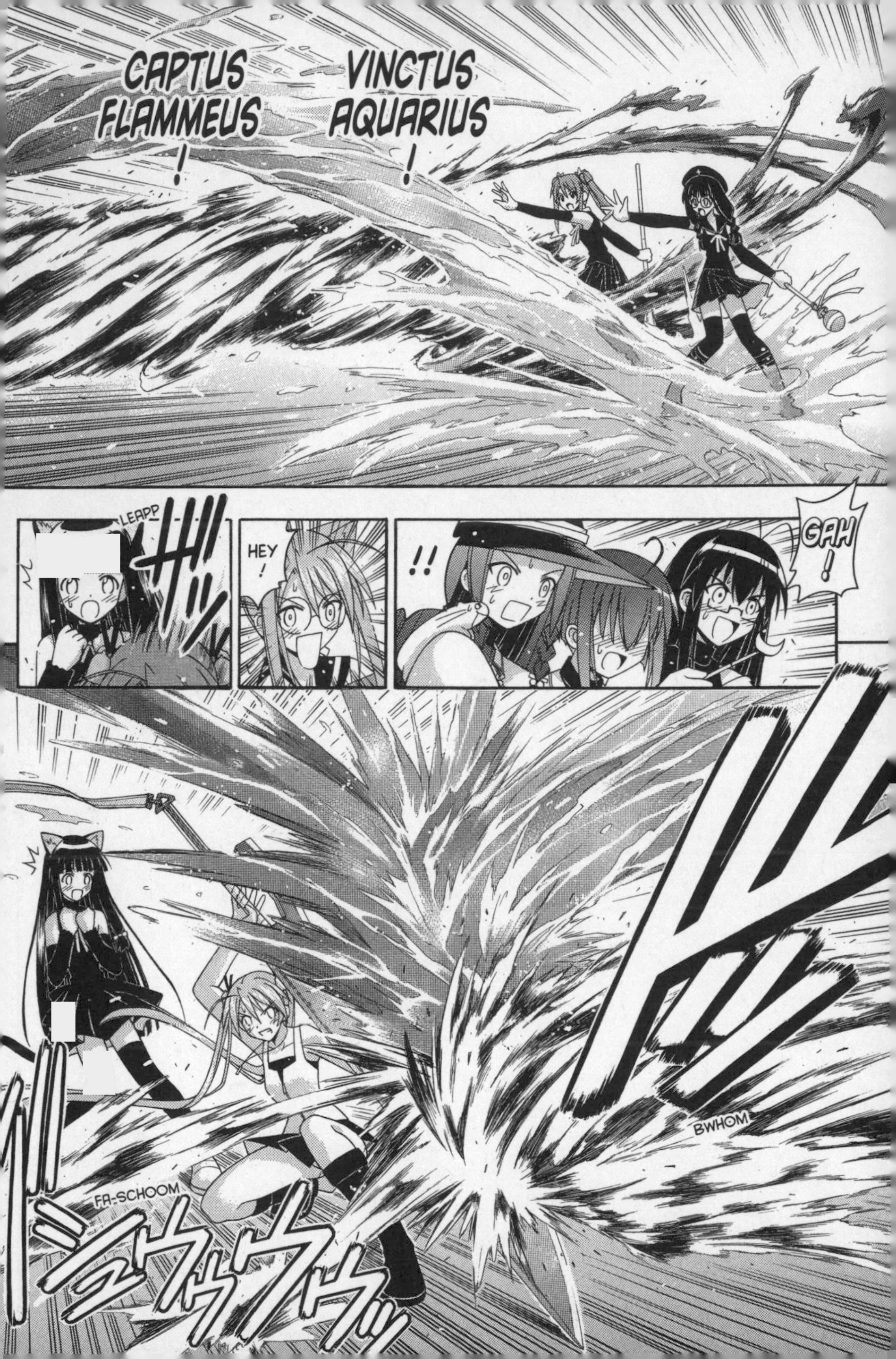
VINCTUS AQUARIUS !
CAPTUS FLAMMEUS !
GAH !
!!
HEY !
LEAPP
BWHOM
FA-SCHOOM

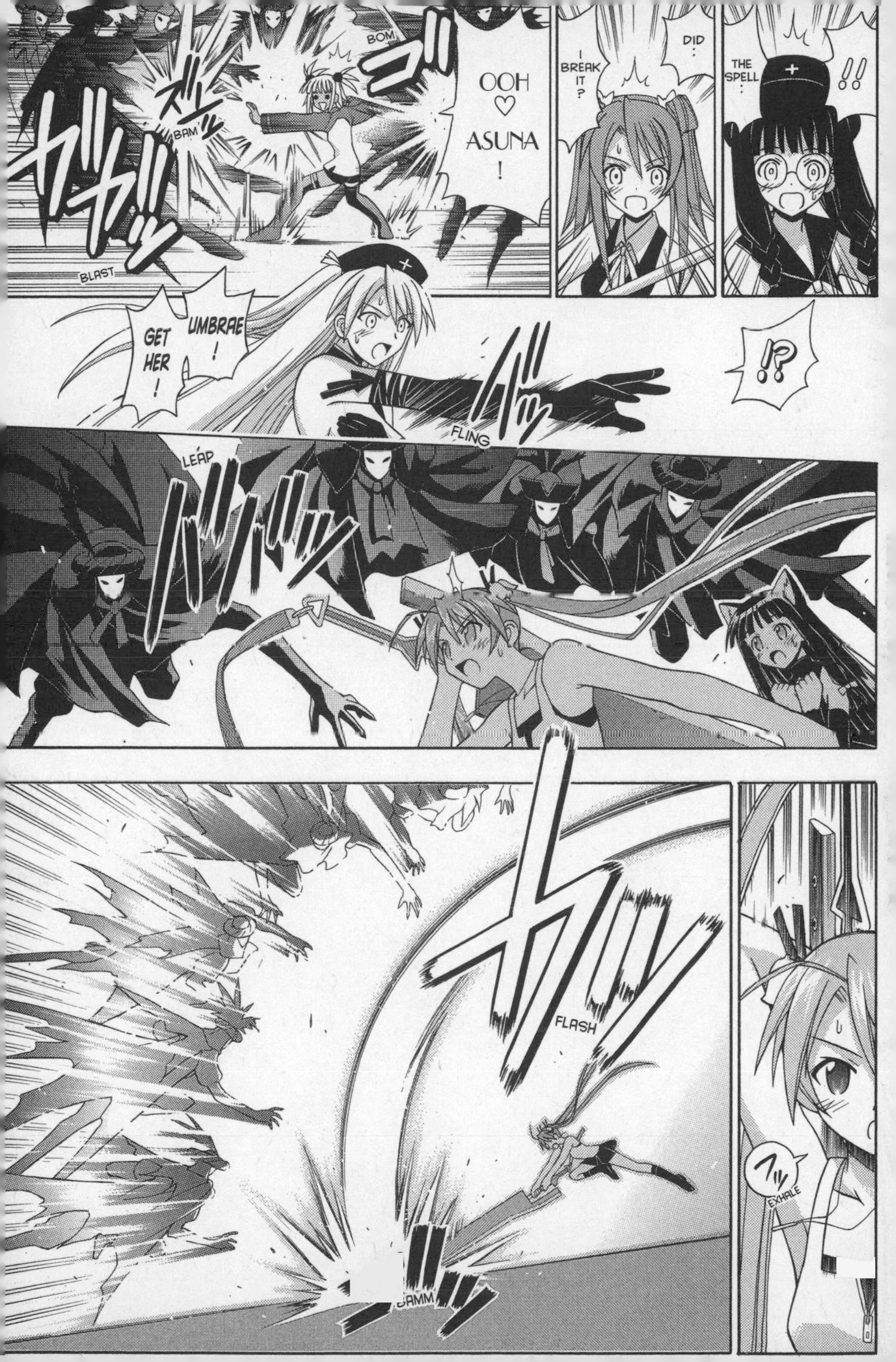
THE SPELL...
!!
DID...
I BREAK IT?
OOH ♡ ASUNA!
BOM
BAM
BLAST
!?
UMBRAE!
GET HER!
FLING
LEAP
EXHALE
FLASH
BAMM

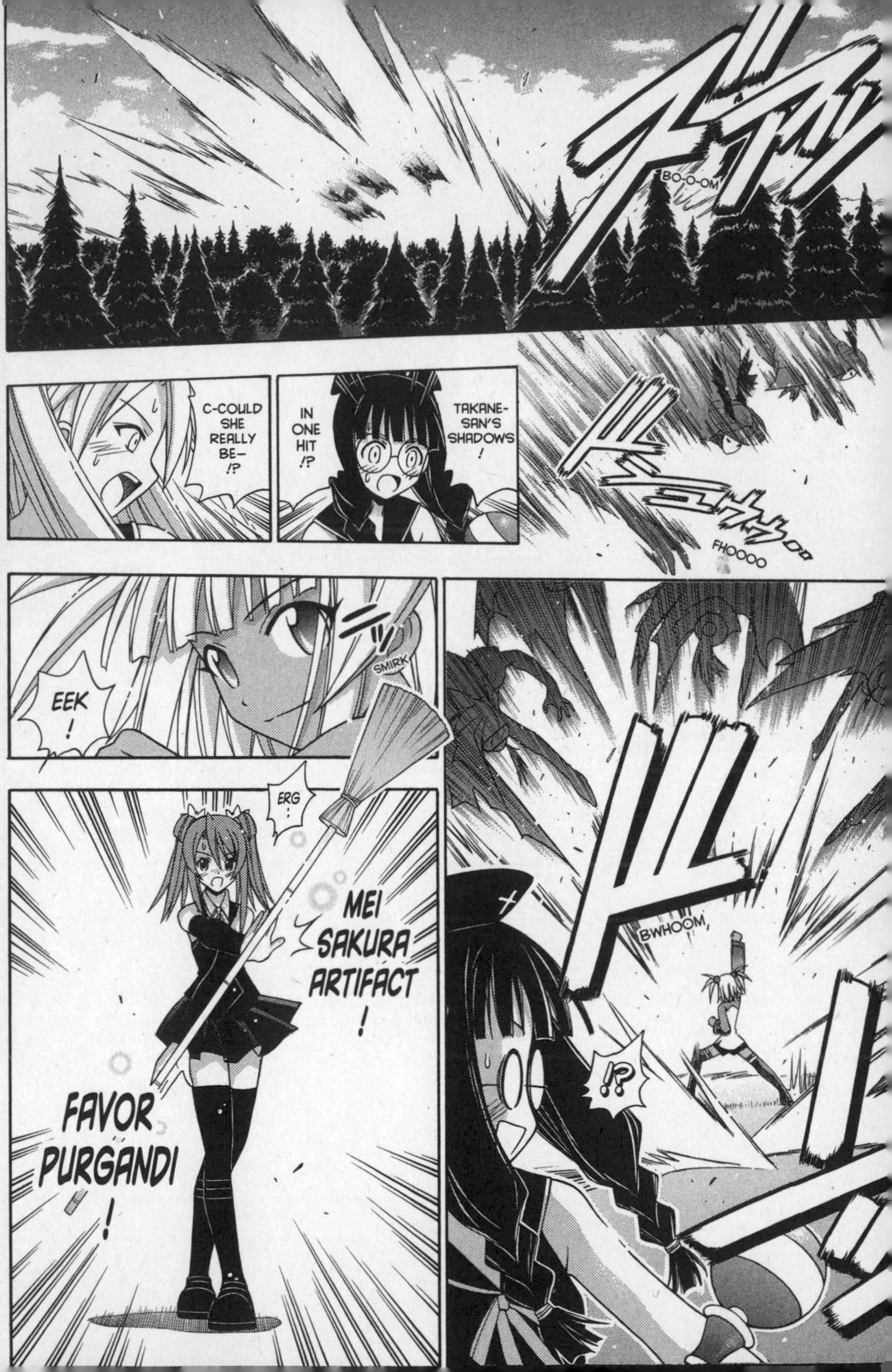
BO-O-OM
FHOOOO
TAKANE-SAN'S SHADOWS!
IN ONE HIT!?
C-COULD SHE REALLY BE—!?
BWHOOM,
!?
SMIRK
EEK!
ERG:
MEI SAKURA ARTIFACT!
FAVOR PURGANDI!

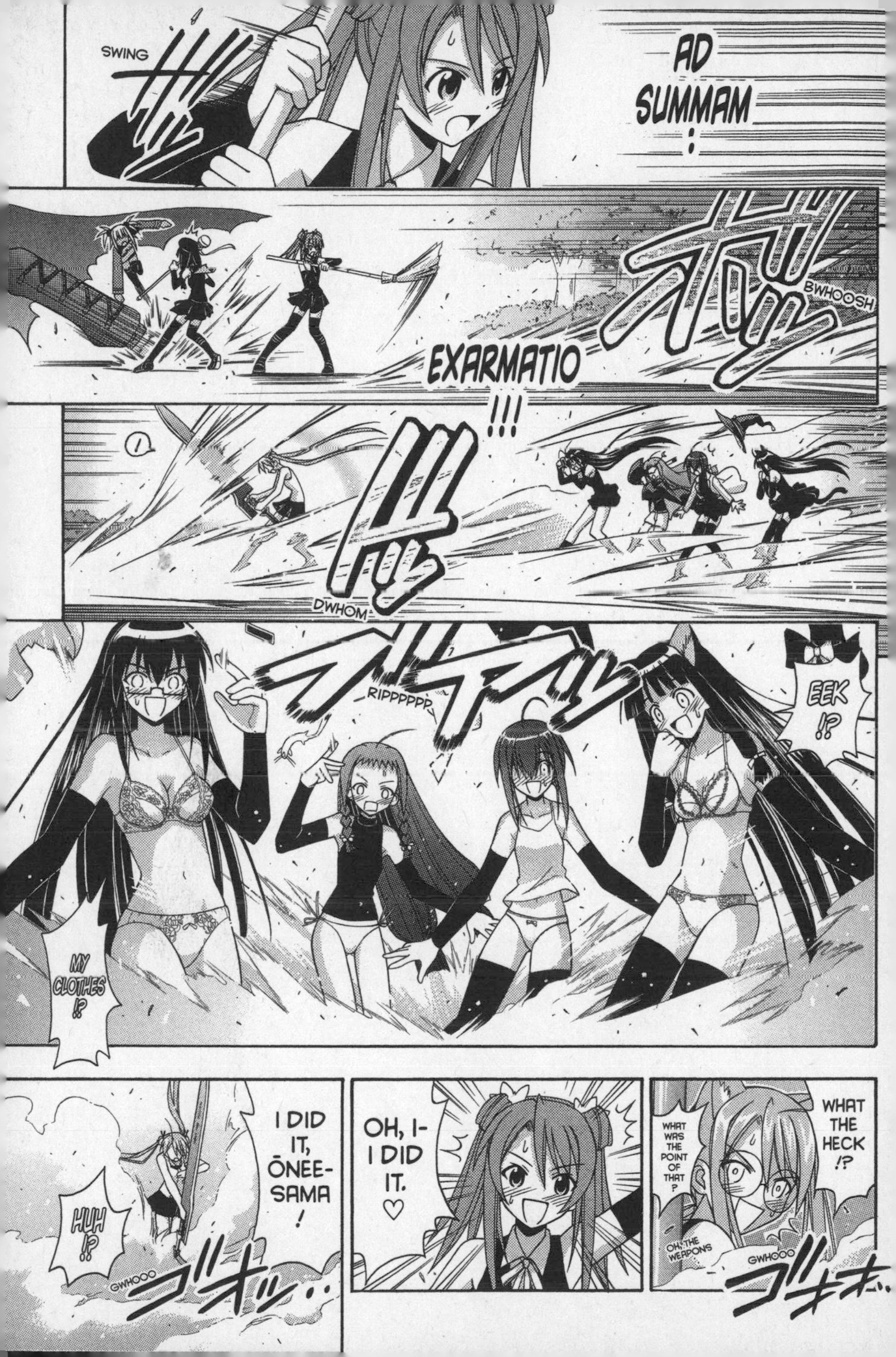
AD SUMMAM!
SWING
BWHOOSH
EXARMATIO!!!
!
DWHOM
EEK!?
RIPPPPPP
MY CLOTHES!?
WHAT THE HECK!?
WHAT WAS THE POINT OF THAT?
OH, THE WEAPONS
GWHOOO
OH, I- I DID IT. ♡
I DID IT, ŌNEE-SAMA!
HUH!?
GWHOOO

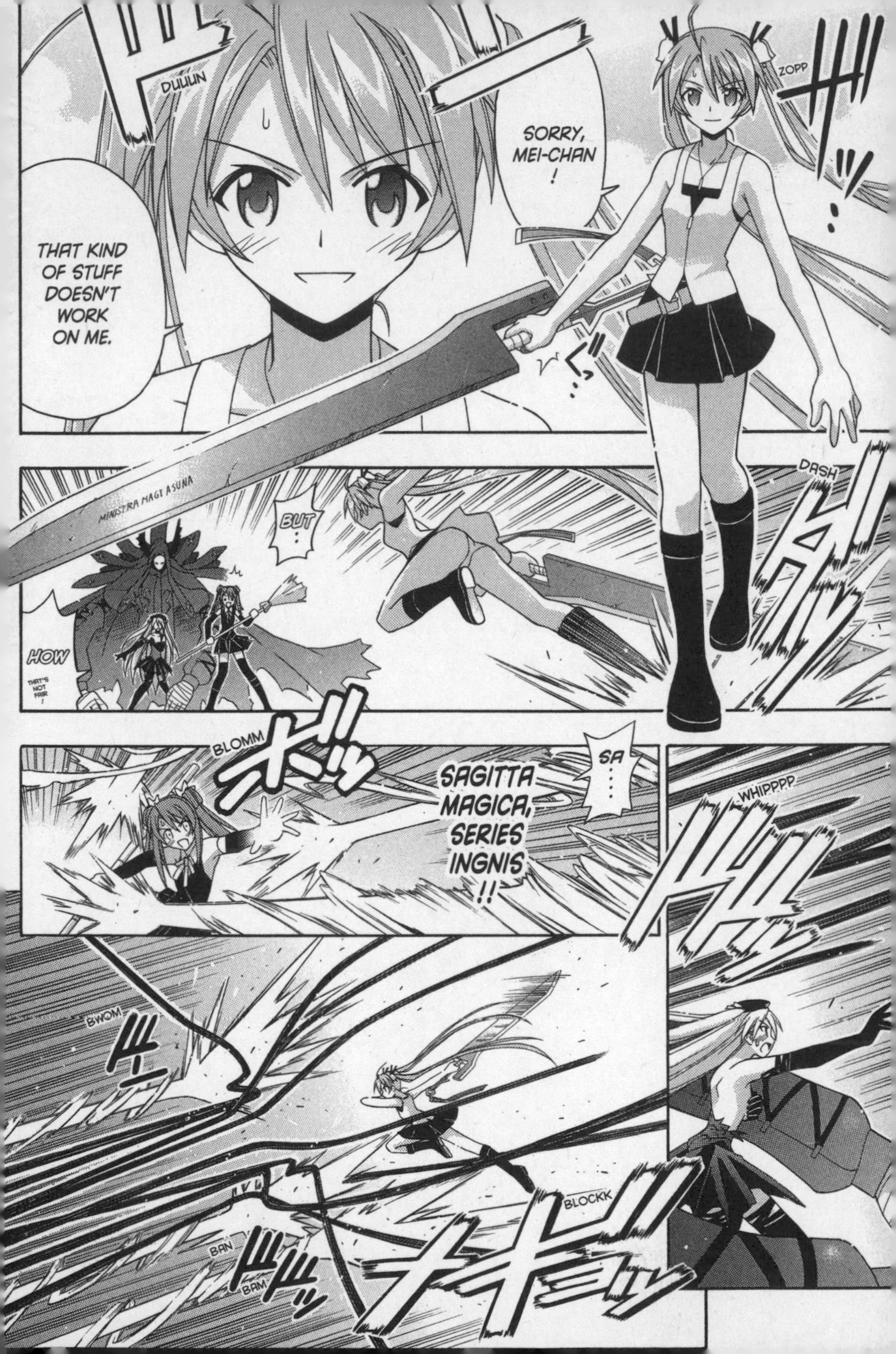
ZOPP
SORRY, MEI-CHAN!
DUUUN
THAT KIND OF STUFF DOESN'T WORK ON ME.
MINISTRA MAGI ASUNA
DASH
BUT...
HOW
THAT'S NOT FAIR!
WHIPPPP
SA...
SAGITTA MAGICA, SERIES INGNIS!!
BLOMM
BLOCKK
BWOM
BAN
BAM

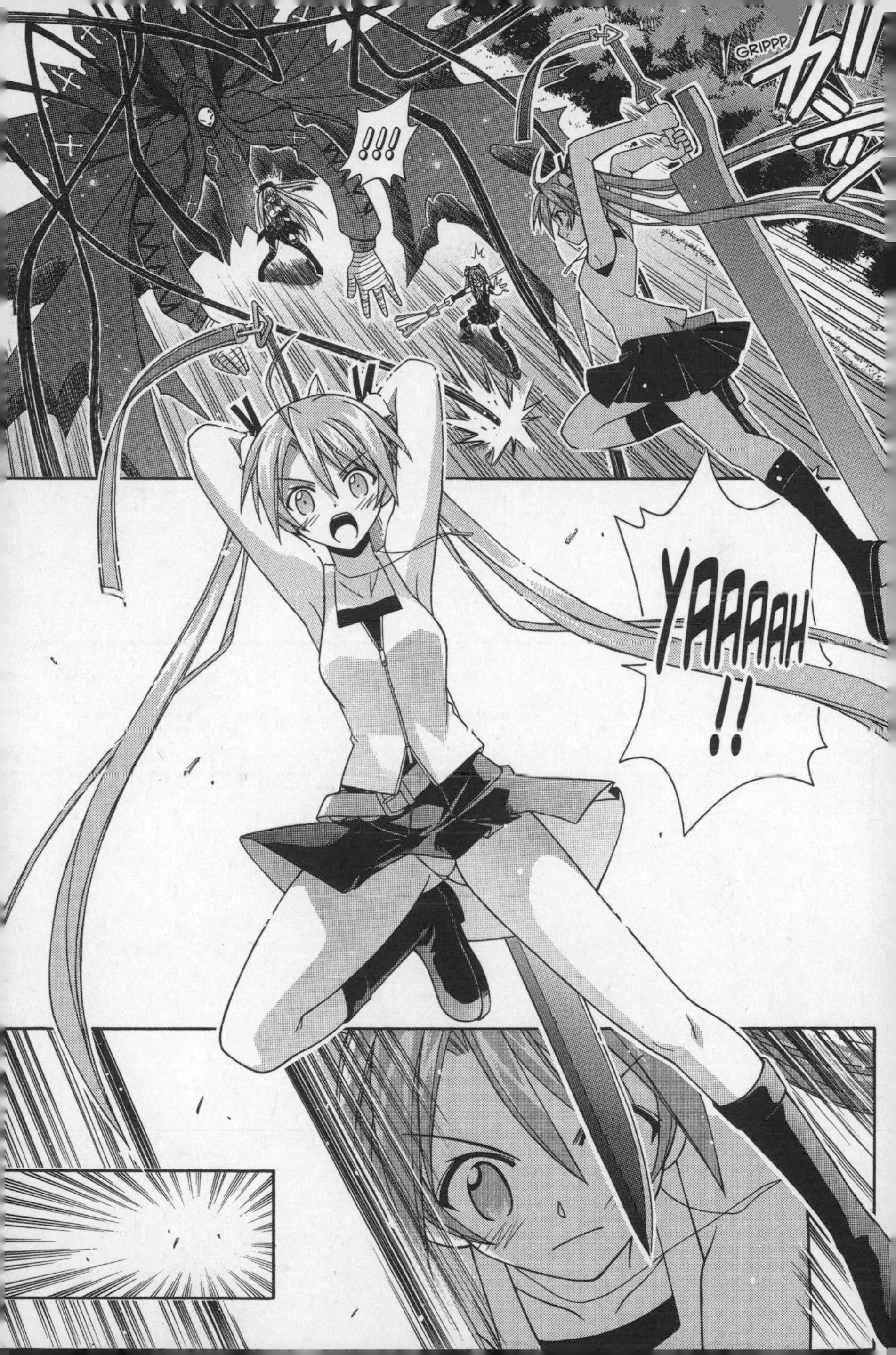
GRIPPP
!!!
YAAAAH !!

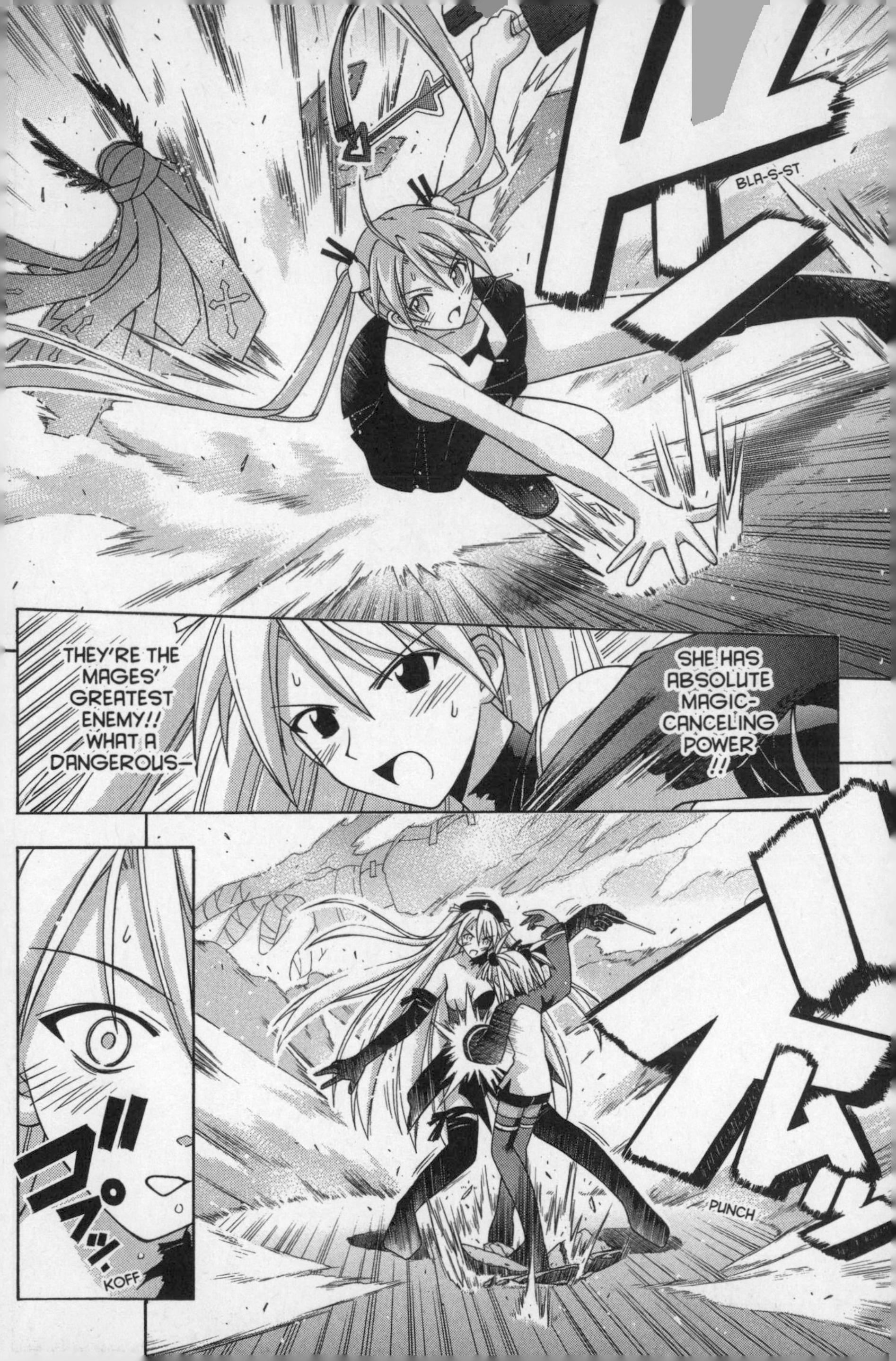
BLA-S-ST
SHE HAS ABSOLUTE MAGIC-CANCELING POWER!!
THEY'RE THE MAGES' GREATEST ENEMY!! WHAT A DANGEROUS—
PUNCH
KOFF

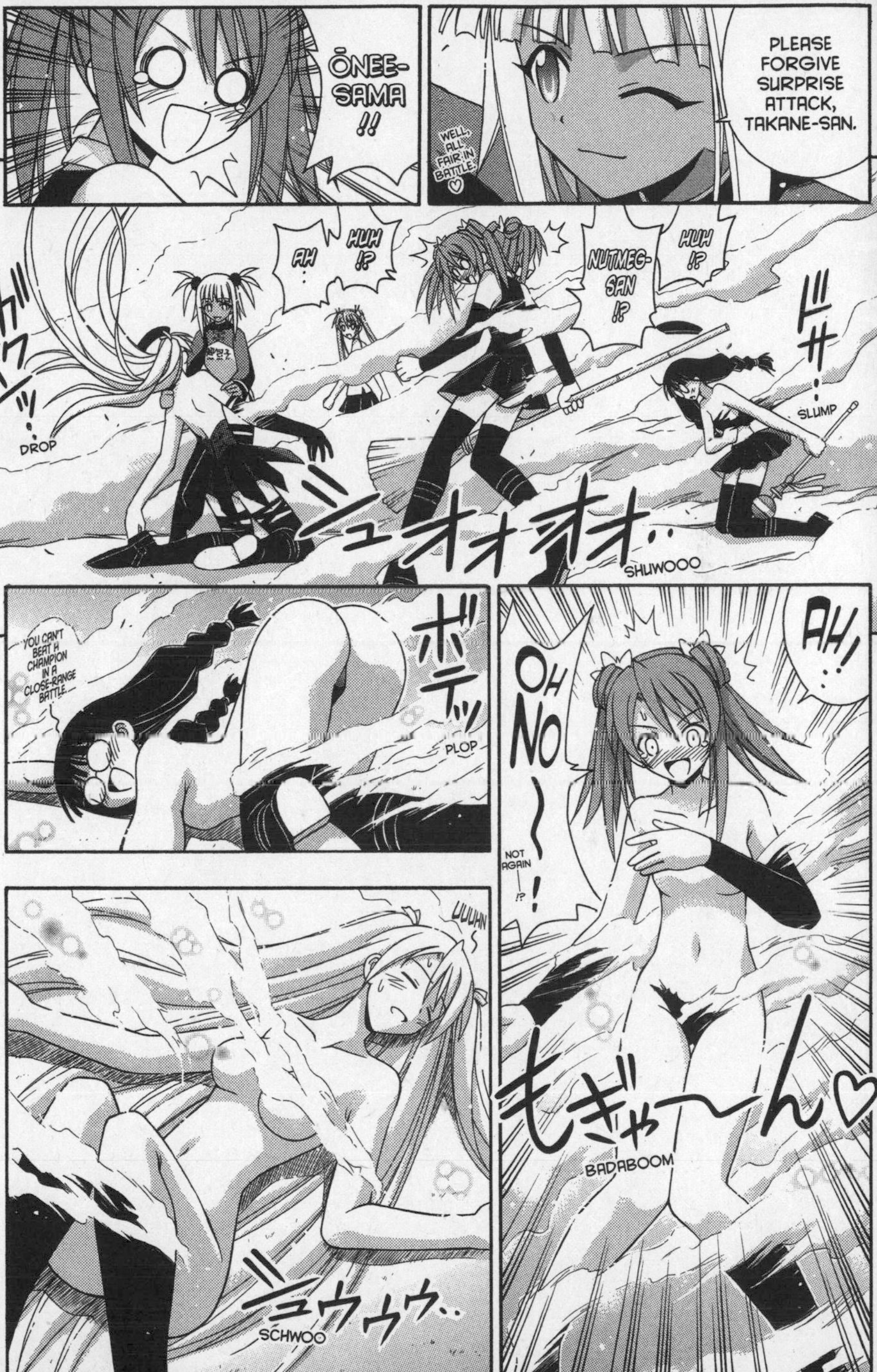
PLEASE FORGIVE SURPRISE ATTACK, TAKANE-SAN.
WELL, ALL FAIR IN BATTLE. ♡
ŌNEE-SAMA !!
ドサ!
SLUMP
HUH !?
NUTMEG-SAN !?
HUH !?
AH...
ガクンッ!
DROP
シュオオオオ..
SHUWOOO
AH!
OH NO~~!
NOT AGAIN !?
もぎゃ〜ん♡
BADABOOM
ボテッ
PLOP
YOU CAN'T BEAT A CHAMPION IN A CLOSE-RANGE BATTLE...
UUUHN
シュウゥウ..
SCHWOO

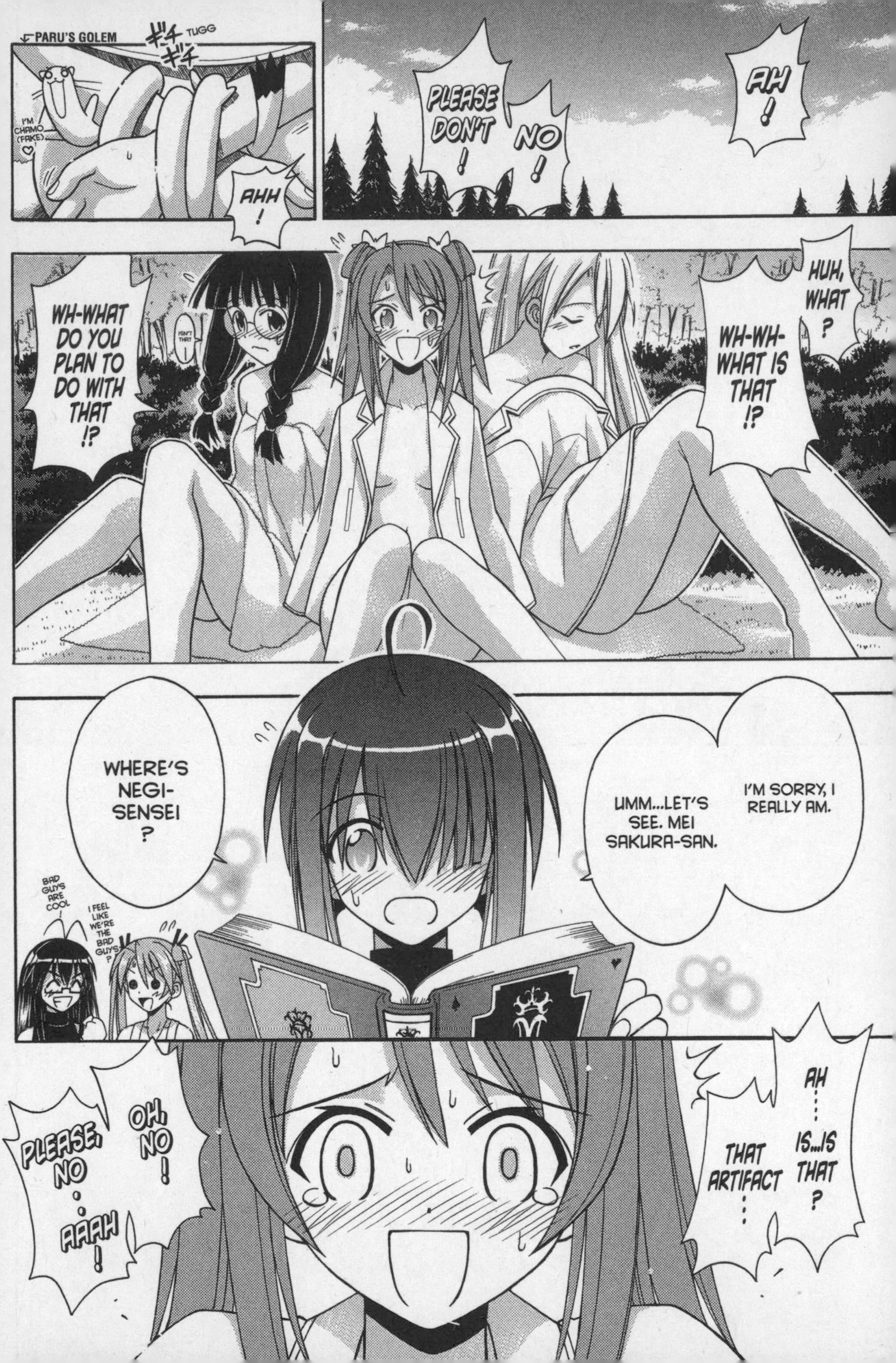
AH !
NO !
PLEASE DON'T !
PARU'S GOLEM
ギチギチ TUGG
I'M CHAMO (FAKE) ♡
AHH !
HUH, WHAT ?
WH-WH-WHAT IS THAT !?
ISN'T THAT
WH-WHAT DO YOU PLAN TO DO WITH THAT !?
I'M SORRY, I REALLY AM.
UMM...LET'S SEE. MEI SAKURA-SAN.
WHERE'S NEGI-SENSEI ?
I FEEL LIKE WE'RE THE BAD GUYS ?
BAD GUYS ARE COOL !
AH... IS...IS THAT ?
THAT ARTIFACT...
OH, NO !
PLEASE, NO... AAAH !

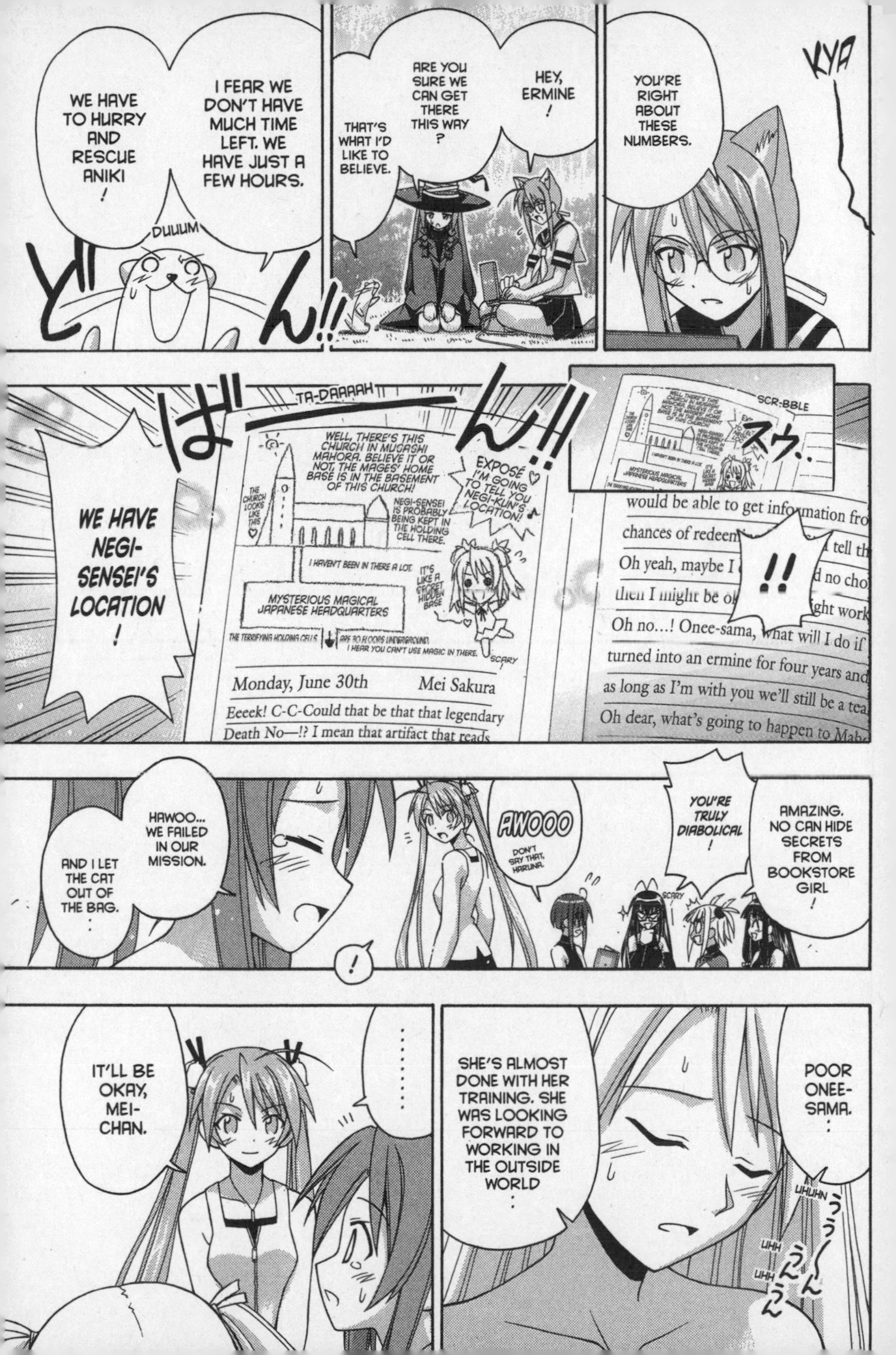

KYA
YOU'RE RIGHT ABOUT THESE NUMBERS.
HEY, ERMINE!
ARE YOU SURE WE CAN GET THERE THIS WAY?
THAT'S WHAT I'D LIKE TO BELIEVE.
I FEAR WE DON'T HAVE MUCH TIME LEFT. WE HAVE JUST A FEW HOURS.
WE HAVE TO HURRY AND RESCUE ANIKI!
DUUUM
どん!!
SCR-BBLE
スウ…
would be able to get information fro
chances of redeem
tell th
Oh yeah, maybe I
d no cho
then I might be ok
ight work
Oh no...! Onee-sama, what will I do if
turned into an ermine for four years and
as long as I'm with you we'll still be a tea
Oh dear, what's going to happen to Mah
!!
TA-DAAAAH
ばーーん!!
WELL, THERE'S THIS CHURCH IN MUGASHI MAHORA. BELIEVE IT OR NOT, THE MAGES' HOME BASE IS IN THE BASEMENT OF THIS CHURCH!
EXPOSÉ I'M GOING TO TELL YOU NEGI-KUN'S LOCATION!
THE CHURCH LOOKS LIKE THIS
NEGI-SENSEI IS PROBABLY BEING KEPT IN THE HOLDING CELL THERE.
I HAVEN'T BEEN IN THERE A LOT.
IT'S LIKE A SECRET HIDDEN BASE
MYSTERIOUS MAGICAL JAPANESE HEADQUARTERS
THE TERRIFYING HOLDING CELLS ARE 30 FLOORS UNDERGROUND.
I HEAR YOU CAN'T USE MAGIC IN THERE.
SCARY!
Monday, June 30th Mei Sakura
Eeeek! C-C-Could that be that that legendary
Death No—!? I mean that artifact that reads
WE HAVE NEGI-SENSEI'S LOCATION!
AMAZING. NO CAN HIDE SECRETS FROM BOOKSTORE GIRL!
YOU'RE TRULY DIABOLICAL!
SCARY
AWOOO
DON'T SAY THAT, HARUNA.
HAWOO... WE FAILED IN OUR MISSION.
AND I LET THE CAT OUT OF THE BAG...
!
POOR ONEE-SAMA...
UHUHN うう～ん
UHH うん
UHH うん
SHE'S ALMOST DONE WITH HER TRAINING. SHE WAS LOOKING FORWARD TO WORKING IN THE OUTSIDE WORLD...
......
IT'LL BE OKAY, MEI-CHAN.

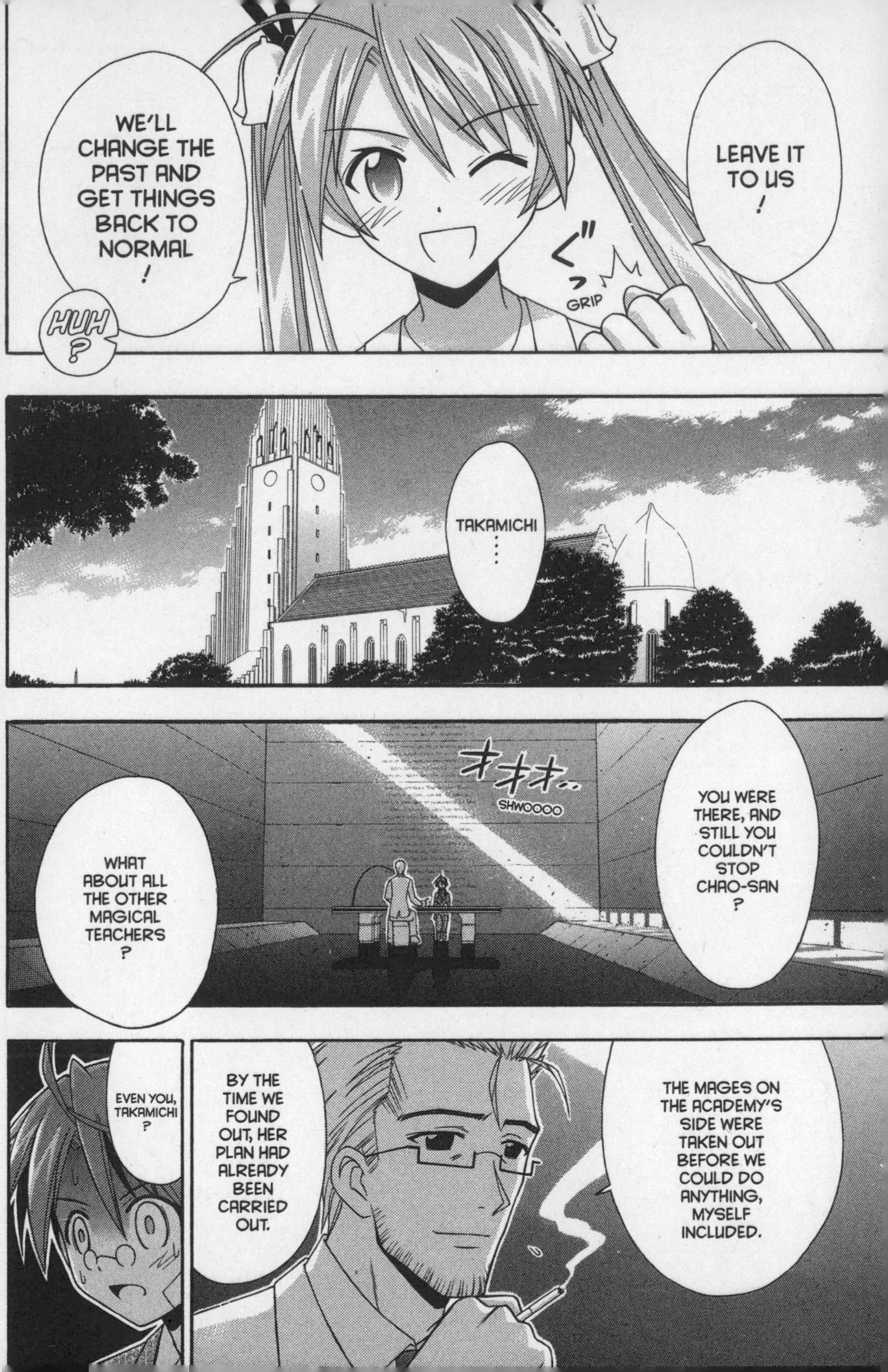

LEAVE IT TO US!
GRIP
WE'LL CHANGE THE PAST AND GET THINGS BACK TO NORMAL!
HUH?
TAKAMICHI...
YOU WERE THERE, AND STILL YOU COULDN'T STOP CHAO-SAN?
オオオ..
SHWOOOO
WHAT ABOUT ALL THE OTHER MAGICAL TEACHERS?
THE MAGES ON THE ACADEMY'S SIDE WERE TAKEN OUT BEFORE WE COULD DO ANYTHING, MYSELF INCLUDED.
BY THE TIME WE FOUND OUT, HER PLAN HAD ALREADY BEEN CARRIED OUT.
EVEN YOU, TAKAMICHI?

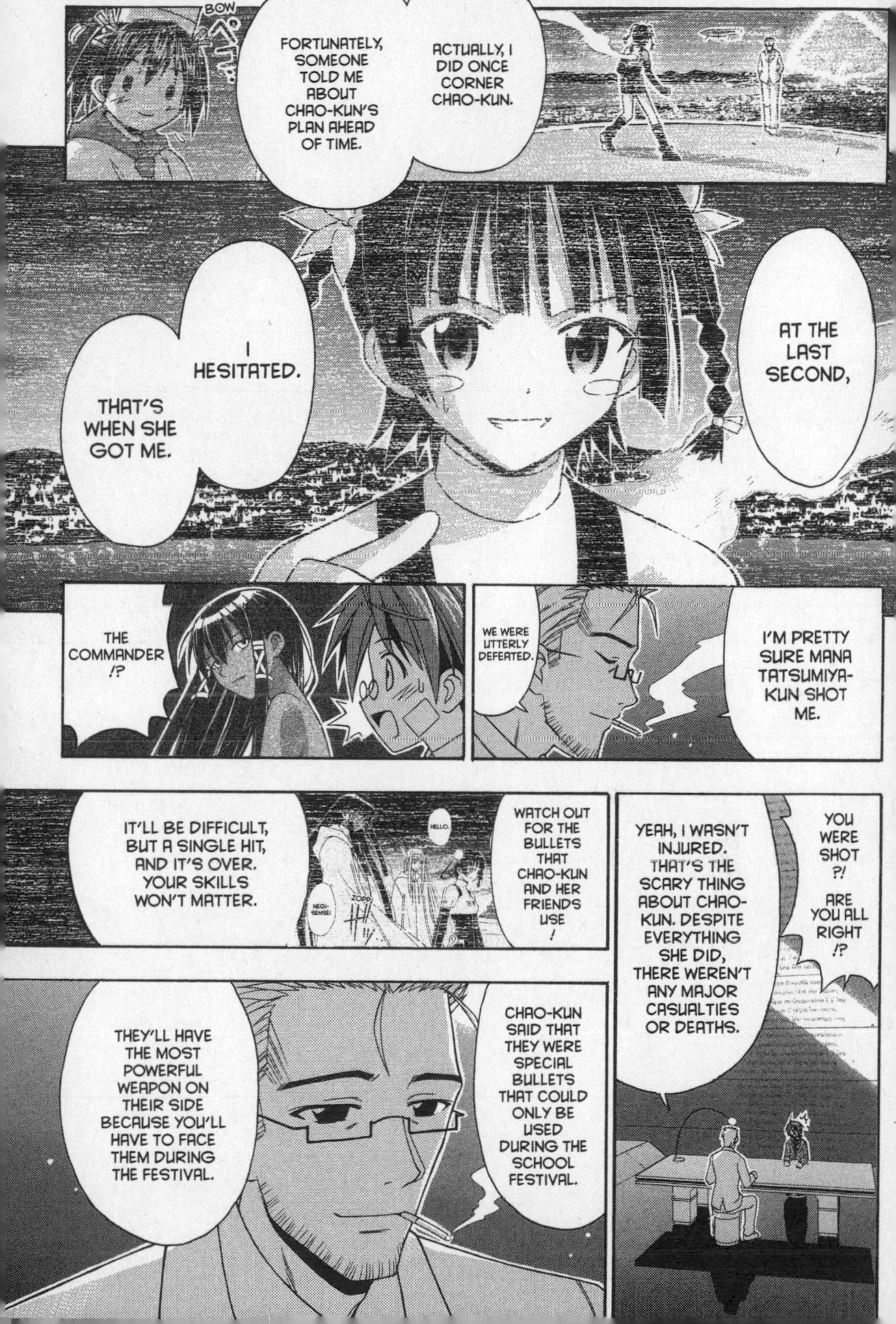

ACTUALLY, I DID ONCE CORNER CHAO-KUN.
FORTUNATELY, SOMEONE TOLD ME ABOUT CHAO-KUN'S PLAN AHEAD OF TIME.
BOW
AT THE LAST SECOND,
I HESITATED.
THAT'S WHEN SHE GOT ME.
I'M PRETTY SURE MANA TATSUMIYA-KUN SHOT ME.
WE WERE UTTERLY DEFEATED.
THE COMMANDER!?
YOU WERE SHOT?!
ARE YOU ALL RIGHT!?
YEAH, I WASN'T INJURED. THAT'S THE SCARY THING ABOUT CHAO-KUN. DESPITE EVERYTHING SHE DID, THERE WEREN'T ANY MAJOR CASUALTIES OR DEATHS.
WATCH OUT FOR THE BULLETS THAT CHAO-KUN AND HER FRIENDS USE!
HELLO.
NEGI-SENSEI
ZOPP
IT'LL BE DIFFICULT, BUT A SINGLE HIT, AND IT'S OVER. YOUR SKILLS WON'T MATTER.
CHAO-KUN SAID THAT THEY WERE SPECIAL BULLETS THAT COULD ONLY BE USED DURING THE SCHOOL FESTIVAL.
THEY'LL HAVE THE MOST POWERFUL WEAPON ON THEIR SIDE BECAUSE YOU'LL HAVE TO FACE THEM DURING THE FESTIVAL.

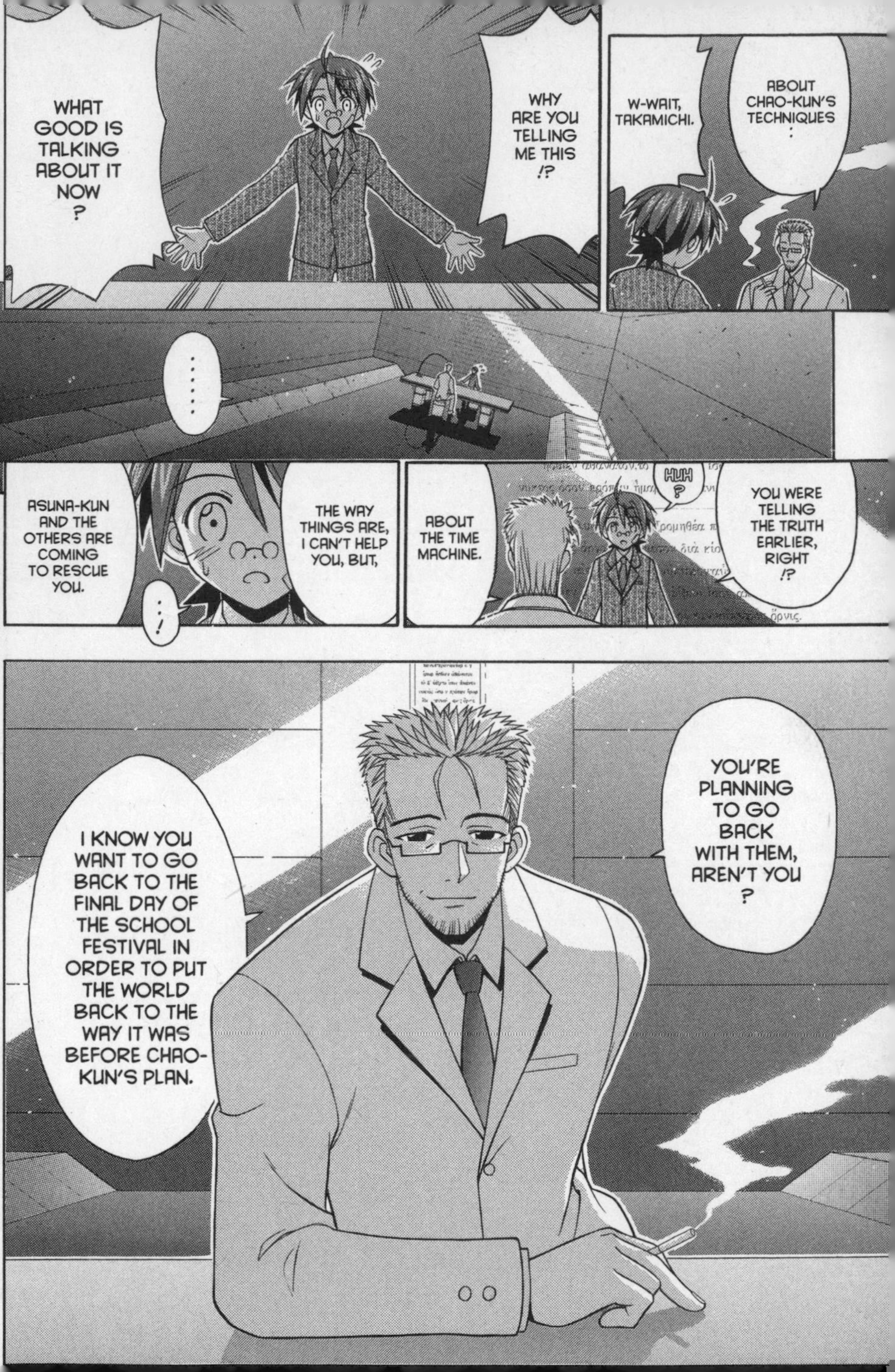
ABOUT CHAO-KUN'S TECHNIQUES :
W-WAIT, TAKAMICHI.
WHY ARE YOU TELLING ME THIS !?
WHAT GOOD IS TALKING ABOUT IT NOW ?
......
YOU WERE TELLING THE TRUTH EARLIER, RIGHT !?
HUH ?
ABOUT THE TIME MACHINE.
THE WAY THINGS ARE, I CAN'T HELP YOU, BUT,
ASUNA-KUN AND THE OTHERS ARE COMING TO RESCUE YOU.
...!
YOU'RE PLANNING TO GO BACK WITH THEM, AREN'T YOU ?
I KNOW YOU WANT TO GO BACK TO THE FINAL DAY OF THE SCHOOL FESTIVAL IN ORDER TO PUT THE WORLD BACK TO THE WAY IT WAS BEFORE CHAO-KUN'S PLAN.

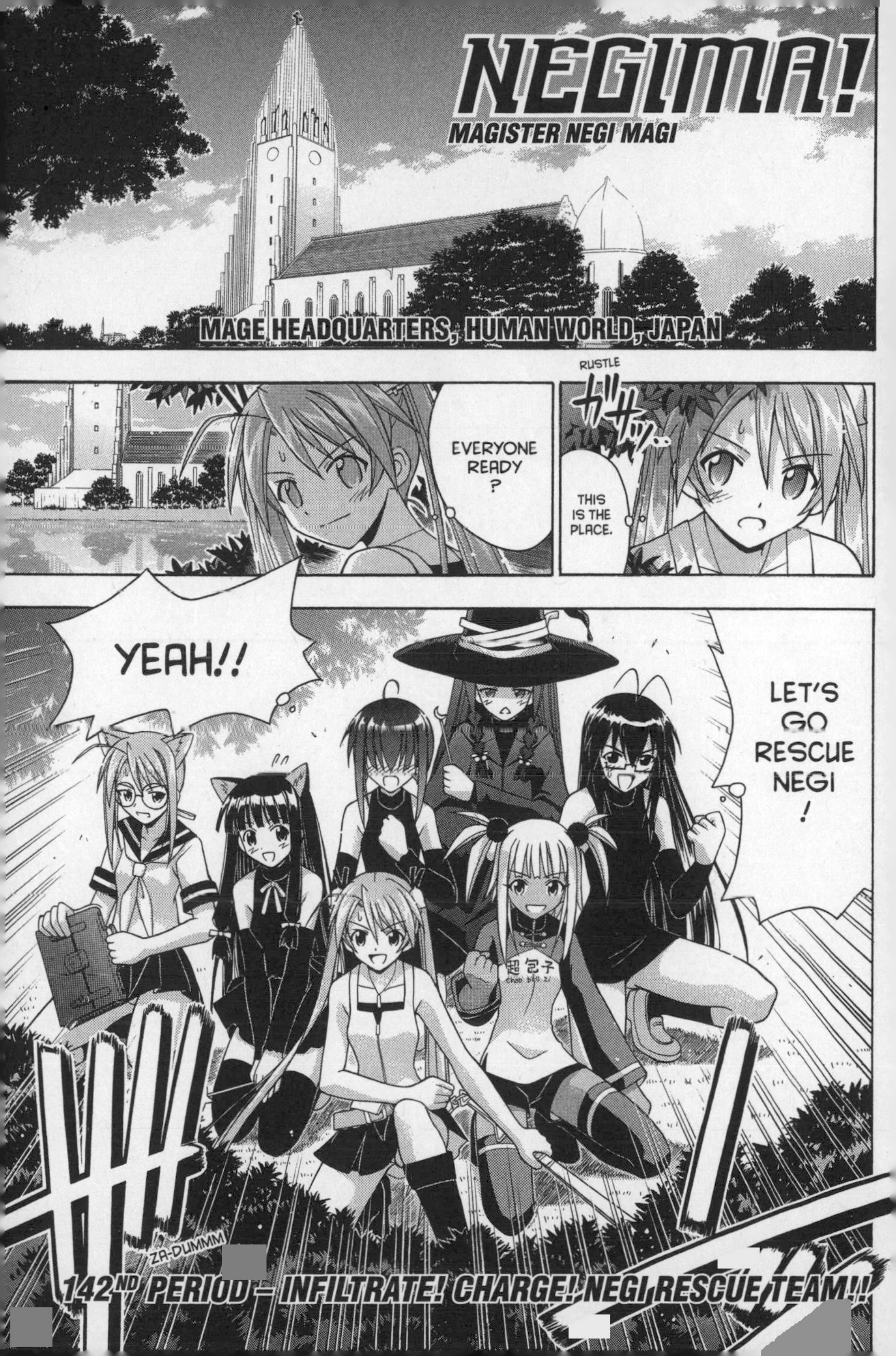
NEGIMA!
MAGISTER NEGI MAGI
MAGE HEADQUARTERS, HUMAN WORLD, JAPAN
RUSTLE
ガサッ
THIS IS THE PLACE.
EVERYONE READY?
LET'S GO RESCUE NEGI!
YEAH!!
超包子
ZA-DUMMM
142ND PERIOD – INFILTRATE! CHARGE! NEGI RESCUE TEAM!!

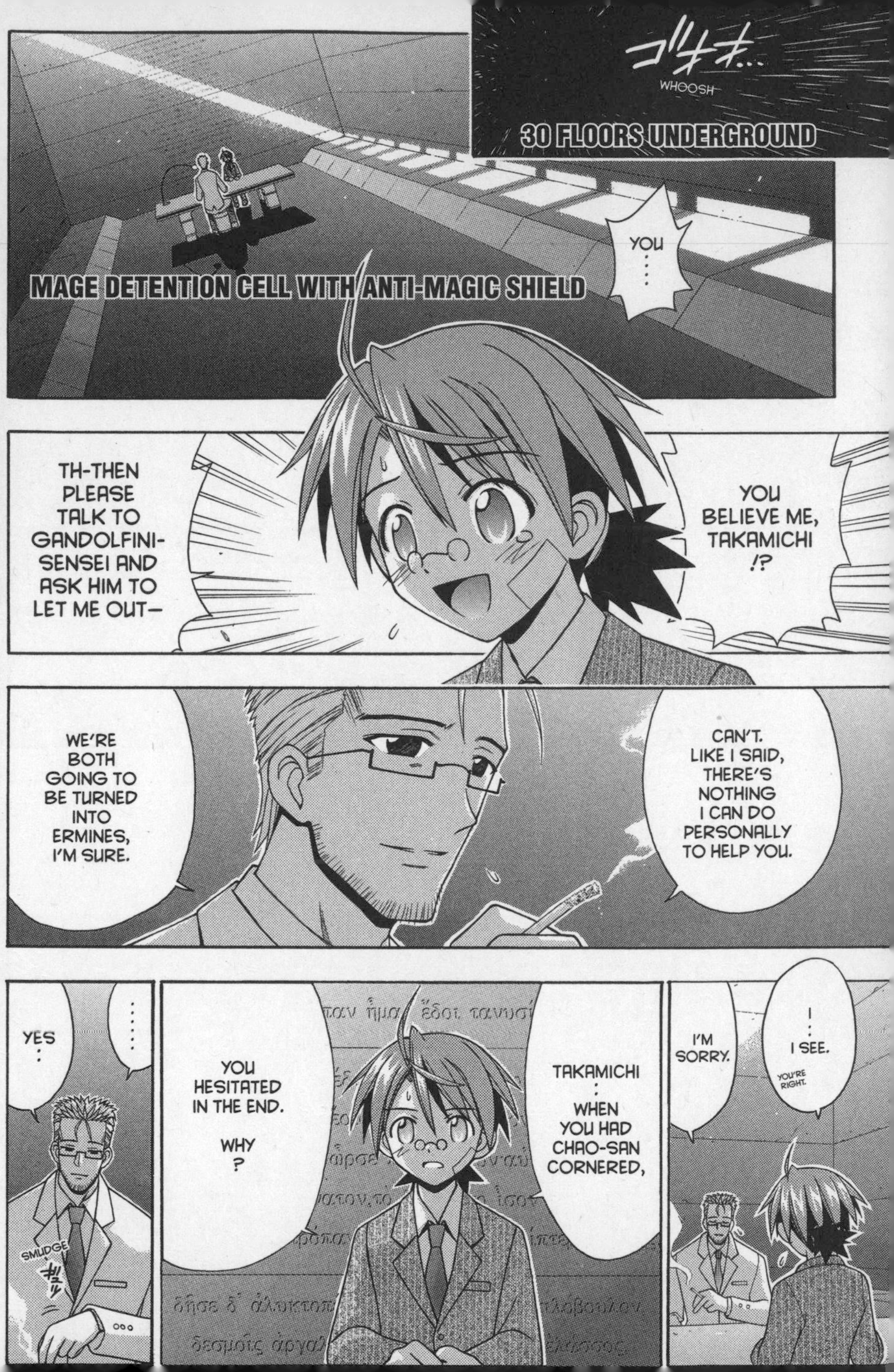
ゴォォ…
WHOOSH
30 FLOORS UNDERGROUND
YOU ......
MAGE DETENTION CELL WITH ANTI-MAGIC SHIELD
YOU BELIEVE ME, TAKAMICHI!?
TH-THEN PLEASE TALK TO GANDOLFINI-SENSEI AND ASK HIM TO LET ME OUT—
CAN'T. LIKE I SAID, THERE'S NOTHING I CAN DO PERSONALLY TO HELP YOU.
WE'RE BOTH GOING TO BE TURNED INTO ERMINES, I'M SURE.
! ... I SEE.
YOU'RE RIGHT.
I'M SORRY.
TAKAMICHI: WHEN YOU HAD CHAO-SAN CORNERED,
YOU HESITATED IN THE END.
WHY?
......
YES:
SMUDGE

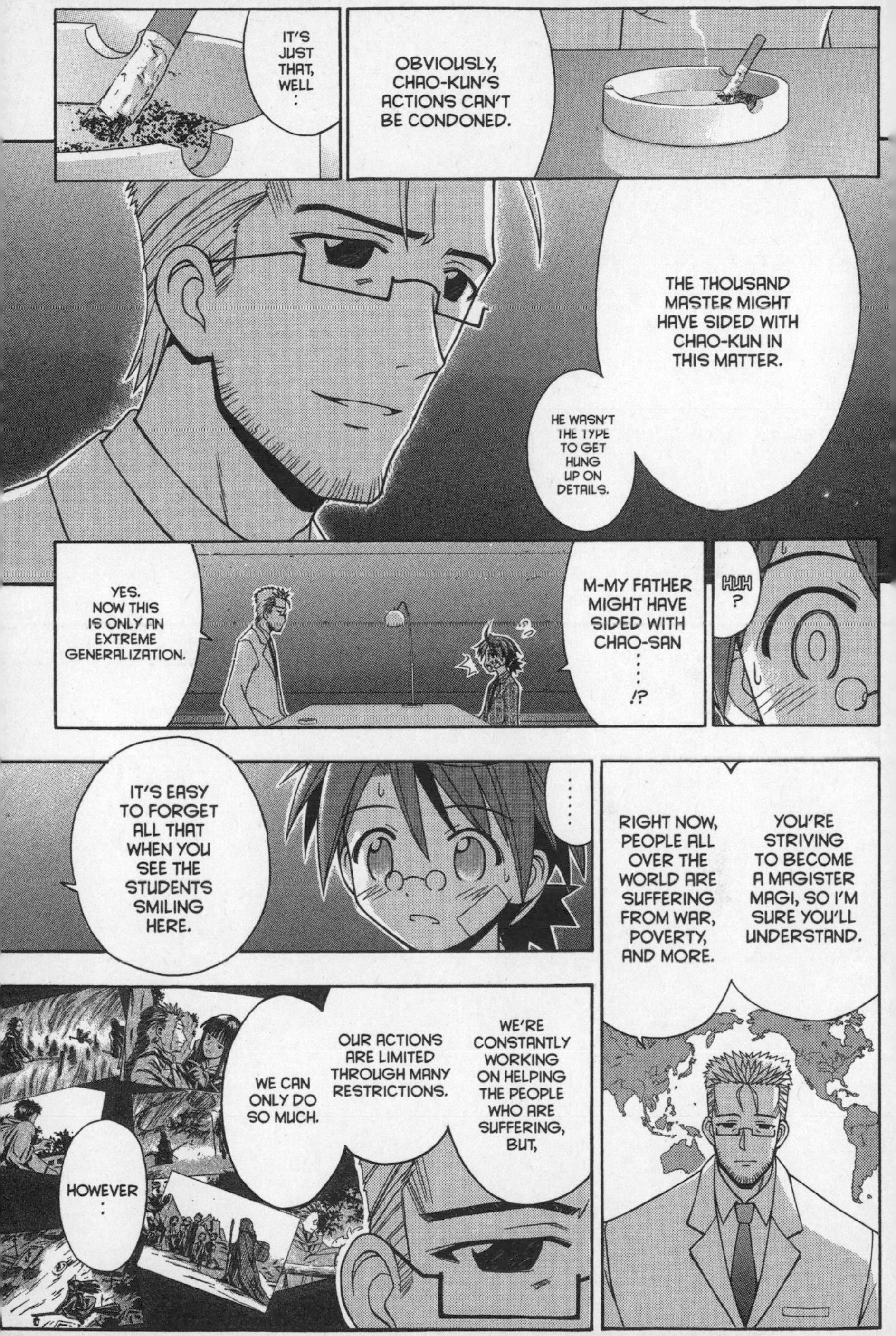
OBVIOUSLY, CHAO-KUN'S ACTIONS CAN'T BE CONDONED.
IT'S JUST THAT, WELL :
THE THOUSAND MASTER MIGHT HAVE SIDED WITH CHAO-KUN IN THIS MATTER.
HE WASN'T THE TYPE TO GET HUNG UP ON DETAILS.
HUH ?
M-MY FATHER MIGHT HAVE SIDED WITH CHAO-SAN ......!?
YES. NOW THIS IS ONLY AN EXTREME GENERALIZATION.
YOU'RE STRIVING TO BECOME A MAGISTER MAGI, SO I'M SURE YOU'LL UNDERSTAND.
RIGHT NOW, PEOPLE ALL OVER THE WORLD ARE SUFFERING FROM WAR, POVERTY, AND MORE.
......
IT'S EASY TO FORGET ALL THAT WHEN YOU SEE THE STUDENTS SMILING HERE.
WE'RE CONSTANTLY WORKING ON HELPING THE PEOPLE WHO ARE SUFFERING, BUT,
OUR ACTIONS ARE LIMITED THROUGH MANY RESTRICTIONS.
WE CAN ONLY DO SO MUCH.
HOWEVER :

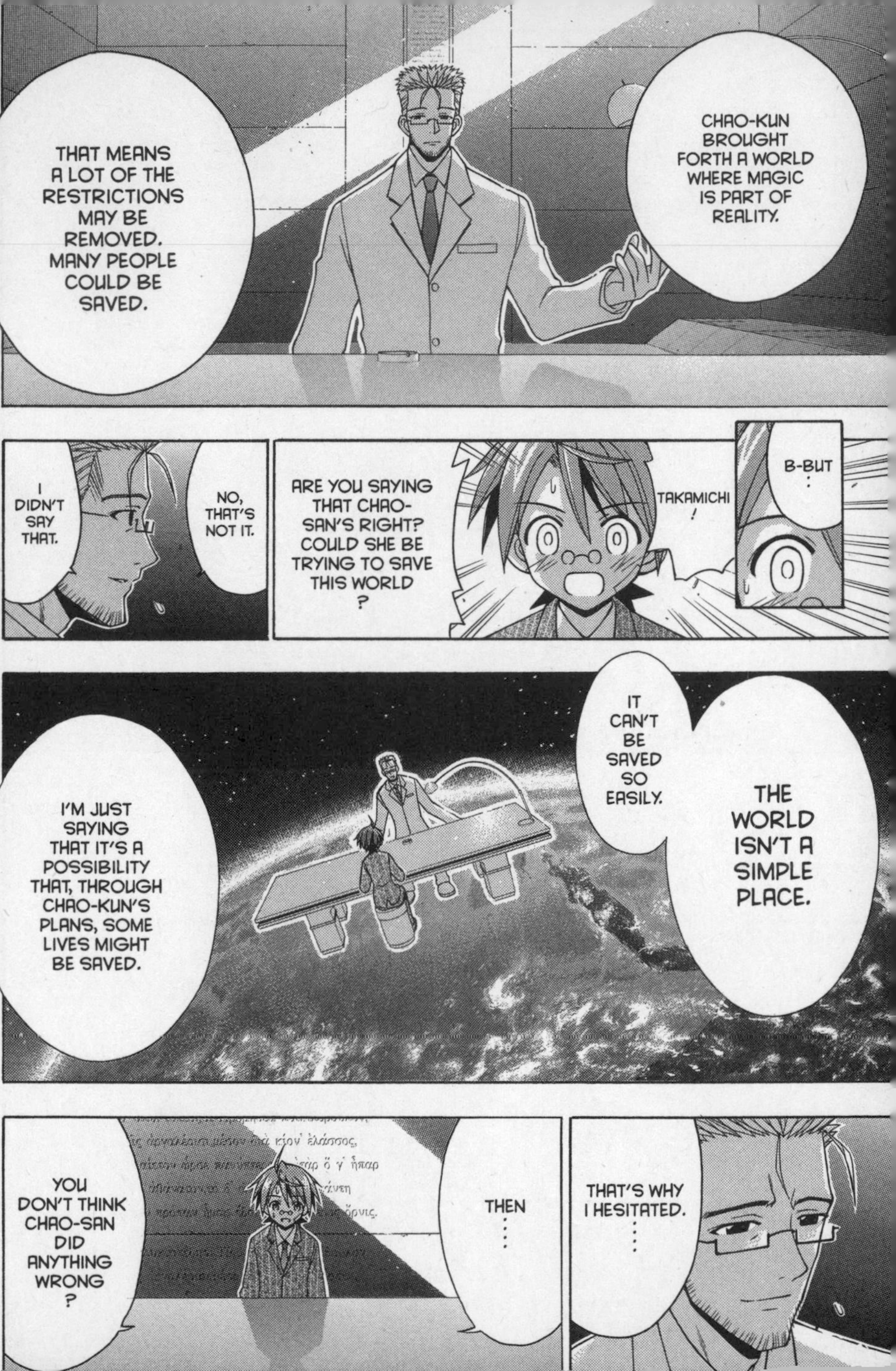
CHAO-KUN BROUGHT FORTH A WORLD WHERE MAGIC IS PART OF REALITY.
THAT MEANS A LOT OF THE RESTRICTIONS MAY BE REMOVED. MANY PEOPLE COULD BE SAVED.
B-BUT...
TAKAMICHI!
ARE YOU SAYING THAT CHAO-SAN'S RIGHT? COULD SHE BE TRYING TO SAVE THIS WORLD?
NO, THAT'S NOT IT.
I DIDN'T SAY THAT.
THE WORLD ISN'T A SIMPLE PLACE.
IT CAN'T BE SAVED SO EASILY.
I'M JUST SAYING THAT IT'S A POSSIBILITY THAT, THROUGH CHAO-KUN'S PLANS, SOME LIVES MIGHT BE SAVED.
THAT'S WHY I HESITATED....
THEN....
YOU DON'T THINK CHAO-SAN DID ANYTHING WRONG?

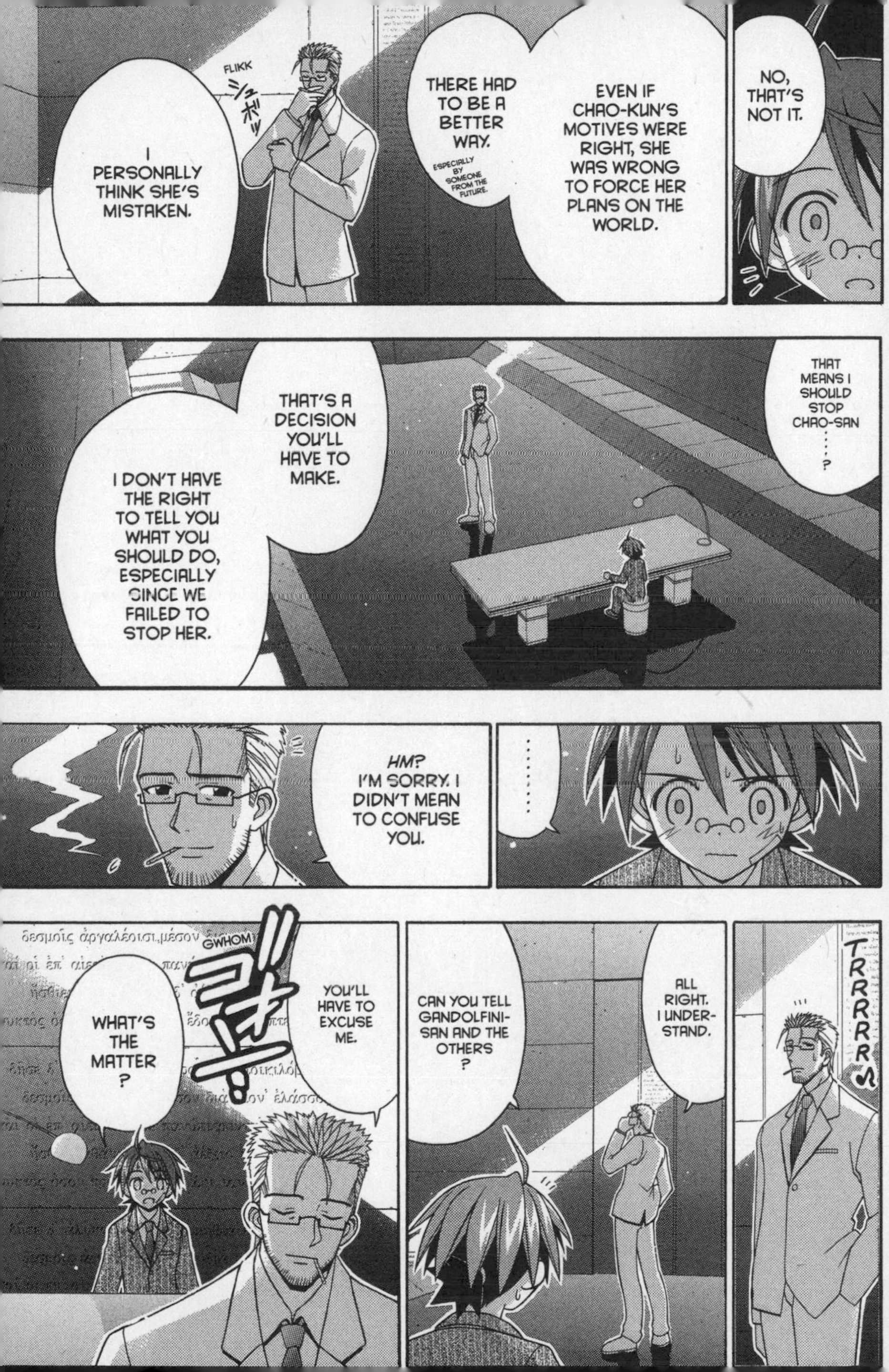
NO, THAT'S NOT IT.
EVEN IF CHAO-KUN'S MOTIVES WERE RIGHT, SHE WAS WRONG TO FORCE HER PLANS ON THE WORLD.
THERE HAD TO BE A BETTER WAY.
ESPECIALLY BY SOMEONE FROM THE FUTURE.
FLIKK
I PERSONALLY THINK SHE'S MISTAKEN.
THAT MEANS I SHOULD STOP CHAO-SAN.....?
THAT'S A DECISION YOU'LL HAVE TO MAKE.
I DON'T HAVE THE RIGHT TO TELL YOU WHAT YOU SHOULD DO, ESPECIALLY SINCE WE FAILED TO STOP HER.
......
HM? I'M SORRY. I DIDN'T MEAN TO CONFUSE YOU.
TRRRR
ALL RIGHT. I UNDERSTAND.
CAN YOU TELL GANDOLFINI-SAN AND THE OTHERS?
YOU'LL HAVE TO EXCUSE ME.
GWHOM
WHAT'S THE MATTER?

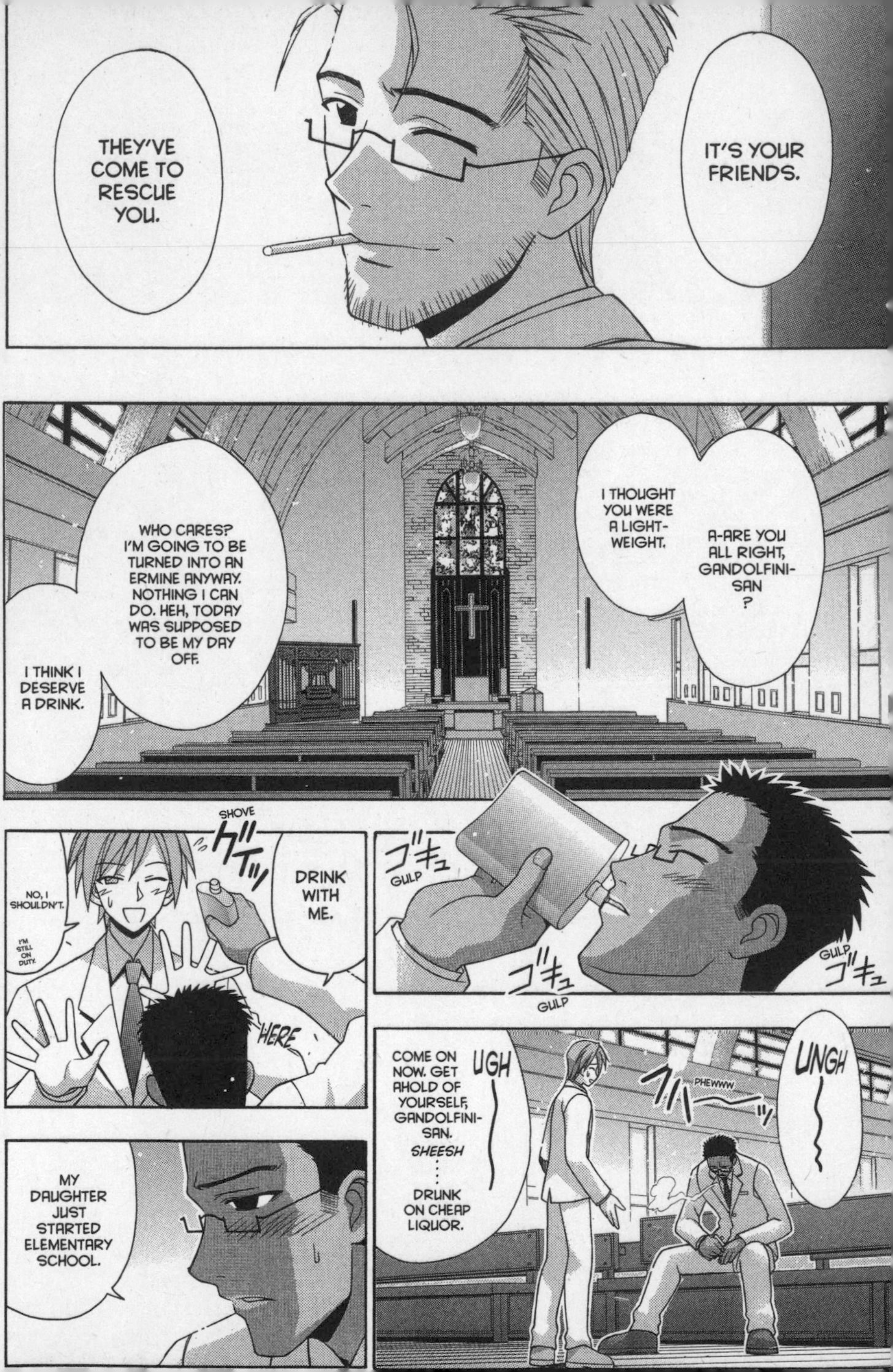
IT'S YOUR FRIENDS.
THEY'VE COME TO RESCUE YOU.
A-ARE YOU ALL RIGHT, GANDOLFINI-SAN ?
I THOUGHT YOU WERE A LIGHT-WEIGHT.
WHO CARES? I'M GOING TO BE TURNED INTO AN ERMINE ANYWAY. NOTHING I CAN DO. HEH, TODAY WAS SUPPOSED TO BE MY DAY OFF.
I THINK I DESERVE A DRINK.
ゴキュ
GULP
ゴキュ
GULP
ゴキュ
GULP
グイッ
SHOVE
DRINK WITH ME.
HERE
NO, I SHOULDN'T.
I'M STILL ON DUTY.
UNGH
ハーッ
PHEWWW
UGH
COME ON NOW. GET AHOLD OF YOURSELF, GANDOLFINI-SAN.
SHEESH
...
DRUNK ON CHEAP LIQUOR.
MY DAUGHTER JUST STARTED ELEMENTARY SCHOOL.

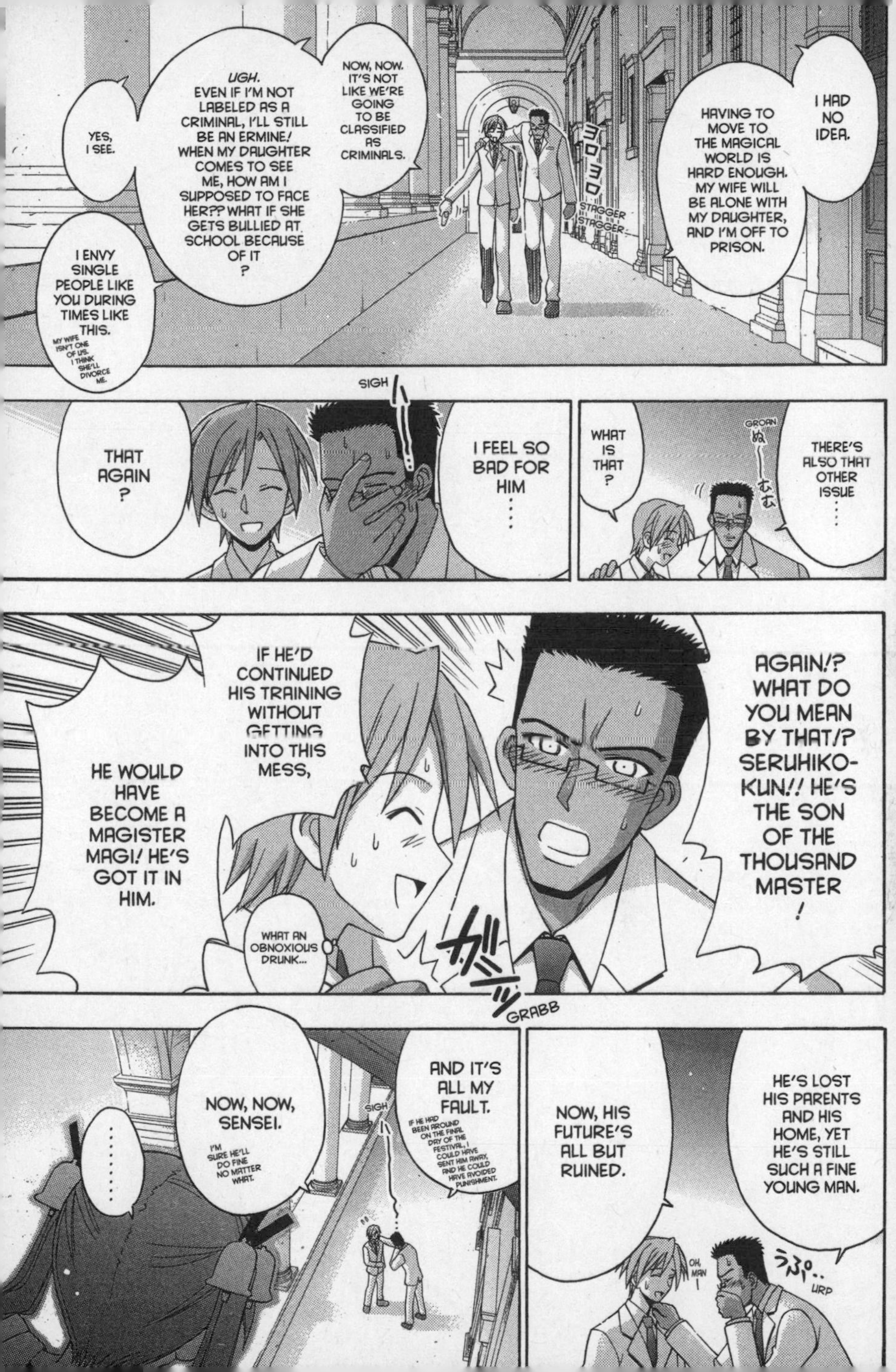

I HAD NO IDEA.
HAVING TO MOVE TO THE MAGICAL WORLD IS HARD ENOUGH. MY WIFE WILL BE ALONE WITH MY DAUGHTER, AND I'M OFF TO PRISON.
ヨロヨロ STAGGER STAGGER
NOW, NOW. IT'S NOT LIKE WE'RE GOING TO BE CLASSIFIED AS CRIMINALS.
UGH. EVEN IF I'M NOT LABELED AS A CRIMINAL, I'LL STILL BE AN ERMINE! WHEN MY DAUGHTER COMES TO SEE ME, HOW AM I SUPPOSED TO FACE HER?? WHAT IF SHE GETS BULLIED AT SCHOOL BECAUSE OF IT?
YES, I SEE.
I ENVY SINGLE PEOPLE LIKE YOU DURING TIMES LIKE THIS.
MY WIFE ISN'T ONE OF US. I THINK SHE'LL DIVORCE ME.
GROAN ぬーむむ
THERE'S ALSO THAT OTHER ISSUE...
WHAT IS THAT?
SIGH
I FEEL SO BAD FOR HIM...
THAT AGAIN?
AGAIN!? WHAT DO YOU MEAN BY THAT!? SERUHIKO-KUN!! HE'S THE SON OF THE THOUSAND MASTER!
IF HE'D CONTINUED HIS TRAINING WITHOUT GETTING INTO THIS MESS,
HE WOULD HAVE BECOME A MAGISTER MAGI! HE'S GOT IT IN HIM.
WHAT AN OBNOXIOUS DRUNK...
ガッ GRABB
HE'S LOST HIS PARENTS AND HIS HOME, YET HE'S STILL SUCH A FINE YOUNG MAN.
NOW, HIS FUTURE'S ALL BUT RUINED.
うぷ.. URP
OH, MAN!
AND IT'S ALL MY FAULT.
SIGH
IF HE HAD BEEN AROUND ON THE FINAL DAY OF THE FESTIVAL, I COULD HAVE SENT HIM AWAY, AND HE COULD HAVE AVOIDED PUNISHMENT.
NOW, NOW, SENSEI.
I'M SURE HE'LL DO FINE NO MATTER WHAT.
......

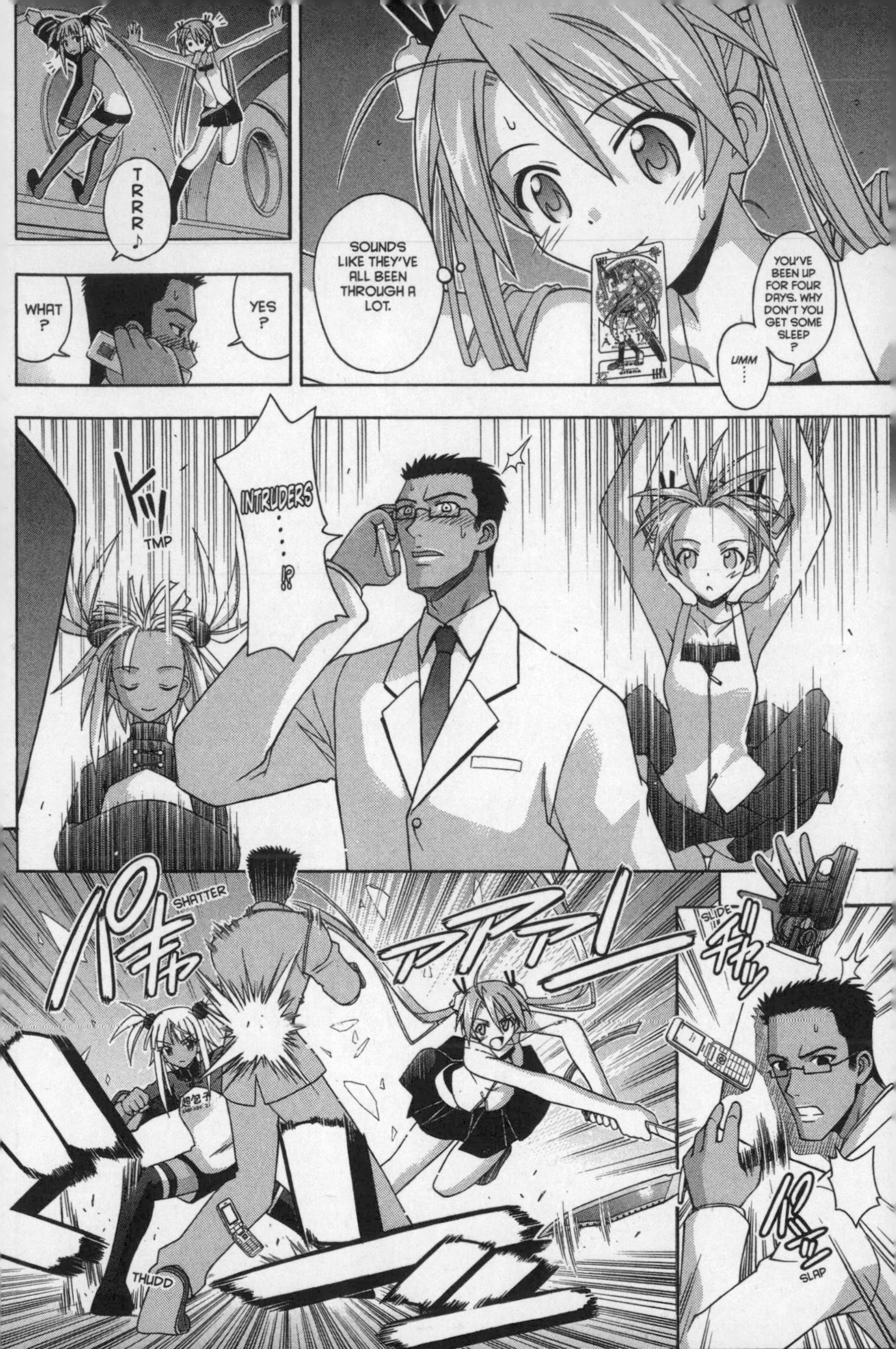
YOU'VE BEEN UP FOR FOUR DAYS. WHY DON'T YOU GET SOME SLEEP?
UMM.....
SOUNDS LIKE THEY'VE ALL BEEN THROUGH A LOT.
TRRR♪
YES?
WHAT?
INTRUDERS.....!?
TMP
SLIDE
SLAP
SHATTER
THUDD

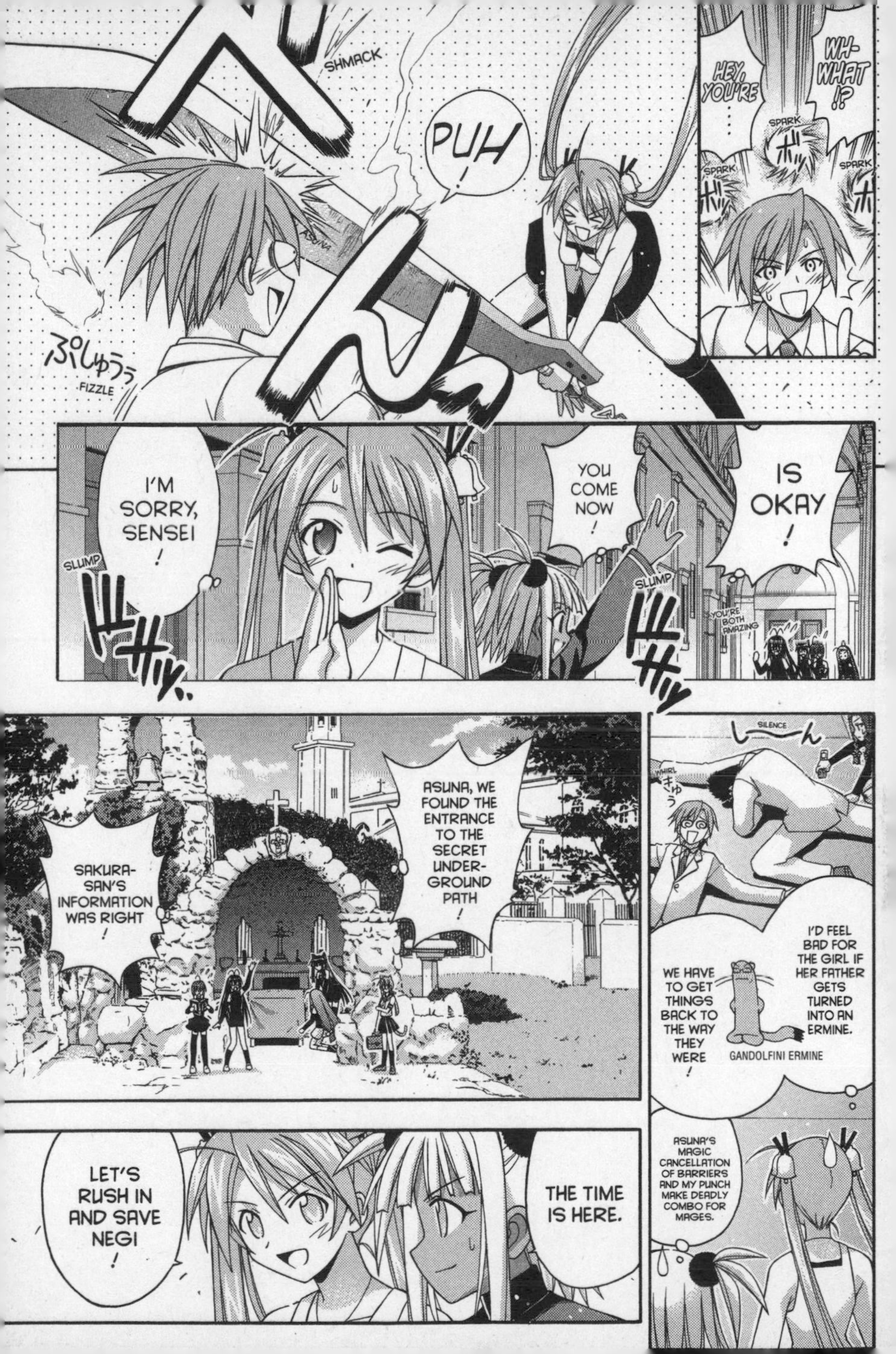
WH-WHAT!?
HEY, YOU'RE...
SPARK
SPARK
SPARK
SHMACK
PUH!
ASUNA
ぷしゅうう
FIZZLE
IS OKAY!
YOU COME NOW!
SLUMP
YOU'RE BOTH AMAZING
I'M SORRY, SENSEI!
SLUMP
SILENCE
しーん
WHIRL
きゅう
I'D FEEL BAD FOR THE GIRL IF HER FATHER GETS TURNED INTO AN ERMINE.
WE HAVE TO GET THINGS BACK TO THE WAY THEY WERE!
GANDOLFINI ERMINE
ASUNA, WE FOUND THE ENTRANCE TO THE SECRET UNDERGROUND PATH!
SAKURA-SAN'S INFORMATION WAS RIGHT!
ASUNA'S MAGIC CANCELLATION OF BARRIERS AND MY PUNCH MAKE DEADLY COMBO FOR MAGES.
THE TIME IS HERE.
LET'S RUSH IN AND SAVE NEGI!

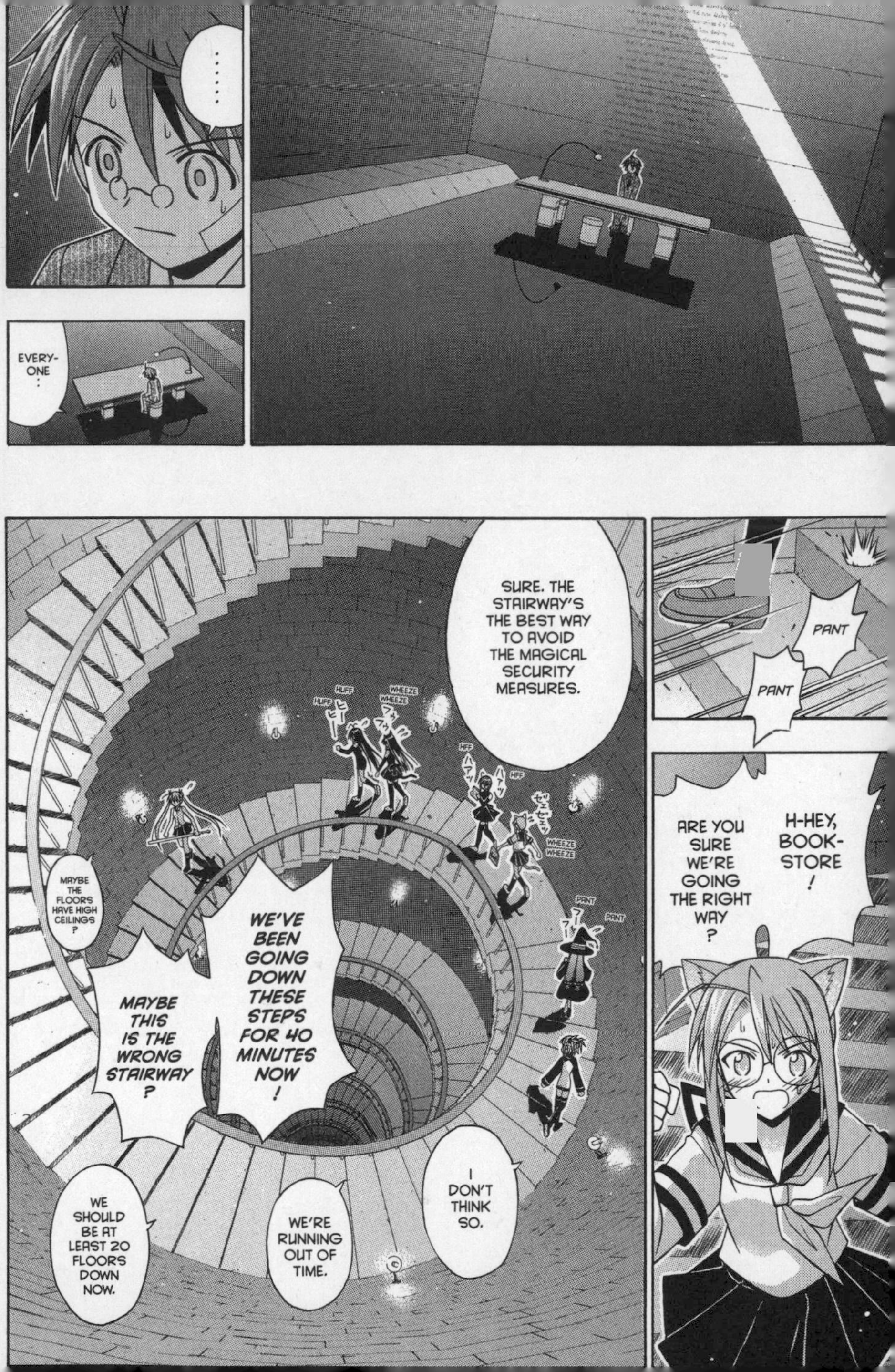
......
EVERY-ONE :
PANT
PANT
H-HEY, BOOK-STORE !
ARE YOU SURE WE'RE GOING THE RIGHT WAY ?
SURE. THE STAIRWAY'S THE BEST WAY TO AVOID THE MAGICAL SECURITY MEASURES.
WHEEZE WHEEZE
HUFF HUFF
HFF HFF
WHEEZE WHEEZE
PANT PANT
WE'VE BEEN GOING DOWN THESE STEPS FOR 40 MINUTES NOW !
MAYBE THIS IS THE WRONG STAIRWAY ?
MAYBE THE FLOORS HAVE HIGH CEILINGS ?
I DON'T THINK SO.
WE'RE RUNNING OUT OF TIME.
WE SHOULD BE AT LEAST 20 FLOORS DOWN NOW.

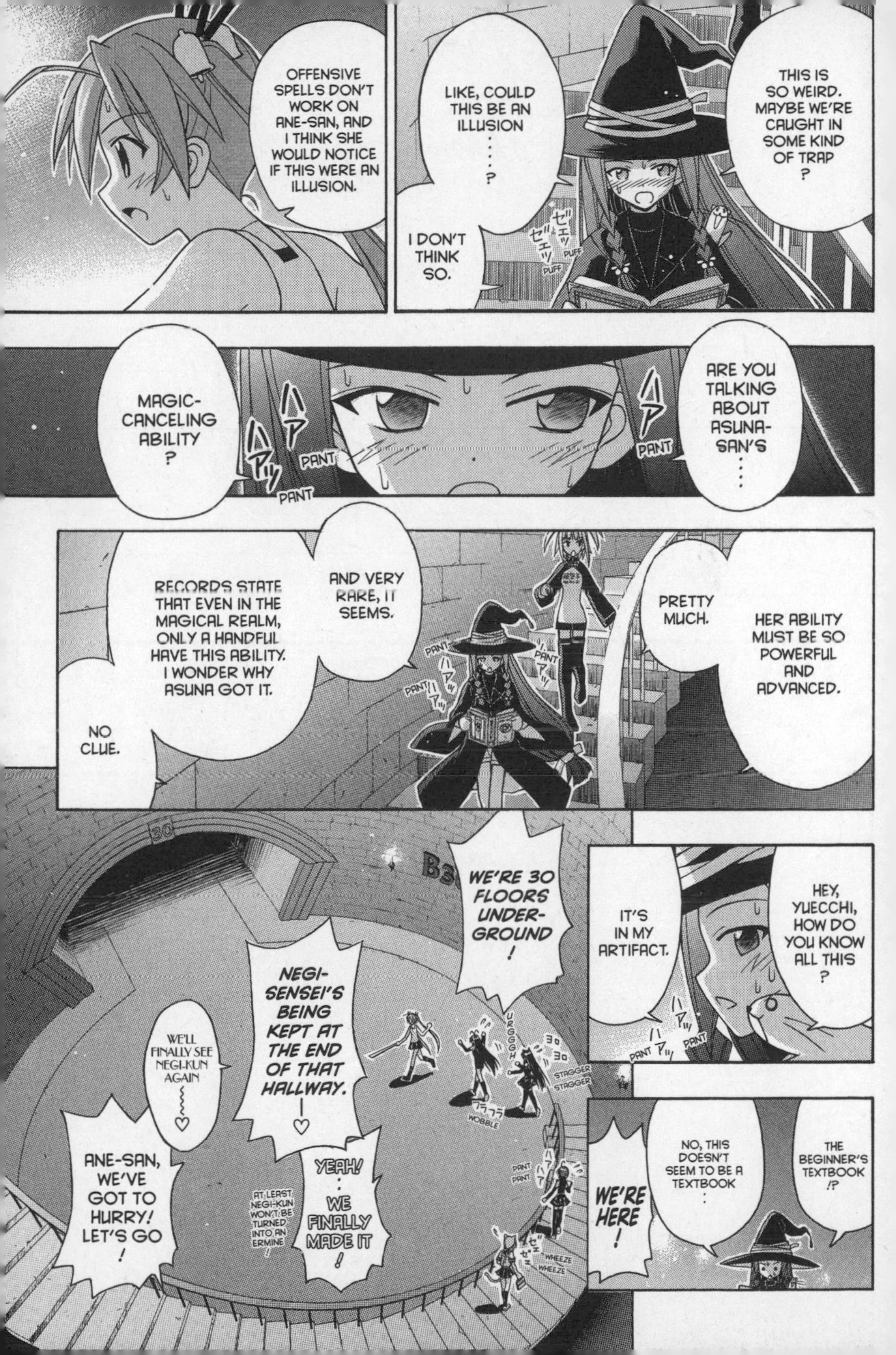
THIS IS SO WEIRD. MAYBE WE'RE CAUGHT IN SOME KIND OF TRAP?
LIKE, COULD THIS BE AN ILLUSION ....?
I DON'T THINK SO.
PUFF PUFF
OFFENSIVE SPELLS DON'T WORK ON ANE-SAN, AND I THINK SHE WOULD NOTICE IF THIS WERE AN ILLUSION.
ARE YOU TALKING ABOUT ASUNA-SAN'S ....
PANT
MAGIC-CANCELING ABILITY?
PANT PANT
HER ABILITY MUST BE SO POWERFUL AND ADVANCED.
PRETTY MUCH.
AND VERY RARE, IT SEEMS.
RECORDS STATE THAT EVEN IN THE MAGICAL REALM, ONLY A HANDFUL HAVE THIS ABILITY. I WONDER WHY ASUNA GOT IT.
NO CLUE.
PANT PANT PANT
HEY, YUECCHI, HOW DO YOU KNOW ALL THIS?
IT'S IN MY ARTIFACT.
PANT PANT
THE BEGINNER'S TEXTBOOK!?
NO, THIS DOESN'T SEEM TO BE A TEXTBOOK :
WE'RE HERE!
WE'RE 30 FLOORS UNDERGROUND!
NEGI-SENSEI'S BEING KEPT AT THE END OF THAT HALLWAY. ♡
URGGGH
STAGGER STAGGER
WOBBLE
WE'LL FINALLY SEE NEGI-KUN AGAIN ♡
YEAH! : WE FINALLY MADE IT!
AT LEAST NEGI-KUN WON'T BE TURNED INTO AN ERMINE!
PANT PANT
WHEEZE WHEEZE
ANE-SAN, WE'VE GOT TO HURRY! LET'S GO!

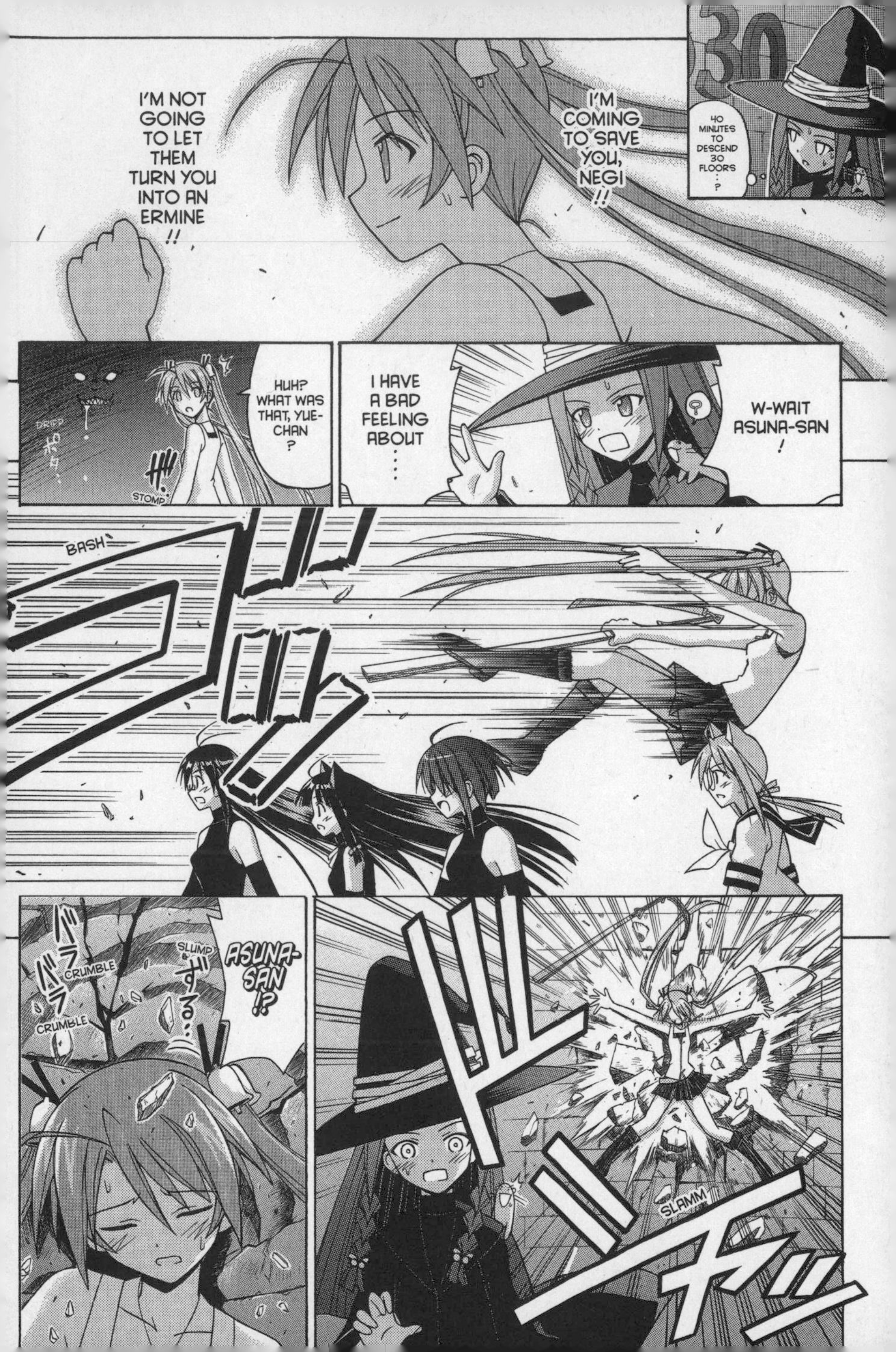
40 MINUTES TO DESCEND 30 FLOORS...?
I'M COMING TO SAVE YOU, NEGI!!
I'M NOT GOING TO LET THEM TURN YOU INTO AN ERMINE!!
W-WAIT ASUNA-SAN!
I HAVE A BAD FEELING ABOUT....
HUH? WHAT WAS THAT, YUE-CHAN?
DRIP
STOMP
BASH
SLAMM
ASUNA-SAN!?
SLUMP
CRUMBLE
CRUMBLE

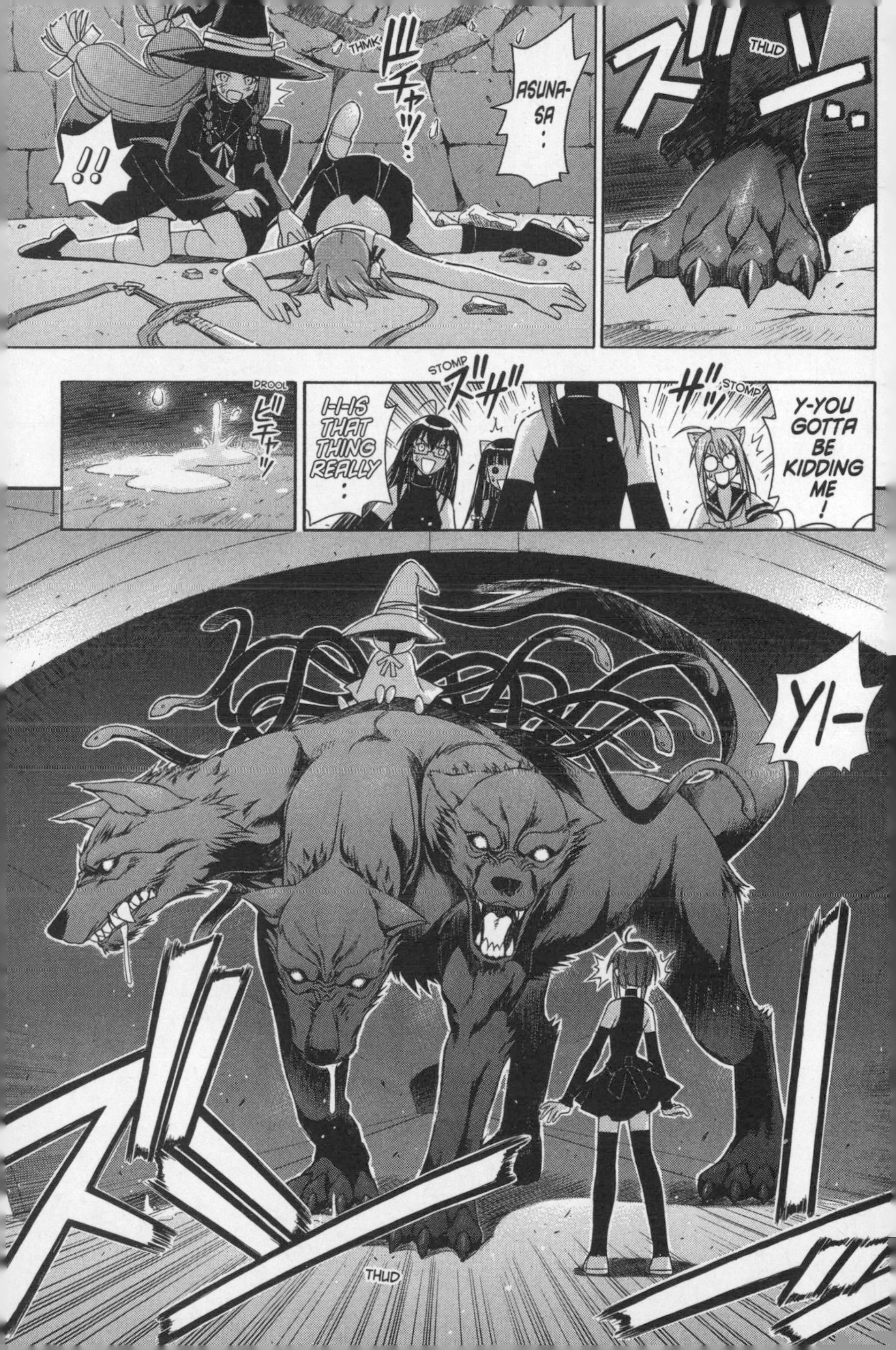
THUD
ASUNA-SA...
THMK
!!
Y-YOU GOTTA BE KIDDING ME!
STOMP
STOMP
I-I-IS THAT THING REALLY...
DROOL
YI-
THUD

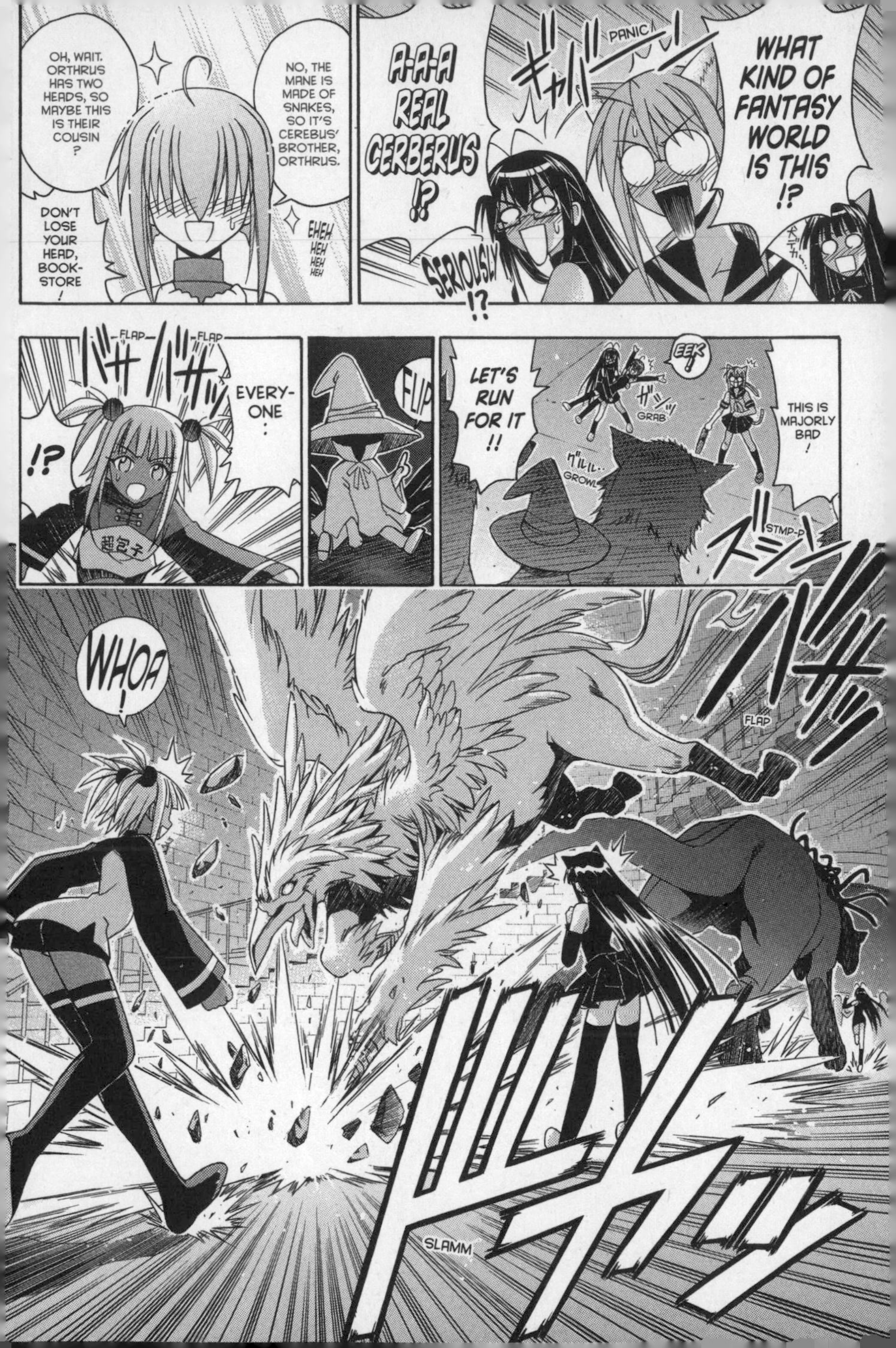
WHAT KIND OF FANTASY WORLD IS THIS!?
PANIC
A-A-A REAL CERBERUS!?
SERIOUSLY!?
NO, THE MANE IS MADE OF SNAKES, SO IT'S CEREBUS' BROTHER, ORTHRUS.
OH, WAIT. ORTHRUS HAS TWO HEADS, SO MAYBE THIS IS THEIR COUSIN?
EHEH HEH HEH HEH
DON'T LOSE YOUR HEAD, BOOK-STORE!
THIS IS MAJORLY BAD!
EEK!
GRAB
LET'S RUN FOR IT!!
GROWL
STMP-P
FLIP
FLAP
FLAP
EVERY-ONE:
!?
FLAP
WHOA!
SLAMM

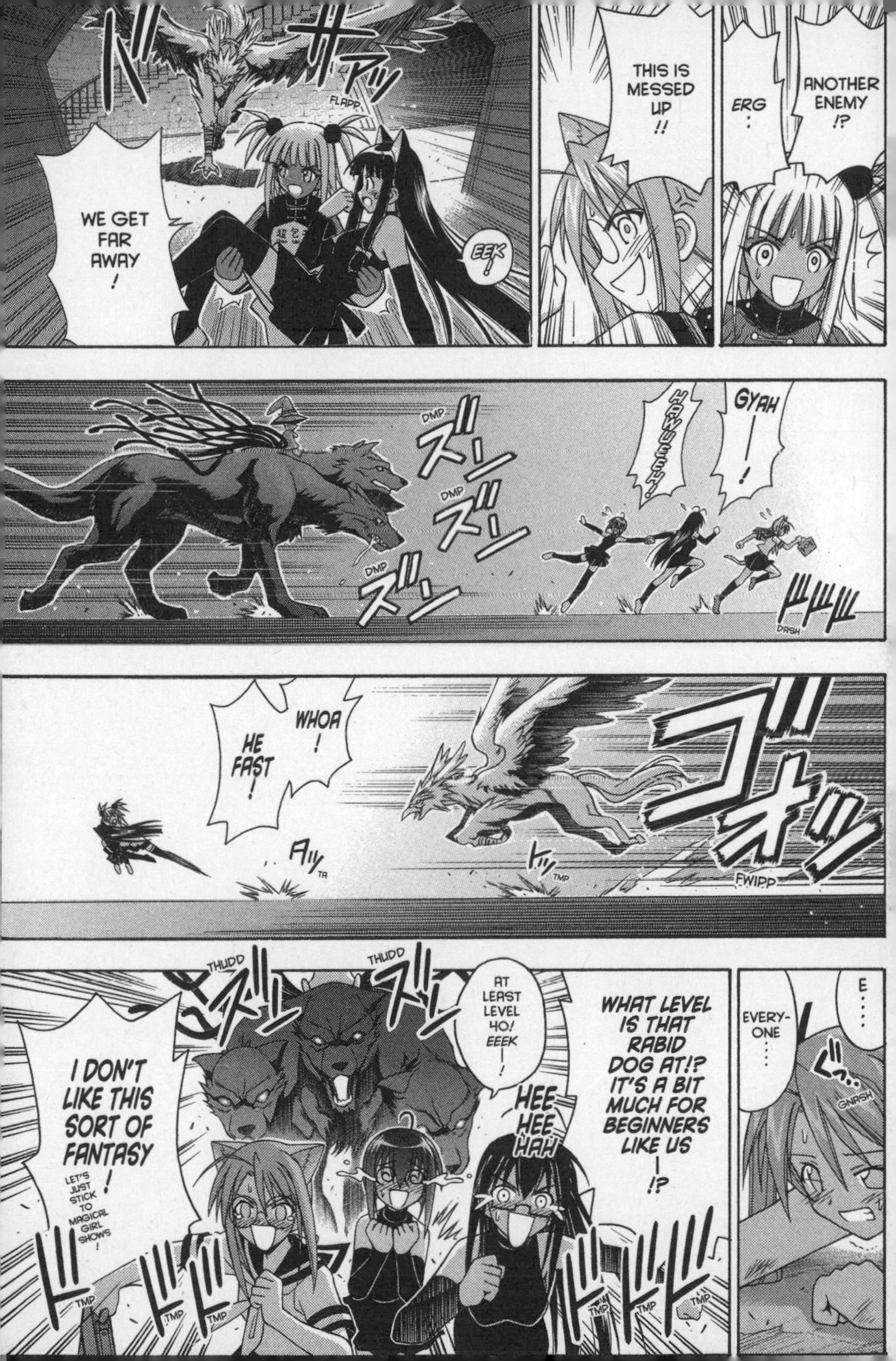

ANOTHER ENEMY !?
ERG :
THIS IS MESSED UP !!
FLAPP
EEK !
WE GET FAR AWAY !
GYAH — !
HAWUEEEH!
DMP
DMP
DMP
DASH
FWIPP
TMP
WHOA !
HE FAST !
TA
E....
EVERY-ONE .....
GNASH
WHAT LEVEL IS THAT RABID DOG AT!? IT'S A BIT MUCH FOR BEGINNERS LIKE US —!?
AT LEAST LEVEL 40! EEEK —!
THUDD
THUDD
HEE HEE HAH
I DON'T LIKE THIS SORT OF FANTASY !
LET'S JUST STICK TO MAGICAL GIRL SHOWS !
TMP
TMP
TMP
TMP
TMP
TMP

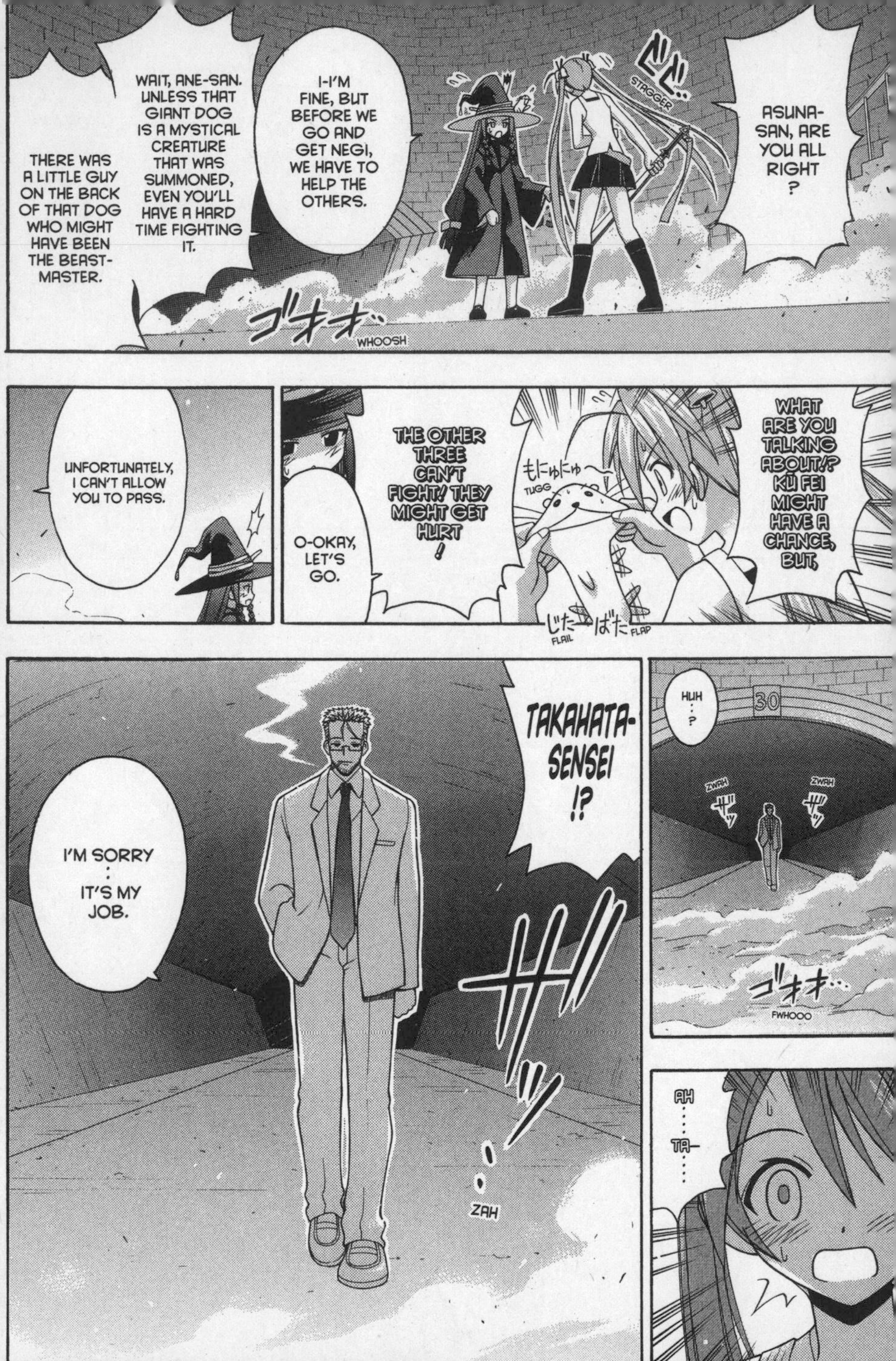
ASUNA-SAN, ARE YOU ALL RIGHT?
STAGGER
I-I'M FINE, BUT BEFORE WE GO AND GET NEGI, WE HAVE TO HELP THE OTHERS.
WAIT, ANE-SAN. UNLESS THAT GIANT DOG IS A MYSTICAL CREATURE THAT WAS SUMMONED, EVEN YOU'LL HAVE A HARD TIME FIGHTING IT.
THERE WAS A LITTLE GUY ON THE BACK OF THAT DOG WHO MIGHT HAVE BEEN THE BEAST-MASTER.
ゴオオ
WHOOSH
WHAT ARE YOU TALKING ABOUT!? KŪ FEI MIGHT HAVE A CHANCE, BUT,
もにゅにゅ〜
TUGG
THE OTHER THREE CAN'T FIGHT! THEY MIGHT GET HURT!
O-OKAY, LET'S GO.
じた ばた
FLAIL FLAP
UNFORTUNATELY, I CAN'T ALLOW YOU TO PASS.
HUH...?
30
ZWAH
ZWAH
ゴオオ…
FWHOOO
AH... TA—...
TAKAHATA-SENSEI!?
I'M SORRY: IT'S MY JOB.
ZAH

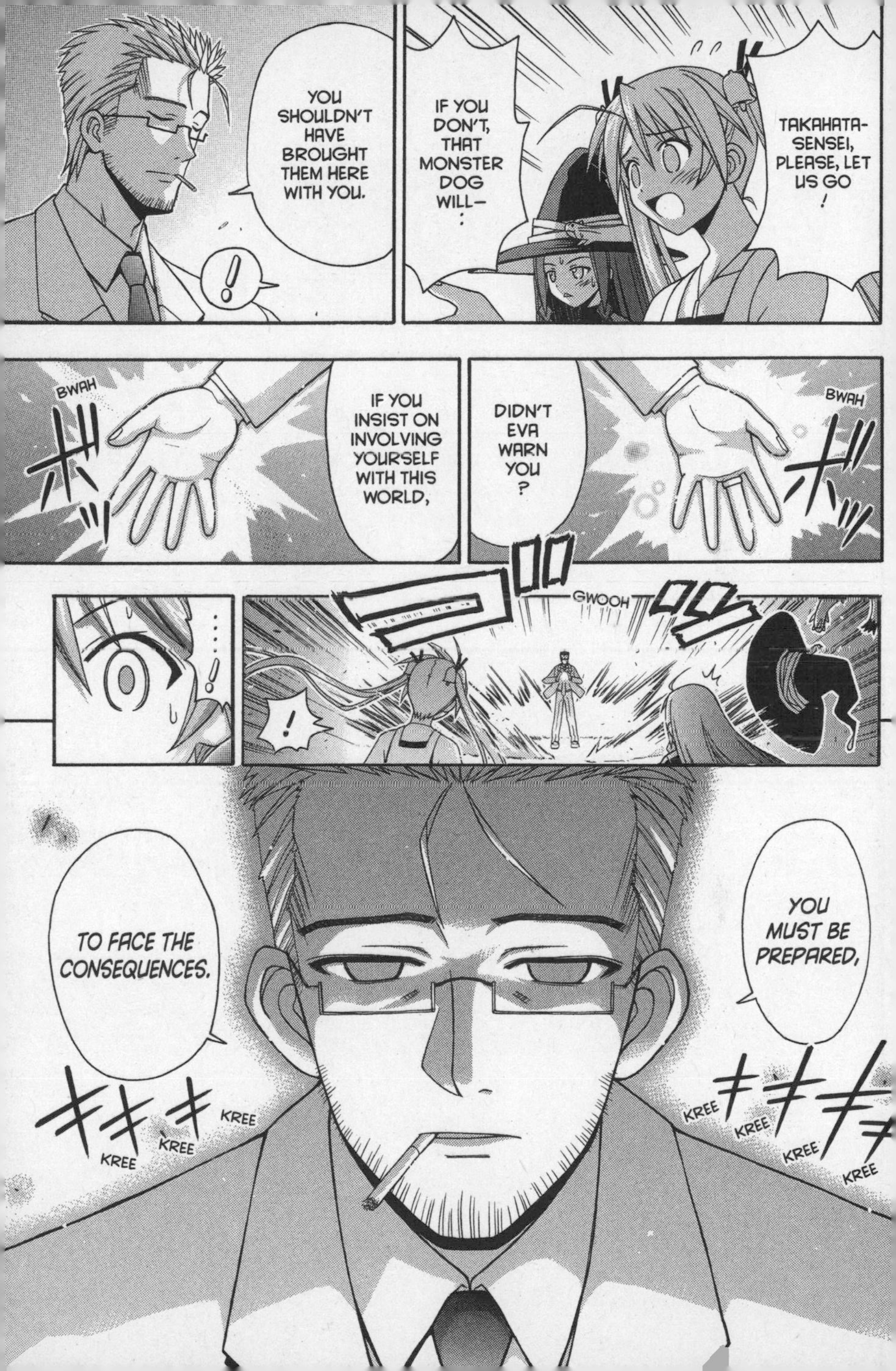
TAKAHATA-SENSEI, PLEASE, LET US GO!
IF YOU DON'T, THAT MONSTER DOG WILL—:
YOU SHOULDN'T HAVE BROUGHT THEM HERE WITH YOU.
!
BWAH
DIDN'T EVA WARN YOU?
IF YOU INSIST ON INVOLVING YOURSELF WITH THIS WORLD,
BWAH
GWOOH
!
......!
YOU MUST BE PREPARED,
KREE KREE KREE KREE
TO FACE THE CONSEQUENCES.
KREE KREE KREE

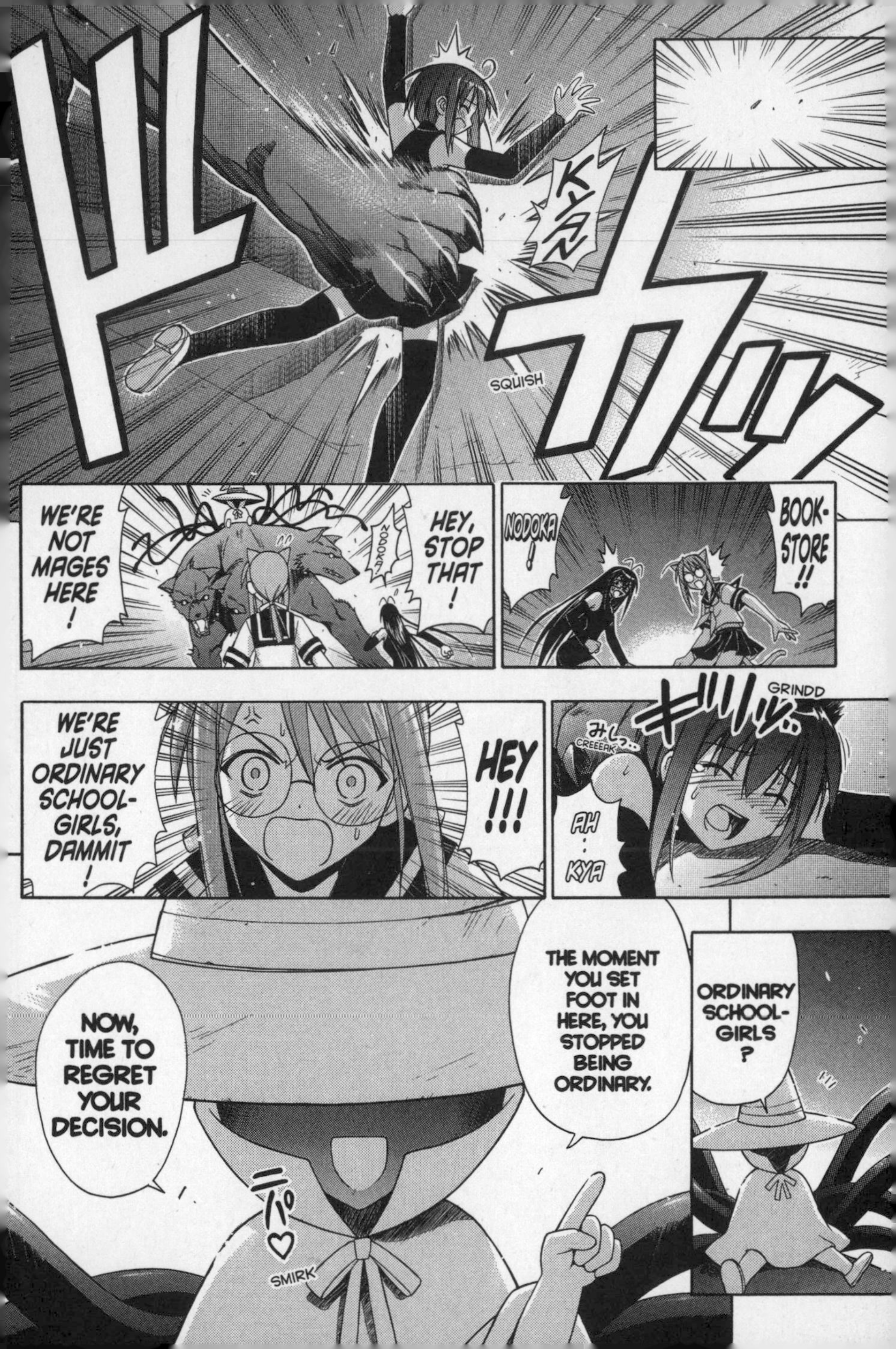

KYAN
SQUISH
BOOK-STORE!!
NODOKA!
HEY, STOP THAT!
NODOKA!
WE'RE NOT MAGES HERE!
GRINDD
みしっ...
CREEEAK
AH... KYA
HEY!!!
WE'RE JUST ORDINARY SCHOOL-GIRLS, DAMMIT!
ORDINARY SCHOOL-GIRLS?
THE MOMENT YOU SET FOOT IN HERE, YOU STOPPED BEING ORDINARY.
NOW, TIME TO REGRET YOUR DECISION.
SMIRK

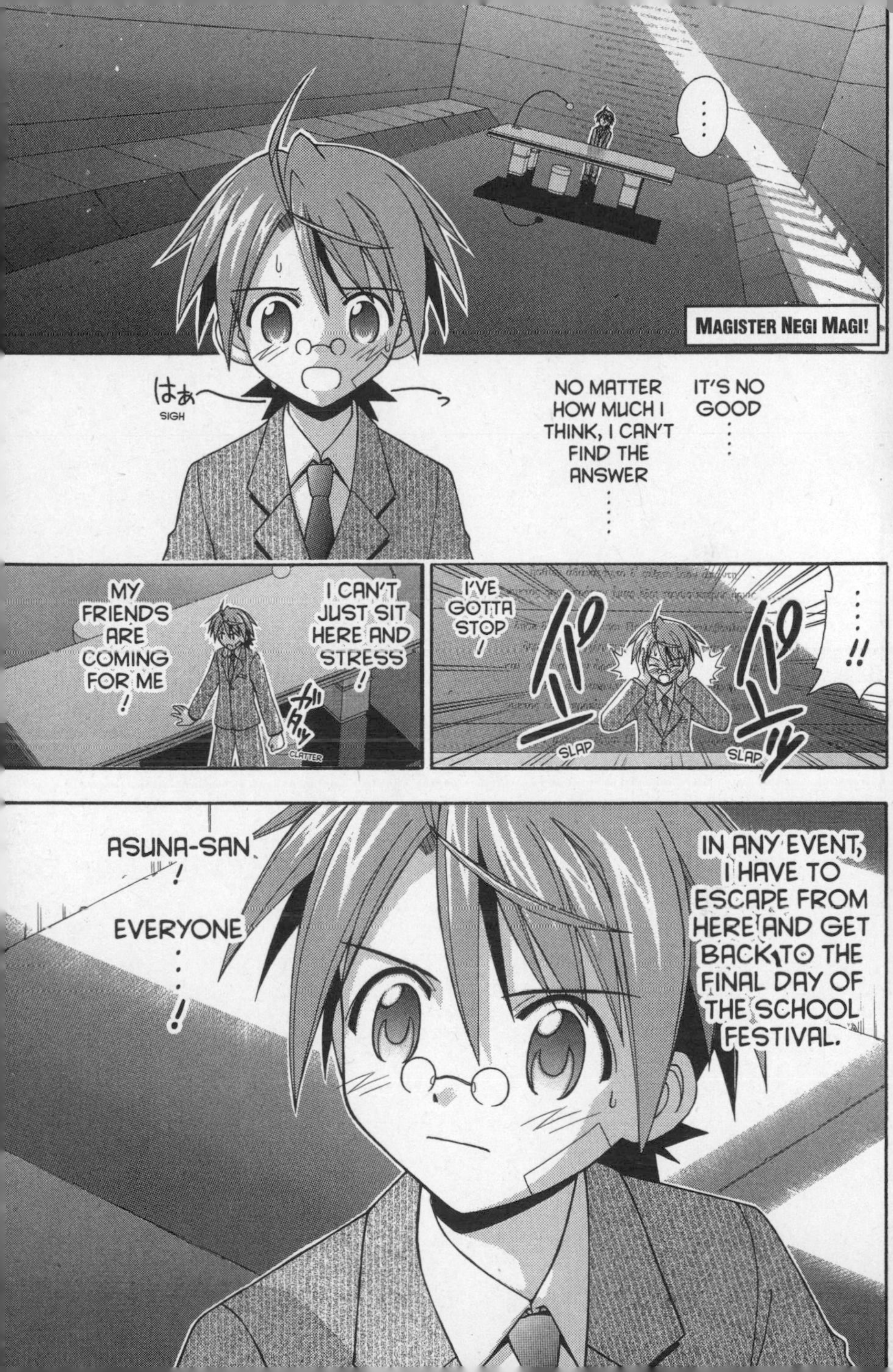
...
MAGISTER NEGI MAGI!
IT'S NO GOOD ...
NO MATTER HOW MUCH I THINK, I CAN'T FIND THE ANSWER ...
はぁ
SIGH
...!!
SLAP
SLAP
I'VE GOTTA STOP!
I CAN'T JUST SIT HERE AND STRESS!
MY FRIENDS ARE COMING FOR ME!
CLATTER
IN ANY EVENT, I HAVE TO ESCAPE FROM HERE AND GET BACK TO THE FINAL DAY OF THE SCHOOL FESTIVAL.
ASUNA-SAN!
EVERYONE ...!

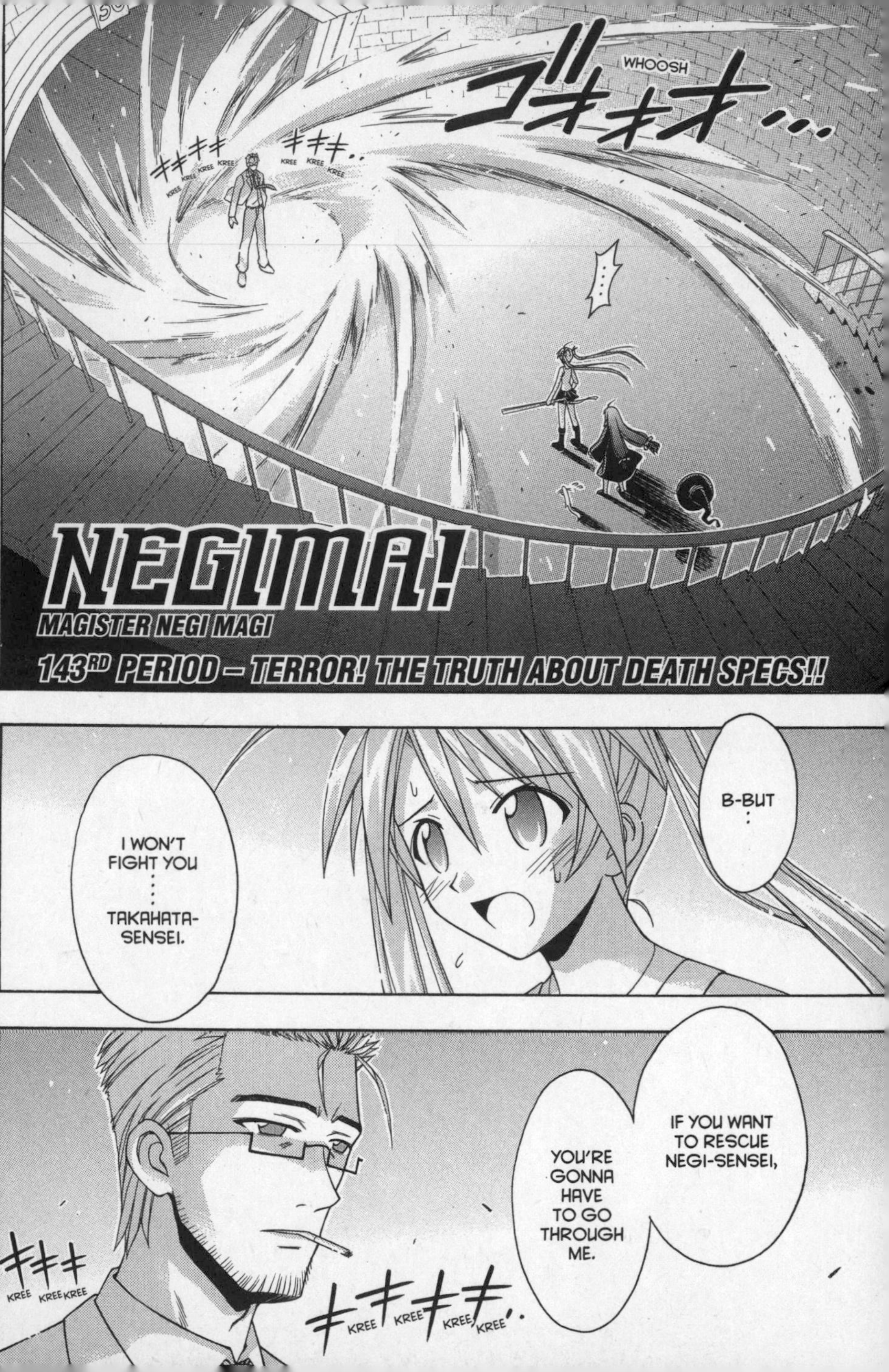
WHOOSH
KREE KREE KREE
KREE KREE KREE
NEGIMA!
MAGISTER NEGI MAGI
143RD PERIOD – TERROR! THE TRUTH ABOUT DEATH SPECS!!
B-BUT...
I WON'T FIGHT YOU... TAKAHATA-SENSEI.
IF YOU WANT TO RESCUE NEGI-SENSEI,
YOU'RE GONNA HAVE TO GO THROUGH ME.
KREE KREE KREE
KREE KREE KREE KREE

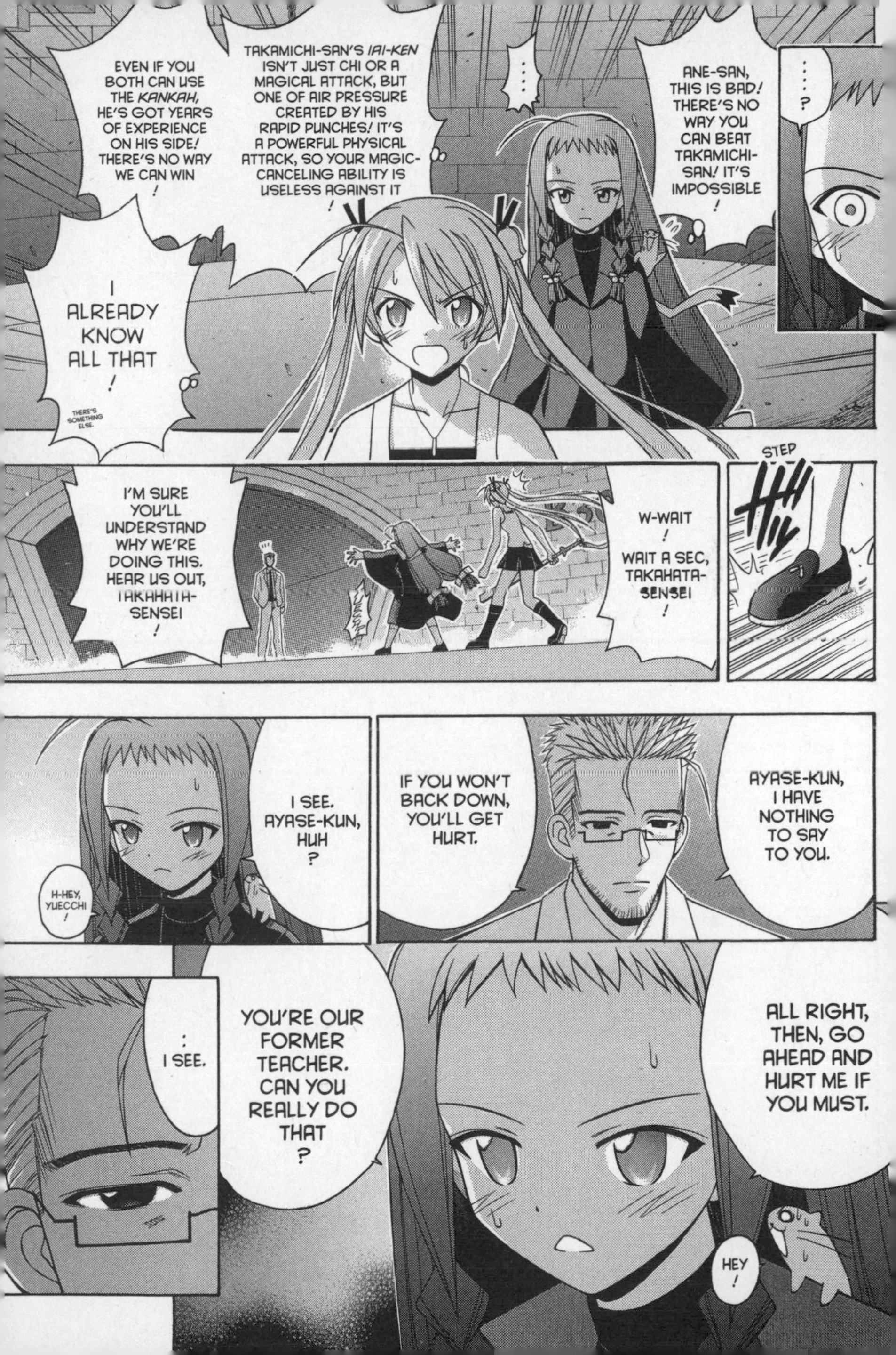
...?
ANE-SAN, THIS IS BAD! THERE'S NO WAY YOU CAN BEAT TAKAMICHI-SAN! IT'S IMPOSSIBLE!
...!
TAKAMICHI-SAN'S *IAI-KEN* ISN'T JUST CHI OR A MAGICAL ATTACK, BUT ONE OF AIR PRESSURE CREATED BY HIS RAPID PUNCHES! IT'S A POWERFUL PHYSICAL ATTACK, SO YOUR MAGIC-CANCELING ABILITY IS USELESS AGAINST IT!
EVEN IF YOU BOTH CAN USE THE *KANKAH*, HE'S GOT YEARS OF EXPERIENCE ON HIS SIDE! THERE'S NO WAY WE CAN WIN!
I ALREADY KNOW ALL THAT!
THERE'S SOMETHING ELSE.
STEP
W-WAIT! WAIT A SEC, TAKAHATA-SENSEI!
I'M SURE YOU'LL UNDERSTAND WHY WE'RE DOING THIS. HEAR US OUT, TAKAHATA-SENSEI!
AYASE-KUN, I HAVE NOTHING TO SAY TO YOU.
IF YOU WON'T BACK DOWN, YOU'LL GET HURT.
I SEE. AYASE-KUN, HUH?
H-HEY, YUECCHI!
ALL RIGHT, THEN, GO AHEAD AND HURT ME IF YOU MUST.
HEY!
YOU'RE OUR FORMER TEACHER. CAN YOU REALLY DO THAT?
: I SEE.

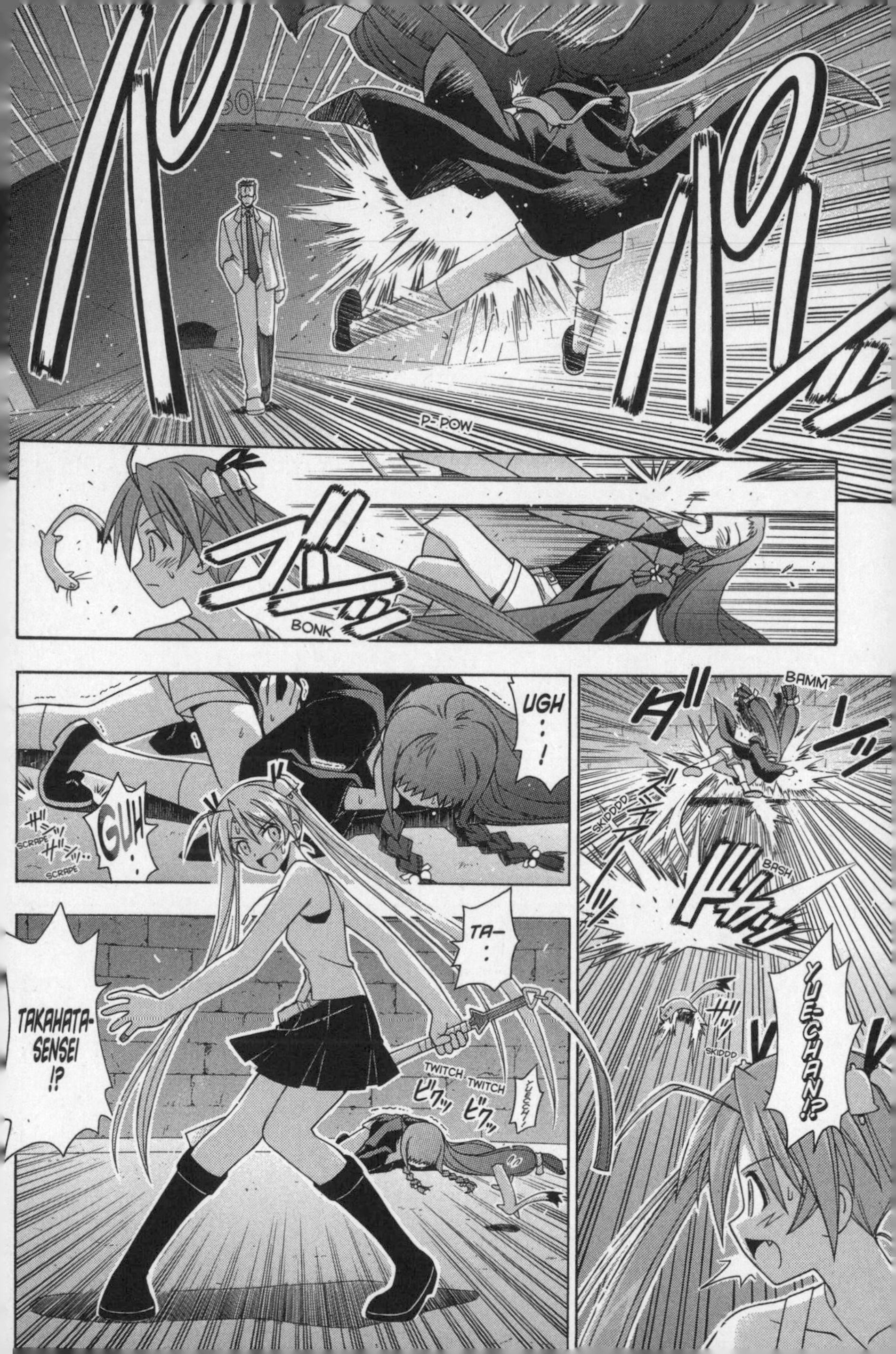
P-POW
BONK
BAMM
SKIDDD
BASH
YUE-CHAN!?
SKIDDD
UGH...!
GUH
SCRAPE
SCRAPE
TA-...
TAKAHATA-SENSEI!?
TWITCH TWITCH

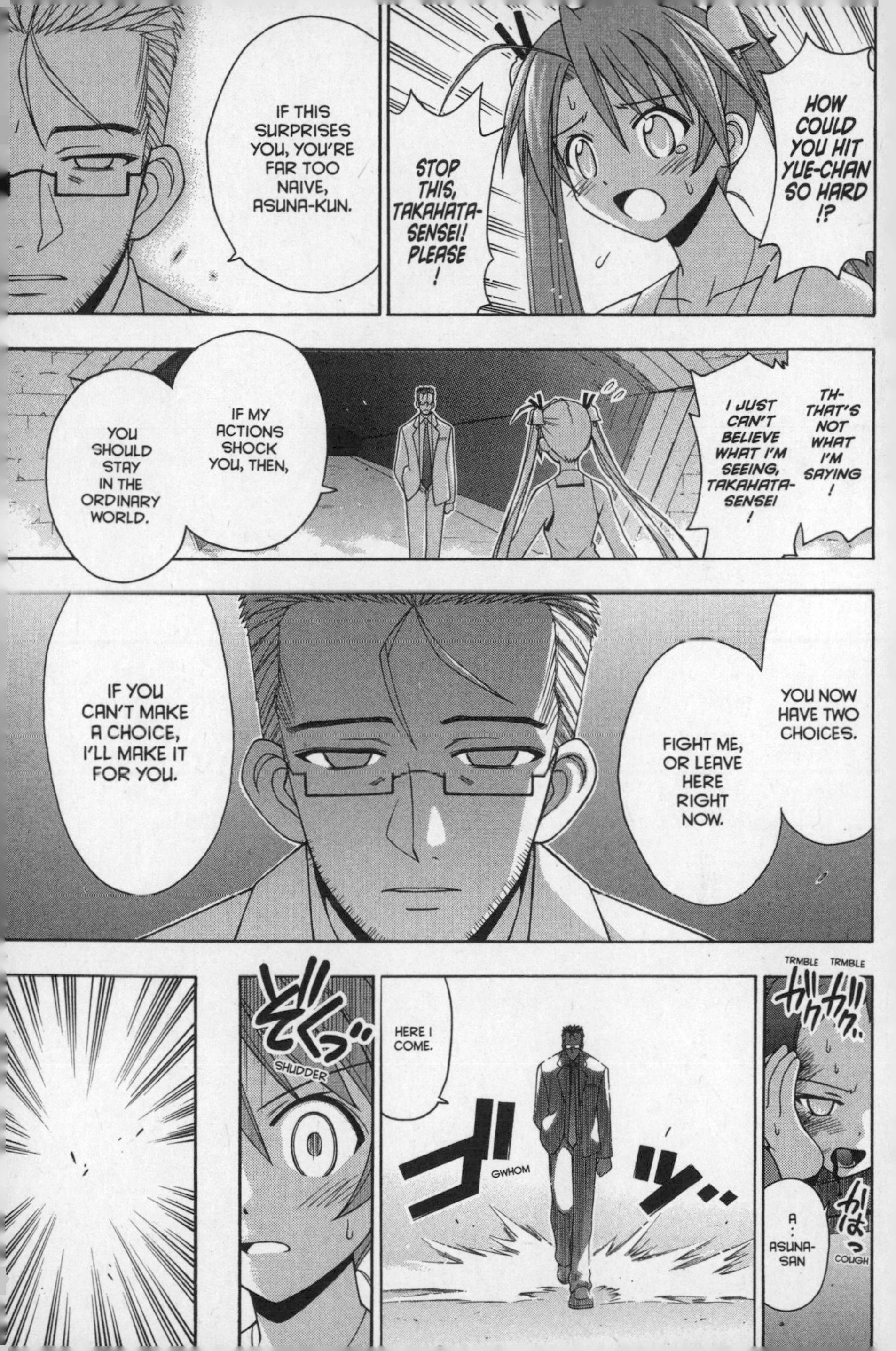
HOW COULD YOU HIT YUE-CHAN SO HARD!?
STOP THIS, TAKAHATA-SENSEI! PLEASE!
IF THIS SURPRISES YOU, YOU'RE FAR TOO NAIVE, ASUNA-KUN.
TH-THAT'S NOT WHAT I'M SAYING!
I JUST CAN'T BELIEVE WHAT I'M SEEING, TAKAHATA-SENSEI!
IF MY ACTIONS SHOCK YOU, THEN,
YOU SHOULD STAY IN THE ORDINARY WORLD.
YOU NOW HAVE TWO CHOICES.
FIGHT ME, OR LEAVE HERE RIGHT NOW.
IF YOU CAN'T MAKE A CHOICE, I'LL MAKE IT FOR YOU.
TRMBLE TRMBLE
COUGH
A... ASUNA-SAN
HERE I COME.
GWHOM
SHUDDER

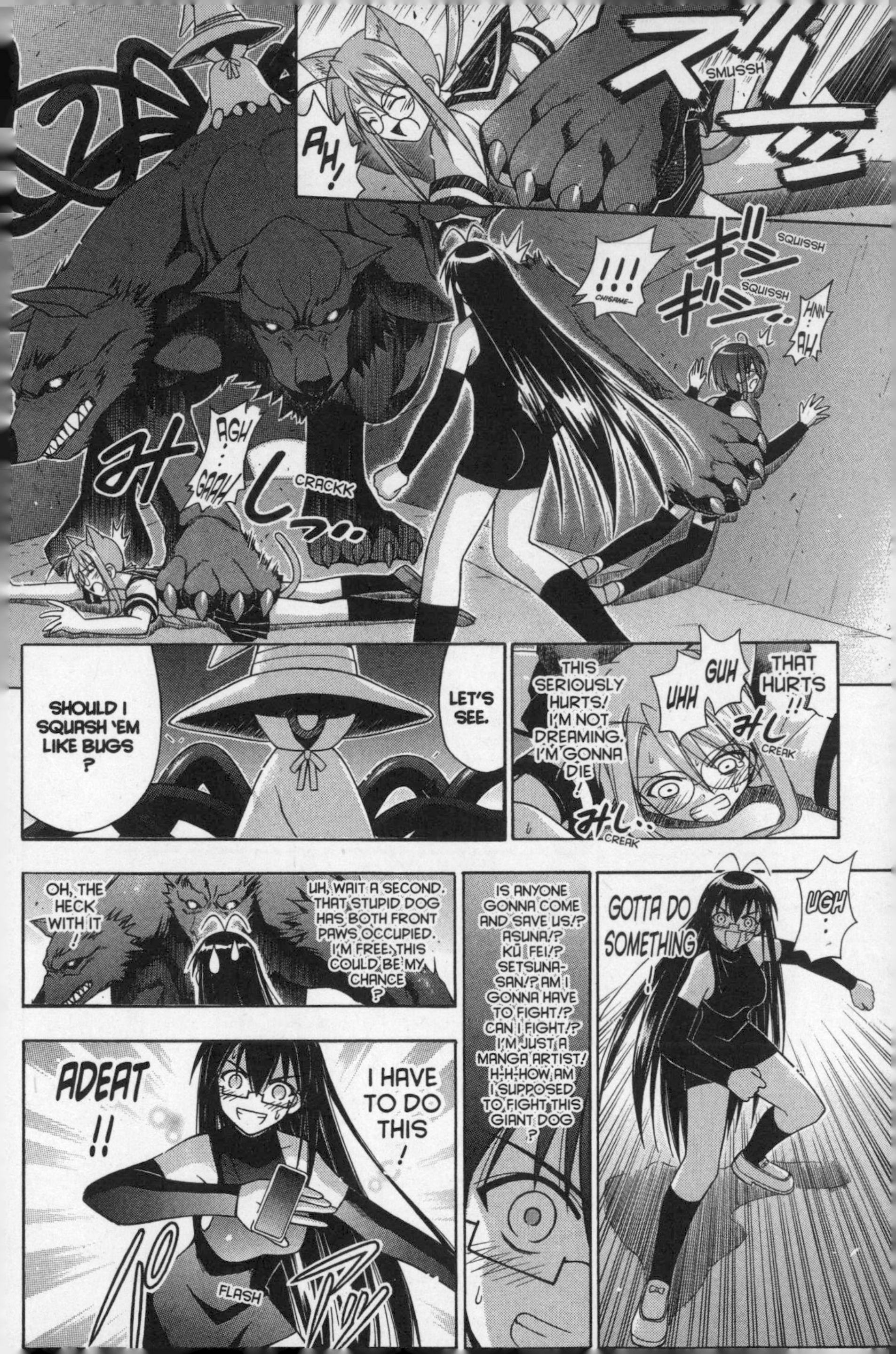
SMUSSH
AH!
!!!
CHISAME—
SQUISSH
SQUISSH
HNN... AH!
AGH... GAAH
CRACKK
THAT HURTS!!
GUH
UHH
THIS SERIOUSLY HURTS! I'M NOT DREAMING. I'M GONNA DIE!
CREAK
CREAK
LET'S SEE.
SHOULD I SQUASH 'EM LIKE BUGS?
UGH...
GOTTA DO SOMETHING!
IS ANYONE GONNA COME AND SAVE US!? ASUNA!? KŪ FEI!? SETSUNA-SAN!? AM I GONNA HAVE TO FIGHT!? CAN I FIGHT!? I'M JUST A MANGA ARTIST! H-H-HOW AM I SUPPOSED TO FIGHT THIS GIANT DOG?
UH, WAIT A SECOND. THAT STUPID DOG HAS BOTH FRONT PAWS OCCUPIED. I'M FREE. THIS COULD BE MY CHANCE?
OH, THE HECK WITH IT!
I HAVE TO DO THIS!
ADEAT!!
FLASH

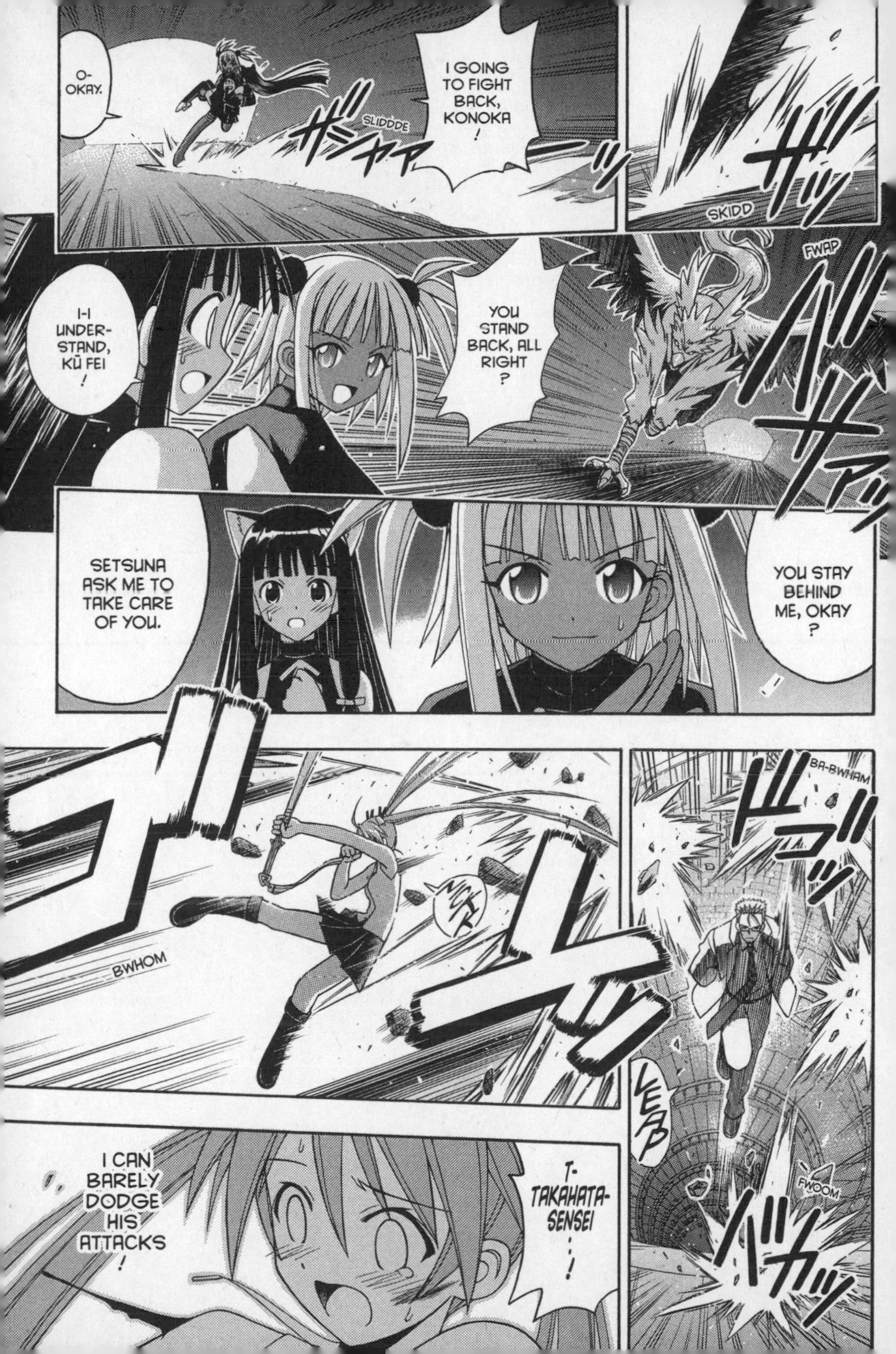
SKIDD
I GOING TO FIGHT BACK, KONOKA!
SLIDDDE
O-OKAY.
FWAP
YOU STAND BACK, ALL RIGHT?
I-I UNDER-STAND, KŪ FEI!
YOU STAY BEHIND ME, OKAY?
SETSUNA ASK ME TO TAKE CARE OF YOU.
BA-BWHAM
LEAP
FWOOM
NICK
BWHOM
T-TAKAHATA-SENSEI...!
I CAN BARELY DODGE HIS ATTACKS!

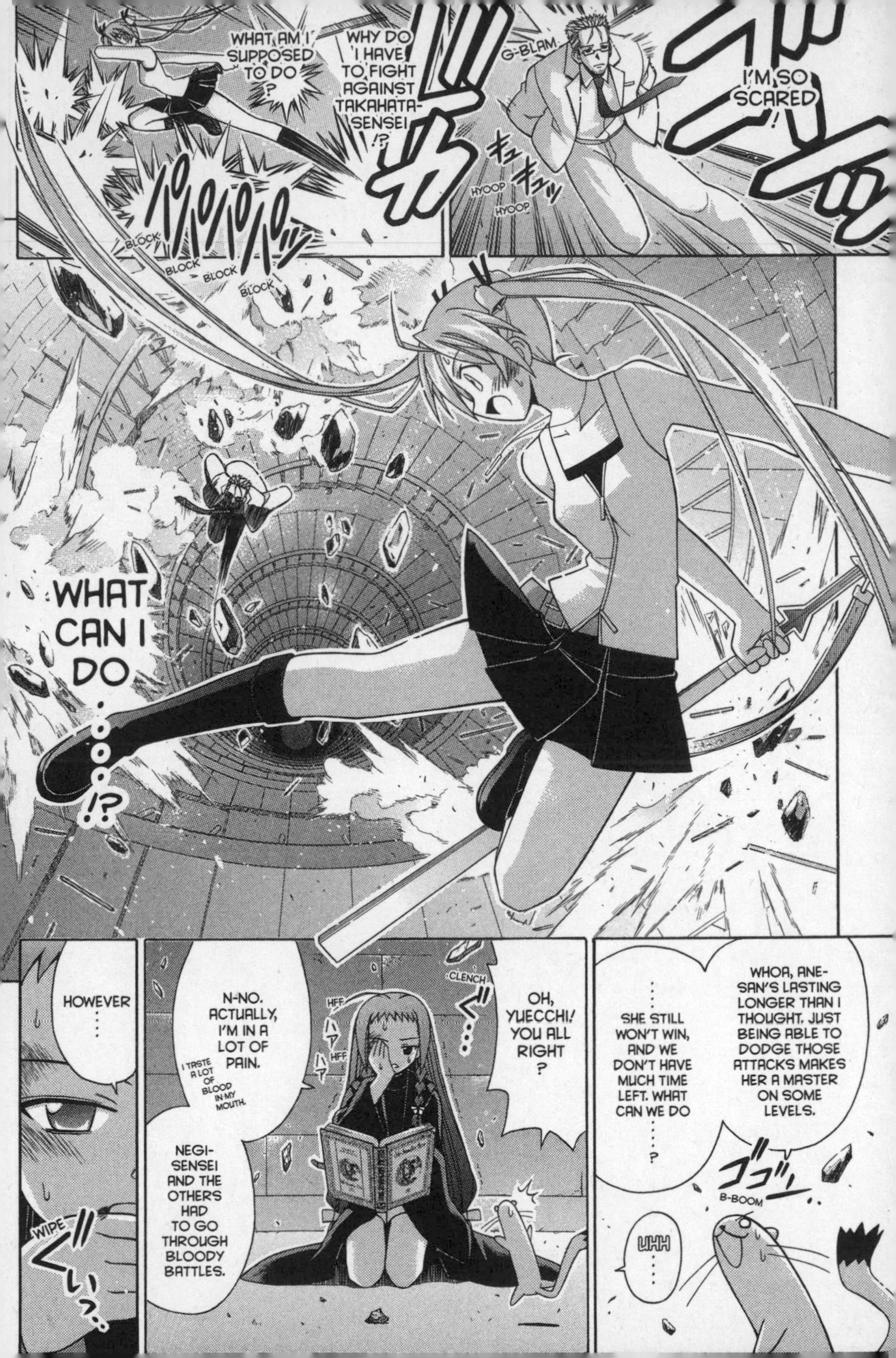
I'M SO SCARED!
G-BLAM
HYOOP
HYOOP
WHY DO I HAVE TO FIGHT AGAINST TAKAHATA-SENSEI!?
WHAT AM I SUPPOSED TO DO?
BLOCK
BLOCK
BLOCK
BLOCK
WHAT CAN I DO......!?
WHOA, ANE-SAN'S LASTING LONGER THAN I THOUGHT. JUST BEING ABLE TO DODGE THOSE ATTACKS MAKES HER A MASTER ON SOME LEVELS.
...SHE STILL WON'T WIN, AND WE DON'T HAVE MUCH TIME LEFT. WHAT CAN WE DO.....?
B-BOOM
UHH.....
CLENCH
OH, YUECCHI! YOU ALL RIGHT?
HFF
HFF
N-NO. ACTUALLY, I'M IN A LOT OF PAIN.
I TASTE A LOT OF BLOOD IN MY MOUTH.
NEGI-SENSEI AND THE OTHERS HAD TO GO THROUGH BLOODY BATTLES.
HOWEVER.....
WIPE

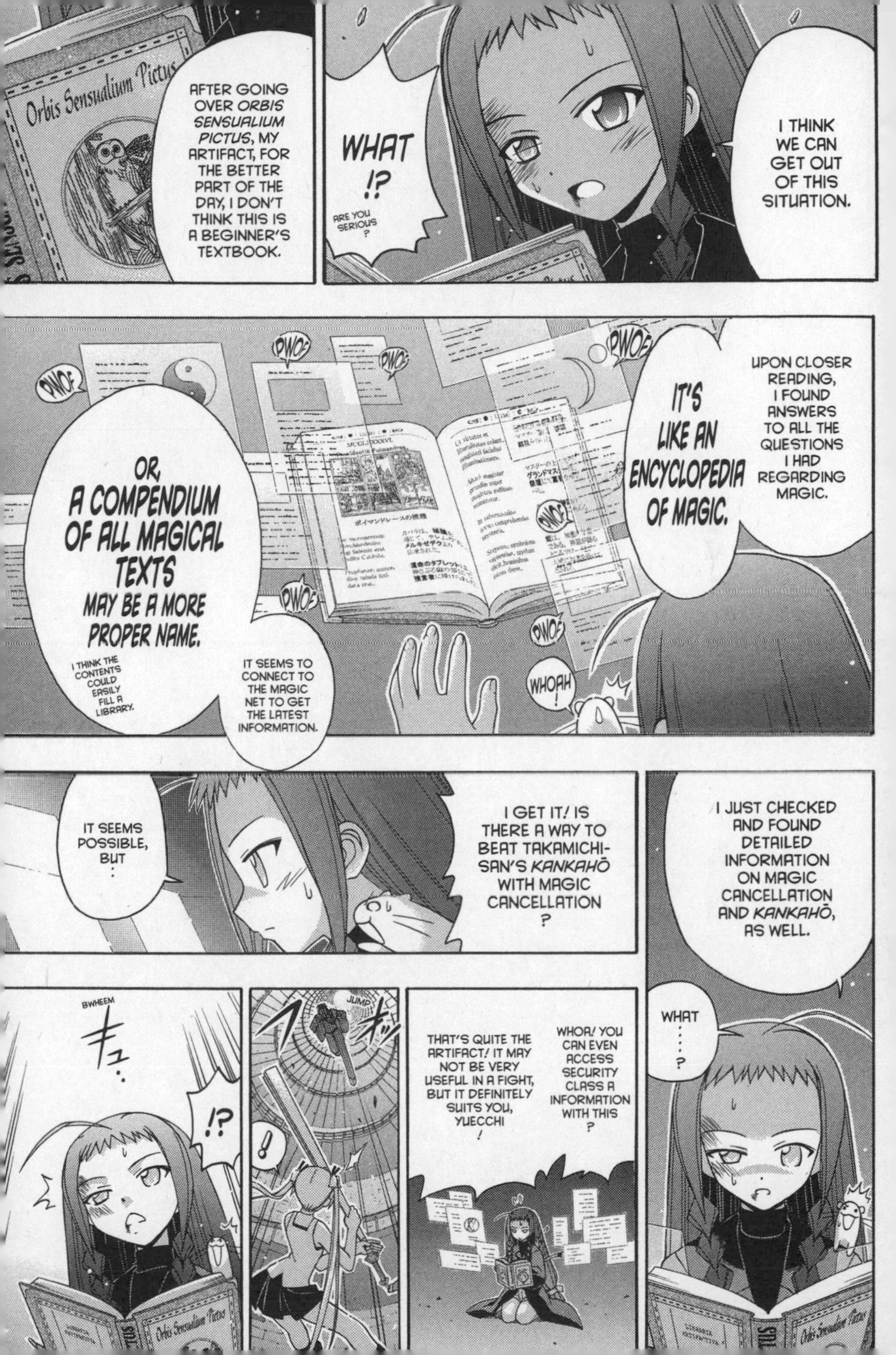
I THINK WE CAN GET OUT OF THIS SITUATION.
WHAT !?
ARE YOU SERIOUS ?
AFTER GOING OVER *ORBIS SENSUALIUM PICTUS*, MY ARTIFACT, FOR THE BETTER PART OF THE DAY, I DON'T THINK THIS IS A BEGINNER'S TEXTBOOK.
UPON CLOSER READING, I FOUND ANSWERS TO ALL THE QUESTIONS I HAD REGARDING MAGIC.
IT'S LIKE AN ENCYCLOPEDIA OF MAGIC.
PWOF
PWOF
PWOF
PWOF
OR, A COMPENDIUM OF ALL MAGICAL TEXTS MAY BE A MORE PROPER NAME.
I THINK THE CONTENTS COULD EASILY FILL A LIBRARY.
PWOF
PWOF
PWOF
IT SEEMS TO CONNECT TO THE MAGIC NET TO GET THE LATEST INFORMATION.
WHOAH !
I JUST CHECKED AND FOUND DETAILED INFORMATION ON MAGIC CANCELLATION AND *KANKAHŌ*, AS WELL.
WHAT ....?
I GET IT! IS THERE A WAY TO BEAT TAKAMICHI-SAN'S *KANKAHŌ* WITH MAGIC CANCELLATION ?
IT SEEMS POSSIBLE, BUT ..
WHOA! YOU CAN EVEN ACCESS SECURITY CLASS A INFORMATION WITH THIS ?
THAT'S QUITE THE ARTIFACT! IT MAY NOT BE VERY USEFUL IN A FIGHT, BUT IT DEFINITELY SUITS YOU, YUECCHI !
JUMP
!
!?
BWHEEM

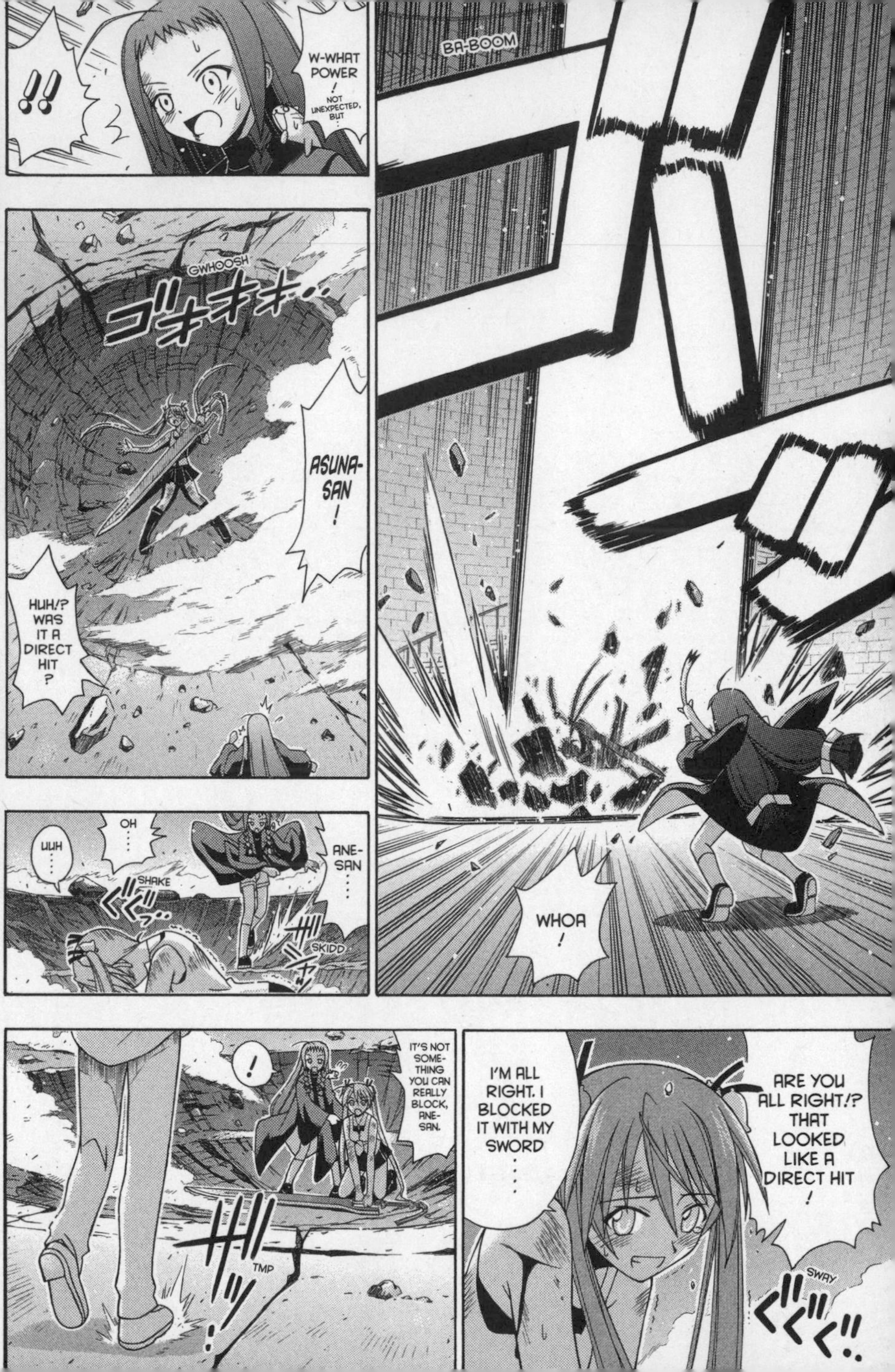
BA-BOOM
WHOA!
W-WHAT POWER! NOT UNEXPECTED, BUT...
!!
GWHOOSH
ASUNA-SAN!
HUH!? WAS IT A DIRECT HIT?
ANE-SAN...
OH...
UUH...
SHAKE
SKIDD
SWAY
ARE YOU ALL RIGHT!? THAT LOOKED LIKE A DIRECT HIT!
I'M ALL RIGHT. I BLOCKED IT WITH MY SWORD...
IT'S NOT SOMETHING YOU CAN REALLY BLOCK, ANE-SAN.
!
TMP

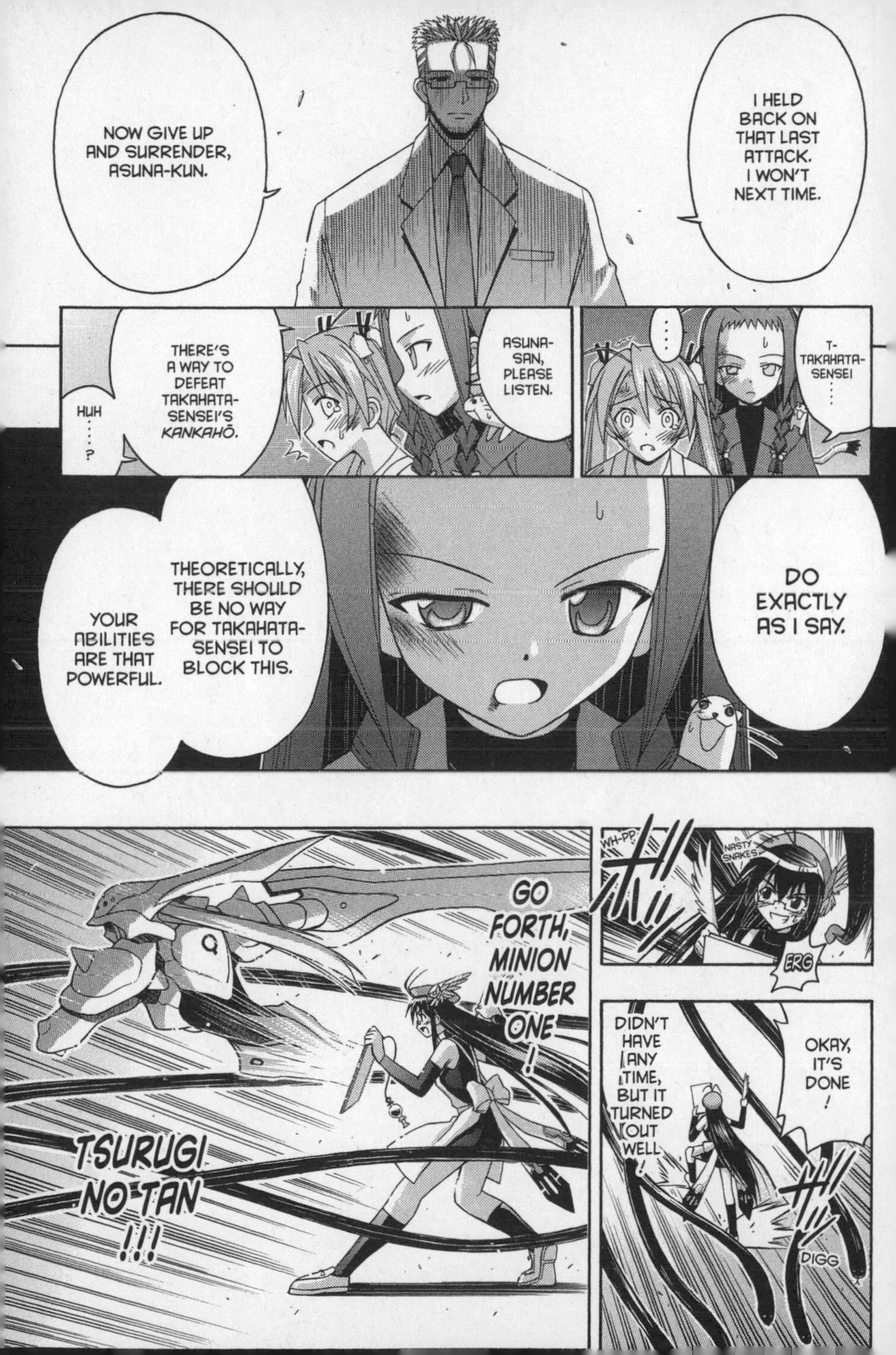
I HELD BACK ON THAT LAST ATTACK. I WON'T NEXT TIME.
NOW GIVE UP AND SURRENDER, ASUNA-KUN.
T-TAKAHATA-SENSEI……
……
ASUNA-SAN, PLEASE LISTEN.
THERE'S A WAY TO DEFEAT TAKAHATA-SENSEI'S *KANKAHŌ*.
HUH……?
DO EXACTLY AS I SAY.
THEORETICALLY, THERE SHOULD BE NO WAY FOR TAKAHATA-SENSEI TO BLOCK THIS.
YOUR ABILITIES ARE THAT POWERFUL.
WH-PP
NASTY SNAKES
ERG
OKAY, IT'S DONE!
DIDN'T HAVE ANY TIME, BUT IT TURNED OUT WELL!
DIGG
GO FORTH, MINION NUMBER ONE!
TSURUGI NO TAN!!!

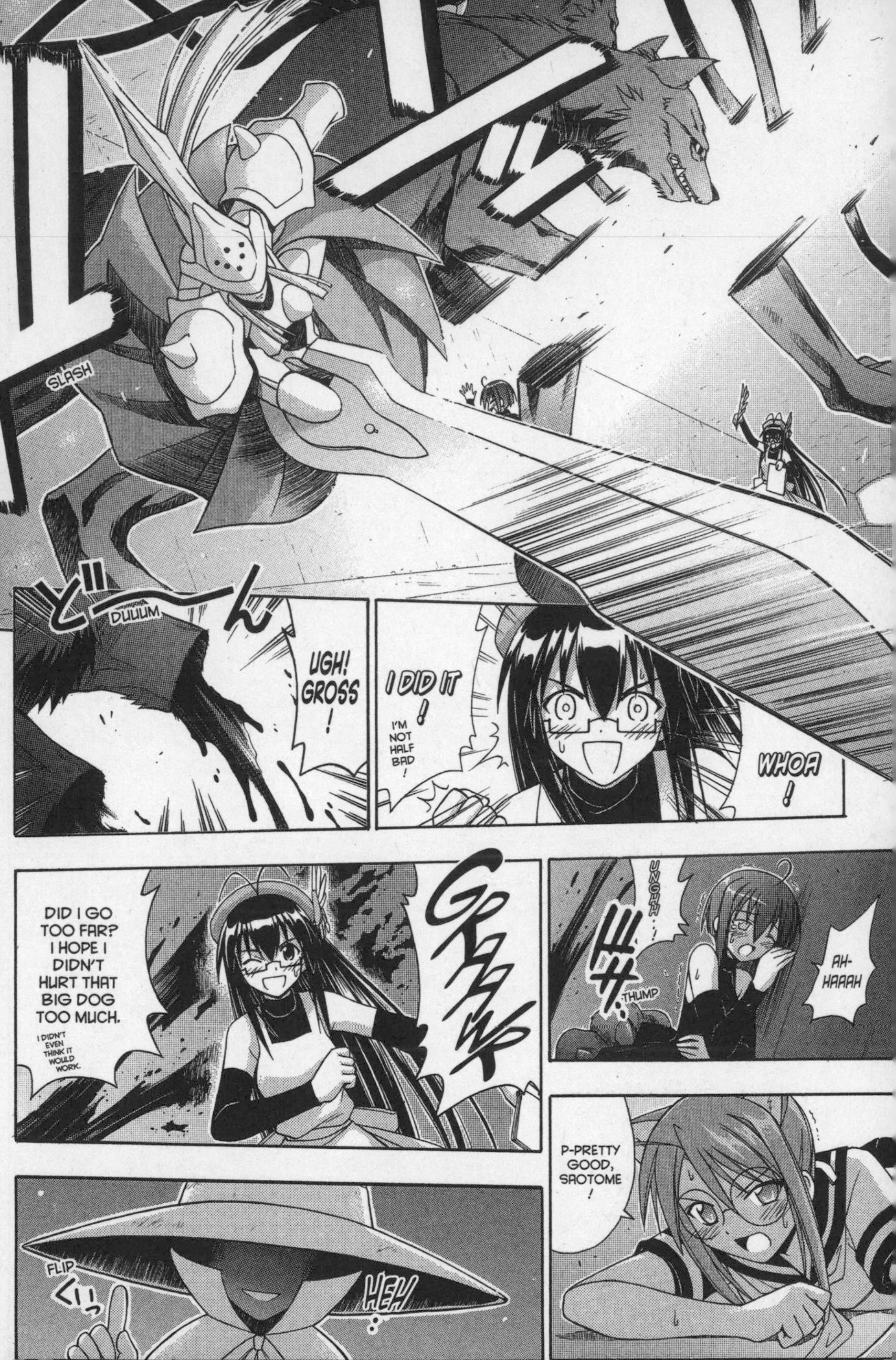

SLASH
どーーん
DUUUM
WHOA!
I DID IT!
I'M NOT HALF BAD!
UGH! GROSS!
UNGHH...!
THUMP
AH-HAAAH
GRAAWR
DID I GO TOO FAR? I HOPE I DIDN'T HURT THAT BIG DOG TOO MUCH.
I DIDN'T EVEN THINK IT WOULD WORK.
P-PRETTY GOOD, SAOTOME!
HEH
FLIP
くいっ

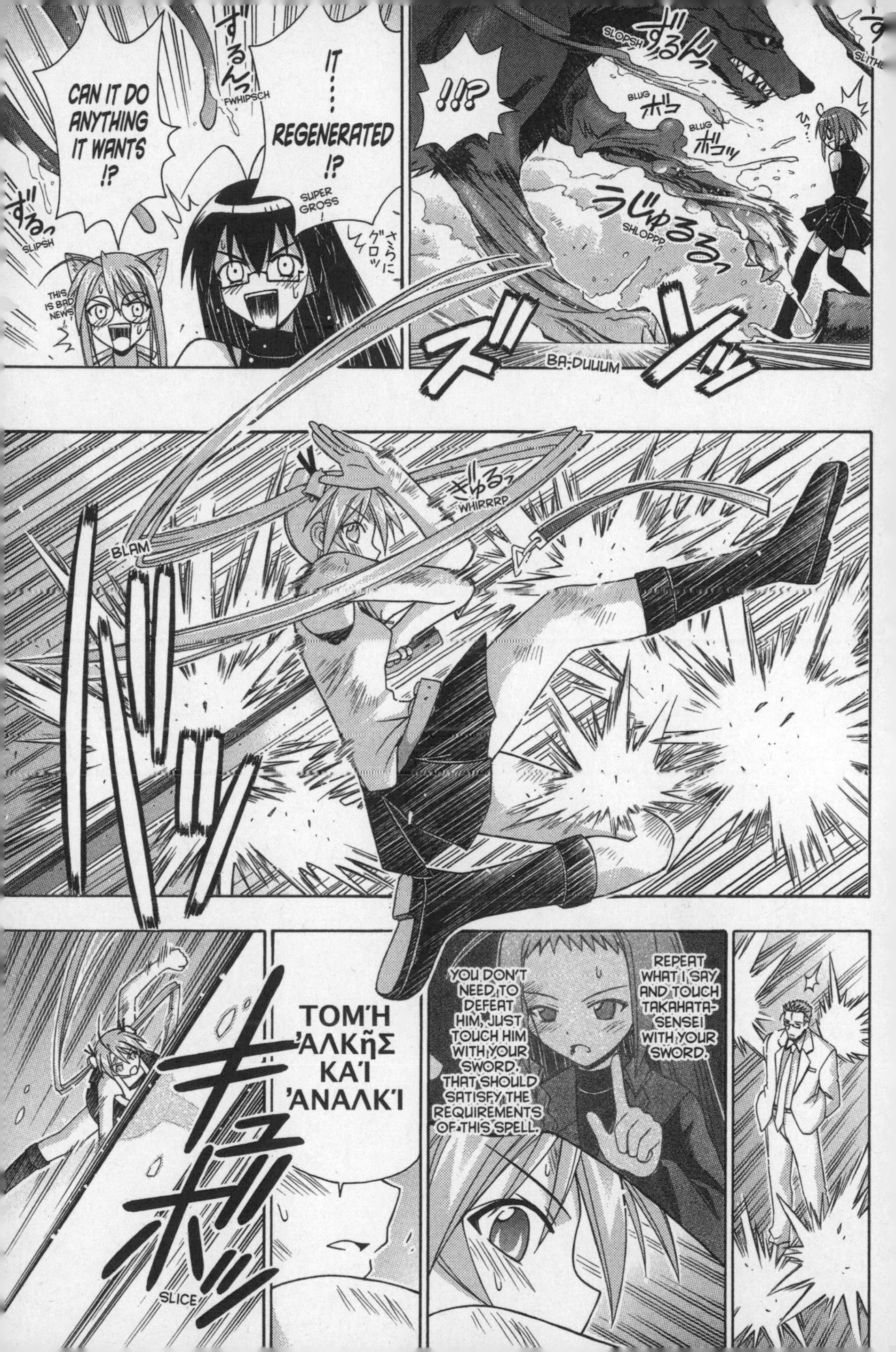

SLOPSH
ずるんっ
!!!?
BLUG
ボコ
BLUG
ボコッ
うじゅるるっ
SHLOPPP
SLITHE
BA-DUUUM
ずるんっ
FWHIPSCH
IT... REGENERATED!?
CAN IT DO ANYTHING IT WANTS!?
SUPER GROSS!
さらにグロッ
ずるっ
SLIPSH
THIS IS BAD NEWS
ぎゅるっ
WHIRRRP
BLAM
REPEAT WHAT I SAY AND TOUCH TAKAHATA-SENSEI WITH YOUR SWORD.
YOU DON'T NEED TO DEFEAT HIM, JUST TOUCH HIM WITH YOUR SWORD. THAT SHOULD SATISFY THE REQUIREMENTS OF THIS SPELL.
ΤΟΜ'Η 'ΑΛΚῆΣ ΚΑ'Ι 'ΑΝΑΛΚ'Ι
SLICE

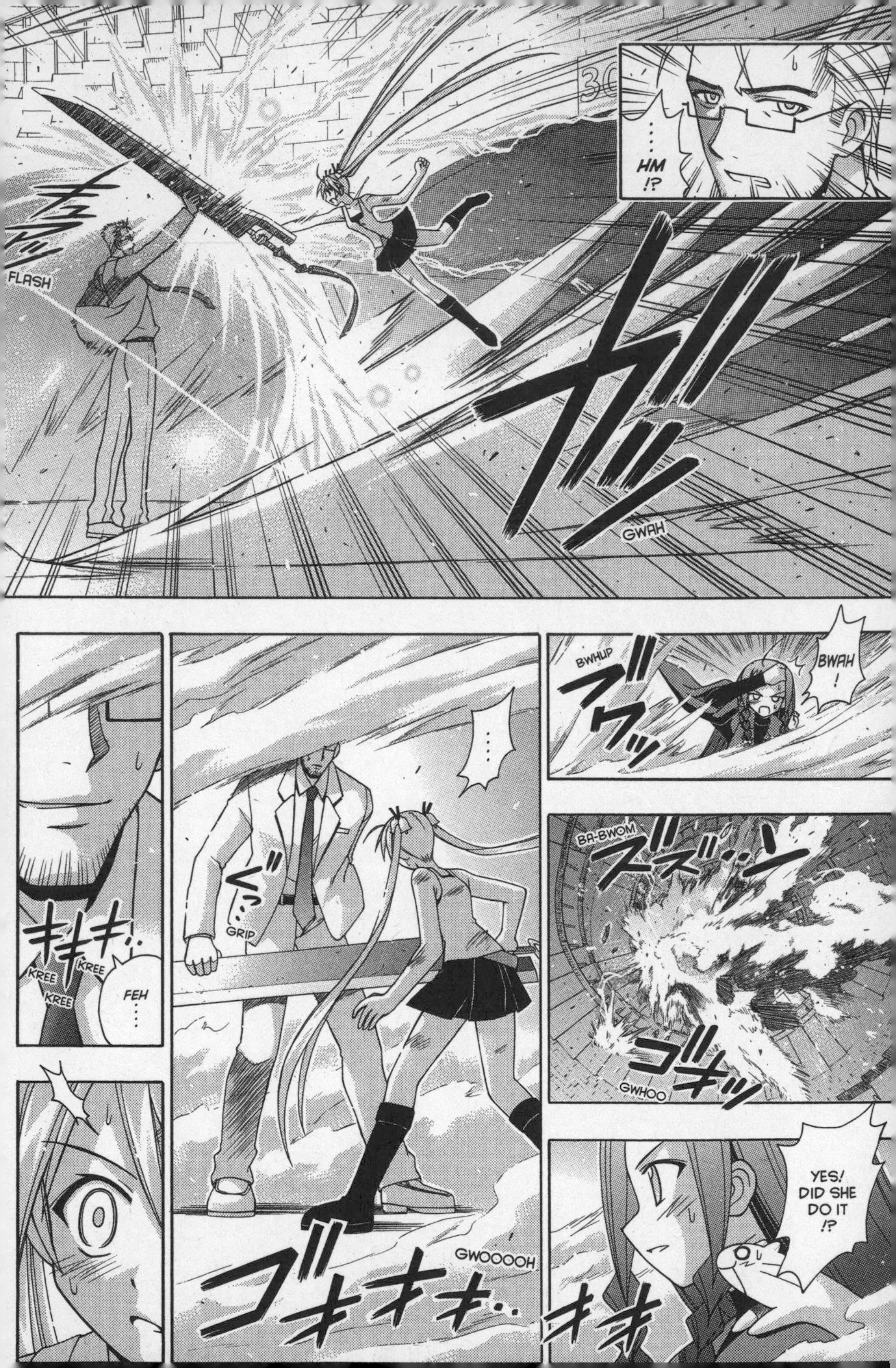

....HM !?
GWAH
FLASH
BWAH !
BWHUP
BA-BWOM
GWHOO
YES! DID SHE DO IT !?
....
GRIP
GWOOOOH
KREE
KREE
KREE
FEH ....

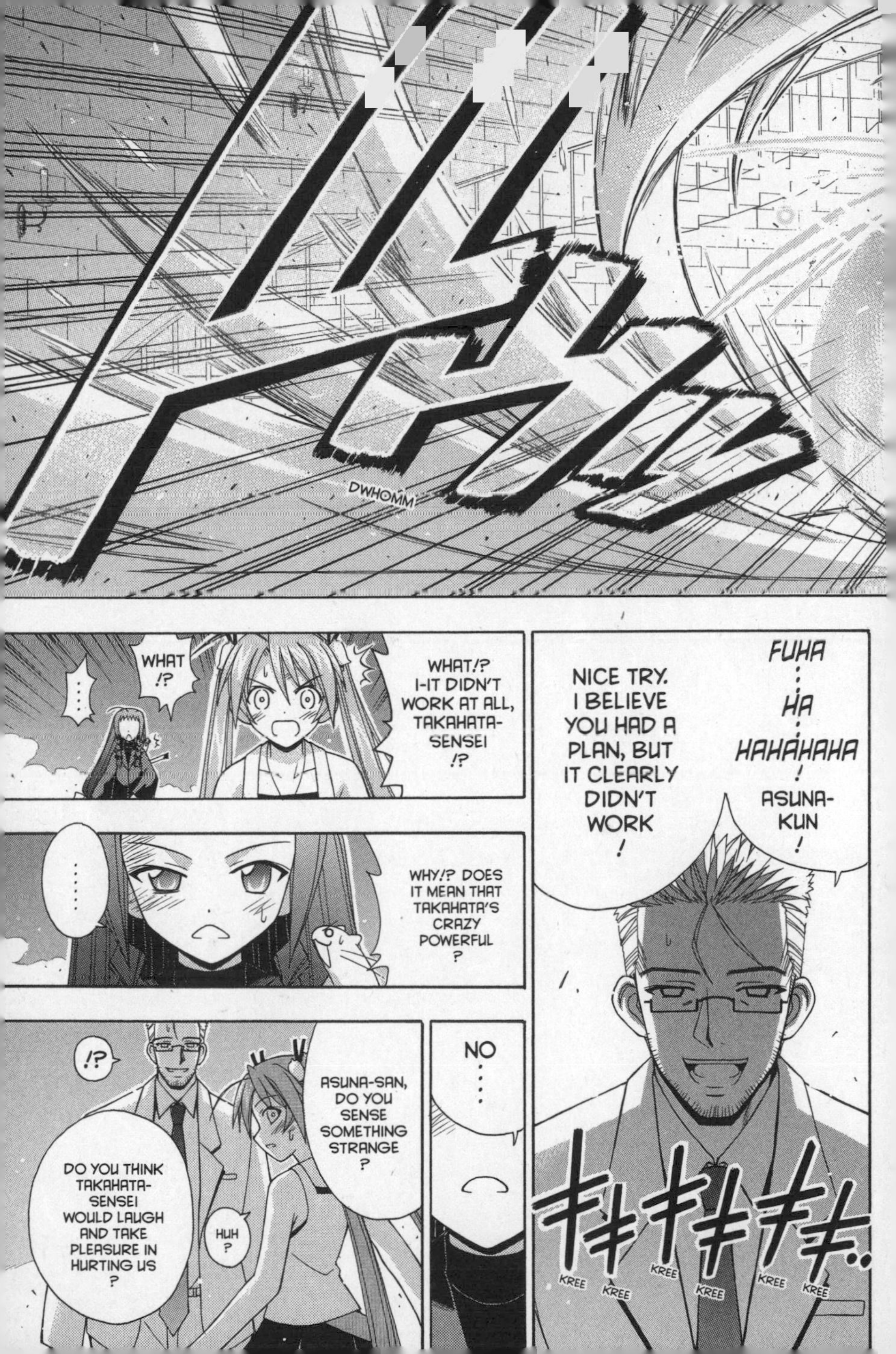
DWHOMM
FUHA... HA... HAHAHAHA! ASUNA-KUN!
NICE TRY. I BELIEVE YOU HAD A PLAN, BUT IT CLEARLY DIDN'T WORK!
KREE KREE KREE KREE KREE KREE
WHAT!? I-IT DIDN'T WORK AT ALL, TAKAHATA-SENSEI!?
WHAT!?
...
WHY!? DOES IT MEAN THAT TAKAHATA'S CRAZY POWERFUL?
......
NO...
ASUNA-SAN, DO YOU SENSE SOMETHING STRANGE?
!?
DO YOU THINK TAKAHATA-SENSEI WOULD LAUGH AND TAKE PLEASURE IN HURTING US?
HUH?

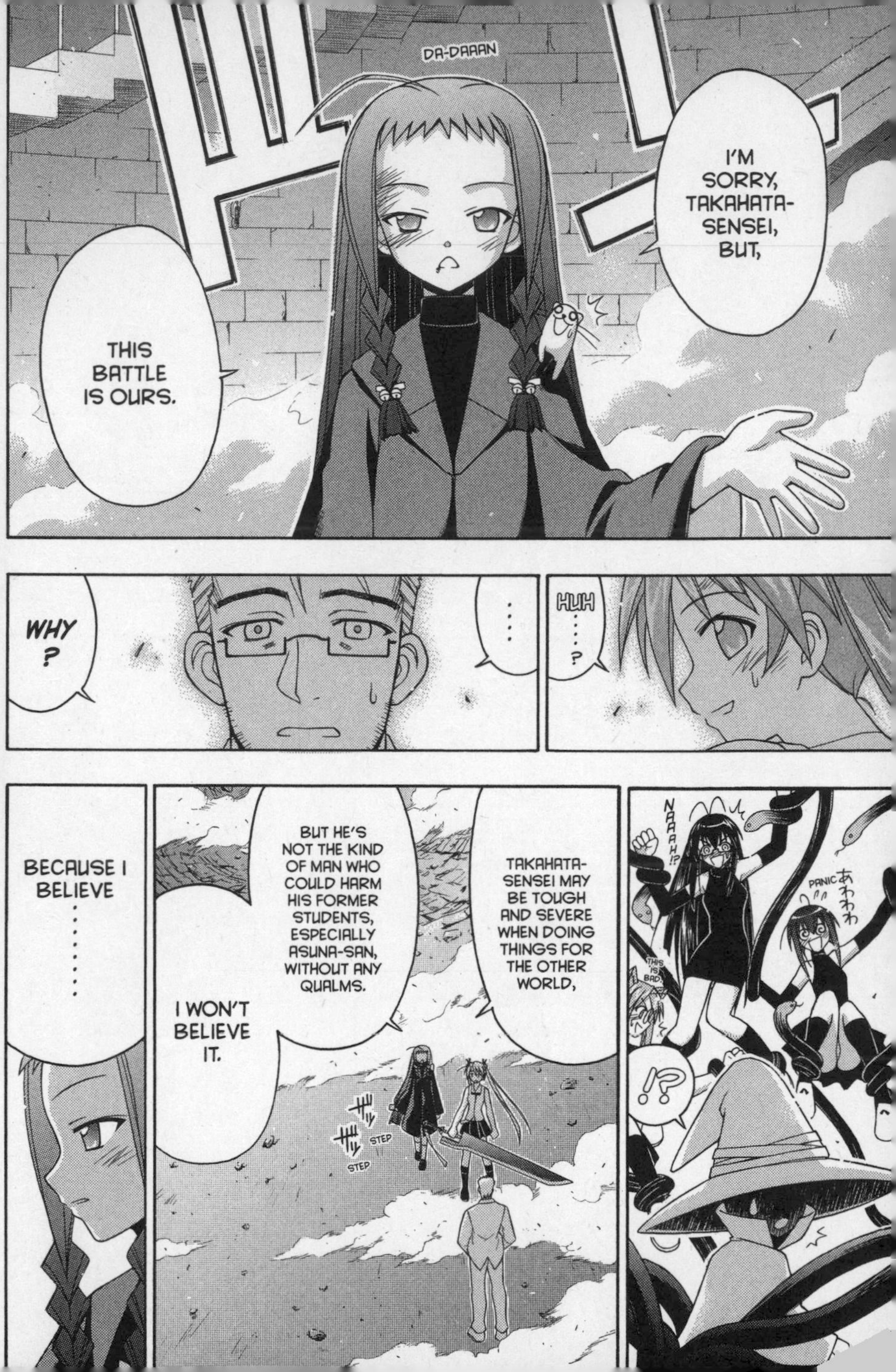
DA-DAAAN
I'M SORRY, TAKAHATA-SENSEI, BUT,
THIS BATTLE IS OURS.
HUH.....?
....
WHY?
NAAAAH!?
PANIC あわわわ
THIS IS BAD.
!?
TAKAHATA-SENSEI MAY BE TOUGH AND SEVERE WHEN DOING THINGS FOR THE OTHER WORLD,
BUT HE'S NOT THE KIND OF MAN WHO COULD HARM HIS FORMER STUDENTS, ESPECIALLY ASUNA-SAN, WITHOUT ANY QUALMS.
I WON'T BELIEVE IT.
ザッ STEP
ザッ STEP
BECAUSE I BELIEVE.......

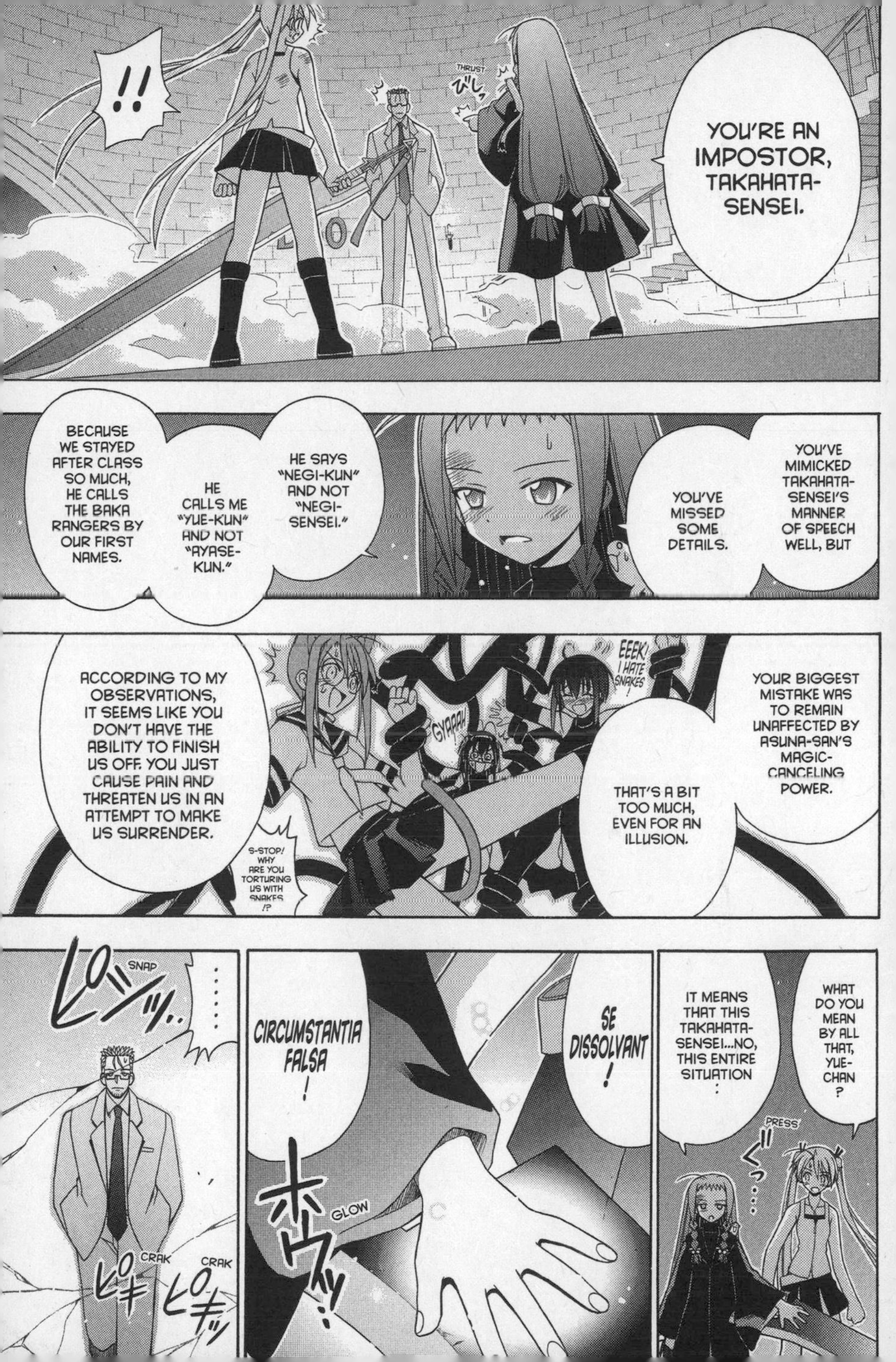
YOU'RE AN IMPOSTOR, TAKAHATA-SENSEI.
THRUST
!!
YOU'VE MIMICKED TAKAHATA-SENSEI'S MANNER OF SPEECH WELL, BUT
YOU'VE MISSED SOME DETAILS.
HE SAYS "NEGI-KUN" AND NOT "NEGI-SENSEI."
HE CALLS ME "YUE-KUN" AND NOT "AYASE-KUN."
BECAUSE WE STAYED AFTER CLASS SO MUCH, HE CALLS THE BAKA RANGERS BY OUR FIRST NAMES.
YOUR BIGGEST MISTAKE WAS TO REMAIN UNAFFECTED BY ASUNA-SAN'S MAGIC-CANCELING POWER.
THAT'S A BIT TOO MUCH, EVEN FOR AN ILLUSION.
EEEK! I HATE SNAKES!
GYAAAH
S-STOP! WHY ARE YOU TORTURING US WITH SNAKES!?
ACCORDING TO MY OBSERVATIONS, IT SEEMS LIKE YOU DON'T HAVE THE ABILITY TO FINISH US OFF. YOU JUST CAUSE PAIN AND THREATEN US IN AN ATTEMPT TO MAKE US SURRENDER.
WHAT DO YOU MEAN BY ALL THAT, YUE-CHAN?
IT MEANS THAT THIS TAKAHATA-SENSEI...NO, THIS ENTIRE SITUATION:
PRESS
SE DISSOLVANT!
CIRCUMSTANTIA FALSA!
GLOW
SNAP
......
CRAK
CRAK

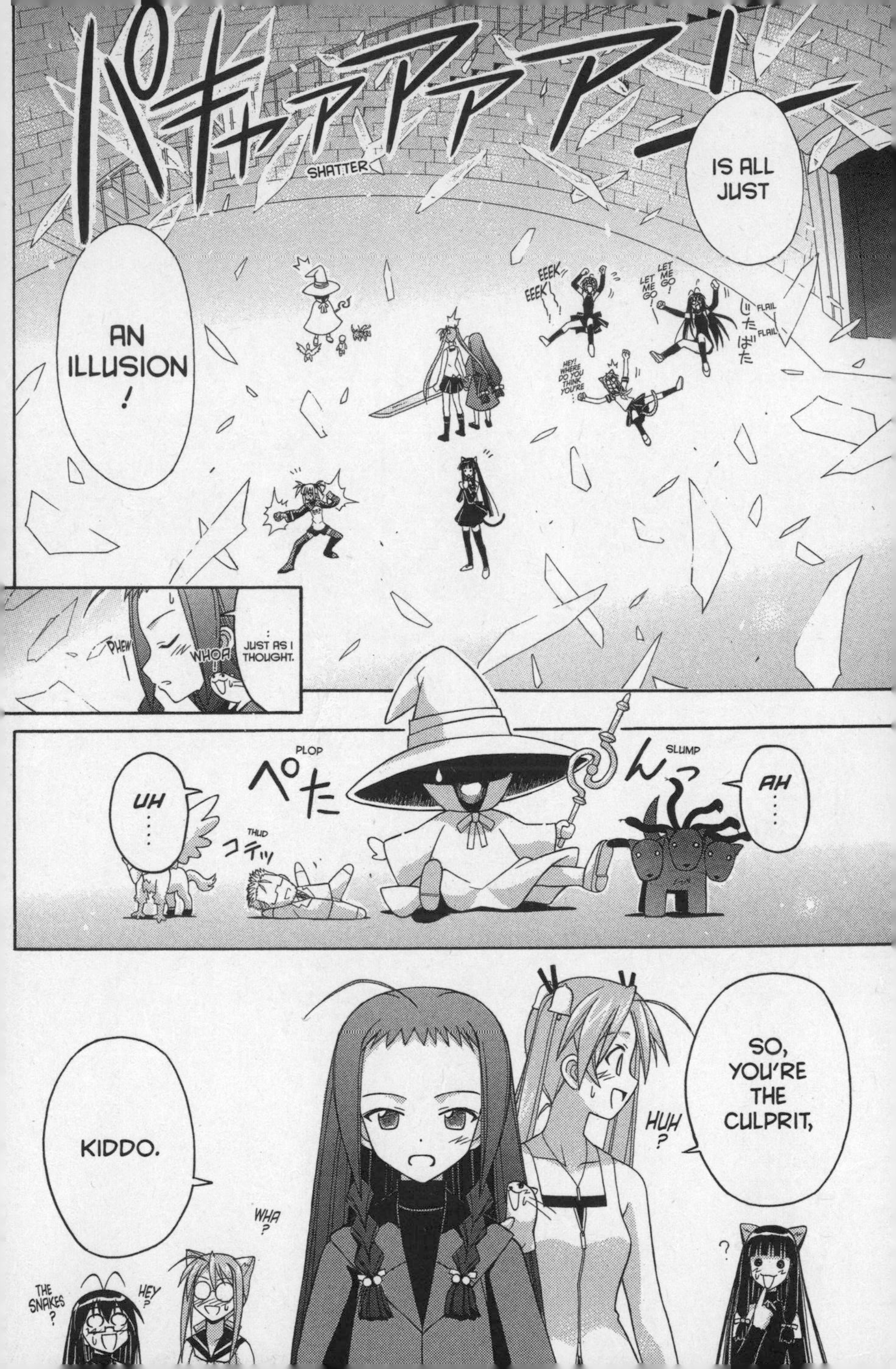
SHATTER
IS ALL JUST
AN ILLUSION!
LET ME GO! LET ME GO!
じたばた
FLAIL FLAIL
EEEK EEEK
HEY! WHERE DO YOU THINK YOU'RE
...JUST AS I THOUGHT.
WHOA!
PHEW
AH...
ん
SLUMP
ぺた
PLOP
コテッ
THUD
UH...
SO, YOU'RE THE CULPRIT,
HUH?
KIDDO.
?
WHA?
HEY?
THE SNAKES?

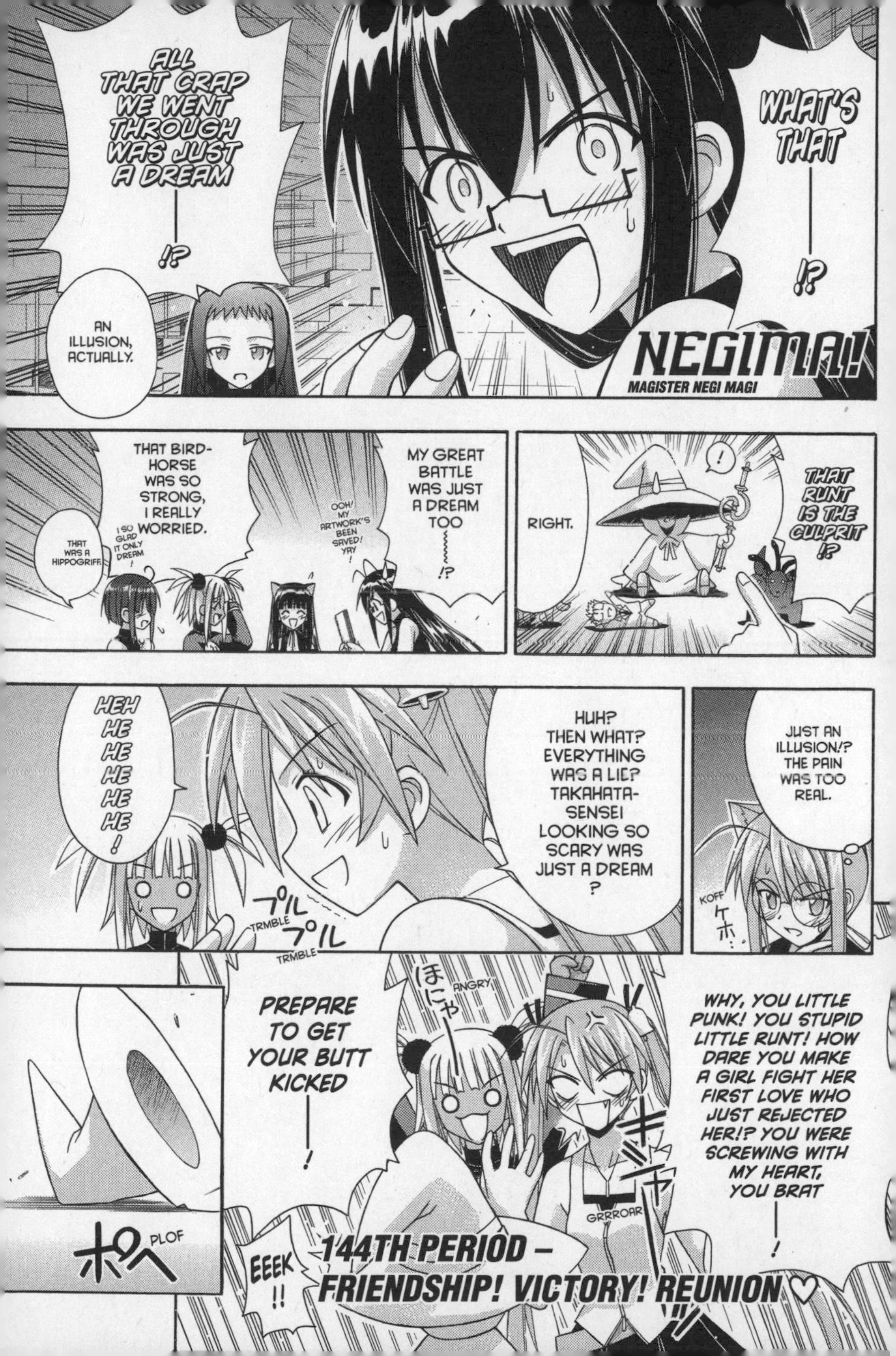
WHAT'S THAT —!?
ALL THAT CRAP WE WENT THROUGH WAS JUST A DREAM —!?
AN ILLUSION, ACTUALLY.
NEGIMA!
MAGISTER NEGI MAGI
THAT RUNT IS THE CULPRIT!?
!
RIGHT.
MY GREAT BATTLE WAS JUST A DREAM TOO ......!?
OOH! MY ARTWORK'S BEEN SAVED! YAY!
THAT BIRD-HORSE WAS SO STRONG, I REALLY WORRIED.
I SO GLAD IT ONLY DREAM!
THAT WAS A HIPPOGRIFF.
JUST AN ILLUSION!? THE PAIN WAS TOO REAL.
ケホ
KOFF
HUH? THEN WHAT? EVERYTHING WAS A LIE? TAKAHATA-SENSEI LOOKING SO SCARY WAS JUST A DREAM?
HEH HE HE HE HE HE!
プル TRMBLE
プル TRMBLE
WHY, YOU LITTLE PUNK! YOU STUPID LITTLE RUNT! HOW DARE YOU MAKE A GIRL FIGHT HER FIRST LOVE WHO JUST REJECTED HER!? YOU WERE SCREWING WITH MY HEART, YOU BRAT —!
GRRROAR
ほにゃ ANGRY
PREPARE TO GET YOUR BUTT KICKED —!
EEEK!!
ポヘ PLOF
144TH PERIOD – FRIENDSHIP! VICTORY! REUNION ♡

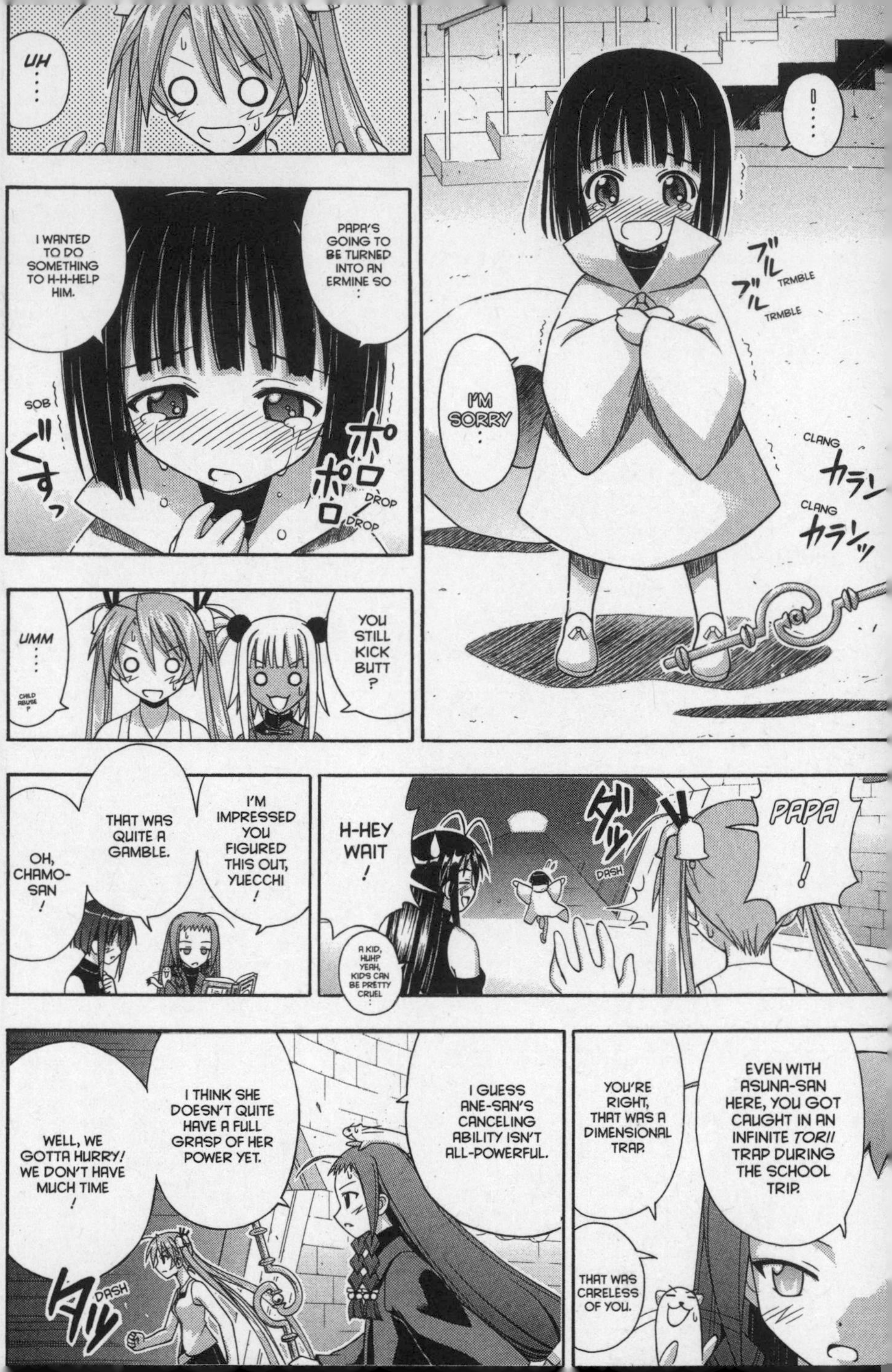
!...
I'M SORRY...
ブル TRMBLE
ブル TRMBLE
カラン CLANG
カランッ CLANG
UH...
PAPA'S GOING TO BE TURNED INTO AN ERMINE SO...
I WANTED TO DO SOMETHING TO H-H-HELP HIM.
ポロ DROP
ポロ DROP
ぐすっ SOB
YOU STILL KICK BUTT?
UMM...
CHILD ABUSE?
PAPA!
ダッ DASH
H-HEY WAIT!
A KID, HUH? YEAH, KIDS CAN BE PRETTY CRUEL...
I'M IMPRESSED YOU FIGURED THIS OUT, YUECCHI!
THAT WAS QUITE A GAMBLE.
OH, CHAMO-SAN!
EVEN WITH ASUNA-SAN HERE, YOU GOT CAUGHT IN AN INFINITE *TORII* TRAP DURING THE SCHOOL TRIP.
YOU'RE RIGHT, THAT WAS A DIMENSIONAL TRAP.
THAT WAS CARELESS OF YOU.
I GUESS ANE-SAN'S CANCELING ABILITY ISN'T ALL-POWERFUL.
I THINK SHE DOESN'T QUITE HAVE A FULL GRASP OF HER POWER YET.
WELL, WE GOTTA HURRY! WE DON'T HAVE MUCH TIME!
ダッ DASH

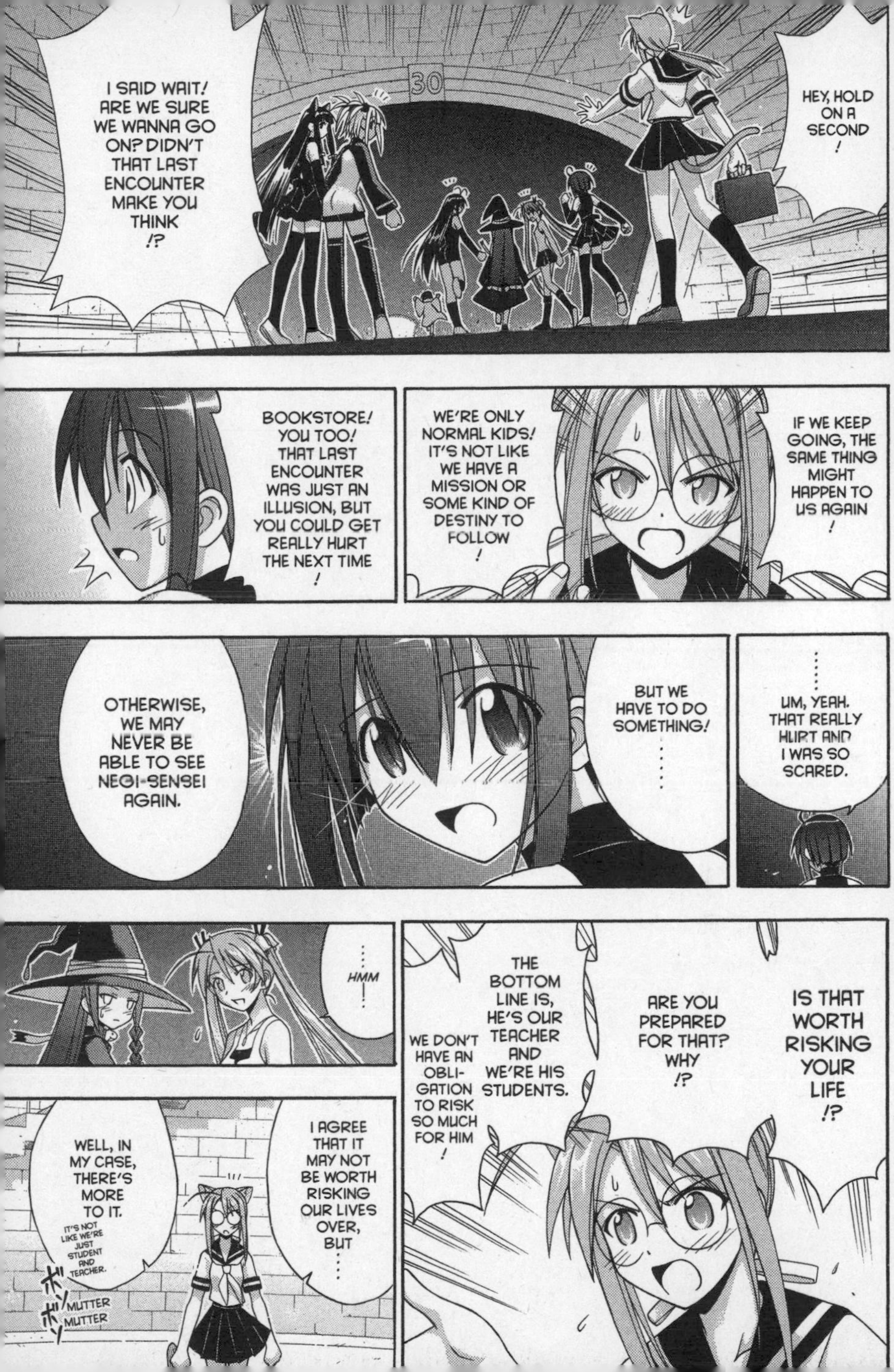
HEY, HOLD ON A SECOND!
I SAID WAIT! ARE WE SURE WE WANNA GO ON? DIDN'T THAT LAST ENCOUNTER MAKE YOU THINK!?
30
IF WE KEEP GOING, THE SAME THING MIGHT HAPPEN TO US AGAIN!
WE'RE ONLY NORMAL KIDS! IT'S NOT LIKE WE HAVE A MISSION OR SOME KIND OF DESTINY TO FOLLOW!
BOOKSTORE! YOU TOO! THAT LAST ENCOUNTER WAS JUST AN ILLUSION, BUT YOU COULD GET REALLY HURT THE NEXT TIME!
......
UM, YEAH. THAT REALLY HURT AND I WAS SO SCARED.
BUT WE HAVE TO DO SOMETHING! ......
OTHERWISE, WE MAY NEVER BE ABLE TO SEE NEGI-SENSEI AGAIN.
IS THAT WORTH RISKING YOUR LIFE!?
ARE YOU PREPARED FOR THAT? WHY!?
THE BOTTOM LINE IS, HE'S OUR TEACHER AND WE'RE HIS STUDENTS.
WE DON'T HAVE AN OBLI-GATION TO RISK SO MUCH FOR HIM!
... HMM ...!
I AGREE THAT IT MAY NOT BE WORTH RISKING OUR LIVES OVER, BUT......
WELL, IN MY CASE, THERE'S MORE TO IT.
IT'S NOT LIKE WE'RE JUST STUDENT AND TEACHER.
MUTTER MUTTER

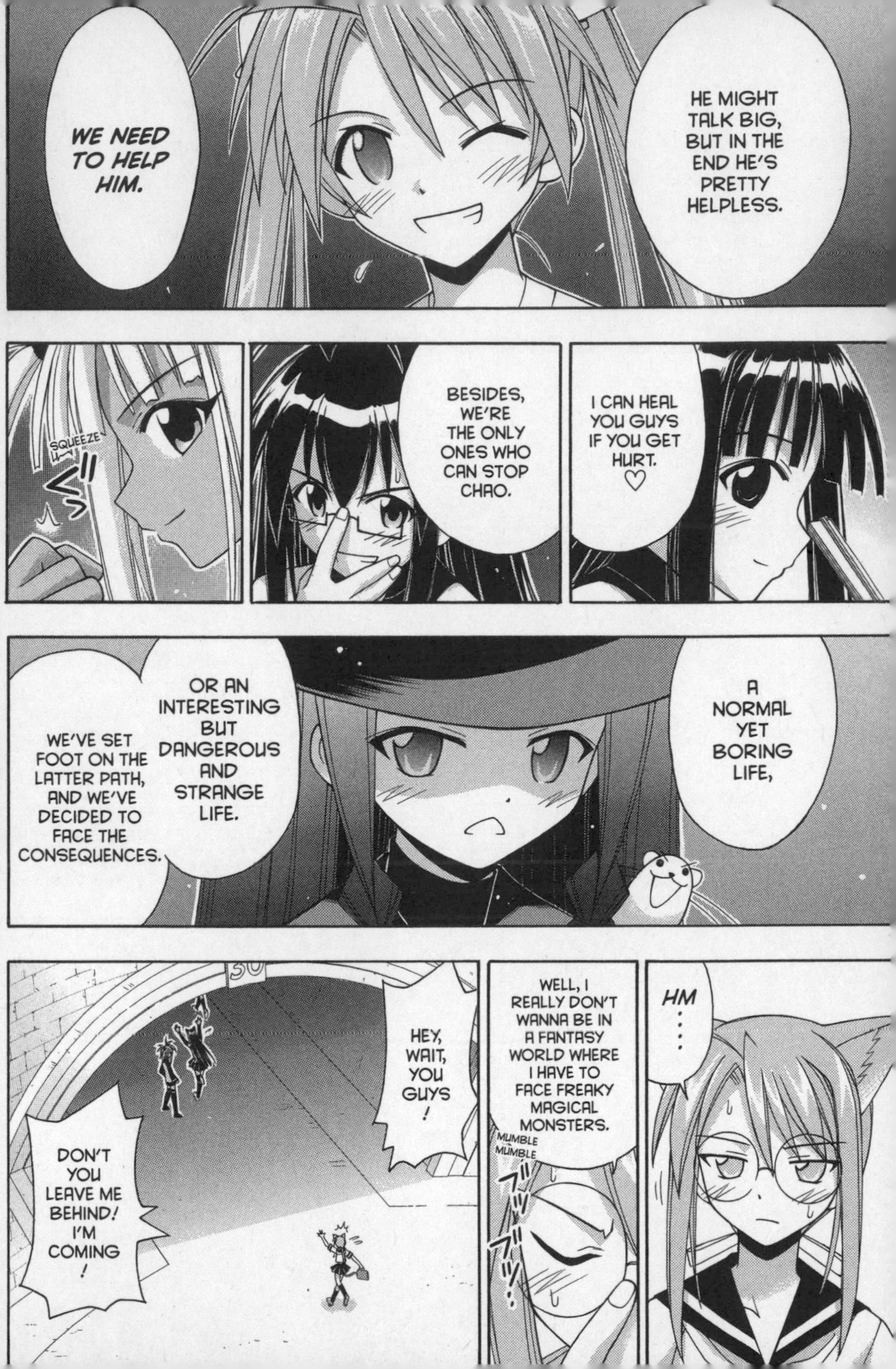
HE MIGHT TALK BIG, BUT IN THE END HE'S PRETTY HELPLESS.
WE NEED TO HELP HIM.
I CAN HEAL YOU GUYS IF YOU GET HURT. ♡
BESIDES, WE'RE THE ONLY ONES WHO CAN STOP CHAO.
SQUEEZE
A NORMAL YET BORING LIFE,
OR AN INTERESTING BUT DANGEROUS AND STRANGE LIFE.
WE'VE SET FOOT ON THE LATTER PATH, AND WE'VE DECIDED TO FACE THE CONSEQUENCES.
HM....
WELL, I REALLY DON'T WANNA BE IN A FANTASY WORLD WHERE I HAVE TO FACE FREAKY MAGICAL MONSTERS.
MUMBLE MUMBLE
HEY, WAIT, YOU GUYS!
DON'T YOU LEAVE ME BEHIND! I'M COMING!

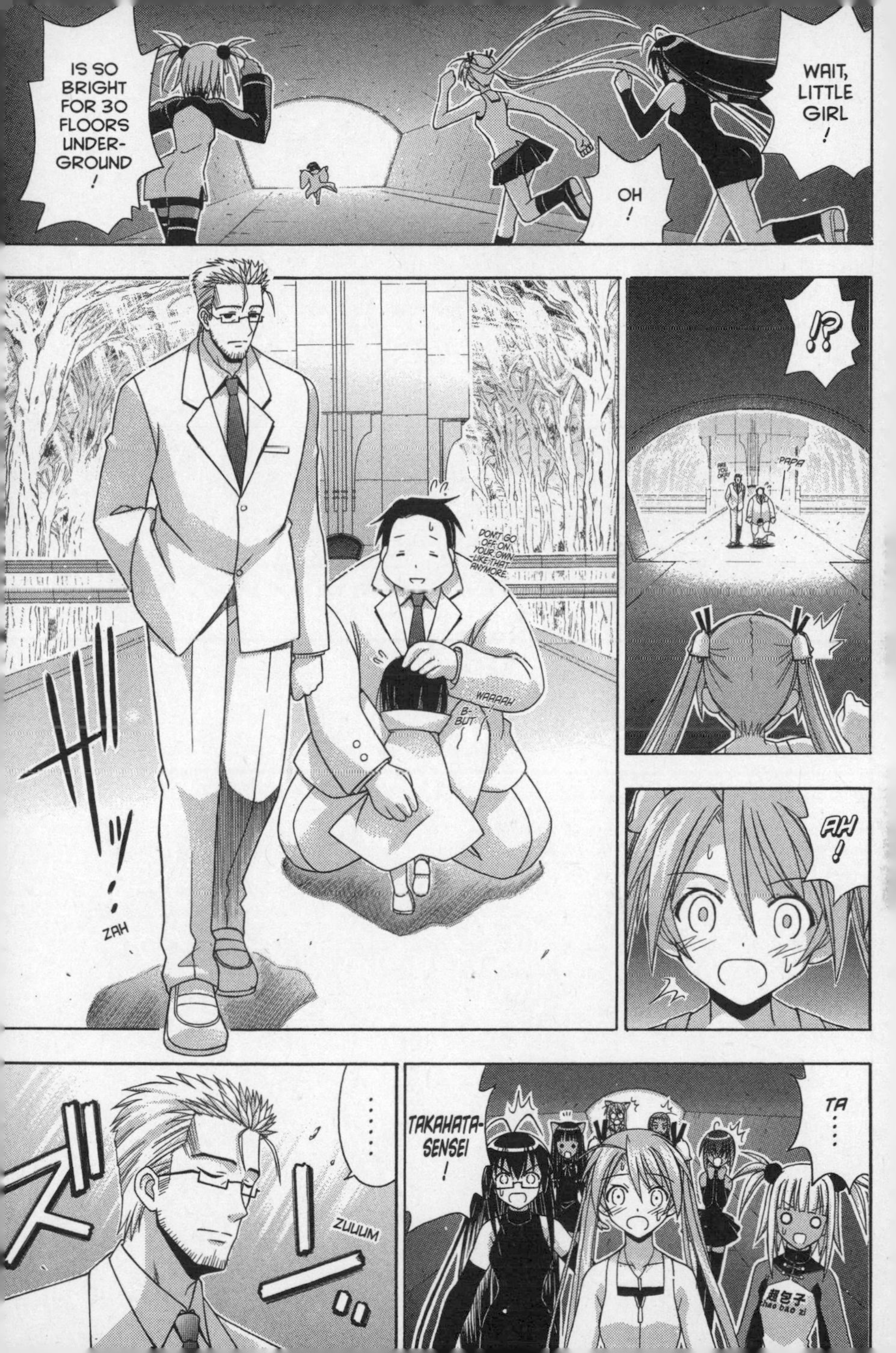
WAIT, LITTLE GIRL !
OH !
IS SO BRIGHT FOR 30 FLOORS UNDER-GROUND !
!?
PAPA
AH !
DON'T GO OFF ON YOUR OWN LIKE THAT ANYMORE.
WAAAAH
B-BUT
ZAH
TA.....
TAKAHATA-SENSEI !
超包子
chao bāo zi
......
ZUUUM

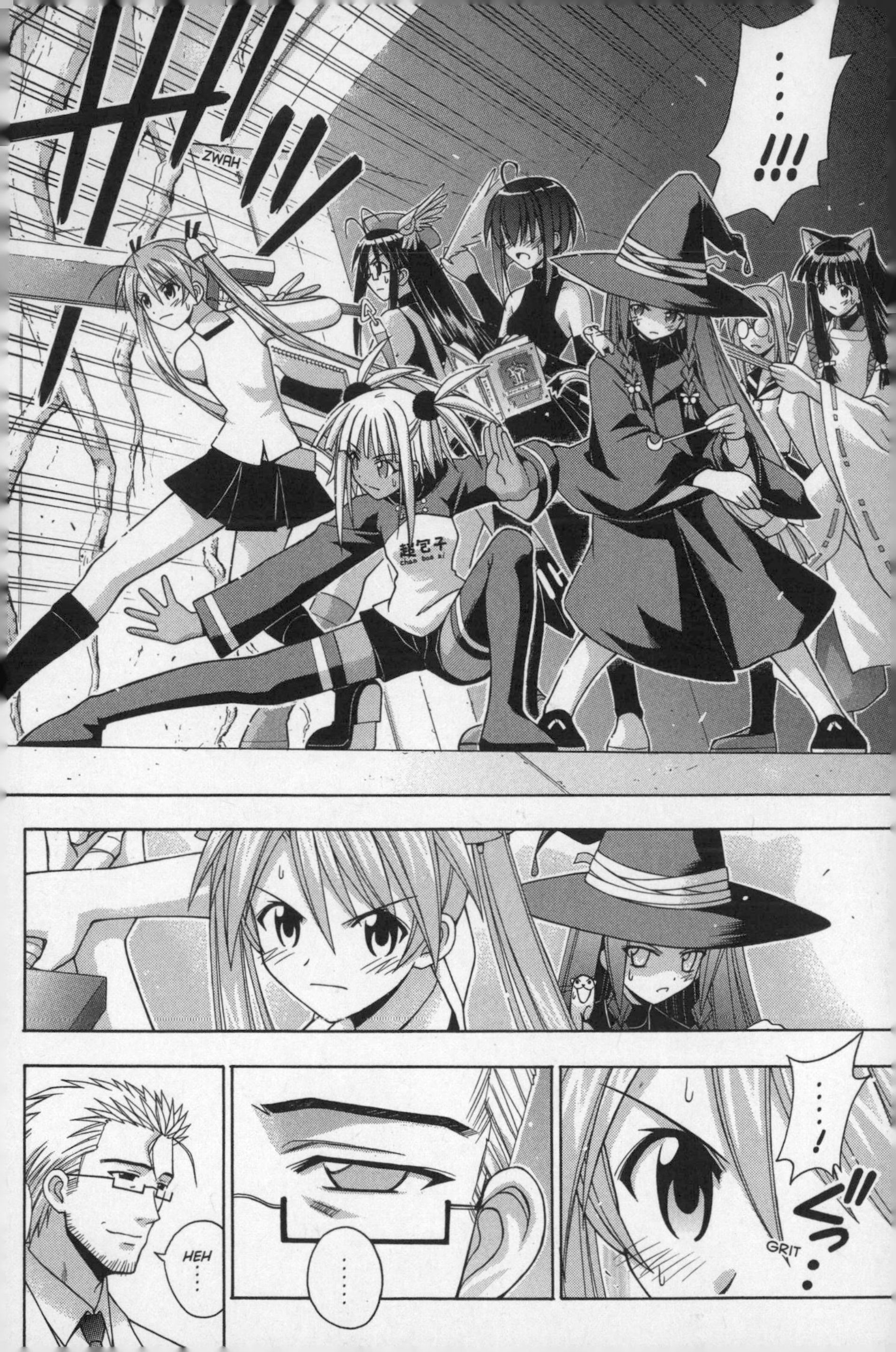
....!!!
ZWAH
....!
ぐっ..
GRIT
......
HEH
....

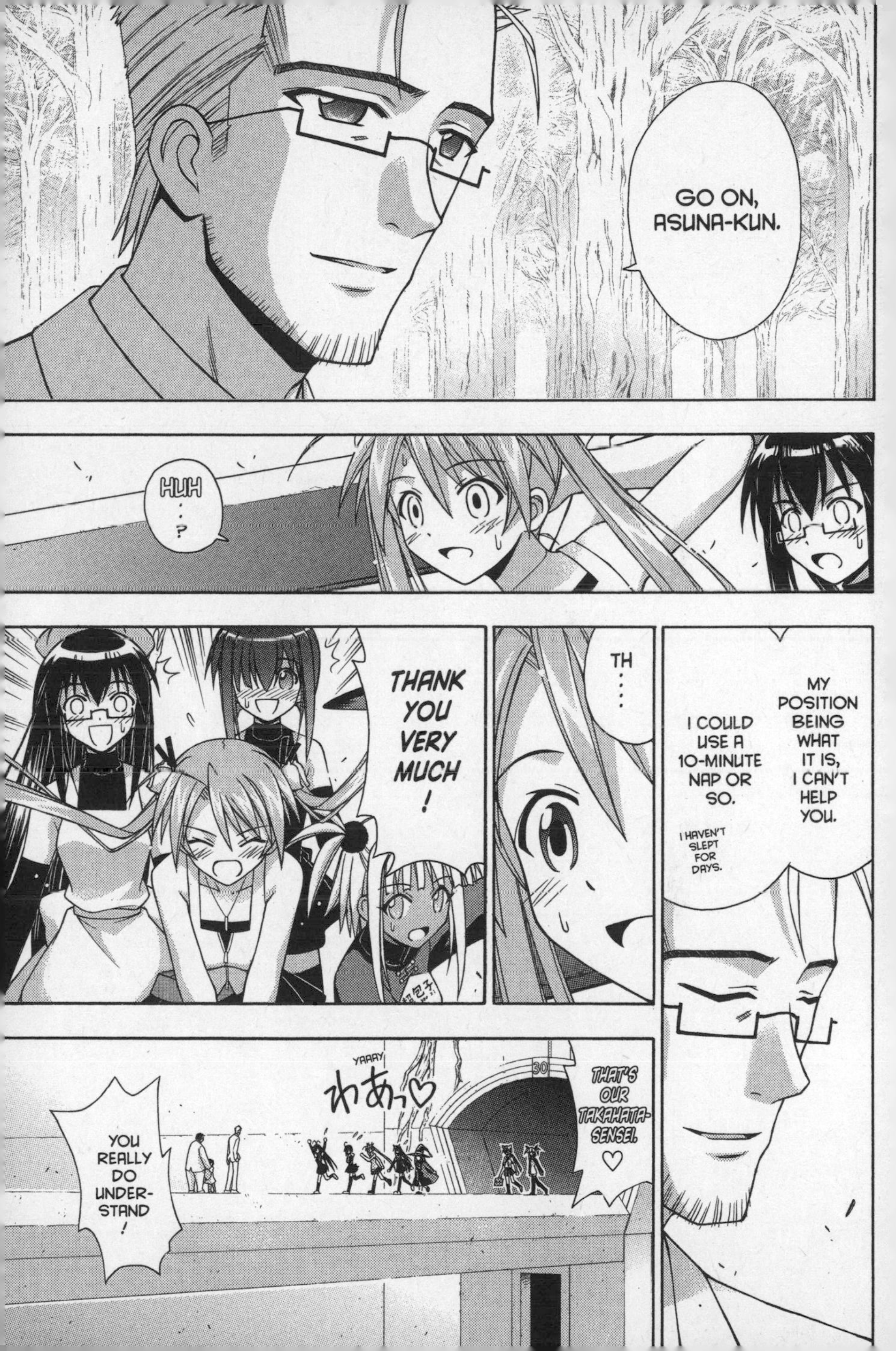
GO ON, ASUNA-KUN.
HUH...?
MY POSITION BEING WHAT IT IS, I CAN'T HELP YOU.
I COULD USE A 10-MINUTE NAP OR SO.
I HAVEN'T SLEPT FOR DAYS.
TH...
THANK YOU VERY MUCH!
THAT'S OUR TAKAHATA-SENSEI. ♡
30
わあっ♡
YAAAY
YOU REALLY DO UNDER-STAND!

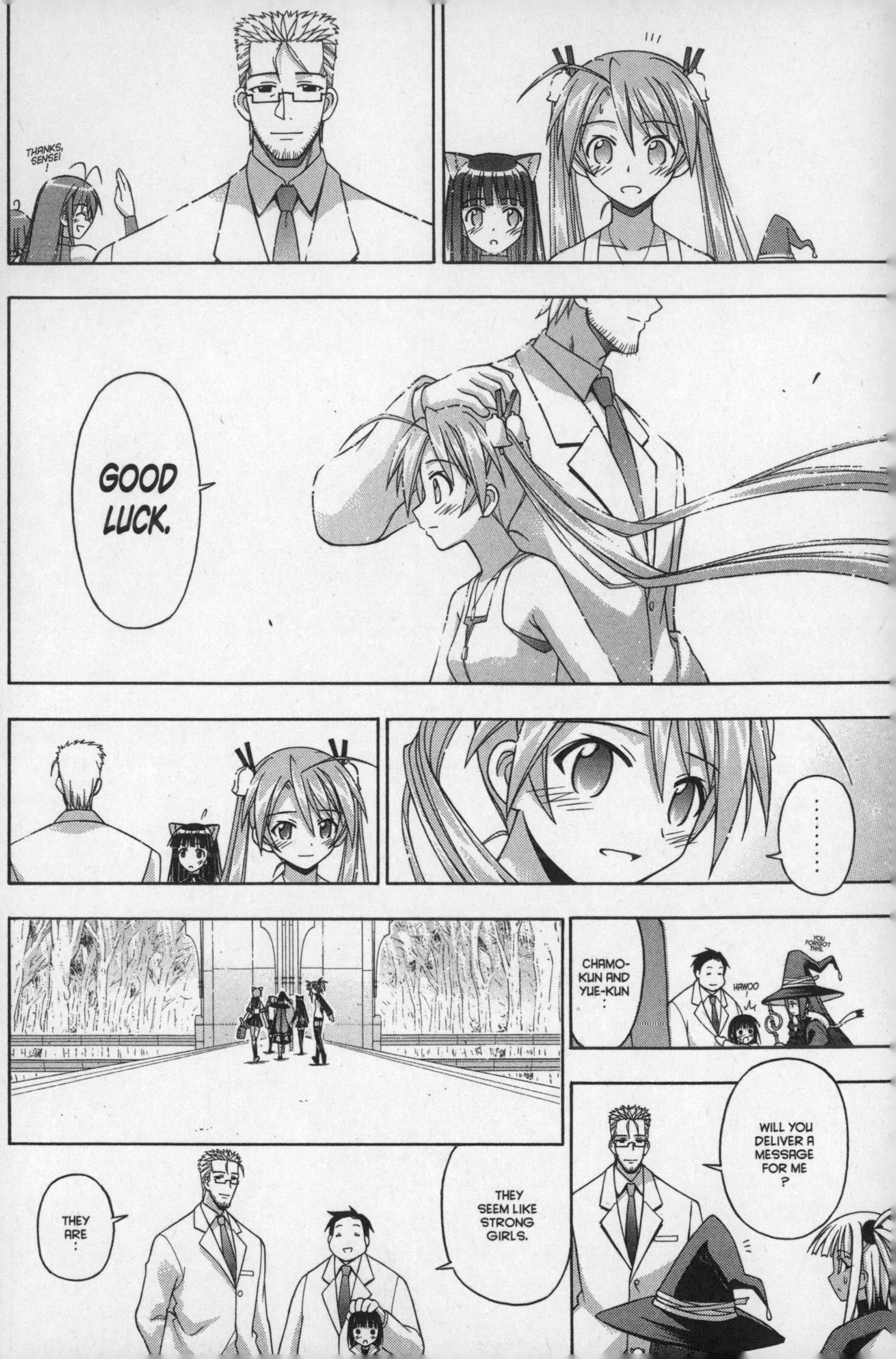
THANKS, SENSEI!
GOOD LUCK.
....
CHAMO-KUN AND YUE-KUN...
YOU FORGOT THIS.
HAWOO!
WILL YOU DELIVER A MESSAGE FOR ME?
THEY SEEM LIKE STRONG GIRLS.
THEY ARE...

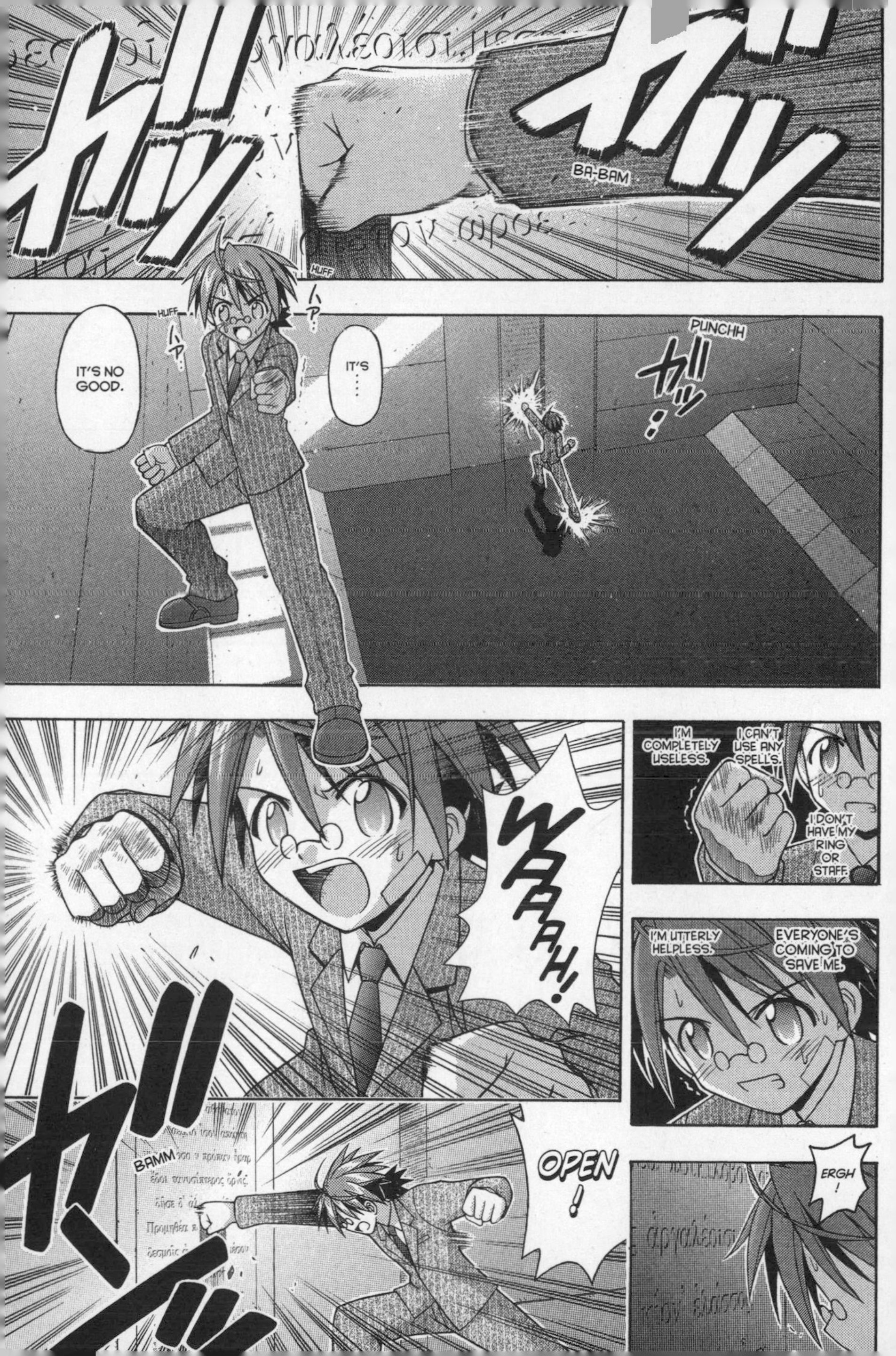
BA-BAM
HUFF
PUNCHH
IT'S ......
IT'S NO GOOD.
HUFF
I CAN'T USE ANY SPELLS.
I'M COMPLETELY USELESS.
I DON'T HAVE MY RING OR STAFF.
EVERYONE'S COMING TO SAVE ME.
I'M UTTERLY HELPLESS.
WAAAH!
ERGH!
OPEN!
BAMM

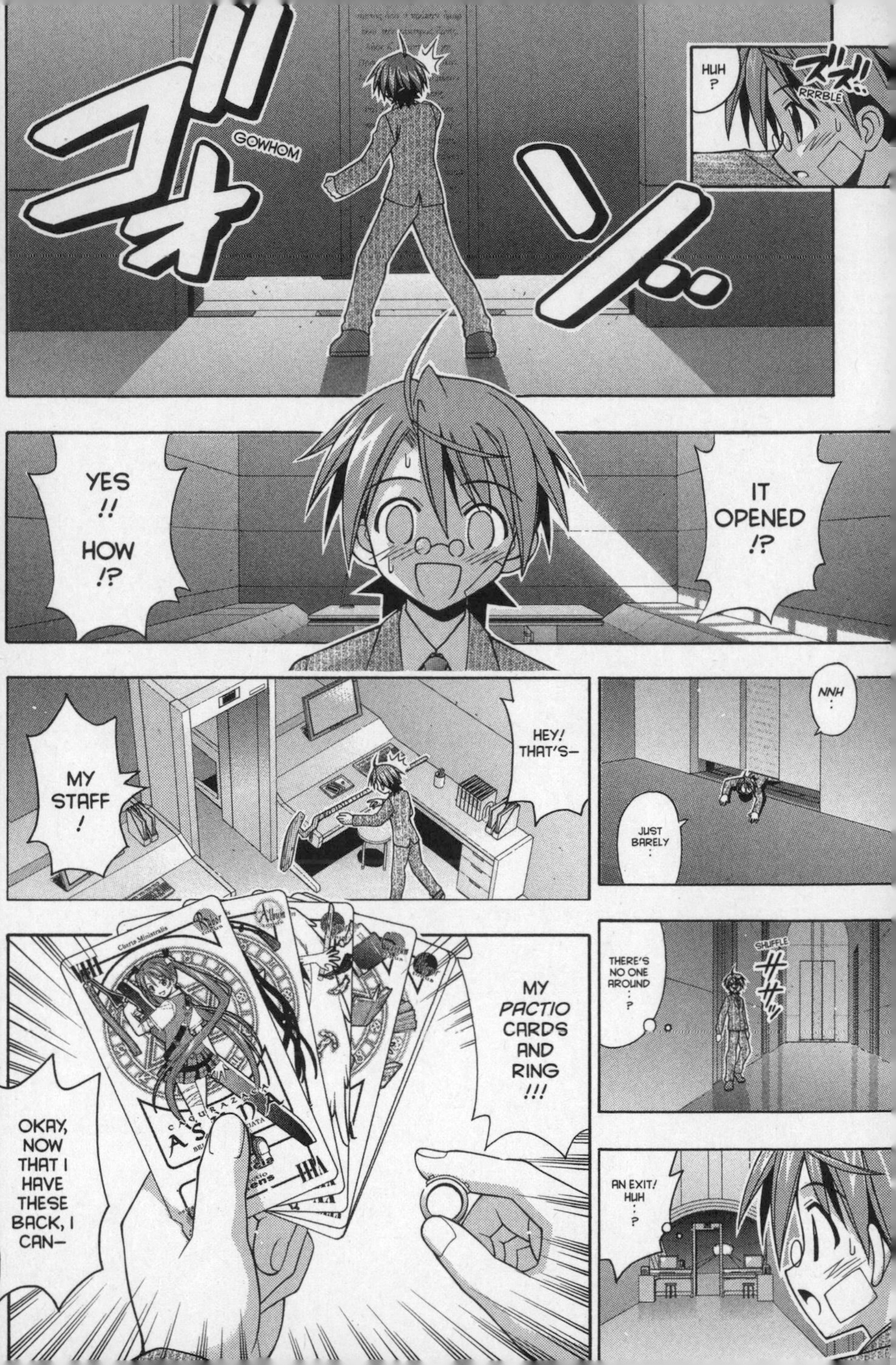
HUH?
ズズ!!
RRRBLE
ゴオン…
GOWHOM
IT OPENED!?
YES!! HOW!?
NNH...
JUST BARELY...
HEY! THAT'S—
MY STAFF!
THERE'S NO ONE AROUND...?
SHUFFLE
AN EXIT! HUH...?
MY PACTIO CARDS AND RING!!!
OKAY, NOW THAT I HAVE THESE BACK, I CAN—

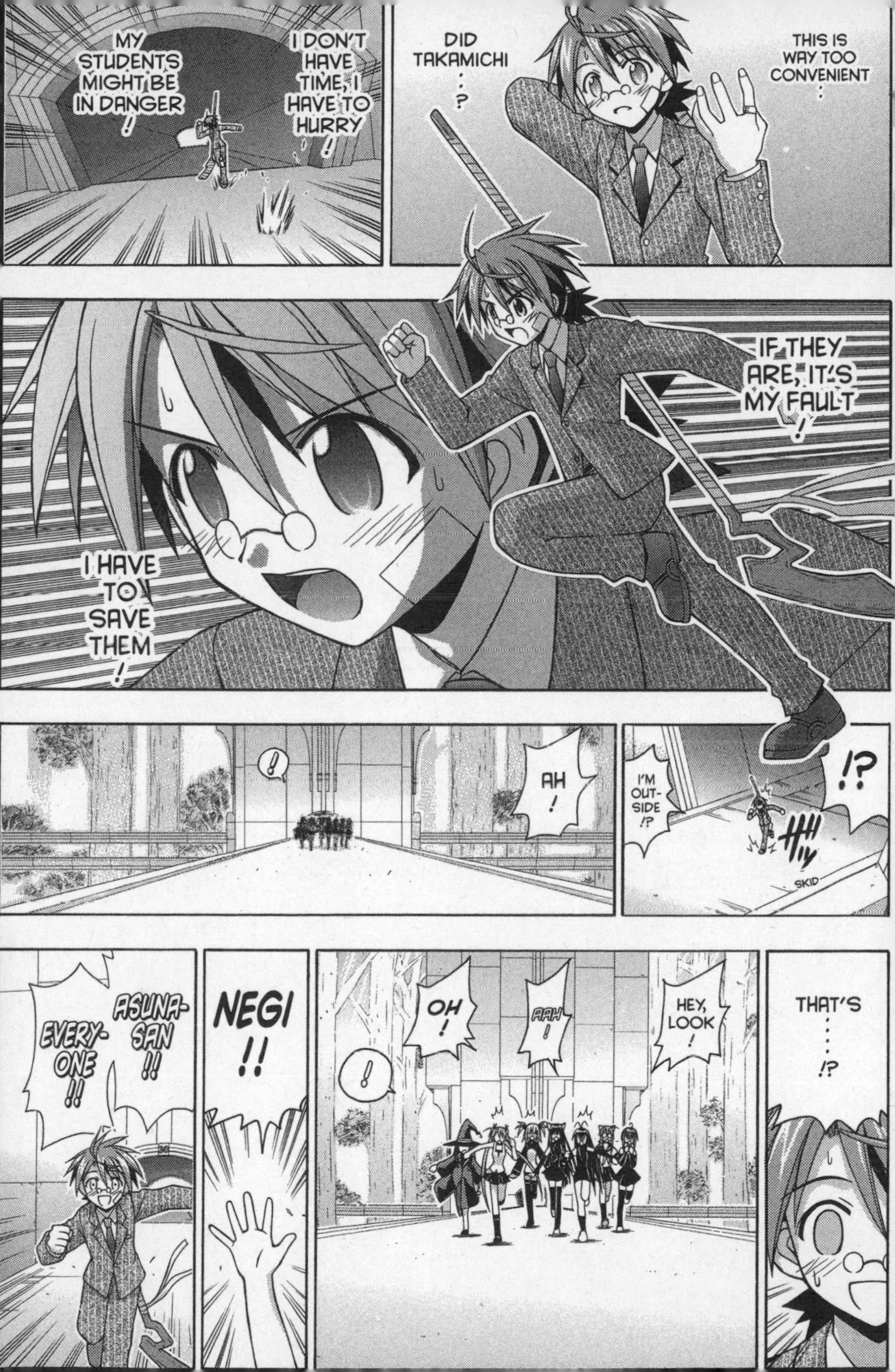
THIS IS WAY TOO CONVENIENT...
DID TAKAMICHI...?
I DON'T HAVE TIME, I HAVE TO HURRY!
MY STUDENTS MIGHT BE IN DANGER!
IF THEY ARE, IT'S MY FAULT!
I HAVE TO SAVE THEM!
!?
I'M OUT-SIDE !?
SKID
AH!
!
THAT'S...!?
HEY, LOOK!
AAH!
OH!
!
NEGI!!
ASUNA-SAN!!
EVERY-ONE!!

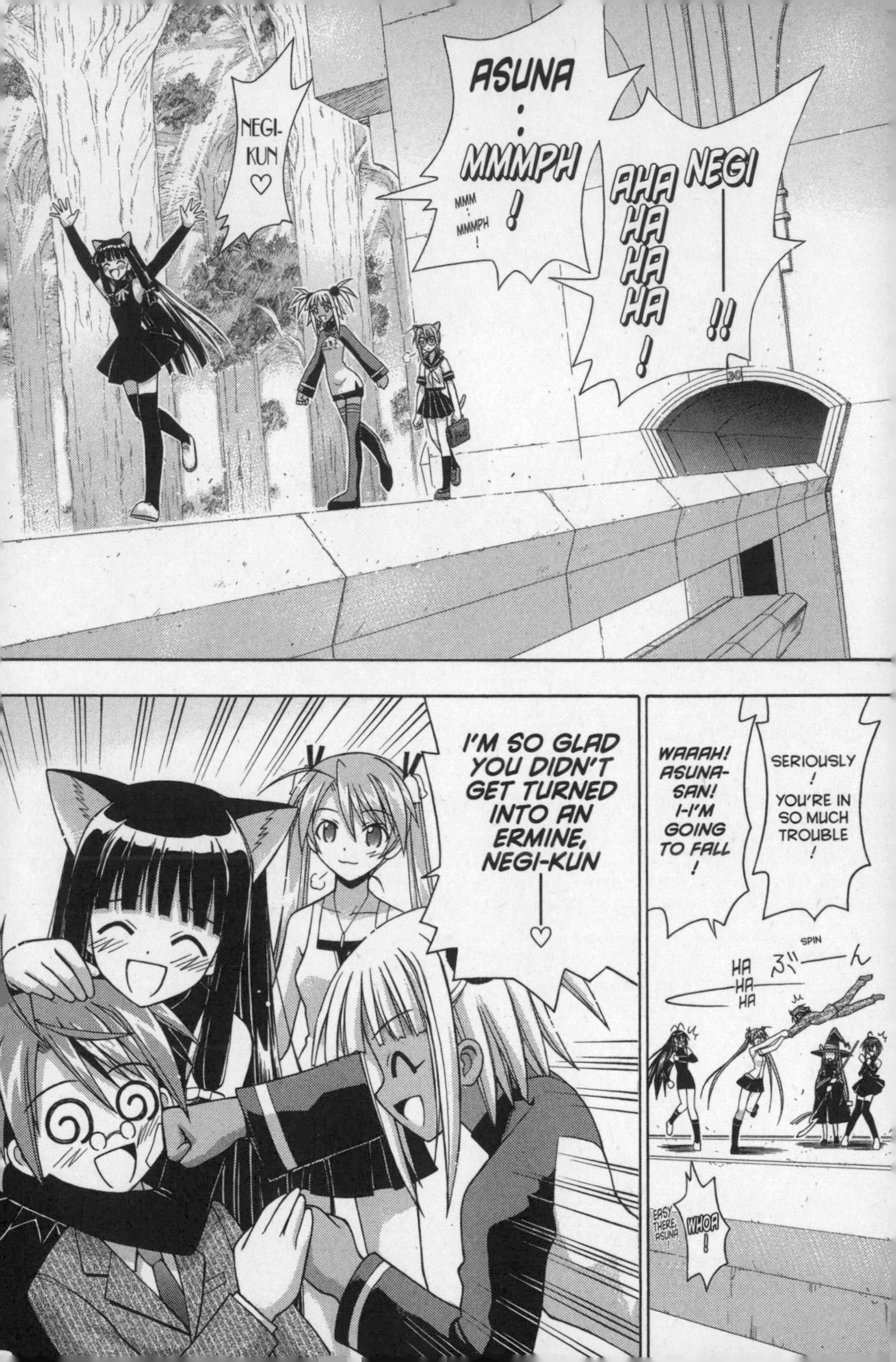
NEGI —— !!
AHA HA HA HA !
ASUNA : MMMPH !
MMM : MMMPH !
NEGI-KUN ♡
SERIOUSLY! YOU'RE IN SO MUCH TROUBLE!
WAAAH! ASUNA-SAN! I-I'M GOING TO FALL!
SPIN
HA HA HA
WHOA!
EASY THERE, ASUNA!
I'M SO GLAD YOU DIDN'T GET TURNED INTO AN ERMINE, NEGI-KUN —— ♡

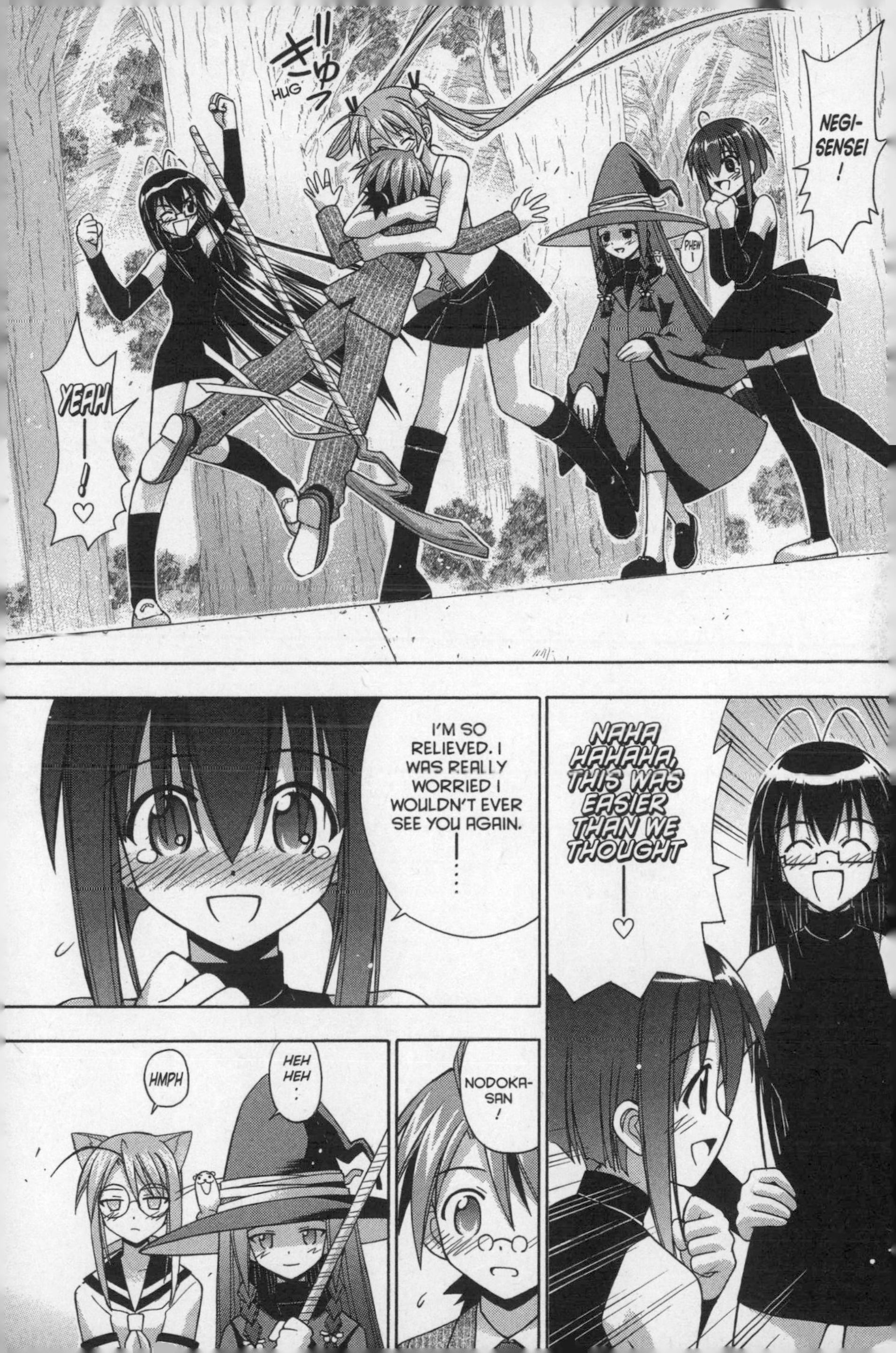
NEGI-SENSEI!
PHEW
きゅっ
HUG
YEAH—!♡
NAHA HAHAHA, THIS WAS EASIER THAN WE THOUGHT—♡
I'M SO RELIEVED. I WAS REALLY WORRIED I WOULDN'T EVER SEE YOU AGAIN.—...
NODOKA-SAN!
HEH HEH..
HMPH

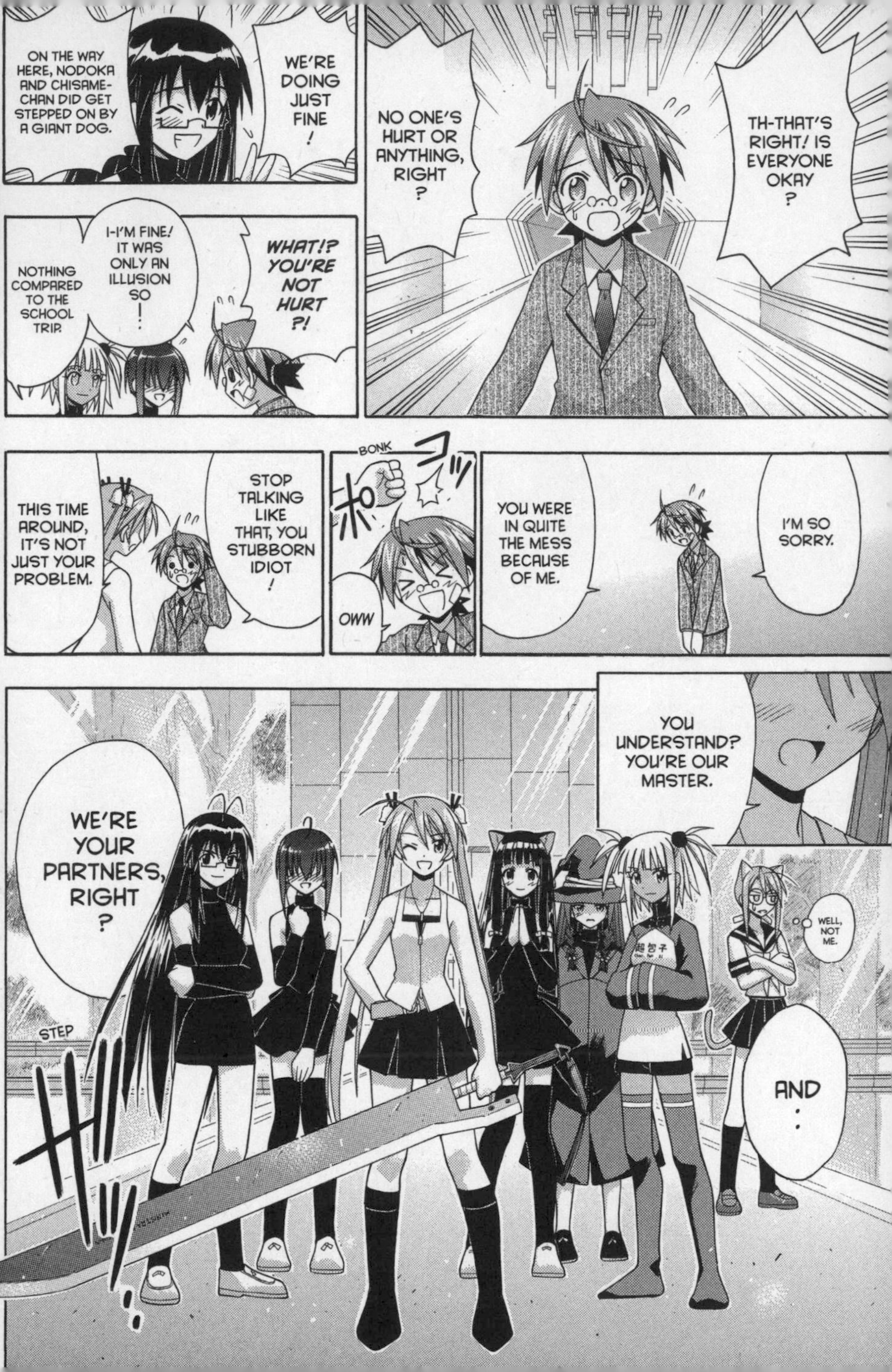
TH-THAT'S RIGHT! IS EVERYONE OKAY?
NO ONE'S HURT OR ANYTHING, RIGHT?
WE'RE DOING JUST FINE!
ON THE WAY HERE, NODOKA AND CHISAME-CHAN DID GET STEPPED ON BY A GIANT DOG.
WHAT!? YOU'RE NOT HURT?!
I-I'M FINE! IT WAS ONLY AN ILLUSION SO...!
NOTHING COMPARED TO THE SCHOOL TRIP.
I'M SO SORRY.
YOU WERE IN QUITE THE MESS BECAUSE OF ME.
BONK
OWW
STOP TALKING LIKE THAT, YOU STUBBORN IDIOT!
THIS TIME AROUND, IT'S NOT JUST YOUR PROBLEM.
YOU UNDERSTAND? YOU'RE OUR MASTER.
WE'RE YOUR PARTNERS, RIGHT?
WELL, NOT ME.
AND...
STEP

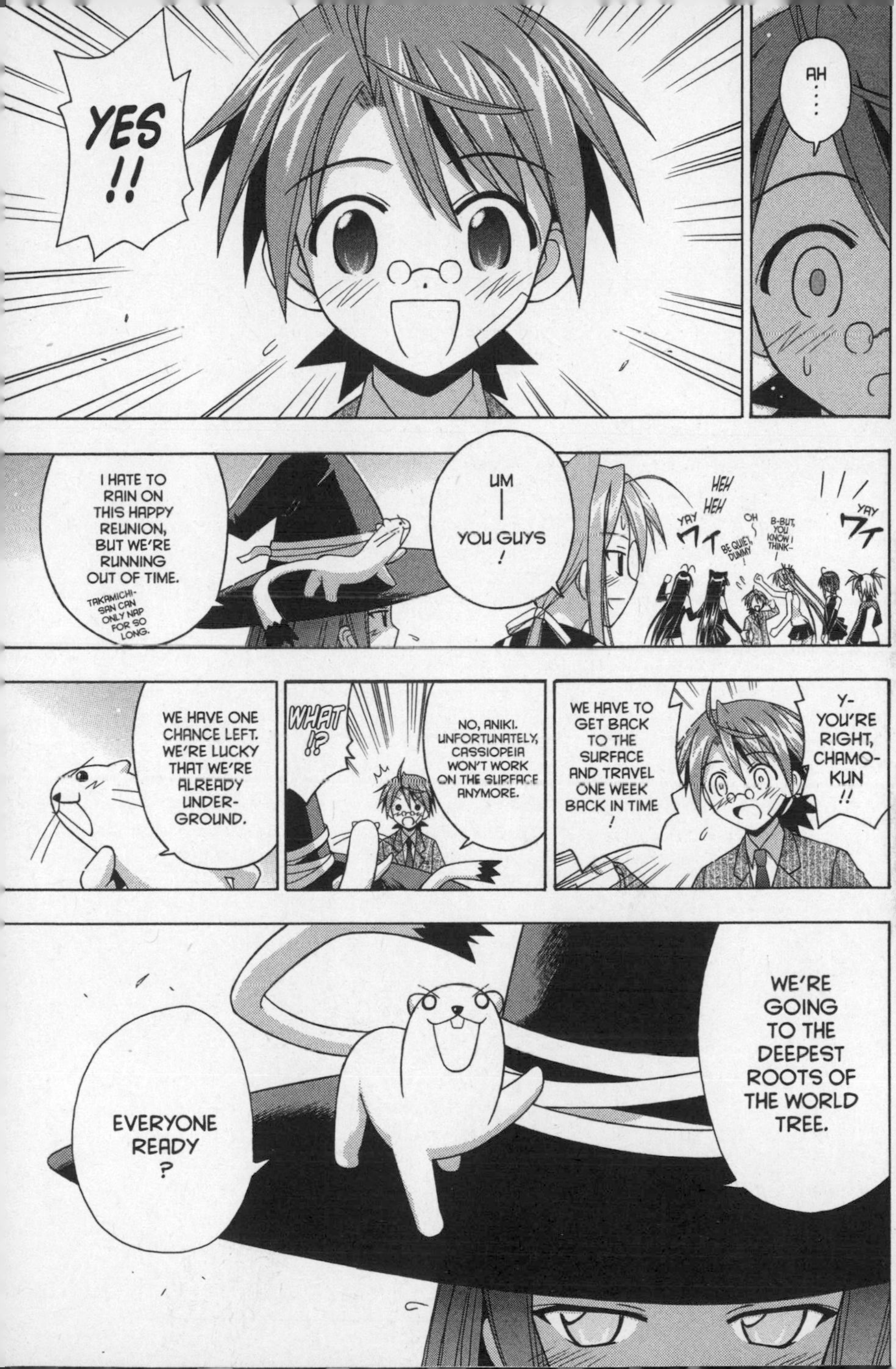
AH...
YES!!
YAY
B-BUT, YOU KNOW I THINK–
OH
BE QUIET, DUMMY!
HEH HEH
YAY
UM — YOU GUYS!
I HATE TO RAIN ON THIS HAPPY REUNION, BUT WE'RE RUNNING OUT OF TIME.
TAKAMICHI-SAN CAN ONLY NAP FOR SO LONG.
Y-YOU'RE RIGHT, CHAMO-KUN!!
WE HAVE TO GET BACK TO THE SURFACE AND TRAVEL ONE WEEK BACK IN TIME!
NO, ANIKI. UNFORTUNATELY, CASSIOPEIA WON'T WORK ON THE SURFACE ANYMORE.
WHAT!?
WE HAVE ONE CHANCE LEFT. WE'RE LUCKY THAT WE'RE ALREADY UNDERGROUND.
WE'RE GOING TO THE DEEPEST ROOTS OF THE WORLD TREE.
EVERYONE READY?

LEXICON MAGICUM NEGIMARIUM

■世界図絵
オルビス・センスアリウム・ピクトゥス

ORBIS SENSUALIUM PICTUS

By the power of the Pactio with Negi, Yue Ayase is awarded this artifact. She also receives a flying broom and a mage's robe and pointed hat.

As shown in the story, this artifact is primarily an encyclopedia of magic. As one reads on, the user is able to follow related links in order to find more and more detailed information, but in order to understand the entries, the reader must already have a basic grasp of the material. So, even before reading, the user must be well versed in magical study in order to properly make use of it.

Although the encyclopedia is a very powerful tool, it has one major flaw. The book is connected to Mage-Net and is therefore constantly being updated, so that old data is always being overwritten by new information. Up-to-date information is indeed a powerful tool, yet something important may be lost in the process. For example, old and yet still significant information about ancient magic (such as rituals performed in the days of yore) might accidentally be deleted to make room for new data. This counters the methodology of nineteenth-century philology of ancient texts. The *Orbis Sensualium Pictus* was not created to emphasize ancient texts with a modern viewpoint but as a book of dynamic writings based on the feudalistic system of the ancient cultures of words.

John Amos Comenius (1592–1670), a Czech educator, created the *Orbis Sensualium Pictus,* a children's textbook, with a guide to some Latin words. It is unknown if the artifact was created first or not. *Orbis Sensualium Pictus,* translated simply, means, "The Visible World in Pictures." The book explains basic pronunciation of the Latin alphabet and lists a series of words over 150 chapters, starting with DEUS (God) and ending with JUDICIUM EXTREMUM (Final Judgment). At the end, an entry reads, "You have now studied the basic Latin vocabulary" and concludes with "now take your leave," encouraging the reader to be independent. As a side note, Comenius was said to have strong connections with the secret societies of Renaissance Magic (Rose) and the Christian Counterreformation (Cross). It is not known whether these were societies of mages.

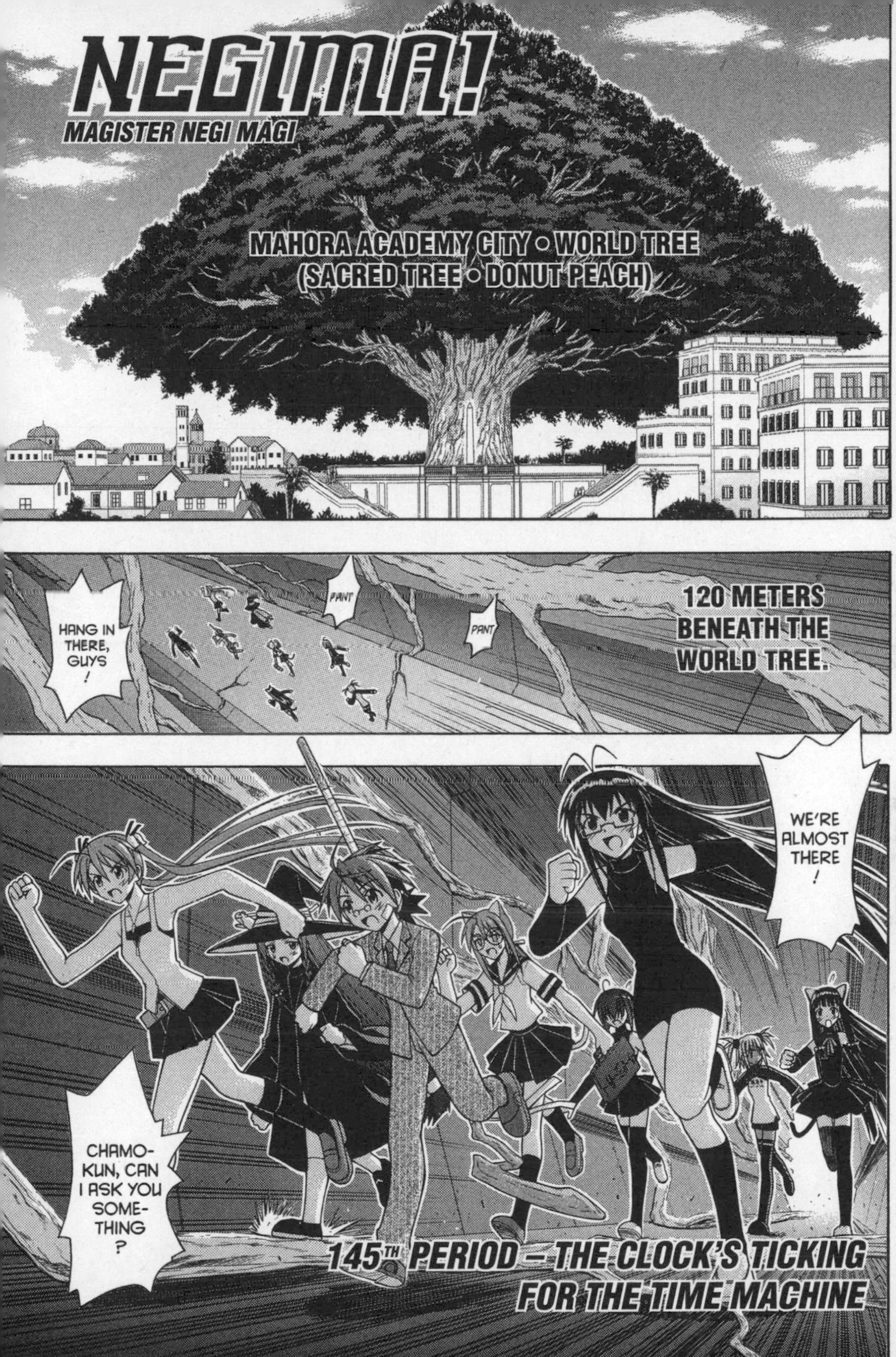
NEGIMA!
MAGISTER NEGI MAGI
MAHORA ACADEMY CITY • WORLD TREE (SACRED TREE • DONUT PEACH)
120 METERS BENEATH THE WORLD TREE.
PANT
PANT
HANG IN THERE, GUYS!
WE'RE ALMOST THERE!
CHAMO-KUN, CAN I ASK YOU SOME-THING?
145TH PERIOD – THE CLOCK'S TICKING FOR THE TIME MACHINE

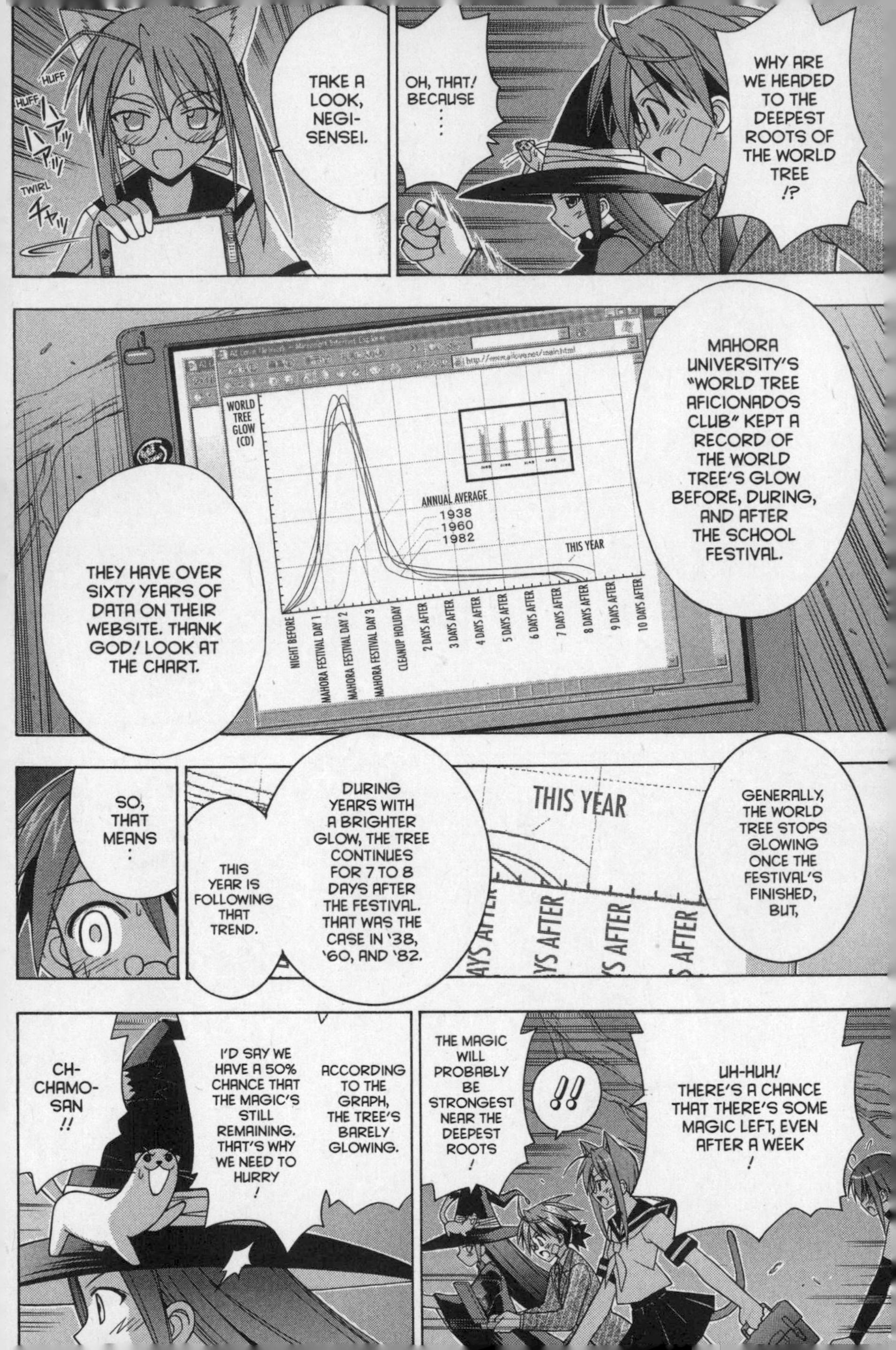
WHY ARE WE HEADED TO THE DEEPEST ROOTS OF THE WORLD TREE !?
OH, THAT! BECAUSE ...
TAKE A LOOK, NEGI-SENSEI.
HUFF
HUFF
TWIRL
MAHORA UNIVERSITY'S "WORLD TREE AFICIONADOS CLUB" KEPT A RECORD OF THE WORLD TREE'S GLOW BEFORE, DURING, AND AFTER THE SCHOOL FESTIVAL.
WORLD TREE GLOW (CD)
ANNUAL AVERAGE
1938
1960
1982
THIS YEAR
NIGHT BEFORE
MAHORA FESTIVAL DAY 1
MAHORA FESTIVAL DAY 2
MAHORA FESTIVAL DAY 3
CLEANUP HOLIDAY
2 DAYS AFTER
3 DAYS AFTER
4 DAYS AFTER
5 DAYS AFTER
6 DAYS AFTER
7 DAYS AFTER
8 DAYS AFTER
9 DAYS AFTER
10 DAYS AFTER
THEY HAVE OVER SIXTY YEARS OF DATA ON THEIR WEBSITE. THANK GOD! LOOK AT THE CHART.
GENERALLY, THE WORLD TREE STOPS GLOWING ONCE THE FESTIVAL'S FINISHED, BUT,
THIS YEAR
DURING YEARS WITH A BRIGHTER GLOW, THE TREE CONTINUES FOR 7 TO 8 DAYS AFTER THE FESTIVAL. THAT WAS THE CASE IN '38, '60, AND '82.
THIS YEAR IS FOLLOWING THAT TREND.
SO, THAT MEANS :
UH-HUH! THERE'S A CHANCE THAT THERE'S SOME MAGIC LEFT, EVEN AFTER A WEEK !
!!
THE MAGIC WILL PROBABLY BE STRONGEST NEAR THE DEEPEST ROOTS !
ACCORDING TO THE GRAPH, THE TREE'S BARELY GLOWING.
I'D SAY WE HAVE A 50% CHANCE THAT THE MAGIC'S STILL REMAINING. THAT'S WHY WE NEED TO HURRY !
CH-CHAMO-SAN !!

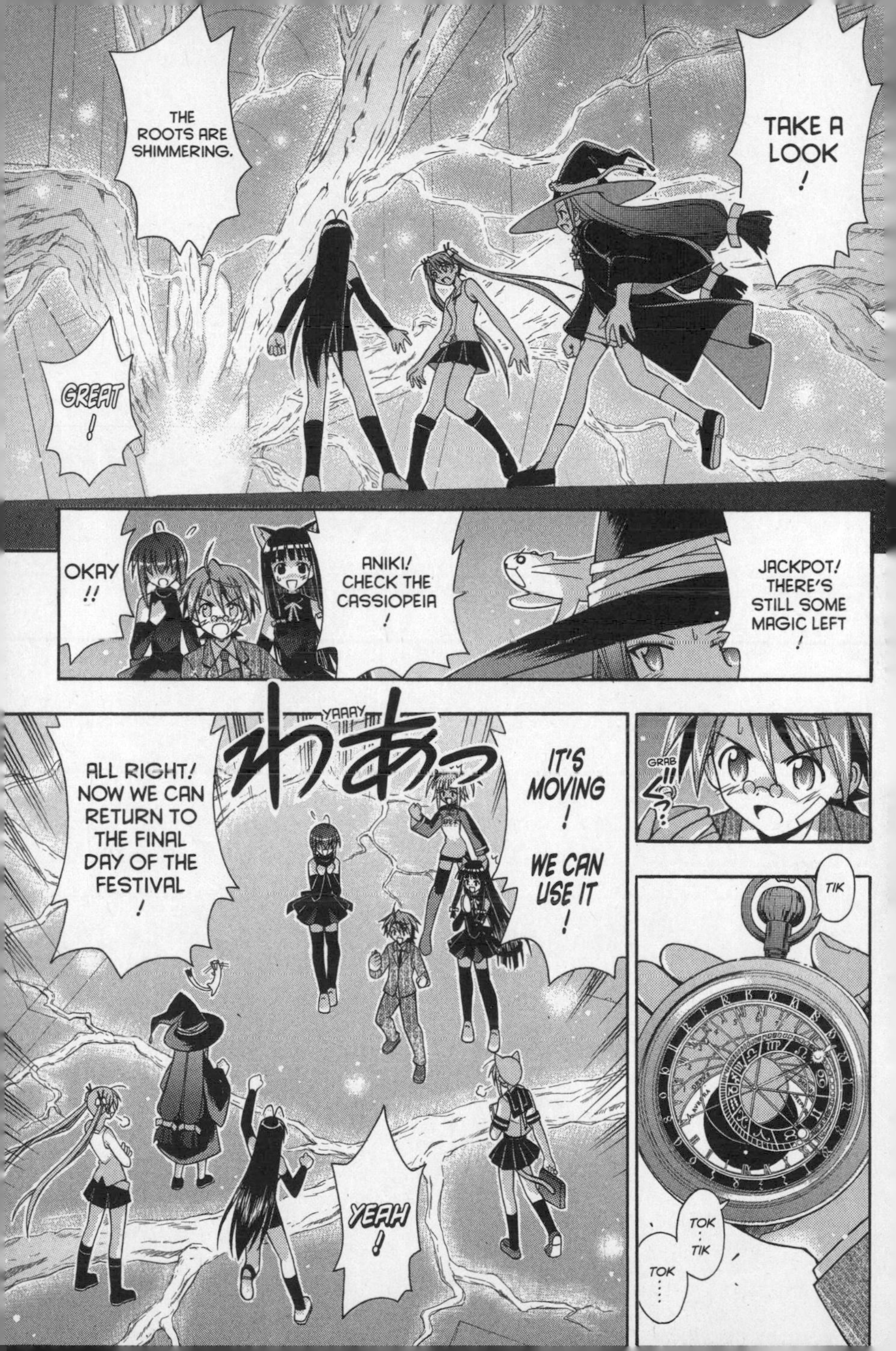
TAKE A LOOK!
THE ROOTS ARE SHIMMERING.
GREAT!
JACKPOT! THERE'S STILL SOME MAGIC LEFT!
ANIKI! CHECK THE CASSIOPEIA!
OKAY!!
GRAB
TIK
TOK... TIK
TOK....
YAAAY
わあっ
IT'S MOVING!
WE CAN USE IT!
ALL RIGHT! NOW WE CAN RETURN TO THE FINAL DAY OF THE FESTIVAL!
YEAH!

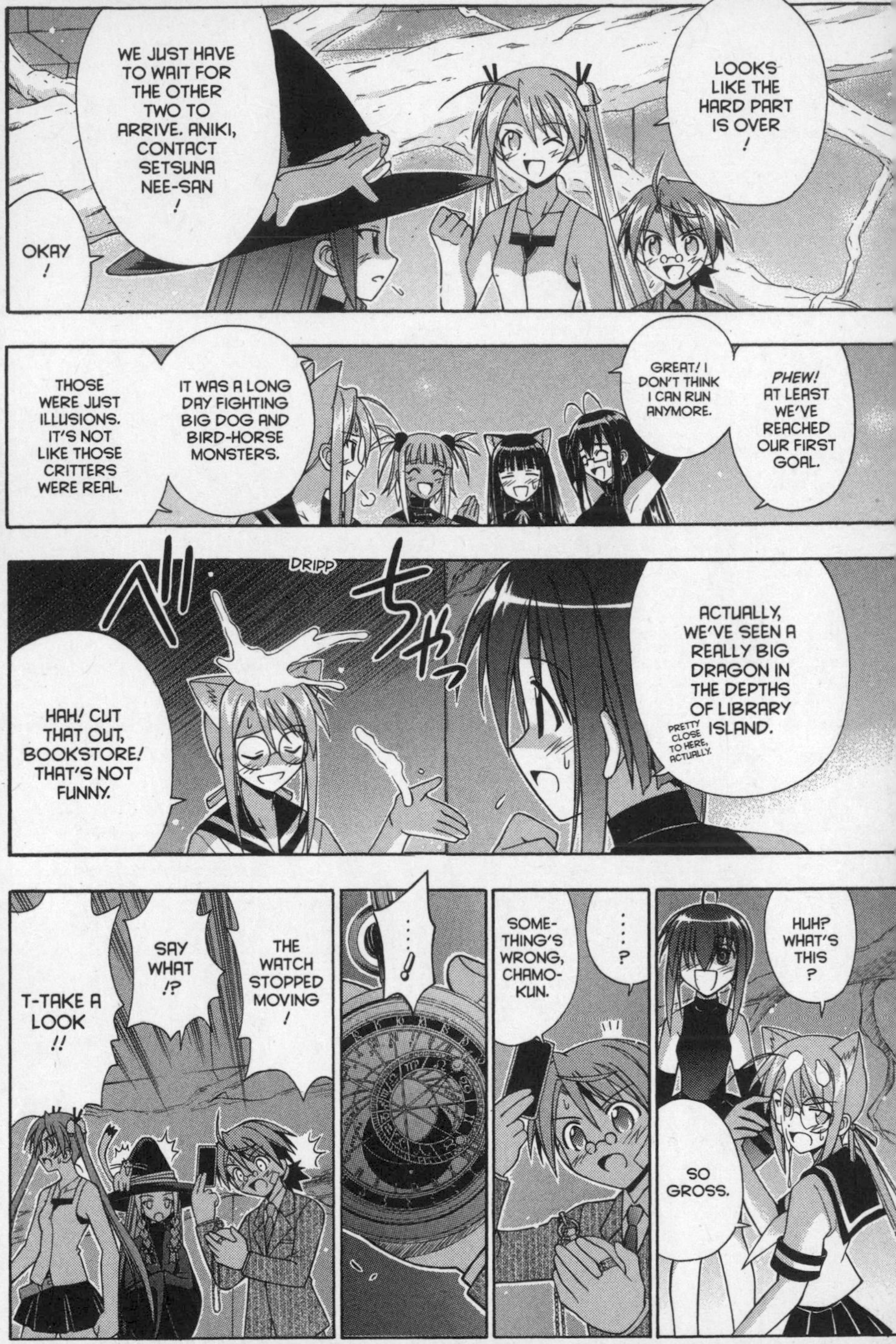
LOOKS LIKE THE HARD PART IS OVER!
WE JUST HAVE TO WAIT FOR THE OTHER TWO TO ARRIVE. ANIKI, CONTACT SETSUNA NEE-SAN!
OKAY!
PHEW! AT LEAST WE'VE REACHED OUR FIRST GOAL.
GREAT! I DON'T THINK I CAN RUN ANYMORE.
IT WAS A LONG DAY FIGHTING BIG DOG AND BIRD-HORSE MONSTERS.
THOSE WERE JUST ILLUSIONS. IT'S NOT LIKE THOSE CRITTERS WERE REAL.
ACTUALLY, WE'VE SEEN A REALLY BIG DRAGON IN THE DEPTHS OF LIBRARY ISLAND.
PRETTY CLOSE TO HERE, ACTUALLY.
DRIPP
HAH! CUT THAT OUT, BOOKSTORE! THAT'S NOT FUNNY.
HUH? WHAT'S THIS?
SO GROSS.
....?
SOME-THING'S WRONG, CHAMO-KUN.
....!
THE WATCH STOPPED MOVING!
SAY WHAT!?
T-TAKE A LOOK!!

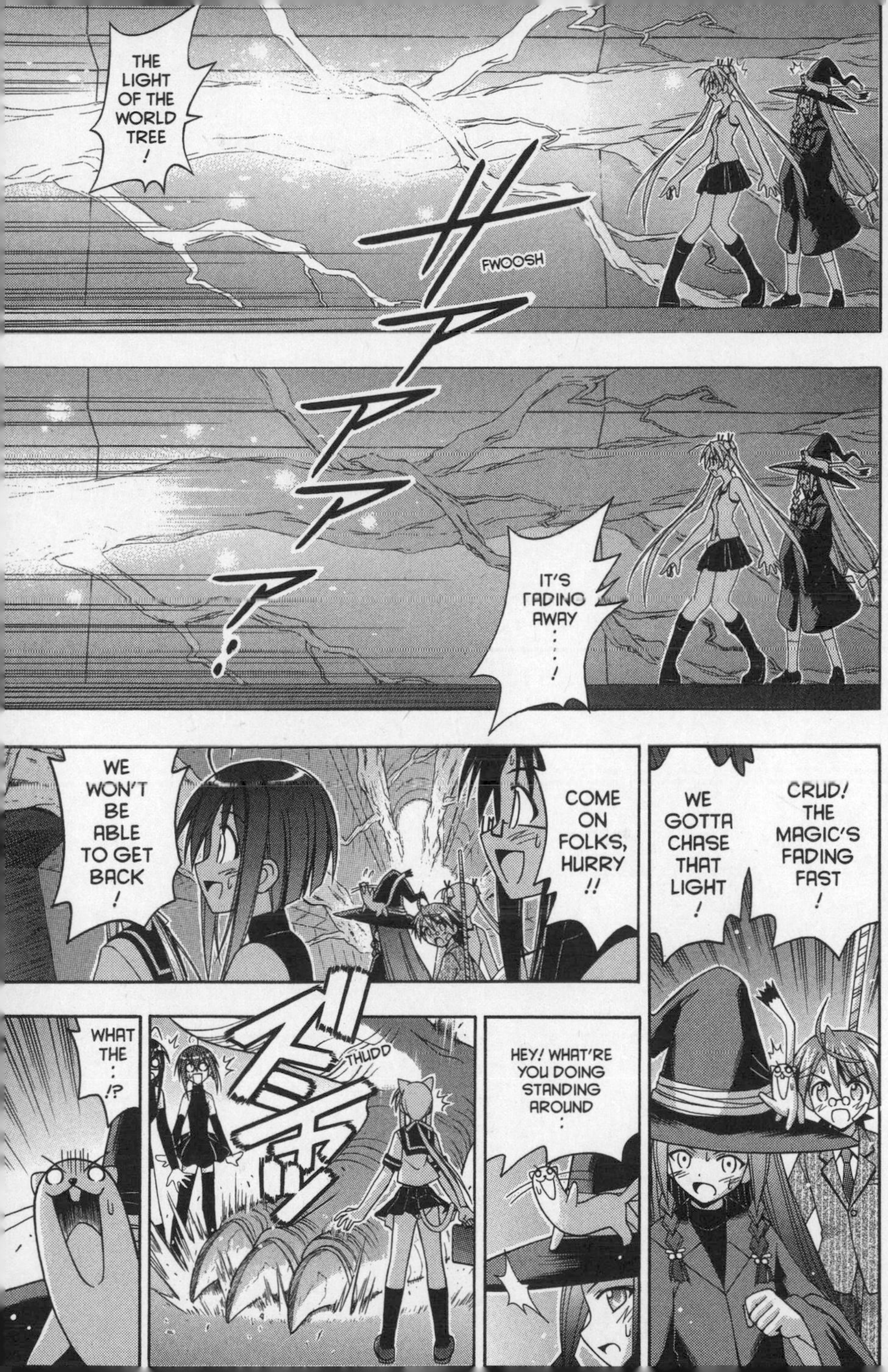

THE LIGHT OF THE WORLD TREE!
FWOOSH
IT'S FADING AWAY.....!
CRUD! THE MAGIC'S FADING FAST!
WE GOTTA CHASE THAT LIGHT!
COME ON FOLKS, HURRY!!
WE WON'T BE ABLE TO GET BACK!
HEY! WHAT'RE YOU DOING STANDING AROUND..
THUDD
WHAT THE..!?

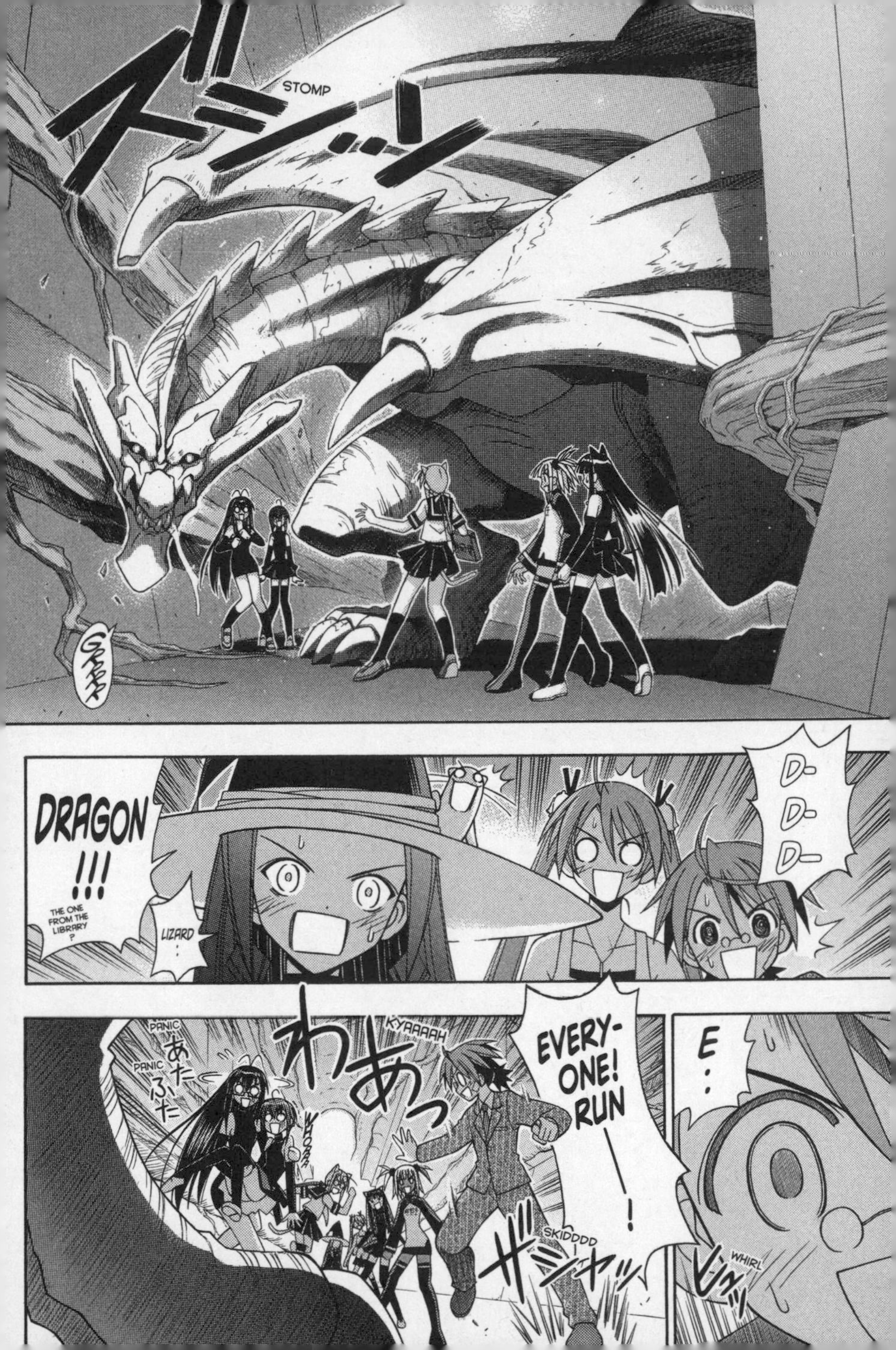
STOMP
D-
D-
D–
LIZARD
...
DRAGON
!!!
THE ONE FROM THE LIBRARY
?
E
..
WHIRL
EVERY-ONE! RUN
—
!
KYAAAAH
わあっ
PANIC
あた
PANIC
ふた
SKIDDDD

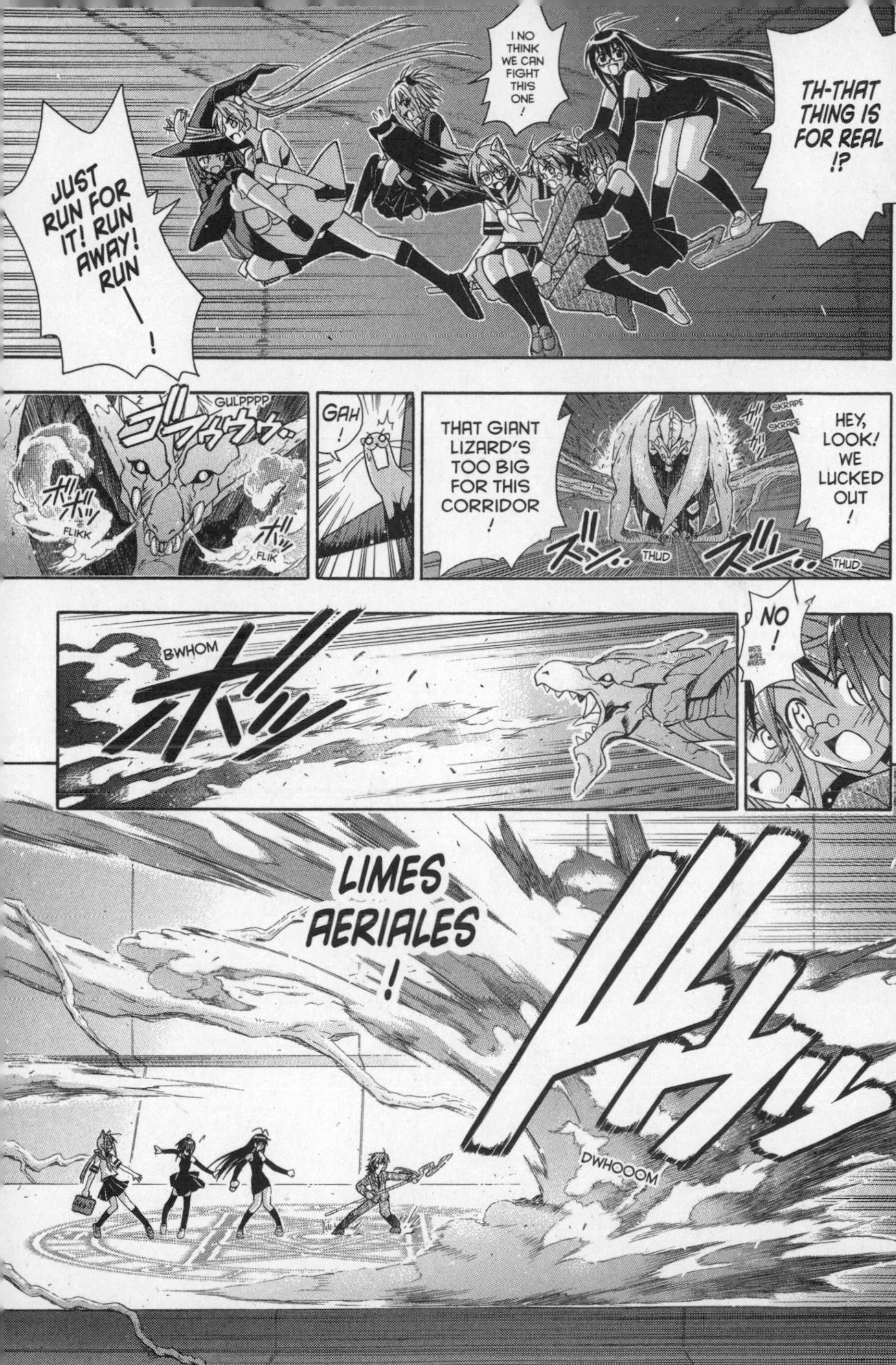

TH-THAT THING IS FOR REAL !?
I NO THINK WE CAN FIGHT THIS ONE !
JUST RUN FOR IT! RUN AWAY! RUN—!
HEY, LOOK! WE LUCKED OUT!
SKRAPE
SKRAPE
THAT GIANT LIZARD'S TOO BIG FOR THIS CORRIDOR!
THUD
THUD
GAH!
GULPPPP
FLIKK
FLIK
NO!
RASTEL MASKIL MAGISTER
BWHOM
LIMES AERIALES!
DWHOOOM

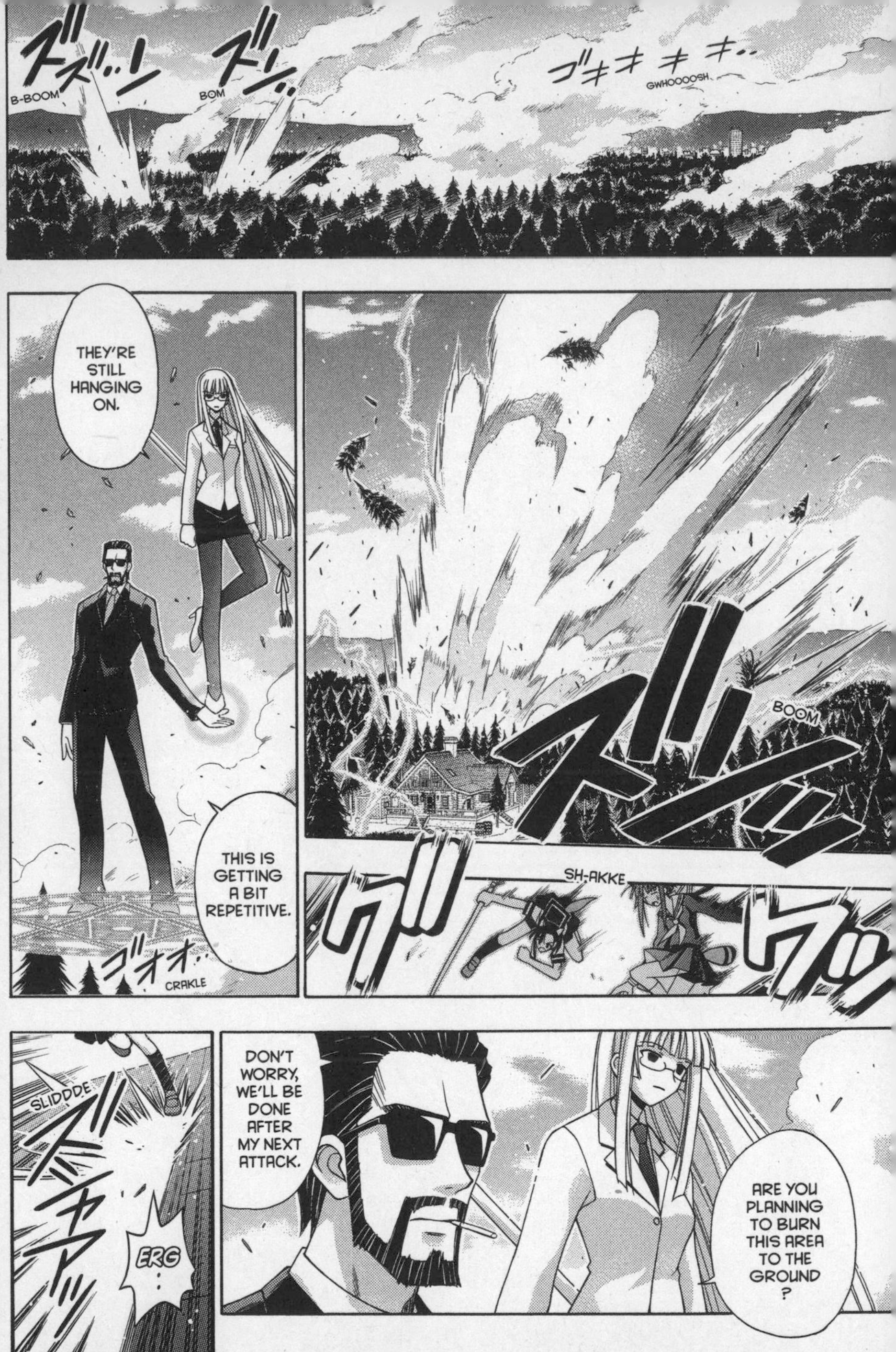
GWHOOOOSH
BOM
B-BOOM
BOOM
SH-AKKE
THEY'RE STILL HANGING ON.
THIS IS GETTING A BIT REPETITIVE.
CRAKLE
ARE YOU PLANNING TO BURN THIS AREA TO THE GROUND ?
DON'T WORRY, WE'LL BE DONE AFTER MY NEXT ATTACK.
SLIDDDE
ERG

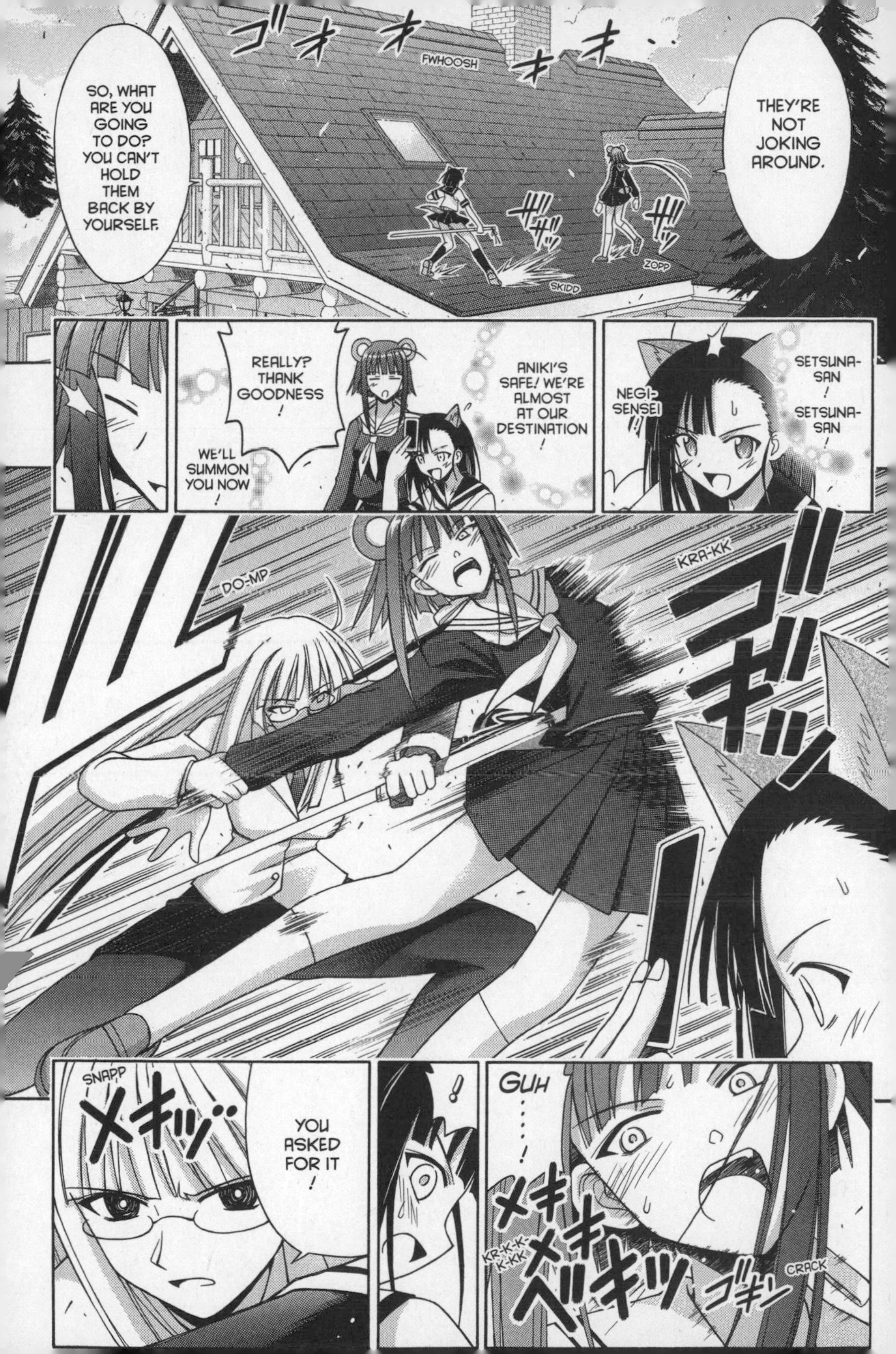

THEY'RE NOT JOKING AROUND.
FWHOOSH
SO, WHAT ARE YOU GOING TO DO? YOU CAN'T HOLD THEM BACK BY YOURSELF.
ZOPP
SKIDD
SETSUNA-SAN! SETSUNA-SAN!
NEGI-SENSEI!!
ANIKI'S SAFE! WE'RE ALMOST AT OUR DESTINATION!
REALLY? THANK GOODNESS!
WE'LL SUMMON YOU NOW!
KRA-KK
DO-MP
GUH...!
KR-K-K-K-KK
CRACK
!
SNAPP!
YOU ASKED FOR IT!

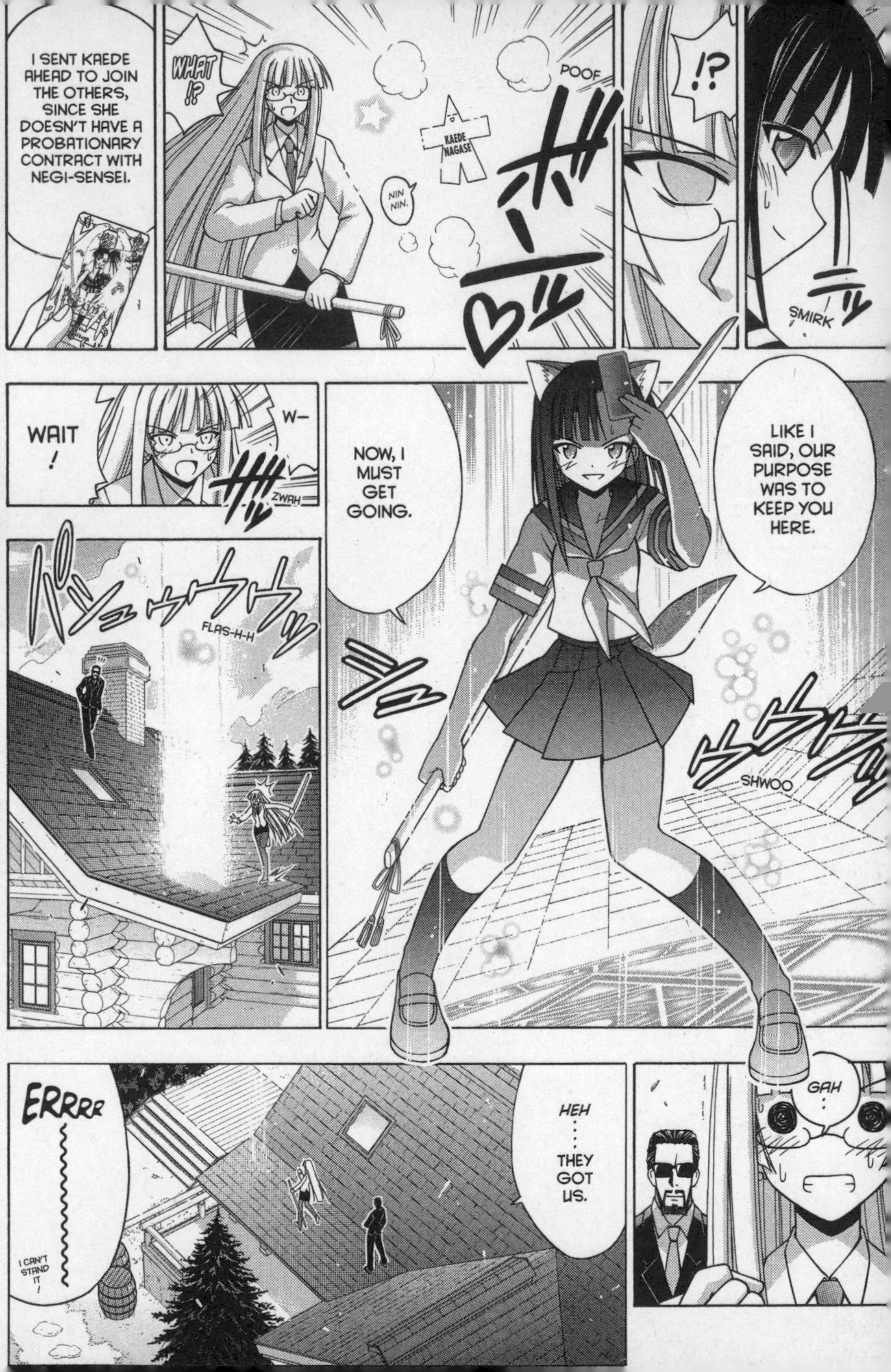
!?
SMIRK
POOF
KAEDE NAGASE
NIN NIN.
WHAT !?
I SENT KAEDE AHEAD TO JOIN THE OTHERS, SINCE SHE DOESN'T HAVE A PROBATIONARY CONTRACT WITH NEGI-SENSEI.
LIKE I SAID, OUR PURPOSE WAS TO KEEP YOU HERE.
NOW, I MUST GET GOING.
SHWOO
W—
WAIT !
ZWAH
FLAS-H-H
GAH ...
HEH ... THEY GOT US.
ERRRR
I CAN'T STAND IT !

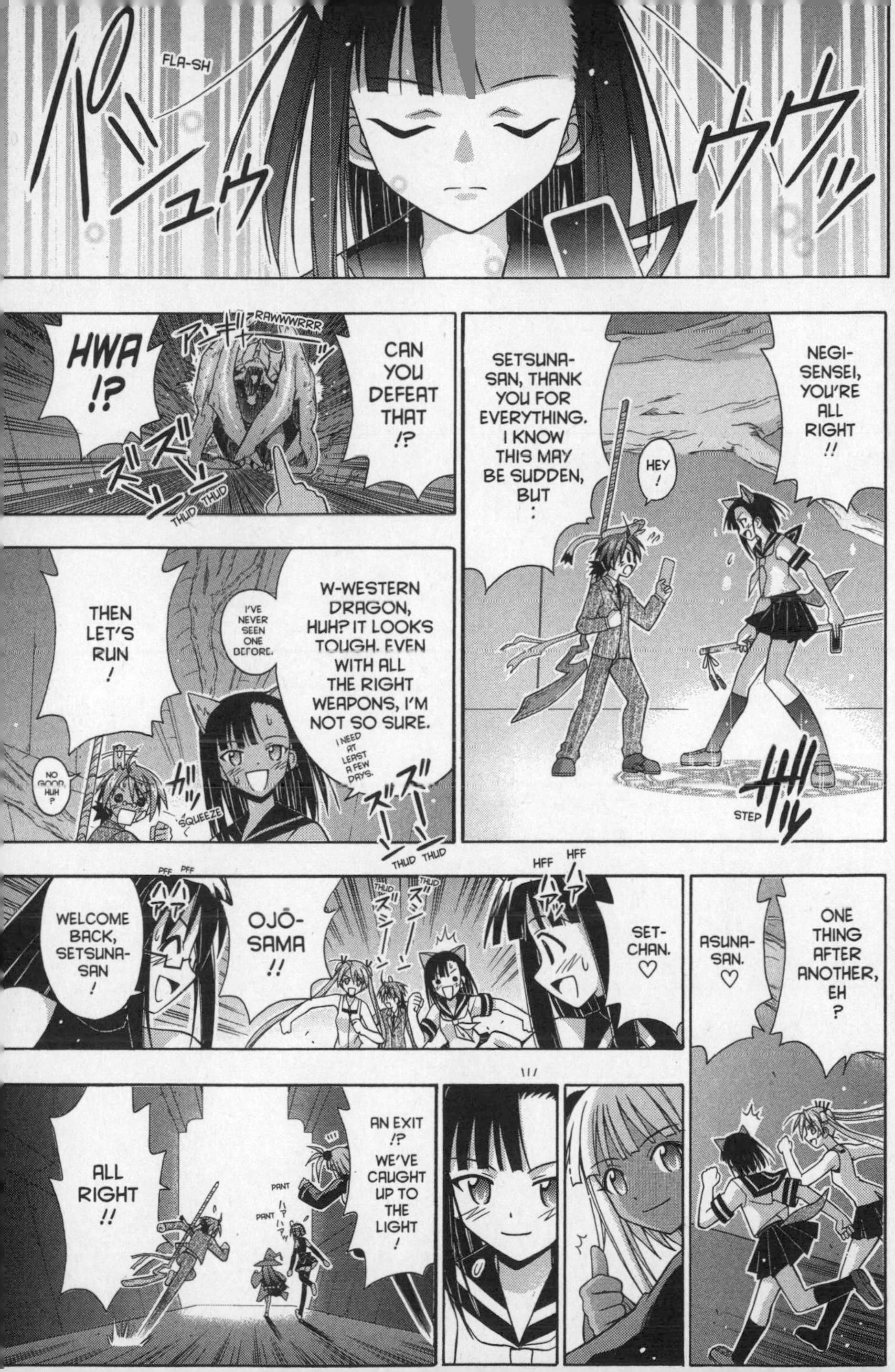
FLA-SH
NEGI-SENSEI, YOU'RE ALL RIGHT!!
SETSUNA-SAN, THANK YOU FOR EVERYTHING. I KNOW THIS MAY BE SUDDEN, BUT:
HEY!
STEP
RAWWWRRR
CAN YOU DEFEAT THAT!?
HWA!?
THUD THUD
W-WESTERN DRAGON, HUH? IT LOOKS TOUGH. EVEN WITH ALL THE RIGHT WEAPONS, I'M NOT SO SURE.
I'VE NEVER SEEN ONE BEFORE.
THEN LET'S RUN!
I NEED AT LEAST A FEW DAYS.
NO GOOD, HUH?
SQUEEZE
THUD THUD
ONE THING AFTER ANOTHER, EH?
ASUNA-SAN. ♡
HFF HFF
SET-CHAN. ♡
THUD THUD
OJŌ-SAMA!!
PFF PFF
WELCOME BACK, SETSUNA-SAN!
AN EXIT!? WE'VE CAUGHT UP TO THE LIGHT!
PANT PANT
ALL RIGHT!!

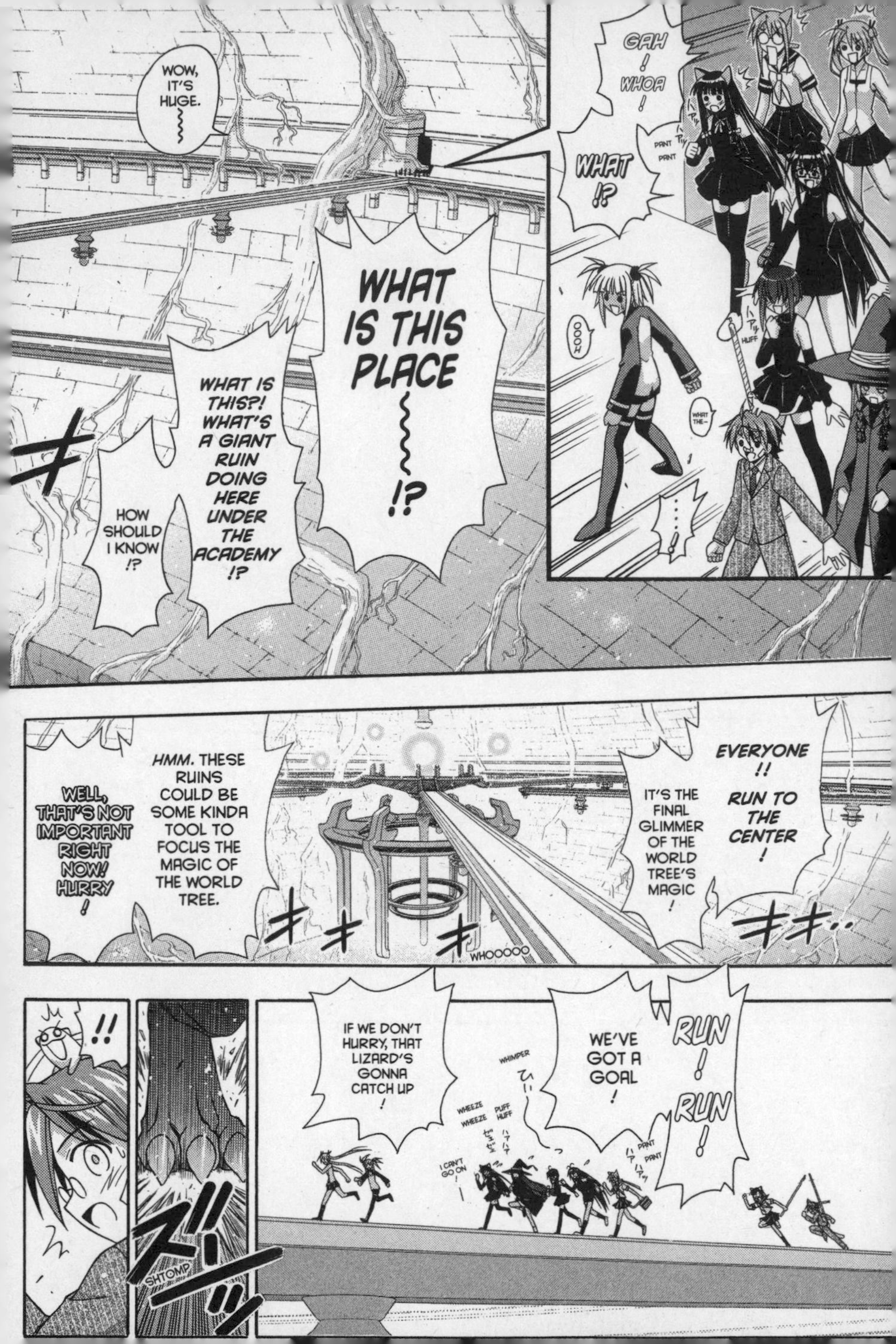
GAH! WHOA!
WHAT!?
PANT PANT
OOOH
WHAT THE—
...!
WOW, IT'S HUGE.
WHAT IS THIS PLACE~~~!?
WHAT IS THIS?! WHAT'S A GIANT RUIN DOING HERE UNDER THE ACADEMY!?
HOW SHOULD I KNOW!?
EVERYONE!! RUN TO THE CENTER!
IT'S THE FINAL GLIMMER OF THE WORLD TREE'S MAGIC!
HMM. THESE RUINS COULD BE SOME KINDA TOOL TO FOCUS THE MAGIC OF THE WORLD TREE.
WELL, THAT'S NOT IMPORTANT RIGHT NOW! HURRY!
WHOOOOO
RUN! RUN!
WE'VE GOT A GOAL!
PANT PANT
IF WE DON'T HURRY, THAT LIZARD'S GONNA CATCH UP!
WHIMPER
WHEEZE WHEEZE
PUFF HUFF
I CAN'T GO ON!
SHTOMP
!!

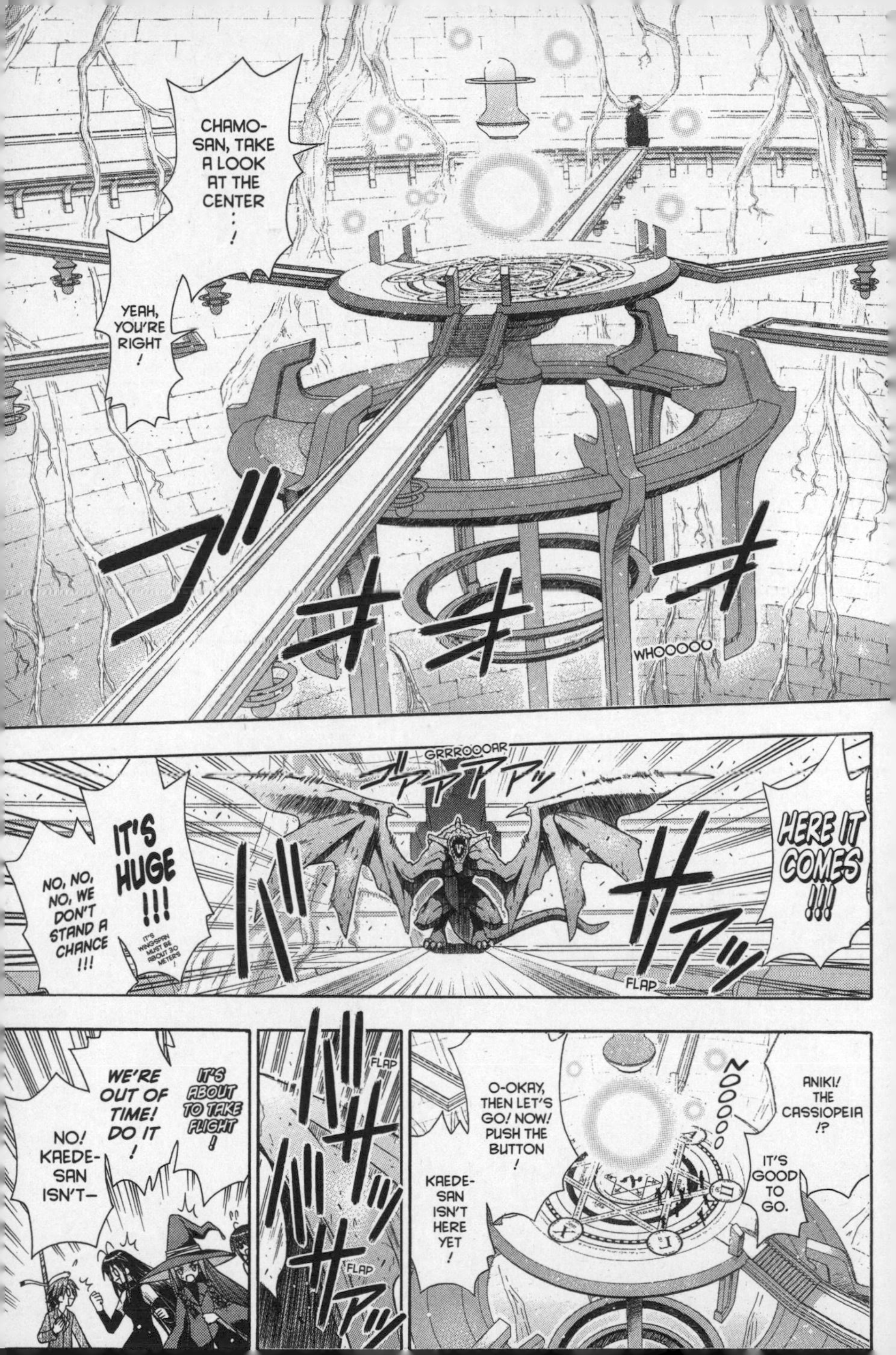
CHAMO-SAN, TAKE A LOOK AT THE CENTER...!
YEAH, YOU'RE RIGHT!
WHOOOOO
HERE IT COMES!!!
GRRROOOAR
FLAP
IT'S HUGE!!!
IT'S WINGSPAN MUST BE ABOUT 30 METERS
NO, NO, NO, WE DON'T STAND A CHANCE!!!
ANIKI! THE CASSIOPEIA!?
IT'S GOOD TO GO.
NOOOOOO
O-OKAY, THEN LET'S GO! NOW! PUSH THE BUTTON!
KAEDE-SAN ISN'T HERE YET!
FLAP
FLAP
IT'S ABOUT TO TAKE FLIGHT!
WE'RE OUT OF TIME! DO IT!
NO! KAEDE-SAN ISN'T—

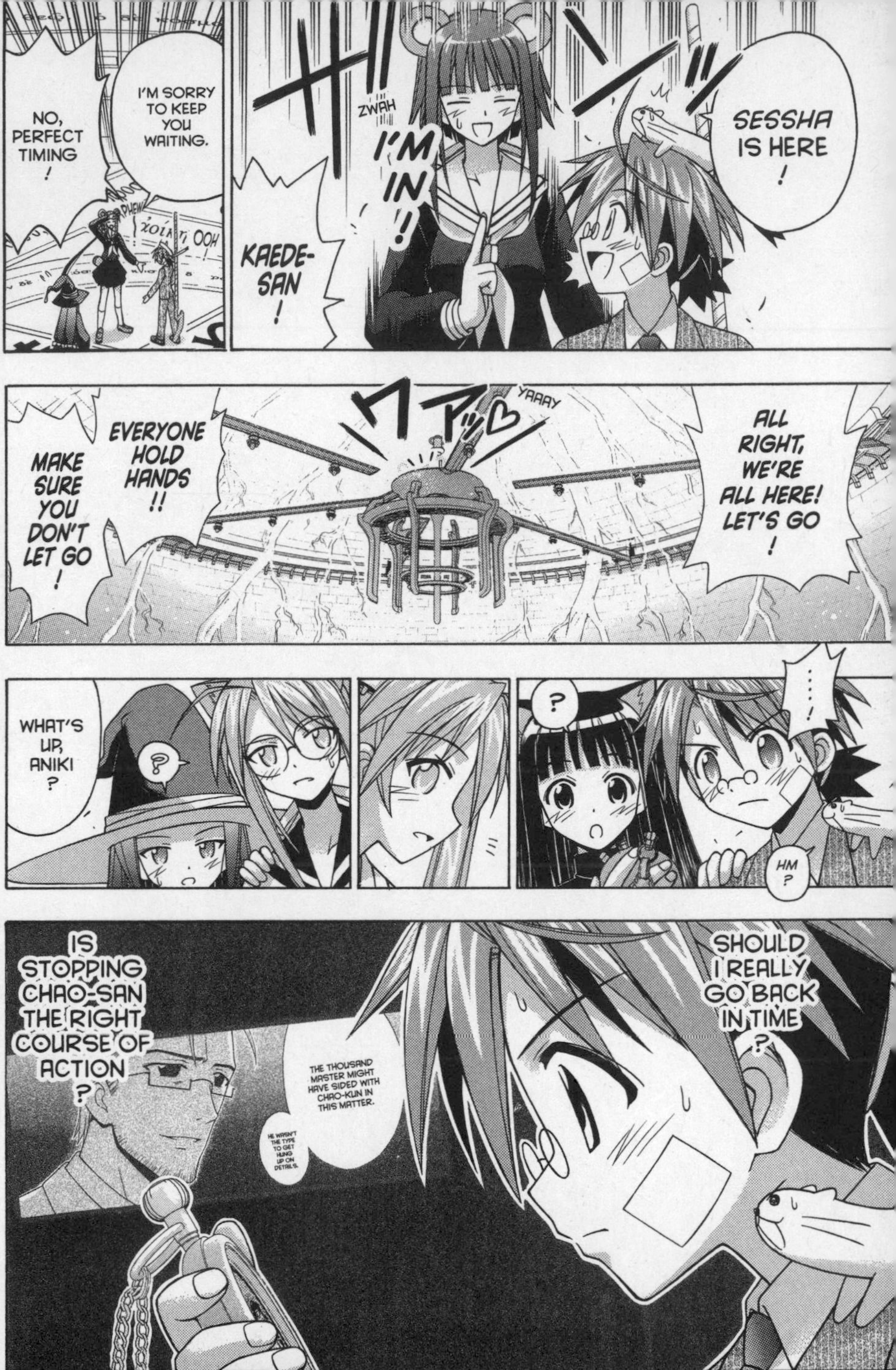
SESSHA IS HERE!
ZWAH
I'M IN!
KAEDE-SAN!
I'M SORRY TO KEEP YOU WAITING.
NO, PERFECT TIMING!
PHEW
OOH
ALL RIGHT, WE'RE ALL HERE! LET'S GO!
YAAAY
EVERYONE HOLD HANDS!!
MAKE SURE YOU DON'T LET GO!
...!
?
HM?
?
WHAT'S UP, ANIKI?
SHOULD I REALLY GO BACK IN TIME?
IS STOPPING CHAO-SAN THE RIGHT COURSE OF ACTION?
THE THOUSAND MASTER MIGHT HAVE SIDED WITH CHAO-KUN IN THIS MATTER.
HE WASN'T THE TYPE TO GET HUNG UP ON DETAILS.

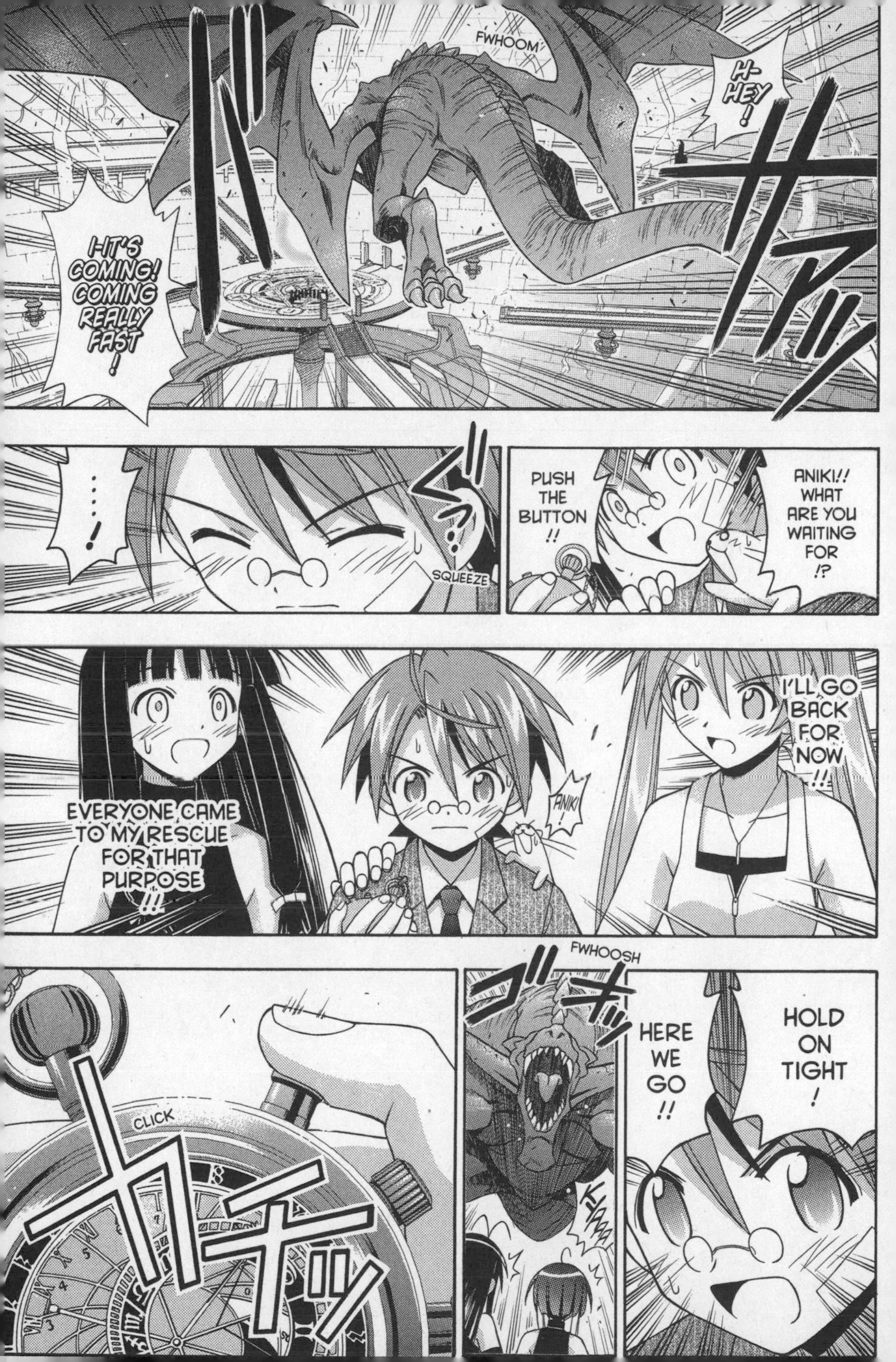
FWHOOM
H-HEY!
I-IT'S COMING! COMING REALLY FAST!
ANIKI!! WHAT ARE YOU WAITING FOR!?
PUSH THE BUTTON!!
SQUEEZE
......!
I'LL GO BACK FOR NOW!!
ANIKI!
EVERYONE CAME TO MY RESCUE FOR THAT PURPOSE!!
HOLD ON TIGHT!
HERE WE GO!!
FWHOOSH
CLICK

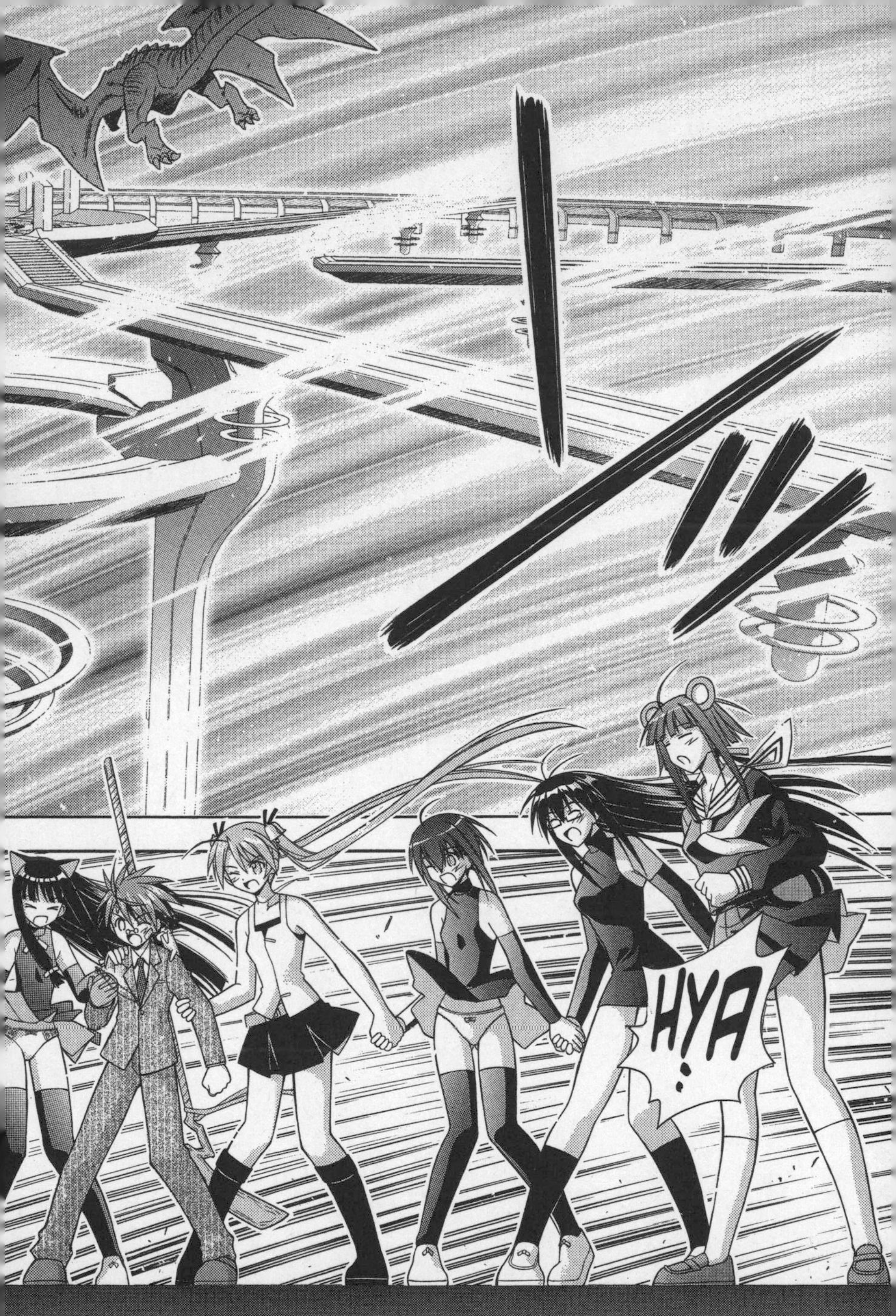
HYA!

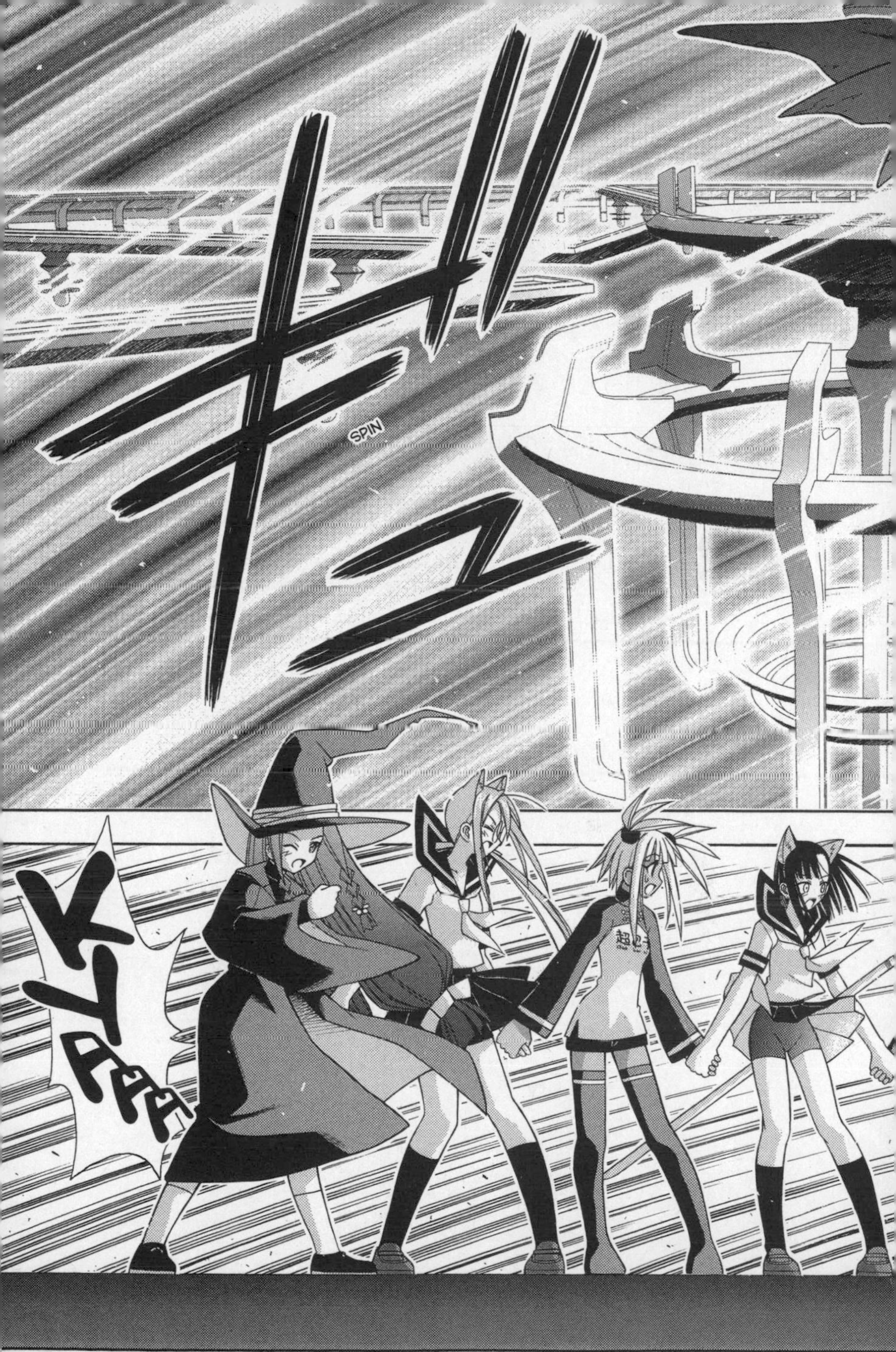
SPIN
KYAAA

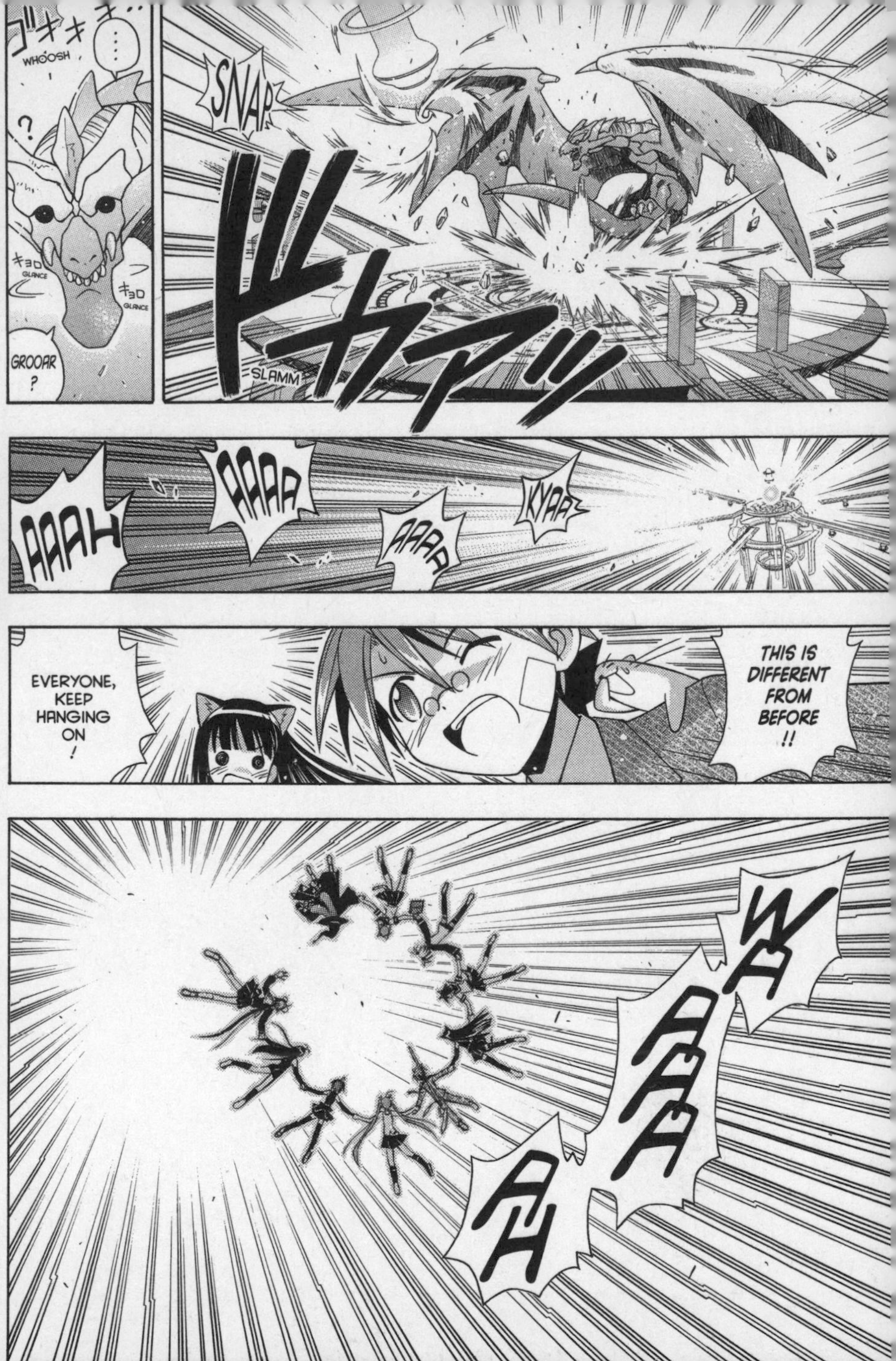
SNAP
ドカァッ
SLAMM
ゴオオオ…
WHOOSH
…
?
キョロ GLANCE
キョロ GLANCE
GROOAR ?
KYAA
AAAA
AAAA
AAAH
THIS IS DIFFERENT FROM BEFORE !!
EVERYONE, KEEP HANGING ON !
WAAAAAAH

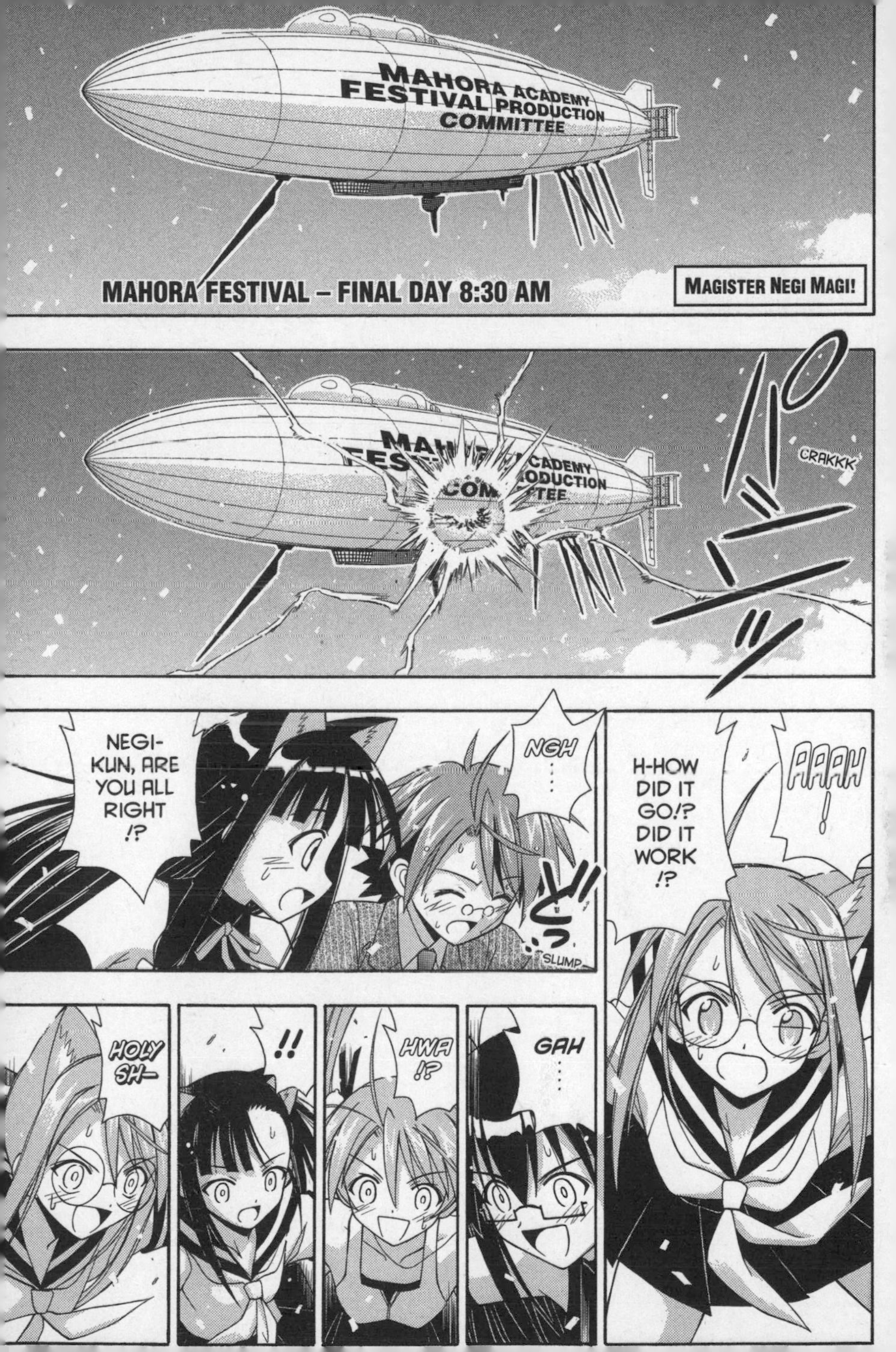
MAHORA ACADEMY FESTIVAL PRODUCTION COMMITTEE
MAGISTER NEGI MAGI!
MAHORA FESTIVAL – FINAL DAY 8:30 AM
CRAKKK
AAAH!
H-HOW DID IT GO!? DID IT WORK!?
NGH......
NEGI-KUN, ARE YOU ALL RIGHT!?
SLUMP
GAH......
HWA!?
!!
HOLY SH—

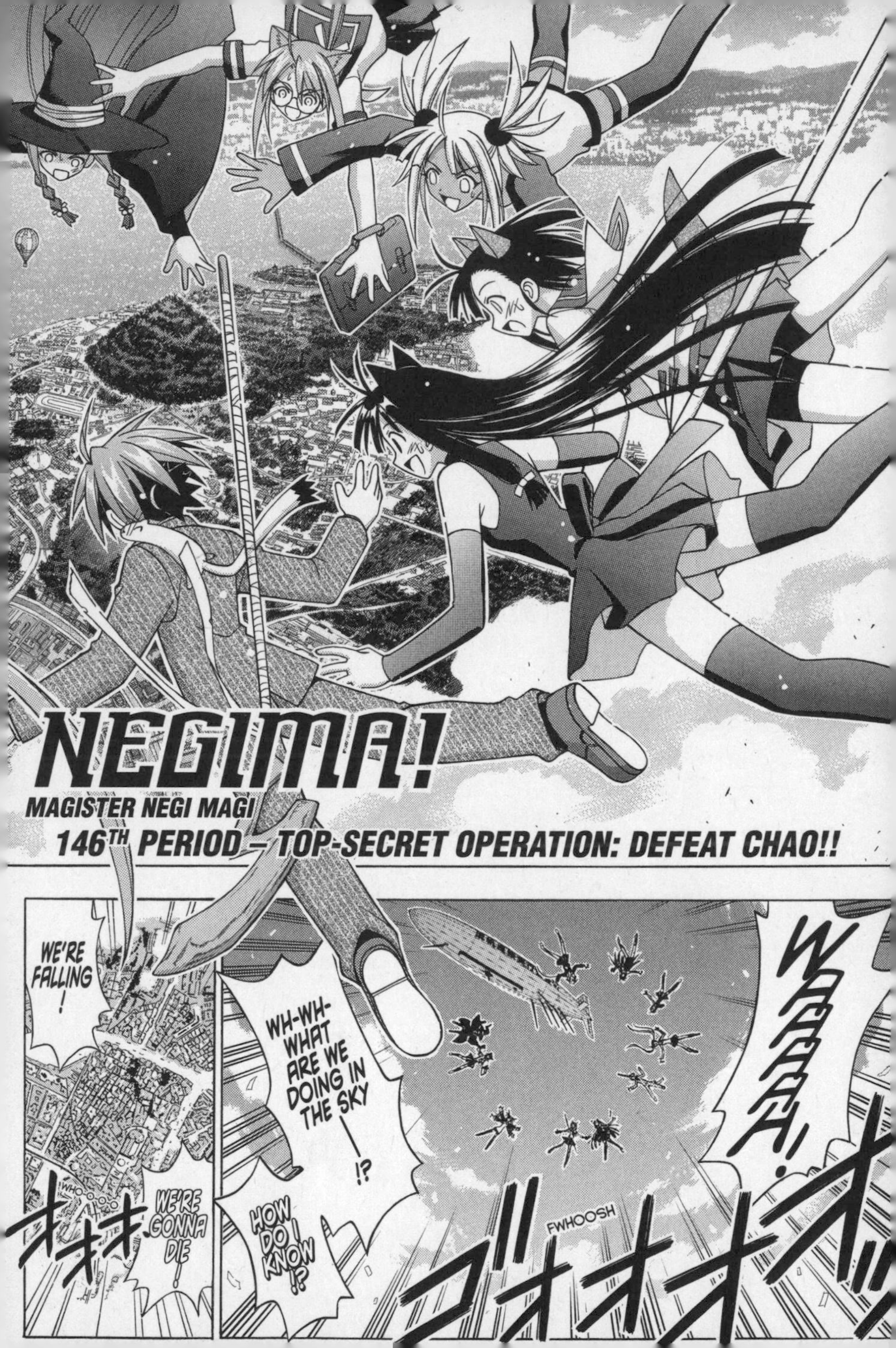
NEGIMA!
MAGISTER NEGI MAGI
146TH PERIOD – TOP-SECRET OPERATION: DEFEAT CHAO!!
WAAAAAH!
WH-WH-WHAT ARE WE DOING IN THE SKY—!?
HOW DO I KNOW!?
FWHOOSH
WE'RE FALLING!
WHO-O-O-O
WE'RE GONNA DIE!

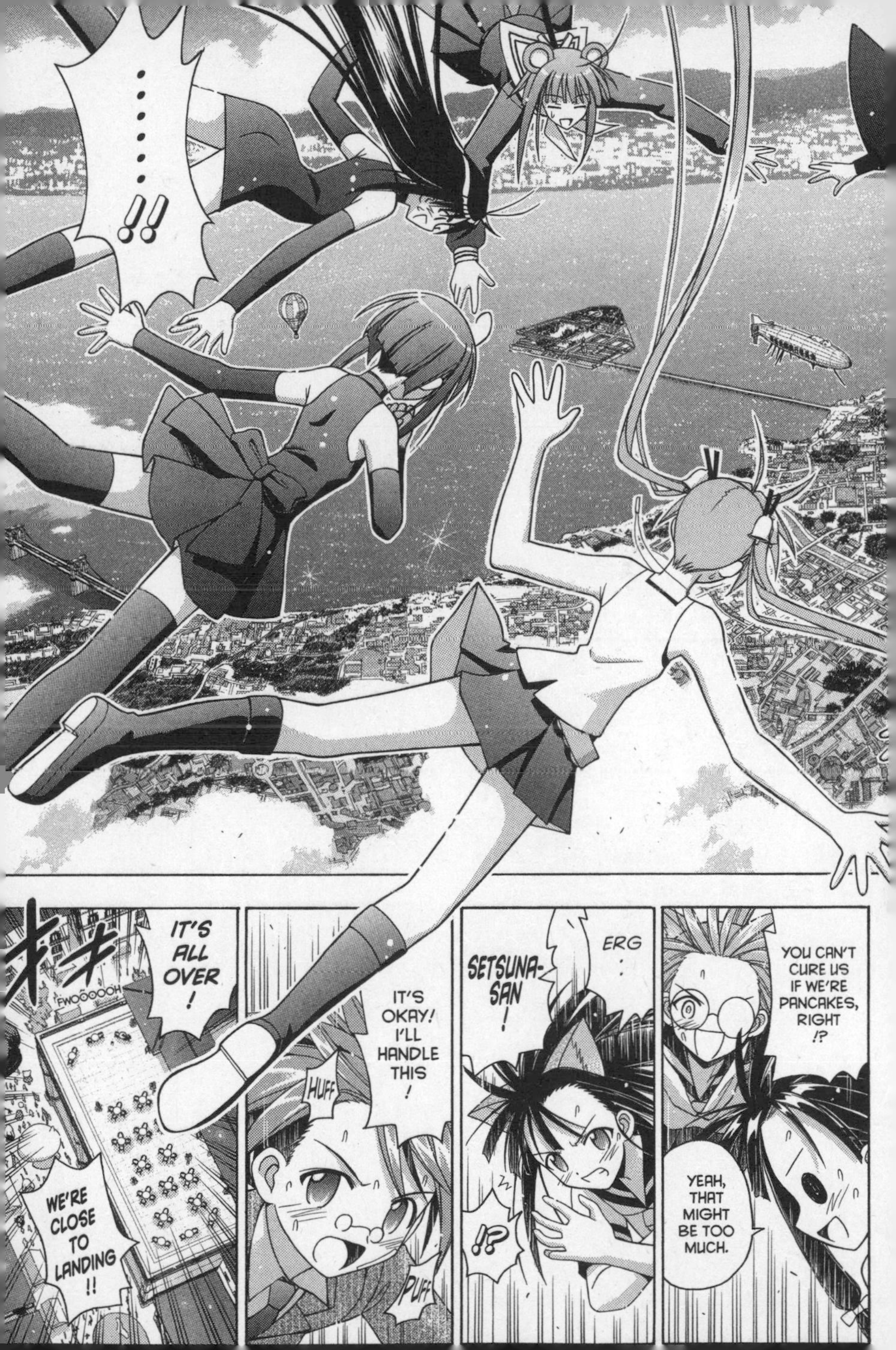

......
!!
YOU CAN'T CURE US IF WE'RE PANCAKES, RIGHT !?
YEAH, THAT MIGHT BE TOO MUCH.
ERG :
SETSUNA-SAN !
!?
IT'S OKAY! I'LL HANDLE THIS !
HUFF
PUFF
IT'S ALL OVER !
FWOOOOOH
WE'RE CLOSE TO LANDING !!

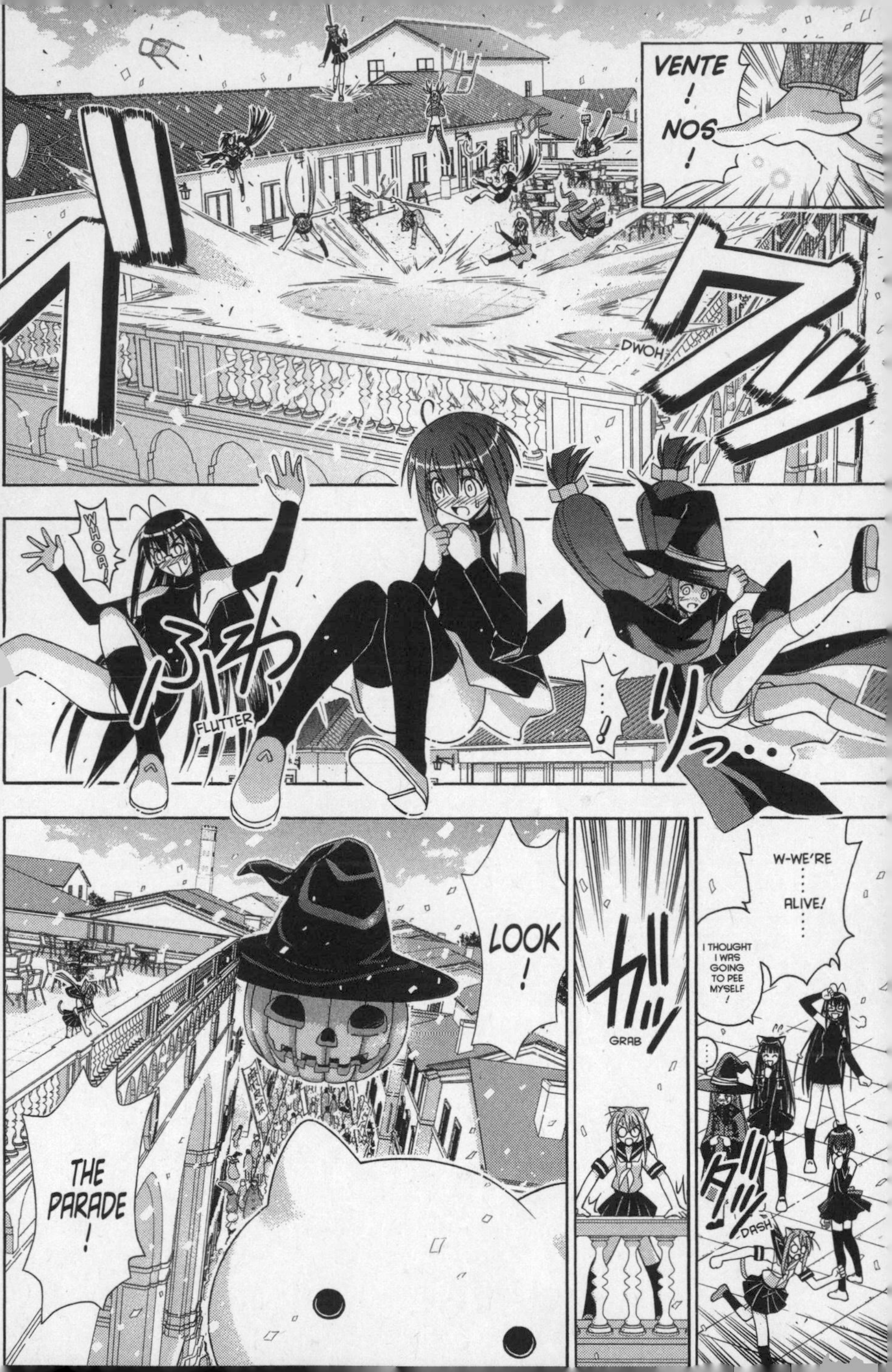
VENTE! NOS!
DWOH
WHOA!
FLUTTER
...!
W-WE'RE ...... ALIVE!
I THOUGHT I WAS GOING TO PEE MYSELF!
...
DASH
GRAB
LOOK!
THE PARADE!

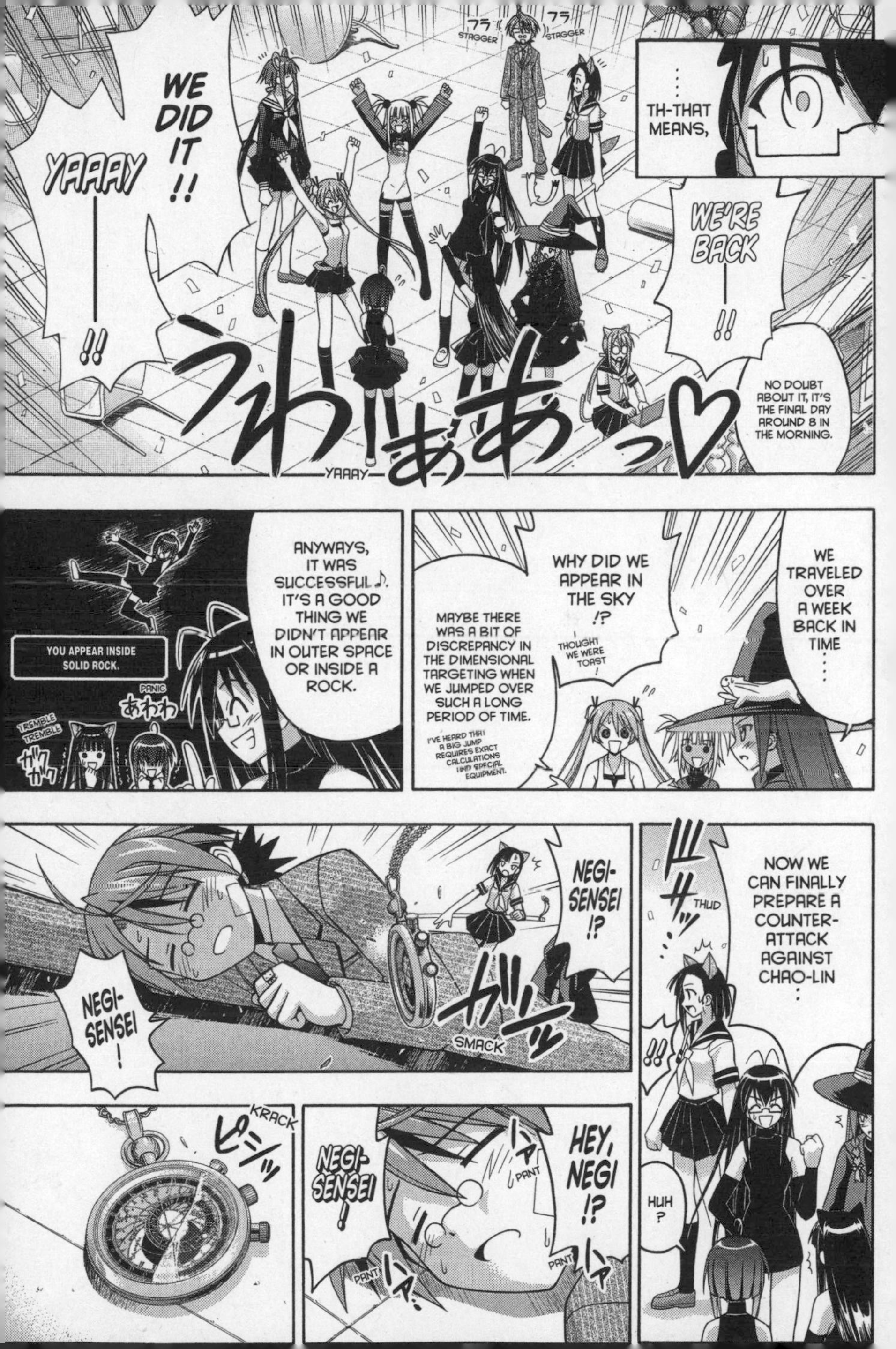

...TH-THAT MEANS,
WE'RE BACK—!!
NO DOUBT ABOUT IT, IT'S THE FINAL DAY AROUND 8 IN THE MORNING.
フラ STAGGER フラ STAGGER
WE DID IT!!
YAAAY—!!
うわぁあっ♡
YAAAY
WE TRAVELED OVER A WEEK BACK IN TIME...
WHY DID WE APPEAR IN THE SKY!?
THOUGHT WE WERE TOAST!
MAYBE THERE WAS A BIT OF DISCREPANCY IN THE DIMENSIONAL TARGETING WHEN WE JUMPED OVER SUCH A LONG PERIOD OF TIME.
I'VE HEARD THAT A BIG JUMP REQUIRES EXACT CALCULATIONS AND SPECIAL EQUIPMENT.
ANYWAYS, IT WAS SUCCESSFUL♪. IT'S A GOOD THING WE DIDN'T APPEAR IN OUTER SPACE OR INSIDE A ROCK.
YOU APPEAR INSIDE SOLID ROCK.
あわわ PANIC
ガクガク TREMBLE TREMBLE
NOW WE CAN FINALLY PREPARE A COUNTER-ATTACK AGAINST CHAO-LIN...
ドサッ THUD
!!
HUH?
NEGI-SENSEI!?
ガシャ SMACK
NEGI-SENSEI!
HEY, NEGI!?
NEGI-SENSEI!
ハァ PANT
ハァ PANT
ハァ PANT
ピシッ KRACK

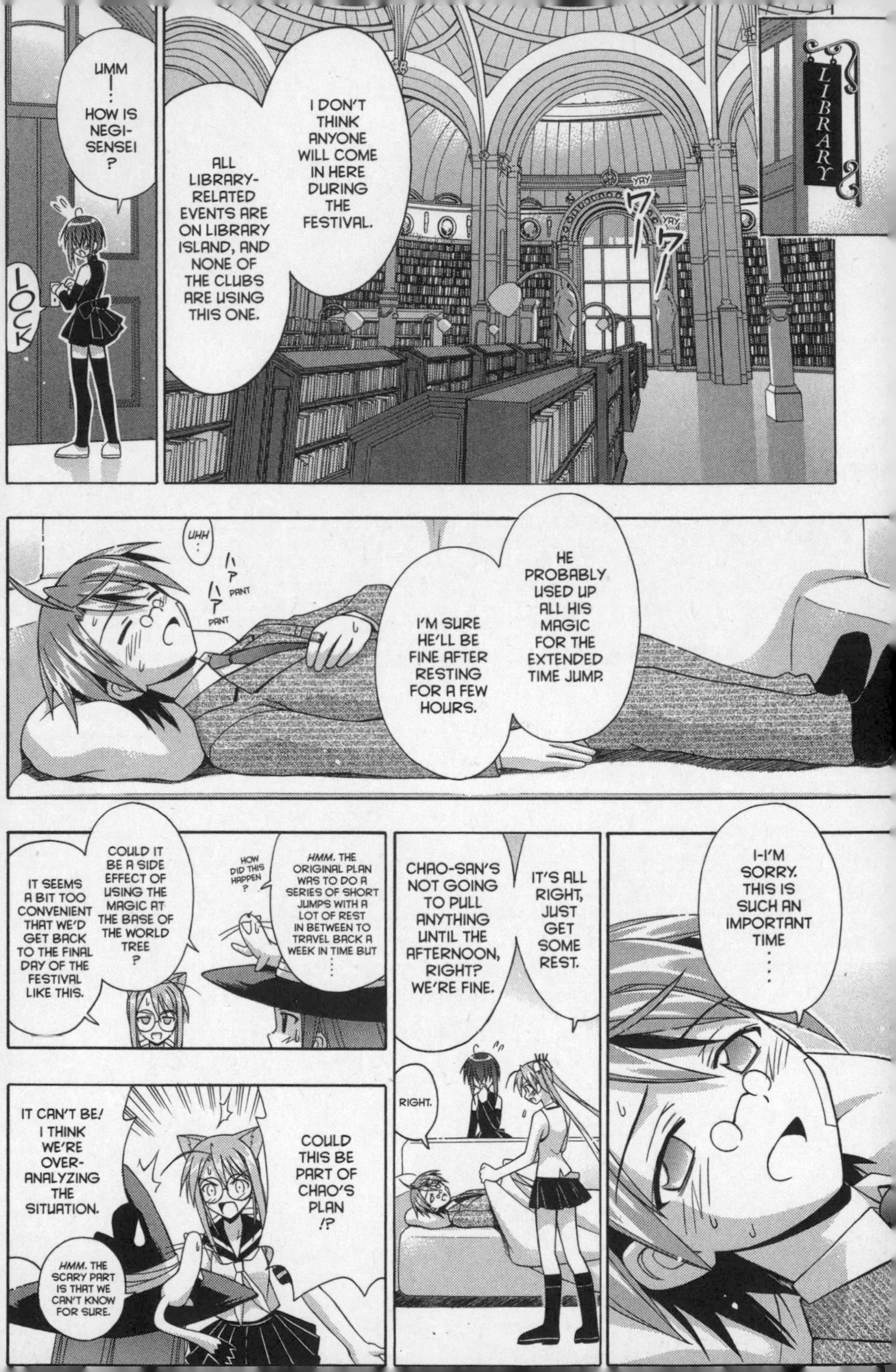
LIBRARY
YAY YAY
I DON'T THINK ANYONE WILL COME IN HERE DURING THE FESTIVAL.
ALL LIBRARY-RELATED EVENTS ARE ON LIBRARY ISLAND, AND NONE OF THE CLUBS ARE USING THIS ONE.
UMM...! HOW IS NEGI-SENSEI?
LOCK
HE PROBABLY USED UP ALL HIS MAGIC FOR THE EXTENDED TIME JUMP.
I'M SURE HE'LL BE FINE AFTER RESTING FOR A FEW HOURS.
UHH...
PANT
PANT
I-I'M SORRY. THIS IS SUCH AN IMPORTANT TIME....
IT'S ALL RIGHT, JUST GET SOME REST.
CHAO-SAN'S NOT GOING TO PULL ANYTHING UNTIL THE AFTERNOON, RIGHT? WE'RE FINE.
RIGHT.
HMM. THE ORIGINAL PLAN WAS TO DO A SERIES OF SHORT JUMPS WITH A LOT OF REST IN BETWEEN TO TRAVEL BACK A WEEK IN TIME BUT....
HOW DID THIS HAPPEN?
COULD IT BE A SIDE EFFECT OF USING THE MAGIC AT THE BASE OF THE WORLD TREE?
IT SEEMS A BIT TOO CONVENIENT THAT WE'D GET BACK TO THE FINAL DAY OF THE FESTIVAL LIKE THIS.
COULD THIS BE PART OF CHAO'S PLAN!?
IT CAN'T BE! I THINK WE'RE OVER-ANALYZING THE SITUATION.
HMM. THE SCARY PART IS THAT WE CAN'T KNOW FOR SURE.

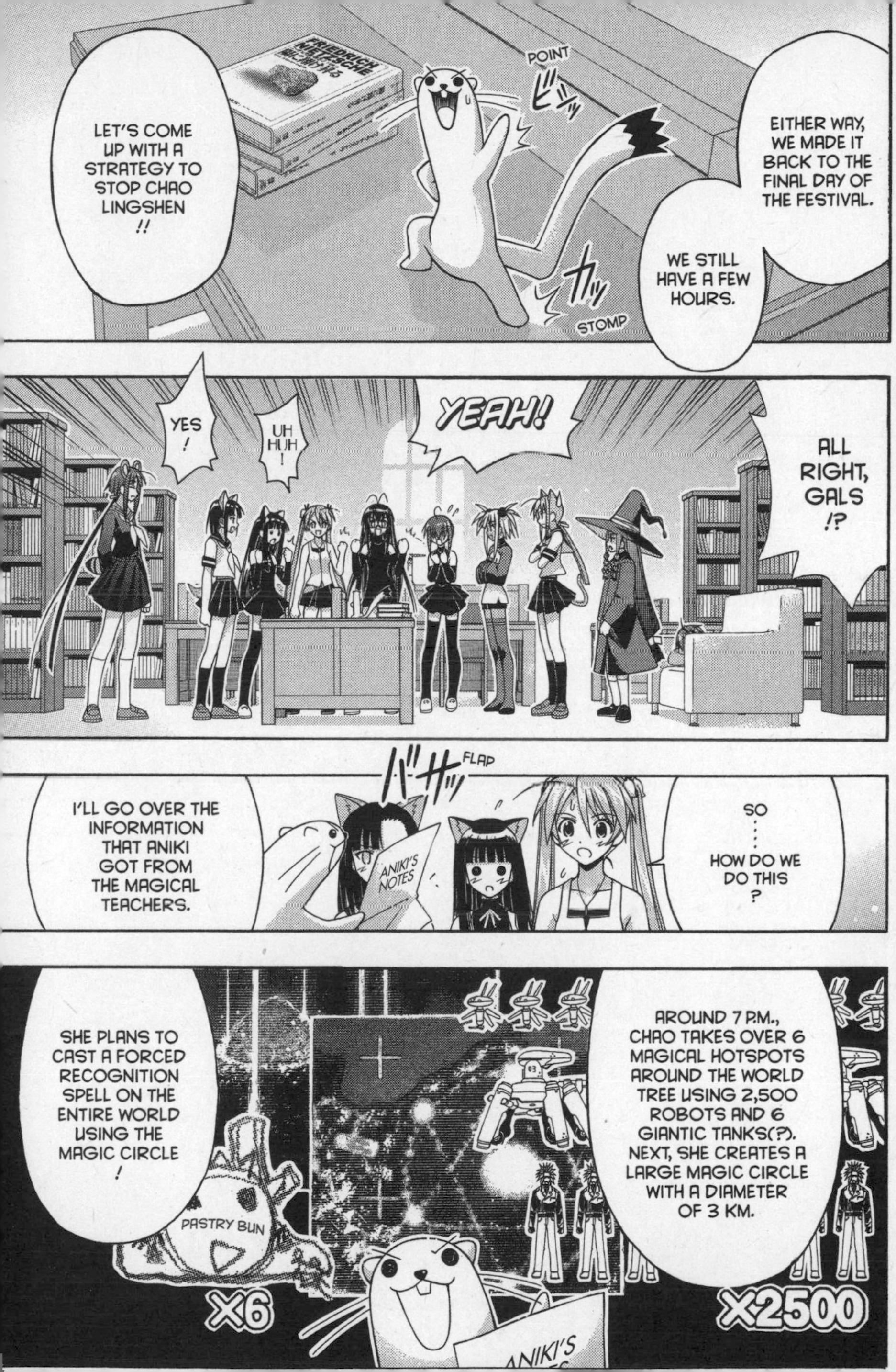

EITHER WAY, WE MADE IT BACK TO THE FINAL DAY OF THE FESTIVAL.
WE STILL HAVE A FEW HOURS.
POINT
STOMP
FRIEDRICH NIETZSCHE
LET'S COME UP WITH A STRATEGY TO STOP CHAO LINGSHEN!!
ALL RIGHT, GALS!?
YEAH!
UH HUH!
YES!
FLAP
SO... HOW DO WE DO THIS?
ANIKI'S NOTES
I'LL GO OVER THE INFORMATION THAT ANIKI GOT FROM THE MAGICAL TEACHERS.
AROUND 7 P.M., CHAO TAKES OVER 6 MAGICAL HOTSPOTS AROUND THE WORLD TREE USING 2,500 ROBOTS AND 6 GIANTIC TANKS(?). NEXT, SHE CREATES A LARGE MAGIC CIRCLE WITH A DIAMETER OF 3 KM.
×2500
SHE PLANS TO CAST A FORCED RECOGNITION SPELL ON THE ENTIRE WORLD USING THE MAGIC CIRCLE!
PASTRY BUN
×6
ANIKI'S

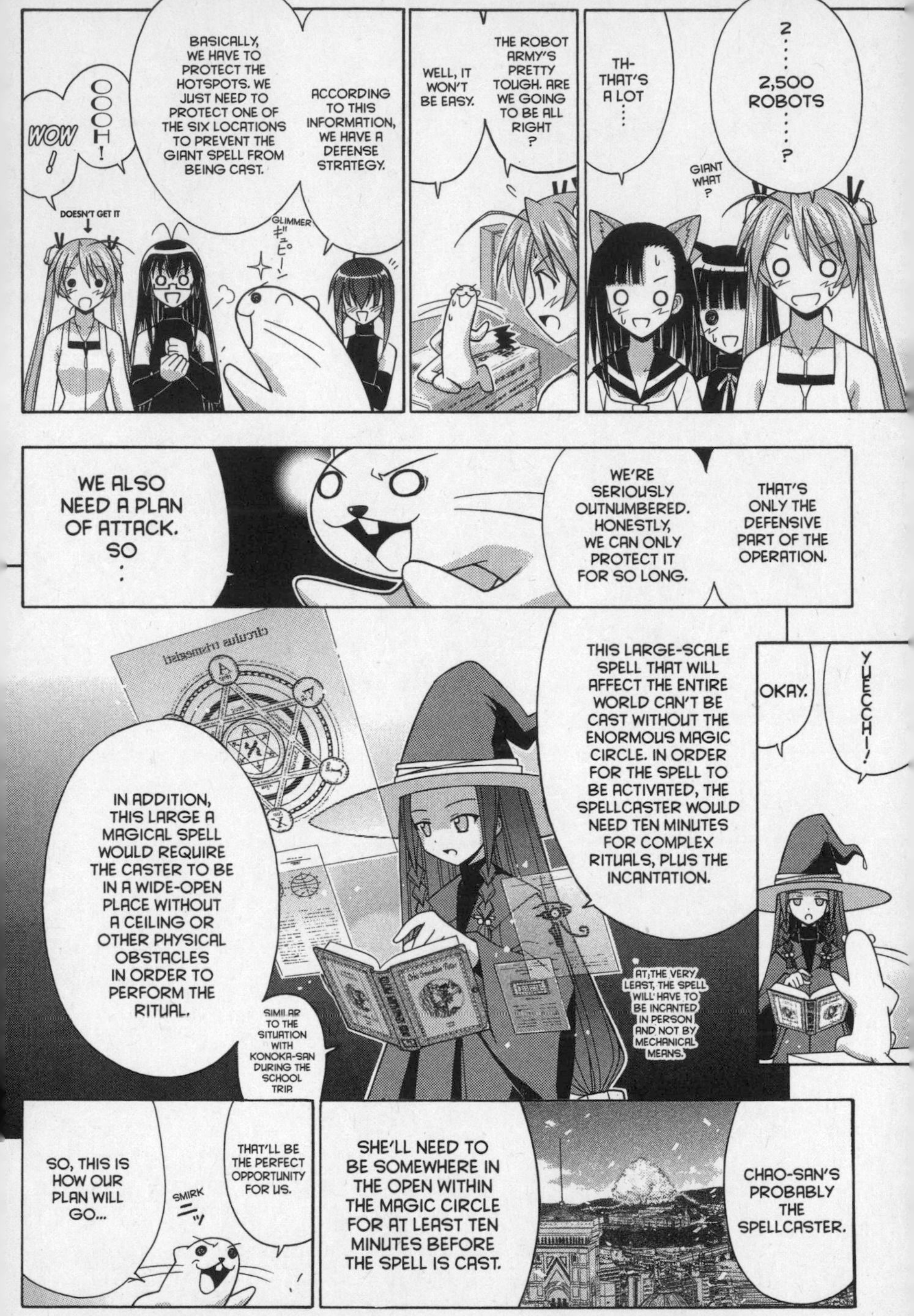
Z.... 2,500 ROBOTS....?
TH- THAT'S A LOT....
GIANT WHAT?
THE ROBOT ARMY'S PRETTY TOUGH. ARE WE GOING TO BE ALL RIGHT?
WELL, IT WON'T BE EASY.
ACCORDING TO THIS INFORMATION, WE HAVE A DEFENSE STRATEGY.
BASICALLY, WE HAVE TO PROTECT THE HOTSPOTS. WE JUST NEED TO PROTECT ONE OF THE SIX LOCATIONS TO PREVENT THE GIANT SPELL FROM BEING CAST.
GLIMMER
OOOH!
WOW!
DOESN'T GET IT
THAT'S ONLY THE DEFENSIVE PART OF THE OPERATION.
WE'RE SERIOUSLY OUTNUMBERED. HONESTLY, WE CAN ONLY PROTECT IT FOR SO LONG.
WE ALSO NEED A PLAN OF ATTACK. SO:
YUECCHI!
OKAY.
THIS LARGE-SCALE SPELL THAT WILL AFFECT THE ENTIRE WORLD CAN'T BE CAST WITHOUT THE ENORMOUS MAGIC CIRCLE. IN ORDER FOR THE SPELL TO BE ACTIVATED, THE SPELLCASTER WOULD NEED TEN MINUTES FOR COMPLEX RITUALS, PLUS THE INCANTATION.
AT THE VERY LEAST, THE SPELL WILL HAVE TO BE INCANTED IN PERSON AND NOT BY MECHANICAL MEANS.
IN ADDITION, THIS LARGE A MAGICAL SPELL WOULD REQUIRE THE CASTER TO BE IN A WIDE-OPEN PLACE WITHOUT A CEILING OR OTHER PHYSICAL OBSTACLES IN ORDER TO PERFORM THE RITUAL.
SIMILAR TO THE SITUATION WITH KONOKA-SAN DURING THE SCHOOL TRIP.
CHAO-SAN'S PROBABLY THE SPELLCASTER.
SHE'LL NEED TO BE SOMEWHERE IN THE OPEN WITHIN THE MAGIC CIRCLE FOR AT LEAST TEN MINUTES BEFORE THE SPELL IS CAST.
THAT'LL BE THE PERFECT OPPORTUNITY FOR US.
SO, THIS IS HOW OUR PLAN WILL GO...
SMIRK

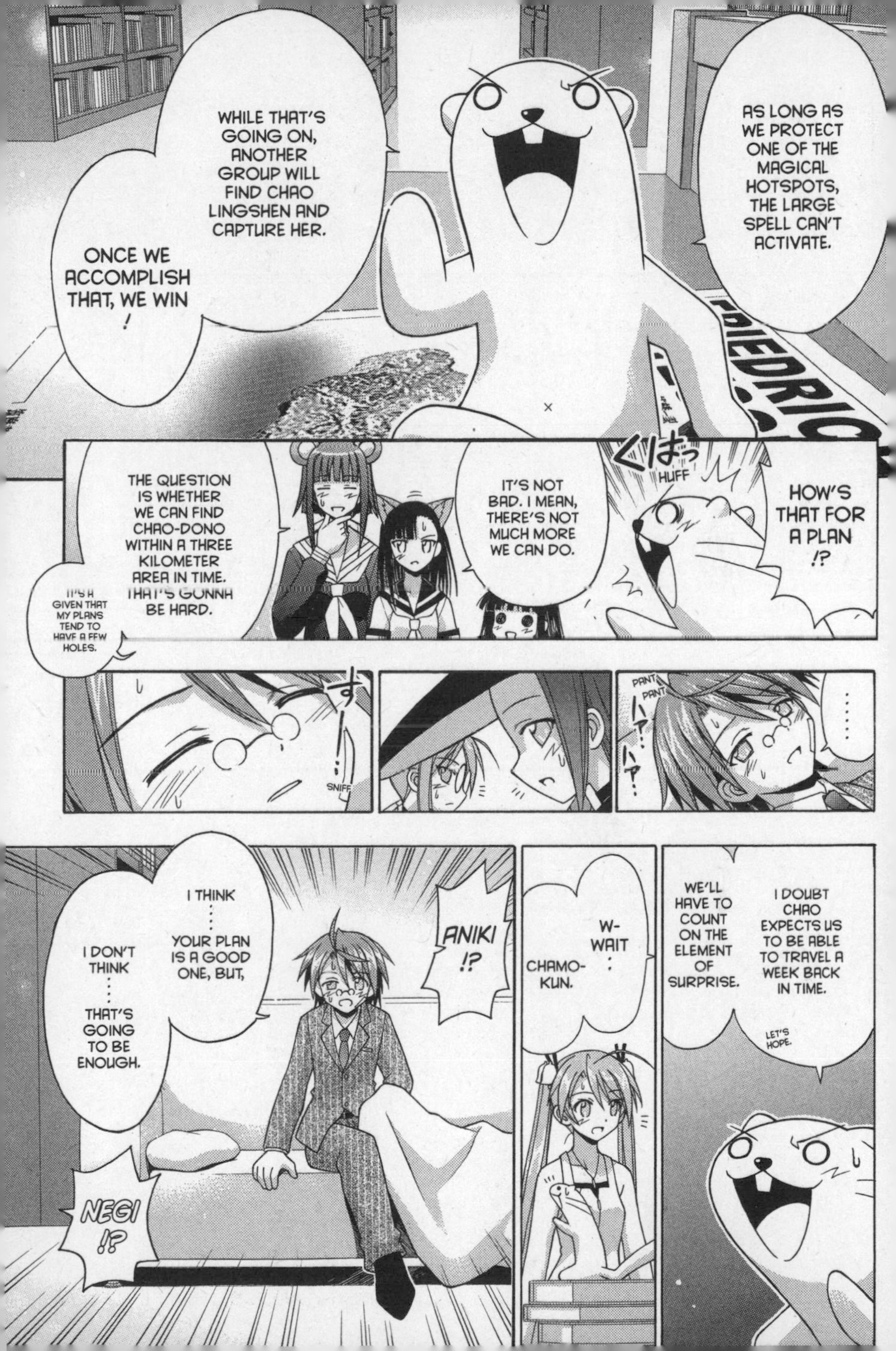
AS LONG AS WE PROTECT ONE OF THE MAGICAL HOTSPOTS, THE LARGE SPELL CAN'T ACTIVATE.
WHILE THAT'S GOING ON, ANOTHER GROUP WILL FIND CHAO LINGSHEN AND CAPTURE HER.
ONCE WE ACCOMPLISH THAT, WE WIN!
HOW'S THAT FOR A PLAN!?
くぱっ
HUFF
IT'S NOT BAD. I MEAN, THERE'S NOT MUCH MORE WE CAN DO.
THE QUESTION IS WHETHER WE CAN FIND CHAO-DONO WITHIN A THREE KILOMETER AREA IN TIME. THAT'S GONNA BE HARD.
IT'S A GIVEN THAT MY PLANS TEND TO HAVE A FEW HOLES.
......
PANT PANT
すー
SNIFF
I DOUBT CHAO EXPECTS US TO BE ABLE TO TRAVEL A WEEK BACK IN TIME.
WE'LL HAVE TO COUNT ON THE ELEMENT OF SURPRISE.
LET'S HOPE.
W-WAIT...
CHAMO-KUN.
ANIKI!?
I THINK... YOUR PLAN IS A GOOD ONE, BUT,
I DON'T THINK... THAT'S GOING TO BE ENOUGH.
NEGI!?

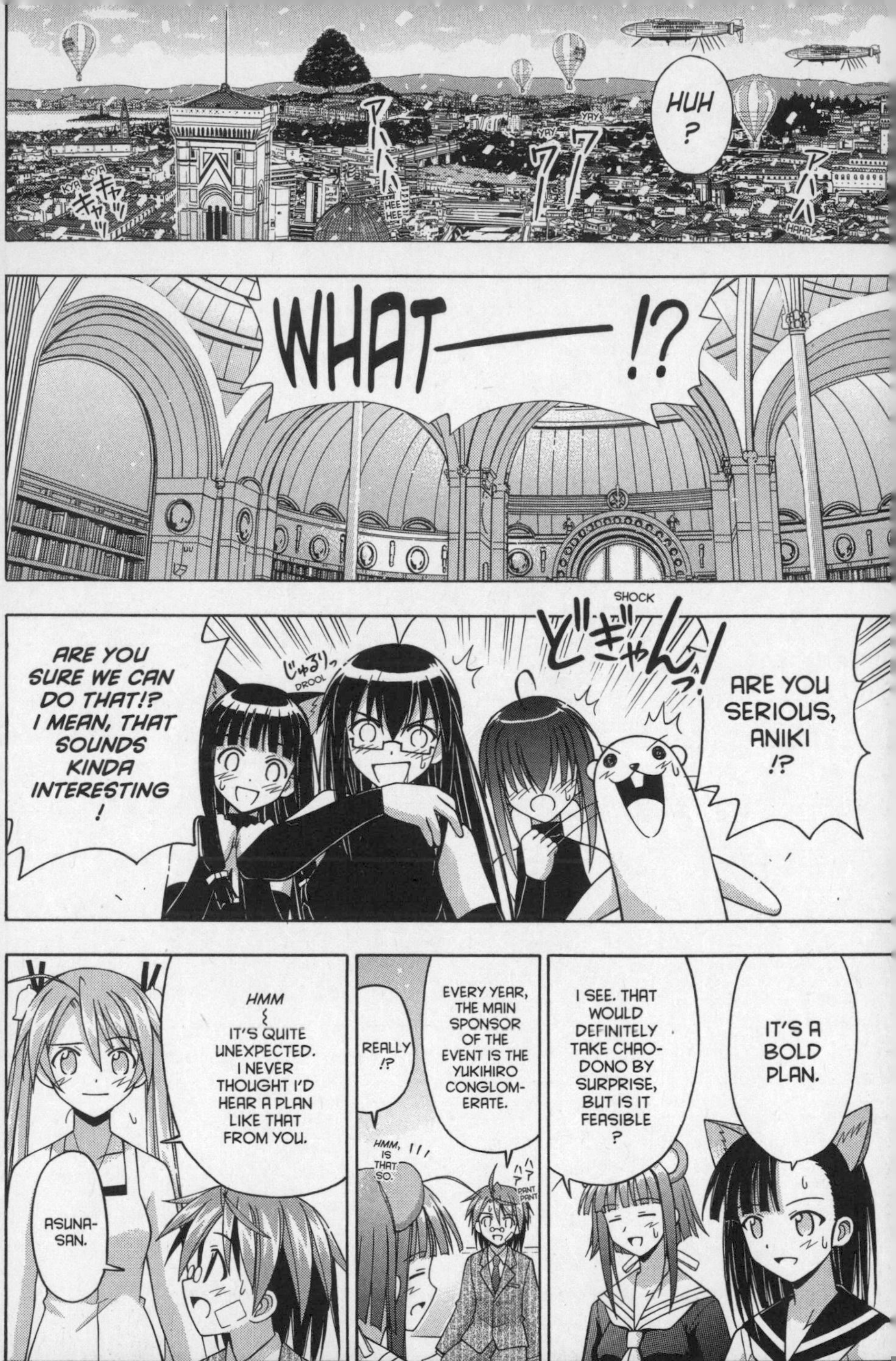
HAHA
HUH ?
YAY
YAY
HEE HEE
KYA
KYA
WHAT——!?
ARE YOU SERIOUS, ANIKI !?
どぎゃんっ
SHOCK
じゅるりっ
DROOL
ARE YOU SURE WE CAN DO THAT!? I MEAN, THAT SOUNDS KINDA INTERESTING !
IT'S A BOLD PLAN.
I SEE. THAT WOULD DEFINITELY TAKE CHAO-DONO BY SURPRISE, BUT IS IT FEASIBLE ?
PANT PANT
EVERY YEAR, THE MAIN SPONSOR OF THE EVENT IS THE YUKIHIRO CONGLOM-ERATE.
REALLY !?
HMM, IS THAT SO.
HMM~ IT'S QUITE UNEXPECTED. I NEVER THOUGHT I'D HEAR A PLAN LIKE THAT FROM YOU.
ASUNA-SAN.

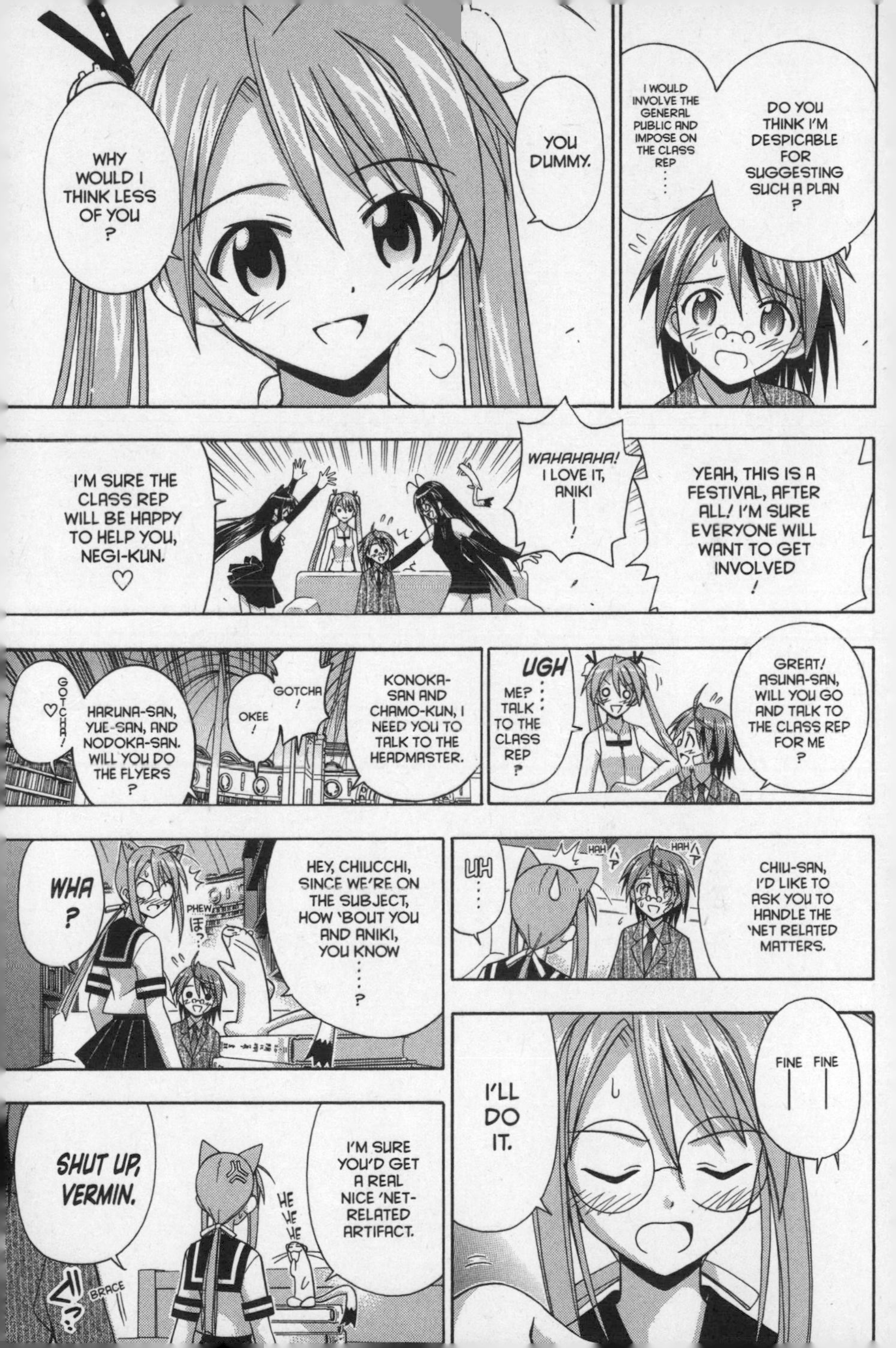
DO YOU THINK I'M DESPICABLE FOR SUGGESTING SUCH A PLAN?
I WOULD INVOLVE THE GENERAL PUBLIC AND IMPOSE ON THE CLASS REP......
YOU DUMMY.
WHY WOULD I THINK LESS OF YOU?
YEAH, THIS IS A FESTIVAL, AFTER ALL! I'M SURE EVERYONE WILL WANT TO GET INVOLVED!
WAHAHAHA! I LOVE IT, ANIKI!
I'M SURE THE CLASS REP WILL BE HAPPY TO HELP YOU, NEGI-KUN. ♡
GREAT! ASUNA-SAN, WILL YOU GO AND TALK TO THE CLASS REP FOR ME?
UGH
ME? TALK TO THE CLASS REP...?
KONOKA-SAN AND CHAMO-KUN, I NEED YOU TO TALK TO THE HEADMASTER.
GOTCHA!
OKEE!
HARUNA-SAN, YUE-SAN, AND NODOKA-SAN. WILL YOU DO THE FLYERS?
GOTCHA! ♡
CHIU-SAN, I'D LIKE TO ASK YOU TO HANDLE THE 'NET RELATED MATTERS.
HAH
HAH
UH...
FINE FINE
I'LL DO IT.
HEY, CHIUCCHI, SINCE WE'RE ON THE SUBJECT, HOW 'BOUT YOU AND ANIKI, YOU KNOW....?
PHEW ほっ
WHA?
I'M SURE YOU'D GET A REAL NICE 'NET-RELATED ARTIFACT.
HE HE HE
SHUT UP, VERMIN.
BRACE

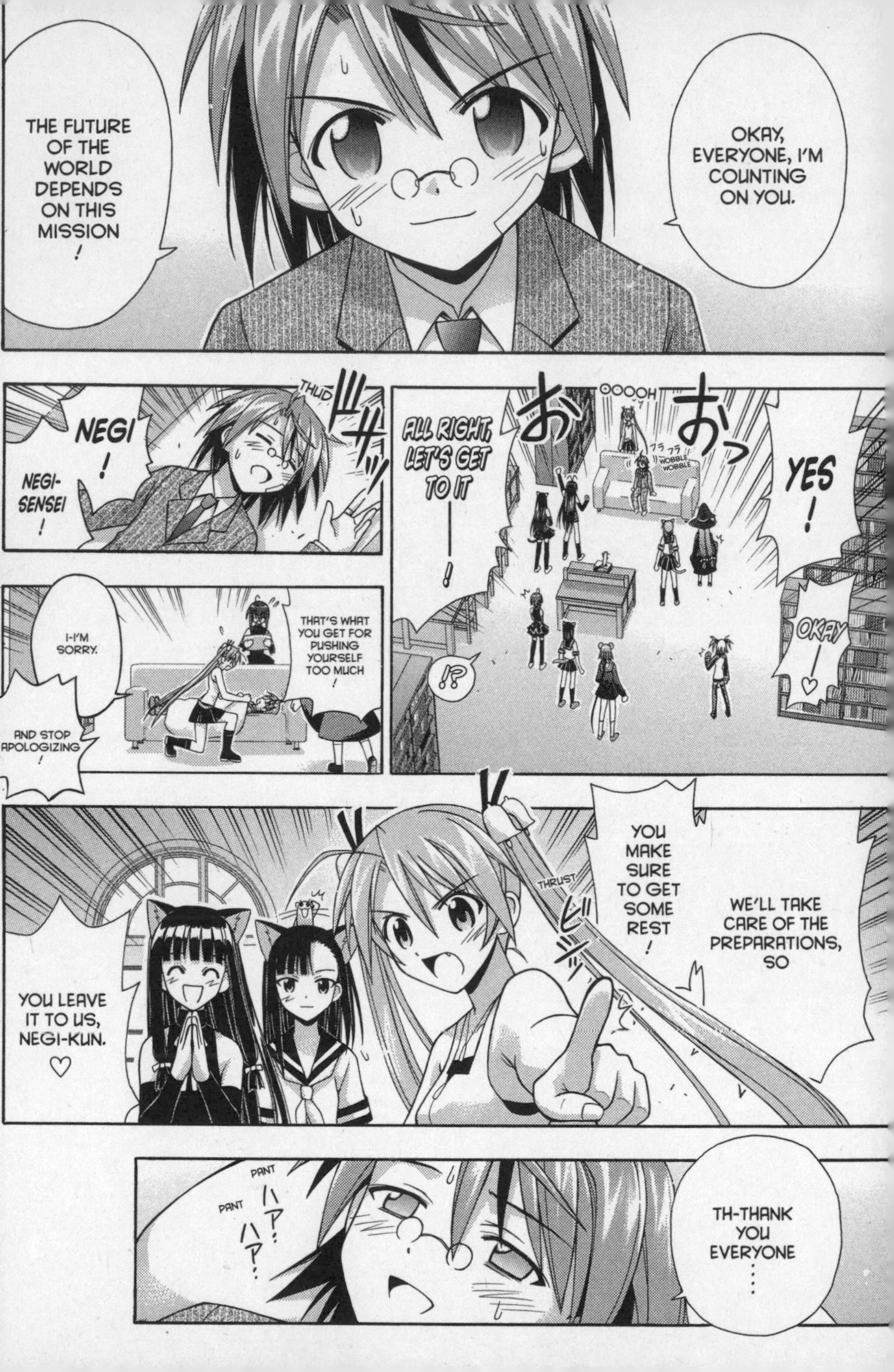

OKAY, EVERYONE, I'M COUNTING ON YOU.
THE FUTURE OF THE WORLD DEPENDS ON THIS MISSION!
YES!
OKAY—♥
おおっ
OOOOH
WOBBLE WOBBLE
ALL RIGHT, LET'S GET TO IT—!
!?
THUD
NEGI!
NEGI-SENSEI!
THAT'S WHAT YOU GET FOR PUSHING YOURSELF TOO MUCH!
I-I'M SORRY.
AND STOP APOLOGIZING!
WE'LL TAKE CARE OF THE PREPARATIONS, SO
YOU MAKE SURE TO GET SOME REST!
THRUST
YOU LEAVE IT TO US, NEGI-KUN. ♡
TH-THANK YOU EVERYONE......
PANT
ハァ!
PANT
ハァ!

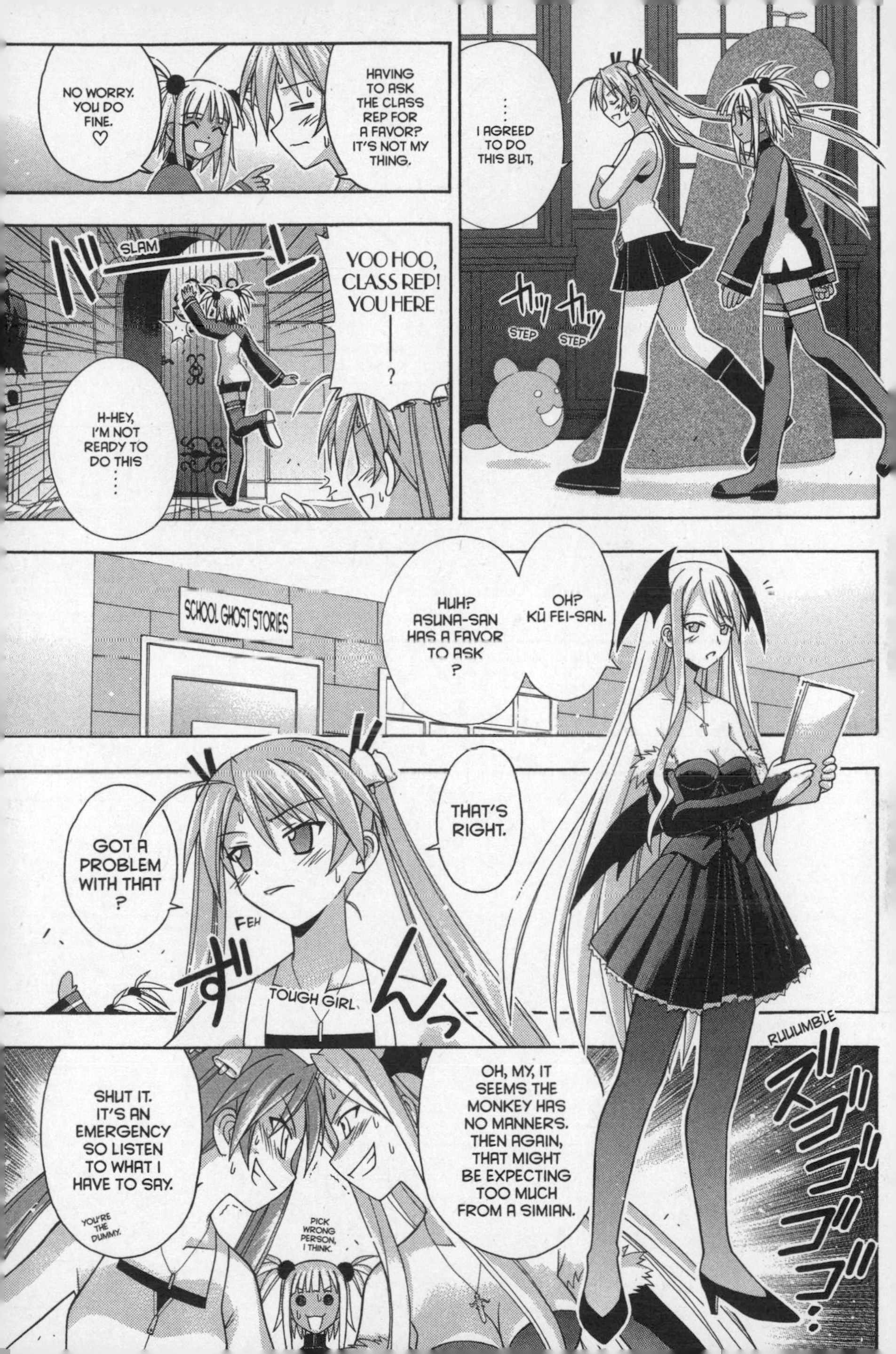
STEP
STEP
...I AGREED TO DO THIS BUT,
HAVING TO ASK THE CLASS REP FOR A FAVOR? IT'S NOT MY THING.
NO WORRY. YOU DO FINE. ♡
YOO HOO, CLASS REP! YOU HERE—?
SLAM
H-HEY, I'M NOT READY TO DO THIS......
OH? KŪ FEI-SAN.
HUH? ASUNA-SAN HAS A FAVOR TO ASK?
SCHOOL GHOST STORIES
THAT'S RIGHT.
GOT A PROBLEM WITH THAT?
FEH
TOUGH GIRL
RUUUMBLE
OH, MY, IT SEEMS THE MONKEY HAS NO MANNERS. THEN AGAIN, THAT MIGHT BE EXPECTING TOO MUCH FROM A SIMIAN.
SHUT IT. IT'S AN EMERGENCY SO LISTEN TO WHAT I HAVE TO SAY.
PICK WRONG PERSON, I THINK.
YOU'RE THE DUMMY.

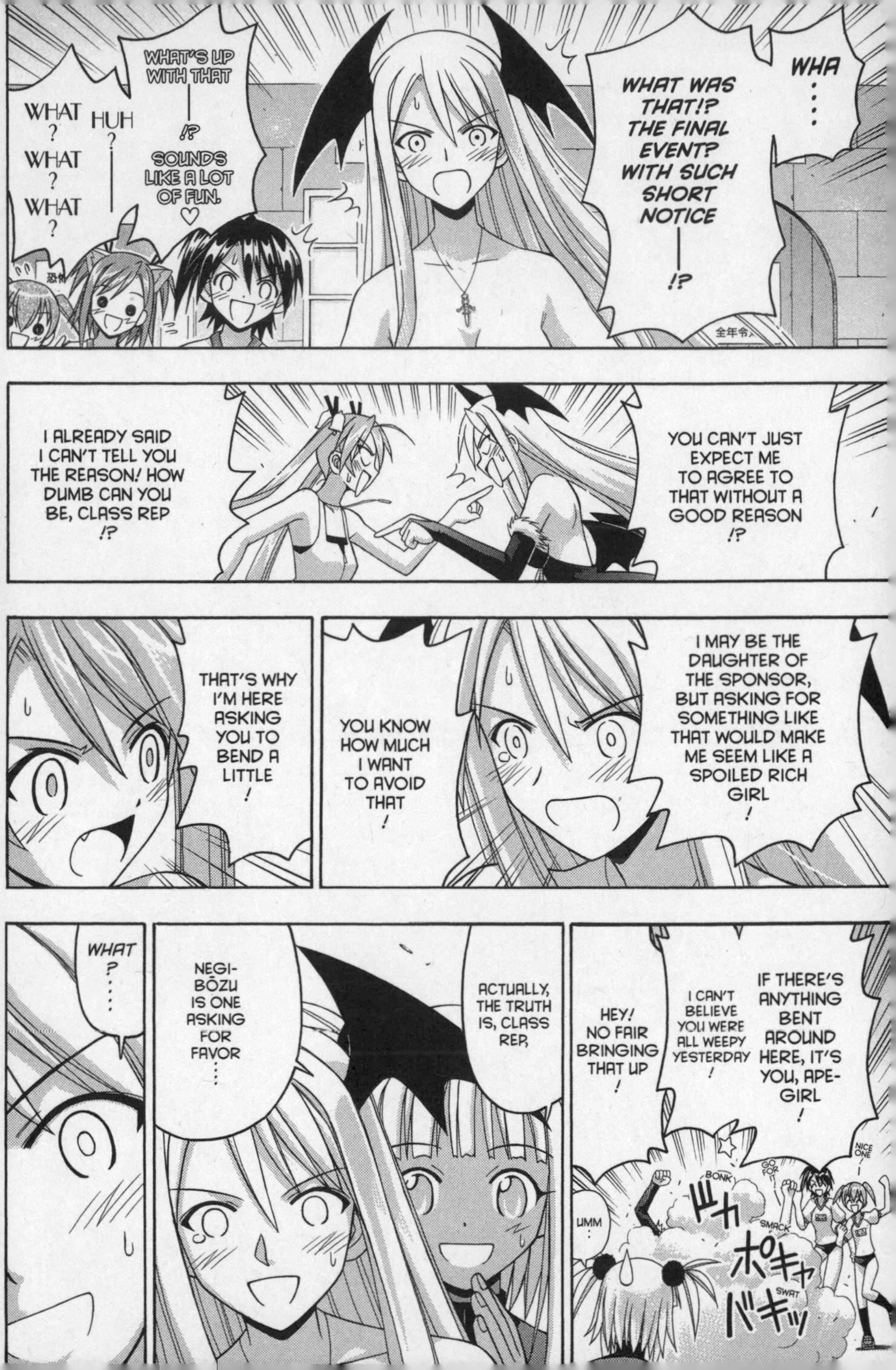

WHA...
WHAT WAS THAT!? THE FINAL EVENT? WITH SUCH SHORT NOTICE—!?
WHAT'S UP WITH THAT—!? SOUNDS LIKE A LOT OF FUN. ♡
HUH?—
WHAT? WHAT? WHAT?
YOU CAN'T JUST EXPECT ME TO AGREE TO THAT WITHOUT A GOOD REASON!?
I ALREADY SAID I CAN'T TELL YOU THE REASON! HOW DUMB CAN YOU BE, CLASS REP!?
I MAY BE THE DAUGHTER OF THE SPONSOR, BUT ASKING FOR SOMETHING LIKE THAT WOULD MAKE ME SEEM LIKE A SPOILED RICH GIRL!
YOU KNOW HOW MUCH I WANT TO AVOID THAT!
THAT'S WHY I'M HERE ASKING YOU TO BEND A LITTLE!
IF THERE'S ANYTHING BENT AROUND HERE, IT'S YOU, APE-GIRL!
I CAN'T BELIEVE YOU WERE ALL WEEPY YESTERDAY!
HEY! NO FAIR BRINGING THAT UP!
NICE ONE!
GO FOR IT!
BONK
ドカ
SMACK
ポキャ
SWAT
バキッ
UMM:
ACTUALLY, THE TRUTH IS, CLASS REP,
NEGI-BŌZU IS ONE ASKING FOR FAVOR...
WHAT?...

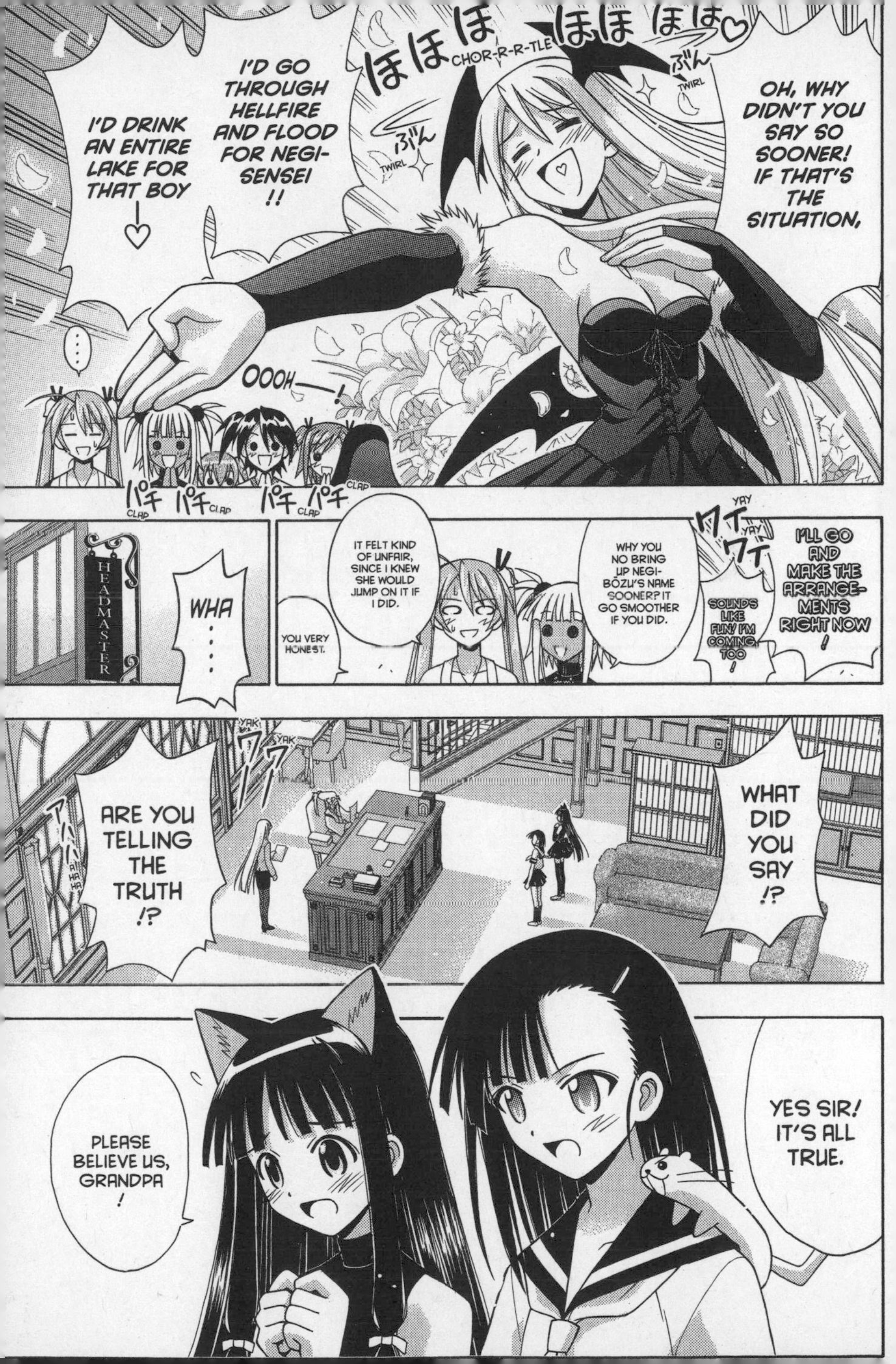
ほほほ CHOR-R-R-TLE ほほ ほほ♡
ぶん TWIRL
OH, WHY DIDN'T YOU SAY SO SOONER! IF THAT'S THE SITUATION,
ぶん TWIRL
I'D GO THROUGH HELLFIRE AND FLOOD FOR NEGI-SENSEI !!
I'D DRINK AN ENTIRE LAKE FOR THAT BOY ♡
...
OOOH—!
パチ CLAP パチ CLAP パチ CLAP パチ CLAP
I'LL GO AND MAKE THE ARRANGEMENTS RIGHT NOW !
ワイ YAY ワイ YAY
SOUND'S LIKE FUN! I'M COMING, TOO !
WHY YOU NO BRING UP NEGI-BÔZU'S NAME SOONER? IT GO SMOOTHER IF YOU DID.
IT FELT KIND OF UNFAIR, SINCE I KNEW SHE WOULD JUMP ON IT IF I DID.
YOU VERY HONEST.
WHA.....
HEADMASTER
WHAT DID YOU SAY !?
ワァ YAK ワァ YAK
ARE YOU TELLING THE TRUTH !?
アハハ AHAHA
YES SIR! IT'S ALL TRUE.
PLEASE BELIEVE US, GRANDPA !

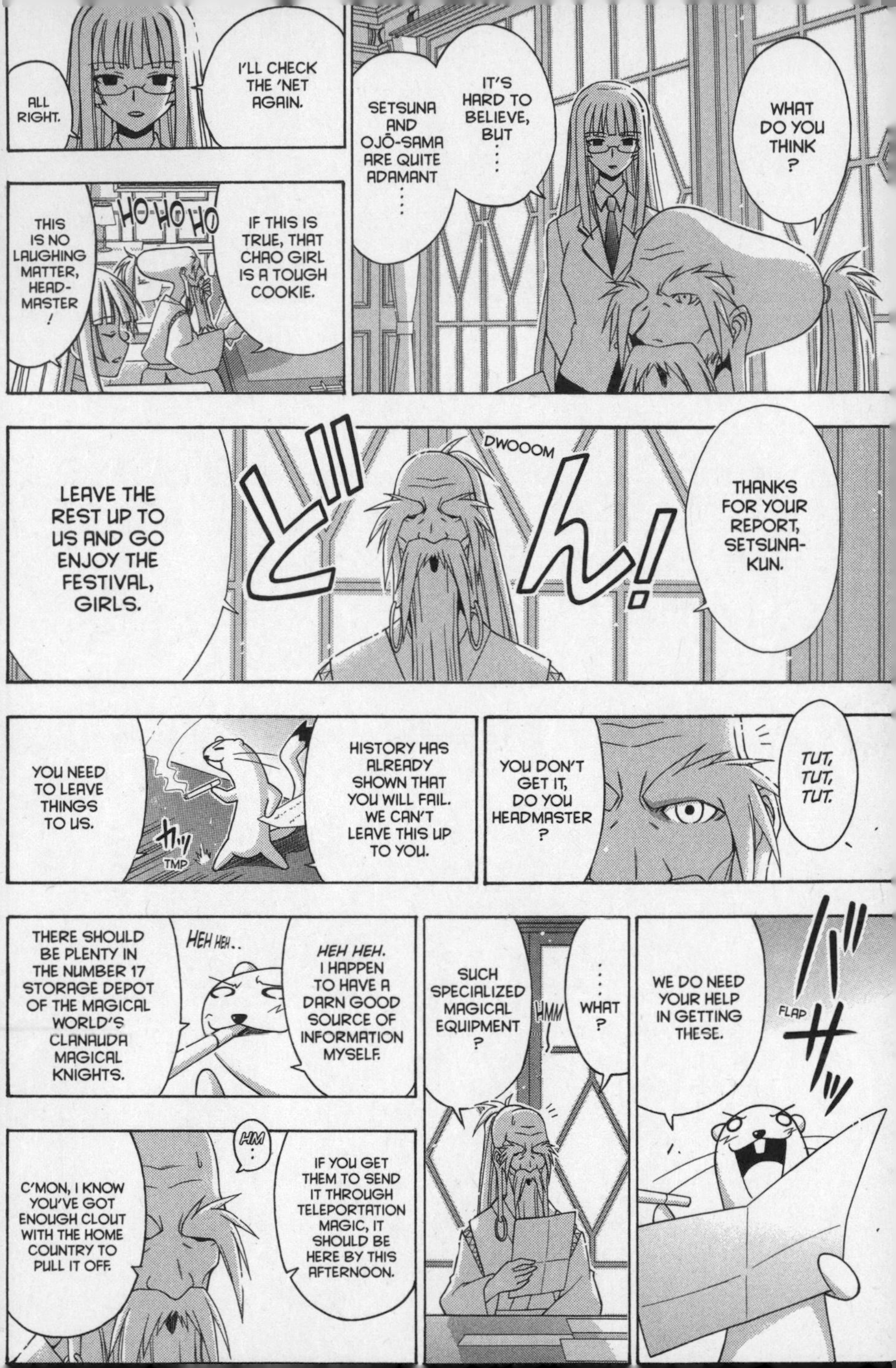
WHAT DO YOU THINK?
IT'S HARD TO BELIEVE, BUT....
SETSUNA AND OJŌ-SAMA ARE QUITE ADAMANT....
I'LL CHECK THE 'NET AGAIN.
ALL RIGHT.
IF THIS IS TRUE, THAT CHAO GIRL IS A TOUGH COOKIE.
HO HO HO
THIS IS NO LAUGHING MATTER, HEAD-MASTER!
DWOOOM
どん!
THANKS FOR YOUR REPORT, SETSUNA-KUN.
LEAVE THE REST UP TO US AND GO ENJOY THE FESTIVAL, GIRLS.
TUT, TUT, TUT.
YOU DON'T GET IT, DO YOU HEADMASTER?
HISTORY HAS ALREADY SHOWN THAT YOU WILL FAIL. WE CAN'T LEAVE THIS UP TO YOU.
カッ
TMP
YOU NEED TO LEAVE THINGS TO US.
バサッ
FLAP
WE DO NEED YOUR HELP IN GETTING THESE.
....WHAT?
HMM
SUCH SPECIALIZED MAGICAL EQUIPMENT?
HEH HEH. I HAPPEN TO HAVE A DARN GOOD SOURCE OF INFORMATION MYSELF.
HEH HEH..
THERE SHOULD BE PLENTY IN THE NUMBER 17 STORAGE DEPOT OF THE MAGICAL WORLD'S CLANAUDA MAGICAL KNIGHTS.
HM...
IF YOU GET THEM TO SEND IT THROUGH TELEPORTATION MAGIC, IT SHOULD BE HERE BY THIS AFTERNOON.
C'MON, I KNOW YOU'VE GOT ENOUGH CLOUT WITH THE HOME COUNTRY TO PULL IT OFF.

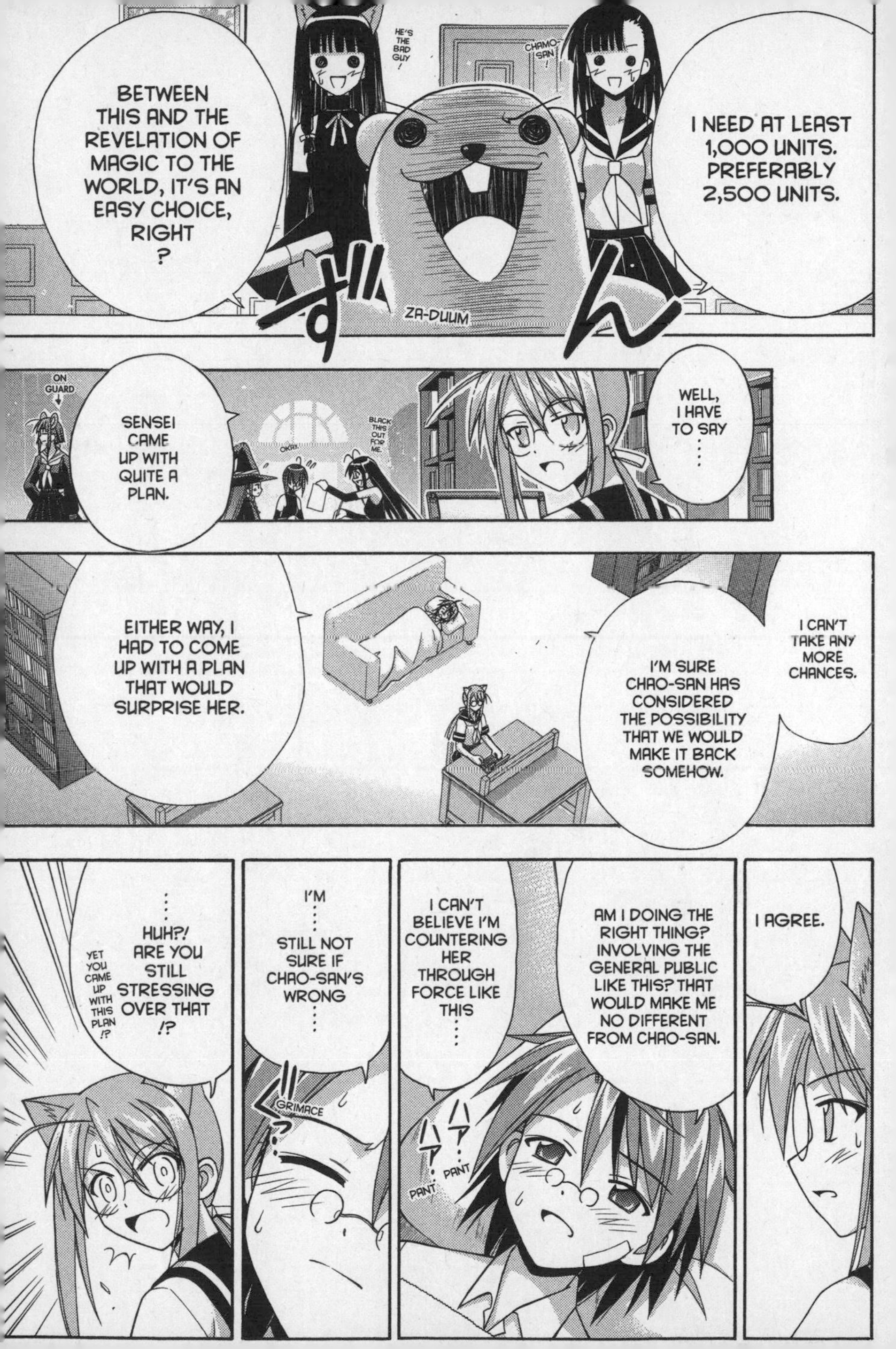
I NEED AT LEAST 1,000 UNITS. PREFERABLY 2,500 UNITS.
CHAMO-SAN!
HE'S THE BAD GUY!
BETWEEN THIS AND THE REVELATION OF MAGIC TO THE WORLD, IT'S AN EASY CHOICE, RIGHT?
ZA-DUUM
WELL, I HAVE TO SAY ...
BLACK THIS OUT FOR ME.
OKAY!
SENSEI CAME UP WITH QUITE A PLAN.
ON GUARD
I CAN'T TAKE ANY MORE CHANCES.
I'M SURE CHAO-SAN HAS CONSIDERED THE POSSIBILITY THAT WE WOULD MAKE IT BACK SOMEHOW.
EITHER WAY, I HAD TO COME UP WITH A PLAN THAT WOULD SURPRISE HER.
I AGREE.
AM I DOING THE RIGHT THING? INVOLVING THE GENERAL PUBLIC LIKE THIS? THAT WOULD MAKE ME NO DIFFERENT FROM CHAO-SAN.
I CAN'T BELIEVE I'M COUNTERING HER THROUGH FORCE LIKE THIS ...
PANT
PANT
I'M ... STILL NOT SURE IF CHAO-SAN'S WRONG ...
GRIMACE
... HUH?! ARE YOU STILL STRESSING OVER THAT!?
YET YOU CAME UP WITH THIS PLAN!?

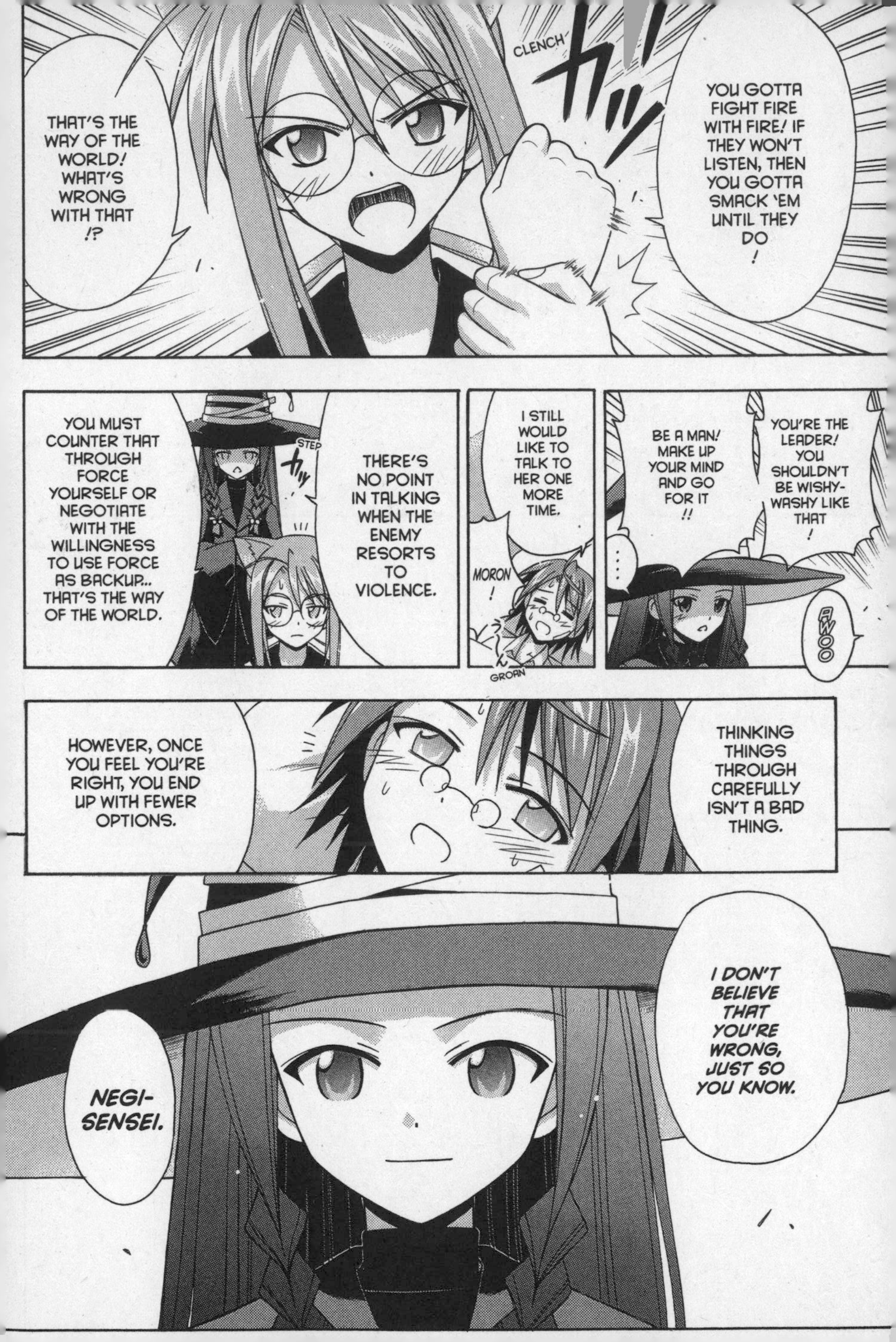

CLENCH
YOU GOTTA FIGHT FIRE WITH FIRE! IF THEY WON'T LISTEN, THEN YOU GOTTA SMACK 'EM UNTIL THEY DO!
THAT'S THE WAY OF THE WORLD! WHAT'S WRONG WITH THAT!?
YOU'RE THE LEADER! YOU SHOULDN'T BE WISHY-WASHY LIKE THAT!
BE A MAN! MAKE UP YOUR MIND AND GO FOR IT!!
...
AWOO
I STILL WOULD LIKE TO TALK TO HER ONE MORE TIME.
MORON!
GROAN
THERE'S NO POINT IN TALKING WHEN THE ENEMY RESORTS TO VIOLENCE.
STEP
YOU MUST COUNTER THAT THROUGH FORCE YOURSELF OR NEGOTIATE WITH THE WILLINGNESS TO USE FORCE AS BACKUP... THAT'S THE WAY OF THE WORLD.
THINKING THINGS THROUGH CAREFULLY ISN'T A BAD THING.
HOWEVER, ONCE YOU FEEL YOU'RE RIGHT, YOU END UP WITH FEWER OPTIONS.
I DON'T BELIEVE THAT YOU'RE WRONG, JUST SO YOU KNOW.
NEGI-SENSEI.

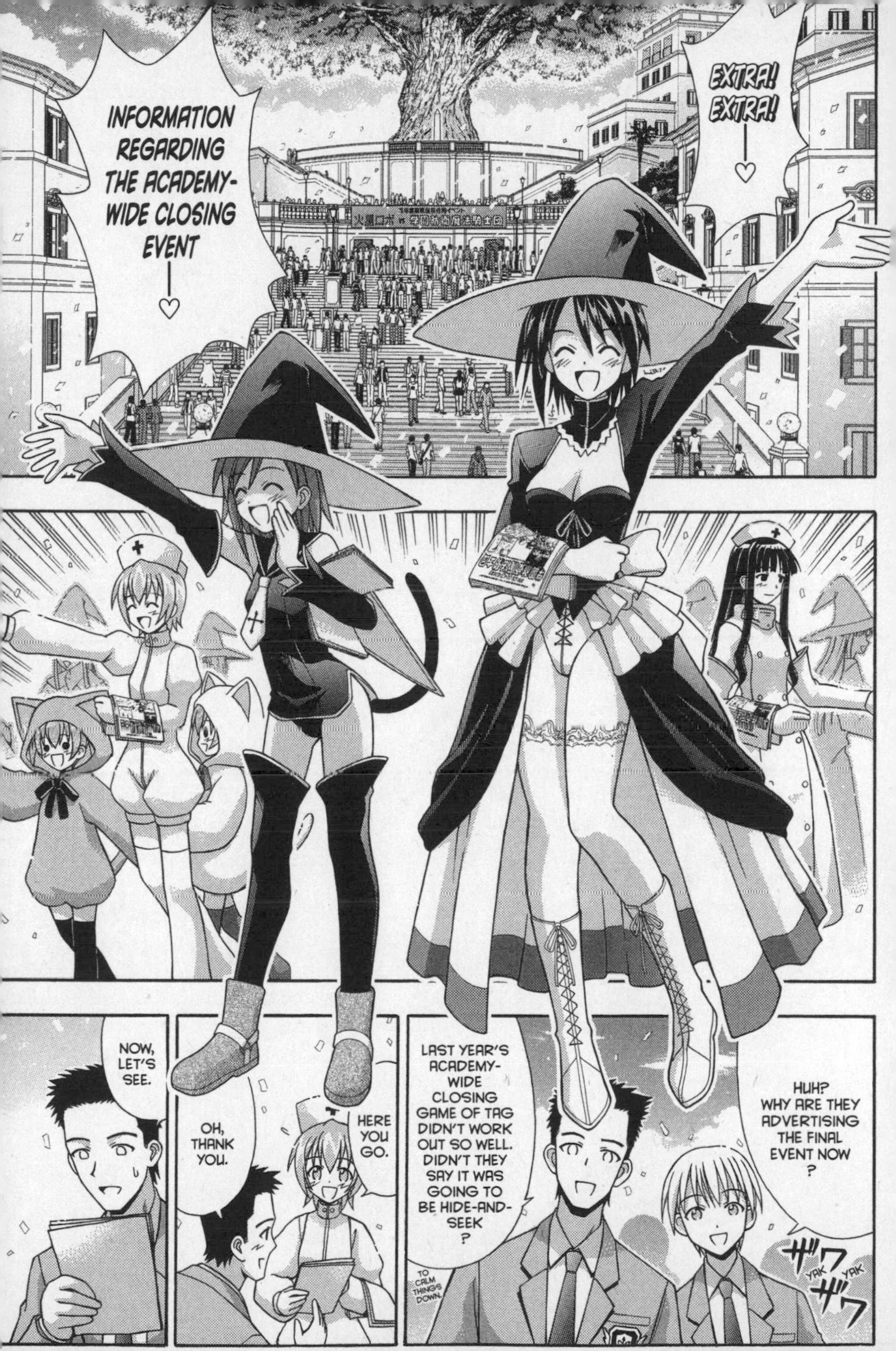
EXTRA! EXTRA! ♡
INFORMATION REGARDING THE ACADEMY-WIDE CLOSING EVENT ♡
HUH? WHY ARE THEY ADVERTISING THE FINAL EVENT NOW?
LAST YEAR'S ACADEMY-WIDE CLOSING GAME OF TAG DIDN'T WORK OUT SO WELL. DIDN'T THEY SAY IT WAS GOING TO BE HIDE-AND-SEEK?
TO CALM THINGS DOWN.
YAK YAK
HERE YOU GO.
OH, THANK YOU.
NOW, LET'S SEE.

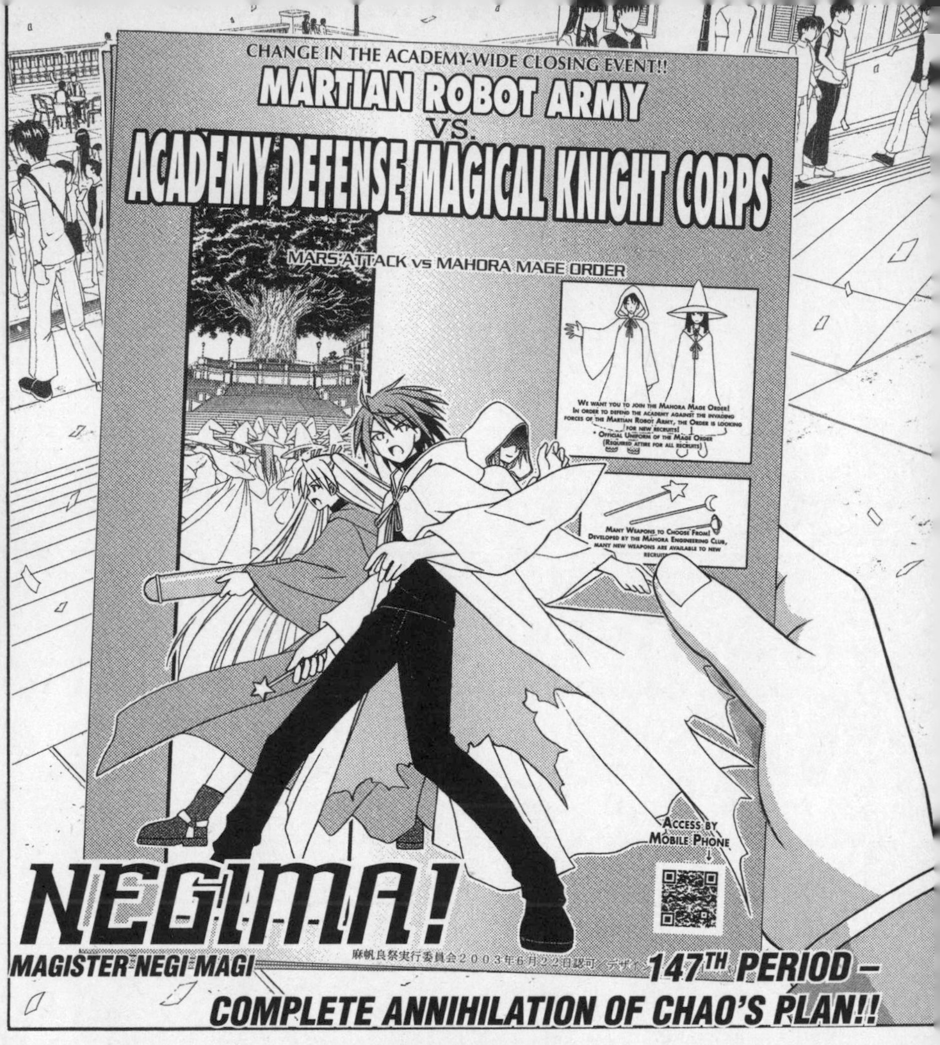
CHANGE IN THE ACADEMY-WIDE CLOSING EVENT!!
MARTIAN ROBOT ARMY VS. ACADEMY DEFENSE MAGICAL KNIGHT CORPS
MARS ATTACK vs MAHORA MAGE ORDER
We want you to join the Mahora Mage Order! In order to defend the academy against the invading forces of the Martian Robot Army, the Order is looking for new recruits!
* Official Uniform of the Mage Order (Required attire for all recruits)
Many Weapons to Choose From! Developed by the Mahora Engineering Club, many new weapons are available to new recruits!
Access by Mobile Phone
麻帆良祭実行委員会2003年6月22日認可
NEGIMA!
MAGISTER NEGI MAGI
147TH PERIOD – COMPLETE ANNIHILATION OF CHAO'S PLAN!!
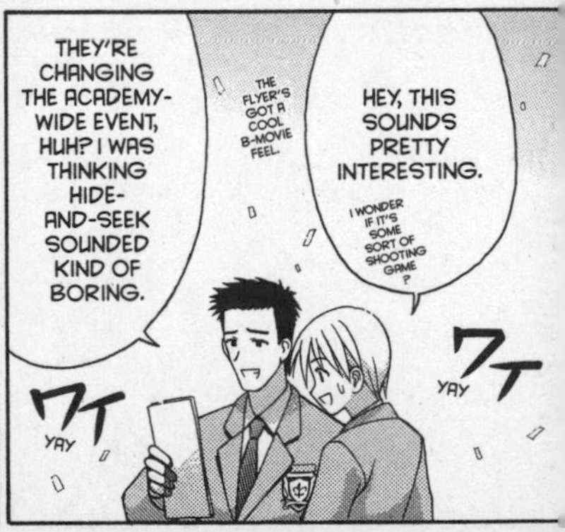
HEY, THIS SOUNDS PRETTY INTERESTING.
I WONDER IF IT'S SOME SORT OF SHOOTING GAME?
THEY'RE CHANGING THE ACADEMY-WIDE EVENT, HUH? I WAS THINKING HIDE-AND-SEEK SOUNDED KIND OF BORING.
THE FLYER'S GOT A COOL B-MOVIE FEEL.
ワイ YAY
ワイ YAY
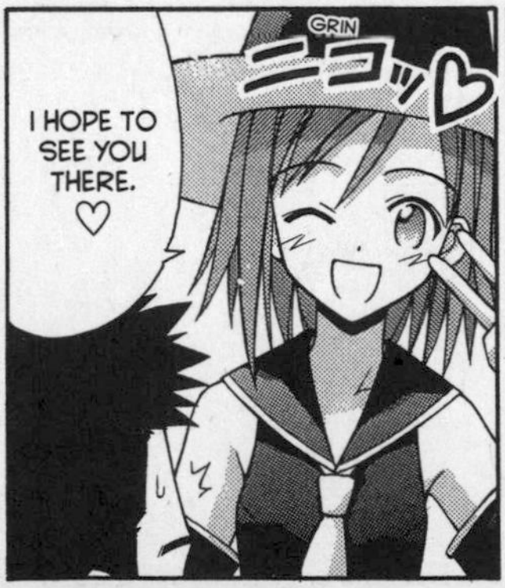
ニコッ♡ GRIN
I HOPE TO SEE YOU THERE. ♡
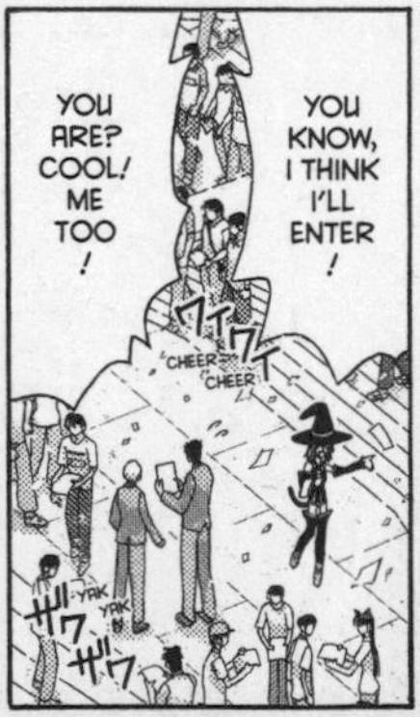
YOU KNOW, I THINK I'LL ENTER!
YOU ARE? COOL! ME TOO!
ワイワイ CHEER CHEER
ザワザワ YAK YAK

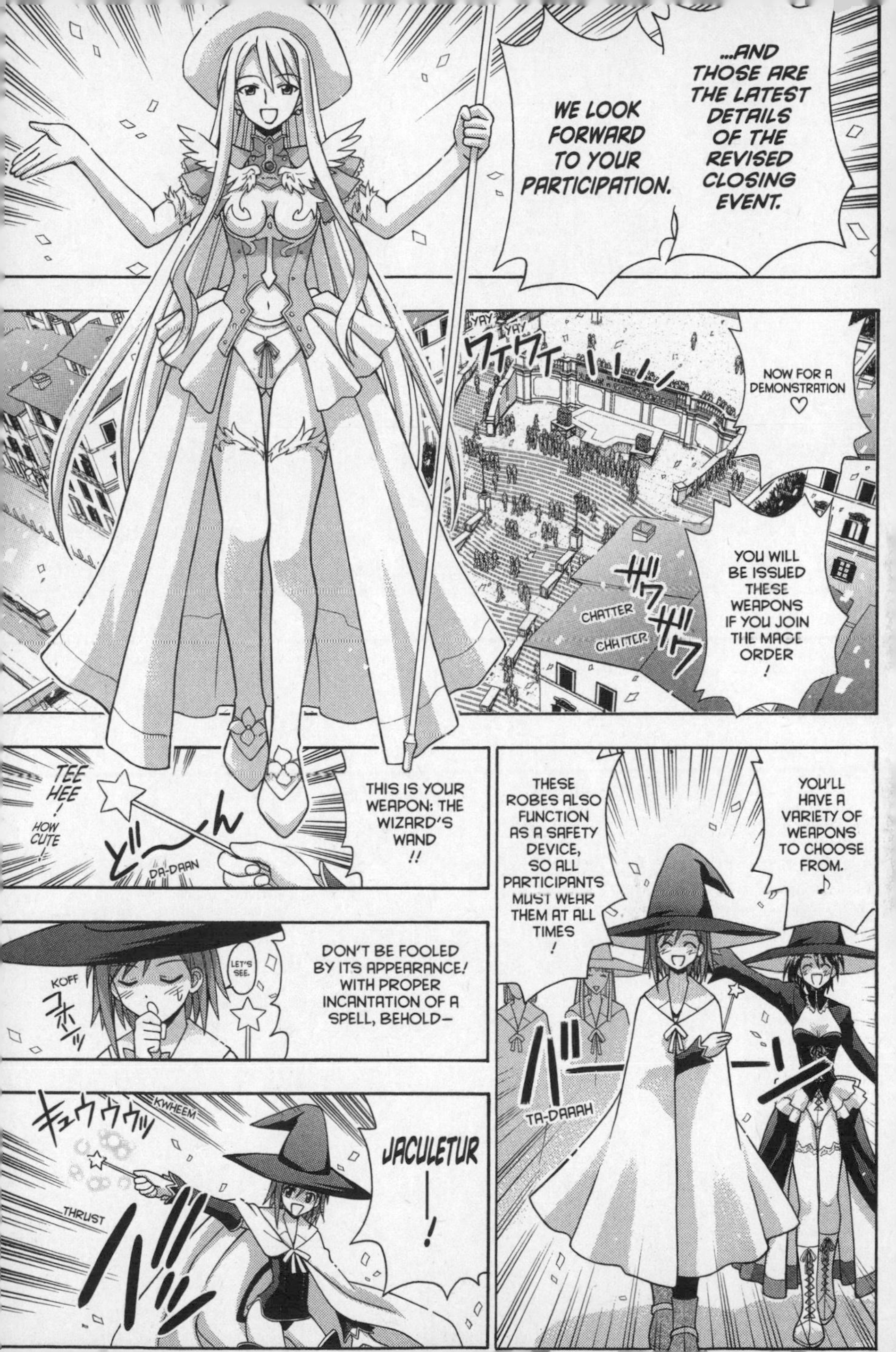
...AND THOSE ARE THE LATEST DETAILS OF THE REVISED CLOSING EVENT.
WE LOOK FORWARD TO YOUR PARTICIPATION.
YAY YAY
ワイワイ
NOW FOR A DEMONSTRATION ♡
ザワザワ
CHATTER CHATTER
YOU WILL BE ISSUED THESE WEAPONS IF YOU JOIN THE MAGE ORDER!
YOU'LL HAVE A VARIETY OF WEAPONS TO CHOOSE FROM. ♪
THESE ROBES ALSO FUNCTION AS A SAFETY DEVICE, SO ALL PARTICIPANTS MUST WEAR THEM AT ALL TIMES!
TA-DAAAH
THIS IS YOUR WEAPON: THE WIZARD'S WAND!!
DA-DAAN
TEE HEE! HOW CUTE!
DON'T BE FOOLED BY ITS APPEARANCE! WITH PROPER INCANTATION OF A SPELL, BEHOLD—
LET'S SEE.
KOFF
JACULETUR—!
KWHEEM
THRUST

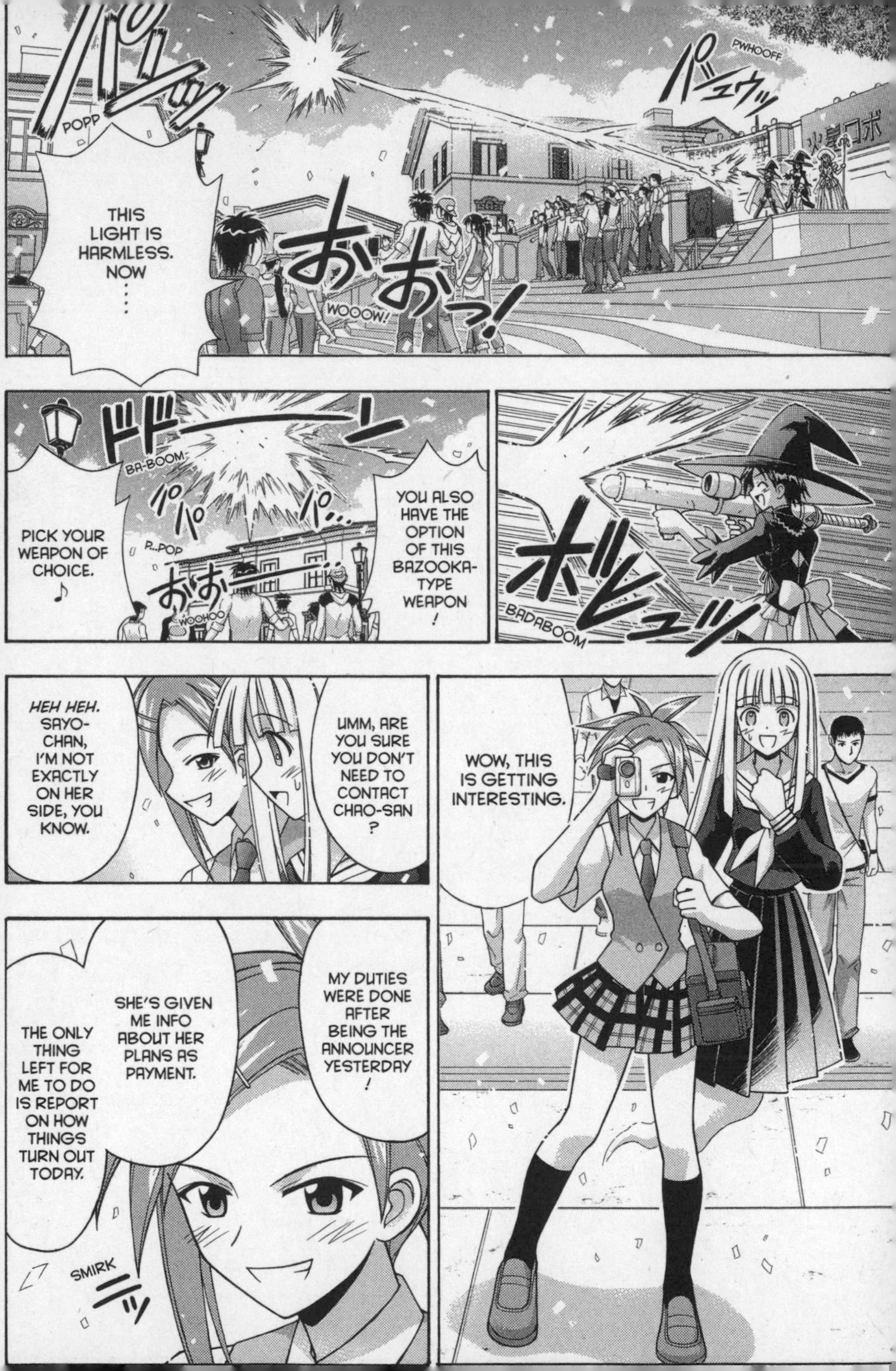
PWHOOFF
POPP
THIS LIGHT IS HARMLESS. NOW......
WOOOW!
BADABOOM
BA-BOOM
P...POP
WOOHOO
YOU ALSO HAVE THE OPTION OF THIS BAZOOKA-TYPE WEAPON!
PICK YOUR WEAPON OF CHOICE. ♪
WOW, THIS IS GETTING INTERESTING.
UMM, ARE YOU SURE YOU DON'T NEED TO CONTACT CHAO-SAN?
HEH HEH. SAYO-CHAN, I'M NOT EXACTLY ON HER SIDE, YOU KNOW.
MY DUTIES WERE DONE AFTER BEING THE ANNOUNCER YESTERDAY!
SHE'S GIVEN ME INFO ABOUT HER PLANS AS PAYMENT.
THE ONLY THING LEFT FOR ME TO DO IS REPORT ON HOW THINGS TURN OUT TODAY.
SMIRK

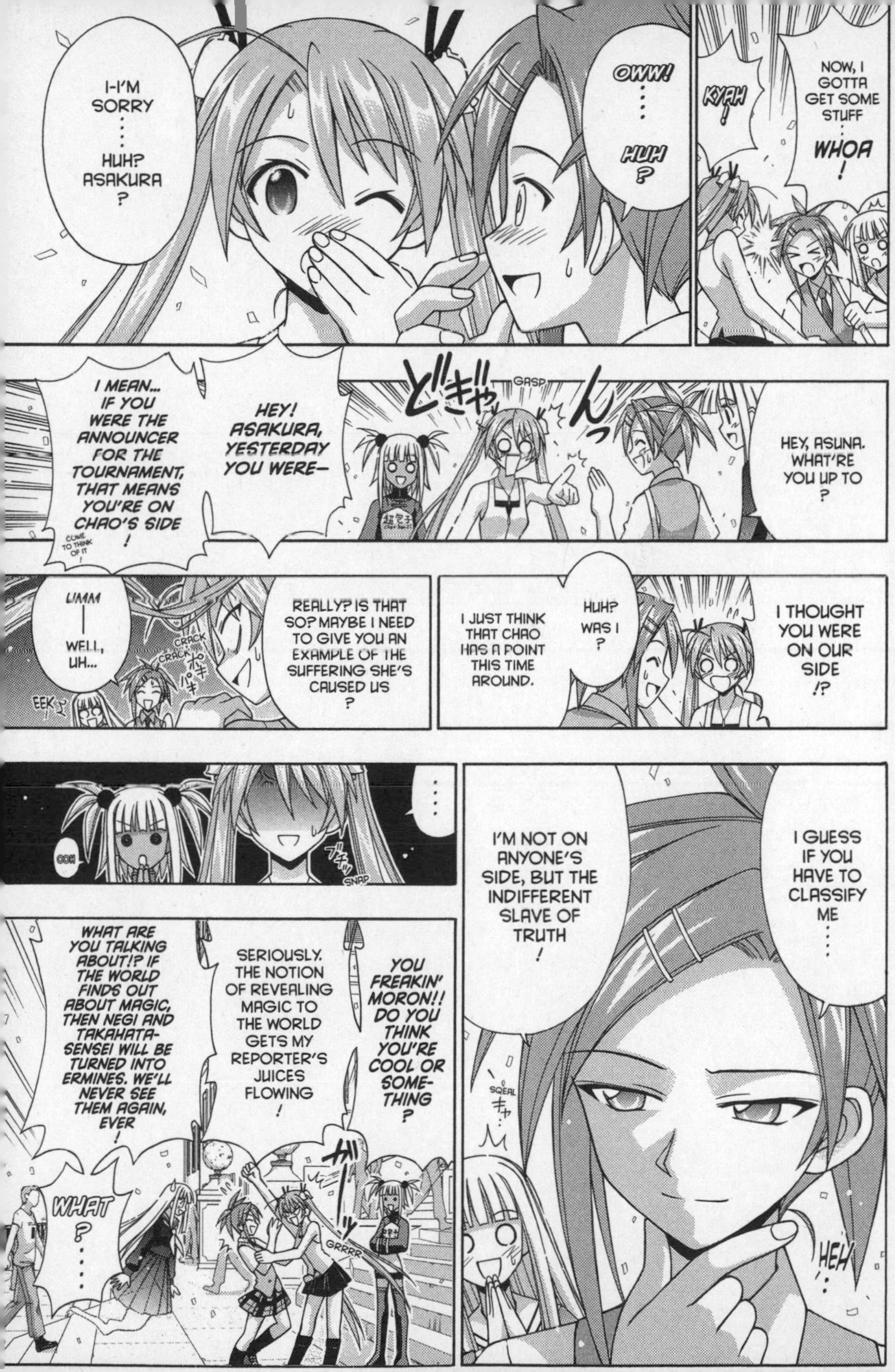

NOW, I GOTTA GET SOME STUFF...
WHOA!
KYAH!
OWW!...
HUH?
I-I'M SORRY...
HUH? ASAKURA?
HEY, ASUNA. WHAT'RE YOU UP TO?
どぎゃん
GASP
HEY! ASAKURA, YESTERDAY YOU WERE—
I MEAN... IF YOU WERE THE ANNOUNCER FOR THE TOURNAMENT, THAT MEANS YOU'RE ON CHAO'S SIDE!
COME TO THINK OF IT!
I THOUGHT YOU WERE ON OUR SIDE!?
HUH? WAS I?
I JUST THINK THAT CHAO HAS A POINT THIS TIME AROUND.
REALLY? IS THAT SO? MAYBE I NEED TO GIVE YOU AN EXAMPLE OF THE SUFFERING SHE'S CAUSED US?
CRACK CRACK
ポキ パキ
UMM — WELL, UH...
EEK
I GUESS IF YOU HAVE TO CLASSIFY ME...
I'M NOT ON ANYONE'S SIDE, BUT THE INDIFFERENT SLAVE OF TRUTH!
SQEAL
キャ
HEH
...
ブチッ
SNAP
OOH
YOU FREAKIN' MORON!! DO YOU THINK YOU'RE COOL OR SOMETHING?
SERIOUSLY. THE NOTION OF REVEALING MAGIC TO THE WORLD GETS MY REPORTER'S JUICES FLOWING!
WHAT ARE YOU TALKING ABOUT!? IF THE WORLD FINDS OUT ABOUT MAGIC, THEN NEGI AND TAKAHATA-SENSEI WILL BE TURNED INTO ERMINES. WE'LL NEVER SEE THEM AGAIN, EVER!
GRRRR
WHAT?...

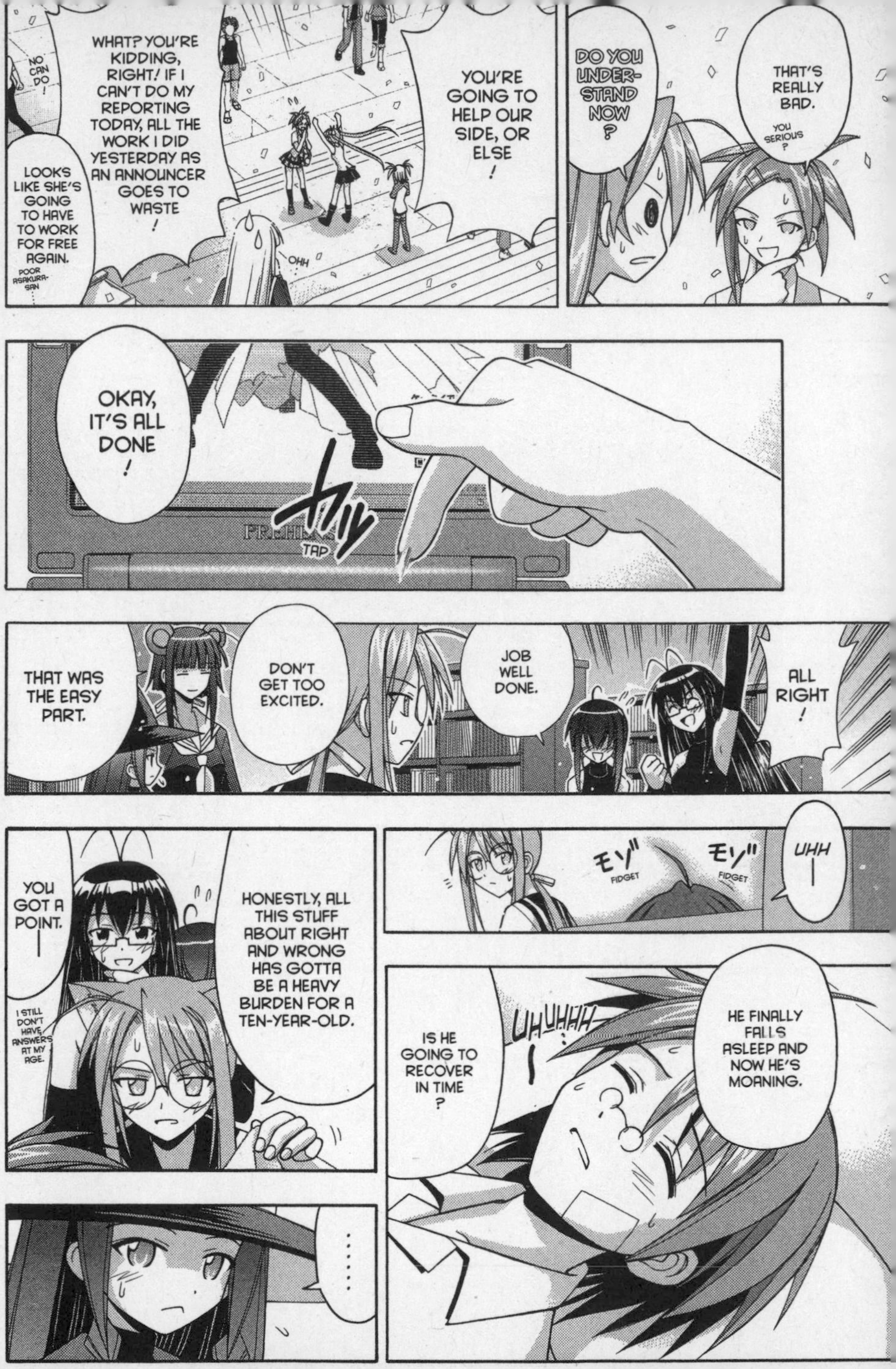
THAT'S REALLY BAD.
YOU SERIOUS?
DO YOU UNDERSTAND NOW?
YOU'RE GOING TO HELP OUR SIDE, OR ELSE!
WHAT? YOU'RE KIDDING, RIGHT! IF I CAN'T DO MY REPORTING TODAY, ALL THE WORK I DID YESTERDAY AS AN ANNOUNCER GOES TO WASTE!
NO CAN DO!
OHH
LOOKS LIKE SHE'S GOING TO HAVE TO WORK FOR FREE AGAIN.
POOR ASAKURA-SAN...
OKAY, IT'S ALL DONE!
TAP
ALL RIGHT!
JOB WELL DONE.
DON'T GET TOO EXCITED.
THAT WAS THE EASY PART.
UHH—
FIDGET
FIDGET
HE FINALLY FALLS ASLEEP AND NOW HE'S MOANING.
UHUHHH—!
IS HE GOING TO RECOVER IN TIME?
HONESTLY, ALL THIS STUFF ABOUT RIGHT AND WRONG HAS GOTTA BE A HEAVY BURDEN FOR A TEN-YEAR-OLD.
YOU GOT A POINT.—
I STILL DON'T HAVE ANSWERS AT MY AGE.
......

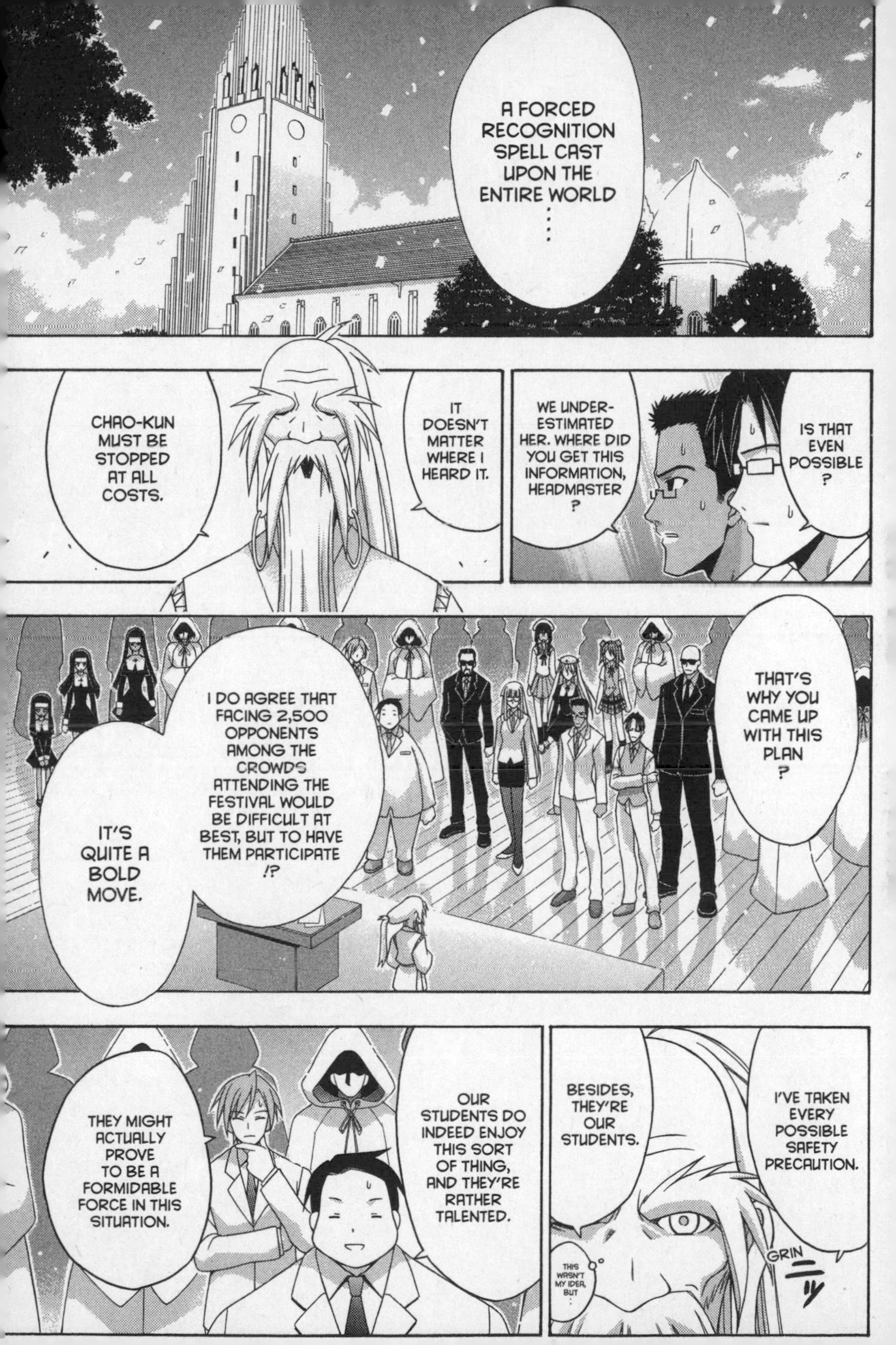
A FORCED RECOGNITION SPELL CAST UPON THE ENTIRE WORLD ...
IS THAT EVEN POSSIBLE ?
WE UNDER-ESTIMATED HER. WHERE DID YOU GET THIS INFORMATION, HEADMASTER ?
IT DOESN'T MATTER WHERE I HEARD IT.
CHAO-KUN MUST BE STOPPED AT ALL COSTS.
THAT'S WHY YOU CAME UP WITH THIS PLAN ?
I DO AGREE THAT FACING 2,500 OPPONENTS AMONG THE CROWDS ATTENDING THE FESTIVAL WOULD BE DIFFICULT AT BEST, BUT TO HAVE THEM PARTICIPATE !?
IT'S QUITE A BOLD MOVE.
I'VE TAKEN EVERY POSSIBLE SAFETY PRECAUTION.
BESIDES, THEY'RE OUR STUDENTS.
THIS WASN'T MY IDEA, BUT ...
GRIN
OUR STUDENTS DO INDEED ENJOY THIS SORT OF THING, AND THEY'RE RATHER TALENTED.
THEY MIGHT ACTUALLY PROVE TO BE A FORMIDABLE FORCE IN THIS SITUATION.

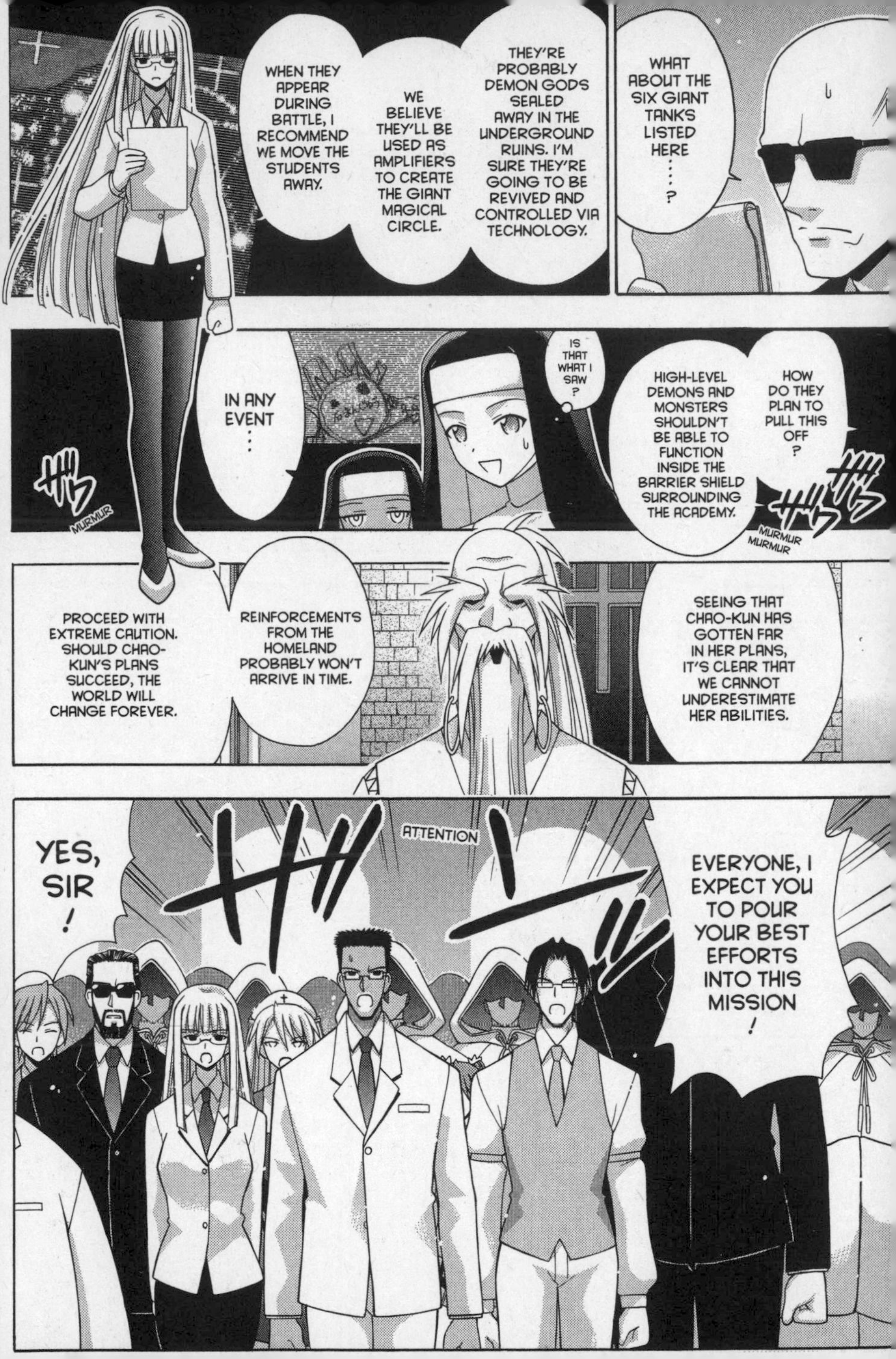
WHAT ABOUT THE SIX GIANT TANKS LISTED HERE....?
THEY'RE PROBABLY DEMON GODS SEALED AWAY IN THE UNDERGROUND RUINS. I'M SURE THEY'RE GOING TO BE REVIVED AND CONTROLLED VIA TECHNOLOGY.
WE BELIEVE THEY'LL BE USED AS AMPLIFIERS TO CREATE THE GIANT MAGICAL CIRCLE.
WHEN THEY APPEAR DURING BATTLE, I RECOMMEND WE MOVE THE STUDENTS AWAY.
HOW DO THEY PLAN TO PULL THIS OFF?
HIGH-LEVEL DEMONS AND MONSTERS SHOULDN'T BE ABLE TO FUNCTION INSIDE THE BARRIER SHIELD SURROUNDING THE ACADEMY.
MURMUR MURMUR
IS THAT WHAT I SAW?
IN ANY EVENT...
MURMUR
SEEING THAT CHAO-KUN HAS GOTTEN FAR IN HER PLANS, IT'S CLEAR THAT WE CANNOT UNDERESTIMATE HER ABILITIES.
REINFORCEMENTS FROM THE HOMELAND PROBABLY WON'T ARRIVE IN TIME.
PROCEED WITH EXTREME CAUTION. SHOULD CHAO-KUN'S PLANS SUCCEED, THE WORLD WILL CHANGE FOREVER.
EVERYONE, I EXPECT YOU TO POUR YOUR BEST EFFORTS INTO THIS MISSION!
ATTENTION
YES, SIR!

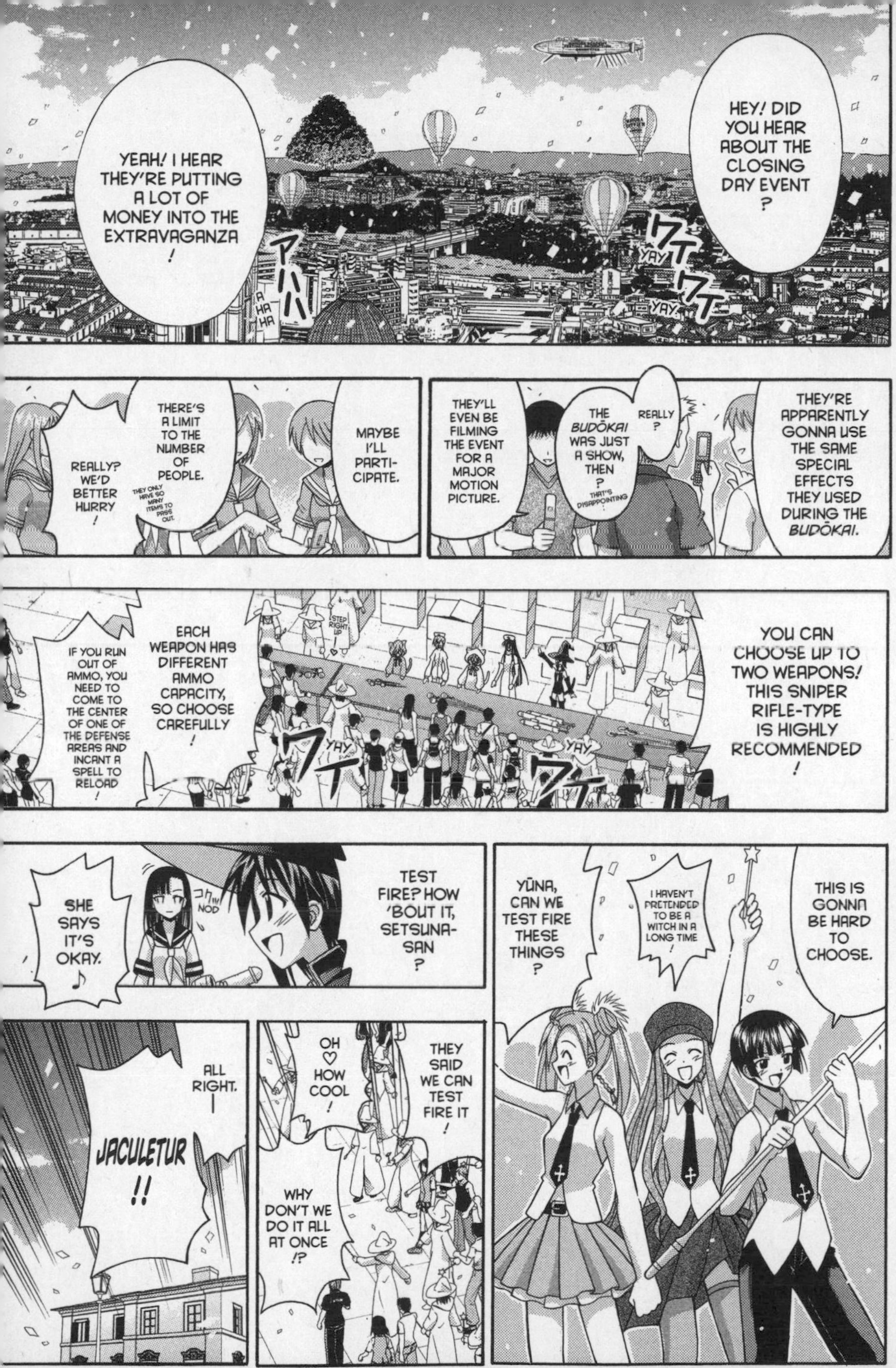
HEY! DID YOU HEAR ABOUT THE CLOSING DAY EVENT?
YAY
YAY
YEAH! I HEAR THEY'RE PUTTING A LOT OF MONEY INTO THE EXTRAVAGANZA!
A HA HA
THEY'RE APPARENTLY GONNA USE THE SAME SPECIAL EFFECTS THEY USED DURING THE *BUDŌKAI*.
REALLY?
THE *BUDŌKAI* WAS JUST A SHOW, THEN?
THAT'S DISAPPOINTING!
THEY'LL EVEN BE FILMING THE EVENT FOR A MAJOR MOTION PICTURE.
MAYBE I'LL PARTI-CIPATE.
THERE'S A LIMIT TO THE NUMBER OF PEOPLE.
THEY ONLY HAVE SO MANY ITEMS TO PASS OUT.
REALLY? WE'D BETTER HURRY!
YOU CAN CHOOSE UP TO TWO WEAPONS! THIS SNIPER RIFLE-TYPE IS HIGHLY RECOMMENDED!
YAY
YAY
STEP RIGHT UP ♡
EACH WEAPON HAS DIFFERENT AMMO CAPACITY, SO CHOOSE CAREFULLY!
IF YOU RUN OUT OF AMMO, YOU NEED TO COME TO THE CENTER OF ONE OF THE DEFENSE AREAS AND INCANT A SPELL TO RELOAD!
THIS IS GONNA BE HARD TO CHOOSE.
I HAVEN'T PRETENDED TO BE A WITCH IN A LONG TIME!
YŪNA, CAN WE TEST FIRE THESE THINGS?
TEST FIRE? HOW 'BOUT IT, SETSUNA-SAN?
NOD
SHE SAYS IT'S OKAY. ♪
THEY SAID WE CAN TEST FIRE IT
OH ♡ HOW COOL!
WHY DON'T WE DO IT ALL AT ONCE!?
ALL RIGHT.
JACULETUR!!

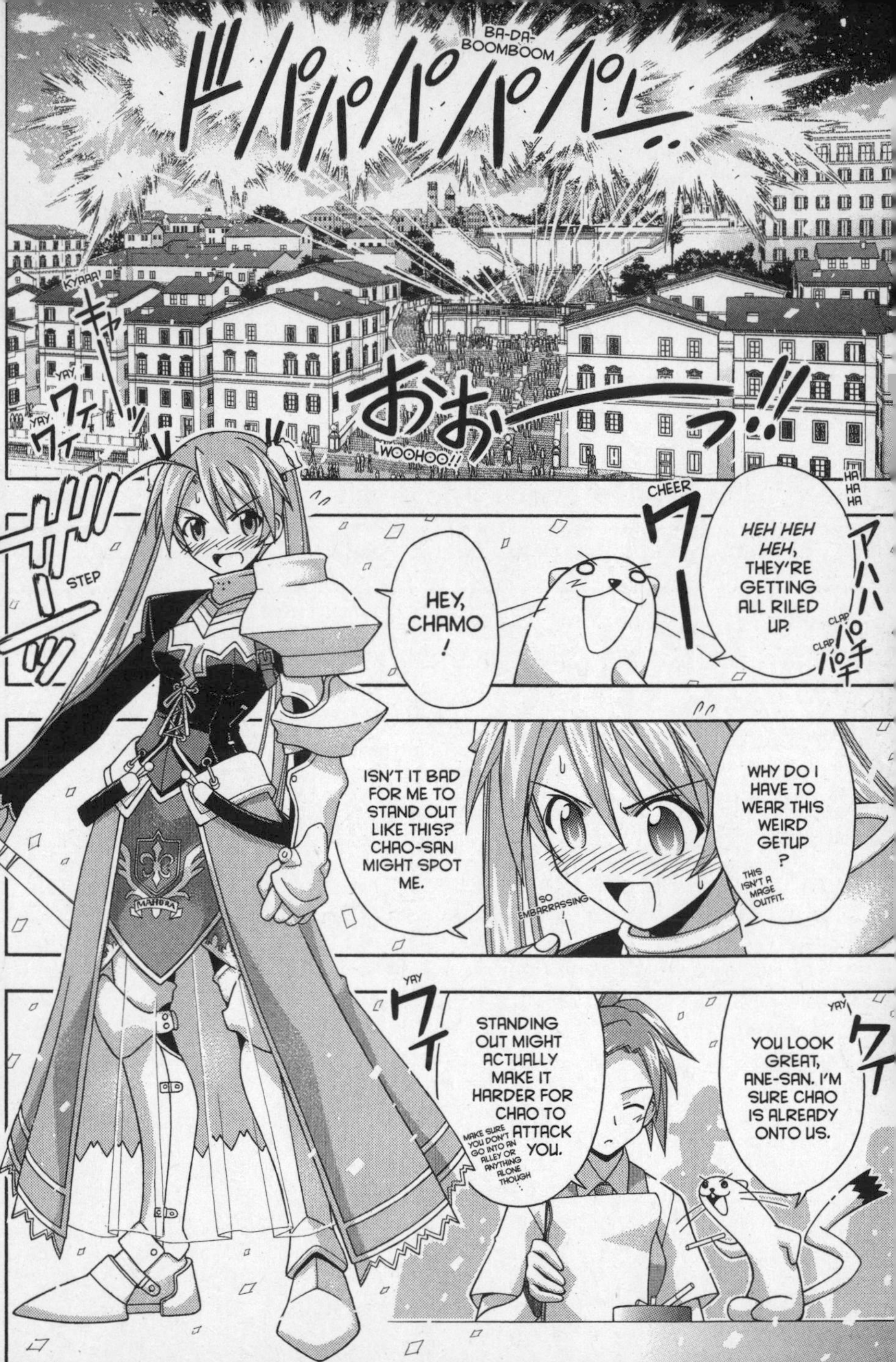

BA-DA-BOOMBOOM
ドパパパパー
KYAAA!
キャー
YAY
ワイ
YAY
ワイ
おおーーっ!!
WOOHOO!!
CHEER
ワー
HA HA HA
アハハ
HEH HEH HEH, THEY'RE GETTING ALL RILED UP.
CLAP CLAP
パチパチ
HEY, CHAMO!
WHY DO I HAVE TO WEAR THIS WEIRD GETUP?
THIS ISN'T A MAGE OUTFIT.
SO EMBARRASSING!
ISN'T IT BAD FOR ME TO STAND OUT LIKE THIS? CHAO-SAN MIGHT SPOT ME.
YAY
ワイ
YOU LOOK GREAT, ANE-SAN. I'M SURE CHAO IS ALREADY ONTO US.
YAY
ワイ
STANDING OUT MIGHT ACTUALLY MAKE IT HARDER FOR CHAO TO ATTACK YOU.
MAKE SURE YOU DON'T GO INTO AN ALLEY OR ANYTHING ALONE THOUGH...
STEP
ザーッ
MAHORA

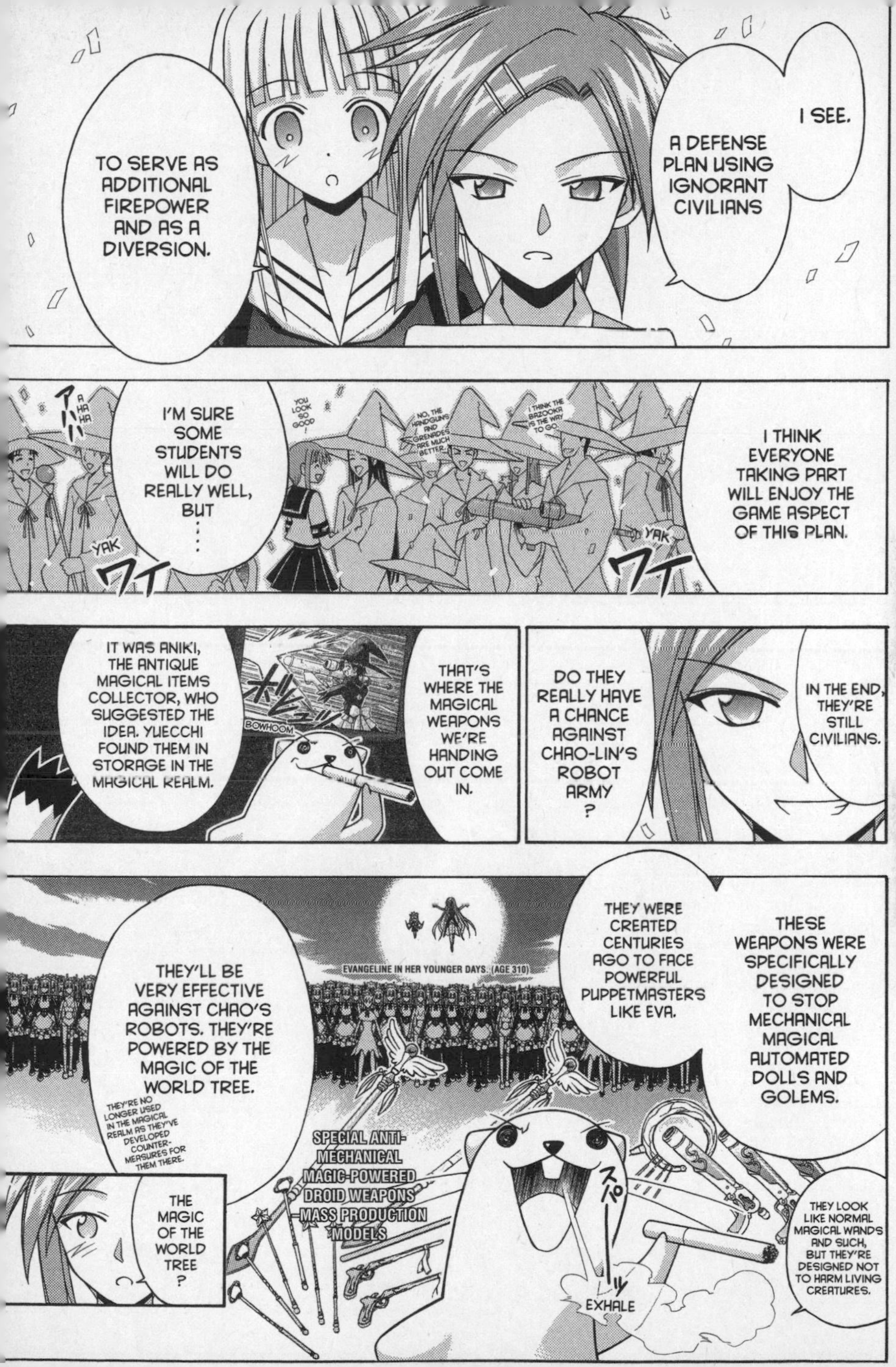
I SEE.
A DEFENSE PLAN USING IGNORANT CIVILIANS
TO SERVE AS ADDITIONAL FIREPOWER AND AS A DIVERSION.
I THINK EVERYONE TAKING PART WILL ENJOY THE GAME ASPECT OF THIS PLAN.
YAK
I THINK THE BAZOOKA IS THE WAY TO GO.
NO, THE HANDGUNS AND GRENADES ARE MUCH BETTER.
YOU LOOK SO GOOD!
I'M SURE SOME STUDENTS WILL DO REALLY WELL, BUT .....
AHAHA
YAK
IN THE END, THEY'RE STILL CIVILIANS.
DO THEY REALLY HAVE A CHANCE AGAINST CHAO-LIN'S ROBOT ARMY?
THAT'S WHERE THE MAGICAL WEAPONS WE'RE HANDING OUT COME IN.
BOWHOOM
IT WAS ANIKI, THE ANTIQUE MAGICAL ITEMS COLLECTOR, WHO SUGGESTED THE IDEA. YUECCHI FOUND THEM IN STORAGE IN THE MAGICAL REALM.
THESE WEAPONS WERE SPECIFICALLY DESIGNED TO STOP MECHANICAL MAGICAL AUTOMATED DOLLS AND GOLEMS.
THEY WERE CREATED CENTURIES AGO TO FACE POWERFUL PUPPETMASTERS LIKE EVA.
EVANGELINE IN HER YOUNGER DAYS. (AGE 310)
THEY'LL BE VERY EFFECTIVE AGAINST CHAO'S ROBOTS. THEY'RE POWERED BY THE MAGIC OF THE WORLD TREE.
THEY'RE NO LONGER USED IN THE MAGICAL REALM AS THEY'VE DEVELOPED COUNTER-MEASURES FOR THEM THERE.
THEY LOOK LIKE NORMAL MAGICAL WANDS AND SUCH, BUT THEY'RE DESIGNED NOT TO HARM LIVING CREATURES.
EXHALE
SPECIAL ANTI-MECHANICAL MAGIC-POWERED DROID WEAPONS —MASS PRODUCTION MODELS
THE MAGIC OF THE WORLD TREE?

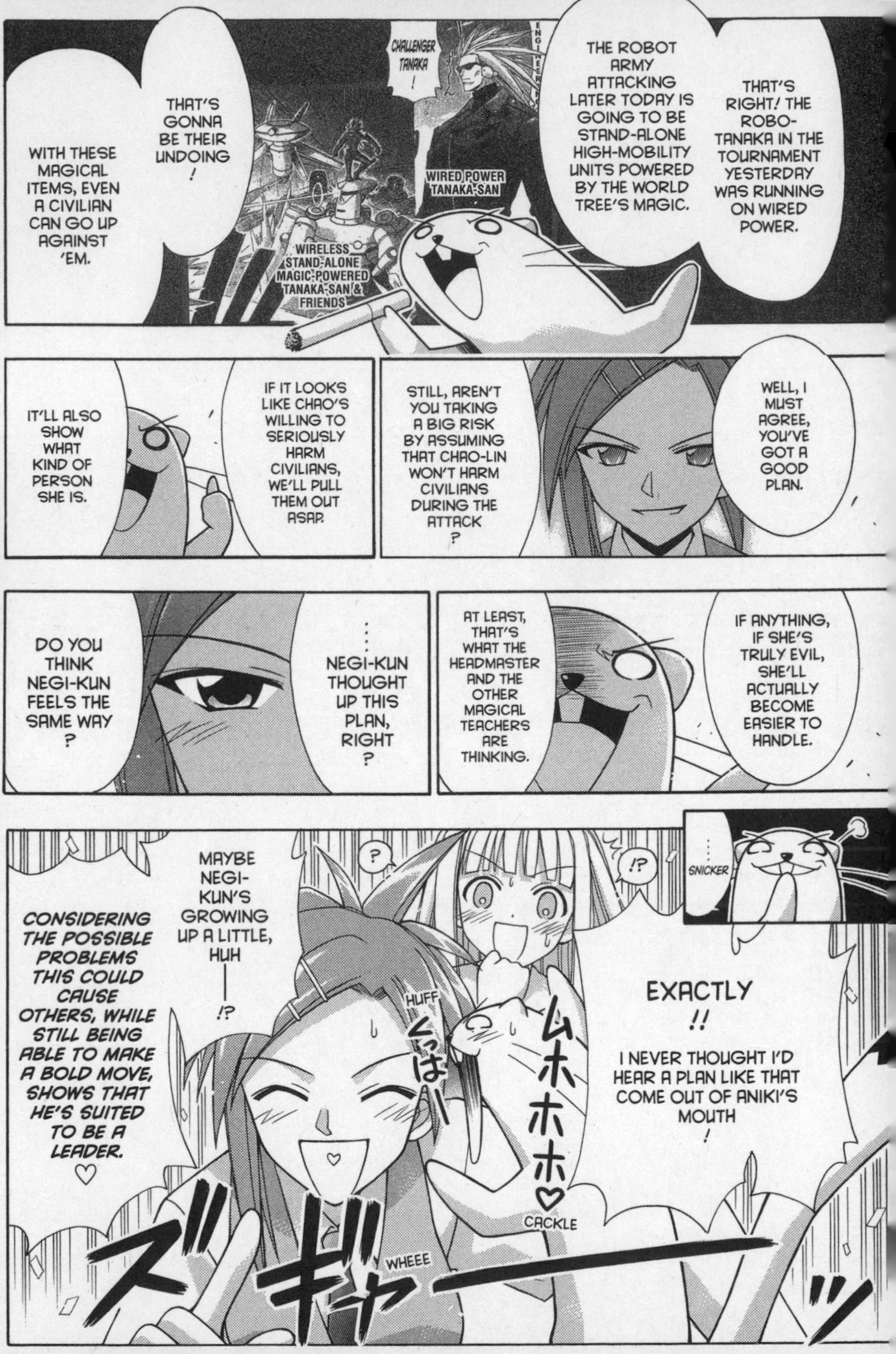

THAT'S RIGHT! THE ROBO-TANAKA IN THE TOURNAMENT YESTERDAY WAS RUNNING ON WIRED POWER.
THE ROBOT ARMY ATTACKING LATER TODAY IS GOING TO BE STAND-ALONE HIGH-MOBILITY UNITS POWERED BY THE WORLD TREE'S MAGIC.
CHALLENGER TANAKA!
WIRED POWER TANAKA-SAN
WIRELESS STAND-ALONE MAGIC-POWERED TANAKA-SAN & FRIENDS
THAT'S GONNA BE THEIR UNDOING!
WITH THESE MAGICAL ITEMS, EVEN A CIVILIAN CAN GO UP AGAINST 'EM.
WELL, I MUST AGREE, YOU'VE GOT A GOOD PLAN.
STILL, AREN'T YOU TAKING A BIG RISK BY ASSUMING THAT CHAO-LIN WON'T HARM CIVILIANS DURING THE ATTACK?
IF IT LOOKS LIKE CHAO'S WILLING TO SERIOUSLY HARM CIVILIANS, WE'LL PULL THEM OUT ASAP.
IT'LL ALSO SHOW WHAT KIND OF PERSON SHE IS.
IF ANYTHING, IF SHE'S TRULY EVIL, SHE'LL ACTUALLY BECOME EASIER TO HANDLE.
AT LEAST, THAT'S WHAT THE HEADMASTER AND THE OTHER MAGICAL TEACHERS ARE THINKING.
... NEGI-KUN THOUGHT UP THIS PLAN, RIGHT?
DO YOU THINK NEGI-KUN FEELS THE SAME WAY?
... SNICKER
EXACTLY!!
I NEVER THOUGHT I'D HEAR A PLAN LIKE THAT COME OUT OF ANIKI'S MOUTH!
ムホホホ♡
CACKLE
!?
?
くっはー
HUFF
MAYBE NEGI-KUN'S GROWING UP A LITTLE, HUH—!?
CONSIDERING THE POSSIBLE PROBLEMS THIS COULD CAUSE OTHERS, WHILE STILL BEING ABLE TO MAKE A BOLD MOVE, SHOWS THAT HE'S SUITED TO BE A LEADER. ♡
ズギャーーッ
WHEEE

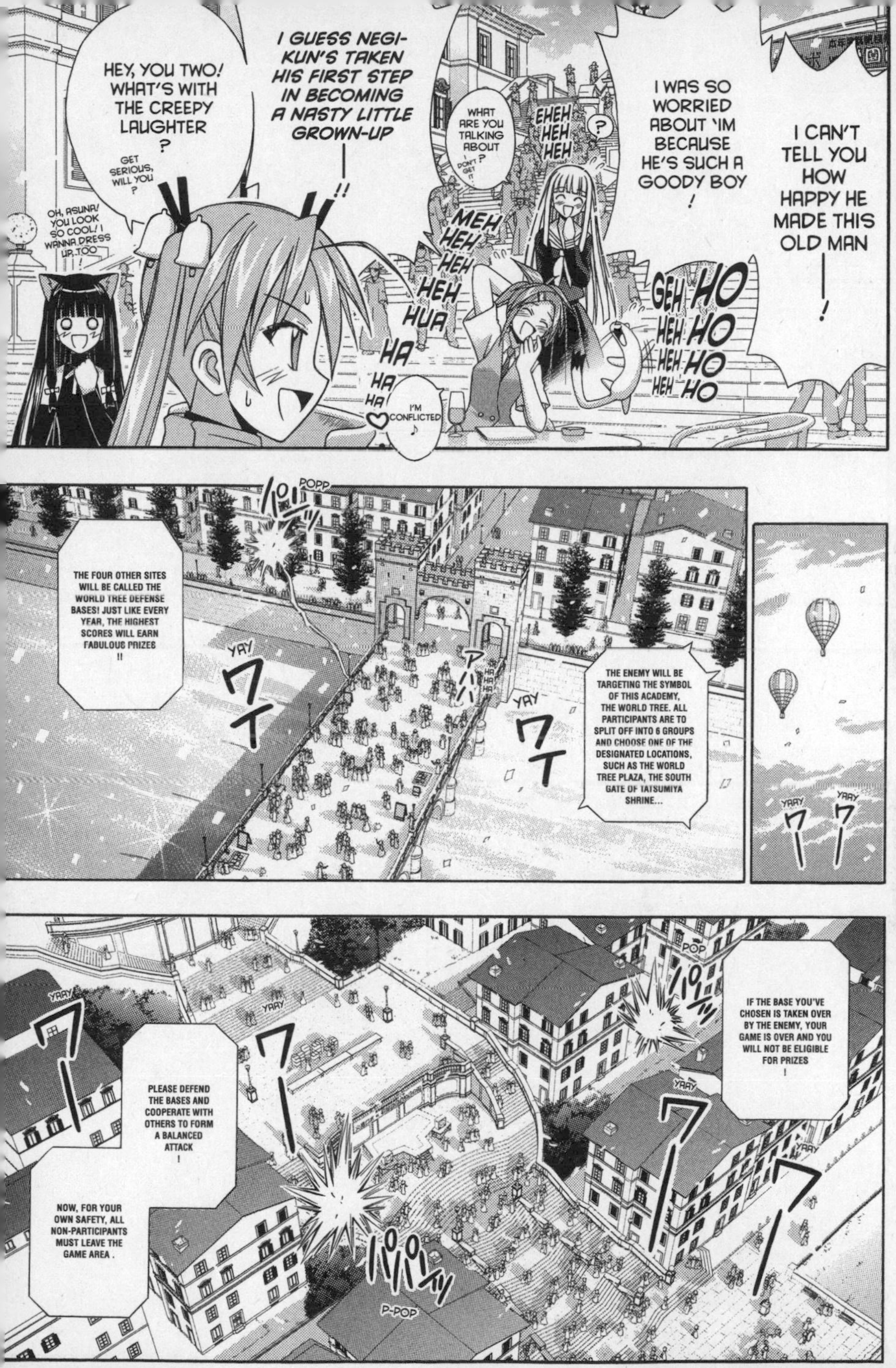

I CAN'T TELL YOU HOW HAPPY HE MADE THIS OLD MAN —!
GEH HEH HEH HEH
HO HO HO HO
I WAS SO WORRIED ABOUT 'IM BECAUSE HE'S SUCH A GOODY BOY!
?
EHEH HEH HEH
WHAT ARE YOU TALKING ABOUT?
I DON'T GET IT
I GUESS NEGI-KUN'S TAKEN HIS FIRST STEP IN BECOMING A NASTY LITTLE GROWN-UP —!!
MEH HEH HEH HEH HUA HA HA HA
I'M CONFLICTED ♪
HEY, YOU TWO! WHAT'S WITH THE CREEPY LAUGHTER?
GET SERIOUS, WILL YOU?
OH, ASUNA! YOU LOOK SO COOL! I WANNA DRESS UP, TOO!
YAAY ワー
YAAY ワー
THE ENEMY WILL BE TARGETING THE SYMBOL OF THIS ACADEMY, THE WORLD TREE. ALL PARTICIPANTS ARE TO SPLIT OFF INTO 6 GROUPS AND CHOOSE ONE OF THE DESIGNATED LOCATIONS, SUCH AS THE WORLD TREE PLAZA, THE SOUTH GATE OF TATSUMIYA SHRINE...
YAY ワイ
アハハ HA HA HA
POPP パンッ
THE FOUR OTHER SITES WILL BE CALLED THE WORLD TREE DEFENSE BASES! JUST LIKE EVERY YEAR, THE HIGHEST SCORES WILL EARN FABULOUS PRIZES!!
YAY ワイ
IF THE BASE YOU'VE CHOSEN IS TAKEN OVER BY THE ENEMY, YOUR GAME IS OVER AND YOU WILL NOT BE ELIGIBLE FOR PRIZES!
YAAY ワー
YAAY ワー
POP パンッ
PLEASE DEFEND THE BASES AND COOPERATE WITH OTHERS TO FORM A BALANCED ATTACK!
YAAY ワー
YAAY ワー
NOW, FOR YOUR OWN SAFETY, ALL NON-PARTICIPANTS MUST LEAVE THE GAME AREA.
P-POP パパパンッ

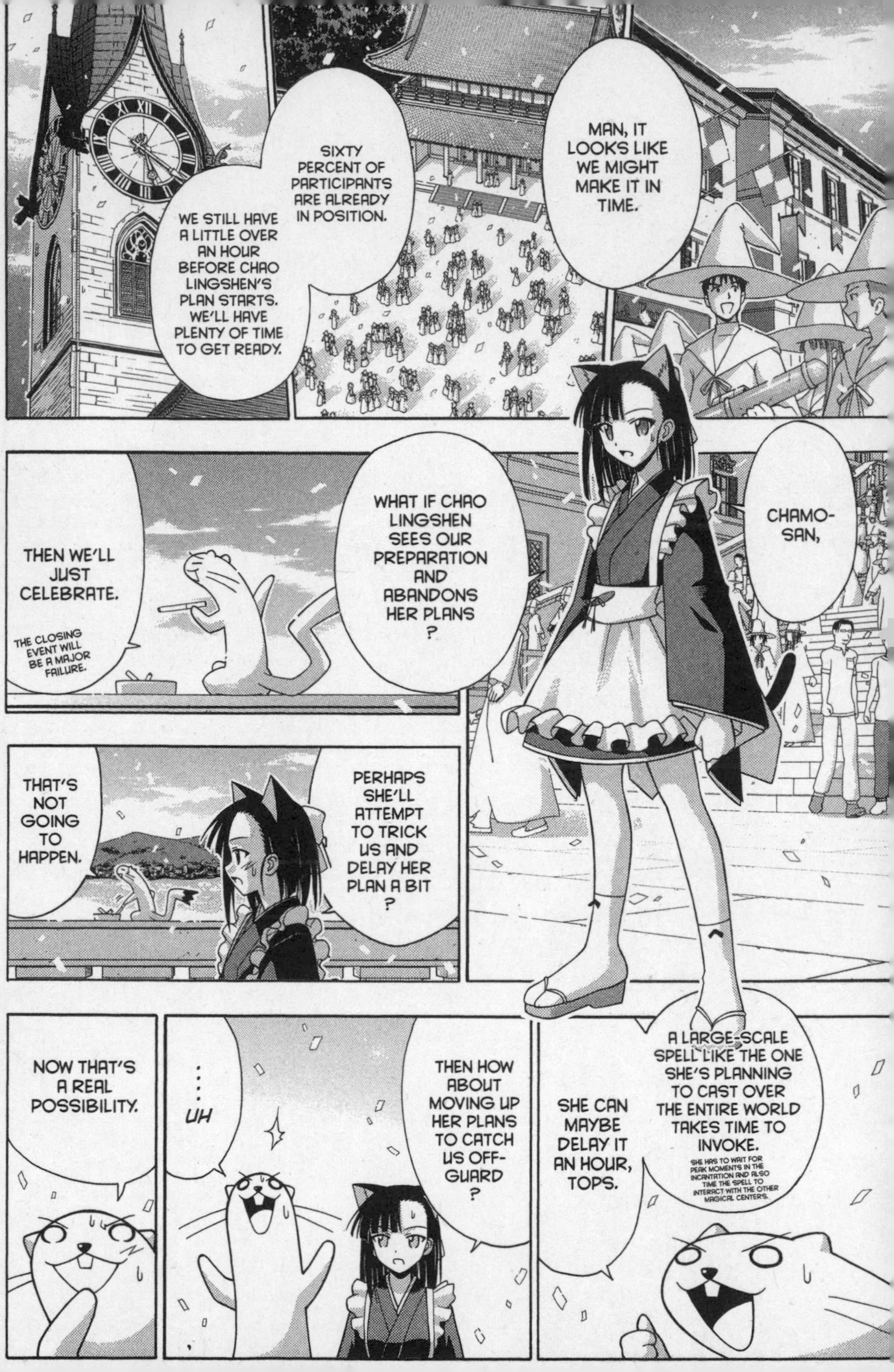
MAN, IT LOOKS LIKE WE MIGHT MAKE IT IN TIME.
SIXTY PERCENT OF PARTICIPANTS ARE ALREADY IN POSITION.
WE STILL HAVE A LITTLE OVER AN HOUR BEFORE CHAO LINGSHEN'S PLAN STARTS. WE'LL HAVE PLENTY OF TIME TO GET READY.
CHAMO-SAN,
WHAT IF CHAO LINGSHEN SEES OUR PREPARATION AND ABANDONS HER PLANS?
THEN WE'LL JUST CELEBRATE.
THE CLOSING EVENT WILL BE A MAJOR FAILURE.
PERHAPS SHE'LL ATTEMPT TO TRICK US AND DELAY HER PLAN A BIT?
THAT'S NOT GOING TO HAPPEN.
A LARGE-SCALE SPELL LIKE THE ONE SHE'S PLANNING TO CAST OVER THE ENTIRE WORLD TAKES TIME TO INVOKE.
SHE HAS TO WAIT FOR PEAK MOMENTS IN THE INCANTATION AND ALSO TIME THE SPELL TO INTERACT WITH THE OTHER MAGICAL CENTERS.
SHE CAN MAYBE DELAY IT AN HOUR, TOPS.
THEN HOW ABOUT MOVING UP HER PLANS TO CATCH US OFF-GUARD?
....UH
NOW THAT'S A REAL POSSIBILITY.

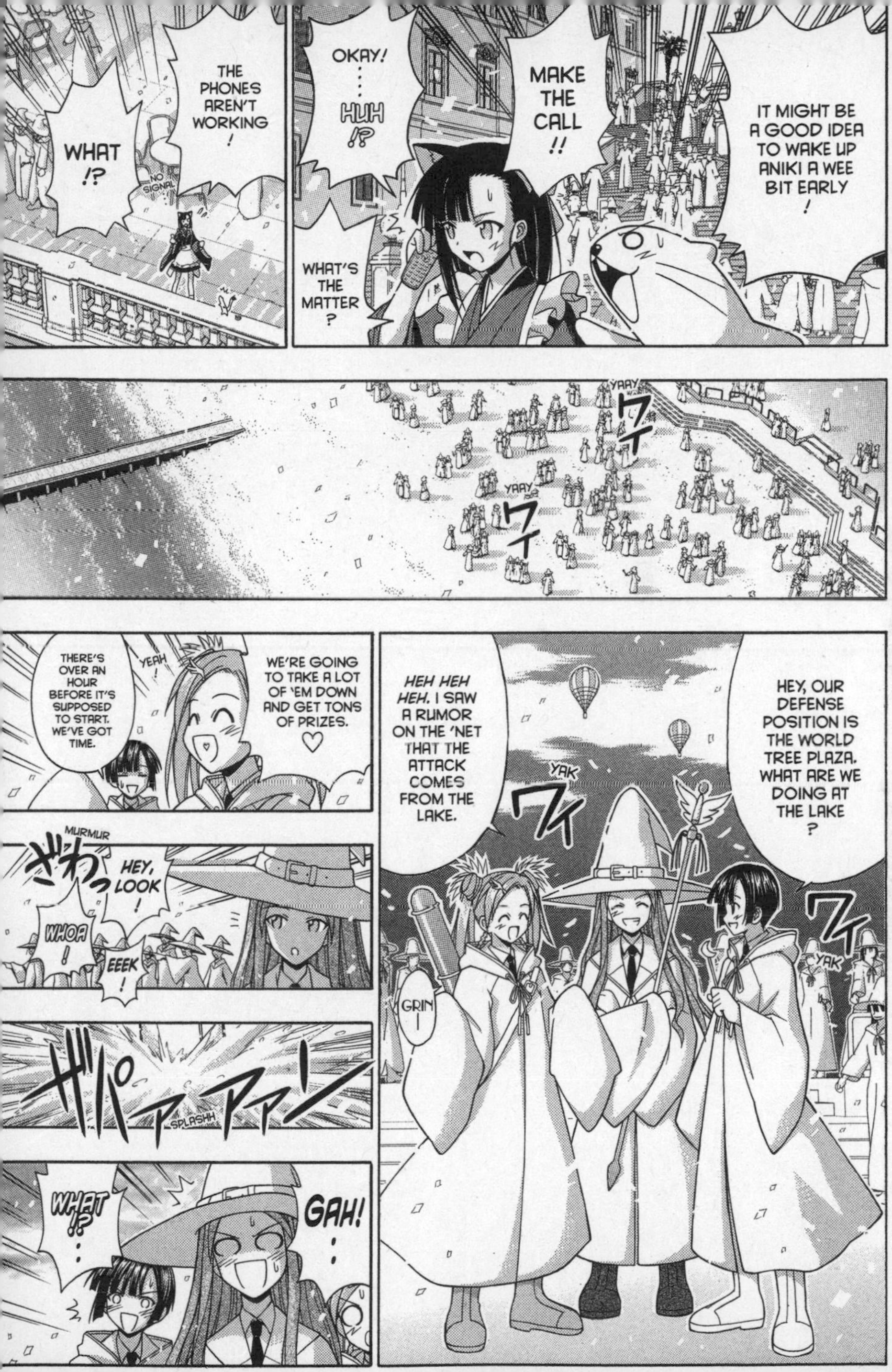
IT MIGHT BE A GOOD IDEA TO WAKE UP ANIKI A WEE BIT EARLY!
MAKE THE CALL!!
OKAY! ... HUH!?
WHAT'S THE MATTER?
THE PHONES AREN'T WORKING!
NO SIGNAL
WHAT!?
ワイ YAAY
ワイ YAAY
HEY, OUR DEFENSE POSITION IS THE WORLD TREE PLAZA. WHAT ARE WE DOING AT THE LAKE?
HEH HEH HEH. I SAW A RUMOR ON THE 'NET THAT THE ATTACK COMES FROM THE LAKE.
ワイ YAK
ワイ YAK
GRIN!
WE'RE GOING TO TAKE A LOT OF 'EM DOWN AND GET TONS OF PRIZES. ♡
YEAH!
THERE'S OVER AN HOUR BEFORE IT'S SUPPOSED TO START. WE'VE GOT TIME.
HEY, LOOK!
ざわっ MURMUR
WHOA!
EEEK!
ザパァアァー SPLASHH
GAH!
WHAT!?

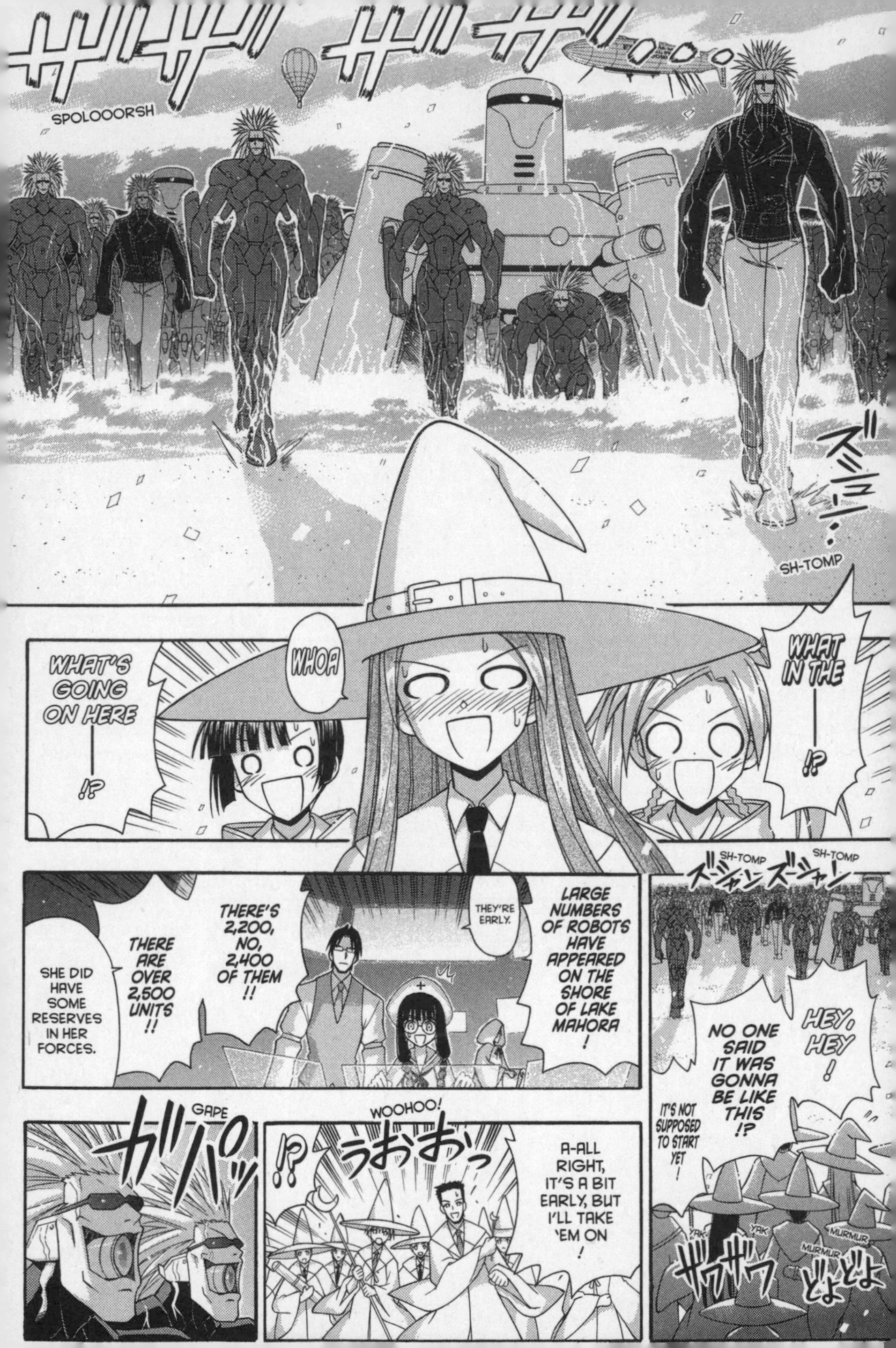

SPOLOOORSH
SH-TOMP
WHAT IN THE —— !?
WHOA
WHAT'S GOING ON HERE —— !?
SH-TOMP SH-TOMP
HEY, HEY!
NO ONE SAID IT WAS GONNA BE LIKE THIS !?
IT'S NOT SUPPOSED TO START YET!
YAK YAK
MURMUR MURMUR
ザワザワ どよどよ
LARGE NUMBERS OF ROBOTS HAVE APPEARED ON THE SHORE OF LAKE MAHORA!
THEY'RE EARLY.
THERE'S 2,200, NO, 2,400 OF THEM!!
THERE ARE OVER 2,500 UNITS!!
SHE DID HAVE SOME RESERVES IN HER FORCES.
A-ALL RIGHT, IT'S A BIT EARLY, BUT I'LL TAKE 'EM ON!
WOOHOO!
うおおっ
!?
GAPE
ガパッ

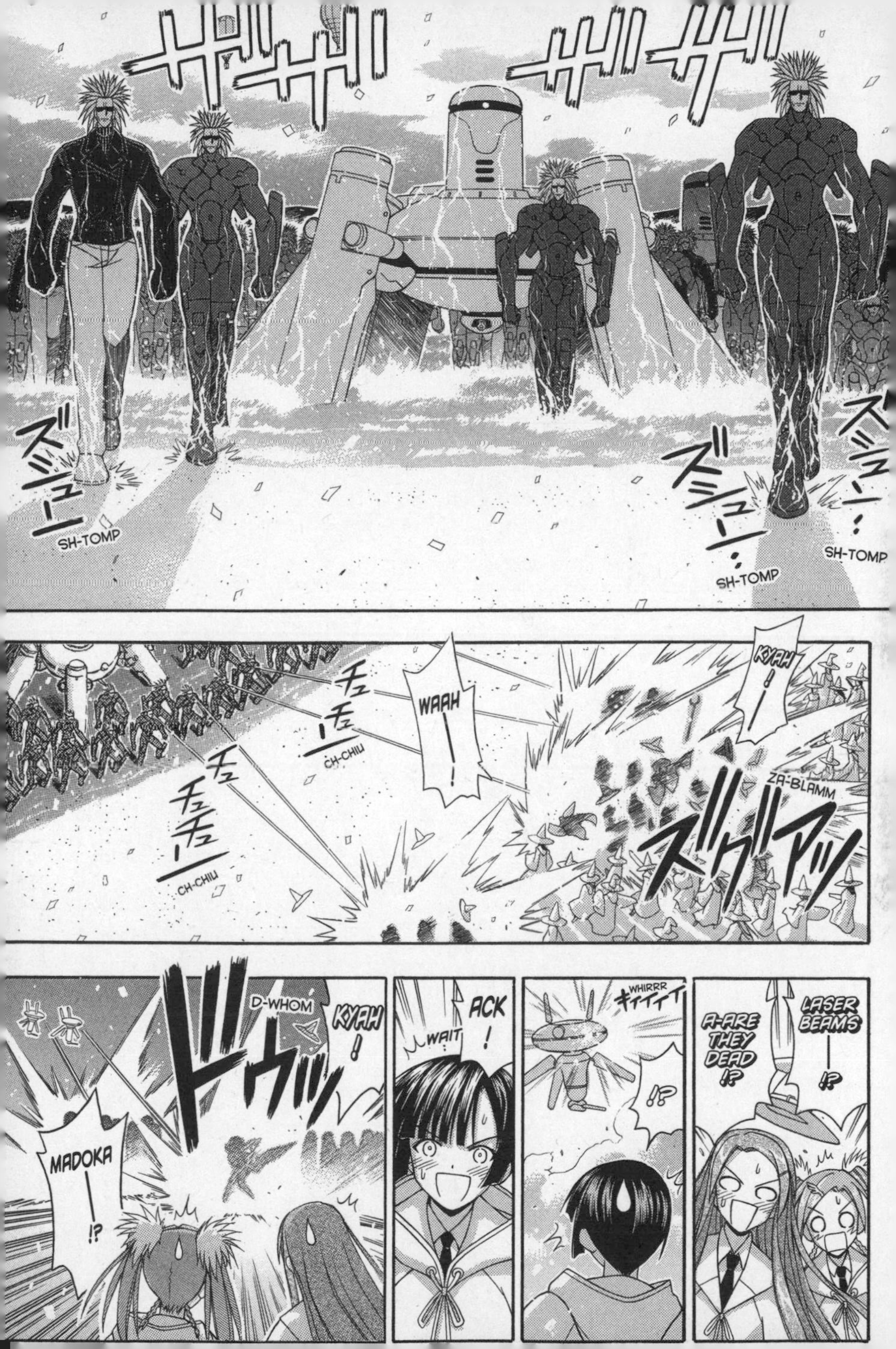
SH-TOMP
SH-TOMP
SH-TOMP
KYAH!
ZA-BLAMM
WAAH!
CH-CHIU
CH-CHIU
LASER BEAMS!?
A-ARE THEY DEAD!?
WHIRRR
!?
ACK!
WAIT
KYAH!
D-WHOM
MADOKA!?

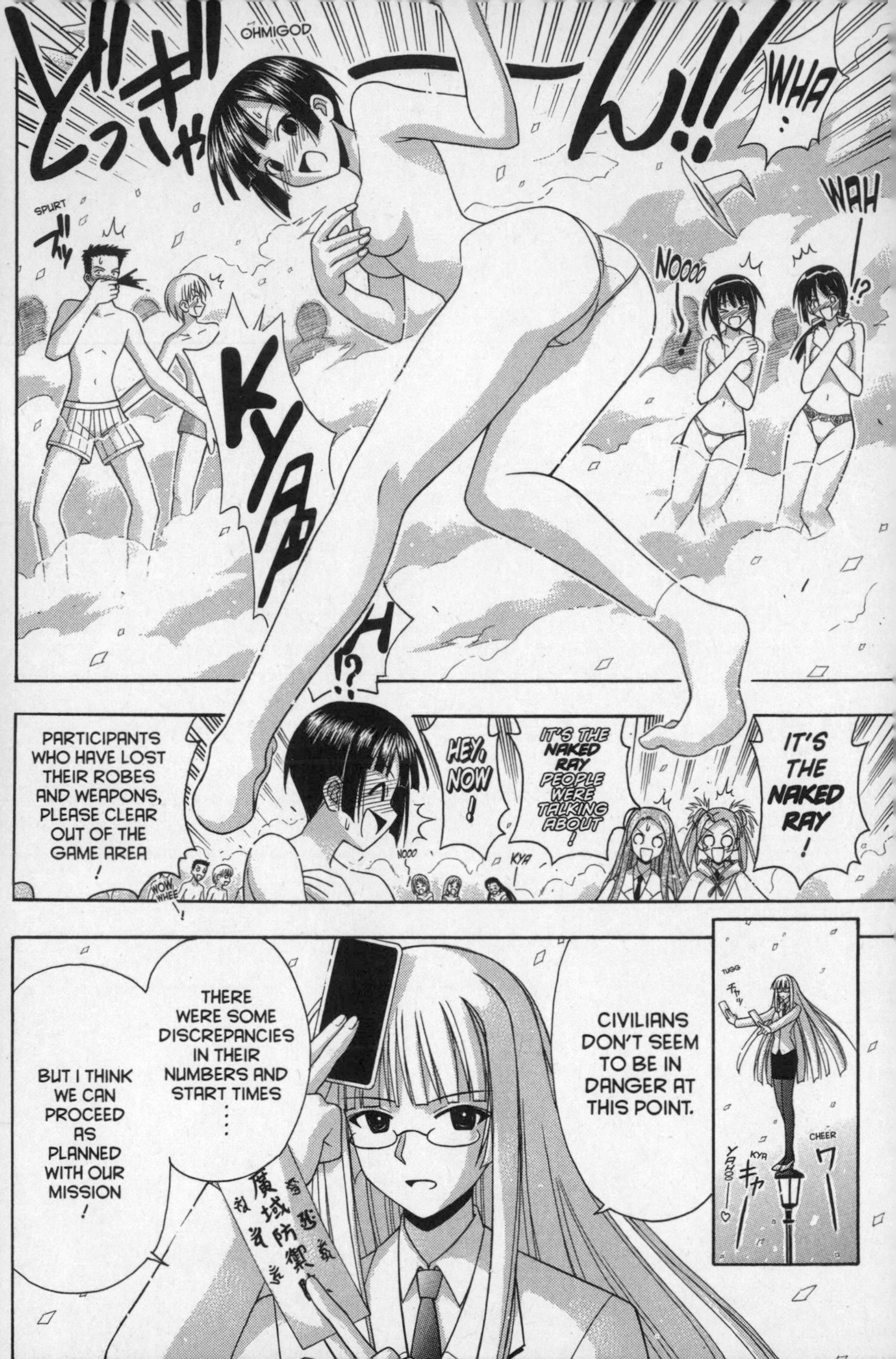
WHA :
WAH !?
NOOOO !
OHMIGOD
KYAAAH !?
SPURT
IT'S THE NAKED RAY !
IT'S THE NAKED RAY PEOPLE WERE TALKING ABOUT !
HEY, NOW !
KYA
NOOO
PARTICIPANTS WHO HAVE LOST THEIR ROBES AND WEAPONS, PLEASE CLEAR OUT OF THE GAME AREA !
WOW WHEE !
TUGG
CHEER
KYA
YAHOO—♡
CIVILIANS DON'T SEEM TO BE IN DANGER AT THIS POINT.
THERE WERE SOME DISCREPANCIES IN THEIR NUMBERS AND START TIMES ......
BUT I THINK WE CAN PROCEED AS PLANNED WITH OUR MISSION !

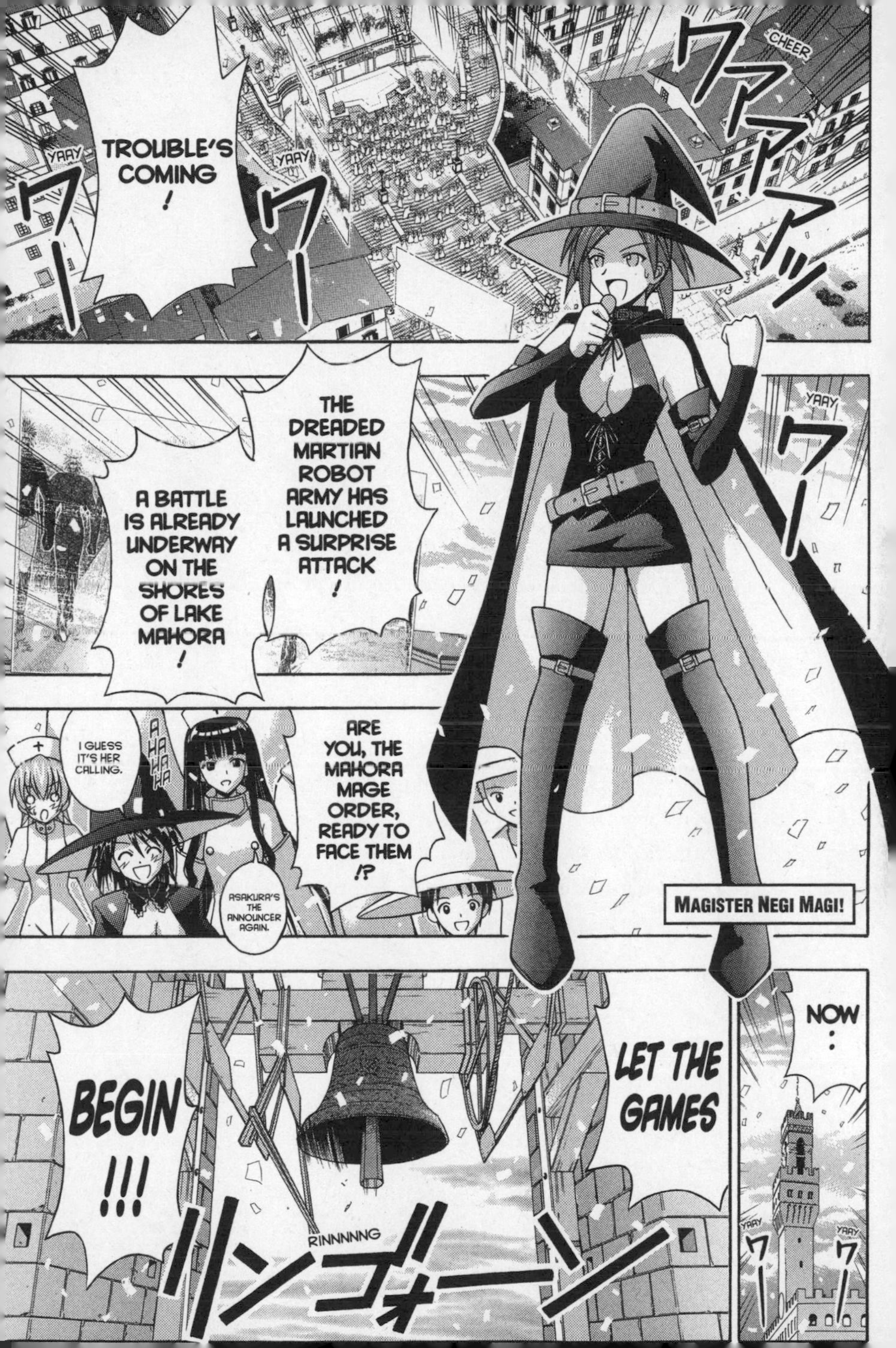
CHEER
ワァァァッ
YAAY
ワー
TROUBLE'S COMING!
YAAY
ワー
YAAY
ワー
THE DREADED MARTIAN ROBOT ARMY HAS LAUNCHED A SURPRISE ATTACK!
A BATTLE IS ALREADY UNDERWAY ON THE SHORES OF LAKE MAHORA!
MAGISTER NEGI MAGI!
ARE YOU, THE MAHORA MAGE ORDER, READY TO FACE THEM!?
ASAKURA'S THE ANNOUNCER AGAIN.
AHAHAHA
I GUESS IT'S HER CALLING.
NOW:
YAAY
ワー
YAAY
ワー
LET THE GAMES
BEGIN!!!
RINNNNG
リンゴォーン

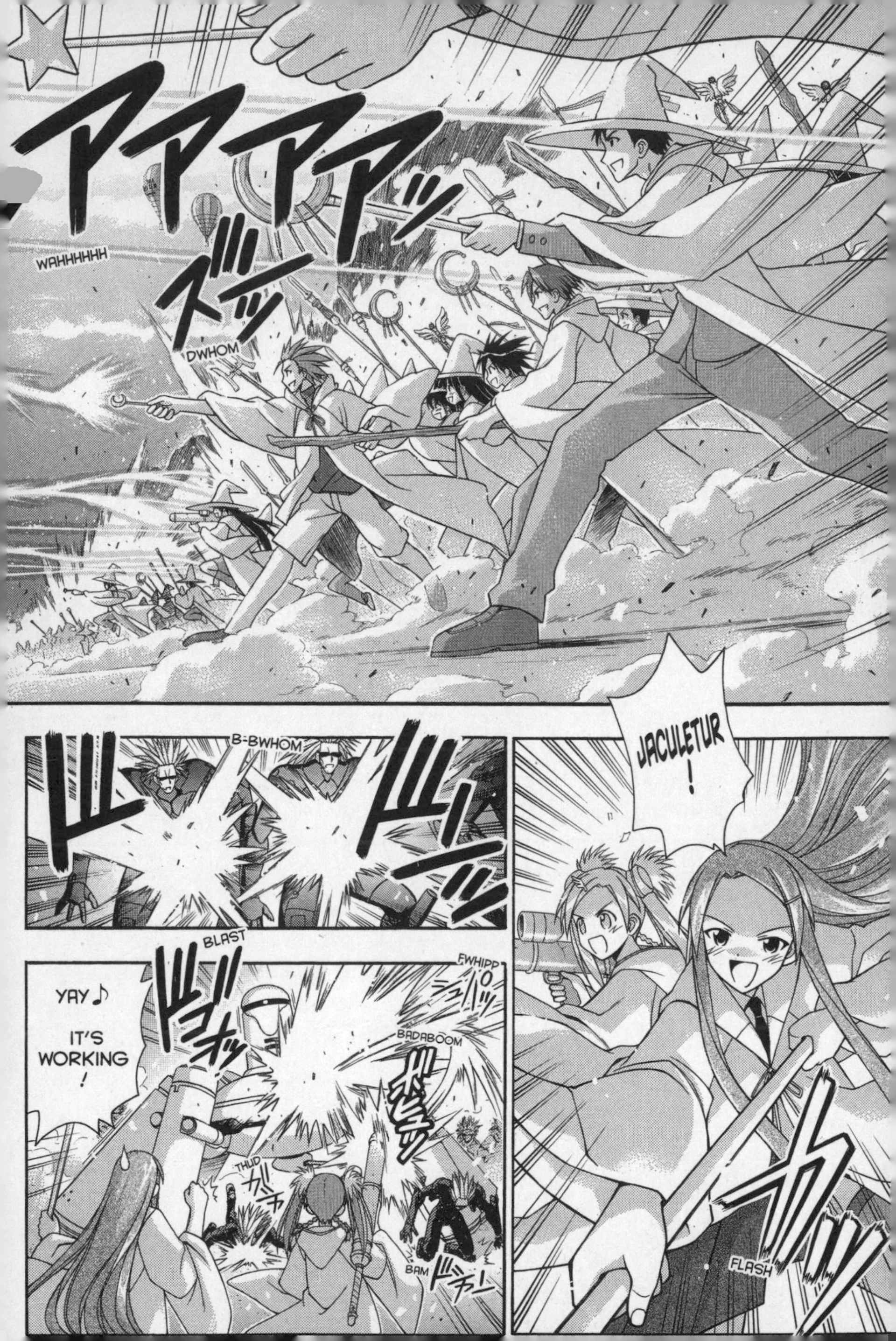
WAHHHHHH
DWHOM
JACULETUR!
FLASH
B-BWHOM
BLAST
FWHIPP
BADABOOM
YAY♪
IT'S WORKING!
THUD
BAM

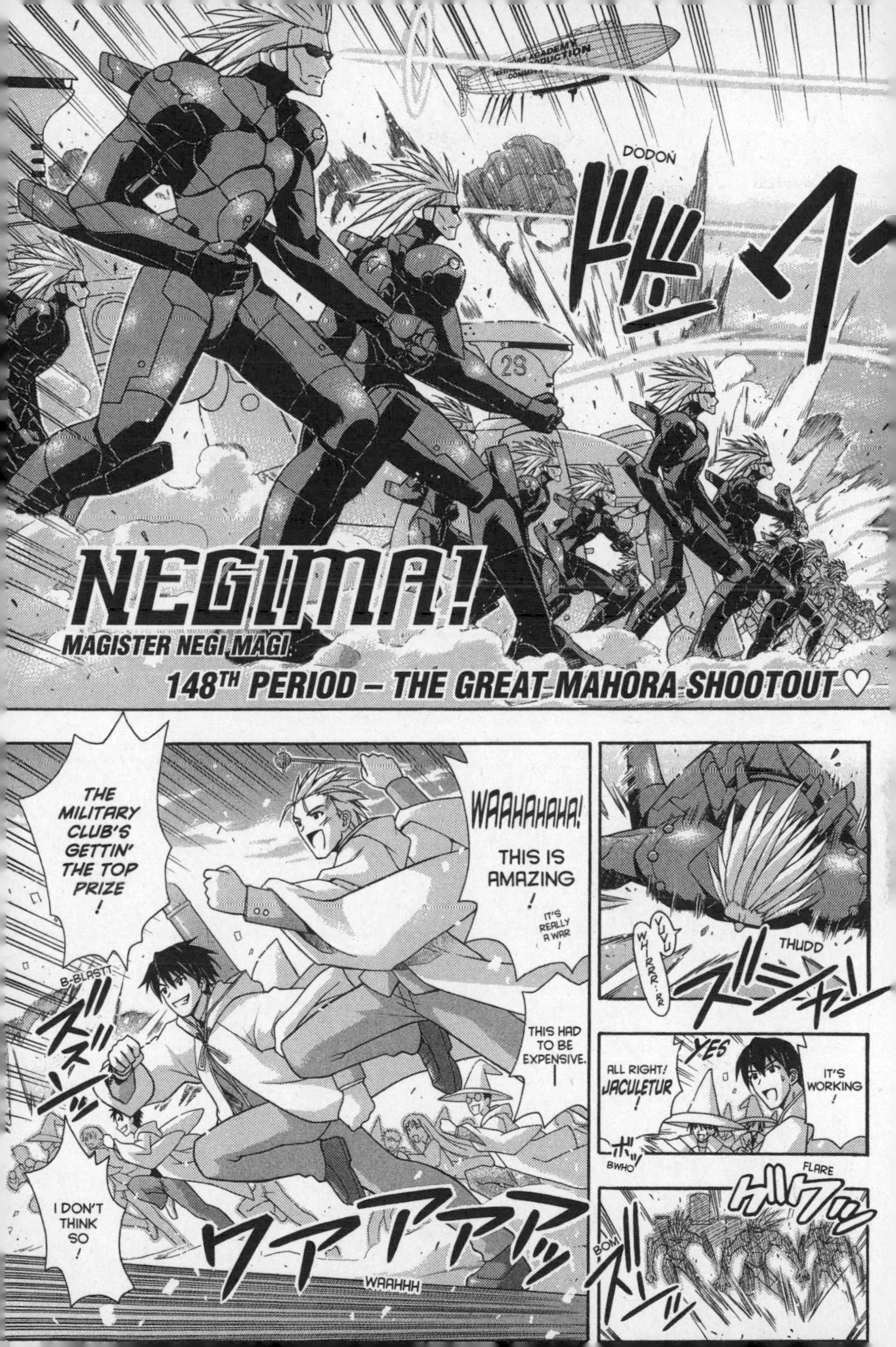
DODON
NEGIMA!
MAGISTER NEGI MAGI
148TH PERIOD – THE GREAT MAHORA SHOOTOUT ♡
YUUU
WHIRRR...RR
THUDD
YES
ALL RIGHT! JACULETUR
IT'S WORKING!
BWHO
FLARE
BOM
THE MILITARY CLUB'S GETTIN' THE TOP PRIZE!
WAAHAHAHA!
THIS IS AMAZING!
IT'S REALLY A WAR!
THIS HAD TO BE EXPENSIVE.
B-BLAST!
I DON'T THINK SO!
WAAHHH

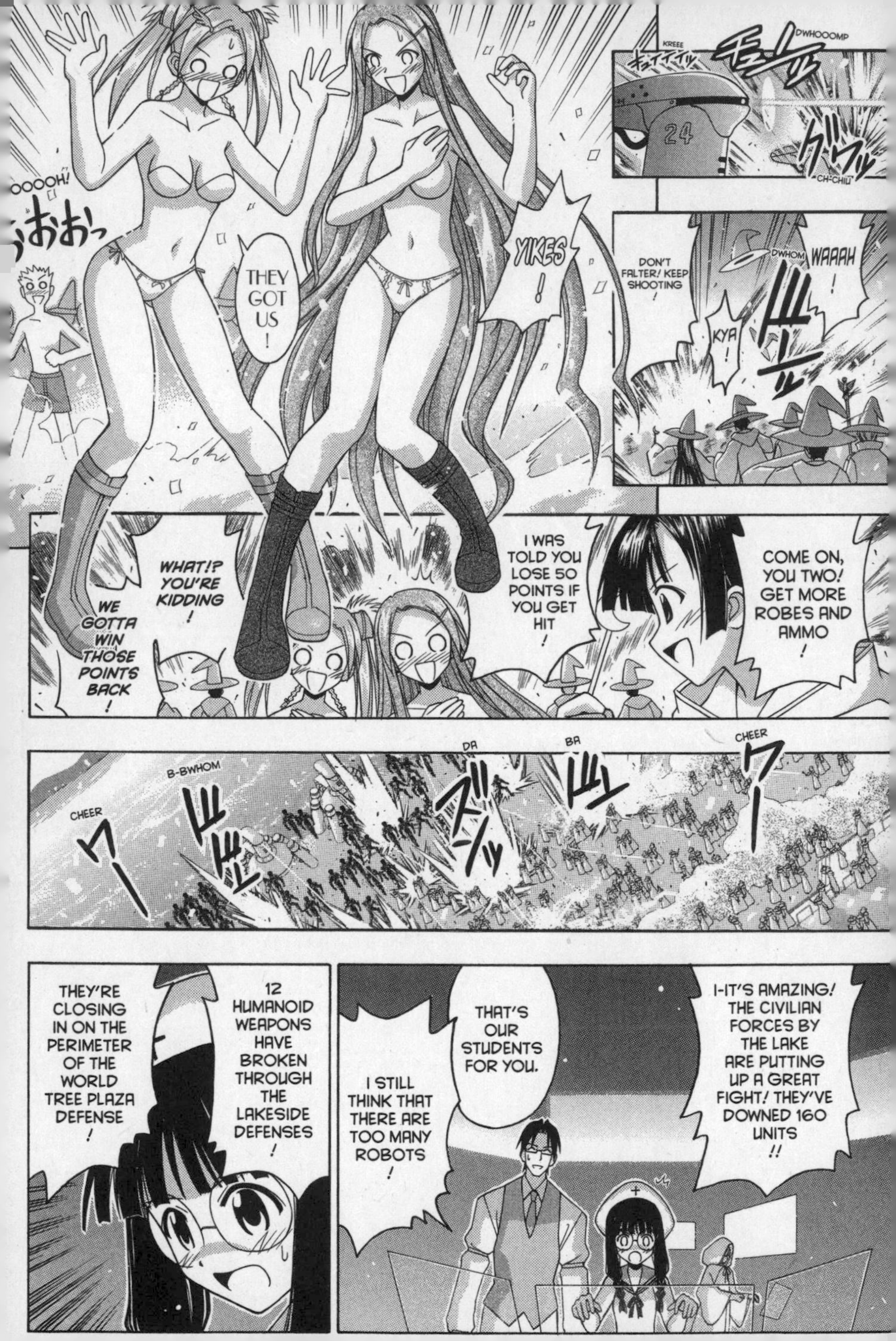
KREEE
DWHOOOMP
CH-CHIU
DON'T FALTER! KEEP SHOOTING!
DWHOM
WAAAH!
KYA!
YIKES!
THEY GOT US!
OOOOH!
COME ON, YOU TWO! GET MORE ROBES AND AMMO!
I WAS TOLD YOU LOSE 50 POINTS IF YOU GET HIT!
WHAT!? YOU'RE KIDDING!
WE GOTTA WIN THOSE POINTS BACK!
CHEER
BA
DA
B-BWHOM
CHEER
I-IT'S AMAZING! THE CIVILIAN FORCES BY THE LAKE ARE PUTTING UP A GREAT FIGHT! THEY'VE DOWNED 160 UNITS!!
THAT'S OUR STUDENTS FOR YOU.
I STILL THINK THAT THERE ARE TOO MANY ROBOTS!
12 HUMANOID WEAPONS HAVE BROKEN THROUGH THE LAKESIDE DEFENSES!
THEY'RE CLOSING IN ON THE PERIMETER OF THE WORLD TREE PLAZA DEFENSE!

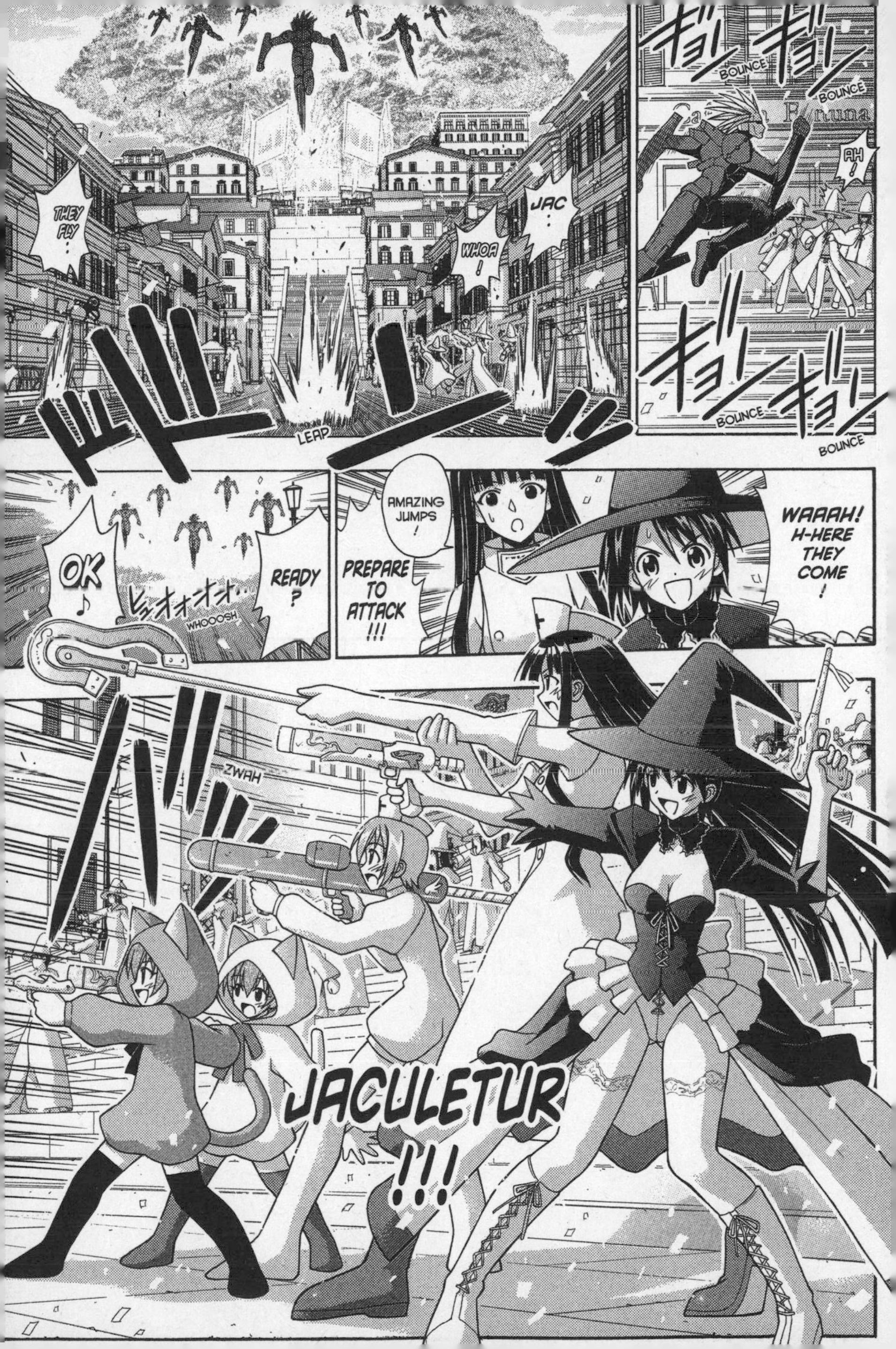

BOUNCE
BOUNCE
AH!
BOUNCE
BOUNCE
JAC...
WHOA!
THEY FLY...
LEAP
WAAAH! H-HERE THEY COME!
AMAZING JUMPS!
PREPARE TO ATTACK!!!
READY?
OK ♪
WHOOOSH
ZWAH
JACULETUR!!!

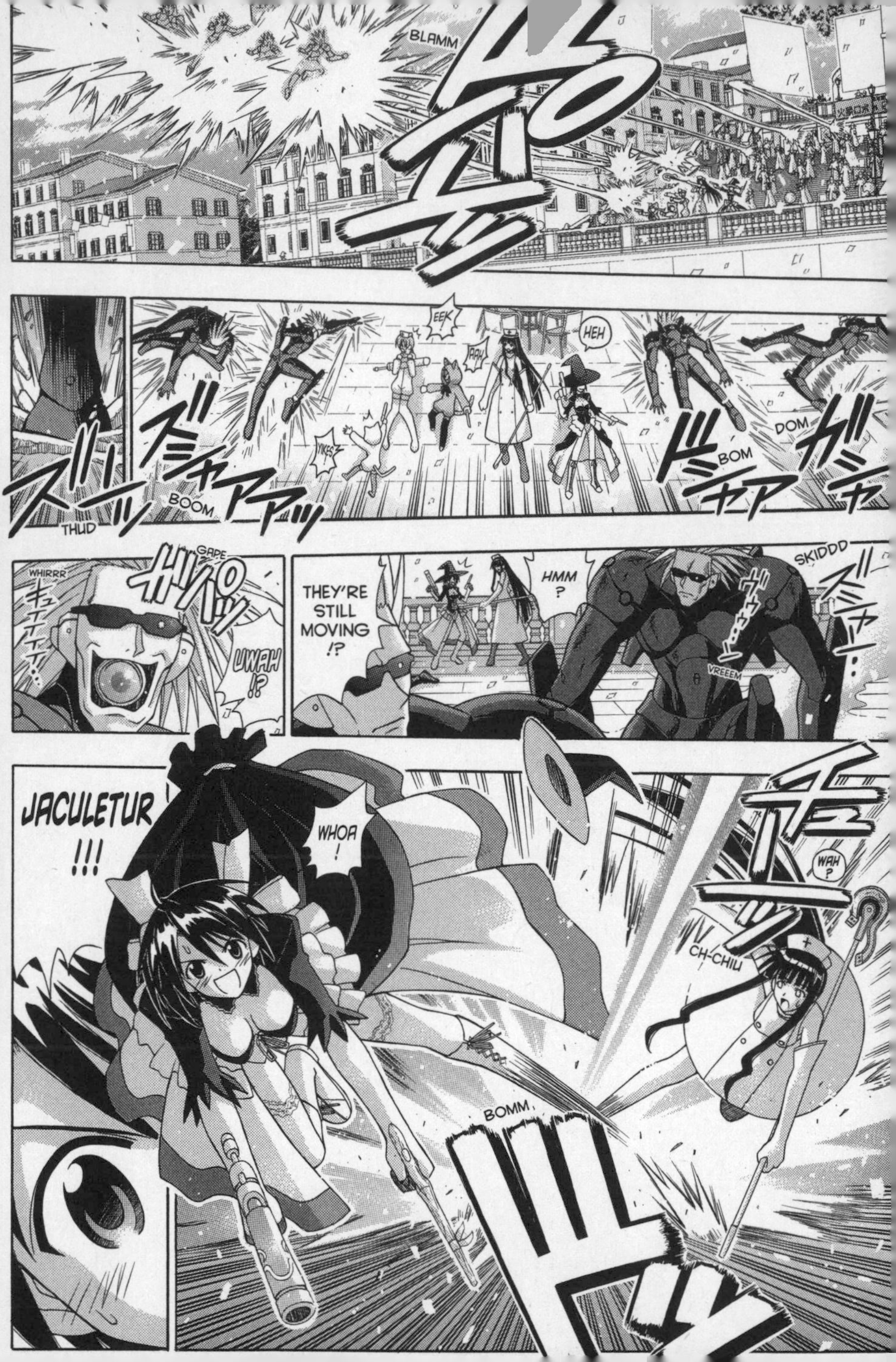
BLAMM
DOM
BOM
HEH
EEK
AAH
YIKES
BOOM
THUD
SKIDDD
VREEEM
HMM ?
THEY'RE STILL MOVING !?
GAPE
WHIRRR
UWAH !?
WAH ?
CH-CHIU
WHOA !
JACULETUR !!!
BOMM

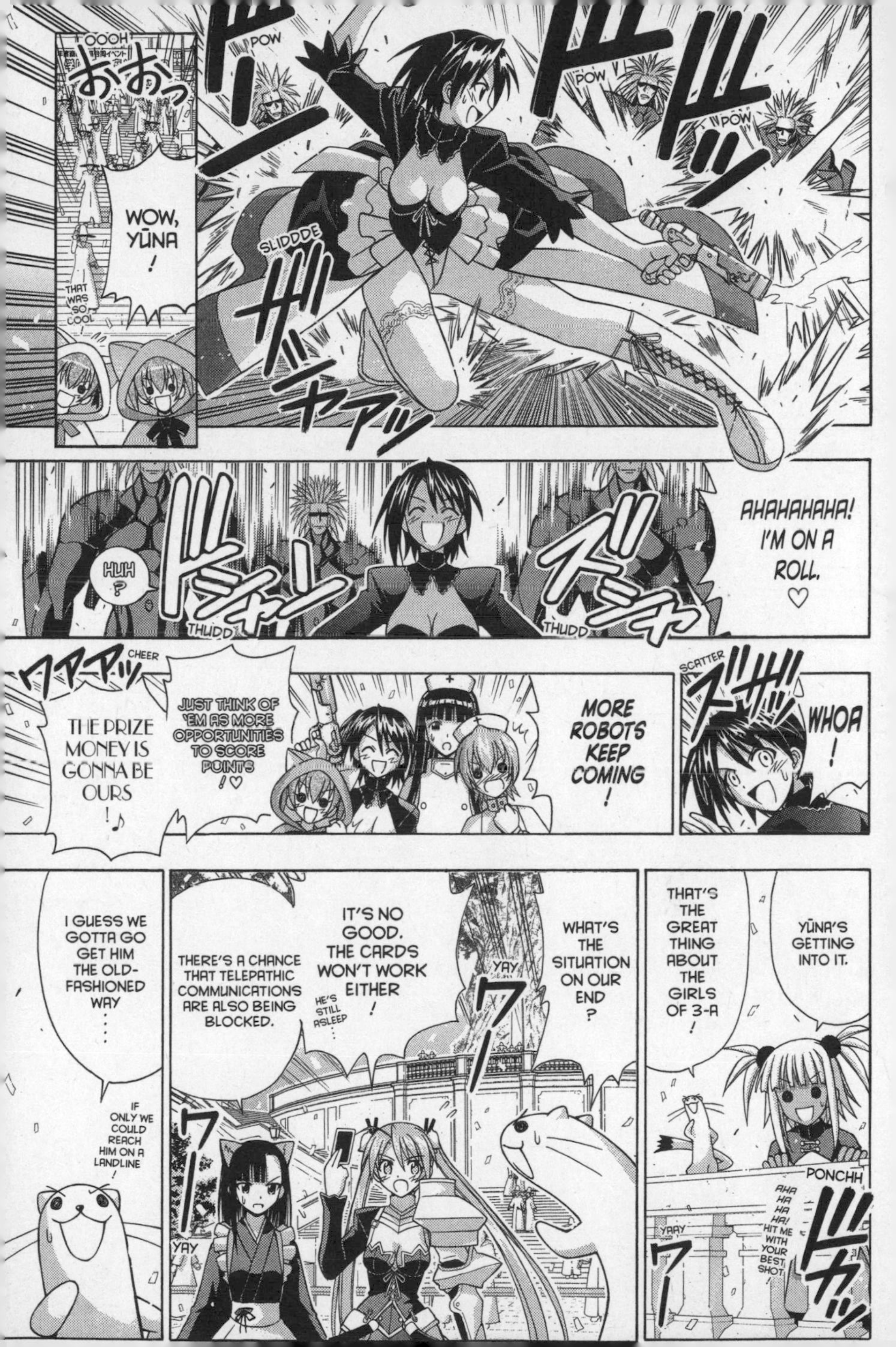
POW
POW
POW
SLIDDDE
OOOH
おおっ
WOW, YŪNA!
THAT WAS SO COOL!
AHAHAHAHA! I'M ON A ROLL. ♡
THUDD
HUH?
THUDD
SCATTER
WHOA!
MORE ROBOTS KEEP COMING!
JUST THINK OF 'EM AS MORE OPPORTUNITIES TO SCORE POINTS! ♡
THE PRIZE MONEY IS GONNA BE OURS! ♪
CHEER
YŪNA'S GETTING INTO IT.
THAT'S THE GREAT THING ABOUT THE GIRLS OF 3-A!
PONCHH
AHA HA HA! HIT ME WITH YOUR BEST SHOT
YAAY
WHAT'S THE SITUATION ON OUR END?
YAY
IT'S NO GOOD. THE CARDS WON'T WORK EITHER!
HE'S STILL ASLEEP...
THERE'S A CHANCE THAT TELEPATHIC COMMUNICATIONS ARE ALSO BEING BLOCKED.
YAY
I GUESS WE GOTTA GO GET HIM THE OLD-FASHIONED WAY...
IF ONLY WE COULD REACH HIM ON A LANDLINE!

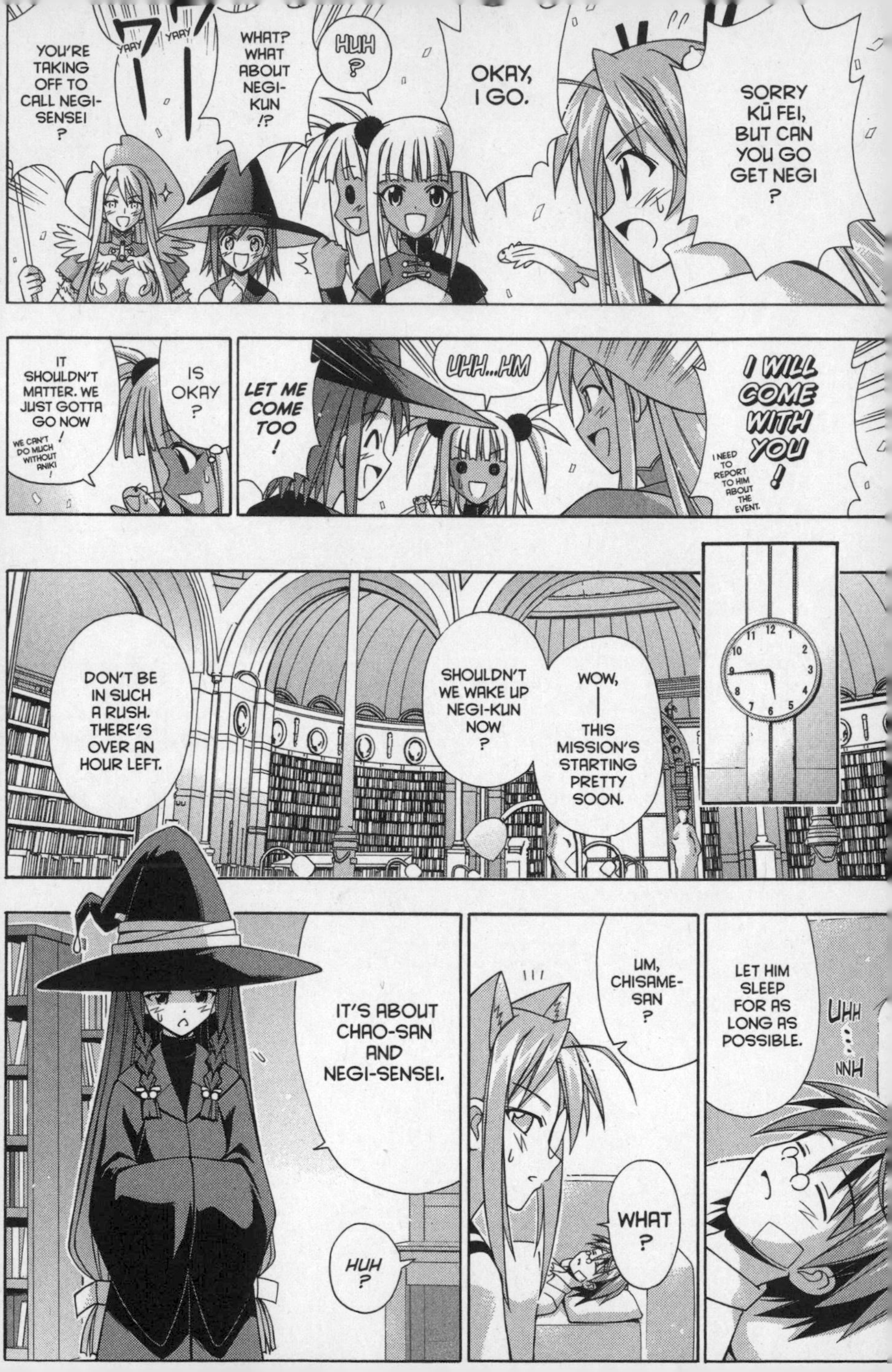

SORRY KŪ FEI, BUT CAN YOU GO GET NEGI?
OKAY, I GO.
HUH?
WHAT? WHAT ABOUT NEGI-KUN!?
YARY YARY
YOU'RE TAKING OFF TO CALL NEGI-SENSEI?
I WILL COME WITH YOU!
I NEED TO REPORT TO HIM ABOUT THE EVENT.
UHH...HM
LET ME COME TOO!
IS OKAY?
IT SHOULDN'T MATTER. WE JUST GOTTA GO NOW!
WE CAN'T DO MUCH WITHOUT ANIKI!
WOW, — THIS MISSION'S STARTING PRETTY SOON.
SHOULDN'T WE WAKE UP NEGI-KUN NOW?
DON'T BE IN SUCH A RUSH. THERE'S OVER AN HOUR LEFT.
LET HIM SLEEP FOR AS LONG AS POSSIBLE.
UHH... NNH
UM, CHISAME-SAN?
WHAT?
IT'S ABOUT CHAO-SAN AND NEGI-SENSEI.
HUH?

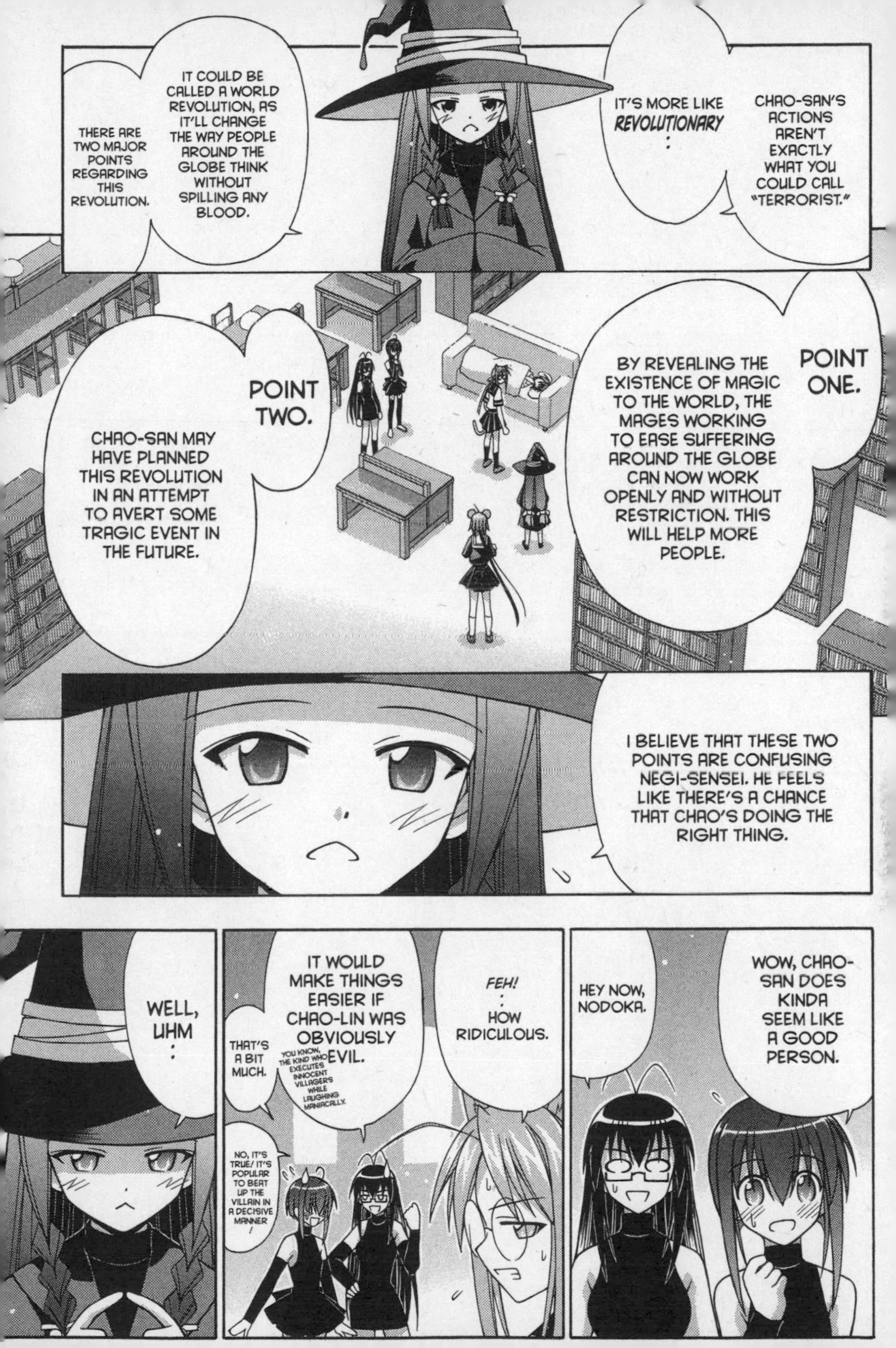
CHAO-SAN'S ACTIONS AREN'T EXACTLY WHAT YOU COULD CALL "TERRORIST."
IT'S MORE LIKE *REVOLUTIONARY* :
IT COULD BE CALLED A WORLD REVOLUTION, AS IT'LL CHANGE THE WAY PEOPLE AROUND THE GLOBE THINK WITHOUT SPILLING ANY BLOOD.
THERE ARE TWO MAJOR POINTS REGARDING THIS REVOLUTION.
POINT ONE.
BY REVEALING THE EXISTENCE OF MAGIC TO THE WORLD, THE MAGES WORKING TO EASE SUFFERING AROUND THE GLOBE CAN NOW WORK OPENLY AND WITHOUT RESTRICTION. THIS WILL HELP MORE PEOPLE.
POINT TWO.
CHAO-SAN MAY HAVE PLANNED THIS REVOLUTION IN AN ATTEMPT TO AVERT SOME TRAGIC EVENT IN THE FUTURE.
I BELIEVE THAT THESE TWO POINTS ARE CONFUSING NEGI-SENSEI. HE FEELS LIKE THERE'S A CHANCE THAT CHAO'S DOING THE RIGHT THING.
WOW, CHAO-SAN DOES KINDA SEEM LIKE A GOOD PERSON.
HEY NOW, NODOKA.
FEH! : HOW RIDICULOUS.
IT WOULD MAKE THINGS EASIER IF CHAO-LIN WAS OBVIOUSLY EVIL.
YOU KNOW, THE KIND WHO EXECUTES INNOCENT VILLAGERS WHILE LAUGHING MANIACALLY.
THAT'S A BIT MUCH.
NO, IT'S TRUE! IT'S POPULAR TO BEAT UP THE VILLAIN IN A DECISIVE MANNER!
WELL, UHM :

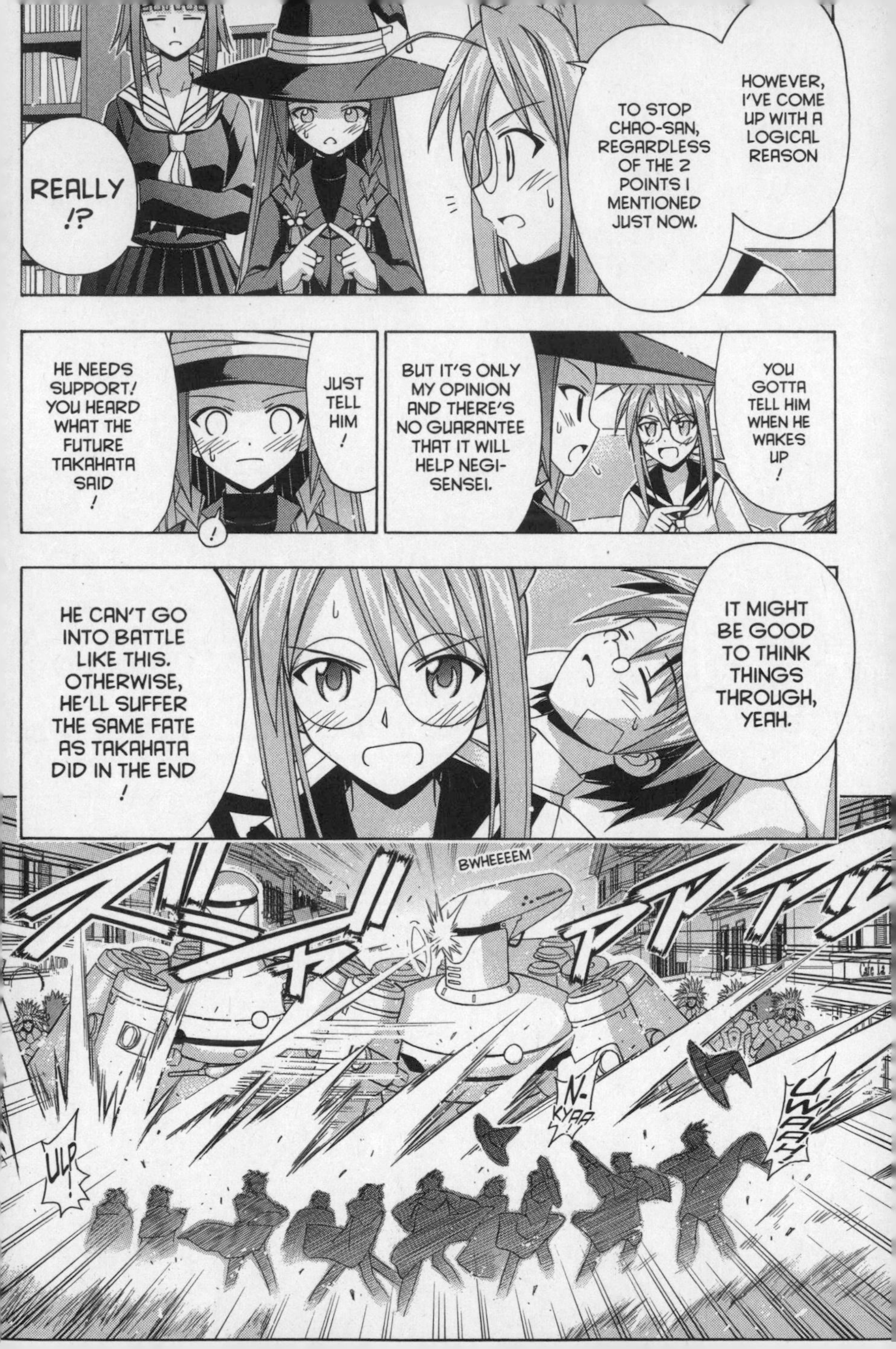
HOWEVER, I'VE COME UP WITH A LOGICAL REASON
TO STOP CHAO-SAN, REGARDLESS OF THE 2 POINTS I MENTIONED JUST NOW.
REALLY !?
YOU GOTTA TELL HIM WHEN HE WAKES UP !
BUT IT'S ONLY MY OPINION AND THERE'S NO GUARANTEE THAT IT WILL HELP NEGI-SENSEI.
JUST TELL HIM !
HE NEEDS SUPPORT! YOU HEARD WHAT THE FUTURE TAKAHATA SAID !
!
IT MIGHT BE GOOD TO THINK THINGS THROUGH, YEAH.
HE CAN'T GO INTO BATTLE LIKE THIS. OTHERWISE, HE'LL SUFFER THE SAME FATE AS TAKAHATA DID IN THE END !
BWHEEEEM
U-WAAH!
N-KYAA!
ULP!

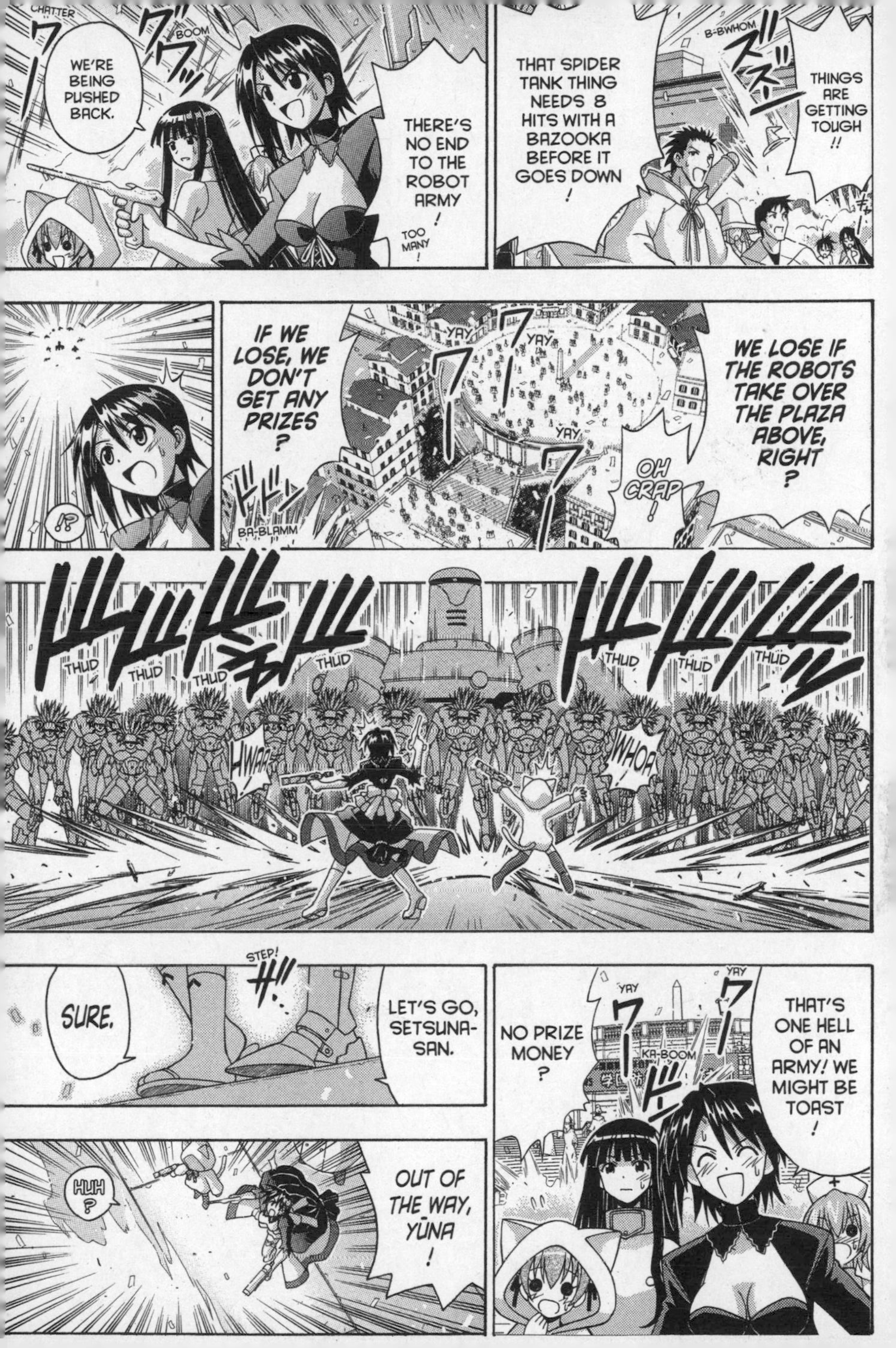
B-BWHOM
THINGS ARE GETTING TOUGH !!
THAT SPIDER TANK THING NEEDS 8 HITS WITH A BAZOOKA BEFORE IT GOES DOWN !
BOOM
THERE'S NO END TO THE ROBOT ARMY !
TOO MANY !
WE'RE BEING PUSHED BACK.
CHATTER
WE LOSE IF THE ROBOTS TAKE OVER THE PLAZA ABOVE, RIGHT ?
OH CRAP !
YAY
YAY
YAY
IF WE LOSE, WE DON'T GET ANY PRIZES ?
BA-BLAMM
!?
THUD
THUD
THUD
THUD
THUD
THUD
WHOA
HWAA
YAY
THAT'S ONE HELL OF AN ARMY! WE MIGHT BE TOAST !
YAY
KA-BOOM
NO PRIZE MONEY ?
STEP!
LET'S GO, SETSUNA-SAN.
SURE.
OUT OF THE WAY, YŪNA !
HUH ?

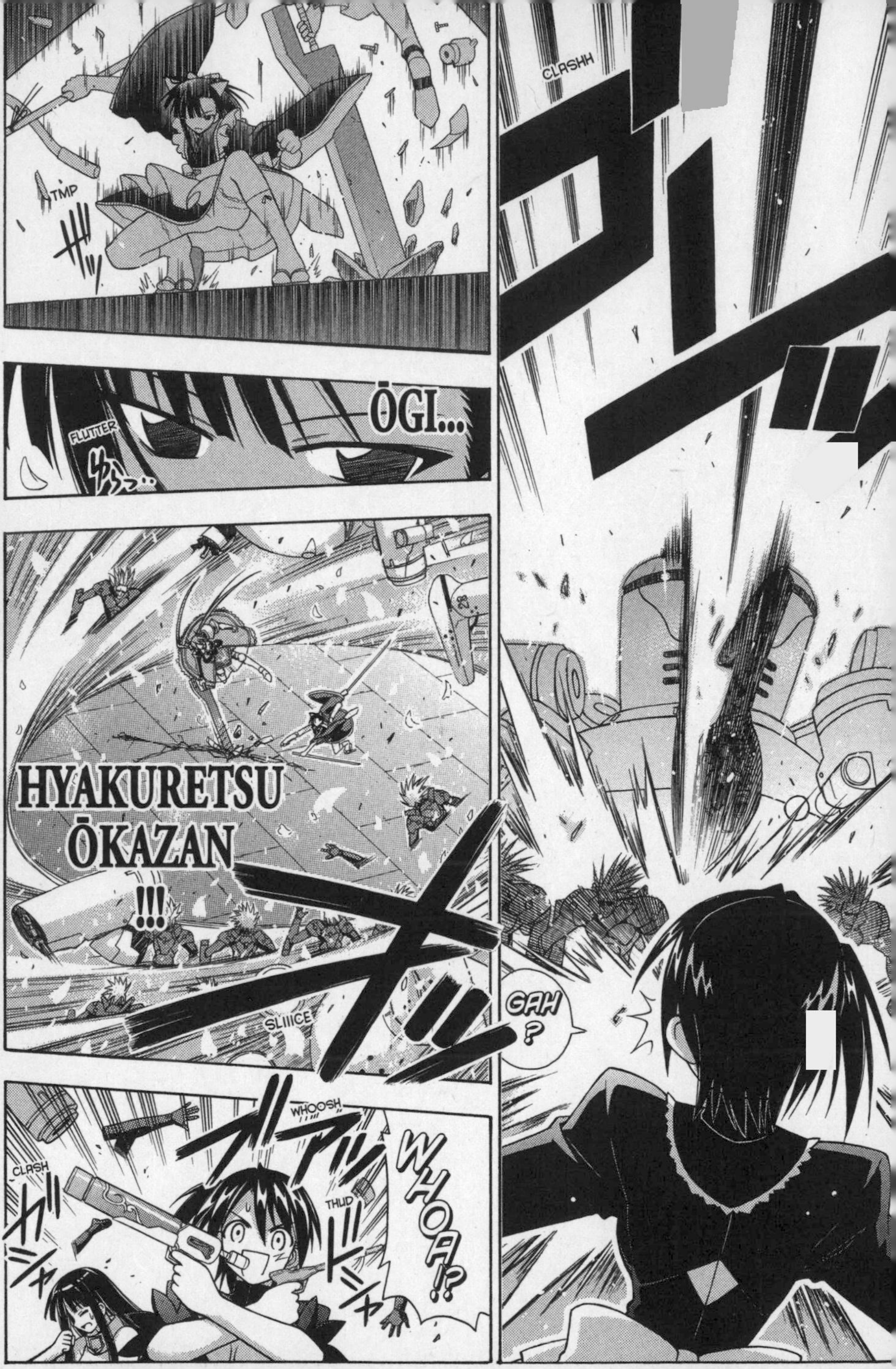
CLASHH
GAH ?
TMP
ŌGI...
FLUTTER
HYAKURETSU ŌKAZAN !!!
SLIIICE
WHOOSH
WHOA!?
THUD
CLASH

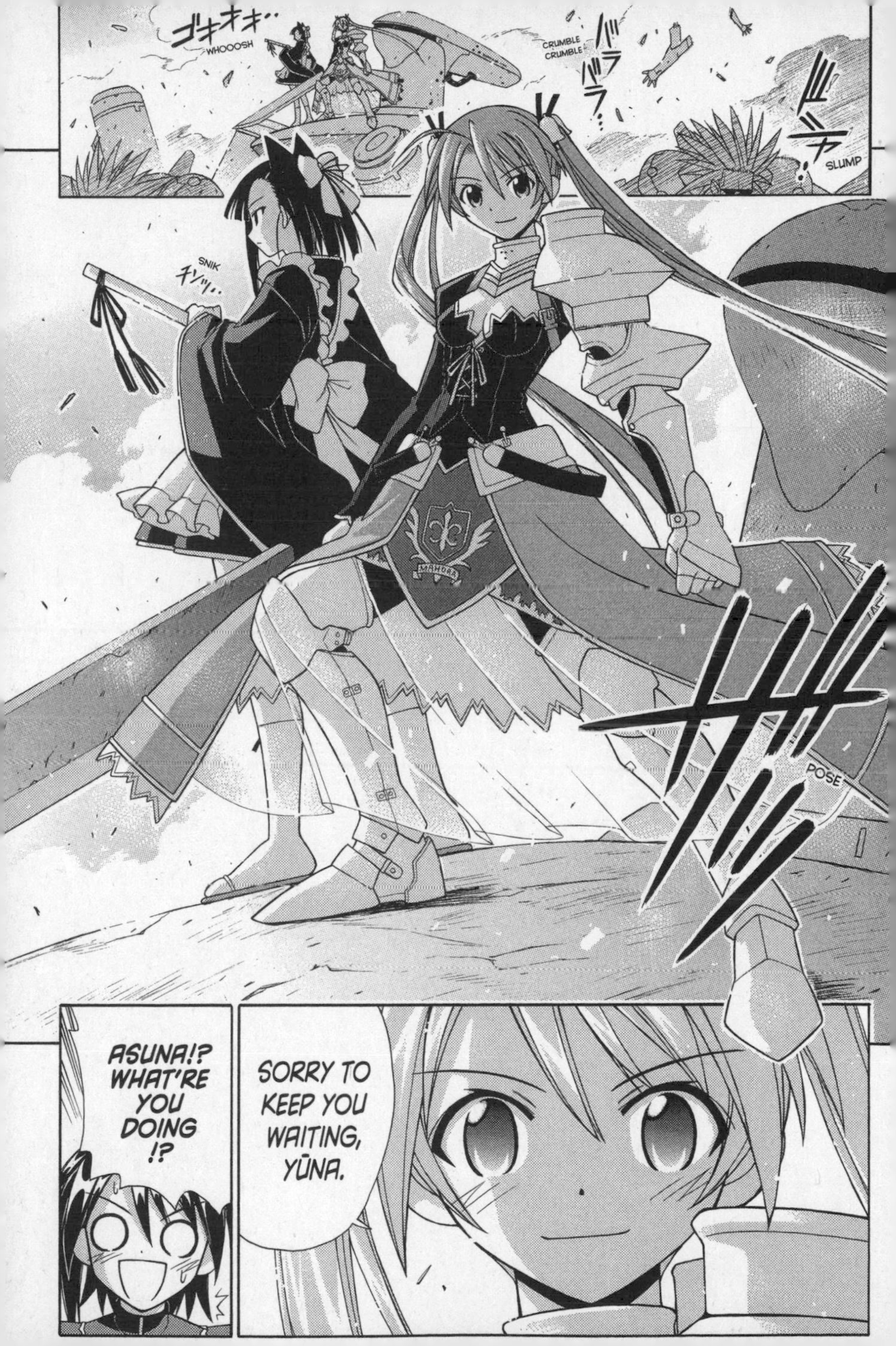
SLUMP
CRUMBLE CRUMBLE
WHOOOSH
SNIK
POSE
SORRY TO KEEP YOU WAITING, YŪNA.
ASUNA!? WHAT'RE YOU DOING !?

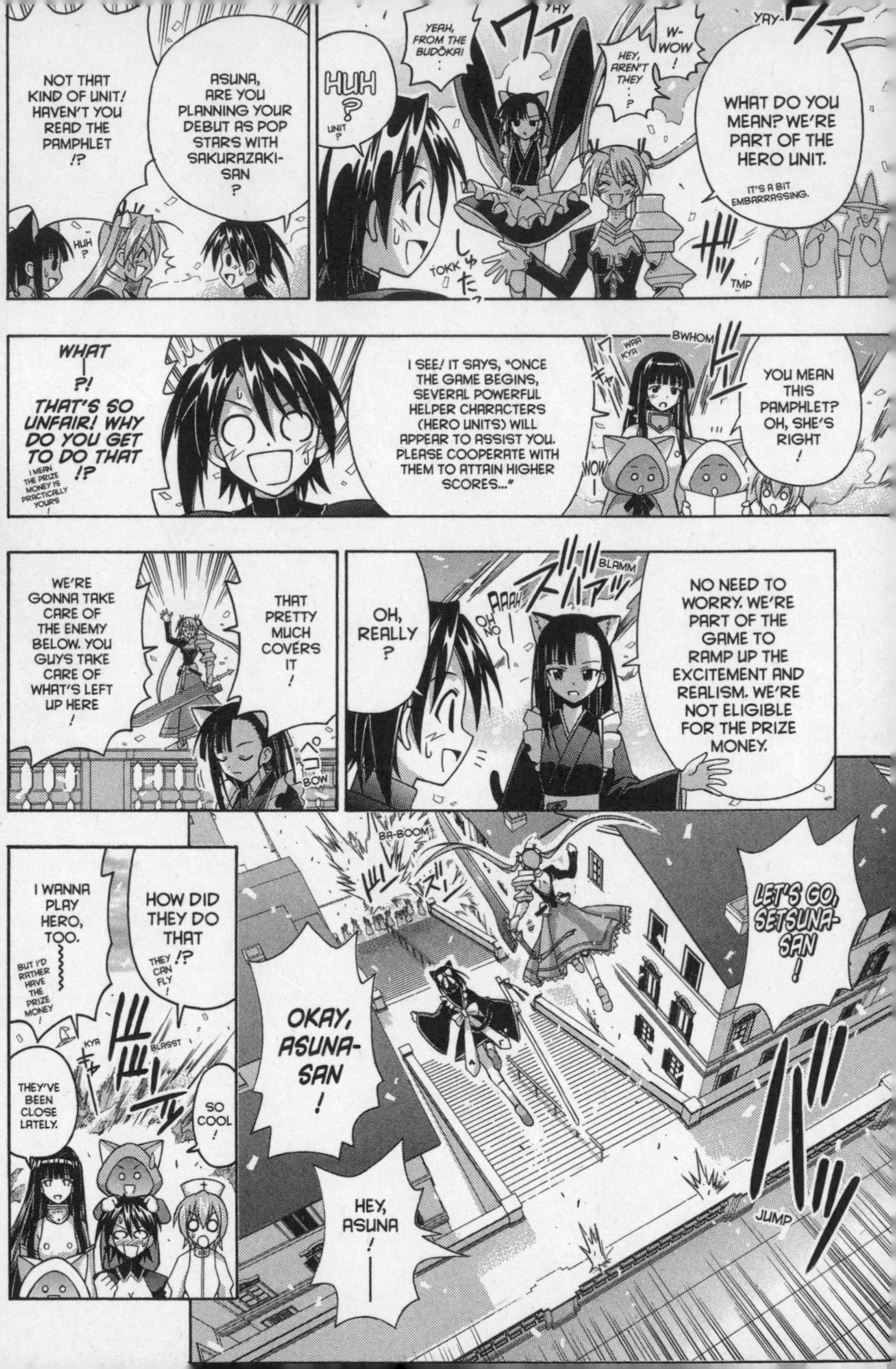
YAY
WHAT DO YOU MEAN? WE'RE PART OF THE HERO UNIT.
IT'S A BIT EMBARRASSING.
W-WOW!
HEY, AREN'T THEY...?
YEAH, FROM THE BUDŌKAI!
YAY
HUH?
UNIT?
TMP
TOKK
ASUNA, ARE YOU PLANNING YOUR DEBUT AS POP STARS WITH SAKURAZAKI-SAN?
NOT THAT KIND OF UNIT! HAVEN'T YOU READ THE PAMPHLET!?
HUH?
BWHOM
YOU MEAN THIS PAMPHLET? OH, SHE'S RIGHT!
WAA KYA
WOW!
I SEE! IT SAYS, "ONCE THE GAME BEGINS, SEVERAL POWERFUL HELPER CHARACTERS (HERO UNITS) WILL APPEAR TO ASSIST YOU. PLEASE COOPERATE WITH THEM TO ATTAIN HIGHER SCORES..."
WHAT?! THAT'S SO UNFAIR! WHY DO YOU GET TO DO THAT!?
I MEAN THE PRIZE MONEY IS PRACTICALLY YOURS!
BLAMM
NO NEED TO WORRY. WE'RE PART OF THE GAME TO RAMP UP THE EXCITEMENT AND REALISM. WE'RE NOT ELIGIBLE FOR THE PRIZE MONEY.
AAAH!
OH NO
OH, REALLY?
THAT PRETTY MUCH COVERS IT!
WE'RE GONNA TAKE CARE OF THE ENEMY BELOW. YOU GUYS TAKE CARE OF WHAT'S LEFT UP HERE!
BOW
LET'S GO, SETSUNA-SAN!
BA-BOOM
OKAY, ASUNA-SAN!
JUMP
HEY, ASUNA!
HOW DID THEY DO THAT!?
THEY CAN FLY
I WANNA PLAY HERO, TOO.
BUT I'D RATHER HAVE THE PRIZE MONEY
BLASST
KYA
SO COOL!
THEY'VE BEEN CLOSE LATELY.

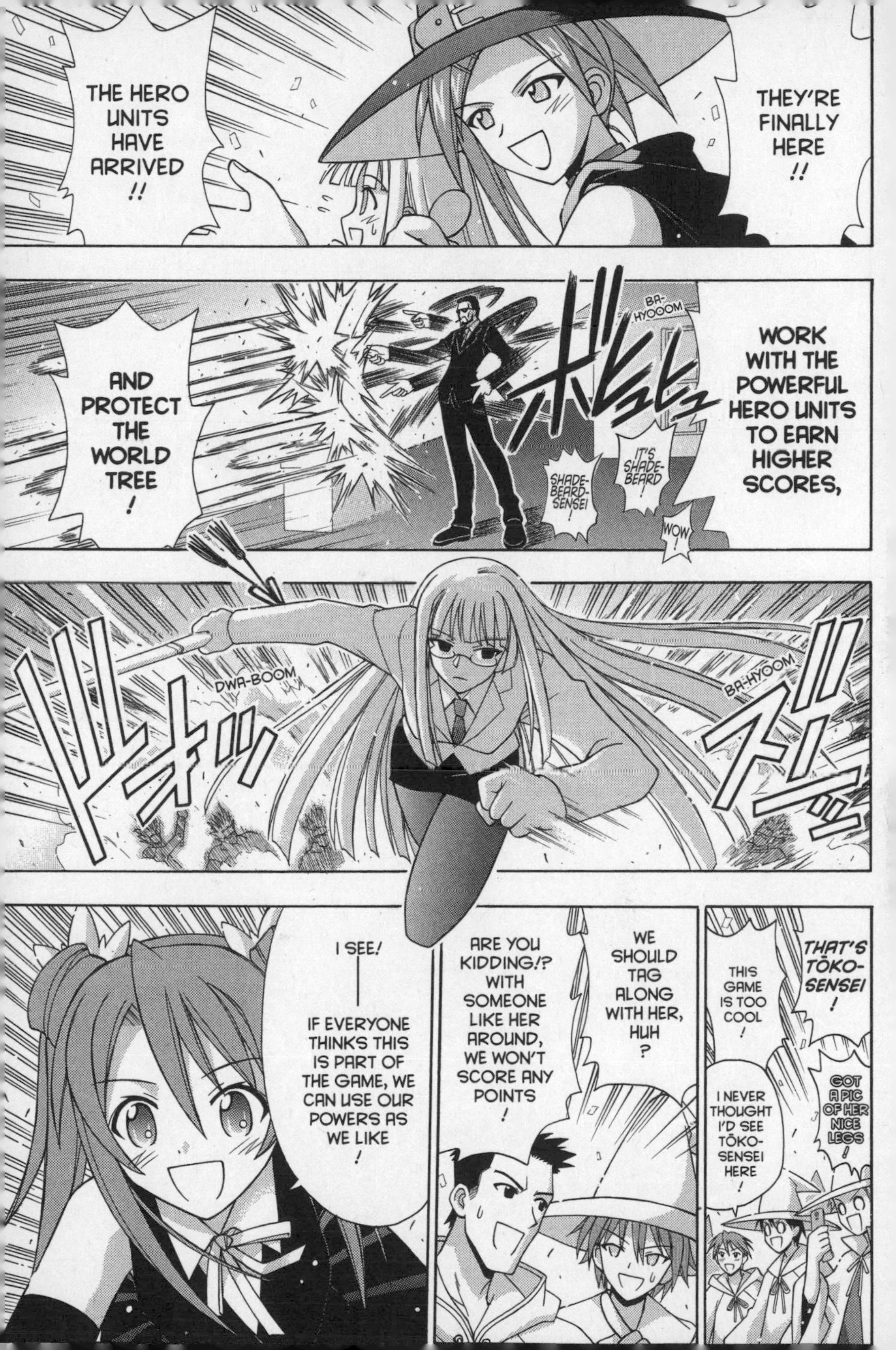
THEY'RE FINALLY HERE!!
THE HERO UNITS HAVE ARRIVED!!
BA-HYOOOM
WORK WITH THE POWERFUL HERO UNITS TO EARN HIGHER SCORES,
AND PROTECT THE WORLD TREE!
IT'S SHADEBEARD!
SHADEBEARD-SENSEI!
WOW!
BA-HYOOM
DWA-BOOM
THAT'S TŌKO-SENSEI!
THIS GAME IS TOO COOL!
GOT A PIC OF HER NICE LEGS!
I NEVER THOUGHT I'D SEE TŌKO-SENSEI HERE!
WE SHOULD TAG ALONG WITH HER, HUH?
ARE YOU KIDDING!? WITH SOMEONE LIKE HER AROUND, WE WON'T SCORE ANY POINTS!
I SEE!
IF EVERYONE THINKS THIS IS PART OF THE GAME, WE CAN USE OUR POWERS AS WE LIKE!

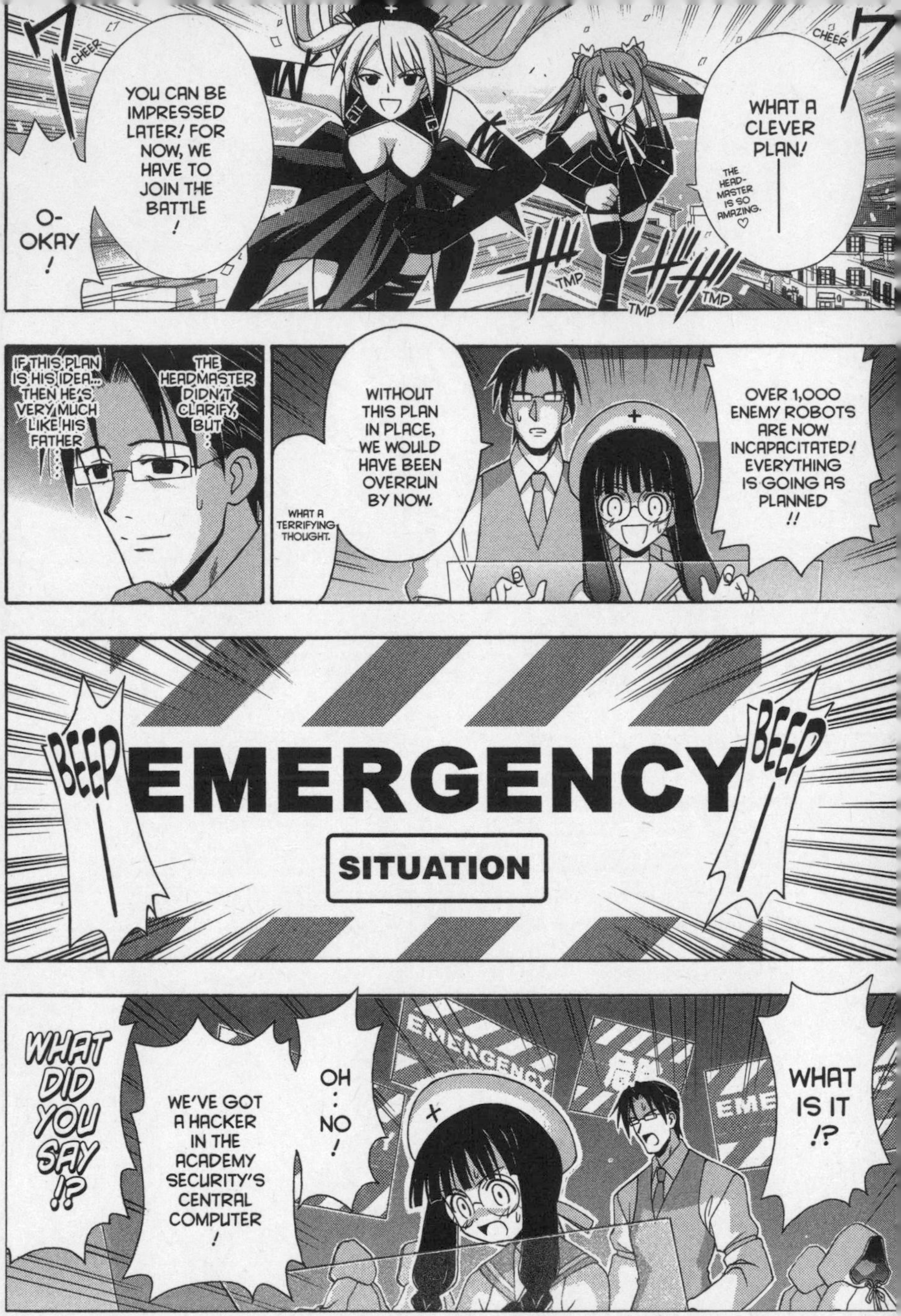
CHEER
WHAT A CLEVER PLAN!
THE HEAD-MASTER IS SO AMAZING. ♡
CHEER
YOU CAN BE IMPRESSED LATER! FOR NOW, WE HAVE TO JOIN THE BATTLE!
O-OKAY!
TMP
TMP
TMP
OVER 1,000 ENEMY ROBOTS ARE NOW INCAPACITATED! EVERYTHING IS GOING AS PLANNED!!
WITHOUT THIS PLAN IN PLACE, WE WOULD HAVE BEEN OVERRUN BY NOW.
WHAT A TERRIFYING THOUGHT.
THE HEADMASTER DIDN'T CLARIFY, BUT...
IF THIS PLAN IS HIS IDEA... THEN HE'S VERY MUCH LIKE HIS FATHER
BEEP
EMERGENCY
SITUATION
BEEP
WHAT IS IT!?
OH... NO!
WE'VE GOT A HACKER IN THE ACADEMY SECURITY'S CENTRAL COMPUTER!
WHAT DID YOU SAY!?

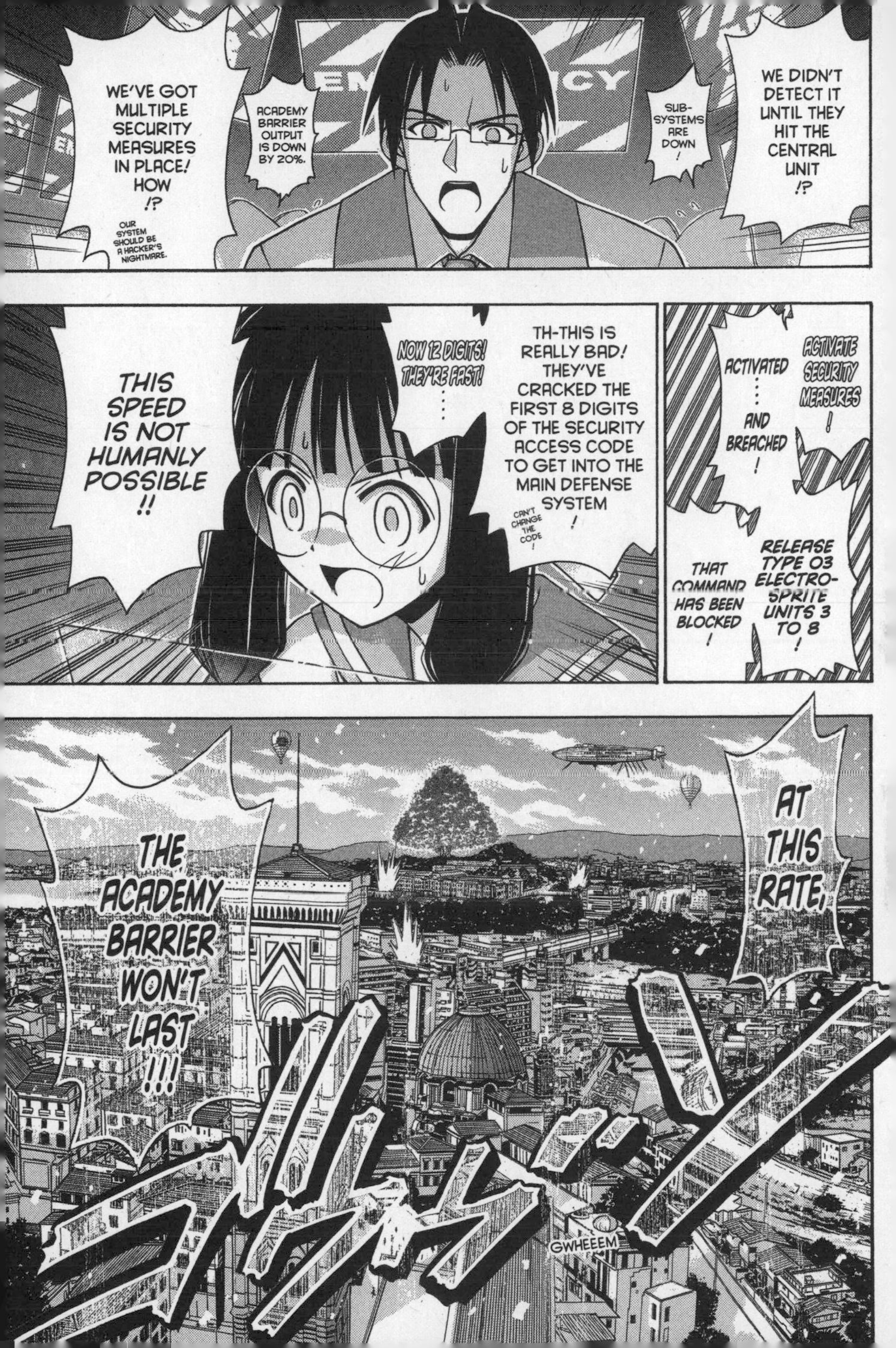
WE DIDN'T DETECT IT UNTIL THEY HIT THE CENTRAL UNIT !?
SUB-SYSTEMS ARE DOWN !
ACADEMY BARRIER OUTPUT IS DOWN BY 20%.
WE'VE GOT MULTIPLE SECURITY MEASURES IN PLACE! HOW !?
OUR SYSTEM SHOULD BE A HACKER'S NIGHTMARE.
ACTIVATE SECURITY MEASURES !
ACTIVATED ... AND BREACHED !
RELEASE TYPE 03 ELECTRO-SPRITE UNITS 3 TO 8 !
THAT COMMAND HAS BEEN BLOCKED !
TH-THIS IS REALLY BAD! THEY'VE CRACKED THE FIRST 8 DIGITS OF THE SECURITY ACCESS CODE TO GET INTO THE MAIN DEFENSE SYSTEM !
NOW 12 DIGITS! THEY'RE FAST! ...
CAN'T CHANGE THE CODE !
THIS SPEED IS NOT HUMANLY POSSIBLE !!
AT THIS RATE,
THE ACADEMY BARRIER WON'T LAST !!!
GWHEEEM

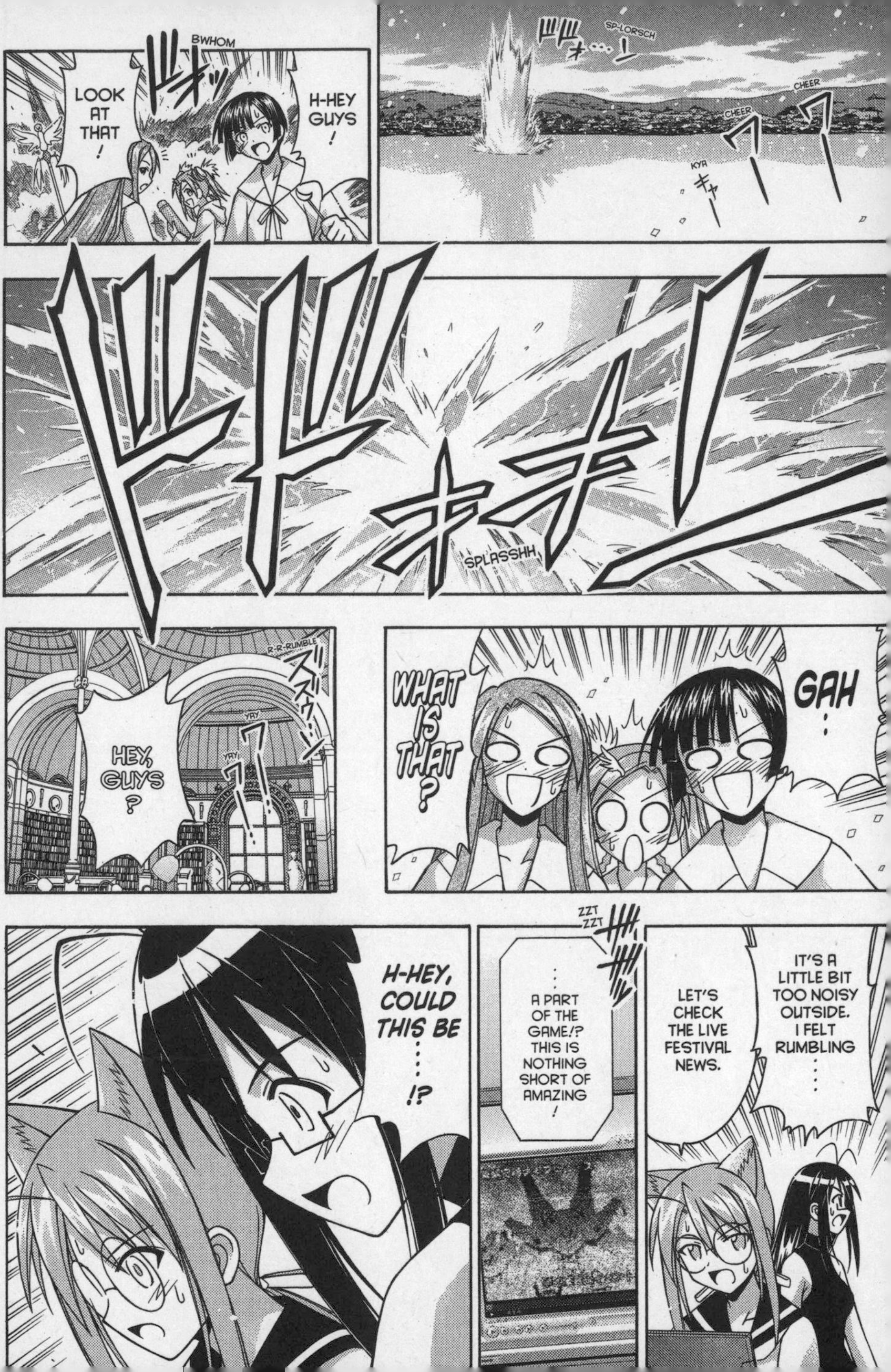
SP-LORSCH
CHEER
CHEER
KYA
BWHOM
H-HEY GUYS !
LOOK AT THAT !
SPLASSHH
GAH . . .
WHAT IS THAT ?
R-R-RUMBLE
YRY
YRY
HEY, GUYS ?
IT'S A LITTLE BIT TOO NOISY OUTSIDE. I FELT RUMBLING . . . .
LET'S CHECK THE LIVE FESTIVAL NEWS.
ZZT
ZZT
. . . A PART OF THE GAME!? THIS IS NOTHING SHORT OF AMAZING !
H-HEY, COULD THIS BE . . . . . !?

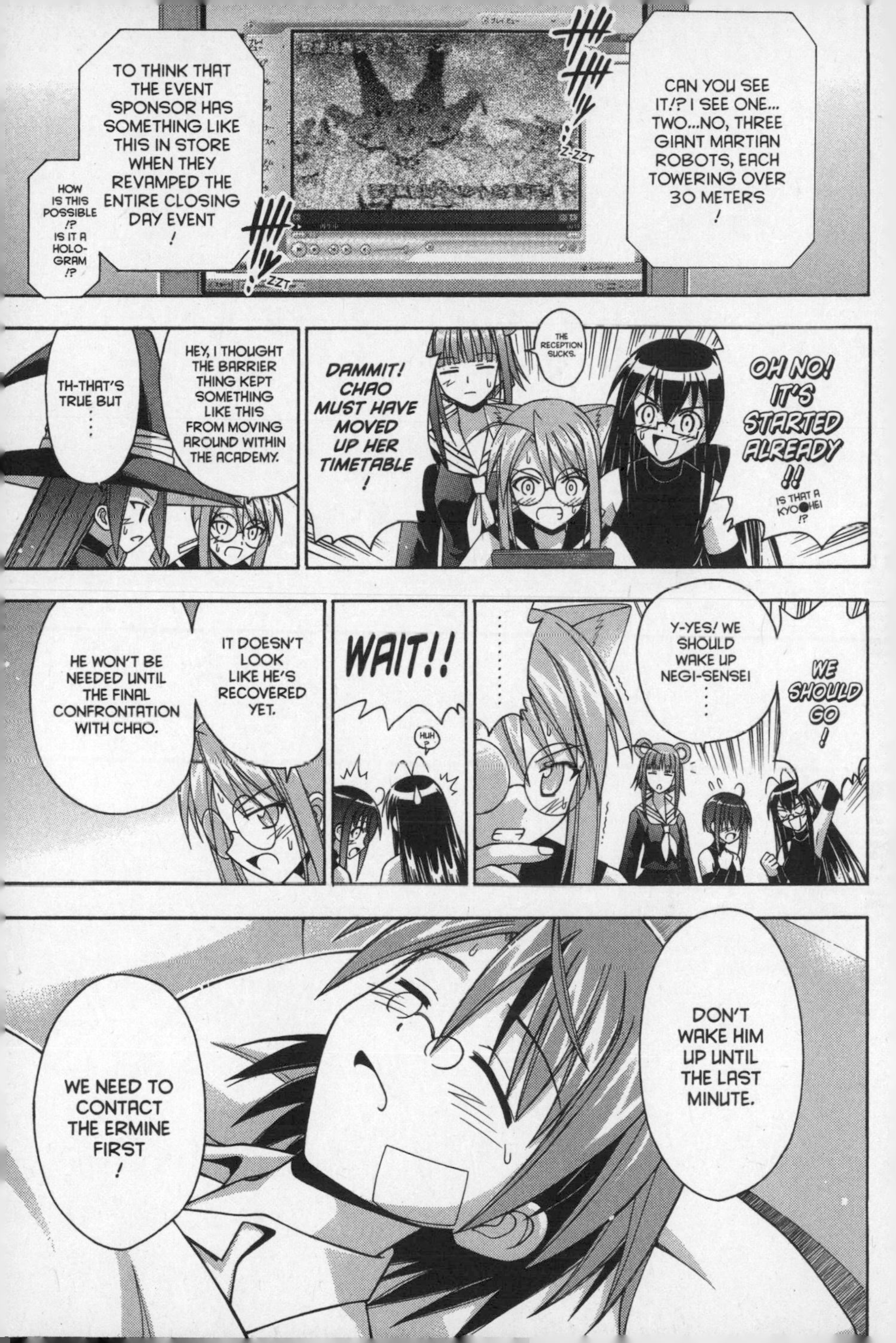
CAN YOU SEE IT!? I SEE ONE... TWO...NO, THREE GIANT MARTIAN ROBOTS, EACH TOWERING OVER 30 METERS!
Z-ZZT
TO THINK THAT THE EVENT SPONSOR HAS SOMETHING LIKE THIS IN STORE WHEN THEY REVAMPED THE ENTIRE CLOSING DAY EVENT!
ZZZT
HOW IS THIS POSSIBLE!? IS IT A HOLO-GRAM!?
OH NO! IT'S STARTED ALREADY!!
IS THAT A KYO●HEI!?
THE RECEPTION SUCKS.
DAMMIT! CHAO MUST HAVE MOVED UP HER TIMETABLE!
HEY, I THOUGHT THE BARRIER THING KEPT SOMETHING LIKE THIS FROM MOVING AROUND WITHIN THE ACADEMY.
TH-THAT'S TRUE BUT......
WE SHOULD GO!
Y-YES! WE SHOULD WAKE UP NEGI-SENSEI...
......
WAIT!!
HUH?
IT DOESN'T LOOK LIKE HE'S RECOVERED YET.
HE WON'T BE NEEDED UNTIL THE FINAL CONFRONTATION WITH CHAO.
DON'T WAKE HIM UP UNTIL THE LAST MINUTE.
WE NEED TO CONTACT THE ERMINE FIRST!

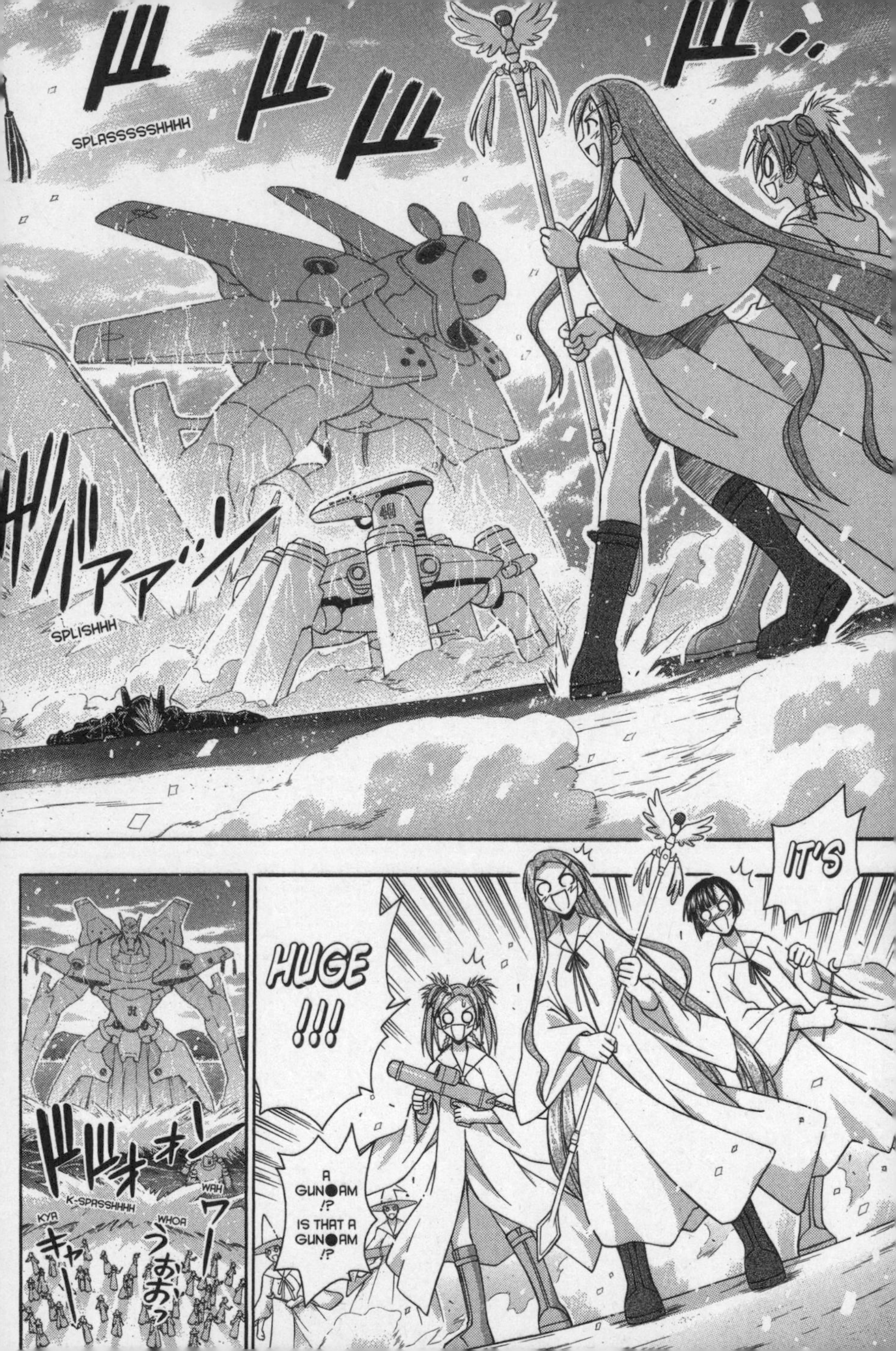
SPLASSSSSHHHH
SPLISHHH
IT'S
HUGE
!!!
A GUN●AM !?
IS THAT A GUN●AM !?
K-SPASSHHHH
WAH
ワー
WHOA
うおおっ
KYA
キャー

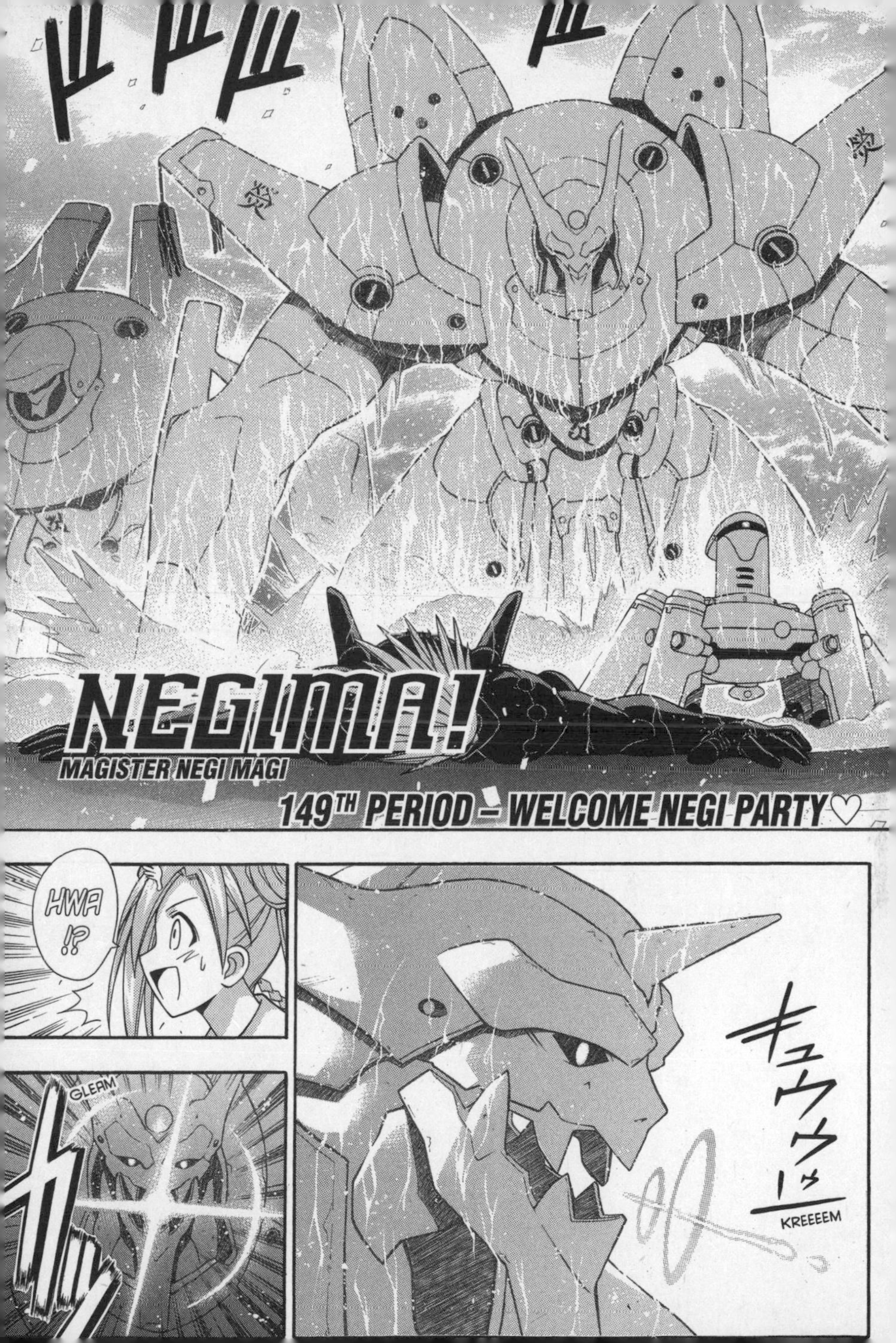

NEGIMA!
MAGISTER NEGI MAGI
149TH PERIOD – WELCOME NEGI PARTY♡
KREEEEM
HWA !?
GLEAM

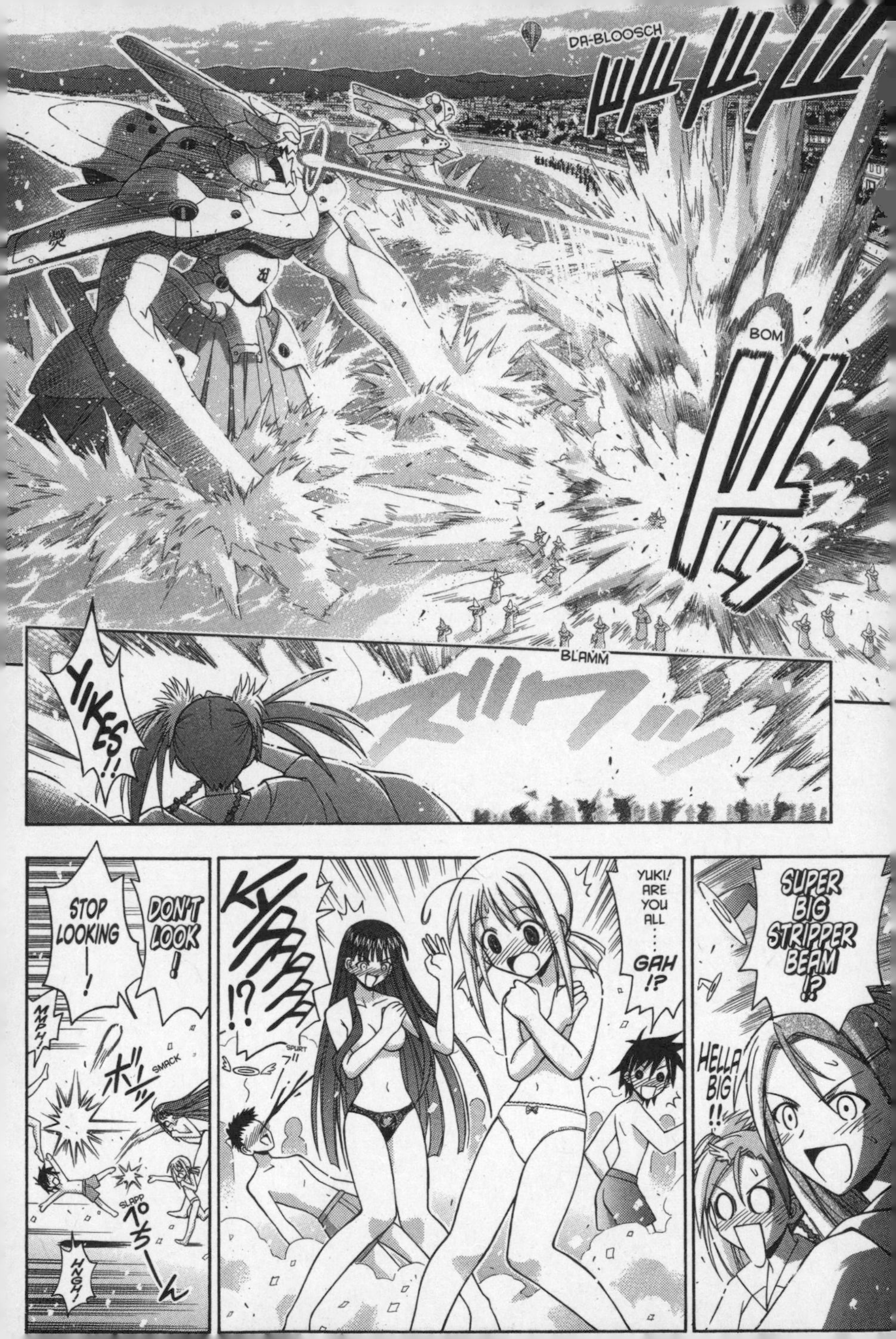

DA-BLOOSCH
BOM
BLAMM
YIKES!!
SUPER BIG STRIPPER BEAM!?
HELLA BIG!!
YUKI! ARE YOU ALL.... GAH!?
KYAAAA!?
SPURT
DON'T LOOK!
STOP LOOKING!!
MMPH!
SMACK
SLAPP
HNGH!

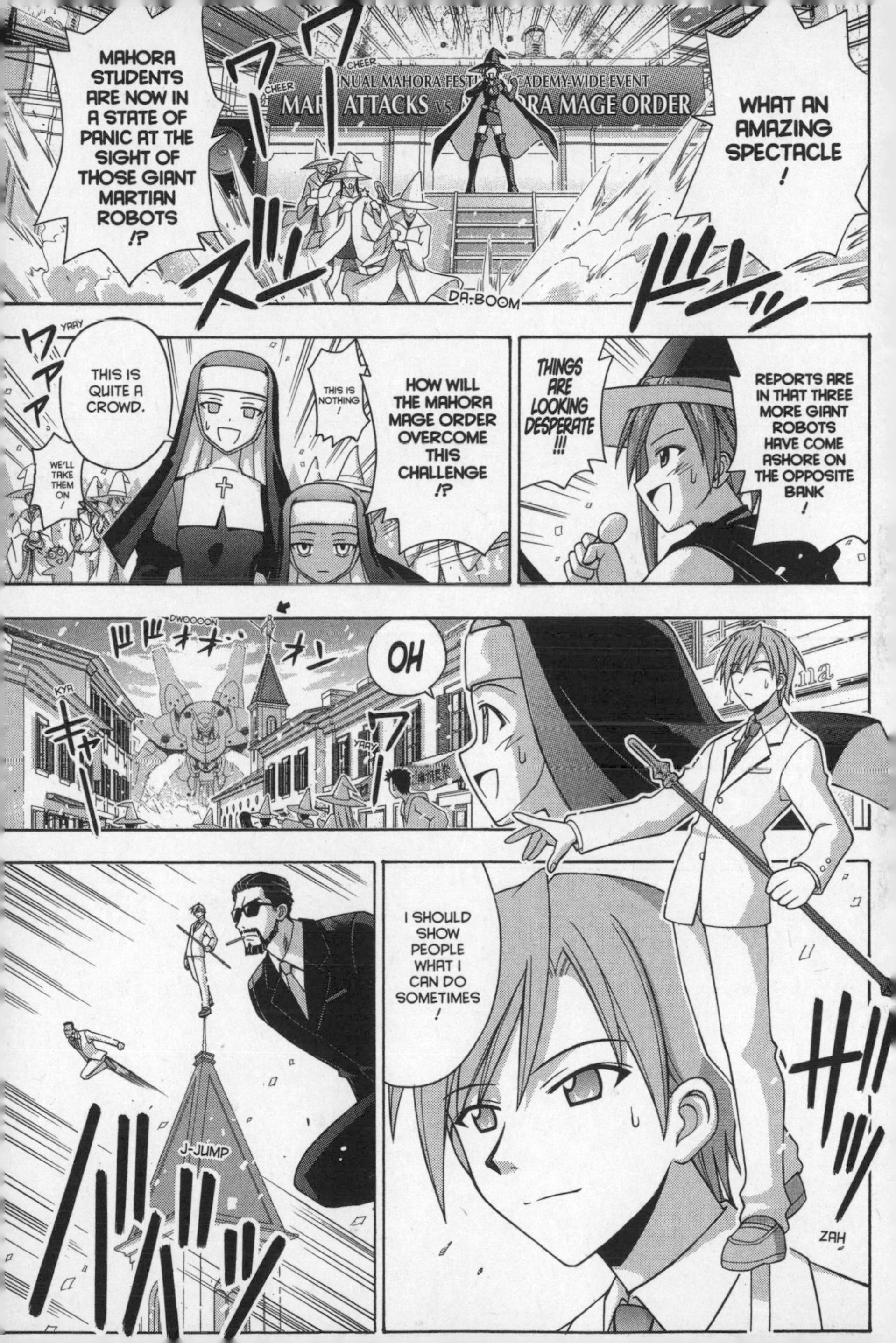
WHAT AN AMAZING SPECTACLE!
CHEER
CHEER
MAHORA STUDENTS ARE NOW IN A STATE OF PANIC AT THE SIGHT OF THOSE GIANT MARTIAN ROBOTS!?
DA-BOOM
REPORTS ARE IN THAT THREE MORE GIANT ROBOTS HAVE COME ASHORE ON THE OPPOSITE BANK!
THINGS ARE LOOKING DESPERATE!!!
HOW WILL THE MAHORA MAGE ORDER OVERCOME THIS CHALLENGE!?
THIS IS NOTHING!
THIS IS QUITE A CROWD.
YAAY
WE'LL TAKE THEM ON!
OH
DWOOOON
YAAY
KYA
I SHOULD SHOW PEOPLE WHAT I CAN DO SOMETIMES!
ZAH
J-JUMP

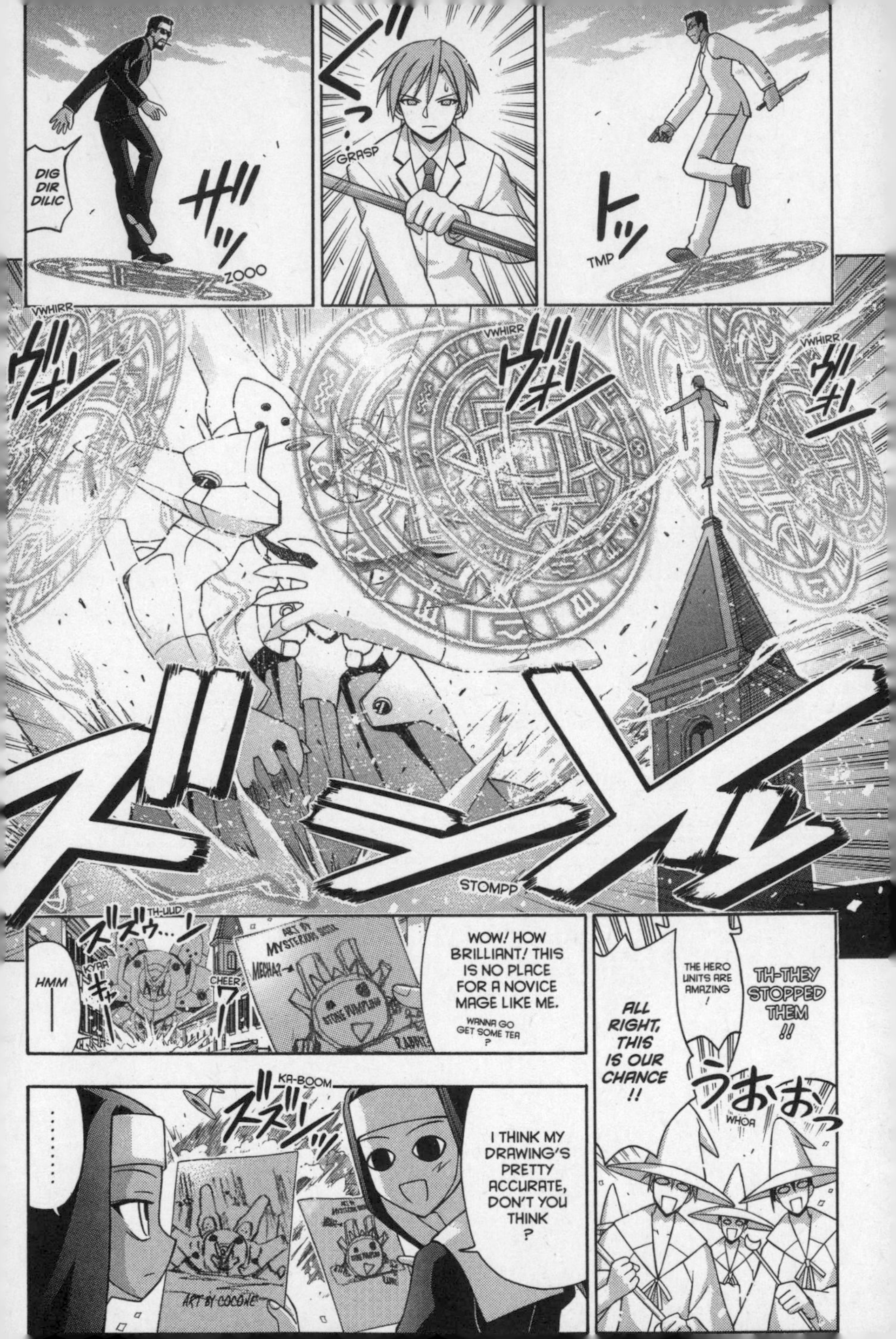
トッ
TMP
ぐっ
GRASP
DIG DIR DILIC
ザッ
ZOOO
VWHIRR
ヴォン
VWHIRR
ヴォン
VWHIRR
ヴォン
ズシン
STOMPP
TH-THEY STOPPED THEM!!
THE HERO UNITS ARE AMAZING!
ALL RIGHT, THIS IS OUR CHANCE!!
うおおっ
WHOA
WOW! HOW BRILLIANT! THIS IS NO PLACE FOR A NOVICE MAGE LIKE ME.
WANNA GO GET SOME TEA?
ART BY MYSTERIOUS SISTER
MECHA?
CHEER
KYAA
HMM
ズズゥ…ン
TH-UUD
KA-BOOM
I THINK MY DRAWING'S PRETTY ACCURATE, DON'T YOU THINK?
……
ART BY COCONE

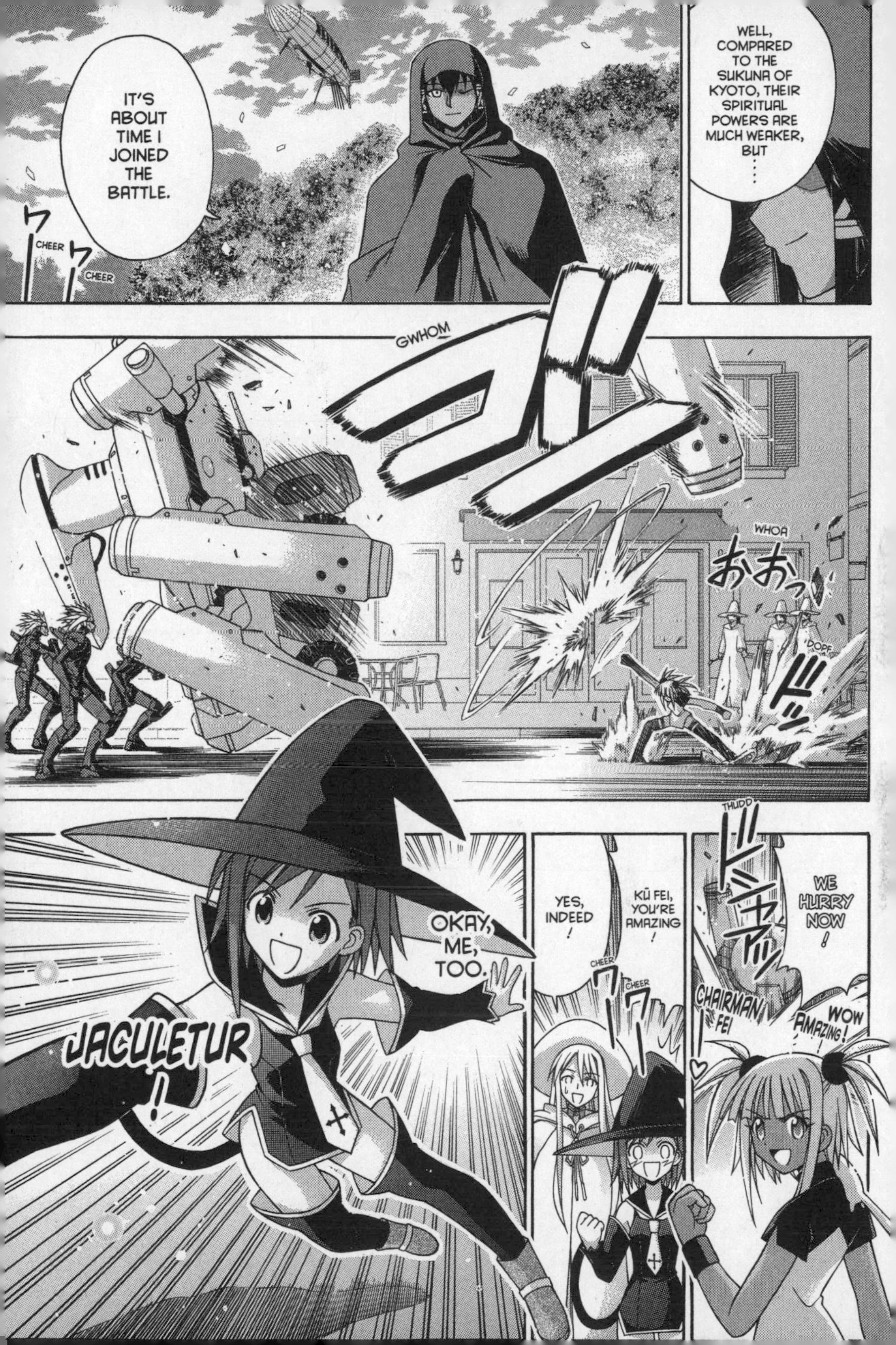
WELL, COMPARED TO THE SUKUNA OF KYOTO, THEIR SPIRITUAL POWERS ARE MUCH WEAKER, BUT . . .
IT'S ABOUT TIME I JOINED THE BATTLE.
CHEER
CHEER
GWHOM
WHOA
おおっ
DOPF
ドッ
THUDD
ドシャアッ
WE HURRY NOW!
CHAIRMAN FEI
WOW AMAZING!
KŪ FEI, YOU'RE AMAZING!
YES, INDEED!
CHEER
CHEER
OKAY, ME, TOO.
JACULETUR!

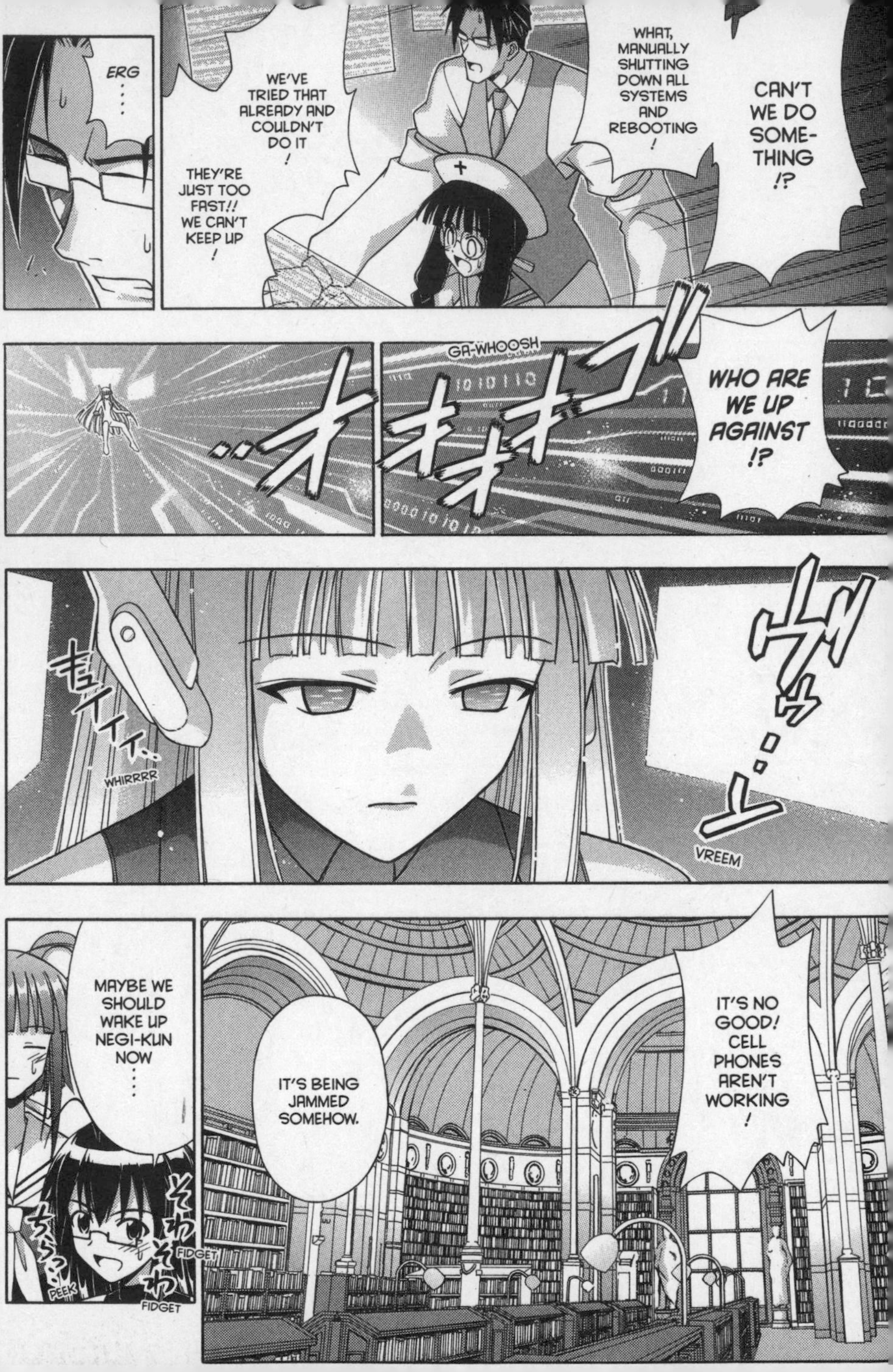
CAN'T WE DO SOME-THING!?
WHAT, MANUALLY SHUTTING DOWN ALL SYSTEMS AND REBOOTING!
WE'VE TRIED THAT ALREADY AND COULDN'T DO IT!
THEY'RE JUST TOO FAST!! WE CAN'T KEEP UP!
ERG.....
WHO ARE WE UP AGAINST!?
GA-WHOOSH
VREEM
WHIRRRR
IT'S NO GOOD! CELL PHONES AREN'T WORKING!
IT'S BEING JAMMED SOMEHOW.
MAYBE WE SHOULD WAKE UP NEGI-KUN NOW.....
FIDGET
FIDGET
PEEK

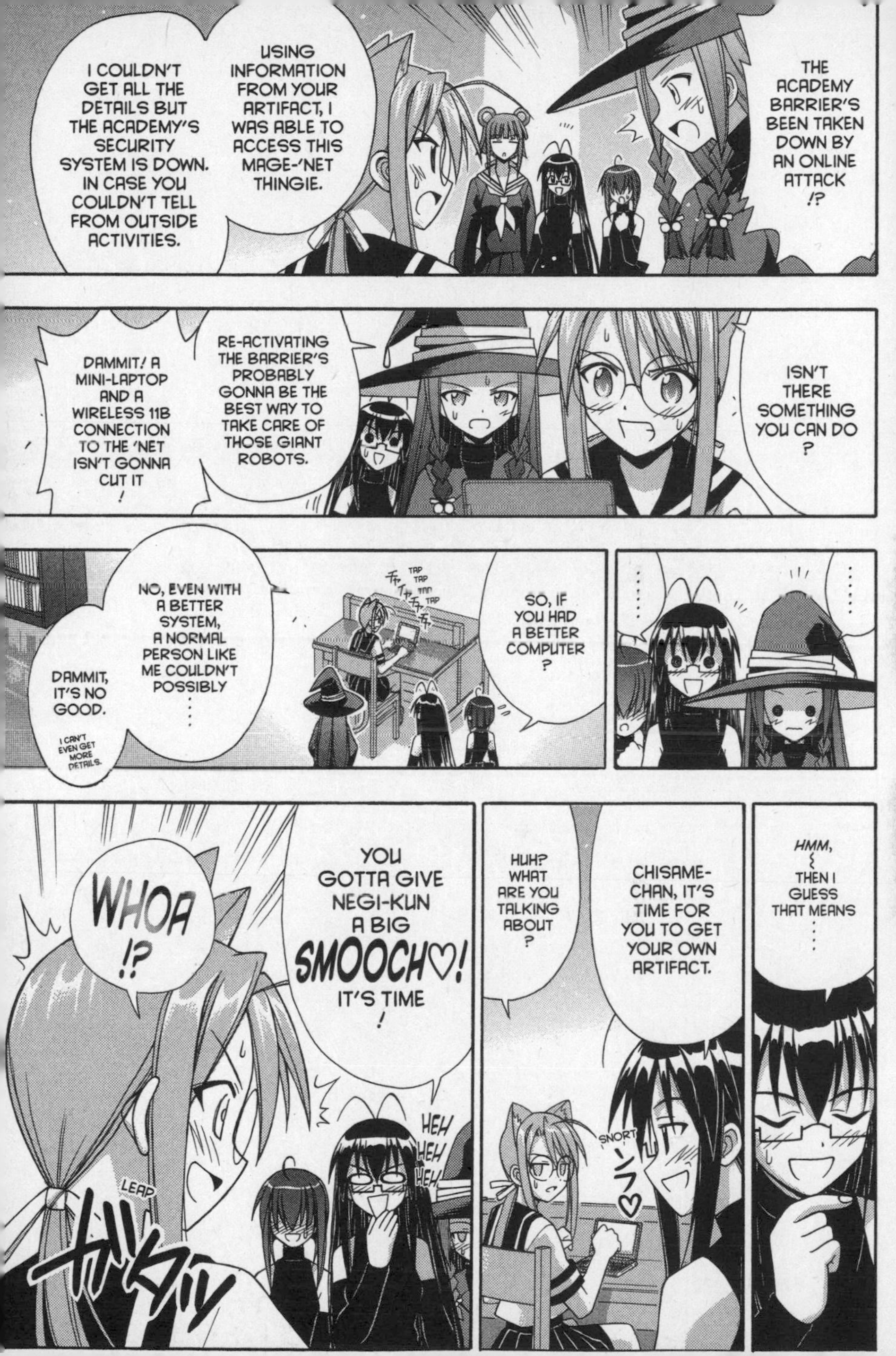
THE ACADEMY BARRIER'S BEEN TAKEN DOWN BY AN ONLINE ATTACK !?
USING INFORMATION FROM YOUR ARTIFACT, I WAS ABLE TO ACCESS THIS MAGE-'NET THINGIE.
I COULDN'T GET ALL THE DETAILS BUT THE ACADEMY'S SECURITY SYSTEM IS DOWN. IN CASE YOU COULDN'T TELL FROM OUTSIDE ACTIVITIES.
ISN'T THERE SOMETHING YOU CAN DO ?
RE-ACTIVATING THE BARRIER'S PROBABLY GONNA BE THE BEST WAY TO TAKE CARE OF THOSE GIANT ROBOTS.
DAMMIT! A MINI-LAPTOP AND A WIRELESS 11B CONNECTION TO THE 'NET ISN'T GONNA CUT IT !
......
......
SO, IF YOU HAD A BETTER COMPUTER ?
TAP TAP TAP TAP
NO, EVEN WITH A BETTER SYSTEM, A NORMAL PERSON LIKE ME COULDN'T POSSIBLY ...
DAMMIT, IT'S NO GOOD.
I CAN'T EVEN GET MORE DETAILS.
HMM, THEN I GUESS THAT MEANS ...
CHISAME-CHAN, IT'S TIME FOR YOU TO GET YOUR OWN ARTIFACT.
HUH? WHAT ARE YOU TALKING ABOUT ?
SNORT
YOU GOTTA GIVE NEGI-KUN A BIG SMOOCH♡! IT'S TIME !
HEH HEH HEH
WHOA !?
LEAP

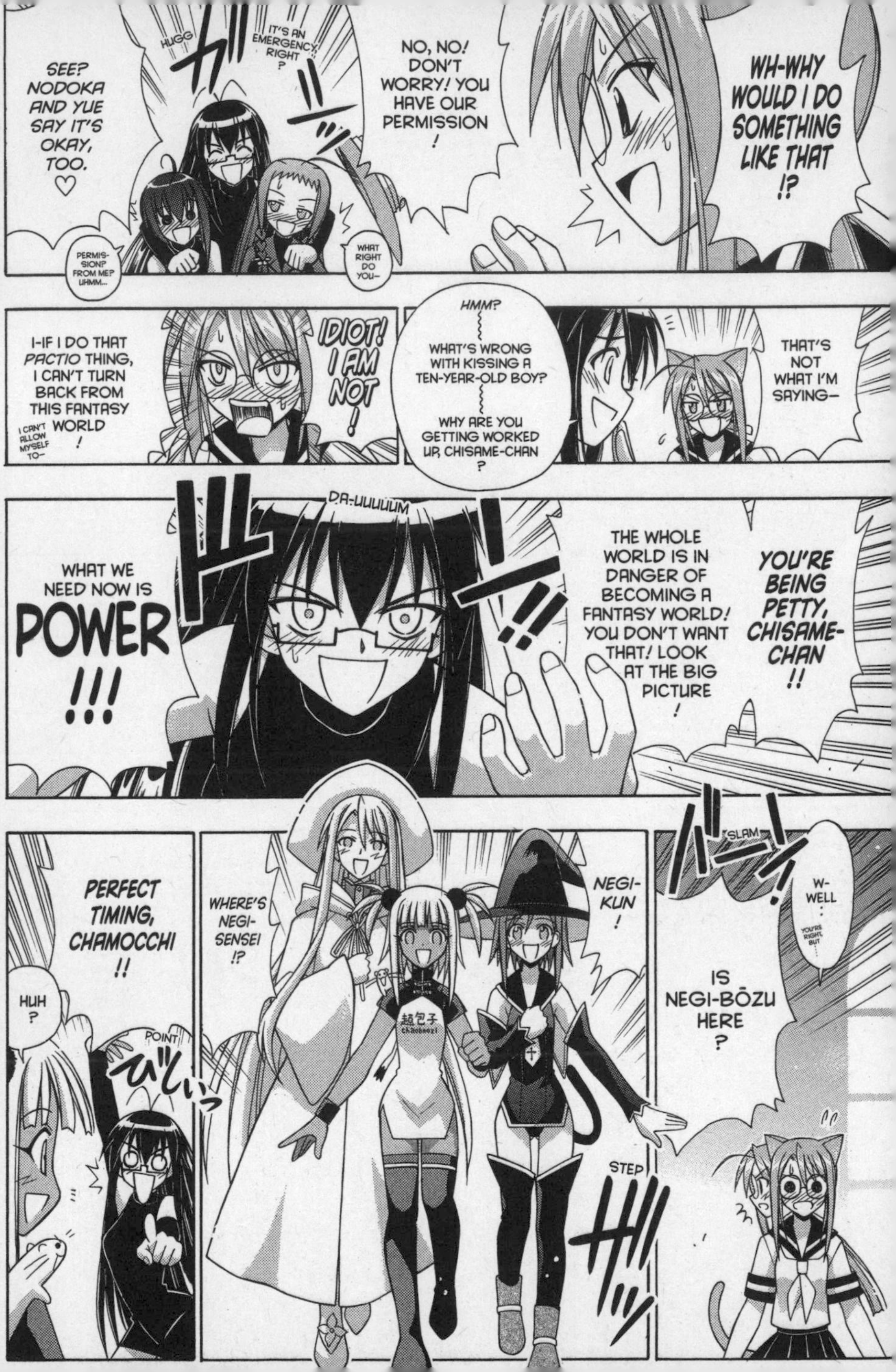
WH-WHY WOULD I DO SOMETHING LIKE THAT !?
NO, NO! DON'T WORRY! YOU HAVE OUR PERMISSION !
IT'S AN EMERGENCY, RIGHT ?
HUGG
SEE? NODOKA AND YUE SAY IT'S OKAY, TOO. ♡
WHAT RIGHT DO YOU–
PERMISSION? FROM ME? UHMM...
THAT'S NOT WHAT I'M SAYING–
HMM? WHAT'S WRONG WITH KISSING A TEN-YEAR-OLD BOY? WHY ARE YOU GETTING WORKED UP, CHISAME-CHAN ?
IDIOT! I AM NOT !
I-IF I DO THAT *PACTIO* THING, I CAN'T TURN BACK FROM THIS FANTASY WORLD !
I CAN'T ALLOW MYSELF TO–
YOU'RE BEING PETTY, CHISAME-CHAN !!
THE WHOLE WORLD IS IN DANGER OF BECOMING A FANTASY WORLD! YOU DON'T WANT THAT! LOOK AT THE BIG PICTURE !
DA-UUUUUM
WHAT WE NEED NOW IS POWER !!!
SLAM
W-WELL ...
YOU'RE RIGHT, BUT ...
IS NEGI-BŌZU HERE ?
NEGI-KUN !
WHERE'S NEGI-SENSEI !?
STEP
PERFECT TIMING, CHAMOCCHI !!
HUH ?
POINT

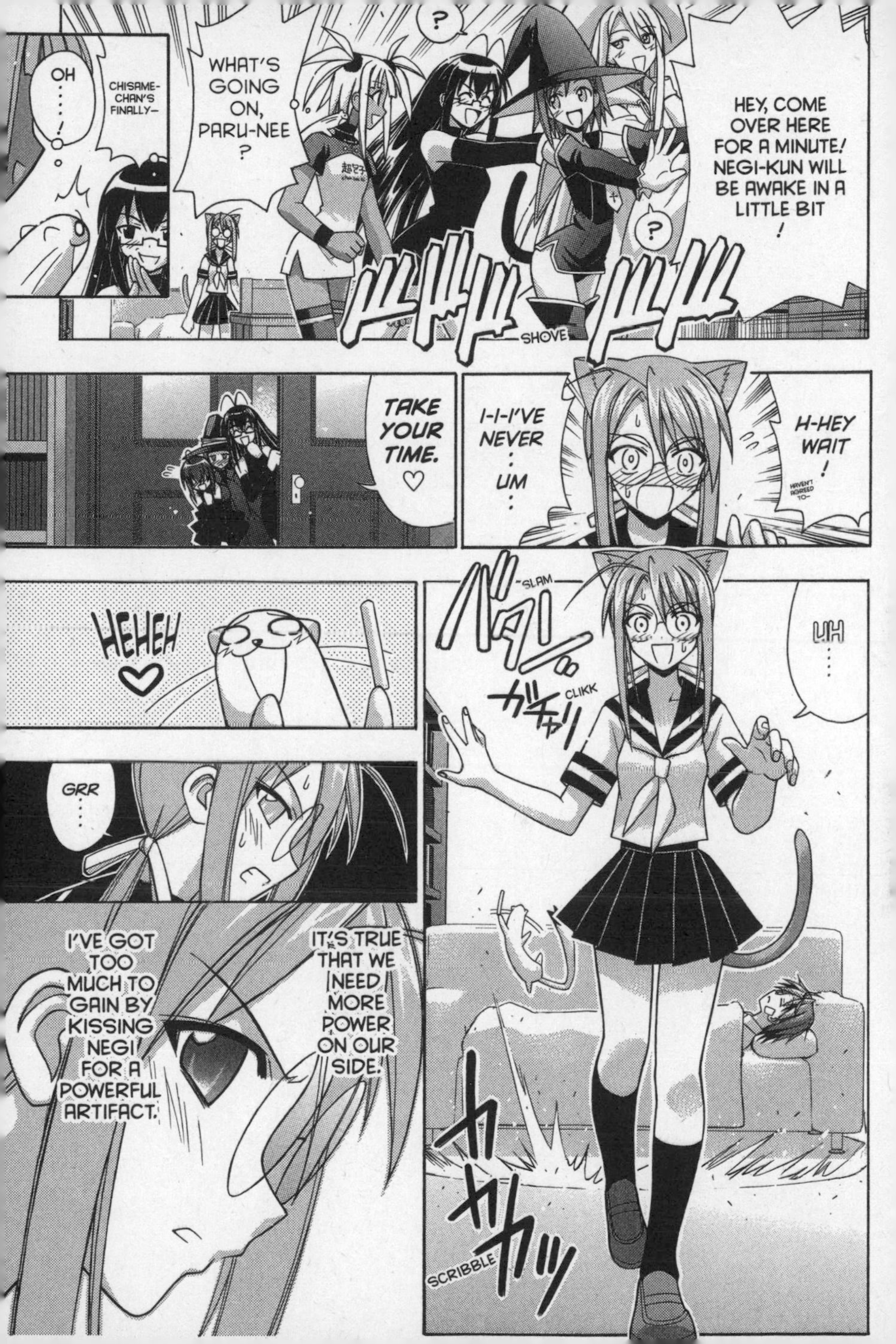
HEY, COME OVER HERE FOR A MINUTE! NEGI-KUN WILL BE AWAKE IN A LITTLE BIT!
?
?
WHAT'S GOING ON, PARU-NEE?
CHISAME-CHAN'S FINALLY—
OH.....!
SHOVE
H-HEY WAIT!
HAVEN'T AGREED TO-
I-I-I'VE NEVER... UM...
TAKE YOUR TIME. ♡
UH....
SLAM
CLIKK
SCRIBBLE
HEHEH ♡
GRR....
IT'S TRUE THAT WE NEED MORE POWER ON OUR SIDE.
I'VE GOT TOO MUCH TO GAIN BY KISSING NEGI FOR A POWERFUL ARTIFACT.

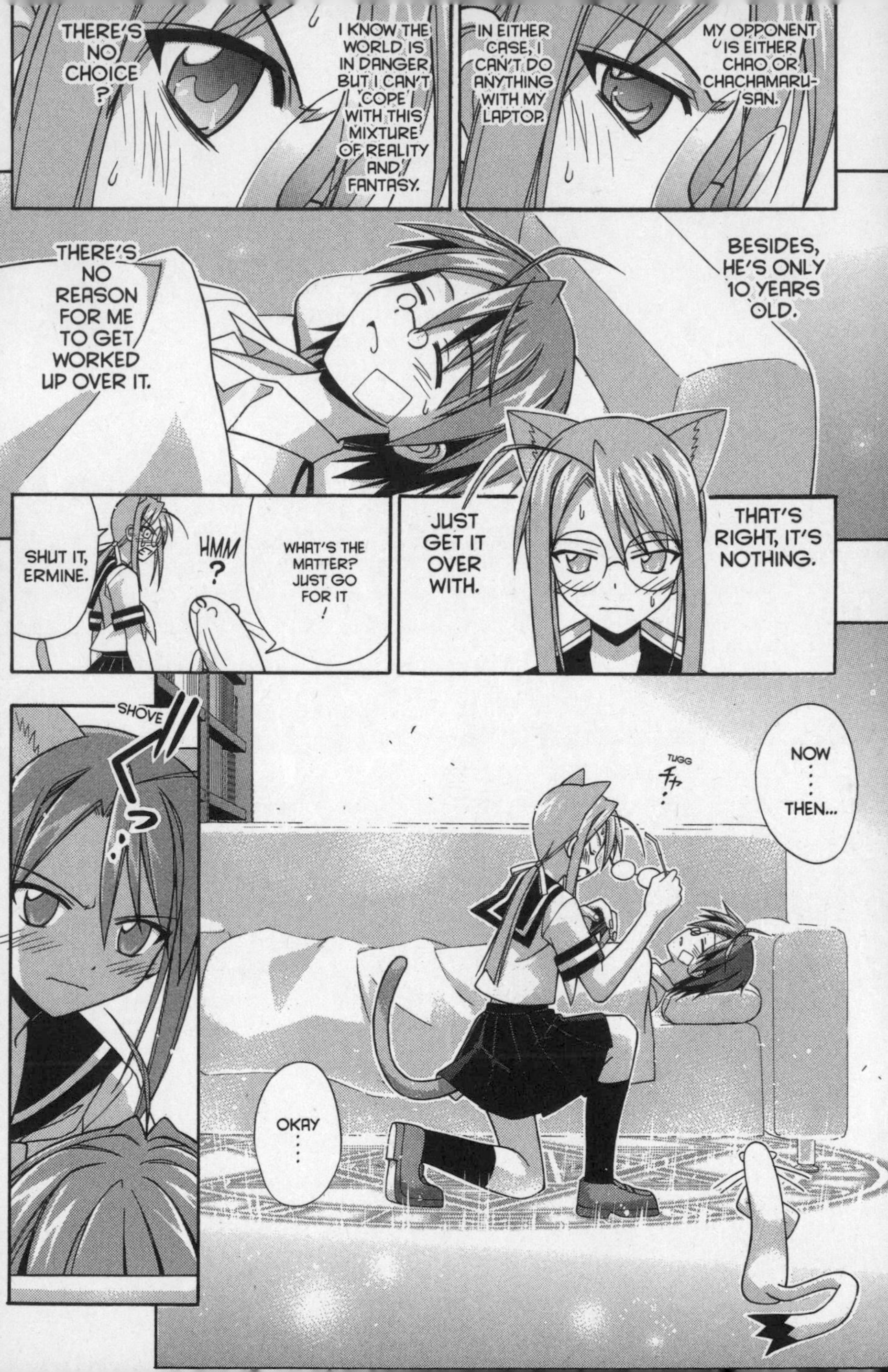
MY OPPONENT IS EITHER CHAO OR CHACHAMARU-SAN.
IN EITHER CASE, I CAN'T DO ANYTHING WITH MY LAPTOP.
I KNOW THE WORLD IS IN DANGER BUT I CAN'T COPE WITH THIS MIXTURE OF REALITY AND FANTASY.
THERE'S NO CHOICE?
BESIDES, HE'S ONLY 10 YEARS OLD.
THERE'S NO REASON FOR ME TO GET WORKED UP OVER IT.
THAT'S RIGHT, IT'S NOTHING.
JUST GET IT OVER WITH.
WHAT'S THE MATTER? JUST GO FOR IT!
HMM?
SHUT IT, ERMINE.
NOW... THEN...
TUGG
OKAY...
SHOVE

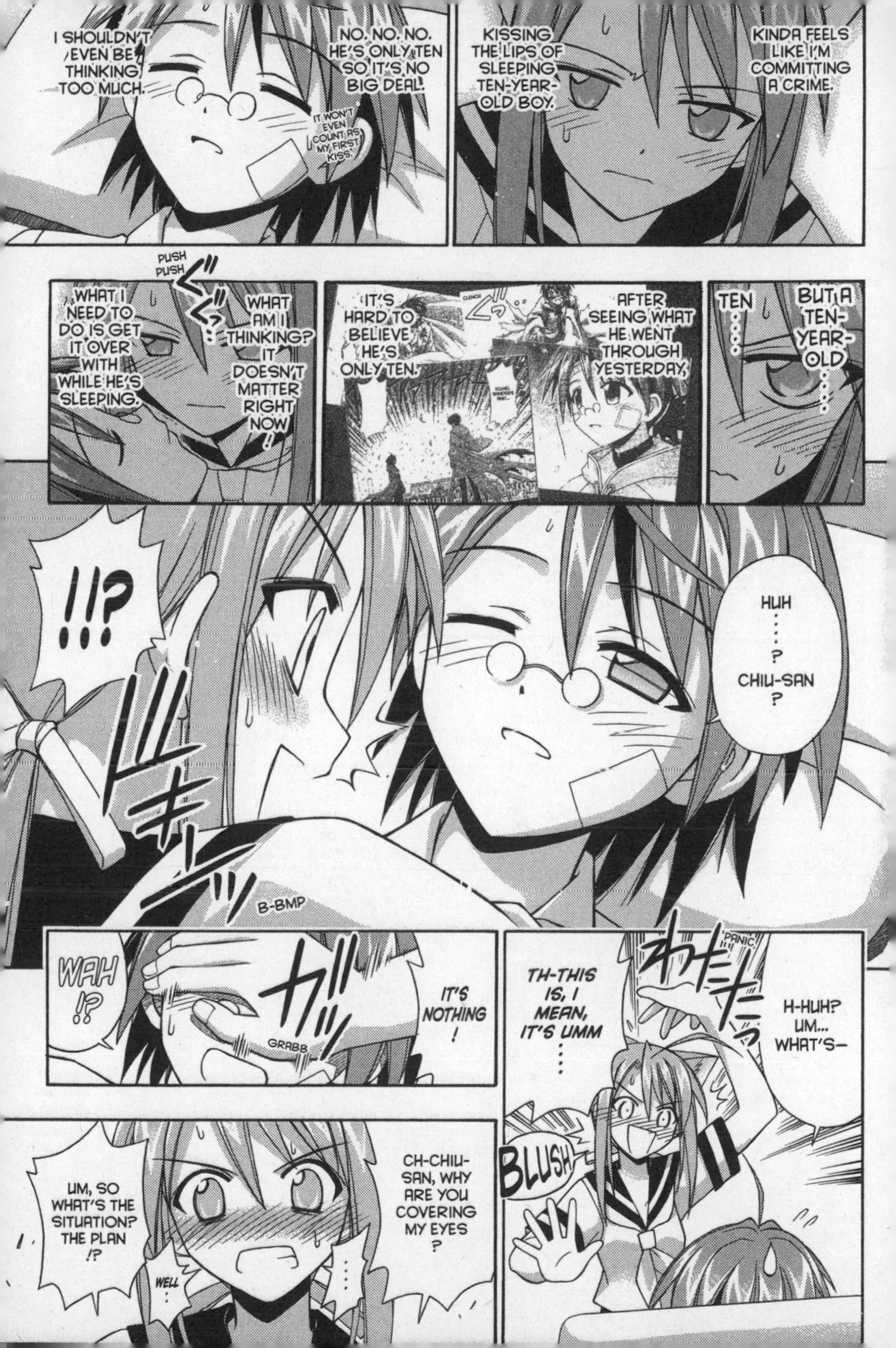

KINDA FEELS LIKE I'M COMMITTING A CRIME.
KISSING THE LIPS OF SLEEPING TEN-YEAR-OLD BOY.
NO. NO. NO. HE'S ONLY TEN SO IT'S NO BIG DEAL.
IT WON'T EVEN COUNT AS MY FIRST KISS.
I SHOULDN'T EVEN BE THINKING TOO MUCH.
BUT A TEN-YEAR-OLD.....
TEN.....
AFTER SEEING WHAT HE WENT THROUGH YESTERDAY,
CLENCH
IT'S HARD TO BELIEVE HE'S ONLY TEN.
WHAT AM I THINKING? IT DOESN'T MATTER RIGHT NOW!
PUSH PUSH
WHAT I NEED TO DO IS GET IT OVER WITH WHILE HE'S SLEEPING.
HUH....? CHIU-SAN?
!!?
B-BMP
H-HUH? UM... WHAT'S—
PANIC
TH-THIS IS, I MEAN, IT'S UMM.....
BLUSH
IT'S NOTHING!
GRABB
WAH!?
CH-CHIU-SAN, WHY ARE YOU COVERING MY EYES?
.....
WELL...
UM, SO WHAT'S THE SITUATION? THE PLAN!?

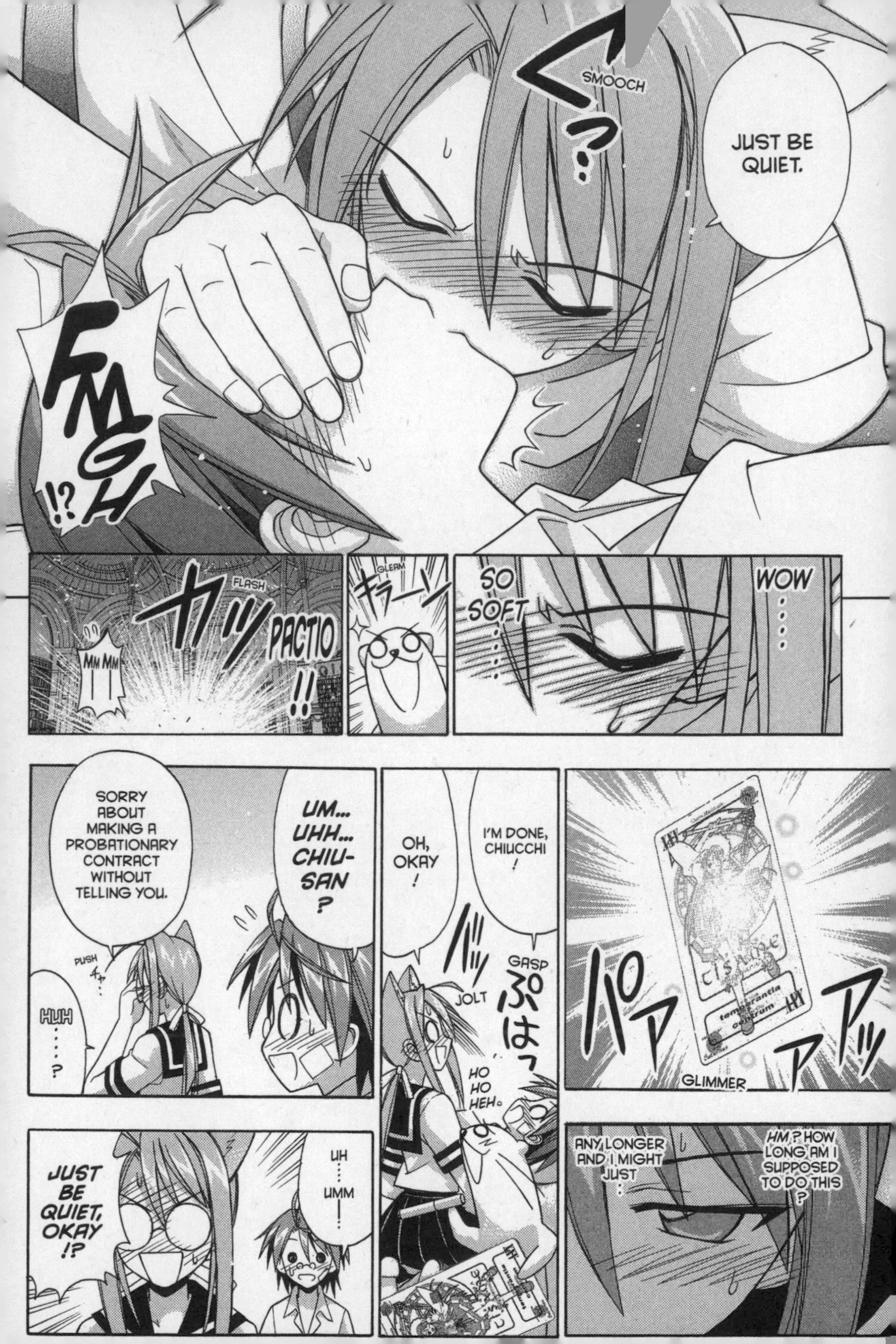
SMOOCH
JUST BE QUIET.
FMGH !?
WOW ....
SO SOFT ....
GLEAM
キラーン
FLASH
カッ
PACTIO !!
MM MM
パァァアッ
GLIMMER
HM? HOW LONG AM I SUPPOSED TO DO THIS?
ANY LONGER AND I MIGHT JUST ...
I'M DONE, CHIUCCHI!
OH, OKAY!
GASP
ぷはっ
JOLT
HO HO HEH。
UM... UHH... CHIU-SAN?
SORRY ABOUT MAKING A PROBATIONARY CONTRACT WITHOUT TELLING YOU.
PUSH
HUH .....?
UH .... UMM ...!
JUST BE QUIET, OKAY!?

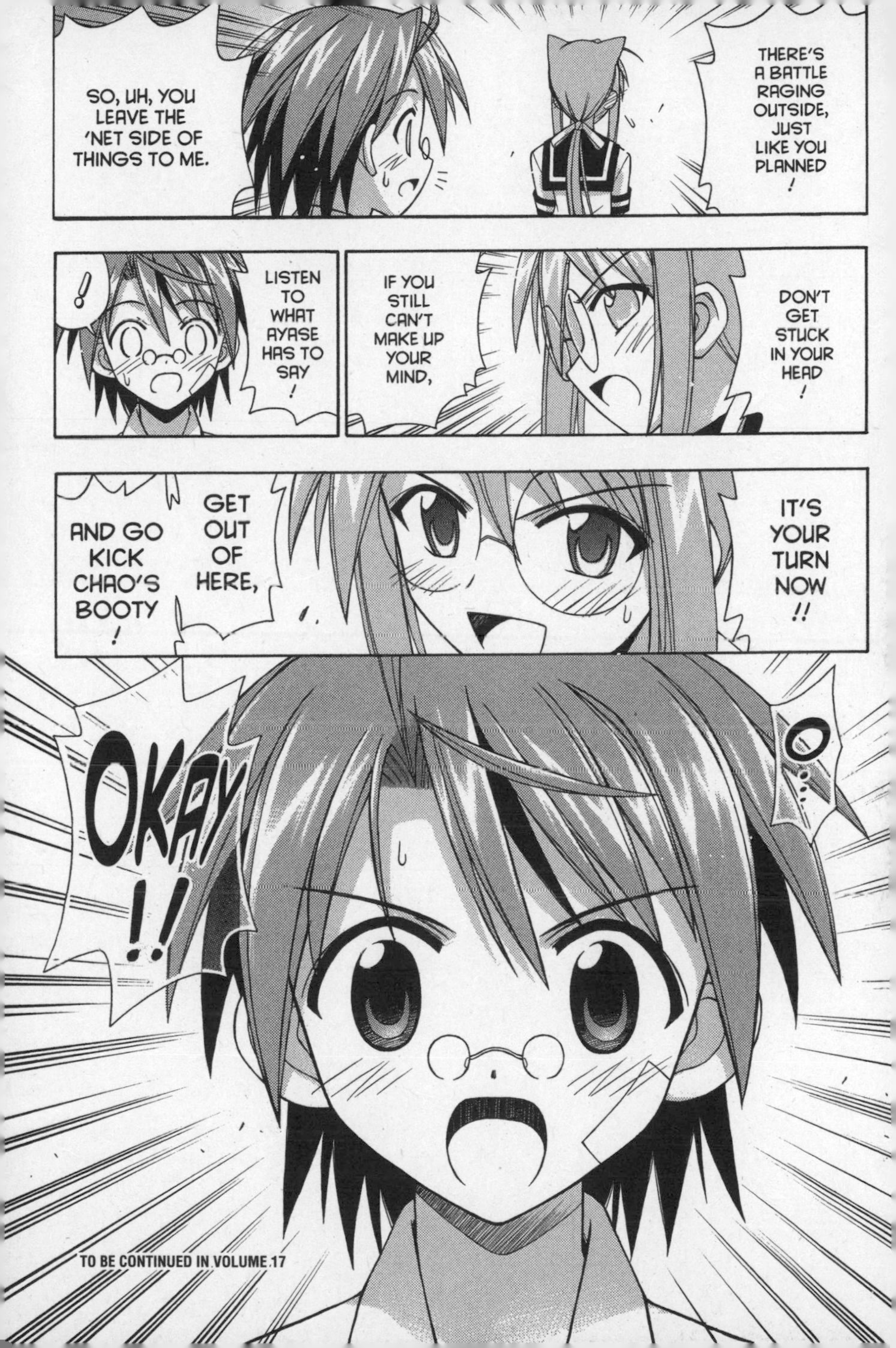
THERE'S A BATTLE RAGING OUTSIDE, JUST LIKE YOU PLANNED!
SO, UH, YOU LEAVE THE 'NET SIDE OF THINGS TO ME.
DON'T GET STUCK IN YOUR HEAD!
IF YOU STILL CAN'T MAKE UP YOUR MIND,
LISTEN TO WHAT AYASE HAS TO SAY!
!
IT'S YOUR TURN NOW!!
GET OUT OF HERE,
AND GO KICK CHAO'S BOOTY!
O...
OKAY!!

TO BE CONTINUED IN VOLUME 17

魔法先生ネギま!

MAGISTER NEGI MAGI

17

Ken Akamatsu

赤松 健

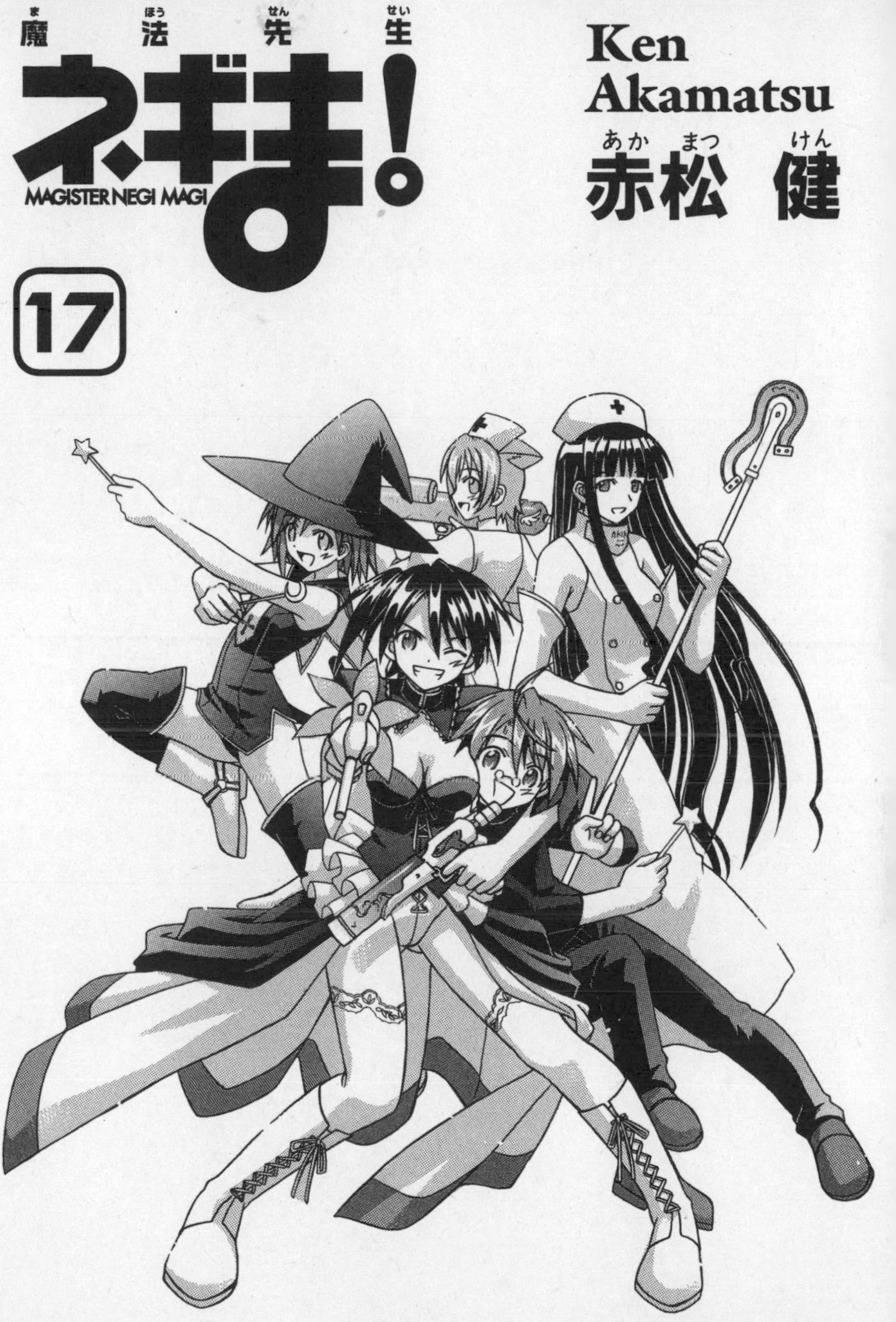

CONTENTS

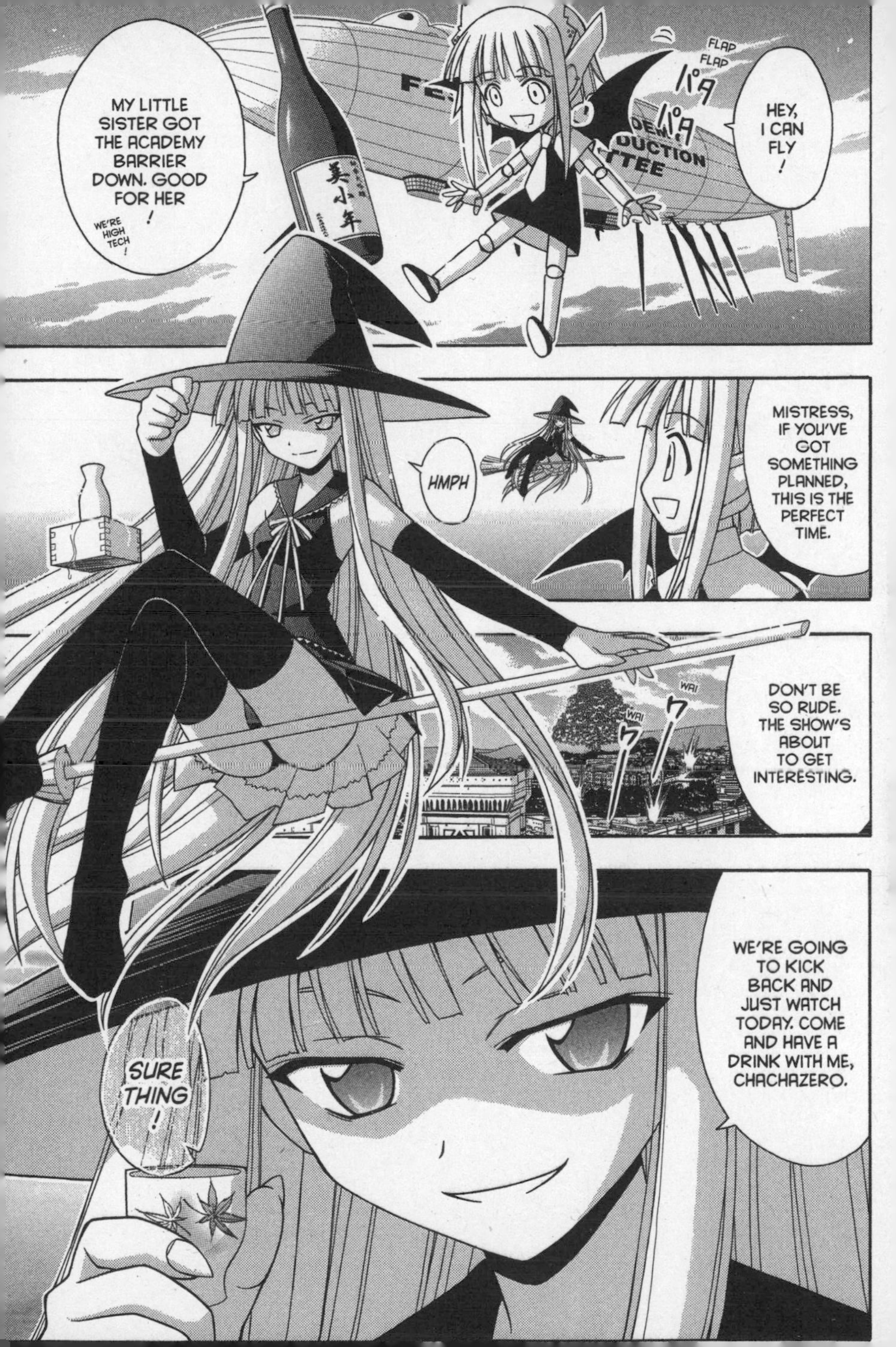
FLAP FLAP
パタパタ
HEY, I CAN FLY!
MY LITTLE SISTER GOT THE ACADEMY BARRIER DOWN. GOOD FOR HER!
WE'RE HIGH TECH!
美少年
MISTRESS, IF YOU'VE GOT SOMETHING PLANNED, THIS IS THE PERFECT TIME.
HMPH
DON'T BE SO RUDE. THE SHOW'S ABOUT TO GET INTERESTING.
WAI WAI
WE'RE GOING TO KICK BACK AND JUST WATCH TODAY. COME AND HAVE A DRINK WITH ME, CHACHAZERO.
SURE THING!

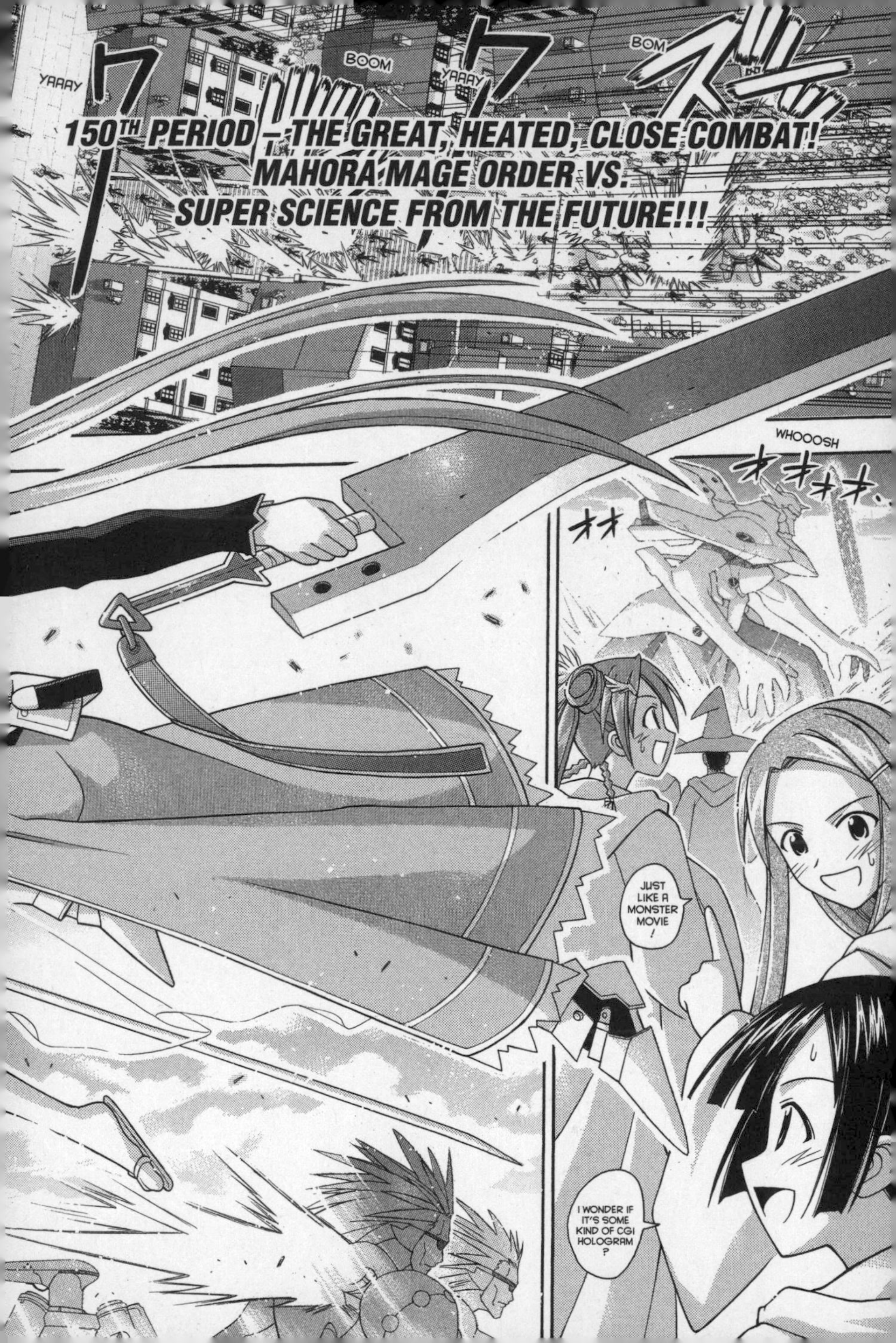

BOM
BOOM
YAAAY
YAAAY
150TH PERIOD – THE GREAT, HEATED, CLOSE COMBAT! MAHORA MAGE ORDER VS. SUPER SCIENCE FROM THE FUTURE!!!
WHOOOSH
JUST LIKE A MONSTER MOVIE!
I WONDER IF IT'S SOME KIND OF CGI HOLOGRAM?

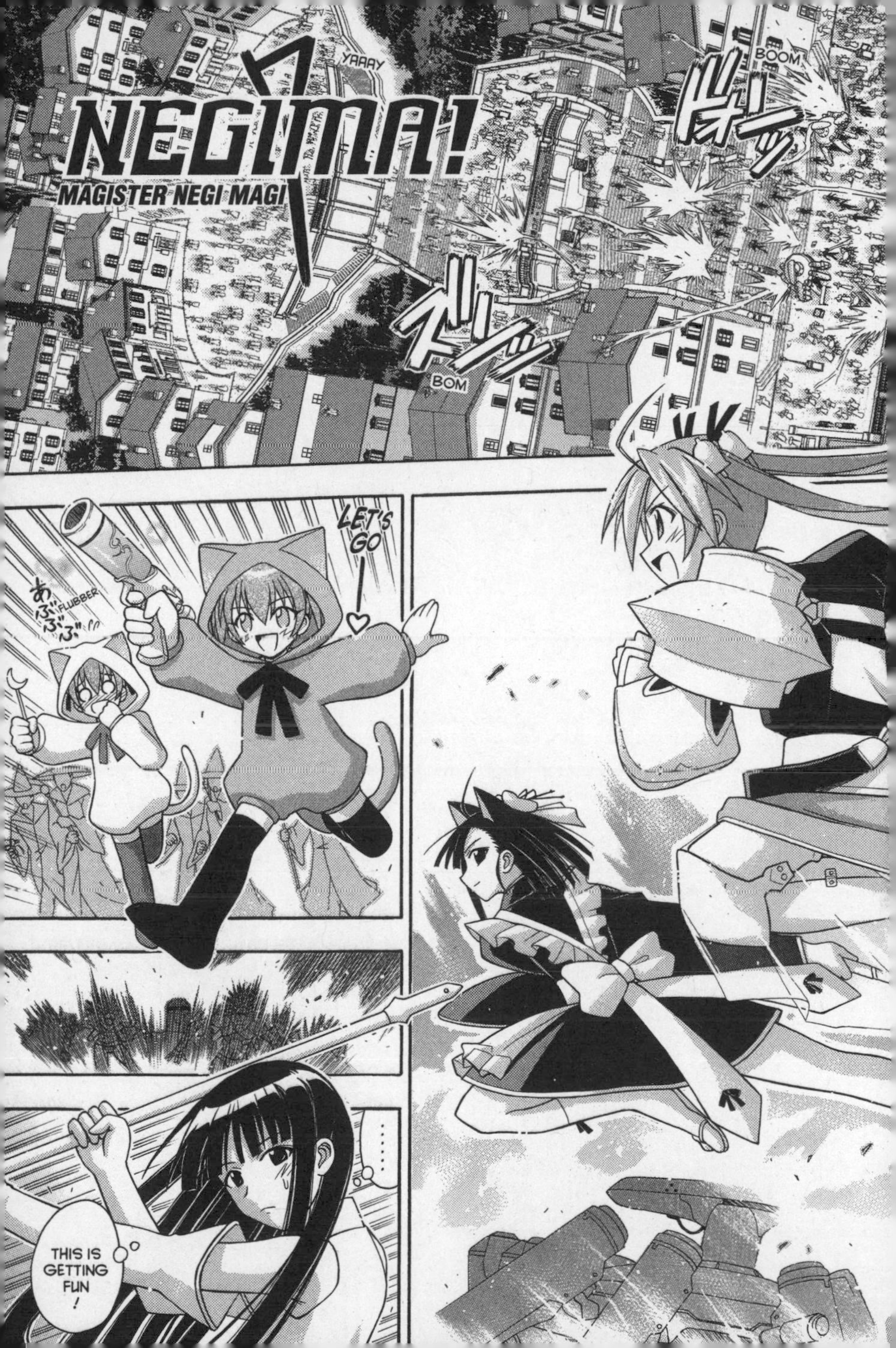

BOOM
YAAAY
NEGIMA!
MAGISTER NEGI MAGI
BOM
LET'S GO ♡
あぶぶぶ FLUBBER
THIS IS GETTING FUN!

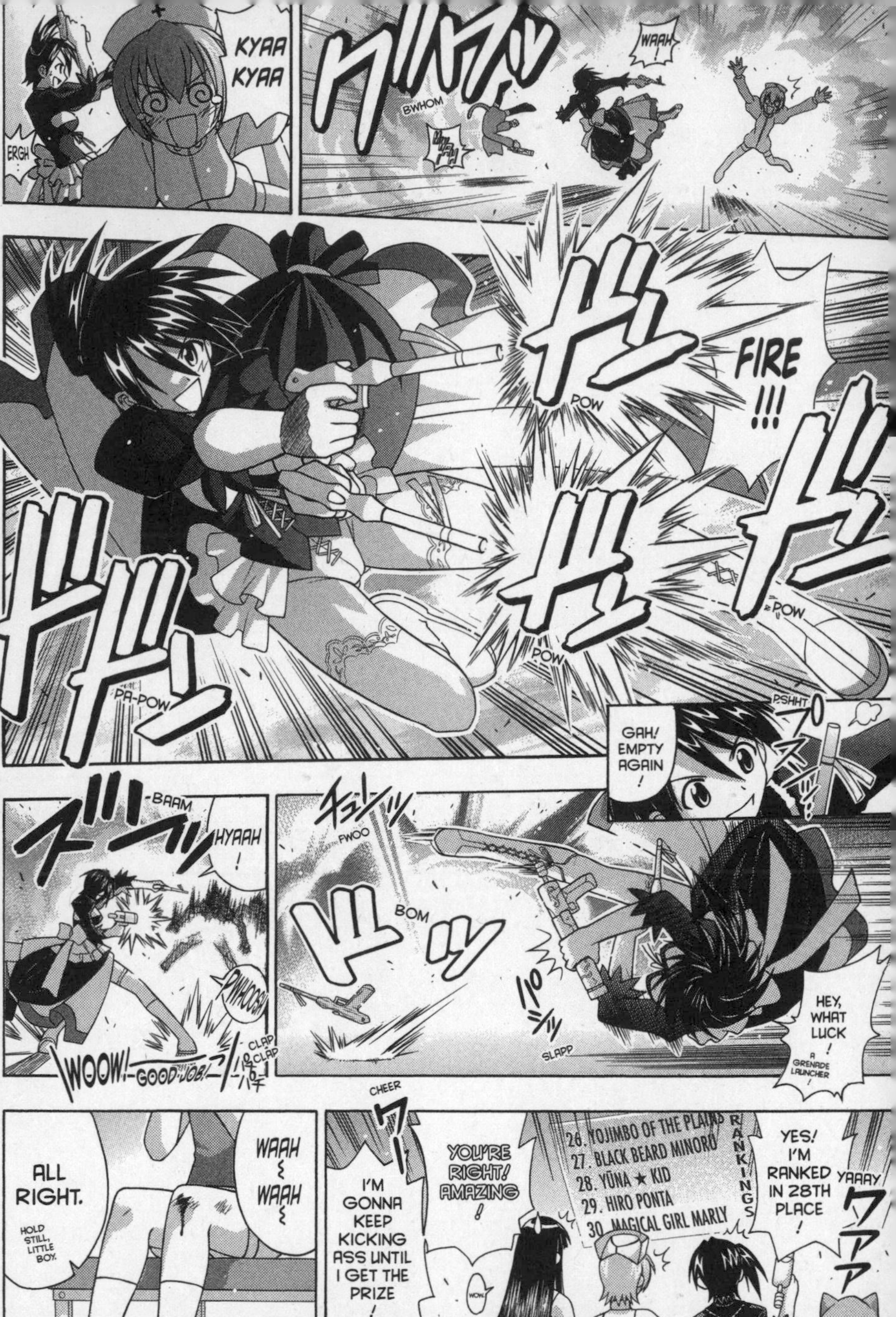
WAAH!
BWHOM
KYAA KYAA
ERGH
FIRE!!!
POW
POW
POW
PA-POW
PSHHT
GAH! EMPTY AGAIN!
FWOO
BOM
HEY, WHAT LUCK!
A GRENADE LAUNCHER!
SLAPP
BAAM
HYAAH!
PWHOOSH
WOOW!
GOOD JOB!
CLAP CLAP
YAAAY
YES! I'M RANKED IN 28TH PLACE!
RANKINGS
26. YOJIMBO OF THE PLAINS
27. BLACK BEARD MINORO
28. YŪNA ★ KID
29. HIRO PONTA
30. MAGICAL GIRL MARLY
YOU'RE RIGHT! AMAZING!
CHEER
I'M GONNA KEEP KICKING ASS UNTIL I GET THE PRIZE!
WOW
WAAH WAAH
ALL RIGHT.
HOLD STILL, LITTLE BOY.

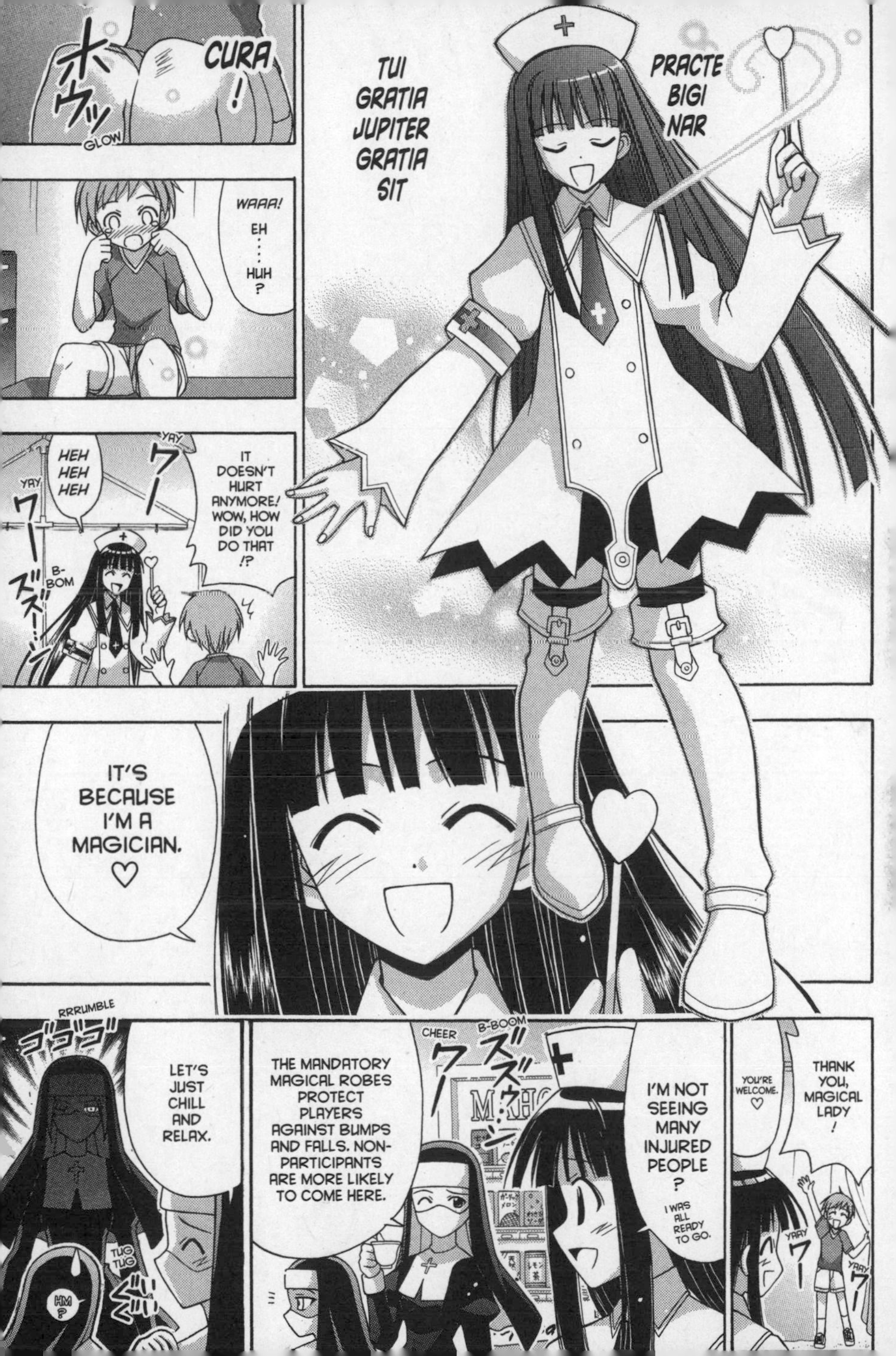
PRACTE BIGI NAR
TUI GRATIA JUPITER GRATIA SIT
CURA!
GLOW
WAAA!
EH... HUH?
IT DOESN'T HURT ANYMORE! WOW, HOW DID YOU DO THAT!?
YAY
HEH HEH HEH
YAY
B-BOM
IT'S BECAUSE I'M A MAGICIAN. ♡
THANK YOU, MAGICAL LADY!
YOU'RE WELCOME. ♡
YAAY
YAAY
I'M NOT SEEING MANY INJURED PEOPLE?
I WAS ALL READY TO GO.
B-BOOM
CHEER
THE MANDATORY MAGICAL ROBES PROTECT PLAYERS AGAINST BUMPS AND FALLS. NON-PARTICIPANTS ARE MORE LIKELY TO COME HERE.
LET'S JUST CHILL AND RELAX.
RRRUMBLE
TUG TUG
HM?

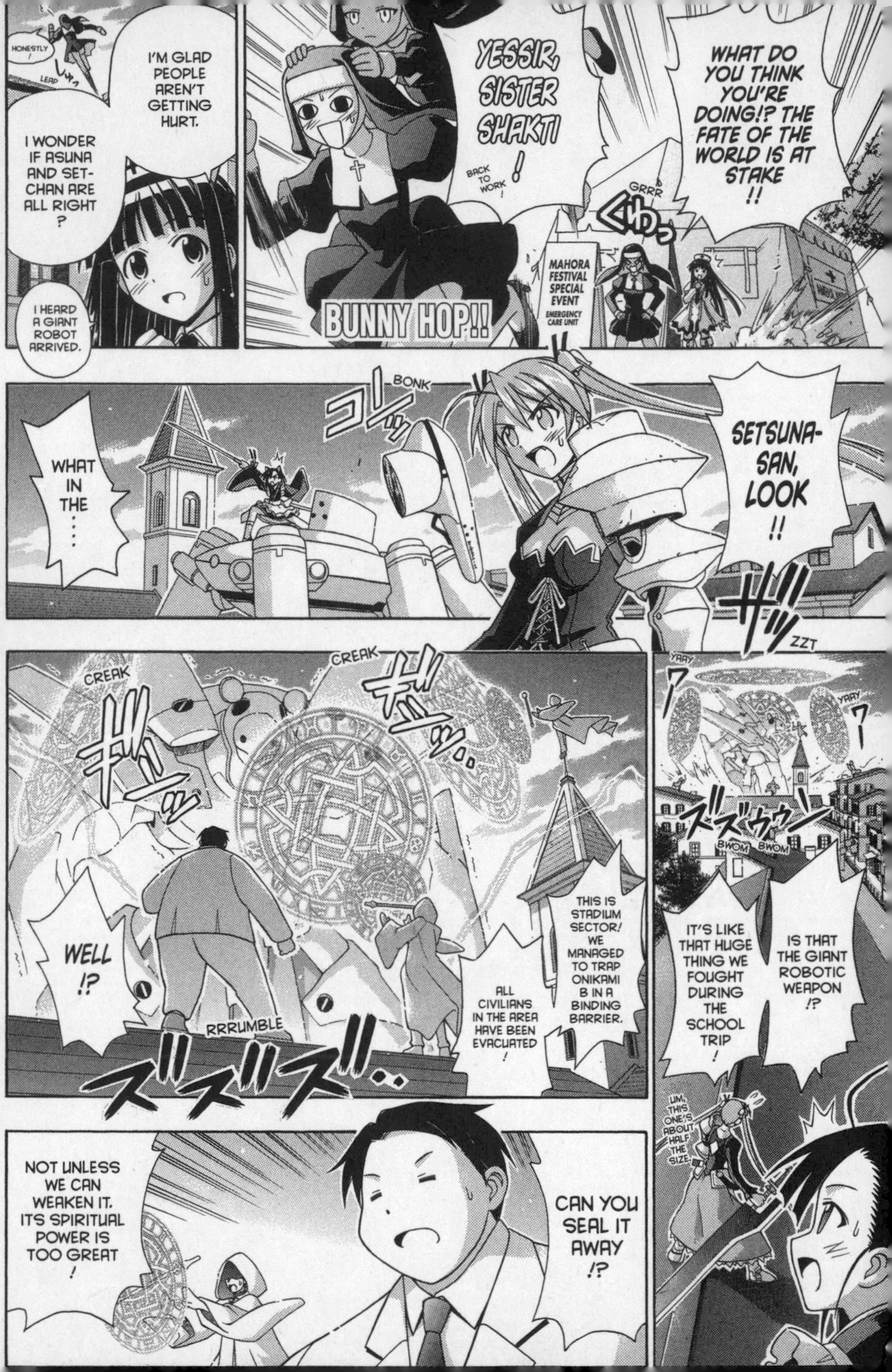
WHAT DO YOU THINK YOU'RE DOING!? THE FATE OF THE WORLD IS AT STAKE!!
GRRR
MAHORA FESTIVAL SPECIAL EVENT
EMERGENCY CARE UNIT
YESSIR, SISTER SHAKTI!
BACK TO WORK!
BUNNY HOP!!
HONESTLY!
LEAP
I'M GLAD PEOPLE AREN'T GETTING HURT.
I WONDER IF ASUNA AND SET-CHAN ARE ALL RIGHT?
I HEARD A GIANT ROBOT ARRIVED.
SETSUNA-SAN, LOOK!!
ZZT
BONK
WHAT IN THE.....
YAAY
YAAY
BWOM BWOM
IS THAT THE GIANT ROBOTIC WEAPON!?
IT'S LIKE THAT HUGE THING WE FOUGHT DURING THE SCHOOL TRIP!
CREAK
CREAK
THIS IS STADIUM SECTOR! WE MANAGED TO TRAP ONIKAMI B IN A BINDING BARRIER.
ALL CIVILIANS IN THE AREA HAVE BEEN EVACUATED!
WELL!?
RRRUMBLE
UM, THIS ONE'S ABOUT HALF THE SIZE.
CAN YOU SEAL IT AWAY!?
NOT UNLESS WE CAN WEAKEN IT. ITS SPIRITUAL POWER IS TOO GREAT!

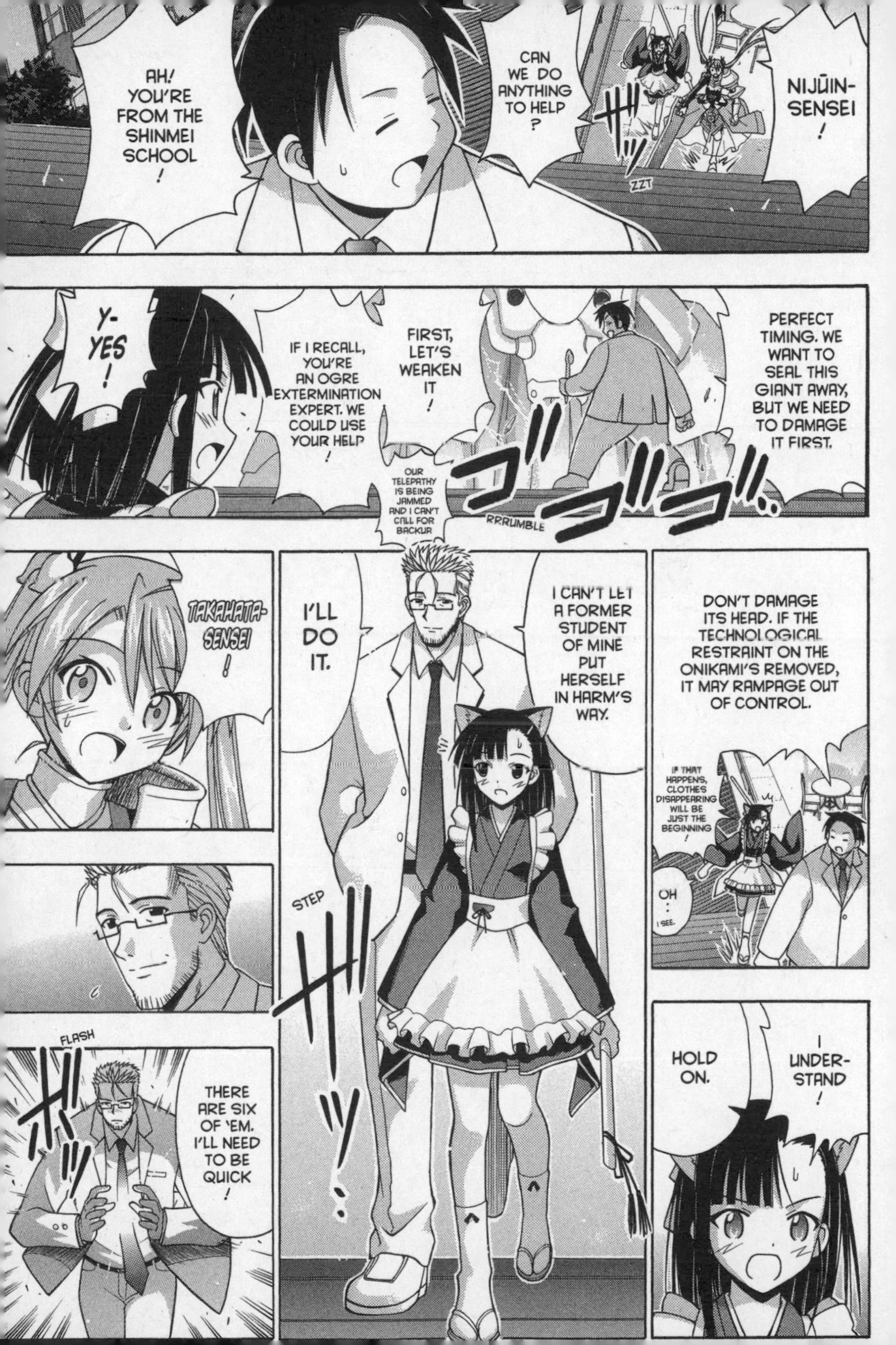
NIJŪIN-SENSEI!
CAN WE DO ANYTHING TO HELP?
ZZT
AH! YOU'RE FROM THE SHINMEI SCHOOL!
PERFECT TIMING. WE WANT TO SEAL THIS GIANT AWAY, BUT WE NEED TO DAMAGE IT FIRST.
FIRST, LET'S WEAKEN IT!
IF I RECALL, YOU'RE AN OGRE EXTERMINATION EXPERT. WE COULD USE YOUR HELP!
Y-YES!
RRRUMBLE
OUR TELEPATHY IS BEING JAMMED AND I CAN'T CALL FOR BACKUP.
DON'T DAMAGE ITS HEAD. IF THE TECHNOLOGICAL RESTRAINT ON THE ONIKAMI'S REMOVED, IT MAY RAMPAGE OUT OF CONTROL.
IF THAT HAPPENS, CLOTHES DISAPPEARING WILL BE JUST THE BEGINNING!
OH... I SEE.
I UNDERSTAND!
HOLD ON.
I CAN'T LET A FORMER STUDENT OF MINE PUT HERSELF IN HARM'S WAY.
I'LL DO IT.
STEP
TAKAHATA-SENSEI!
FLASH
THERE ARE SIX OF 'EM. I'LL NEED TO BE QUICK!

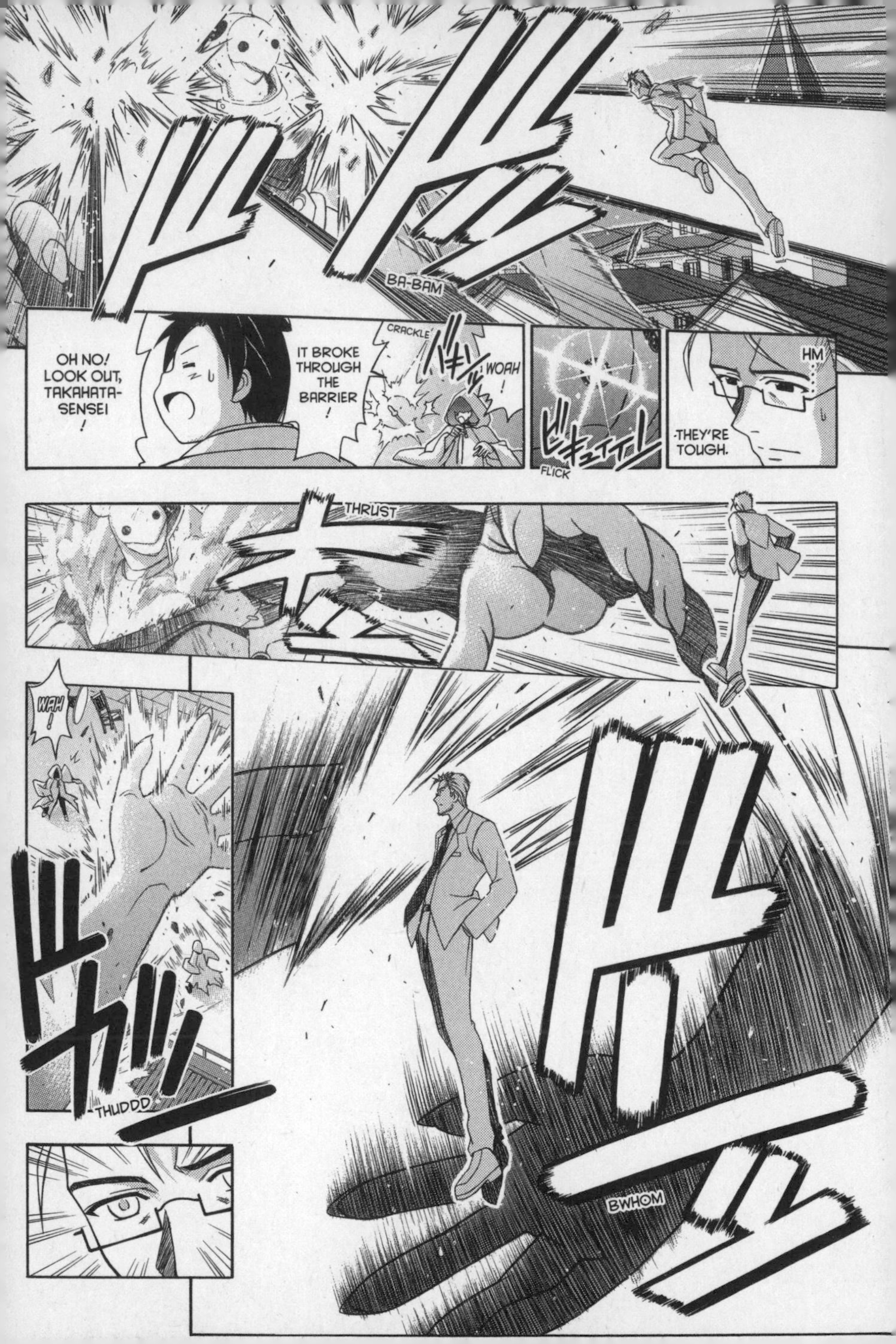
BA-BAM
HM
THEY'RE TOUGH.
FLICK
CRACKLE
WOAH!
IT BROKE THROUGH THE BARRIER!
OH NO! LOOK OUT, TAKAHATA-SENSEI!
THRUST
BWHOM
WAH!
THUDDD

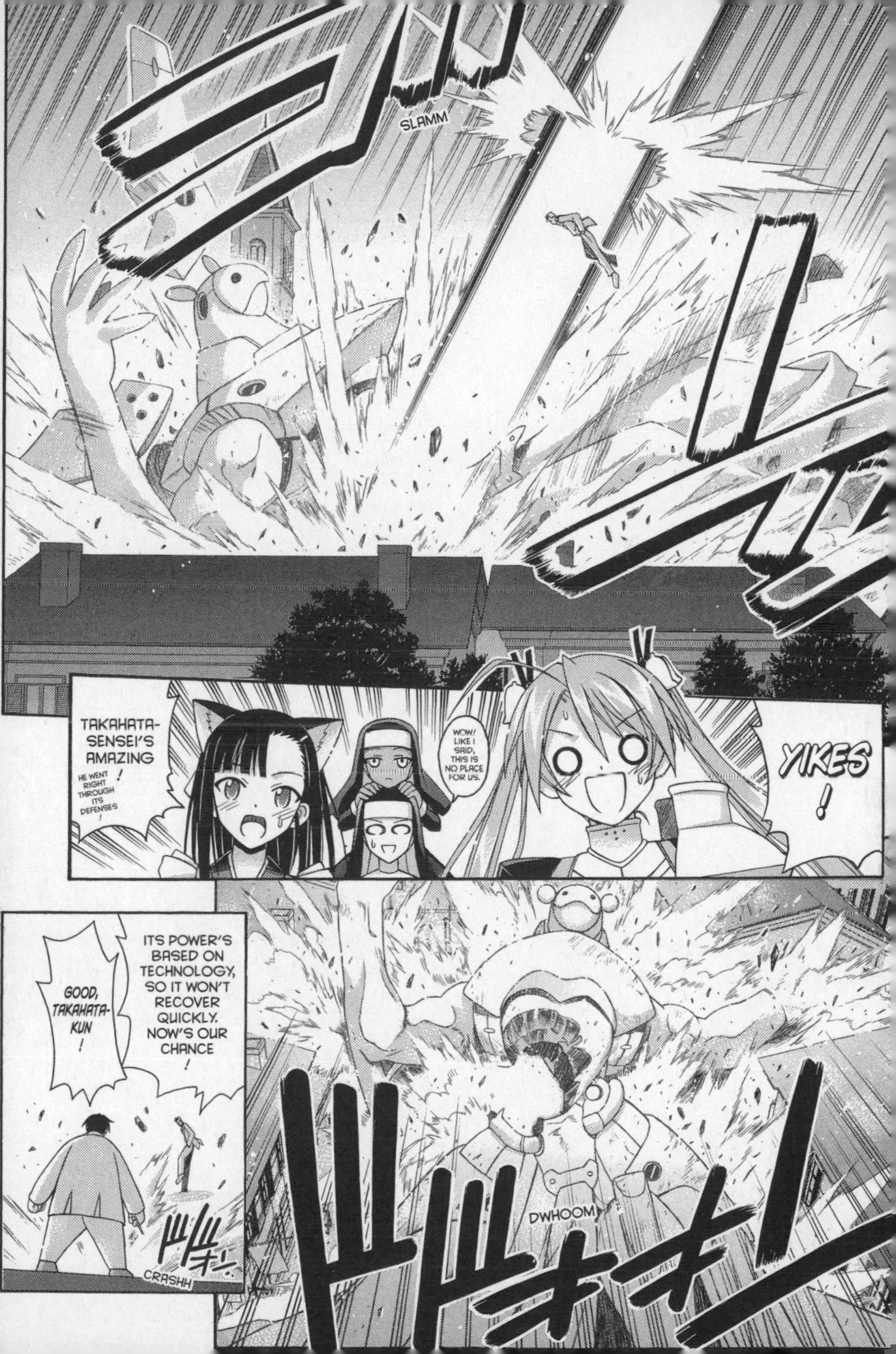
SLAMM
YIKES !
WOW! LIKE I SAID, THIS IS NO PLACE FOR US.
TAKAHATA-SENSEI'S AMAZING !
HE WENT RIGHT THROUGH ITS DEFENSES !
DWHOOM
ITS POWER'S BASED ON TECHNOLOGY, SO IT WON'T RECOVER QUICKLY. NOW'S OUR CHANCE !
GOOD, TAKAHATA-KUN !
CRASHH

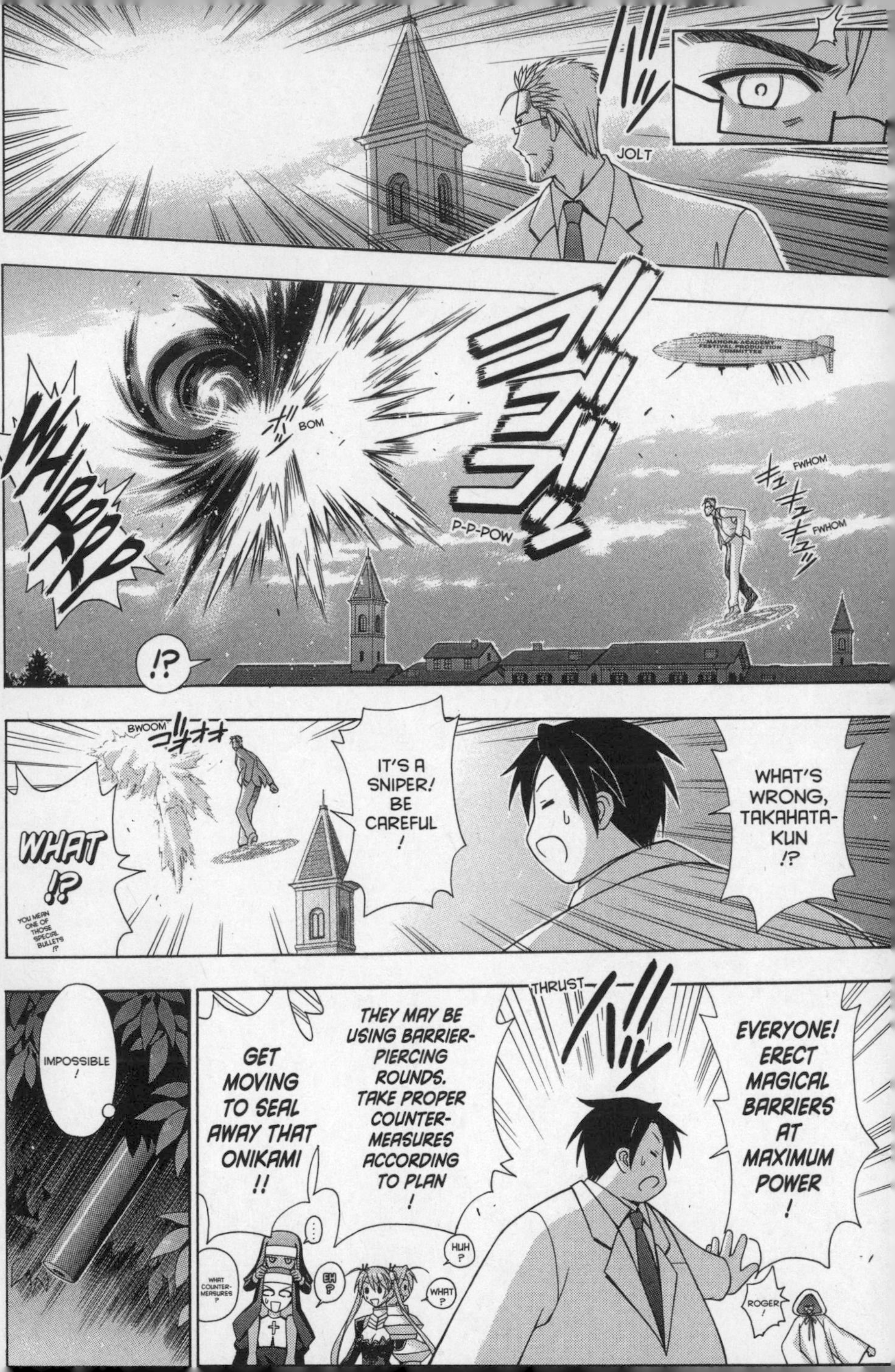
JOLT
FWHOM
FWHOM
P-P-POW
BOM
WHIRRRR!
!?
WHAT'S WRONG, TAKAHATA-KUN!?
IT'S A SNIPER! BE CAREFUL!
BWOOM
WHAT!?
YOU MEAN ONE OF THOSE SPECIAL BULLETS!?
THRUST
EVERYONE! ERECT MAGICAL BARRIERS AT MAXIMUM POWER!
THEY MAY BE USING BARRIER-PIERCING ROUNDS. TAKE PROPER COUNTER-MEASURES ACCORDING TO PLAN!
GET MOVING TO SEAL AWAY THAT ONIKAMI!!
ROGER!
HUH?
WHAT?
EH?
...
WHAT COUNTER-MEASURES?
IMPOSSIBLE!

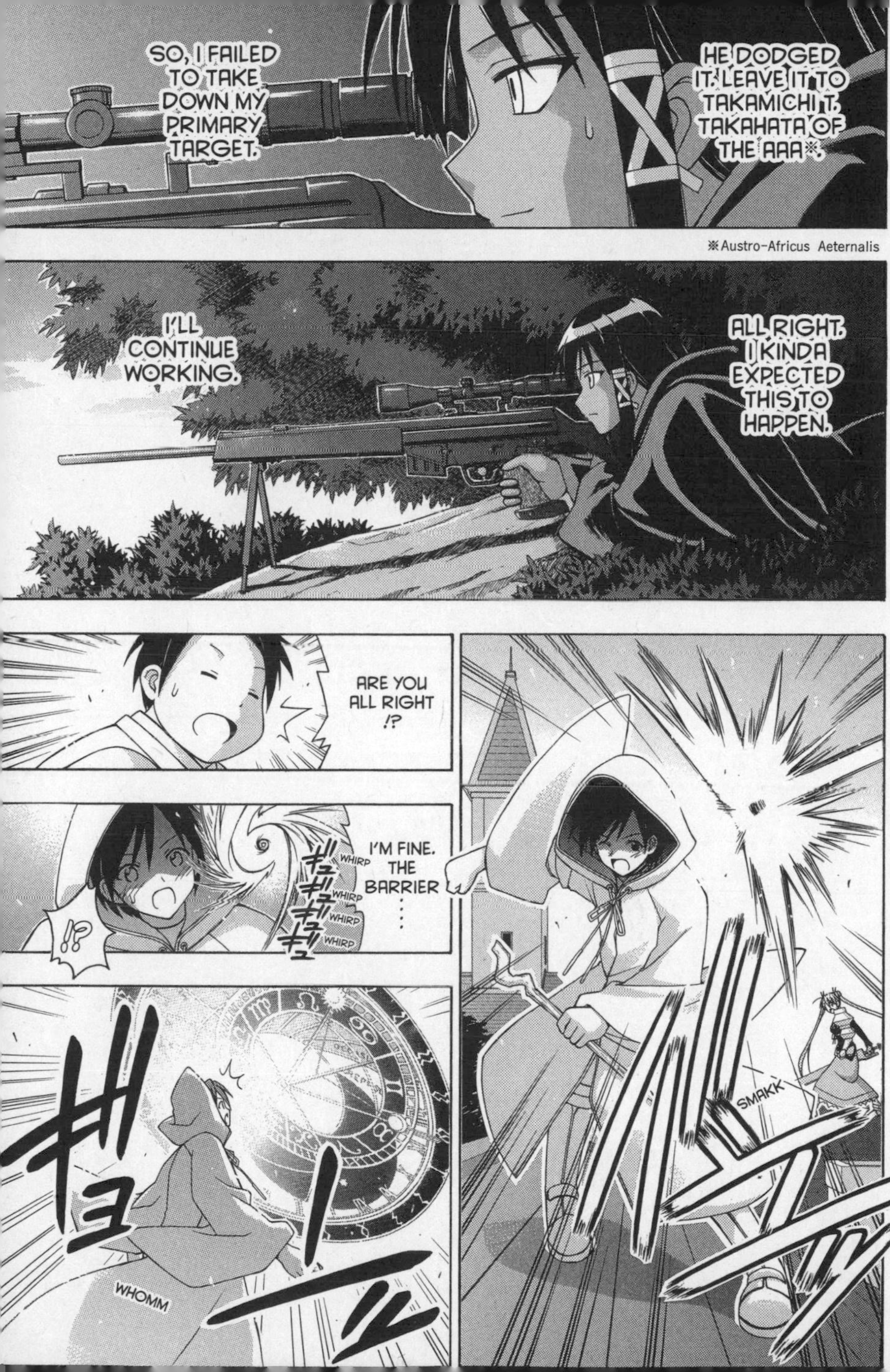
HE DODGED IT. LEAVE IT TO TAKAMICHI T. TAKAHATA OF THE AAA※.
SO, I FAILED TO TAKE DOWN MY PRIMARY TARGET.
ALL RIGHT. I KINDA EXPECTED THIS TO HAPPEN.
I'LL CONTINUE WORKING.
SMAKK
ARE YOU ALL RIGHT !?
I'M FINE. THE BARRIER ...
WHIRP
WHIRP
WHIRP
WHIRP
!!?
WHOMM

※Austro-Africus Aeternalis

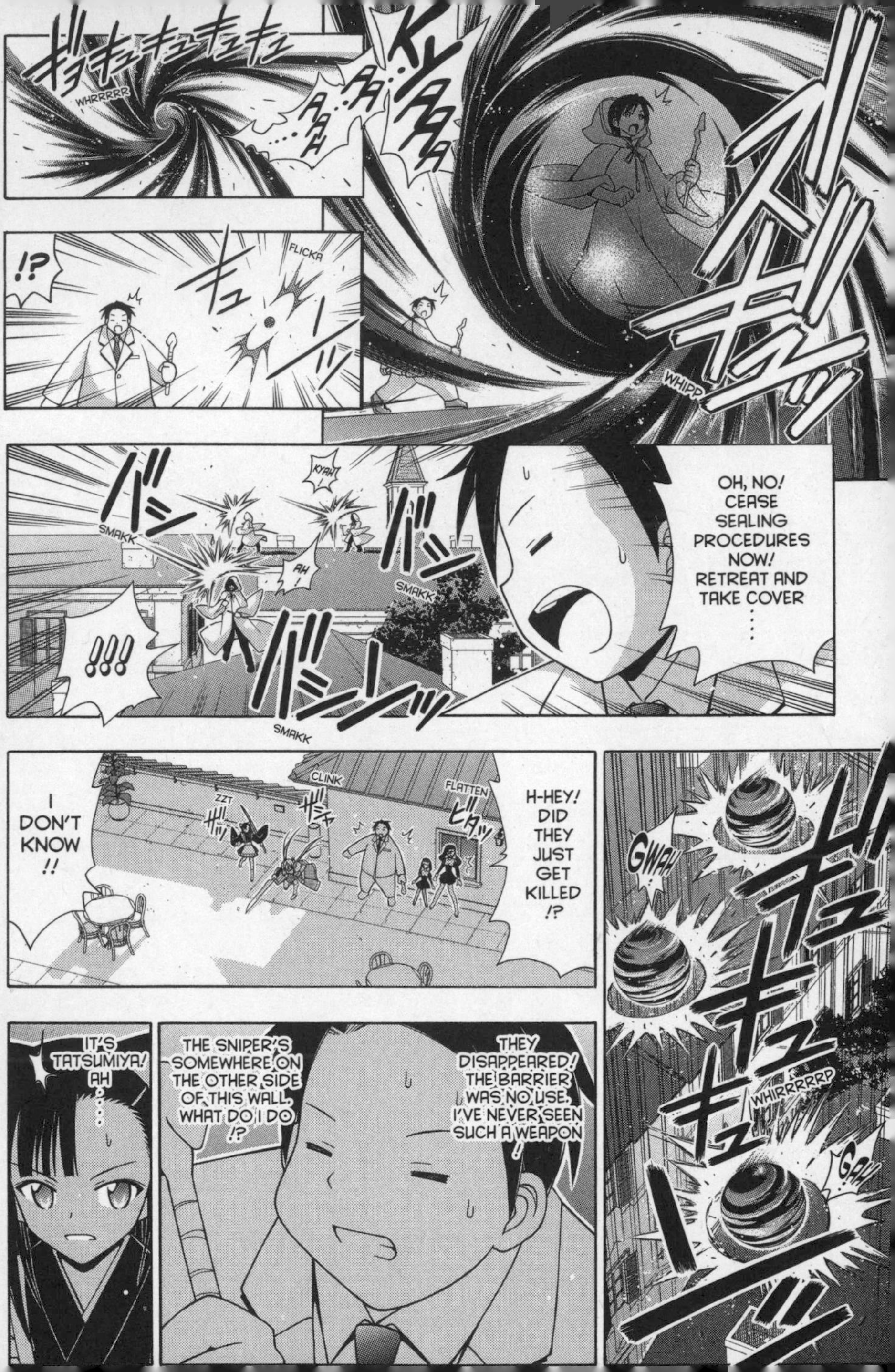

KYAAAAA...AAA...AAA
WHIPP
WHRRRRR
!?
FLICKA
OH, NO! CEASE SEALING PROCEDURES NOW! RETREAT AND TAKE COVER ...
KYAH!
SMAKK
AH!
SMAKK
!!!
SMAKK
GWAH
WHIRRRRP
GAH
H-HEY! DID THEY JUST GET KILLED !?
FLATTEN
CLINK
ZZT
I DON'T KNOW !!
THEY DISAPPEARED! THE BARRIER WAS NO USE. I'VE NEVER SEEN SUCH A WEAPON !
THE SNIPER'S SOMEWHERE ON THE OTHER SIDE OF THIS WALL. WHAT DO I DO !?
IT'S TATSUMIYA! AH ...

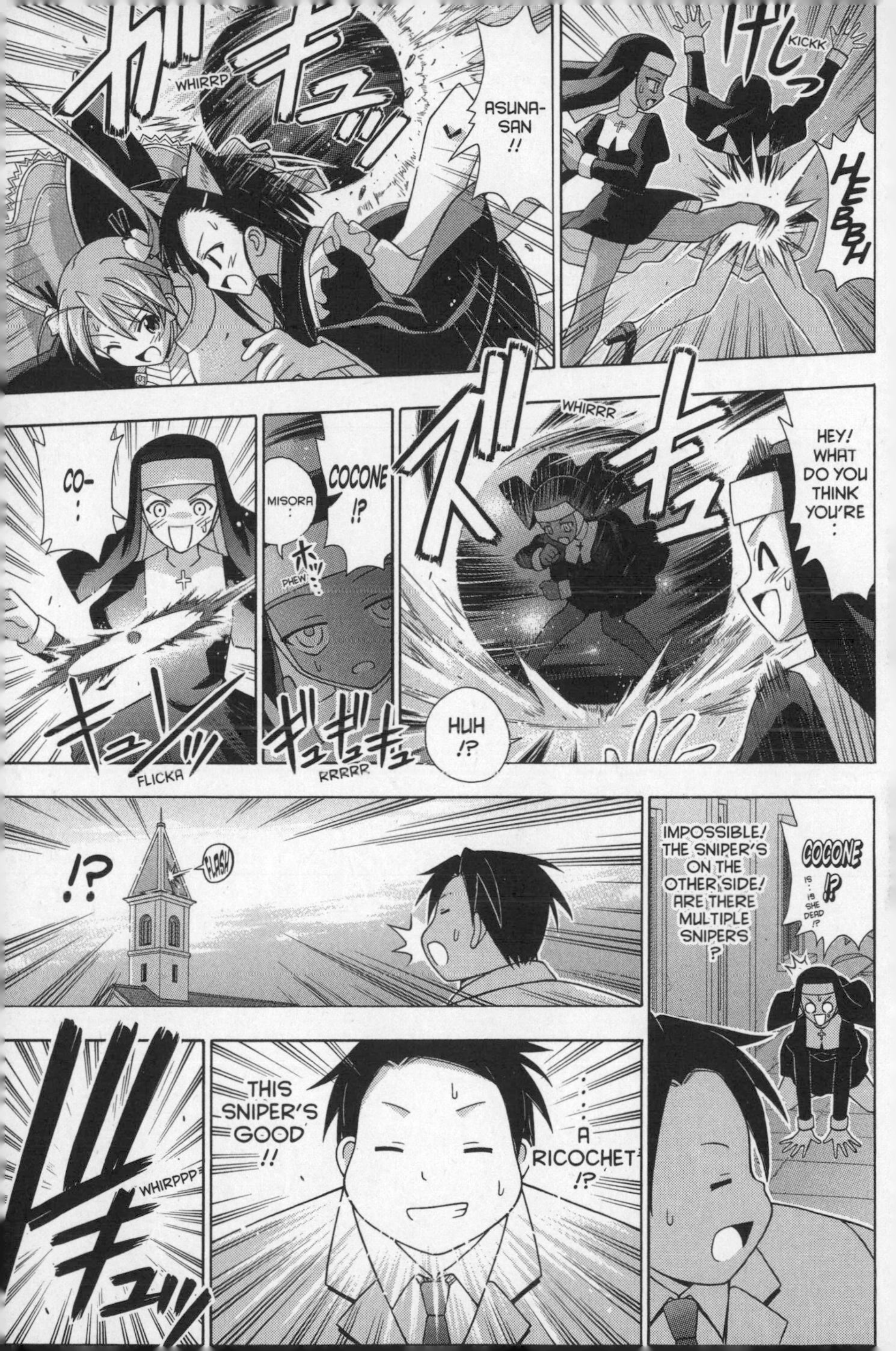
KICKK
HEBBH
WHIRRP
ASUNA-SAN!!
WHIRRR
HEY! WHAT DO YOU THINK YOU'RE...
HUH!?
COCONE!?
MISORA...
PHEW
RRRRR
CO-...
FLICKA
IMPOSSIBLE! THE SNIPER'S ON THE OTHER SIDE! ARE THERE MULTIPLE SNIPERS?
COCONE!?
IS... IS SHE DEAD!?
!?
FLASH
...A RICOCHET!?
THIS SNIPER'S GOOD!!
WHIRPPP

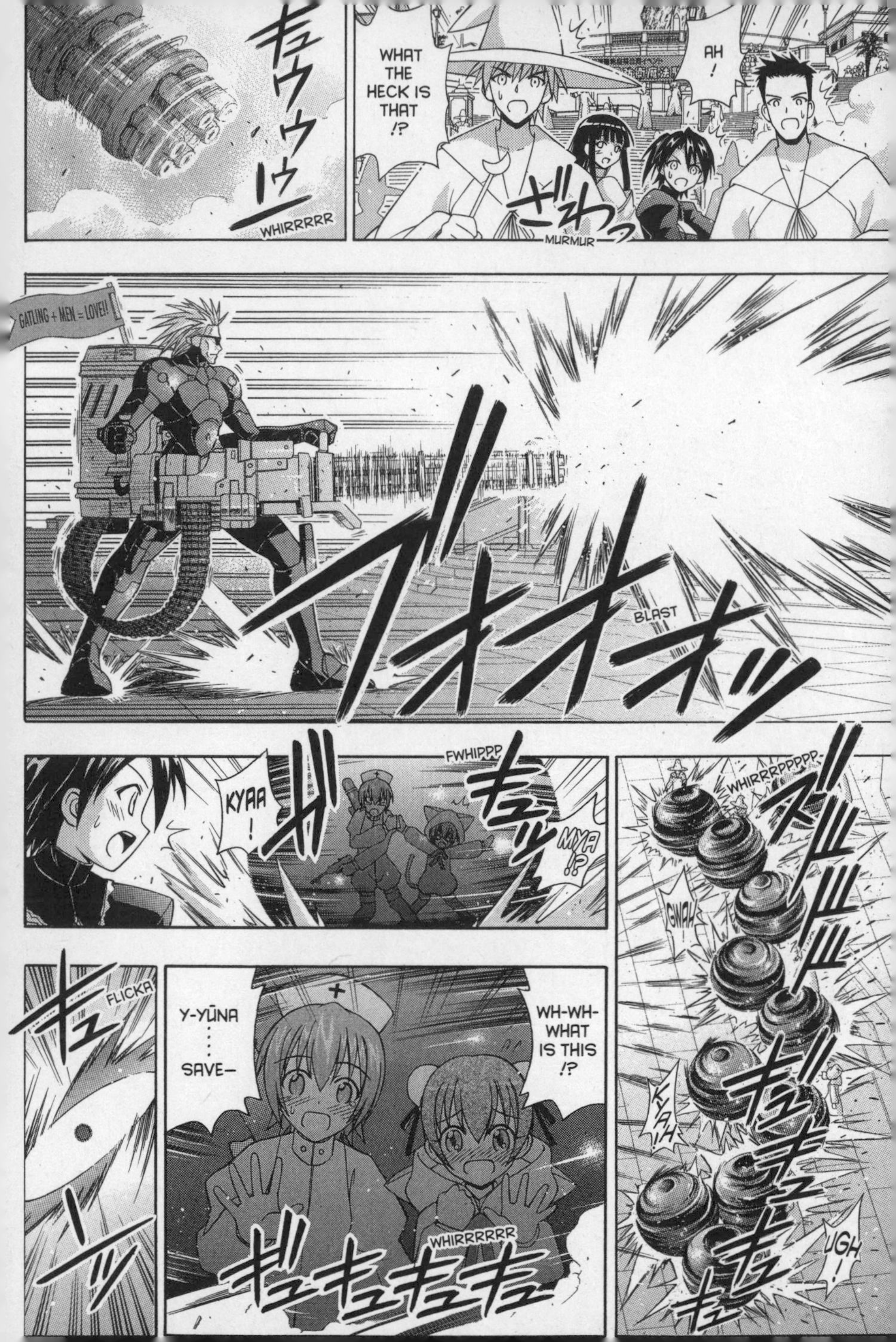
AH!
WHAT THE HECK IS THAT!?
MURMUR
WHIRRRRR
GATLING + MEN = LOVE!!
BLAST
WHIRRRPPPPP
GWAH
KYAH
UGH!
FWHIPPP
MYA!?
KYAA!
WH-WH-WHAT IS THIS!?
Y-YŪNA... SAVE—
WHIRRRRRR
FLICKA

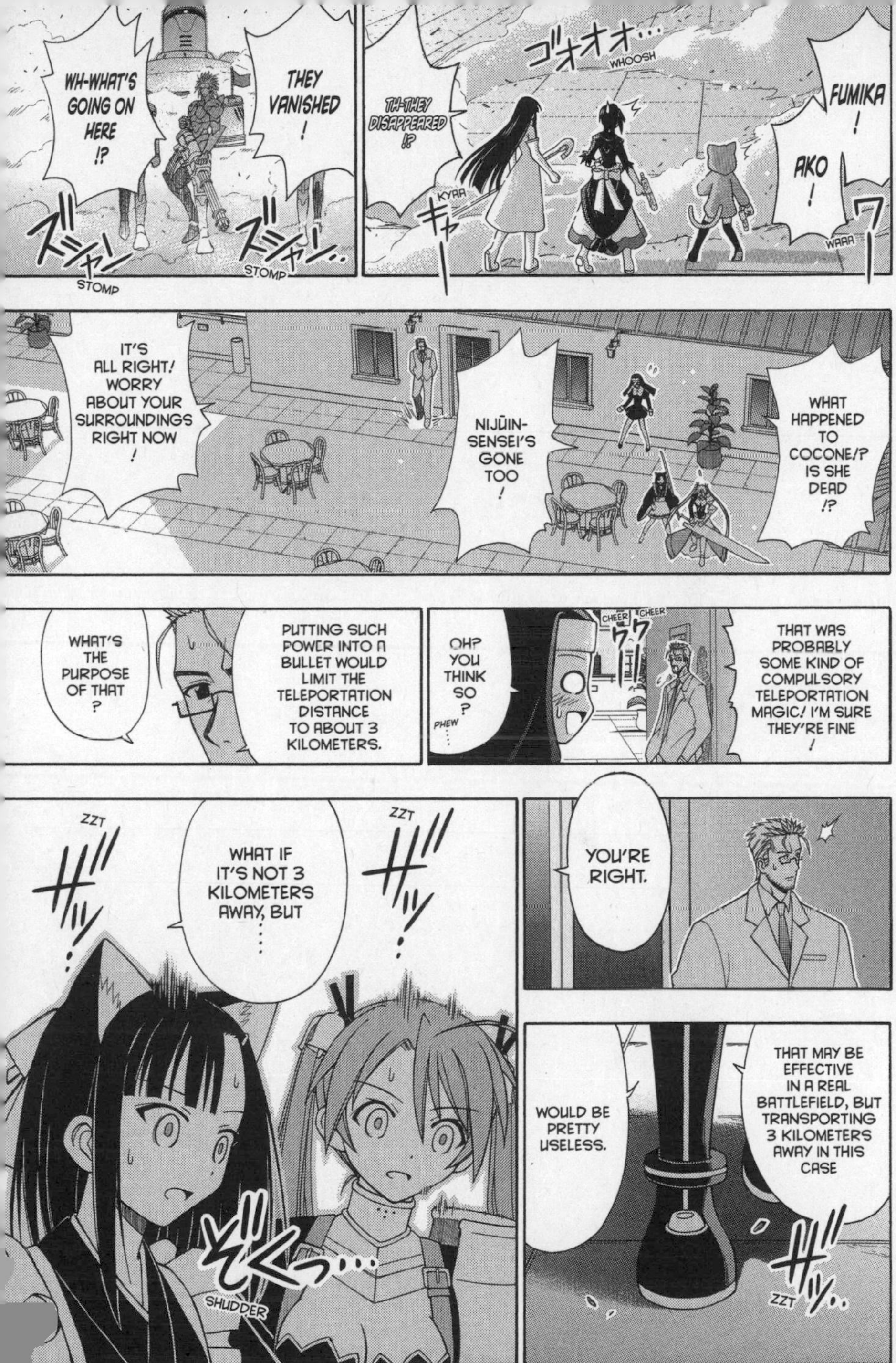
FUMIKA!
AKO!
ワー
WAAA
ゴオオオ…
WHOOSH
TH-THEY DISAPPEARED!?
キャー
KYAA
THEY VANISHED!
WH-WHAT'S GOING ON HERE!?
ズシャーン
STOMP
ズシャーン…
STOMP
WHAT HAPPENED TO COCONE!? IS SHE DEAD!?
NIJŪIN-SENSEI'S GONE TOO!
IT'S ALL RIGHT! WORRY ABOUT YOUR SURROUNDINGS RIGHT NOW!
THAT WAS PROBABLY SOME KIND OF COMPULSORY TELEPORTATION MAGIC! I'M SURE THEY'RE FINE!
ワーワー
CHEER CHEER
OH? YOU THINK SO?
PHEW…
PUTTING SUCH POWER INTO A BULLET WOULD LIMIT THE TELEPORTATION DISTANCE TO ABOUT 3 KILOMETERS.
WHAT'S THE PURPOSE OF THAT?
YOU'RE RIGHT.
THAT MAY BE EFFECTIVE IN A REAL BATTLEFIELD, BUT TRANSPORTING 3 KILOMETERS AWAY IN THIS CASE
WOULD BE PRETTY USELESS.
ザッ..
ZZT
ザッ!
ZZT
WHAT IF IT'S NOT 3 KILOMETERS AWAY, BUT…
ザッ!
ZZT
ぞくっ…
SHUDDER

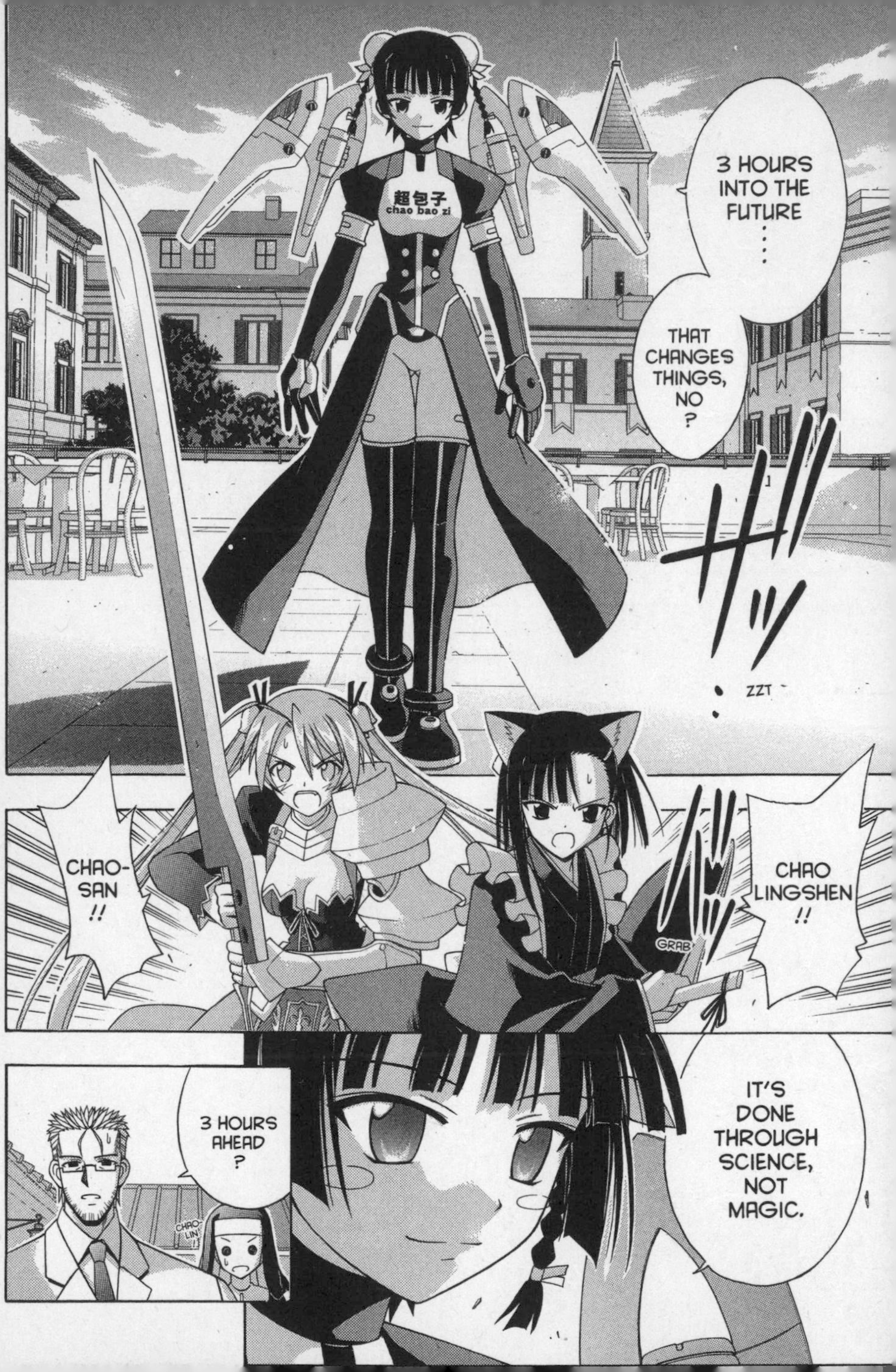

超包子
chao bao zi
3 HOURS INTO THE FUTURE ....
THAT CHANGES THINGS, NO ?
ZZT
CHAO LINGSHEN !!
GRAB
CHAO-SAN !!
IT'S DONE THROUGH SCIENCE, NOT MAGIC.
3 HOURS AHEAD ?
CHAO-LIN

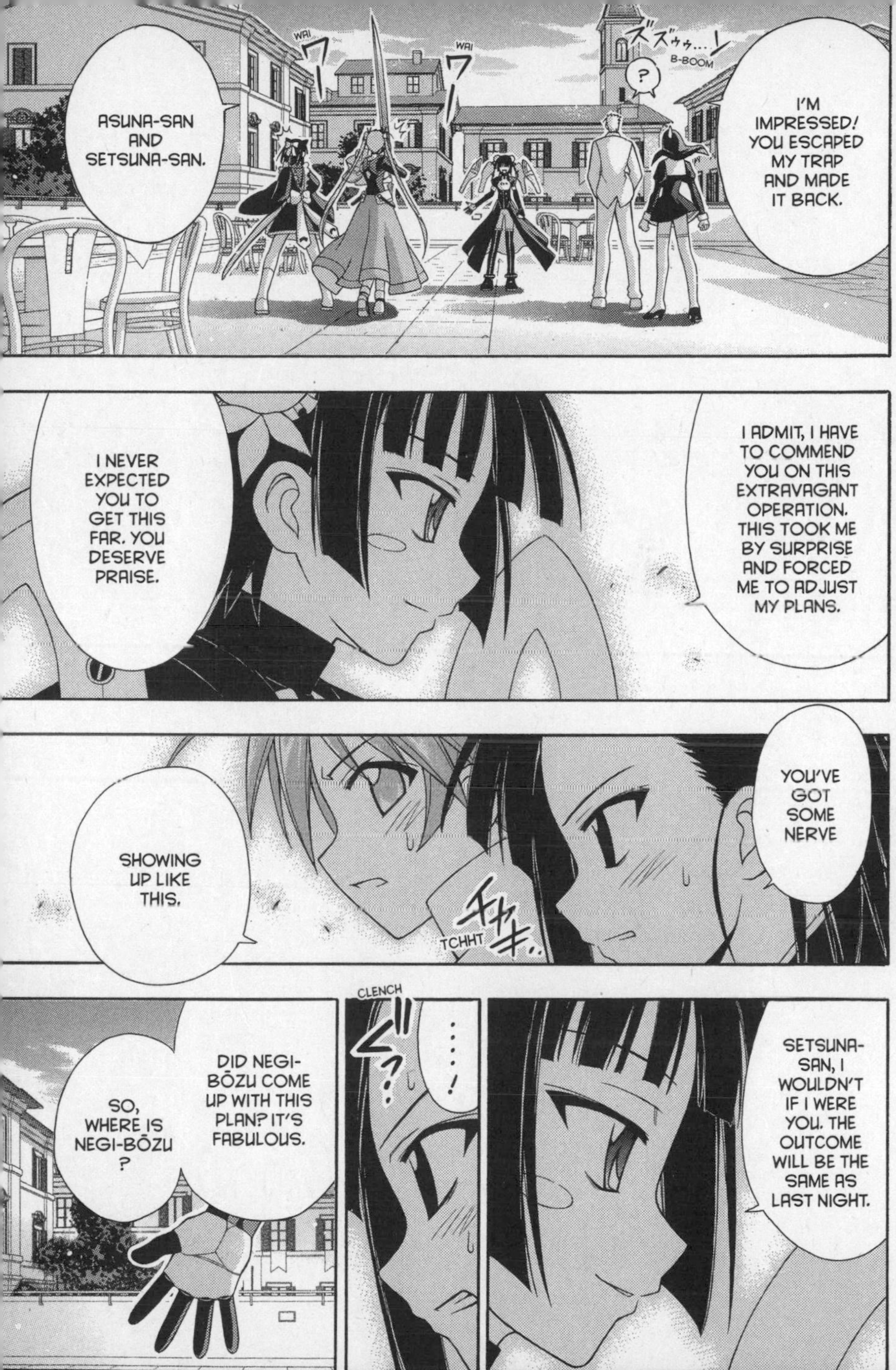
I'M IMPRESSED! YOU ESCAPED MY TRAP AND MADE IT BACK.
B-BOOM
?
WAI
WAI
ASUNA-SAN AND SETSUNA-SAN.
I ADMIT, I HAVE TO COMMEND YOU ON THIS EXTRAVAGANT OPERATION. THIS TOOK ME BY SURPRISE AND FORCED ME TO ADJUST MY PLANS.
I NEVER EXPECTED YOU TO GET THIS FAR. YOU DESERVE PRAISE.
YOU'VE GOT SOME NERVE
SHOWING UP LIKE THIS.
TCHHT
SETSUNA-SAN, I WOULDN'T IF I WERE YOU. THE OUTCOME WILL BE THE SAME AS LAST NIGHT.
CLENCH
...!
DID NEGI-BŌZU COME UP WITH THIS PLAN? IT'S FABULOUS.
SO, WHERE IS NEGI-BŌZU?

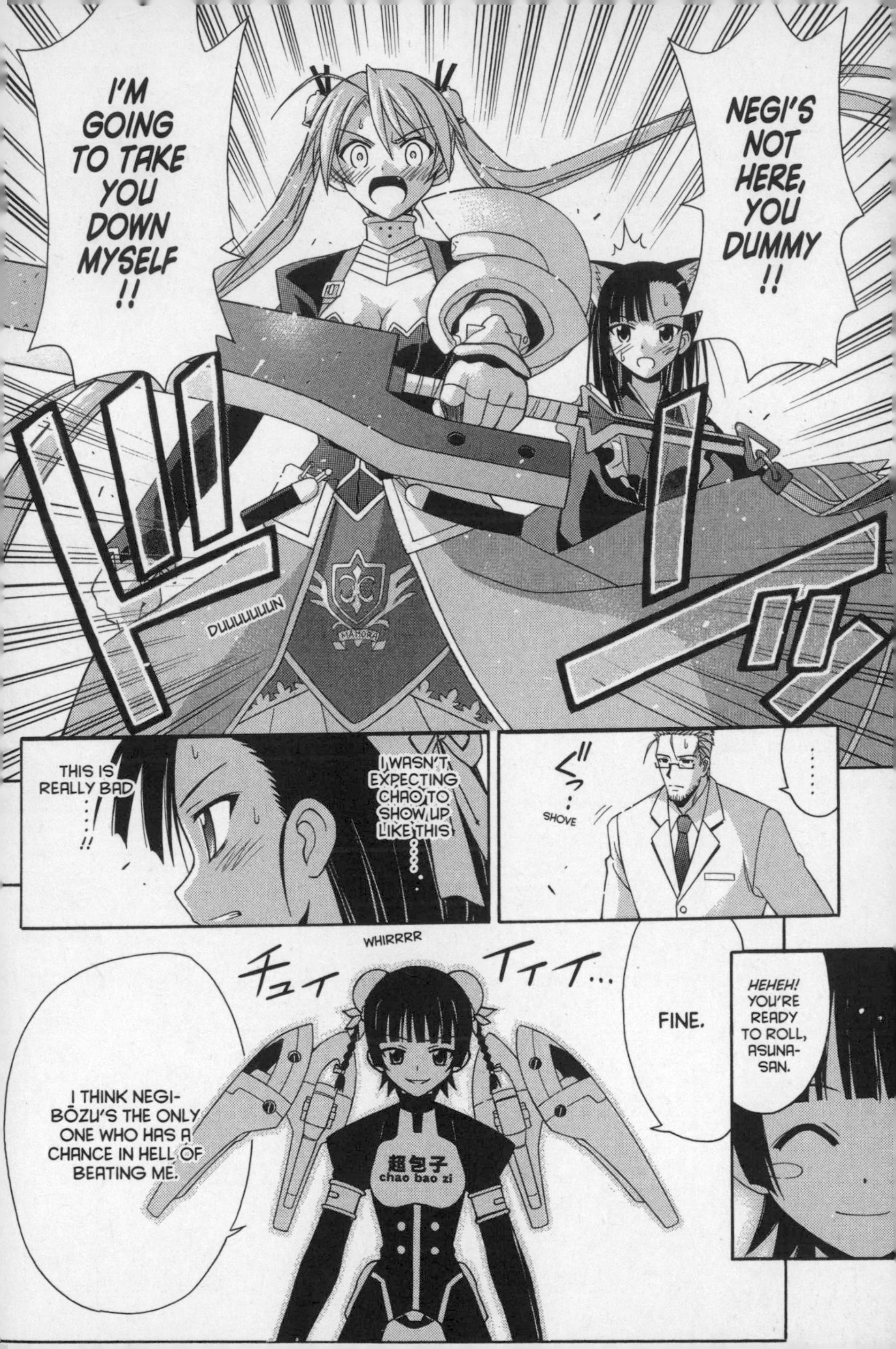
NEGI'S NOT HERE, YOU DUMMY !!
I'M GOING TO TAKE YOU DOWN MYSELF !!
DUUUUUUUN
......
SHOVE
I WASN'T EXPECTING CHAO TO SHOW UP LIKE THIS...
THIS IS REALLY BAD ...!!
HEHEH! YOU'RE READY TO ROLL, ASUNA-SAN.
FINE.
WHIRRRR
チュイイイイ...
I THINK NEGI-BŌZU'S THE ONLY ONE WHO HAS A CHANCE IN HELL OF BEATING ME.
超包子
chao bao zi

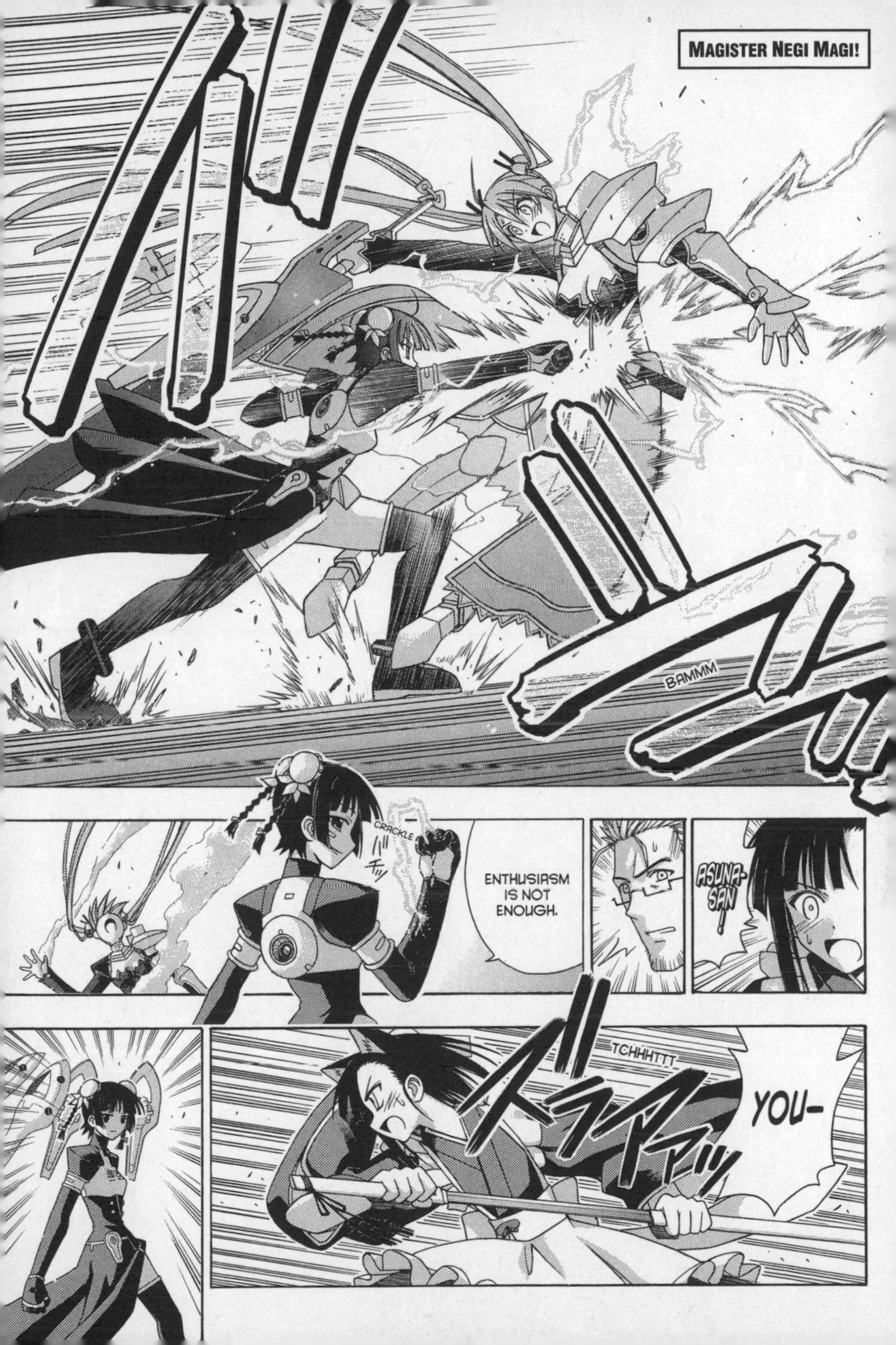
BAMMM
ASUNA-SAN
CRACKLE
ENTHUSIASM IS NOT ENOUGH.
TCHHHTTT
YOU–

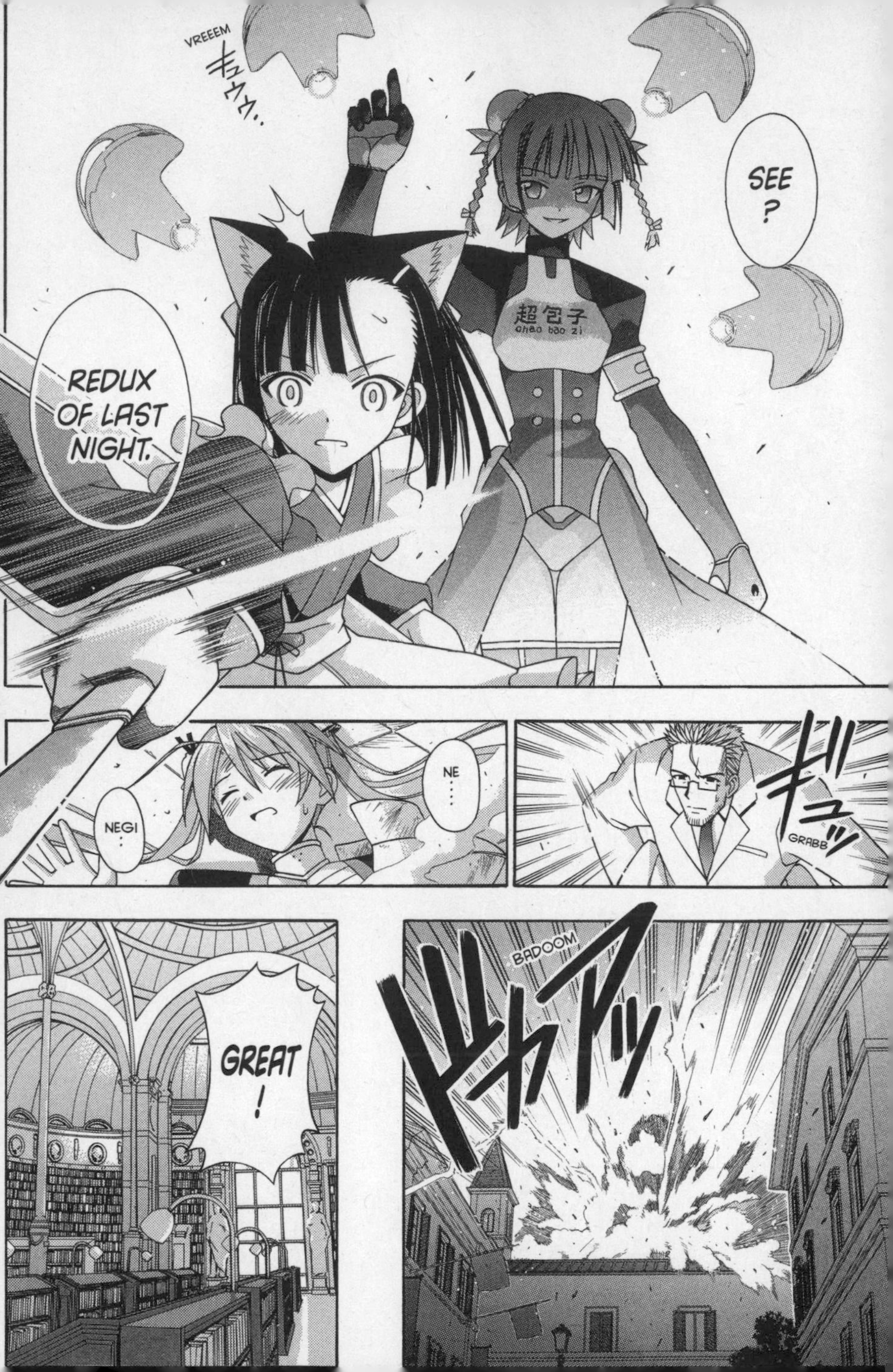
VREEEM
キュウウ..
SEE?
超包子
chao bao zi
REDUX OF LAST NIGHT.
ギュッ
GRABB
NE...
NEGI...
ドォアッ
BADOOM
GREAT!

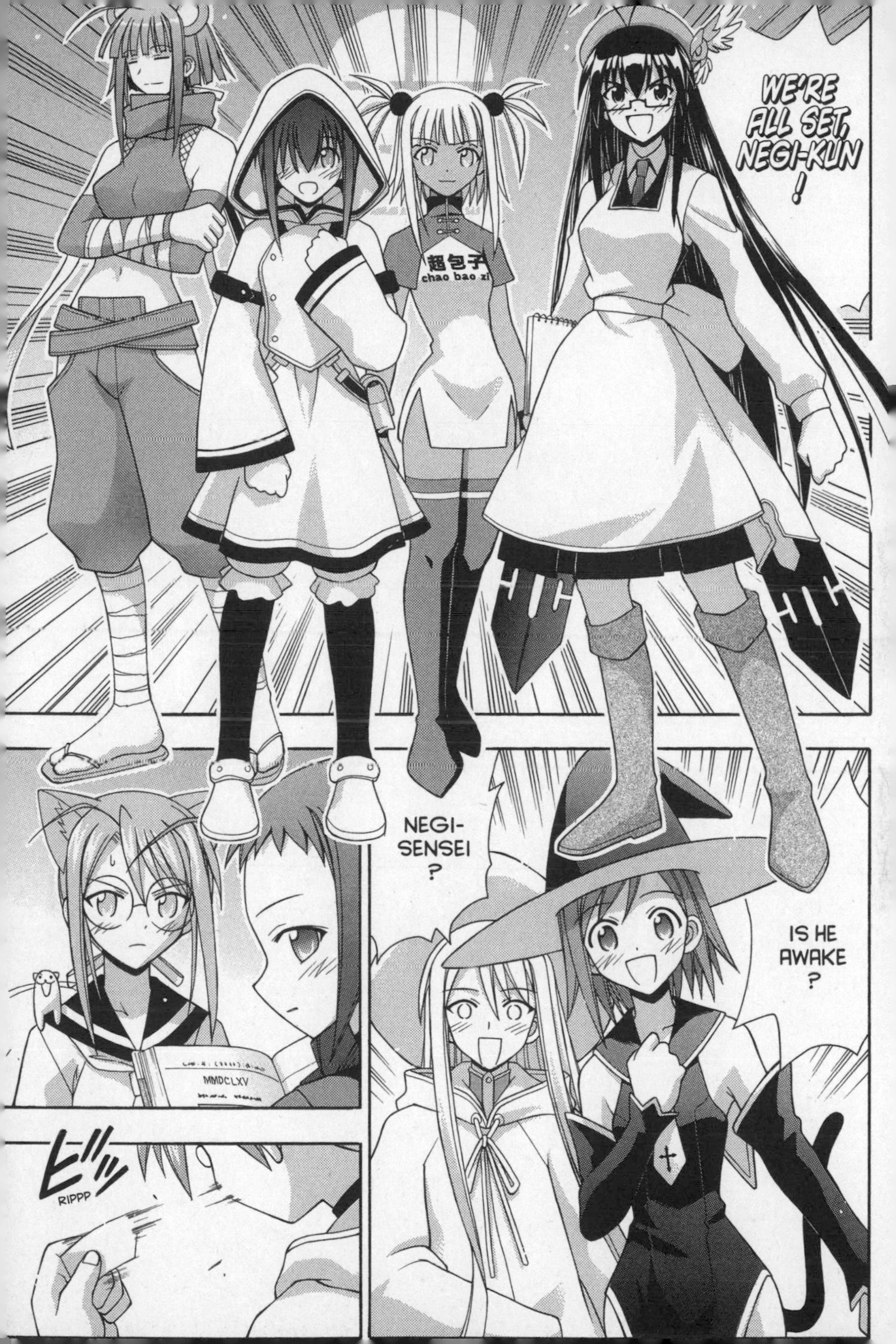
WE'RE ALL SET, NEGI-KUN!
超包子
chao bao zi
NEGI-SENSEI?
IS HE AWAKE?
MMDCLXV
ビッ
RIPPP

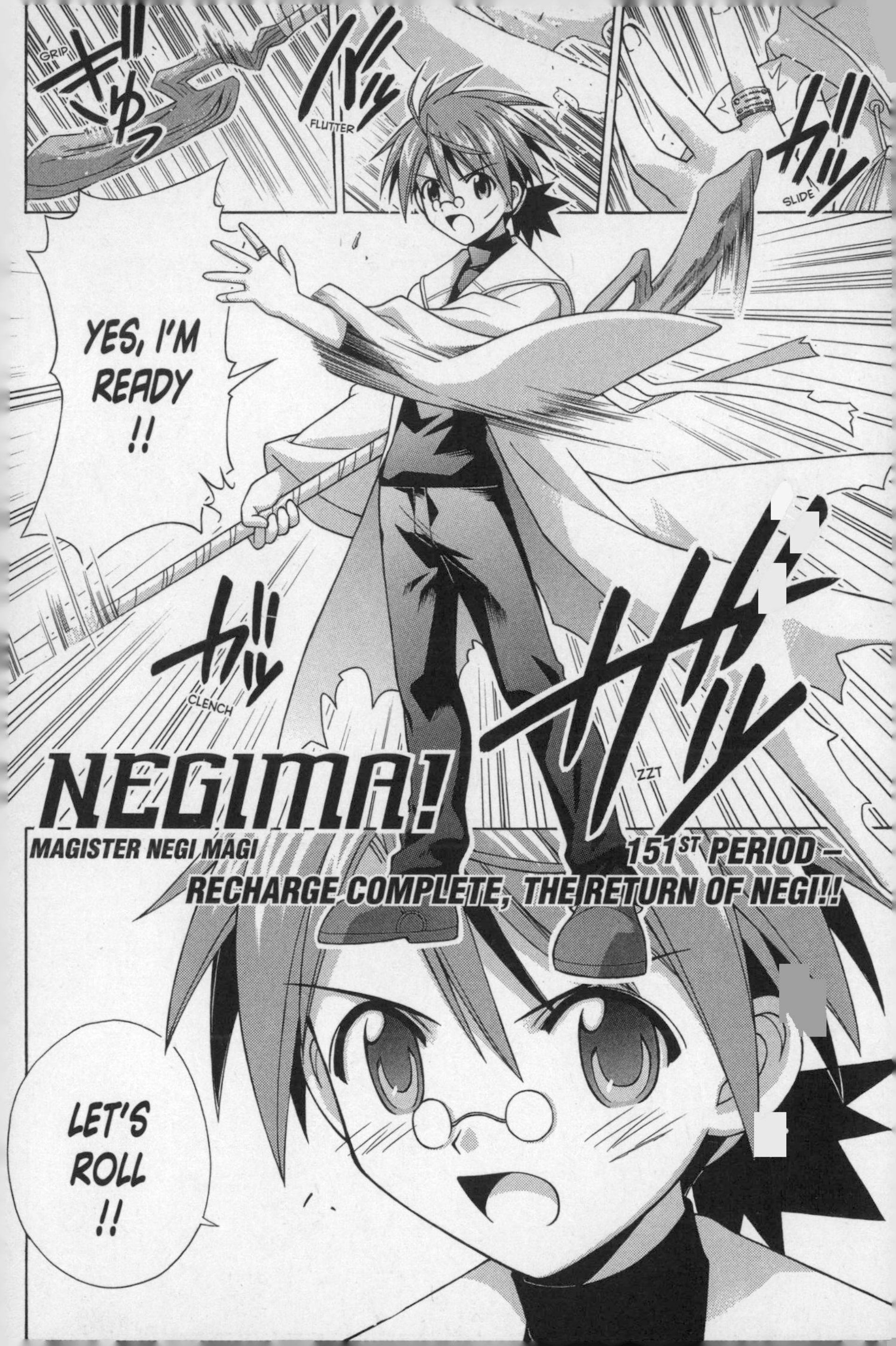
SLIDE
FLUTTER
GRIP
YES, I'M READY!!
CLENCH
ZZT
NEGIMA!
MAGISTER NEGI MAGI
151ST PERIOD – RECHARGE COMPLETE, THE RETURN OF NEGI!!
LET'S ROLL!!

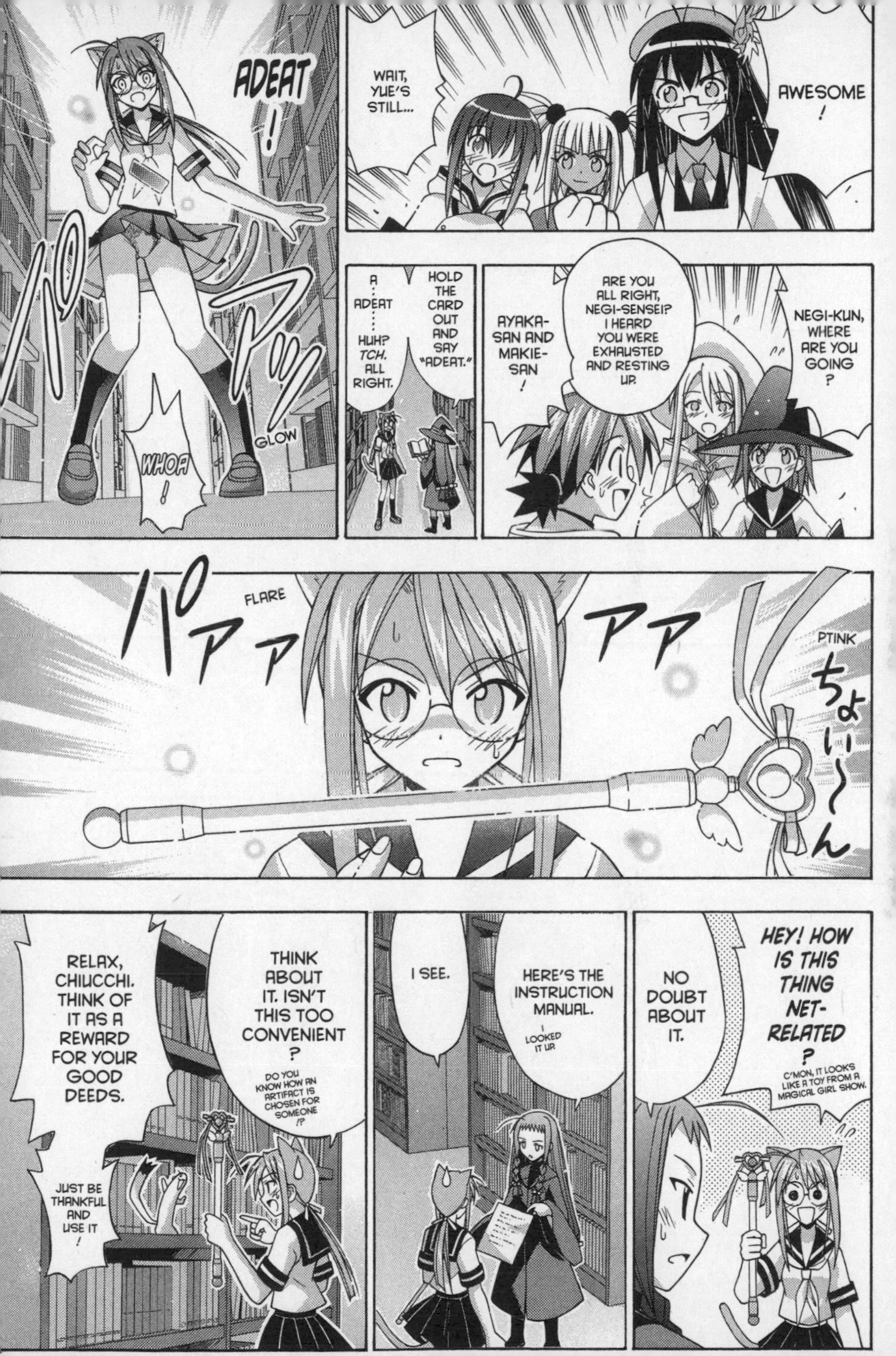
AWESOME!
WAIT, YUE'S STILL...
NEGI-KUN, WHERE ARE YOU GOING?
ARE YOU ALL RIGHT, NEGI-SENSEI? I HEARD YOU WERE EXHAUSTED AND RESTING UP.
AYAKA-SAN AND MAKIE-SAN!
HOLD THE CARD OUT AND SAY "ADEAT."
A... ADEAT... HUH? TCH. ALL RIGHT.
ADEAT!
GLOW
WHOA!
FLARE
PTINK
ちょい～ん
HEY! HOW IS THIS THING NET-RELATED?
C'MON, IT LOOKS LIKE A TOY FROM A MAGICAL GIRL SHOW.
NO DOUBT ABOUT IT.
HERE'S THE INSTRUCTION MANUAL.
I LOOKED IT UP.
I SEE.
THINK ABOUT IT. ISN'T THIS TOO CONVENIENT?
DO YOU KNOW HOW AN ARTIFACT IS CHOSEN FOR SOMEONE!?
RELAX, CHIUCCHI. THINK OF IT AS A REWARD FOR YOUR GOOD DEEDS.
JUST BE THANKFUL AND USE IT!

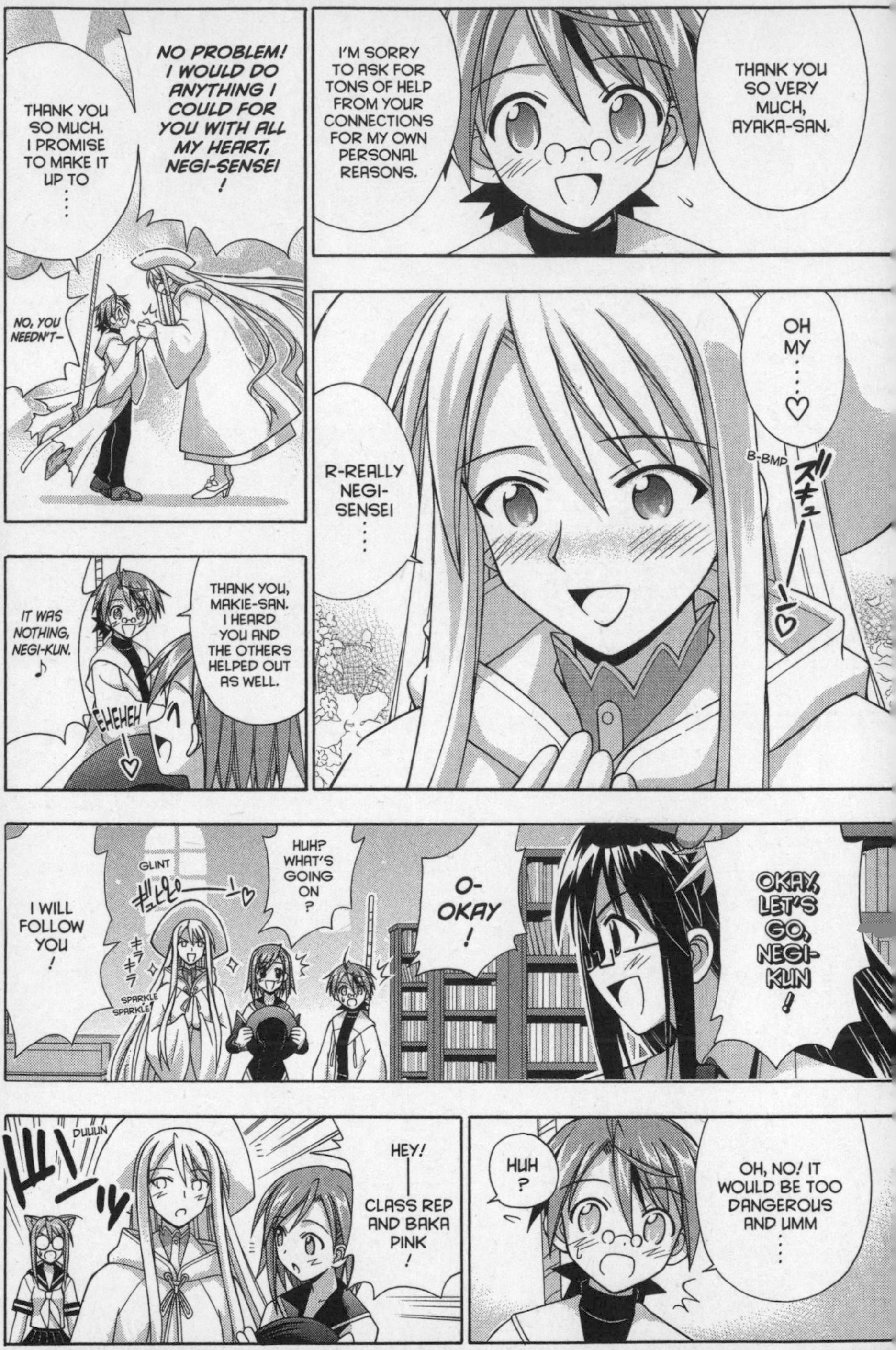
THANK YOU SO VERY MUCH, AYAKA-SAN.
I'M SORRY TO ASK FOR TONS OF HELP FROM YOUR CONNECTIONS FOR MY OWN PERSONAL REASONS.
OH MY ....♡
B-BMP
R-REALLY NEGI-SENSEI ....
NO PROBLEM! I WOULD DO ANYTHING I COULD FOR YOU WITH ALL MY HEART, NEGI-SENSEI!
THANK YOU SO MUCH. I PROMISE TO MAKE IT UP TO ....
NO, YOU NEEDN'T-
THANK YOU, MAKIE-SAN. I HEARD YOU AND THE OTHERS HELPED OUT AS WELL.
IT WAS NOTHING, NEGI-KUN. ♪
EHEHEH ♡
OKAY, LET'S GO, NEGI-KUN!
O-OKAY!
HUH? WHAT'S GOING ON?
GLINT
I WILL FOLLOW YOU!
SPARKLE SPARKLE
OH, NO! IT WOULD BE TOO DANGEROUS AND UMM ....
HUH?
HEY! — CLASS REP AND BAKA PINK!
DUUUN

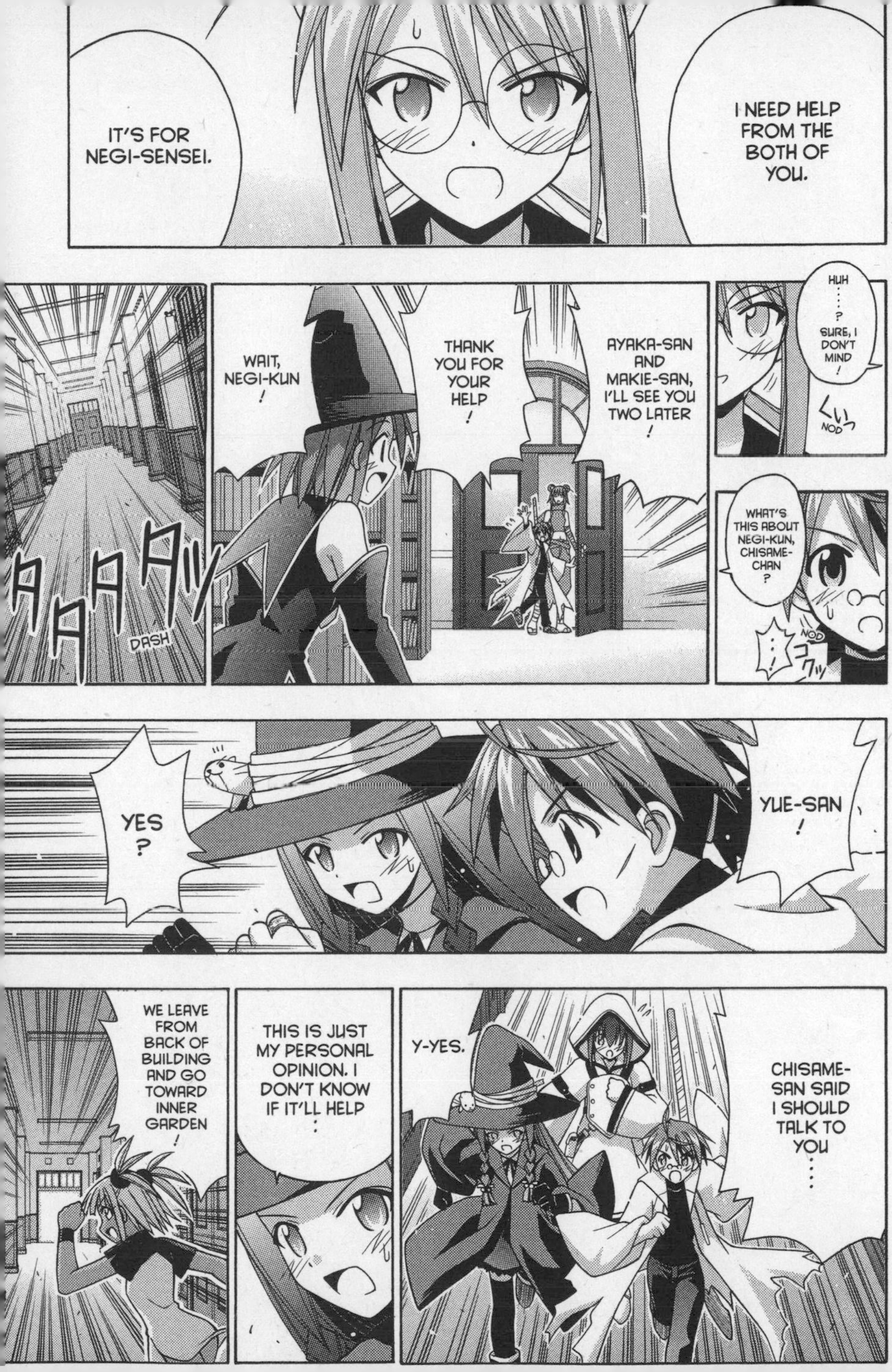
I NEED HELP FROM THE BOTH OF YOU.
IT'S FOR NEGI-SENSEI.
HUH...? SURE, I DON'T MIND!
NOD
WHAT'S THIS ABOUT NEGI-KUN, CHISAME-CHAN?
NOD
AYAKA-SAN AND MAKIE-SAN, I'LL SEE YOU TWO LATER!
THANK YOU FOR YOUR HELP!
WAIT, NEGI-KUN!
DASH
YUE-SAN!
YES?
CHISAME-SAN SAID I SHOULD TALK TO YOU....
Y-YES.
THIS IS JUST MY PERSONAL OPINION. I DON'T KNOW IF IT'LL HELP...
WE LEAVE FROM BACK OF BUILDING AND GO TOWARD INNER GARDEN!

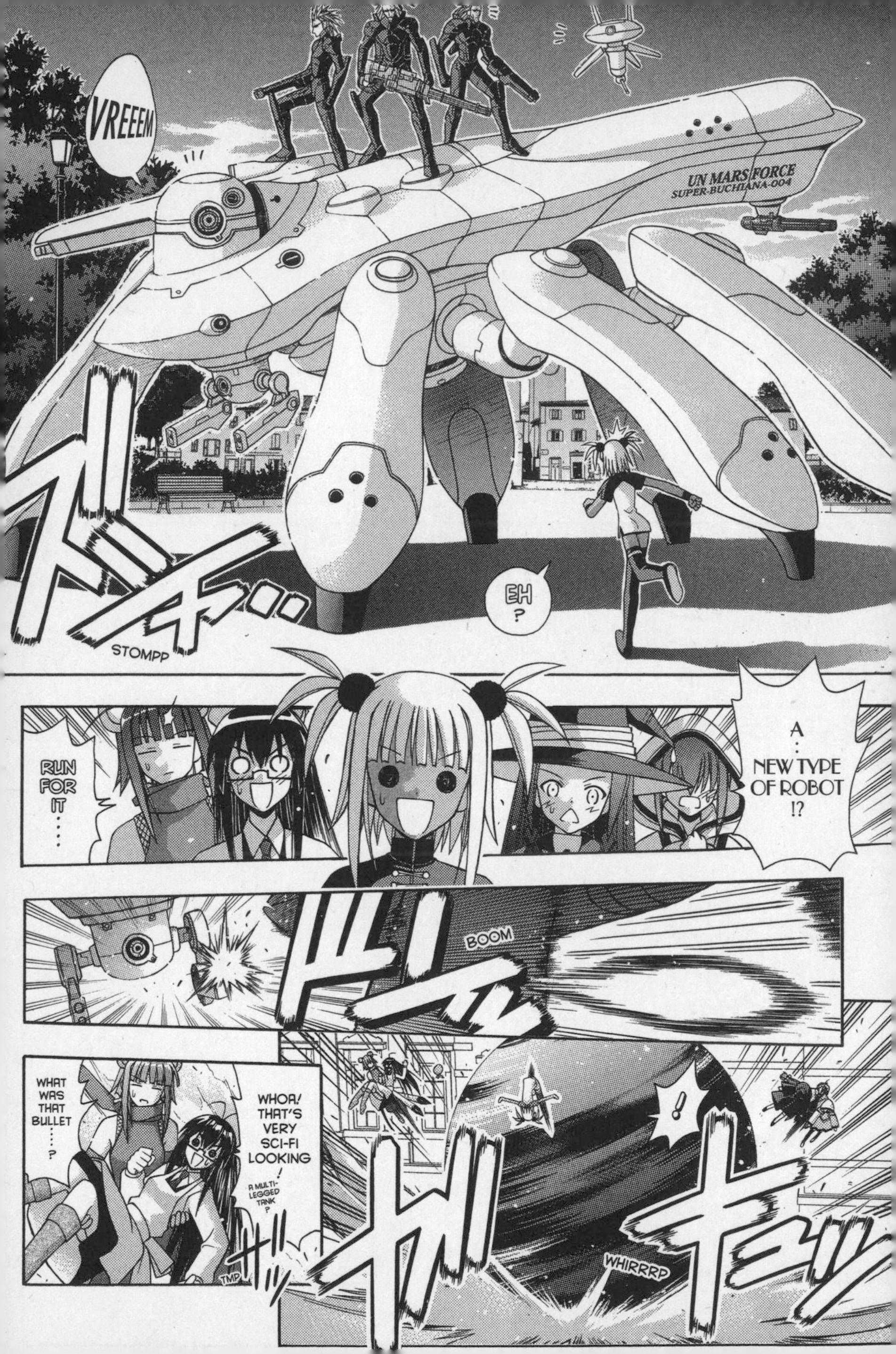
UN MARS FORCE
SUPER-BUCHIANA-004
VREEEM
EH ?
STOMPP
A ... NEW TYPE OF ROBOT !?
RUN FOR IT .....
BOOM
!
WHIRRRP
WHOA! THAT'S VERY SCI-FI LOOKING !
WHAT WAS THAT BULLET .....?
A MULTI-LEGGED TANK ?
TMP

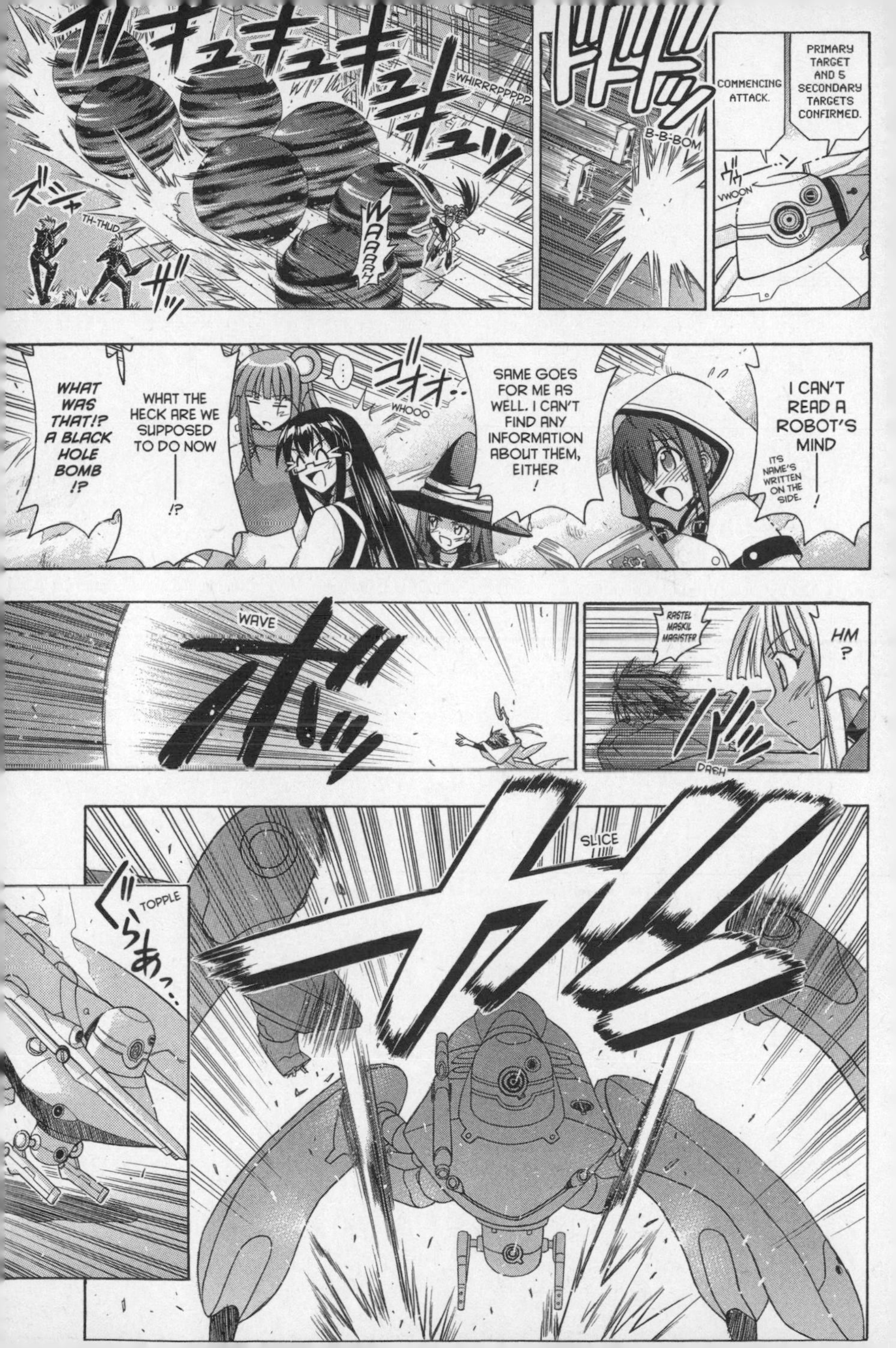
PRIMARY TARGET AND 5 SECONDARY TARGETS CONFIRMED.
COMMENCING ATTACK.
VWOON
B-B-BOM
WHIRRRPPPPP
WAAAAAH!
TH-THUD
I CAN'T READ A ROBOT'S MIND —!
ITS NAME'S WRITTEN ON THE SIDE.
SAME GOES FOR ME AS WELL. I CAN'T FIND ANY INFORMATION ABOUT THEM, EITHER!
WHOOO
...
WHAT THE HECK ARE WE SUPPOSED TO DO NOW —!?
WHAT WAS THAT!? A BLACK HOLE BOMB!?
HM?
RASTEL MASKIL MAGISTER
DASH
WAVE
SLICE
TOPPLE

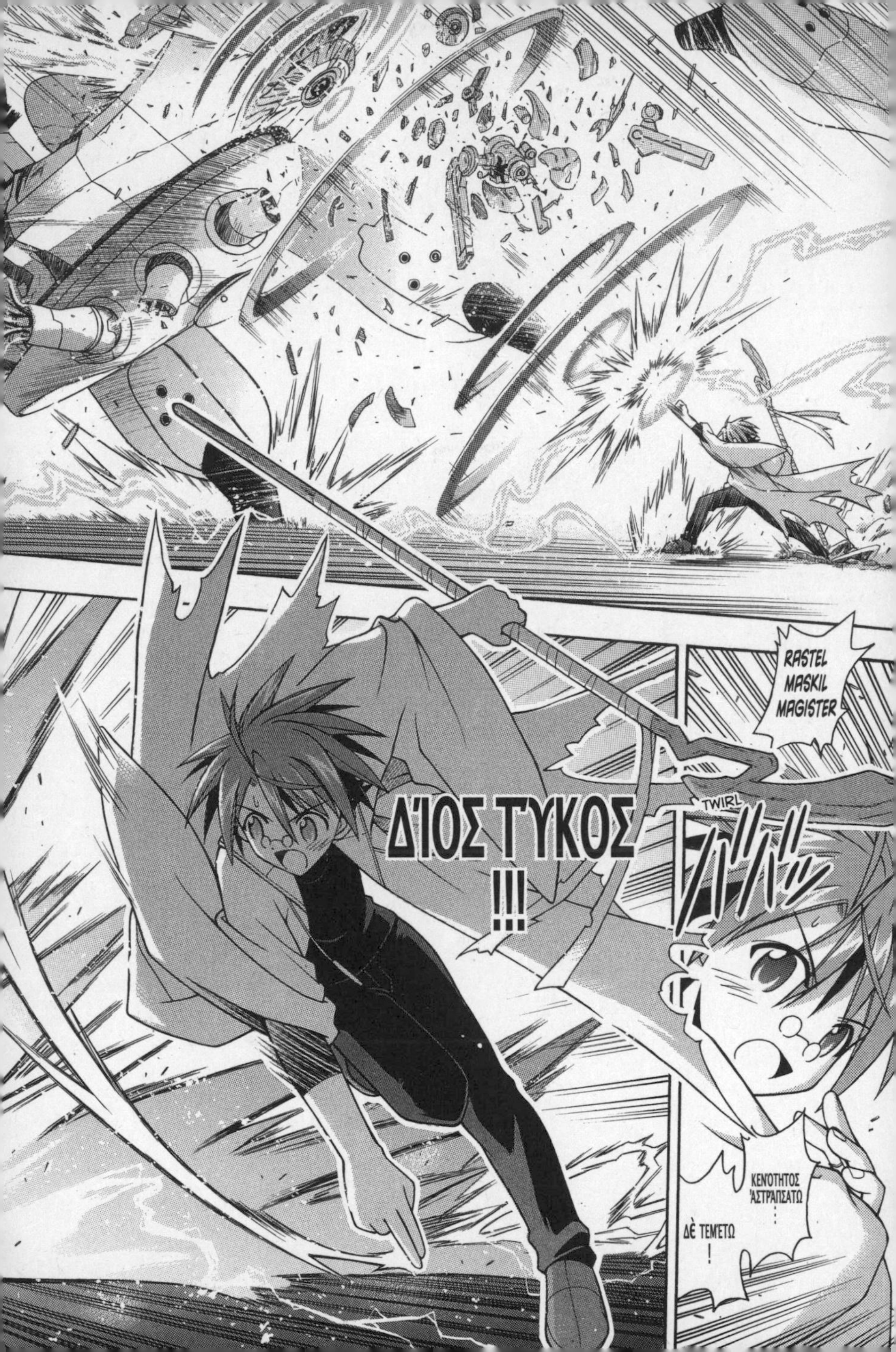
RASTEL MASKIL MAGISTER
TWIRL
ΚΕΝΌΤΗΤΟΣ ἈΣΤΡΆΠΣΑΤΩ ...
ΔΈ ΤΕΜΈΤΩ !
ΔΊΟΣ ΤΥΚΟΣ !!!

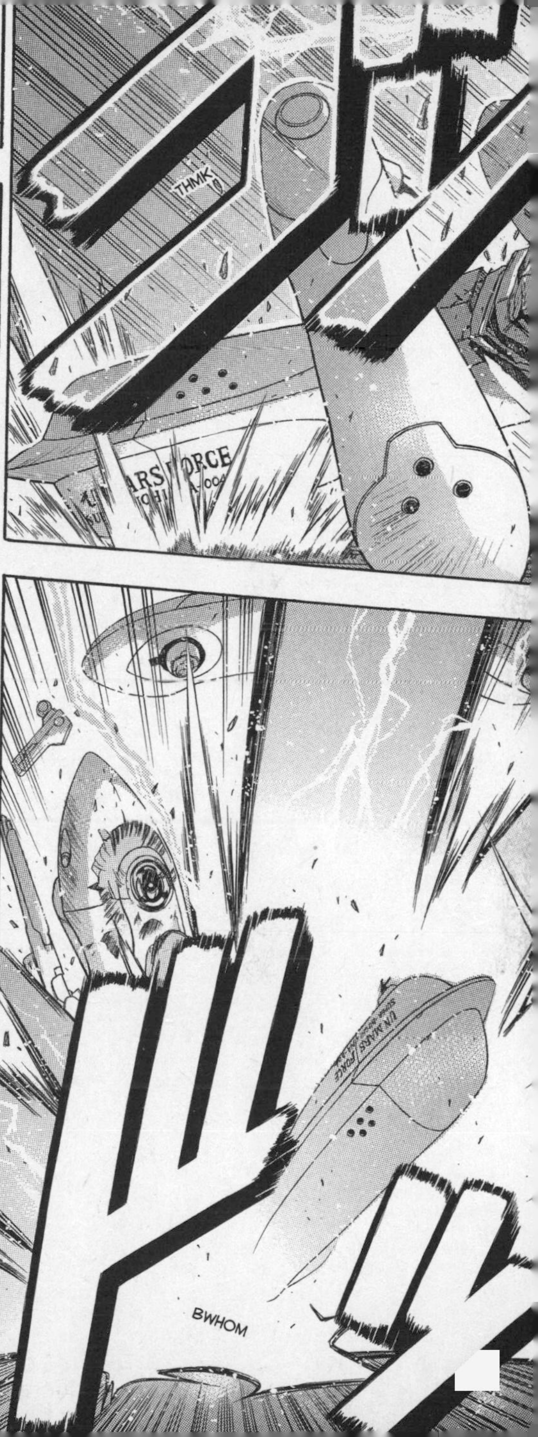
THMK
BWHOM
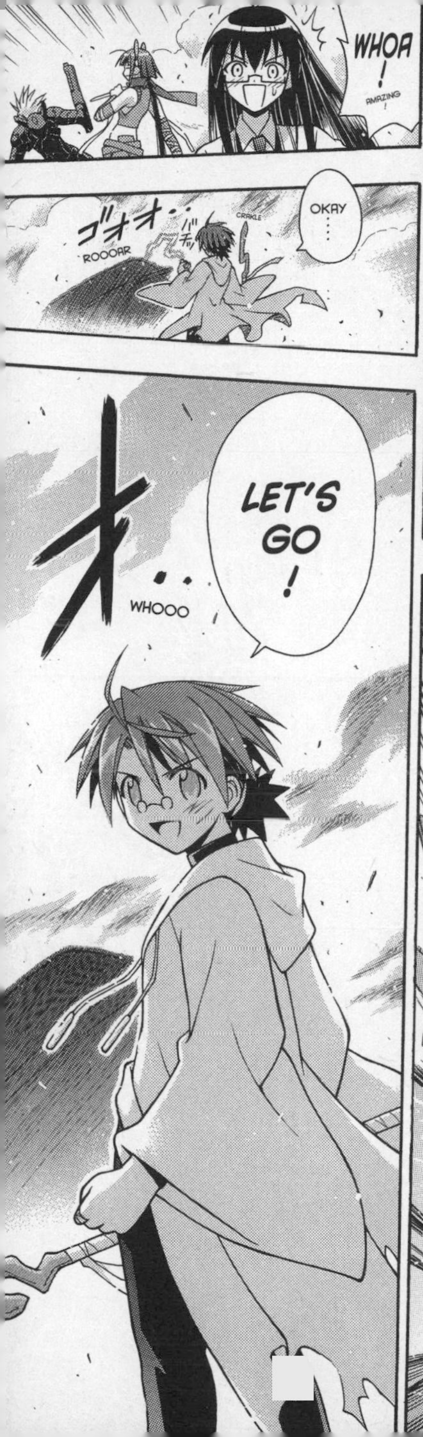
WHOA !
AMAZING !
ゴオオ‥
ROOOAR
バチッ
CRAKLE
OKAY ...
LET'S GO !
WHOOO

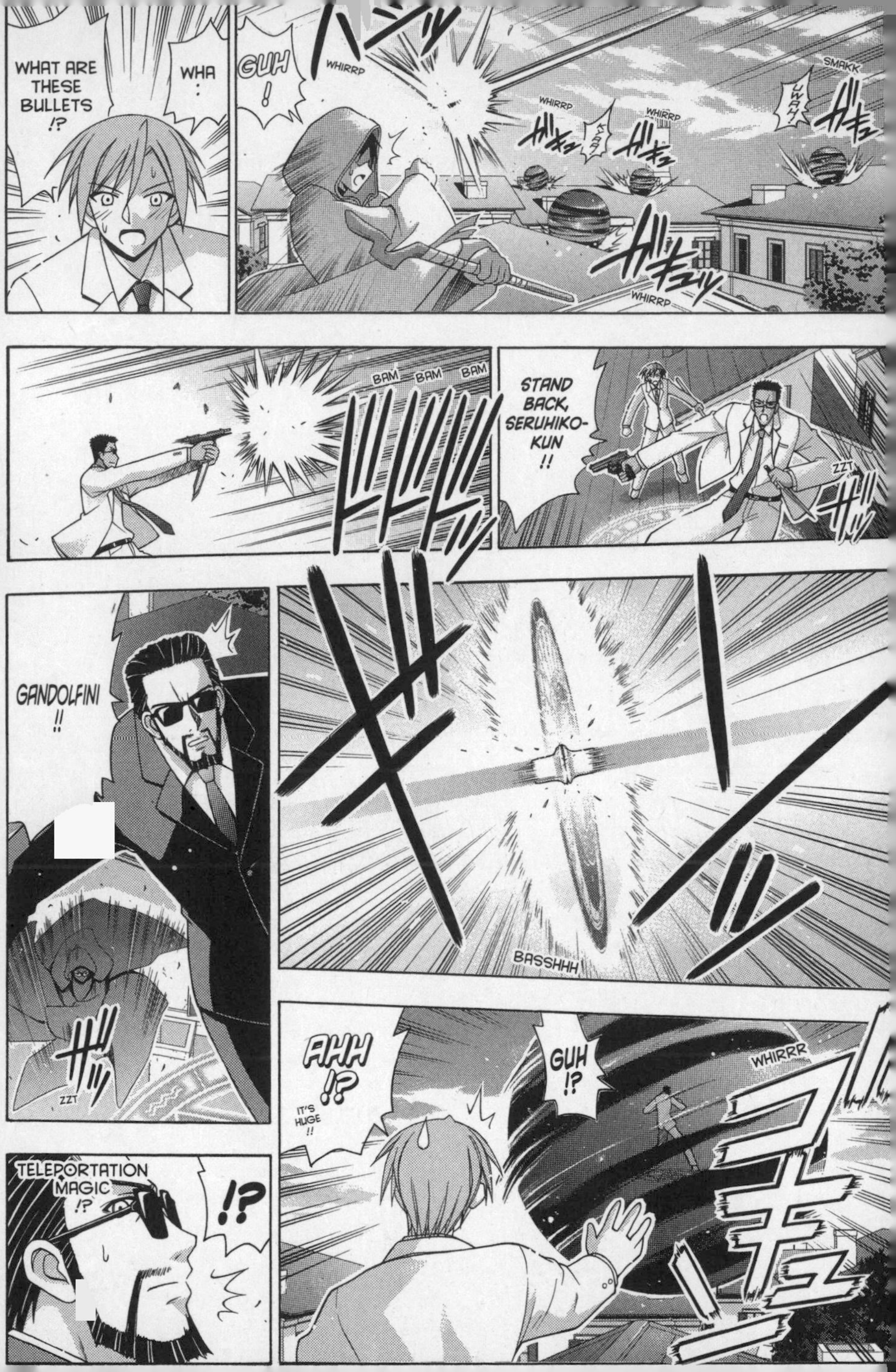
GUH
!
WHIRRP
WHIRRP
WHIRRP
SMAKK
UWAH!
WHIRRP
WHA
:
WHAT ARE THESE BULLETS !?
STAND BACK, SERUHIKO-KUN !!
ZZT
BAM BAM BAM
BASSHHH
GANDOLFINI !!
ZZT
GUH !?
AHH !?
IT'S HUGE !!
WHIRRR
!?
TELEPORTATION MAGIC !?

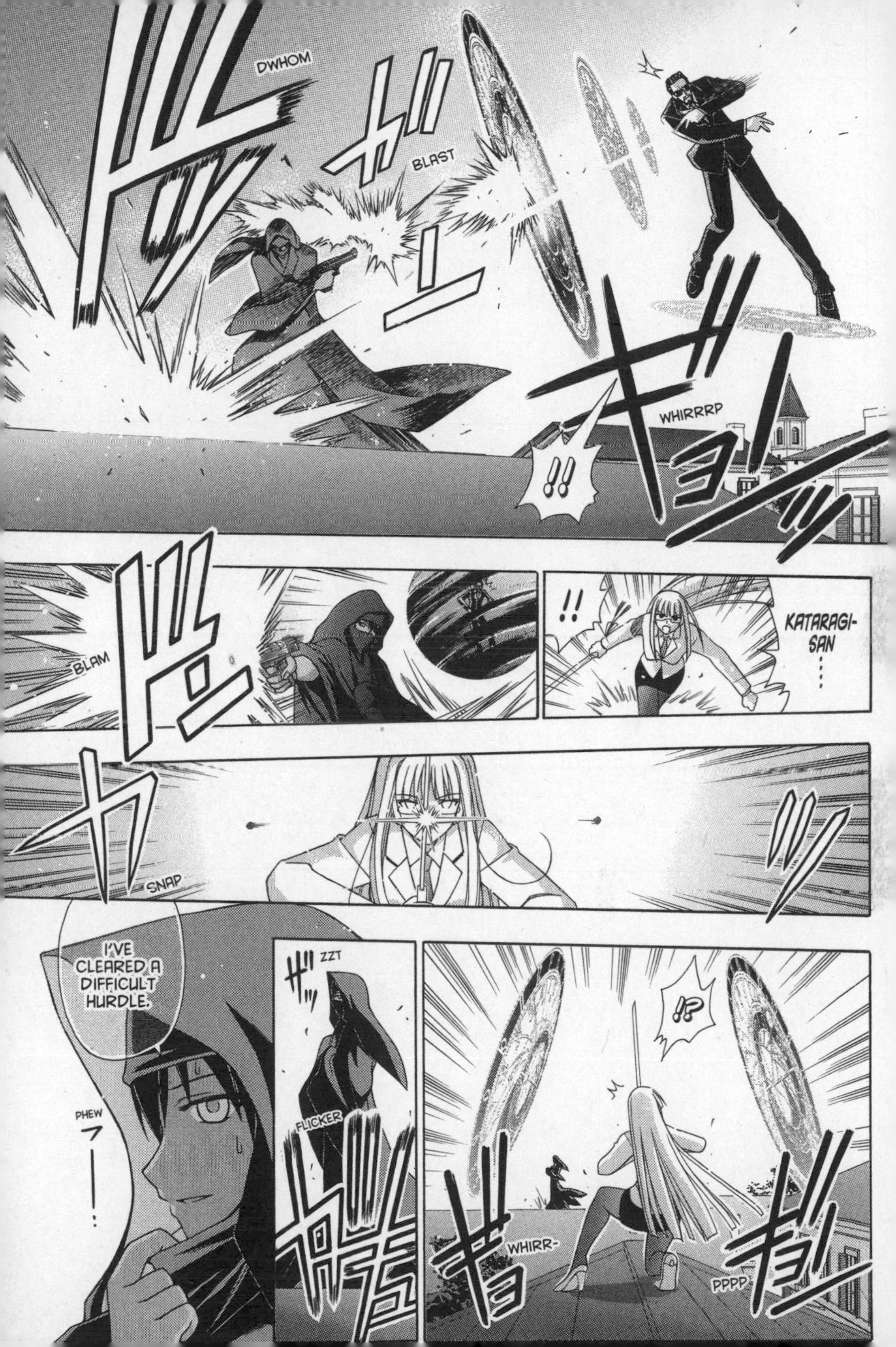
DWHOM
BLAST
WHIRRRP
!!
KATARAGI-SAN ...
!!
BLAM
SNAP
!?
WHIRR-
PPPP
ZZT
FLICKER
I'VE CLEARED A DIFFICULT HURDLE.
PHEW

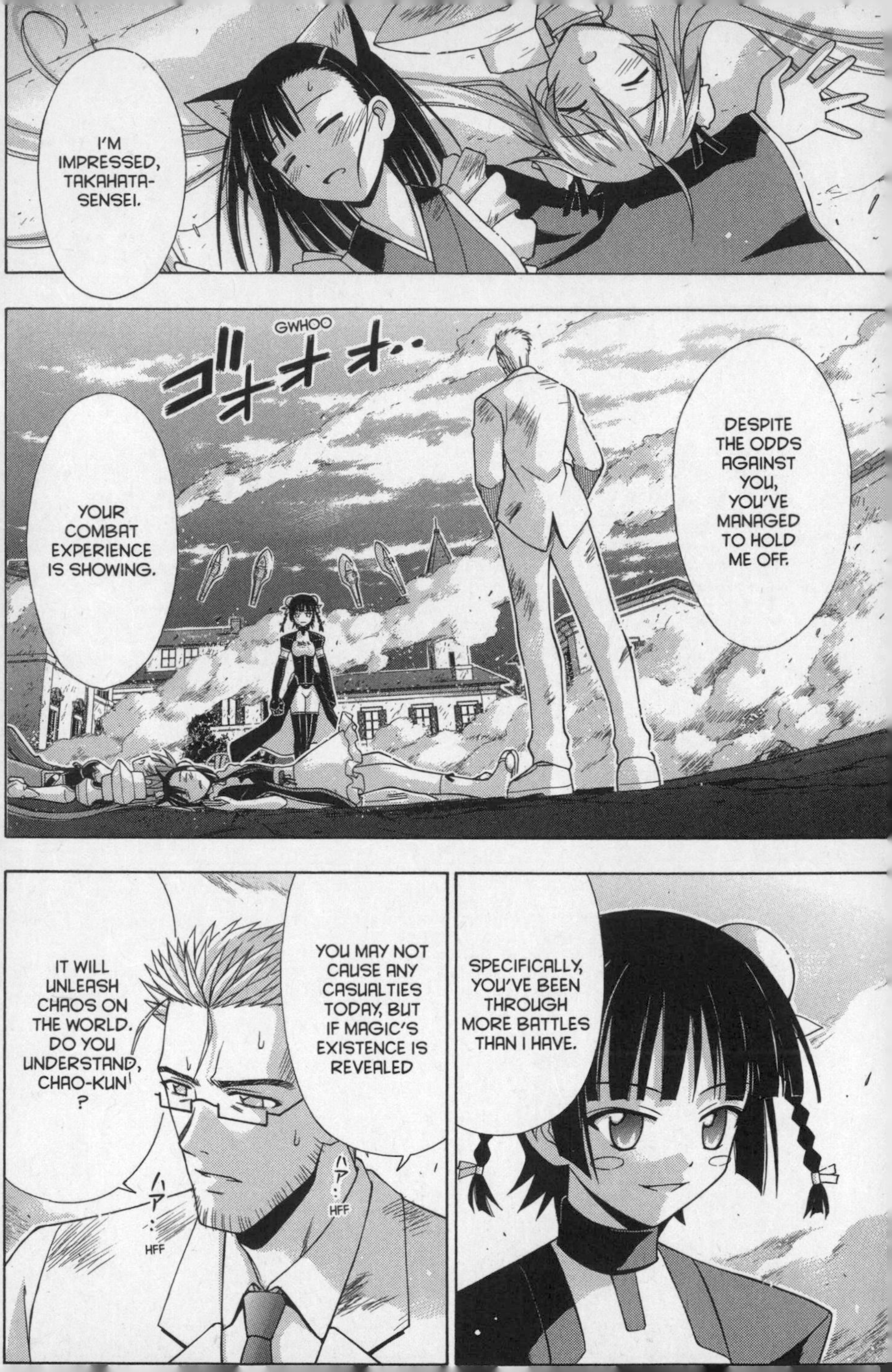

I'M IMPRESSED, TAKAHATA-SENSEI.
DESPITE THE ODDS AGAINST YOU, YOU'VE MANAGED TO HOLD ME OFF.
GWHOO
YOUR COMBAT EXPERIENCE IS SHOWING.
SPECIFICALLY, YOU'VE BEEN THROUGH MORE BATTLES THAN I HAVE.
YOU MAY NOT CAUSE ANY CASUALTIES TODAY, BUT IF MAGIC'S EXISTENCE IS REVEALED
HFF
IT WILL UNLEASH CHAOS ON THE WORLD. DO YOU UNDERSTAND, CHAO-KUN?
HFF

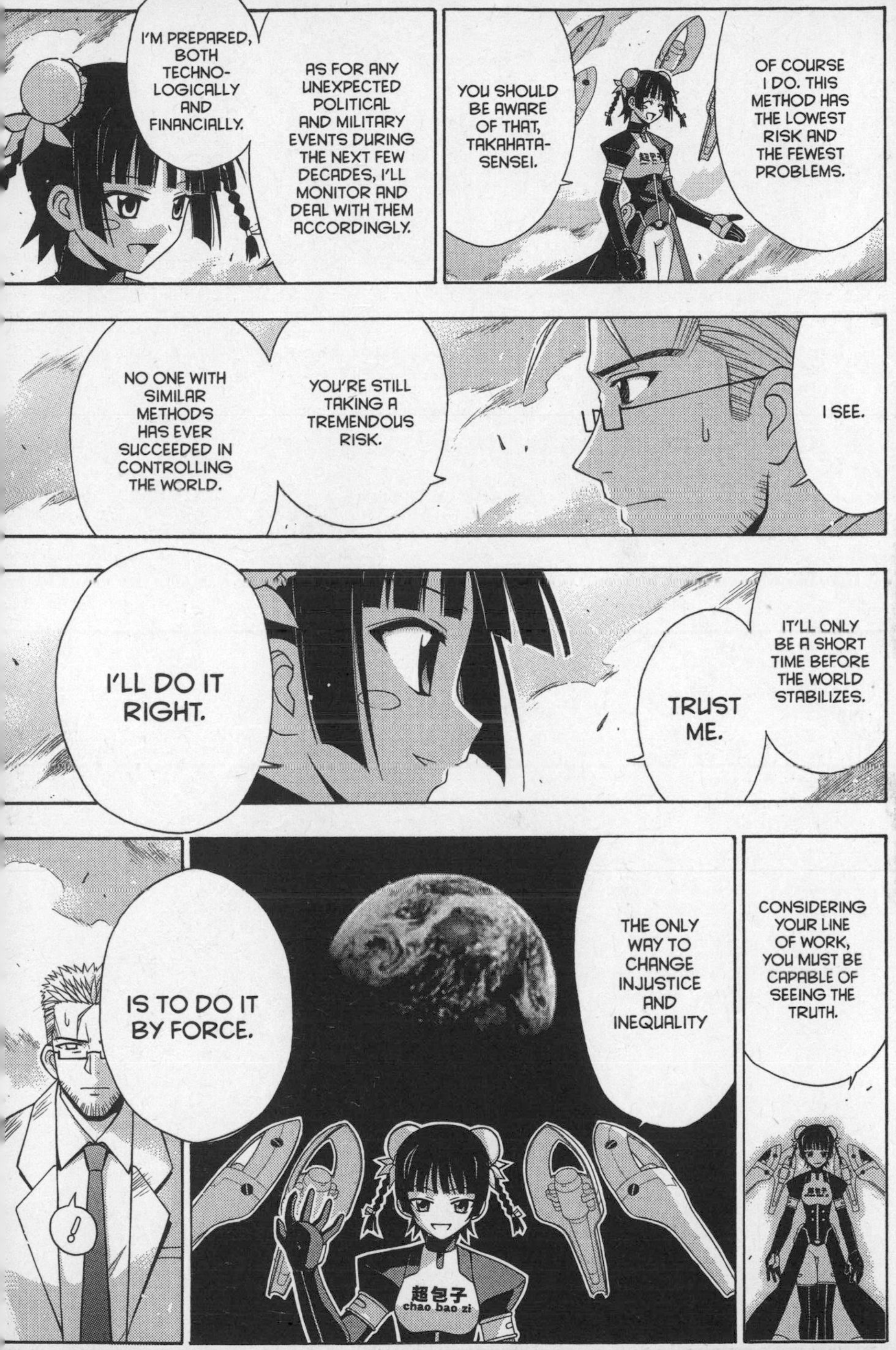
OF COURSE I DO. THIS METHOD HAS THE LOWEST RISK AND THE FEWEST PROBLEMS.
YOU SHOULD BE AWARE OF THAT, TAKAHATA-SENSEI.
AS FOR ANY UNEXPECTED POLITICAL AND MILITARY EVENTS DURING THE NEXT FEW DECADES, I'LL MONITOR AND DEAL WITH THEM ACCORDINGLY.
I'M PREPARED, BOTH TECHNO-LOGICALLY AND FINANCIALLY.
I SEE.
YOU'RE STILL TAKING A TREMENDOUS RISK.
NO ONE WITH SIMILAR METHODS HAS EVER SUCCEEDED IN CONTROLLING THE WORLD.
IT'LL ONLY BE A SHORT TIME BEFORE THE WORLD STABILIZES.
TRUST ME.
I'LL DO IT RIGHT.
CONSIDERING YOUR LINE OF WORK, YOU MUST BE CAPABLE OF SEEING THE TRUTH.
THE ONLY WAY TO CHANGE INJUSTICE AND INEQUALITY
超包子
chao bao zi
IS TO DO IT BY FORCE.
!

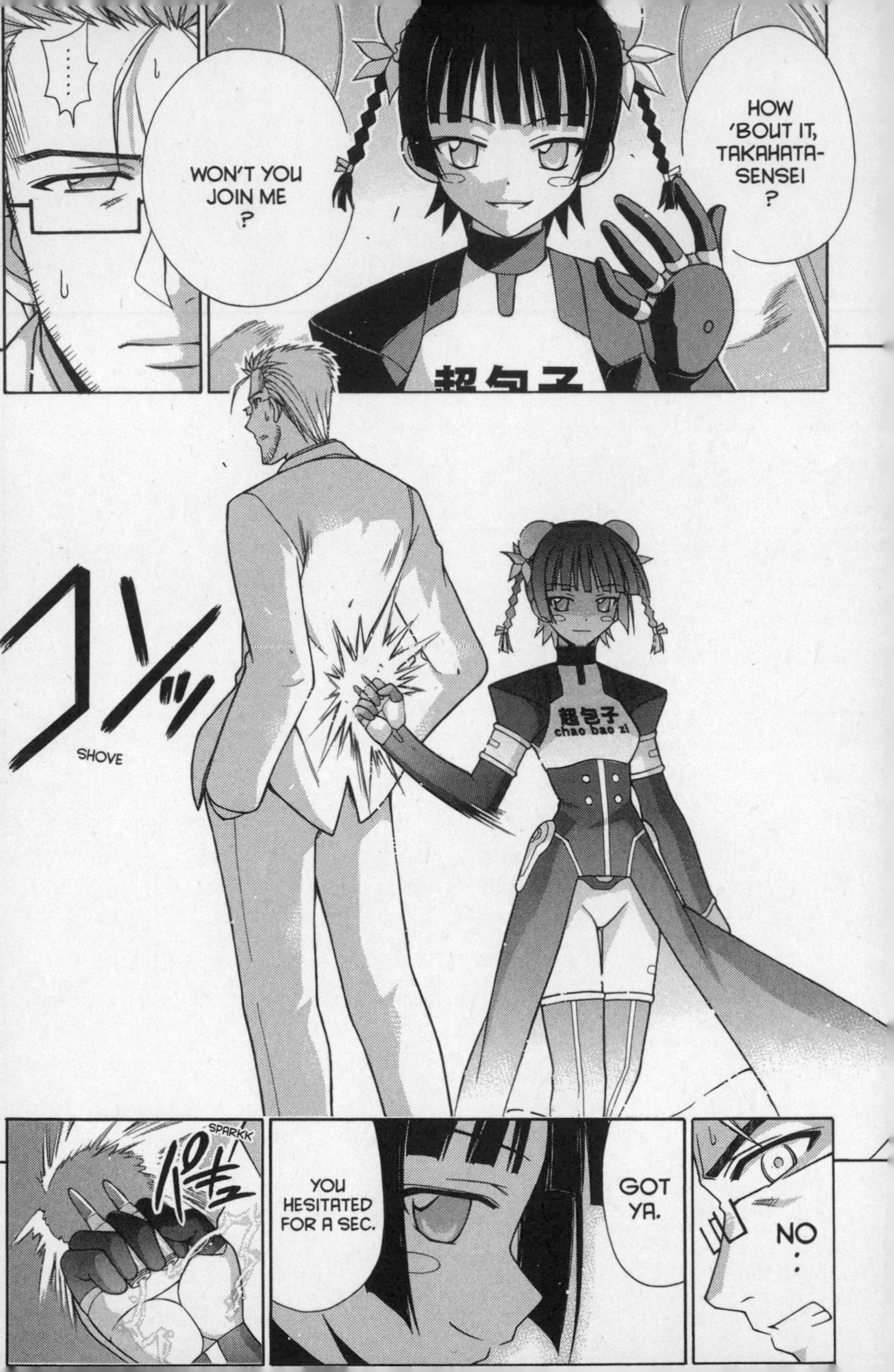
HOW 'BOUT IT, TAKAHATA-SENSEI?
WON'T YOU JOIN ME?
……
超包子
コンッ
SHOVE
超包子
chao bao zi
NO:
GOT YA.
YOU HESITATED FOR A SEC.
パキュ
SPARKK

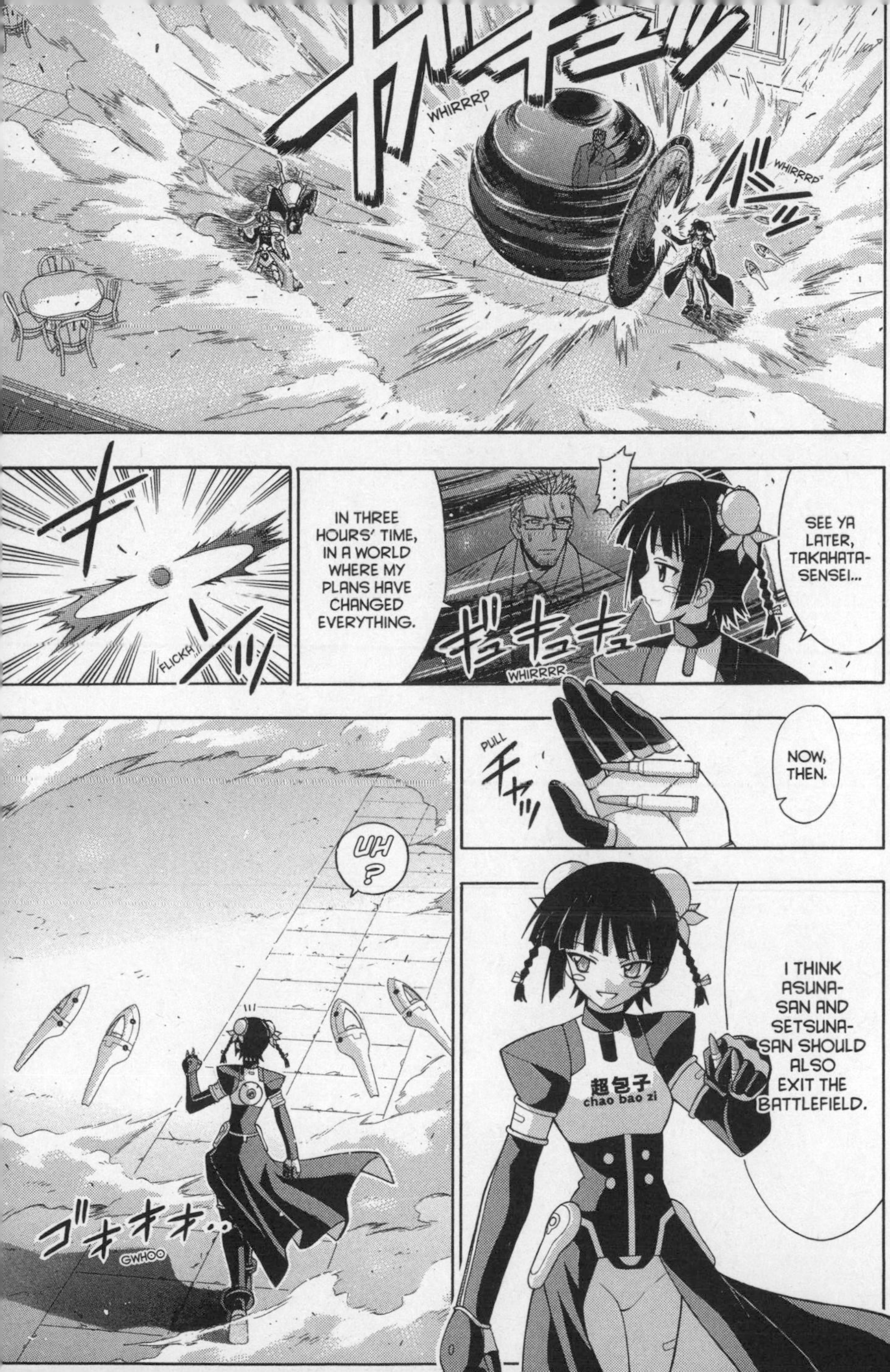

WHIRRRP
WHIRRRP
SEE YA LATER, TAKAHATA-SENSEI...
...
IN THREE HOURS' TIME, IN A WORLD WHERE MY PLANS HAVE CHANGED EVERYTHING.
WHIRRRR
FLICKA
NOW, THEN.
PULL
I THINK ASUNA-SAN AND SETSUNA-SAN SHOULD ALSO EXIT THE BATTLEFIELD.
超包子
chao bao zi
UH?
GWHOO

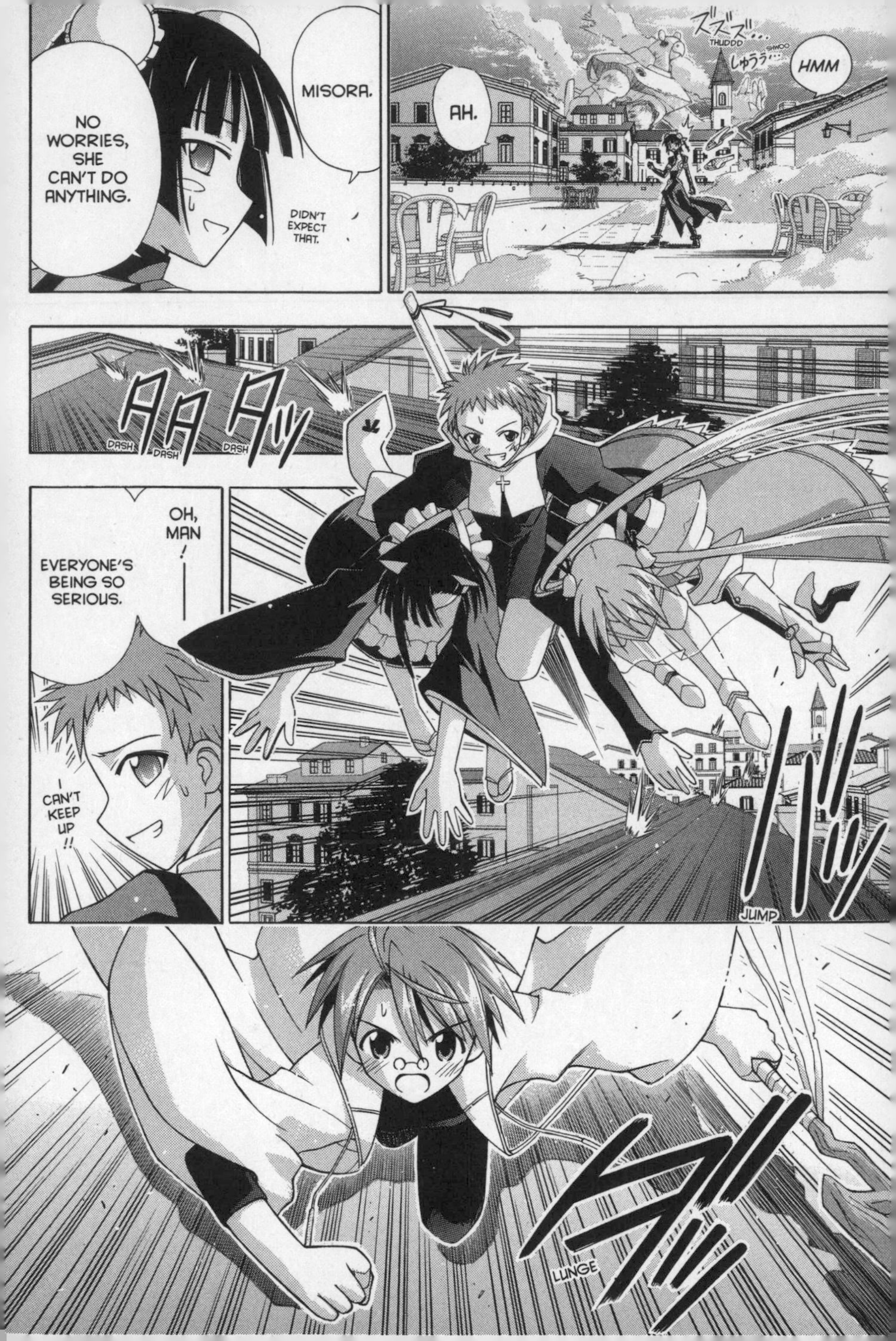

ズズズ…
THUDDD
しゅうう…
SHWOO
HMM
AH.
MISORA.
NO WORRIES, SHE CAN'T DO ANYTHING.
DIDN'T EXPECT THAT.
DASH
DASH
DASH
JUMP
OH, MAN!
EVERYONE'S BEING SO SERIOUS.
I CAN'T KEEP UP!!
LUNGE

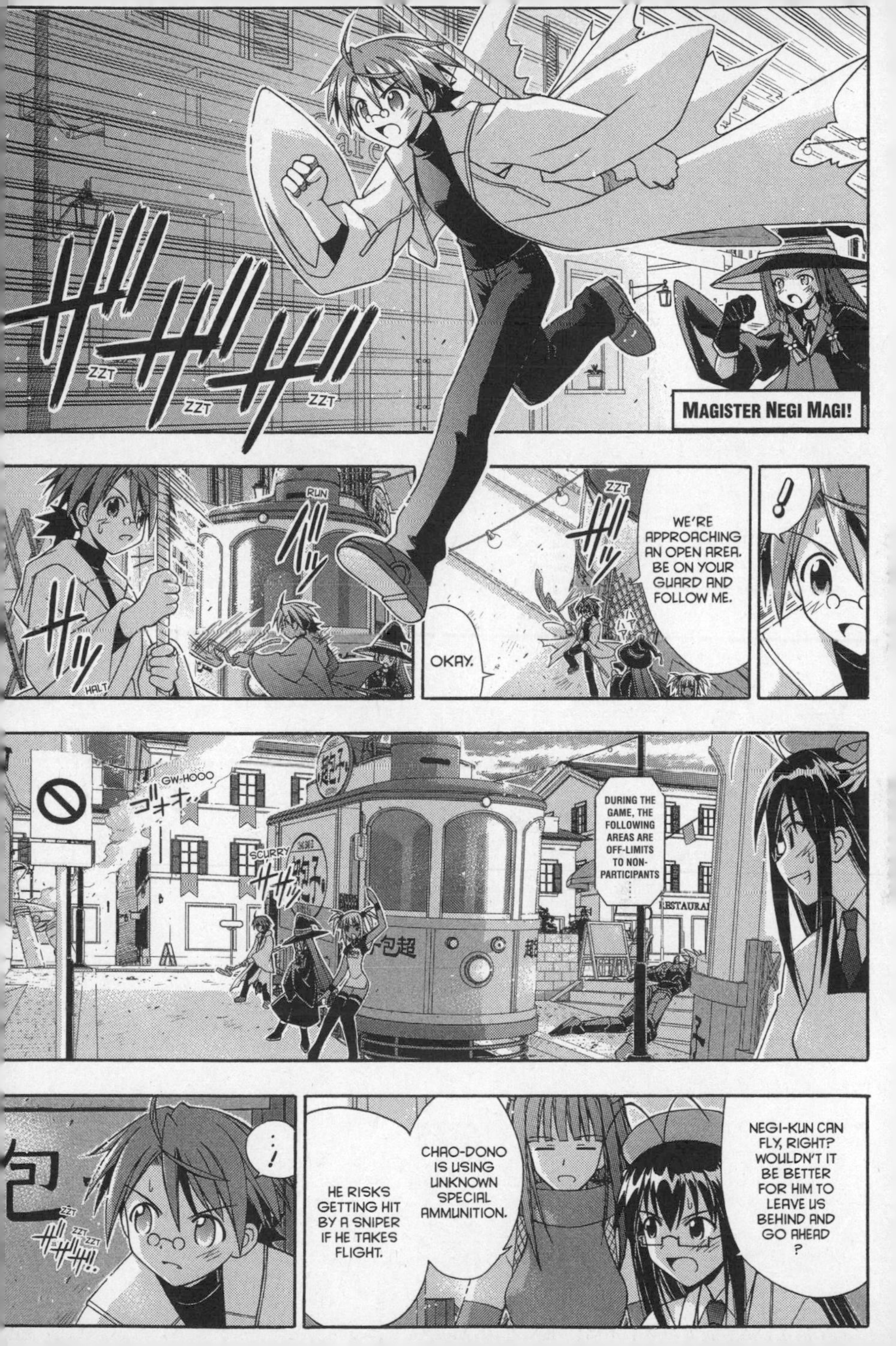
MAGISTER NEGI MAGI!
ZZT
ZZT
ZZT
!
ZZT
WE'RE APPROACHING AN OPEN AREA. BE ON YOUR GUARD AND FOLLOW ME.
OKAY.
RUN
HALT
DURING THE GAME, THE FOLLOWING AREAS ARE OFF-LIMITS TO NON-PARTICIPANTS ......
SCURRY
GW-HOOO
NEGI-KUN CAN FLY, RIGHT? WOULDN'T IT BE BETTER FOR HIM TO LEAVE US BEHIND AND GO AHEAD ?
CHAO-DONO IS USING UNKNOWN SPECIAL AMMUNITION.
HE RISKS GETTING HIT BY A SNIPER IF HE TAKES FLIGHT.
...!
ZZT
ZZT
ZZT

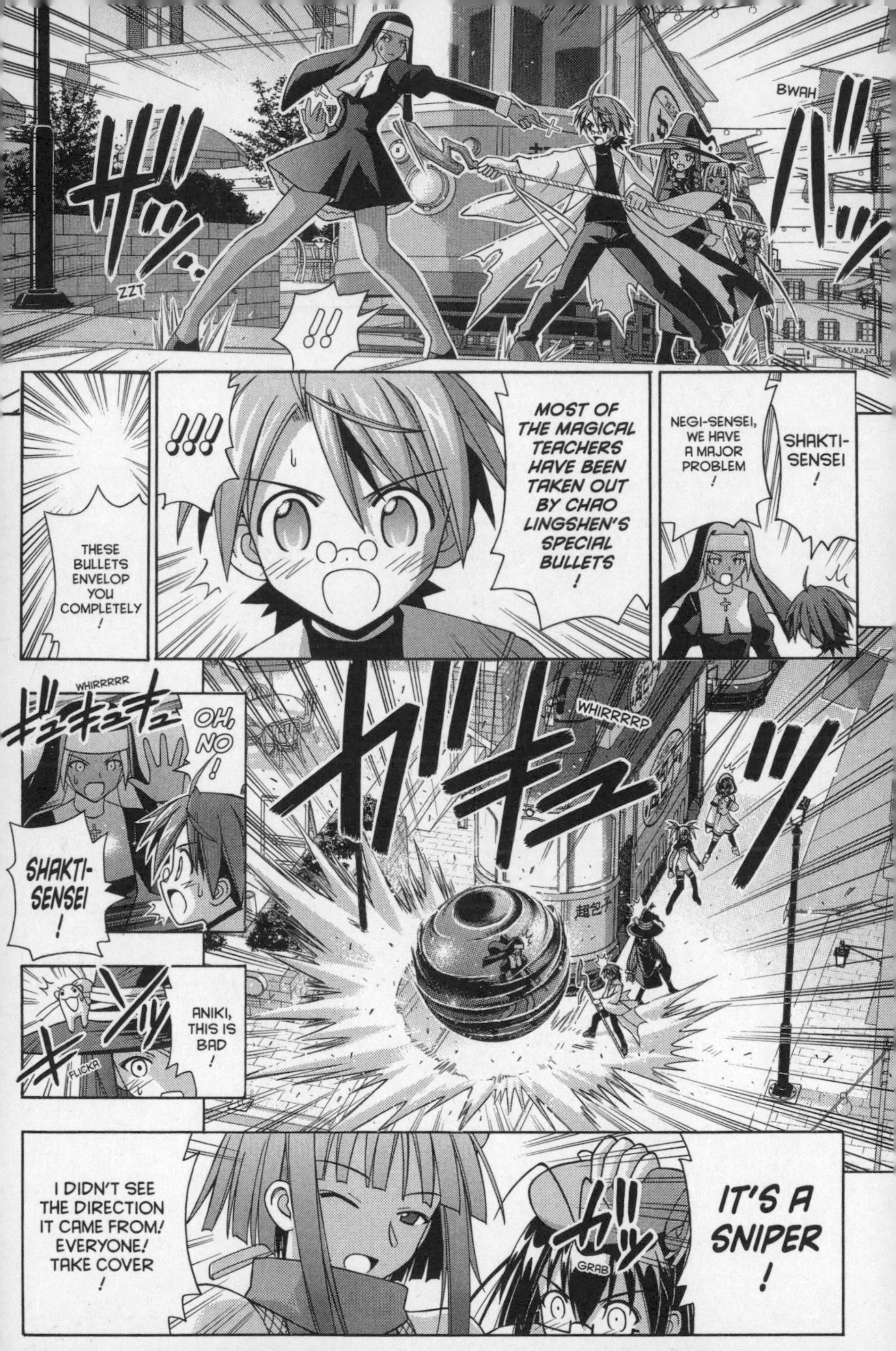
BWAH
ZZT
!!
SHAKTI-SENSEI!
NEGI-SENSEI, WE HAVE A MAJOR PROBLEM!
MOST OF THE MAGICAL TEACHERS HAVE BEEN TAKEN OUT BY CHAO LINGSHEN'S SPECIAL BULLETS!
!!!
THESE BULLETS ENVELOP YOU COMPLETELY!
WHIRRRRP
WHIRRRRR
OH, NO!
SHAKTI-SENSEI!
ANIKI, THIS IS BAD!
FLICKA
IT'S A SNIPER!
GRAB
I DIDN'T SEE THE DIRECTION IT CAME FROM! EVERYONE! TAKE COVER!

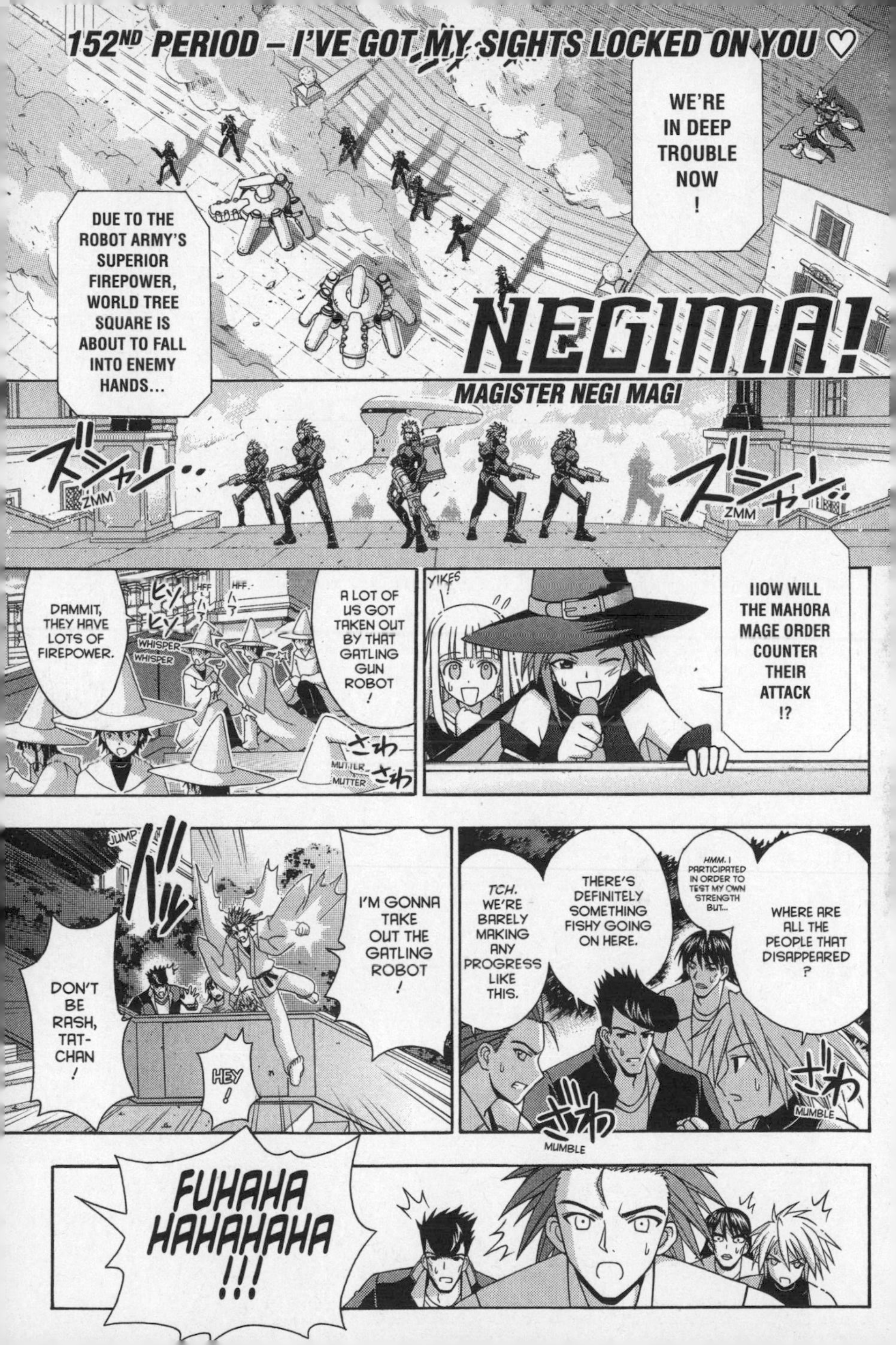

152ND PERIOD – I'VE GOT MY SIGHTS LOCKED ON YOU ♡
WE'RE IN DEEP TROUBLE NOW!
NEGIMA!
MAGISTER NEGI MAGI
DUE TO THE ROBOT ARMY'S SUPERIOR FIREPOWER, WORLD TREE SQUARE IS ABOUT TO FALL INTO ENEMY HANDS...
ZMM
ZMM
YIKES
HOW WILL THE MAHORA MAGE ORDER COUNTER THEIR ATTACK!?
A LOT OF US GOT TAKEN OUT BY THAT GATLING GUN ROBOT!
HFF HFF
DAMMIT, THEY HAVE LOTS OF FIREPOWER.
WHISPER WHISPER
MUTTER MUTTER
WHERE ARE ALL THE PEOPLE THAT DISAPPEARED?
HMM. I PARTICIPATED IN ORDER TO TEST MY OWN STRENGTH BUT...
THERE'S DEFINITELY SOMETHING FISHY GOING ON HERE.
TCH. WE'RE BARELY MAKING ANY PROGRESS LIKE THIS.
MUMBLE
MUMBLE
I'M GONNA TAKE OUT THE GATLING ROBOT!
JUMP
HEY!
DON'T BE RASH, TAT-CHAN!
FUHAHA HAHAHAHA!!!

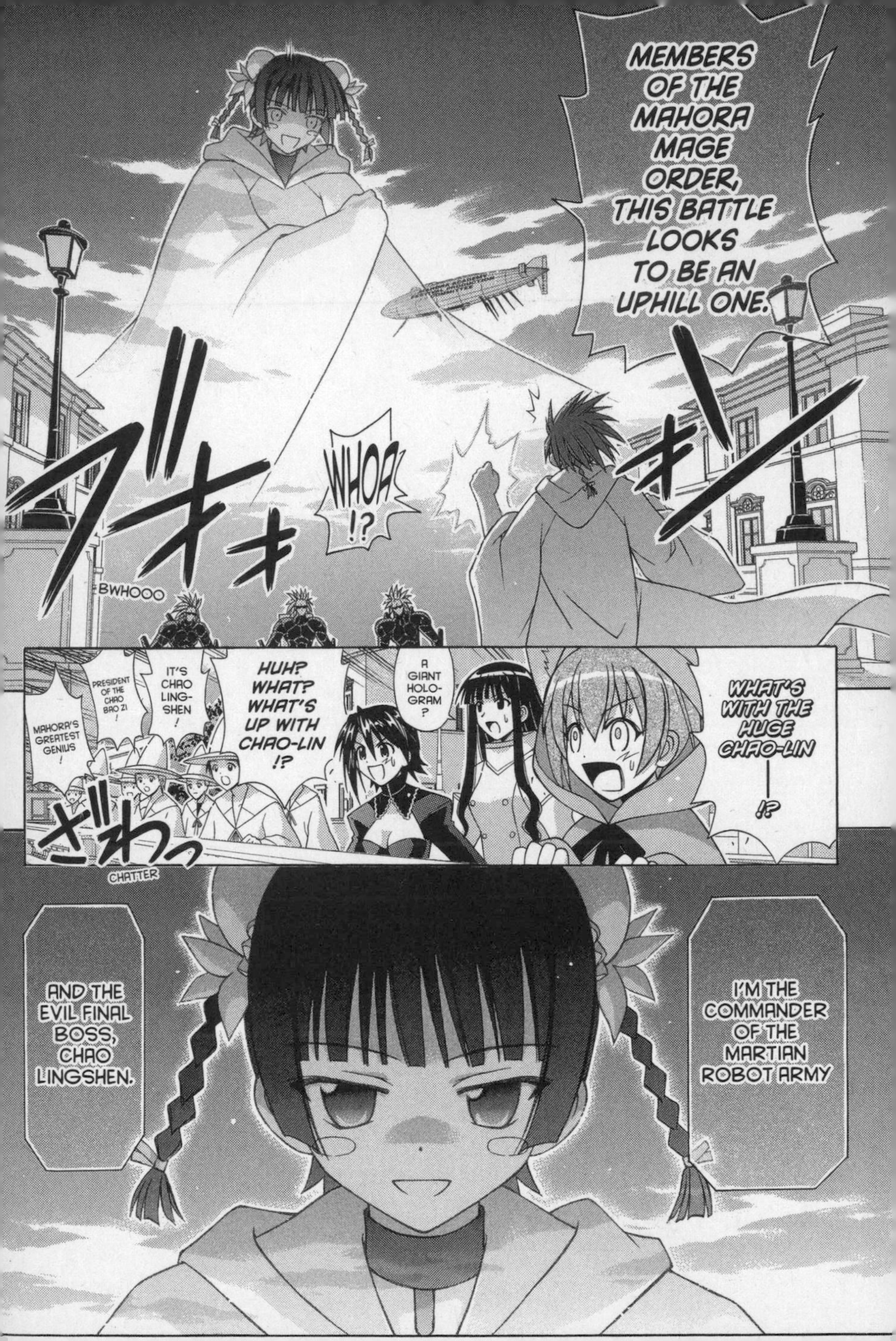
MEMBERS OF THE MAHORA MAGE ORDER, THIS BATTLE LOOKS TO BE AN UPHILL ONE.
BWHOOO
WHOA!?
WHAT'S WITH THE HUGE CHAO-LIN —!?
A GIANT HOLOGRAM?
HUH? WHAT? WHAT'S UP WITH CHAO-LIN!?
IT'S CHAO LINGSHEN!
PRESIDENT OF THE CHAO BAO ZI!
MAHORA'S GREATEST GENIUS!
CHATTER
I'M THE COMMANDER OF THE MARTIAN ROBOT ARMY
AND THE EVIL FINAL BOSS, CHAO LINGSHEN.

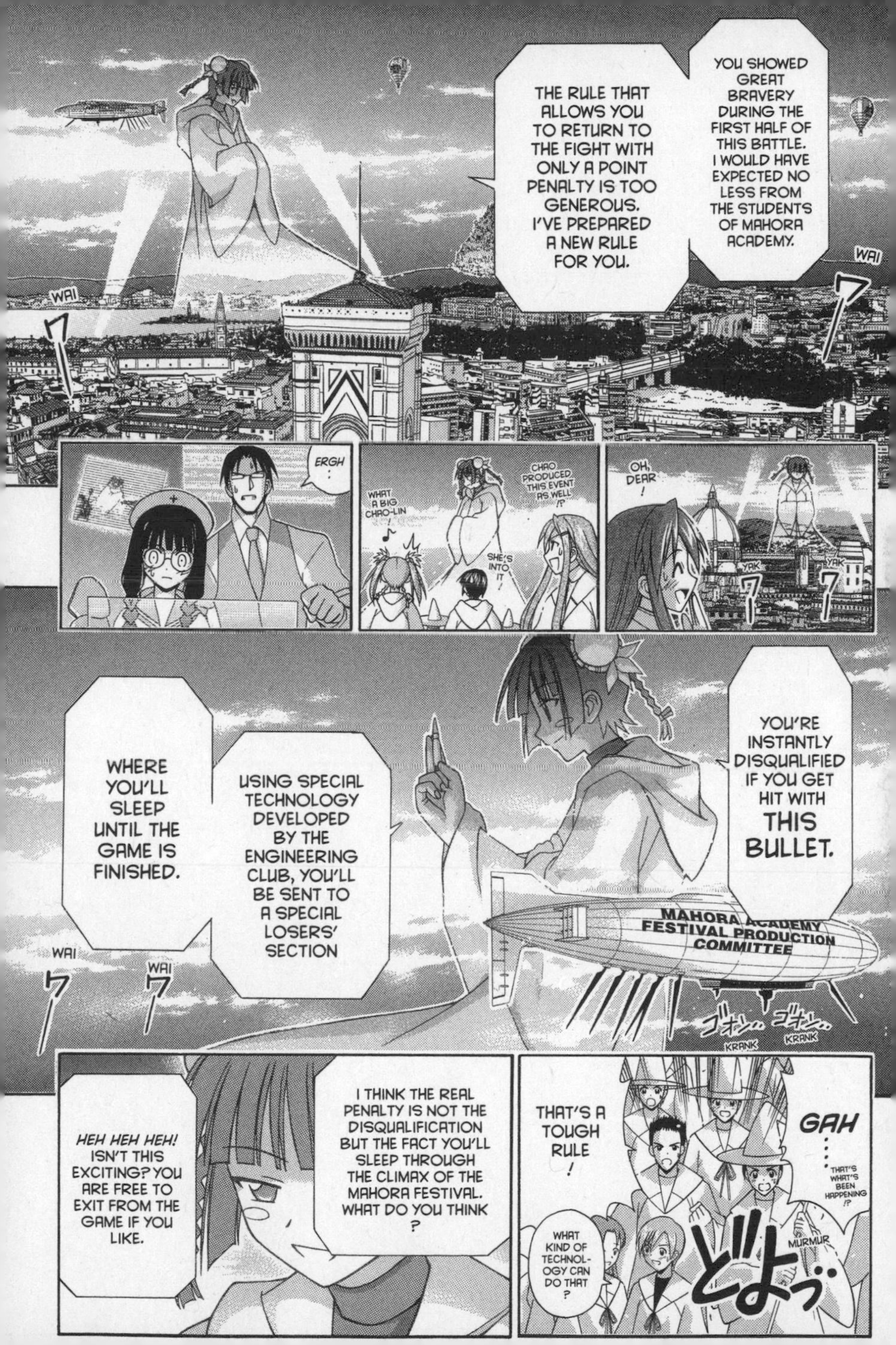
YOU SHOWED GREAT BRAVERY DURING THE FIRST HALF OF THIS BATTLE. I WOULD HAVE EXPECTED NO LESS FROM THE STUDENTS OF MAHORA ACADEMY.
THE RULE THAT ALLOWS YOU TO RETURN TO THE FIGHT WITH ONLY A POINT PENALTY IS TOO GENEROUS. I'VE PREPARED A NEW RULE FOR YOU.
WAI
WAI
OH, DEAR!
YAK
YAK
CHAO PRODUCED THIS EVENT AS WELL!?
WHAT A BIG CHAO-LIN
SHE'S INTO IT!
ERGH...
YOU'RE INSTANTLY DISQUALIFIED IF YOU GET HIT WITH THIS BULLET.
USING SPECIAL TECHNOLOGY DEVELOPED BY THE ENGINEERING CLUB, YOU'LL BE SENT TO A SPECIAL LOSERS' SECTION
WHERE YOU'LL SLEEP UNTIL THE GAME IS FINISHED.
MAHORA ACADEMY FESTIVAL PRODUCTION COMMITTEE
KRANK
KRANK
WAI
WAI
THAT'S A TOUGH RULE!
GAH...
THAT'S WHAT'S BEEN HAPPENING!?
MURMUR
WHAT KIND OF TECHNOLOGY CAN DO THAT?
どよっ
I THINK THE REAL PENALTY IS NOT THE DISQUALIFICATION BUT THE FACT YOU'LL SLEEP THROUGH THE CLIMAX OF THE MAHORA FESTIVAL. WHAT DO YOU THINK?
HEH HEH HEH! ISN'T THIS EXCITING? YOU ARE FREE TO EXIT FROM THE GAME IF YOU LIKE.

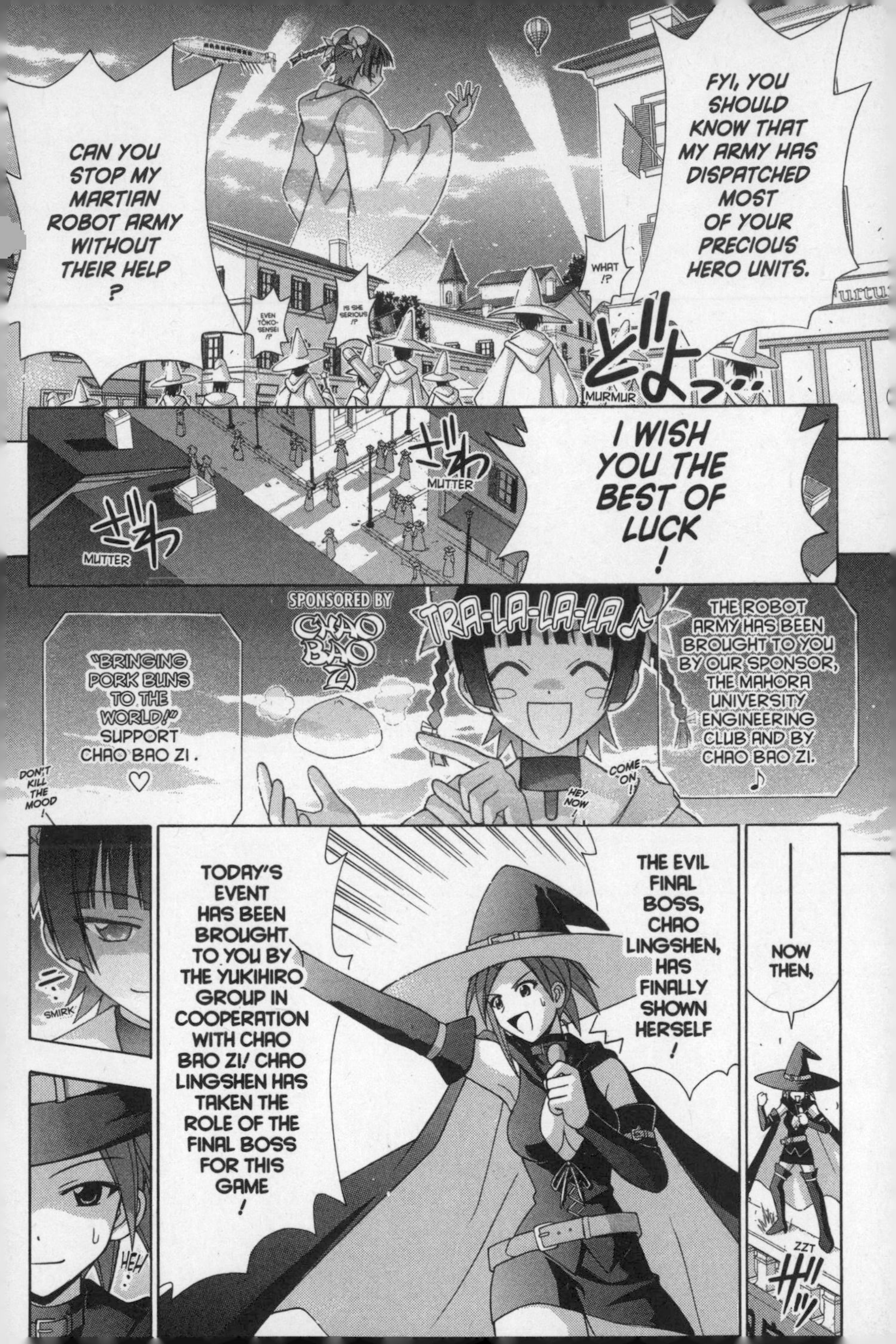
FYI, YOU SHOULD KNOW THAT MY ARMY HAS DISPATCHED MOST OF YOUR PRECIOUS HERO UNITS.
WHAT !?
MURMUR
IS SHE SERIOUS !?
EVEN TŌKO-SENSEI !?
CAN YOU STOP MY MARTIAN ROBOT ARMY WITHOUT THEIR HELP ?
I WISH YOU THE BEST OF LUCK !
MUTTER
MUTTER
THE ROBOT ARMY HAS BEEN BROUGHT TO YOU BY OUR SPONSOR, THE MAHORA UNIVERSITY ENGINEERING CLUB AND BY CHAO BAO ZI. ♪
TRA-LA-LA-LA♪
COME ON !
HEY NOW !
SPONSORED BY
CHAO BAO ZI
"BRINGING PORK BUNS TO THE WORLD!" SUPPORT CHAO BAO ZI. ♡
DON'T KILL THE MOOD !
NOW THEN,
ZZT
THE EVIL FINAL BOSS, CHAO LINGSHEN, HAS FINALLY SHOWN HERSELF !
TODAY'S EVENT HAS BEEN BROUGHT TO YOU BY THE YUKIHIRO GROUP IN COOPERATION WITH CHAO BAO ZI! CHAO LINGSHEN HAS TAKEN THE ROLE OF THE FINAL BOSS FOR THIS GAME !
SMIRK
HEH

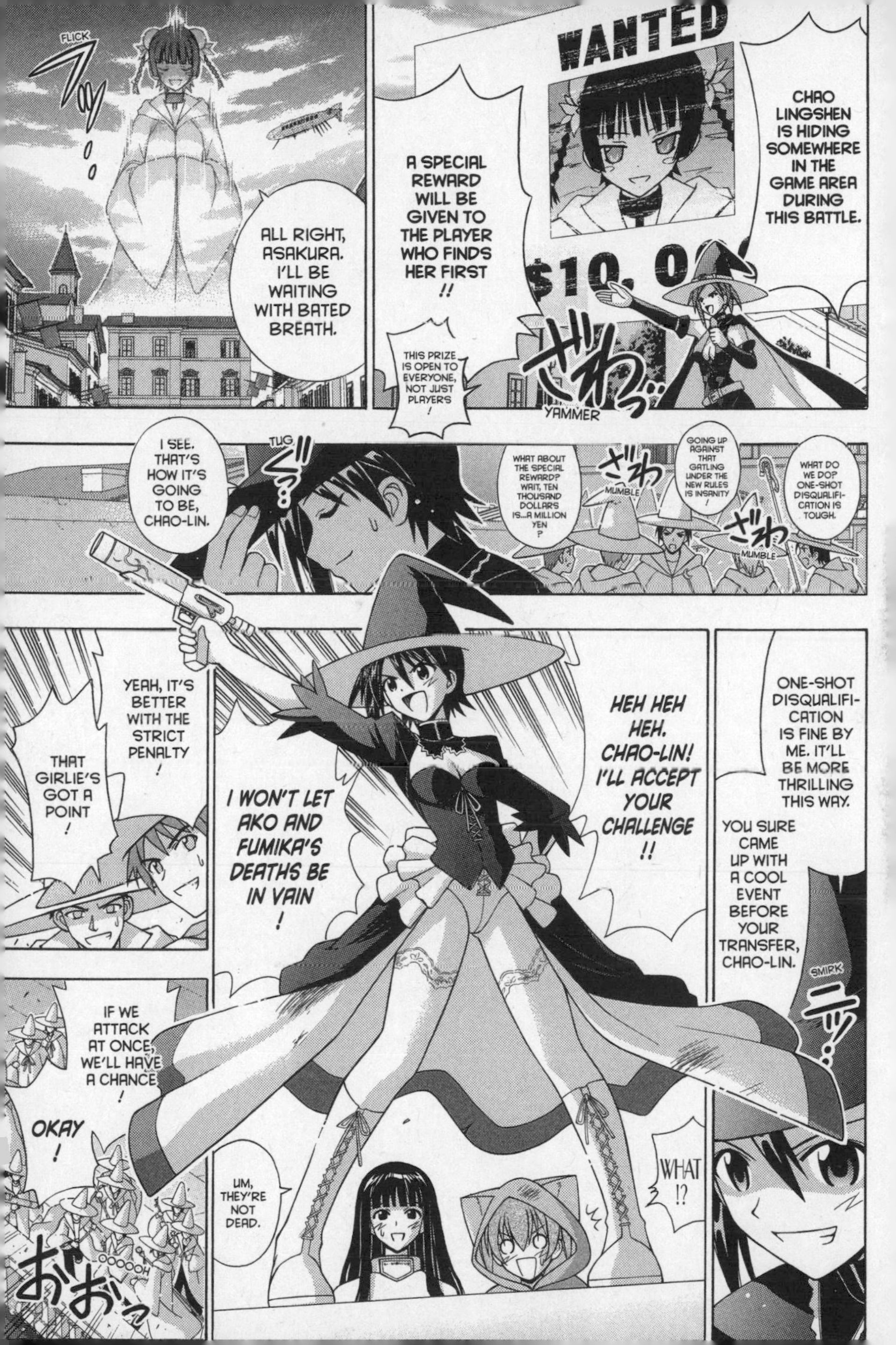
WANTED
CHAO LINGSHEN IS HIDING SOMEWHERE IN THE GAME AREA DURING THIS BATTLE.
A SPECIAL REWARD WILL BE GIVEN TO THE PLAYER WHO FINDS HER FIRST !!
$10,00
YAMMER
THIS PRIZE IS OPEN TO EVERYONE, NOT JUST PLAYERS !
FLICK
ALL RIGHT, ASAKURA. I'LL BE WAITING WITH BATED BREATH.
WHAT DO WE DO? ONE-SHOT DISQUALIFICATION IS TOUGH.
MUMBLE
GOING UP AGAINST THAT GATLING UNDER THE NEW RULES IS INSANITY !
MUMBLE
WHAT ABOUT THE SPECIAL REWARD? WAIT, TEN THOUSAND DOLLARS IS...A MILLION YEN ?
TUG
I SEE. THAT'S HOW IT'S GOING TO BE, CHAO-LIN.
ONE-SHOT DISQUALIFICATION IS FINE BY ME. IT'LL BE MORE THRILLING THIS WAY.
YOU SURE CAME UP WITH A COOL EVENT BEFORE YOUR TRANSFER, CHAO-LIN.
SMIRK
HEH HEH HEH. CHAO-LIN! I'LL ACCEPT YOUR CHALLENGE !!
I WON'T LET AKO AND FUMIKA'S DEATHS BE IN VAIN !
WHAT !?
UM, THEY'RE NOT DEAD.
YEAH, IT'S BETTER WITH THE STRICT PENALTY !
THAT GIRLIE'S GOT A POINT !
IF WE ATTACK AT ONCE, WE'LL HAVE A CHANCE !
OKAY !
OOOOOH

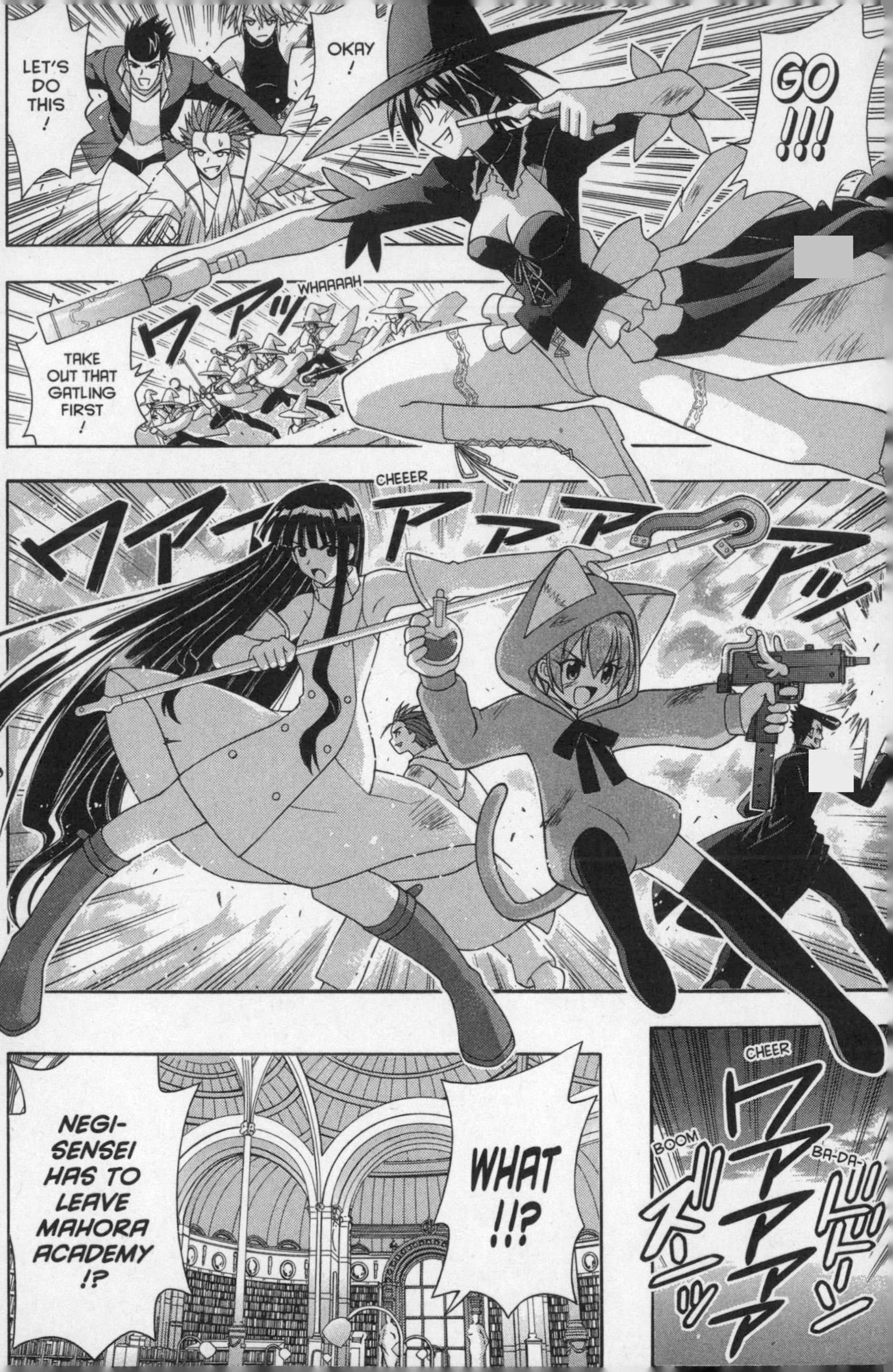
GO!!!
OKAY!
LET'S DO THIS!
WHAAAAH
TAKE OUT THAT GATLING FIRST!
CHEEER
CHEER
BA-DA-
BOOM
WHAT!!?
NEGI-SENSEI HAS TO LEAVE MAHORA ACADEMY!?

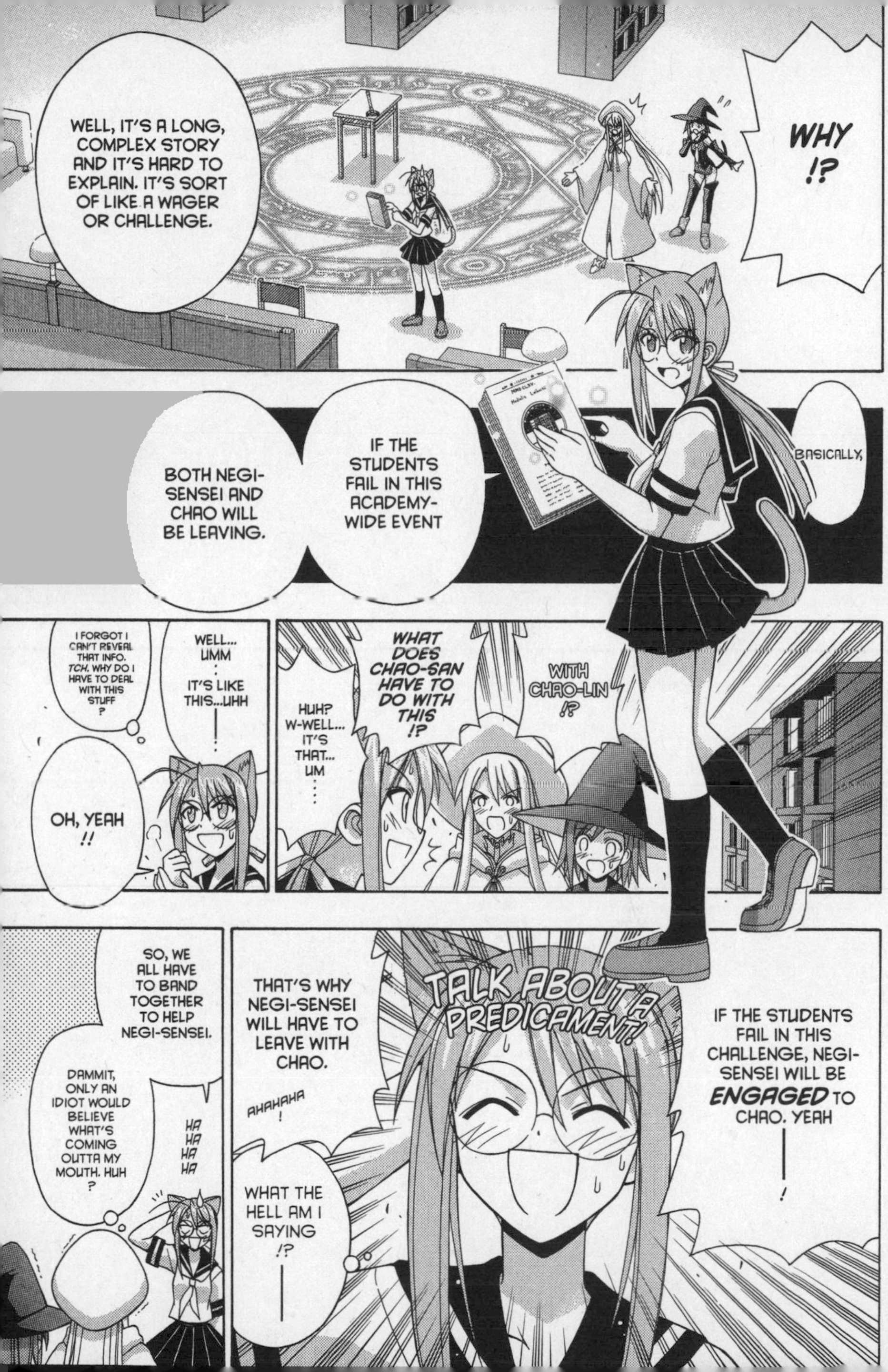
WHY !?
WELL, IT'S A LONG, COMPLEX STORY AND IT'S HARD TO EXPLAIN. IT'S SORT OF LIKE A WAGER OR CHALLENGE.
BASICALLY,
IF THE STUDENTS FAIL IN THIS ACADEMY-WIDE EVENT
BOTH NEGI-SENSEI AND CHAO WILL BE LEAVING.
WITH CHAO-LIN !?
WHAT DOES CHAO-SAN HAVE TO DO WITH THIS !?
HUH? W-WELL... IT'S THAT... UM
WELL... UMM IT'S LIKE THIS...UHH
I FORGOT I CAN'T REVEAL THAT INFO. TCH. WHY DO I HAVE TO DEAL WITH THIS STUFF ?
OH, YEAH !!
IF THE STUDENTS FAIL IN THIS CHALLENGE, NEGI-SENSEI WILL BE ENGAGED TO CHAO. YEAH
TALK ABOUT A PREDICAMENT!
THAT'S WHY NEGI-SENSEI WILL HAVE TO LEAVE WITH CHAO.
AHAHAHA !
WHAT THE HELL AM I SAYING !?
SO, WE ALL HAVE TO BAND TOGETHER TO HELP NEGI-SENSEI.
HA HA HA HA
DAMMIT, ONLY AN IDIOT WOULD BELIEVE WHAT'S COMING OUTTA MY MOUTH. HUH ?

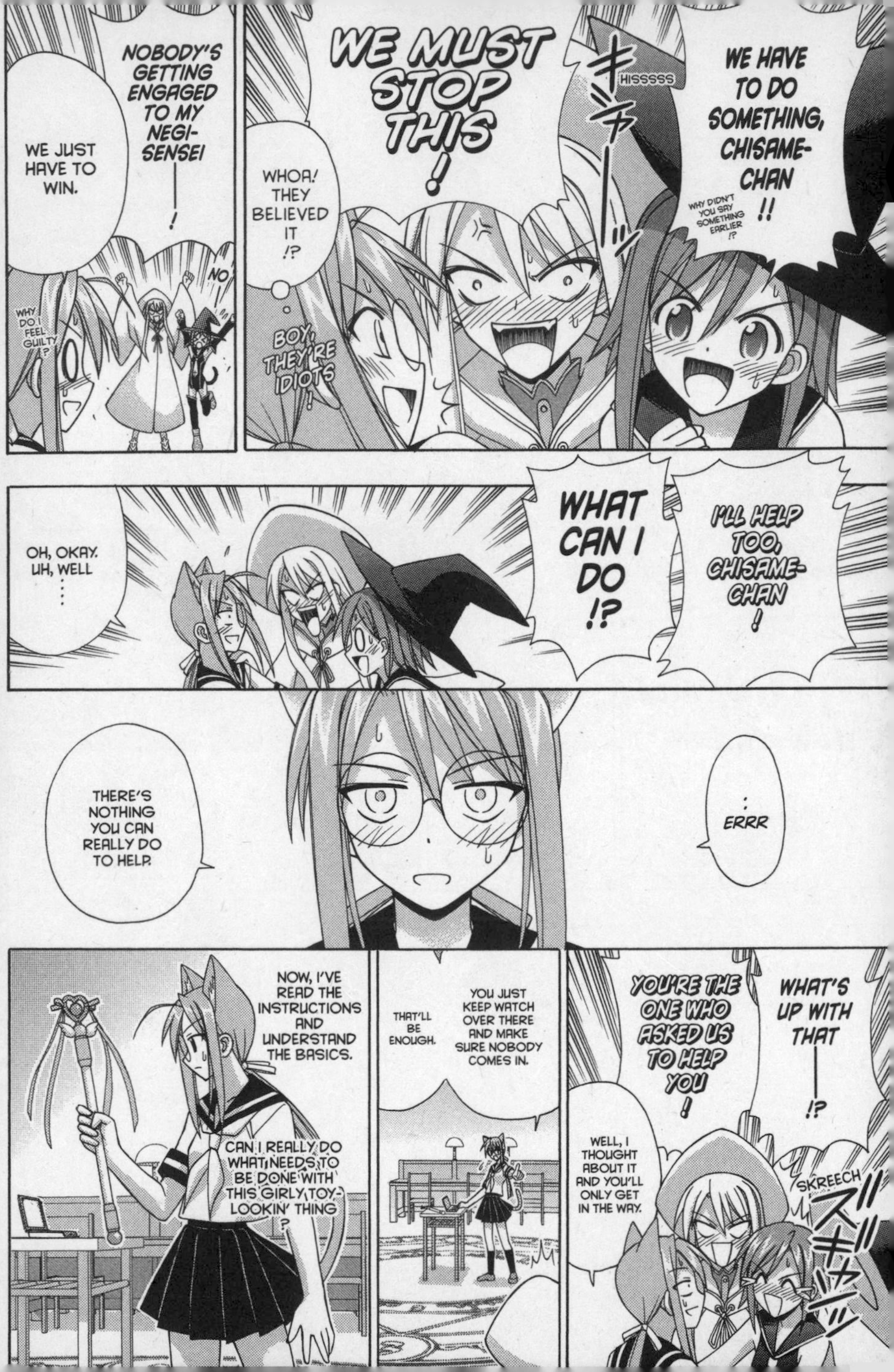
WE HAVE TO DO SOMETHING, CHISAME-CHAN!!
WHY DIDN'T YOU SAY SOMETHING EARLIER!?
HISSSSS
WE MUST STOP THIS!
WHOA! THEY BELIEVED IT!?
BOY, THEY'RE IDIOTS!
NOBODY'S GETTING ENGAGED TO MY NEGI-SENSEI—!
WE JUST HAVE TO WIN.
NO!
WHY DO I FEEL GUILTY!?
I'LL HELP TOO, CHISAME-CHAN!
WHAT CAN I DO!?
OH, OKAY. UH, WELL.....
: ERRR
THERE'S NOTHING YOU CAN REALLY DO TO HELP.
WHAT'S UP WITH THAT—!?
YOU'RE THE ONE WHO ASKED US TO HELP YOU!
SKREECH
WELL, I THOUGHT ABOUT IT AND YOU'LL ONLY GET IN THE WAY.
YOU JUST KEEP WATCH OVER THERE AND MAKE SURE NOBODY COMES IN.
THAT'LL BE ENOUGH.
NOW, I'VE READ THE INSTRUCTIONS AND UNDERSTAND THE BASICS.
CAN I REALLY DO WHAT NEEDS TO BE DONE WITH THIS GIRLY TOY-LOOKIN' THING?

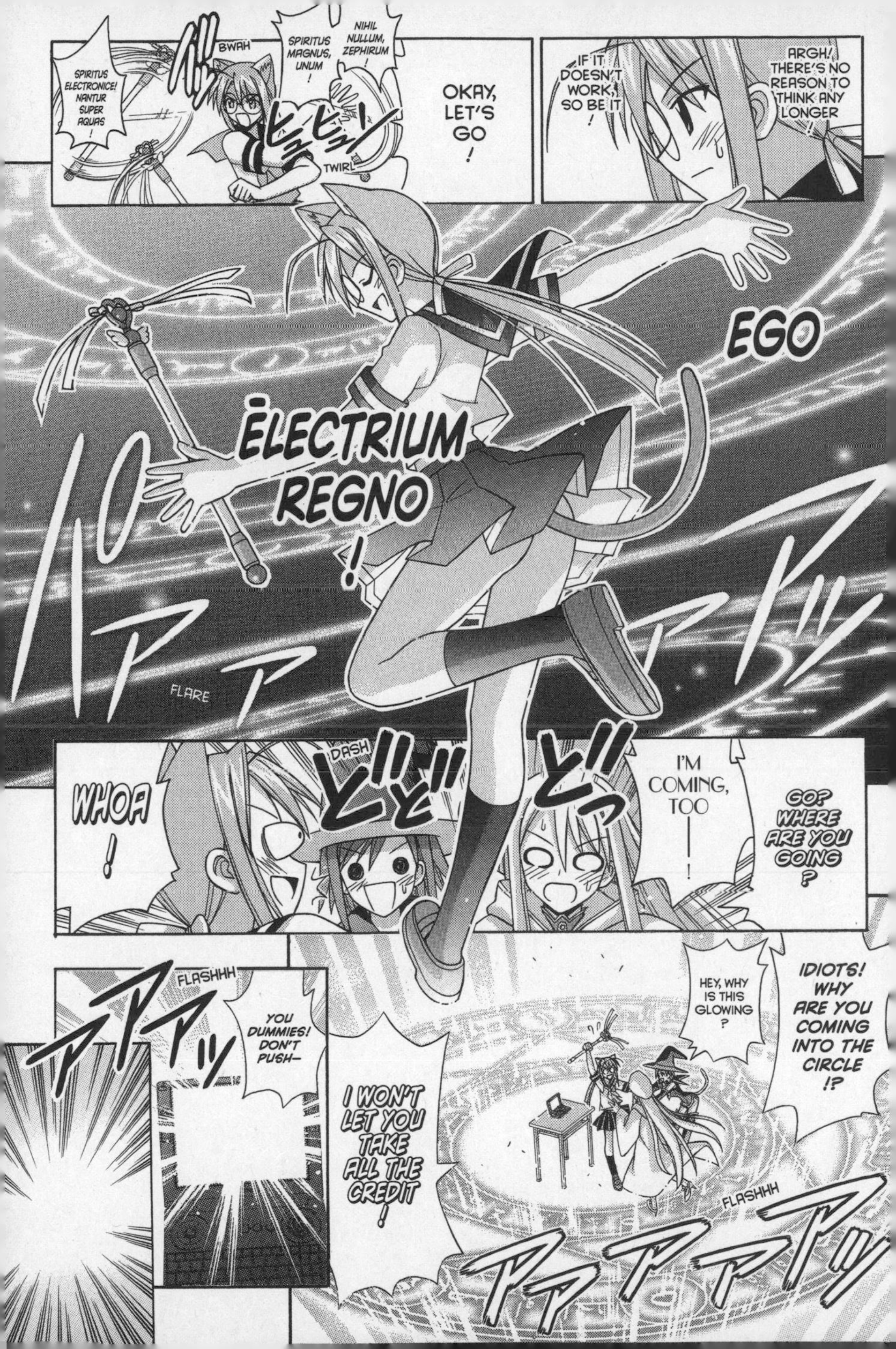
ARGH! THERE'S NO REASON TO THINK ANY LONGER!
IF IT DOESN'T WORK, SO BE IT!
OKAY, LET'S GO!
NIHIL NULLUM, ZEPHIRUM!
SPIRITUS MAGNUS, UNUM!
BWAH
SPIRITUS ELECTRONICE! NANTUR SUPER AQUAS!
TWIRL
EGO
ĒLECTRIUM REGNO!
FLARE
GO? WHERE ARE YOU GOING?
I'M COMING, TOO!
DASH
WHOA!
IDIOTS! WHY ARE YOU COMING INTO THE CIRCLE!?
HEY, WHY IS THIS GLOWING?
I WON'T LET YOU TAKE ALL THE CREDIT!
FLASHHH
FLASHHH
YOU DUMMIES! DON'T PUSH—

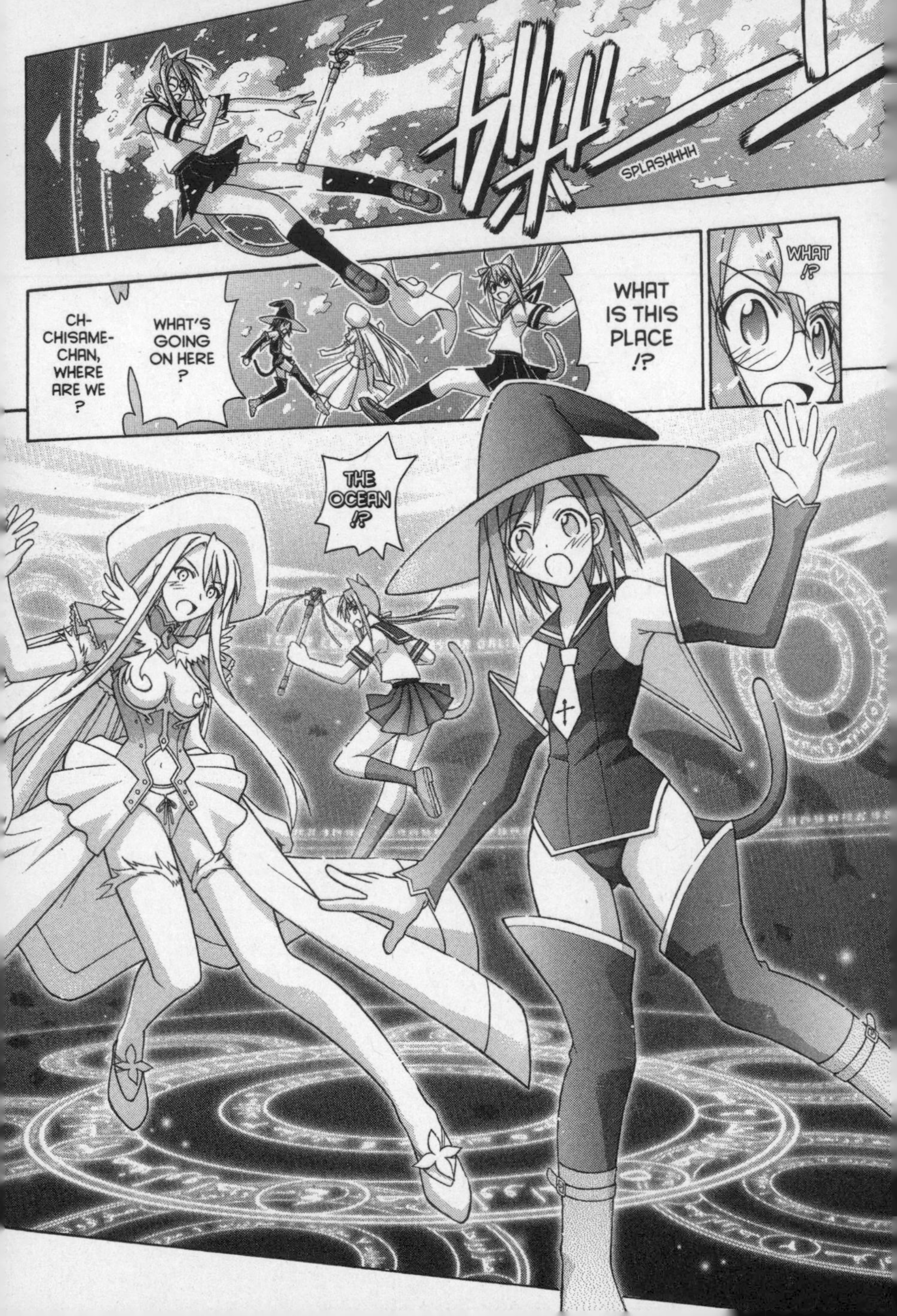
SPLASHHHH
WHAT !?
WHAT IS THIS PLACE !?
WHAT'S GOING ON HERE ?
CH-CHISAME-CHAN, WHERE ARE WE ?
THE OCEAN !?

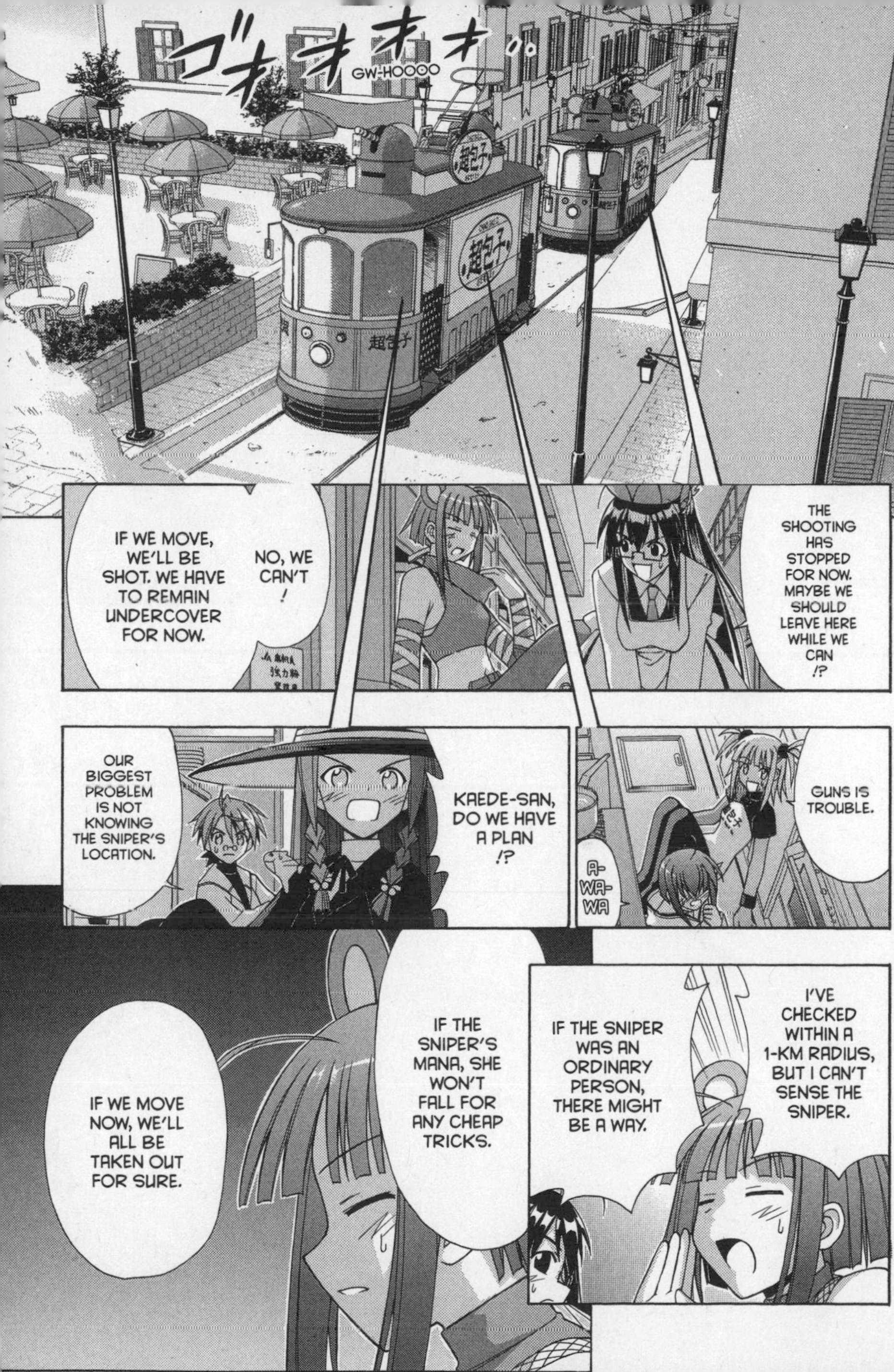
GW-HOOOO
THE SHOOTING HAS STOPPED FOR NOW. MAYBE WE SHOULD LEAVE HERE WHILE WE CAN!?
NO, WE CAN'T!
IF WE MOVE, WE'LL BE SHOT. WE HAVE TO REMAIN UNDERCOVER FOR NOW.
GUNS IS TROUBLE.
A-WA-WA
KAEDE-SAN, DO WE HAVE A PLAN!?
OUR BIGGEST PROBLEM IS NOT KNOWING THE SNIPER'S LOCATION.
I'VE CHECKED WITHIN A 1-KM RADIUS, BUT I CAN'T SENSE THE SNIPER.
IF THE SNIPER WAS AN ORDINARY PERSON, THERE MIGHT BE A WAY.
IF THE SNIPER'S MANA, SHE WON'T FALL FOR ANY CHEAP TRICKS.
IF WE MOVE NOW, WE'LL ALL BE TAKEN OUT FOR SURE.

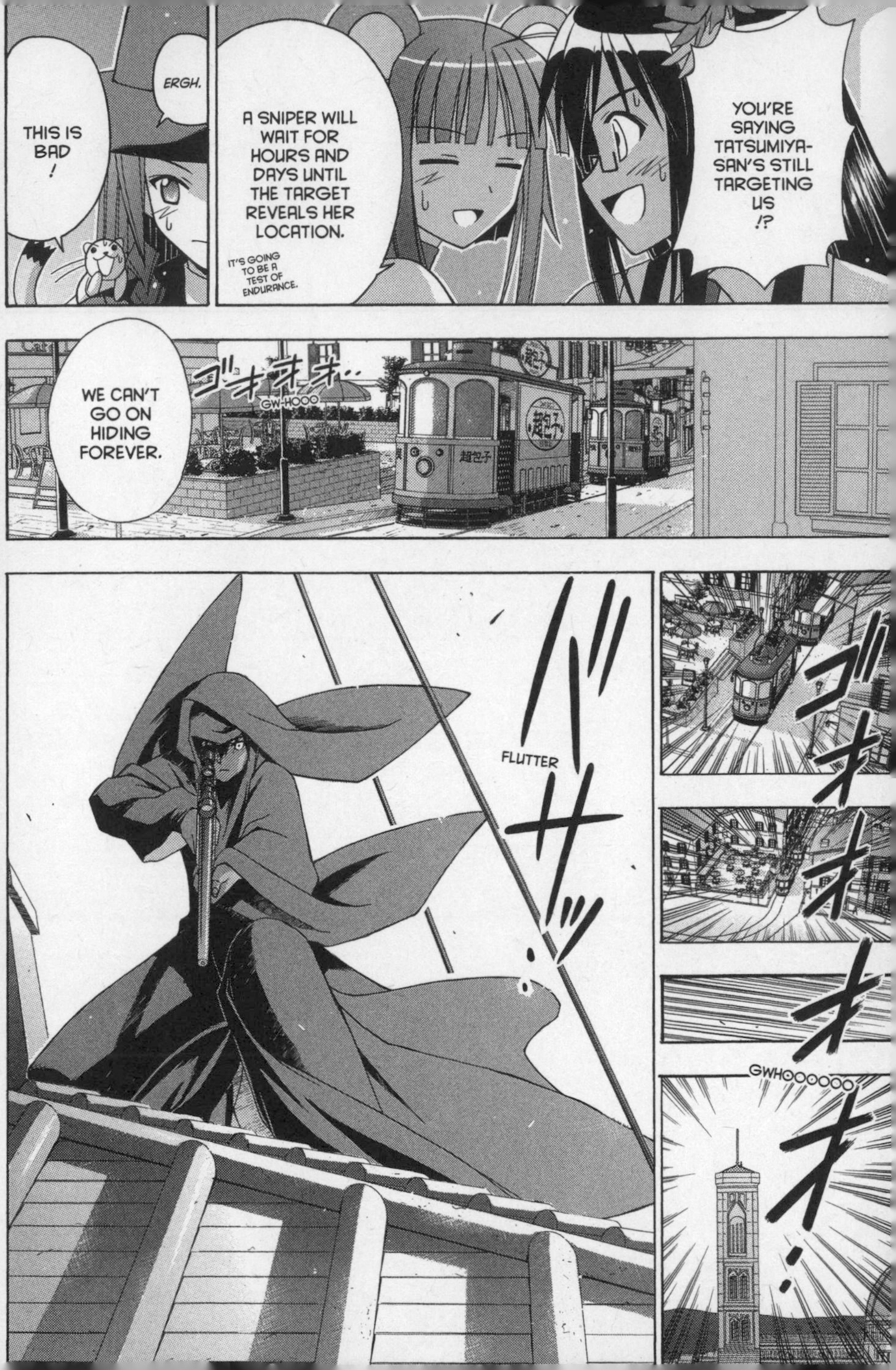
YOU'RE SAYING TATSUMIYA-SAN'S STILL TARGETING US !?
A SNIPER WILL WAIT FOR HOURS AND DAYS UNTIL THE TARGET REVEALS HER LOCATION.
IT'S GOING TO BE A TEST OF ENDURANCE.
ERGH.
THIS IS BAD !
GW-HOOO
WE CAN'T GO ON HIDING FOREVER.
GWHOOOOOOO
FLUTTER

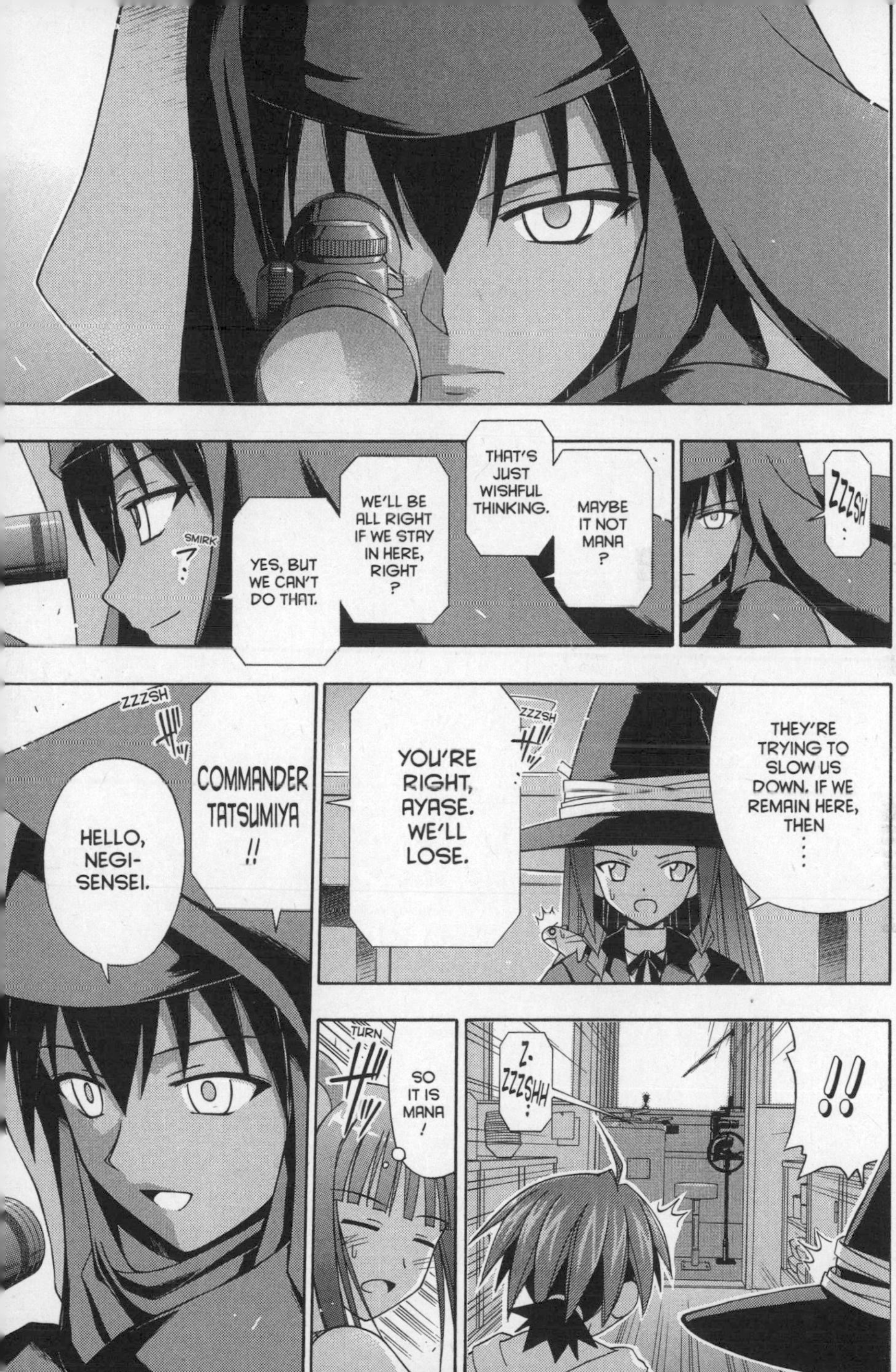
ZZZSH :
MAYBE IT NOT MANA ?
THAT'S JUST WISHFUL THINKING.
WE'LL BE ALL RIGHT IF WE STAY IN HERE, RIGHT ?
YES, BUT WE CAN'T DO THAT.
SMIRK
THEY'RE TRYING TO SLOW US DOWN. IF WE REMAIN HERE, THEN ....
ZZZSH
YOU'RE RIGHT, AYASE. WE'LL LOSE.
!!
Z-ZZZSHH :
TURN
SO IT IS MANA !
ZZZSH
COMMANDER TATSUMIYA !!
HELLO, NEGI-SENSEI.

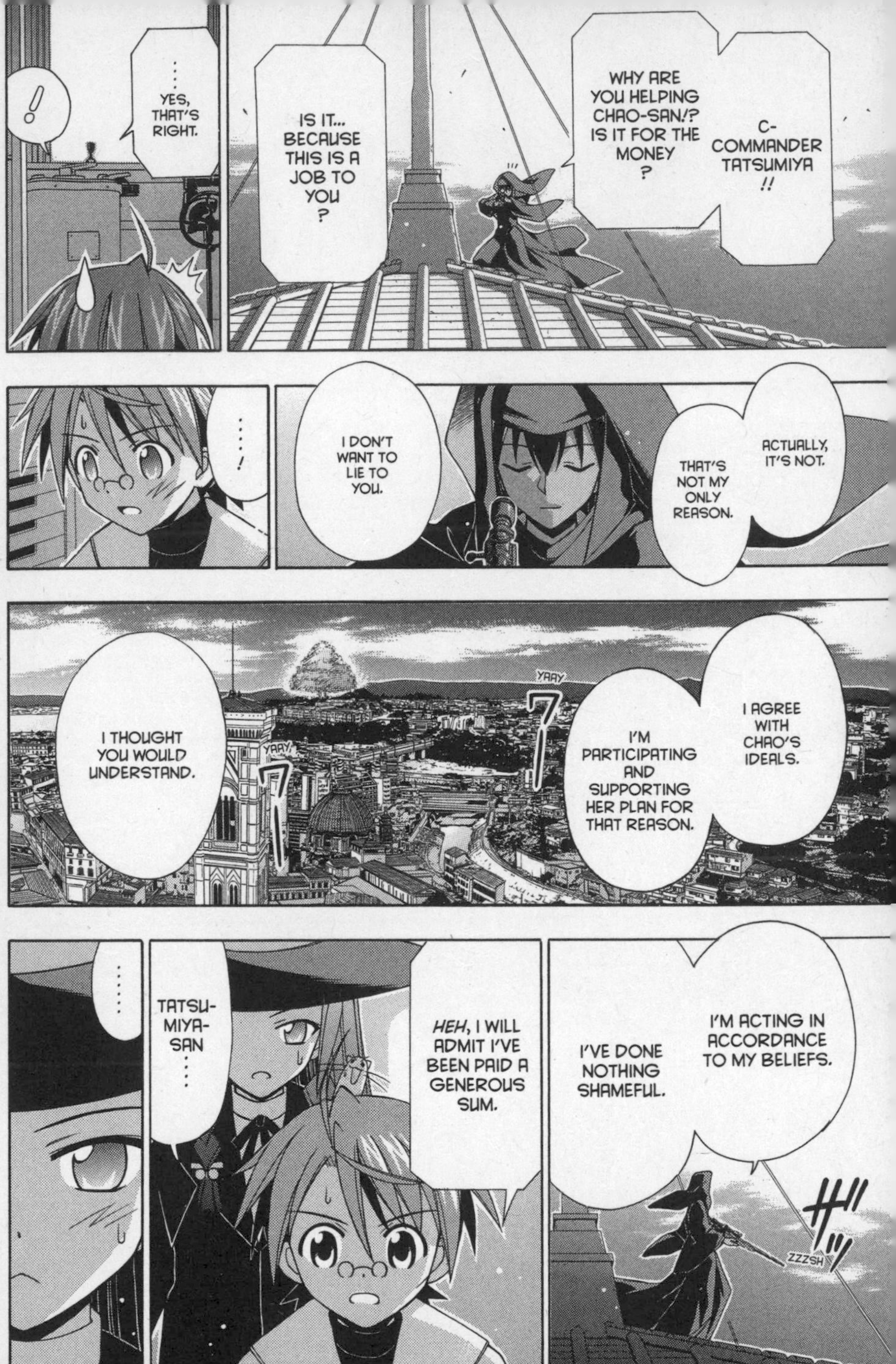
C-COMMANDER TATSUMIYA!!
WHY ARE YOU HELPING CHAO-SAN!? IS IT FOR THE MONEY?
IS IT... BECAUSE THIS IS A JOB TO YOU?
...YES, THAT'S RIGHT.
!
ACTUALLY, IT'S NOT.
THAT'S NOT MY ONLY REASON.
I DON'T WANT TO LIE TO YOU.
...!
I AGREE WITH CHAO'S IDEALS.
I'M PARTICIPATING AND SUPPORTING HER PLAN FOR THAT REASON.
YAAY
YAAY
I THOUGHT YOU WOULD UNDERSTAND.
I'M ACTING IN ACCORDANCE TO MY BELIEFS.
I'VE DONE NOTHING SHAMEFUL.
ZZZSH
HEH, I WILL ADMIT I'VE BEEN PAID A GENEROUS SUM.
TATSU-MIYA-SAN....
......

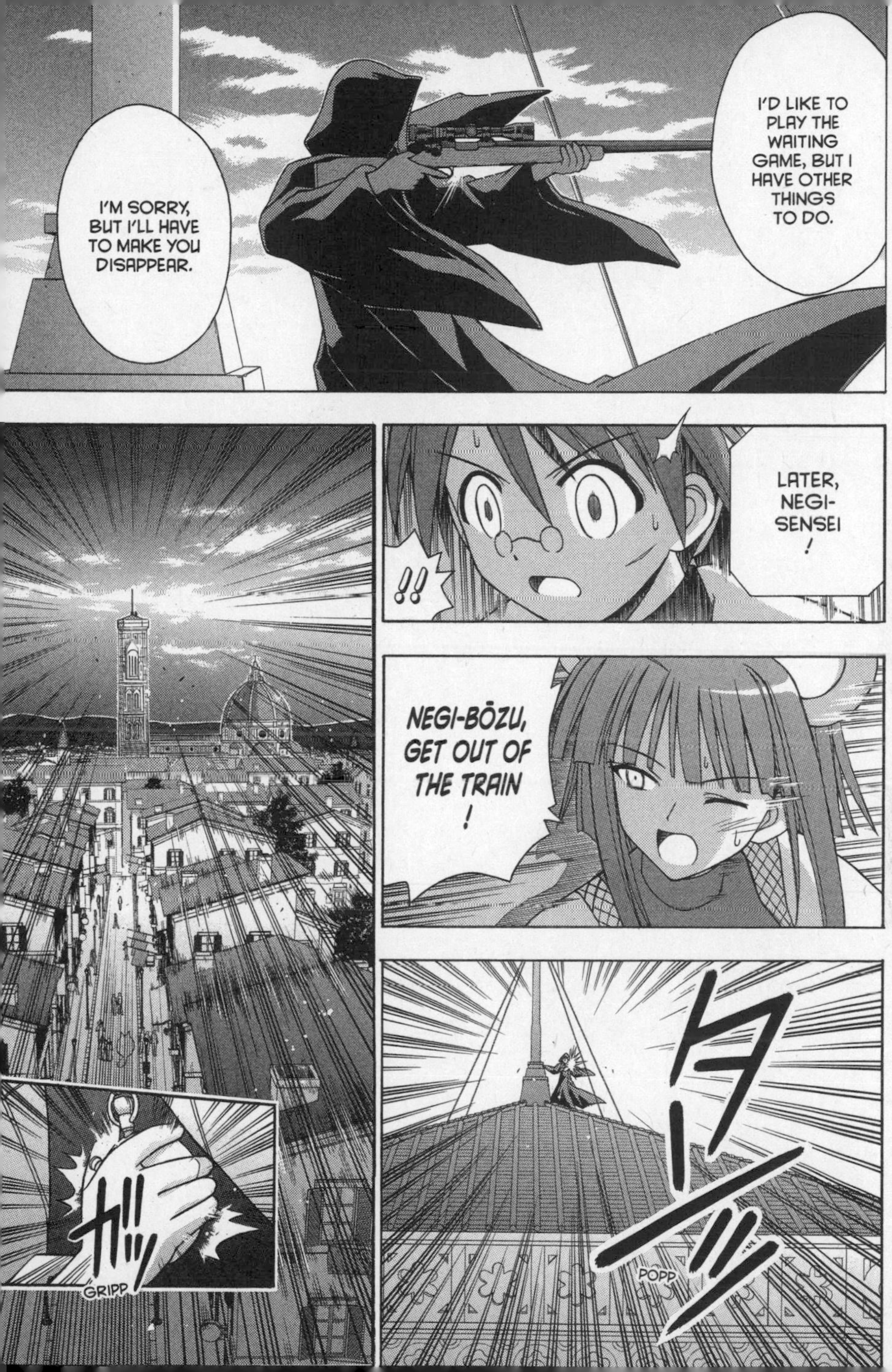
I'D LIKE TO PLAY THE WAITING GAME, BUT I HAVE OTHER THINGS TO DO.
I'M SORRY, BUT I'LL HAVE TO MAKE YOU DISAPPEAR.
LATER, NEGI-SENSEI!
!!
NEGI-BŌZU, GET OUT OF THE TRAIN!
POPP
GRIPP

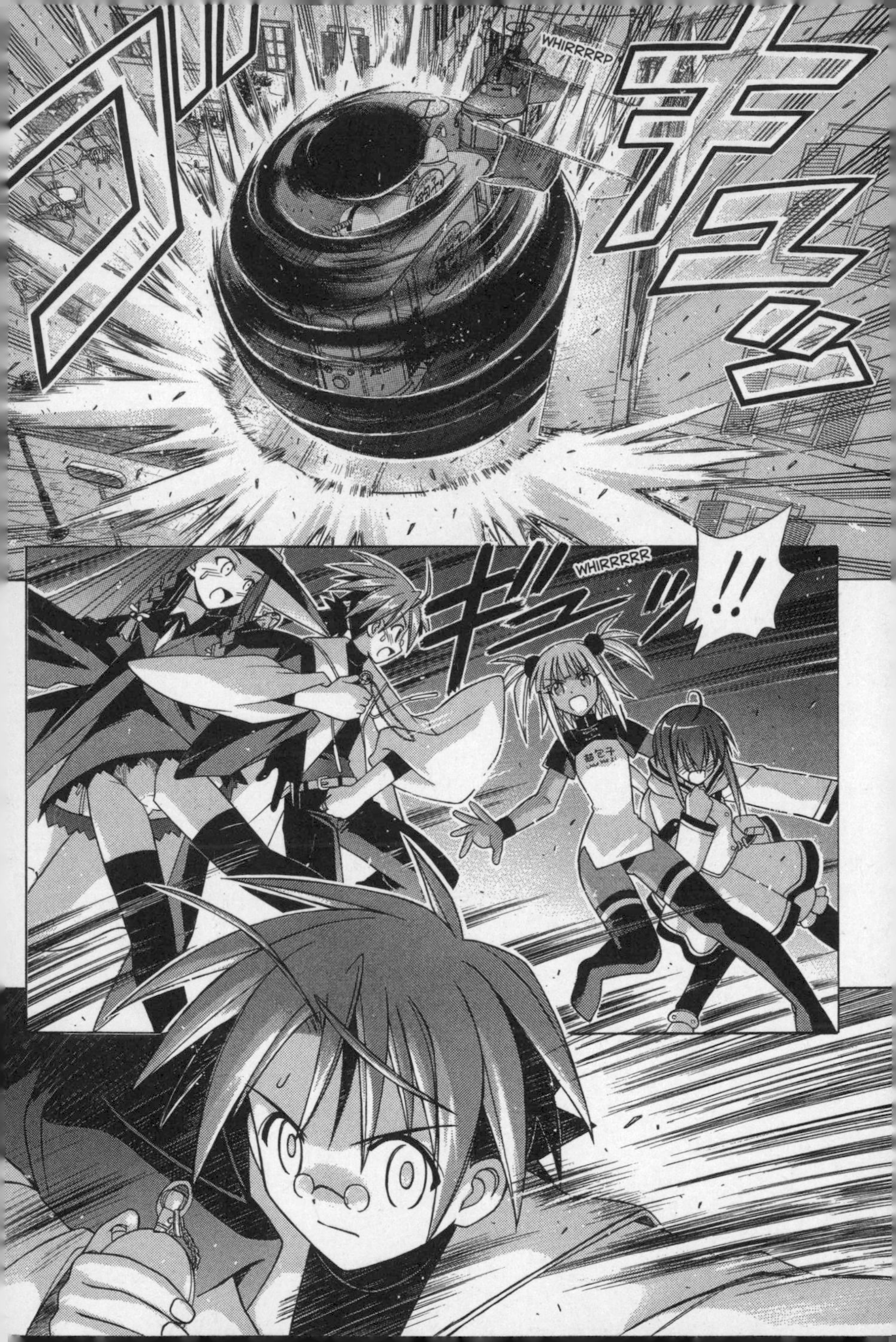
WHIRRRRP
!!
WHIRRRRR

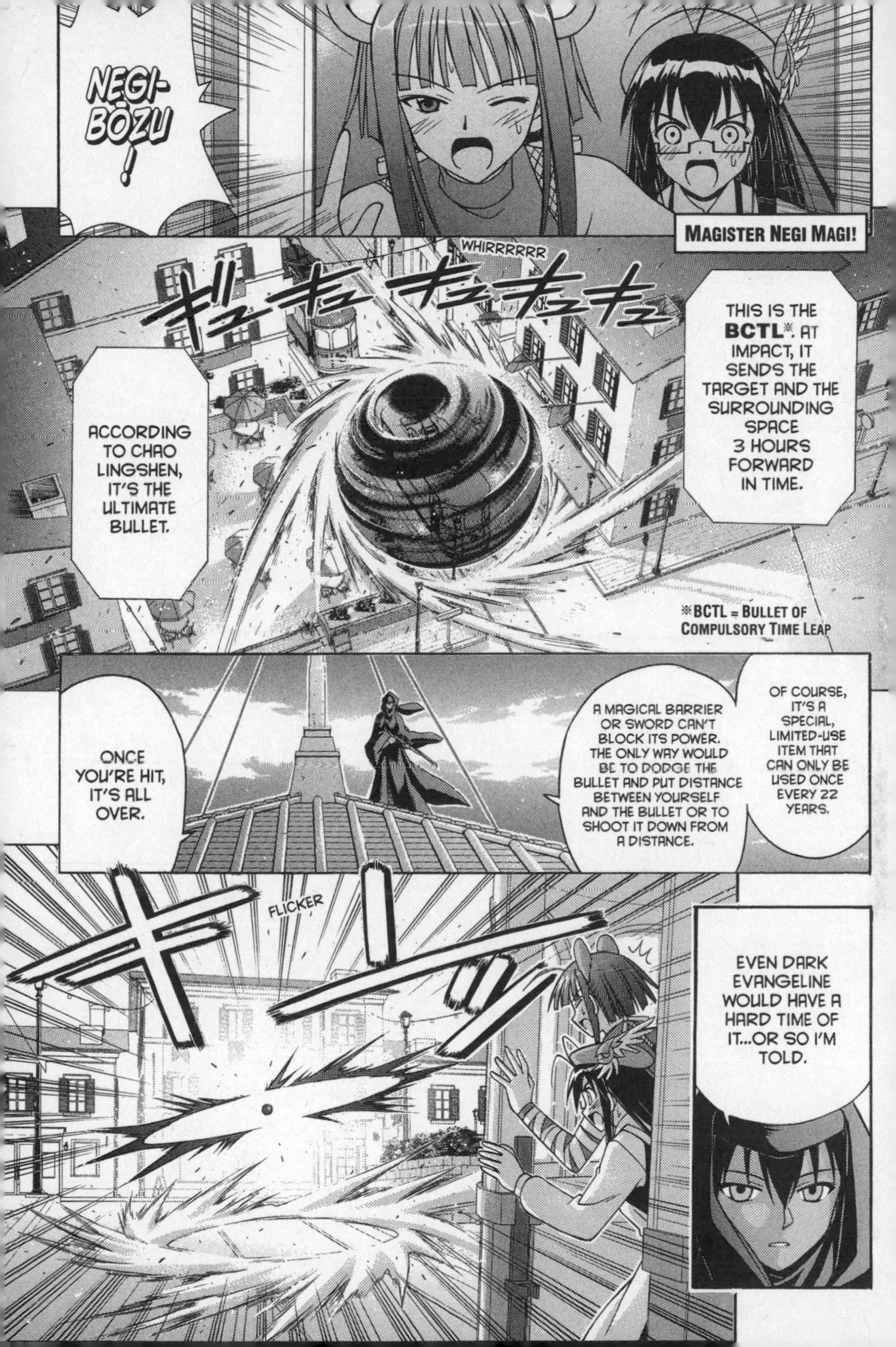

NEGI-BŌZU!
MAGISTER NEGI MAGI!
WHIRRRRRR
THIS IS THE BCTL※. AT IMPACT, IT SENDS THE TARGET AND THE SURROUNDING SPACE 3 HOURS FORWARD IN TIME.
ACCORDING TO CHAO LINGSHEN, IT'S THE ULTIMATE BULLET.
※BCTL = BULLET OF COMPULSORY TIME LEAP
OF COURSE, IT'S A SPECIAL, LIMITED-USE ITEM THAT CAN ONLY BE USED ONCE EVERY 22 YEARS.
A MAGICAL BARRIER OR SWORD CAN'T BLOCK ITS POWER. THE ONLY WAY WOULD BE TO DODGE THE BULLET AND PUT DISTANCE BETWEEN YOURSELF AND THE BULLET OR TO SHOOT IT DOWN FROM A DISTANCE.
ONCE YOU'RE HIT, IT'S ALL OVER.
EVEN DARK EVANGELINE WOULD HAVE A HARD TIME OF IT...OR SO I'M TOLD.
FLICKER

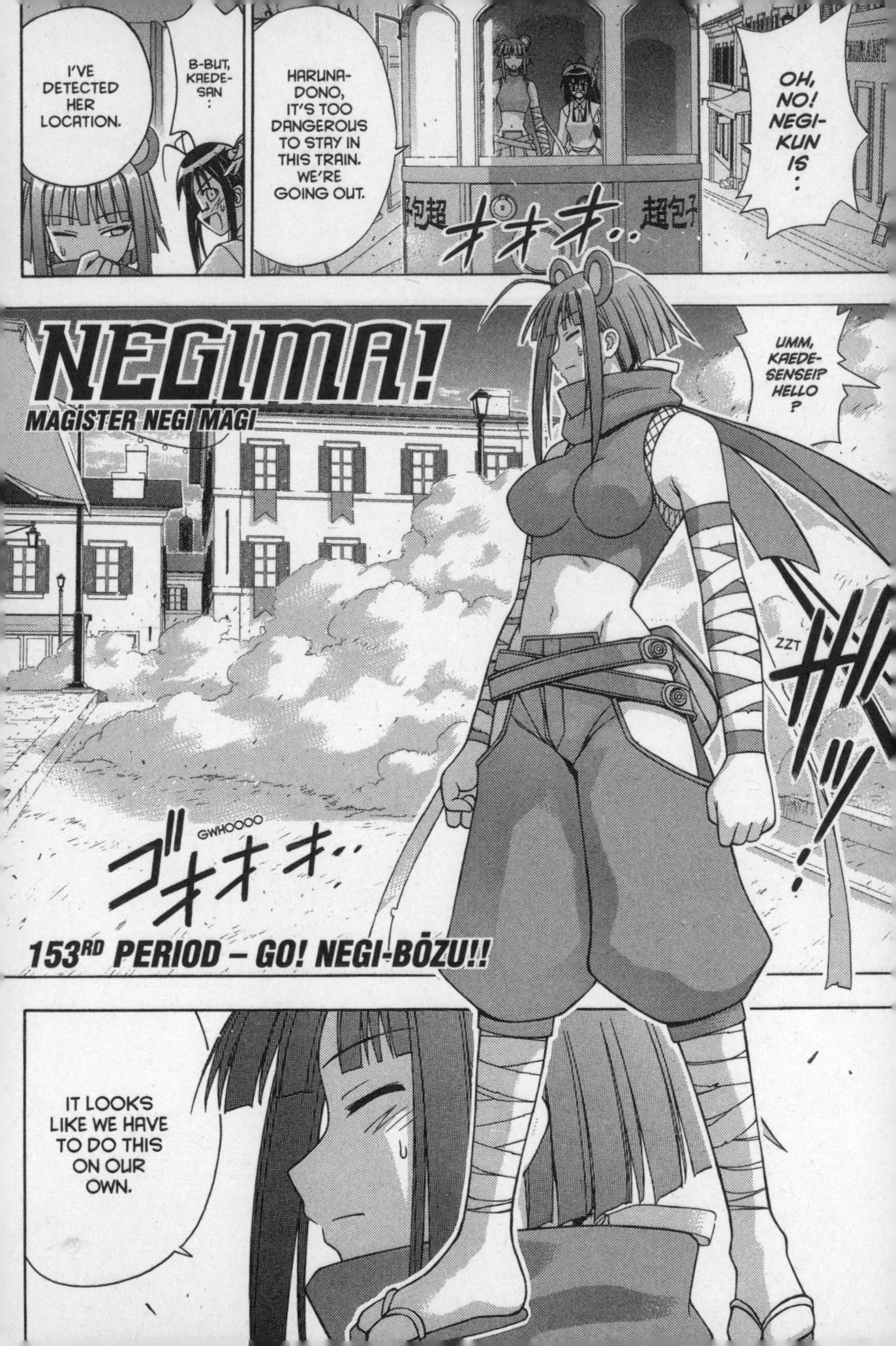

OH, NO! NEGI-KUN IS...
オォォ..
HARUNA-DONO, IT'S TOO DANGEROUS TO STAY IN THIS TRAIN. WE'RE GOING OUT.
B-BUT, KAEDE-SAN...
I'VE DETECTED HER LOCATION.
UMM, KAEDE-SENSEI? HELLO?
ZZT
ザザッ!!
NEGIMA!
MAGISTER NEGI MAGI
GWHOOOO
ゴォォォ..
153RD PERIOD – GO! NEGI-BŌZU!!
IT LOOKS LIKE WE HAVE TO DO THIS ON OUR OWN.

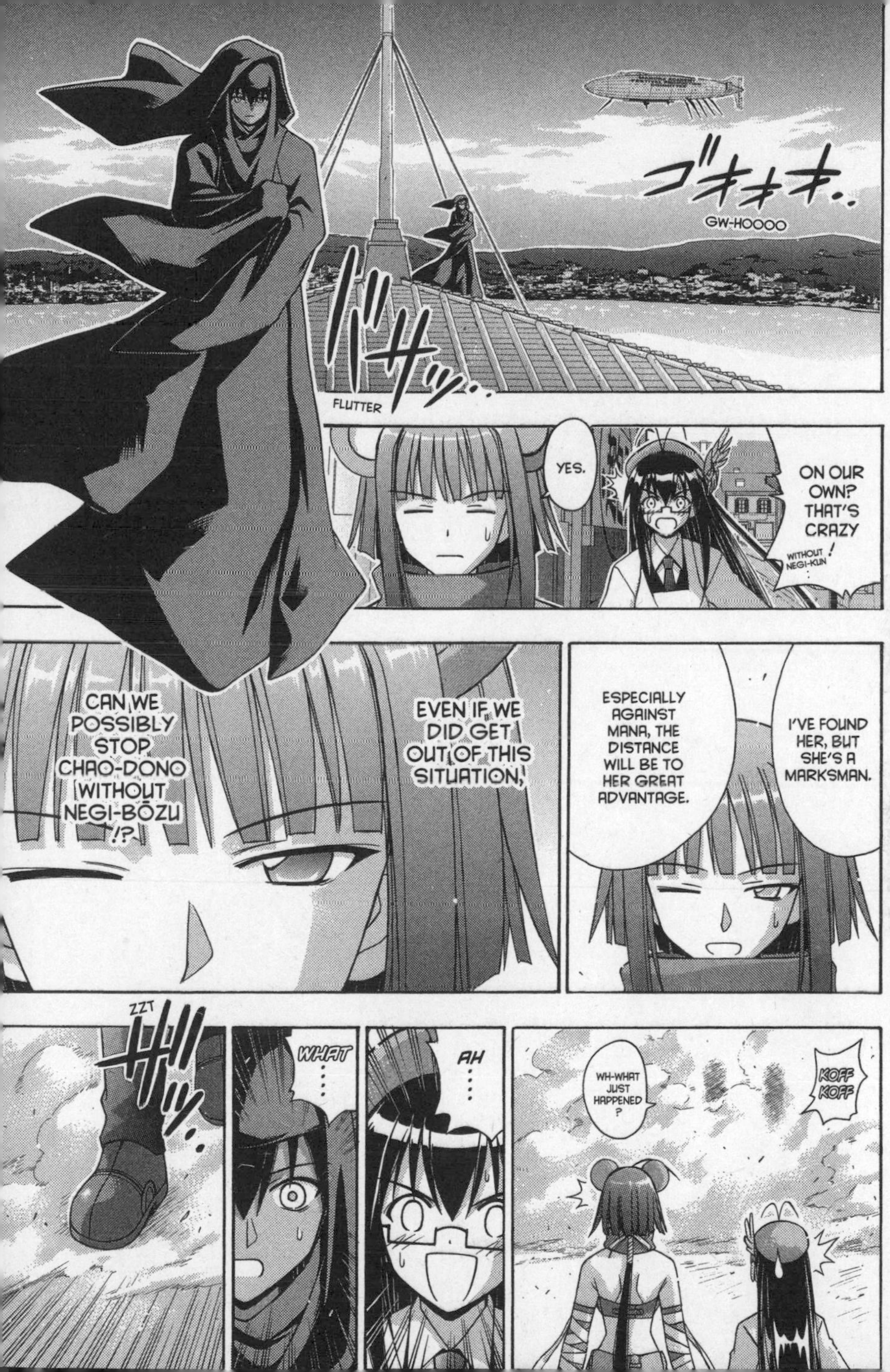
GW-HOOOO
FLUTTER
ON OUR OWN? THAT'S CRAZY
WITHOUT NEGI-KUN!
YES.
I'VE FOUND HER, BUT SHE'S A MARKSMAN.
ESPECIALLY AGAINST MANA, THE DISTANCE WILL BE TO HER GREAT ADVANTAGE.
EVEN IF WE DID GET OUT OF THIS SITUATION,
CAN WE POSSIBLY STOP CHAO-DONO WITHOUT NEGI-BŌZU !?
KOFF KOFF
WH-WHAT JUST HAPPENED?
AH ....
WHAT ....
ZZT

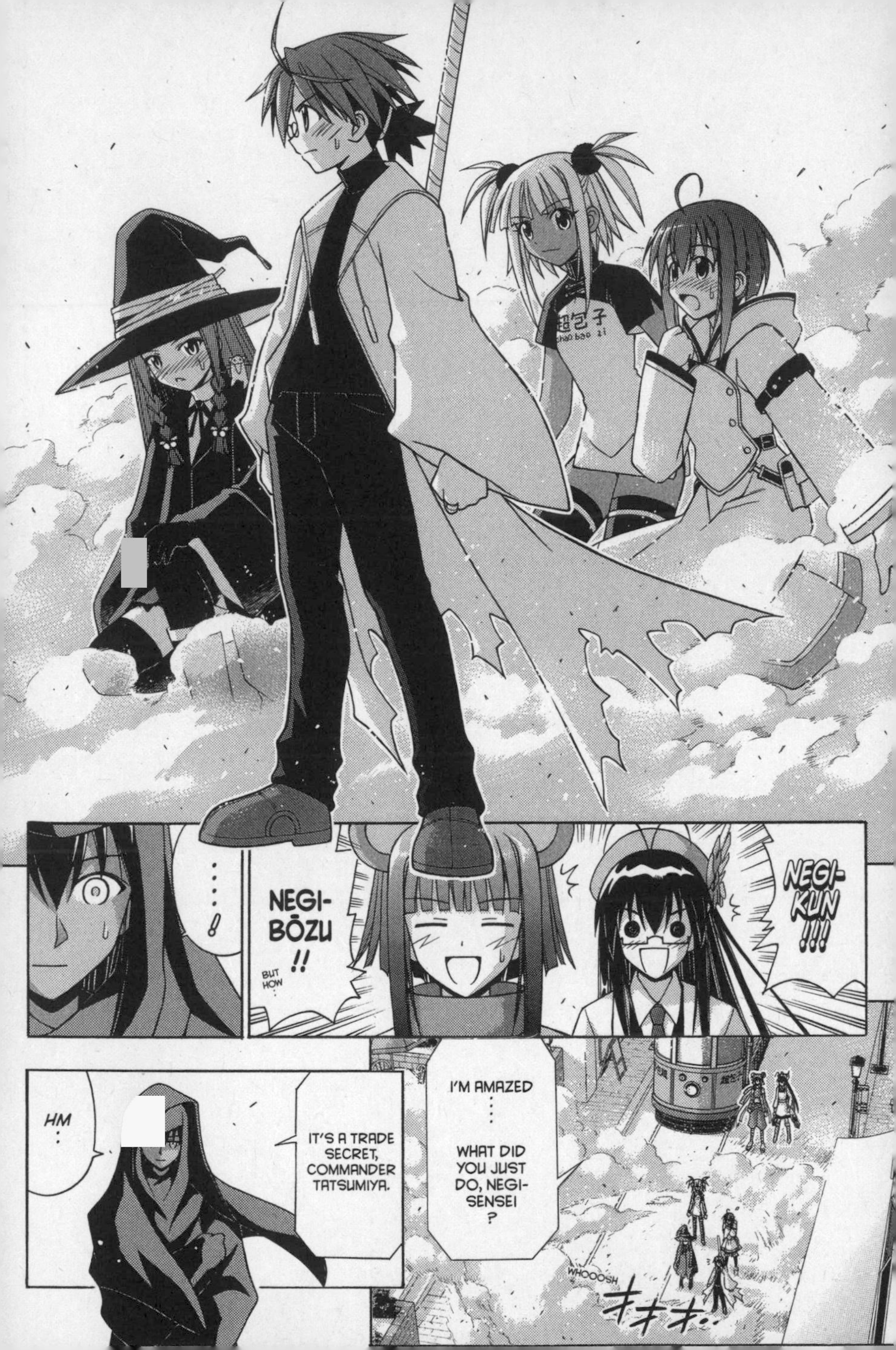
NEGI-KUN!!!
NEGI-BŌZU!!
BUT HOW
....!
I'M AMAZED...
WHAT DID YOU JUST DO, NEGI-SENSEI?
WHOOOSH
IT'S A TRADE SECRET, COMMANDER TATSUMIYA.
HM...

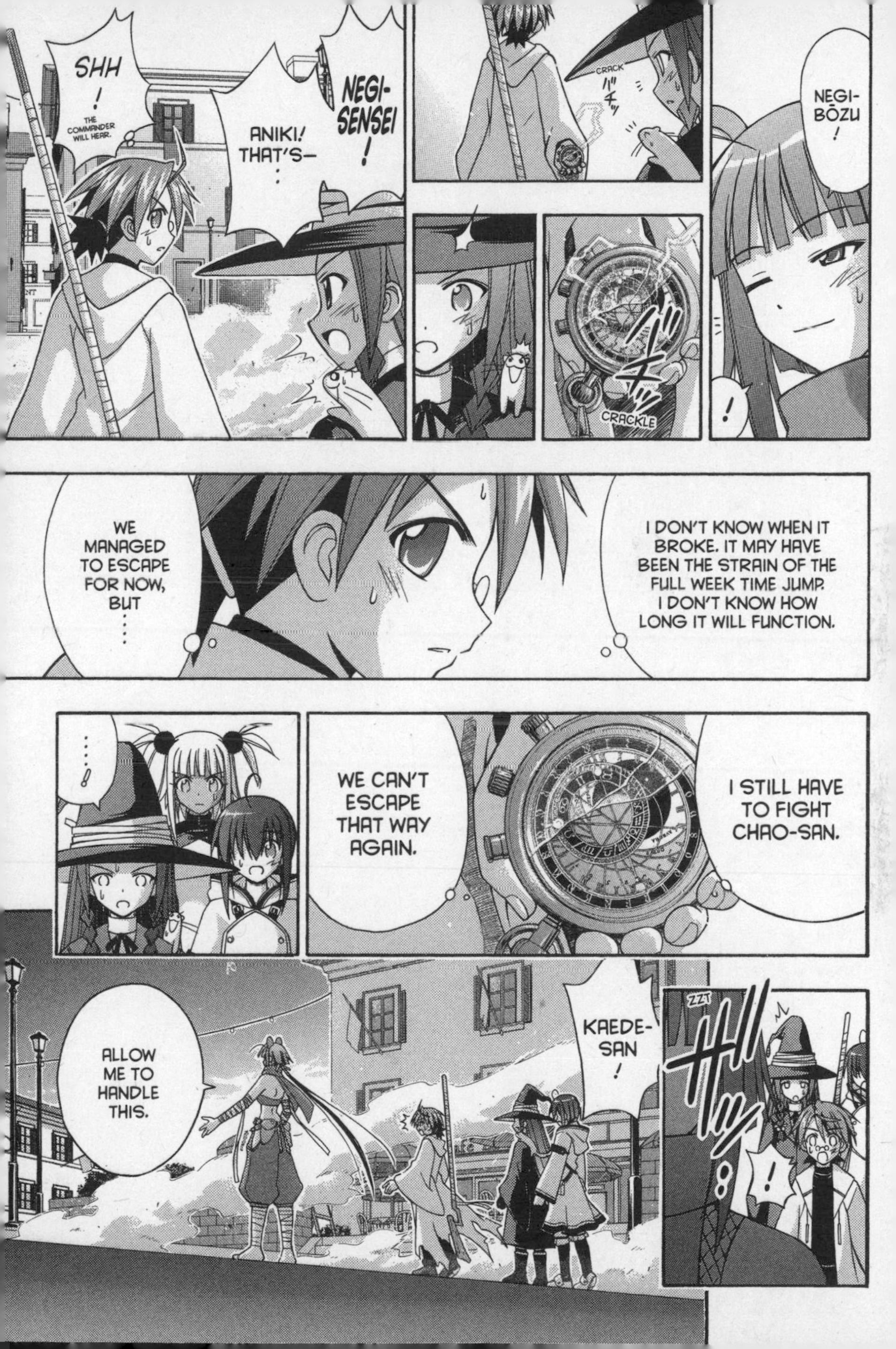
NEGI-BŌZU!
!
CRACK
CRACKLE
NEGI-SENSEI!
ANIKI! THAT'S—...
SHH! THE COMMANDER WILL HEAR.
I DON'T KNOW WHEN IT BROKE. IT MAY HAVE BEEN THE STRAIN OF THE FULL WEEK TIME JUMP. I DON'T KNOW HOW LONG IT WILL FUNCTION.
WE MANAGED TO ESCAPE FOR NOW, BUT...
I STILL HAVE TO FIGHT CHAO-SAN.
WE CAN'T ESCAPE THAT WAY AGAIN.
...!
ZZT
!
!
KAEDE-SAN!
ALLOW ME TO HANDLE THIS.

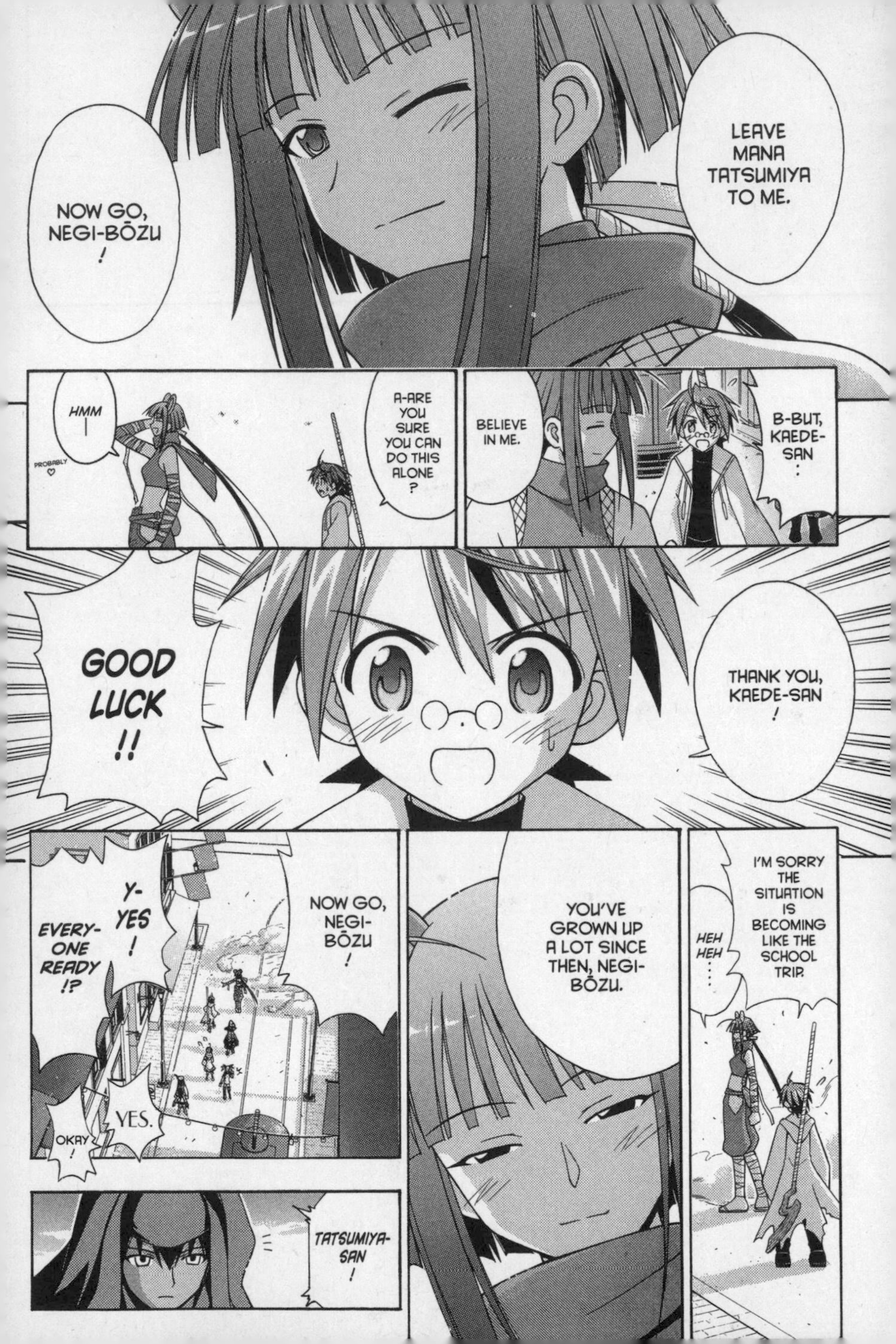

LEAVE MANA TATSUMIYA TO ME.
NOW GO, NEGI-BŌZU!
B-BUT, KAEDE-SAN...
BELIEVE IN ME.
A-ARE YOU SURE YOU CAN DO THIS ALONE?
HMM!
PROBABLY ♡
THANK YOU, KAEDE-SAN!
GOOD LUCK!!
I'M SORRY THE SITUATION IS BECOMING LIKE THE SCHOOL TRIP.
HEH HEH...
YOU'VE GROWN UP A LOT SINCE THEN, NEGI-BŌZU.
NOW GO, NEGI-BŌZU!
Y-YES!
EVERYONE READY!?
YES.
OKAY!
TATSUMIYA-SAN!

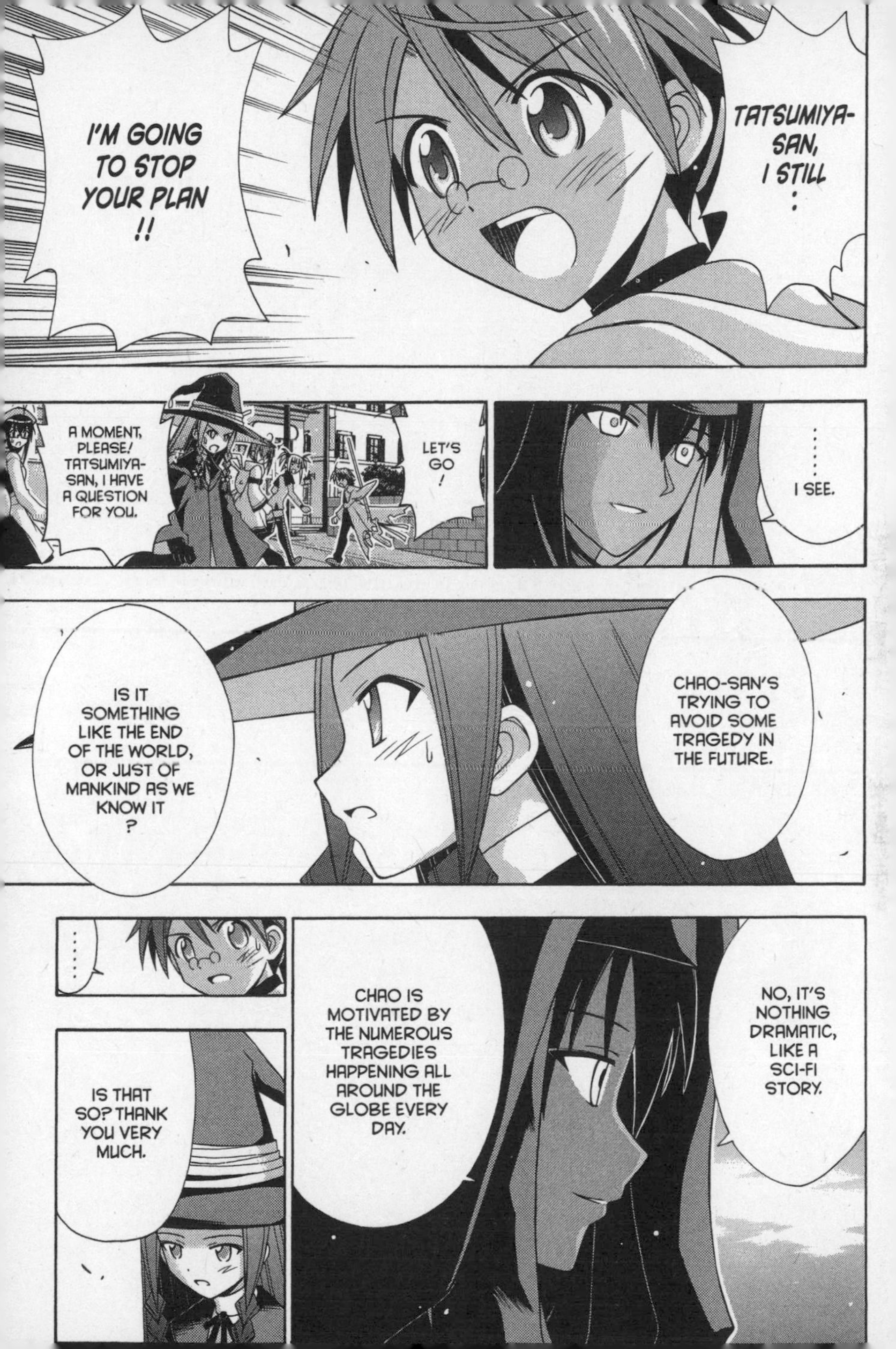
TATSUMIYA-SAN, I STILL :
I'M GOING TO STOP YOUR PLAN !!
...... I SEE.
LET'S GO!
A MOMENT, PLEASE! TATSUMIYA-SAN, I HAVE A QUESTION FOR YOU.
CHAO-SAN'S TRYING TO AVOID SOME TRAGEDY IN THE FUTURE.
IS IT SOMETHING LIKE THE END OF THE WORLD, OR JUST OF MANKIND AS WE KNOW IT ?
NO, IT'S NOTHING DRAMATIC, LIKE A SCI-FI STORY.
CHAO IS MOTIVATED BY THE NUMEROUS TRAGEDIES HAPPENING ALL AROUND THE GLOBE EVERY DAY.
......
IS THAT SO? THANK YOU VERY MUCH.

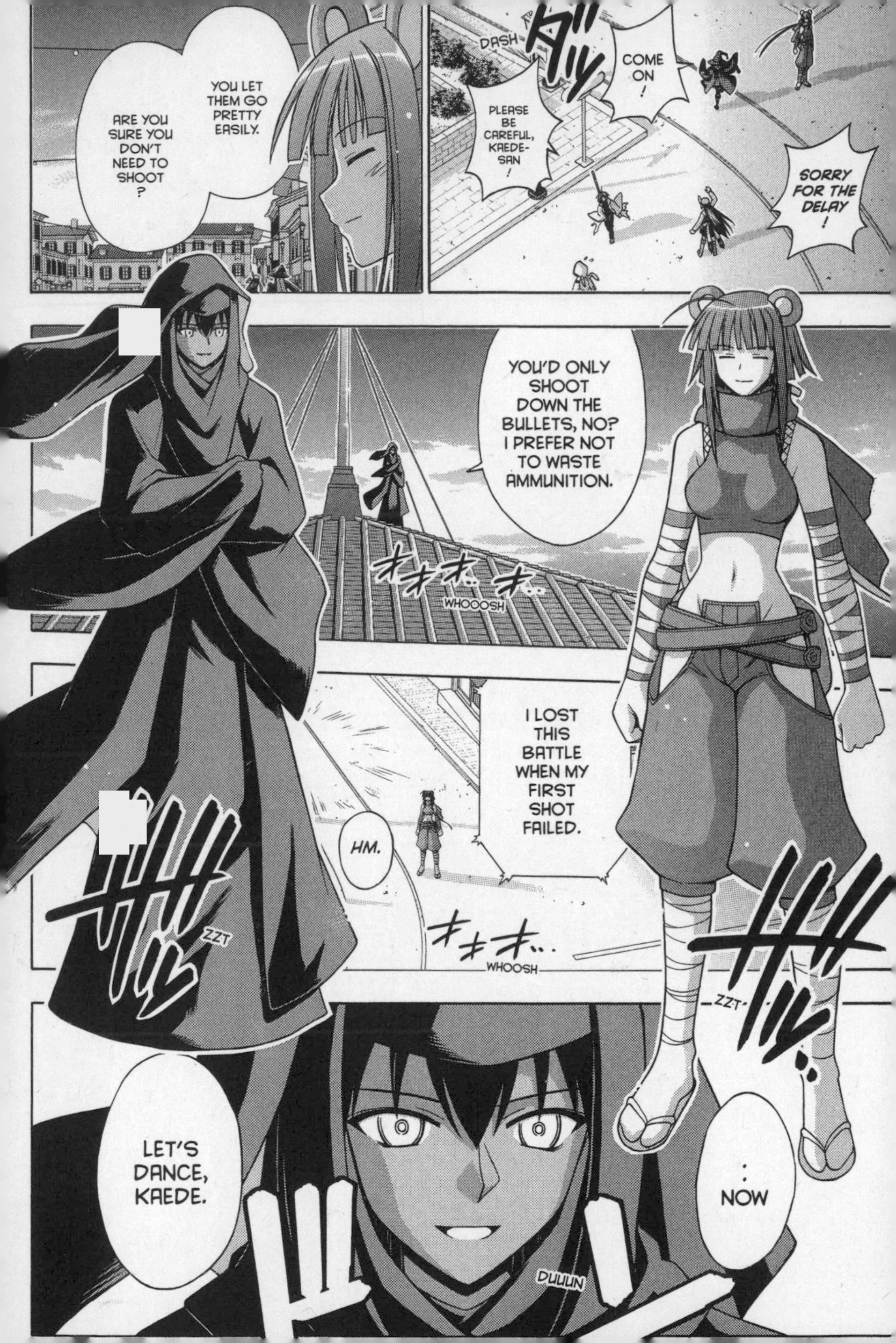

COME ON!
SORRY FOR THE DELAY!
DASH
PLEASE BE CAREFUL, KAEDE-SAN!
YOU LET THEM GO PRETTY EASILY.
ARE YOU SURE YOU DON'T NEED TO SHOOT?
YOU'D ONLY SHOOT DOWN THE BULLETS, NO? I PREFER NOT TO WASTE AMMUNITION.
WHOOOSH
I LOST THIS BATTLE WHEN MY FIRST SHOT FAILED.
HM.
WHOOSH
ZZ-T
ZZ-T
...NOW
LET'S DANCE, KAEDE.
DUUUN

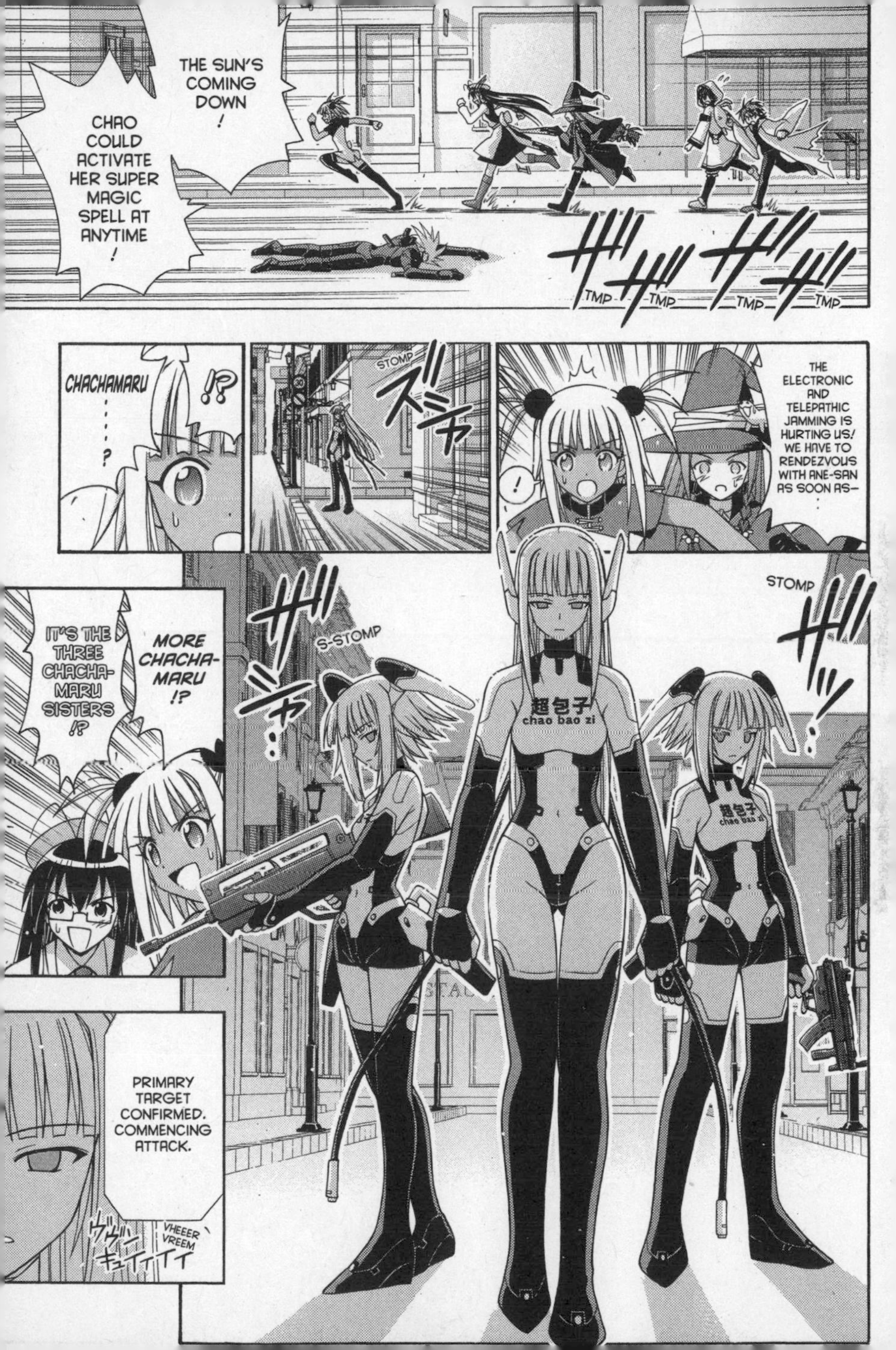
THE SUN'S COMING DOWN!
CHAO COULD ACTIVATE HER SUPER MAGIC SPELL AT ANYTIME!
TMP TMP TMP TMP
THE ELECTRONIC AND TELEPATHIC JAMMING IS HURTING US! WE HAVE TO RENDEZVOUS WITH ANE-SAN AS SOON AS—
!
STOMP
!?
CHACHAMARU.....?
STOMP
S-STOMP
超包子
chao bao zi
超包子
chao bao zi
MORE CHACHA-MARU!?
IT'S THE THREE CHACHA-MARU SISTERS!?
PRIMARY TARGET CONFIRMED. COMMENCING ATTACK.
VHEEER VREEM

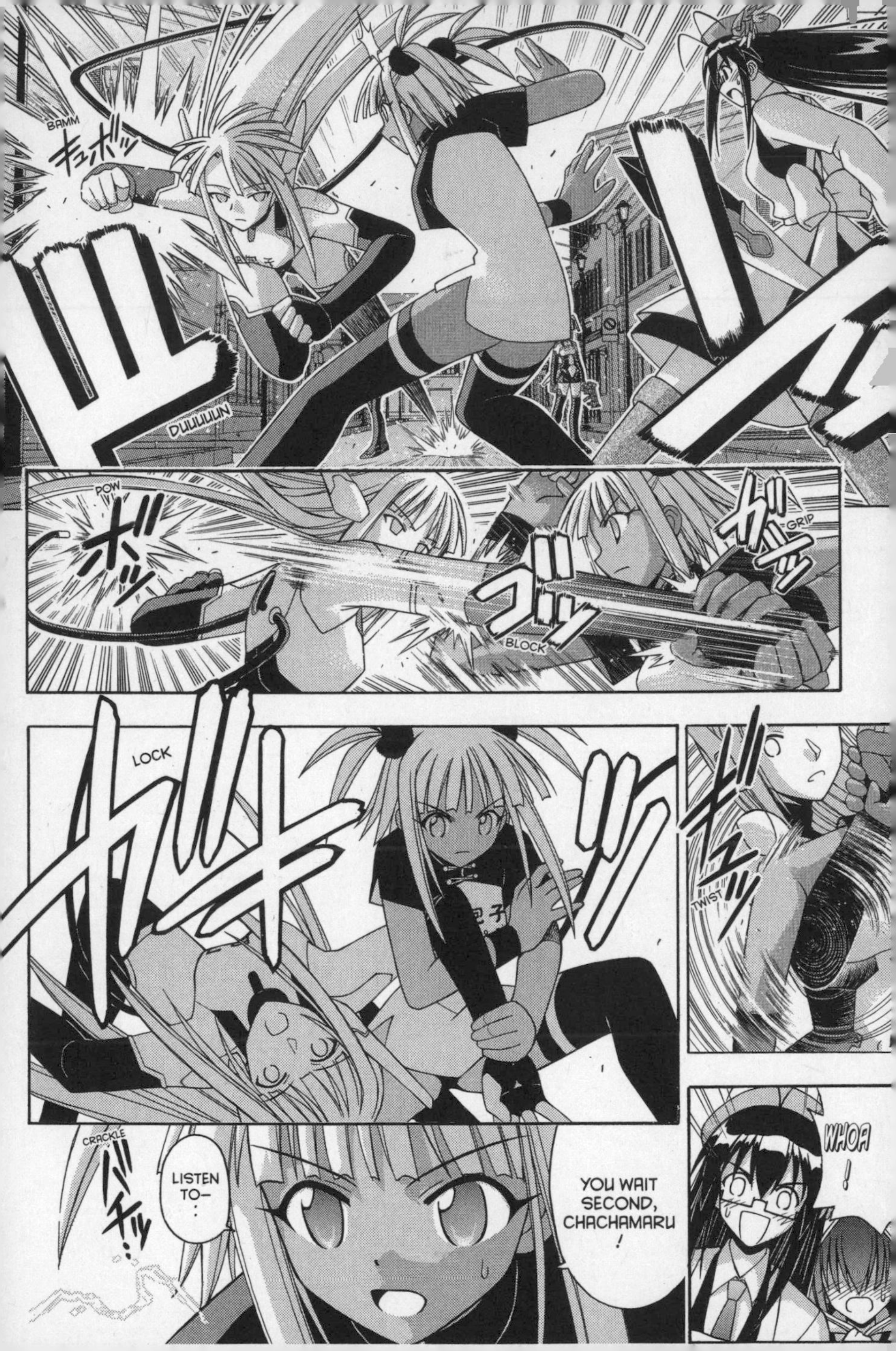
BAMM
DUUUUUUN
GRIP
BLOCK
POW
TWIST
LOCK
WHOA!
YOU WAIT SECOND, CHACHAMARU!
LISTEN TO—...
CRACKLE

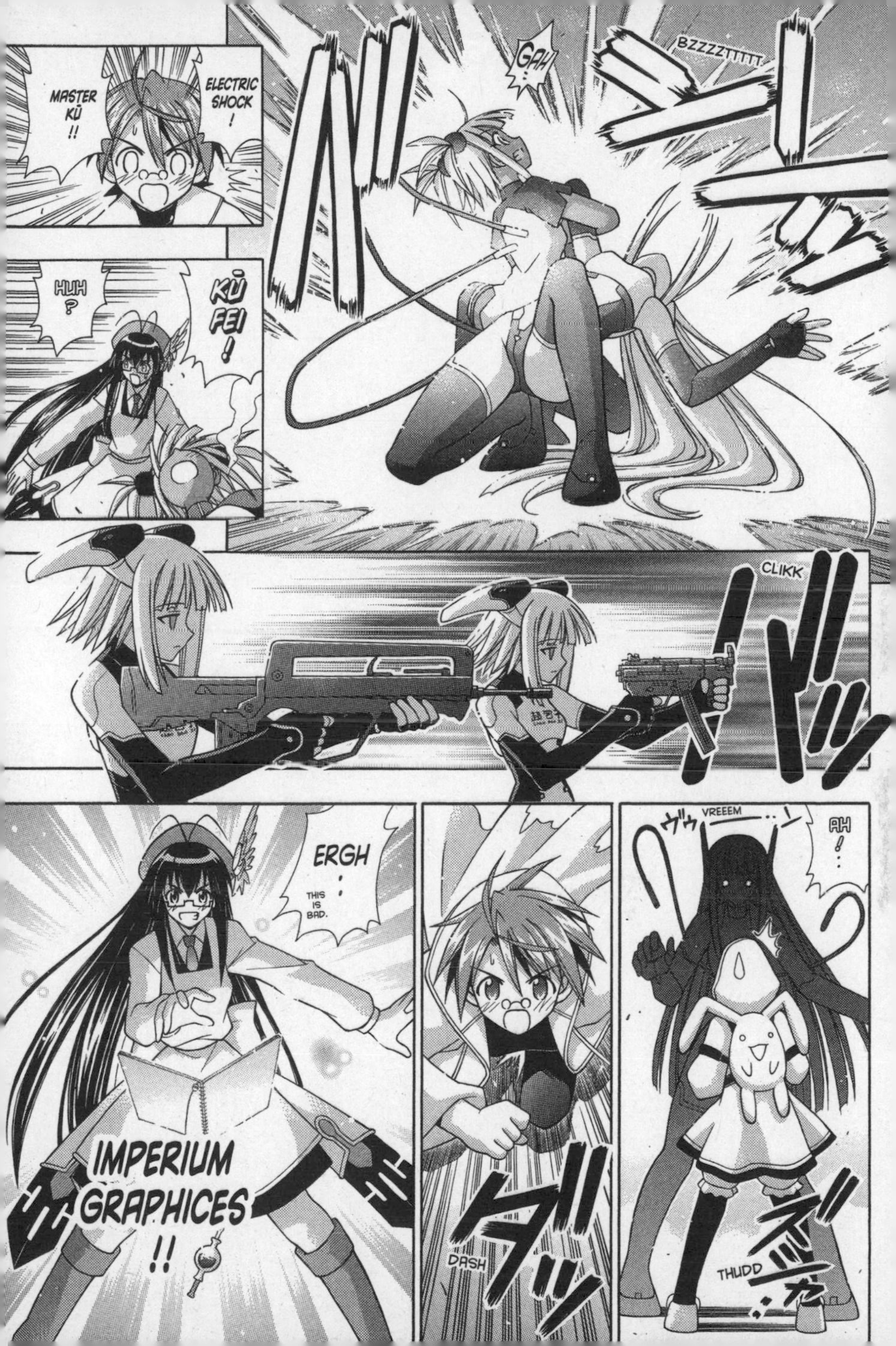
BZZZZTTTTT
GAH
ELECTRIC SHOCK !
MASTER KŪ !!
KŪ FEI !
HUH ?
CLIKK
ヴゥ
VREEEM
AH ! . .
THUDD
DASH
ERGH :
THIS IS BAD.
IMPERIUM GRAPHICES !!

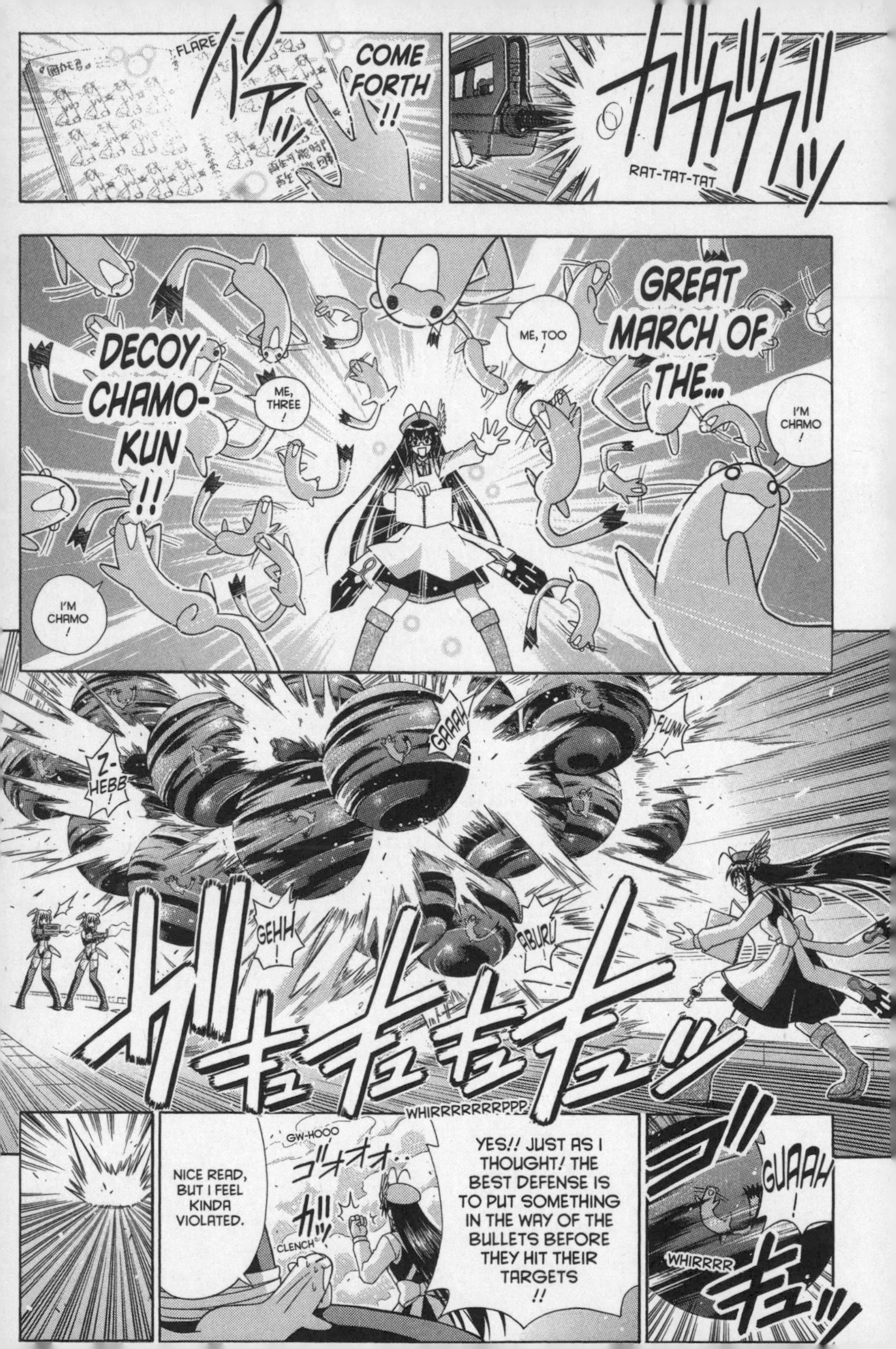
RAT-TAT-TAT
FLARE
COME FORTH!!
GREAT MARCH OF THE...
I'M CHAMO!
ME, TOO!
ME, THREE!
DECOY CHAMO-KUN!!
I'M CHAMO!
FLUN!
GAAAH
Z-HEBB!
ABURU!
GEHH!
WHIRRRRRRRPPP
GUAAH!
WHIRRRR
YES!! JUST AS I THOUGHT! THE BEST DEFENSE IS TO PUT SOMETHING IN THE WAY OF THE BULLETS BEFORE THEY HIT THEIR TARGETS!!
GW-HOOO
CLENCH
NICE READ, BUT I FEEL KINDA VIOLATED.

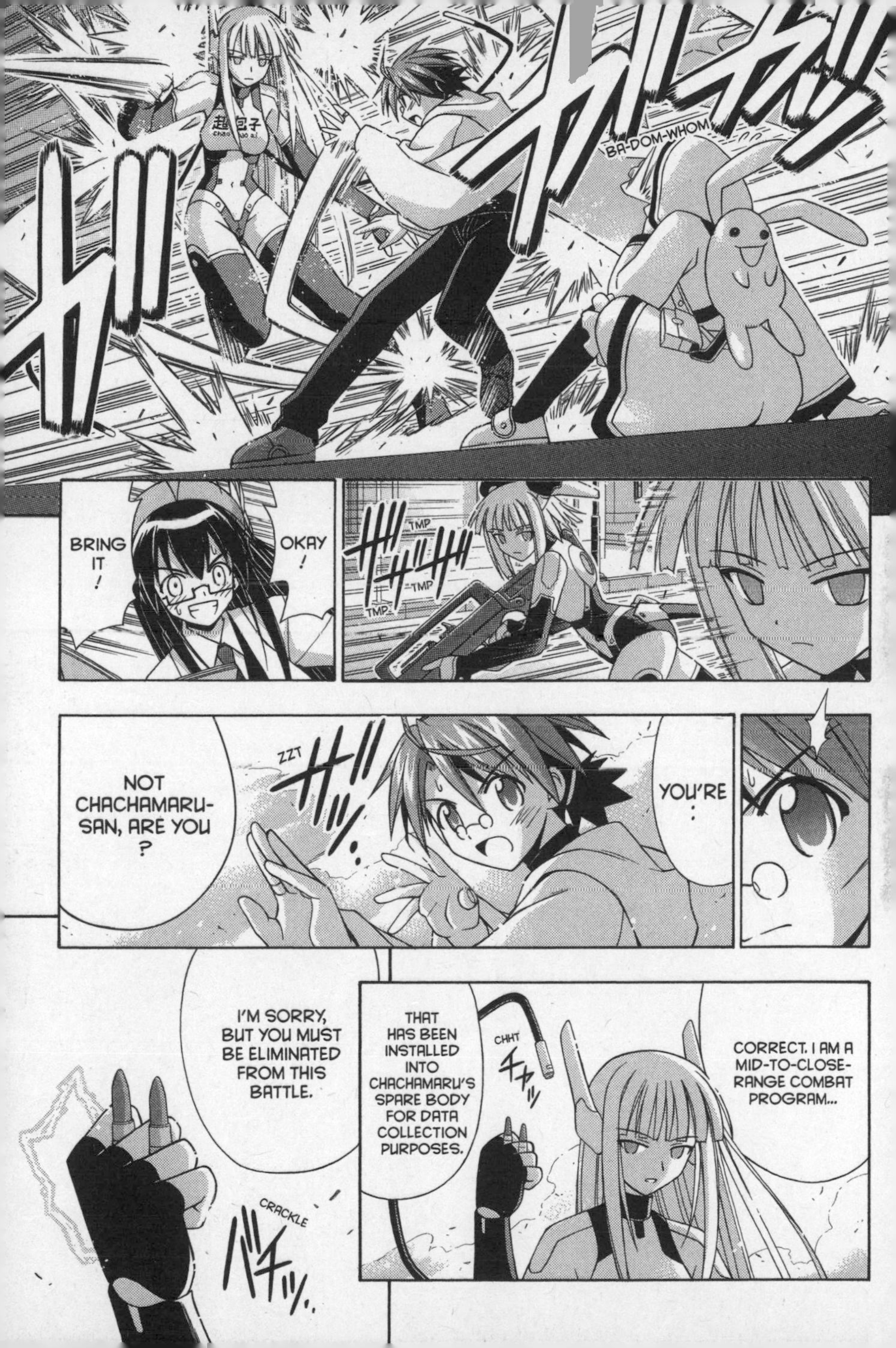
BA-DOM-WHOM
TMP
TMP
TMP
OKAY!
BRING IT!
YOU'RE...
NOT CHACHAMARU-SAN, ARE YOU?
ZZT
CORRECT. I AM A MID-TO-CLOSE-RANGE COMBAT PROGRAM...
THAT HAS BEEN INSTALLED INTO CHACHAMARU'S SPARE BODY FOR DATA COLLECTION PURPOSES.
CHHT
I'M SORRY, BUT YOU MUST BE ELIMINATED FROM THIS BATTLE.
CRACKLE

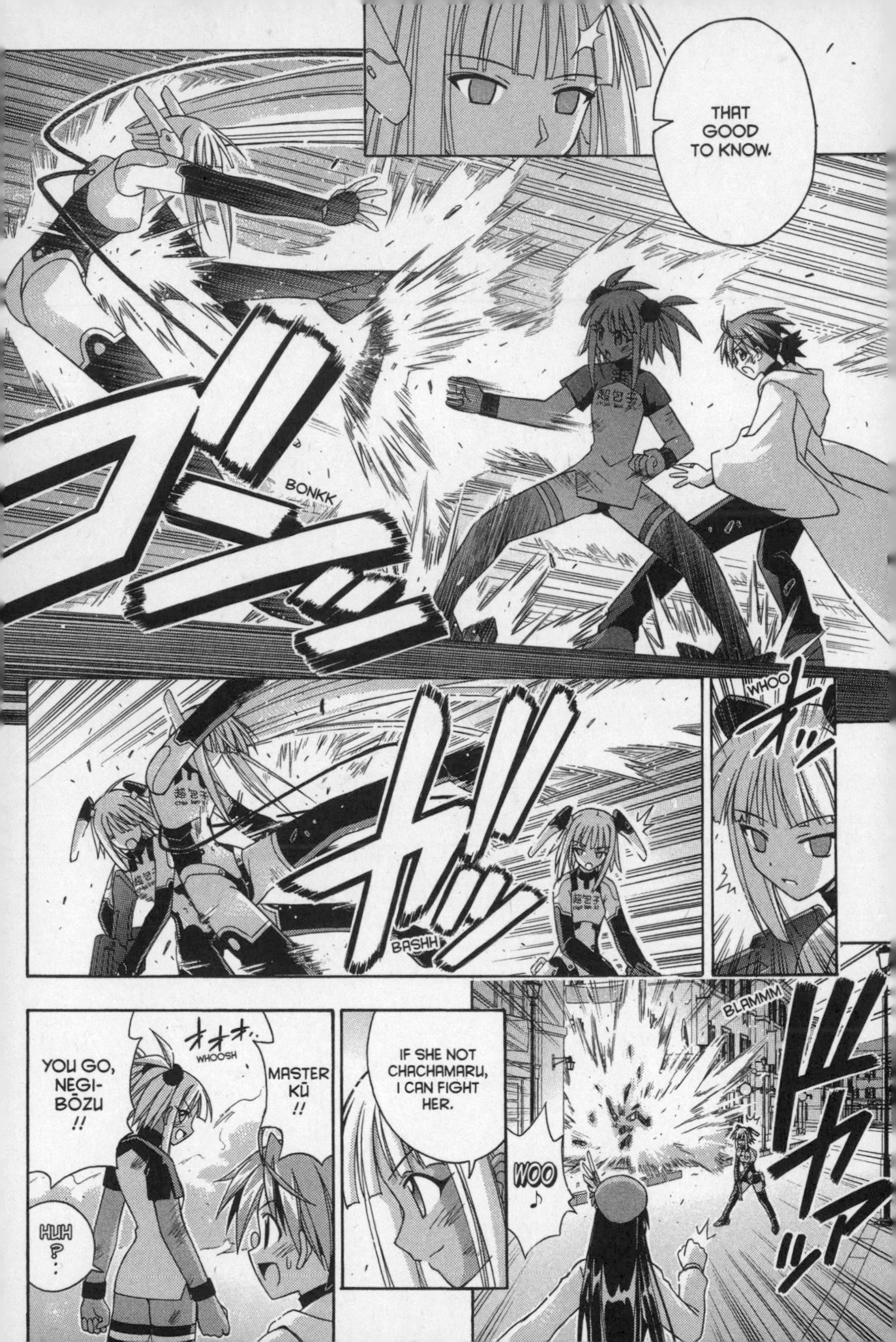
THAT GOOD TO KNOW.
BONKK
WHOO
BASHH
BLAMMM
WOO ♪
IF SHE NOT CHACHAMARU, I CAN FIGHT HER.
MASTER KŪ !!
WHOOSH
YOU GO, NEGI-BŌZU !!
HUH ?

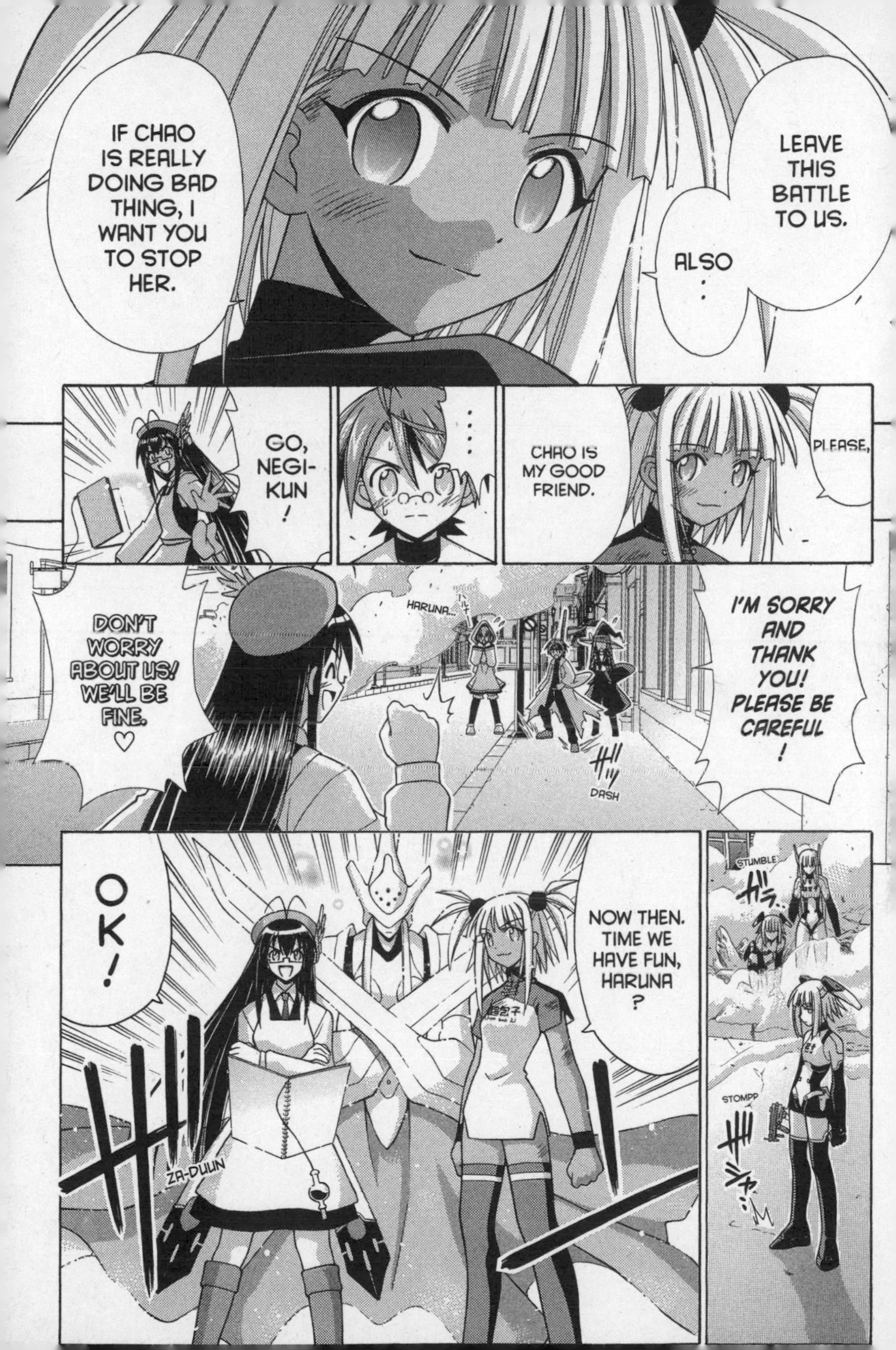
LEAVE THIS BATTLE TO US.
ALSO :
IF CHAO IS REALLY DOING BAD THING, I WANT YOU TO STOP HER.
PLEASE,
CHAO IS MY GOOD FRIEND.
...
GO, NEGI-KUN!
I'M SORRY AND THANK YOU! PLEASE BE CAREFUL!
HARUNA...
DASH
DON'T WORRY ABOUT US! WE'LL BE FINE. ♡
STUMBLE
STOMPP
NOW THEN. TIME WE HAVE FUN, HARUNA?
OK!
ZA-DUUN

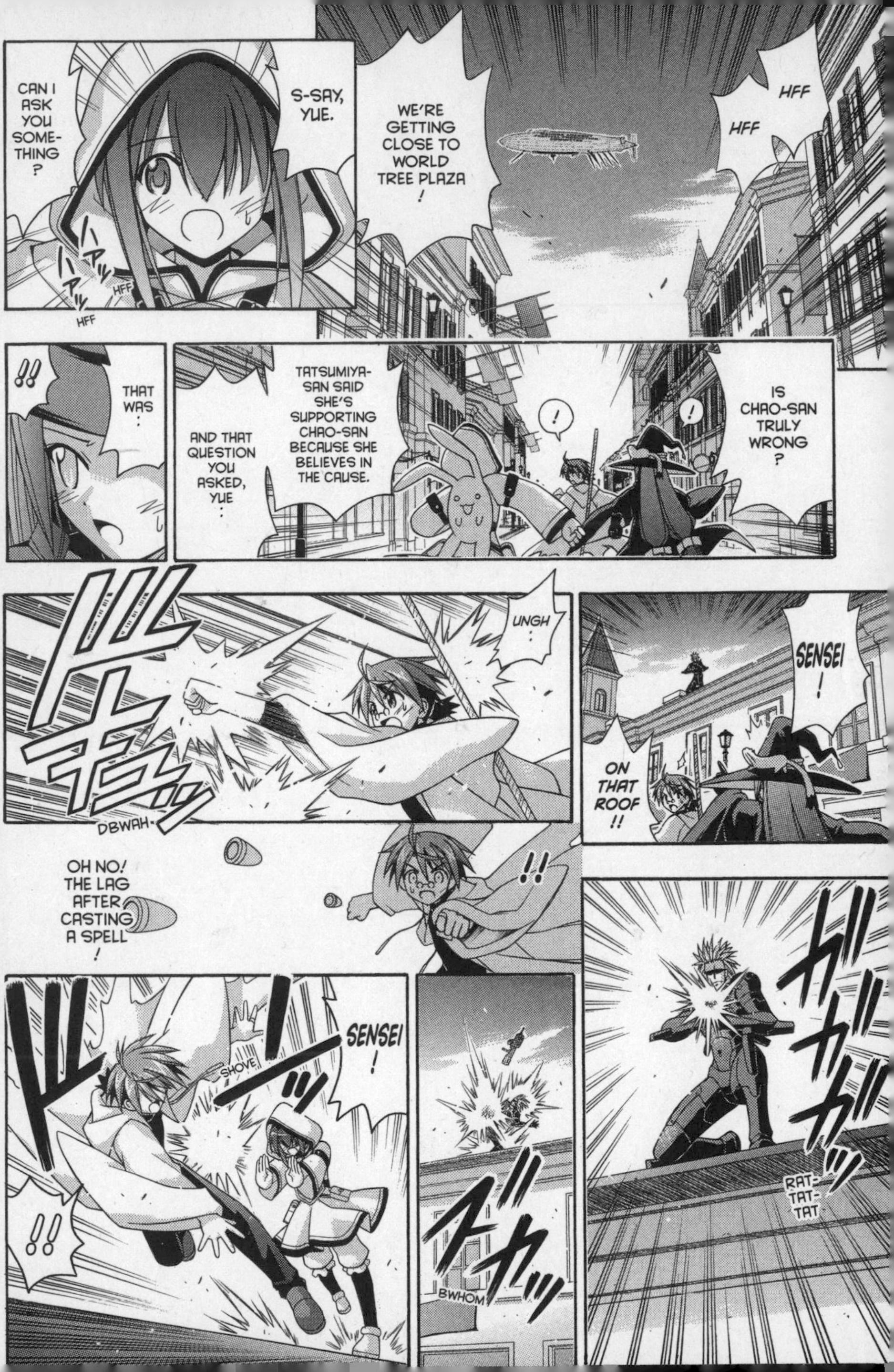

HFF
HFF
WE'RE GETTING CLOSE TO WORLD TREE PLAZA!
S-SAY, YUE.
CAN I ASK YOU SOMETHING?
HFF
HFF
IS CHAO-SAN TRULY WRONG?
!
!
TATSUMIYA-SAN SAID SHE'S SUPPORTING CHAO-SAN BECAUSE SHE BELIEVES IN THE CAUSE.
AND THAT QUESTION YOU ASKED, YUE:
!!
THAT WAS:
SENSEI!
ON THAT ROOF!!
UNGH:
DBWAH
RAT-TAT-TAT
!!
OH NO! THE LAG AFTER CASTING A SPELL!
BWHOM
SENSEI!
SHOVE
!!

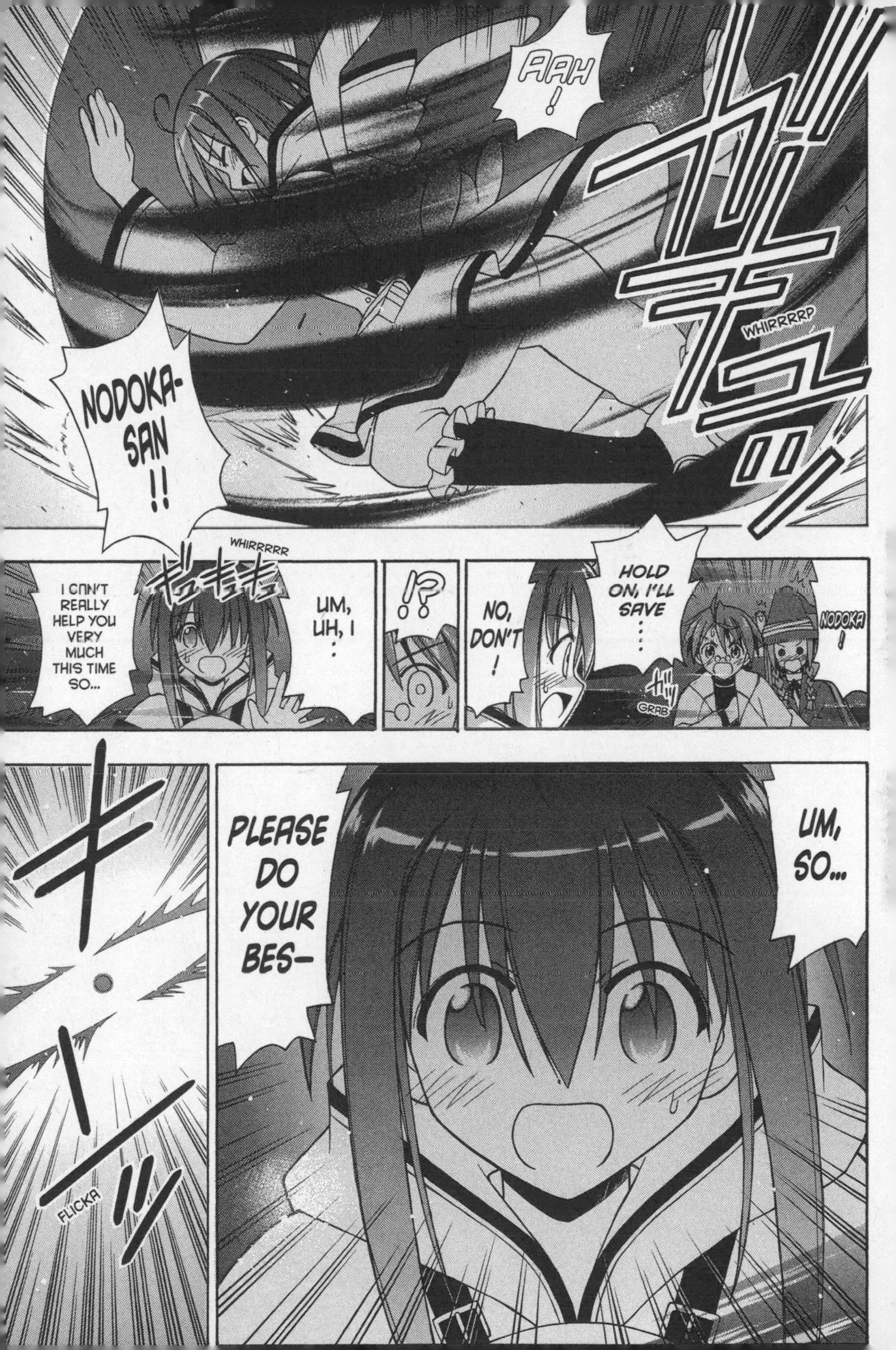
WHIRRRRP
AAH!
NODOKA-SAN!!
NODOKA!
GRAB
HOLD ON, I'LL SAVE ....
NO, DON'T!
!?
UM, UH, I :
WHIRRRRR
I CAN'T REALLY HELP YOU VERY MUCH THIS TIME SO...
UM, SO...
PLEASE DO YOUR BES-
FLICKA

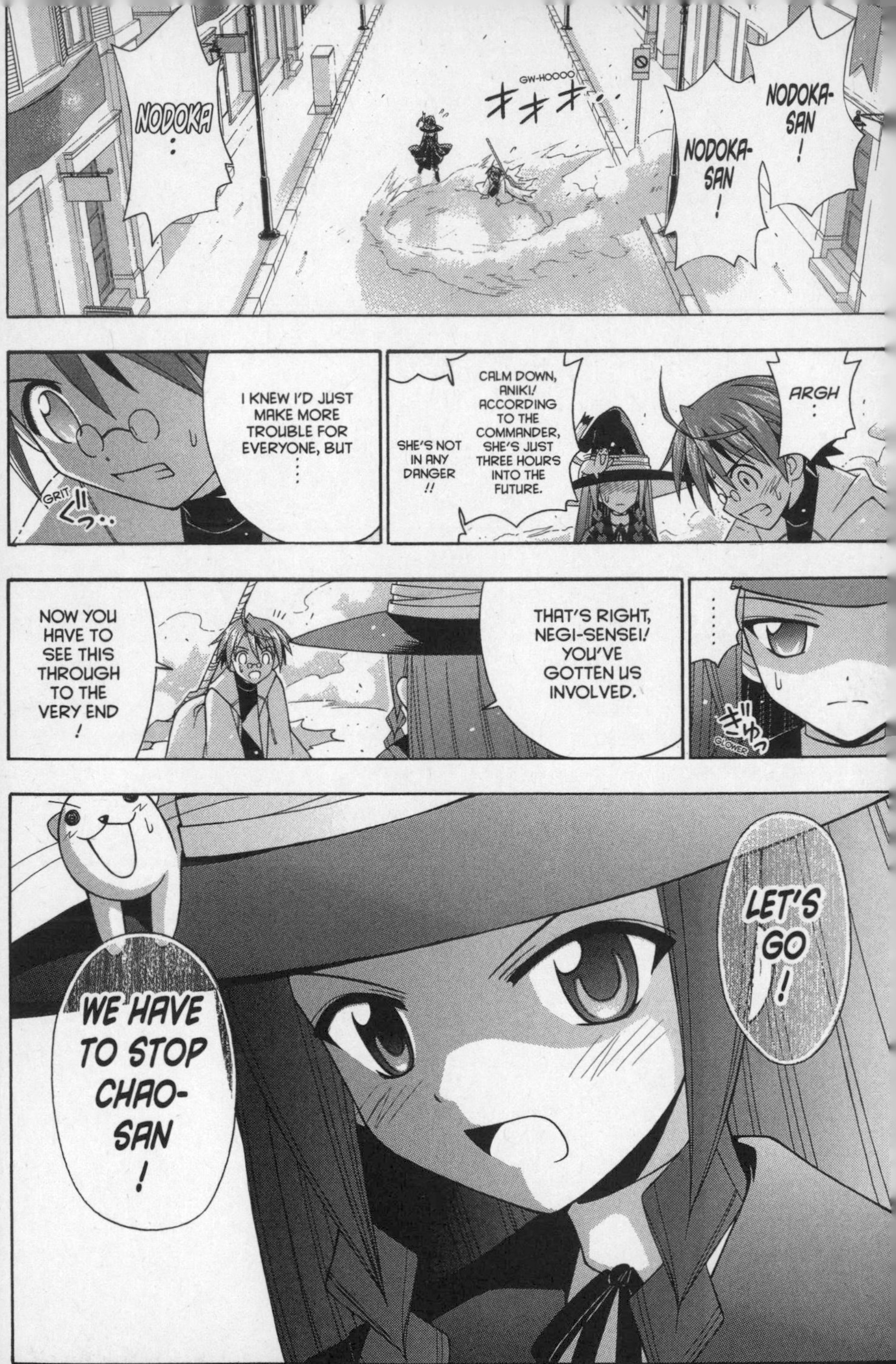

NODOKA-SAN!
NODOKA-SAN!
GW-HOOOO
オォォ
NODOKA...
ARGH...
CALM DOWN, ANIKI! ACCORDING TO THE COMMANDER, SHE'S JUST THREE HOURS INTO THE FUTURE.
SHE'S NOT IN ANY DANGER!!
I KNEW I'D JUST MAKE MORE TROUBLE FOR EVERYONE, BUT...
GRIT
くっ...
......
ぎゅっ
THAT'S RIGHT, NEGI-SENSEI! YOU'VE GOTTEN US INVOLVED.
NOW YOU HAVE TO SEE THIS THROUGH TO THE VERY END!
LET'S GO!
WE HAVE TO STOP CHAO-SAN!

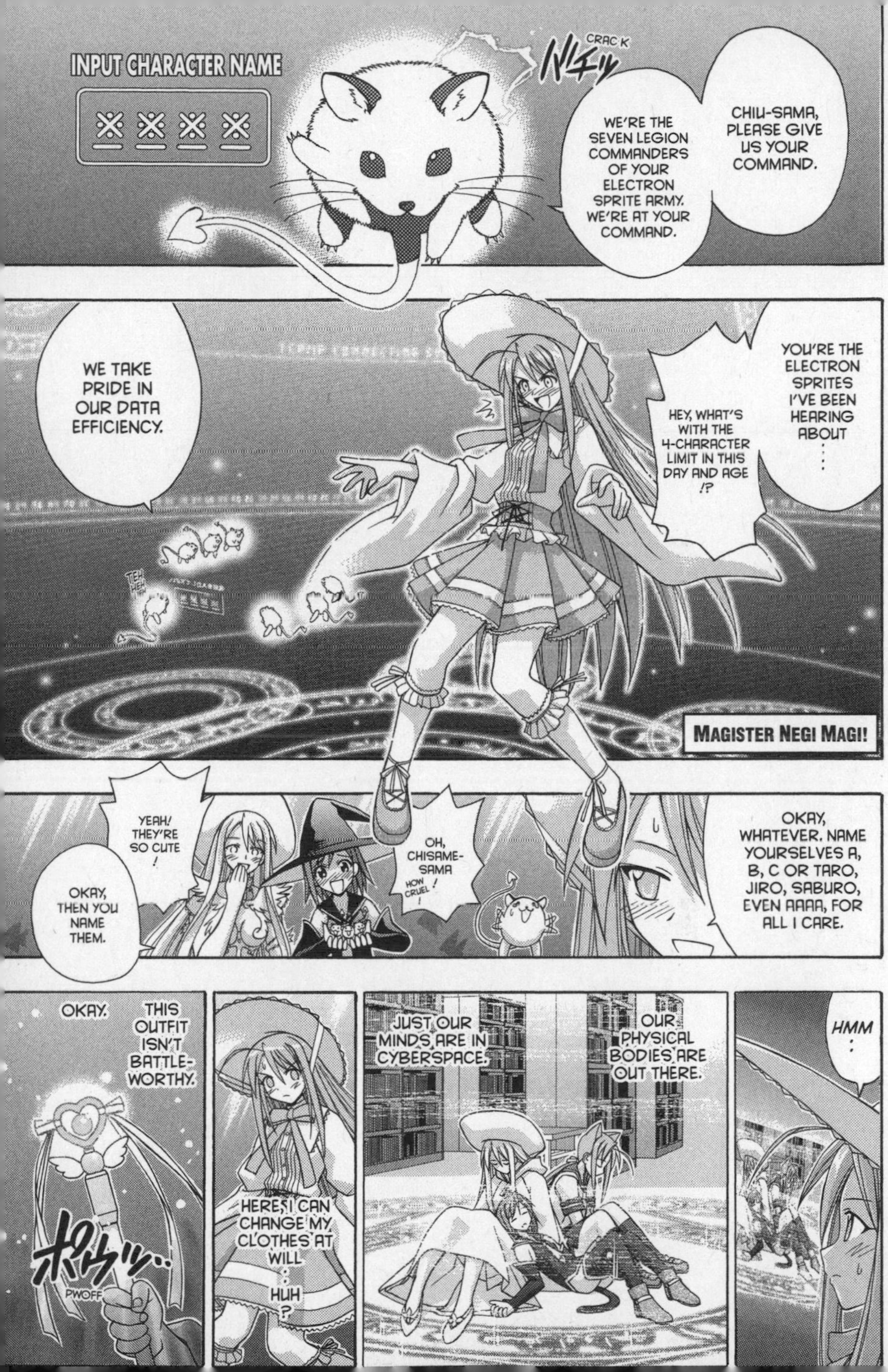

INPUT CHARACTER NAME
※※※※
CRAC K
CHIU-SAMA, PLEASE GIVE US YOUR COMMAND.
WE'RE THE SEVEN LEGION COMMANDERS OF YOUR ELECTRON SPRITE ARMY. WE'RE AT YOUR COMMAND.
YOU'RE THE ELECTRON SPRITES I'VE BEEN HEARING ABOUT...
HEY, WHAT'S WITH THE 4-CHARACTER LIMIT IN THIS DAY AND AGE!?
WE TAKE PRIDE IN OUR DATA EFFICIENCY.
TEH HEH
MAGISTER NEGI MAGI!
OKAY, WHATEVER. NAME YOURSELVES A, B, C OR TARO, JIRO, SABURO, EVEN AAAA, FOR ALL I CARE.
OH, CHISAME-SAMA
HOW CRUEL!
YEAH! THEY'RE SO CUTE!
OKAY, THEN YOU NAME THEM.
HMM:
OUR PHYSICAL BODIES ARE OUT THERE.
JUST OUR MINDS ARE IN CYBERSPACE.
HERE, I CAN CHANGE MY CLOTHES AT WILL::
HUH?
THIS OUTFIT ISN'T BATTLE-WORTHY.
OKAY.
PWOFF

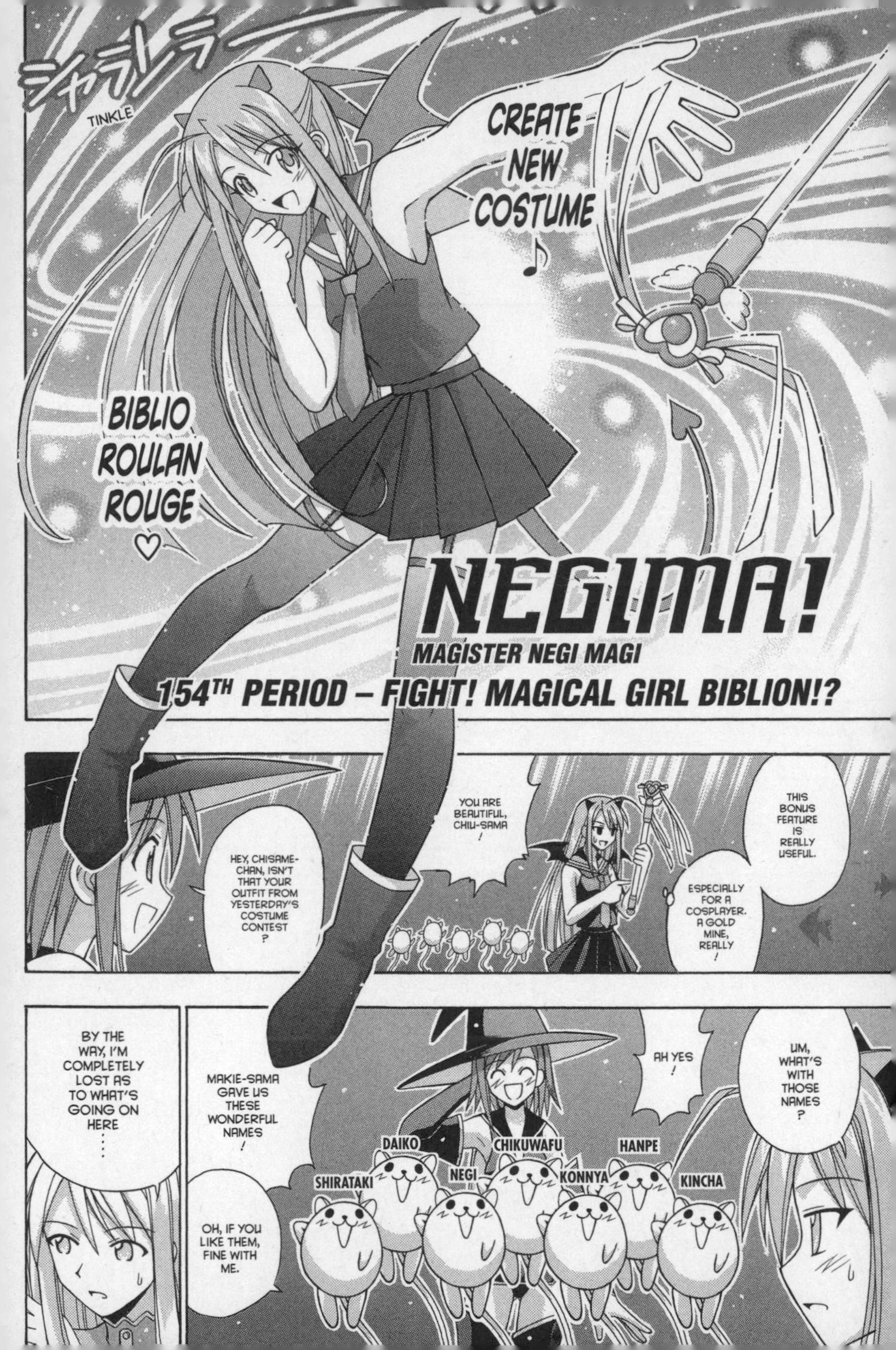
シャラレラー
TINKLE
CREATE NEW COSTUME ♪
BIBLIO ROULAN ROUGE ♡
NEGIMA!
MAGISTER NEGI MAGI
154TH PERIOD – FIGHT! MAGICAL GIRL BIBLION!?
THIS BONUS FEATURE IS REALLY USEFUL.
ESPECIALLY FOR A COSPLAYER. A GOLD MINE, REALLY!
YOU ARE BEAUTIFUL, CHIU-SAMA!
HEY, CHISAME-CHAN, ISN'T THAT YOUR OUTFIT FROM YESTERDAY'S COSTUME CONTEST?
UM, WHAT'S WITH THOSE NAMES?
AH YES!
MAKIE-SAMA GAVE US THESE WONDERFUL NAMES!
KINCHA
HANPE
KONNYA
CHIKUWAFU
NEGI
DAIKO
SHIRATAKI
OH, IF YOU LIKE THEM, FINE WITH ME.
BY THE WAY, I'M COMPLETELY LOST AS TO WHAT'S GOING ON HERE....

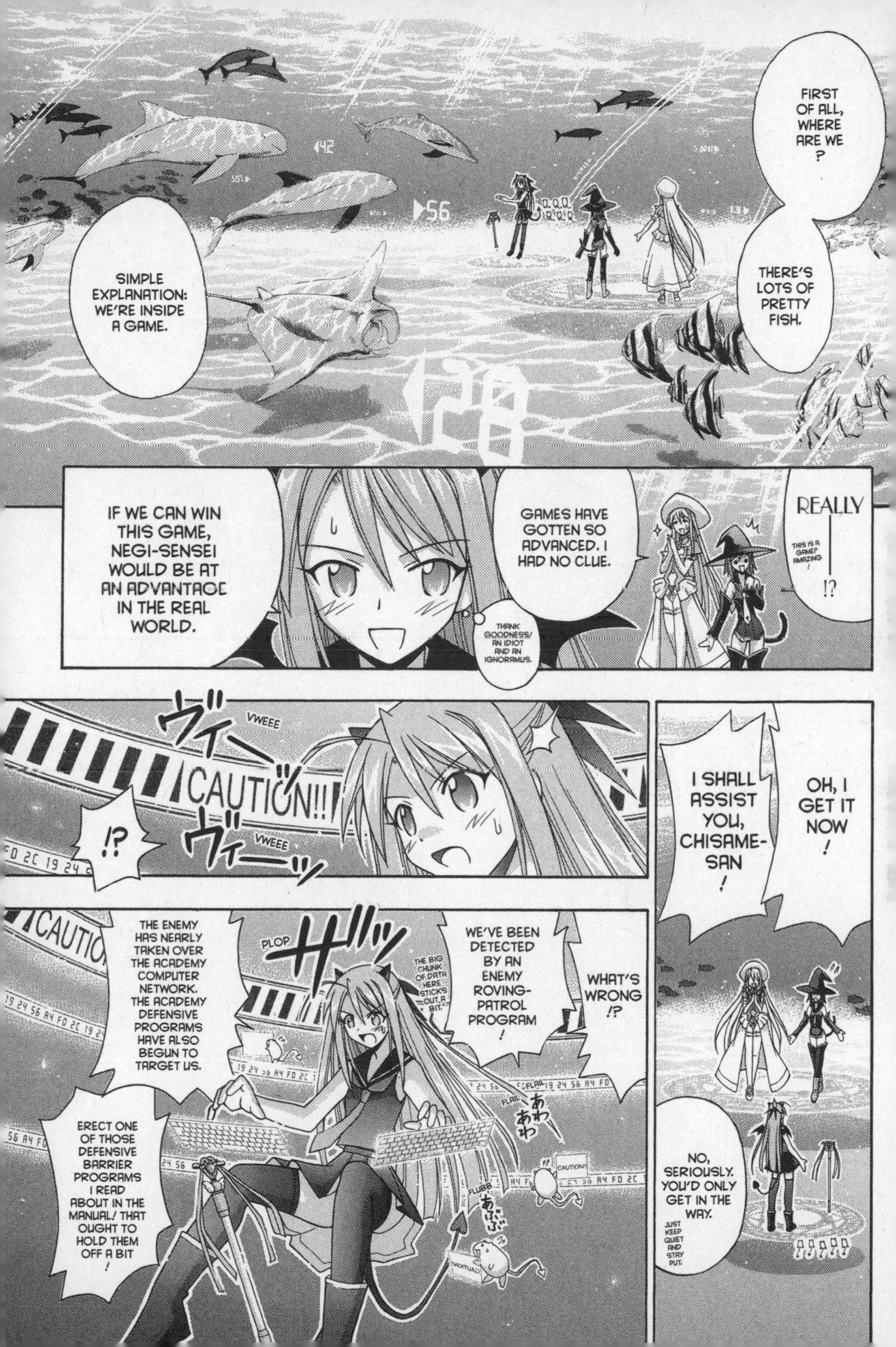
FIRST OF ALL, WHERE ARE WE ?
THERE'S LOTS OF PRETTY FISH.
SIMPLE EXPLANATION: WE'RE INSIDE A GAME.
REALLY —!?
THIS IS A GAME? AMAZING!
GAMES HAVE GOTTEN SO ADVANCED. I HAD NO CLUE.
THANK GOODNESS! AN IDIOT AND AN IGNORAMUS.
IF WE CAN WIN THIS GAME, NEGI-SENSEI WOULD BE AT AN ADVANTAGE IN THE REAL WORLD.
OH, I GET IT NOW!
I SHALL ASSIST YOU, CHISAME-SAN!
NO, SERIOUSLY. YOU'D ONLY GET IN THE WAY.
JUST KEEP QUIET AND STAY PUT.
ヴィー VWEEE
CAUTION!!
ヴィーッ VWEEE
!?
WHAT'S WRONG !?
WE'VE BEEN DETECTED BY AN ENEMY ROVING-PATROL PROGRAM!
THE BIG CHUNK OF DATA HERE STICKS OUT A BIT.
PLOP ザッ
THE ENEMY HAS NEARLY TAKEN OVER THE ACADEMY COMPUTER NETWORK. THE ACADEMY DEFENSIVE PROGRAMS HAVE ALSO BEGUN TO TARGET US.
FLAIL あわあわ
ERECT ONE OF THOSE DEFENSIVE BARRIER PROGRAMS I READ ABOUT IN THE MANUAL! THAT OUGHT TO HOLD THEM OFF A BIT!
FLUBB あぷぷ
CAUTION!

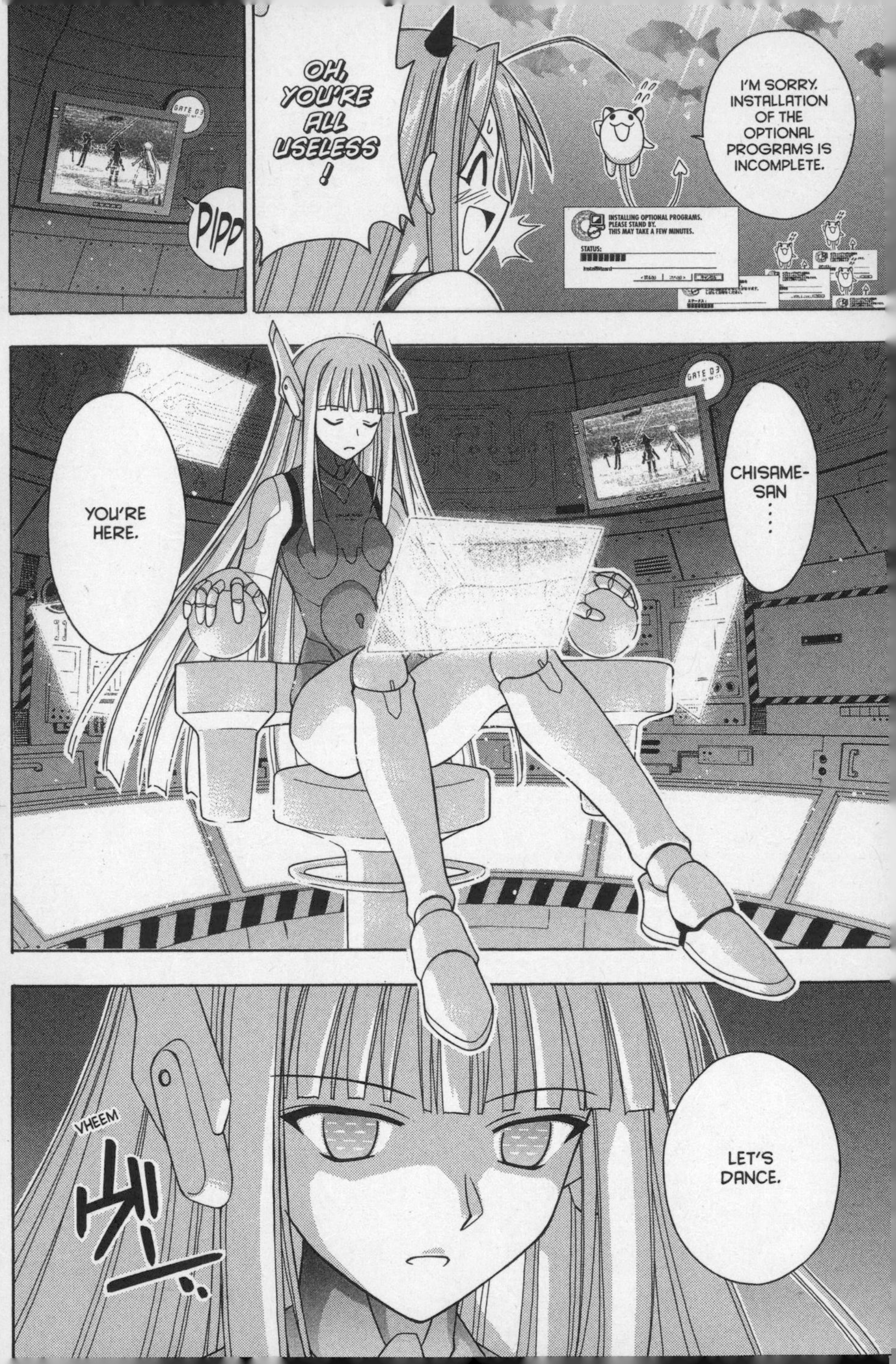

I'M SORRY. INSTALLATION OF THE OPTIONAL PROGRAMS IS INCOMPLETE.
OH, YOU'RE ALL USELESS!
INSTALLING OPTIONAL PROGRAMS. PLEASE STAND BY. THIS MAY TAKE A FEW MINUTES.
STATUS:
InstallWizard
PIPP
GATE 03
CHISAME-SAN.....
YOU'RE HERE.
GATE 03
LET'S DANCE.
VHEEM

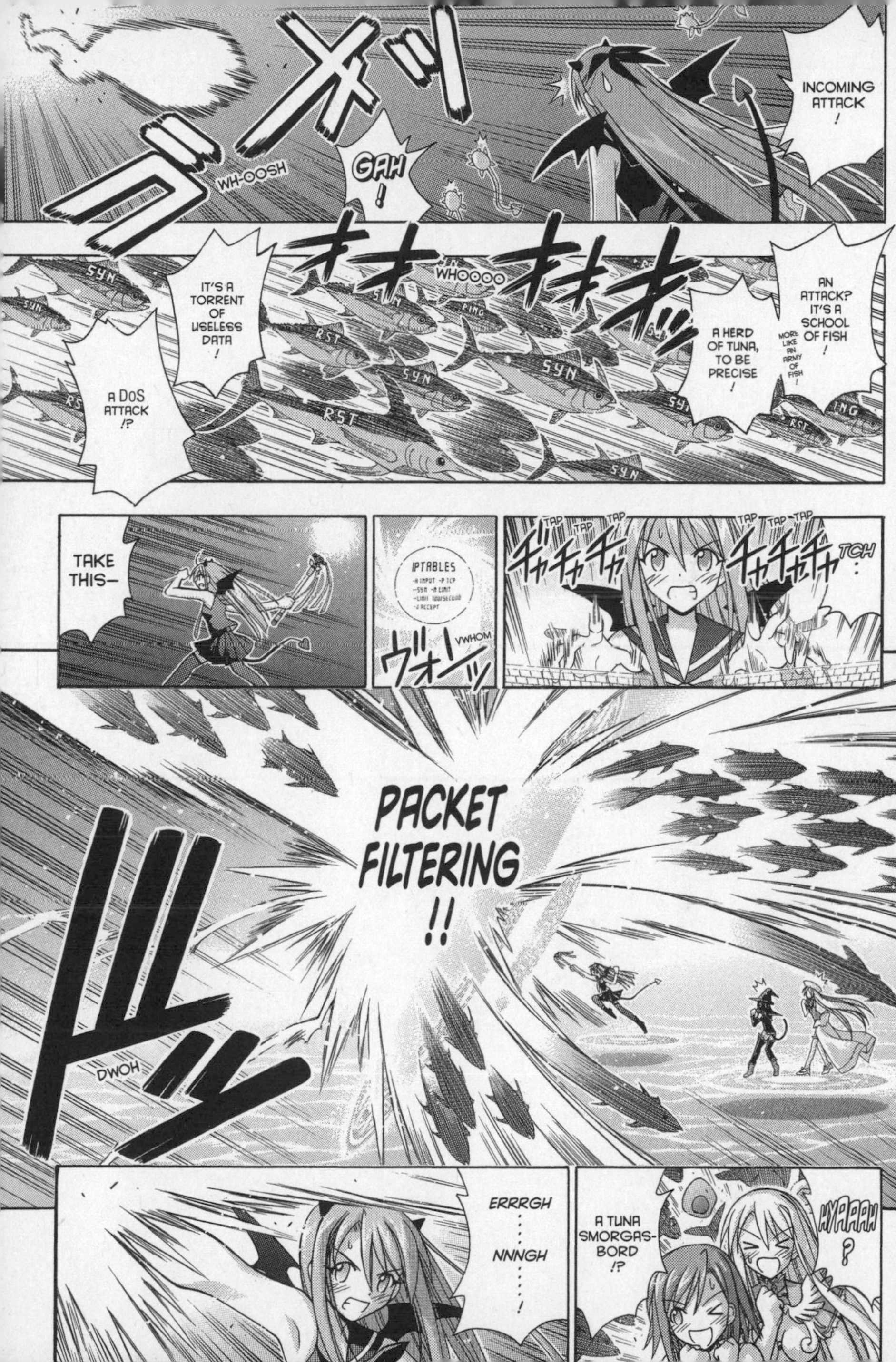
INCOMING ATTACK!
GAH!
WH-OOSH
AN ATTACK? IT'S A SCHOOL OF FISH!
MORE LIKE AN ARMY OF FISH!
A HERD OF TUNA, TO BE PRECISE!
WHOOOO
IT'S A TORRENT OF USELESS DATA!
A DoS ATTACK!?
TAP TAP TAP
TAP TAP TAP
TCH
IPTABLES
-A INPUT -P TCP
--SYN -M LIMIT
--LIMIT 10/SECOND
-J ACCEPT
VWHOM
TAKE THIS—
PACKET FILTERING!!
DWOH
HYAAAH?
A TUNA SMORGAS-BORD!?
ERRRGH......
NNNGH......!

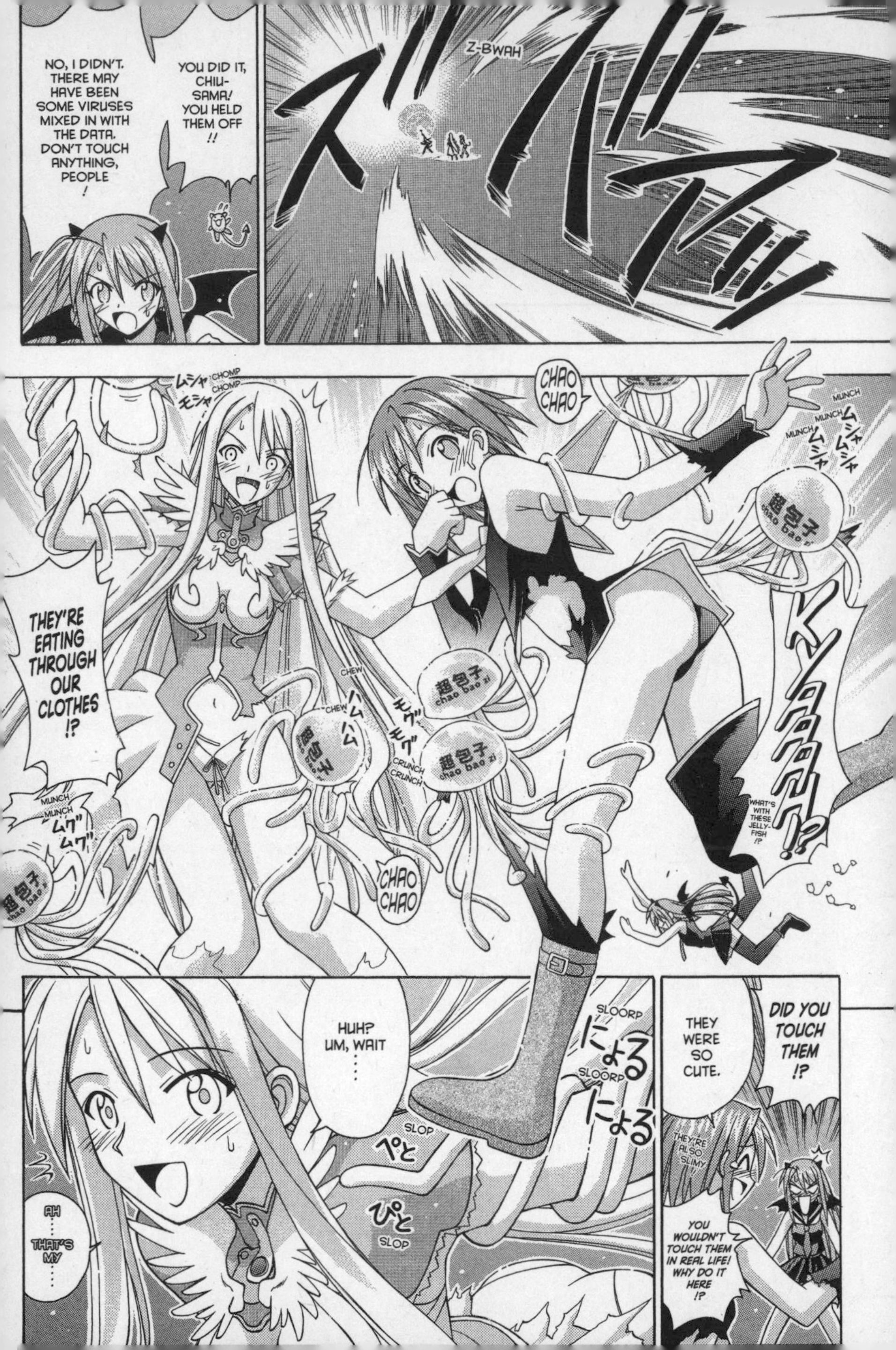

Z-BWAH
ズバァァ
YOU DID IT, CHIU-SAMA! YOU HELD THEM OFF !!
NO, I DIDN'T. THERE MAY HAVE BEEN SOME VIRUSES MIXED IN WITH THE DATA. DON'T TOUCH ANYTHING, PEOPLE !
MUNCH MUNCH MUNCH
ムシャムシャムシャ
CHAO CHAO
超包子 chao bao zi
WHAT'S WITH THESE JELLY-FISH !?
CHOMP CHOMP
ムシャモシャ
THEY'RE EATING THROUGH OUR CLOTHES !?
CHEW CHEW
ハムハム
モグモグ
CRUNCH CRUNCH
超包子 chao bao zi
超包子 chao bao zi
MUNCH MUNCH
ムグムグ
超包子 chao bao zi
CHAO CHAO
DID YOU TOUCH THEM !?
THEY WERE SO CUTE.
THEY'RE ALSO SLIMY.
YOU WOULDN'T TOUCH THEM IN REAL LIFE! WHY DO IT HERE !?
SLOORP
によ
SLOORP
による
HUH? UM, WAIT ...
SLOP
ぺと
ぴと
SLOP
AH ... THAT'S MY ...

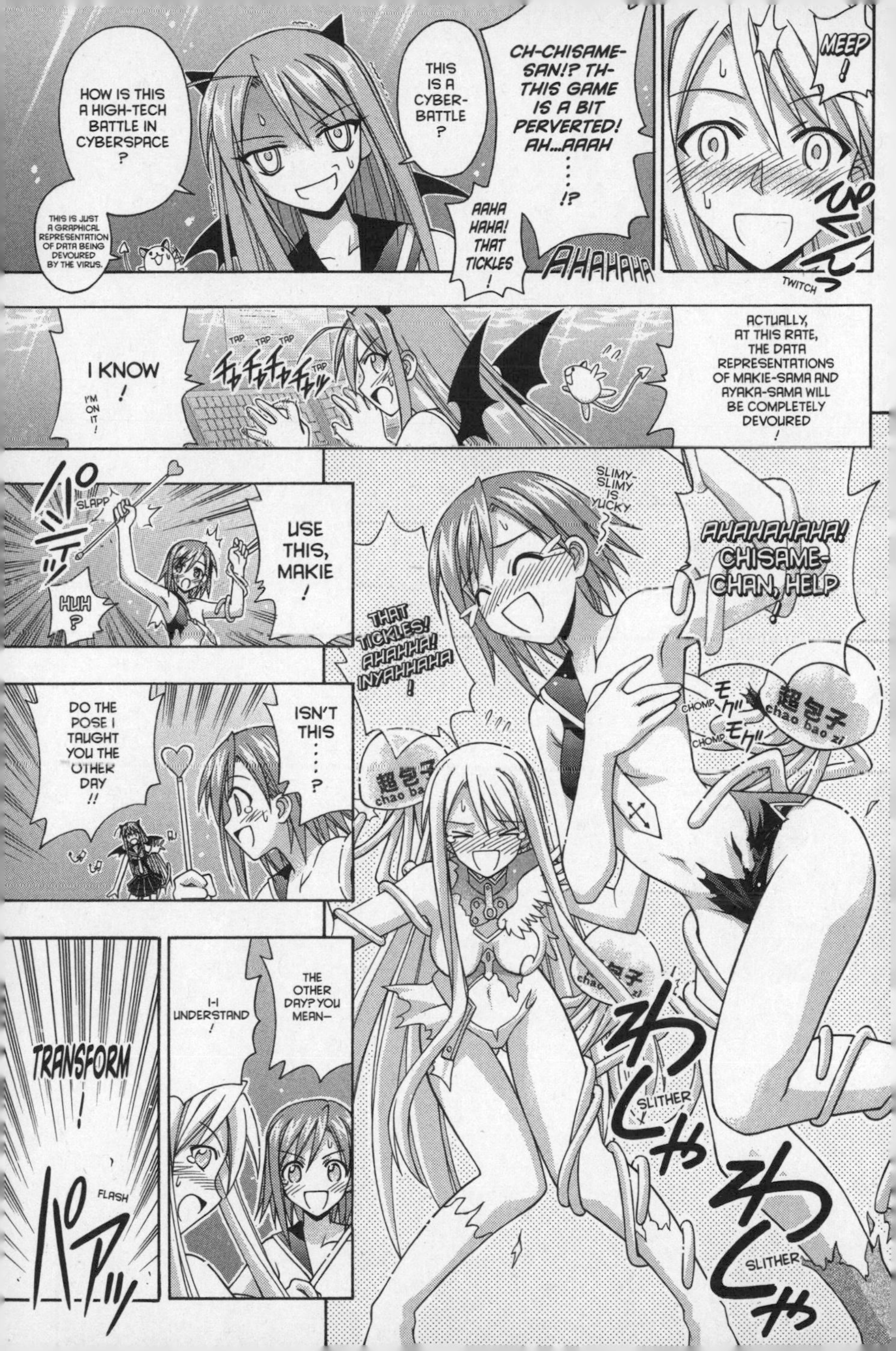
MEEP!
TWITCH
CH-CHISAME-SAN!? TH-THIS GAME IS A BIT PERVERTED! AH...AAAH ......!?
AAHA HAHA! THAT TICKLES!
AHAHAHAHA
THIS IS A CYBER-BATTLE?
HOW IS THIS A HIGH-TECH BATTLE IN CYBERSPACE?
THIS IS JUST A GRAPHICAL REPRESENTATION OF DATA BEING DEVOURED BY THE VIRUS.
ACTUALLY, AT THIS RATE, THE DATA REPRESENTATIONS OF MAKIE-SAMA AND AYAKA-SAMA WILL BE COMPLETELY DEVOURED!
TAP TAP TAP TAP
I KNOW!
I'M ON IT!
AHAHAHAHA! CHISAME-CHAN, HELP!
SLIMY-SLIMY IS YUCKY
CHOMP
CHOMP
超包子 chao bao zi
THAT TICKLES! AHAHHA! INYAHHAHA!
SLITHER
SLITHER
SLAPP
USE THIS, MAKIE!
HUH?
ISN'T THIS......?
DO THE POSE I TAUGHT YOU THE OTHER DAY!!
THE OTHER DAY? YOU MEAN—
I-I UNDERSTAND!
TRANSFORM!
FLASH

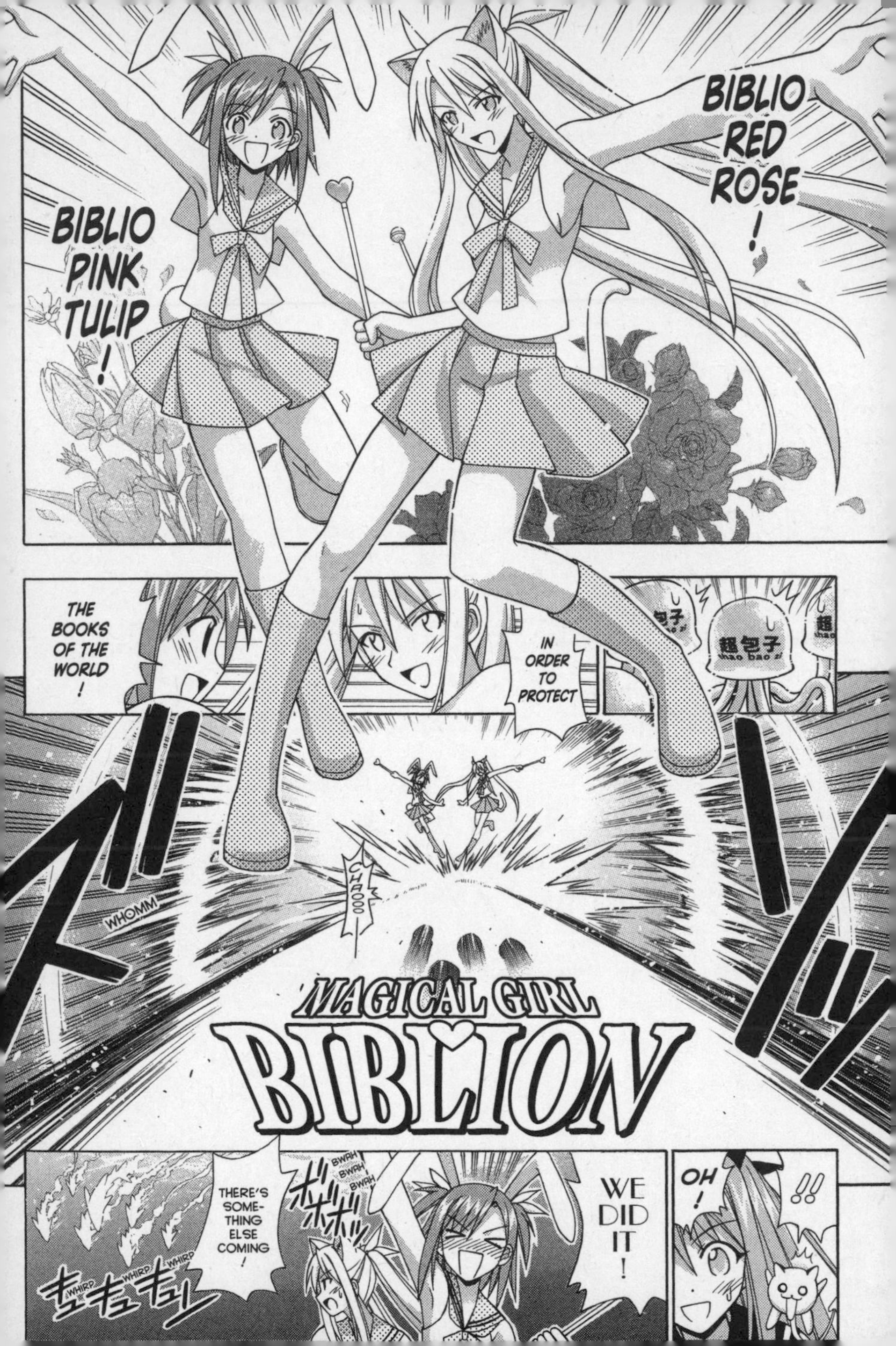
BIBLIO RED ROSE!
BIBLIO PINK TULIP!
超包子
chao bao zi
IN ORDER TO PROTECT
THE BOOKS OF THE WORLD!
CHAOOO
WHOMM
MAGICAL GIRL
BIBLION
OH!
!!
WE DID IT!
BWAH BWAH BWAH
THERE'S SOME-THING ELSE COMING!
WHIRP WHIRP WHIRP

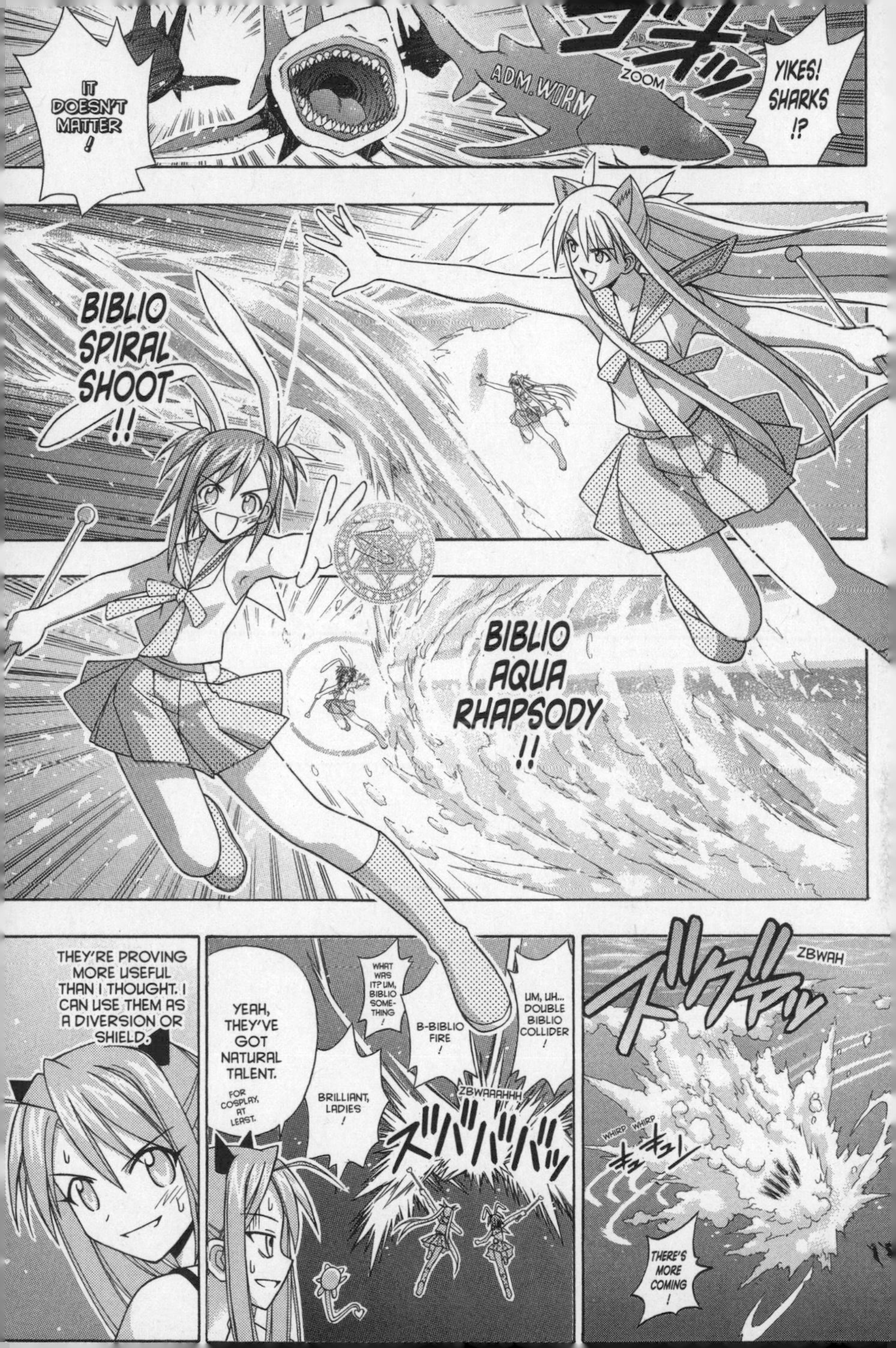
YIKES! SHARKS !?
ZOOM
ADM. WORM
IT DOESN'T MATTER !
BIBLIO AQUA RHAPSODY !!
BIBLIO SPIRAL SHOOT !!
ZBWAH
WHIRP WHIRP
THERE'S MORE COMING !
UM, UH... DOUBLE BIBLIO COLLIDER !
B-BIBLIO FIRE !
WHAT WAS IT? UM, BIBLIO SOME-THING !
ZBWAAAAHHH
BRILLIANT, LADIES !
YEAH, THEY'VE GOT NATURAL TALENT.
FOR COSPLAY, AT LEAST.
THEY'RE PROVING MORE USEFUL THAN I THOUGHT. I CAN USE THEM AS A DIVERSION OR SHIELD.

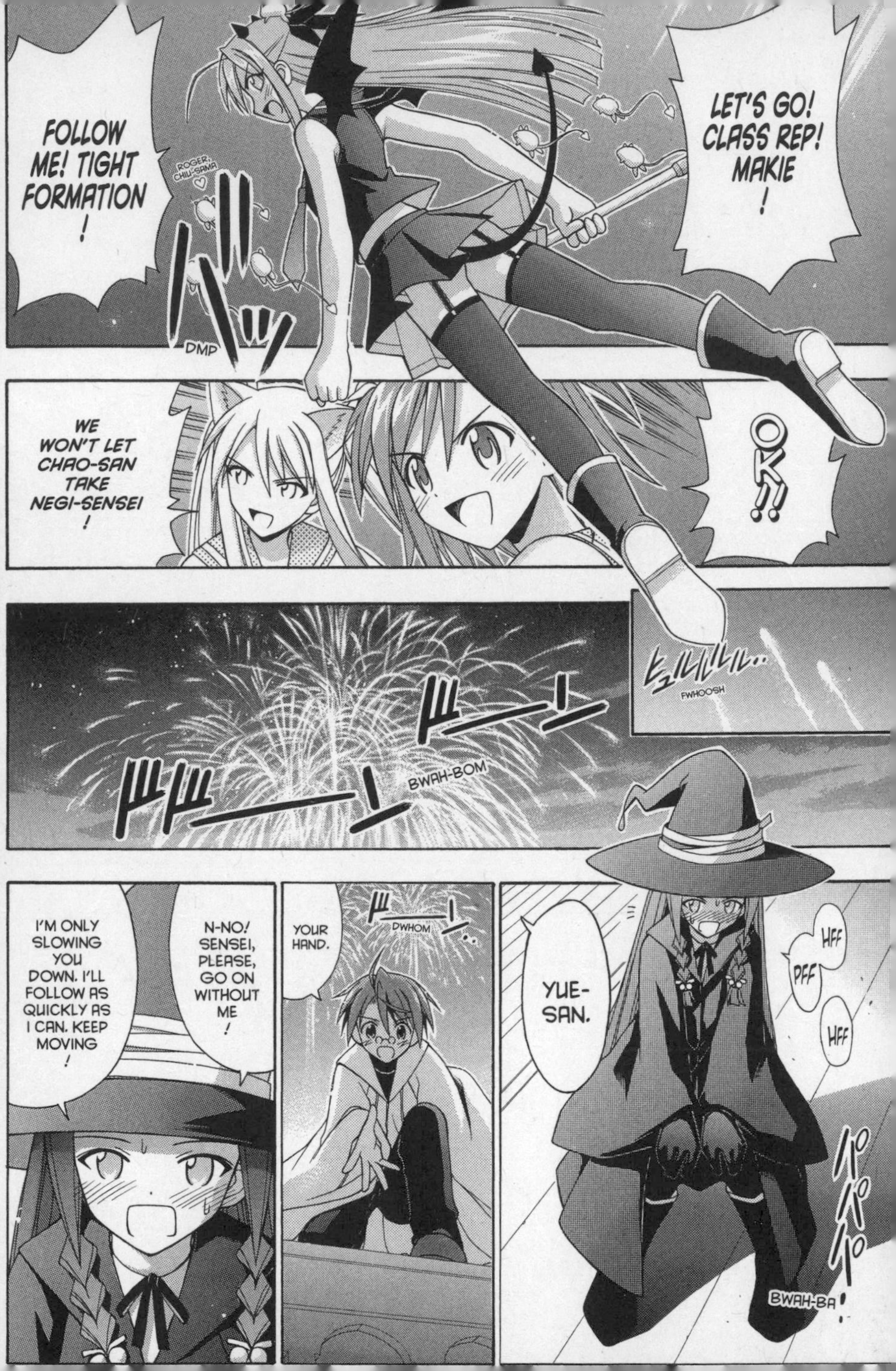
LET'S GO! CLASS REP! MAKIE!
FOLLOW ME! TIGHT FORMATION!
ROGER, CHIU-SAMA ♡
DMP
OK!!
WE WON'T LET CHAO-SAN TAKE NEGI-SENSEI!
FWHOOSH
BWAH-BOM
YUE-SAN.
HFF
PFF
HFF
BWAH-BA!
DWHOM
YOUR HAND.
N-NO! SENSEI, PLEASE, GO ON WITHOUT ME!
I'M ONLY SLOWING YOU DOWN. I'LL FOLLOW AS QUICKLY AS I CAN. KEEP MOVING!

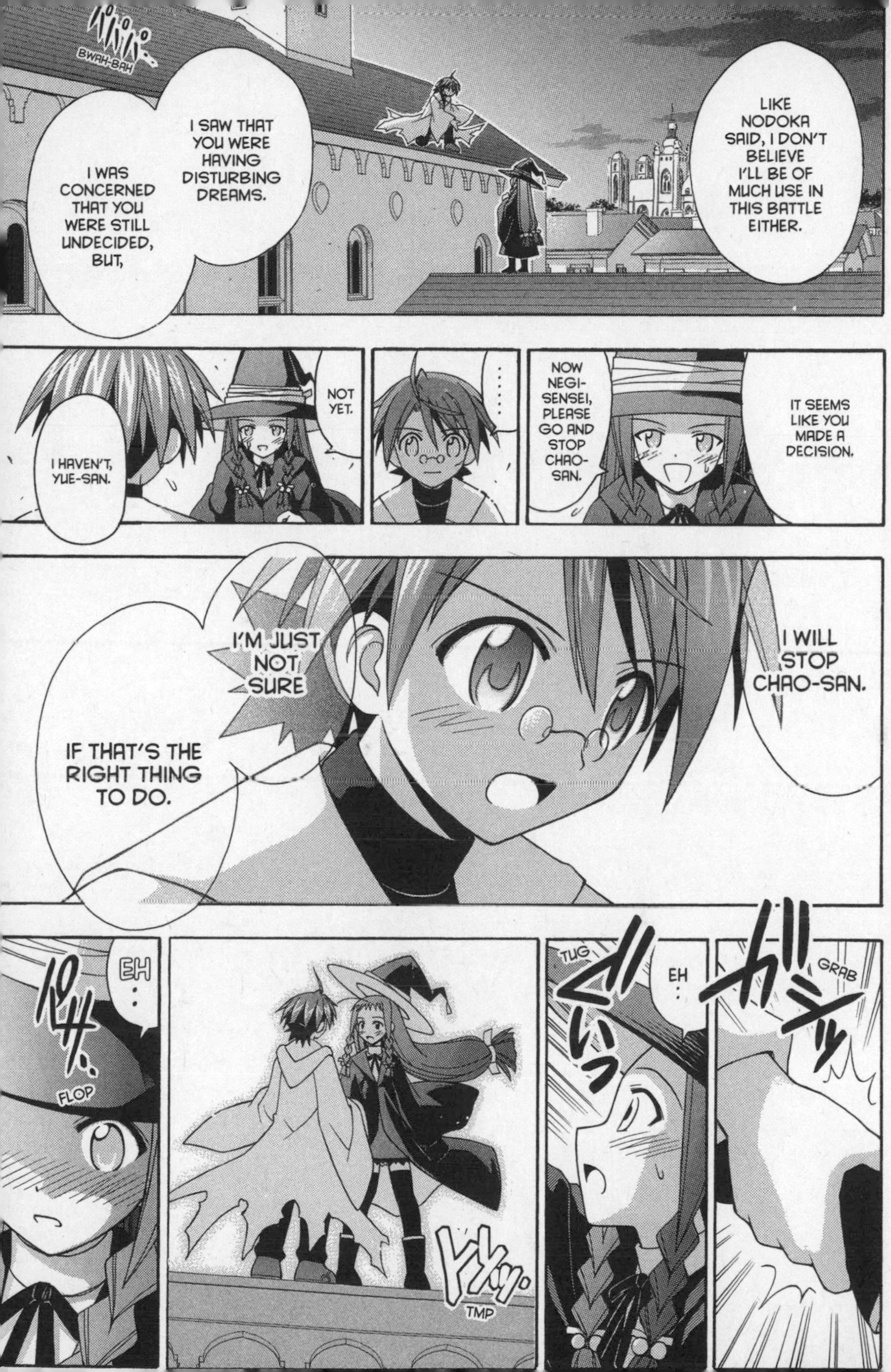
BWAH-BAH
LIKE NODOKA SAID, I DON'T BELIEVE I'LL BE OF MUCH USE IN THIS BATTLE EITHER.
I SAW THAT YOU WERE HAVING DISTURBING DREAMS.
I WAS CONCERNED THAT YOU WERE STILL UNDECIDED, BUT,
IT SEEMS LIKE YOU MADE A DECISION.
NOW NEGI-SENSEI, PLEASE GO AND STOP CHAO-SAN.
.....
NOT YET.
I HAVEN'T, YUE-SAN.
I WILL STOP CHAO-SAN.
I'M JUST NOT SURE
IF THAT'S THE RIGHT THING TO DO.
GRAB
TUG
EH..
TMP
EH..
FLOP

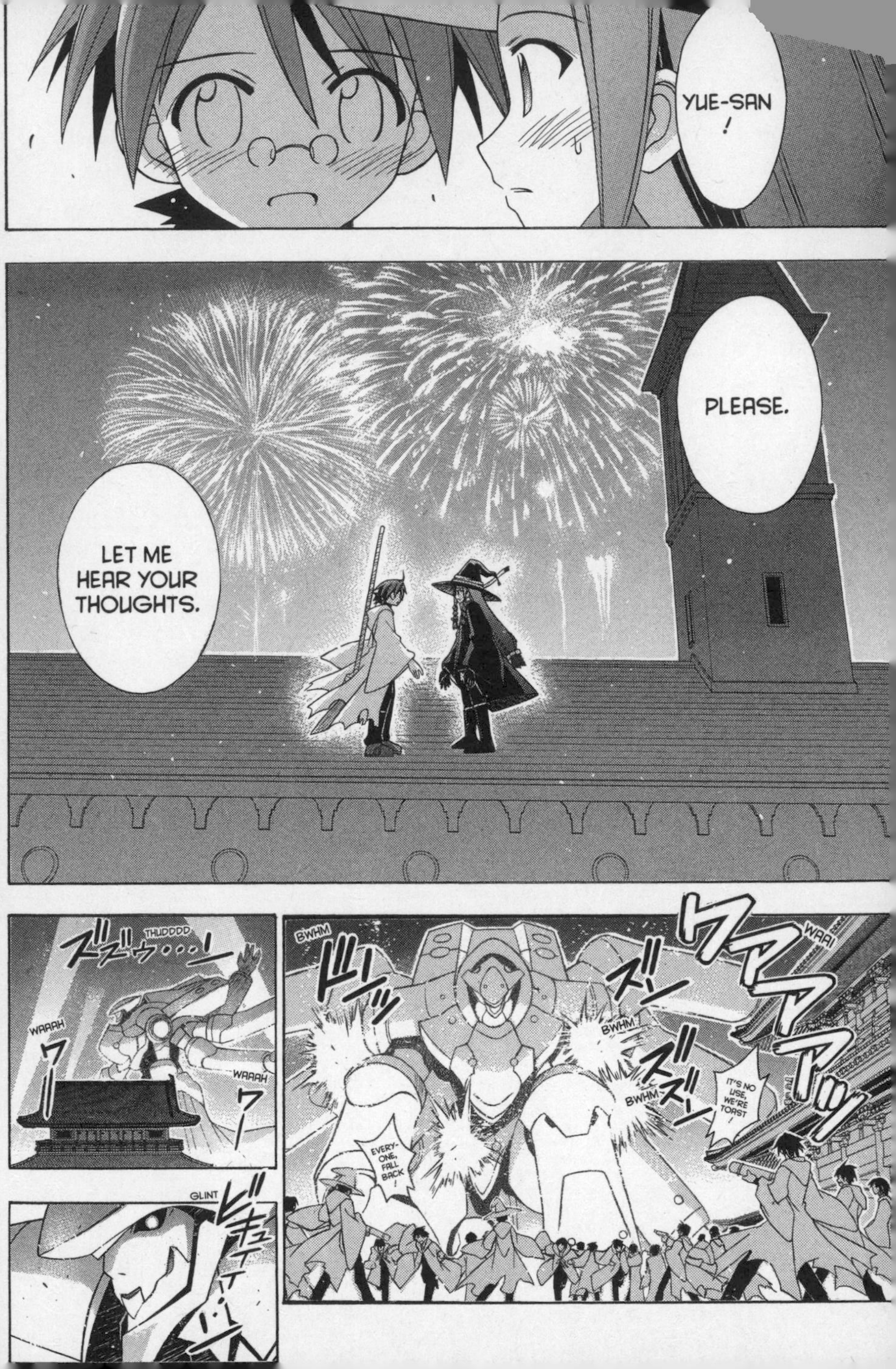

YUE-SAN!
PLEASE.
LET ME HEAR YOUR THOUGHTS.
WAAI
BWHM
BWHM
BWHM
IT'S NO USE, WE'RE TOAST!
EVERYONE, FALL BACK!
THUDDDD
WAAAH
WAAAH
GLINT

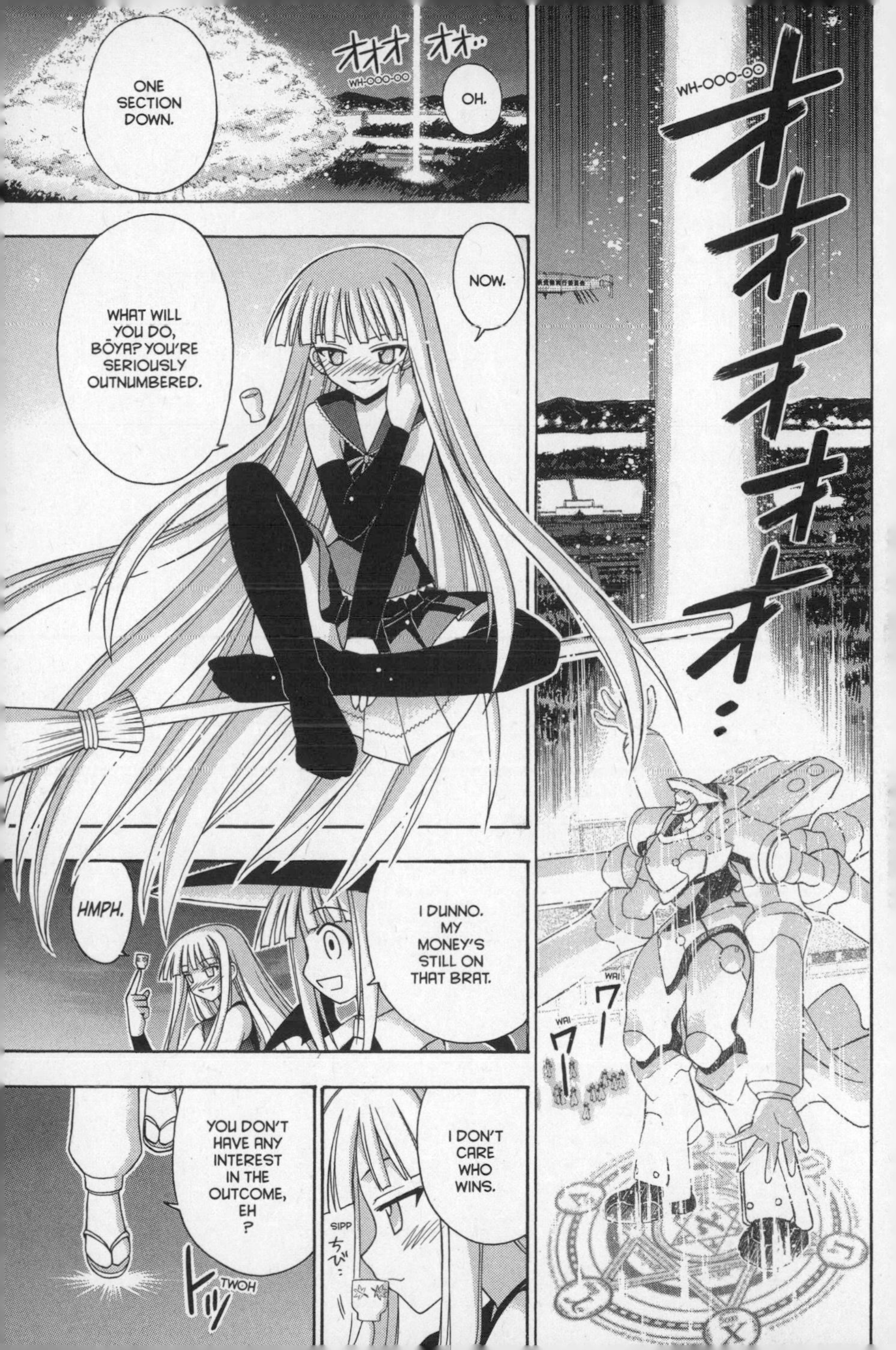
WH-OOO-OO
オォォォォ
WAI
ワー
WAI
ワー
オオオ オオ゛
WH-OOO-OO
OH.
ONE SECTION DOWN.
NOW.
WHAT WILL YOU DO, BŌYA? YOU'RE SERIOUSLY OUTNUMBERED.
I DUNNO. MY MONEY'S STILL ON THAT BRAT.
HMPH.
I DON'T CARE WHO WINS.
SIPP
ちびっ
YOU DON'T HAVE ANY INTEREST IN THE OUTCOME, EH?
トッ
TWOH

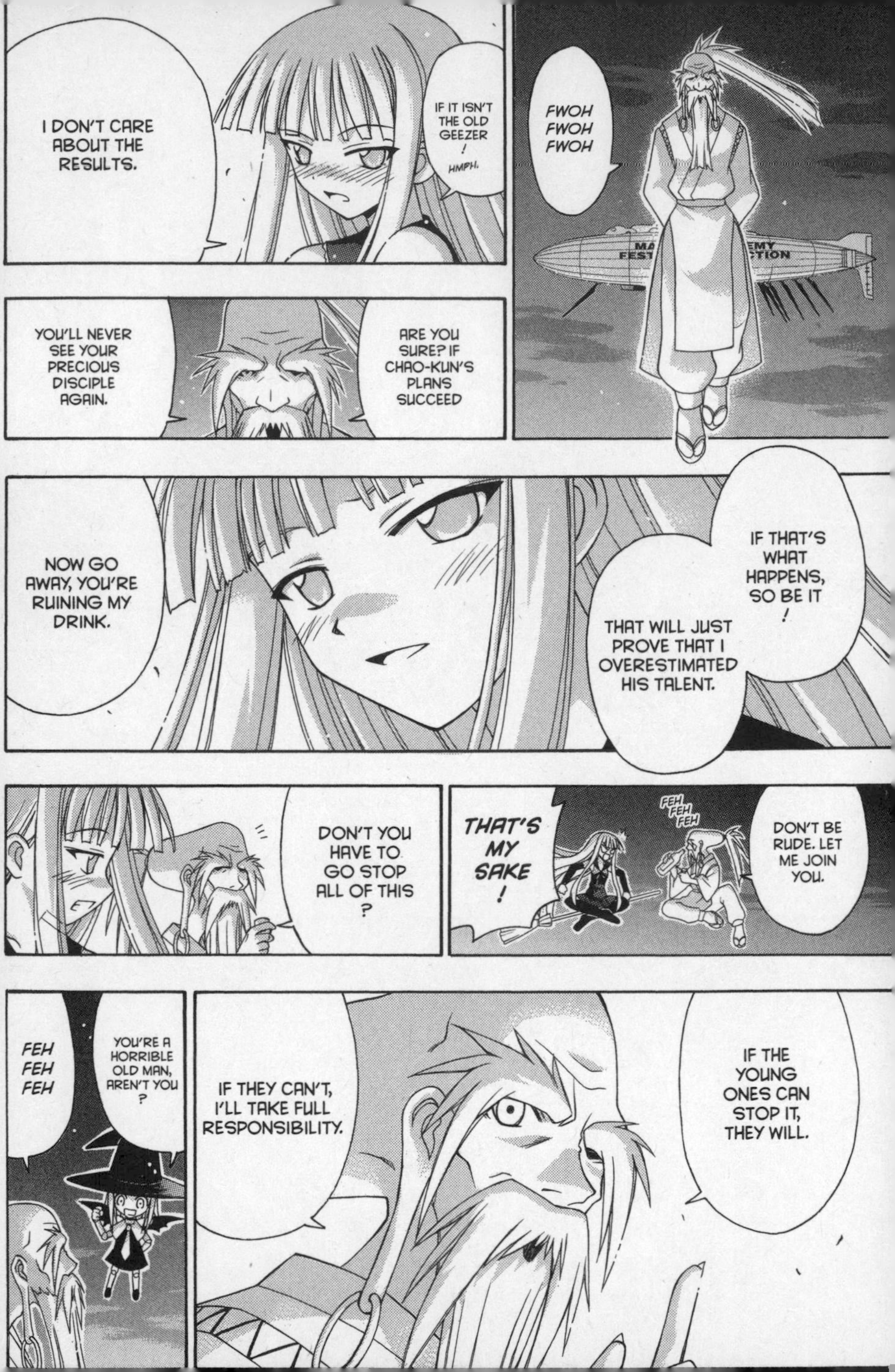
FWOH FWOH FWOH
IF IT ISN'T THE OLD GEEZER!
HMPH.
I DON'T CARE ABOUT THE RESULTS.
ARE YOU SURE? IF CHAO-KUN'S PLANS SUCCEED
YOU'LL NEVER SEE YOUR PRECIOUS DISCIPLE AGAIN.
IF THAT'S WHAT HAPPENS, SO BE IT!
THAT WILL JUST PROVE THAT I OVERESTIMATED HIS TALENT.
NOW GO AWAY, YOU'RE RUINING MY DRINK.
DON'T BE RUDE. LET ME JOIN YOU.
FEH FEH FEH
THAT'S MY SAKE!
DON'T YOU HAVE TO GO STOP ALL OF THIS?
IF THE YOUNG ONES CAN STOP IT, THEY WILL.
IF THEY CAN'T, I'LL TAKE FULL RESPONSIBILITY.
YOU'RE A HORRIBLE OLD MAN, AREN'T YOU?
FEH FEH FEH

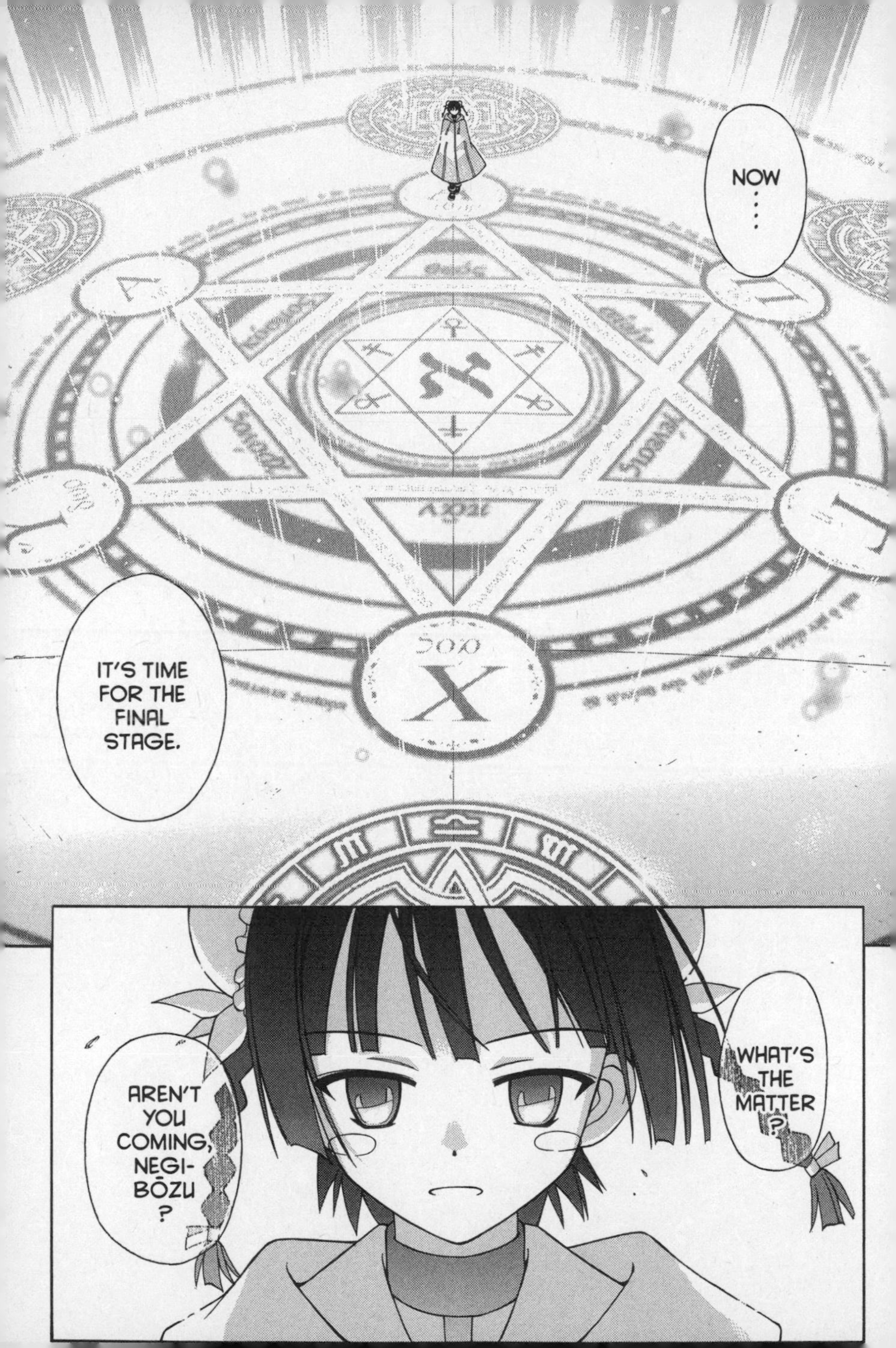
NOW....
IT'S TIME FOR THE FINAL STAGE.
WHAT'S THE MATTER?
AREN'T YOU COMING, NEGI-BŌZU?

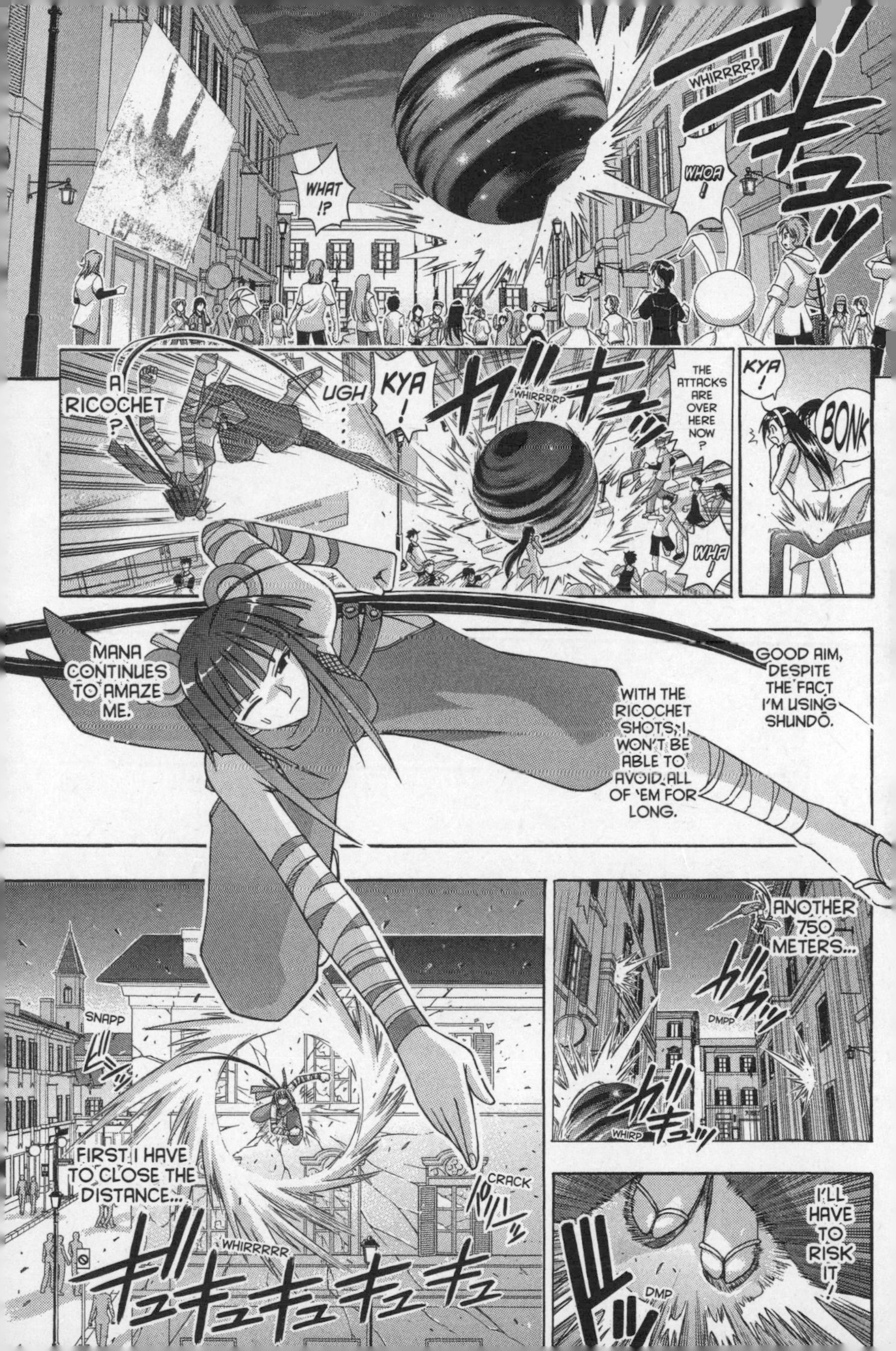
WHIRRRRP
WHOA !
WHAT !?
KYA !
BONK
THE ATTACKS ARE OVER HERE NOW ?
WHIRRRRP
KYA !
UGH ....
WHA !
A RICOCHET ?
GOOD AIM, DESPITE THE FACT I'M USING SHUNDŌ.
WITH THE RICOCHET SHOTS, I WON'T BE ABLE TO AVOID ALL OF 'EM FOR LONG.
MANA CONTINUES TO AMAZE ME.
ANOTHER 750 METERS...
DMPP
WHIRP
I'LL HAVE TO RISK IT !
DMP
SNAPP
FIRST I HAVE TO CLOSE THE DISTANCE...
CRACK
WHIRRRRR

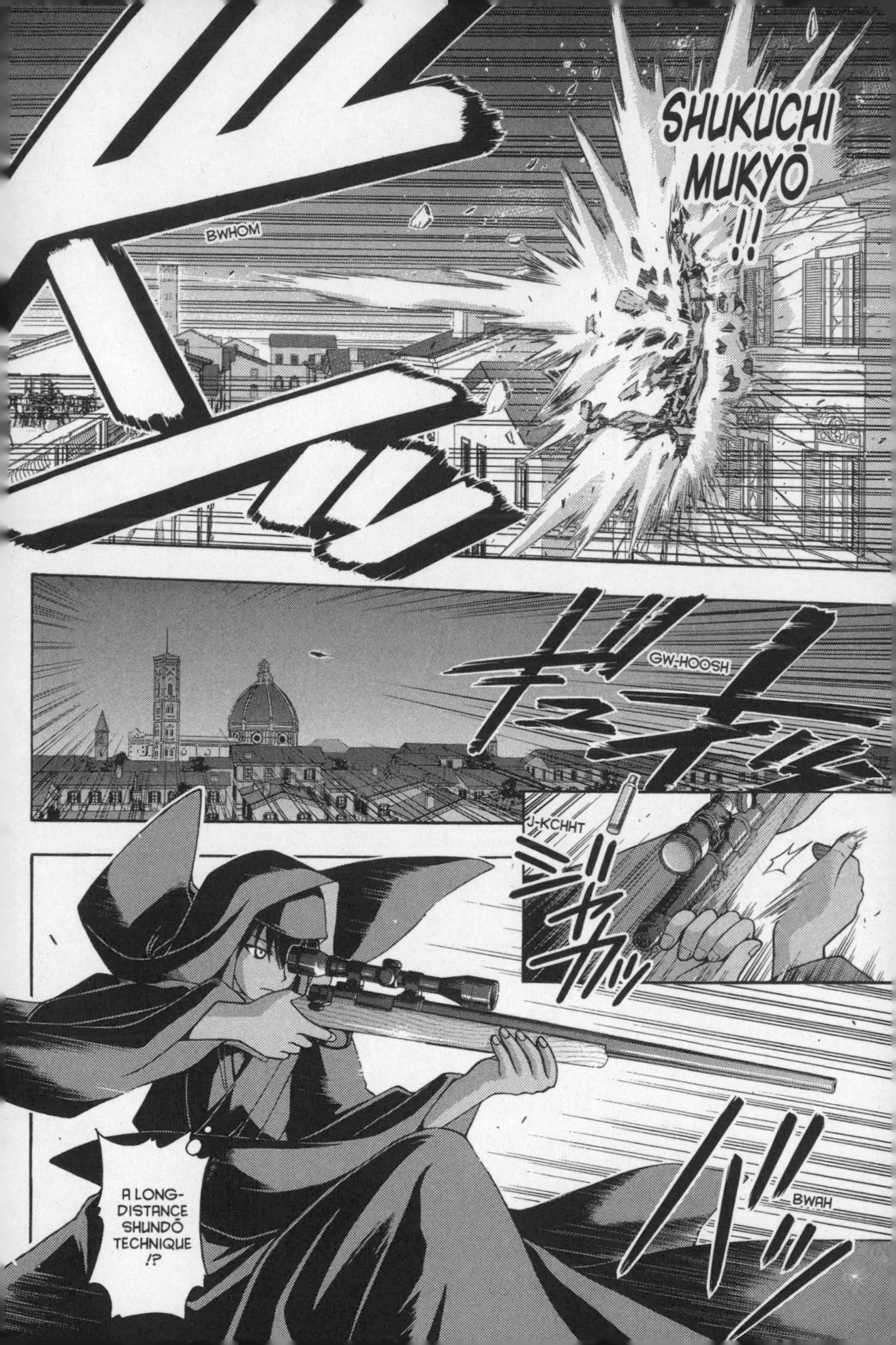

SHUKUCHI MUKYŌ !!
BWHOM
GW-HOOSH
J-KCHHT
BWAH
A LONG-DISTANCE SHUNDŌ TECHNIQUE !?

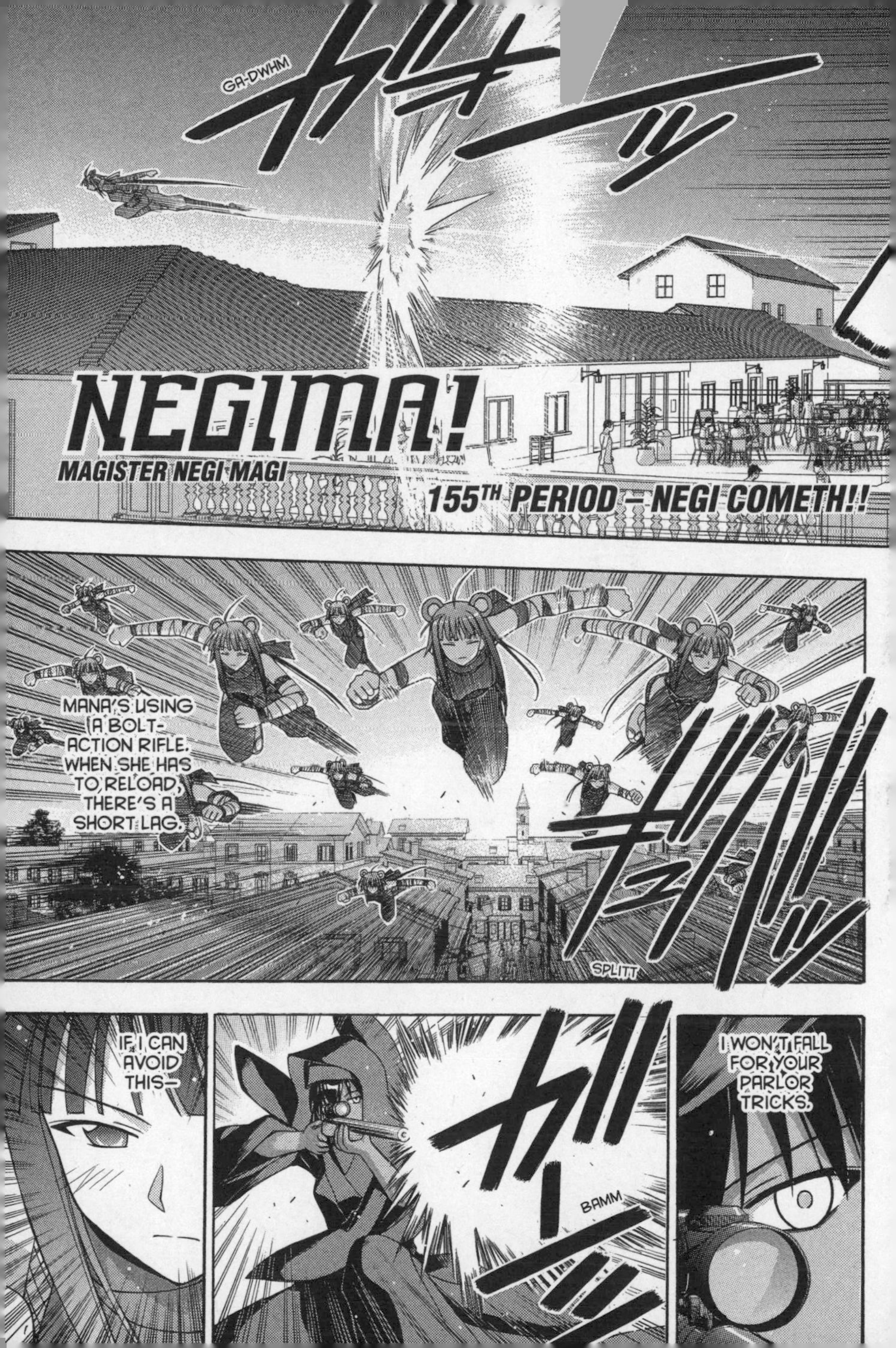
GA-DWHM
NEGIMA!
MAGISTER NEGI MAGI
155TH PERIOD – NEGI COMETH!!
SPLITT
MANA'S USING A BOLT-ACTION RIFLE. WHEN SHE HAS TO RELOAD, THERE'S A SHORT LAG.
I WON'T FALL FOR YOUR PARLOR TRICKS.
BAMM
IF I CAN AVOID THIS—

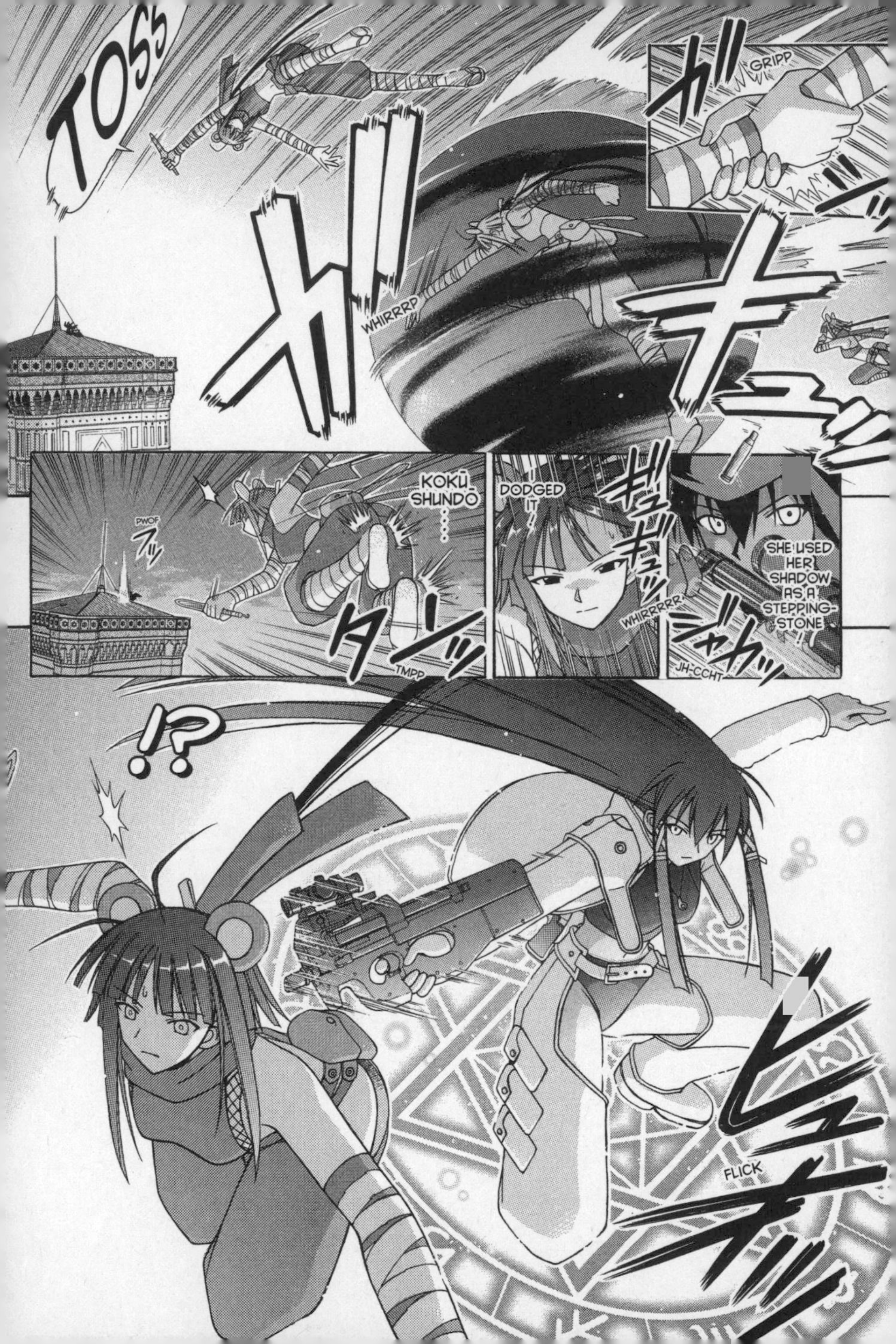
GRIPP
WHIRRRP
TOSS
SHE USED HER SHADOW AS A STEPPING-STONE!
JH-CCHT
DODGED IT!
WHIRRRR
KOKŪ SHUNDŌ......
PWOF
TMPP
!?
FLICK

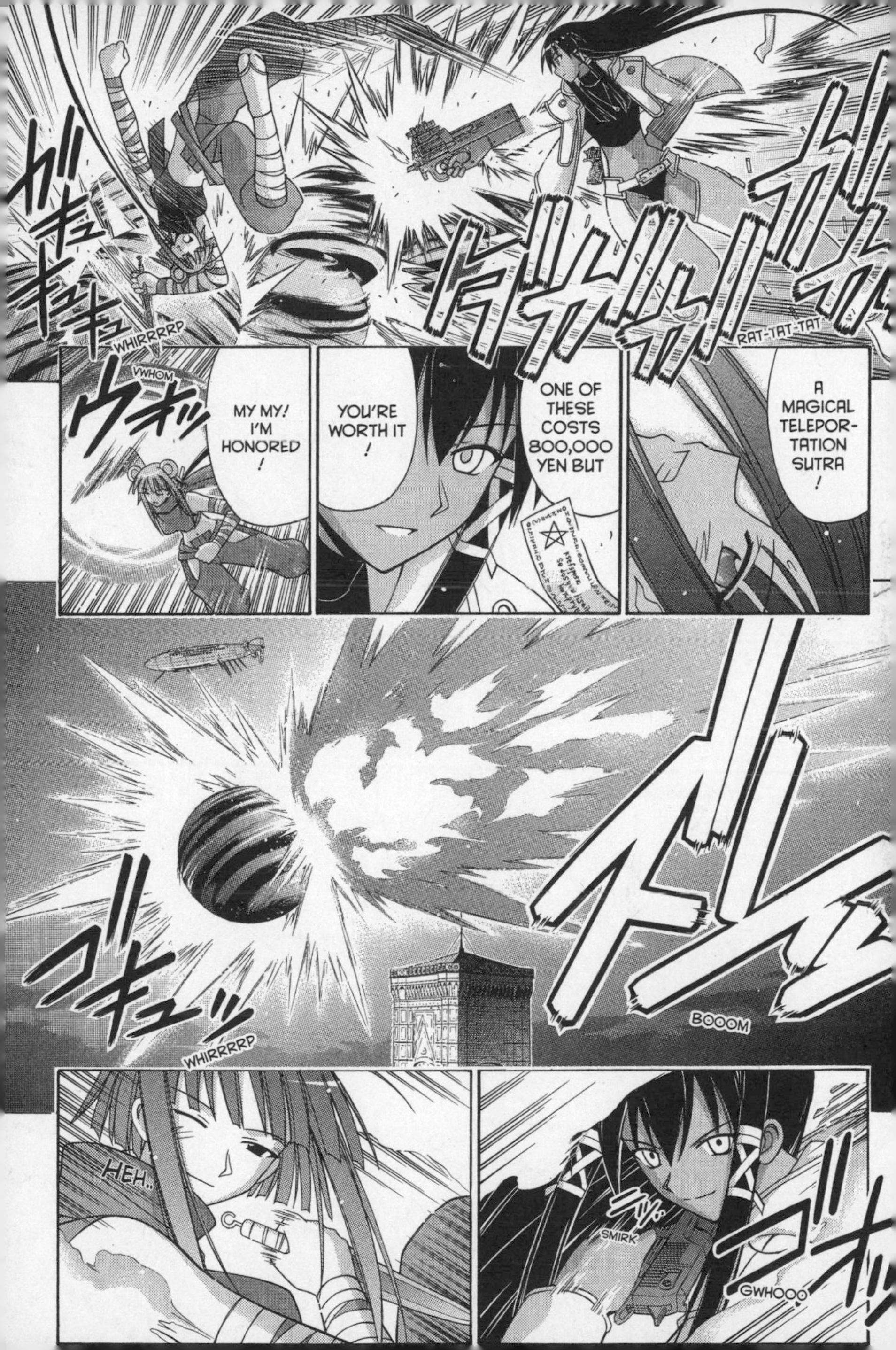
RAT-TAT-TAT
WHIRRRP
A MAGICAL TELEPOR-TATION SUTRA!
ONE OF THESE COSTS 800,000 YEN BUT
YOU'RE WORTH IT!
MY MY! I'M HONORED!
VWHOM
BOOOM
WHIRRRP
SMIRK
GWHOOO
HEH..

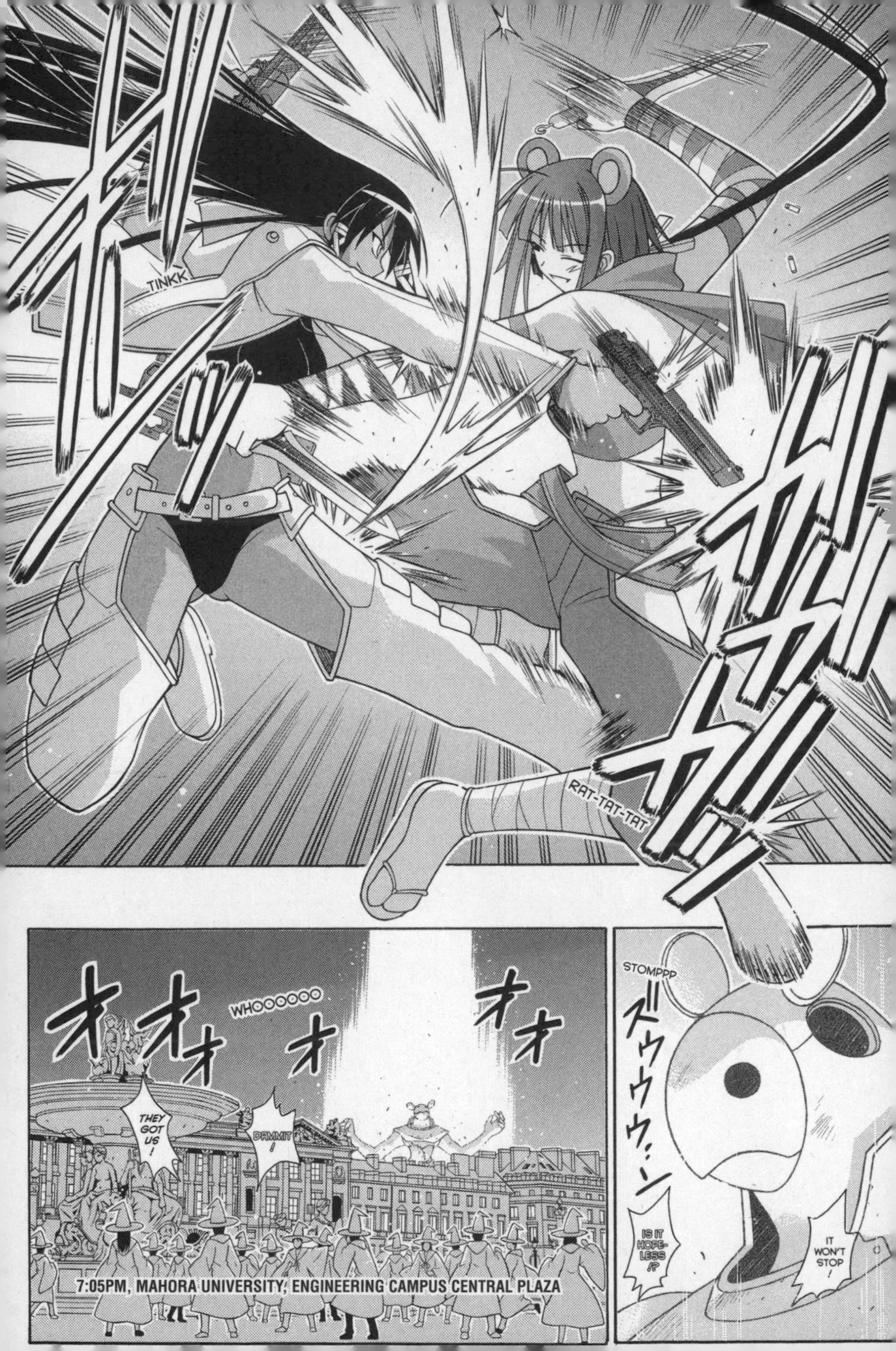

TINKK
RAT-TAT-TAT
STOMPPP
IT WON'T STOP!
IS IT HOPELESS!?
WHOOOOOO
DAMMIT!
THEY GOT US!
7:05PM, MAHORA UNIVERSITY, ENGINEERING CAMPUS CENTRAL PLAZA

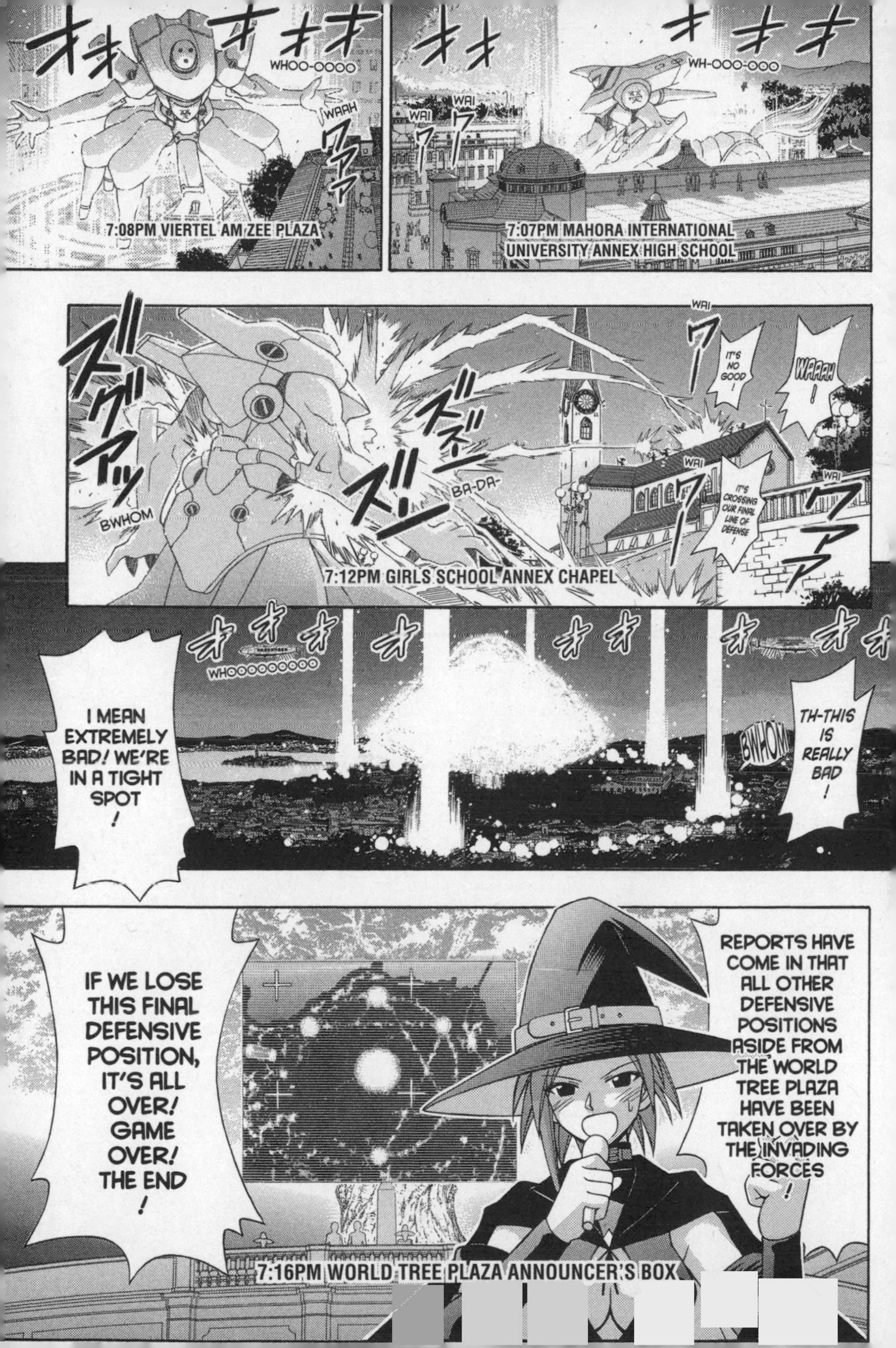
WH-OOO-OOO
WAI
WAI
7:07PM MAHORA INTERNATIONAL UNIVERSITY ANNEX HIGH SCHOOL
WHOO-OOOO
WAAH
7:08PM VIERTEL AM ZEE PLAZA
WAI
IT'S NO GOOD!
WAAAH!
WAI
IT'S CROSSING OUR FINAL LINE OF DEFENSE!
WAI
BA-DA-
BWHOM
7:12PM GIRLS SCHOOL ANNEX CHAPEL
TH-THIS IS REALLY BAD!
BWHOM
I MEAN EXTREMELY BAD! WE'RE IN A TIGHT SPOT!
WHOOOOOOOOOO
REPORTS HAVE COME IN THAT ALL OTHER DEFENSIVE POSITIONS ASIDE FROM THE WORLD TREE PLAZA HAVE BEEN TAKEN OVER BY THE INVADING FORCES!
IF WE LOSE THIS FINAL DEFENSIVE POSITION, IT'S ALL OVER! GAME OVER! THE END!
7:16PM WORLD TREE PLAZA ANNOUNCER'S BOX

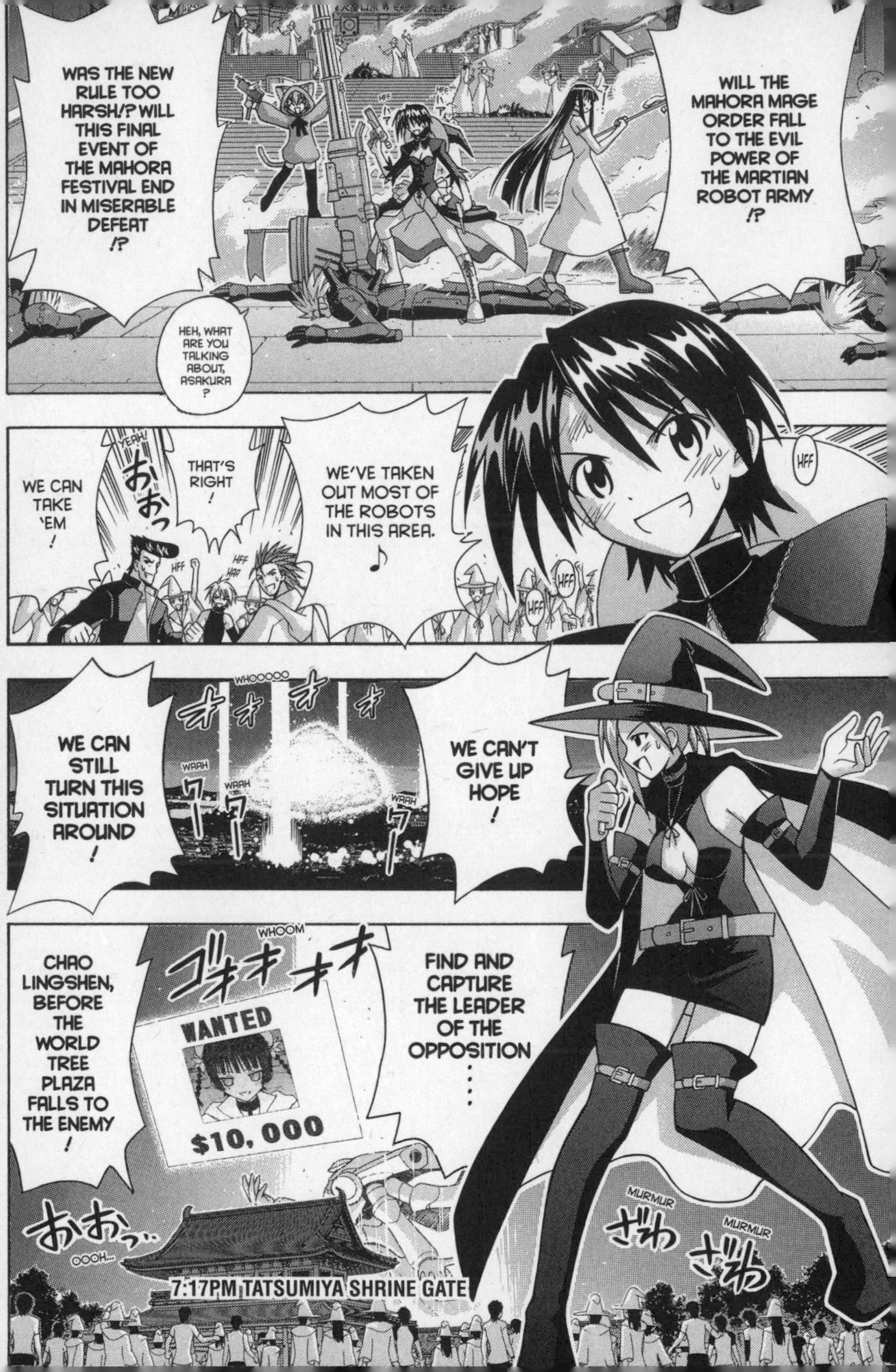
WILL THE MAHORA MAGE ORDER FALL TO THE EVIL POWER OF THE MARTIAN ROBOT ARMY !?
WAS THE NEW RULE TOO HARSH!? WILL THIS FINAL EVENT OF THE MAHORA FESTIVAL END IN MISERABLE DEFEAT !?
HFF
HFF
HEH, WHAT ARE YOU TALKING ABOUT, ASAKURA ?
HFF
WE'VE TAKEN OUT MOST OF THE ROBOTS IN THIS AREA. ♪
HFF
HFF
THAT'S RIGHT !
YEAH!
おおっ
WE CAN TAKE 'EM !
HFF
HAA
WE CAN'T GIVE UP HOPE !
WHOOOOO
WAAH
WAAH
WAAH
WE CAN STILL TURN THIS SITUATION AROUND !
FIND AND CAPTURE THE LEADER OF THE OPPOSITION ...
WHOOM
WANTED
$10, 000
CHAO LINGSHEN, BEFORE THE WORLD TREE PLAZA FALLS TO THE ENEMY !
MURMUR
ざわ
MURMUR
ざわ
おおっ
OOOH...
7:17PM TATSUMIYA SHRINE GATE

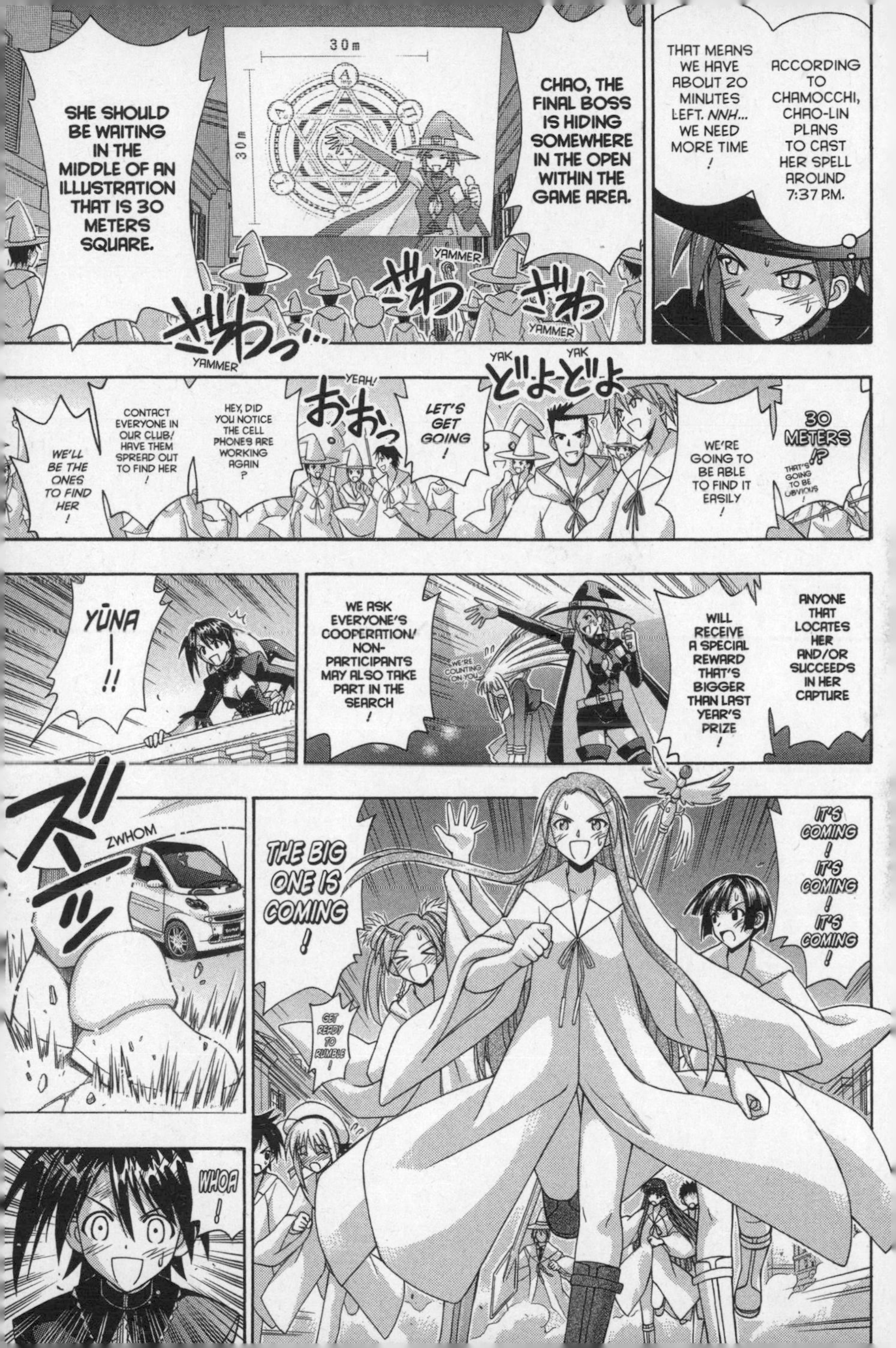
ACCORDING TO CHAMOCCHI, CHAO-LIN PLANS TO CAST HER SPELL AROUND 7:37 P.M.
THAT MEANS WE HAVE ABOUT 20 MINUTES LEFT. NNH... WE NEED MORE TIME!
CHAO, THE FINAL BOSS IS HIDING SOMEWHERE IN THE OPEN WITHIN THE GAME AREA.
30m
30m
SHE SHOULD BE WAITING IN THE MIDDLE OF AN ILLUSTRATION THAT IS 30 METERS SQUARE.
ざわ YAMMER
ざわ YAMMER
ざわっ YAMMER
30 METERS!?
THAT'S GOING TO BE OBVIOUS!
WE'RE GOING TO BE ABLE TO FIND IT EASILY!
どよどよ YAK YAK
LET'S GET GOING!
おおっ YEAH!
HEY, DID YOU NOTICE THE CELL PHONES ARE WORKING AGAIN?
CONTACT EVERYONE IN OUR CLUB! HAVE THEM SPREAD OUT TO FIND HER!
WE'LL BE THE ONES TO FIND HER!
ANYONE THAT LOCATES HER AND/OR SUCCEEDS IN HER CAPTURE
WILL RECEIVE A SPECIAL REWARD THAT'S BIGGER THAN LAST YEAR'S PRIZE!
WE'RE COUNTING ON YOU
WE ASK EVERYONE'S COOPERATION! NON-PARTICIPANTS MAY ALSO TAKE PART IN THE SEARCH!
YŪNA—!!
IT'S COMING! IT'S COMING! IT'S COMING!
THE BIG ONE IS COMING!
GET READY TO RUMBLE!
ズーッ ZWHOM
WHOA!

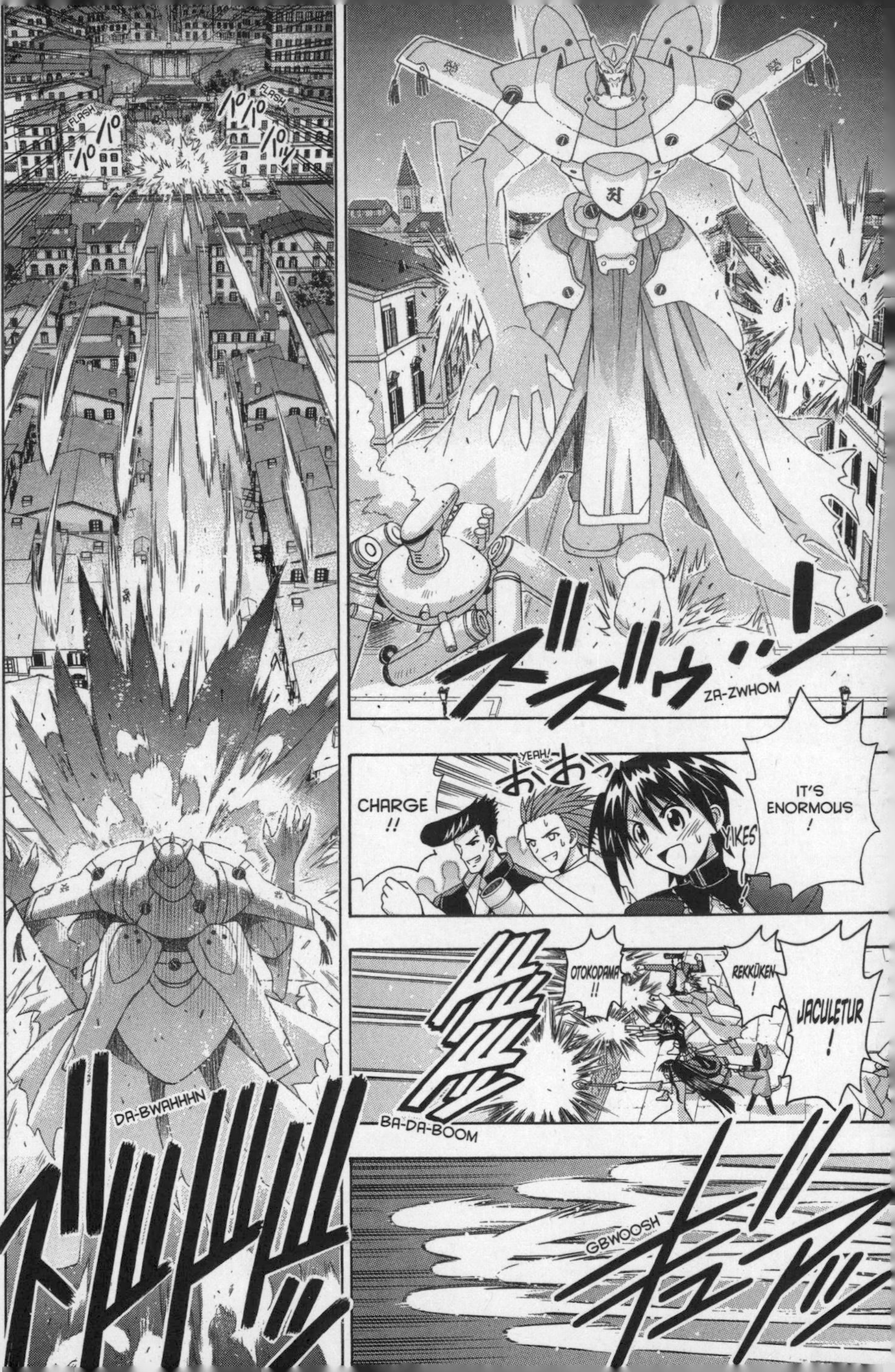
ZA-ZWHOM
IT'S ENORMOUS!
YIKES
YEAH!
CHARGE!!
JACULETUR!
REKKŪKEN!
OTOKODAMA!!
BA-DA-BOOM
GBWOOSH
FLASH
FLASH
DA-BWAHHHN

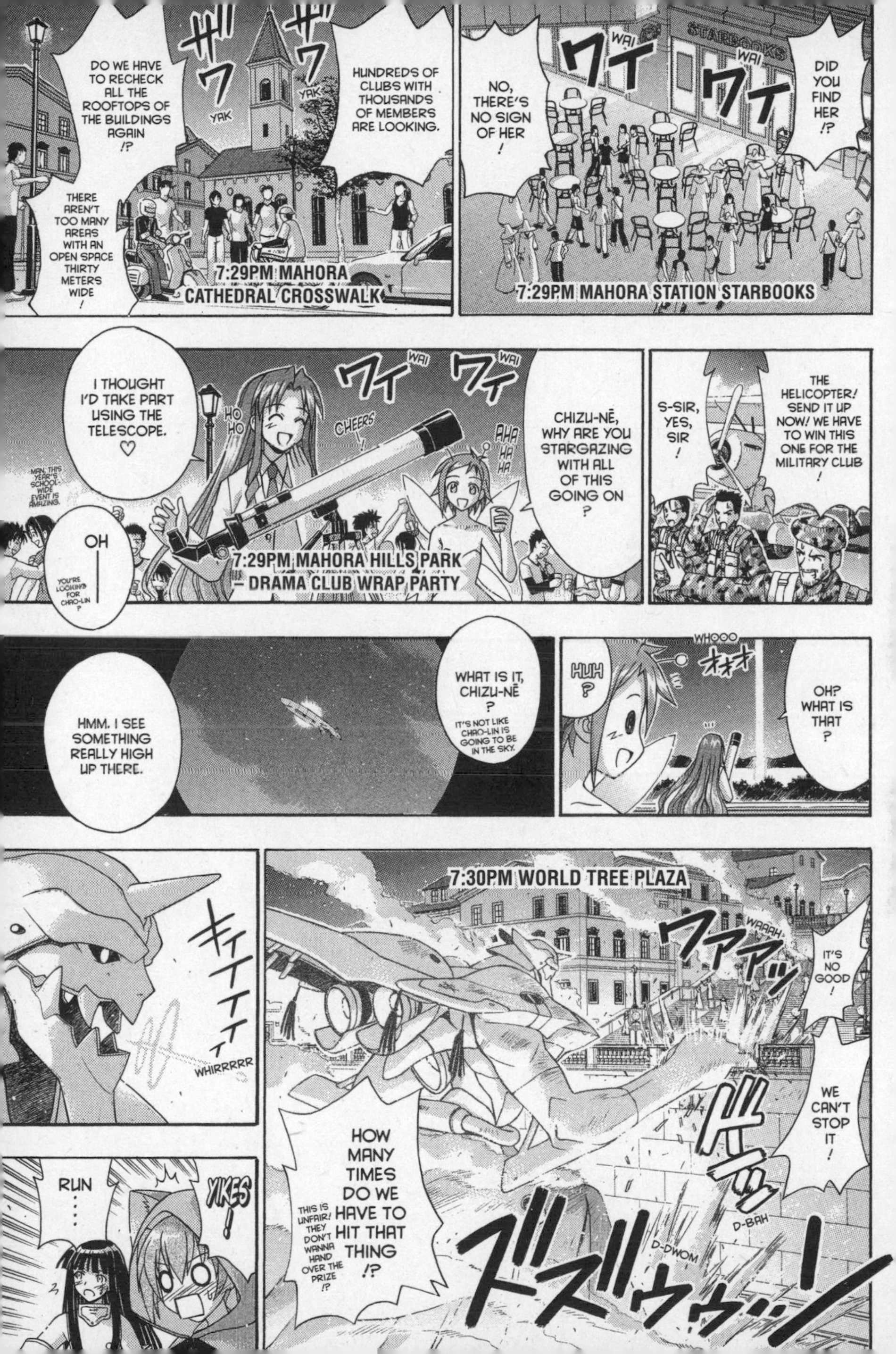
DID YOU FIND HER !?
WAI WAI
NO, THERE'S NO SIGN OF HER !
7:29PM MAHORA STATION STARBOOKS
HUNDREDS OF CLUBS WITH THOUSANDS OF MEMBERS ARE LOOKING.
YAK YAK
DO WE HAVE TO RECHECK ALL THE ROOFTOPS OF THE BUILDINGS AGAIN !?
THERE AREN'T TOO MANY AREAS WITH AN OPEN SPACE THIRTY METERS WIDE !
7:29PM MAHORA CATHEDRAL CROSSWALK
THE HELICOPTER! SEND IT UP NOW! WE HAVE TO WIN THIS ONE FOR THE MILITARY CLUB !
S-SIR, YES, SIR !
CHIZU-NĒ, WHY ARE YOU STARGAZING WITH ALL OF THIS GOING ON ?
WAI WAI
AHA HA HA
CHEERS !
I THOUGHT I'D TAKE PART USING THE TELESCOPE. ♡
HO HO
MAN, THIS YEAR'S SCHOOL-WIDE EVENT IS AMAZING.
OH —
YOU'RE LOOKING FOR CHAO-LIN ?
7:29PM MAHORA HILLS PARK – DRAMA CLUB WRAP PARTY
OH? WHAT IS THAT ?
WHOOO
HUH ?
WHAT IS IT, CHIZU-NĒ ?
IT'S NOT LIKE CHAO-LIN IS GOING TO BE IN THE SKY.
HMM. I SEE SOMETHING REALLY HIGH UP THERE.
7:30PM WORLD TREE PLAZA
WAAAH
IT'S NO GOOD !
WE CAN'T STOP IT !
D-BAH
D-DWOM
HOW MANY TIMES DO WE HAVE TO HIT THAT THING !?
THIS IS UNFAIR! THEY DON'T WANNA HAND OVER THE PRIZE !?
WHIRRRRR
YIKES !
RUN ....

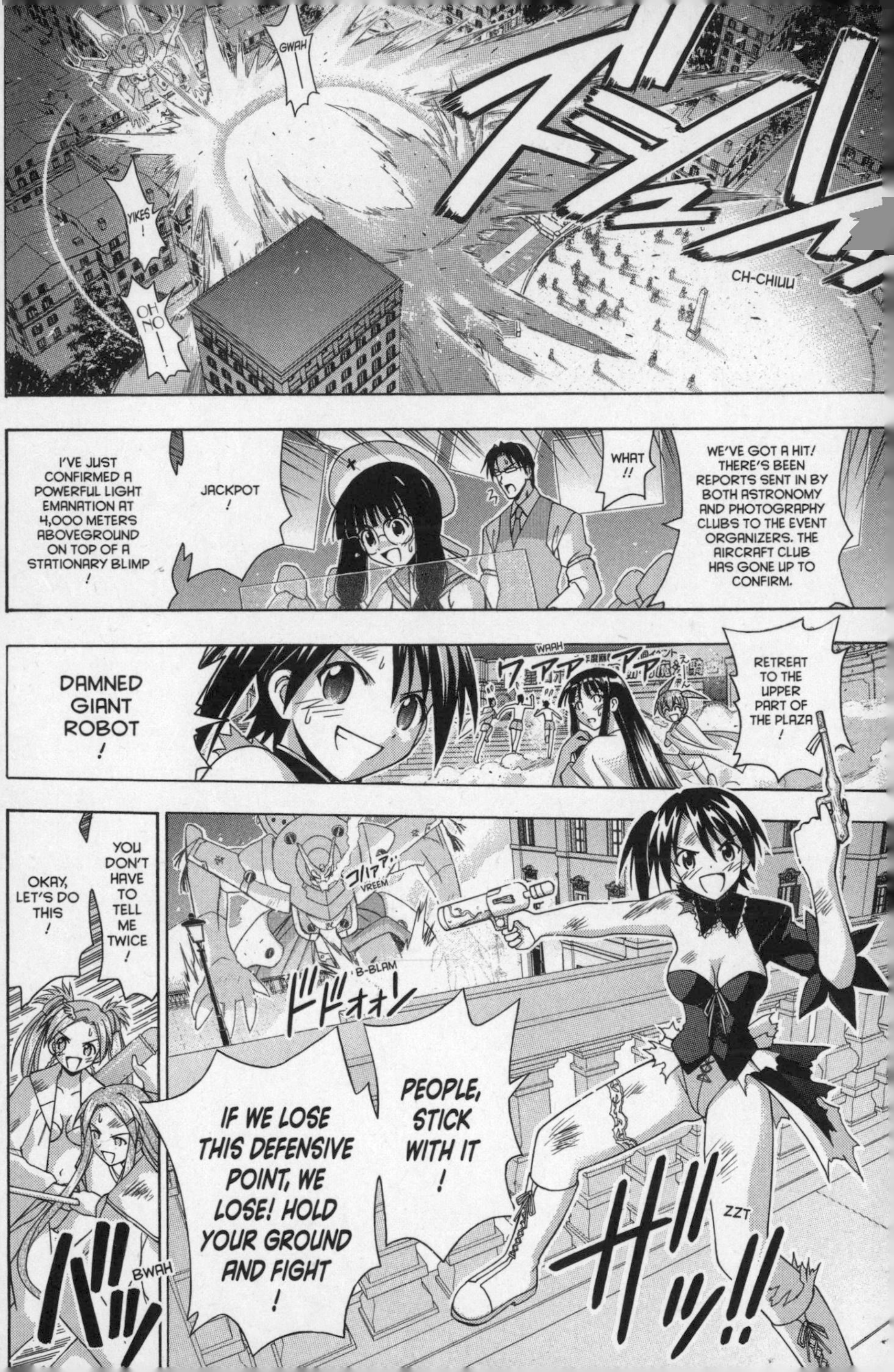
CH-CHIUU
GWAH!
YIKES!
OH NO!!
WE'VE GOT A HIT! THERE'S BEEN REPORTS SENT IN BY BOTH ASTRONOMY AND PHOTOGRAPHY CLUBS TO THE EVENT ORGANIZERS. THE AIRCRAFT CLUB HAS GONE UP TO CONFIRM.
WHAT!!
JACKPOT!
I'VE JUST CONFIRMED A POWERFUL LIGHT EMANATION AT 4,000 METERS ABOVEGROUND ON TOP OF A STATIONARY BLIMP!
RETREAT TO THE UPPER PART OF THE PLAZA!
WAAH
DAMNED GIANT ROBOT!
ZZT
PEOPLE, STICK WITH IT!
IF WE LOSE THIS DEFENSIVE POINT, WE LOSE! HOLD YOUR GROUND AND FIGHT!
VREEM
B-BLAM
YOU DON'T HAVE TO TELL ME TWICE!
OKAY, LET'S DO THIS!
BWAH

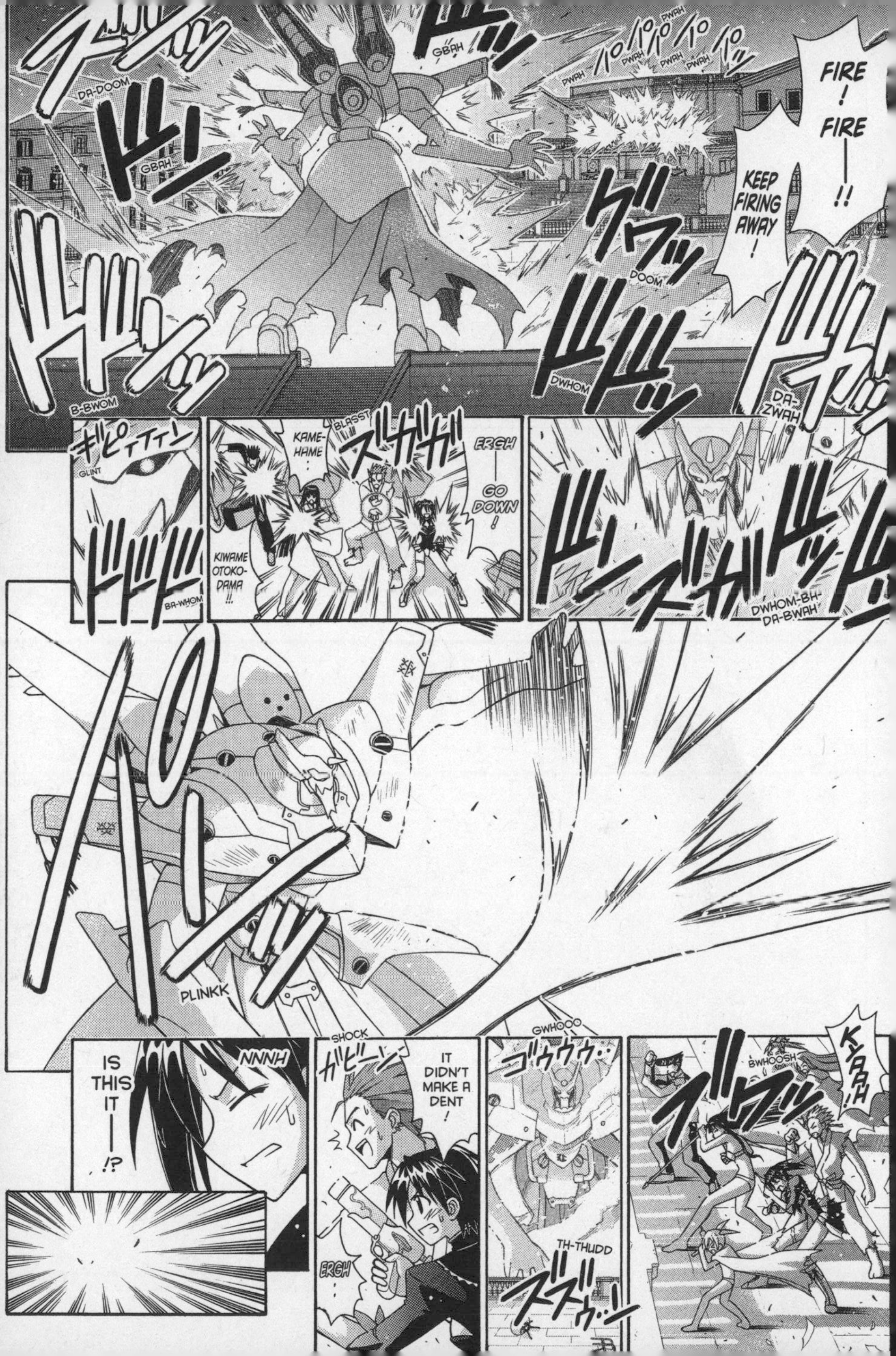
FIRE! FIRE—!!
KEEP FIRING AWAY!
PWAH PWAH PWAH PWAH PWAH
GBAH
DOOM
DA-DOOM
GBAH
DWHOM
DA-ZWAH
B-BWOM
DWHOM-BH-DA-BWAH
ERGH — GO DOWN!
BLASST
KAME-HAME
KIWAME OTOKO-DAMA!!!
GLINT
BA-WHOM
PLINKK
KYAAH!
BWHOOSH
GWHOOO
TH-THUDD
SHOCK
IT DIDN'T MAKE A DENT!
ERGH
NNNH
IS THIS IT—!?

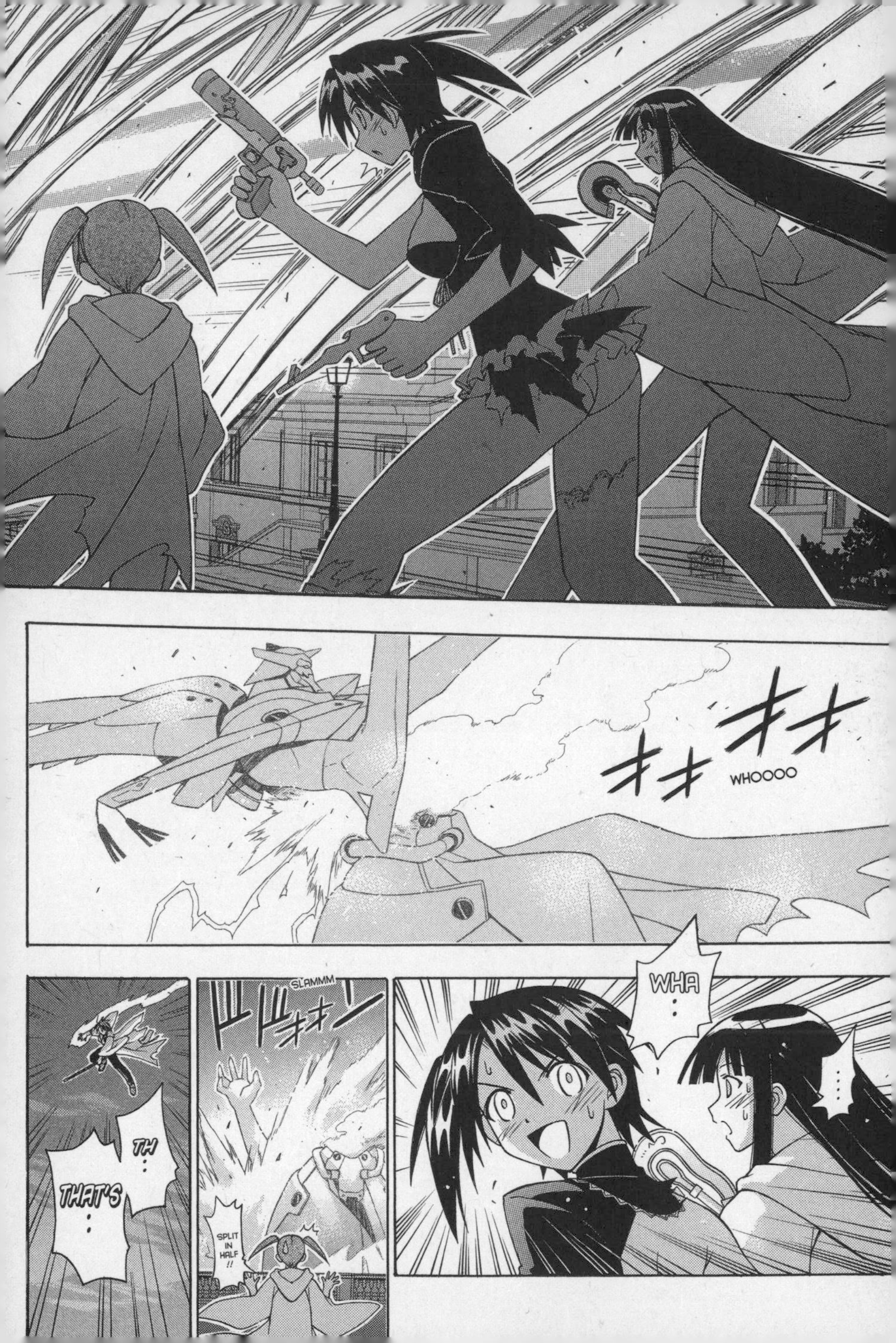

WHOOOO
WHA
...
SLAMMM
SPLIT IN HALF !!
TH... THAT'S...

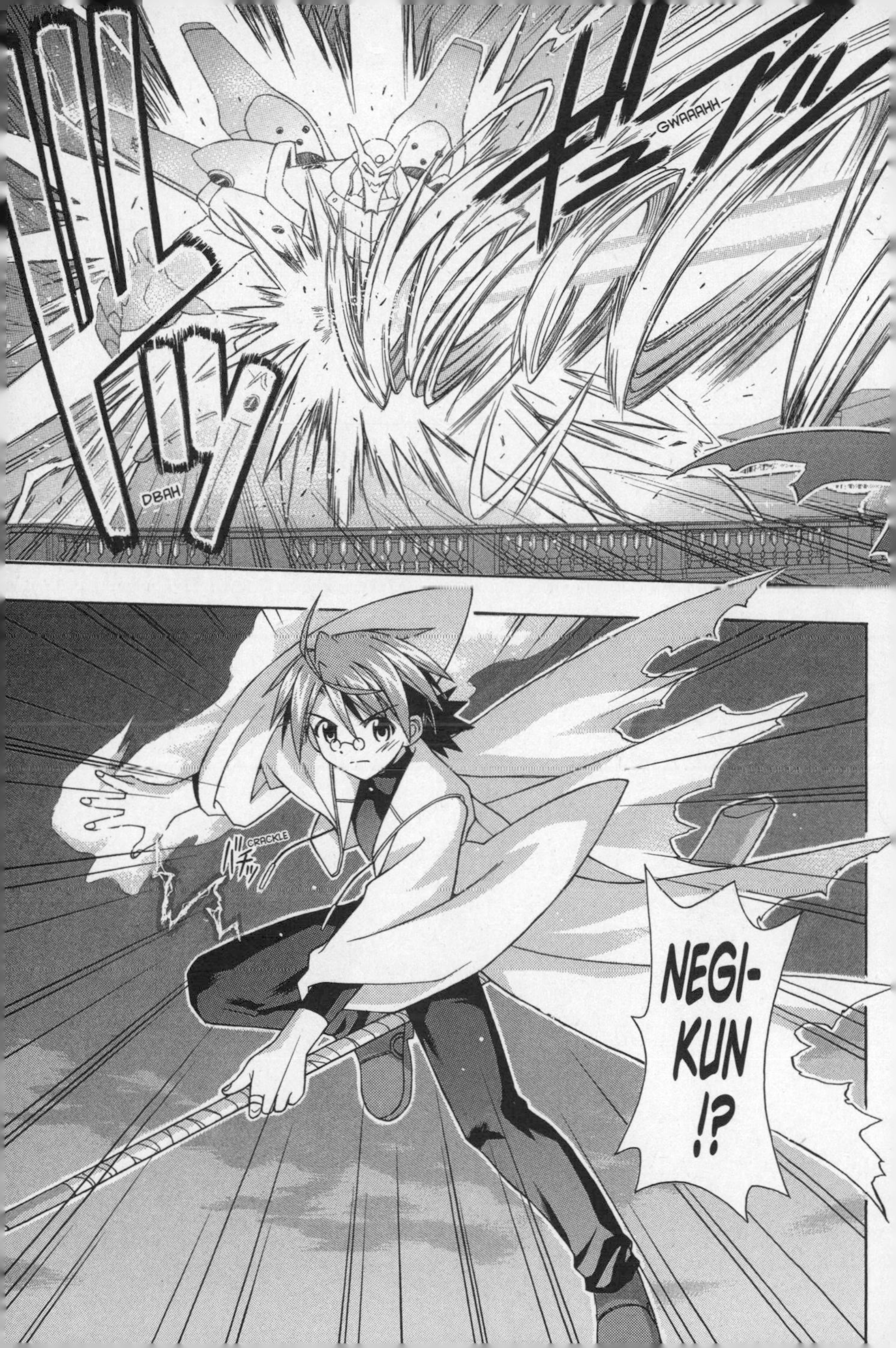
GWAAAHH
DBAH
CRACKLE
NEGI-KUN!?

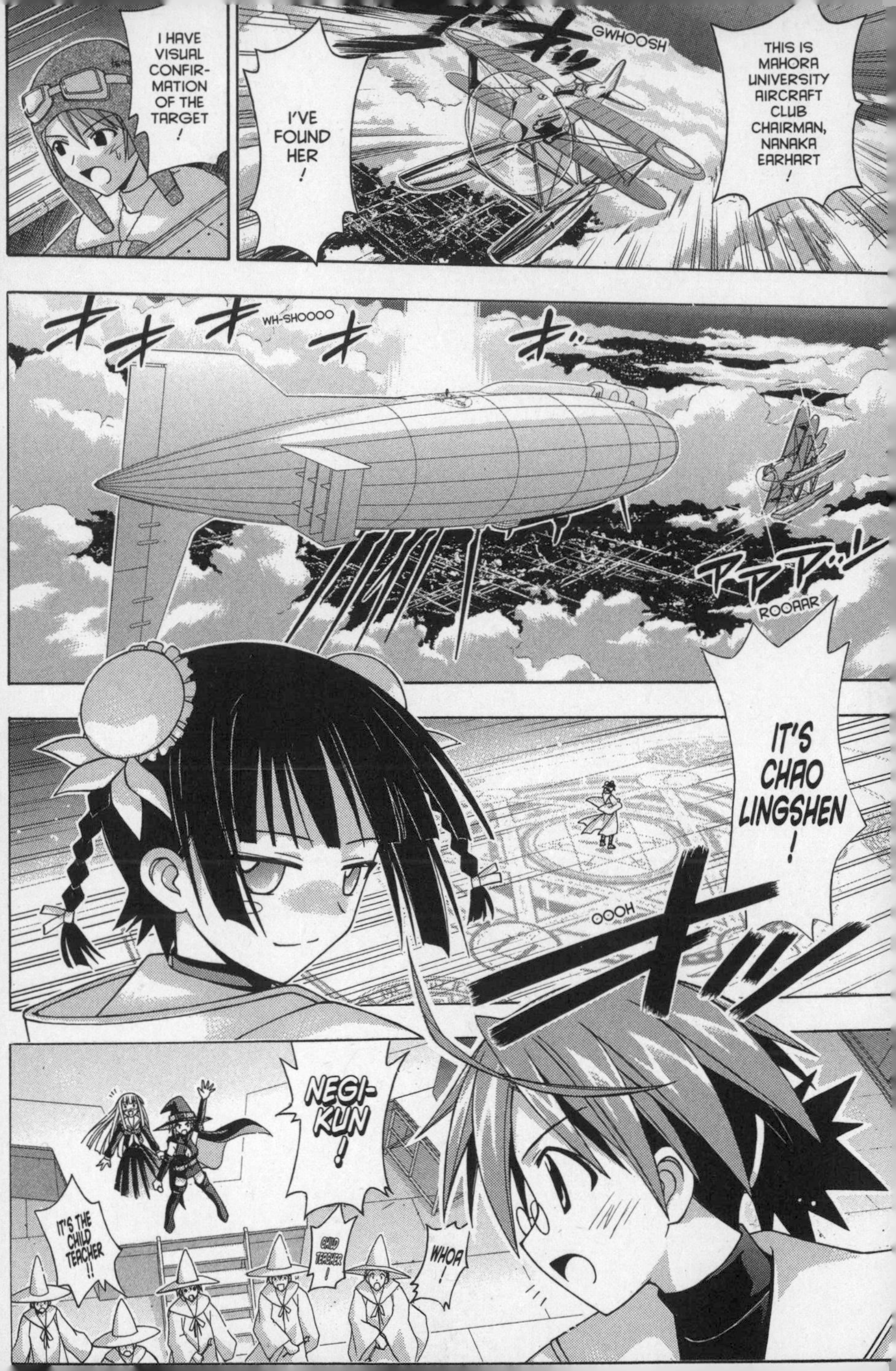
THIS IS MAHORA UNIVERSITY AIRCRAFT CLUB CHAIRMAN, NANAKA EARHART!
GWHOOSH
I'VE FOUND HER!
I HAVE VISUAL CONFIRMATION OF THE TARGET!
WH-SHOOOO
ROOAAR
IT'S CHAO LINGSHEN!
OOOH
NEGI-KUN!
WHOA!
CHILD TEACHER!
IT'S THE CHILD TEACHER!!

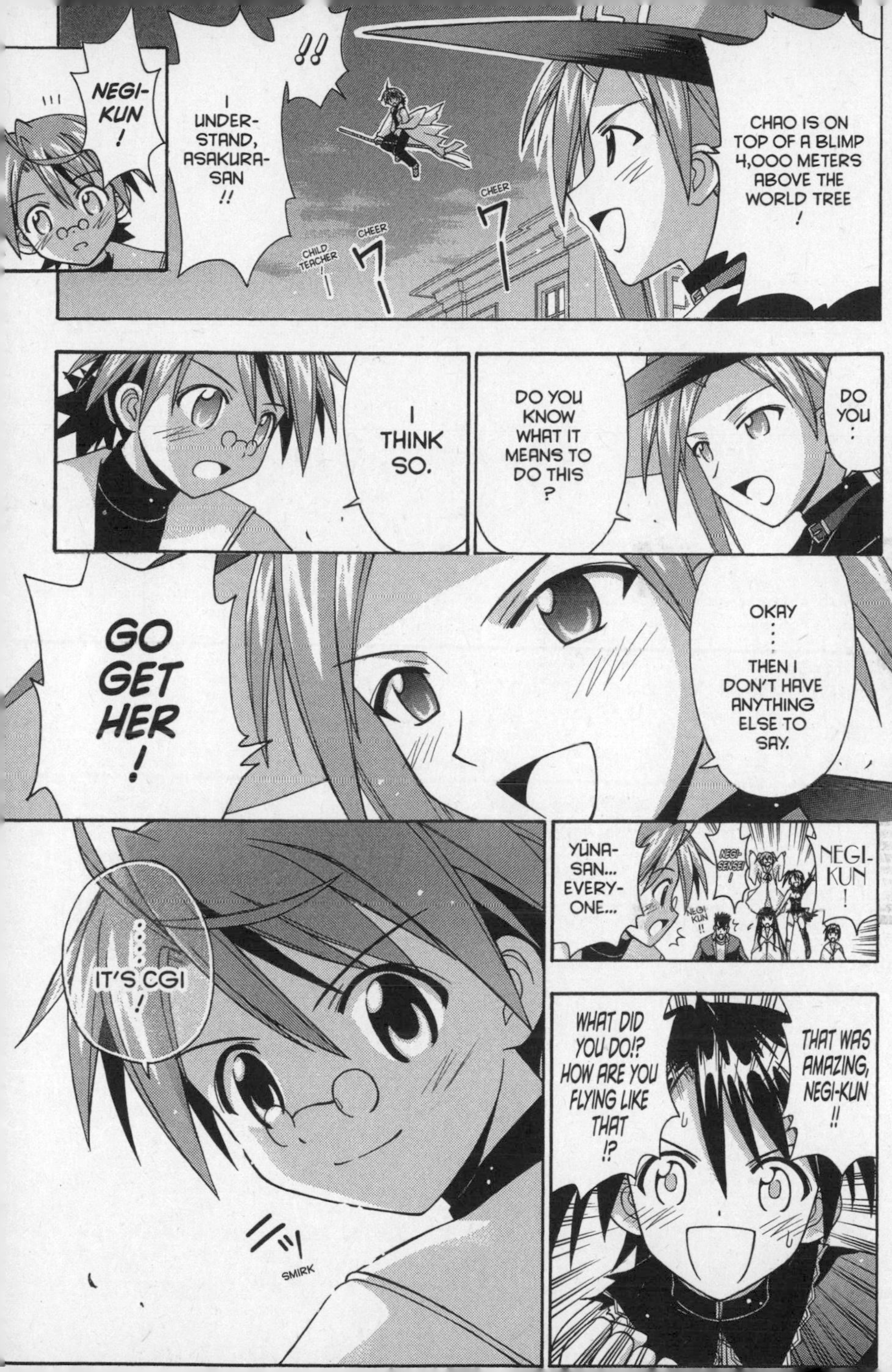
CHAO IS ON TOP OF A BLIMP 4,000 METERS ABOVE THE WORLD TREE!
CHEER
CHEER
CHILD TEACHER!
!!
I UNDERSTAND, ASAKURA-SAN!!
NEGI-KUN!
DO YOU...
DO YOU KNOW WHAT IT MEANS TO DO THIS?
I THINK SO.
OKAY... THEN I DON'T HAVE ANYTHING ELSE TO SAY.
GO GET HER!
NEGI-KUN!
NEGI-SENSEI!
NEGI-KUN!!
YŪNA-SAN... EVERYONE...
THAT WAS AMAZING, NEGI-KUN!!
WHAT DID YOU DO!? HOW ARE YOU FLYING LIKE THAT!?
...... IT'S CGI!
SMIRK

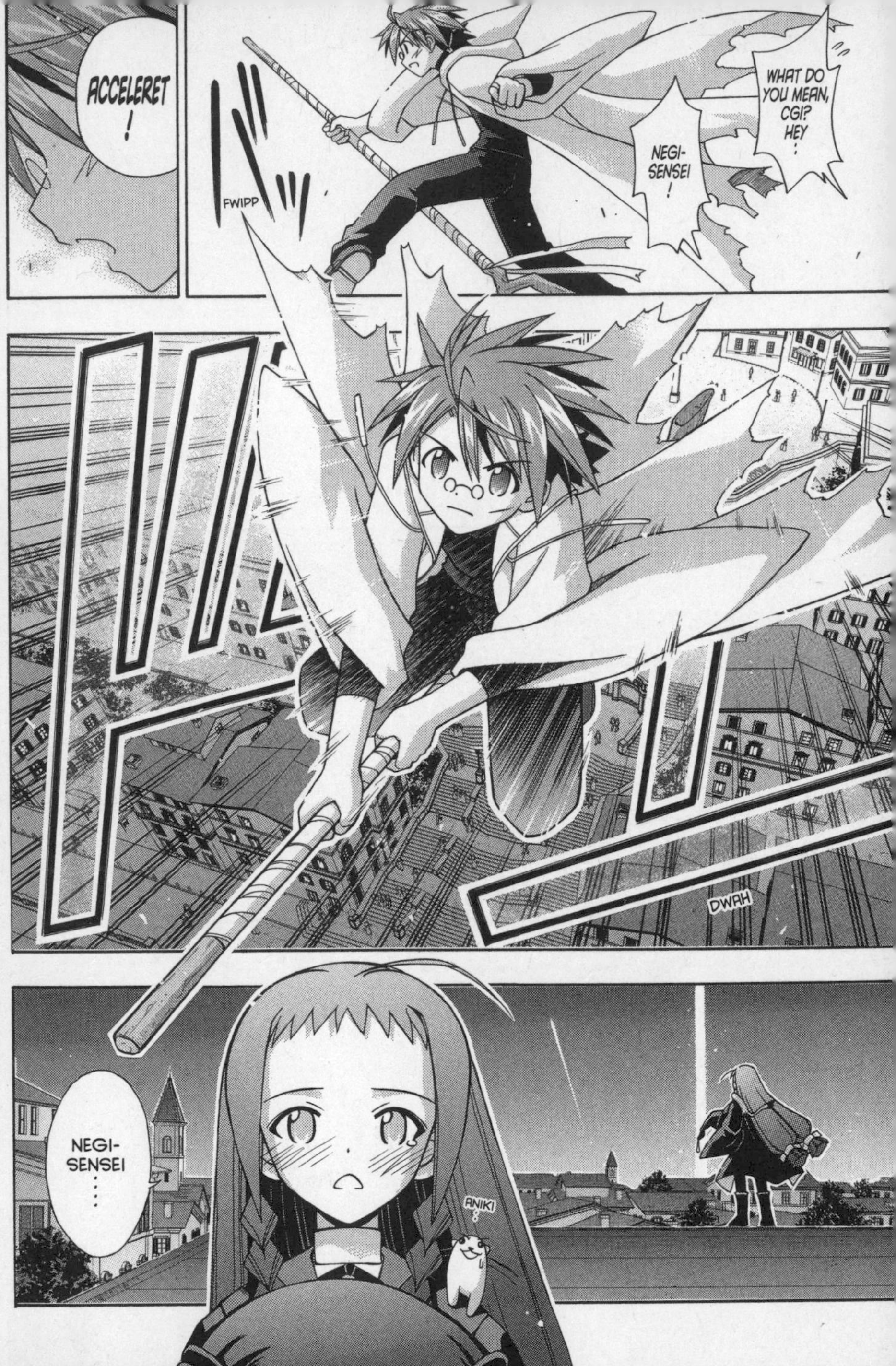
WHAT DO YOU MEAN, CGI? HEY...
NEGI-SENSEI!
FWIPP
ACCELERET!
DWAH
ANIKI
NEGI-SENSEI.....

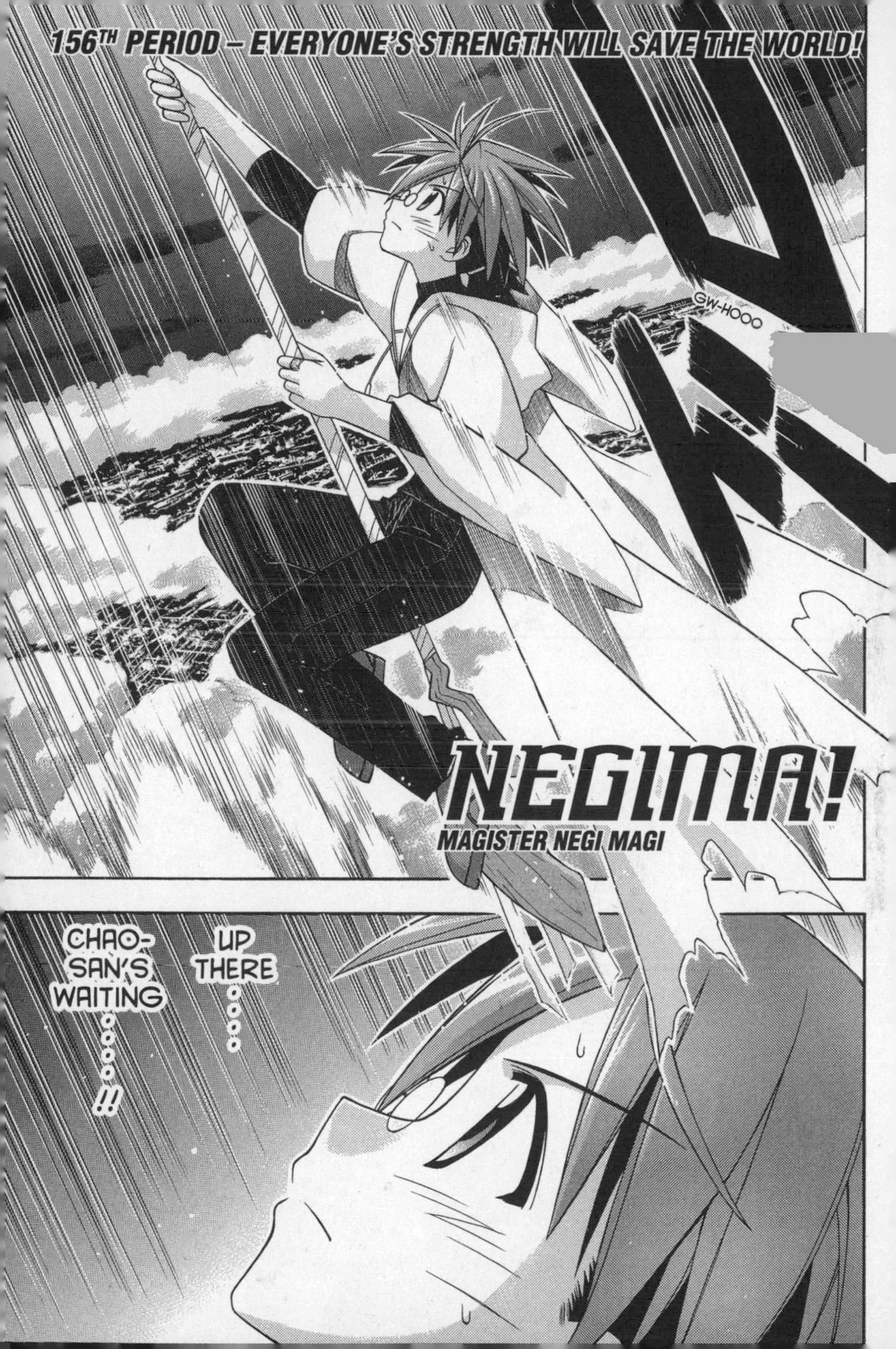
156TH PERIOD – EVERYONE'S STRENGTH WILL SAVE THE WORLD!
GW-HOOO
NEGIMA!
MAGISTER NEGI MAGI
UP THERE....
CHAO-SAN'S WAITING......!!

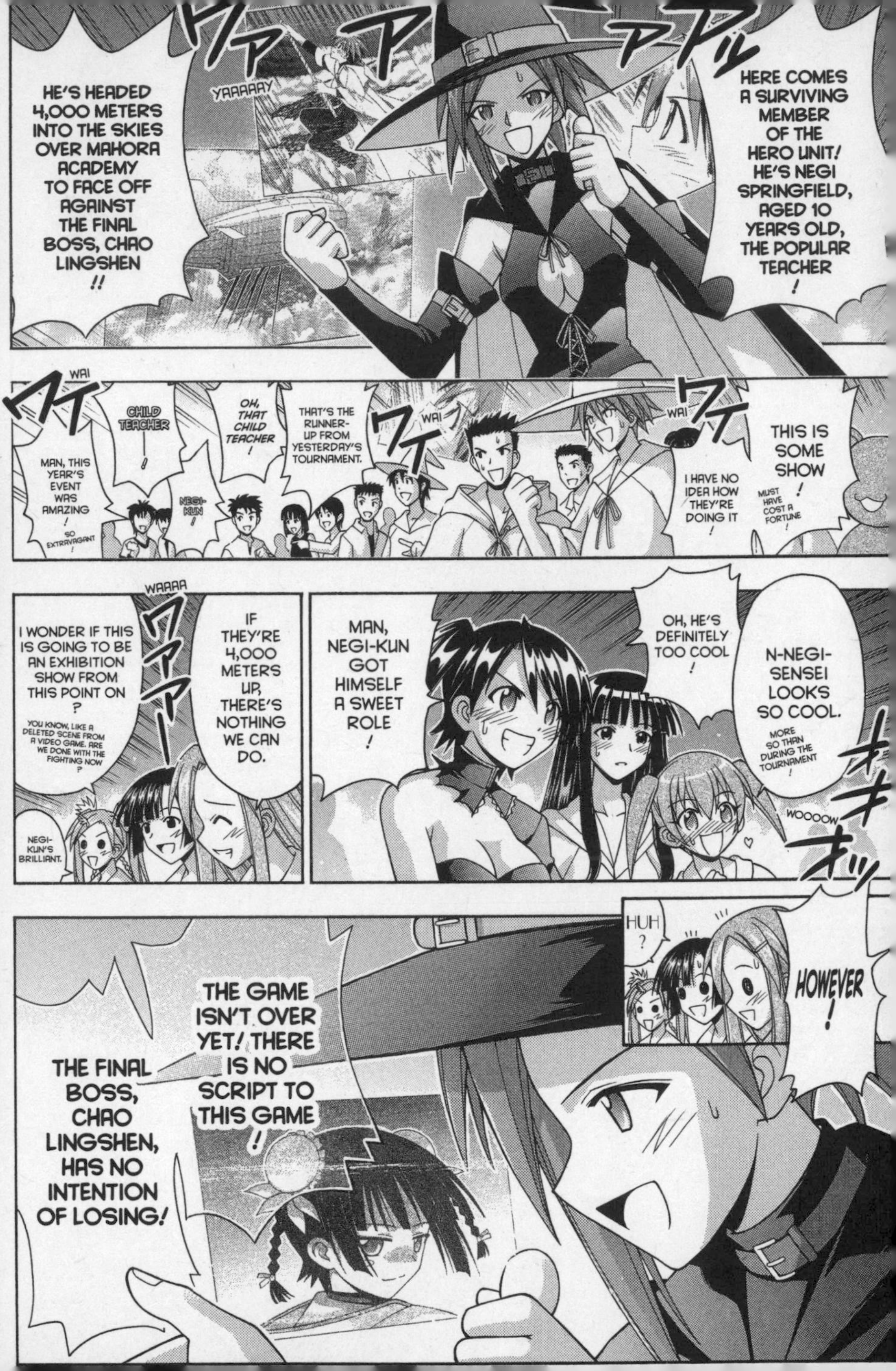
HERE COMES A SURVIVING MEMBER OF THE HERO UNIT! HE'S NEGI SPRINGFIELD, AGED 10 YEARS OLD, THE POPULAR TEACHER!
YAAAAAY
HE'S HEADED 4,000 METERS INTO THE SKIES OVER MAHORA ACADEMY TO FACE OFF AGAINST THE FINAL BOSS, CHAO LINGSHEN!!
THIS IS SOME SHOW!
MUST HAVE COST A FORTUNE!
WAI
I HAVE NO IDEA HOW THEY'RE DOING IT!
WAI
THAT'S THE RUNNER-UP FROM YESTERDAY'S TOURNAMENT.
OH, THAT CHILD TEACHER!
CHILD TEACHER!
NEGI-KUN!
MAN, THIS YEAR'S EVENT WAS AMAZING
SO EXTRAVAGANT!
WAI
N-NEGI-SENSEI LOOKS SO COOL.
MORE SO THAN DURING THE TOURNAMENT!
WOOOOW
OH, HE'S DEFINITELY TOO COOL!
MAN, NEGI-KUN GOT HIMSELF A SWEET ROLE!
IF THEY'RE 4,000 METERS UP, THERE'S NOTHING WE CAN DO.
WAAAAA
I WONDER IF THIS IS GOING TO BE AN EXHIBITION SHOW FROM THIS POINT ON?
YOU KNOW, LIKE A DELETED SCENE FROM A VIDEO GAME. ARE WE DONE WITH THE FIGHTING NOW?
NEGI-KUN'S BRILLIANT.
HOWEVER!
HUH?
THE GAME ISN'T OVER YET! THERE IS NO SCRIPT TO THIS GAME!
THE FINAL BOSS, CHAO LINGSHEN, HAS NO INTENTION OF LOSING!

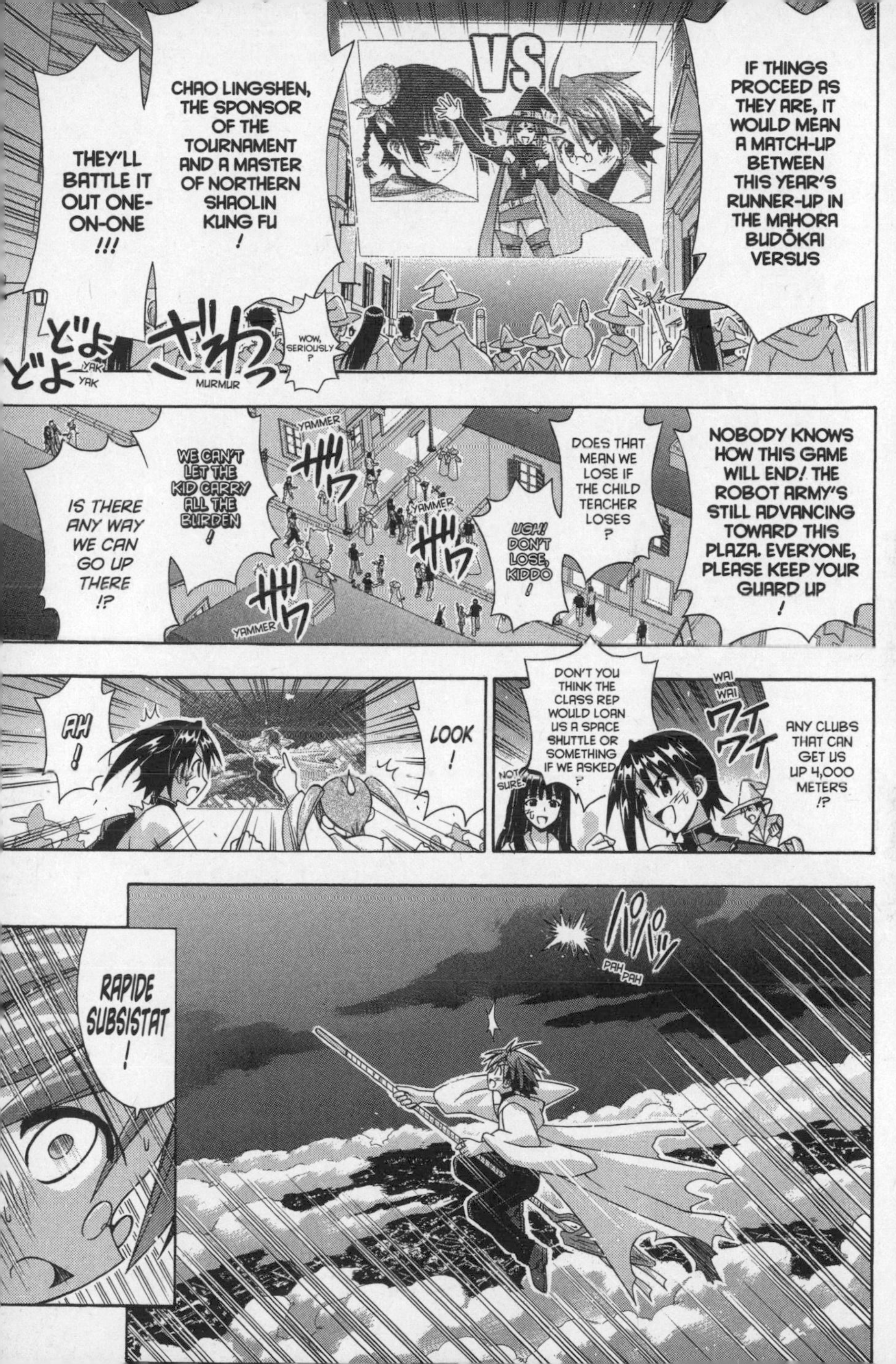

IF THINGS PROCEED AS THEY ARE, IT WOULD MEAN A MATCH-UP BETWEEN THIS YEAR'S RUNNER-UP IN THE MAHORA BUDŌKAI VERSUS
CHAO LINGSHEN, THE SPONSOR OF THE TOURNAMENT AND A MASTER OF NORTHERN SHAOLIN KUNG FU!
THEY'LL BATTLE IT OUT ONE-ON-ONE!!!
VS
WOW, SERIOUSLY?
ざわっ
MURMUR
どよどよ
YAK YAK
NOBODY KNOWS HOW THIS GAME WILL END! THE ROBOT ARMY'S STILL ADVANCING TOWARD THIS PLAZA. EVERYONE, PLEASE KEEP YOUR GUARD UP!
DOES THAT MEAN WE LOSE IF THE CHILD TEACHER LOSES?
UGH! DON'T LOSE, KIDDO!
ザワ
YAMMER
WE CAN'T LET THE KID CARRY ALL THE BURDEN!
IS THERE ANY WAY WE CAN GO UP THERE!?
ワイワイ
WAI WAI
ANY CLUBS THAT CAN GET US UP 4,000 METERS!?
DON'T YOU THINK THE CLASS REP WOULD LOAN US A SPACE SHUTTLE OR SOMETHING IF WE ASKED?
NOT SURE
LOOK!
AH!
パパッ
PAH PAH
RAPIDE SUBSISTAT!

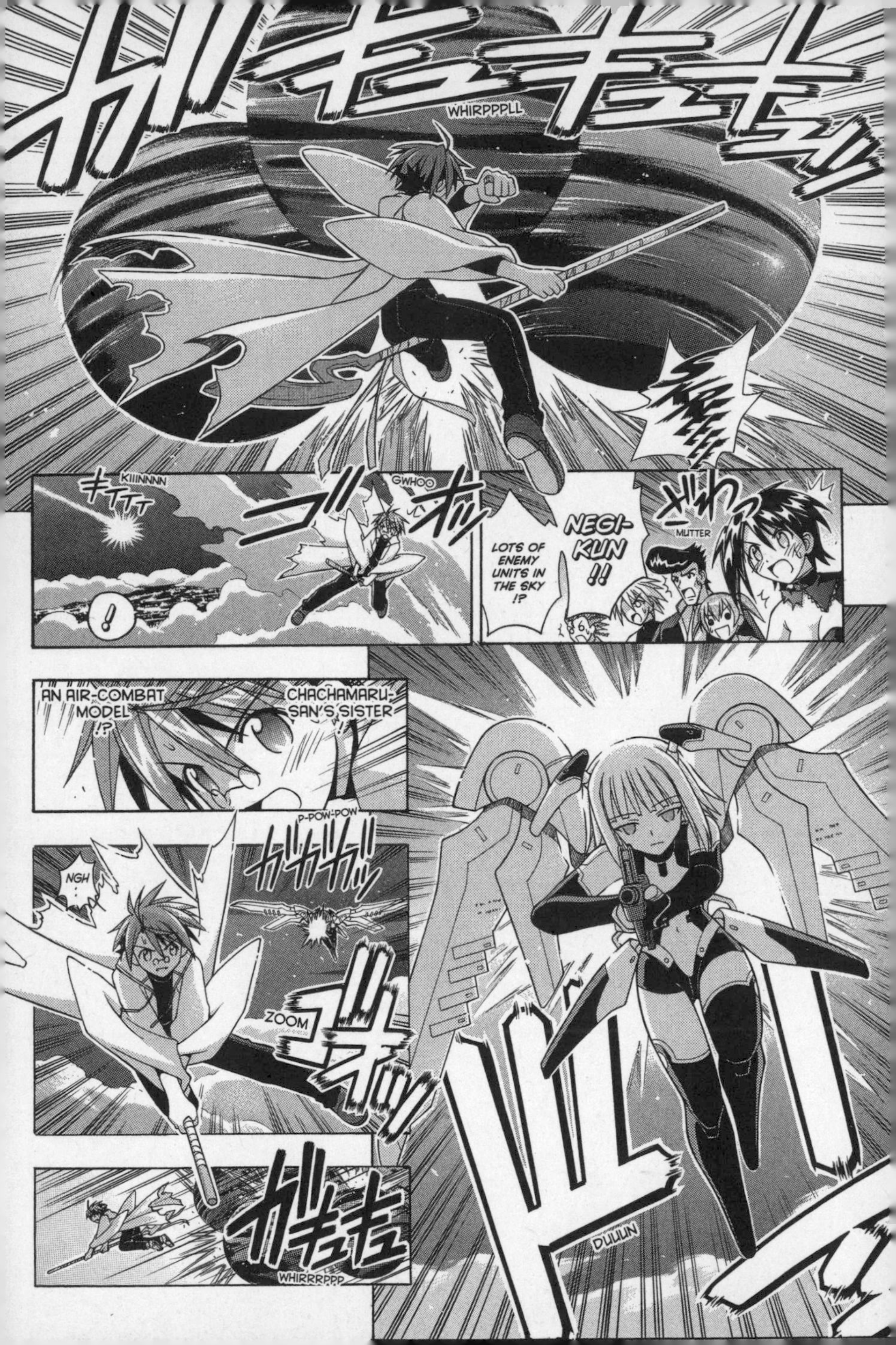
WHIRPPPLL
NEGI-KUN!!
LOTS OF ENEMY UNITS IN THE SKY!?
MUTTER
GWHOO
KIIINNNN
!
DUUUN
CHACHAMARU-SAN'S SISTER
AN AIR-COMBAT MODEL!?
P-POW-POW
ZOOM
NGH...
WHIRRRPPP

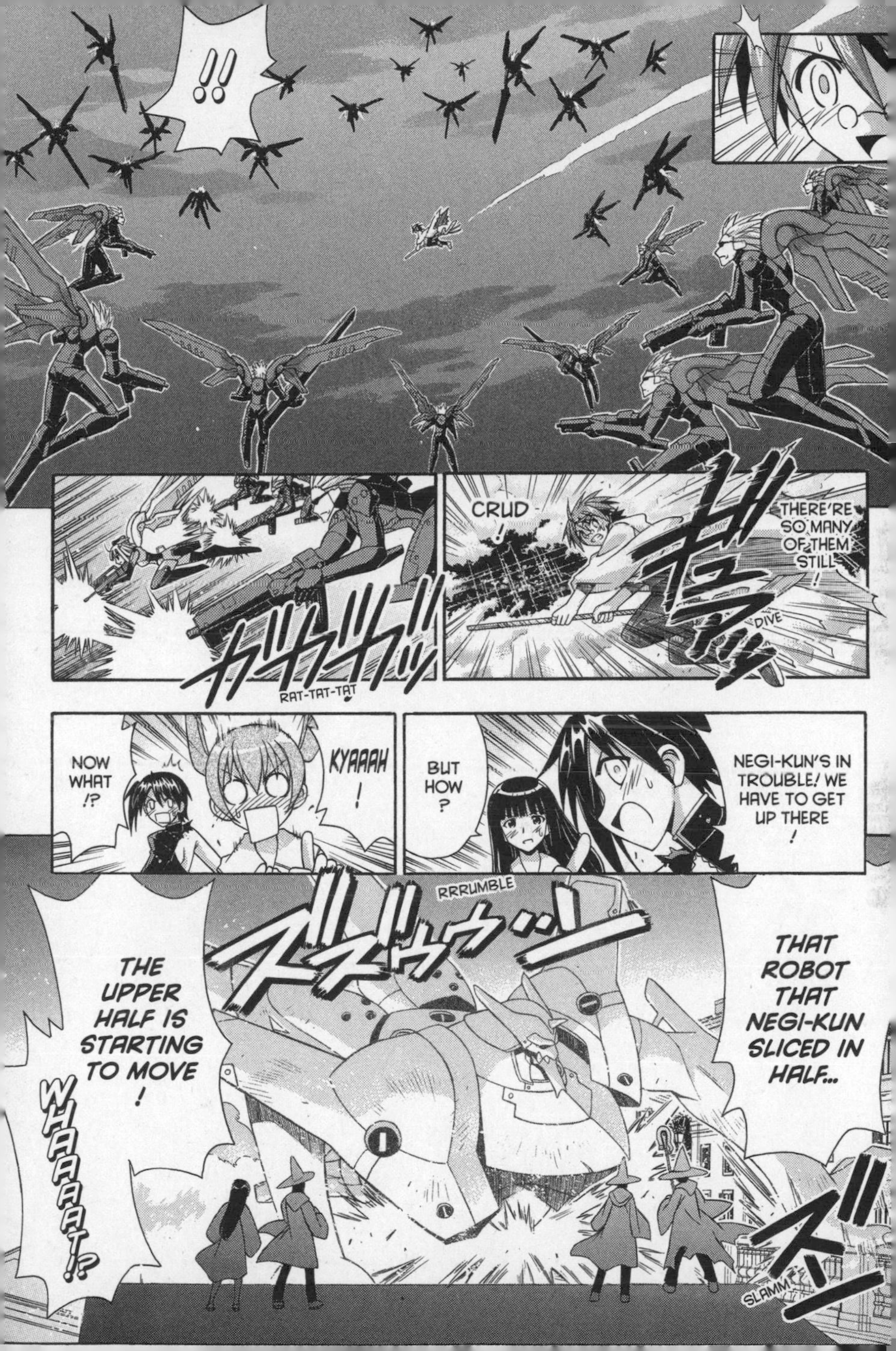
!!
THERE'RE SO MANY OF THEM STILL!
DIVE
CRUD!
RAT-TAT-TAT
NEGI-KUN'S IN TROUBLE! WE HAVE TO GET UP THERE!
BUT HOW?
KYAAAH!
NOW WHAT!?
THAT ROBOT THAT NEGI-KUN SLICED IN HALF...
RRRUMBLE
THE UPPER HALF IS STARTING TO MOVE!
SLAMM
WHAAAAAT!?

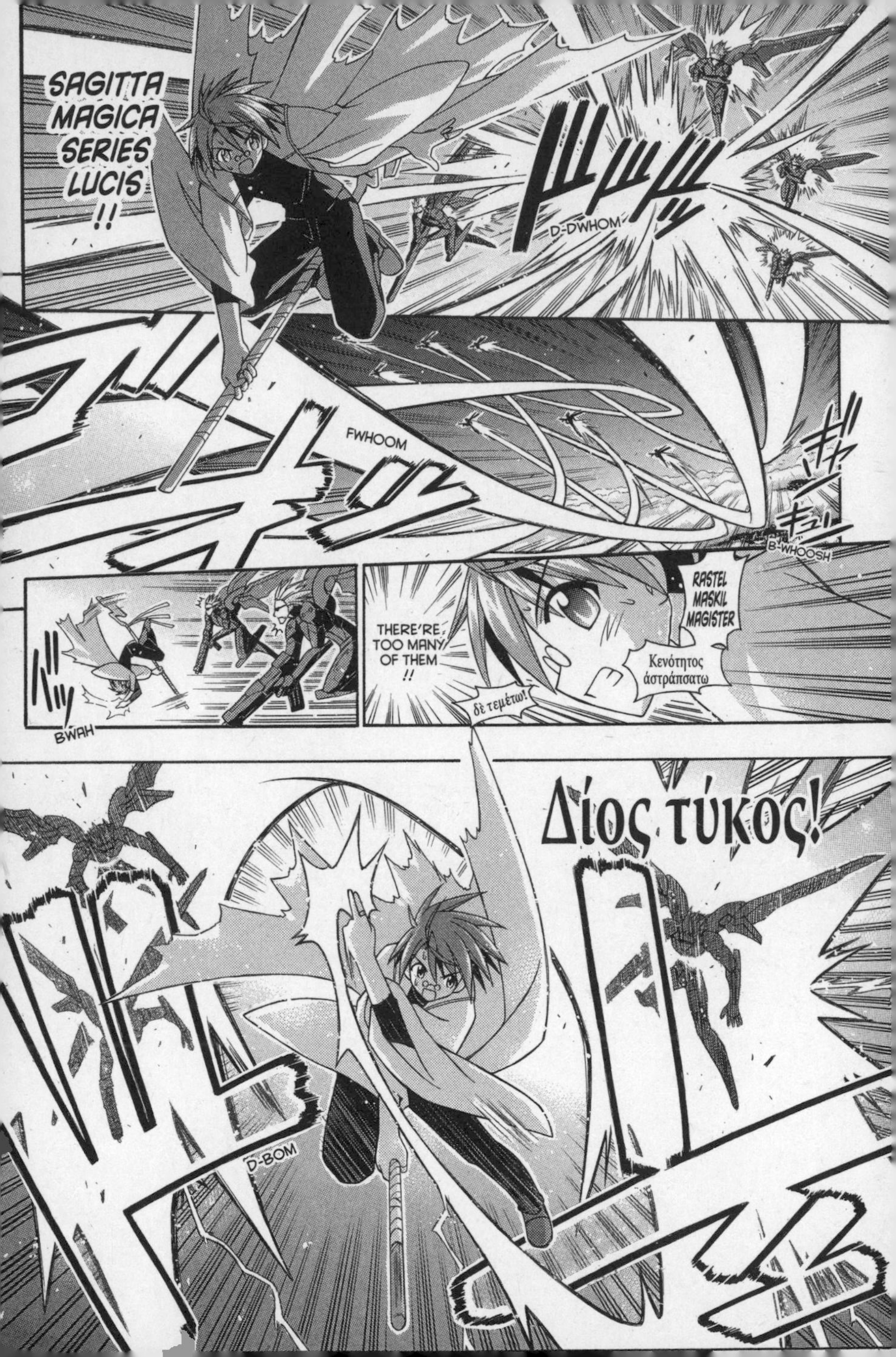
SAGITTA MAGICA SERIES LUCIS !!
D-DWHOM
B-WHOOSH
FWHOOM
RASTEL MASKIL MAGISTER
Κενότητος ἀστράπσατω
δὲ τεμέτω!
THERE'RE TOO MANY OF THEM !!
BWAH
Δίος τύκος!
D-BOM

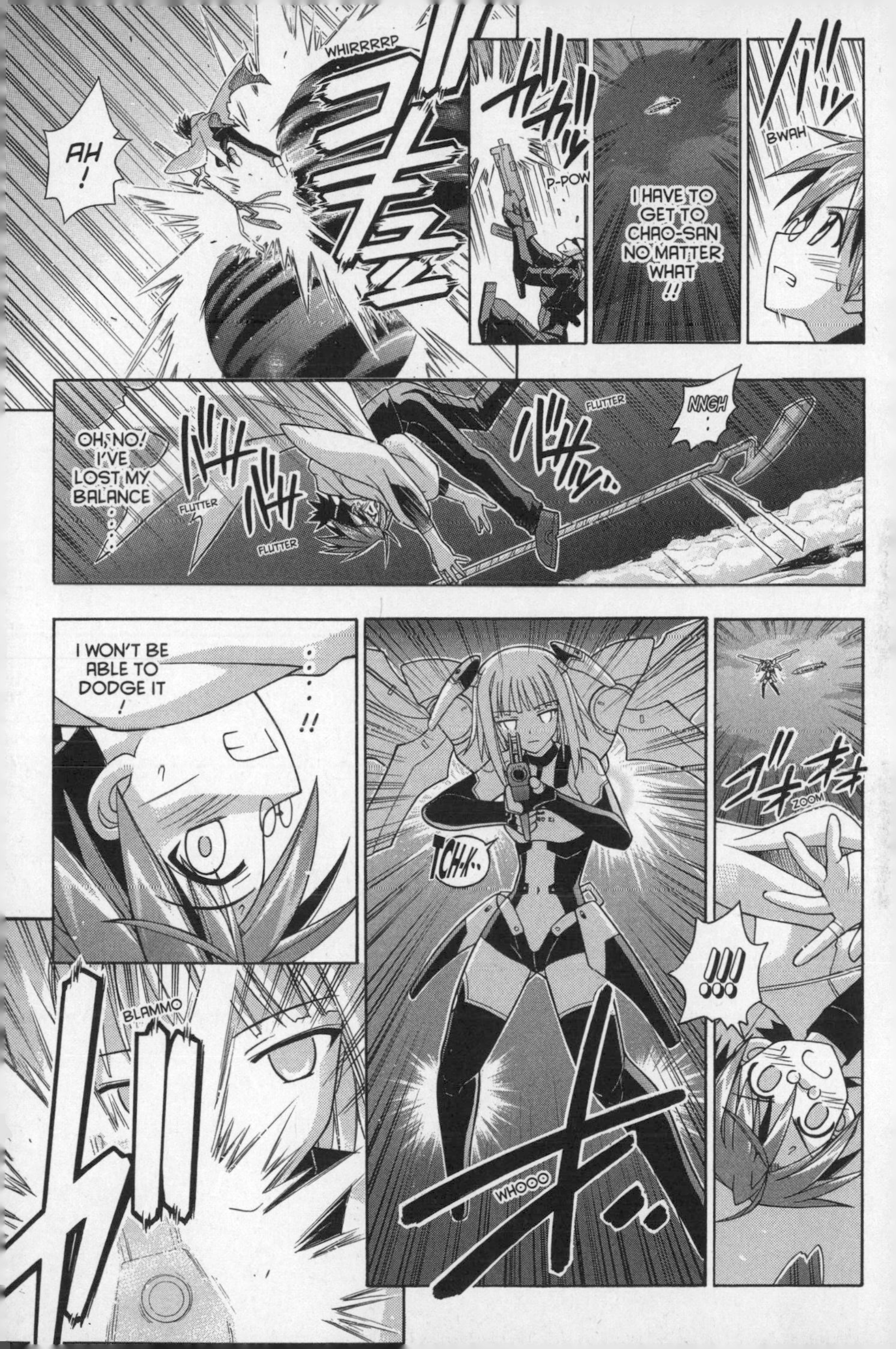
BWAH
I HAVE TO GET TO CHAO-SAN NO MATTER WHAT!!
P-POW
WHIRRRRP
AH!
NNGH...
FLUTTER
OH, NO! I'VE LOST MY BALANCE...
FLUTTER
FLUTTER
ZOOM
!!!...
TCH-K..
WHOOO
I WON'T BE ABLE TO DODGE IT...!!
BLAMMO

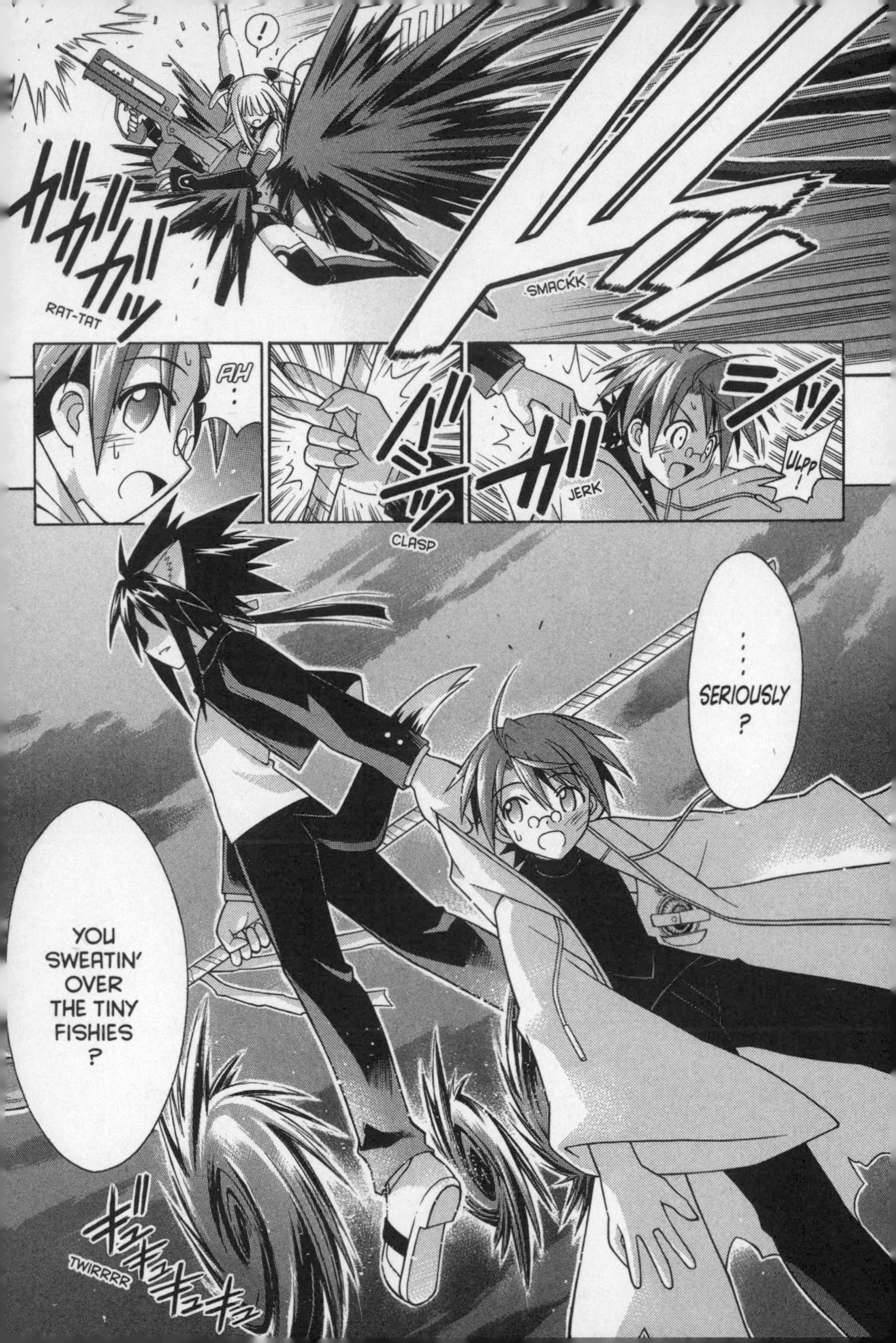
SMACKK
!
RAT-TAT
ULPP!
JERK
CLASP
AH...
...SERIOUSLY?
YOU SWEATIN' OVER THE TINY FISHIES?
TWIRRRR

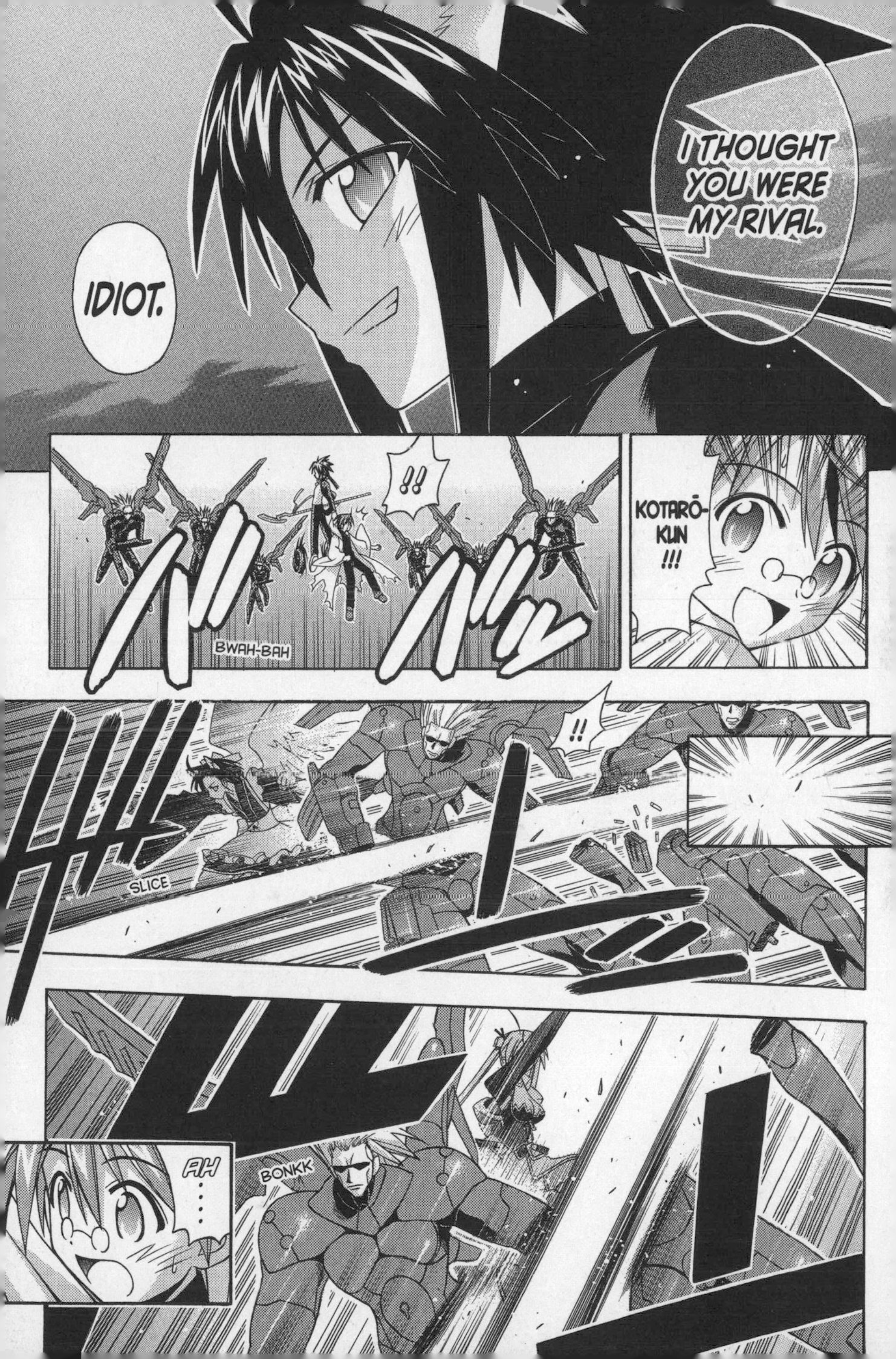
I THOUGHT YOU WERE MY RIVAL.
IDIOT.
KOTARŌ-KUN !!!
!!
BWAH-BAH
!!
SLICE
BONKK
AH .....

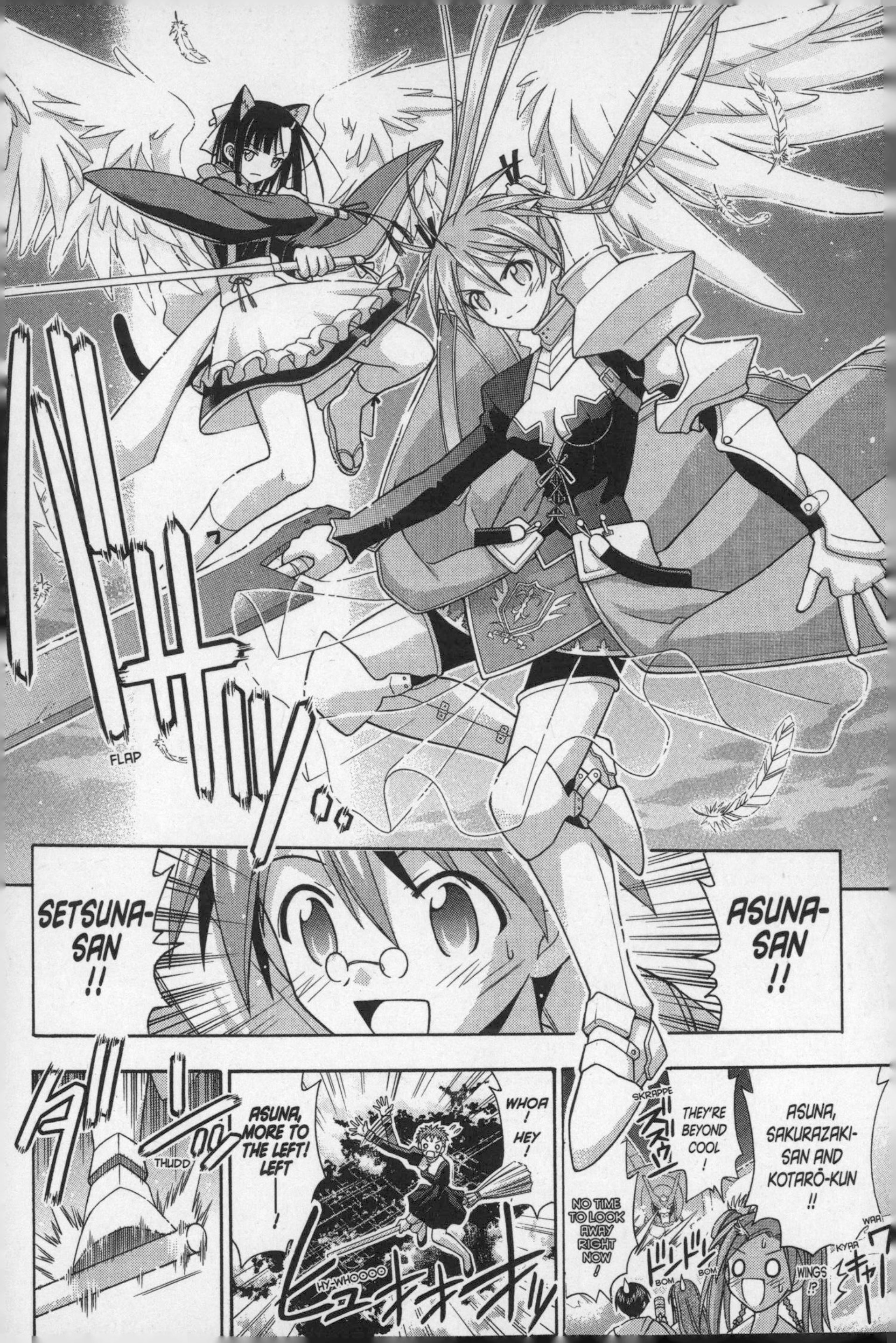
FLAP
ASUNA-SAN !!
SETSUNA-SAN !!
ASUNA, SAKURAZAKI-SAN AND KOTARŌ-KUN !!
WAA
KYAA
WINGS !?
THEY'RE BEYOND COOL !
SKRAPPE
BOM
BOM
NO TIME TO LOOK AWAY RIGHT NOW !
WHOA ! HEY !
ASUNA, MORE TO THE LEFT! LEFT —!
HY-WHOOOO
THUDD

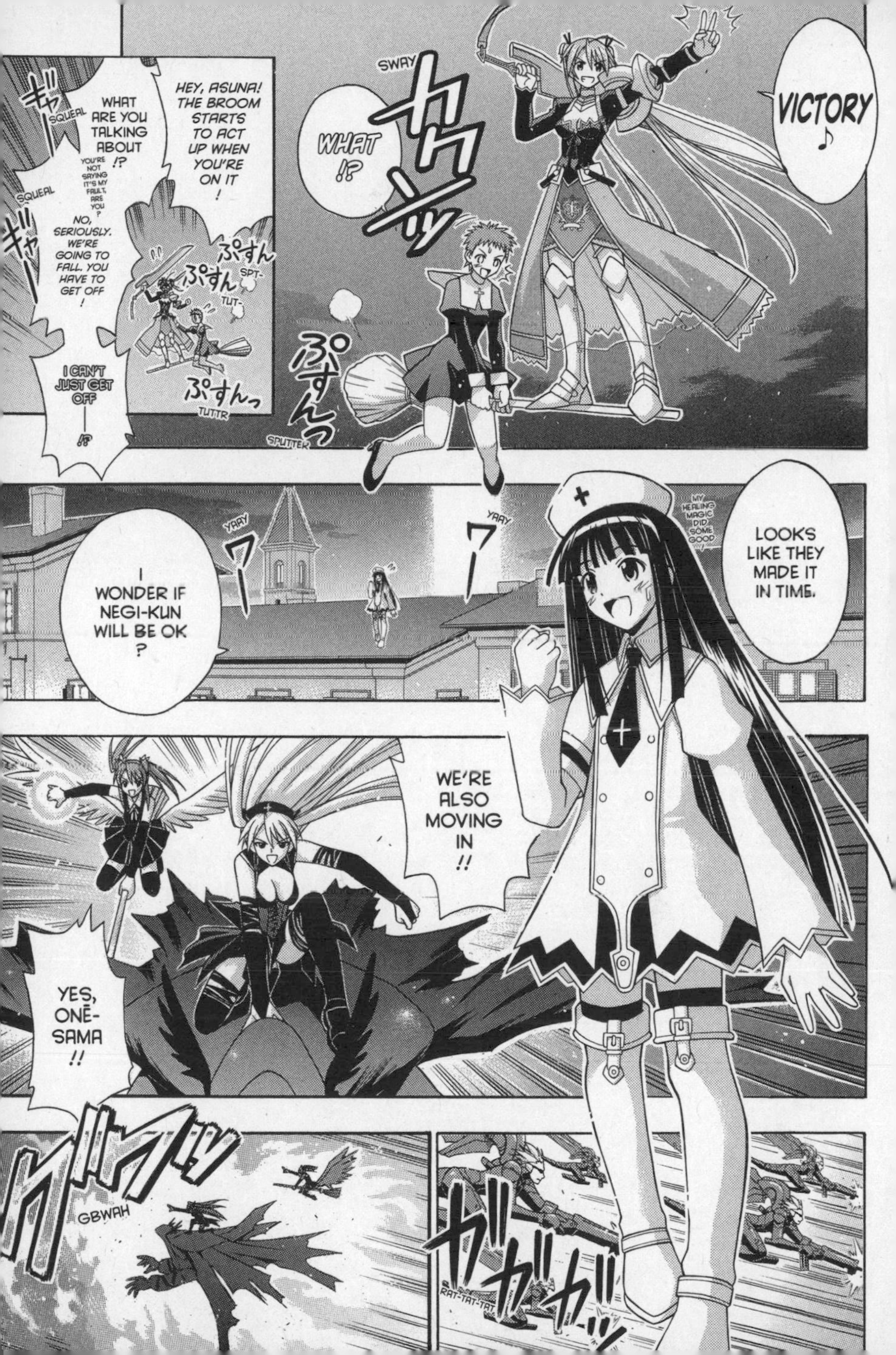
VICTORY ♪
SWAY
WHAT !?
HEY, ASUNA! THE BROOM STARTS TO ACT UP WHEN YOU'RE ON IT !
WHAT ARE YOU TALKING ABOUT !?
YOU'RE NOT SAYING IT'S MY FAULT, ARE YOU ?
SQUEAL
SQUEAL
NO, SERIOUSLY. WE'RE GOING TO FALL. YOU HAVE TO GET OFF !
SPT-
TUT-
TUTTR
I CAN'T JUST GET OFF —— !?
SPUTTER
LOOKS LIKE THEY MADE IT IN TIME.
MY HEALING MAGIC DID SOME GOOD
YAAY
YAAY
I WONDER IF NEGI-KUN WILL BE OK ?
WE'RE ALSO MOVING IN !!
YES, ONĒ-SAMA !!
RAT-TAT-TAT
GBWAH

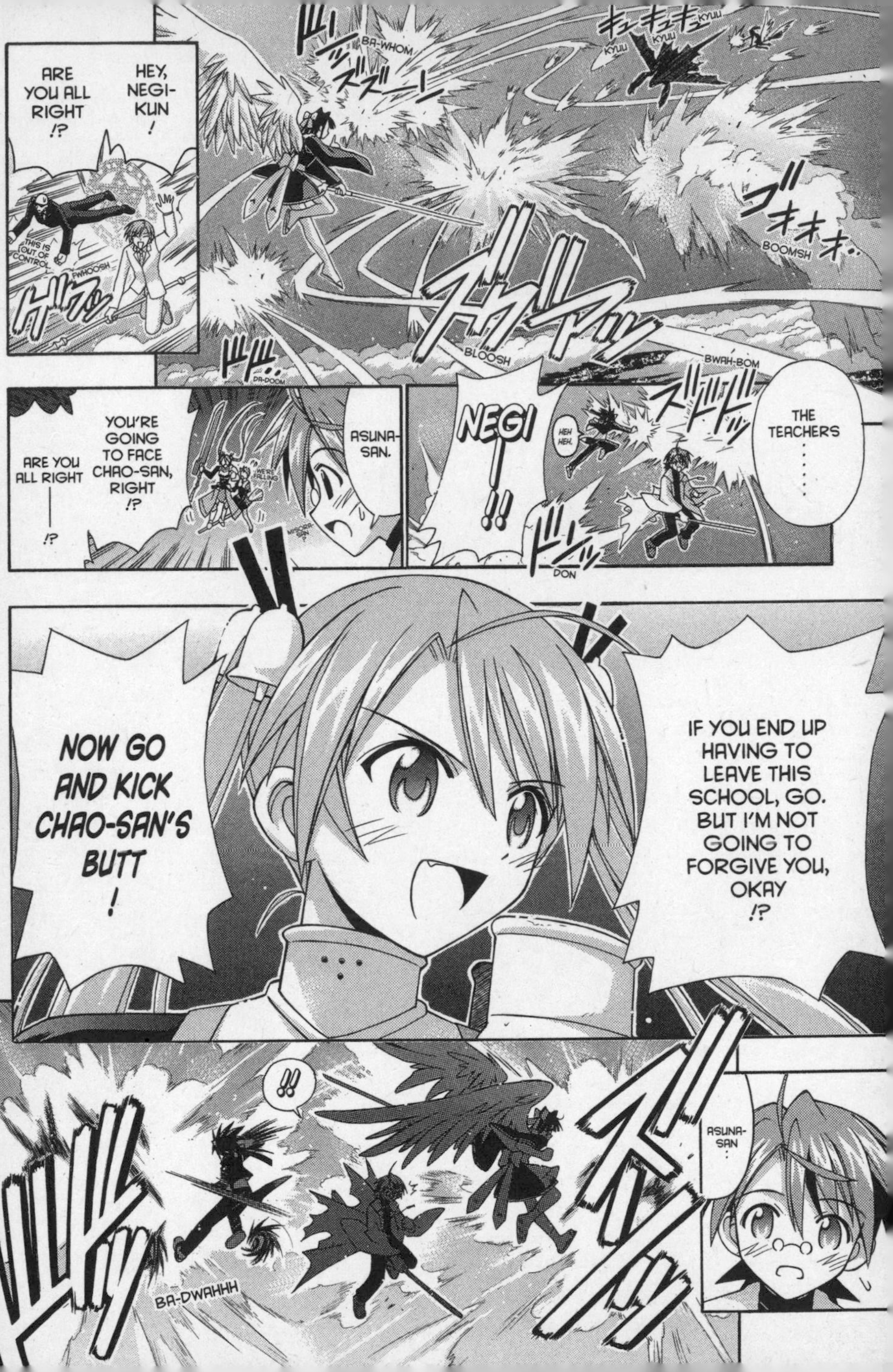
KYUU KYUU KYUU
BA-WHOM
BOOMSH
BLOOSH
DA-DOOM
HEY, NEGI-KUN!
ARE YOU ALL RIGHT!?
THIS IS OUT OF CONTROL
PWHOOSH
THE TEACHERS......
HEH HEH.
BWAH-BOM
NEGI!!!
DON
ASUNA-SAN.
YOU'RE GOING TO FACE CHAO-SAN, RIGHT!?
ARE YOU ALL RIGHT——!?
WE'RE FALLING
IF YOU END UP HAVING TO LEAVE THIS SCHOOL, GO. BUT I'M NOT GOING TO FORGIVE YOU, OKAY!?
NOW GO AND KICK CHAO-SAN'S BUTT!
ASUNA-SAN...
!!
BA-DWAHHH

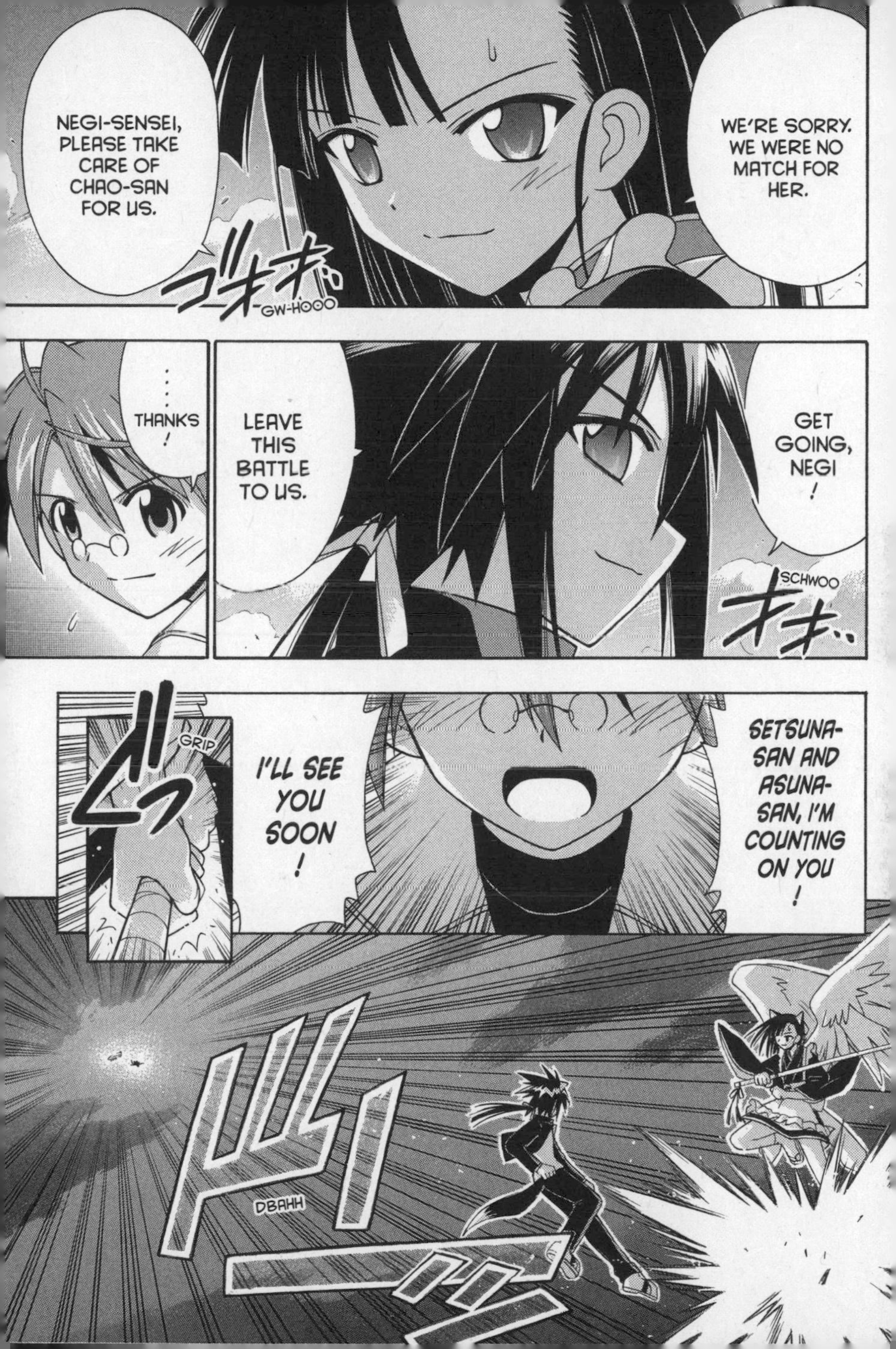
WE'RE SORRY. WE WERE NO MATCH FOR HER.
NEGI-SENSEI, PLEASE TAKE CARE OF CHAO-SAN FOR US.
GW-HOOO
GET GOING, NEGI!
SCHWOO
LEAVE THIS BATTLE TO US.
...THANKS!
SETSUNA-SAN AND ASUNA-SAN, I'M COUNTING ON YOU!
I'LL SEE YOU SOON!
GRIP
DBAHH

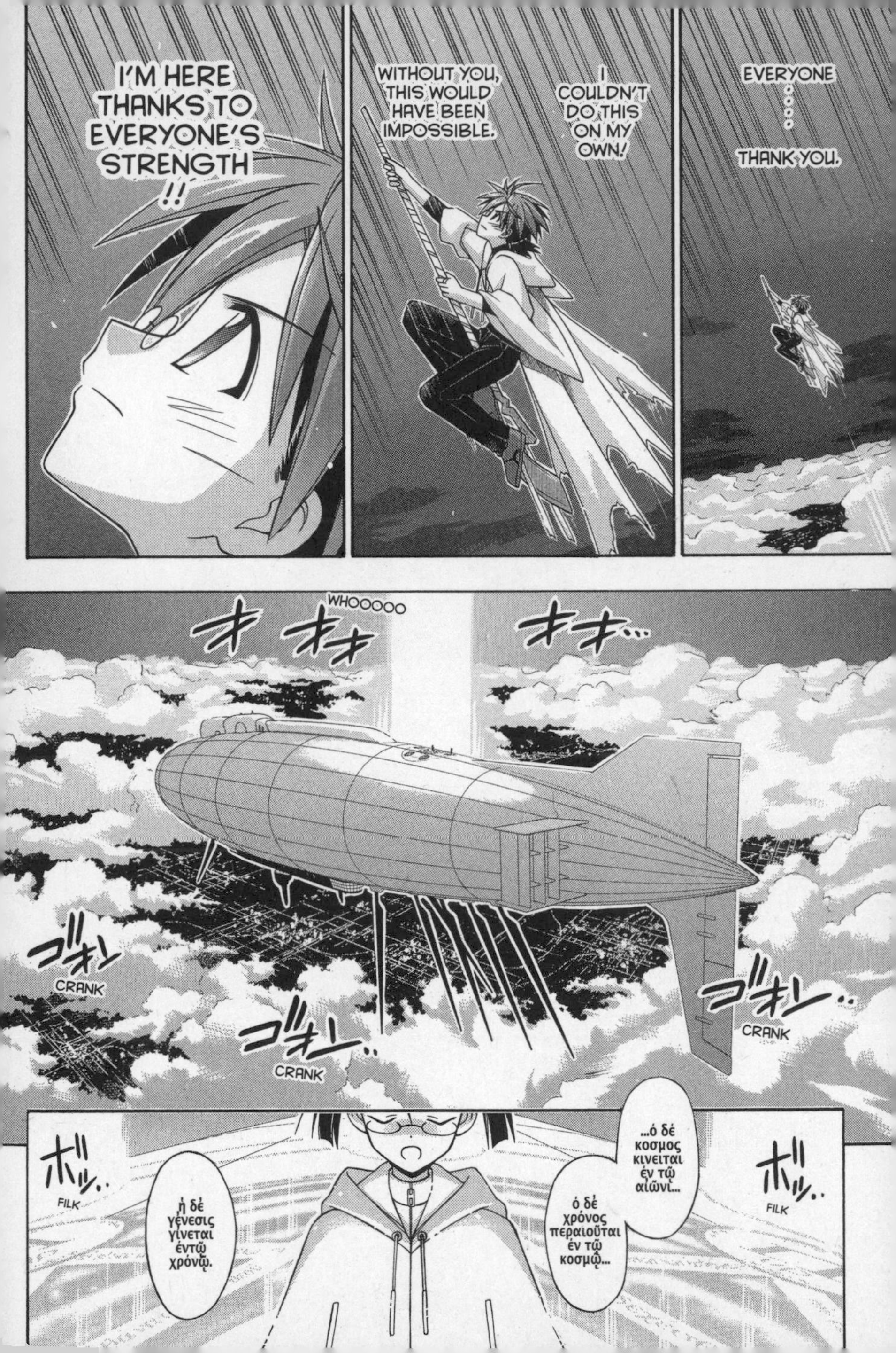
EVERYONE ....
THANK YOU.
I COULDN'T DO THIS ON MY OWN!
WITHOUT YOU, THIS WOULD HAVE BEEN IMPOSSIBLE.
I'M HERE THANKS TO EVERYONE'S STRENGTH!!
オオ…
オ オオ
WHOOOOO
ゴォン..
CRANK
ゴォン..
CRANK
ゴォン
CRANK
ボッ..
FILK
...ό δέ κοσμος κινειται έν τῷ αἰῶνι...
ό δέ χρόνος περαιοῦται έν τῷ κοσμῷ...
ἡ δέ γένεσις γίνεται έντῷ χρόνῳ.
ボッ..
FILK

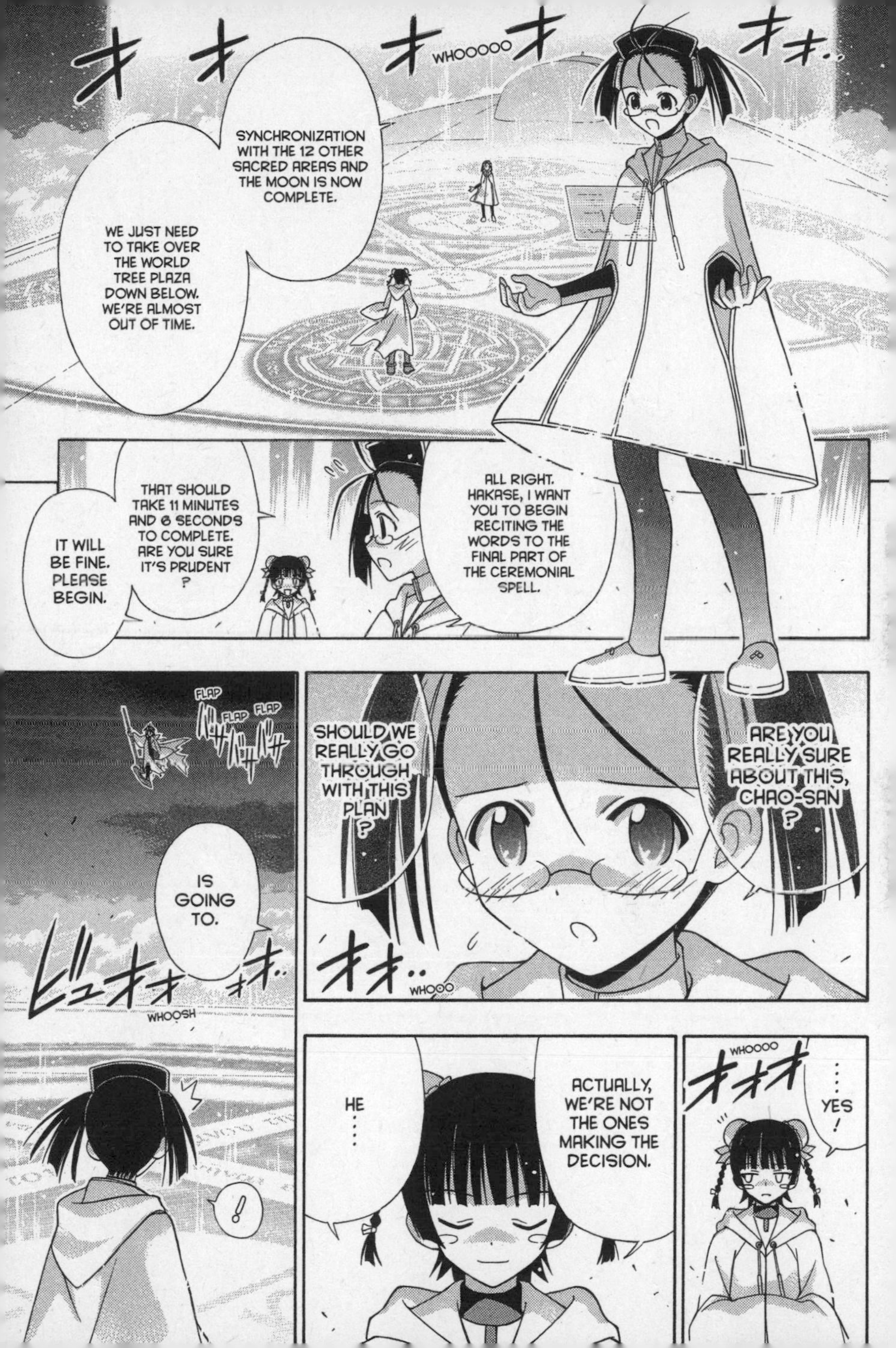
WHOOOOO
SYNCHRONIZATION WITH THE 12 OTHER SACRED AREAS AND THE MOON IS NOW COMPLETE.
WE JUST NEED TO TAKE OVER THE WORLD TREE PLAZA DOWN BELOW. WE'RE ALMOST OUT OF TIME.
ALL RIGHT. HAKASE, I WANT YOU TO BEGIN RECITING THE WORDS TO THE FINAL PART OF THE CEREMONIAL SPELL.
THAT SHOULD TAKE 11 MINUTES AND 6 SECONDS TO COMPLETE. ARE YOU SURE IT'S PRUDENT?
IT WILL BE FINE. PLEASE BEGIN.
ARE YOU REALLY SURE ABOUT THIS, CHAO-SAN?
SHOULD WE REALLY GO THROUGH WITH THIS PLAN?
WHOOO
FLAP FLAP FLAP
IS GOING TO.
WHOOSH
WHOOOO
...YES!
ACTUALLY, WE'RE NOT THE ONES MAKING THE DECISION.
HE...
!

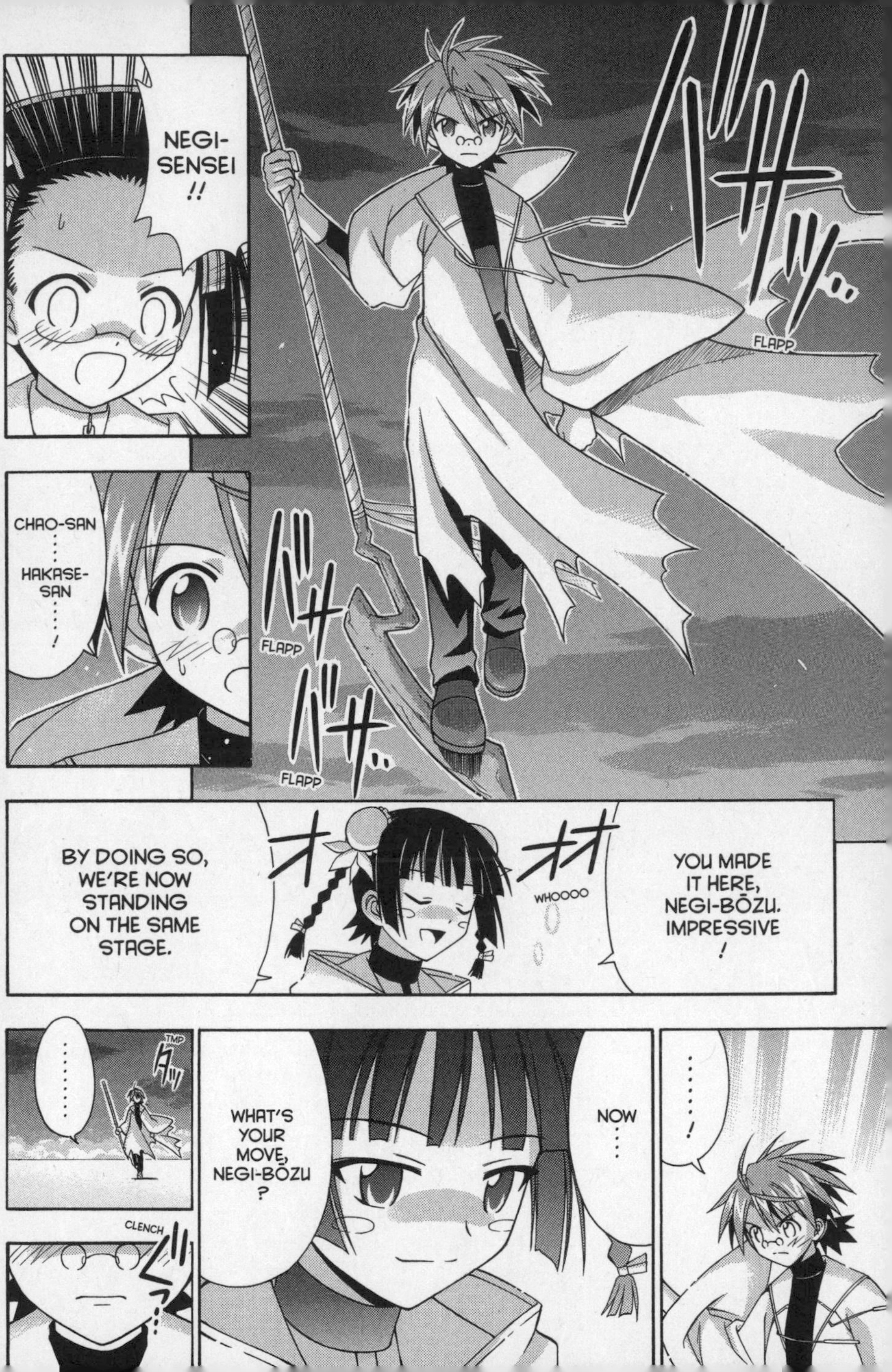

バサッ
FLAPP
バサ
FLAPP
バサ
FLAPP
NEGI-SENSEI!!
CHAO-SAN... HAKASE-SAN......!
YOU MADE IT HERE, NEGI-BŌZU. IMPRESSIVE!
オオ
WHOOOO
BY DOING SO, WE'RE NOW STANDING ON THE SAME STAGE.
......!
NOW...
WHAT'S YOUR MOVE, NEGI-BŌZU?
......
ダッ
TMP
グッ
CLENCH

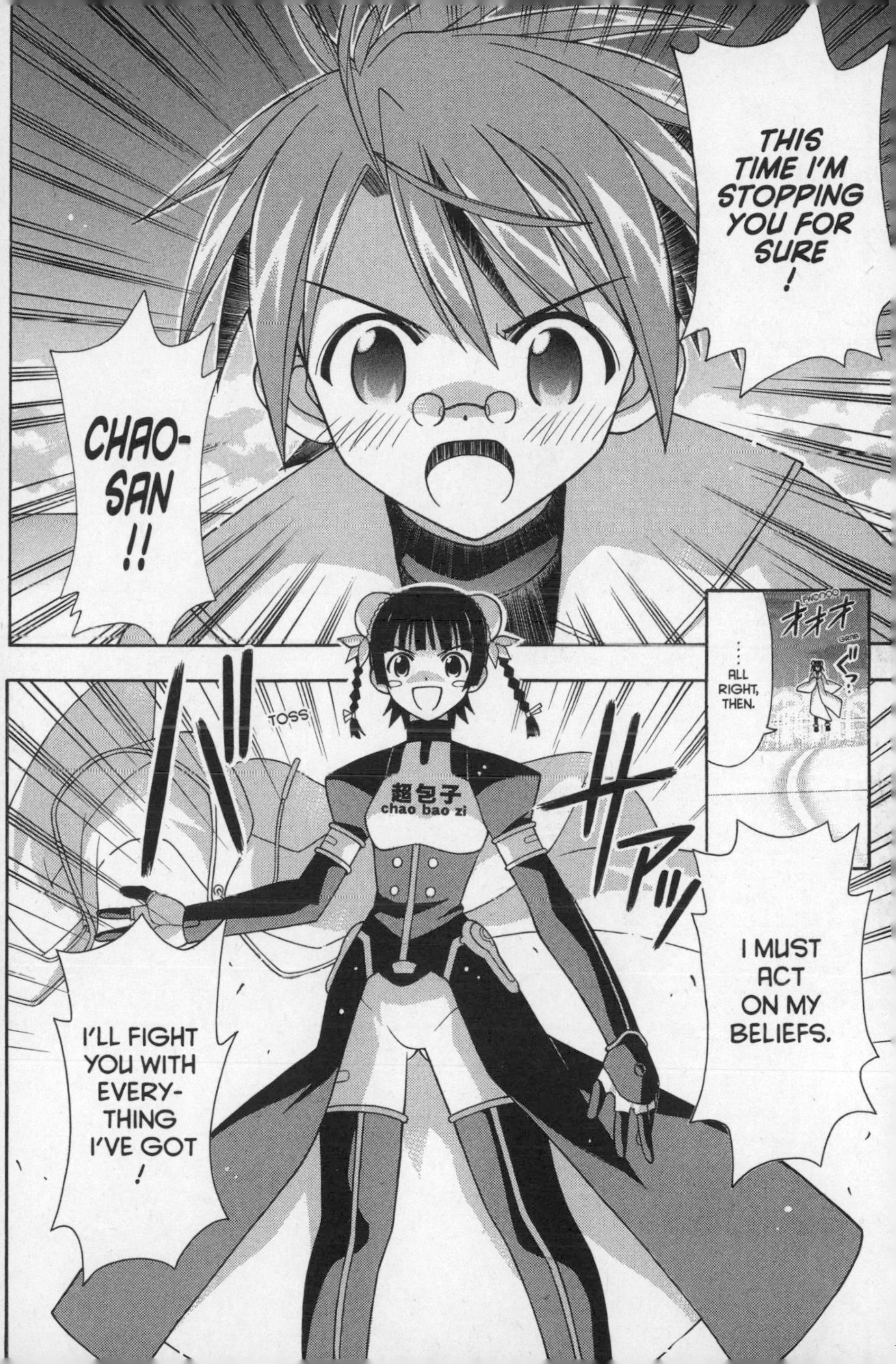
THIS TIME I'M STOPPING YOU FOR SURE!
CHAO-SAN!!
FWOOOO
オオオ
GRNR
ぐっ…
……ALL RIGHT, THEN.
I MUST ACT ON MY BELIEFS.
TOSS
バサァッ
超包子
chao bao zi
I'LL FIGHT YOU WITH EVERY-THING I'VE GOT!

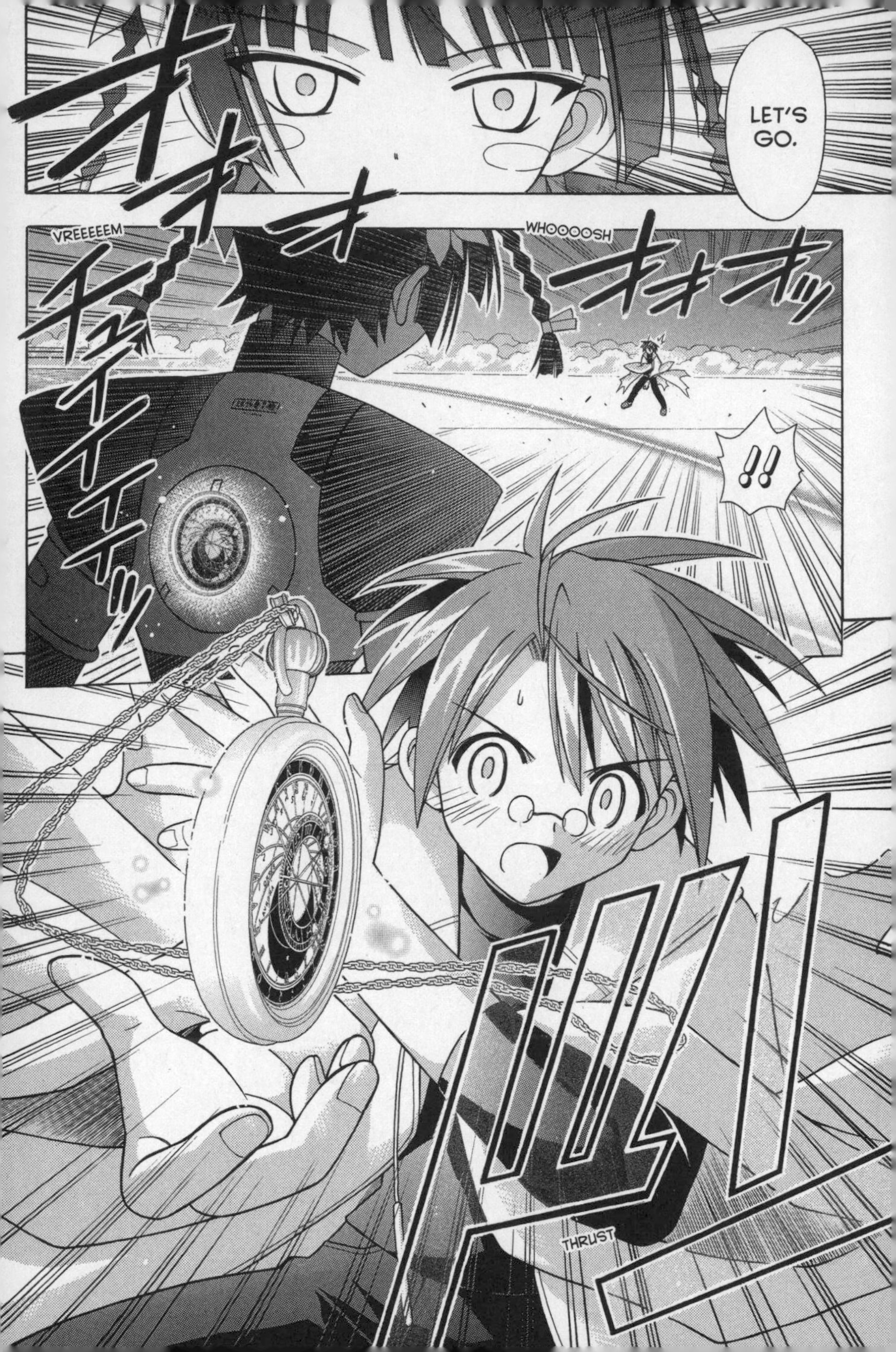

LET'S GO.
WHOOOOSH
VREEEEEM
!!
THRUST

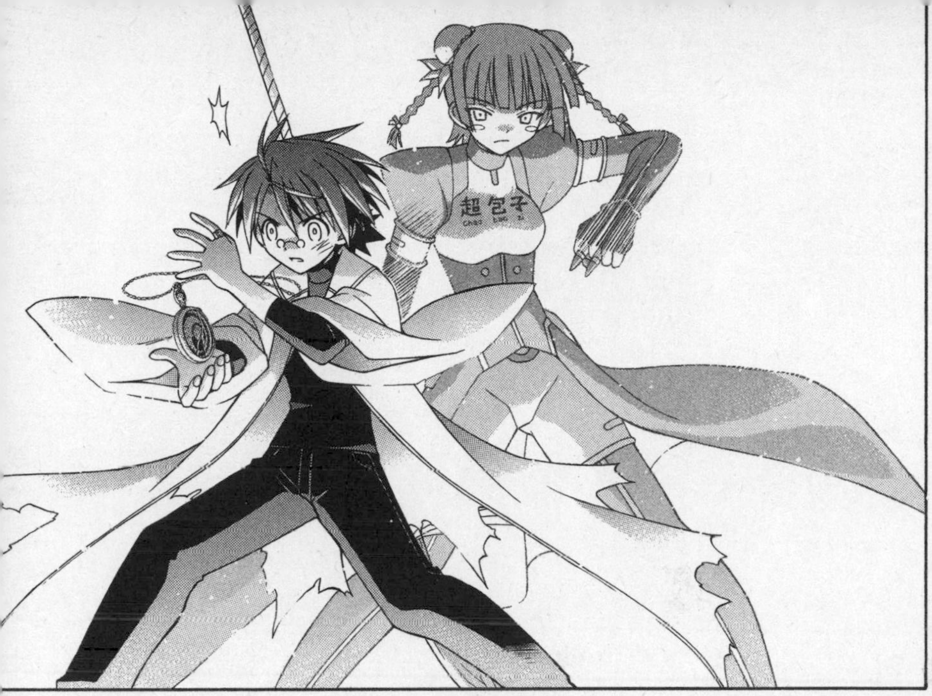
超包子

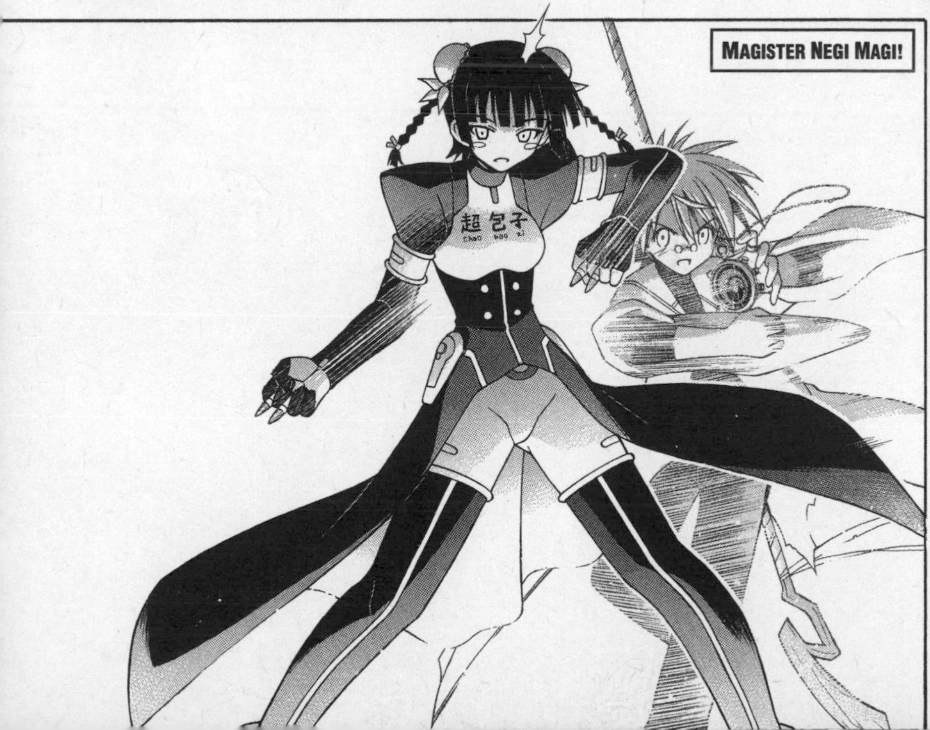
MAGISTER NEGI MAGI!
超包子

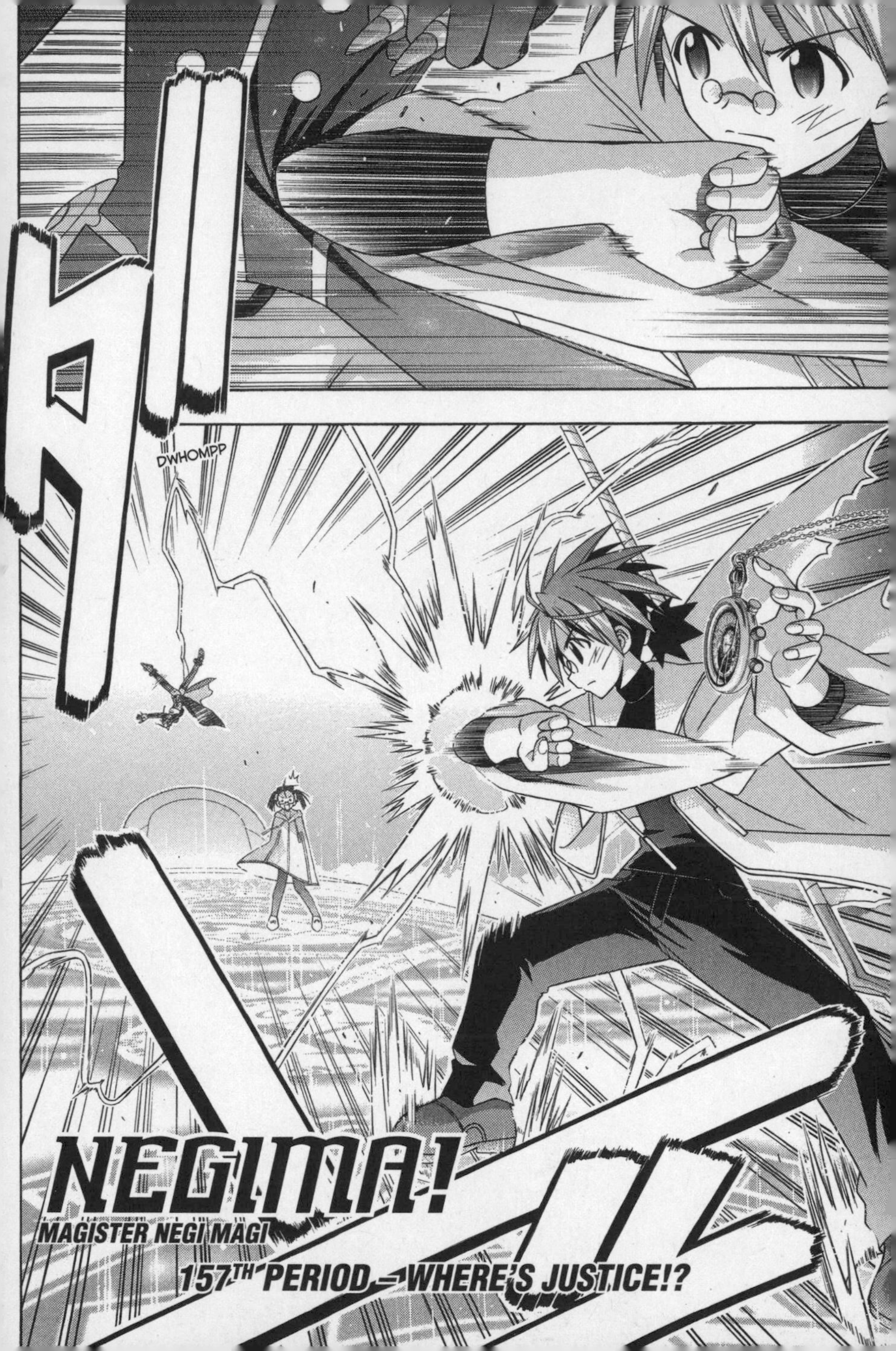
DWHOMPP
NEGIMA!
MAGISTER NEGI MAGI
157TH PERIOD – WHERE'S JUSTICE!?

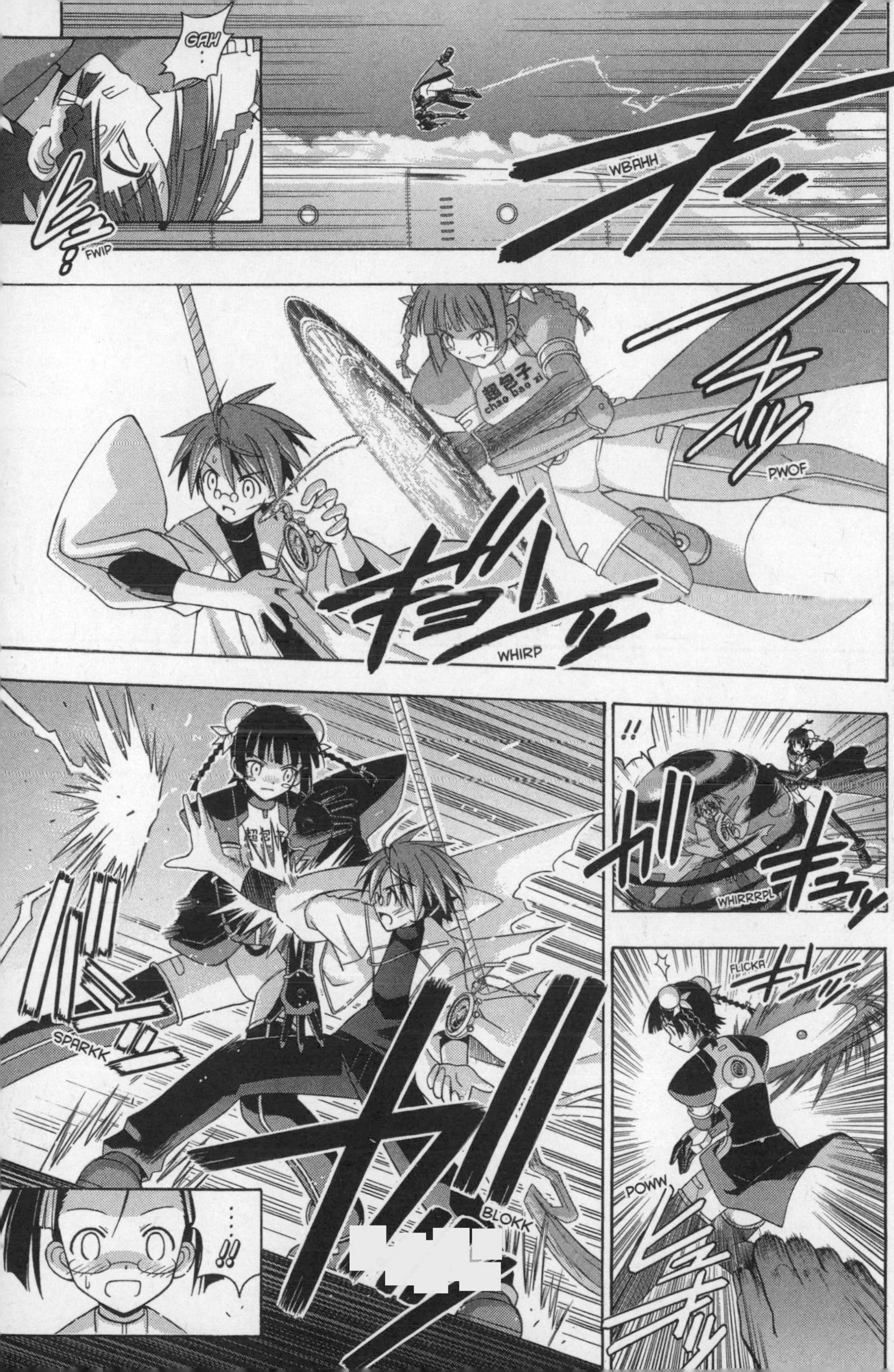
WBAHH
GAH
...
FWIP
PWOF
WHIRP
!!
WHIRRRPL
FLICKA
POWW
SPARKK
BLOKK
......
!!

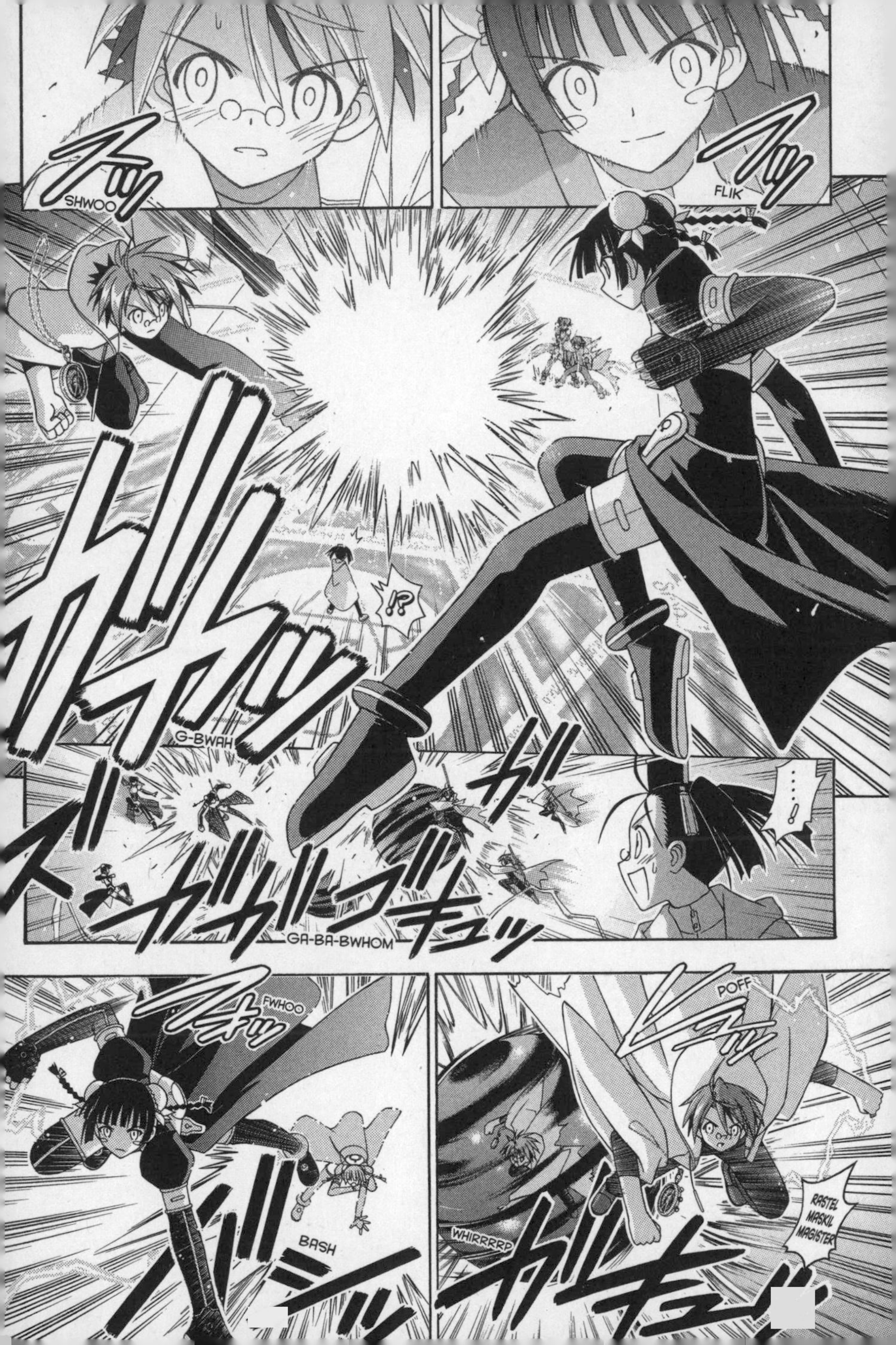

FLIK
SHWOO
!?
G-BWAH
....!
GA-BA-BWHOM
POFF
RASTEL MASKIL MAGISTER
WHIRRRRP
FWHOO
BASH

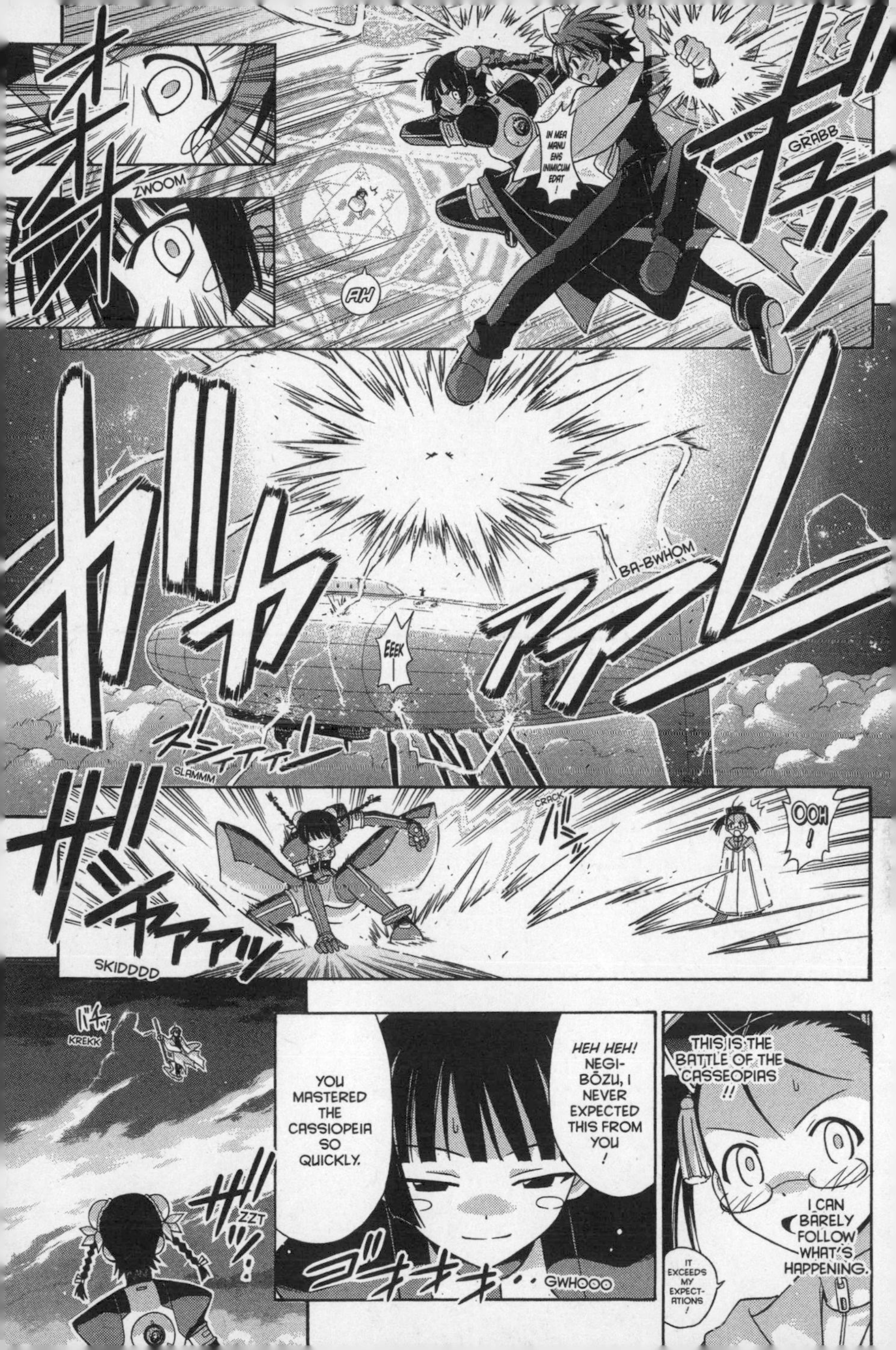
GRABB
IN MEA MANU ENS INIMICUM EDAT!
AH
ZWOOM
BA-BWHOM
EEEK!
SLAMMM
OOH!
CRACK
SKIDDDD
THIS IS THE BATTLE OF THE CASSEOPIAS!!
I CAN BARELY FOLLOW WHAT'S HAPPENING.
IT EXCEEDS MY EXPECT-ATIONS!
HEH HEH! NEGI-BŌZU, I NEVER EXPECTED THIS FROM YOU!
YOU MASTERED THE CASSIOPEIA SO QUICKLY.
GWHOOO
KREKK
ZZT

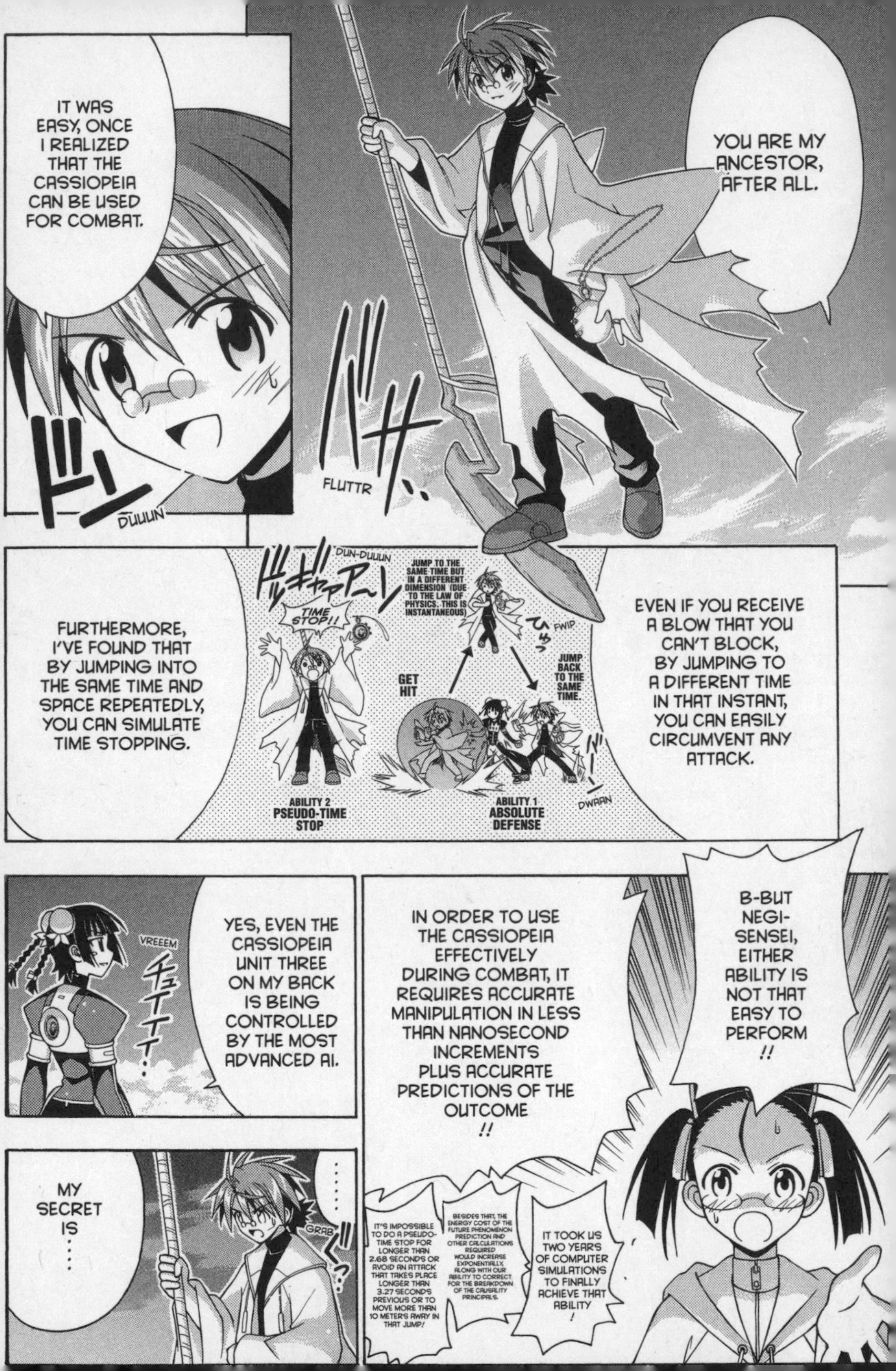

YOU ARE MY ANCESTOR, AFTER ALL.
FLUTTR
IT WAS EASY, ONCE I REALIZED THAT THE CASSIOPEIA CAN BE USED FOR COMBAT.
DUUUN
EVEN IF YOU RECEIVE A BLOW THAT YOU CAN'T BLOCK, BY JUMPING TO A DIFFERENT TIME IN THAT INSTANT, YOU CAN EASILY CIRCUMVENT ANY ATTACK.
FWIP
JUMP TO THE SAME TIME BUT IN A DIFFERENT DIMENSION (DUE TO THE LAW OF PHYSICS. THIS IS INSTANTANEOUS)
JUMP BACK TO THE SAME TIME.
GET HIT
DWAAN
ABILITY 1 ABSOLUTE DEFENSE
DUN-DUUUN
TIME STOP!!
ABILITY 2 PSEUDO-TIME STOP
FURTHERMORE, I'VE FOUND THAT BY JUMPING INTO THE SAME TIME AND SPACE REPEATEDLY, YOU CAN SIMULATE TIME STOPPING.
B-BUT NEGI-SENSEI, EITHER ABILITY IS NOT THAT EASY TO PERFORM!!
IN ORDER TO USE THE CASSIOPEIA EFFECTIVELY DURING COMBAT, IT REQUIRES ACCURATE MANIPULATION IN LESS THAN NANOSECOND INCREMENTS PLUS ACCURATE PREDICTIONS OF THE OUTCOME!!
IT TOOK US TWO YEARS OF COMPUTER SIMULATIONS TO FINALLY ACHIEVE THAT ABILITY!
BESIDES THAT, THE ENERGY COST OF THE FUTURE PHENOMENON PREDICTION AND OTHER CALCULATIONS REQUIRED WOULD INCREASE EXPONENTIALLY, ALONG WITH OUR ABILITY TO CORRECT FOR THE BREAKDOWN OF THE CAUSALITY PRINCIPALS.
IT'S IMPOSSIBLE TO DO A PSEUDO-TIME STOP FOR LONGER THAN 2.68 SECONDS OR AVOID AN ATTACK THAT TAKES PLACE LONGER THAN 3.27 SECONDS PREVIOUS OR TO MOVE MORE THAN 10 METERS AWAY IN THAT JUMP!
YES, EVEN THE CASSIOPEIA UNIT THREE ON MY BACK IS BEING CONTROLLED BY THE MOST ADVANCED AI.
VREEEM
......
GRAB
MY SECRET IS......

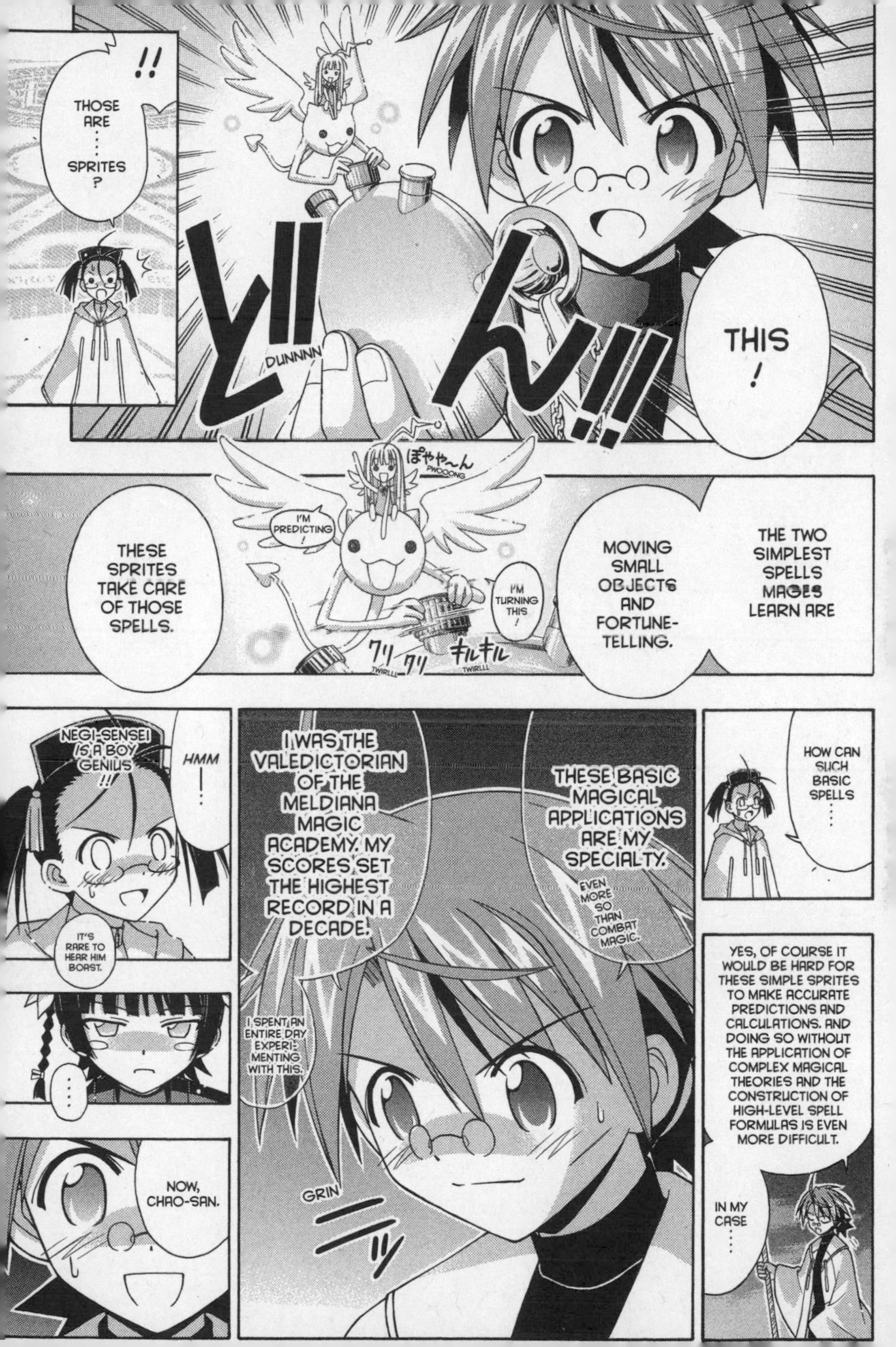
THIS!
どーん!!
DUNNNN
!!
THOSE ARE.... SPRITES?
THE TWO SIMPLEST SPELLS MAGES LEARN ARE
MOVING SMALL OBJECTS AND FORTUNE-TELLING.
ぽややーん
PWOOONG
I'M TURNING THIS!
I'M PREDICTING!
キルキル
TWIRLLL
クリクリ
TWIRLLL
THESE SPRITES TAKE CARE OF THOSE SPELLS.
HOW CAN SUCH BASIC SPELLS....
YES, OF COURSE IT WOULD BE HARD FOR THESE SIMPLE SPRITES TO MAKE ACCURATE PREDICTIONS AND CALCULATIONS. AND DOING SO WITHOUT THE APPLICATION OF COMPLEX MAGICAL THEORIES AND THE CONSTRUCTION OF HIGH-LEVEL SPELL FORMULAS IS EVEN MORE DIFFICULT.
IN MY CASE....
THESE BASIC MAGICAL APPLICATIONS ARE MY SPECIALTY.
EVEN MORE SO THAN COMBAT MAGIC.
I WAS THE VALEDICTORIAN OF THE MELDIANA MAGIC ACADEMY. MY SCORES SET THE HIGHEST RECORD IN A DECADE.
I SPENT AN ENTIRE DAY EXPERI-MENTING WITH THIS.
GRIN
ニッ
HMM!
NEGI-SENSEI IS A BOY GENIUS!!
IT'S RARE TO HEAR HIM BOAST.
....
NOW, CHAO-SAN.

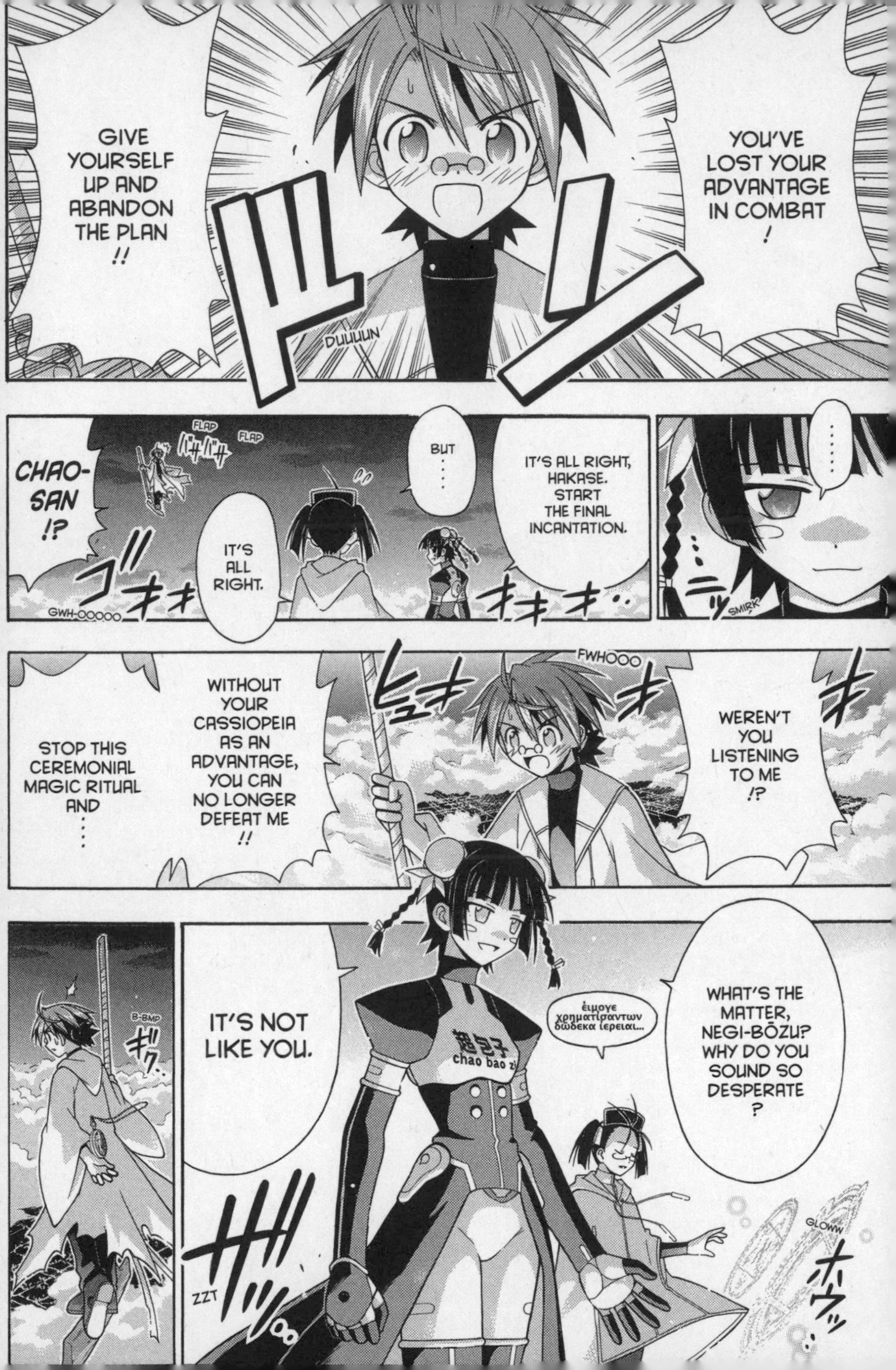

YOU'VE LOST YOUR ADVANTAGE IN COMBAT !
GIVE YOURSELF UP AND ABANDON THE PLAN !!
DUUUUN
......
SMIRK
IT'S ALL RIGHT, HAKASE. START THE FINAL INCANTATION.
BUT .....
IT'S ALL RIGHT.
FLAP FLAP
CHAO-SAN !?
GWH-OOOOO
WEREN'T YOU LISTENING TO ME !?
FWHOOO
WITHOUT YOUR CASSIOPEIA AS AN ADVANTAGE, YOU CAN NO LONGER DEFEAT ME !!
STOP THIS CEREMONIAL MAGIC RITUAL AND .....
WHAT'S THE MATTER, NEGI-BŌZU? WHY DO YOU SOUND SO DESPERATE ?
έιμογε χρηματίσαντων δώδεκα ιερειαι...
IT'S NOT LIKE YOU.
chao bao zi
GLOWW
ZZT
B-BMP

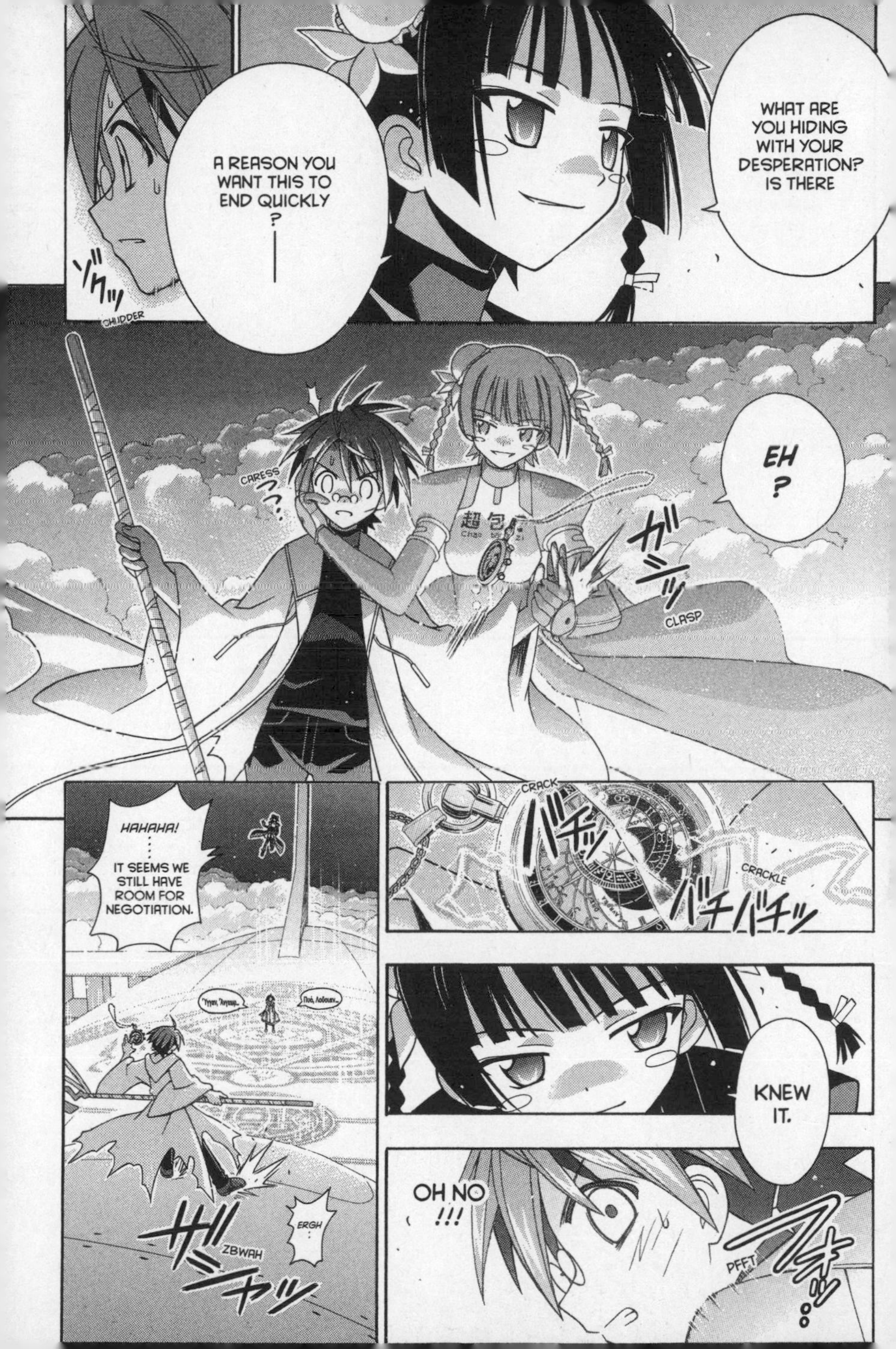
WHAT ARE YOU HIDING WITH YOUR DESPERATION? IS THERE
A REASON YOU WANT THIS TO END QUICKLY ?—
SHUDDER
EH ?
CARESS
CLASP
CRACK
CRACKLE
KNEW IT.
OH NO !!!
PFFT
HAHAHA! ... IT SEEMS WE STILL HAVE ROOM FOR NEGOTIATION.
ERGH ...
ZBWAH

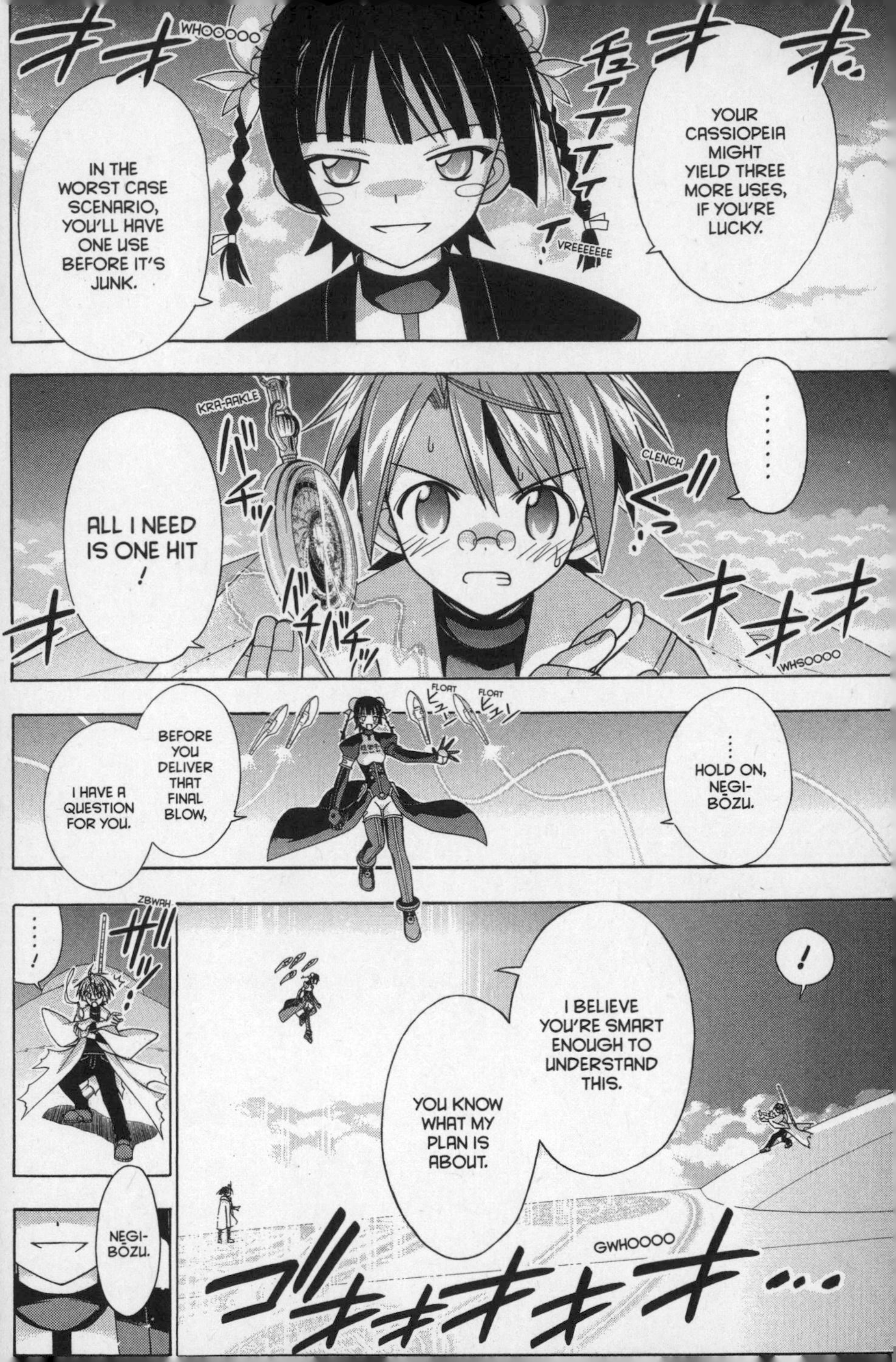

YOUR CASSIOPEIA MIGHT YIELD THREE MORE USES, IF YOU'RE LUCKY.
VREEEEEEE
WHOOOOOO
IN THE WORST CASE SCENARIO, YOU'LL HAVE ONE USE BEFORE IT'S JUNK.
......
CLENCH
KRA-AAKLE
ALL I NEED IS ONE HIT!
WHSOOOO
...HOLD ON, NEGI-BŌZU.
FLOAT
FLOAT
BEFORE YOU DELIVER THAT FINAL BLOW,
I HAVE A QUESTION FOR YOU.
!
I BELIEVE YOU'RE SMART ENOUGH TO UNDERSTAND THIS.
YOU KNOW WHAT MY PLAN IS ABOUT.
GWHOOOO
....!
ZBWAH
NEGI-BŌZU.

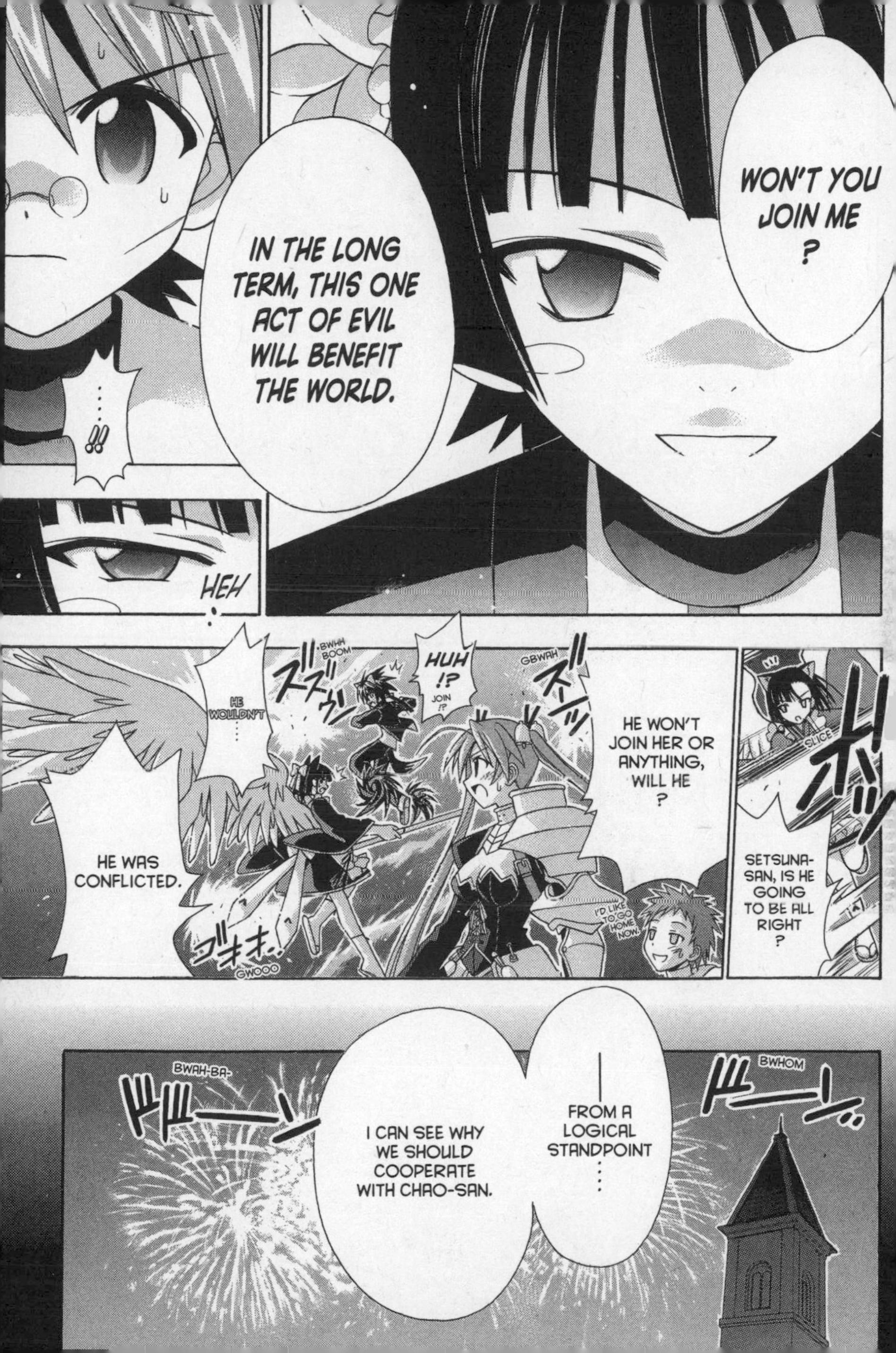
WON'T YOU JOIN ME?
IN THE LONG TERM, THIS ONE ACT OF EVIL WILL BENEFIT THE WORLD.
......!!
HEH
SETSUNA-SAN, IS HE GOING TO BE ALL RIGHT?
SLICE
HE WON'T JOIN HER OR ANYTHING, WILL HE?
GBWAH
HUH!?
JOIN!?
BWHH BOOM
HE WOULDN'T...
I'D LIKE TO GO HOME NOW.
HE WAS CONFLICTED.
GWOOO
BWHOM
—FROM A LOGICAL STANDPOINT...
I CAN SEE WHY WE SHOULD COOPERATE WITH CHAO-SAN.
BWAH-BA-

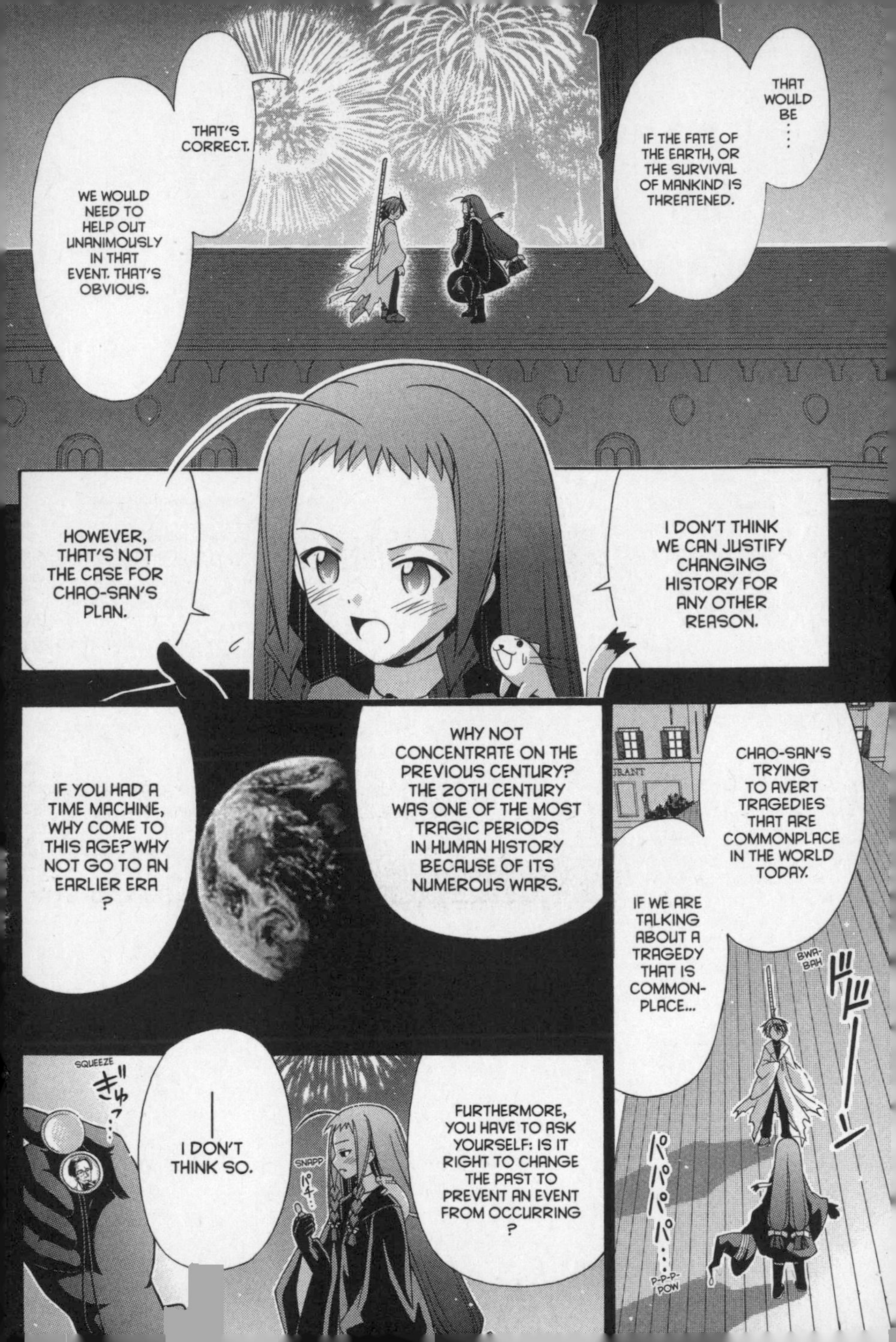
THAT WOULD BE ....
IF THE FATE OF THE EARTH, OR THE SURVIVAL OF MANKIND IS THREATENED.
THAT'S CORRECT.
WE WOULD NEED TO HELP OUT UNANIMOUSLY IN THAT EVENT. THAT'S OBVIOUS.
I DON'T THINK WE CAN JUSTIFY CHANGING HISTORY FOR ANY OTHER REASON.
HOWEVER, THAT'S NOT THE CASE FOR CHAO-SAN'S PLAN.
CHAO-SAN'S TRYING TO AVERT TRAGEDIES THAT ARE COMMONPLACE IN THE WORLD TODAY.
IF WE ARE TALKING ABOUT A TRAGEDY THAT IS COMMON-PLACE...
BWA-BAH
ドドーー
パパパパ…
P-P-P-POW
WHY NOT CONCENTRATE ON THE PREVIOUS CENTURY? THE 20TH CENTURY WAS ONE OF THE MOST TRAGIC PERIODS IN HUMAN HISTORY BECAUSE OF ITS NUMEROUS WARS.
IF YOU HAD A TIME MACHINE, WHY COME TO THIS AGE? WHY NOT GO TO AN EARLIER ERA ?
FURTHERMORE, YOU HAVE TO ASK YOURSELF: IS IT RIGHT TO CHANGE THE PAST TO PREVENT AN EVENT FROM OCCURRING ?
SNAPP
パチ
— I DON'T THINK SO.
SQUEEZE
ぎゅっ…

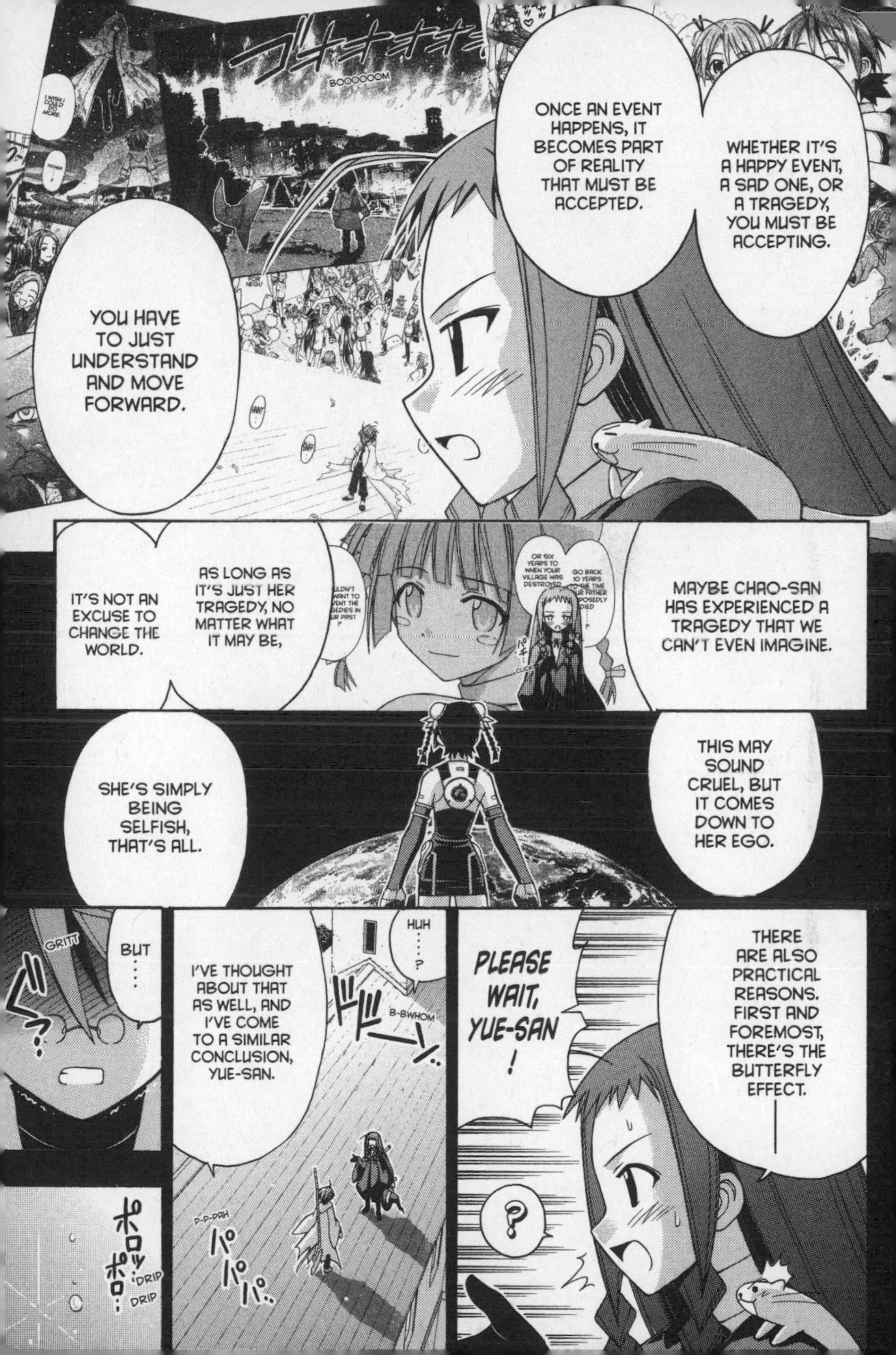
BOOOOOOM
I WISH I COULD DO MORE.
FATHER
ONCE AN EVENT HAPPENS, IT BECOMES PART OF REALITY THAT MUST BE ACCEPTED.
WHETHER IT'S A HAPPY EVENT, A SAD ONE, OR A TRAGEDY, YOU MUST BE ACCEPTING.
YOU HAVE TO JUST UNDERSTAND AND MOVE FORWARD.
AAH!
SWIP
MAYBE CHAO-SAN HAS EXPERIENCED A TRAGEDY THAT WE CAN'T EVEN IMAGINE.
GO BACK 10 YEARS TO THE TIME YOUR FATHER SUPPOSEDLY DIED ...?
OR SIX YEARS TO WHEN YOUR VILLAGE WAS DESTROYED
CLICK
AS LONG AS IT'S JUST HER TRAGEDY, NO MATTER WHAT IT MAY BE,
IT'S NOT AN EXCUSE TO CHANGE THE WORLD.
THIS MAY SOUND CRUEL, BUT IT COMES DOWN TO HER EGO.
SHE'S SIMPLY BEING SELFISH, THAT'S ALL.
THERE ARE ALSO PRACTICAL REASONS. FIRST AND FOREMOST, THERE'S THE BUTTERFLY EFFECT. —
PLEASE WAIT, YUE-SAN!
?
HUH ...?
B-BWHOM
I'VE THOUGHT ABOUT THAT AS WELL, AND I'VE COME TO A SIMILAR CONCLUSION, YUE-SAN.
P-P-PAH
GRITT
BUT ....
DRIP DRIP

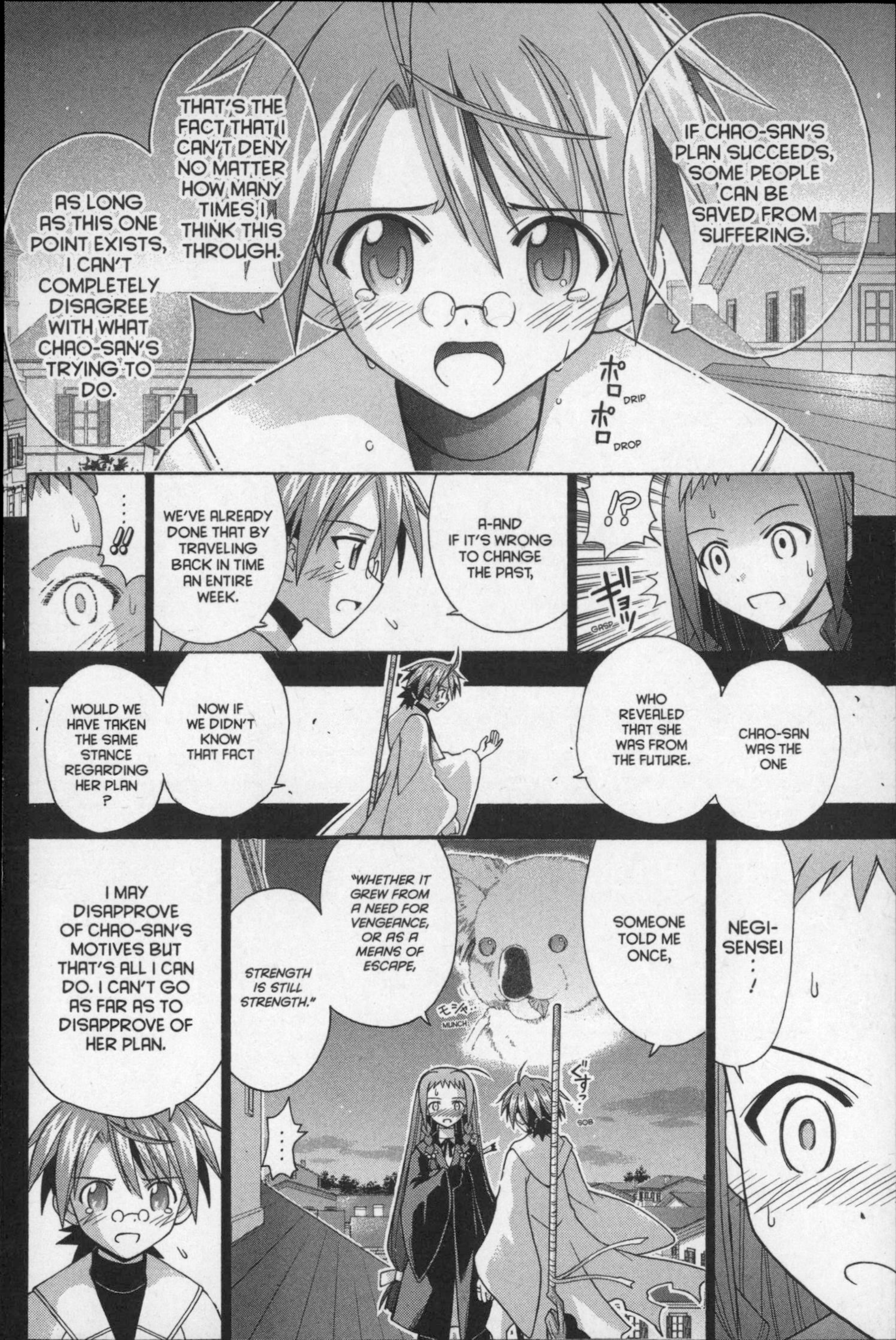
IF CHAO-SAN'S PLAN SUCCEEDS, SOME PEOPLE CAN BE SAVED FROM SUFFERING.
THAT'S THE FACT THAT I CAN'T DENY NO MATTER HOW MANY TIMES I THINK THIS THROUGH.
AS LONG AS THIS ONE POINT EXISTS, I CAN'T COMPLETELY DISAGREE WITH WHAT CHAO-SAN'S TRYING TO DO.
ポロ DRIP
ポロ DROP
!?
ギョッ GASP
A-AND IF IT'S WRONG TO CHANGE THE PAST,
WE'VE ALREADY DONE THAT BY TRAVELING BACK IN TIME AN ENTIRE WEEK.
...!!
CHAO-SAN WAS THE ONE
WHO REVEALED THAT SHE WAS FROM THE FUTURE.
NOW IF WE DIDN'T KNOW THAT FACT
WOULD WE HAVE TAKEN THE SAME STANCE REGARDING HER PLAN?
NEGI-SENSEI...!
SOMEONE TOLD ME ONCE,
"WHETHER IT GREW FROM A NEED FOR VENGEANCE, OR AS A MEANS OF ESCAPE,
STRENGTH IS STILL STRENGTH."
モシャ MUNCH
ぐすっ... SOB
...!
I MAY DISAPPROVE OF CHAO-SAN'S MOTIVES BUT THAT'S ALL I CAN DO. I CAN'T GO AS FAR AS TO DISAPPROVE OF HER PLAN.

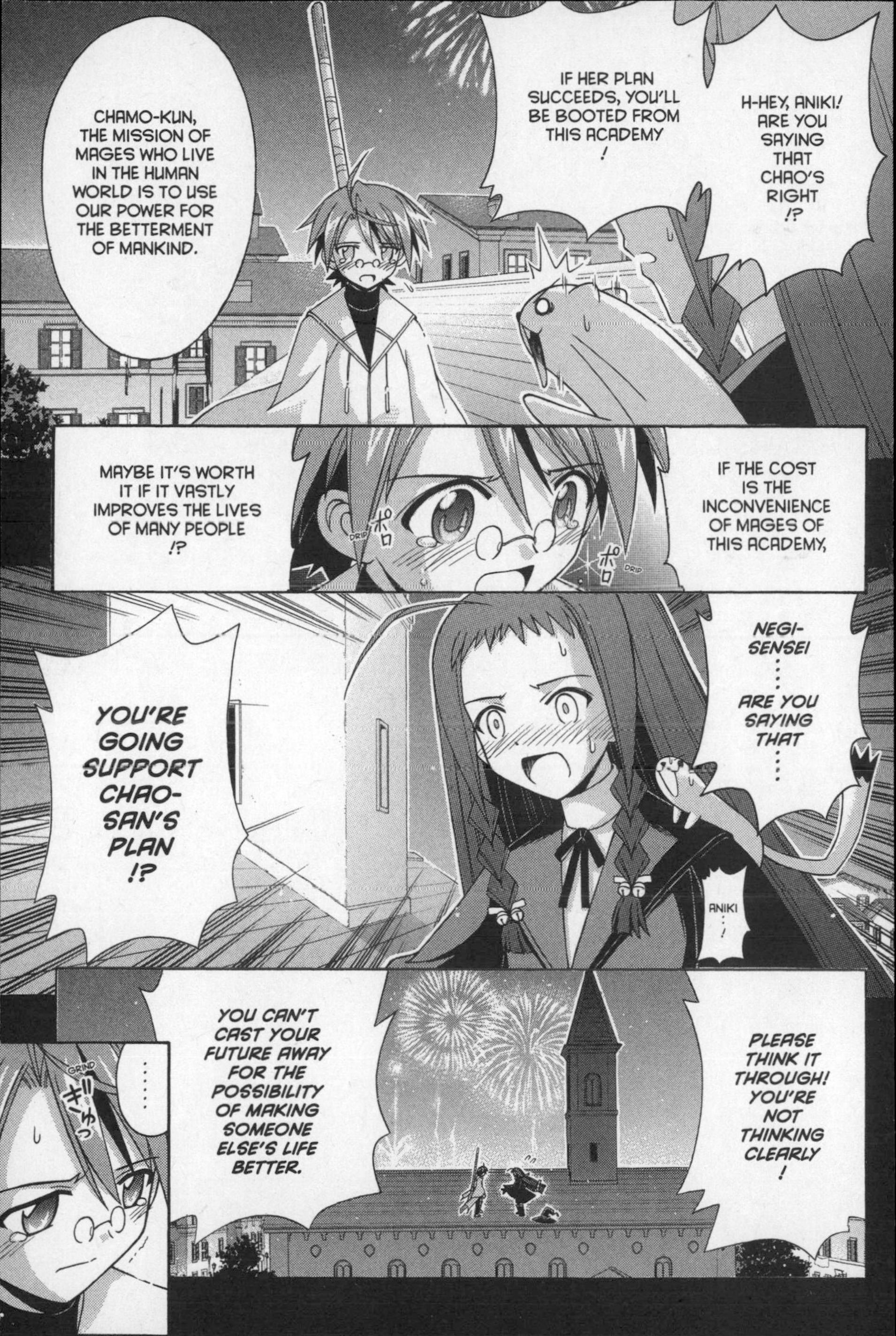
H-HEY, ANIKI! ARE YOU SAYING THAT CHAO'S RIGHT !?
IF HER PLAN SUCCEEDS, YOU'LL BE BOOTED FROM THIS ACADEMY !
CHAMO-KUN, THE MISSION OF MAGES WHO LIVE IN THE HUMAN WORLD IS TO USE OUR POWER FOR THE BETTERMENT OF MANKIND.
IF THE COST IS THE INCONVENIENCE OF MAGES OF THIS ACADEMY,
DRIP
DRIP
MAYBE IT'S WORTH IT IF IT VASTLY IMPROVES THE LIVES OF MANY PEOPLE !?
NEGI-SENSEI ..... ARE YOU SAYING THAT .....
ANIKI ...!
YOU'RE GOING SUPPORT CHAO-SAN'S PLAN !?
PLEASE THINK IT THROUGH! YOU'RE NOT THINKING CLEARLY !
YOU CAN'T CAST YOUR FUTURE AWAY FOR THE POSSIBILITY OF MAKING SOMEONE ELSE'S LIFE BETTER.
GRIND
......

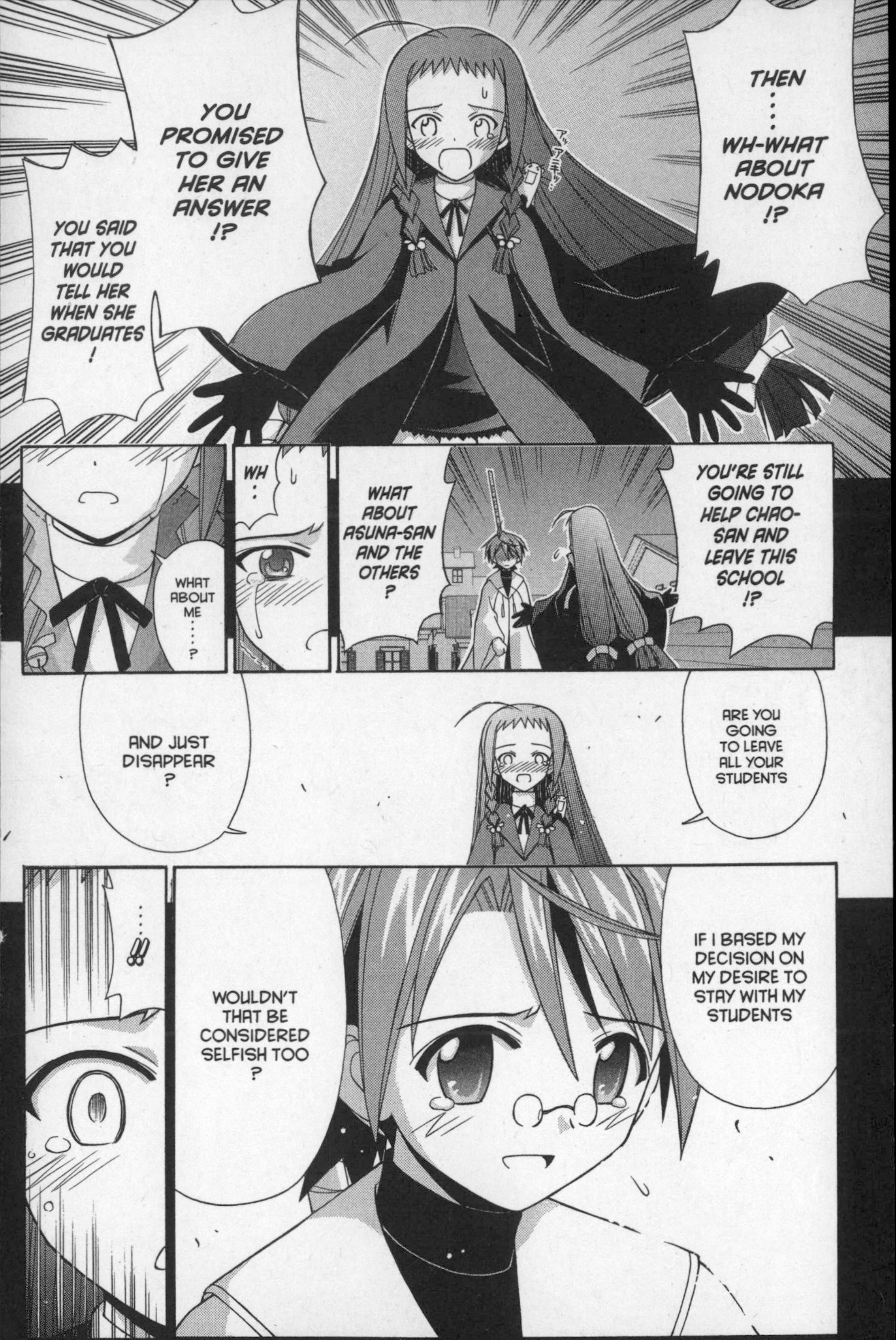
THEN... WH-WHAT ABOUT NODOKA!?
YOU PROMISED TO GIVE HER AN ANSWER!?
YOU SAID THAT YOU WOULD TELL HER WHEN SHE GRADUATES!
YOU'RE STILL GOING TO HELP CHAO-SAN AND LEAVE THIS SCHOOL!?
WHAT ABOUT ASUNA-SAN AND THE OTHERS?
WH...
WHAT ABOUT ME.....?
ARE YOU GOING TO LEAVE ALL YOUR STUDENTS
AND JUST DISAPPEAR?
IF I BASED MY DECISION ON MY DESIRE TO STAY WITH MY STUDENTS
WOULDN'T THAT BE CONSIDERED SELFISH TOO?
...!!

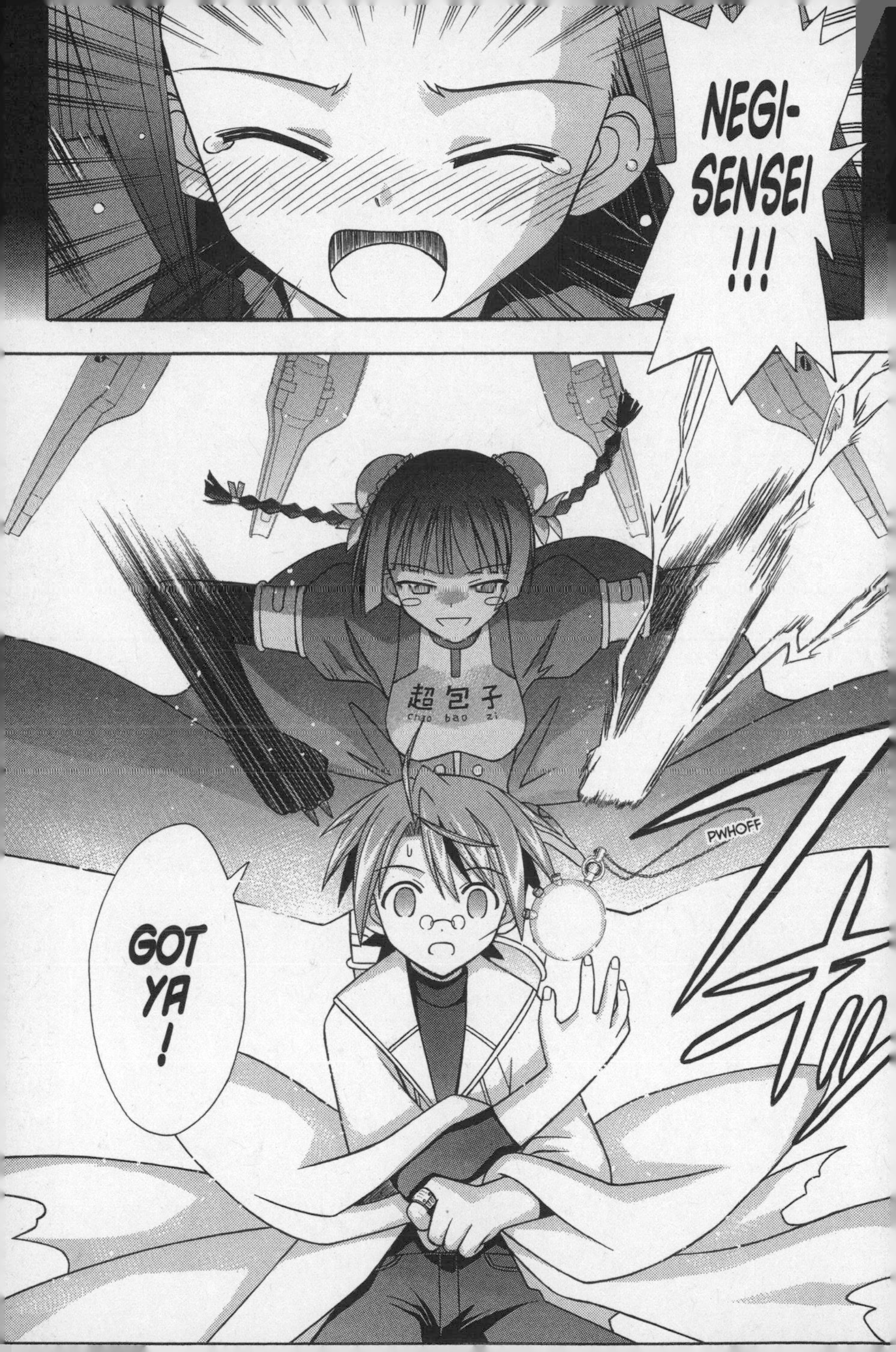
NEGI-SENSEI !!!
超包子
Chao bao zi
PWHOFF
GOT YA!

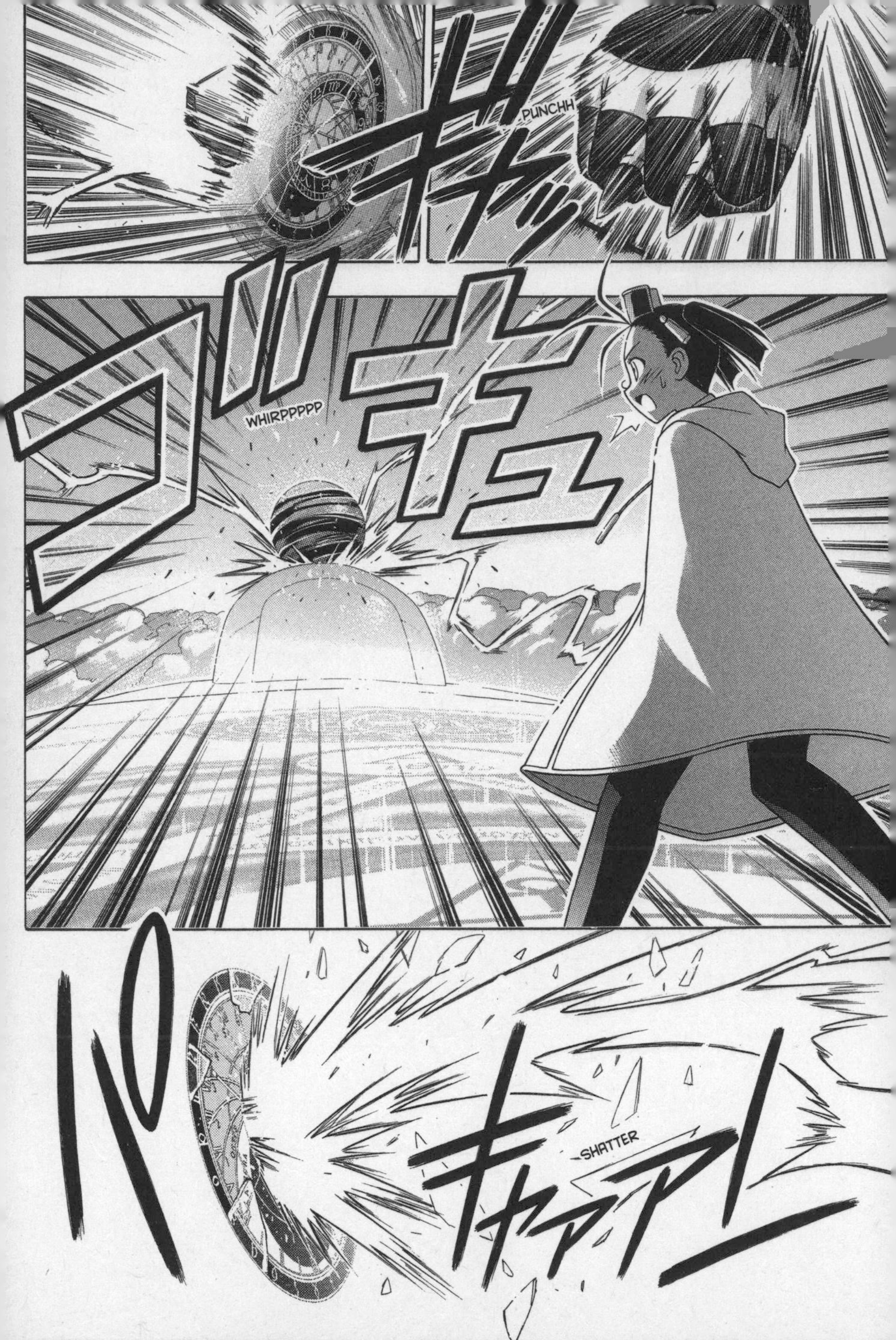
PUNCHH
WHIRPPPPP
SHATTER

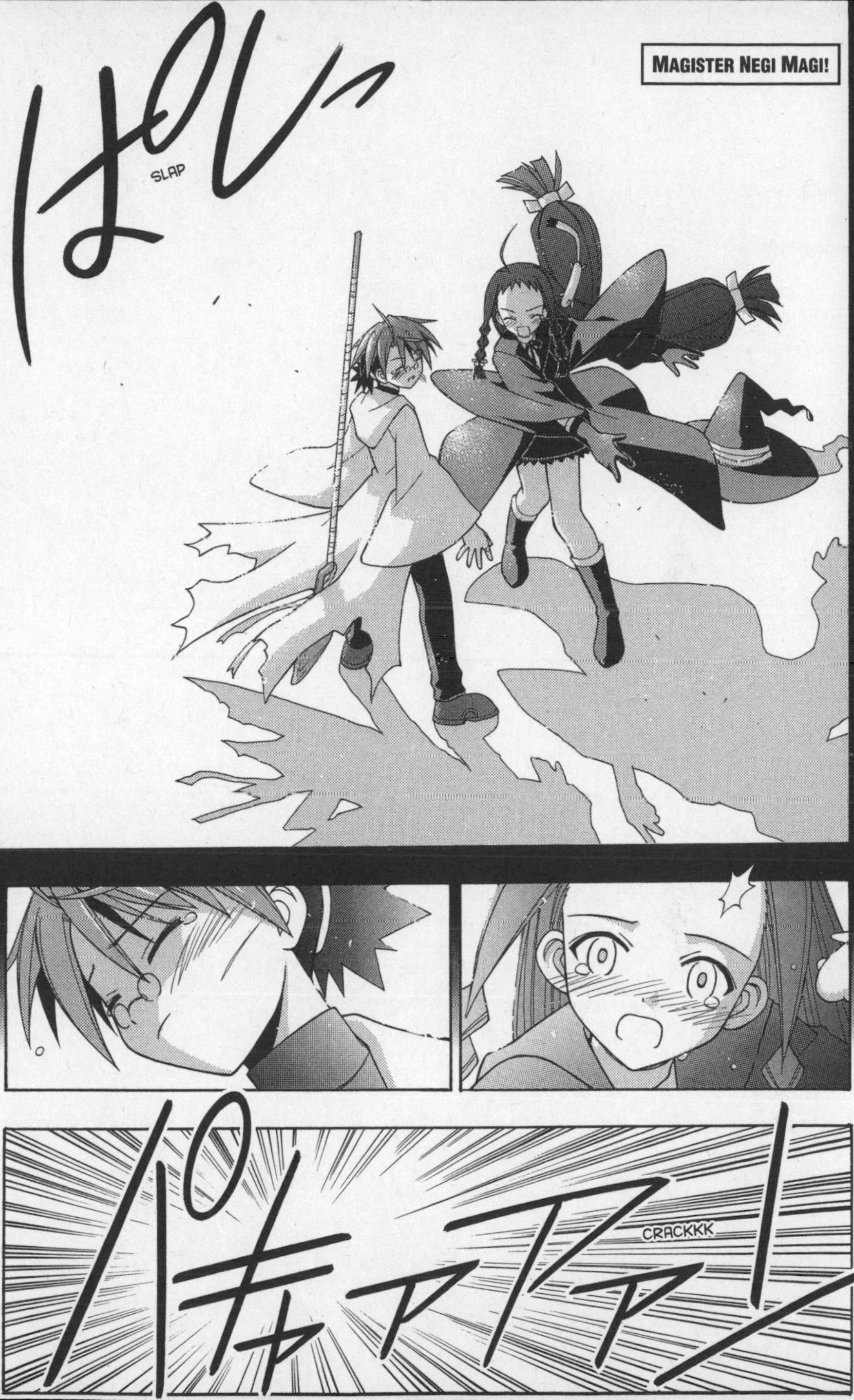
SLAP
CRACKKK

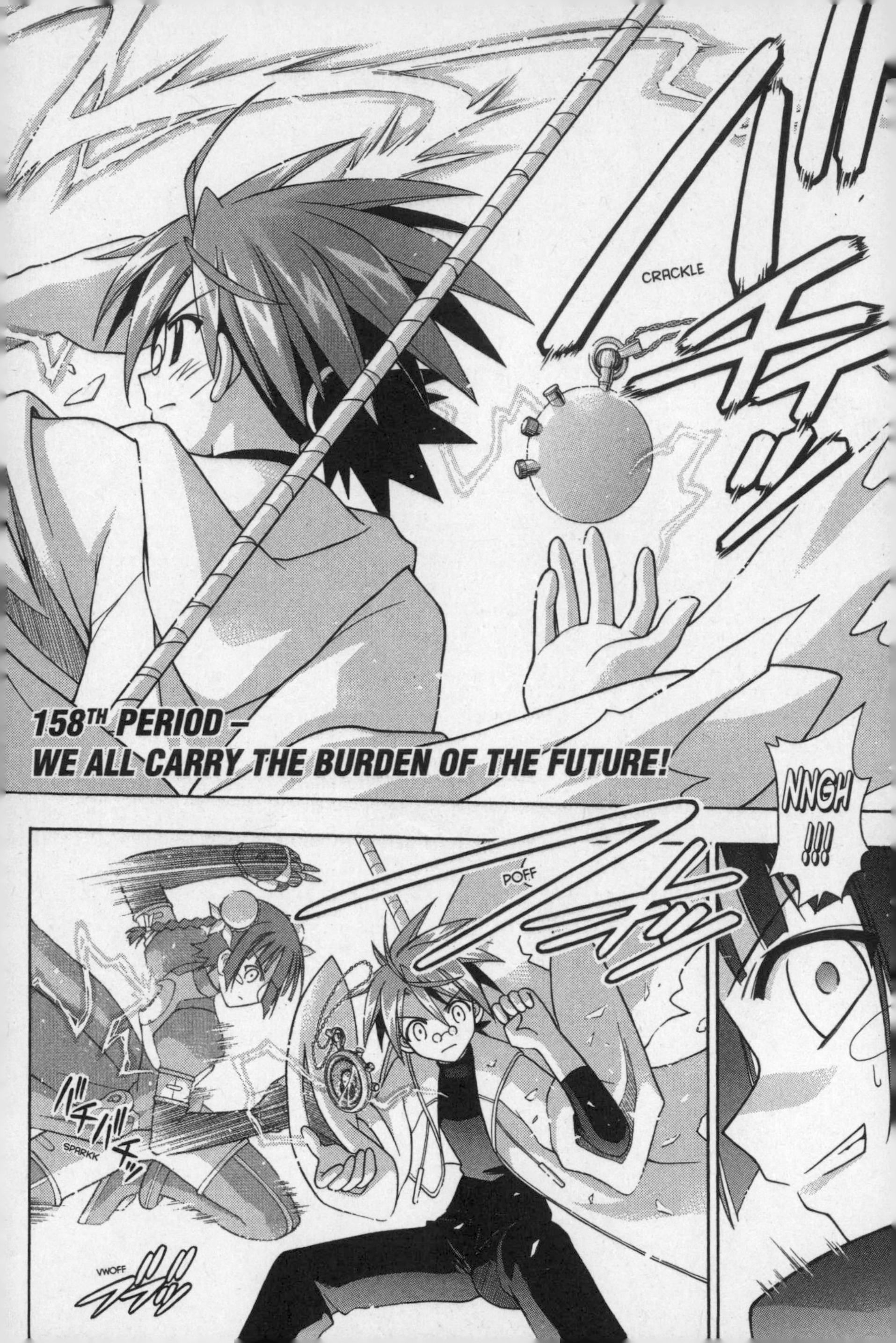
CRACKLE
158TH PERIOD –
WE ALL CARRY THE BURDEN OF THE FUTURE!
NNGH!!!
POFF
SPARKK
VWOFF

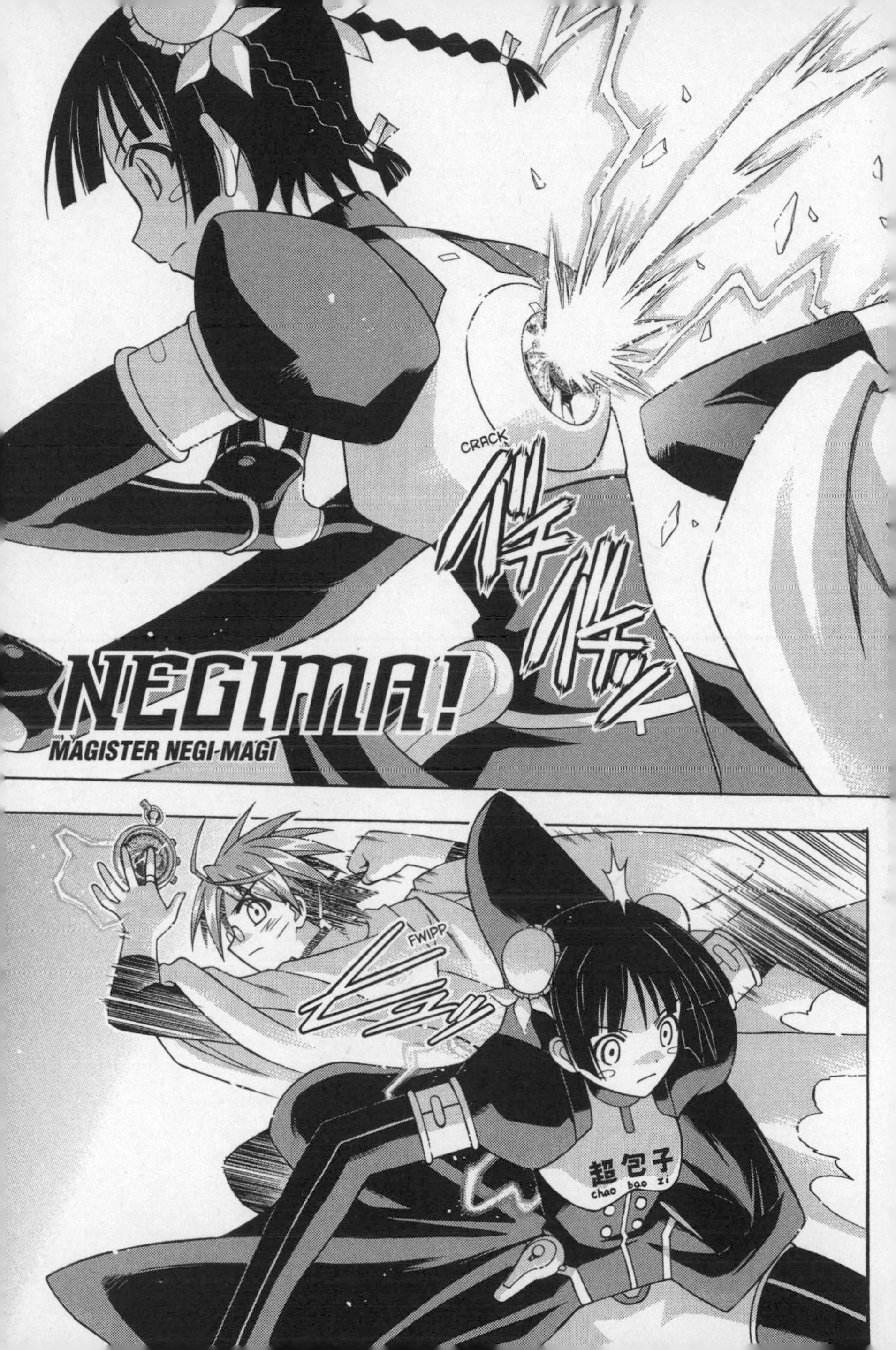
CRACK
NEGIMA!
MAGISTER NEGI-MAGI
FWIPP
超包子
chao bao zi

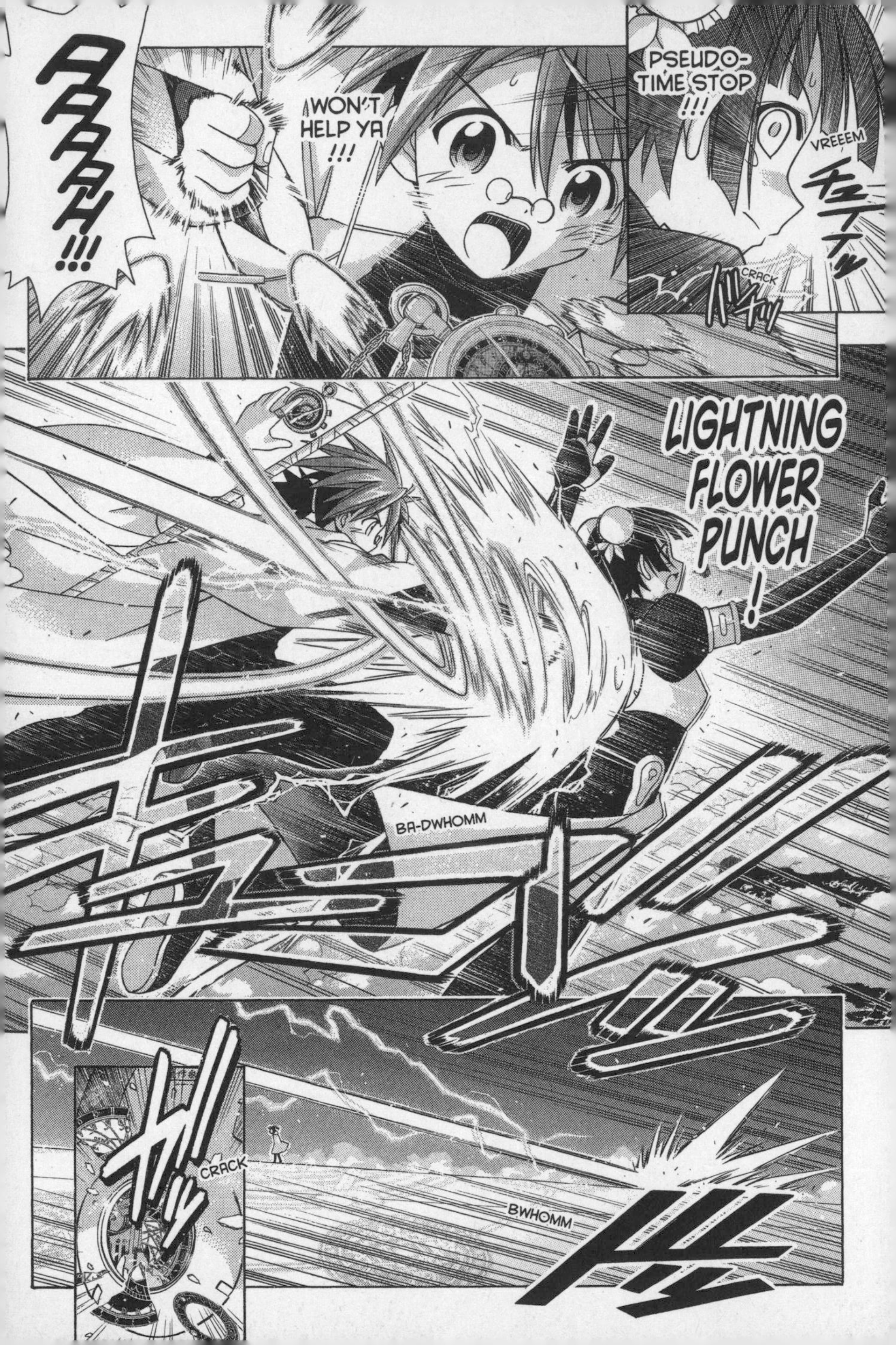
PSEUDO-TIME STOP!!!
VREEEM
CRACK
WON'T HELP YA!!!
LIGHTNING FLOWER PUNCH!
BA-DWHOMM
BWHOMM
CRACK

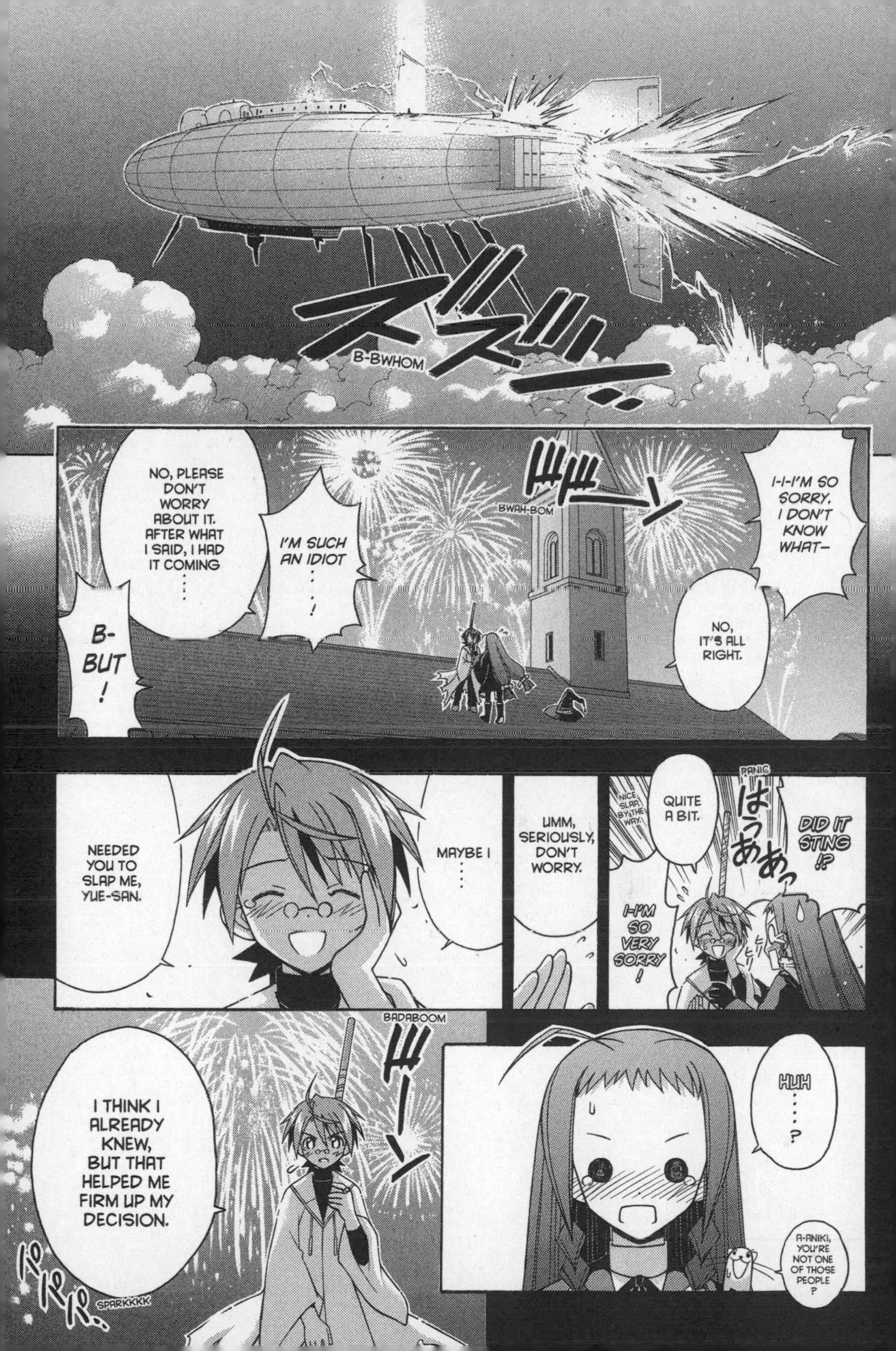
B-BWHOM
I-I-I'M SO SORRY. I DON'T KNOW WHAT—
NO, IT'S ALL RIGHT.
BWAH-BOM
I'M SUCH AN IDIOT ...!
NO, PLEASE DON'T WORRY ABOUT IT. AFTER WHAT I SAID, I HAD IT COMING ...
B-BUT!
PANIC
DID IT STING!?
QUITE A BIT.
NICE SLAP, BY THE WAY.
I-I'M SO VERY SORRY!
UMM, SERIOUSLY, DON'T WORRY.
MAYBE I ...
NEEDED YOU TO SLAP ME, YUE-SAN.
HUH ...?
A-ANIKI, YOU'RE NOT ONE OF THOSE PEOPLE?
BADABOOM
I THINK I ALREADY KNEW, BUT THAT HELPED ME FIRM UP MY DECISION.
SPARKKKK

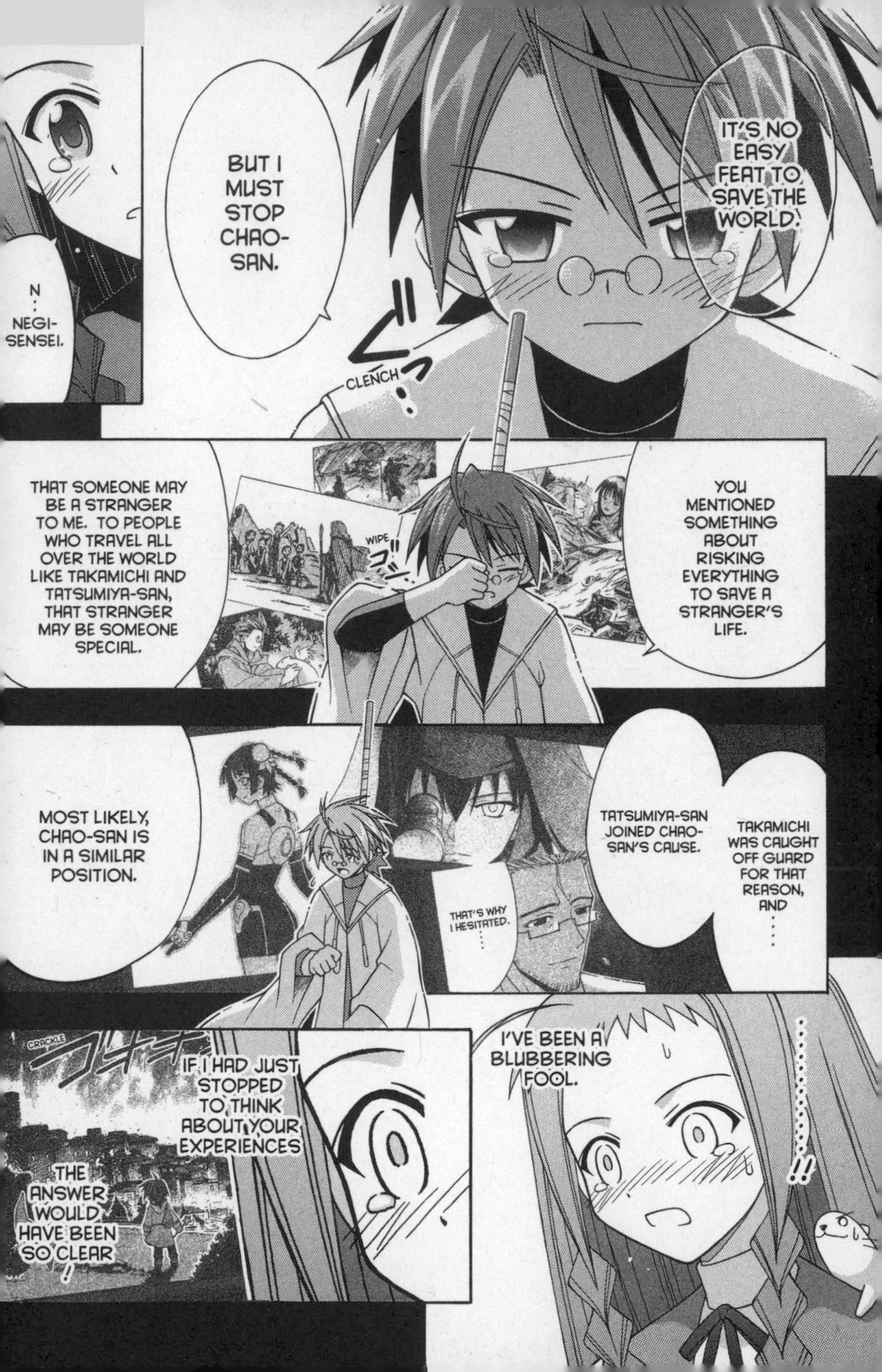
IT'S NO EASY FEAT TO SAVE THE WORLD.
BUT I MUST STOP CHAO-SAN.
CLENCH
N... NEGI-SENSEI.
YOU MENTIONED SOMETHING ABOUT RISKING EVERYTHING TO SAVE A STRANGER'S LIFE.
WIPE
THAT SOMEONE MAY BE A STRANGER TO ME. TO PEOPLE WHO TRAVEL ALL OVER THE WORLD LIKE TAKAMICHI AND TATSUMIYA-SAN, THAT STRANGER MAY BE SOMEONE SPECIAL.
TAKAMICHI WAS CAUGHT OFF GUARD FOR THAT REASON, AND...
TATSUMIYA-SAN JOINED CHAO-SAN'S CAUSE.
THAT'S WHY I HESITATED...
MOST LIKELY, CHAO-SAN IS IN A SIMILAR POSITION.
.........!!
I'VE BEEN A BLUBBERING FOOL.
IF I HAD JUST STOPPED TO THINK ABOUT YOUR EXPERIENCES
THE ANSWER WOULD HAVE BEEN SO CLEAR!
CRACKLE

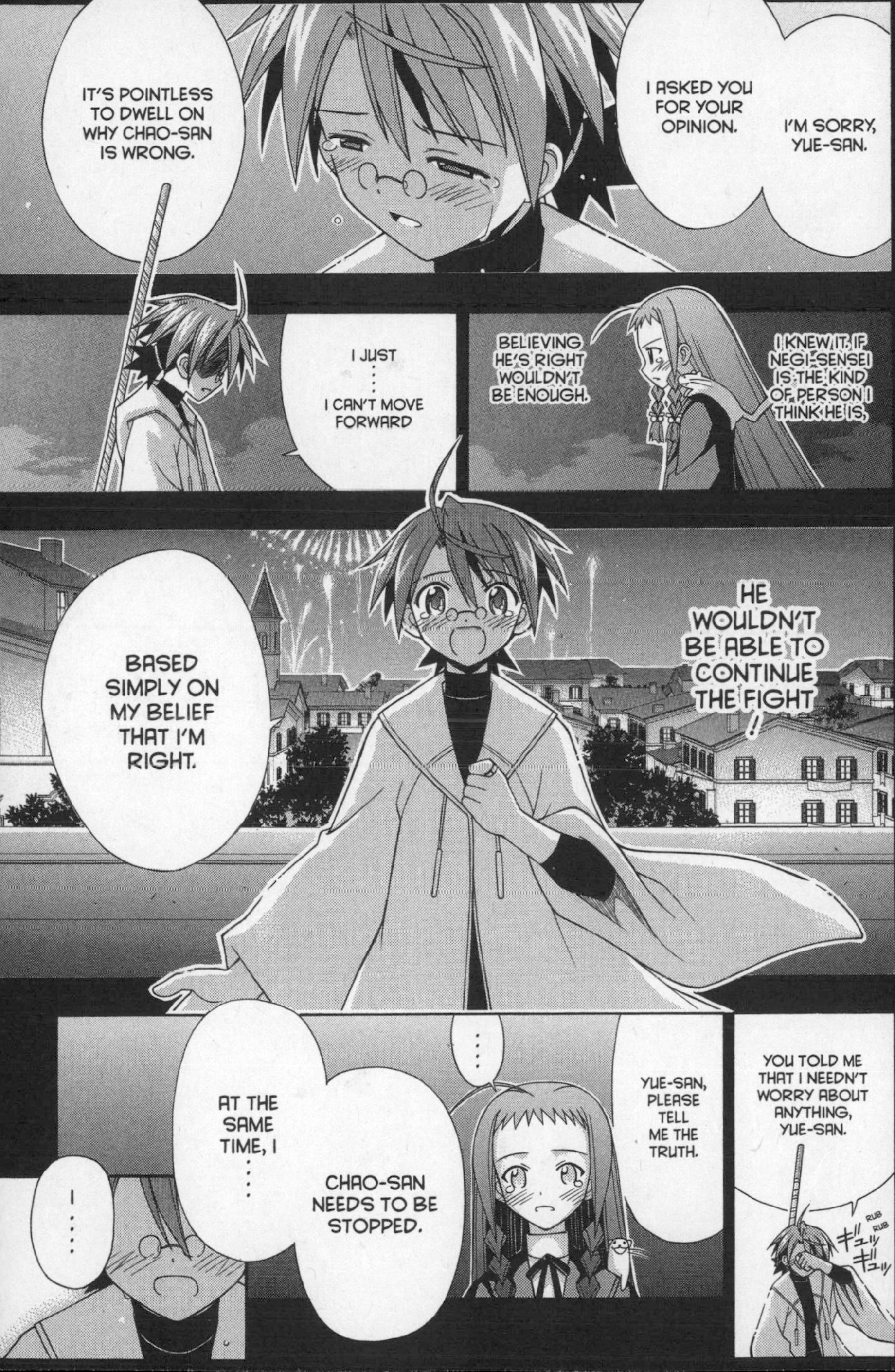
I'M SORRY, YUE-SAN.
I ASKED YOU FOR YOUR OPINION.
IT'S POINTLESS TO DWELL ON WHY CHAO-SAN IS WRONG.
I KNEW IT. IF NEGI-SENSEI IS THE KIND OF PERSON I THINK HE IS,
BELIEVING HE'S RIGHT WOULDN'T BE ENOUGH.
I JUST ... I CAN'T MOVE FORWARD
HE WOULDN'T BE ABLE TO CONTINUE THE FIGHT!
BASED SIMPLY ON MY BELIEF THAT I'M RIGHT.
YOU TOLD ME THAT I NEEDN'T WORRY ABOUT ANYTHING, YUE-SAN.
RUB RUB
YUE-SAN, PLEASE TELL ME THE TRUTH.
....
AT THE SAME TIME, I ....
CHAO-SAN NEEDS TO BE STOPPED.
I ....

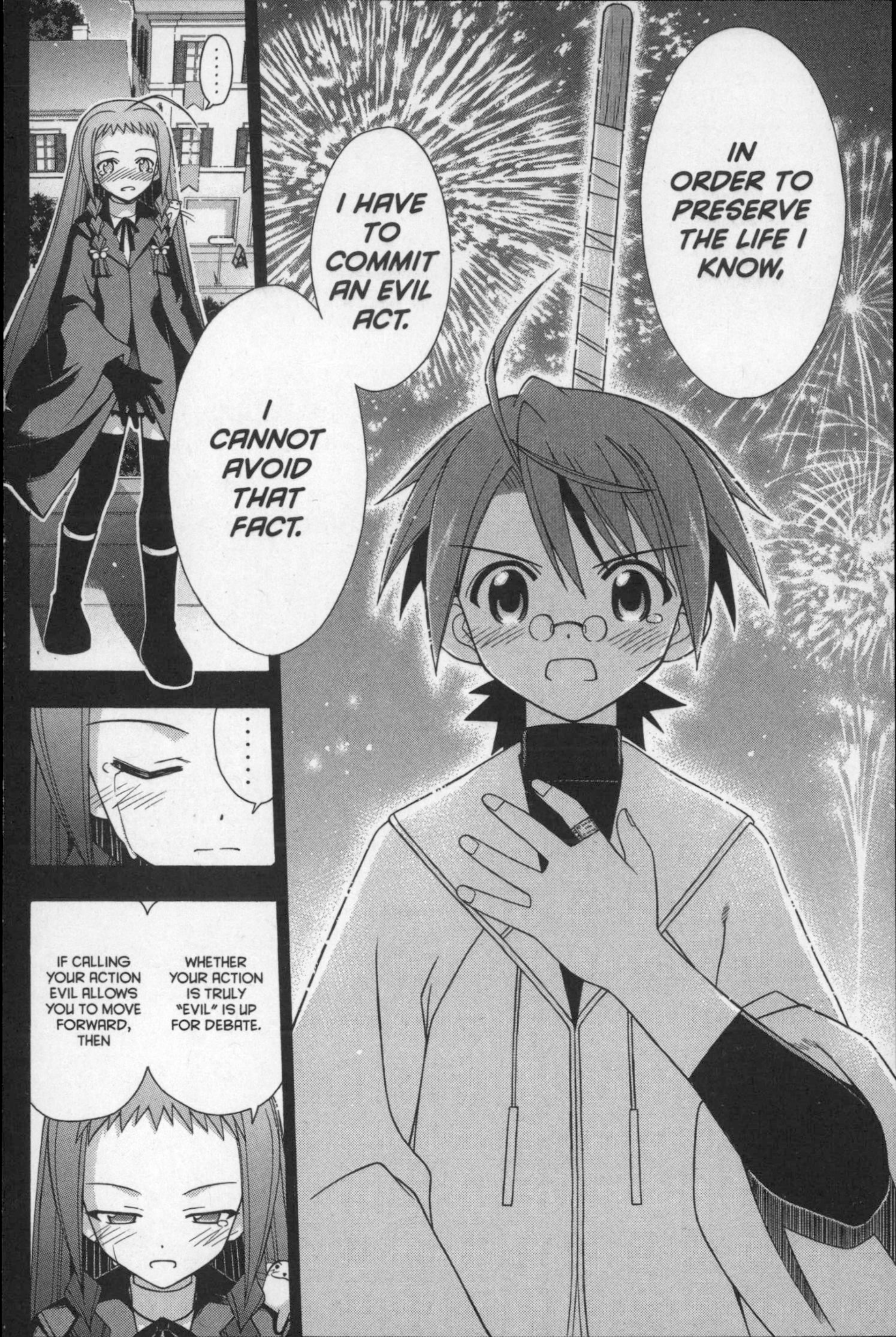
IN ORDER TO PRESERVE THE LIFE I KNOW,
I HAVE TO COMMIT AN EVIL ACT.
I CANNOT AVOID THAT FACT.
......
......
WHETHER YOUR ACTION IS TRULY "EVIL" IS UP FOR DEBATE.
IF CALLING YOUR ACTION EVIL ALLOWS YOU TO MOVE FORWARD, THEN

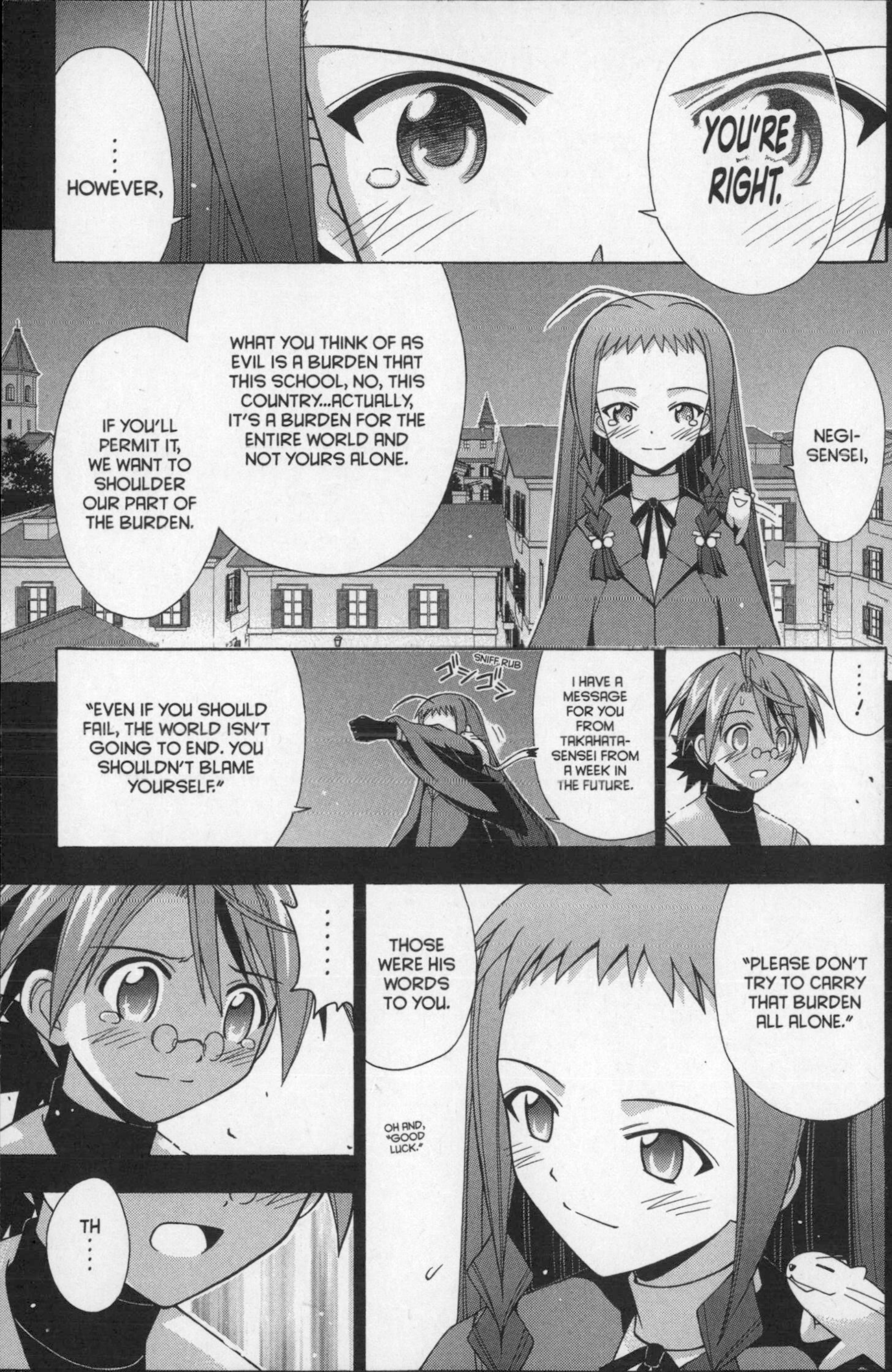
YOU'RE RIGHT.
...HOWEVER,
NEGI-SENSEI,
WHAT YOU THINK OF AS EVIL IS A BURDEN THAT THIS SCHOOL, NO, THIS COUNTRY...ACTUALLY, IT'S A BURDEN FOR THE ENTIRE WORLD AND NOT YOURS ALONE.
IF YOU'LL PERMIT IT, WE WANT TO SHOULDER OUR PART OF THE BURDEN.
....!
I HAVE A MESSAGE FOR YOU FROM TAKAHATA-SENSEI FROM A WEEK IN THE FUTURE.
SNIFF RUB
"EVEN IF YOU SHOULD FAIL, THE WORLD ISN'T GOING TO END. YOU SHOULDN'T BLAME YOURSELF."
"PLEASE DON'T TRY TO CARRY THAT BURDEN ALL ALONE."
THOSE WERE HIS WORDS TO YOU.
OH AND, "GOOD LUCK."
......
TH....

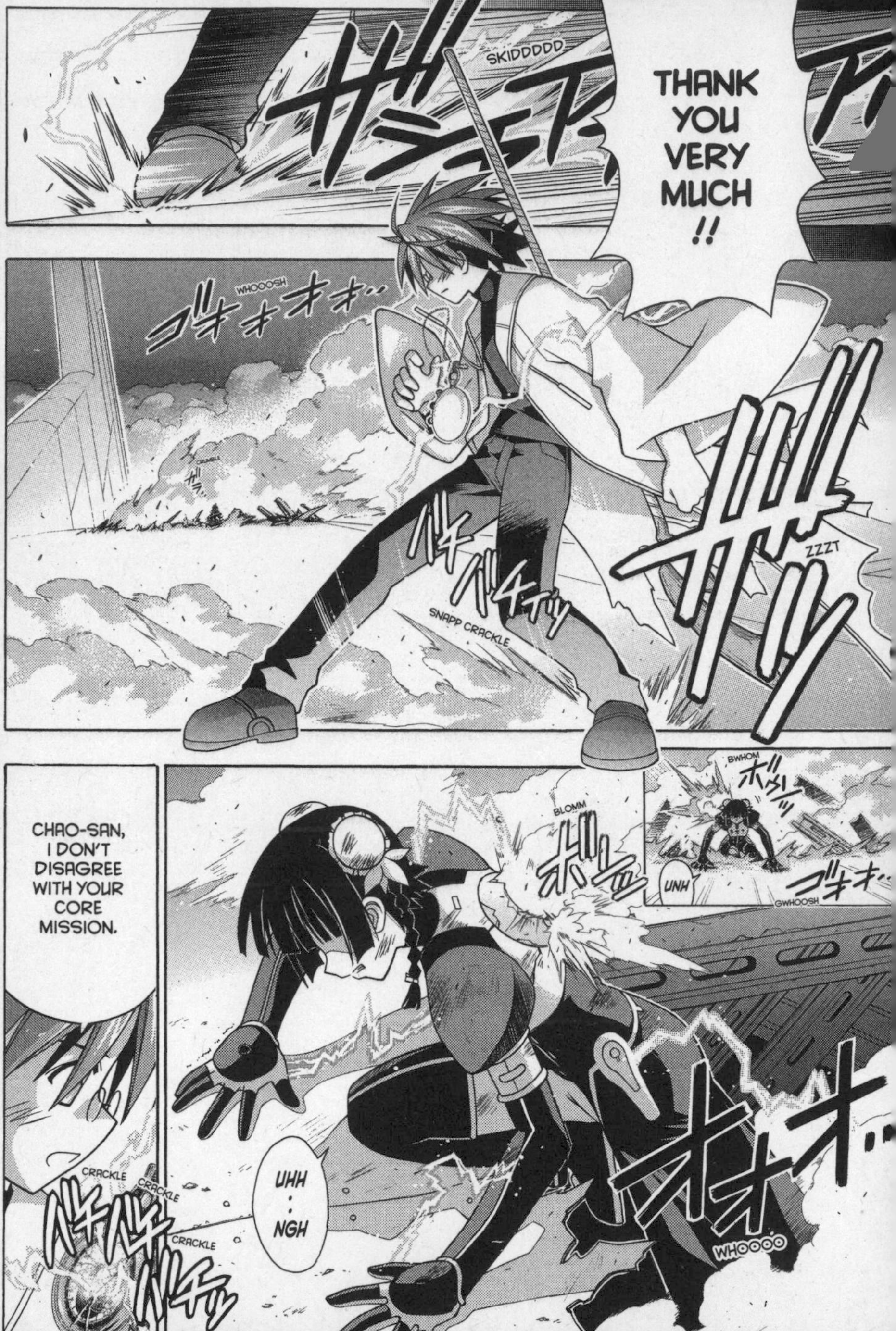
THANK YOU VERY MUCH !!
SKIDDDDD
ZZZT
WHOOOSH
SNAPP CRACKLE
BWHOM
GWHOOSH
UNH
BLOMM
WHOOOO
UHH
:
NGH
CHAO-SAN, I DON'T DISAGREE WITH YOUR CORE MISSION.
CRACKLE
CRACKLE
CRACKLE

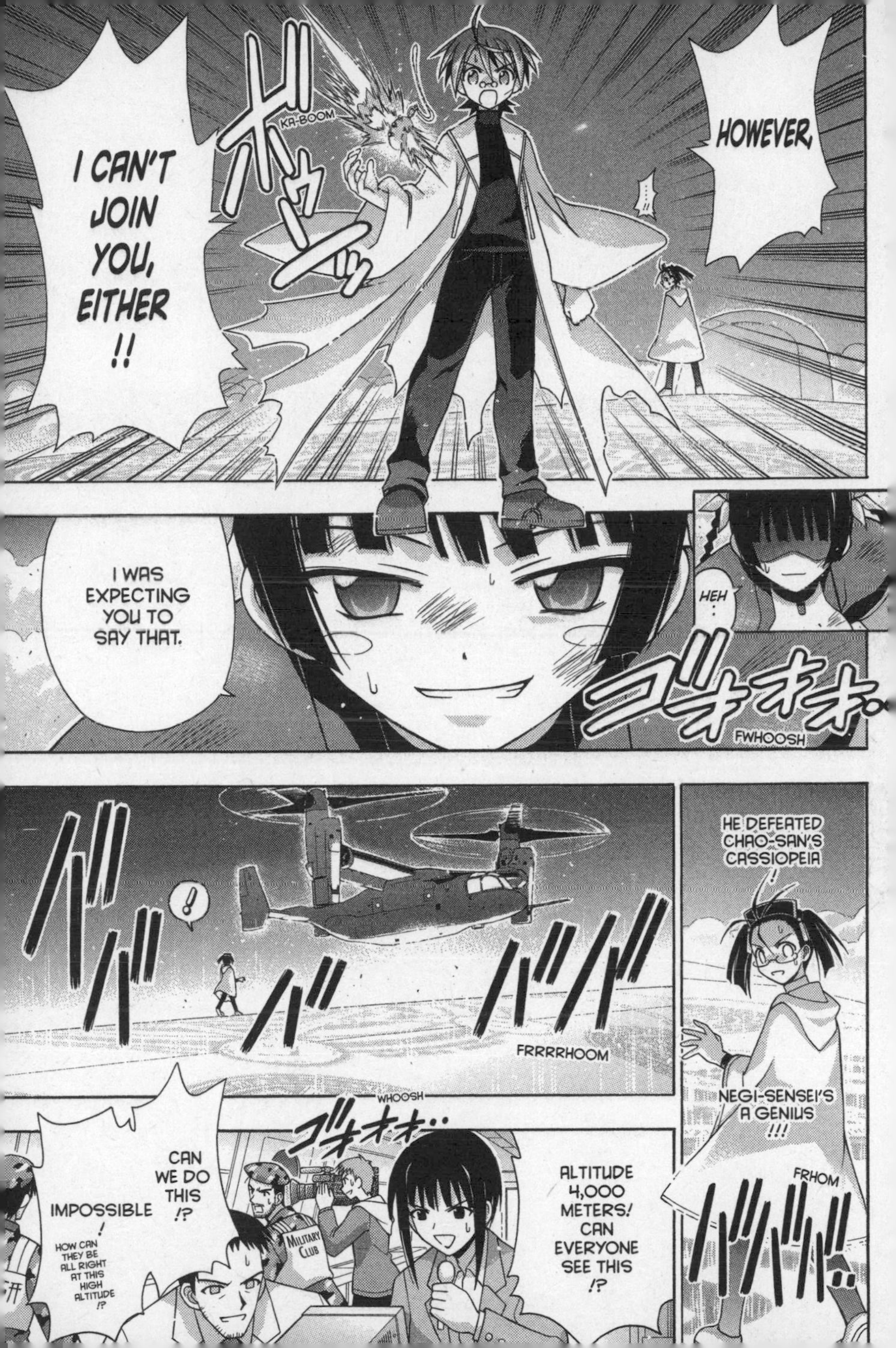
HOWEVER,
...!!
KA-BOOM
I CAN'T JOIN YOU, EITHER !!
HEH :
I WAS EXPECTING YOU TO SAY THAT.
FWHOOSH
HE DEFEATED CHAO-SAN'S CASSIOPEIA !
NEGI-SENSEI'S A GENIUS !!!
FRHOM
!
FRRRRHOOM
WHOOSH
ALTITUDE 4,000 METERS! CAN EVERYONE SEE THIS !?
CAN WE DO THIS !?
MILITARY CLUB
IMPOSSIBLE !
HOW CAN THEY BE ALL RIGHT AT THIS HIGH ALTITUDE !?

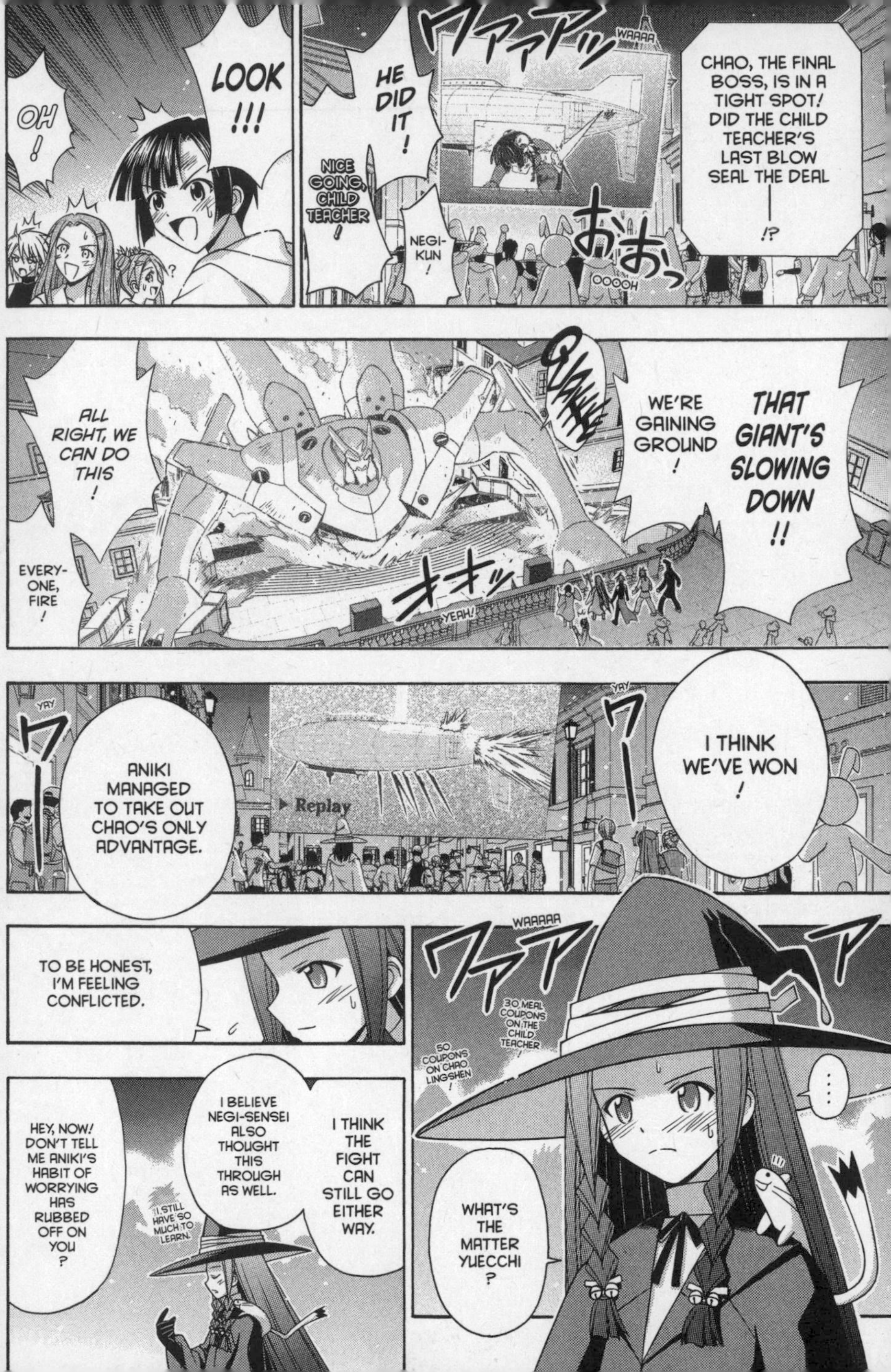

WAAAA
CHAO, THE FINAL BOSS, IS IN A TIGHT SPOT! DID THE CHILD TEACHER'S LAST BLOW SEAL THE DEAL —!?
OOOOH
HE DID IT!
NICE GOING, CHILD TEACHER!
NEGI-KUN!
LOOK!!!
OH!
THAT GIANT'S SLOWING DOWN!!
WE'RE GAINING GROUND!
ALL RIGHT, WE CAN DO THIS!
EVERYONE, FIRE!
YEAH!
YAY
I THINK WE'VE WON!
YAY
ANIKI MANAGED TO TAKE OUT CHAO'S ONLY ADVANTAGE.
Replay
WAAAAA
30 MEAL COUPONS ON THE CHILD TEACHER
50 COUPONS ON CHAO LINGSHEN!
...
WHAT'S THE MATTER YUECCHI?
TO BE HONEST, I'M FEELING CONFLICTED.
I THINK THE FIGHT CAN STILL GO EITHER WAY.
I BELIEVE NEGI-SENSEI ALSO THOUGHT THIS THROUGH AS WELL.
I STILL HAVE SO MUCH TO LEARN.
HEY, NOW! DON'T TELL ME ANIKI'S HABIT OF WORRYING HAS RUBBED OFF ON YOU?

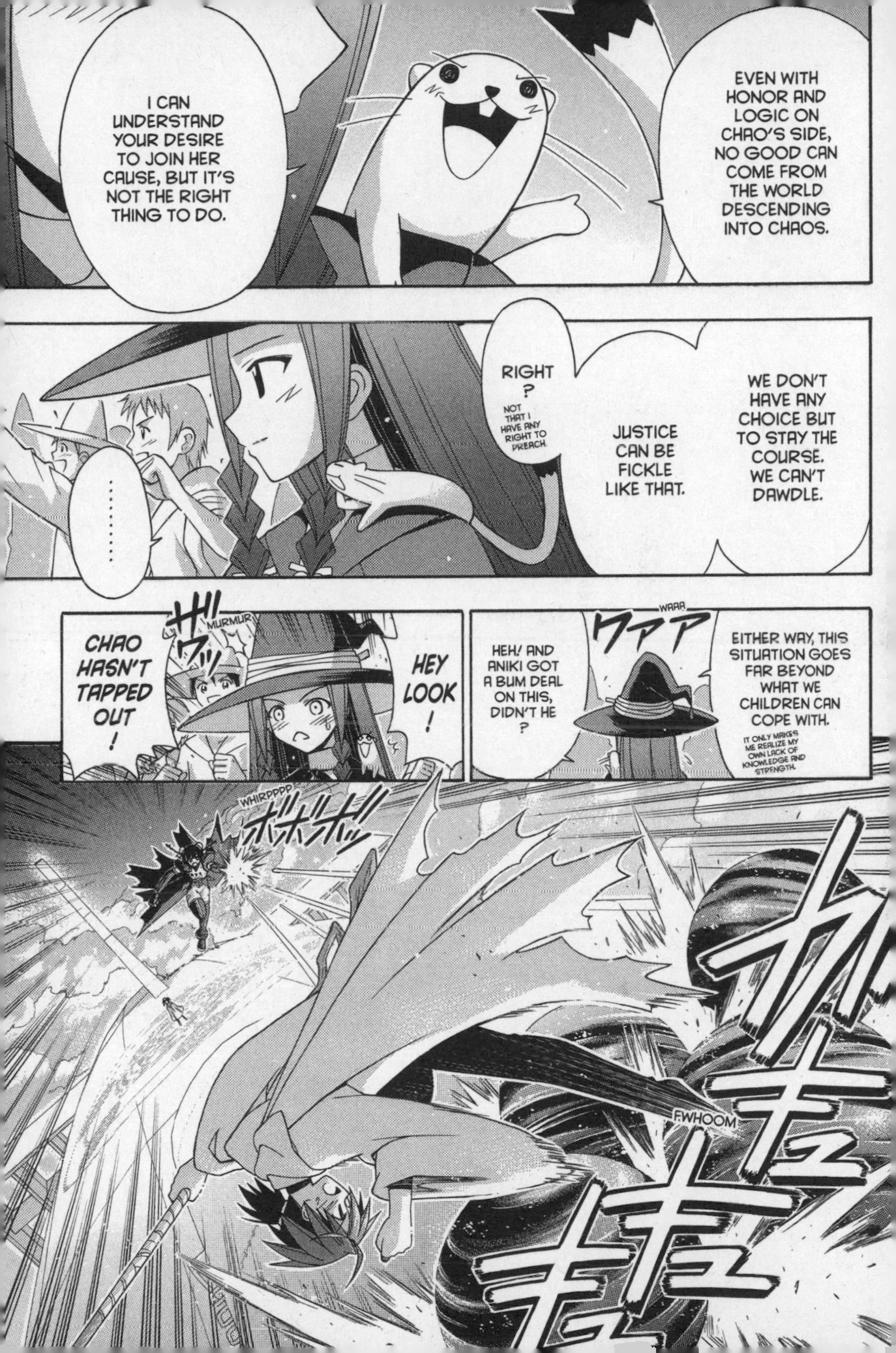
EVEN WITH HONOR AND LOGIC ON CHAO'S SIDE, NO GOOD CAN COME FROM THE WORLD DESCENDING INTO CHAOS.
I CAN UNDERSTAND YOUR DESIRE TO JOIN HER CAUSE, BUT IT'S NOT THE RIGHT THING TO DO.
WE DON'T HAVE ANY CHOICE BUT TO STAY THE COURSE. WE CAN'T DAWDLE.
JUSTICE CAN BE FICKLE LIKE THAT.
RIGHT?
NOT THAT I HAVE ANY RIGHT TO PREACH.
......
WAAA
EITHER WAY, THIS SITUATION GOES FAR BEYOND WHAT WE CHILDREN CAN COPE WITH.
IT ONLY MAKES ME REALIZE MY OWN LACK OF KNOWLEDGE AND STRENGTH.
HEH! AND ANIKI GOT A BUM DEAL ON THIS, DIDN'T HE?
HEY LOOK!
MURMUR
CHAO HASN'T TAPPED OUT!
FWHOOM
WHIRPPPP

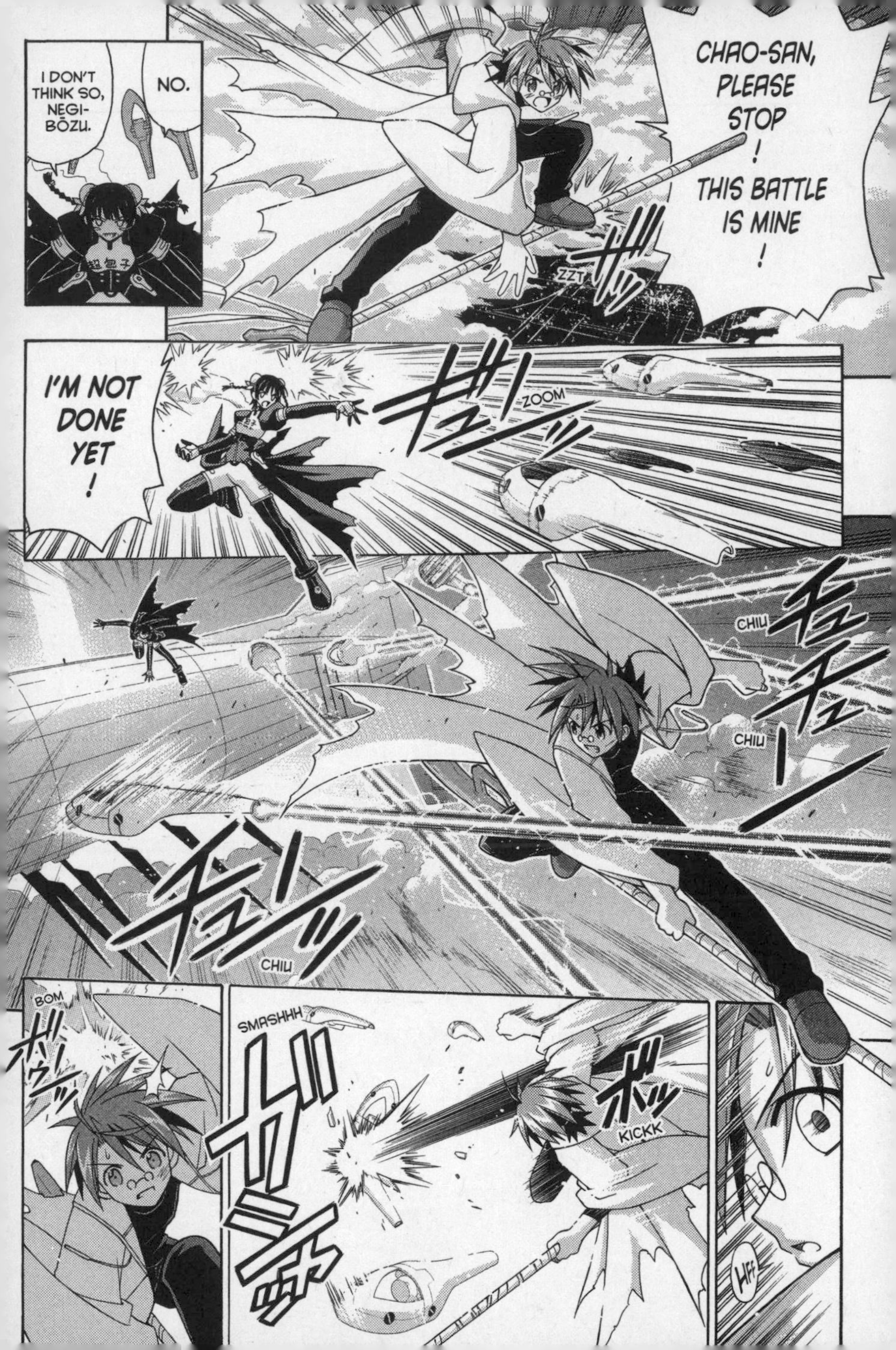
CHAO-SAN, PLEASE STOP!
THIS BATTLE IS MINE!
ZZT
NO.
I DON'T THINK SO, NEGI-BŌZU.
ZOOM
I'M NOT DONE YET!
CHIU
CHIU
CHIU
KICKK
SMASHHH
BOM
HFF

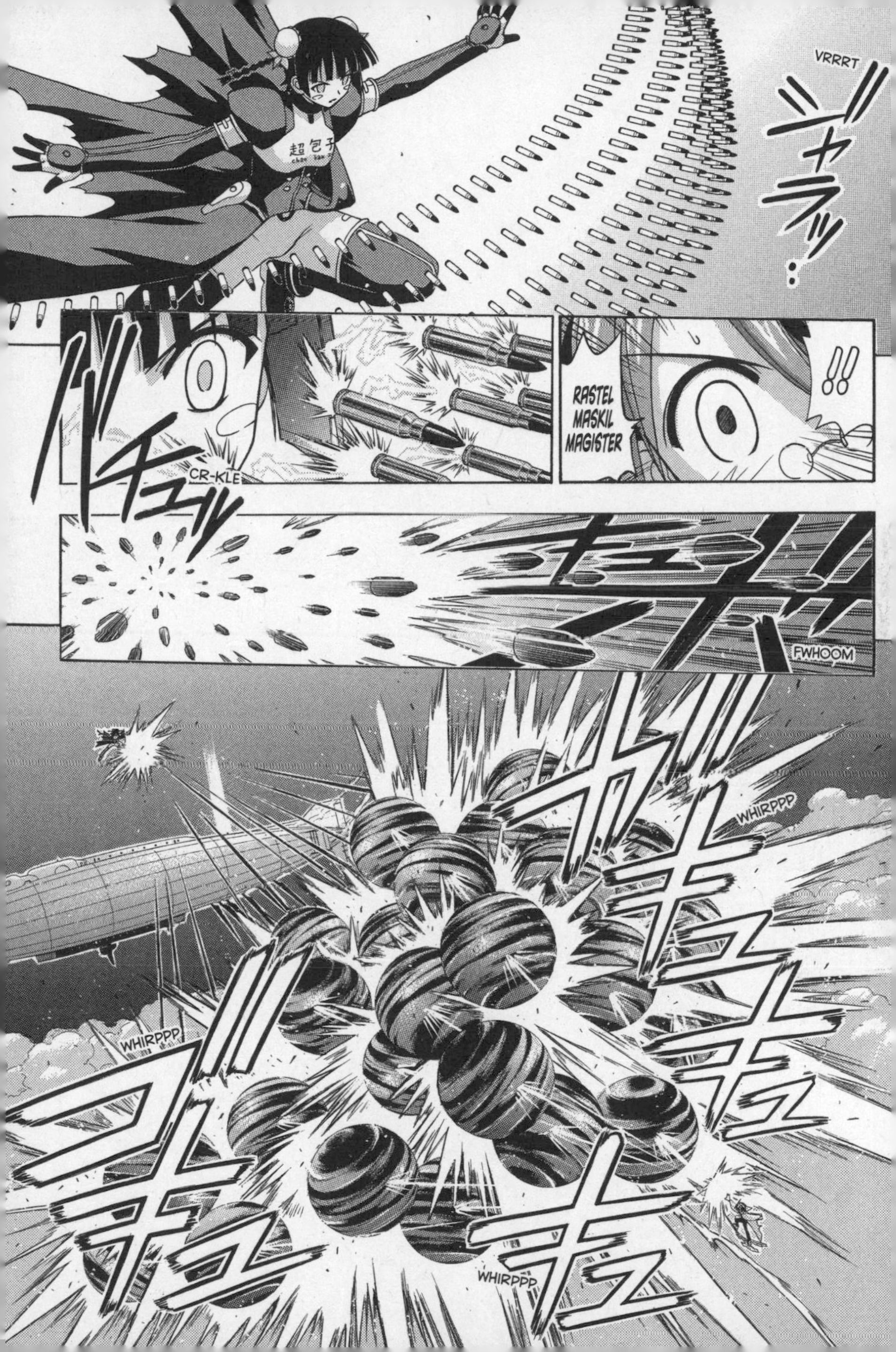

VRRRT
超包子
!!
RASTEL MASKIL MAGISTER
CR-KLE
FWHOOM
WHIRPPP
WHIRPPP
WHIRPPP

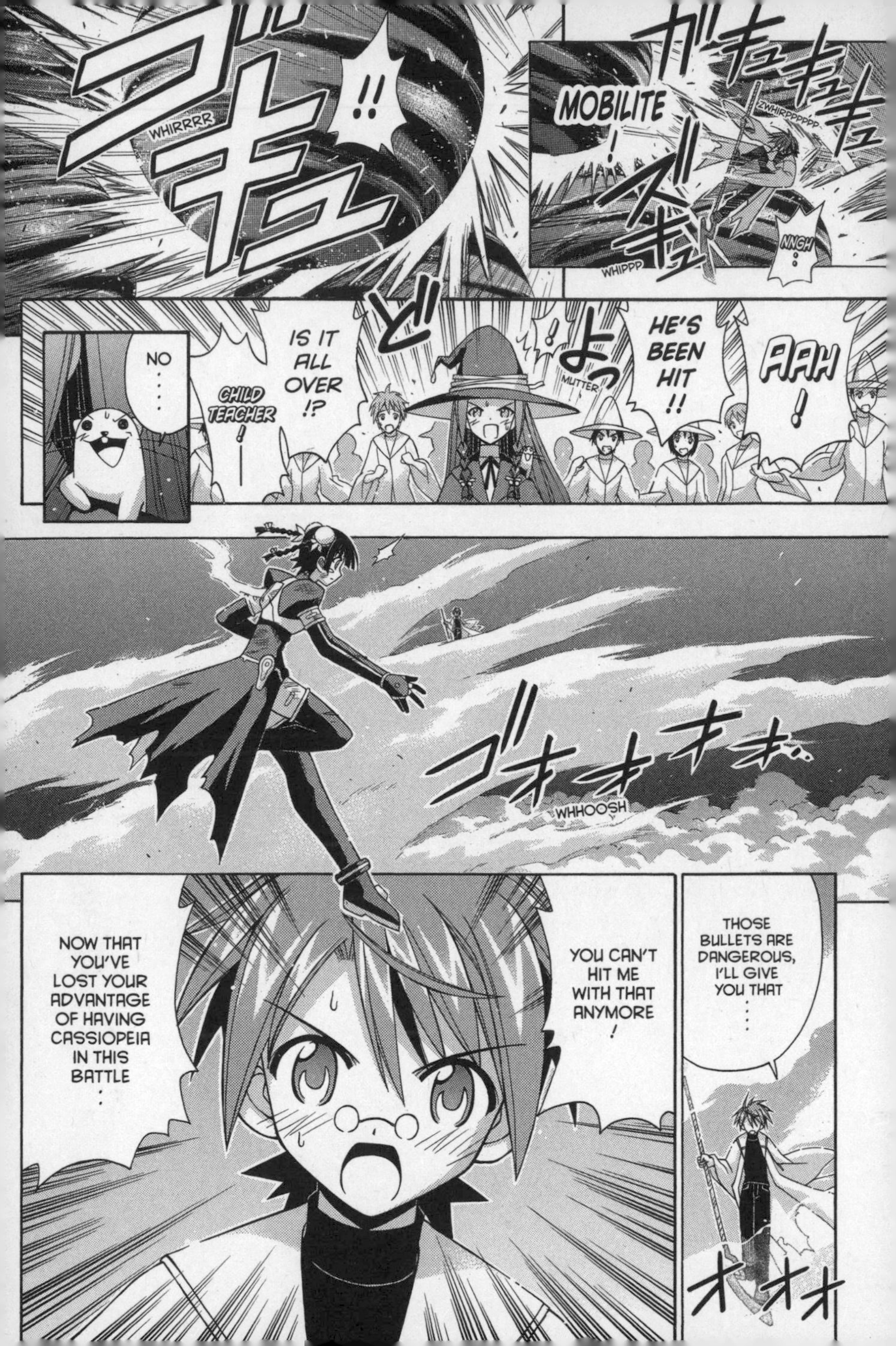
MOBILITE
!
ZWHIRPPPPPP
WHIPPP
NNGH
..
WHIRRRR
!!
AAH
!
HE'S BEEN HIT !!
MUTTER
!
IS IT ALL OVER !?
CHILD TEACHER
! —
NO
....
WHHOOSH
THOSE BULLETS ARE DANGEROUS, I'LL GIVE YOU THAT
....
YOU CAN'T HIT ME WITH THAT ANYMORE
!
NOW THAT YOU'VE LOST YOUR ADVANTAGE OF HAVING CASSIOPEIA IN THIS BATTLE
...

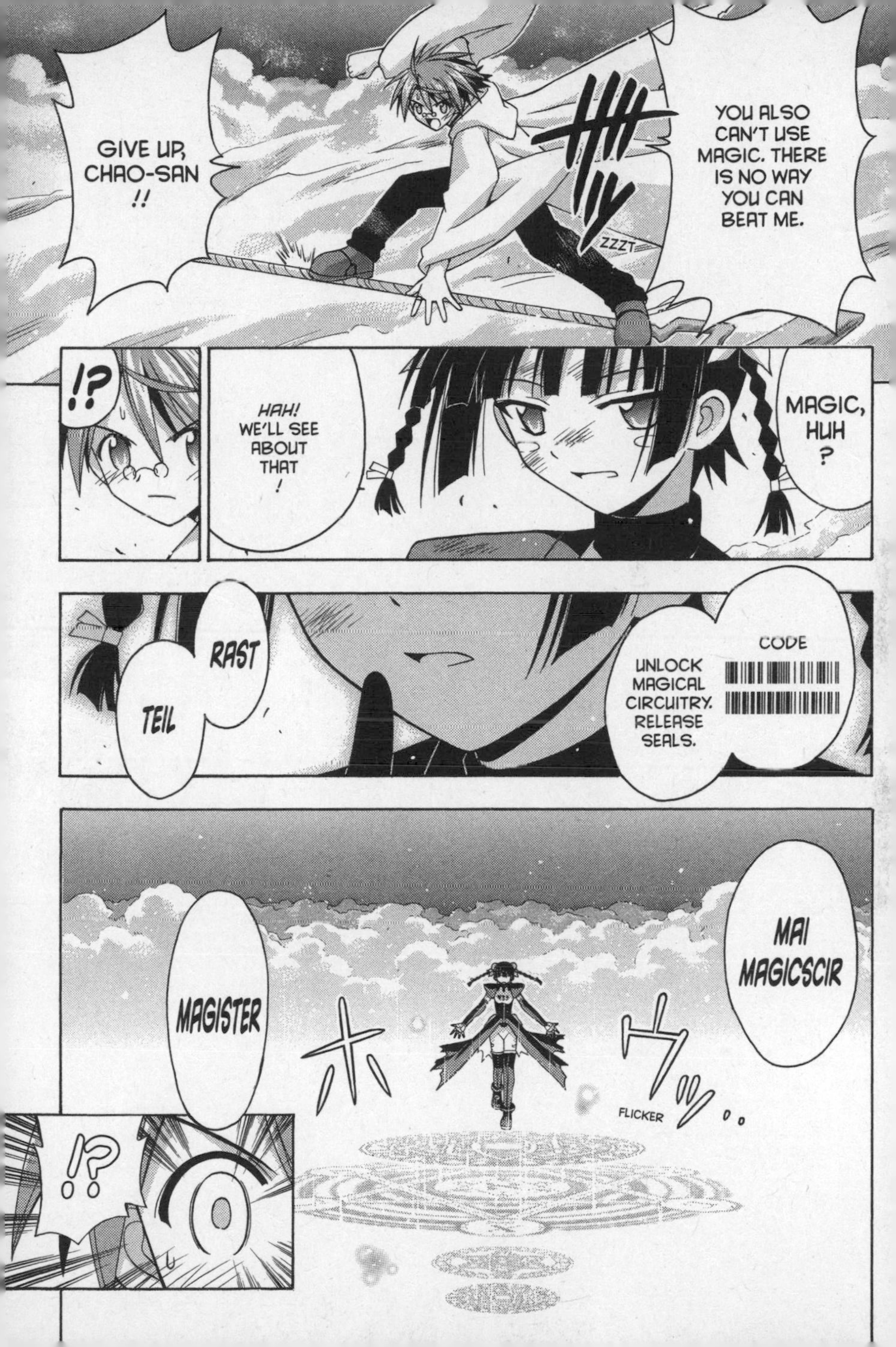

YOU ALSO CAN'T USE MAGIC. THERE IS NO WAY YOU CAN BEAT ME.
ZZZT
GIVE UP, CHAO-SAN !!
MAGIC, HUH ?
HAH! WE'LL SEE ABOUT THAT !
!?
CODE
UNLOCK MAGICAL CIRCUITRY. RELEASE SEALS.
RAST
TEIL
MAI MAGICSCIR
MAGISTER
FLICKER
!?

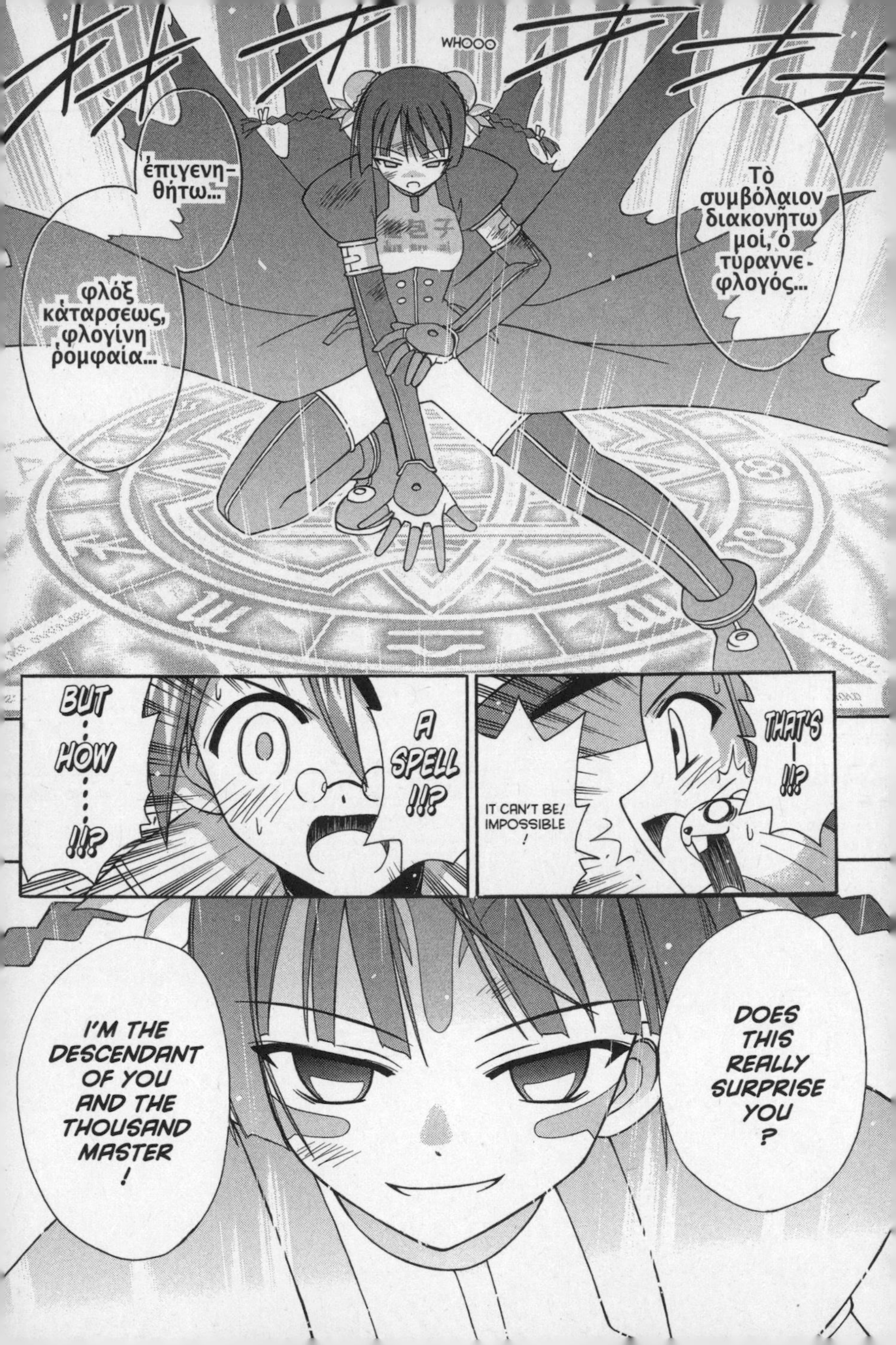
WHOOO
Τὸ συμβόλαιον διακονήτω μοί, ὁ τυραννε-φλογός...
ἐπιγενηθήτω...
φλόξ κάταρσεως, φλογίνη ῥομφαία...
THAT'S—!!?
IT CAN'T BE! IMPOSSIBLE!
A SPELL!!?
BUT... HOW...!!?
DOES THIS REALLY SURPRISE YOU?
I'M THE DESCENDANT OF YOU AND THE THOUSAND MASTER!

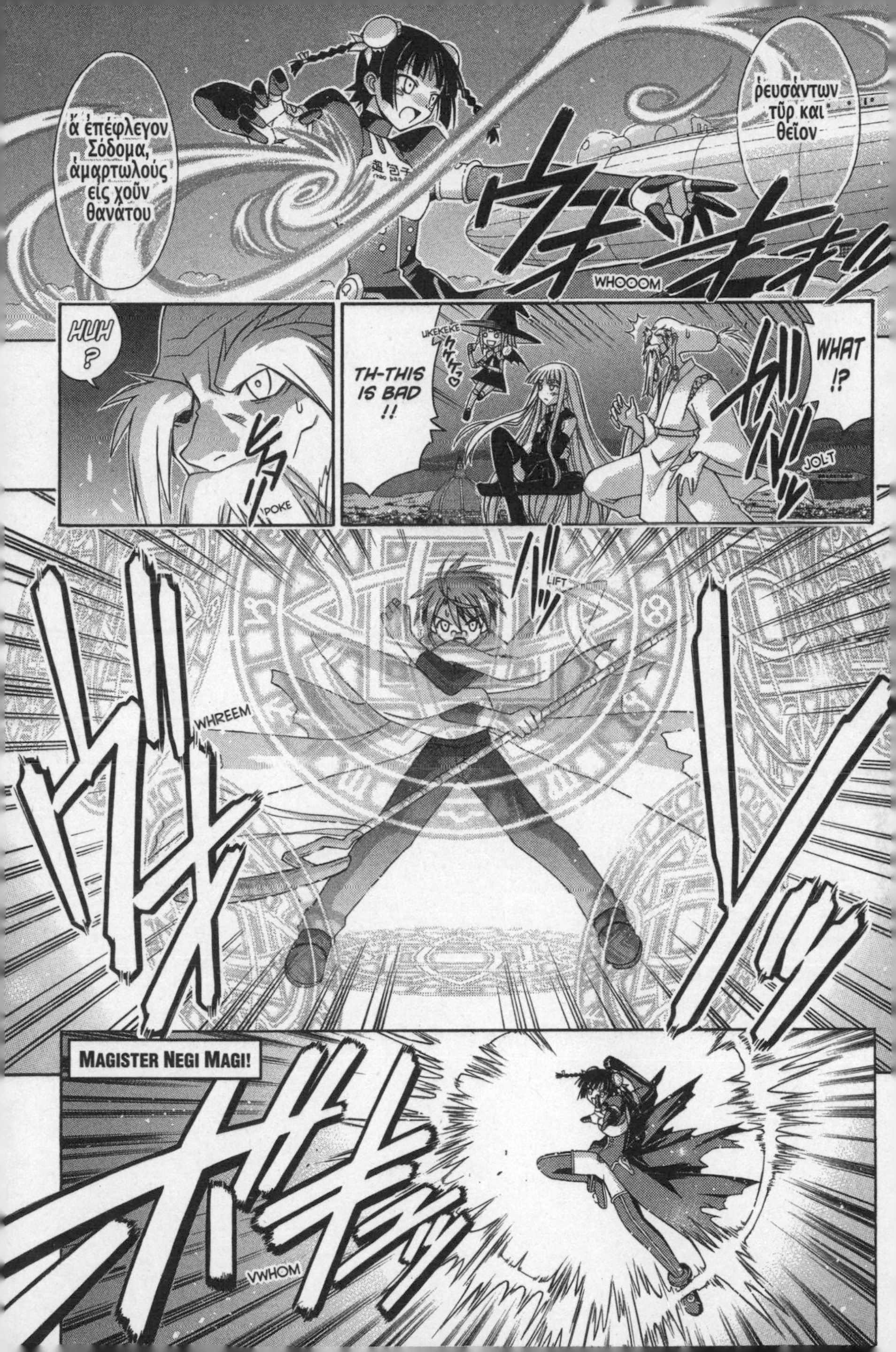
ῥευσάντων
τῦρ και
θεῖον
ἅ ἐπέφλεγον
Σόδομα,
ἁμαρτωλούς
εις χοῦν
θανάτου
WHOOOM
WHAT !?
JOLT
TH-THIS IS BAD !!
UKEKEKE
HUH ?
POKE
LIFT
WHREEM
MAGISTER NEGI MAGI!
VWHOM

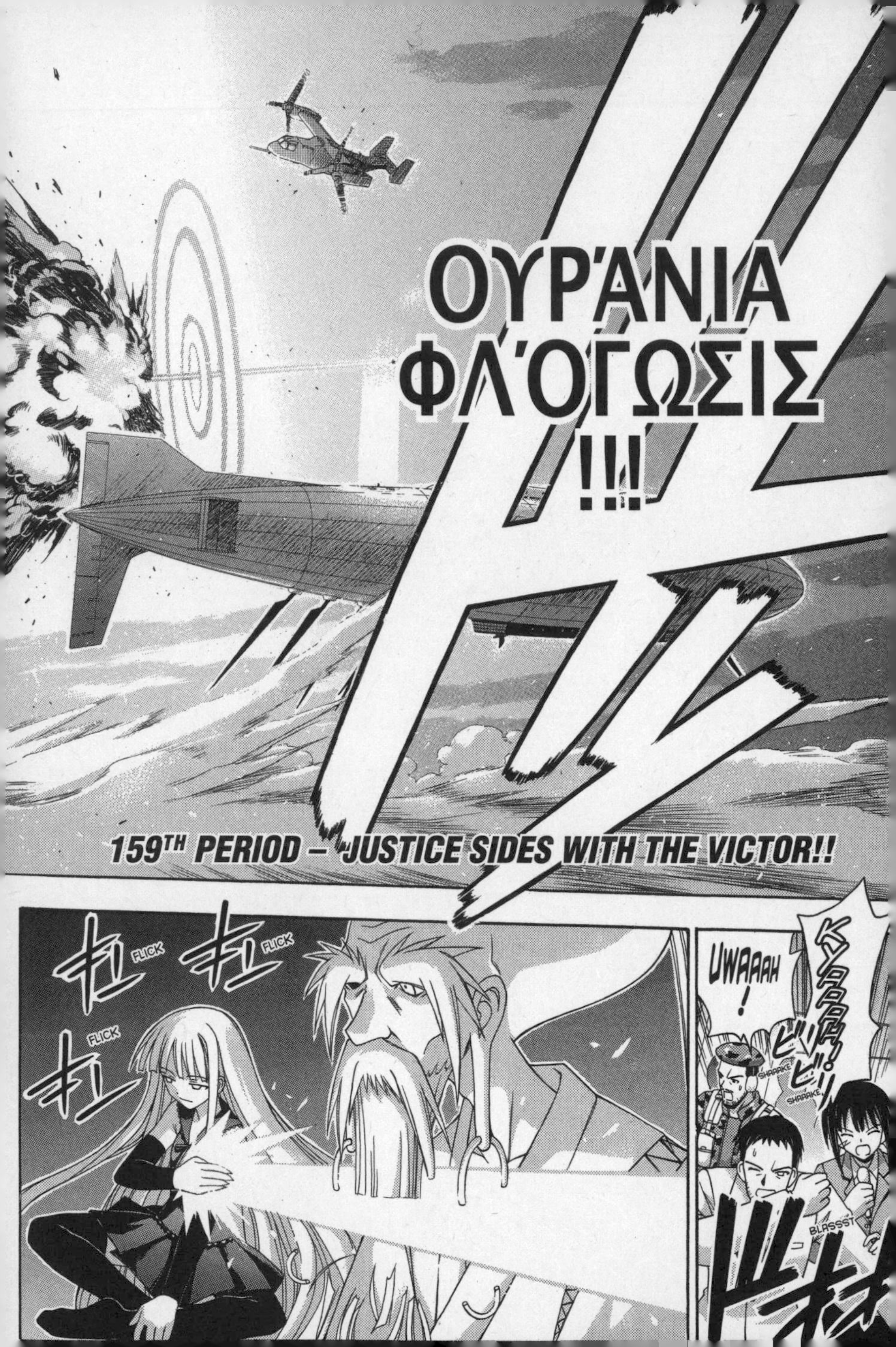
ΟΥΡΆΝΙΑ ΦΛΌΓΩΣΙΣ !!!
159TH PERIOD – JUSTICE SIDES WITH THE VICTOR!!
KYAAAAH!!
UWAAAH!
SHRAAKE
SHRAAKE
BLASSST
FLICK
FLICK
FLICK

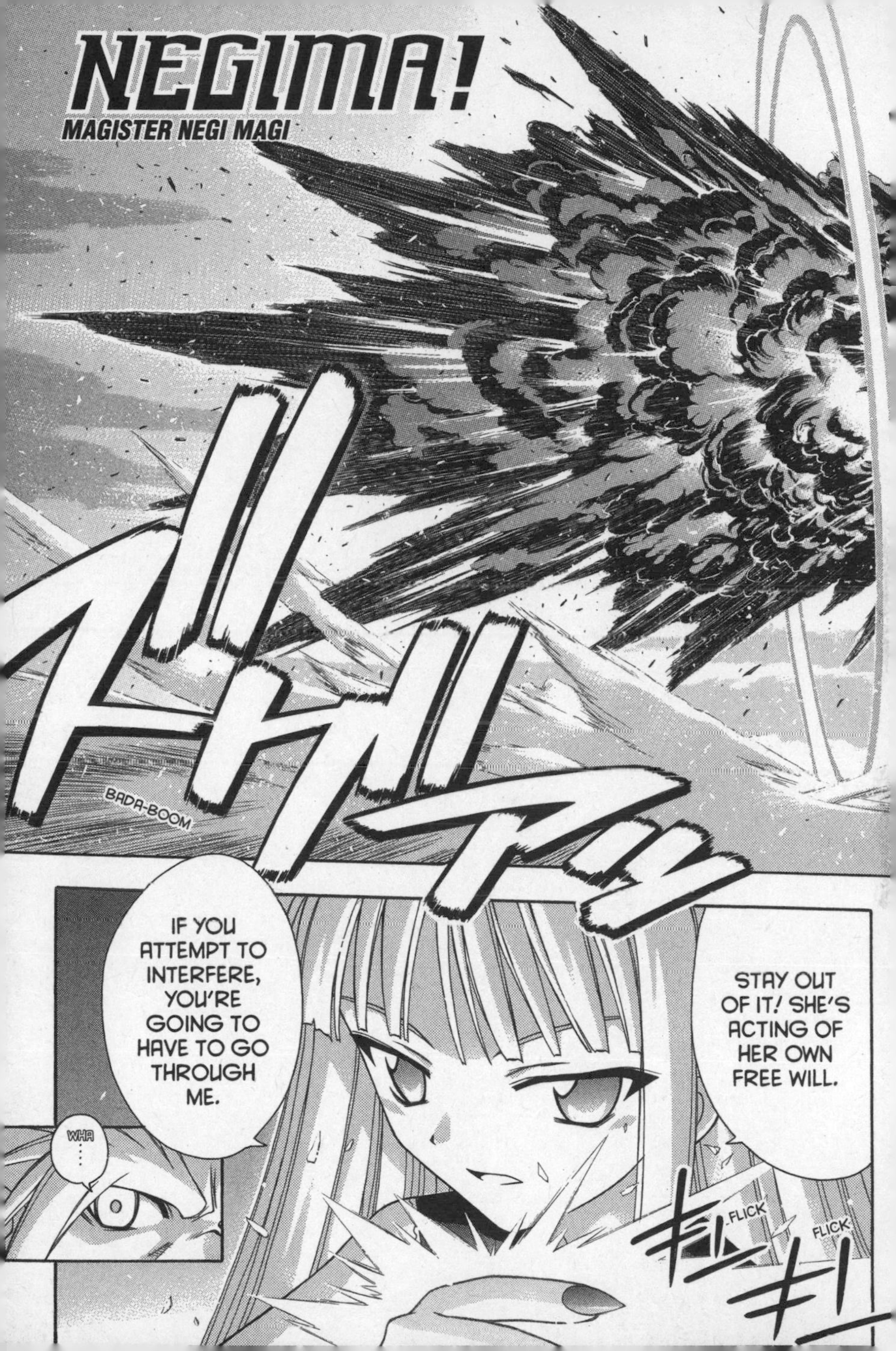
NEGIMA!
MAGISTER NEGI MAGI
BADA-BOOM
STAY OUT OF IT! SHE'S ACTING OF HER OWN FREE WILL.
IF YOU ATTEMPT TO INTERFERE, YOU'RE GOING TO HAVE TO GO THROUGH ME.
FLICK
FLICK
WHA......

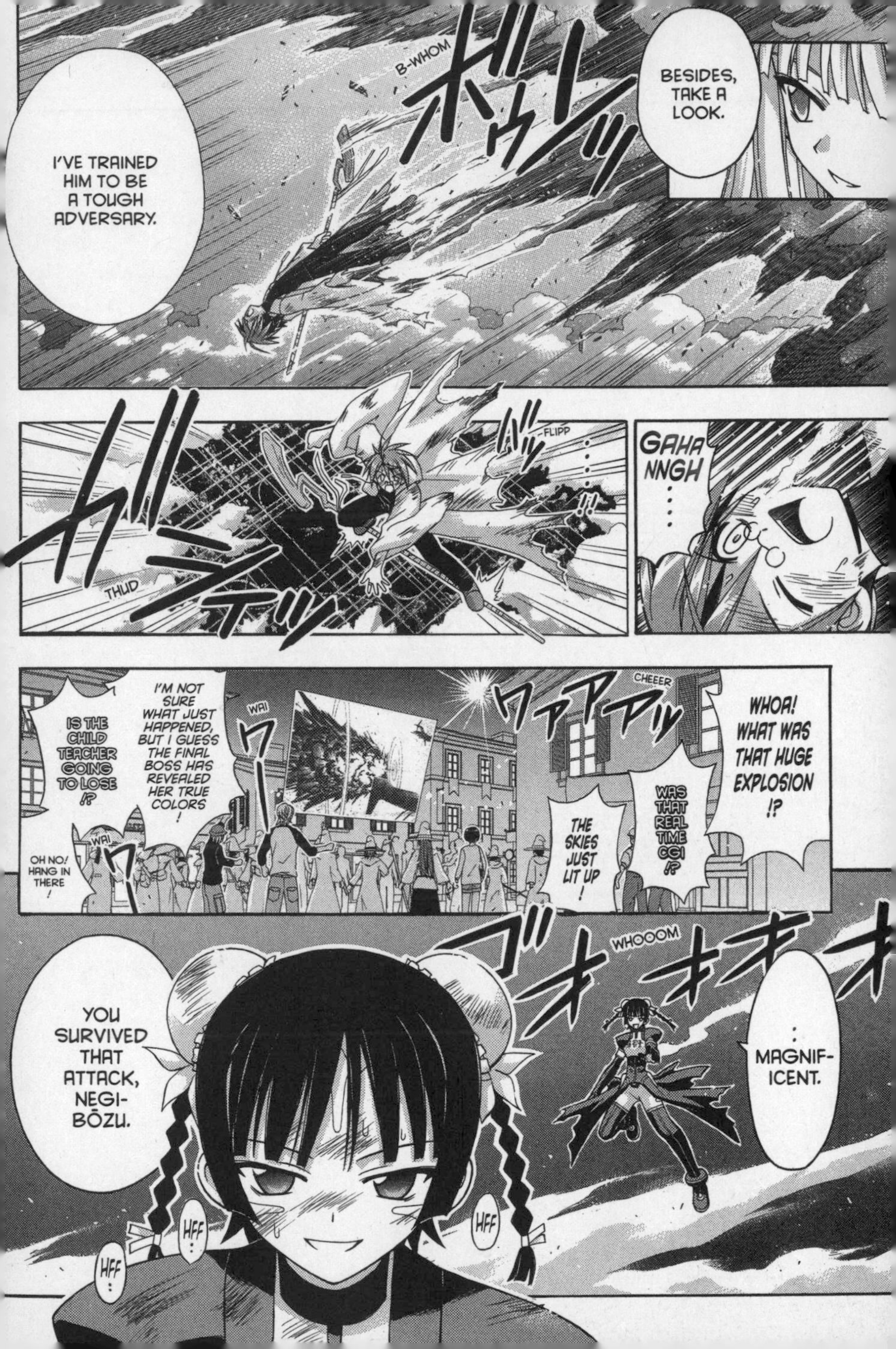
BESIDES, TAKE A LOOK.
B-WHOM
I'VE TRAINED HIM TO BE A TOUGH ADVERSARY.
GAHANNGH ...
FLIPP
...!!
THUD
WHOA! WHAT WAS THAT HUGE EXPLOSION!?
CHEEER
WAS THAT REAL TIME CGI!?
THE SKIES JUST LIT UP!
WAI
I'M NOT SURE WHAT JUST HAPPENED, BUT I GUESS THE FINAL BOSS HAS REVEALED HER TRUE COLORS!
IS THE CHILD TEACHER GOING TO LOSE!?
WAI
OH NO! HANG IN THERE!
WHOOOM
...MAGNIFICENT.
YOU SURVIVED THAT ATTACK, NEGI-BŌZU.
HFF...
HFF...
HFF...

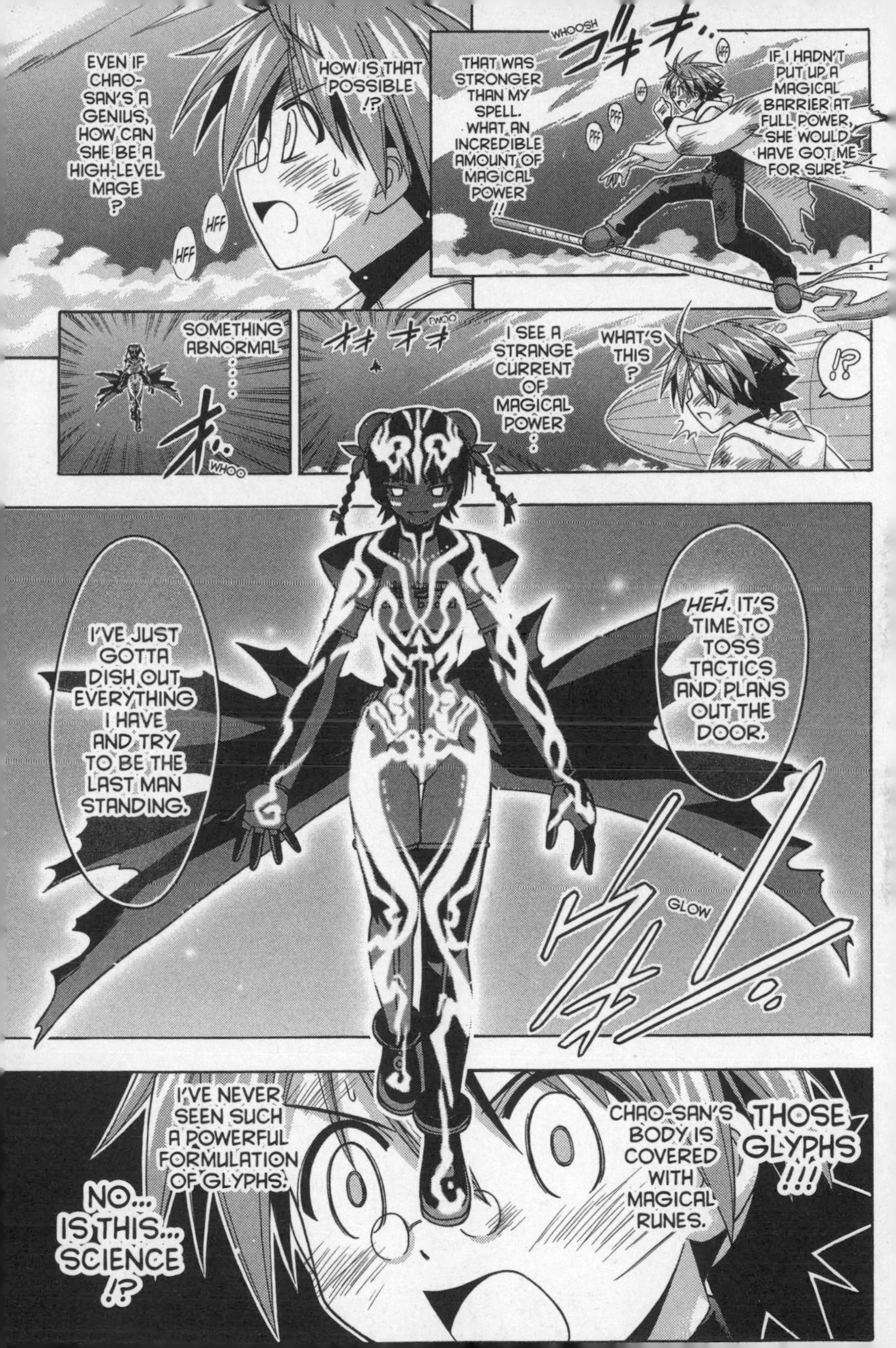
WHOOSH
HFF
PFF
PFF
HFF
IF I HADN'T PUT UP A MAGICAL BARRIER AT FULL POWER, SHE WOULD HAVE GOT ME FOR SURE.
THAT WAS STRONGER THAN MY SPELL. WHAT AN INCREDIBLE AMOUNT OF MAGICAL POWER!!
HOW IS THAT POSSIBLE!?
EVEN IF CHAO-SAN'S A GENIUS, HOW CAN SHE BE A HIGH-LEVEL MAGE?
HFF
HFF
!?
WHAT'S THIS?
I SEE A STRANGE CURRENT OF MAGICAL POWER...
TWOO
SOMETHING ABNORMAL....
WHOO
HEH. IT'S TIME TO TOSS TACTICS AND PLANS OUT THE DOOR.
I'VE JUST GOTTA DISH OUT EVERYTHING I HAVE AND TRY TO BE THE LAST MAN STANDING.
GLOW
THOSE GLYPHS!!!
CHAO-SAN'S BODY IS COVERED WITH MAGICAL RUNES.
I'VE NEVER SEEN SUCH A POWERFUL FORMULATION OF GLYPHS.
NO... IS THIS... SCIENCE!?

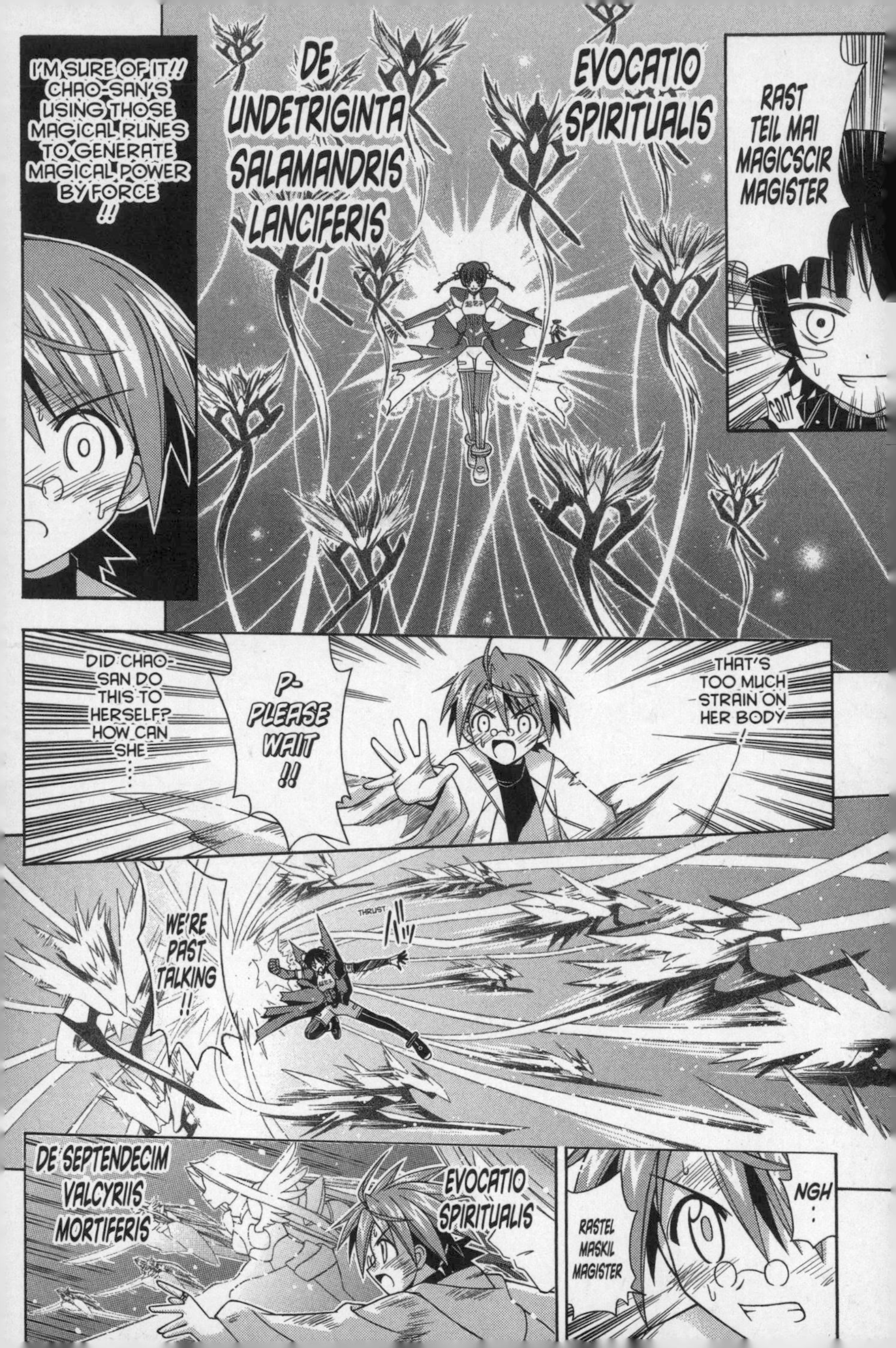

RAST TEIL MAI MAGICSCIR MAGISTER
GRIT
EVOCATIO SPIRITUALIS
DE UNDETRIGINTA SALAMANDRIS LANCIFERIS !
I'M SURE OF IT!! CHAO-SAN'S USING THOSE MAGICAL RUNES TO GENERATE MAGICAL POWER BY FORCE !!
THAT'S TOO MUCH STRAIN ON HER BODY !
P-PLEASE WAIT !!
DID CHAO-SAN DO THIS TO HERSELF? HOW CAN SHE ...
THRUST
WE'RE PAST TALKING !!
NGH :
RASTEL MASKIL MAGISTER
EVOCATIO SPIRITUALIS
DE SEPTENDECIM VALCYRIIS MORTIFERIS

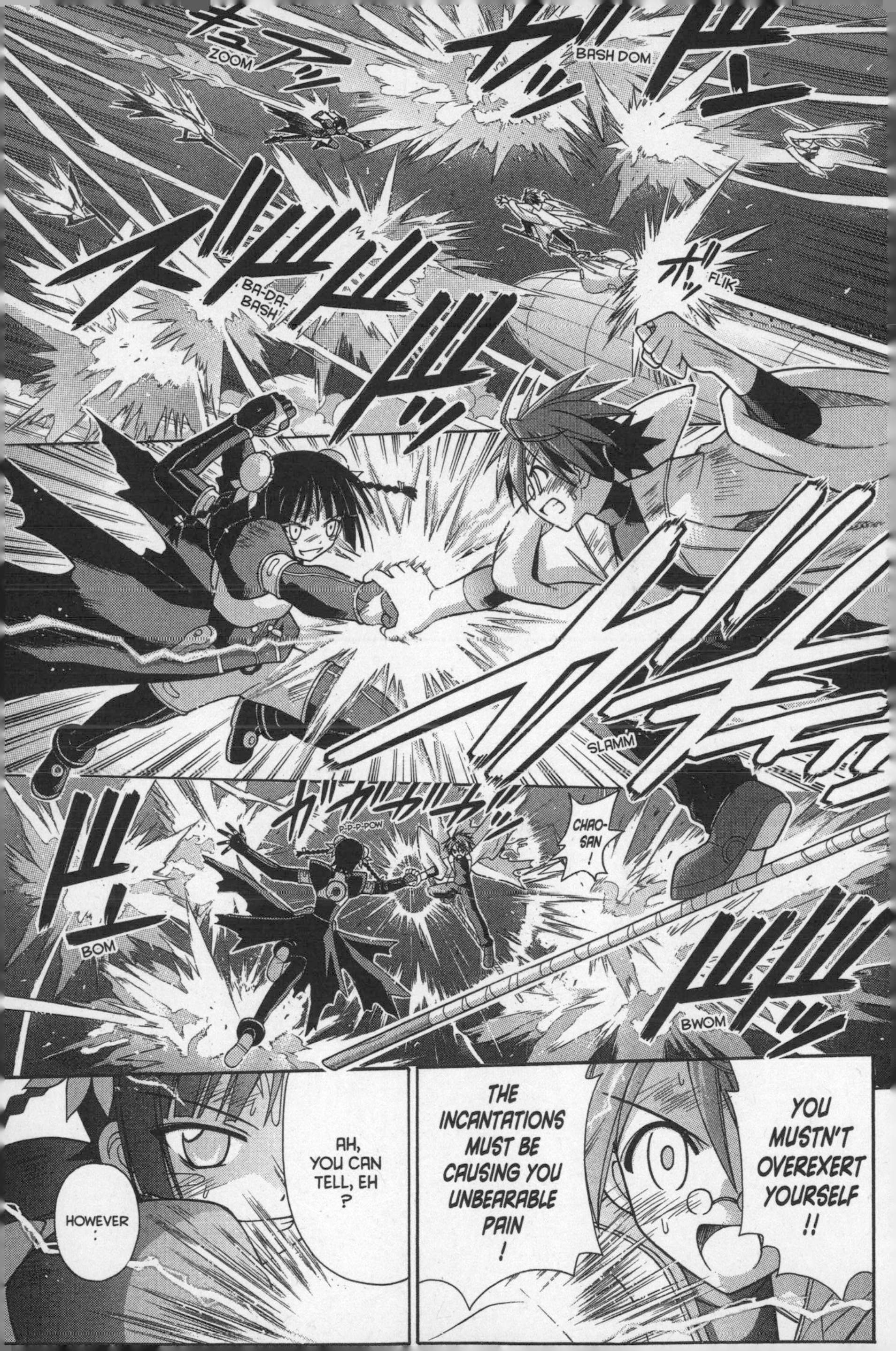
BASH DOM
ZOOM
FLIK
BA-DA-BASH
SLAMM
CHAO-SAN!
BWOM
P-P-P-POW
BOM
YOU MUSTN'T OVEREXERT YOURSELF!!
THE INCANTATIONS MUST BE CAUSING YOU UNBEARABLE PAIN!
AH, YOU CAN TELL, EH?
HOWEVER:

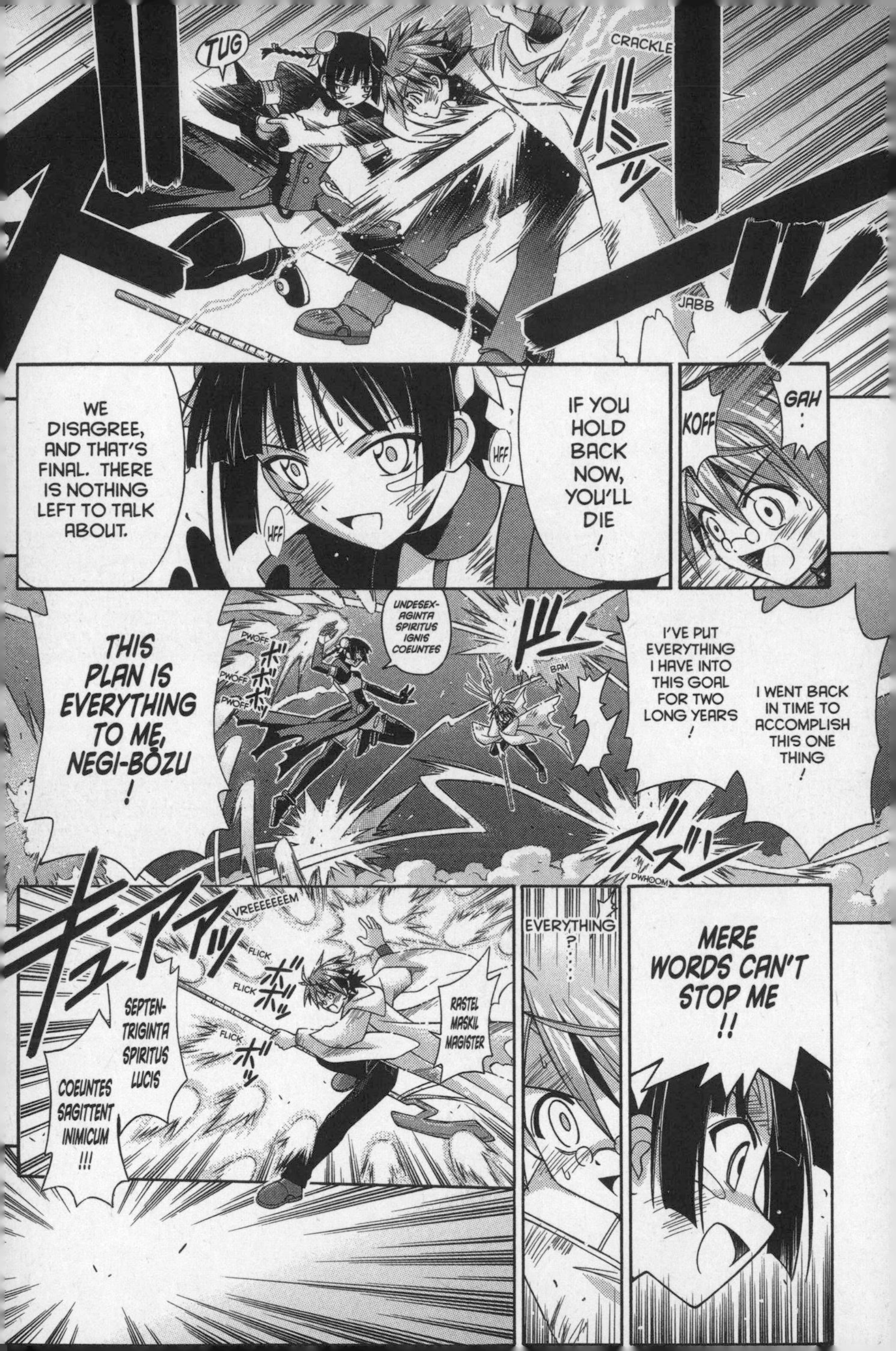
CRACKLE
TUG
JABB
GAH
KOFF
IF YOU HOLD BACK NOW, YOU'LL DIE!
HFF
HFF
WE DISAGREE, AND THAT'S FINAL. THERE IS NOTHING LEFT TO TALK ABOUT.
I WENT BACK IN TIME TO ACCOMPLISH THIS ONE THING!
I'VE PUT EVERYTHING I HAVE INTO THIS GOAL FOR TWO LONG YEARS!
BAM
UNDESEX-AGINTA SPIRITUS IGNIS COEUNTES
PWOFF
PWOFF
PWOFF
THIS PLAN IS EVERYTHING TO ME, NEGI-BÔZU!
DWHOOM
MERE WORDS CAN'T STOP ME!!
EVERYTHING?.....
RASTEL MASKIL MAGISTER
VREEEEEEEM
FLICK
FLICK
FLICK
SEPTEN-TRIGINTA SPIRITUS LUCIS
COEUNTES SAGITTENT INIMICUM!!!

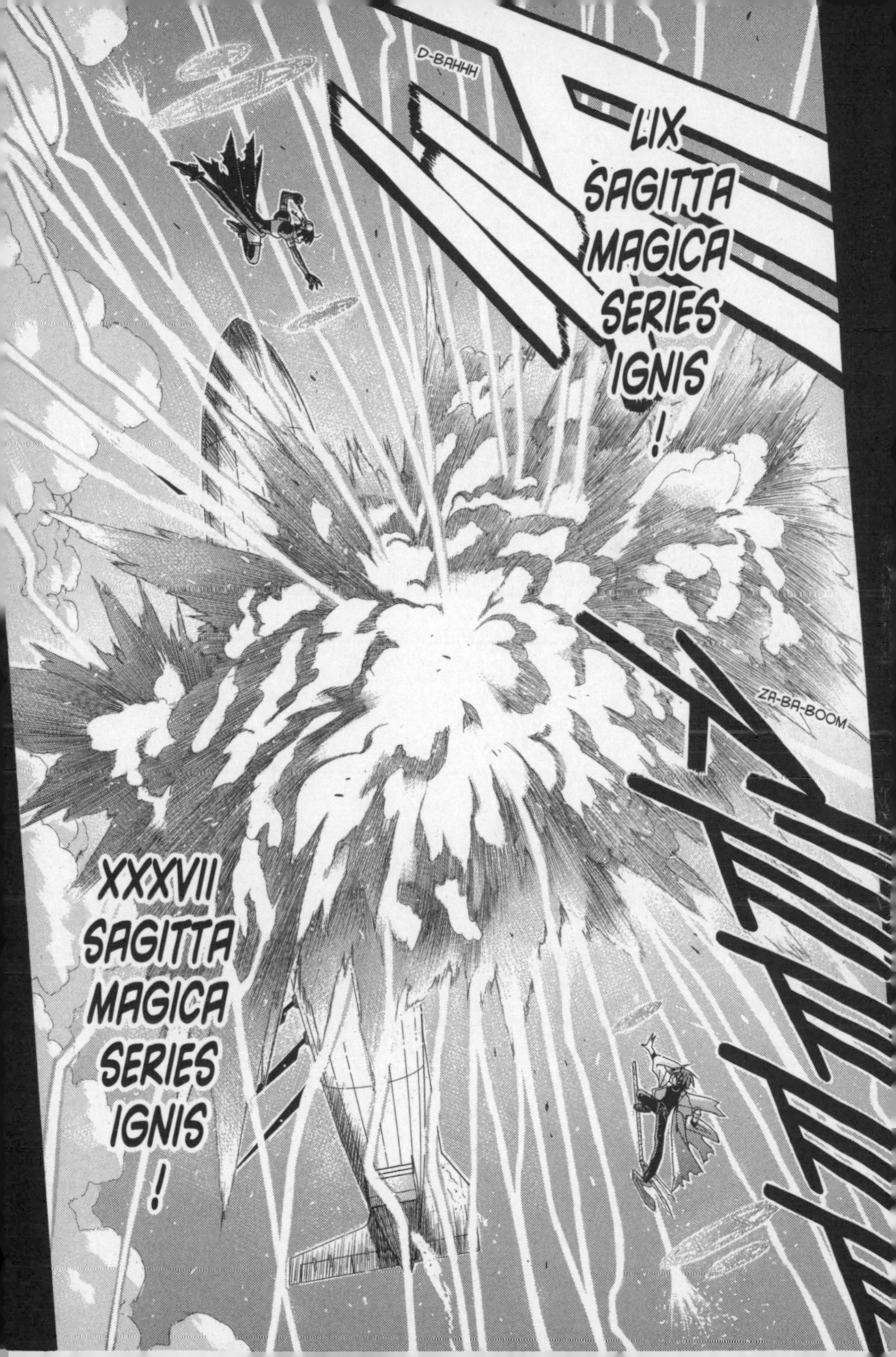
D-BAHHH
LIX SAGITTA MAGICA SERIES IGNIS !
ZA-BA-BOOM
XXXVII SAGITTA MAGICA SERIES IGNIS !

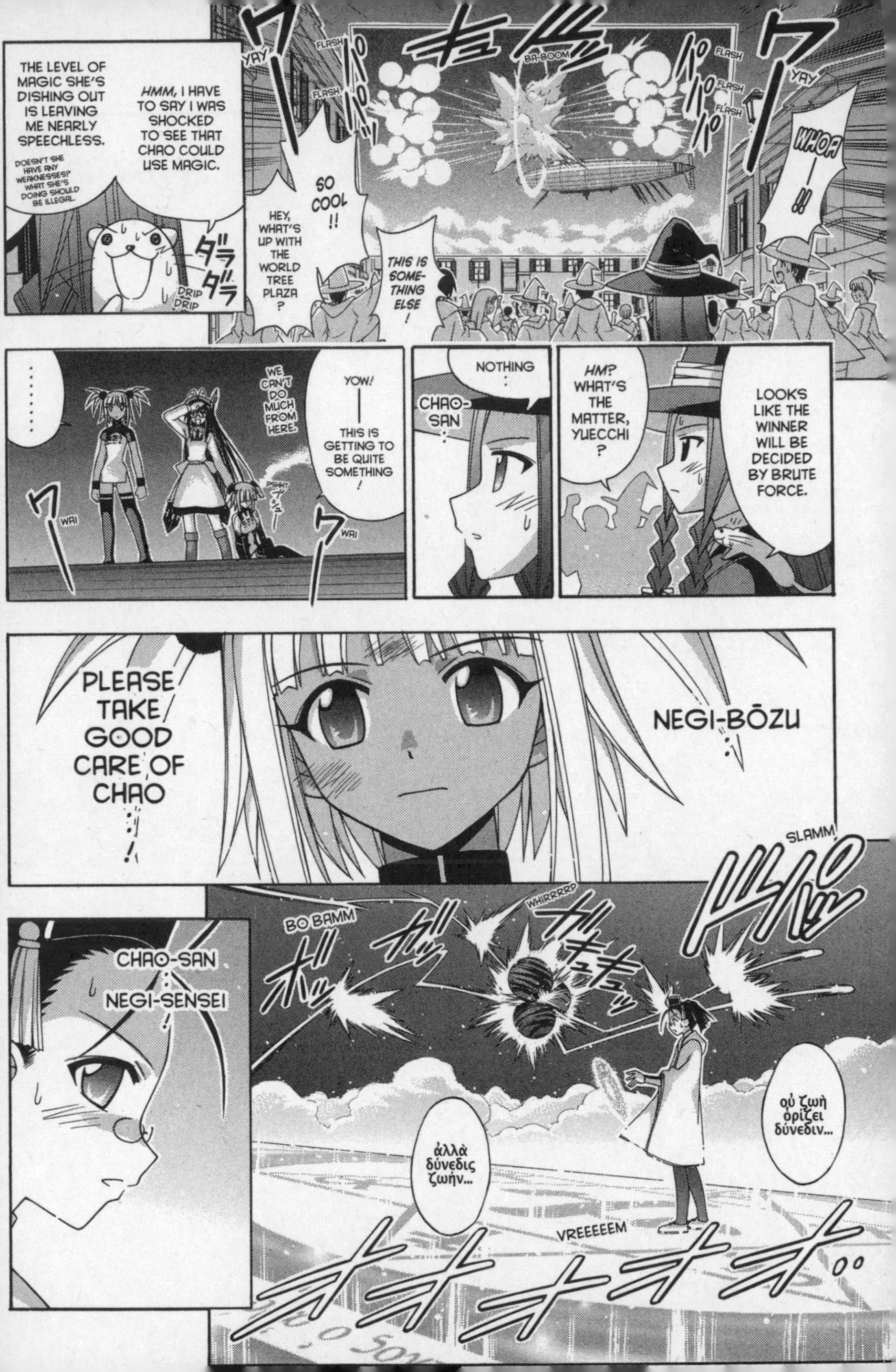

YAY
FLASH
FLASH
BA-BOOM
FLASH
FLASH
FLASH
YAY
WHOA—!!
THIS IS SOMETHING ELSE!
HEY, WHAT'S UP WITH THE WORLD TREE PLAZA?
SO COOL!!
HMM, I HAVE TO SAY I WAS SHOCKED TO SEE THAT CHAO COULD USE MAGIC.
THE LEVEL OF MAGIC SHE'S DISHING OUT IS LEAVING ME NEARLY SPEECHLESS.
DOESN'T SHE HAVE ANY WEAKNESSES? WHAT SHE'S DOING SHOULD BE ILLEGAL.
DRIP DRIP
LOOKS LIKE THE WINNER WILL BE DECIDED BY BRUTE FORCE.
HM? WHAT'S THE MATTER, YUECCHI?
CHAO-SAN...
NOTHING...
YOW! — THIS IS GETTING TO BE QUITE SOMETHING!
WAI
PSHHT
WE CAN'T DO MUCH FROM HERE.
......
WAI
NEGI-BŌZU...
PLEASE TAKE GOOD CARE OF CHAO...!!
SLAMM
WHIRRRRP
BO BAMM
οὐ ζωὴ ὁρίζει δύνεδιν...
ἀλλὰ δύνεδις ζωήν...
VREEEEEM
CHAO-SAN...
NEGI-SENSEI...!

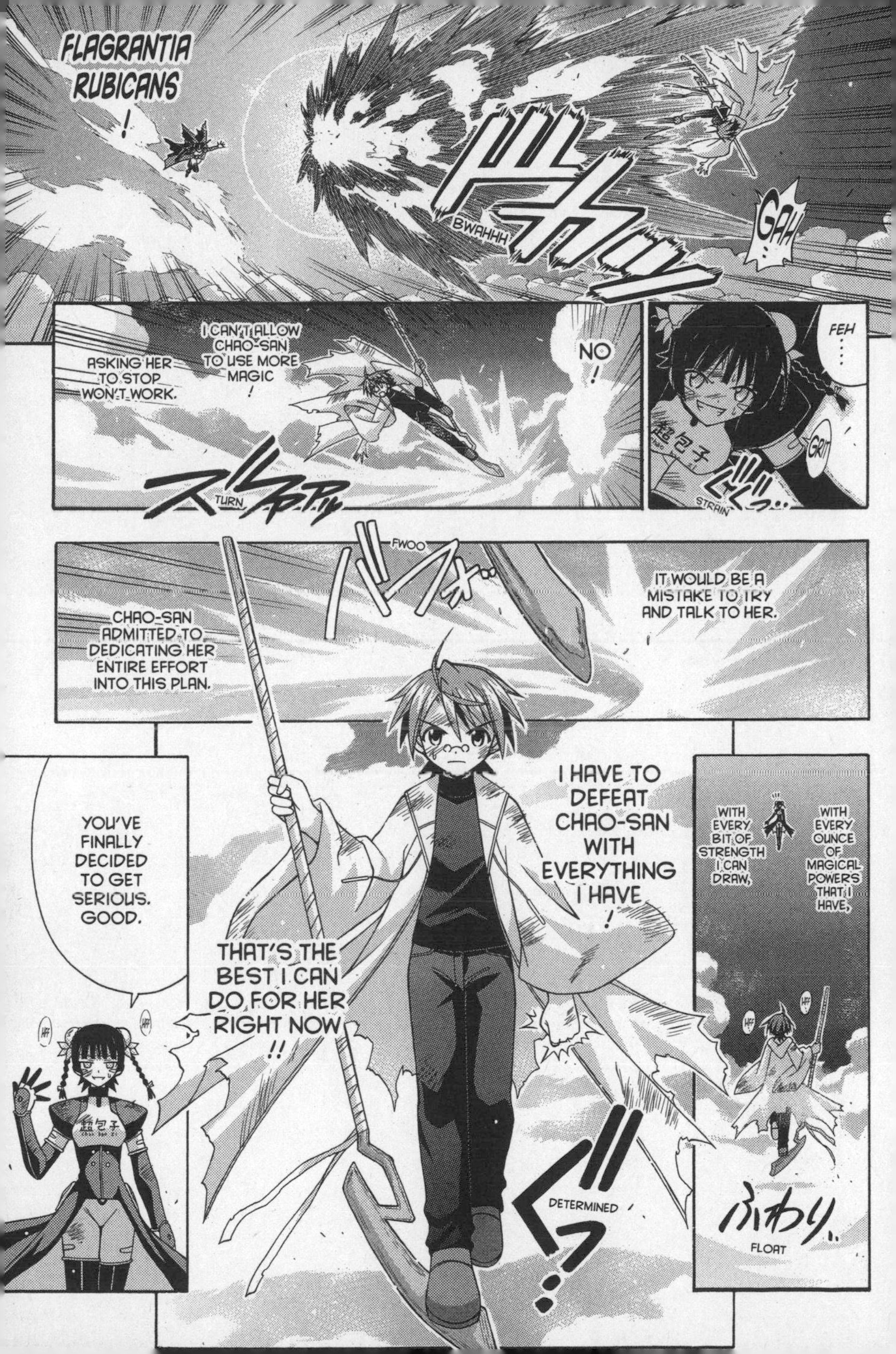
FLAGRANTIA RUBICANS!
BWAHHH
GAH...
FEH...
GRIT
STRAIN
NO!
I CAN'T ALLOW CHAO-SAN TO USE MORE MAGIC!
ASKING HER TO STOP WON'T WORK.
TURN
FWOO
IT WOULD BE A MISTAKE TO TRY AND TALK TO HER.
CHAO-SAN ADMITTED TO DEDICATING HER ENTIRE EFFORT INTO THIS PLAN.
WITH EVERY OUNCE OF MAGICAL POWERS THAT I HAVE,
WITH EVERY BIT OF STRENGTH I CAN DRAW,
FLOAT
I HAVE TO DEFEAT CHAO-SAN WITH EVERYTHING I HAVE!
THAT'S THE BEST I CAN DO FOR HER RIGHT NOW!!
DETERMINED
YOU'VE FINALLY DECIDED TO GET SERIOUS. GOOD.

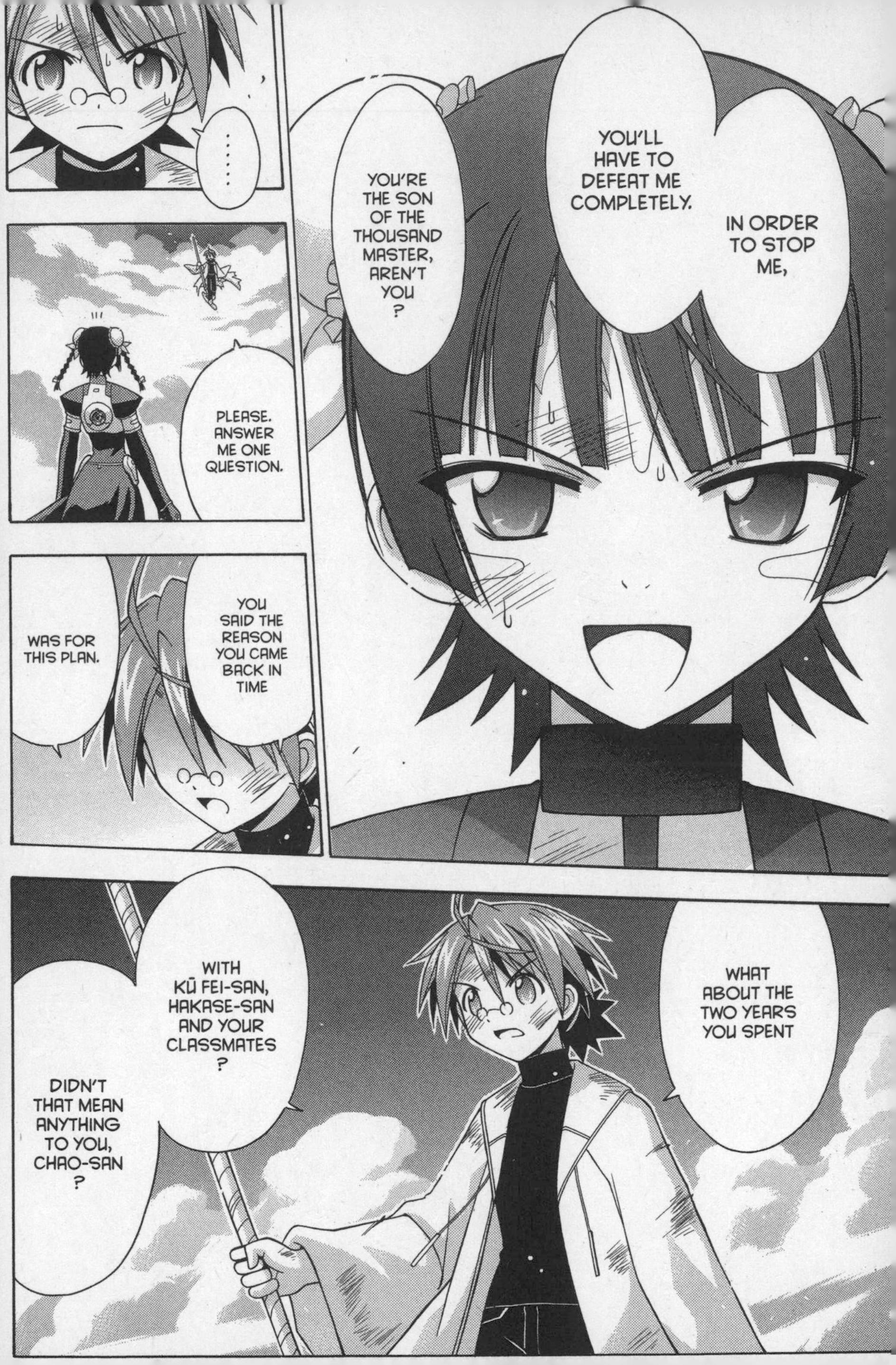
IN ORDER TO STOP ME,
YOU'LL HAVE TO DEFEAT ME COMPLETELY.
YOU'RE THE SON OF THE THOUSAND MASTER, AREN'T YOU?
......
PLEASE. ANSWER ME ONE QUESTION.
YOU SAID THE REASON YOU CAME BACK IN TIME
WAS FOR THIS PLAN.
WHAT ABOUT THE TWO YEARS YOU SPENT
WITH KŪ FEI-SAN, HAKASE-SAN AND YOUR CLASSMATES?
DIDN'T THAT MEAN ANYTHING TO YOU, CHAO-SAN?

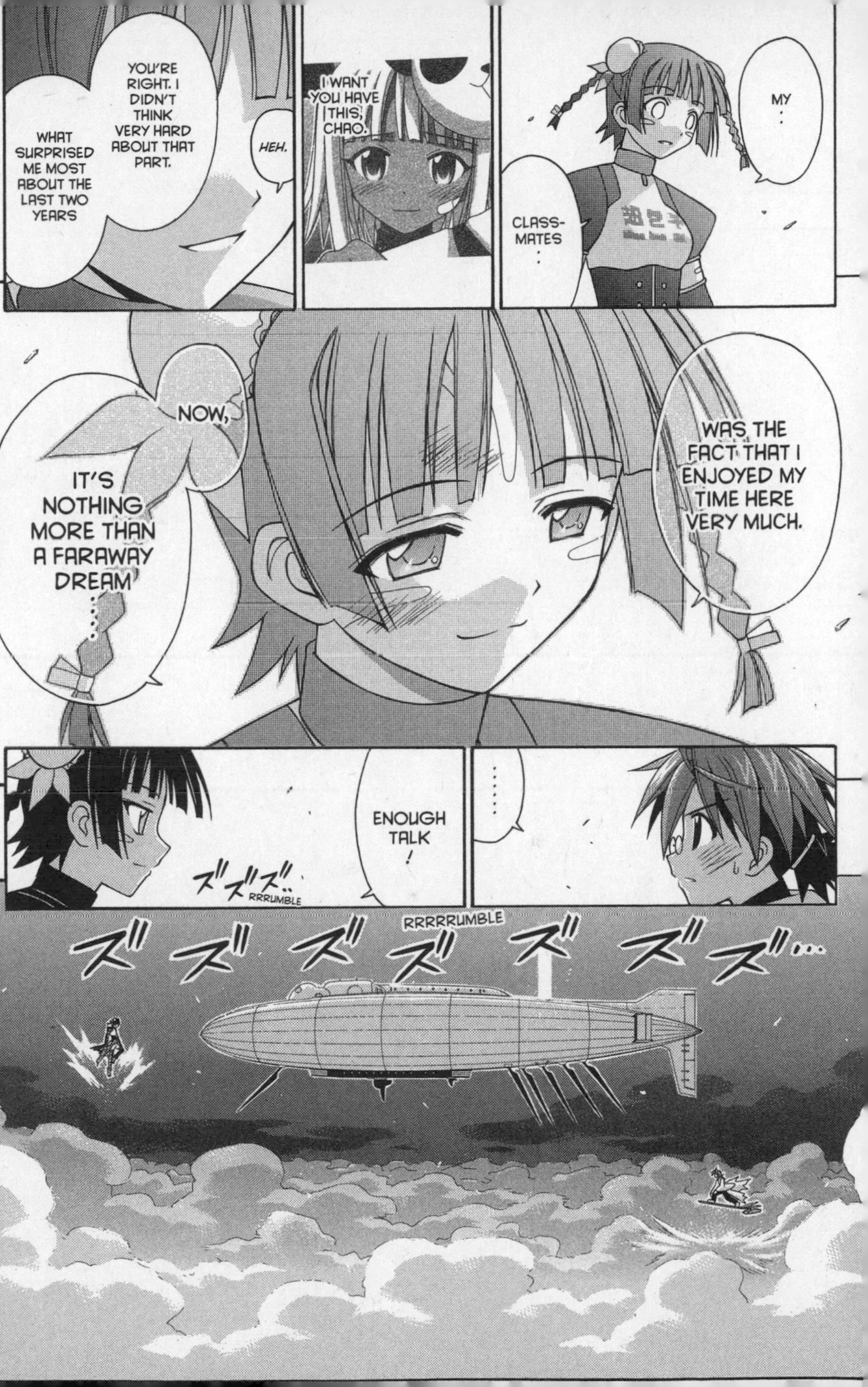
MY . . CLASS-MATES . .
I WANT YOU HAVE THIS, CHAO.
HEH.
YOU'RE RIGHT. I DIDN'T THINK VERY HARD ABOUT THAT PART.
WHAT SURPRISED ME MOST ABOUT THE LAST TWO YEARS
WAS THE FACT THAT I ENJOYED MY TIME HERE VERY MUCH.
NOW,
IT'S NOTHING MORE THAN A FARAWAY DREAM . . .
......
ENOUGH TALK!
ズズズ.. RRRUMBLE
RRRRRUMBLE
ズズズズズズ...

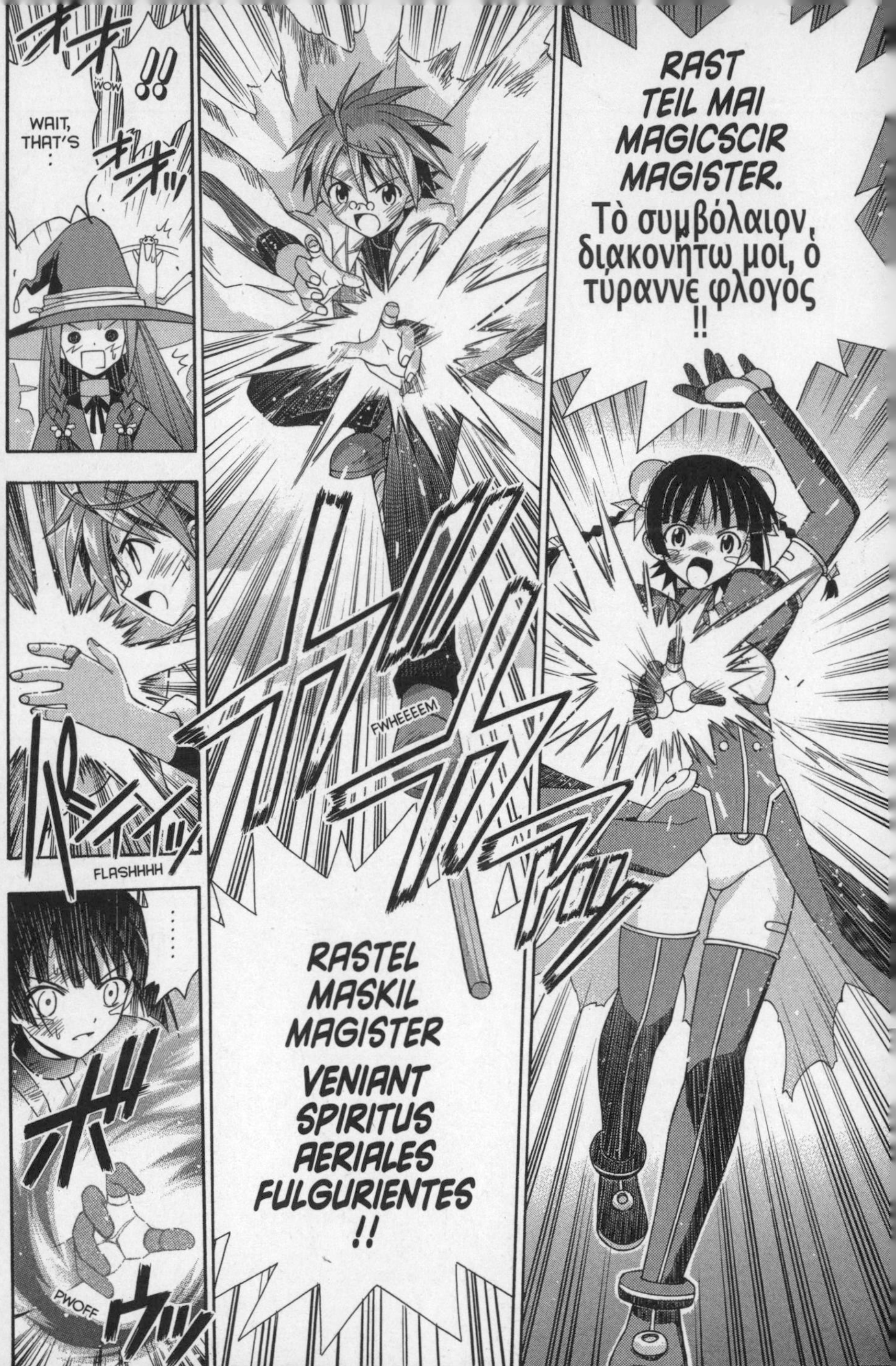
RAST TEIL MAI MAGICSCIR MAGISTER.
Τὸ συμβόλαιον, διακονήτω μοι, ὁ τύραννε φλογός !!
RASTEL MASKIL MAGISTER
VENIANT SPIRITUS AERIALES FULGURIENTES !!
FWHEEEM
WOW
WAIT, THAT'S
FLASHHHH
......
PWOFF

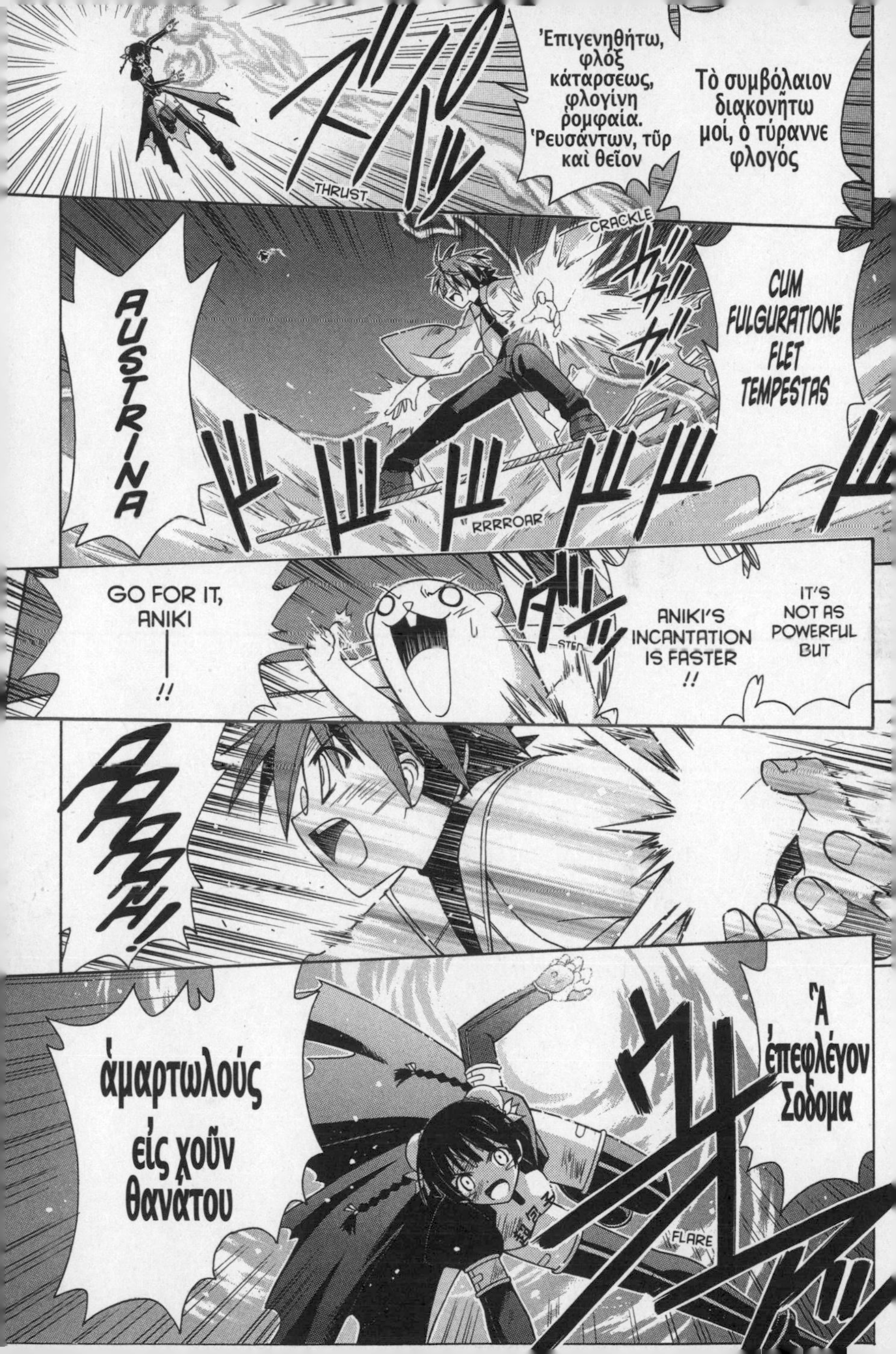
Τὸ συμβόλαιον διακονῆτω μοί, ὁ τύραννε φλογός
Ἐπιγενηθήτω, φλὸξ κάταρσεως, φλογίνη ῥομφαία. Ῥευσάντων, τῦρ καὶ θεῖον
THRUST
CRACKLE
CUM FULGURATIONE FLET TEMPESTAS
AUSTRINA
RRRROAR
IT'S NOT AS POWERFUL BUT
ANIKI'S INCANTATION IS FASTER !!
GO FOR IT, ANIKI —— !!
Ἁ ἐπεφλέγον Σοδομα
FLARE
ἁμαρτωλούς εἰς χοῦν θανάτου

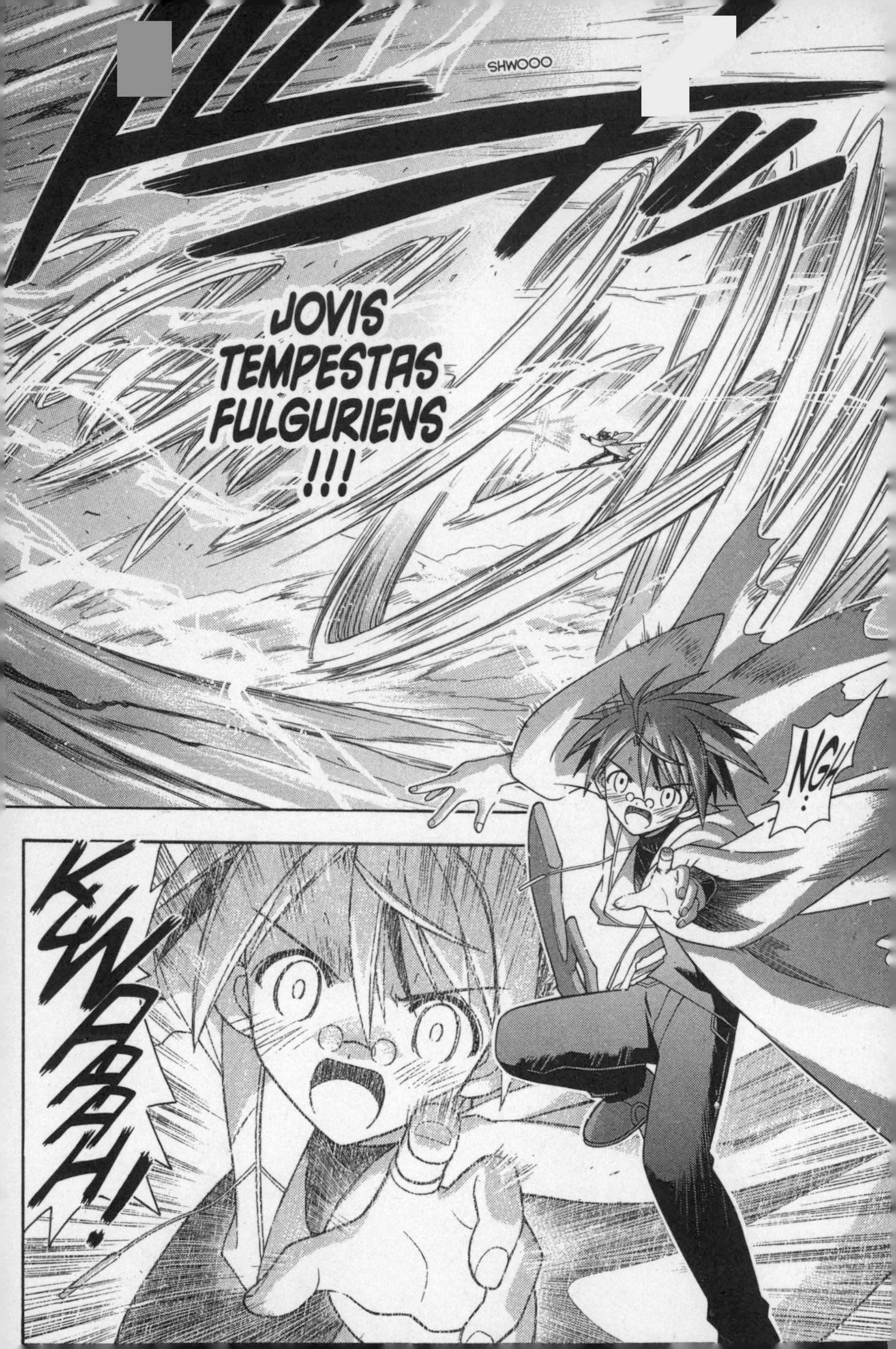
SHWOOO
JOVIS TEMPESTAS FULGURIENS !!!
NGH!
KWAAAH!

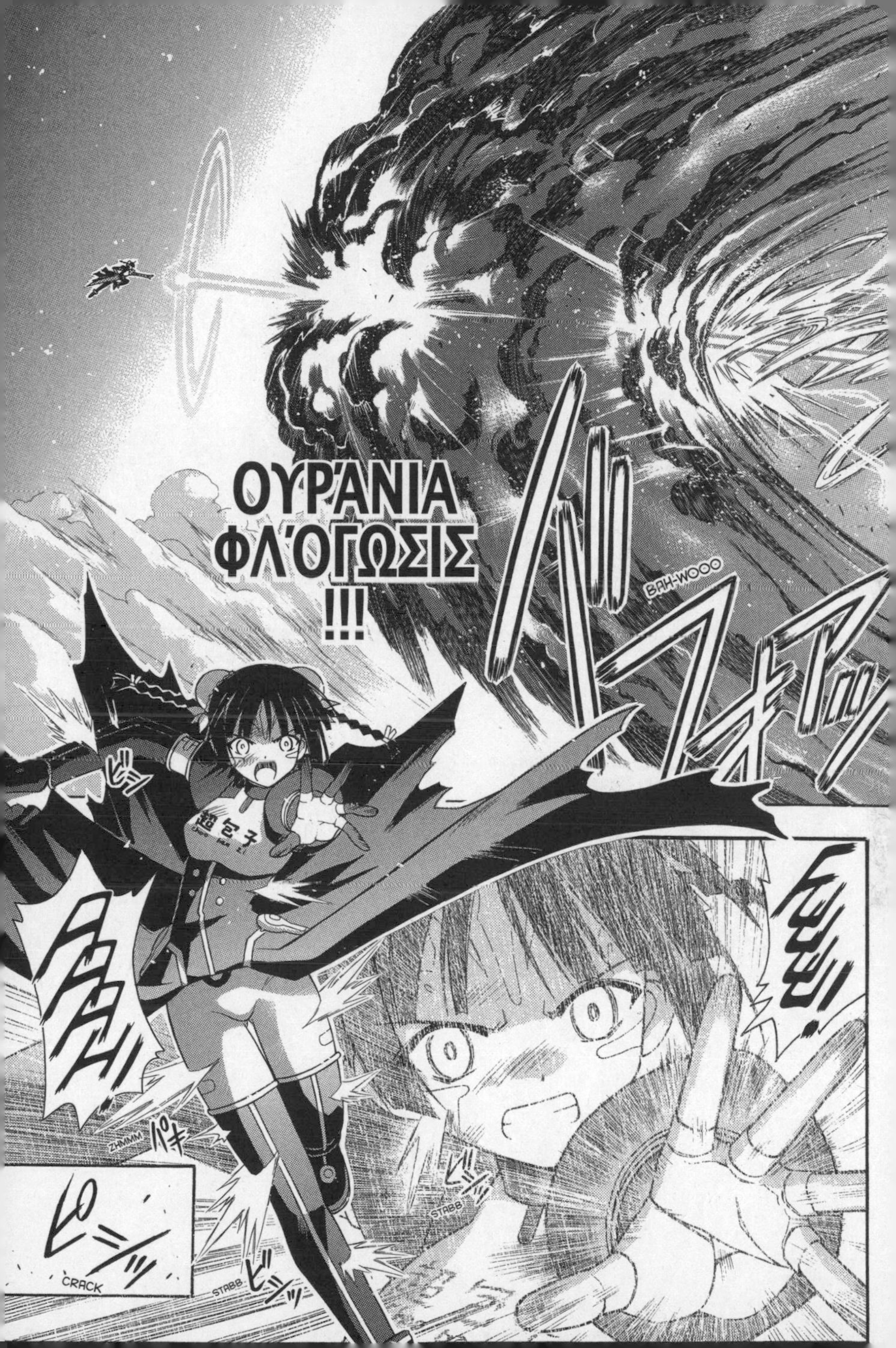

ΟΥΡΆΝΙΑ ΦΛΌΓΩΣΙΣ!!!
BAH-WOOO
STABB
AAAH!
ZHMMM
CRACK
STABB

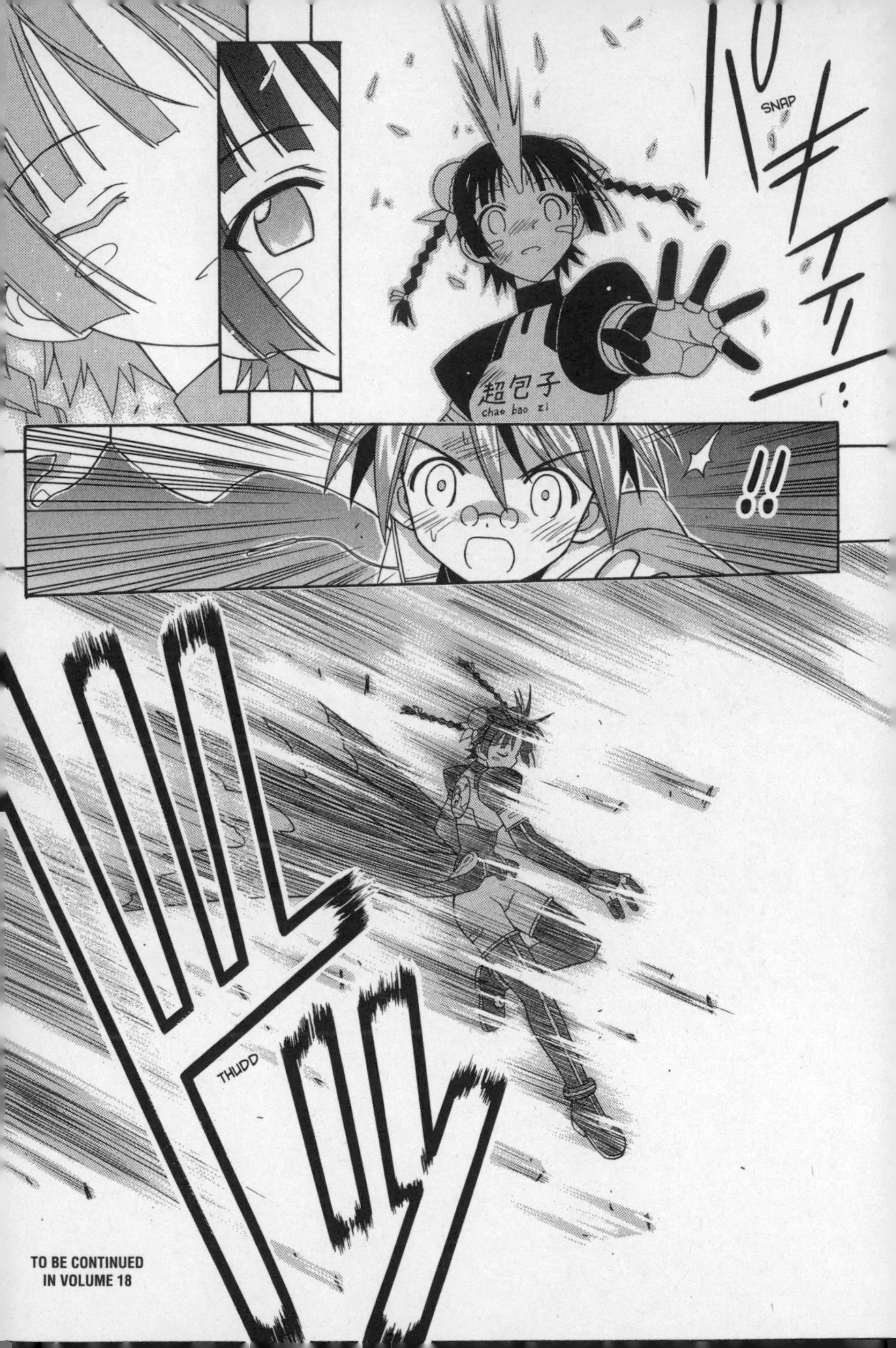
SNAP
超包子
chao bao zi
!!
THUDD
TO BE CONTINUED
IN VOLUME 18

魔法先生ネギま！

MAGISTER NEGI MAGI

18

Ken Akamatsu

赤松 健

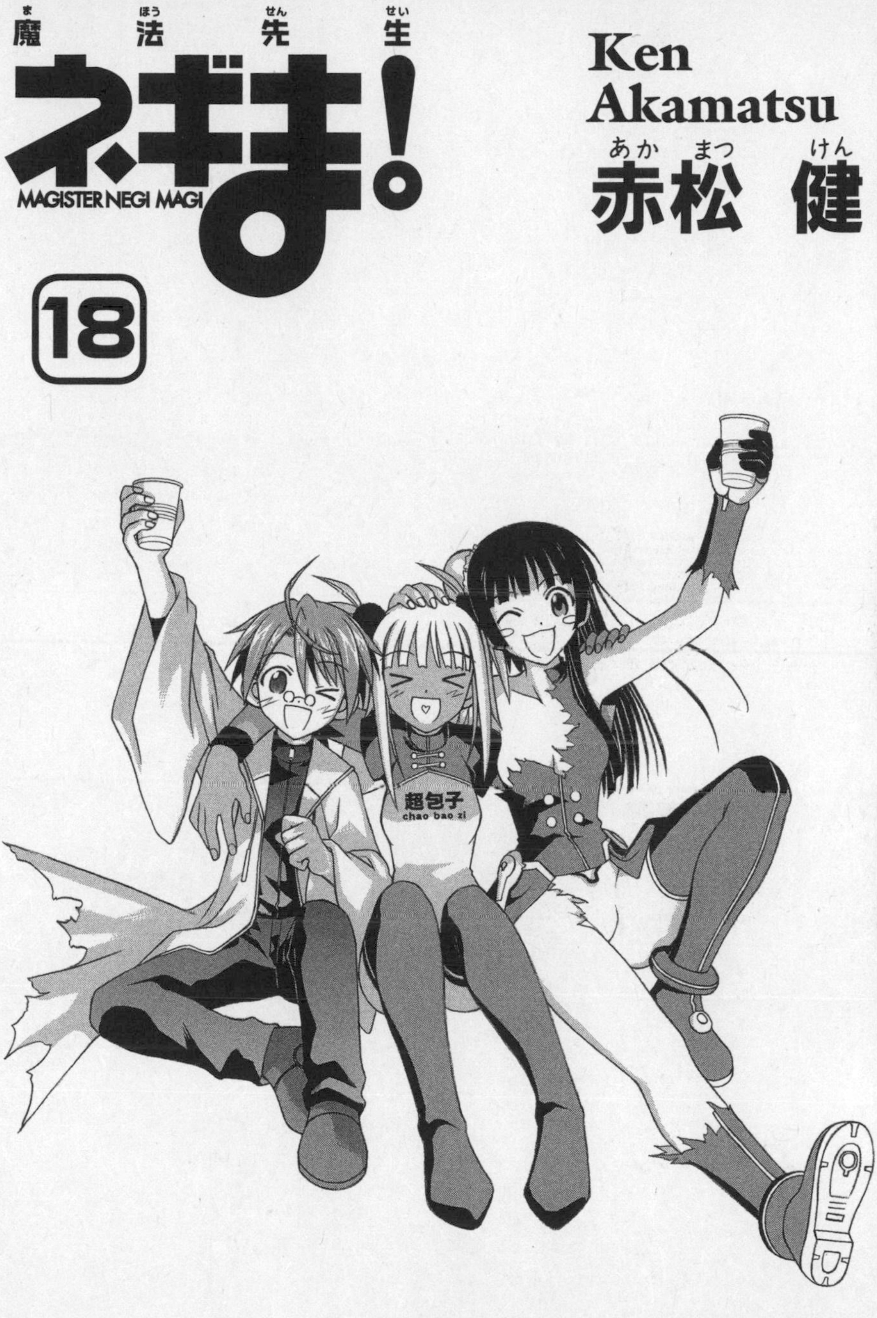
超包子
chao bao zi

CONTENTS

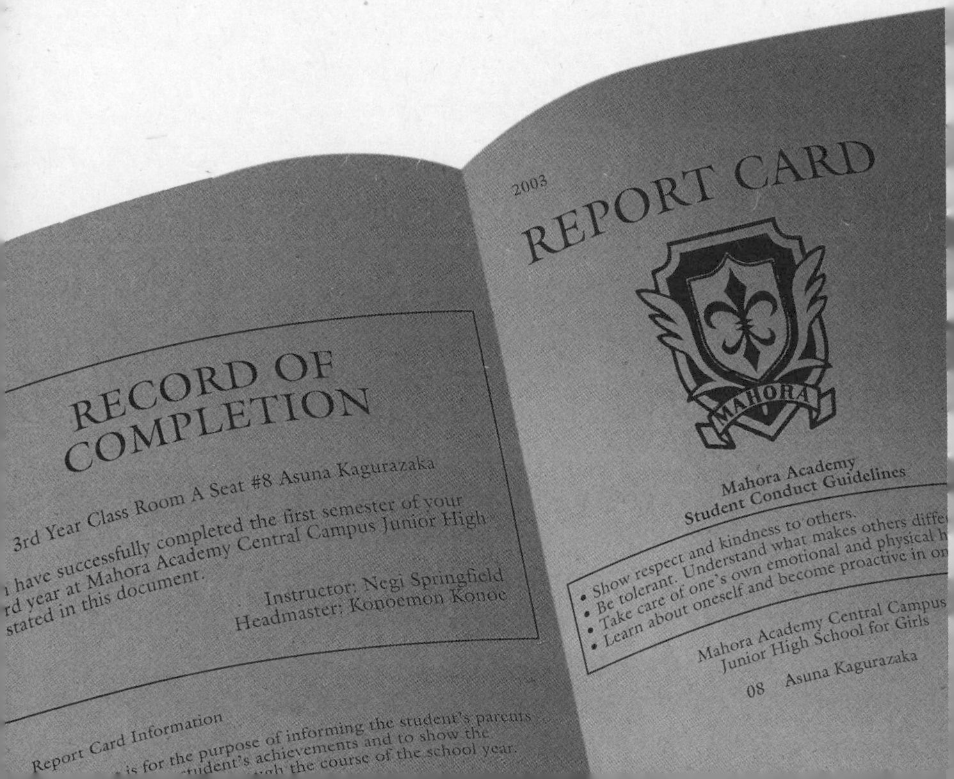

2003
REPORT CARD
MAHORA
Mahora Academy
Student Conduct Guidelines
• Show respect and kindness to others.
• Be tolerant. Understand what makes others diffe
• Take care of one's own emotional and physical h
• Learn about oneself and become proactive in on
Mahora Academy Central Campus
Junior High School for Girls
08 Asuna Kagurazaka
RECORD OF COMPLETION
3rd Year Class Room A Seat #8 Asuna Kagurazaka
have successfully completed the first semester of your
rd year at Mahora Academy Central Campus Junior High
stated in this document.
Instructor: Negi Springfield
Headmaster: Konoemon Konoe
Report Card Information

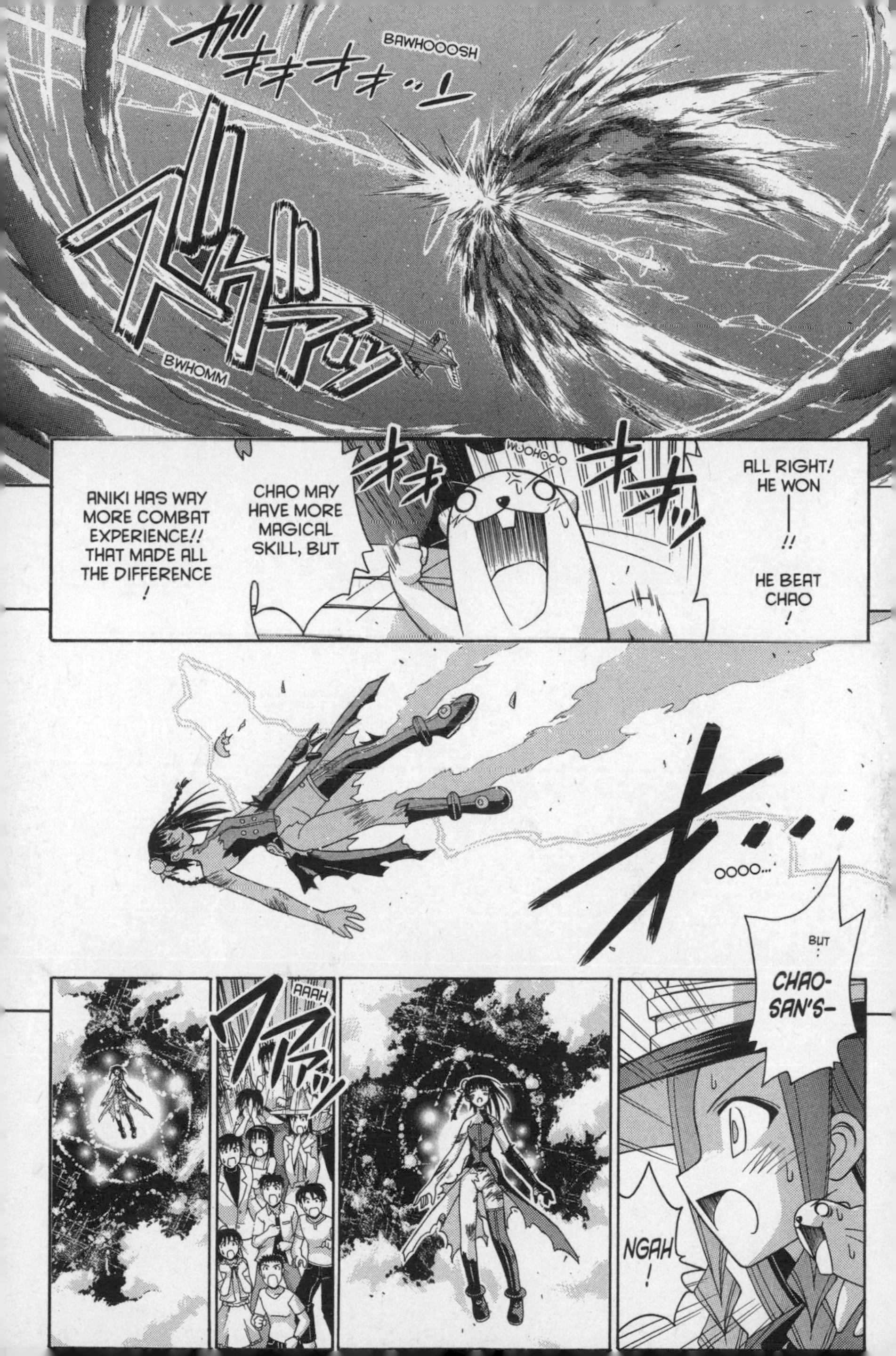
BAWHOOOSH
BWHOMM
ALL RIGHT! HE WON —!!
HE BEAT CHAO!
WOHOOO
CHAO MAY HAVE MORE MAGICAL SKILL, BUT
ANIKI HAS WAY MORE COMBAT EXPERIENCE!! THAT MADE ALL THE DIFFERENCE!
OOOO...
BUT:
CHAO-SAN'S-
NGAH!
AAAH

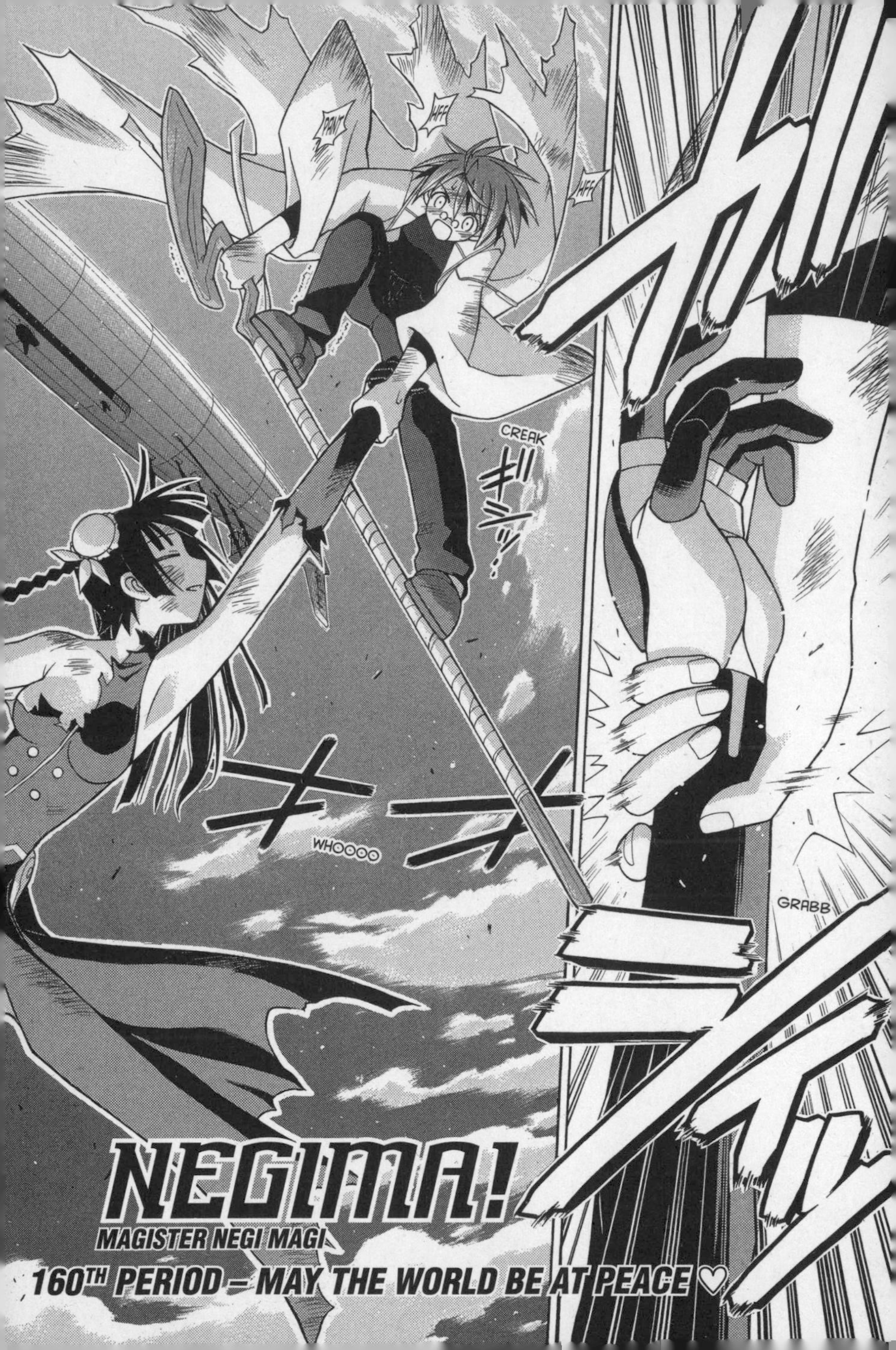
PANT
HFF
HFF
CREAK
WHOOOO
GRABB
NEGIMA!
MAGISTER NEGI MAGI
160TH PERIOD – MAY THE WORLD BE AT PEACE ♡

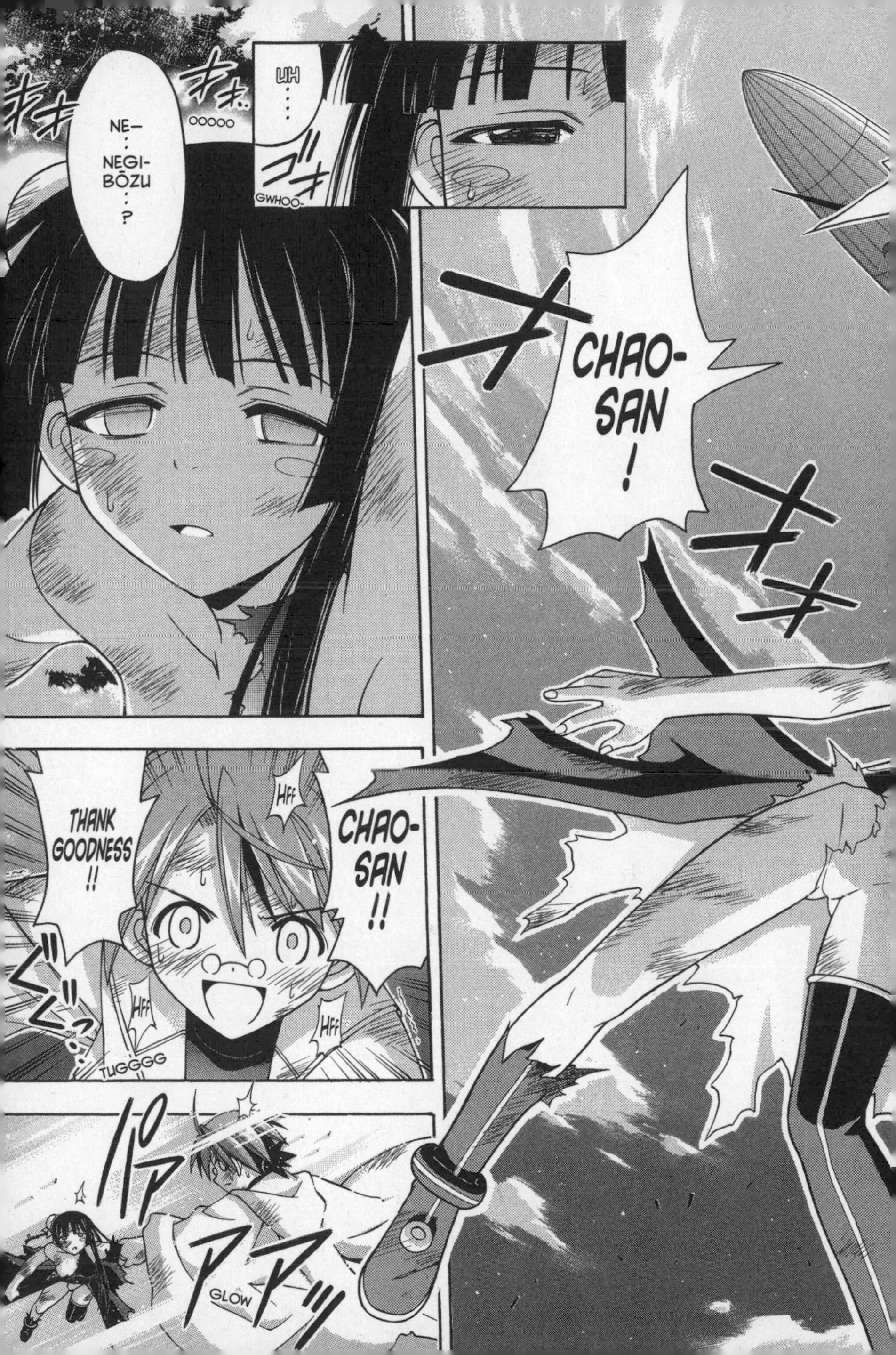
CHAO-SAN!
UH......
GWHOO-
OOOOO
NE—...NEGI-BŌZU...?
CHAO-SAN!!
HFF
THANK GOODNESS!!
HFF
HFF
TUGGGG
GLOW

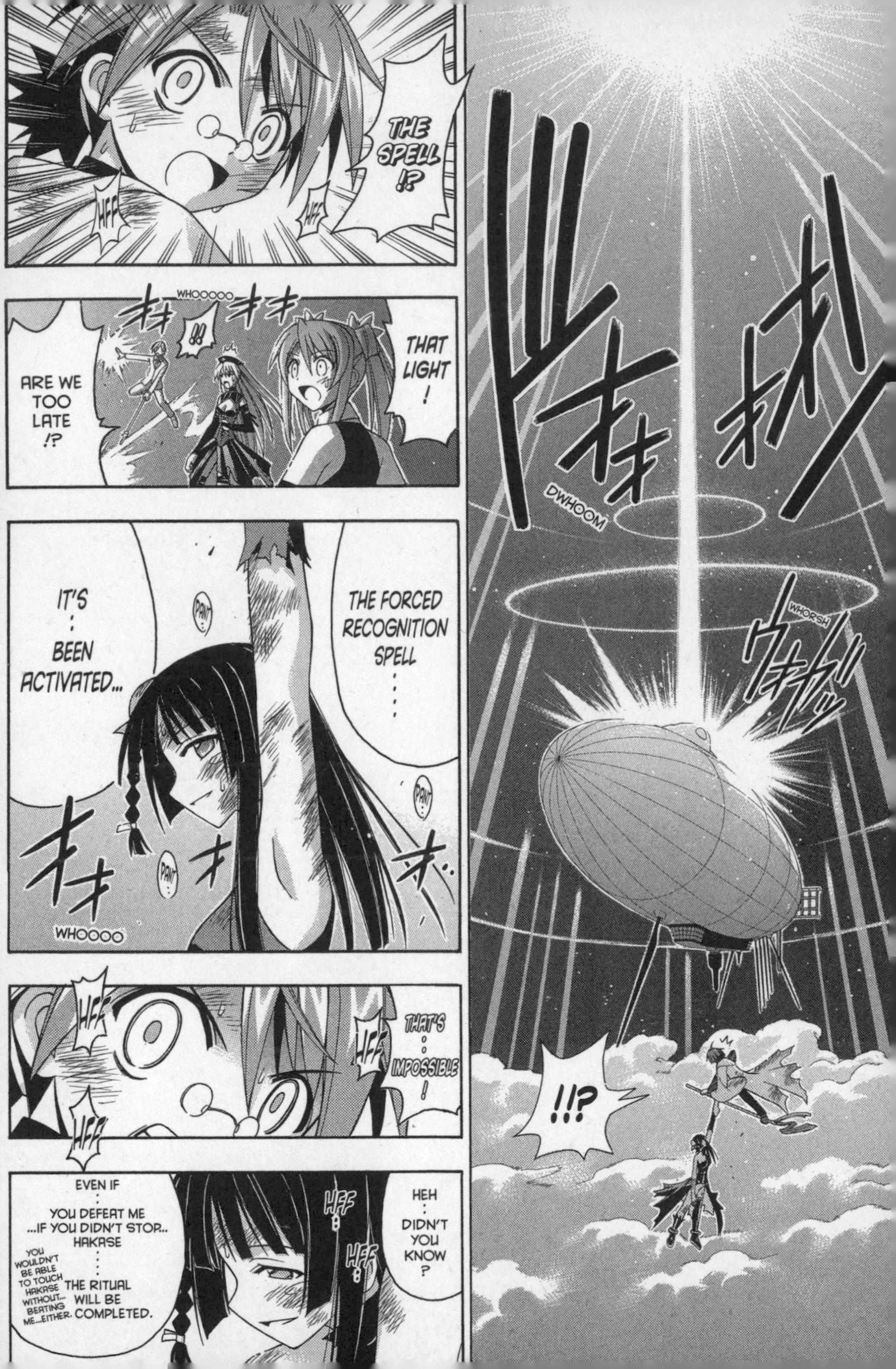
DWHOOM
WHORSH
!!?
THE SPELL !?
HFF
HFF
WHOOOOO
THAT LIGHT !
!!
ARE WE TOO LATE !?
THE FORCED RECOGNITION SPELL ....
PANT
IT'S : BEEN ACTIVATED...
PANT
PANT
WHOOOO
THAT'S : IMPOSSIBLE !
HFF
HFF
HFF
HEH : DIDN'T YOU KNOW ?
HFF
HFF
EVEN IF : YOU DEFEAT ME ...IF YOU DIDN'T STOP.. HAKASE : THE RITUAL WILL BE COMPLETED.
YOU WOULDN'T BE ABLE TO TOUCH HAKASE WITHOUT... BEATING ME...EITHER.

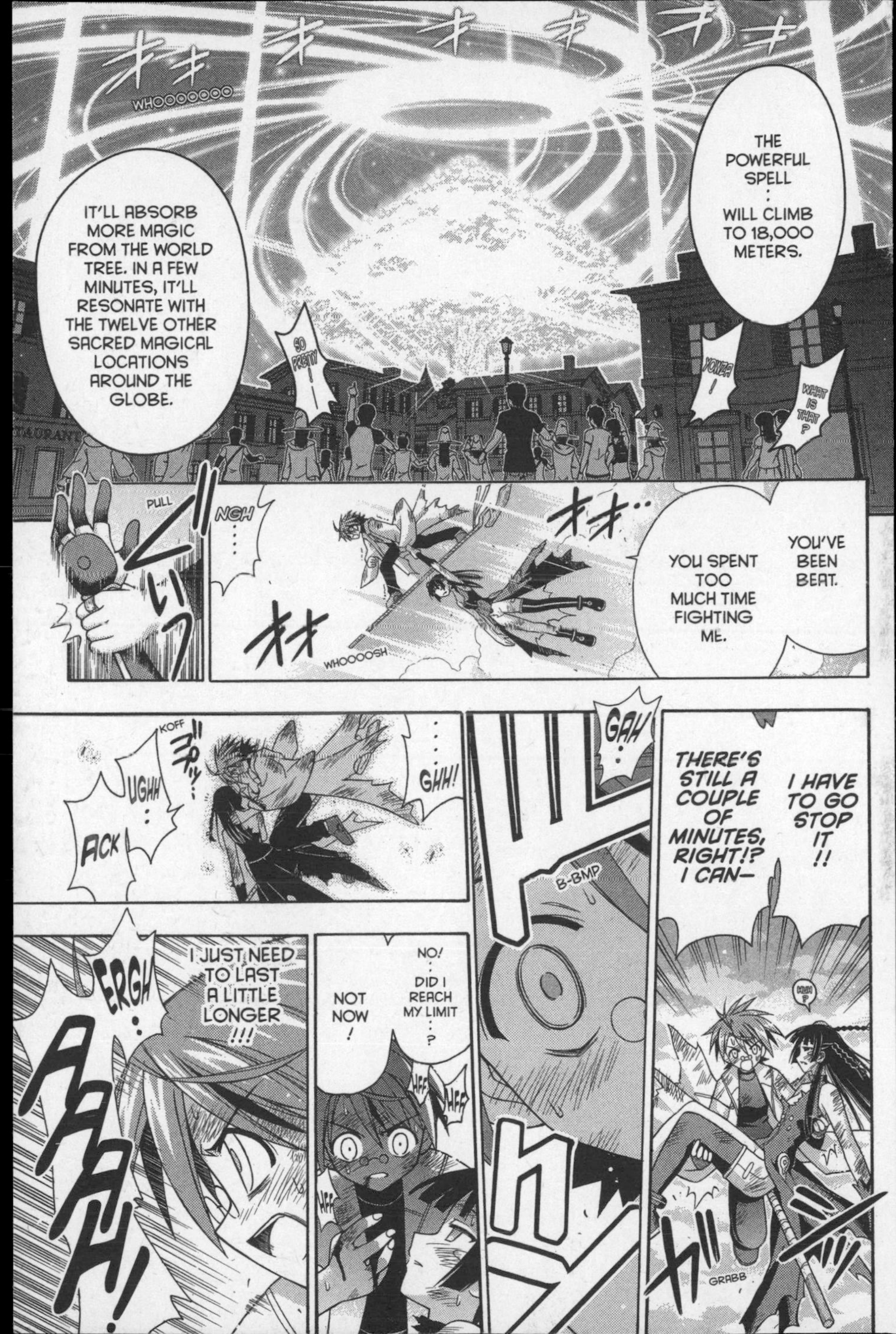
THE POWERFUL SPELL : WILL CLIMB TO 18,000 METERS.
WHAT IS THAT?
YOWZA!
SO PRETTY!
WHOOOOOOOO
IT'LL ABSORB MORE MAGIC FROM THE WORLD TREE. IN A FEW MINUTES, IT'LL RESONATE WITH THE TWELVE OTHER SACRED MAGICAL LOCATIONS AROUND THE GLOBE.
YOU'VE BEEN BEAT.
YOU SPENT TOO MUCH TIME FIGHTING ME.
NGH...
WHOOOOSH
PULL
I HAVE TO GO STOP IT!!
THERE'S STILL A COUPLE OF MINUTES, RIGHT!? I CAN—
GAH!
B-BMP
GHH!
KOFF
UGHH: ACK
HUH?
GRABB
NO! DID I REACH MY LIMIT...?
NOT NOW!
HFF
HFF
HFF
I JUST NEED TO LAST A LITTLE LONGER!!!
ERGH...
AAAAH!!

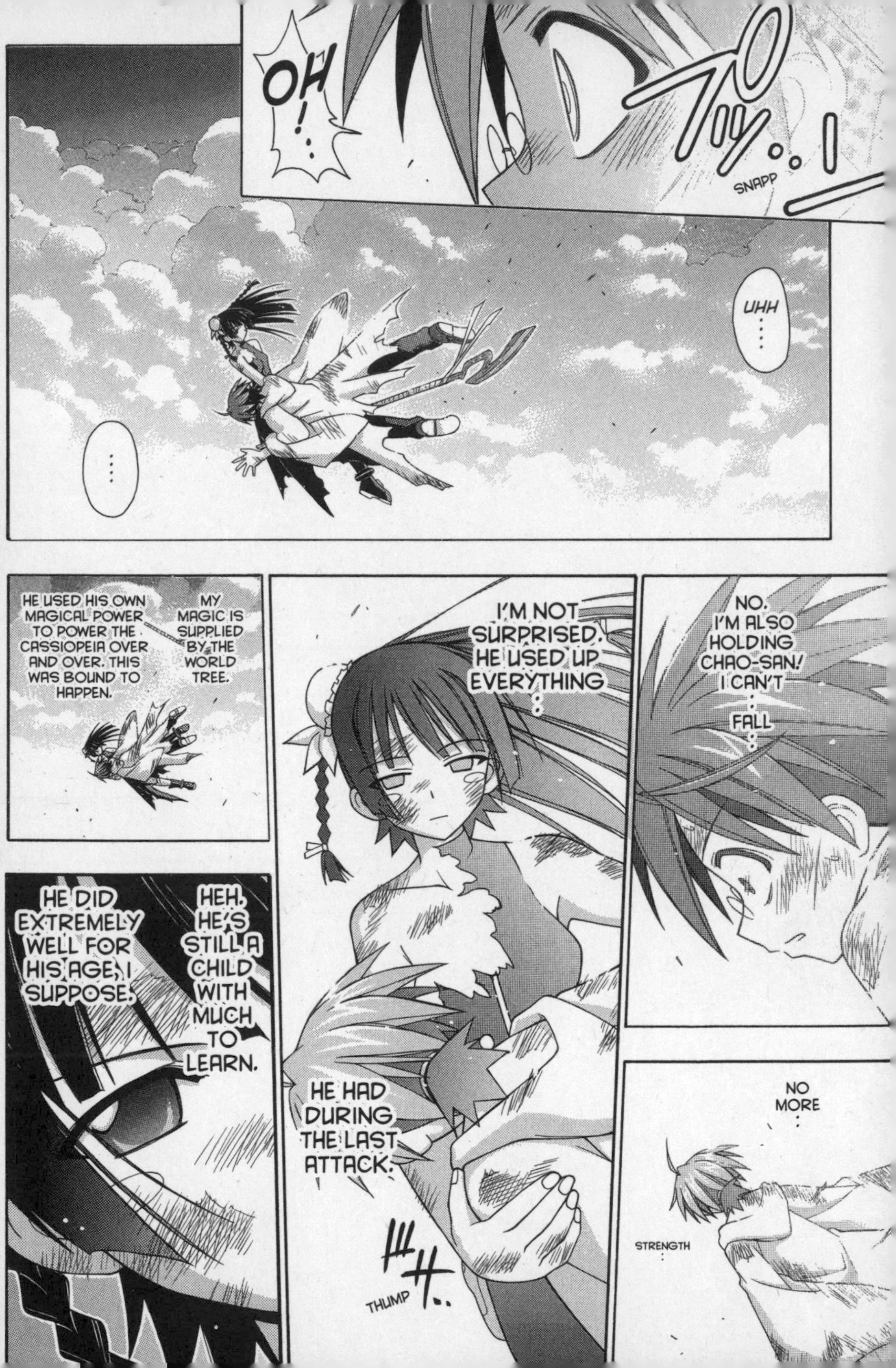
SNAPP
OH! ...
UHH ...
...
NO. I'M ALSO HOLDING CHAO-SAN! I CAN'T ... FALL ...
NO MORE ...
STRENGTH ...
I'M NOT SURPRISED. HE USED UP EVERYTHING ...
HE HAD DURING THE LAST ATTACK.
THUMP
MY MAGIC IS SUPPLIED BY THE WORLD TREE.
HE USED HIS OWN MAGICAL POWER TO POWER THE CASSIOPEIA OVER AND OVER. THIS WAS BOUND TO HAPPEN.
HEH. HE'S STILL A CHILD WITH MUCH TO LEARN.
HE DID EXTREMELY WELL FOR HIS AGE, I SUPPOSE.

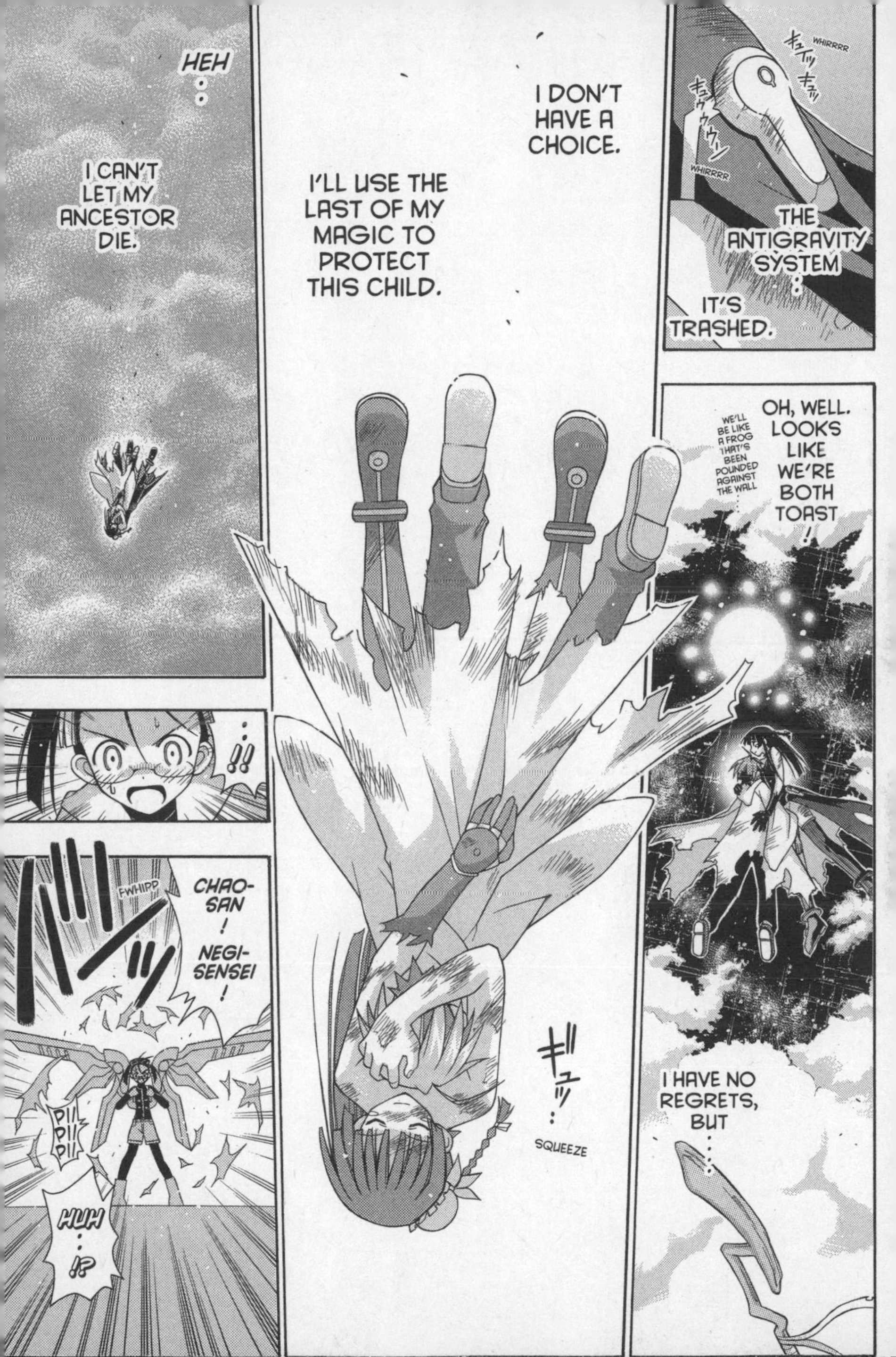
WHIRRRR
WHIRRRR
THE ANTIGRAVITY SYSTEM...
IT'S TRASHED.
OH, WELL. LOOKS LIKE WE'RE BOTH TOAST!
WE'LL BE LIKE A FROG THAT'S BEEN POUNDED AGAINST THE WALL...
I HAVE NO REGRETS, BUT...
I DON'T HAVE A CHOICE.
I'LL USE THE LAST OF MY MAGIC TO PROTECT THIS CHILD.
ギュッ
SQUEEZE
HEH...
I CAN'T LET MY ANCESTOR DIE.
...!!
FWHIPP
CHAO-SAN! NEGI-SENSEI!
P!! P!! P!!
HUH...!?

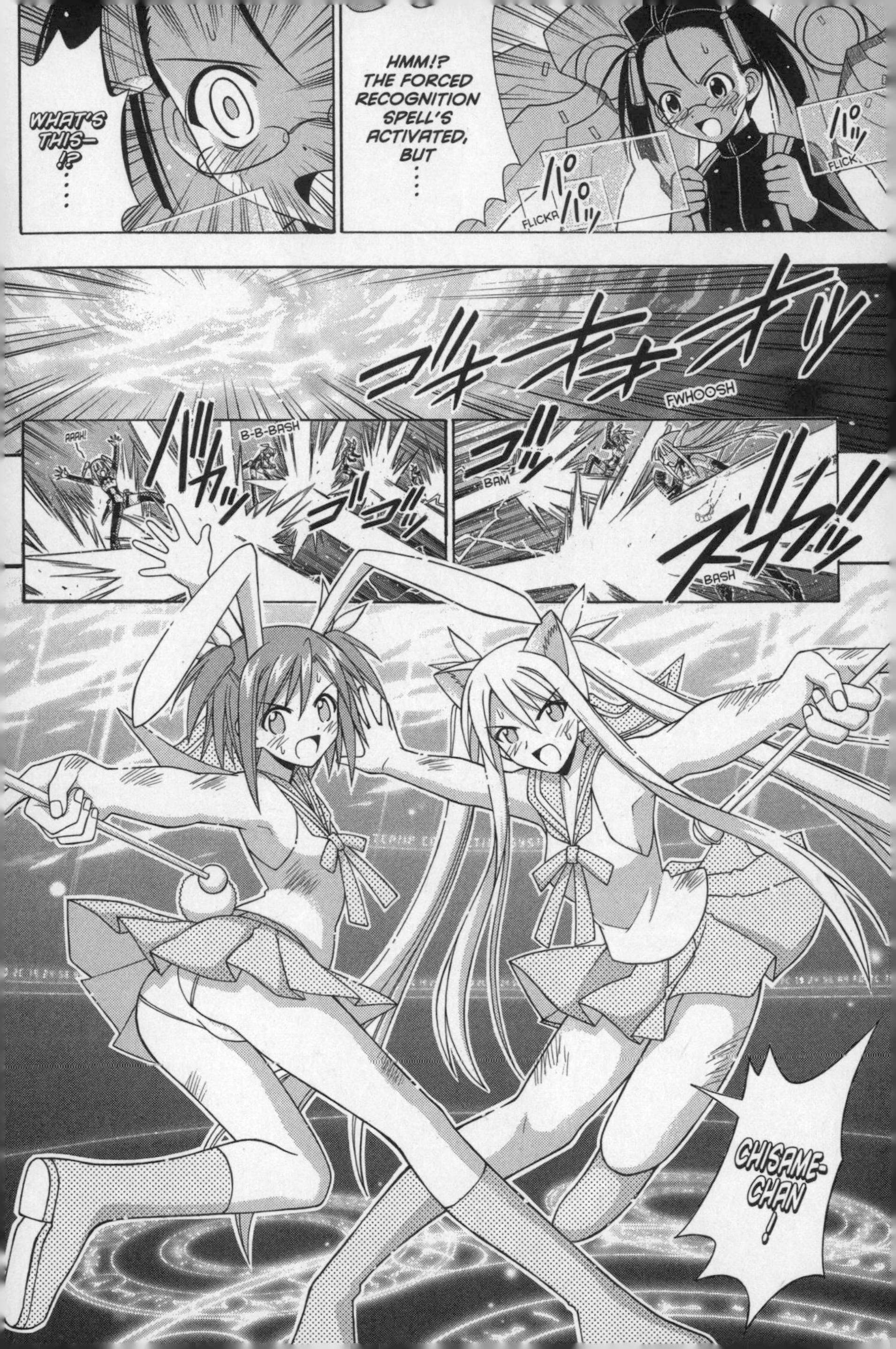
HMM!? THE FORCED RECOGNITION SPELL'S ACTIVATED, BUT ......
FLICK
FLICKA
WHAT'S THIS—!? ......
FWHOOSH
BAM
BASH
B-B-BASH
AAAH!
CHISAME-CHAN!

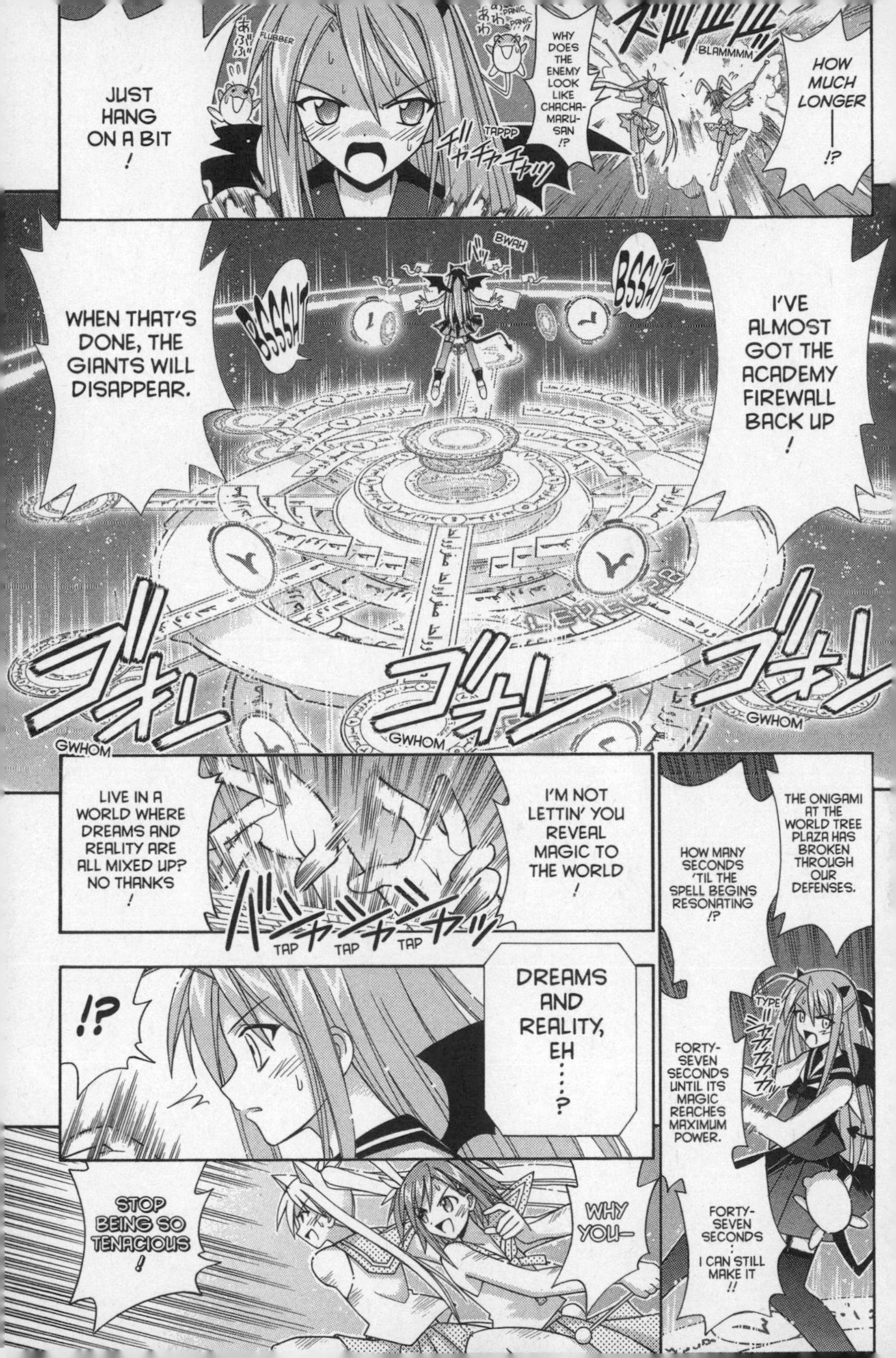

HOW MUCH LONGER——!?
BLAMMMM
WHY DOES THE ENEMY LOOK LIKE CHACHA-MARU-SAN!?
PANIC PANIC
FLUBBER
TAPPP
JUST HANG ON A BIT!
I'VE ALMOST GOT THE ACADEMY FIREWALL BACK UP!
BSSHT
BWAH
BSSSHT
WHEN THAT'S DONE, THE GIANTS WILL DISAPPEAR.
GWHOM
GWHOM
GWHOM
THE ONIGAMI AT THE WORLD TREE PLAZA HAS BROKEN THROUGH OUR DEFENSES.
HOW MANY SECONDS 'TIL THE SPELL BEGINS RESONATING!?
TYPE
FORTY-SEVEN SECONDS UNTIL ITS MAGIC REACHES MAXIMUM POWER.
FORTY-SEVEN SECONDS...
I CAN STILL MAKE IT!!
I'M NOT LETTIN' YOU REVEAL MAGIC TO THE WORLD!
LIVE IN A WORLD WHERE DREAMS AND REALITY ARE ALL MIXED UP? NO THANKS!
TAP TAP TAP
DREAMS AND REALITY, EH.....?
!?
WHY YOU—
STOP BEING SO TENACIOUS!

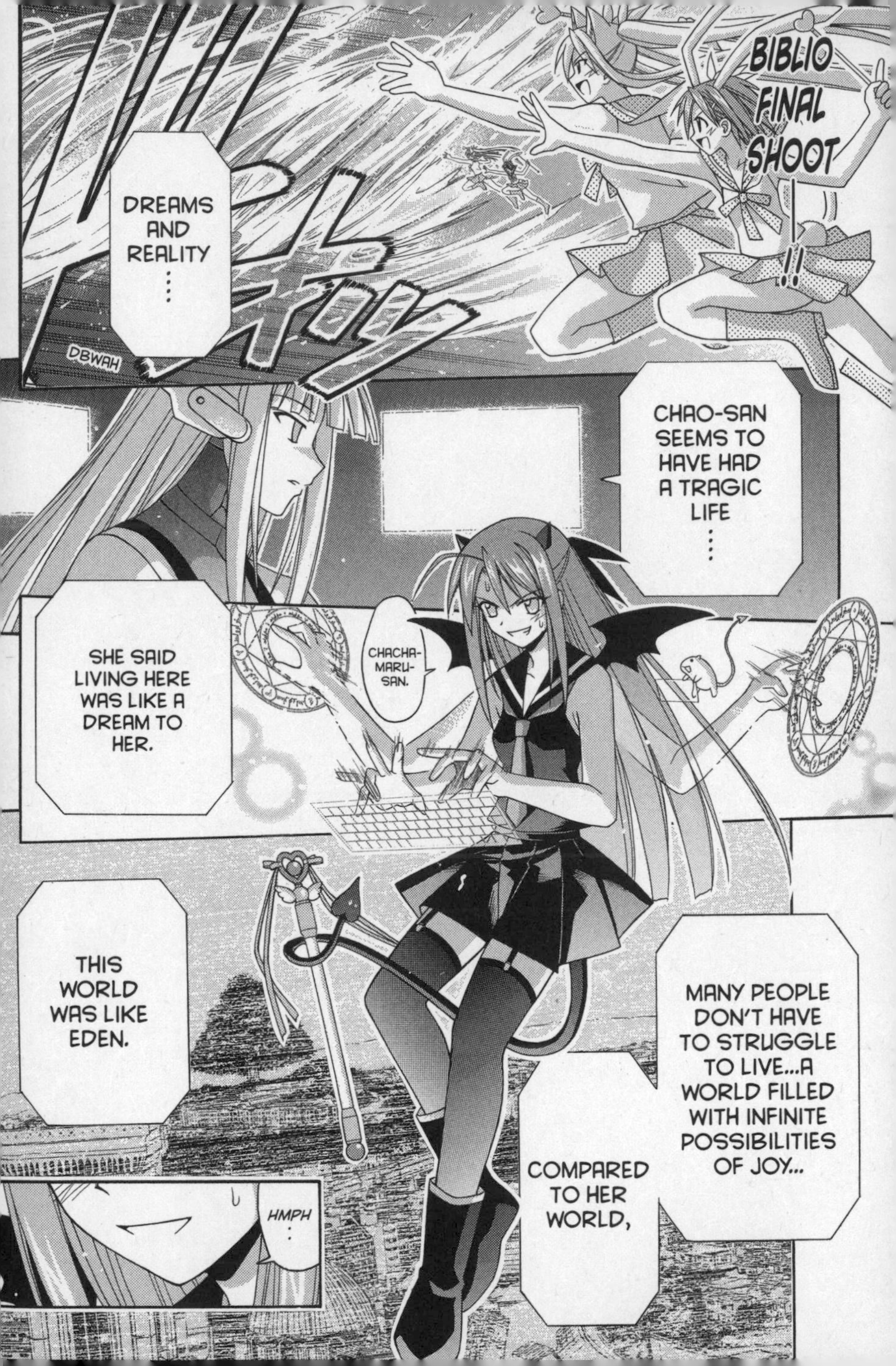

BIBLIO FINAL SHOOT !!
DREAMS AND REALITY ...
DBWAH
CHAO-SAN SEEMS TO HAVE HAD A TRAGIC LIFE ...
CHACHA-MARU-SAN.
SHE SAID LIVING HERE WAS LIKE A DREAM TO HER.
MANY PEOPLE DON'T HAVE TO STRUGGLE TO LIVE...A WORLD FILLED WITH INFINITE POSSIBILITIES OF JOY...
COMPARED TO HER WORLD,
THIS WORLD WAS LIKE EDEN.
HMPH ...

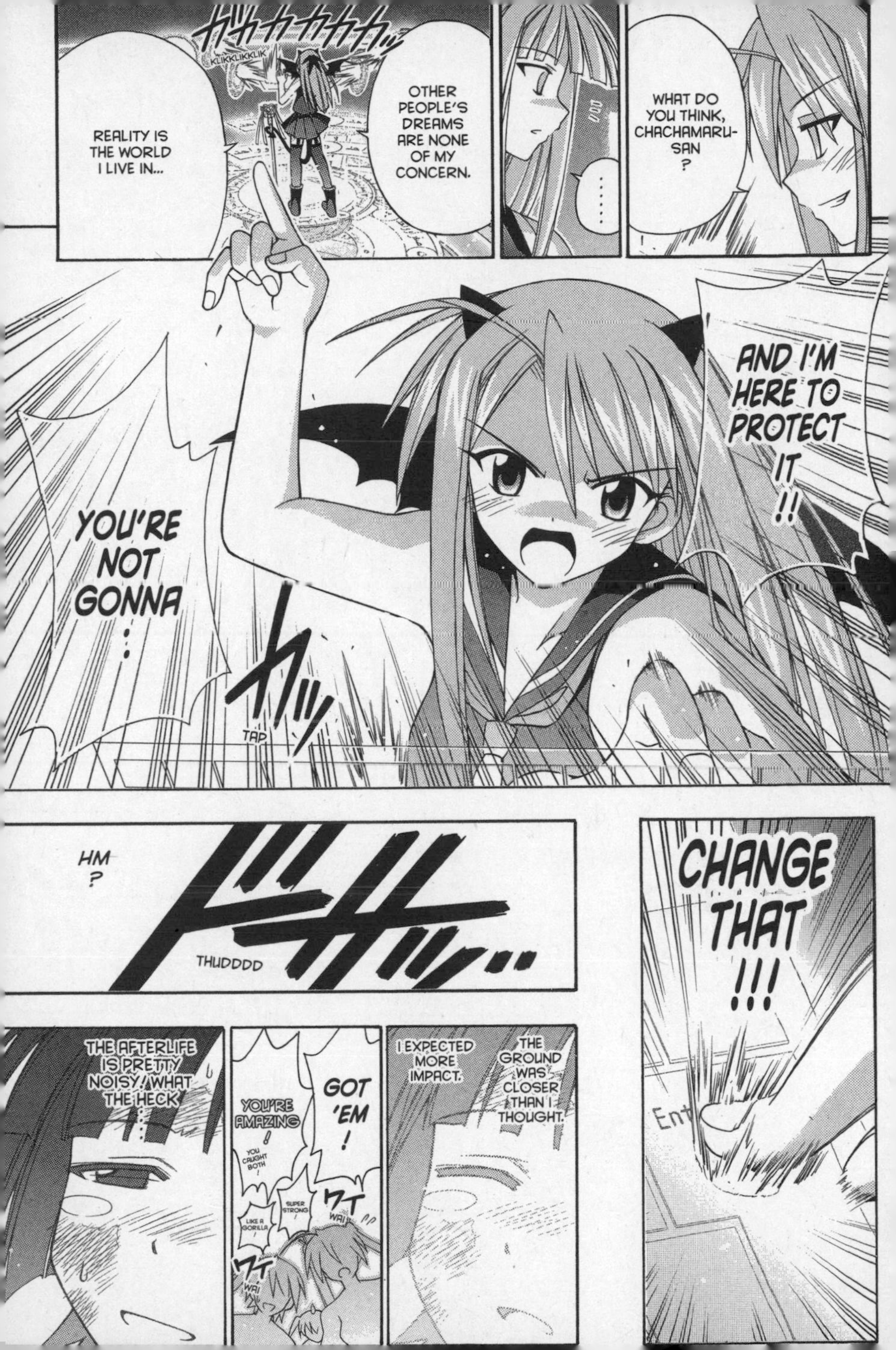
WHAT DO YOU THINK, CHACHAMARU-SAN?
......
KLIKKLIKKLIK
OTHER PEOPLE'S DREAMS ARE NONE OF MY CONCERN.
REALITY IS THE WORLD I LIVE IN...
AND I'M HERE TO PROTECT IT!!
YOU'RE NOT GONNA...
TAP
CHANGE THAT!!!
Ent
HM?
THUDDDD
THE GROUND WAS CLOSER THAN I THOUGHT.
I EXPECTED MORE IMPACT.
GOT 'EM!
YOU'RE AMAZING
YOU CAUGHT BOTH!
WAI
SUPER STRONG!
LIKE A GORILLA
WAI
THE AFTERLIFE IS PRETTY NOISY. WHAT THE HECK...

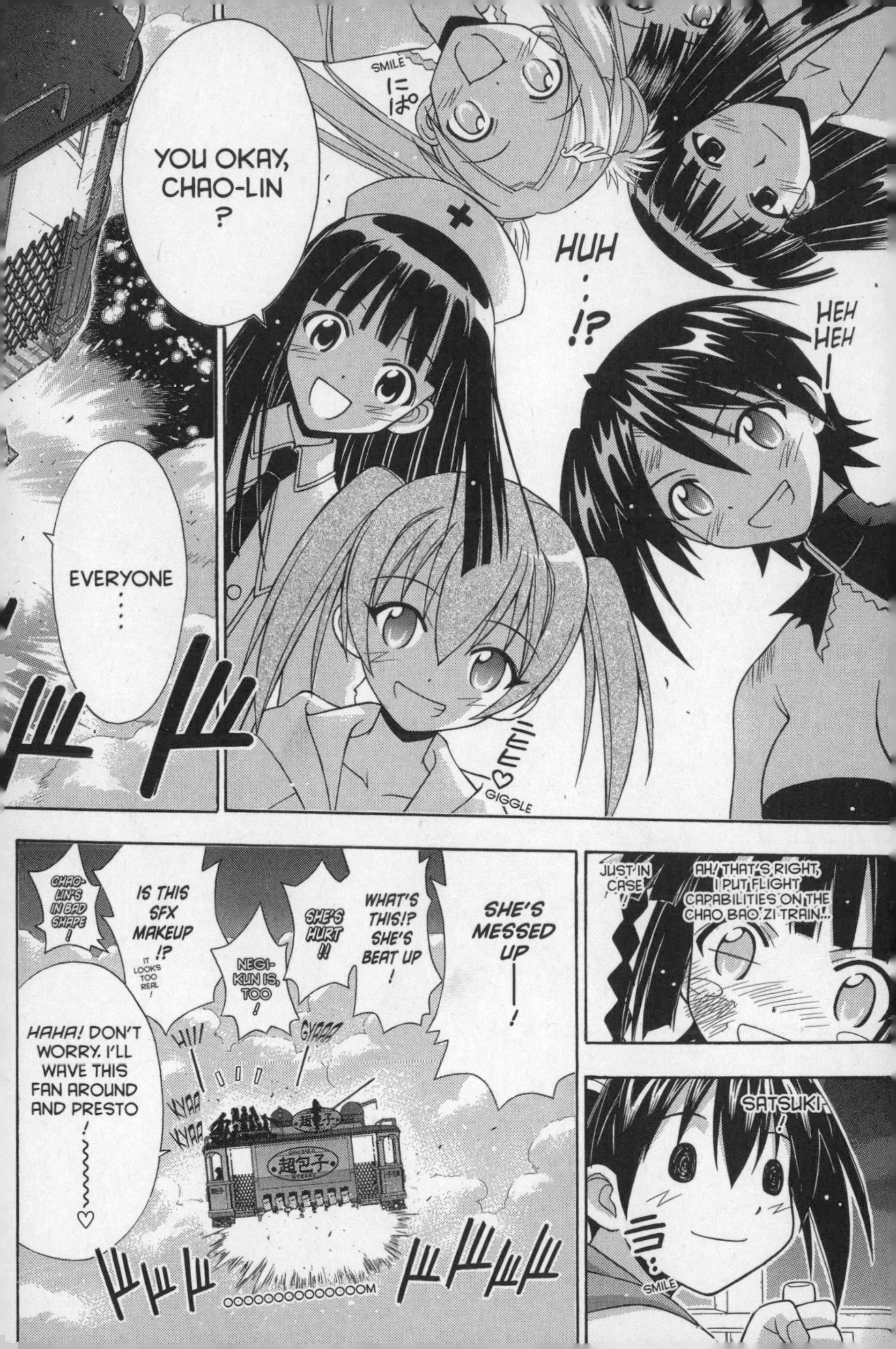
SMILE
にぱ
YOU OKAY, CHAO-LIN?
HUH...!?
HEH HEH!
EVERYONE....
GIGGLE
AH! THAT'S RIGHT, I PUT FLIGHT CAPABILITIES ON THE CHAO BAO ZI TRAIN...
JUST IN CASE..!
SATSUKI-!
SMILE
SHE'S MESSED UP—!
WHAT'S THIS!? SHE'S BEAT UP!
SHE'S HURT!!
NEGI-KUN IS, TOO!
IS THIS SFX MAKEUP!?
IT LOOKS TOO REAL!
CHAO-LIN'S IN BAD SHAPE!
GYAAA
HII!
KYAA KYAA
超包子
HAHA! DON'T WORRY. I'LL WAVE THIS FAN AROUND AND PRESTO!~~~~♡
OOOOOOOOOOOOOOOOM

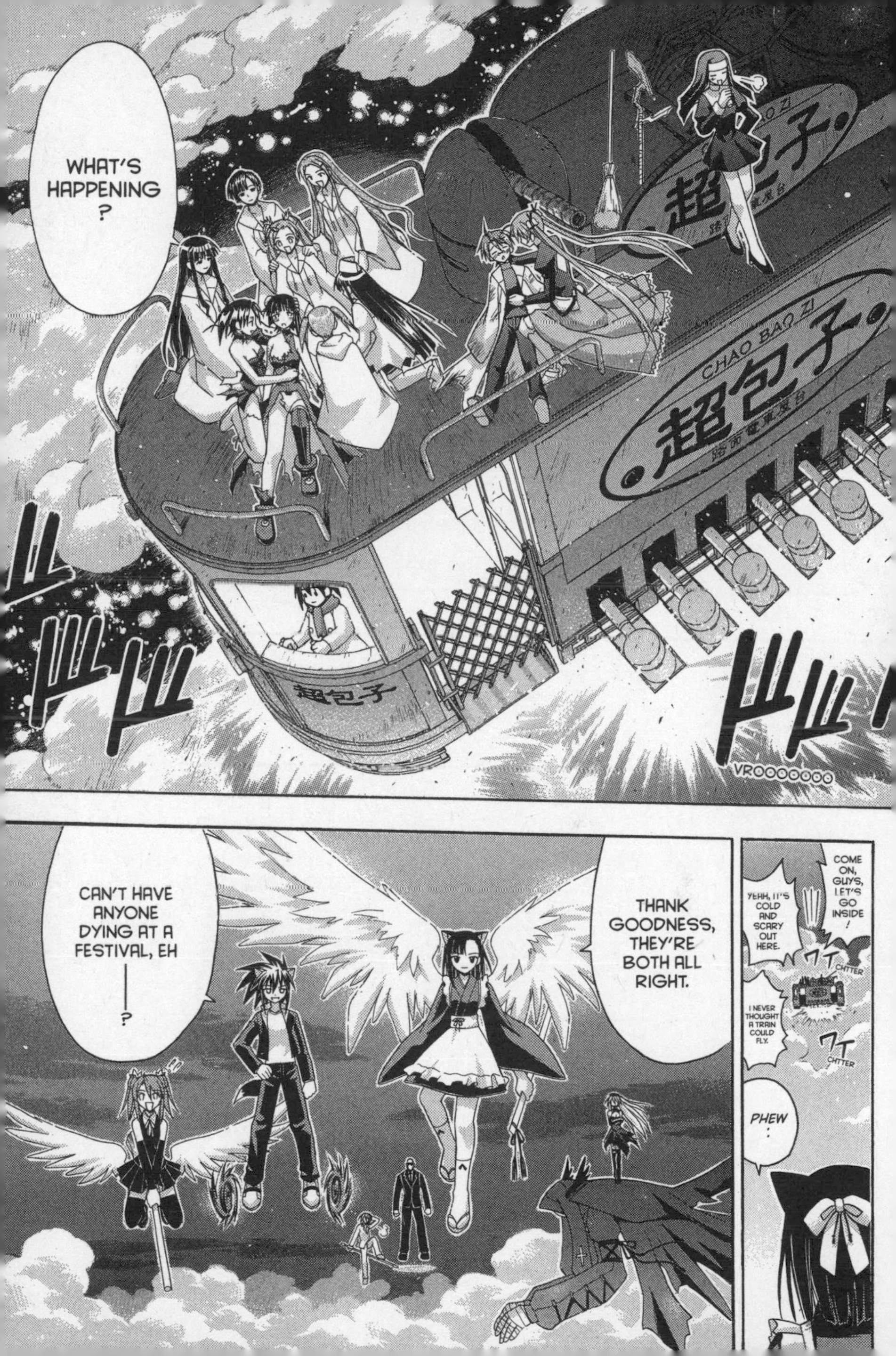
WHAT'S HAPPENING?
CHAO BAO ZI
超包子
超包子
VROOOOOOOO
COME ON, GUYS, LET'S GO INSIDE!
YEAH, IT'S COLD AND SCARY OUT HERE.
CHTTER
I NEVER THOUGHT A TRAIN COULD FLY.
CHTTER
PHEW :
THANK GOODNESS, THEY'RE BOTH ALL RIGHT.
CAN'T HAVE ANYONE DYING AT A FESTIVAL, EH——?

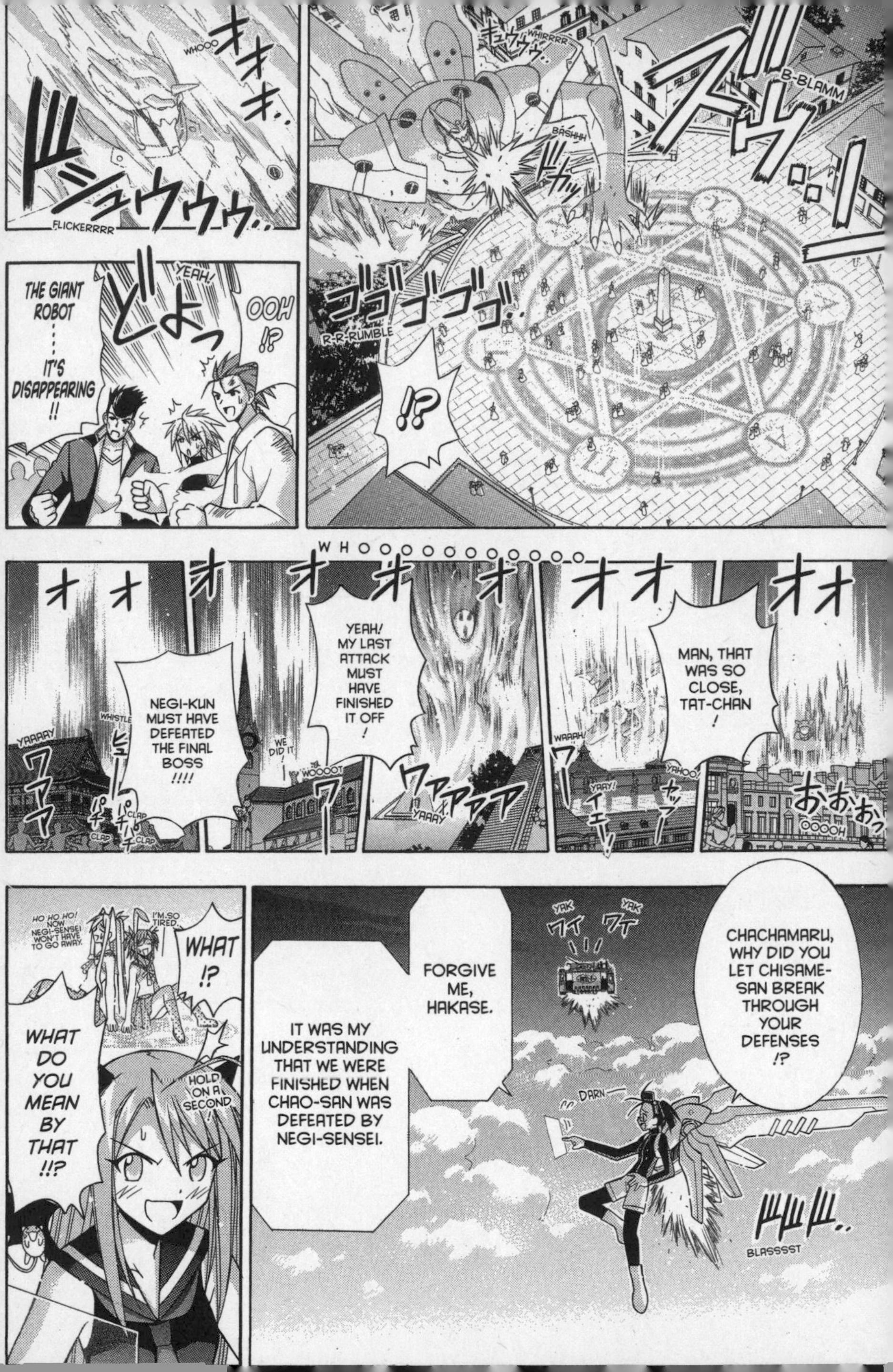
WHIRRRR
B-BLAMM
BASHHH
R-R-RUMBLE
!?
WHOOO
FLICKERRRR
YEAH!
OOH !?
THE GIANT ROBOT...... IT'S DISAPPEARING !!
WHOOOOOOOOOOOOOO
MAN, THAT WAS SO CLOSE, TAT-CHAN!
YAHOO!
YAAY!
WAAAH!
OOOOH
YEAH! MY LAST ATTACK MUST HAVE FINISHED IT OFF!
WOOOOT
YAAAY
WE DID IT!
NEGI-KUN MUST HAVE DEFEATED THE FINAL BOSS !!!!
WHISTLE
YAAAAY
CLAP
CLAP
CLAP
CHACHAMARU, WHY DID YOU LET CHISAME-SAN BREAK THROUGH YOUR DEFENSES !?
YAK
YAK
FORGIVE ME, HAKASE.
IT WAS MY UNDERSTANDING THAT WE WERE FINISHED WHEN CHAO-SAN WAS DEFEATED BY NEGI-SENSEI.
DARN
BLASSSST
WHAT !?
HO HO HO! NOW NEGI-SENSEI WON'T HAVE TO GO AWAY.
I'M SO TIRED...
HOLD ON A SECOND!
WHAT DO YOU MEAN BY THAT !!?

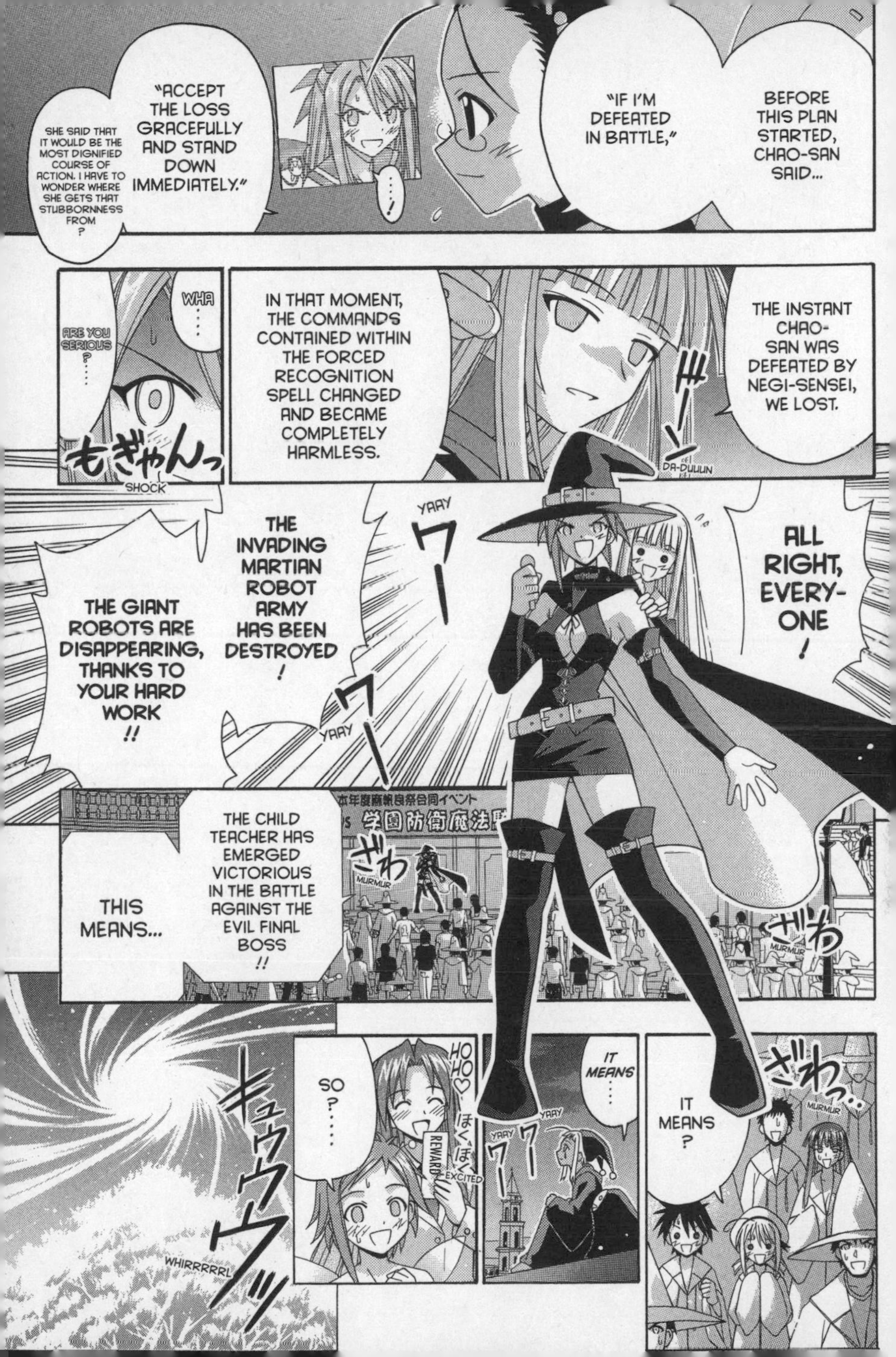
BEFORE THIS PLAN STARTED, CHAO-SAN SAID...
"IF I'M DEFEATED IN BATTLE,"
"ACCEPT THE LOSS GRACEFULLY AND STAND DOWN IMMEDIATELY."
...!
SHE SAID THAT IT WOULD BE THE MOST DIGNIFIED COURSE OF ACTION. I HAVE TO WONDER WHERE SHE GETS THAT STUBBORNNESS FROM?
THE INSTANT CHAO-SAN WAS DEFEATED BY NEGI-SENSEI, WE LOST.
DA-DUUUN
IN THAT MOMENT, THE COMMANDS CONTAINED WITHIN THE FORCED RECOGNITION SPELL CHANGED AND BECAME COMPLETELY HARMLESS.
WHA...
ARE YOU SERIOUS?...
もぎゃんっ
SHOCK
ALL RIGHT, EVERY-ONE!
YAAY
THE INVADING MARTIAN ROBOT ARMY HAS BEEN DESTROYED!
YAAY
THE GIANT ROBOTS ARE DISAPPEARING, THANKS TO YOUR HARD WORK!!
ざわ
MURMUR
ざわ
MURMUR
THE CHILD TEACHER HAS EMERGED VICTORIOUS IN THE BATTLE AGAINST THE EVIL FINAL BOSS!!
THIS MEANS...
ざわっ...
MURMUR
IT MEANS?
IT MEANS....
YAAY
YAAY
HOHO♡
SO?....
ほくほく
EXCITED
REWARD
WHIRRRRRL

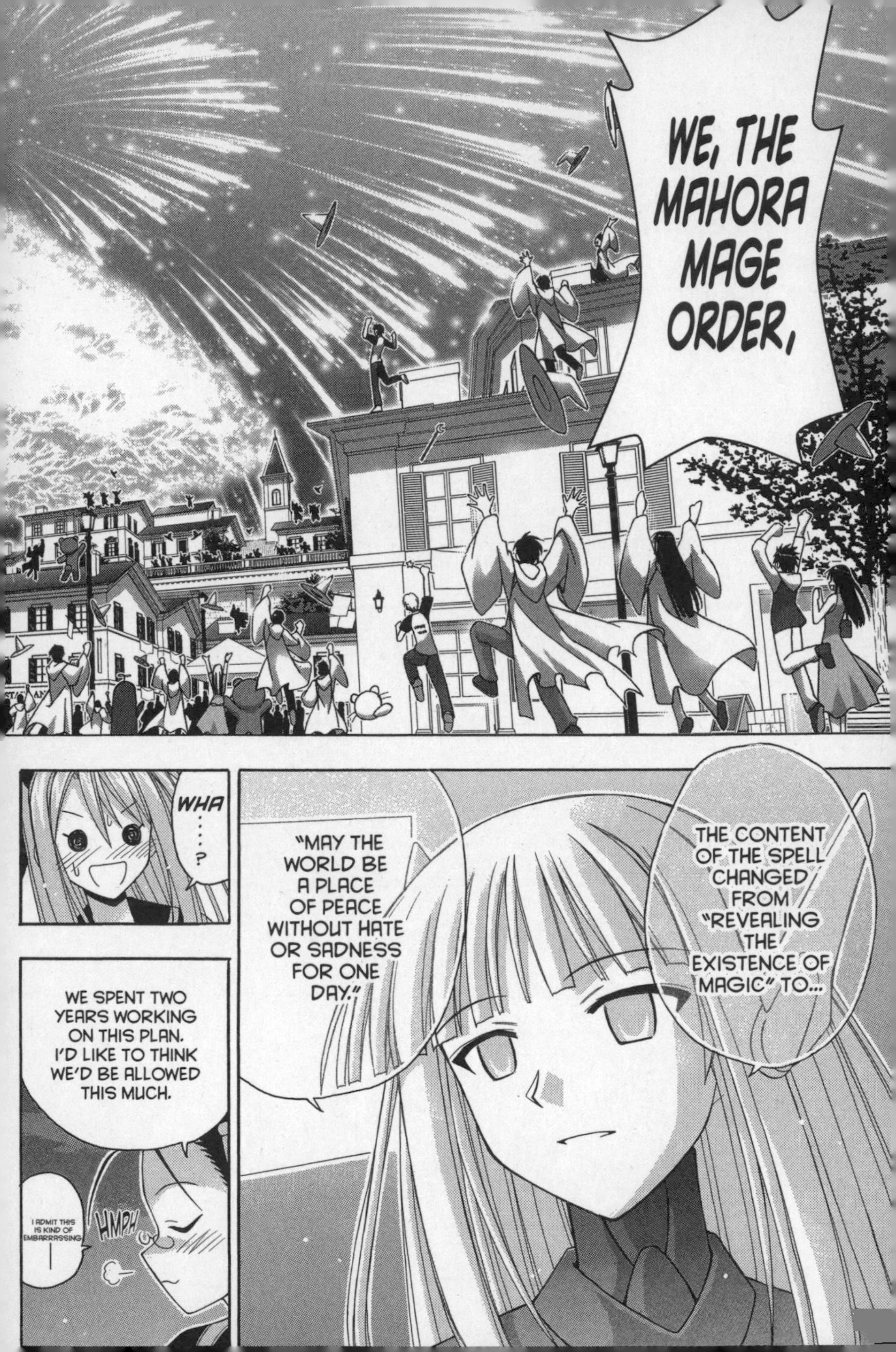
WE, THE MAHORA MAGE ORDER,
THE CONTENT OF THE SPELL CHANGED FROM "REVEALING THE EXISTENCE OF MAGIC" TO...
"MAY THE WORLD BE A PLACE OF PEACE WITHOUT HATE OR SADNESS FOR ONE DAY."
WHA.....?
WE SPENT TWO YEARS WORKING ON THIS PLAN. I'D LIKE TO THINK WE'D BE ALLOWED THIS MUCH.
HMPH
I ADMIT THIS IS KIND OF EMBARRASSING.

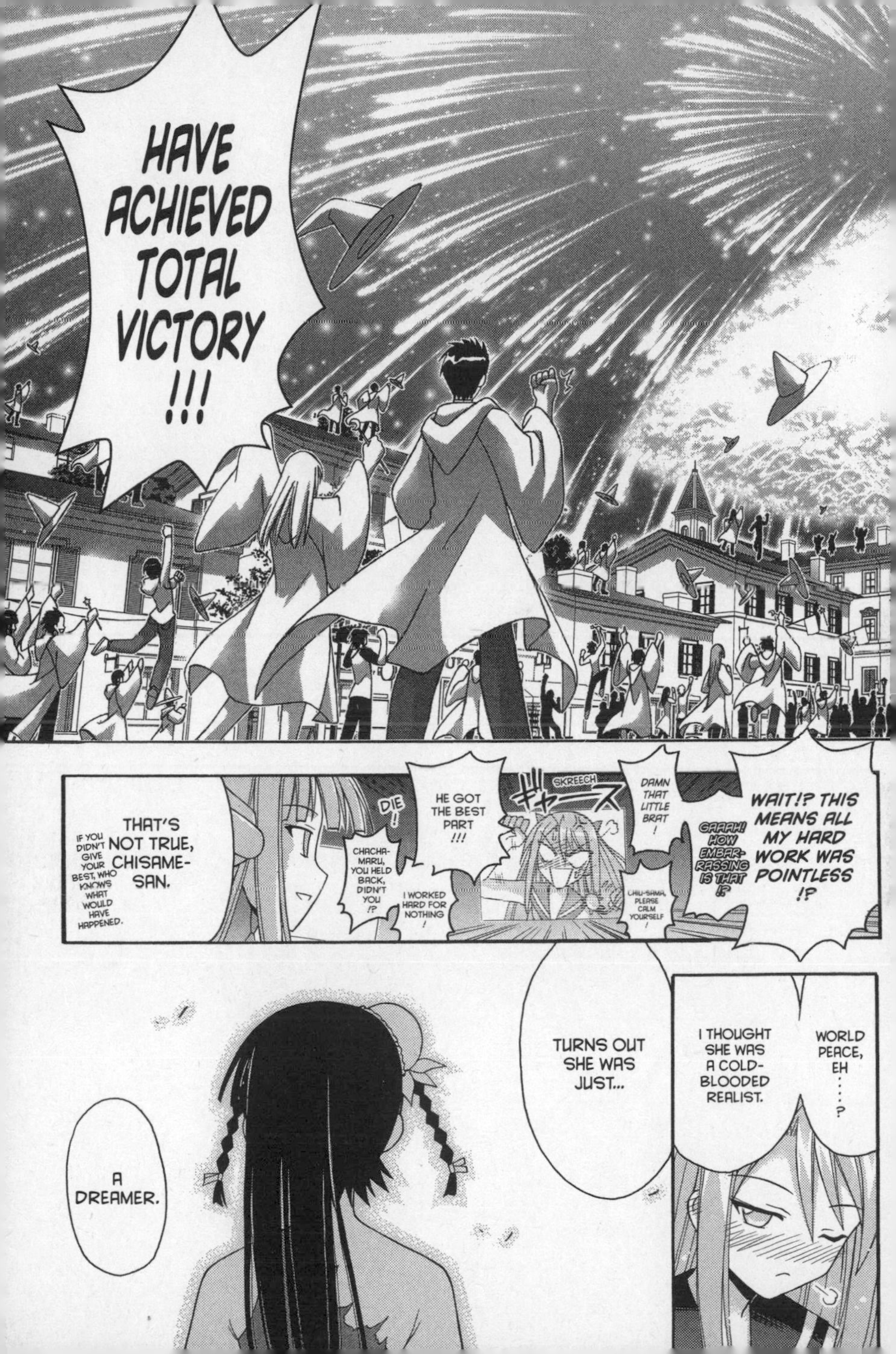
HAVE ACHIEVED TOTAL VICTORY !!!
WAIT!? THIS MEANS ALL MY HARD WORK WAS POINTLESS !?
GAAAH! HOW EMBARRASSING IS THAT !?
DAMN THAT LITTLE BRAT !
CHU-SAMA, PLEASE CALM YOURSELF !
SKREECH
HE GOT THE BEST PART !!!
DIE !
I WORKED HARD FOR NOTHING !
CHACHAMARU, YOU HELD BACK, DIDN'T YOU !?
THAT'S NOT TRUE, CHISAME-SAN.
IF YOU DIDN'T GIVE YOUR BEST, WHO KNOWS WHAT WOULD HAVE HAPPENED.
WORLD PEACE, EH ....?
I THOUGHT SHE WAS A COLD-BLOODED REALIST.
TURNS OUT SHE WAS JUST...
A DREAMER.

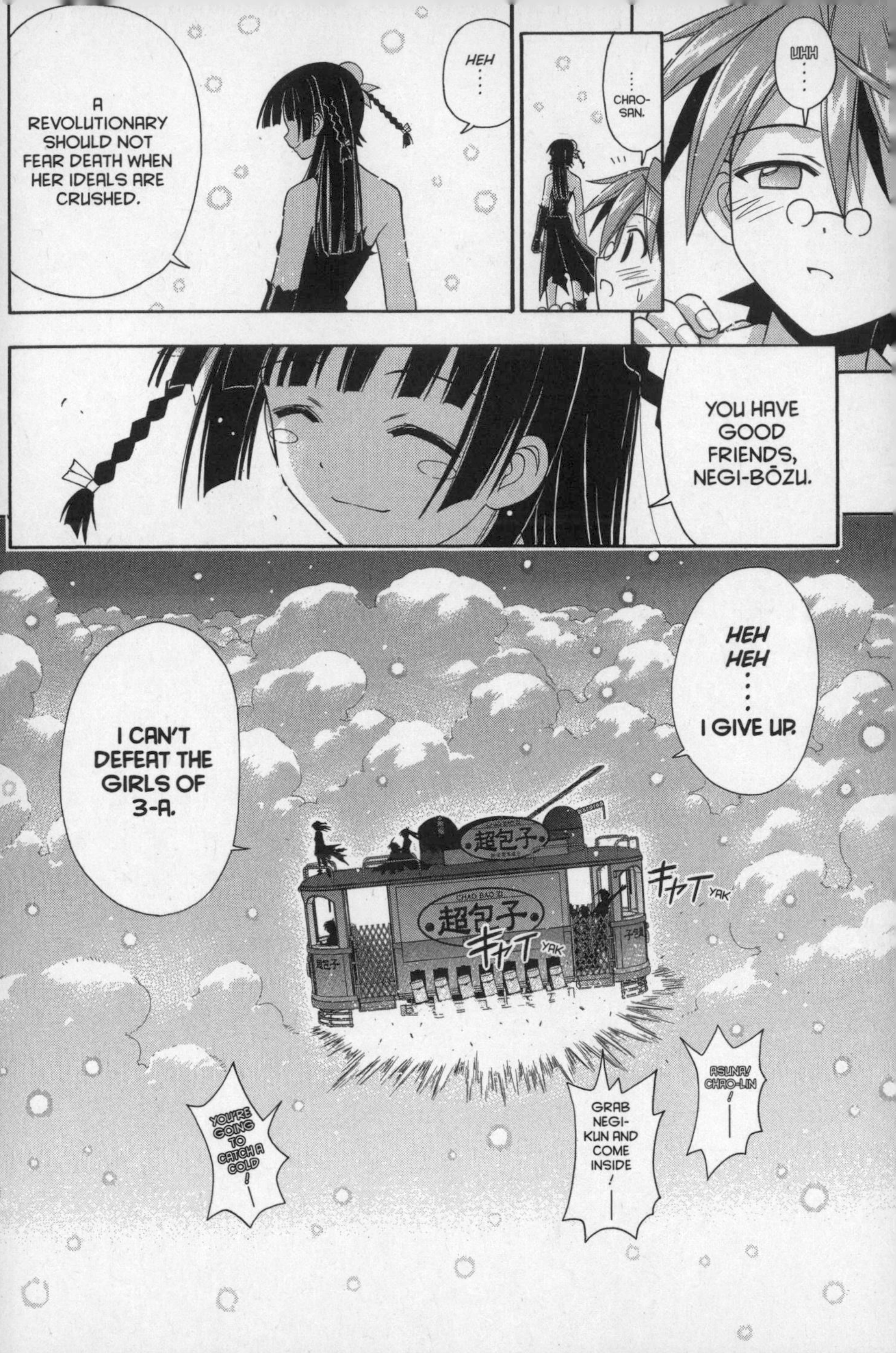

UHH...
...CHAO-SAN.
HEH...
A REVOLUTIONARY SHOULD NOT FEAR DEATH WHEN HER IDEALS ARE CRUSHED.
YOU HAVE GOOD FRIENDS, NEGI-BŌZU.
HEH HEH... I GIVE UP.
I CAN'T DEFEAT THE GIRLS OF 3-A.
超包子
キャア YAK
超包子
キャア YAK
ASUNA/ CHAO-LIN!
GRAB NEGI-KUN AND COME INSIDE!
YOU'RE GOING TO CATCH A COLD!

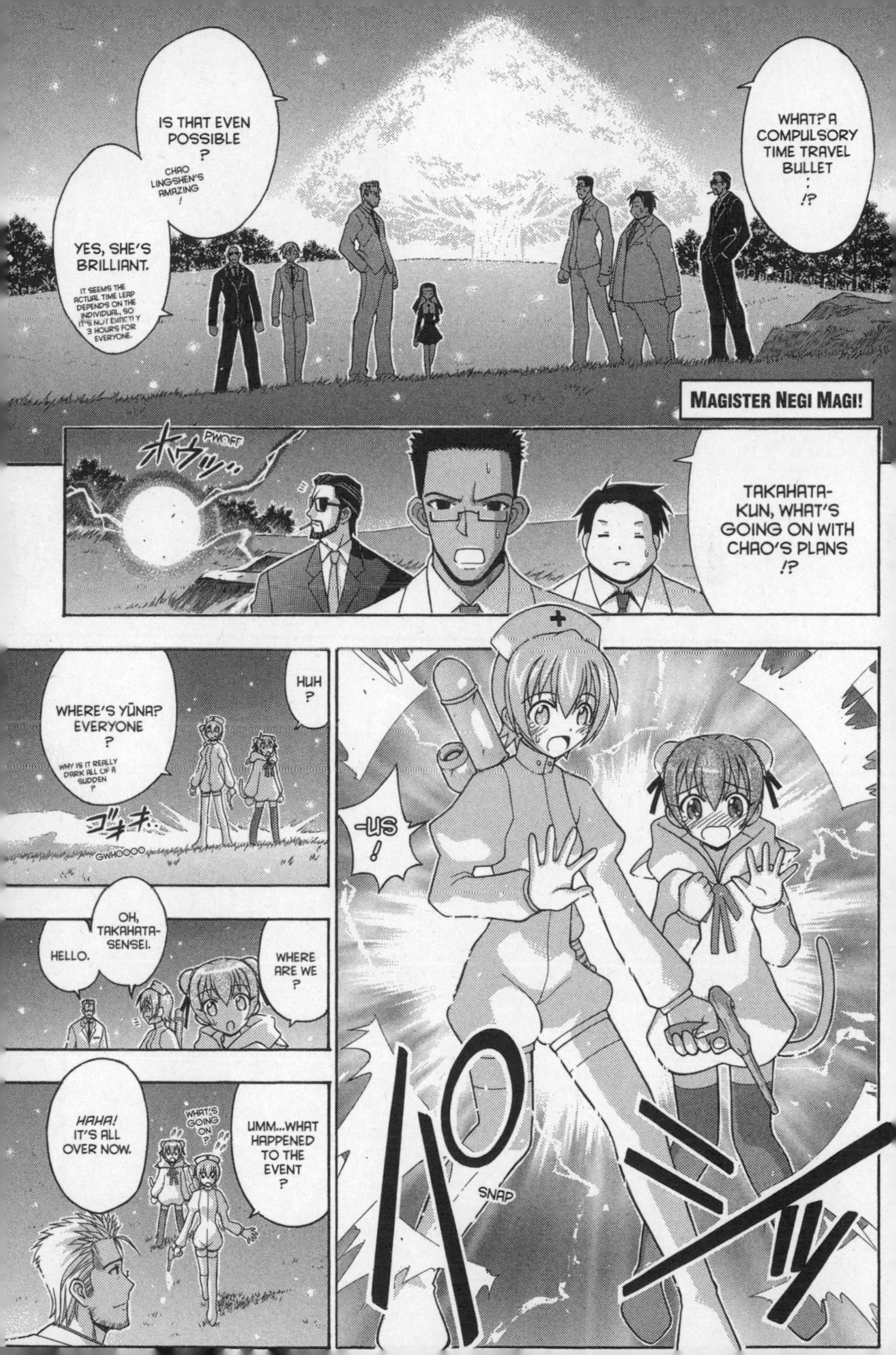
WHAT? A COMPULSORY TIME TRAVEL BULLET...!?
IS THAT EVEN POSSIBLE?
CHAO LINGSHEN'S AMAZING!
YES, SHE'S BRILLIANT.
IT SEEMS THE ACTUAL TIME LEAP DEPENDS ON THE INDIVIDUAL, SO IT'S NOT EXACTLY 3 HOURS FOR EVERYONE.
MAGISTER NEGI MAGI!
TAKAHATA-KUN, WHAT'S GOING ON WITH CHAO'S PLANS!?
PWOFF
-US!
SNAP
HUH?
WHERE'S YŪNA? EVERYONE?
WHY IS IT REALLY DARK ALL OF A SUDDEN?
GWHOOOO
OH, TAKAHATA-SENSEI.
WHERE ARE WE?
HELLO.
UMM...WHAT HAPPENED TO THE EVENT?
WHAT'S GOING ON?
HAHA! IT'S ALL OVER NOW.

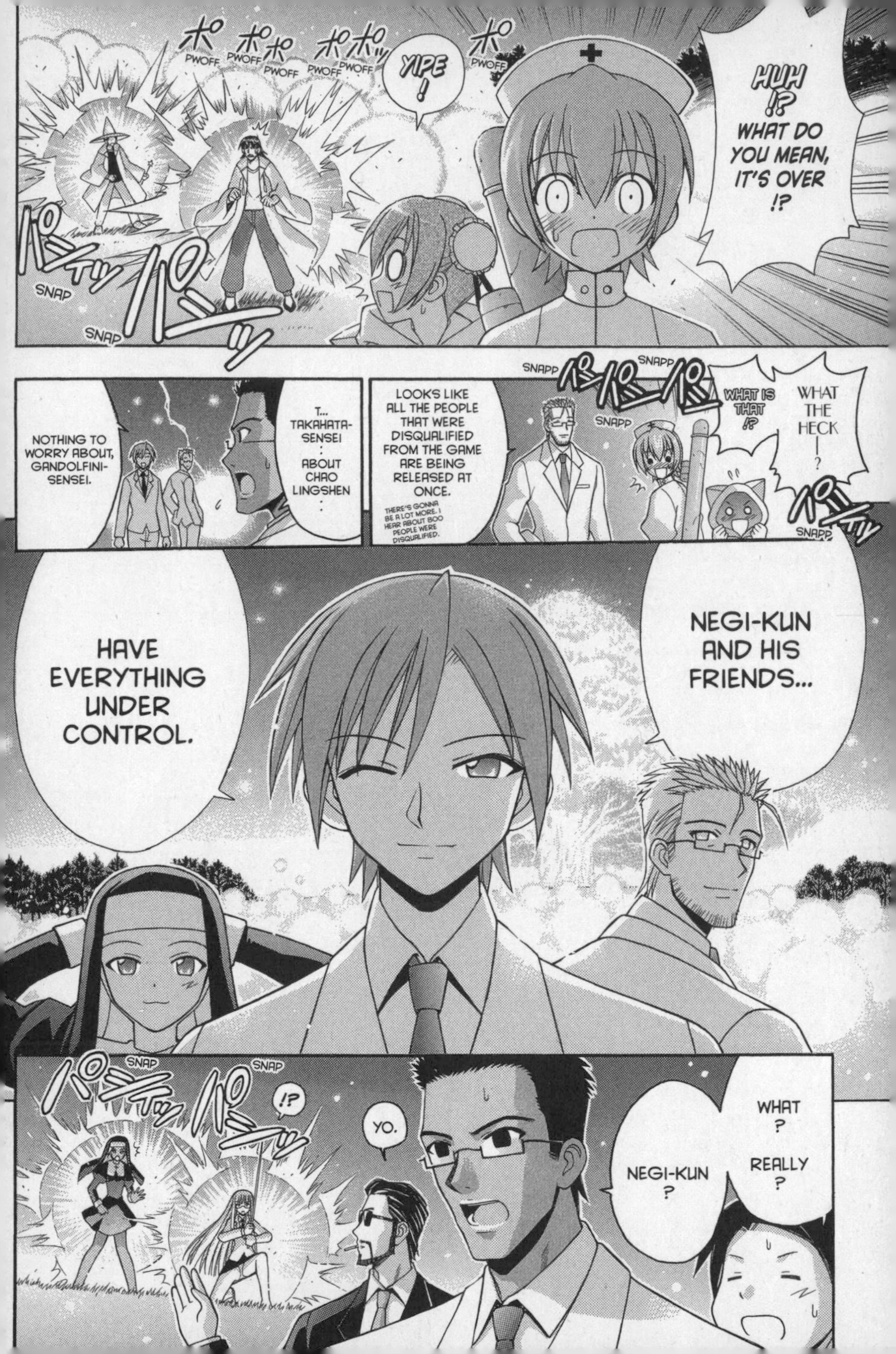
HUH !? WHAT DO YOU MEAN, IT'S OVER !?
PWOFF
YIPE !
PWOFF PWOFF PWOFF PWOFF PWOFF
SNAP
SNAP
SNAPP SNAPP SNAPP SNAPP
WHAT THE HECK !?
WHAT IS THAT !?
LOOKS LIKE ALL THE PEOPLE THAT WERE DISQUALIFIED FROM THE GAME ARE BEING RELEASED AT ONCE.
THERE'S GONNA BE A LOT MORE. I HEAR ABOUT 800 PEOPLE WERE DISQUALIFIED.
T... TAKAHATA-SENSEI : ABOUT CHAO LINGSHEN :
NOTHING TO WORRY ABOUT, GANDOLFINI-SENSEI.
NEGI-KUN AND HIS FRIENDS...
HAVE EVERYTHING UNDER CONTROL.
WHAT ? REALLY ?
NEGI-KUN ?
YO.
!?
SNAP
SNAP

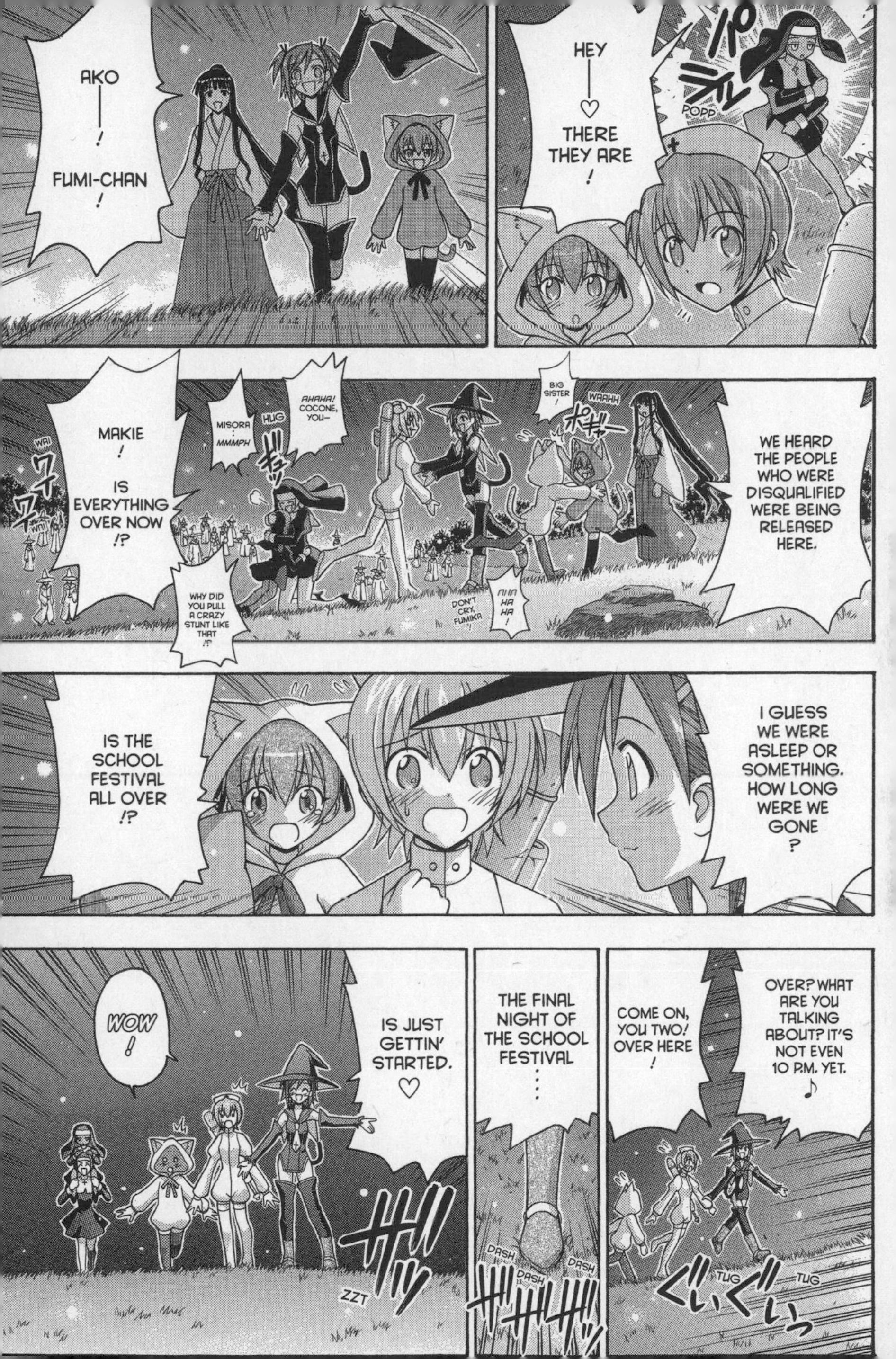

POPP
HEY— ♡ THERE THEY ARE!
AKO—! FUMI-CHAN!
WE HEARD THE PEOPLE WHO WERE DISQUALIFIED WERE BEING RELEASED HERE.
BIG SISTER!
WAAHH
AHAHA! COCONE, YOU—
MISORA: MMMPH
HUG
MAKIE! IS EVERYTHING OVER NOW!?
WAI
NIIN HA HA!
DON'T CRY, FUMIKA!
WHY DID YOU PULL A CRAZY STUNT LIKE THAT!?
I GUESS WE WERE ASLEEP OR SOMETHING. HOW LONG WERE WE GONE?
IS THE SCHOOL FESTIVAL ALL OVER!?
OVER? WHAT ARE YOU TALKING ABOUT? IT'S NOT EVEN 10 P.M. YET. ♪
COME ON, YOU TWO! OVER HERE!
TUG
TUG
THE FINAL NIGHT OF THE SCHOOL FESTIVAL....
DASH
DASH
DASH
IS JUST GETTIN' STARTED. ♡
WOW!
ZZT

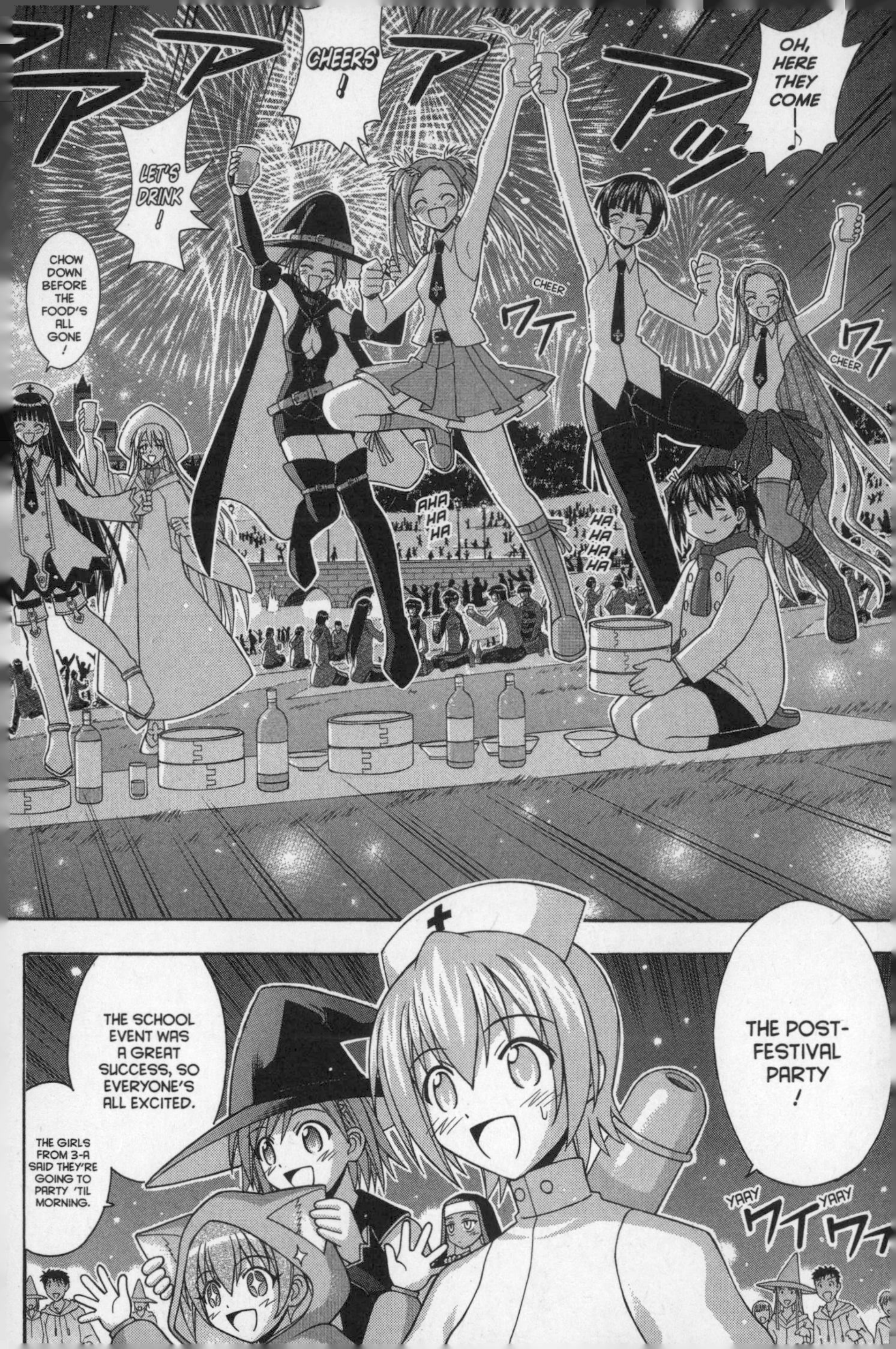

OH, HERE THEY COME!♪
CHEERS!
アアアアッ
LET'S DRINK!
CHEER ワイ
CHEER ワイ
CHOW DOWN BEFORE THE FOOD'S ALL GONE!
HA HA HA HA
AHA HA HA
THE POST-FESTIVAL PARTY!
THE SCHOOL EVENT WAS A GREAT SUCCESS, SO EVERYONE'S ALL EXCITED.
YAAY YAAY ワイワイ
THE GIRLS FROM 3-A SAID THEY'RE GOING TO PARTY 'TIL MORNING.

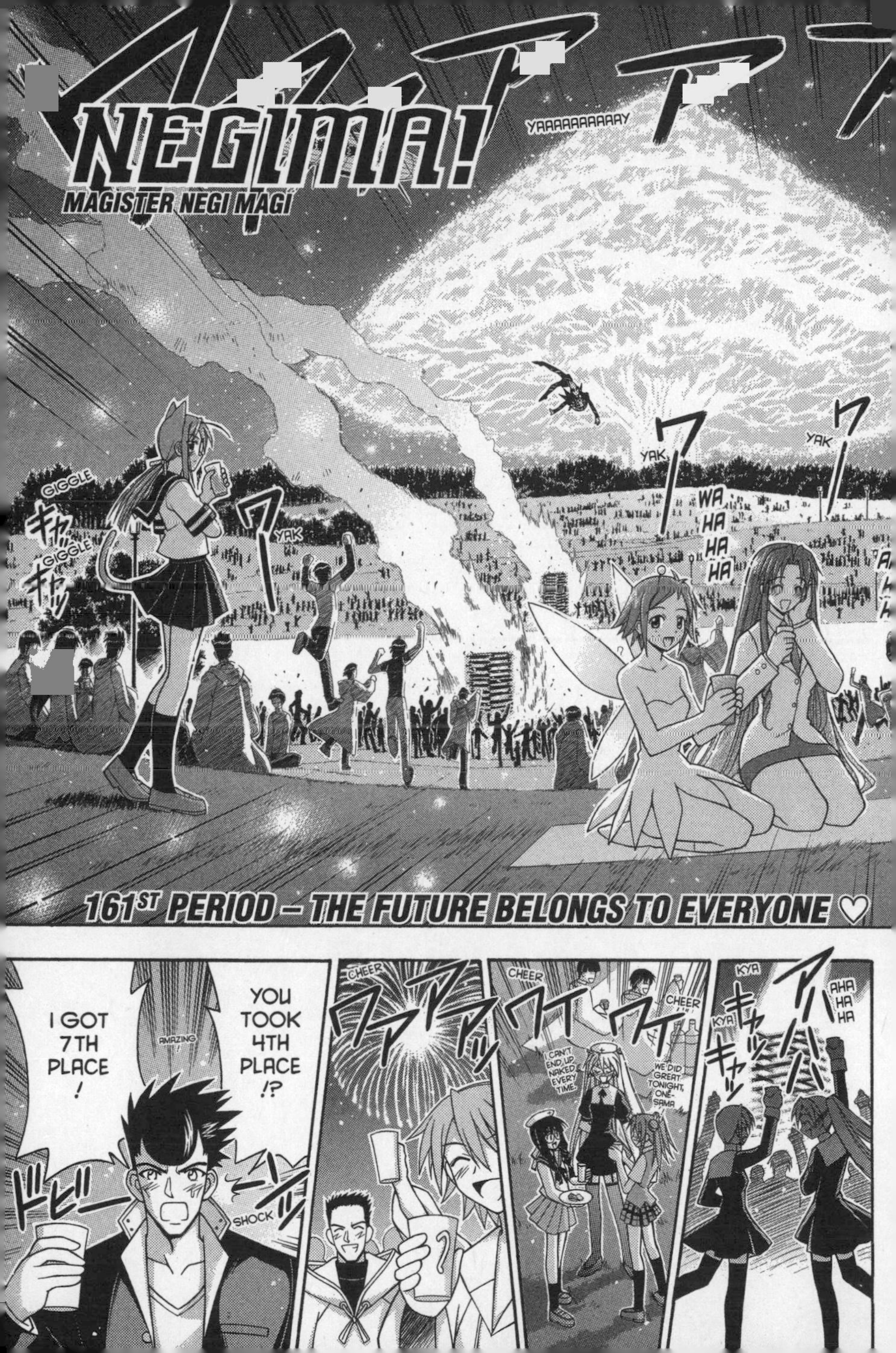

YAAAAAAAAAAAY
NEGIMA!
MAGISTER NEGI MAGI
YAK
YAK
WA HA HA HA
YAK
GIGGLE
GIGGLE
161ST PERIOD – THE FUTURE BELONGS TO EVERYONE ♡
KYA
AHA HA HA
KYA
CHEER
CHEER
WE DID GREAT TONIGHT, ONE-SAMA
CAN'T END UP NAKED EVERY TIME
CHEER
YOU TOOK 4TH PLACE !?
AMAZING
I GOT 7TH PLACE !
SHOCK

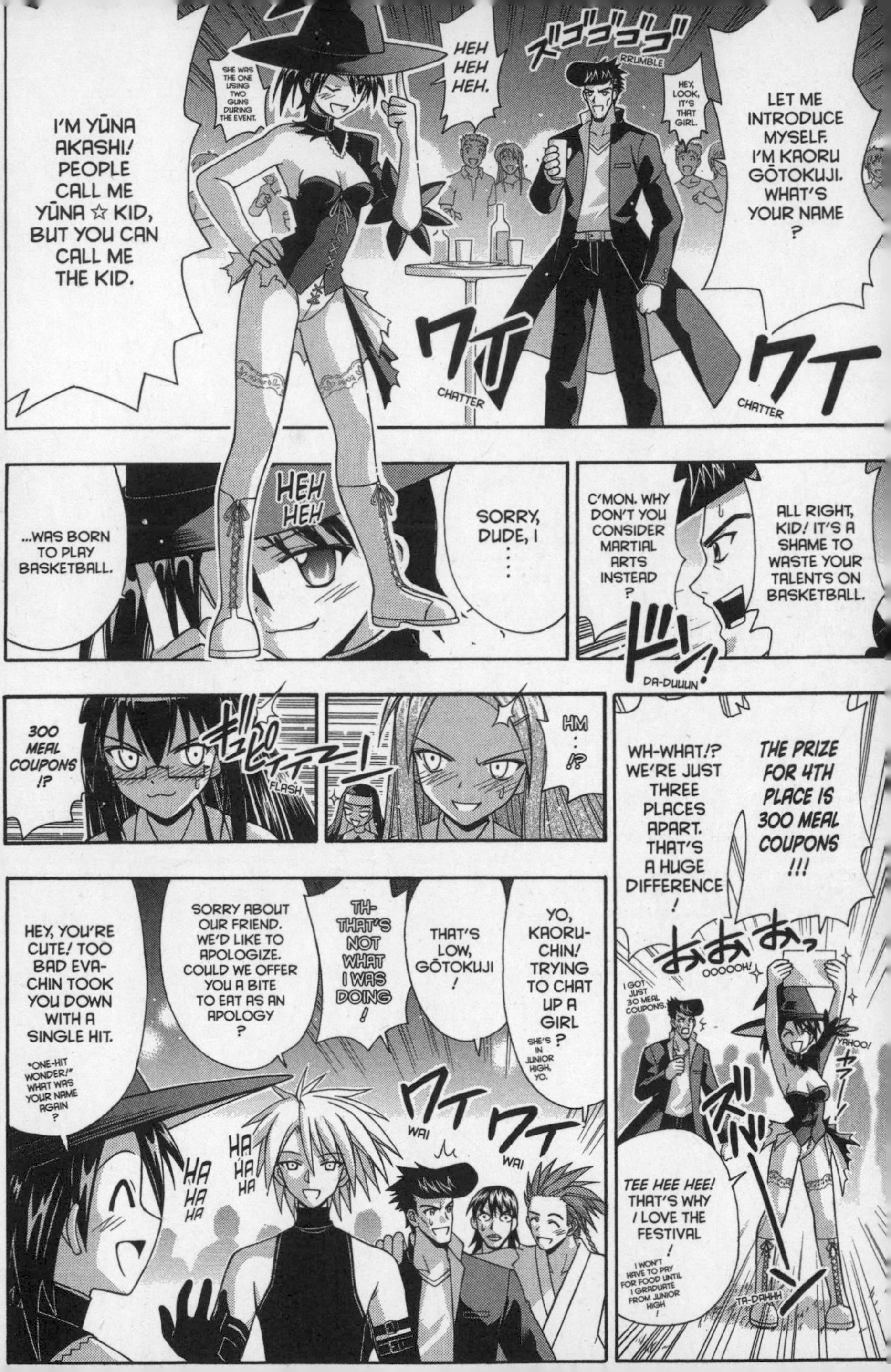
LET ME INTRODUCE MYSELF. I'M KAORU GŌTOKUJI. WHAT'S YOUR NAME ?
HEY, LOOK, IT'S THAT GIRL.
RRUMBLE
HEH HEH HEH.
SHE WAS THE ONE USING TWO GUNS DURING THE EVENT.
I'M YŪNA AKASHI! PEOPLE CALL ME YŪNA ☆ KID, BUT YOU CAN CALL ME THE KID.
CHATTER
CHATTER
ALL RIGHT, KID! IT'S A SHAME TO WASTE YOUR TALENTS ON BASKETBALL.
C'MON. WHY DON'T YOU CONSIDER MARTIAL ARTS INSTEAD ?
DA-DUUUN!
SORRY, DUDE, I ....
HEH HEH
...WAS BORN TO PLAY BASKETBALL.
THE PRIZE FOR 4TH PLACE IS 300 MEAL COUPONS !!!
WH-WHAT!? WE'RE JUST THREE PLACES APART. THAT'S A HUGE DIFFERENCE !
OOOOOH!
I GOT JUST 30 MEAL COUPONS.
YAHOO!
TEE HEE HEE! THAT'S WHY I LOVE THE FESTIVAL !
I WON'T HAVE TO PRY FOR FOOD UNTIL I GRADUATE FROM JUNIOR HIGH !
TA-DAHHH
HM...!?
FLASH
300 MEAL COUPONS !?
YO, KAORU-CHIN! TRYING TO CHAT UP A GIRL ?
SHE'S IN JUNIOR HIGH, YO.
THAT'S LOW, GŌTOKUJI !
TH-THAT'S NOT WHAT I WAS DOING !
SORRY ABOUT OUR FRIEND. WE'D LIKE TO APOLOGIZE. COULD WE OFFER YOU A BITE TO EAT AS AN APOLOGY ?
HEY, YOU'RE CUTE! TOO BAD EVA-CHIN TOOK YOU DOWN WITH A SINGLE HIT.
"ONE-HIT WONDER!" WHAT WAS YOUR NAME AGAIN ?
WAI
WAI
HA HA HA HA
HA HA HA HA

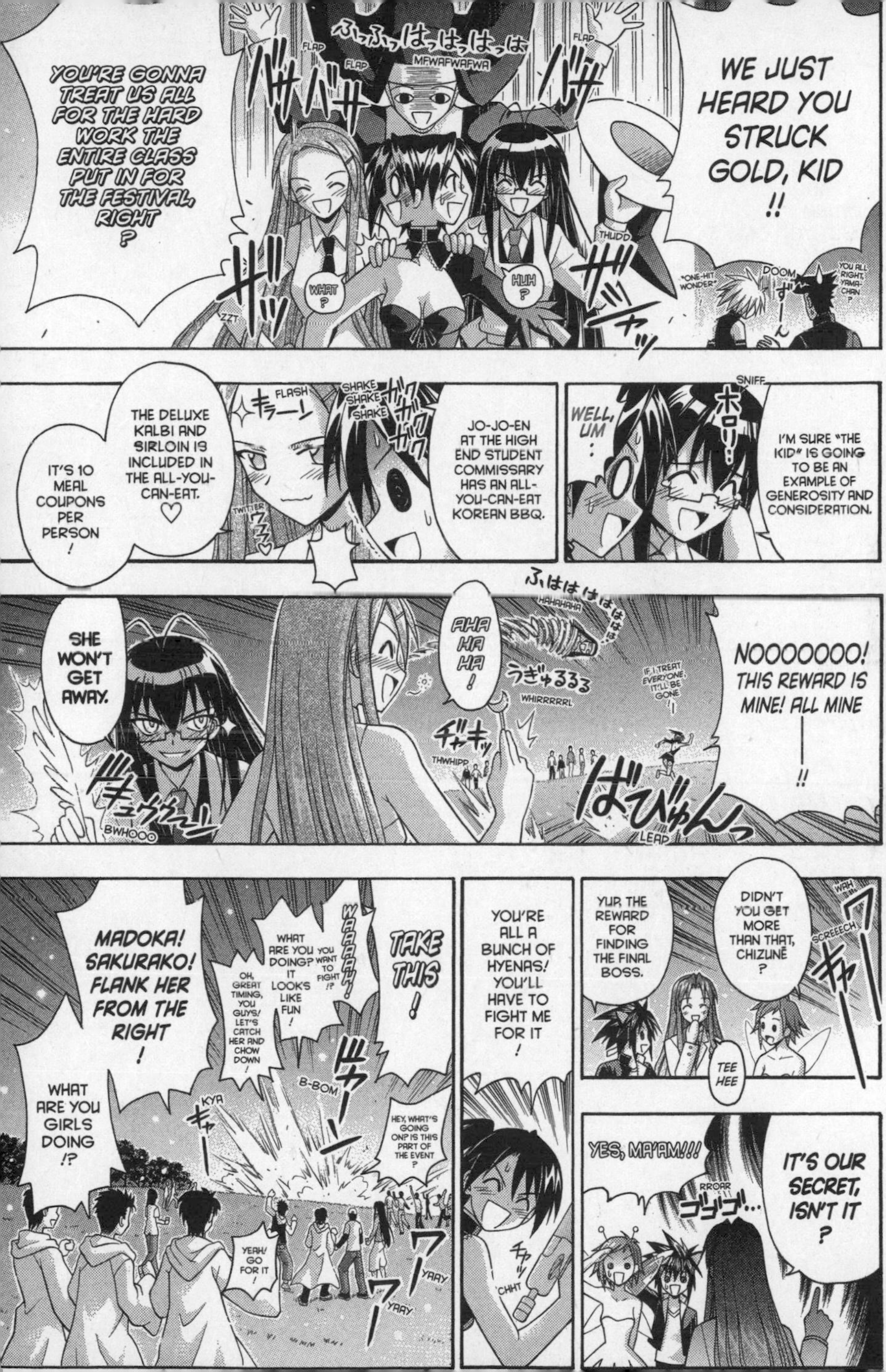
WE JUST HEARD YOU STRUCK GOLD, KID !!
ふっふっはっはっはっは
MFWAFWAFWA
FLAP
FLAP
FLAP
YOU'RE GONNA TREAT US ALL FOR THE HARD WORK THE ENTIRE CLASS PUT IN FOR THE FESTIVAL, RIGHT ?
YOU ALL RIGHT, YAMA-CHAN ?
DOOM
"ONE-HIT WONDER"
THUDD
HUH ?
WHAT ?
ZZT
I'M SURE "THE KID" IS GOING TO BE AN EXAMPLE OF GENEROSITY AND CONSIDERATION.
SNIFF
WELL, UM :
JO-JO-EN AT THE HIGH END STUDENT COMMISSARY HAS AN ALL-YOU-CAN-EAT KOREAN BBQ.
SHAKE SHAKE SHAKE
FLASH
THE DELUXE KALBI AND SIRLOIN IS INCLUDED IN THE ALL-YOU-CAN-EAT. ♡
IT'S 10 MEAL COUPONS PER PERSON !
TWITTER
NOOOOOOO! THIS REWARD IS MINE! ALL MINE ——— !!
IF I TREAT EVERYONE, IT'LL BE GONE !
LEAP
ふははははははは
HAHAHAHA
AHA HA HA !
うぎゅるるる
WHIRRRRRL
THWHIPP
SHE WON'T GET AWAY.
BWHOOO
DIDN'T YOU GET MORE THAN THAT, CHIZUNE ?
WAH
SCREEECH
YUP, THE REWARD FOR FINDING THE FINAL BOSS.
TEE HEE
IT'S OUR SECRET, ISN'T IT ?
YES, MA'AM!!!
RROAR
YOU'RE ALL A BUNCH OF HYENAS! YOU'LL HAVE TO FIGHT ME FOR IT !
CHHT
TAKE THIS !
YOU WANT TO FIGHT !?
WHAT ARE YOU DOING? IT LOOKS LIKE FUN !
MADOKA! SAKURAKO! FLANK HER FROM THE RIGHT !
OH, GREAT TIMING, YOU GUYS! LET'S CATCH HER AND CHOW DOWN !
B-BOM
HEY, WHAT'S GOING ON? IS THIS PART OF THE EVENT ?
KYA
WHAT ARE YOU GIRLS DOING !?
YAAY
YAAY
YEAH! GO FOR IT !

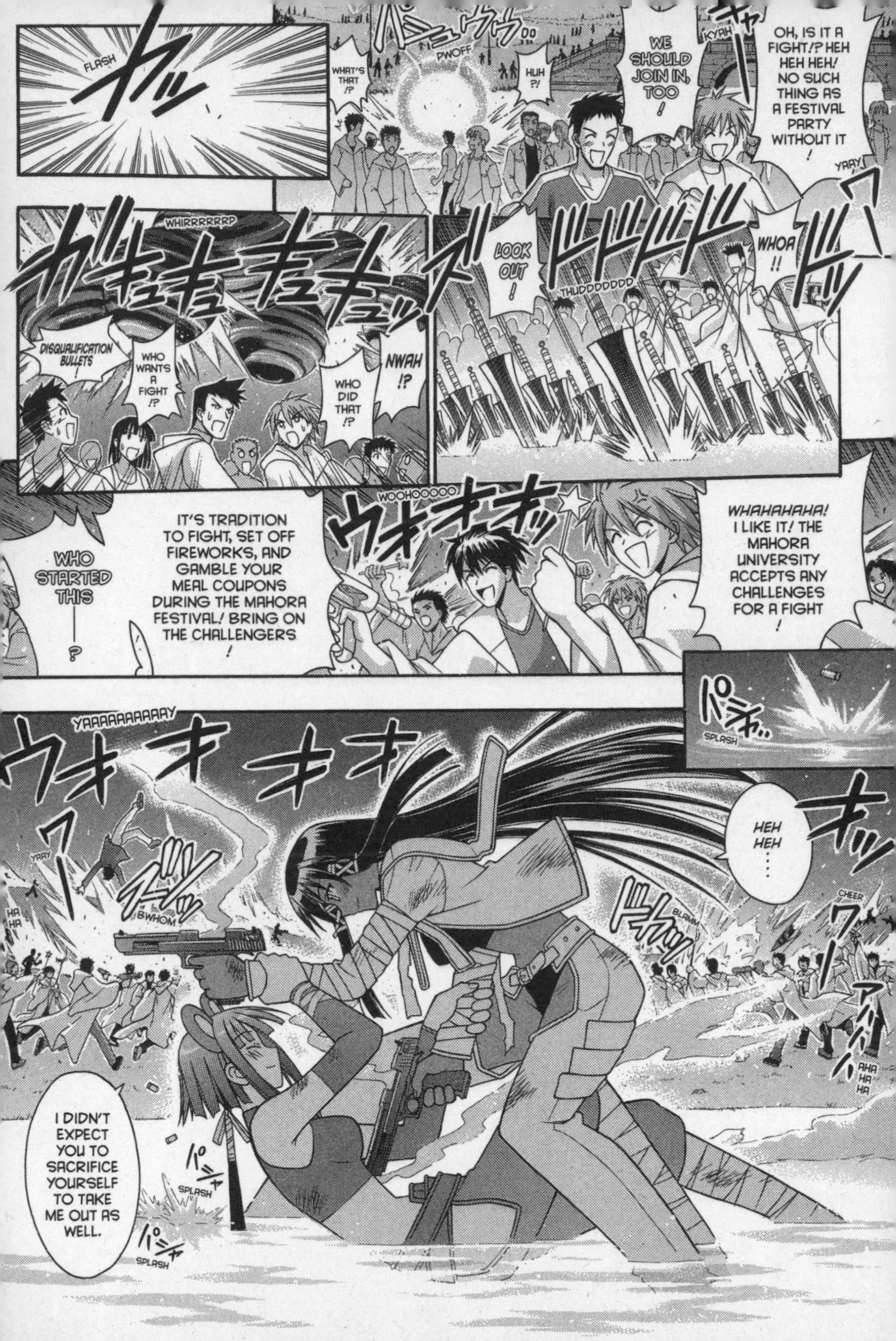
OH, IS IT A FIGHT!? HEH HEH HEH! NO SUCH THING AS A FESTIVAL PARTY WITHOUT IT!
KYAH
WE SHOULD JOIN IN, TOO!
YAAY
HUH?!
WHAT'S THAT!?
PWOFF
FLASH
WHOA!!
LOOK OUT!
THUDDDDDDD
WHIRRRRRRP
NWAH!?
WHO DID THAT!?
WHO WANTS A FIGHT!?
DISQUALIFICATION BULLETS!
WHAHAHAHA! I LIKE IT! THE MAHORA UNIVERSITY ACCEPTS ANY CHALLENGES FOR A FIGHT!
WOOHOOOOO
IT'S TRADITION TO FIGHT, SET OFF FIREWORKS, AND GAMBLE YOUR MEAL COUPONS DURING THE MAHORA FESTIVAL! BRING ON THE CHALLENGERS!
WHO STARTED THIS--?
SPLASH
YAAAAAAAAAAAY
HEH HEH.....
CHEER
AHA HA HA
BLAMM
BWHOM
YAAY
HA HA
I DIDN'T EXPECT YOU TO SACRIFICE YOURSELF TO TAKE ME OUT AS WELL.
SPLASH
SPLASH

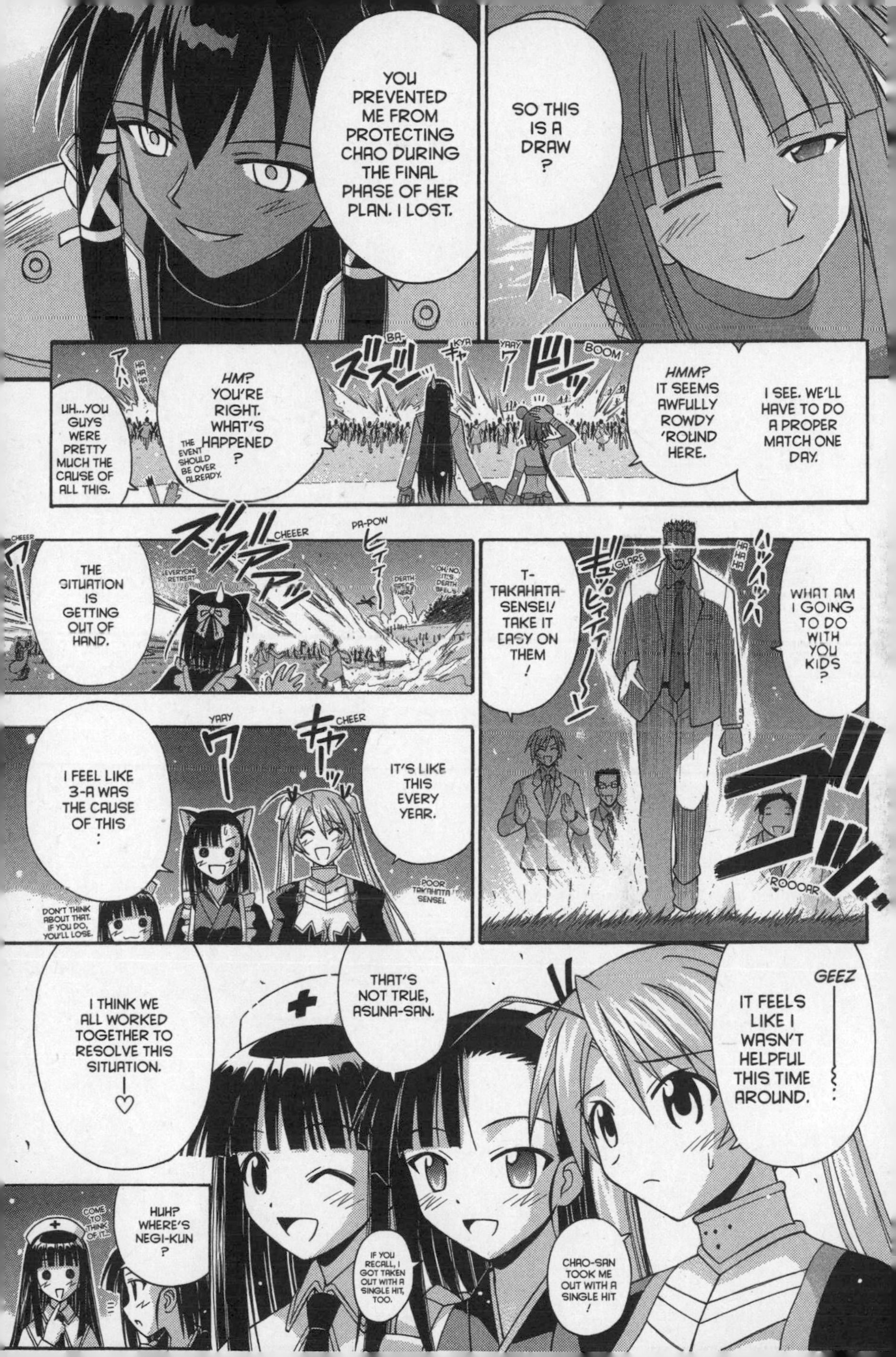
SO THIS IS A DRAW?
YOU PREVENTED ME FROM PROTECTING CHAO DURING THE FINAL PHASE OF HER PLAN. I LOST.
I SEE. WE'LL HAVE TO DO A PROPER MATCH ONE DAY.
HMM? IT SEEMS AWFULLY ROWDY 'ROUND HERE.
BOOM
YAAY
KYA
BA-
HM? YOU'RE RIGHT. WHAT'S HAPPENED?
THE EVENT SHOULD BE OVER ALREADY.
HA HA HA
UH...YOU GUYS WERE PRETTY MUCH THE CAUSE OF ALL THIS.
WHAT AM I GOING TO DO WITH YOU KIDS?
HA HA HA
GLARE
T-TAKAHATA-SENSEI! TAKE IT EASY ON THEM!
ROOOAR
PA-POW
CHEEER
EVERYONE RETREAT
THE SITUATION IS GETTING OUT OF HAND.
CHEEER
CHEER
IT'S LIKE THIS EVERY YEAR.
POOR TAKAHATA SENSEI.
YAAY
I FEEL LIKE 3-A WAS THE CAUSE OF THIS :
DON'T THINK ABOUT THAT. IF YOU DO, YOU'LL LOSE.
GEEZ
IT FEELS LIKE I WASN'T HELPFUL THIS TIME AROUND.
CHAO-SAN TOOK ME OUT WITH A SINGLE HIT!
THAT'S NOT TRUE, ASUNA-SAN.
IF YOU RECALL, I GOT TAKEN OUT WITH A SINGLE HIT, TOO.
I THINK WE ALL WORKED TOGETHER TO RESOLVE THIS SITUATION. —♡
HUH? WHERE'S NEGI-KUN?
COME TO THINK OF IT...

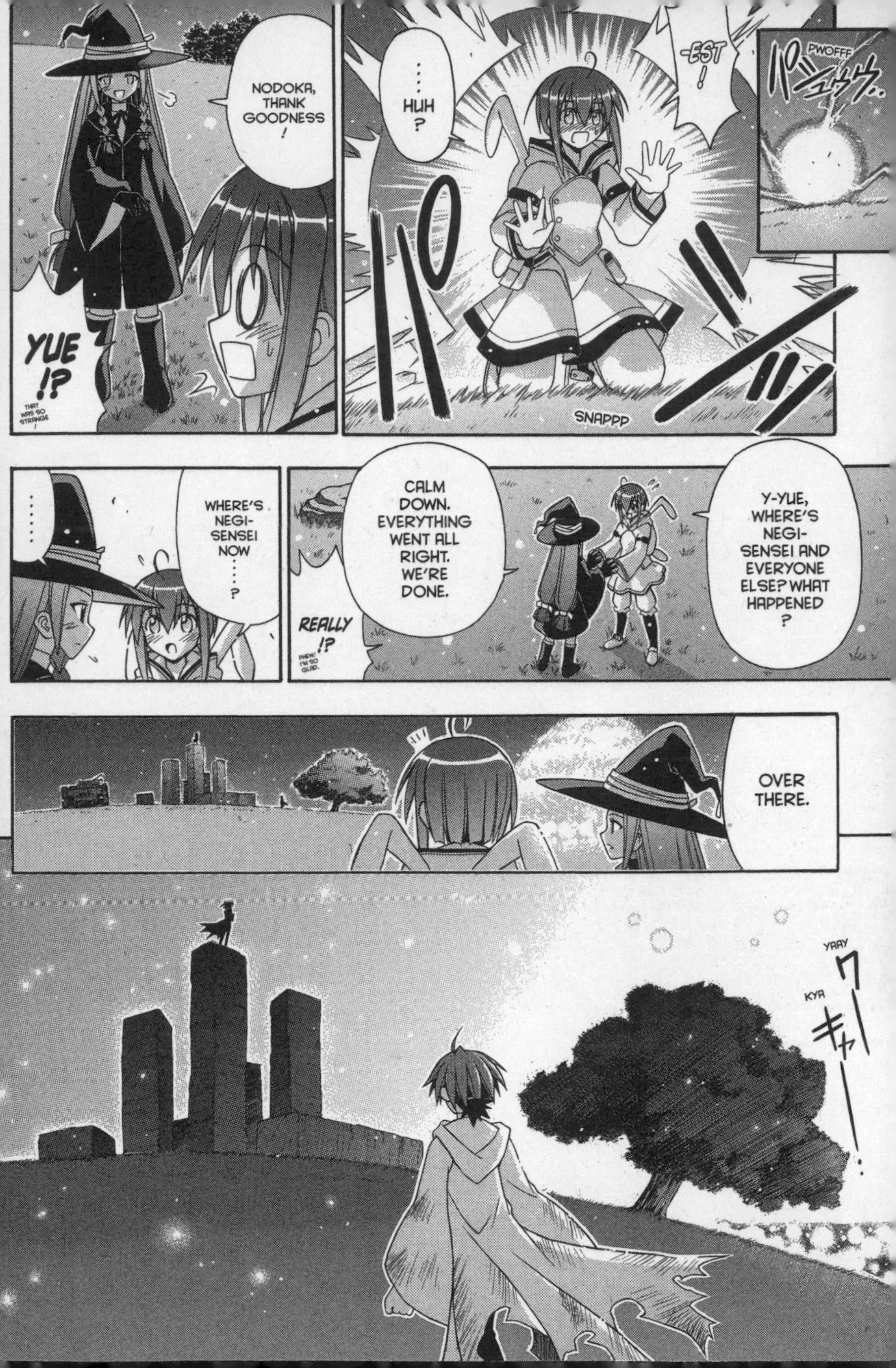

PWOFFF
-EST!
...HUH?
SNAPPP
NODOKA, THANK GOODNESS!
YUE!?
THAT WAS SO STRANGE!
Y-YUE, WHERE'S NEGI-SENSEI AND EVERYONE ELSE? WHAT HAPPENED?
CALM DOWN. EVERYTHING WENT ALL RIGHT. WE'RE DONE.
REALLY!?
PHEW! I'M SO GLAD.
WHERE'S NEGI-SENSEI NOW.....?
......
OVER THERE.
YAAY
KYA

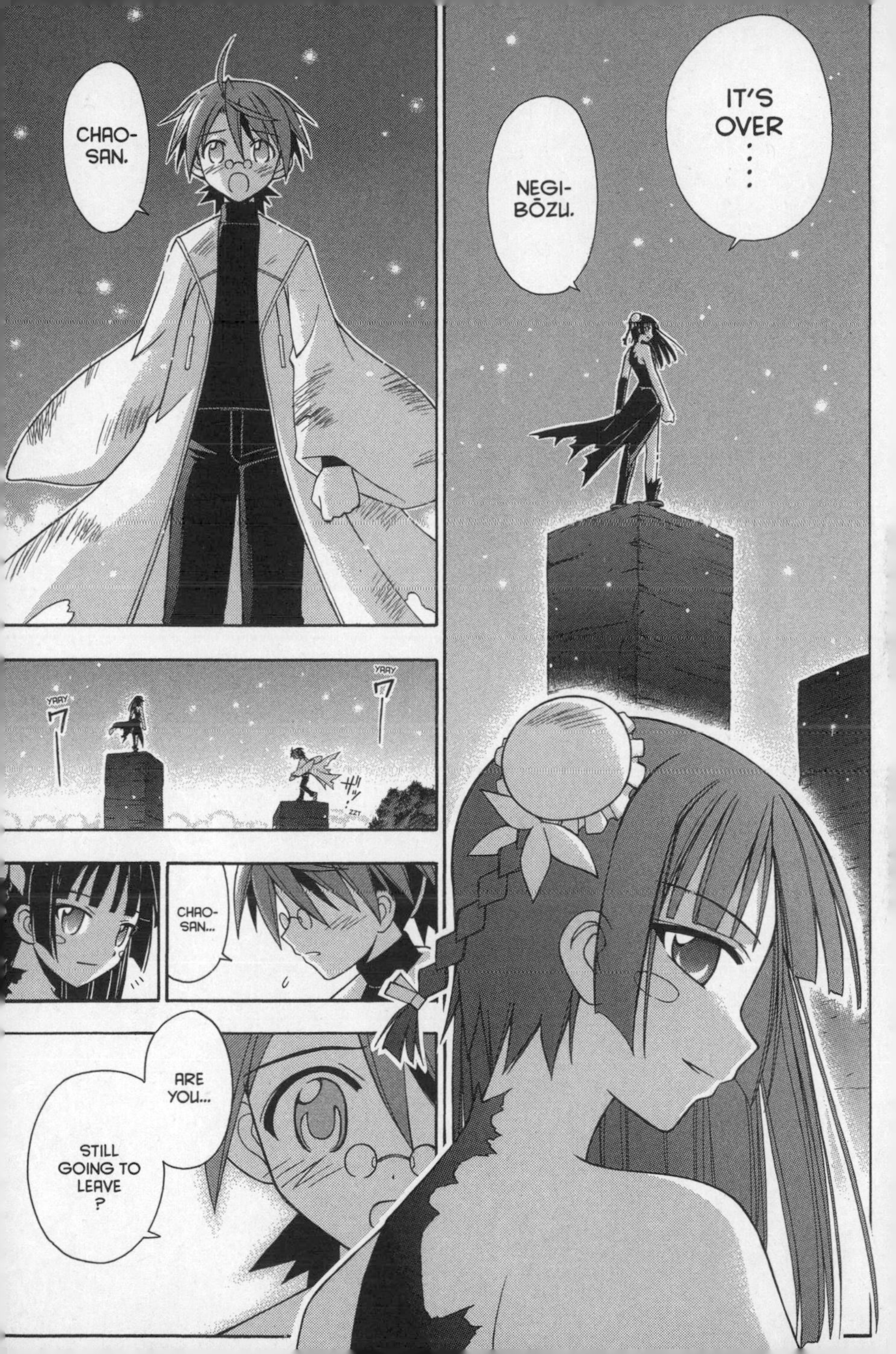
IT'S OVER . . .
NEGI-BŌZU.
CHAO-SAN.
YAAY
YAAY
ZZT
CHAO-SAN...
ARE YOU...
STILL GOING TO LEAVE ?

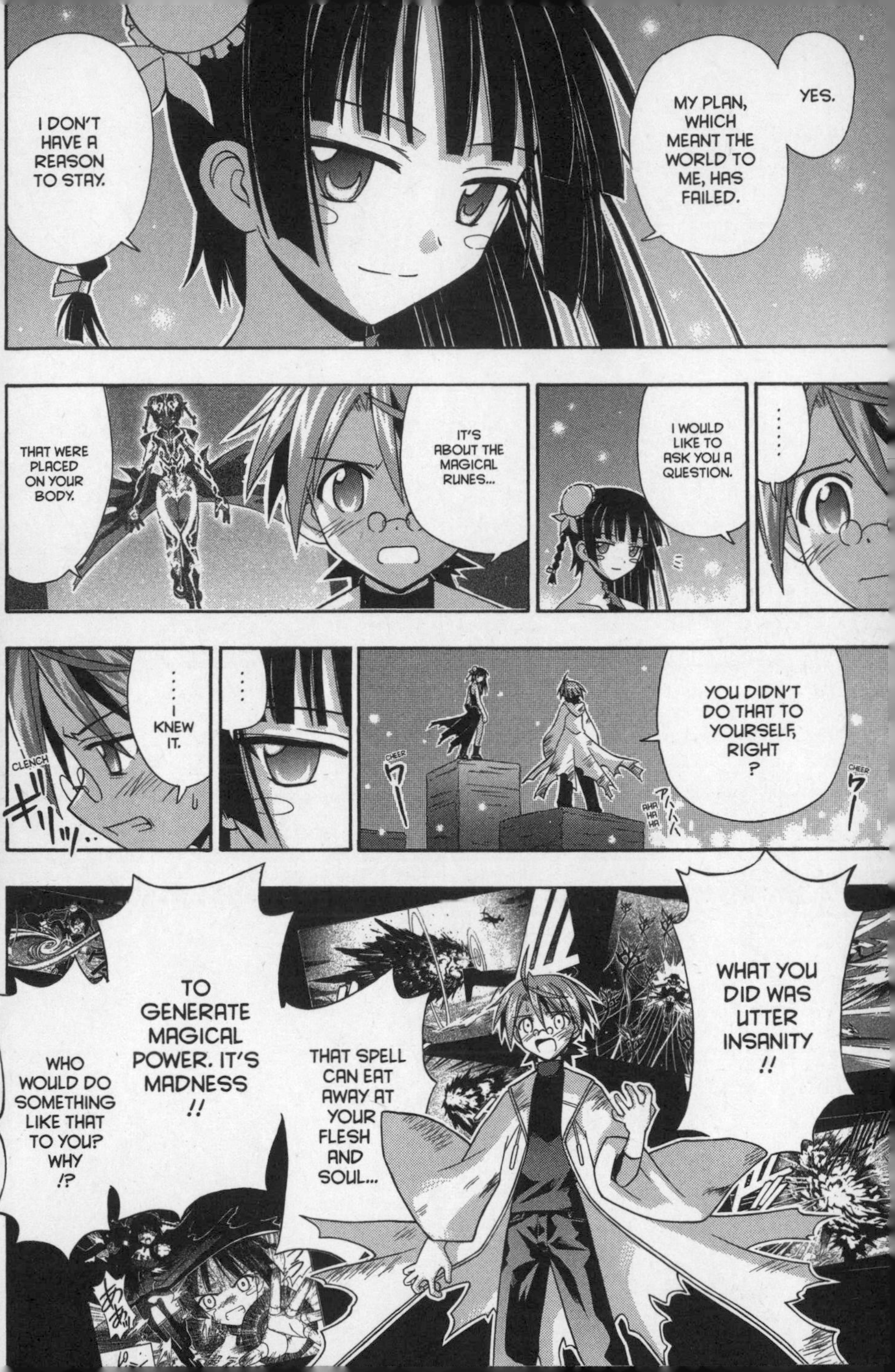
YES.
MY PLAN, WHICH MEANT THE WORLD TO ME, HAS FAILED.
I DON'T HAVE A REASON TO STAY.
......
I WOULD LIKE TO ASK YOU A QUESTION.
IT'S ABOUT THE MAGICAL RUNES...
THAT WERE PLACED ON YOUR BODY.
YOU DIDN'T DO THAT TO YOURSELF, RIGHT?
CHEER
AHA HA HA
CHEER
....
.... I KNEW IT.
CLENCH
WHAT YOU DID WAS UTTER INSANITY!!
THAT SPELL CAN EAT AWAY AT YOUR FLESH AND SOUL...
TO GENERATE MAGICAL POWER. IT'S MADNESS!!
WHO WOULD DO SOMETHING LIKE THAT TO YOU? WHY!?

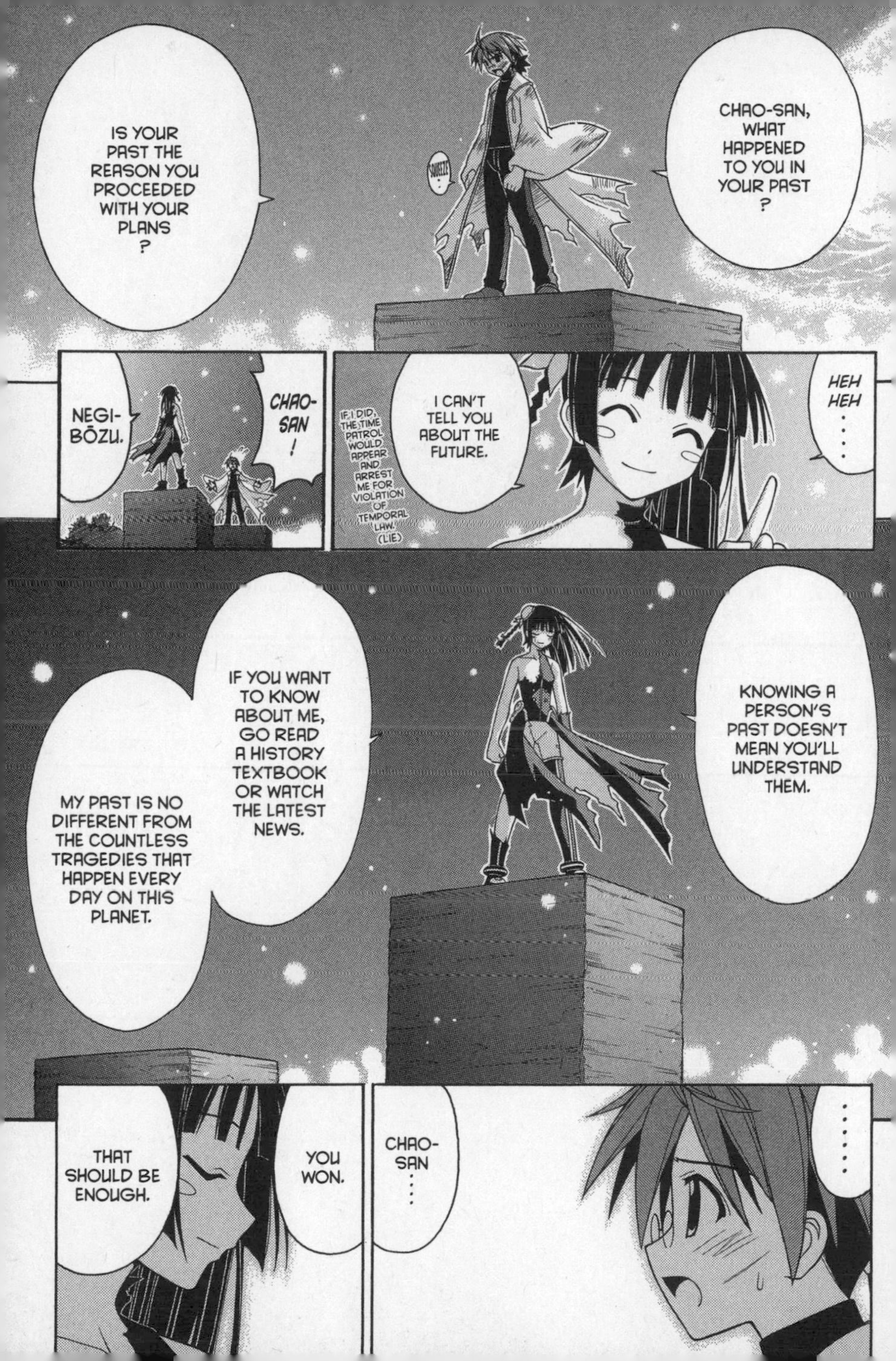

CHAO-SAN, WHAT HAPPENED TO YOU IN YOUR PAST?
SQUEEZE
IS YOUR PAST THE REASON YOU PROCEEDED WITH YOUR PLANS?
HEH HEH ....
I CAN'T TELL YOU ABOUT THE FUTURE.
IF I DID, THE TIME PATROL WOULD APPEAR AND ARREST ME FOR VIOLATION OF TEMPORAL LAW. (LIE)
CHAO-SAN!
NEGI-BŌZU.
KNOWING A PERSON'S PAST DOESN'T MEAN YOU'LL UNDERSTAND THEM.
IF YOU WANT TO KNOW ABOUT ME, GO READ A HISTORY TEXTBOOK OR WATCH THE LATEST NEWS.
MY PAST IS NO DIFFERENT FROM THE COUNTLESS TRAGEDIES THAT HAPPEN EVERY DAY ON THIS PLANET.
......
CHAO-SAN ....
YOU WON.
THAT SHOULD BE ENOUGH.

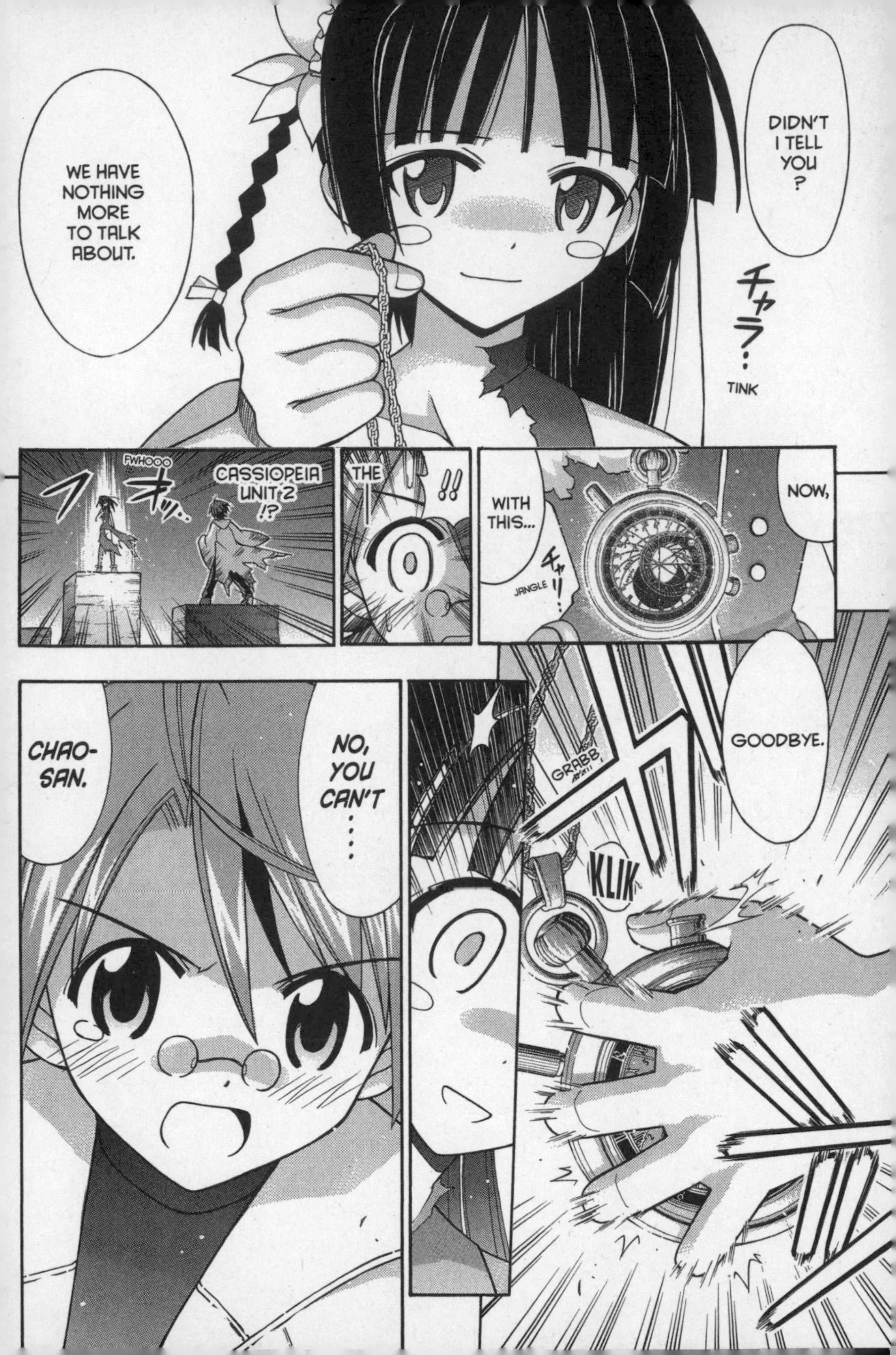
DIDN'T I TELL YOU ?
WE HAVE NOTHING MORE TO TALK ABOUT.
チャラ…
TINK
NOW,
WITH THIS...
JANGLE
THE
!!
FWHOOO
CASSIOPEIA UNIT 2 !?
GOODBYE.
GRABB
KLIK
NO, YOU CAN'T ...
CHAO-SAN.

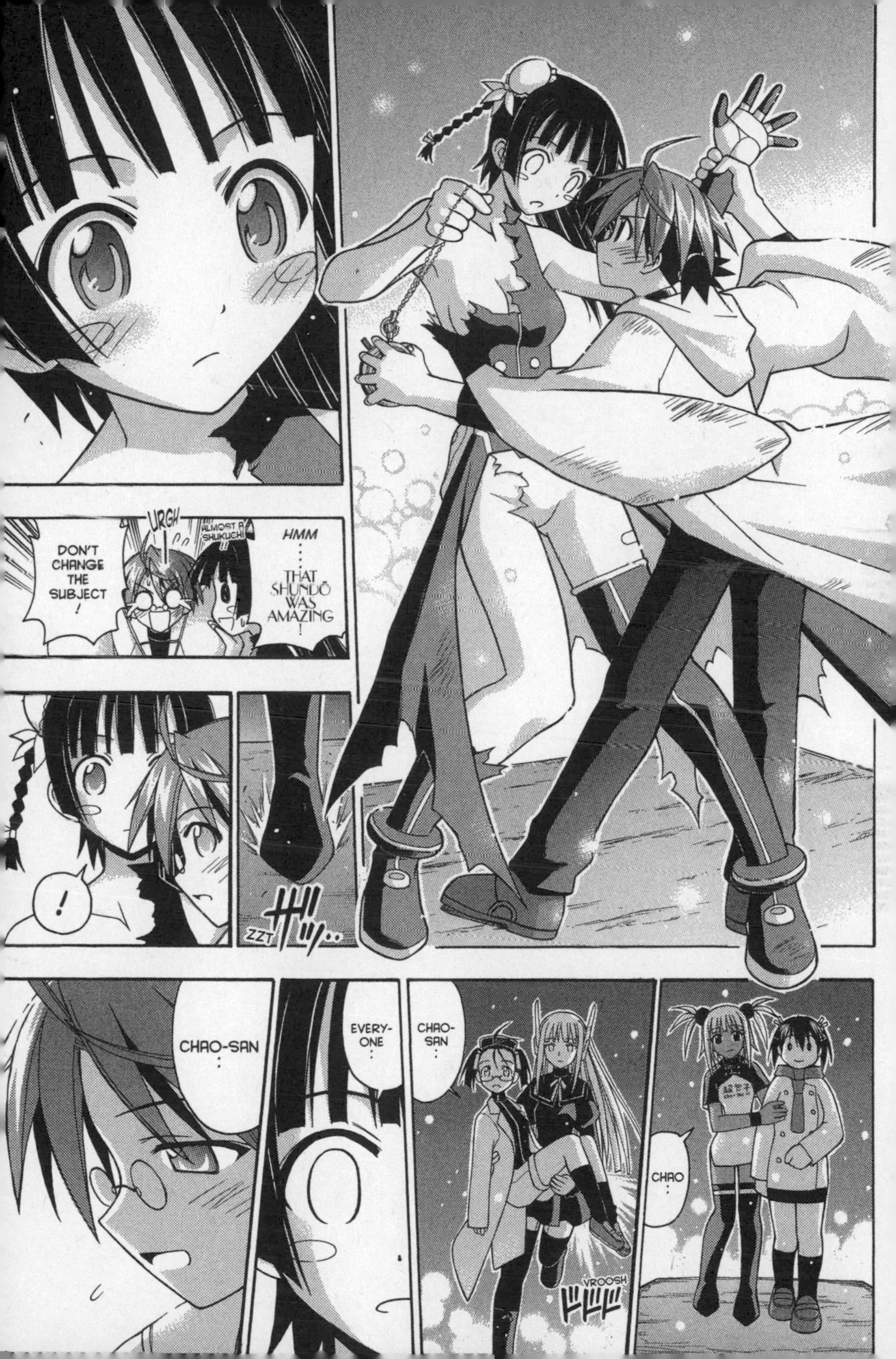
HMM... THAT SHUNDŌ WAS AMAZING!
ALMOST A SHUKUCHI!!
URGH
DON'T CHANGE THE SUBJECT!
ZZT
!
CHAO...
CHAO-SAN
VROOSH
EVERY-ONE...
CHAO-SAN...

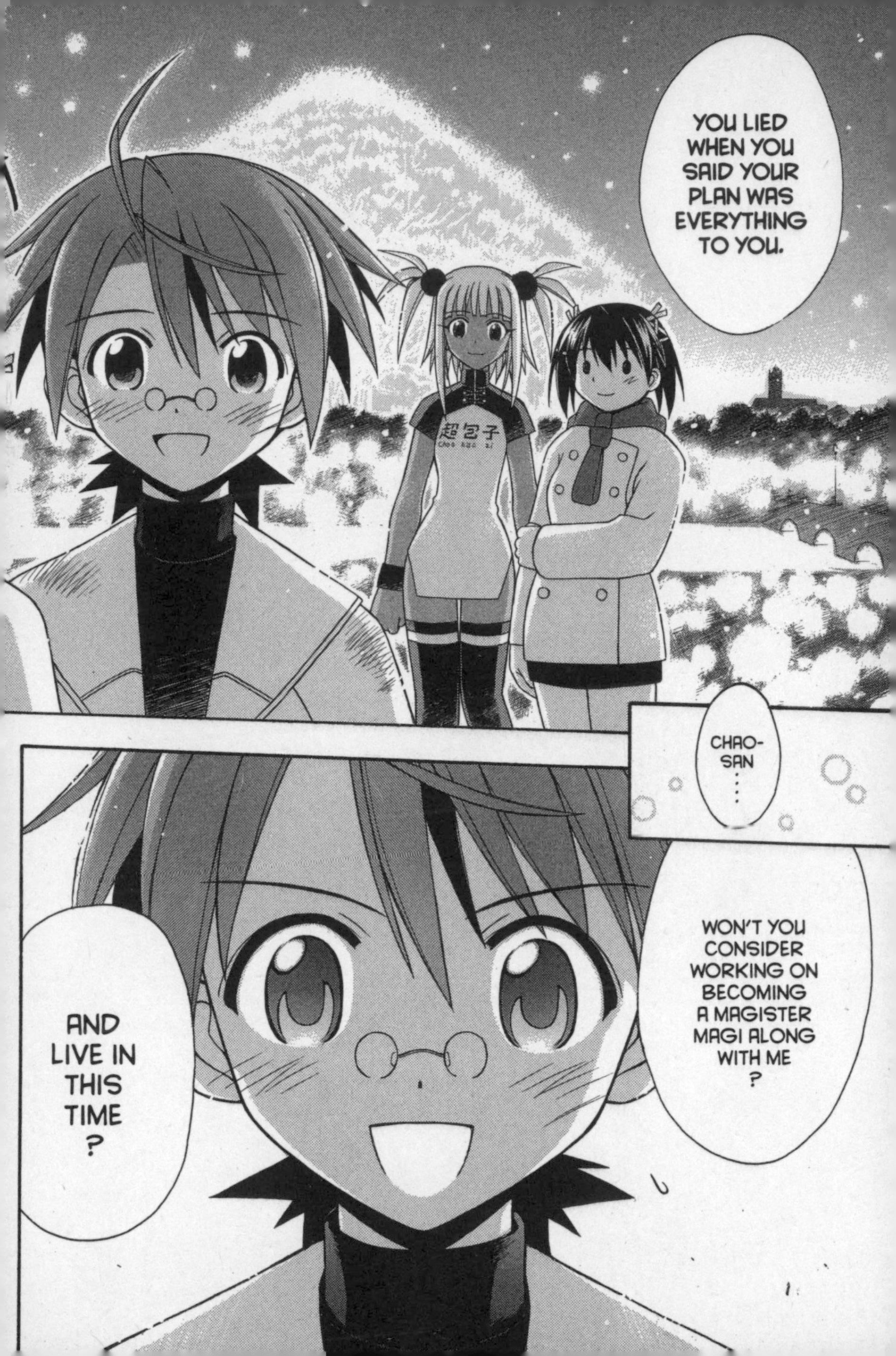
YOU LIED WHEN YOU SAID YOUR PLAN WAS EVERYTHING TO YOU.
超包子
CHAO-SAN ....
WON'T YOU CONSIDER WORKING ON BECOMING A MAGISTER MAGI ALONG WITH ME ?
AND LIVE IN THIS TIME ?

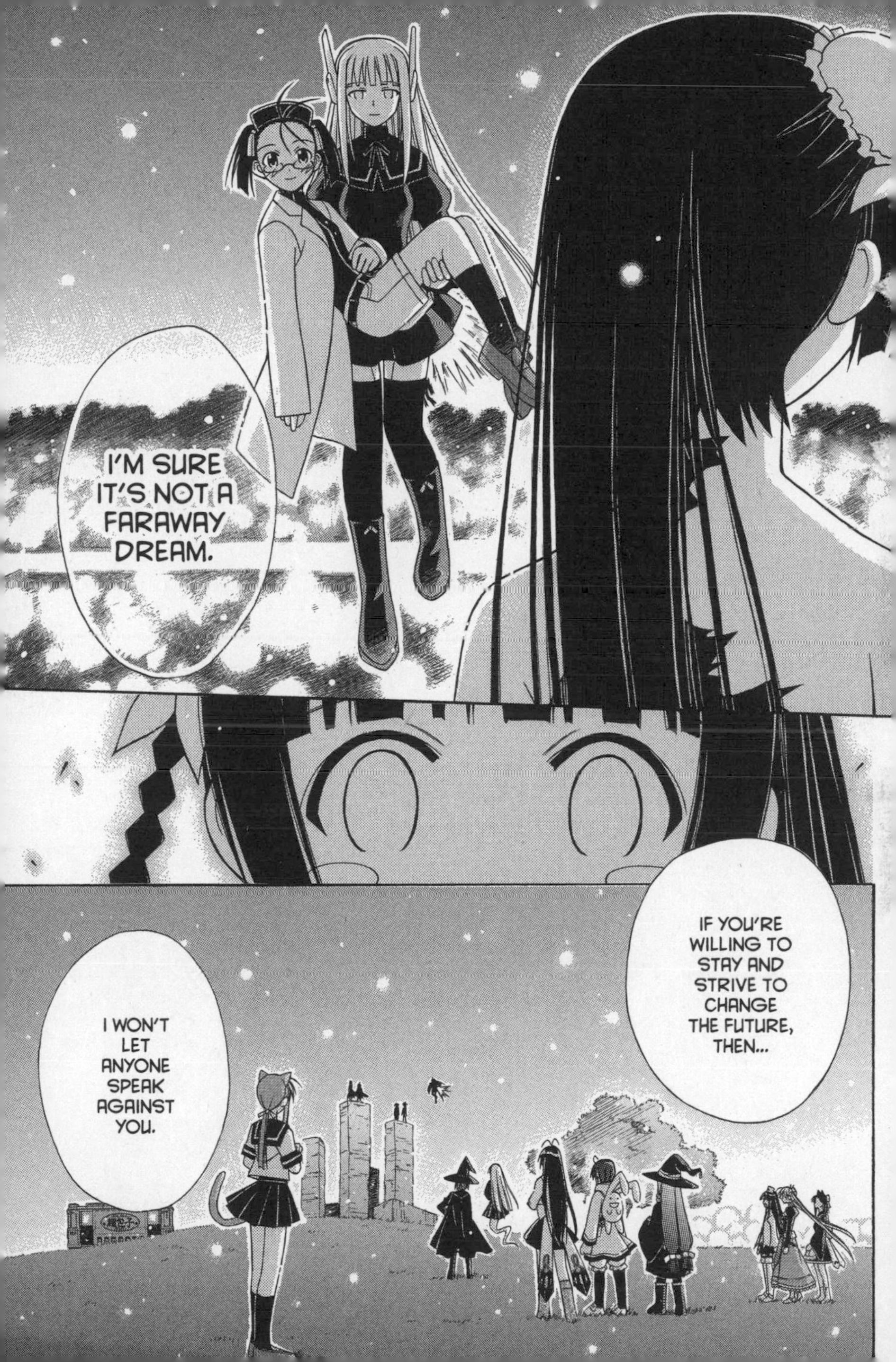
I'M SURE IT'S NOT A FARAWAY DREAM.
IF YOU'RE WILLING TO STAY AND STRIVE TO CHANGE THE FUTURE, THEN...
I WON'T LET ANYONE SPEAK AGAINST YOU.

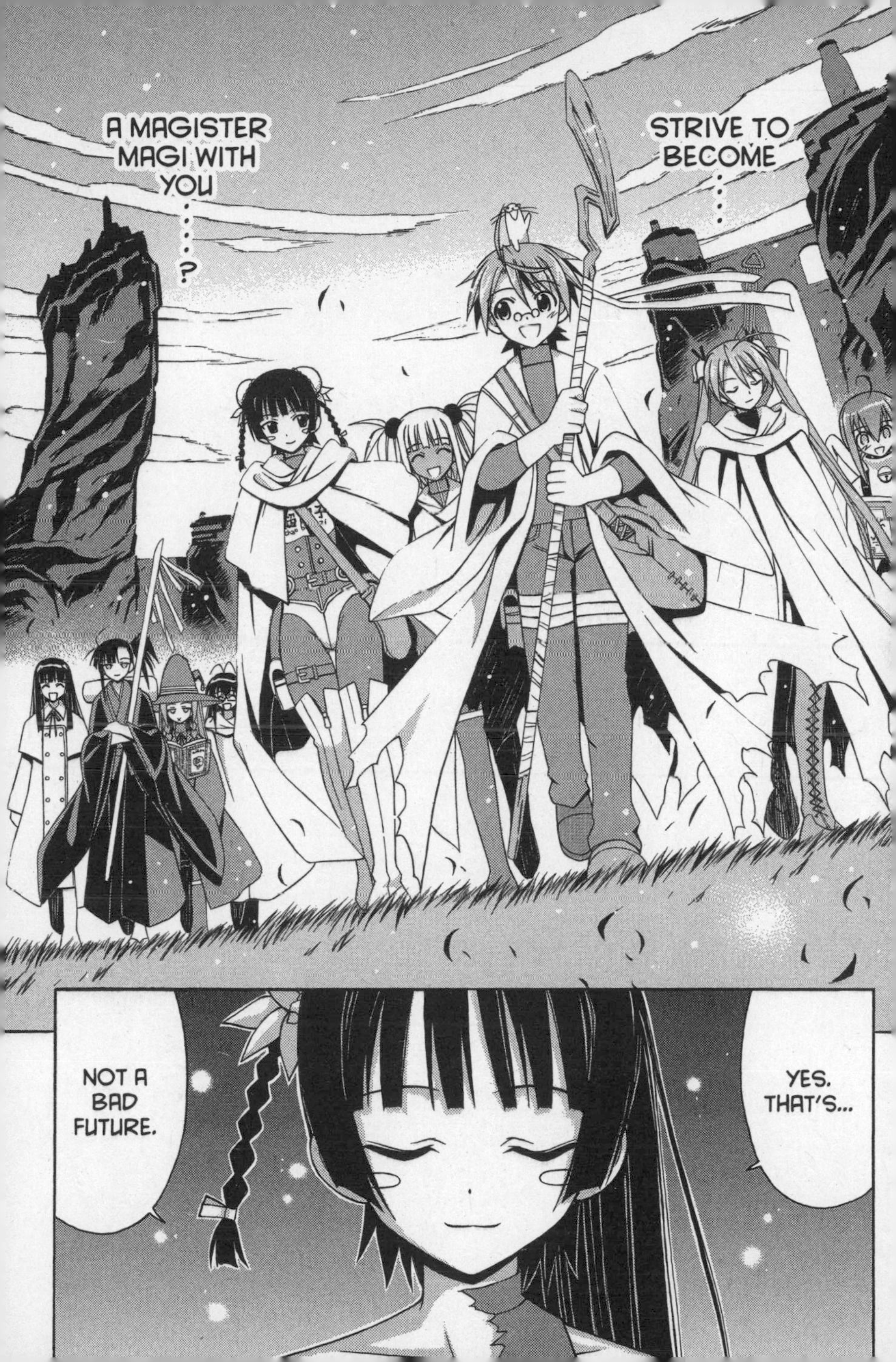
STRIVE TO BECOME...
A MAGISTER MAGI WITH YOU...?
YES. THAT'S...
NOT A BAD FUTURE.

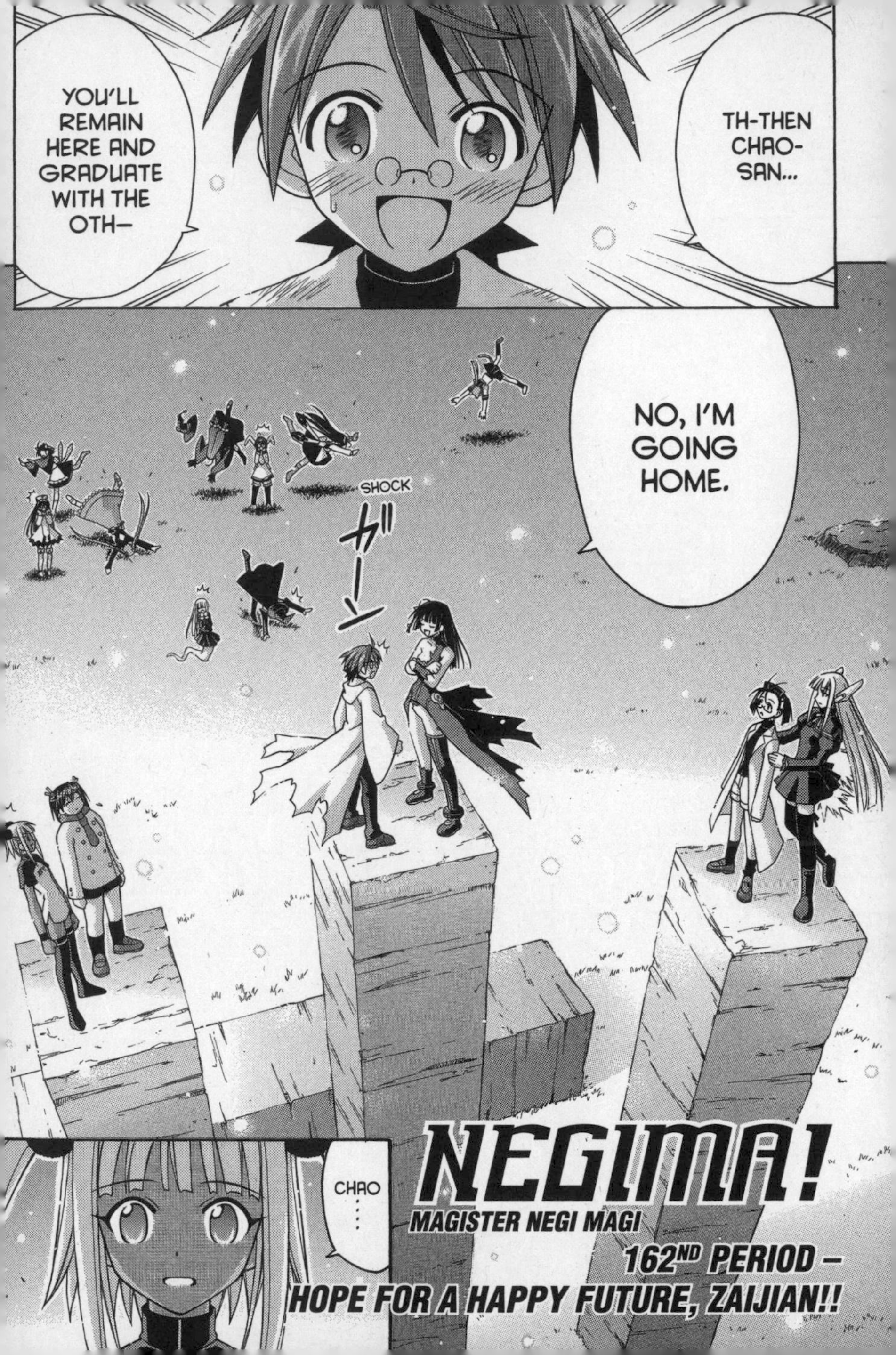
TH-THEN CHAO-SAN...
YOU'LL REMAIN HERE AND GRADUATE WITH THE OTH—
NO, I'M GOING HOME.
SHOCK
NEGIMA!
MAGISTER NEGI MAGI
162ND PERIOD –
HOPE FOR A HAPPY FUTURE, ZAIJIAN!!
CHAO ...

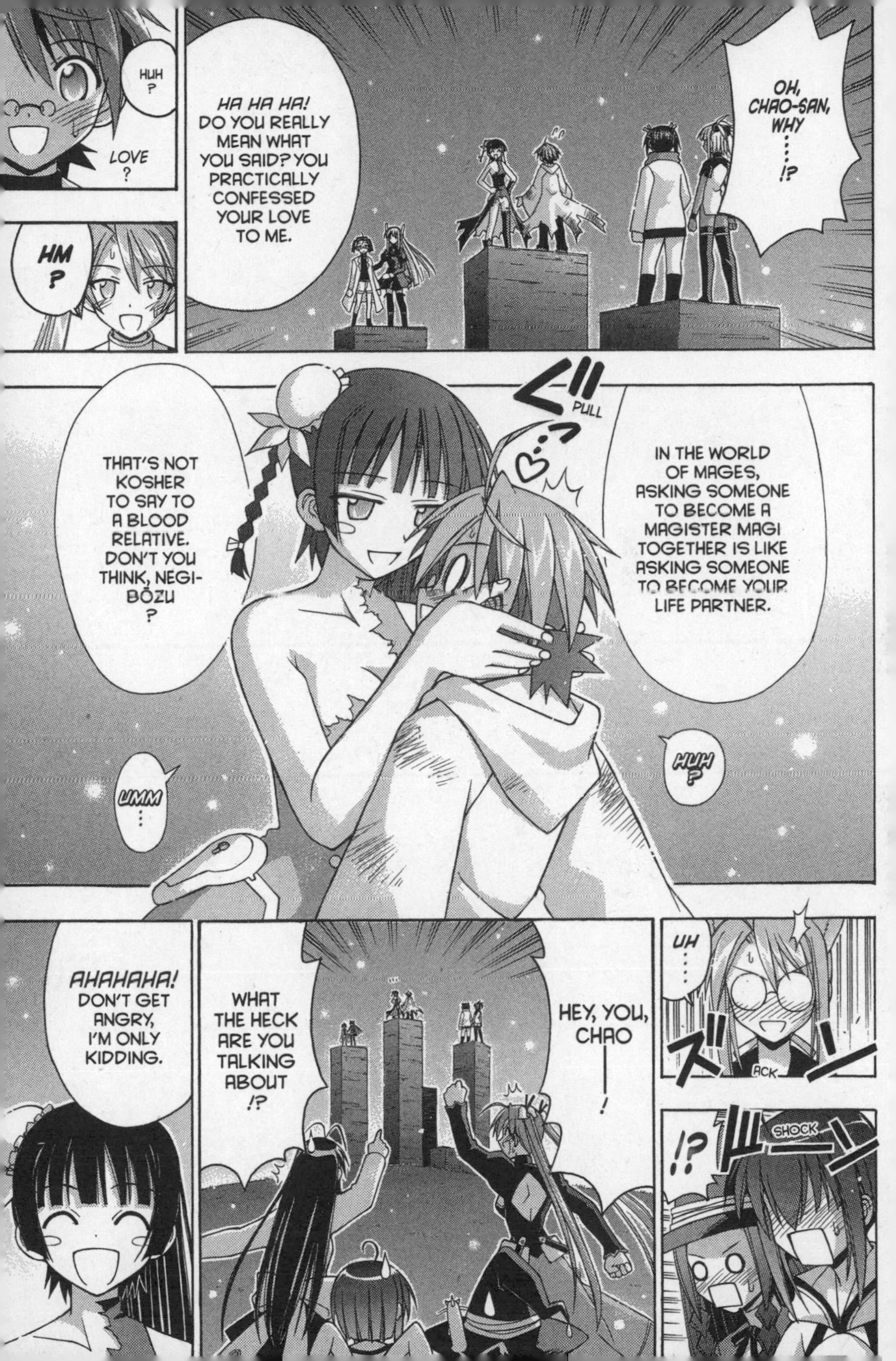
OH, CHAO-SAN, WHY ....!?
HA HA HA! DO YOU REALLY MEAN WHAT YOU SAID? YOU PRACTICALLY CONFESSED YOUR LOVE TO ME.
HUH ?
LOVE ?
HM ?
PULL
IN THE WORLD OF MAGES, ASKING SOMEONE TO BECOME A MAGISTER MAGI TOGETHER IS LIKE ASKING SOMEONE TO BECOME YOUR LIFE PARTNER.
HUH ?
THAT'S NOT KOSHER TO SAY TO A BLOOD RELATIVE. DON'T YOU THINK, NEGI-BŌZU ?
UMM ...
UH ....
ACK
SHOCK
!?
HEY, YOU, CHAO —!
WHAT THE HECK ARE YOU TALKING ABOUT !?
AHAHAHA! DON'T GET ANGRY, I'M ONLY KIDDING.

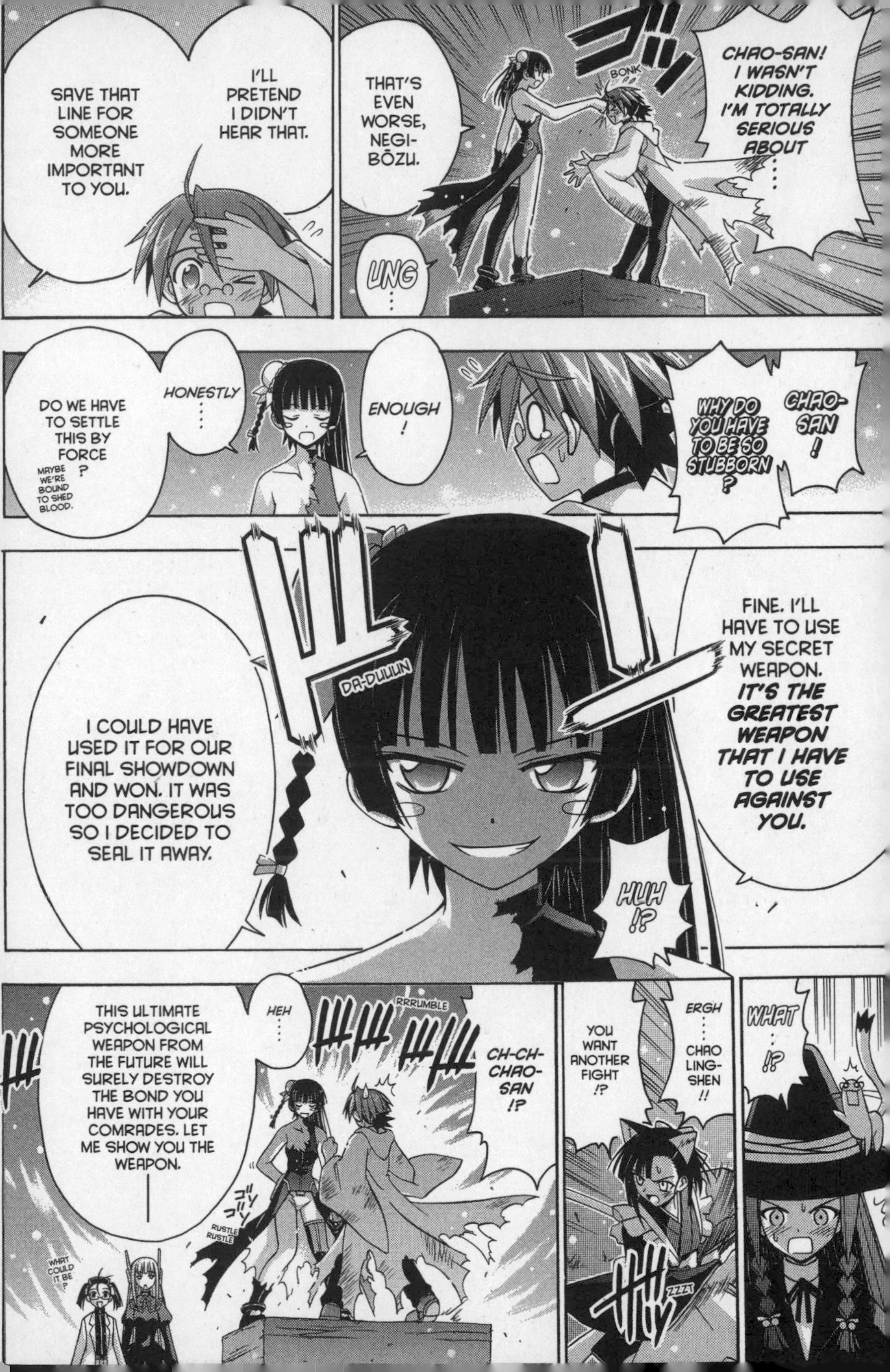
CHAO-SAN! I WASN'T KIDDING. I'M TOTALLY SERIOUS ABOUT ...
BONK
THAT'S EVEN WORSE, NEGI-BŌZU.
UNG ...
I'LL PRETEND I DIDN'T HEAR THAT.
SAVE THAT LINE FOR SOMEONE MORE IMPORTANT TO YOU.
CHAO-SAN!
WHY DO YOU HAVE TO BE SO STUBBORN?
ENOUGH!
HONESTLY...
DO WE HAVE TO SETTLE THIS BY FORCE?
MAYBE WE'RE BOUND TO SHED BLOOD.
FINE. I'LL HAVE TO USE MY SECRET WEAPON. IT'S THE GREATEST WEAPON THAT I HAVE TO USE AGAINST YOU.
DA-DUUUN
HUH!?
I COULD HAVE USED IT FOR OUR FINAL SHOWDOWN AND WON. IT WAS TOO DANGEROUS SO I DECIDED TO SEAL IT AWAY.
WHAT...!?
ERGH... CHAO LING-SHEN!!
YOU WANT ANOTHER FIGHT!?
CH-CH-CHAO-SAN!?
RRRUMBLE
HEH...
THIS ULTIMATE PSYCHOLOGICAL WEAPON FROM THE FUTURE WILL SURELY DESTROY THE BOND YOU HAVE WITH YOUR COMRADES. LET ME SHOW YOU THE WEAPON.
RUSTLE RUSTLE
WHAT COULD IT BE?

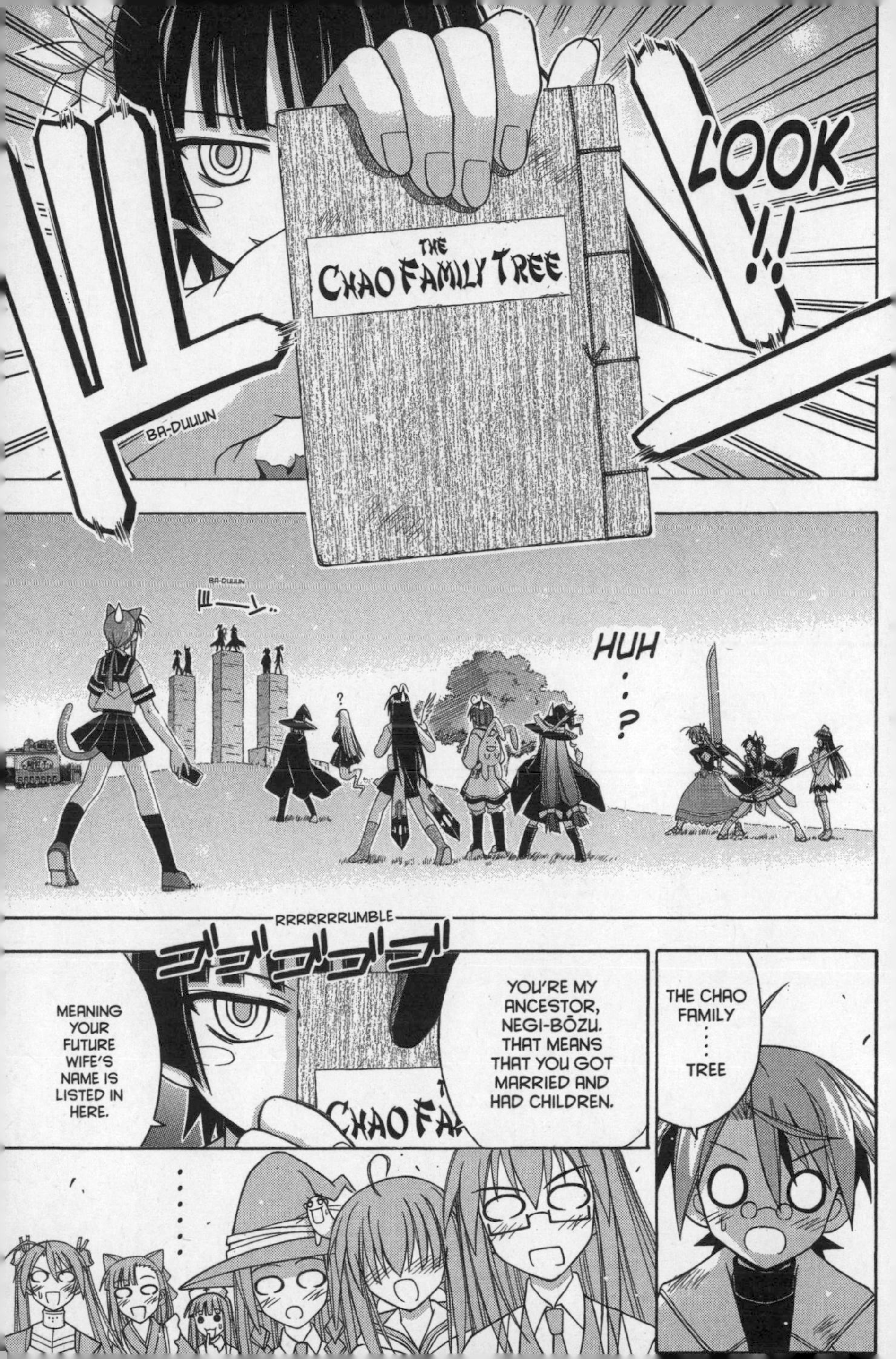
LOOK!!
THE CHAO FAMILY TREE
BA-DUUUN
HUH...?
BA-DUUUN
THE CHAO FAMILY... TREE
RRRRRRRUMBLE
YOU'RE MY ANCESTOR, NEGI-BŌZU. THAT MEANS THAT YOU GOT MARRIED AND HAD CHILDREN.
MEANING YOUR FUTURE WIFE'S NAME IS LISTED IN HERE.

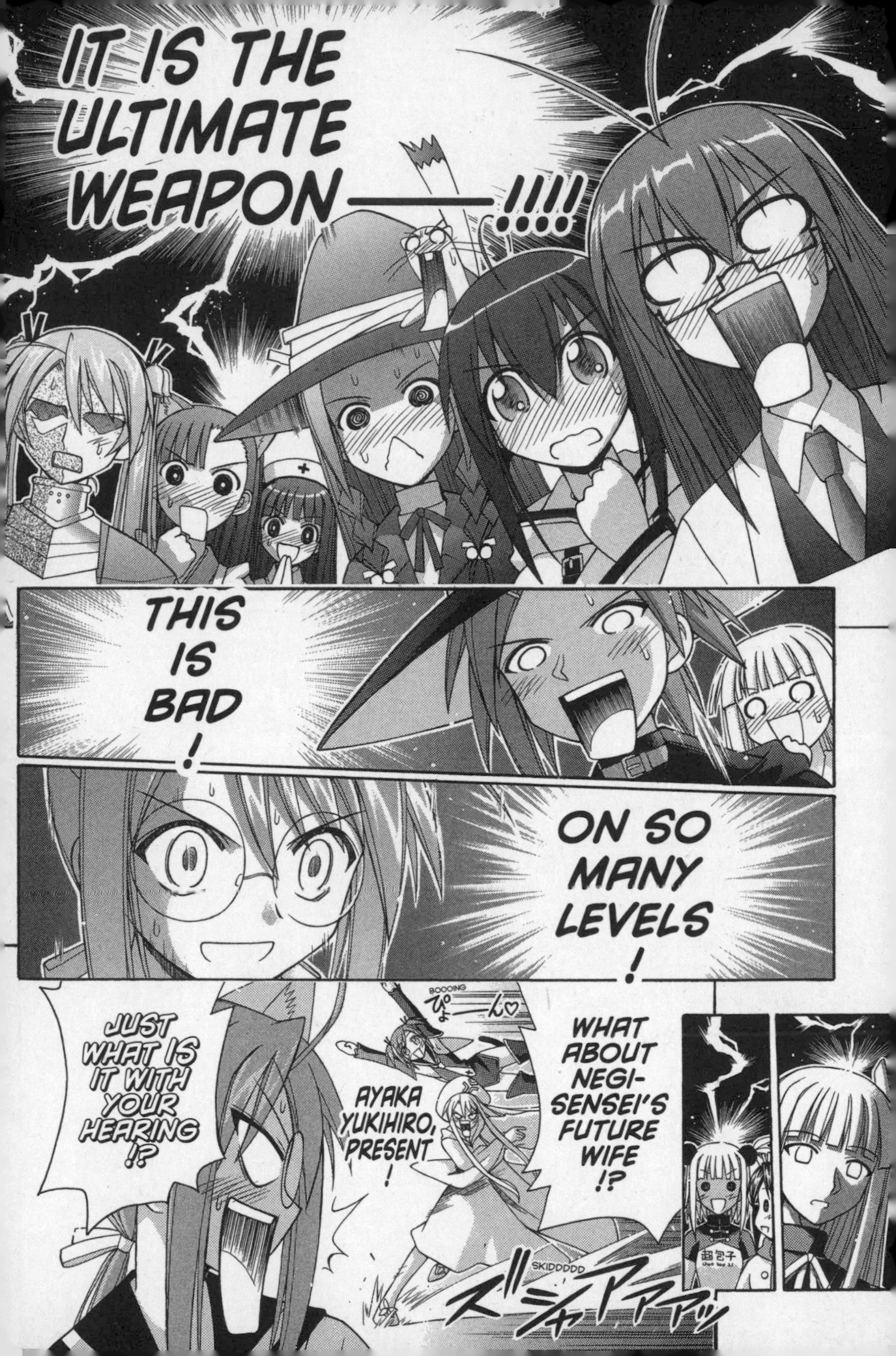
IT IS THE ULTIMATE WEAPON——!!!!
THIS IS BAD!
ON SO MANY LEVELS!
WHAT ABOUT NEGI-SENSEI'S FUTURE WIFE!?
BOOOING
ぴょーん♡
AYAKA YUKIHIRO, PRESENT!
JUST WHAT IS IT WITH YOUR HEARING!?
超包子
SKIDDDDD
ズシャアアッ

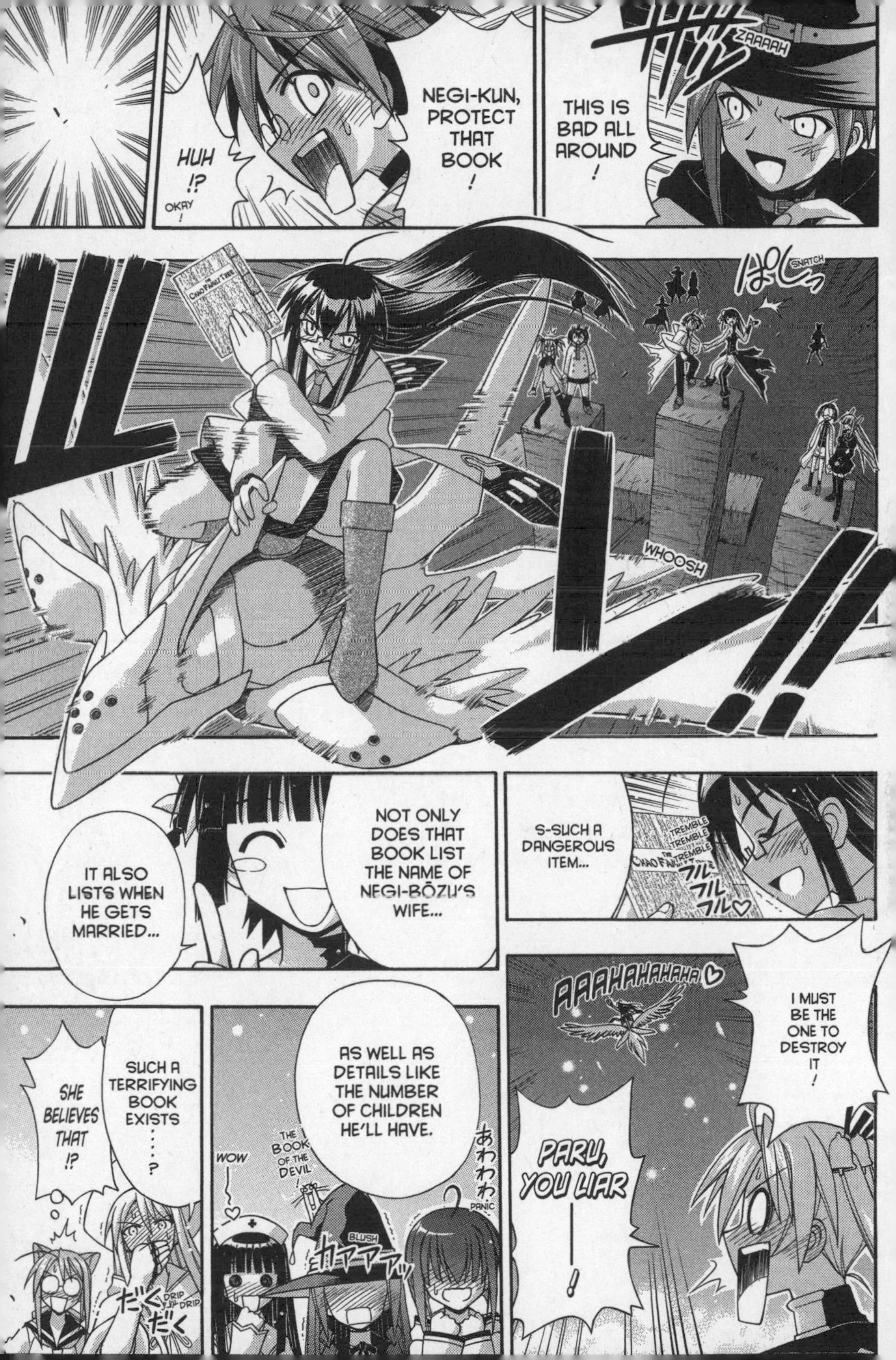
ZAAAAH
THIS IS BAD ALL AROUND!
NEGI-KUN, PROTECT THAT BOOK!
!
HUH !?
OKAY!
SNATCH
THE CHAO FAMILY TREE
WHOOSH
S-SUCH A DANGEROUS ITEM...
TREMBLE TREMBLE TREMBLE
フルフルフル♡
NOT ONLY DOES THAT BOOK LIST THE NAME OF NEGI-BŌZU'S WIFE...
IT ALSO LISTS WHEN HE GETS MARRIED...
AAAHAHAHAHA♡
I MUST BE THE ONE TO DESTROY IT!
PARU, YOU LIAR—!
AS WELL AS DETAILS LIKE THE NUMBER OF CHILDREN HE'LL HAVE.
あわわわ
PANIC
THE BOOK OF THE DEVIL!
WOW
BLUSH
カアアアッ
SUCH A TERRIFYING BOOK EXISTS.....?
SHE BELIEVES THAT!?
DRIP DRIP
だくだく

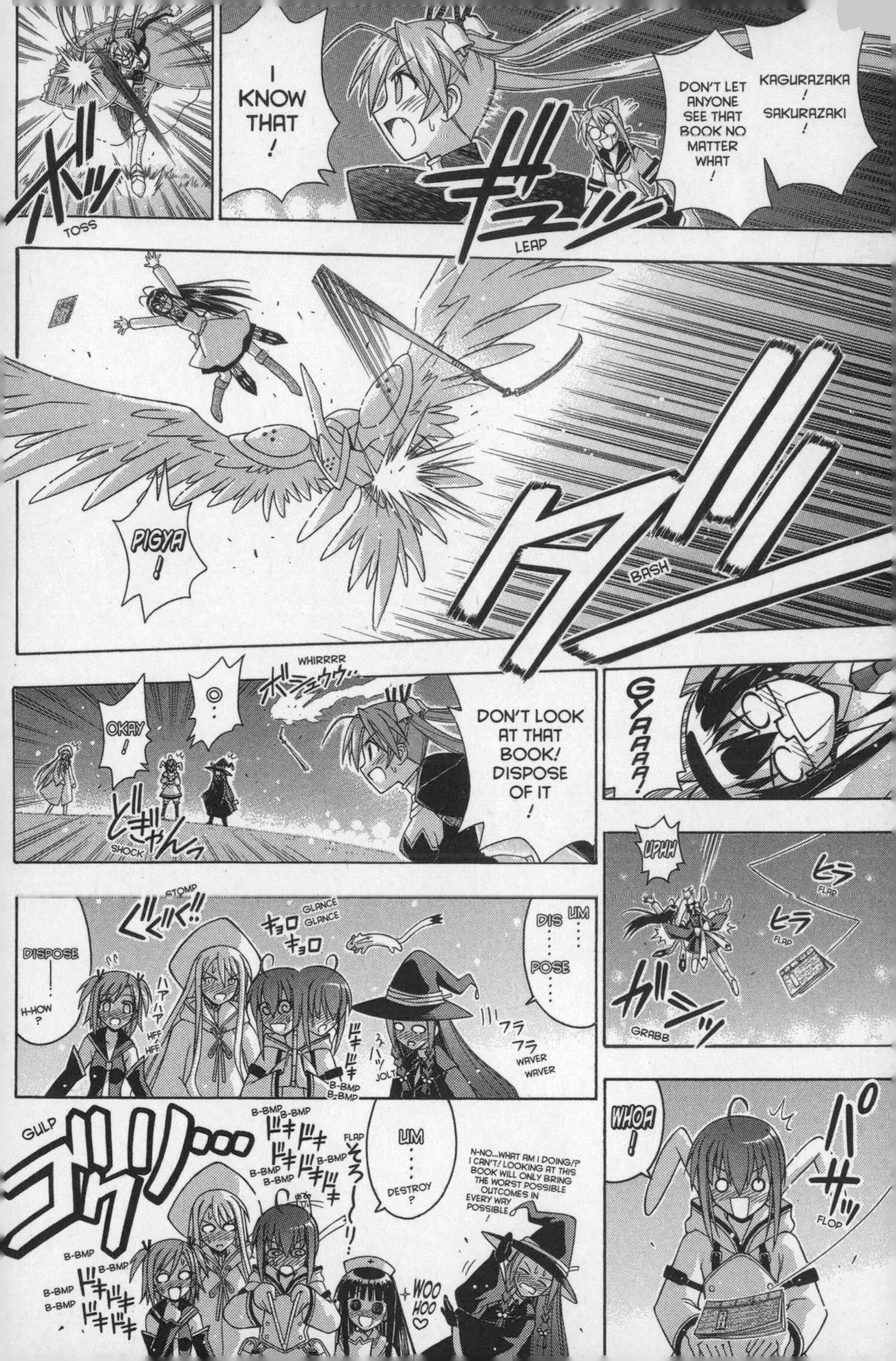
KAGURAZAKA! SAKURAZAKI!
DON'T LET ANYONE SEE THAT BOOK NO MATTER WHAT!
I KNOW THAT!
LEAP
TOSS
PIGYA!
BASH
GYAAAA!
DON'T LOOK AT THAT BOOK! DISPOSE OF IT!
O...
OKAY!
WHIRRRR
SHOCK
UPHH
FLAP
FLAP
GRABB
UM...
DIS...POSE...
GLANCE GLANCE
STOMP
DISPOSE! H-HOW?
HFF HFF
B-BMP B-BMP
JOLT
WAVER WAVER
WHOA!
FLOP
N-NO...WHAT AM I DOING!? I CAN'T! LOOKING AT THIS BOOK WILL ONLY BRING THE WORST POSSIBLE OUTCOMES IN EVERY WAY POSSIBLE!
UM... DESTROY?
FLAP
B-BMP B-BMP
B-BMP B-BMP
GULP
B-BMP B-BMP
B-BMP
WOO HOO

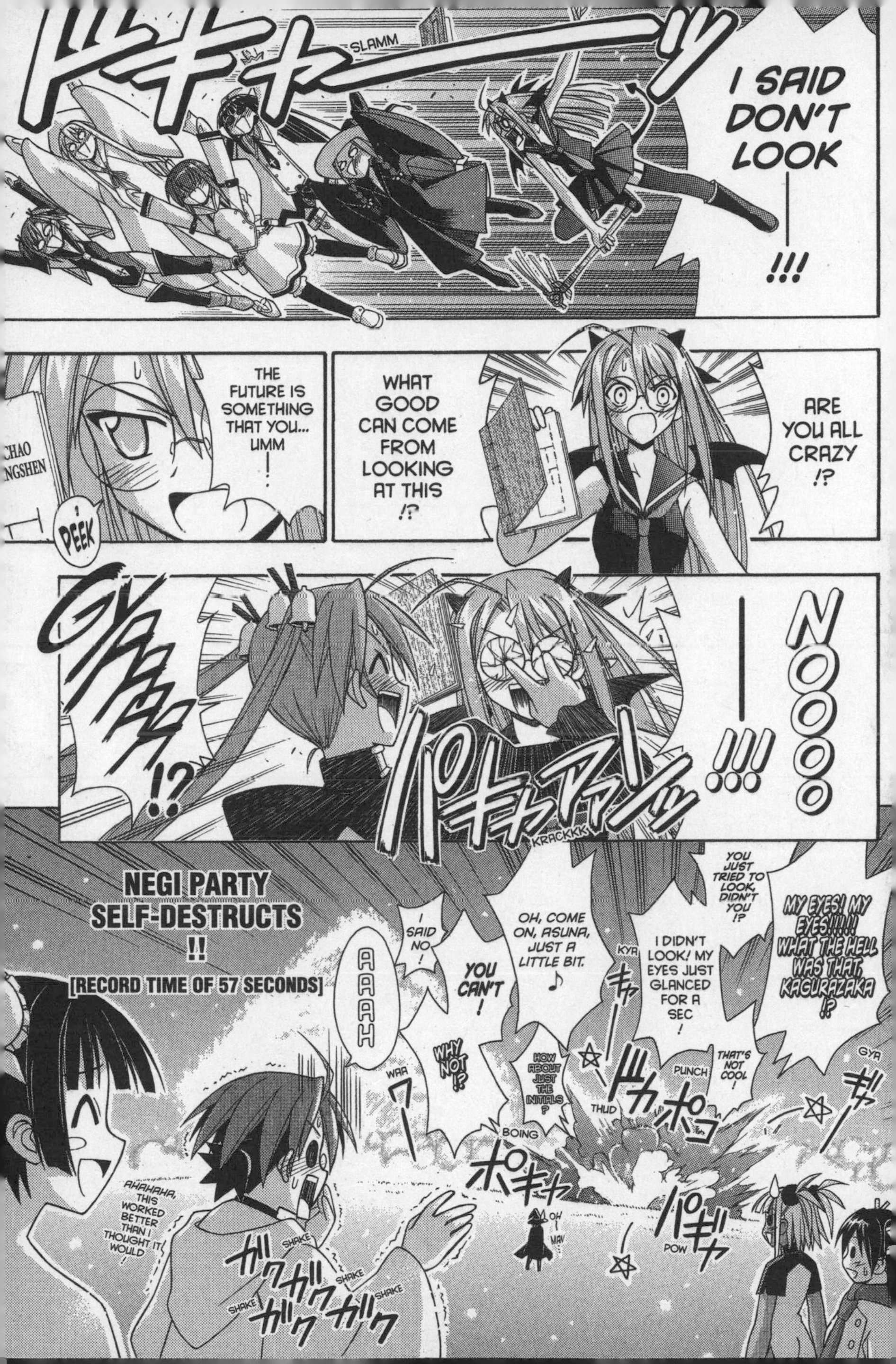
SLAMM
I SAID DON'T LOOK—!!!
ARE YOU ALL CRAZY!?
WHAT GOOD CAN COME FROM LOOKING AT THIS!?
THE FUTURE IS SOMETHING THAT YOU... UMM!
CHAO
PEEK
NOOOO—!!!
KRACKKK
GYAAAA!?
MY EYES! MY EYES!!!!! WHAT THE HELL WAS THAT, KAGURAZAKA!?
GYA
YOU JUST TRIED TO LOOK, DIDN'T YOU!?
I DIDN'T LOOK! MY EYES JUST GLANCED FOR A SEC!
KYA
THAT'S NOT COOL!
PUNCH
THUD
POW
OH, COME ON, ASUNA, JUST A LITTLE BIT. ♪
HOW ABOUT JUST THE INITIALS?
BOING
OH MAN
YOU CAN'T!
WHY NOT!?
I SAID NO!
AAAAH
WAA
NEGI PARTY SELF-DESTRUCTS!!
[RECORD TIME OF 57 SECONDS]
SHAKE SHAKE SHAKE SHAKE
AHAHAHA, THIS WORKED BETTER THAN I THOUGHT IT WOULD!

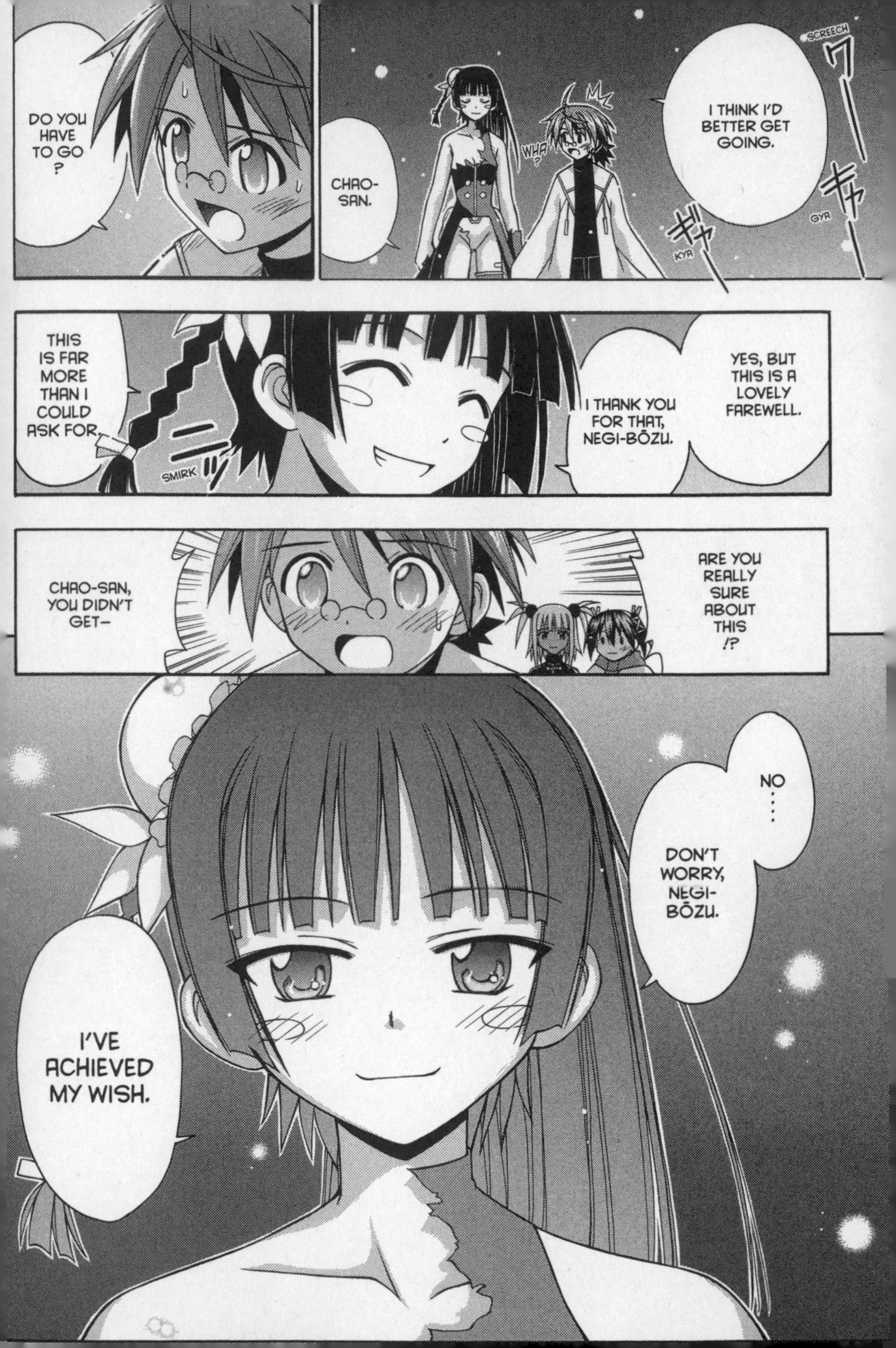
SCREECH
I THINK I'D BETTER GET GOING.
GYA
KYA
WHA?
CHAO-SAN.
DO YOU HAVE TO GO?
YES, BUT THIS IS A LOVELY FAREWELL.
I THANK YOU FOR THAT, NEGI-BŌZU.
SMIRK
THIS IS FAR MORE THAN I COULD ASK FOR.
ARE YOU REALLY SURE ABOUT THIS!?
CHAO-SAN, YOU DIDN'T GET—
NO....
DON'T WORRY, NEGI-BŌZU.
I'VE ACHIEVED MY WISH.

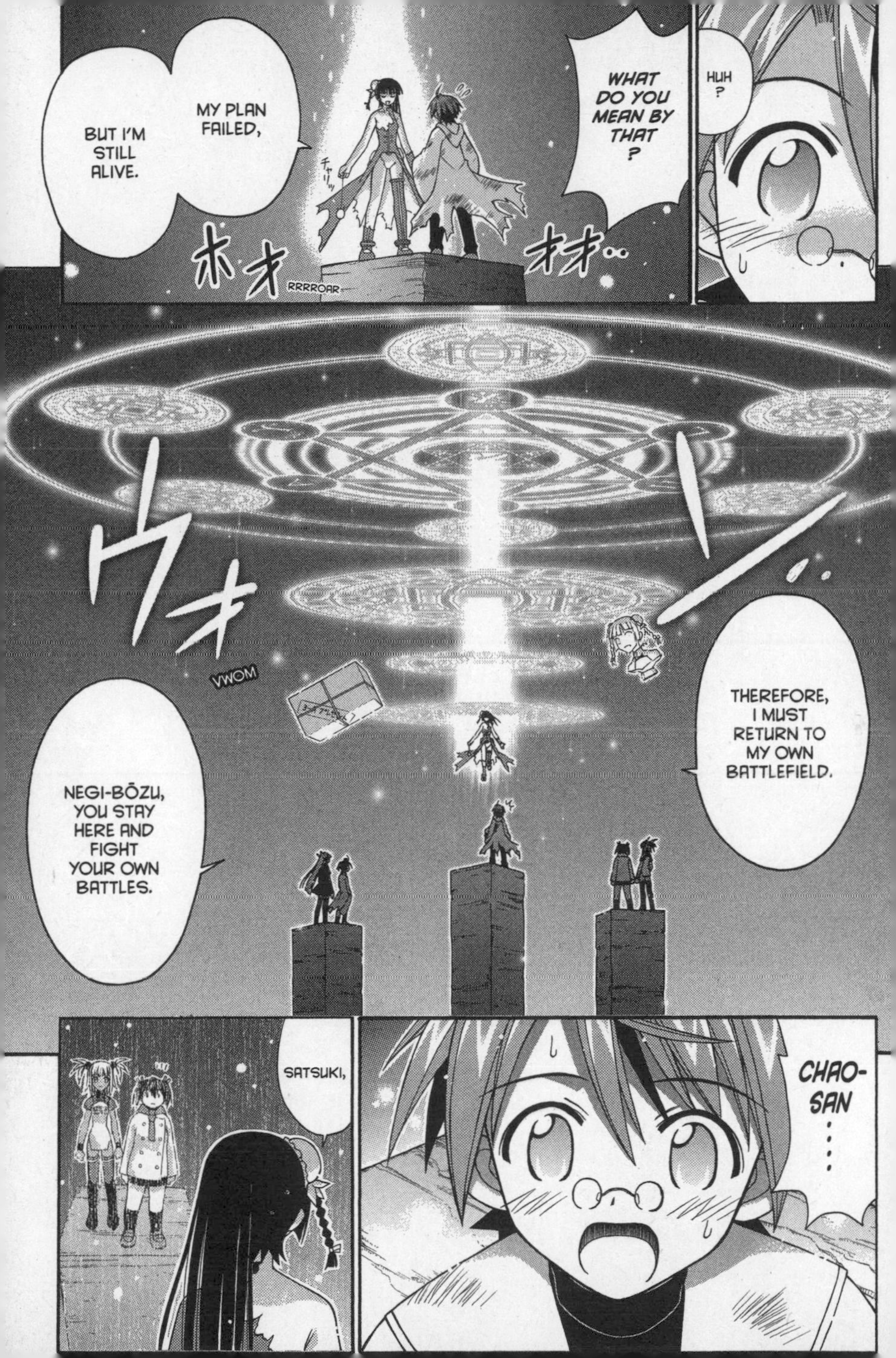
HUH ?
WHAT DO YOU MEAN BY THAT ?
MY PLAN FAILED,
BUT I'M STILL ALIVE.
RRRROAR
VWOM
THEREFORE, I MUST RETURN TO MY OWN BATTLEFIELD.
NEGI-BŌZU, YOU STAY HERE AND FIGHT YOUR OWN BATTLES.
CHAO-SAN ...
SATSUKI,

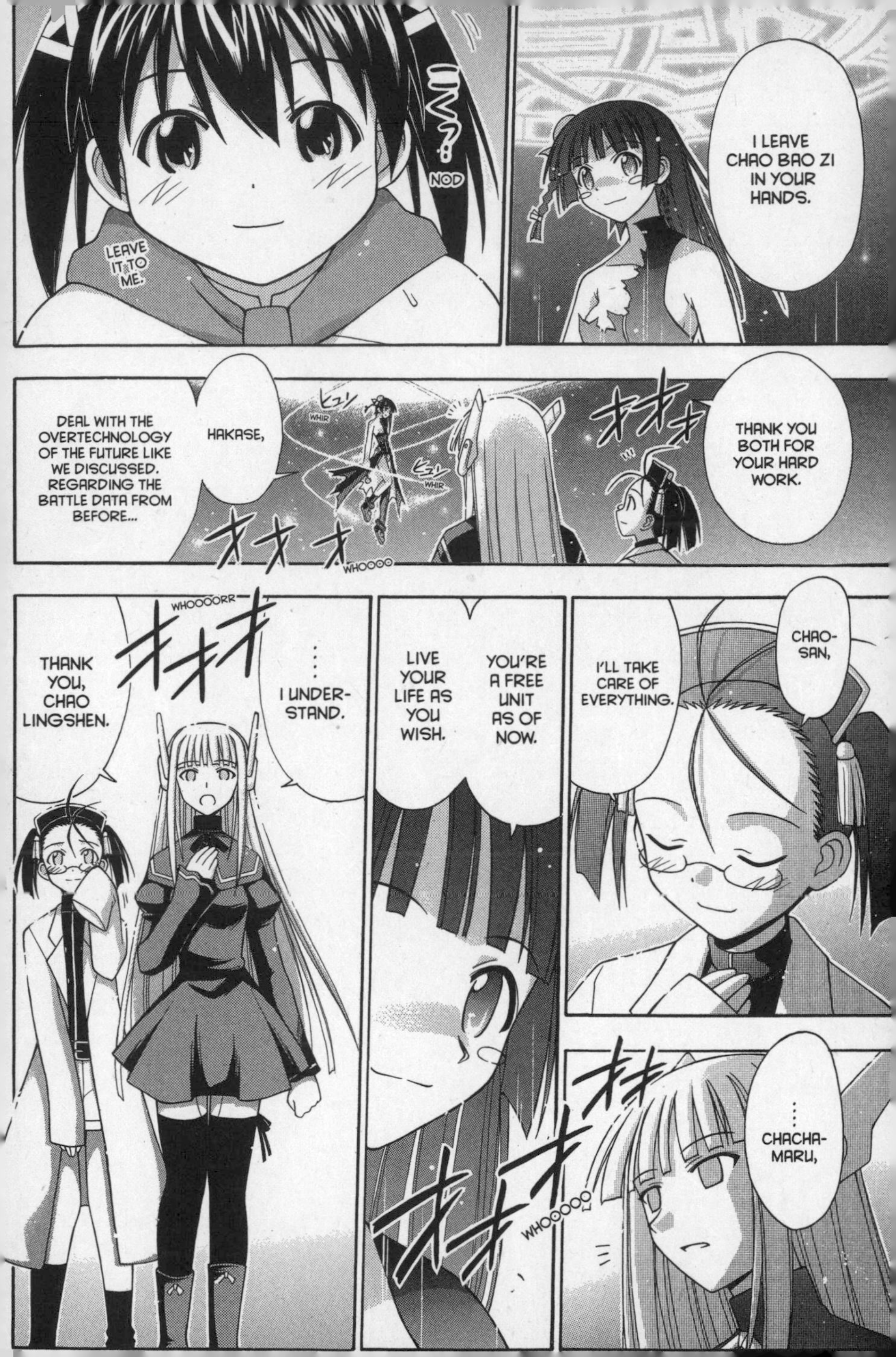

I LEAVE CHAO BAO ZI IN YOUR HANDS.
NOD
LEAVE IT TO ME.
THANK YOU BOTH FOR YOUR HARD WORK.
WHIR
WHIR
HAKASE,
DEAL WITH THE OVERTECHNOLOGY OF THE FUTURE LIKE WE DISCUSSED. REGARDING THE BATTLE DATA FROM BEFORE...
WHOOOO
CHAO-SAN,
I'LL TAKE CARE OF EVERYTHING.
... CHACHA-MARU,
WHOOOOO
YOU'RE A FREE UNIT AS OF NOW.
LIVE YOUR LIFE AS YOU WISH.
... I UNDER-STAND.
WHOOOORR
THANK YOU, CHAO LINGSHEN.

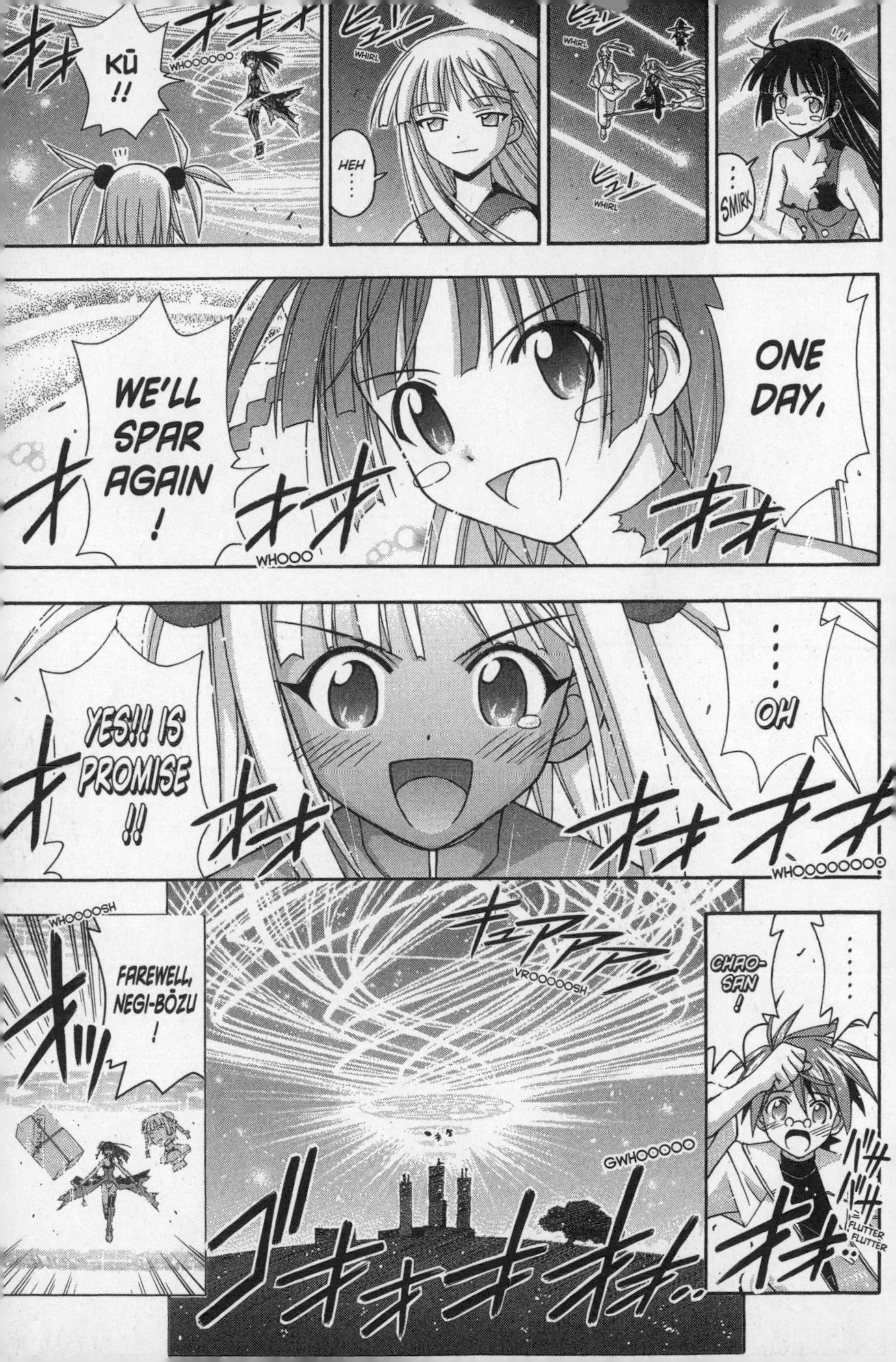

...
SMIRK
WHIRL
WHIRL
WHIRL
HEH...
KŪ!!
WHOOOOOOO
ONE DAY,
WE'LL SPAR AGAIN!
WHOOO
...OH
YES!! IS PROMISE!!
WHOOOOOOOOO
......
CHAO-SAN!
FLUTTER FLUTTER
VROOOOOSH
GWHOOOOO
WHOOOOSH
FAREWELL, NEGI-BŌZU!

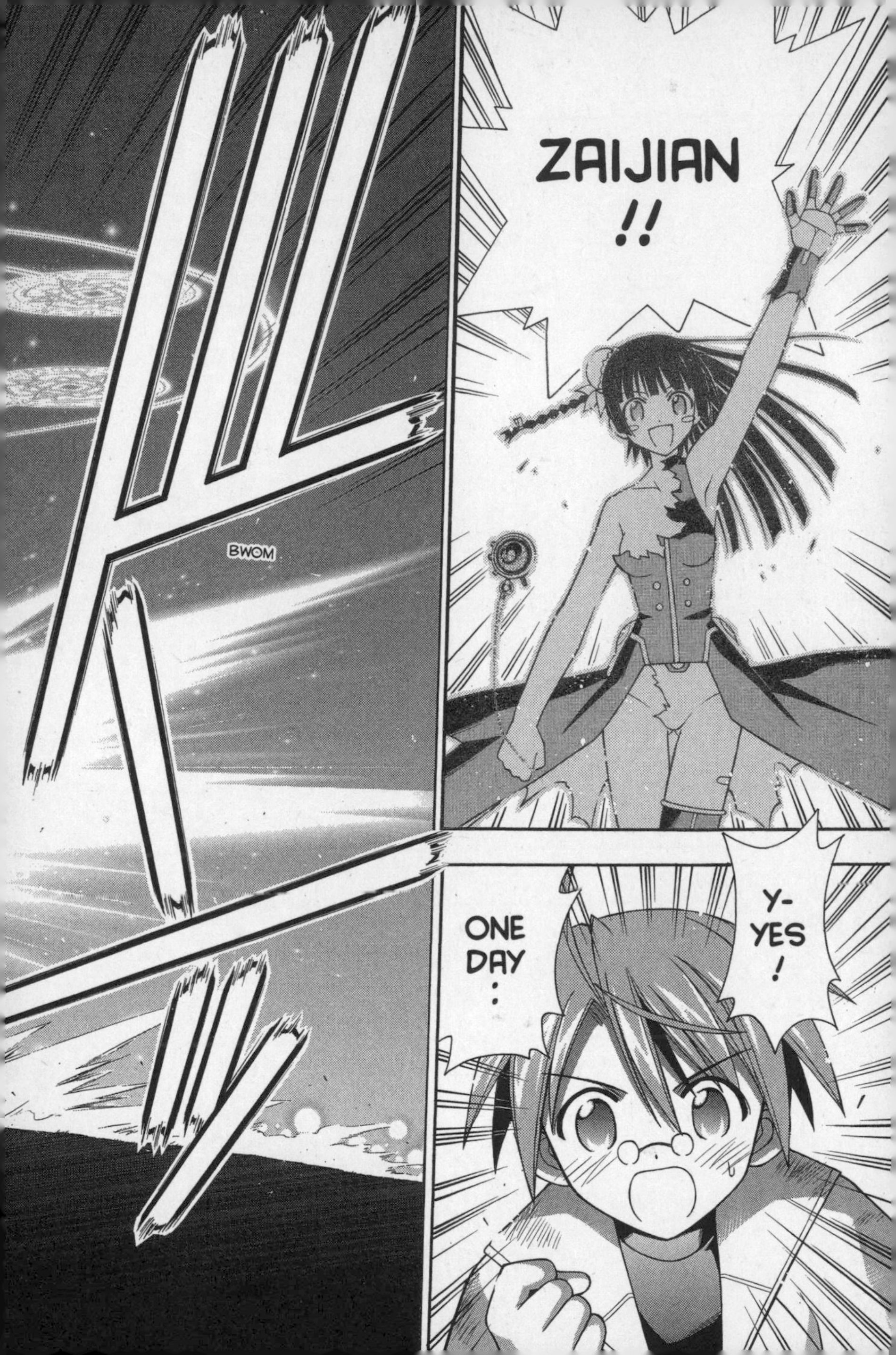
ZAIJIAN !!
Y-YES!
ONE DAY...
BWOM

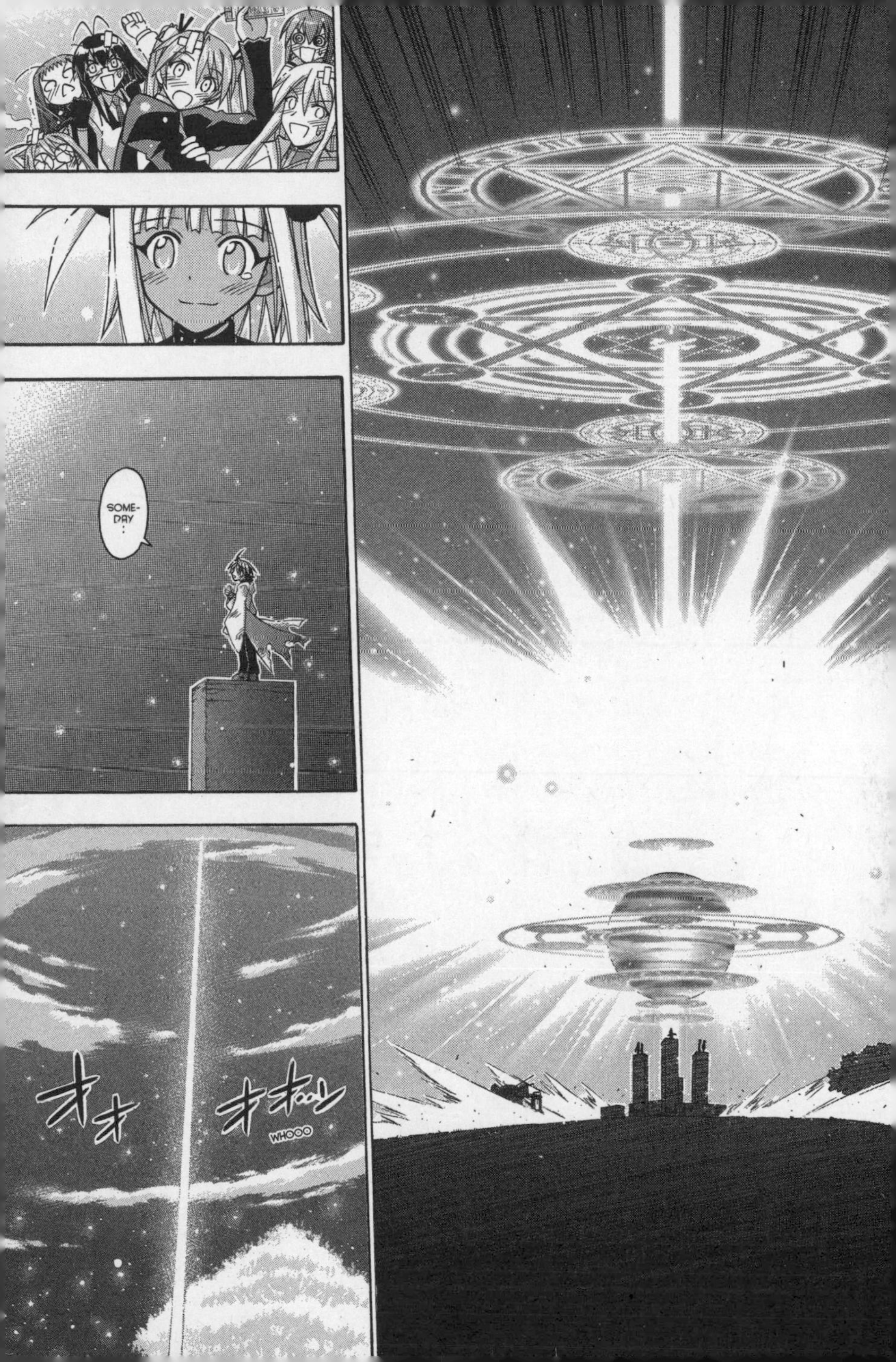

SOME-DAY…
WHOOO

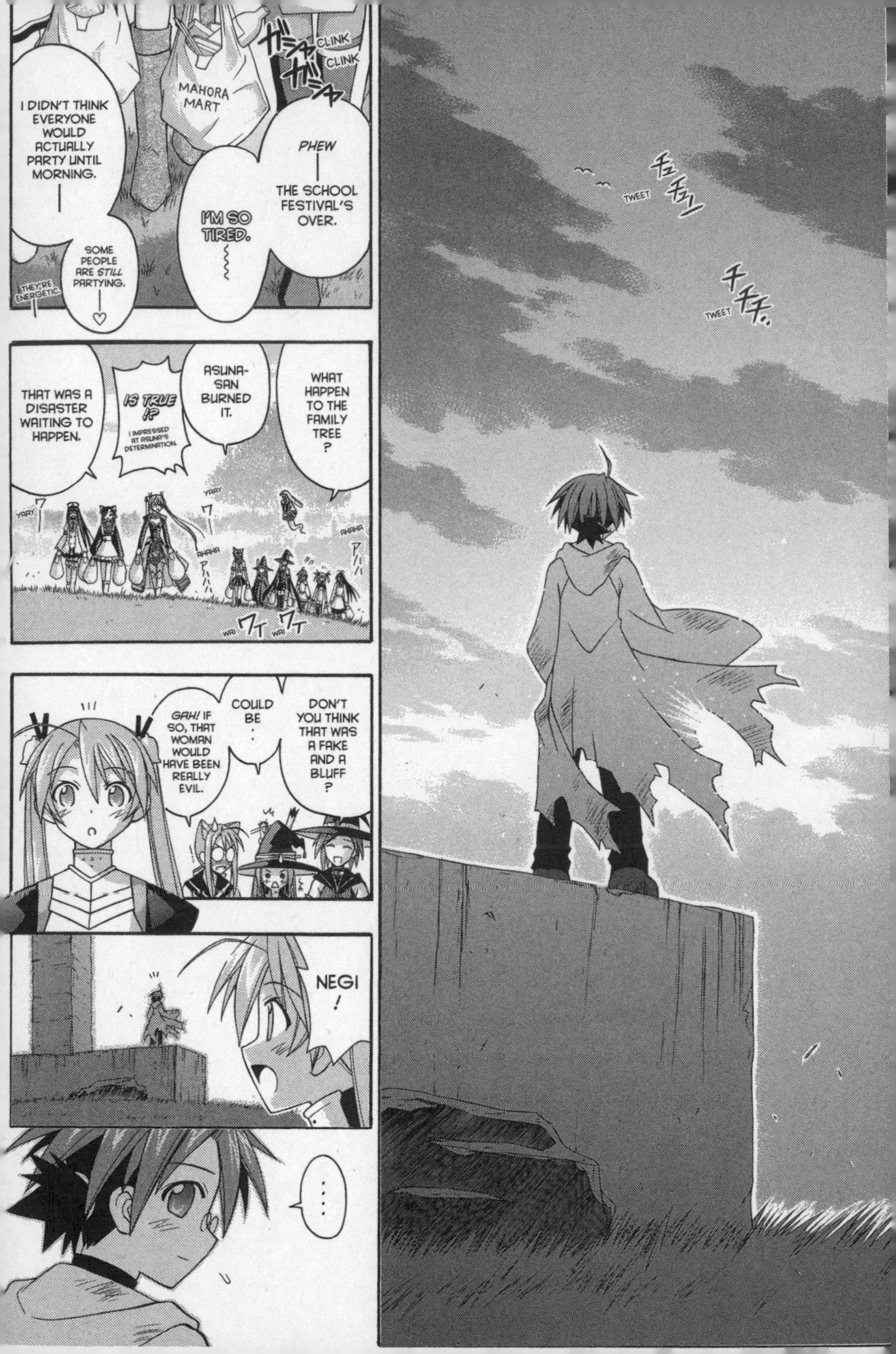

チュチュン
TWEET
チチチ…
TWEET
ガシャ ガシャ
CLINK CLINK
MAHORA MART
PHEW — THE SCHOOL FESTIVAL'S OVER.
I'M SO TIRED.
I DIDN'T THINK EVERYONE WOULD ACTUALLY PARTY UNTIL MORNING.
SOME PEOPLE ARE *STILL* PARTYING.
THEY'RE ENERGETIC.
WHAT HAPPEN TO THE FAMILY TREE?
ASUNA-SAN BURNED IT.
IS TRUE!?
I IMPRESSED AT ASUNA'S DETERMINATION.
THAT WAS A DISASTER WAITING TO HAPPEN.
YAAY
YAAY
AHAHA
AHAHA
WAI WAI
DON'T YOU THINK THAT WAS A FAKE AND A BLUFF?
COULD BE...
GAH! IF SO, THAT WOMAN WOULD HAVE BEEN REALLY EVIL.
NEGI!
....

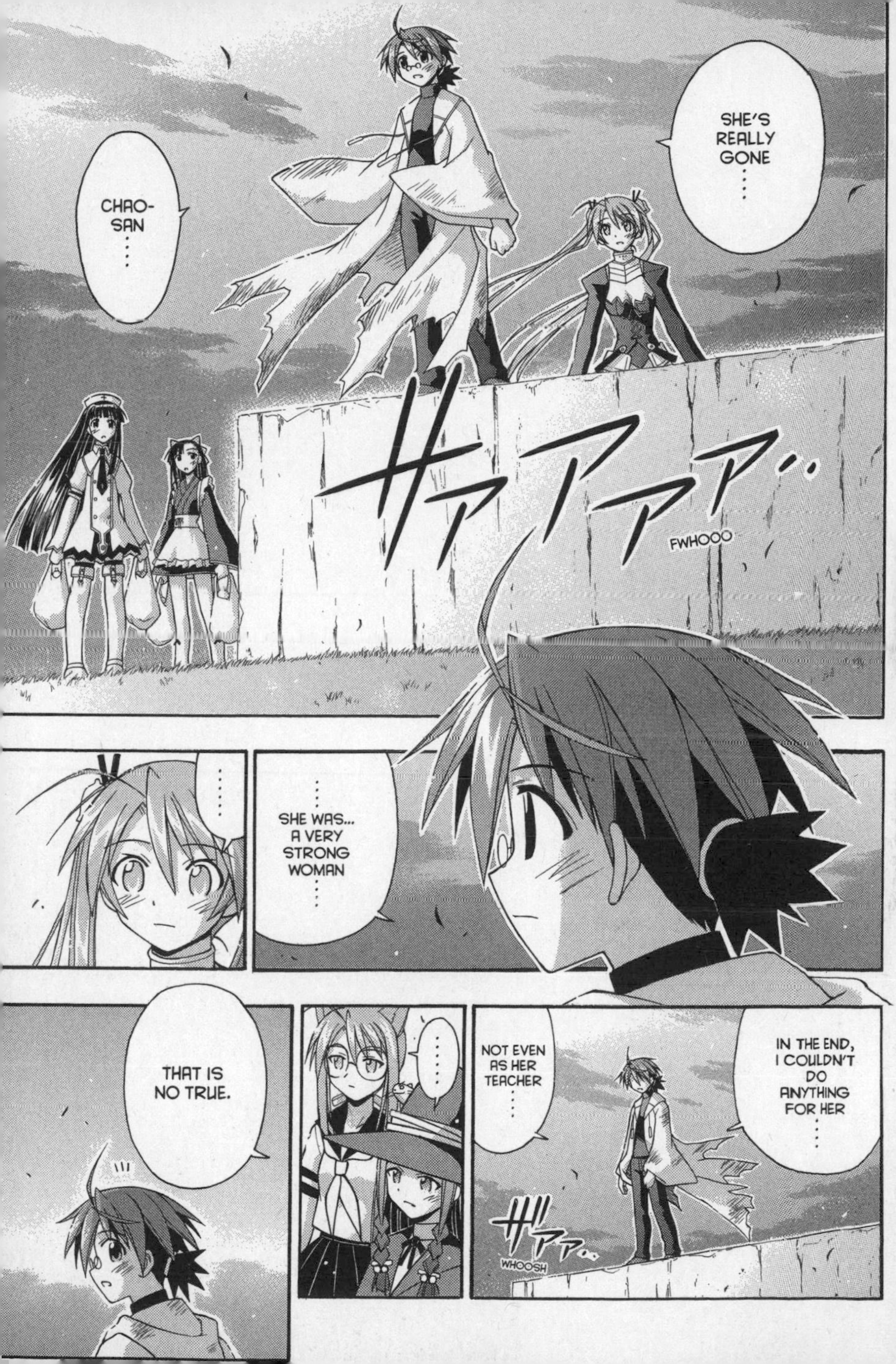
SHE'S REALLY GONE ....
CHAO-SAN ....
FWHOOO
......
SHE WAS... A VERY STRONG WOMAN ......
......
IN THE END, I COULDN'T DO ANYTHING FOR HER ....
NOT EVEN AS HER TEACHER ....
WHOOSH
......
THAT IS NO TRUE.

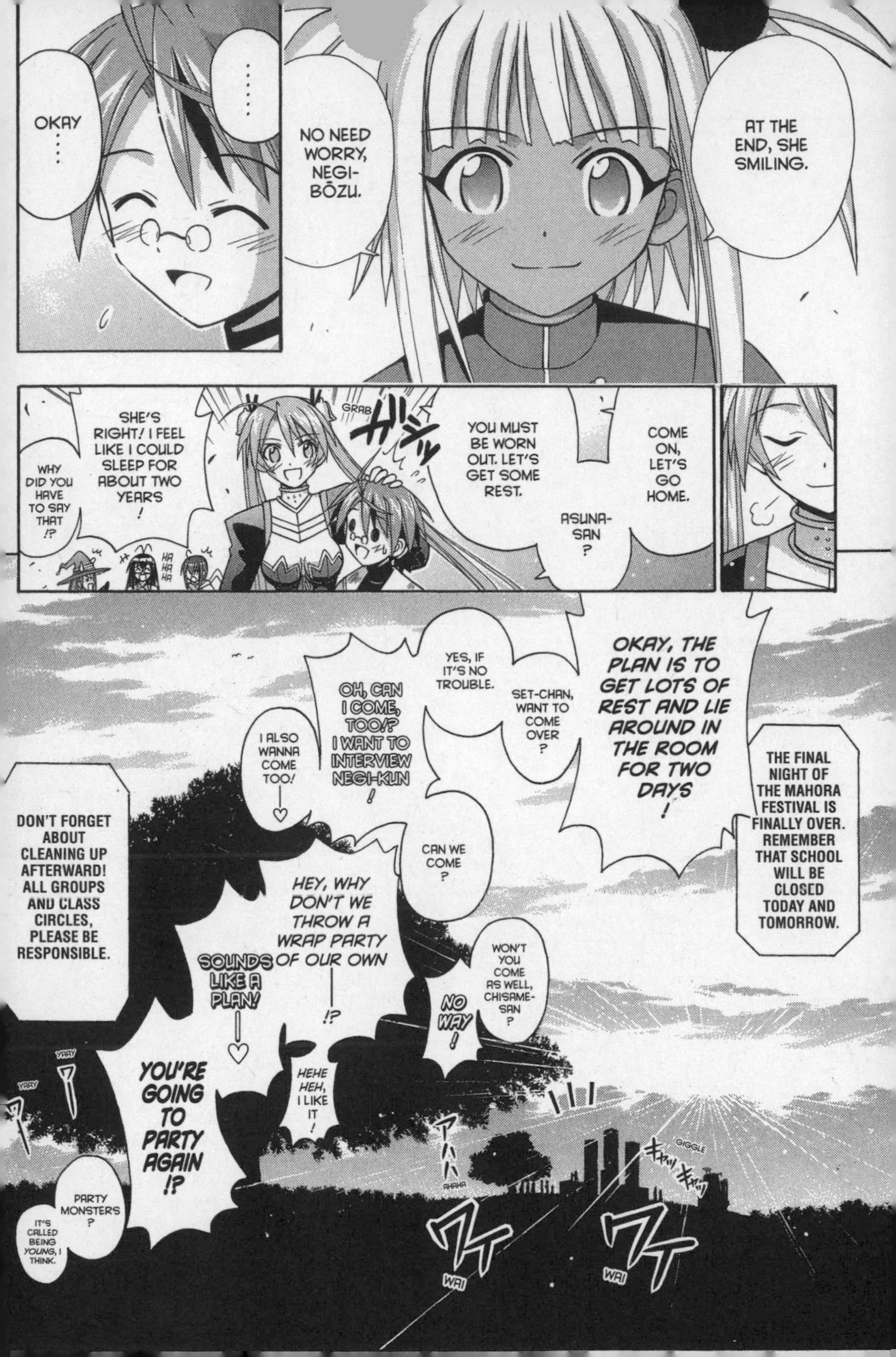
AT THE END, SHE SMILING.
NO NEED WORRY, NEGI-BŌZU.
.....
OKAY.....
COME ON, LET'S GO HOME.
ASUNA-SAN?
YOU MUST BE WORN OUT. LET'S GET SOME REST.
GRAB
SHE'S RIGHT! I FEEL LIKE I COULD SLEEP FOR ABOUT TWO YEARS!
WHY DID YOU HAVE TO SAY THAT!?
HA HA HA
THE FINAL NIGHT OF THE MAHORA FESTIVAL IS FINALLY OVER. REMEMBER THAT SCHOOL WILL BE CLOSED TODAY AND TOMORROW.
OKAY, THE PLAN IS TO GET LOTS OF REST AND LIE AROUND IN THE ROOM FOR TWO DAYS!
SET-CHAN, WANT TO COME OVER?
YES, IF IT'S NO TROUBLE.
OH, CAN I COME, TOO!? I WANT TO INTERVIEW NEGI-KUN!
I ALSO WANNA COME TOO! ♡
CAN WE COME?
WON'T YOU COME AS WELL, CHISAME-SAN?
NO WAY!
HEY, WHY DON'T WE THROW A WRAP PARTY OF OUR OWN!?
SOUNDS LIKE A PLAN! ♡
HEHEHEH, I LIKE IT!
YOU'RE GOING TO PARTY AGAIN!?
GIGGLE
AHAHA
WAI
WAI
DON'T FORGET ABOUT CLEANING UP AFTERWARD! ALL GROUPS AND CLASS CIRCLES, PLEASE BE RESPONSIBLE.
YAAY
YAAY
PARTY MONSTERS?
IT'S CALLED BEING YOUNG, I THINK.

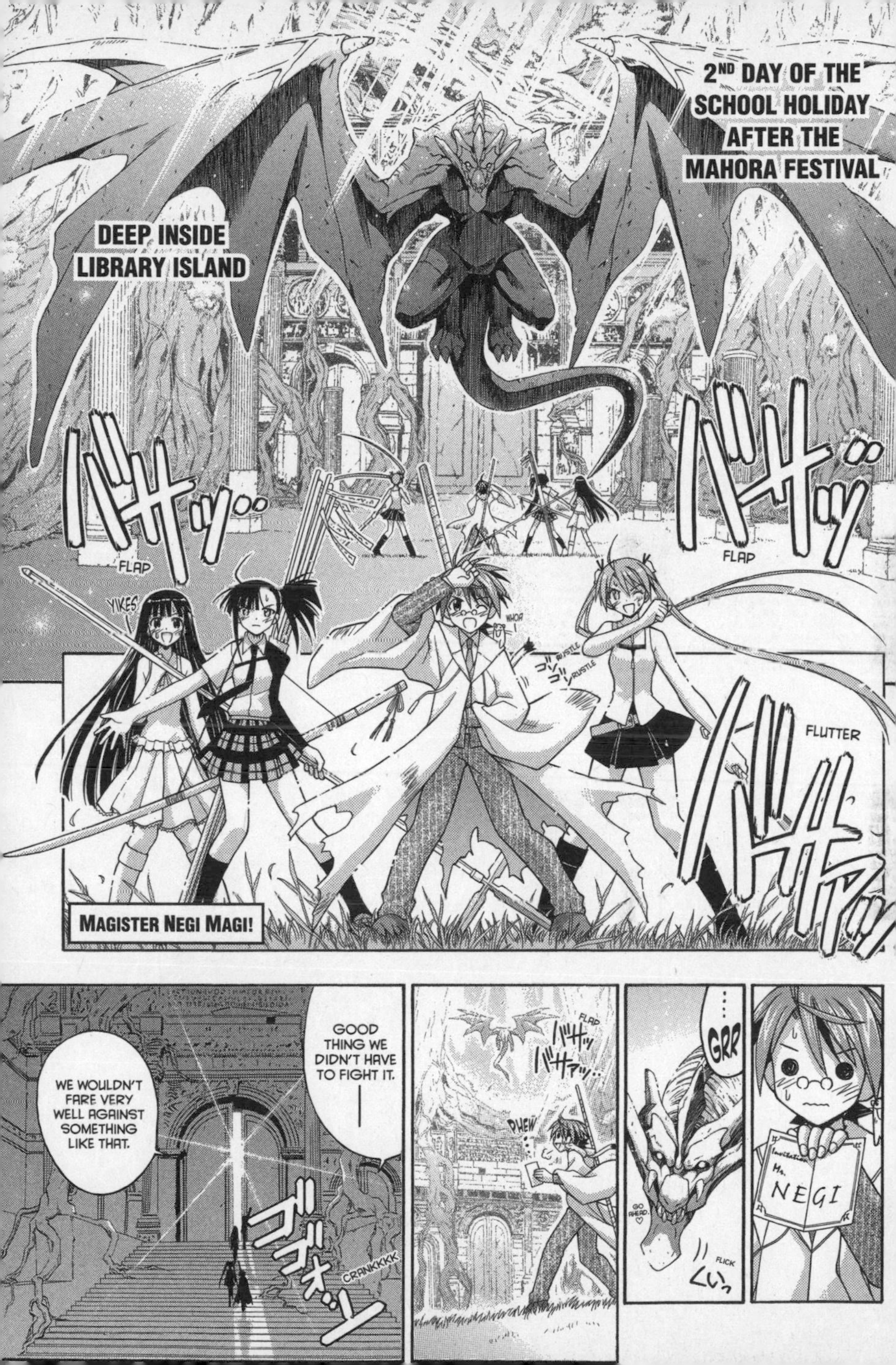

2ND DAY OF THE SCHOOL HOLIDAY AFTER THE MAHORA FESTIVAL
DEEP INSIDE LIBRARY ISLAND
FLAP
FLAP
FLUTTER
RUSTLE
RUSTLE
WHOA
YIKES
MAGISTER NEGI MAGI!
Invitation Mr. NEGI
... GRR
GO AHEAD. ♡
FLICK
FLAP
PHEW
GOOD THING WE DIDN'T HAVE TO FIGHT IT.
WE WOULDN'T FARE VERY WELL AGAINST SOMETHING LIKE THAT.
CRANKKKK

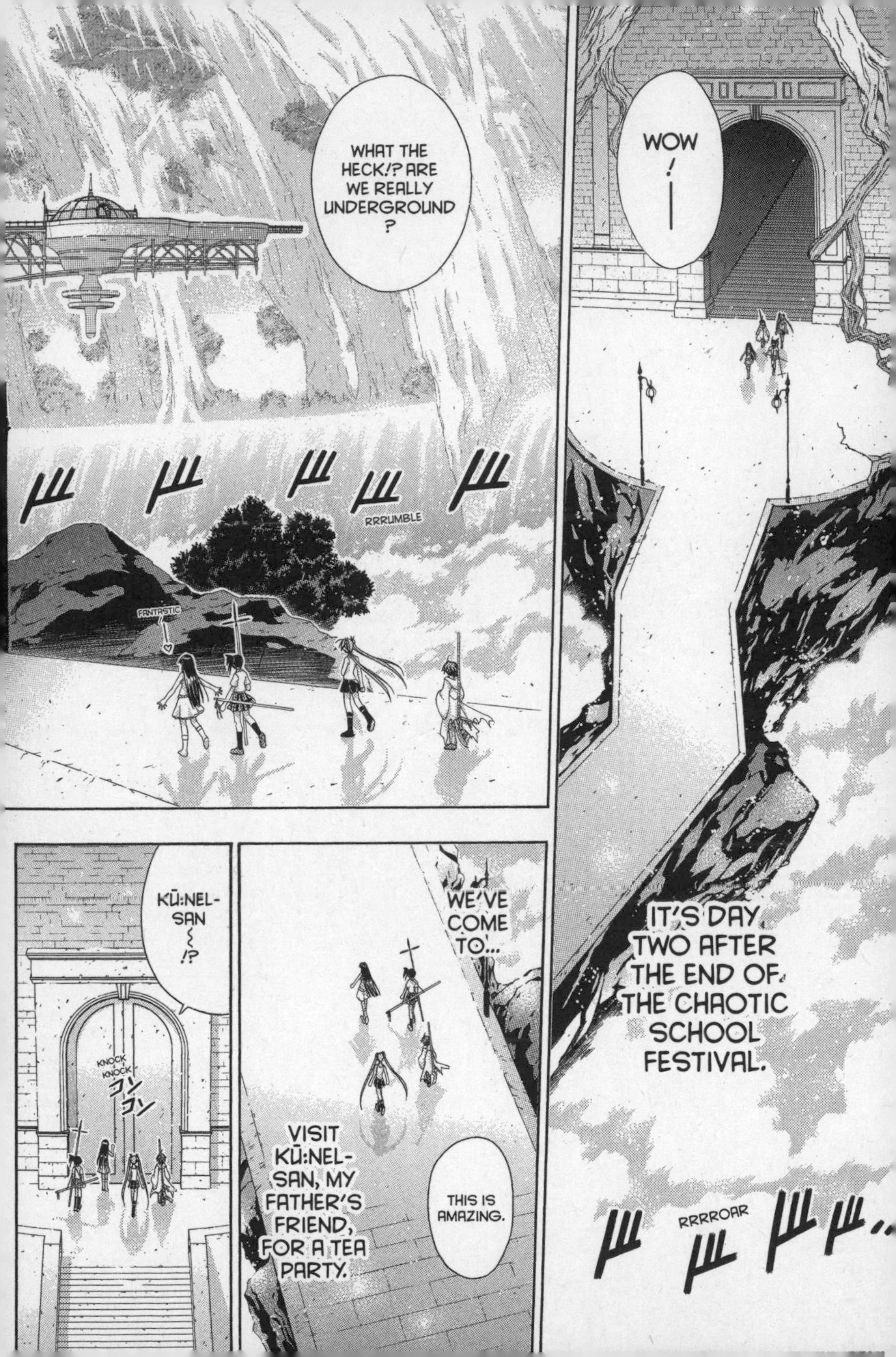
WOW!—
IT'S DAY TWO AFTER THE END OF THE CHAOTIC SCHOOL FESTIVAL.
RRRROAR
WHAT THE HECK!? ARE WE REALLY UNDERGROUND?
RRRUMBLE
FANTASTIC
WE'VE COME TO...
VISIT KŪ:NEL-SAN, MY FATHER'S FRIEND, FOR A TEA PARTY.
THIS IS AMAZING.
KŪ:NEL-SAN~!?
KNOCK KNOCK
コンコン

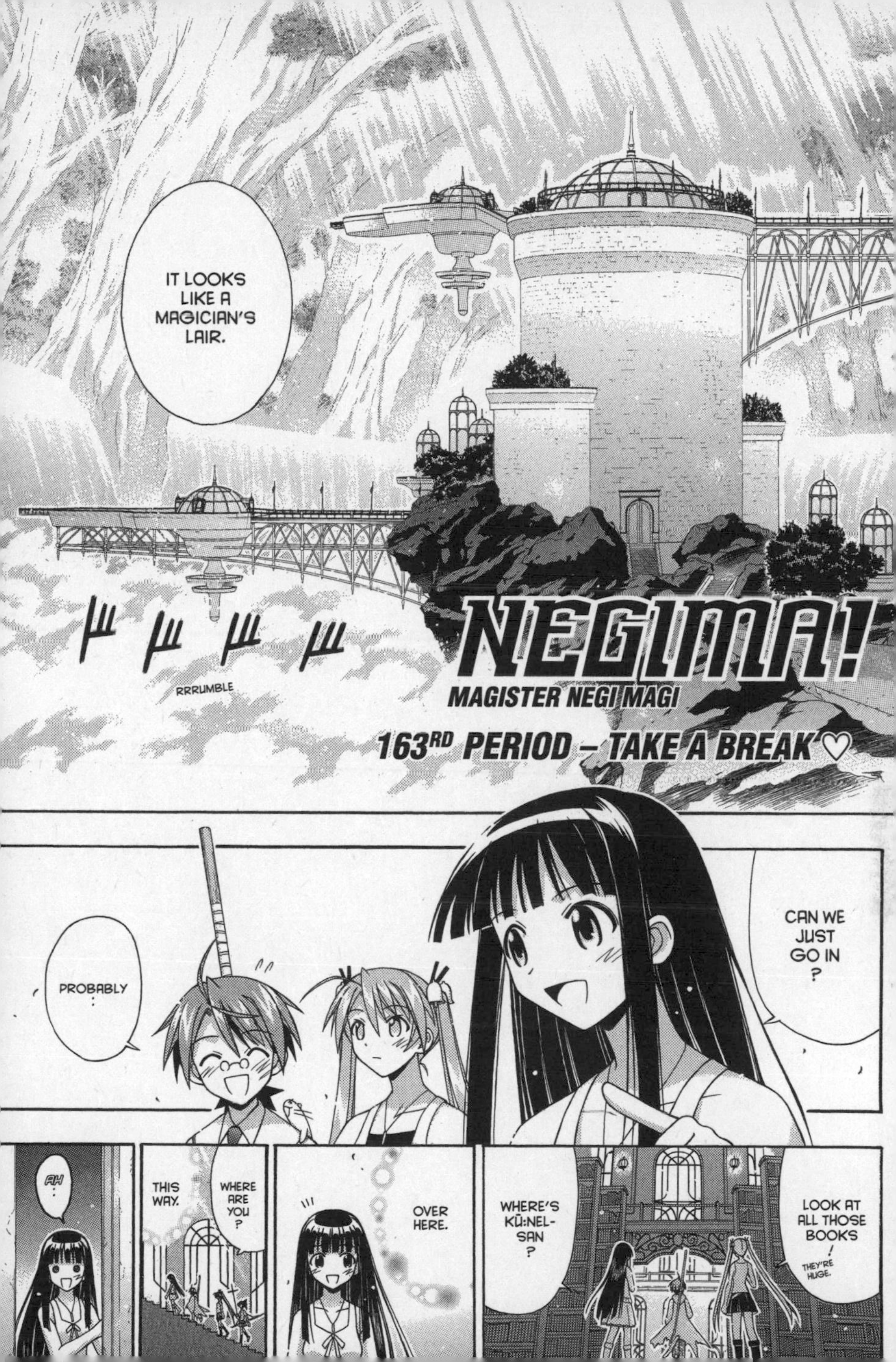
IT LOOKS LIKE A MAGICIAN'S LAIR.
RRRUMBLE
NEGIMA!
MAGISTER NEGI MAGI
163RD PERIOD – TAKE A BREAK♡
CAN WE JUST GO IN?
PROBABLY...
LOOK AT ALL THOSE BOOKS!
THEY'RE HUGE.
WHERE'S KŪ:NEL-SAN?
OVER HERE.
WHERE ARE YOU?
THIS WAY.
AH...

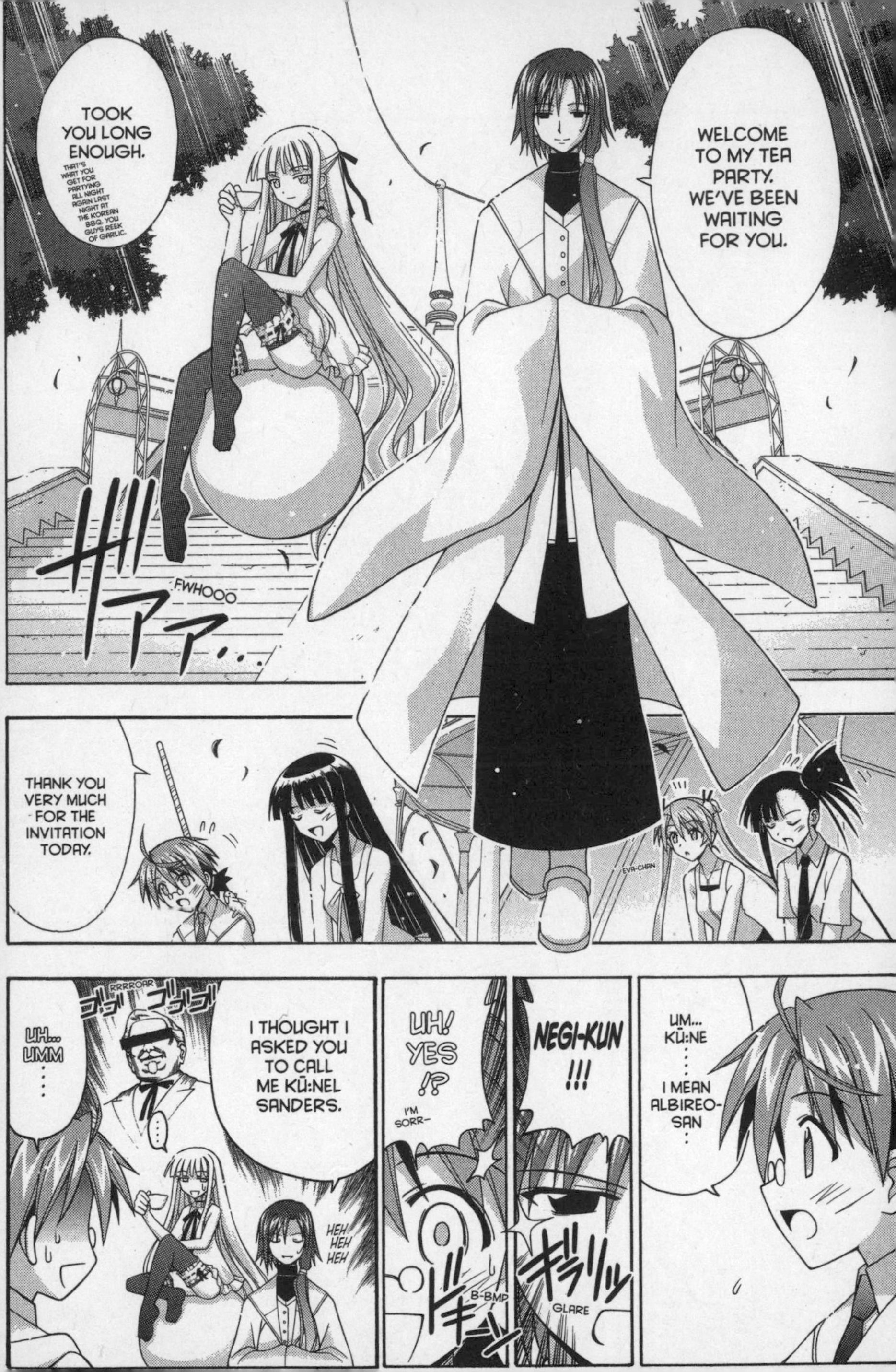
WELCOME TO MY TEA PARTY. WE'VE BEEN WAITING FOR YOU.
TOOK YOU LONG ENOUGH.
THAT'S WHAT YOU GET FOR PARTYING ALL NIGHT AGAIN LAST NIGHT AT THE KOREAN BBQ. YOU GUYS REEK OF GARLIC.
FWHOOO
EVA-CHAN
THANK YOU VERY MUCH FOR THE INVITATION TODAY.
UM... KŪ:NE ... I MEAN ALBIREO-SAN ...
NEGI-KUN !!!
GLARE
UH! YES !?
I'M SORR–
B-BMP
I THOUGHT I ASKED YOU TO CALL ME KŪ:NEL SANDERS.
RRRROAR
UH... UMM ...
...
HEH HEH HEH

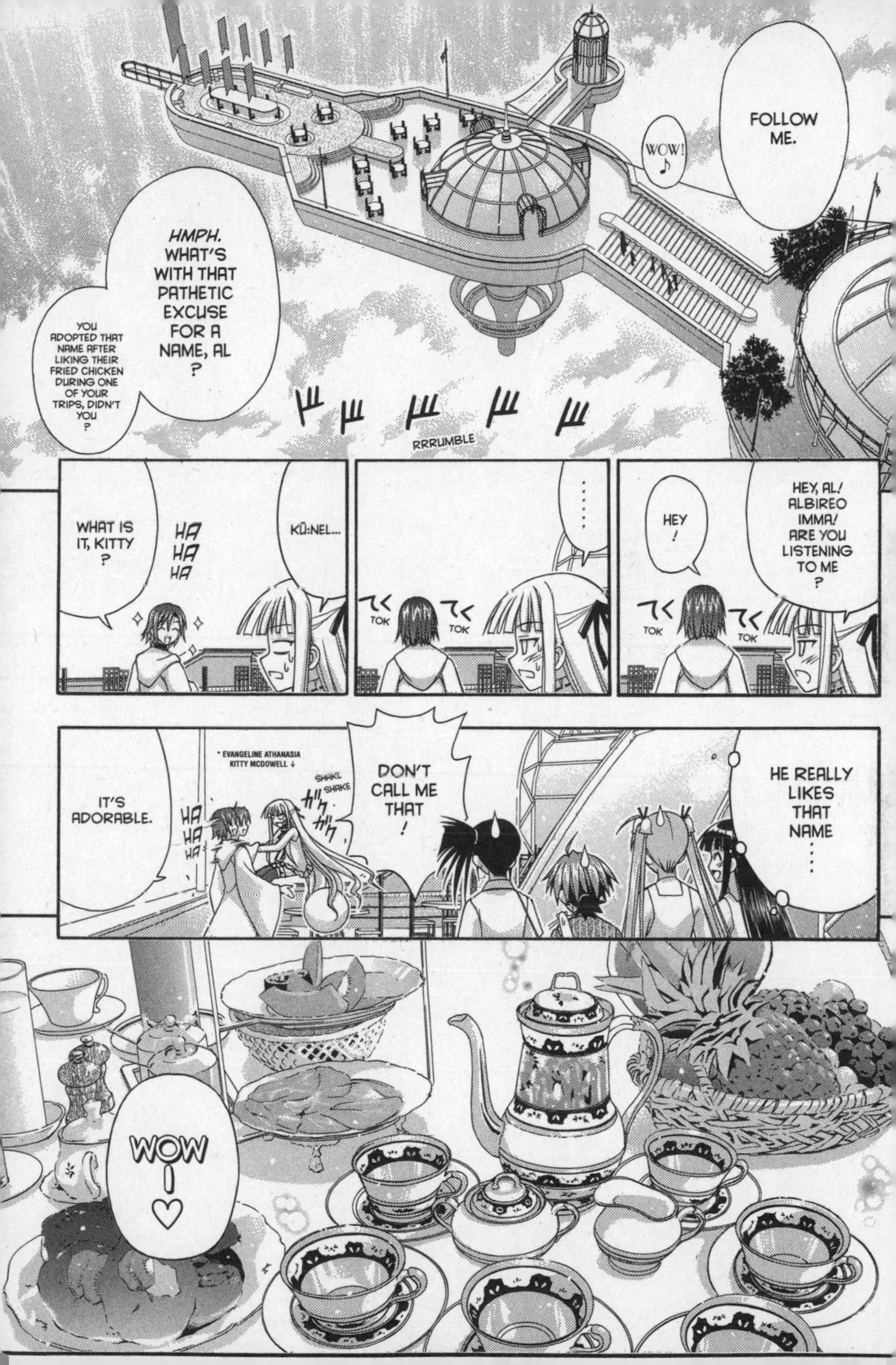
FOLLOW ME.
WOW! ♪
HMPH. WHAT'S WITH THAT PATHETIC EXCUSE FOR A NAME, AL?
YOU ADOPTED THAT NAME AFTER LIKING THEIR FRIED CHICKEN DURING ONE OF YOUR TRIPS, DIDN'T YOU?
RRRUMBLE
HEY, AL! ALBIREO IMMA! ARE YOU LISTENING TO ME?
HEY!
TOK
TOK
......
TOK
TOK
KŪ:NEL...
HA HA HA
WHAT IS IT, KITTY?
HE REALLY LIKES THAT NAME ....
DON'T CALL ME THAT!
SHAKE SHAKE
* EVANGELINE ATHANASIA KITTY MCDOWELL ↓
HA HA HA
IT'S ADORABLE.
WOW ♡

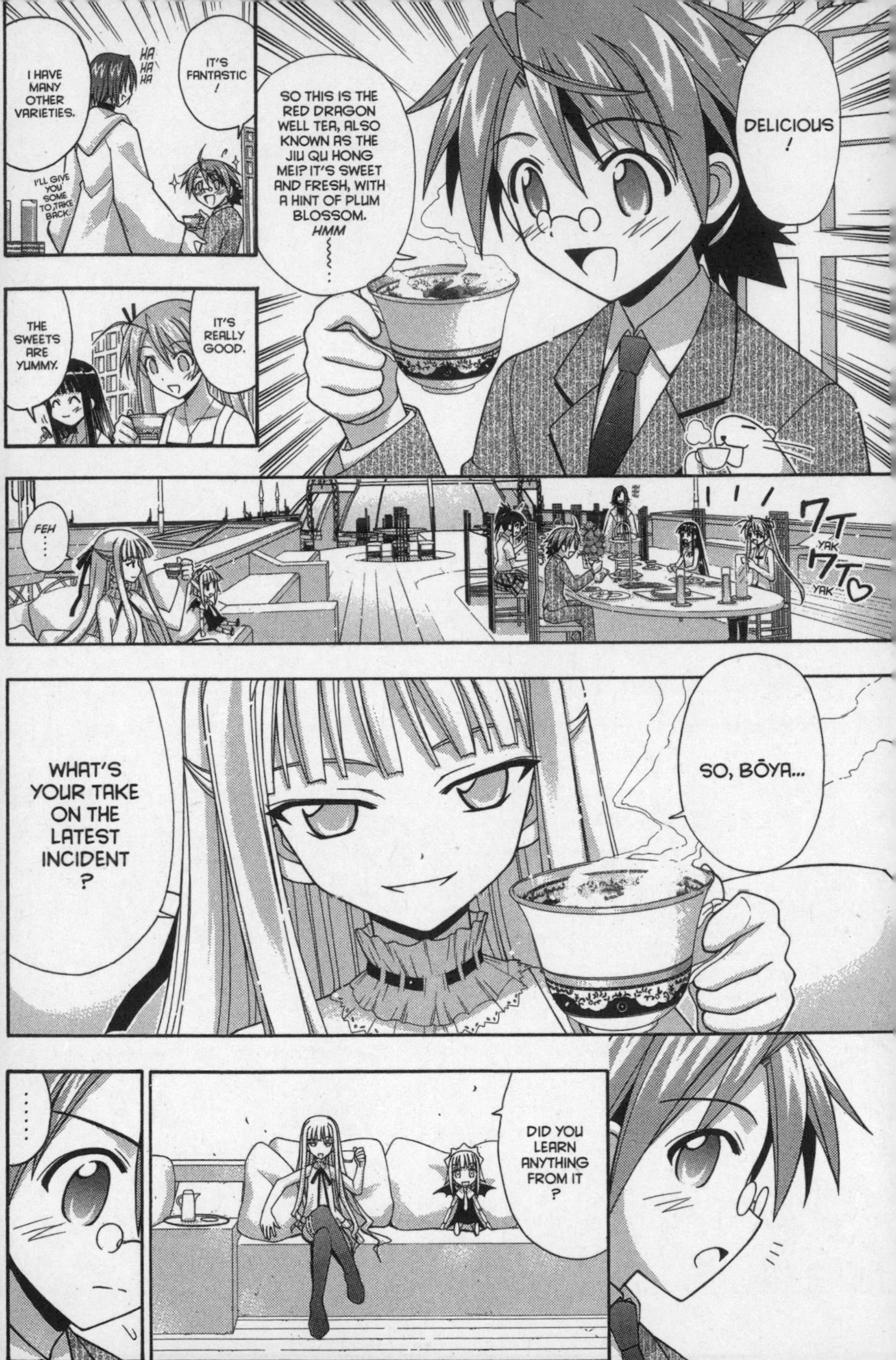
DELICIOUS!
SO THIS IS THE RED DRAGON WELL TEA, ALSO KNOWN AS THE JIU QU HONG MEI? IT'S SWEET AND FRESH, WITH A HINT OF PLUM BLOSSOM. HMM......
IT'S FANTASTIC!
HA HA HA
I HAVE MANY OTHER VARIETIES.
I'LL GIVE YOU SOME TO TAKE BACK.
IT'S REALLY GOOD.
THE SWEETS ARE YUMMY.
YAK YAK ♡
FEH......
SO, BŌYA...
WHAT'S YOUR TAKE ON THE LATEST INCIDENT?
DID YOU LEARN ANYTHING FROM IT?
......

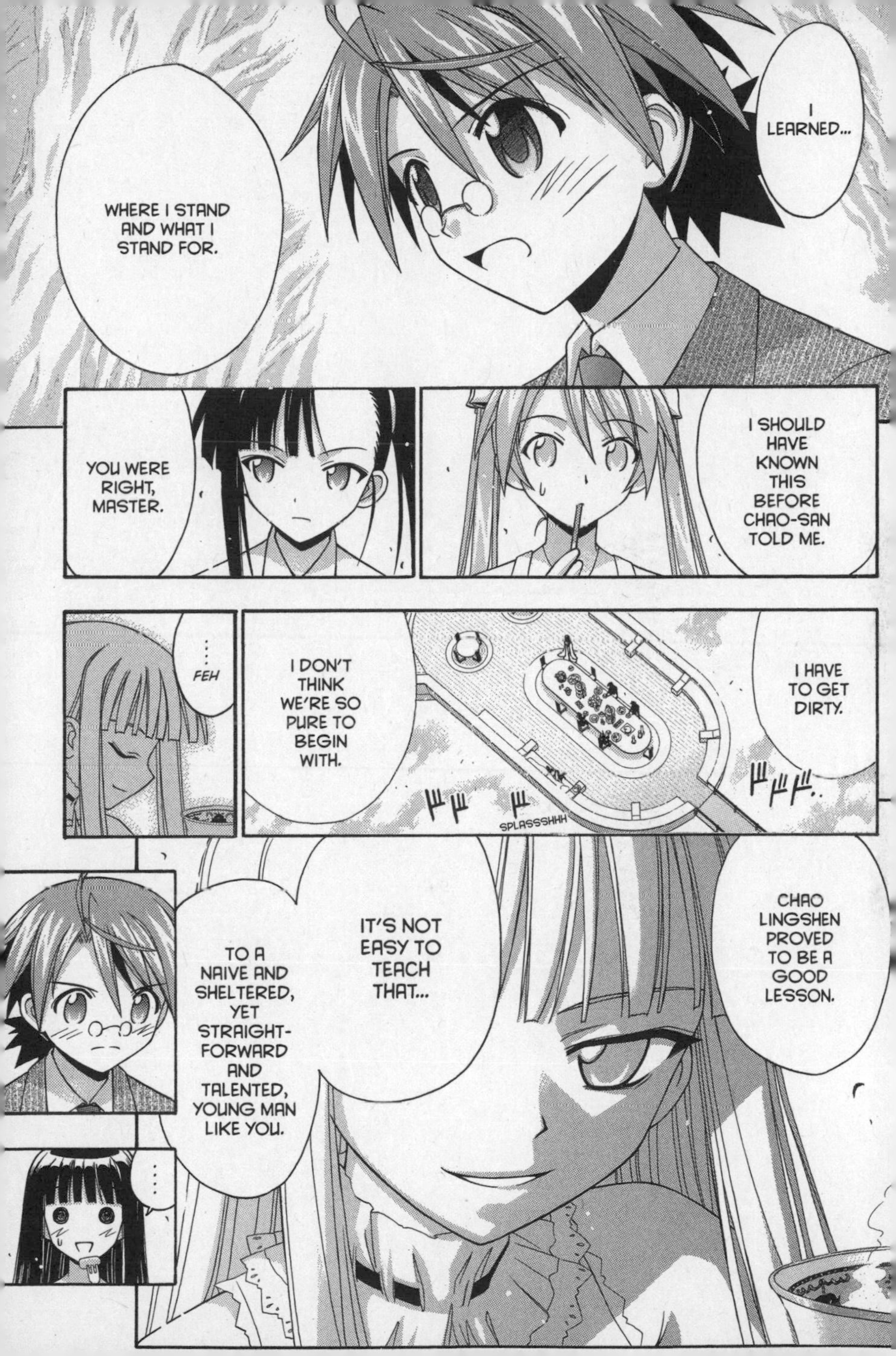
I LEARNED...
WHERE I STAND AND WHAT I STAND FOR.
I SHOULD HAVE KNOWN THIS BEFORE CHAO-SAN TOLD ME.
YOU WERE RIGHT, MASTER.
I HAVE TO GET DIRTY.
I DON'T THINK WE'RE SO PURE TO BEGIN WITH.
SPLASSSHHH
... FEH
CHAO LINGSHEN PROVED TO BE A GOOD LESSON.
IT'S NOT EASY TO TEACH THAT...
TO A NAIVE AND SHELTERED, YET STRAIGHT-FORWARD AND TALENTED, YOUNG MAN LIKE YOU.
...

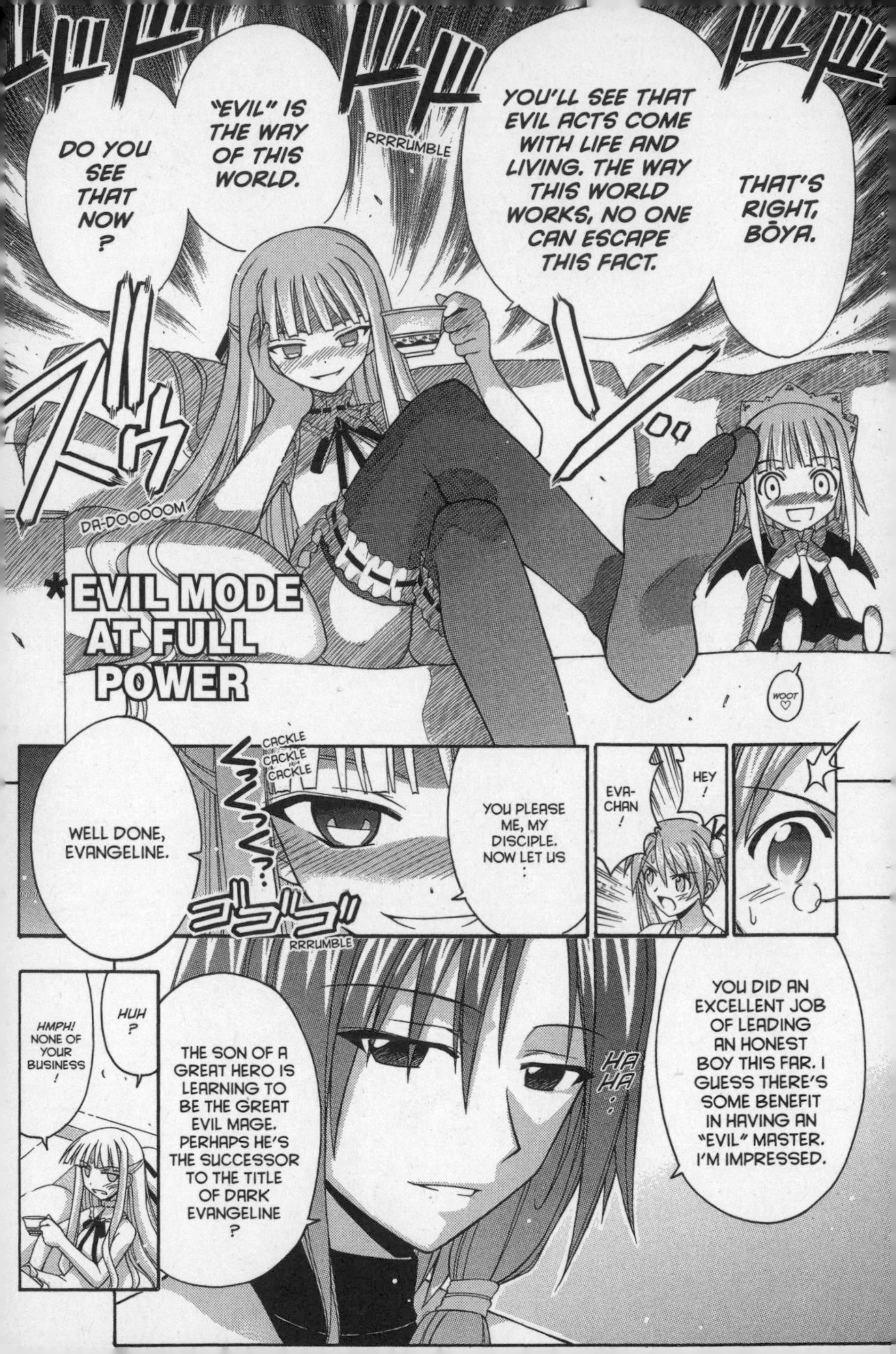
THAT'S RIGHT, BŌYA.
YOU'LL SEE THAT EVIL ACTS COME WITH LIFE AND LIVING. THE WAY THIS WORLD WORKS, NO ONE CAN ESCAPE THIS FACT.
RRRRUMBLE
"EVIL" IS THE WAY OF THIS WORLD.
DO YOU SEE THAT NOW?
DA-DOOOOOM
*EVIL MODE AT FULL POWER
WOOT ♡
HEY!
EVA-CHAN!
YOU PLEASE ME, MY DISCIPLE. NOW LET US :
CACKLE CACKLE CACKLE
WELL DONE, EVANGELINE.
RRRUMBLE
YOU DID AN EXCELLENT JOB OF LEADING AN HONEST BOY THIS FAR. I GUESS THERE'S SOME BENEFIT IN HAVING AN "EVIL" MASTER. I'M IMPRESSED.
HA HA
THE SON OF A GREAT HERO IS LEARNING TO BE THE GREAT EVIL MAGE. PERHAPS HE'S THE SUCCESSOR TO THE TITLE OF DARK EVANGELINE?
HUH?
HMPH! NONE OF YOUR BUSINESS!

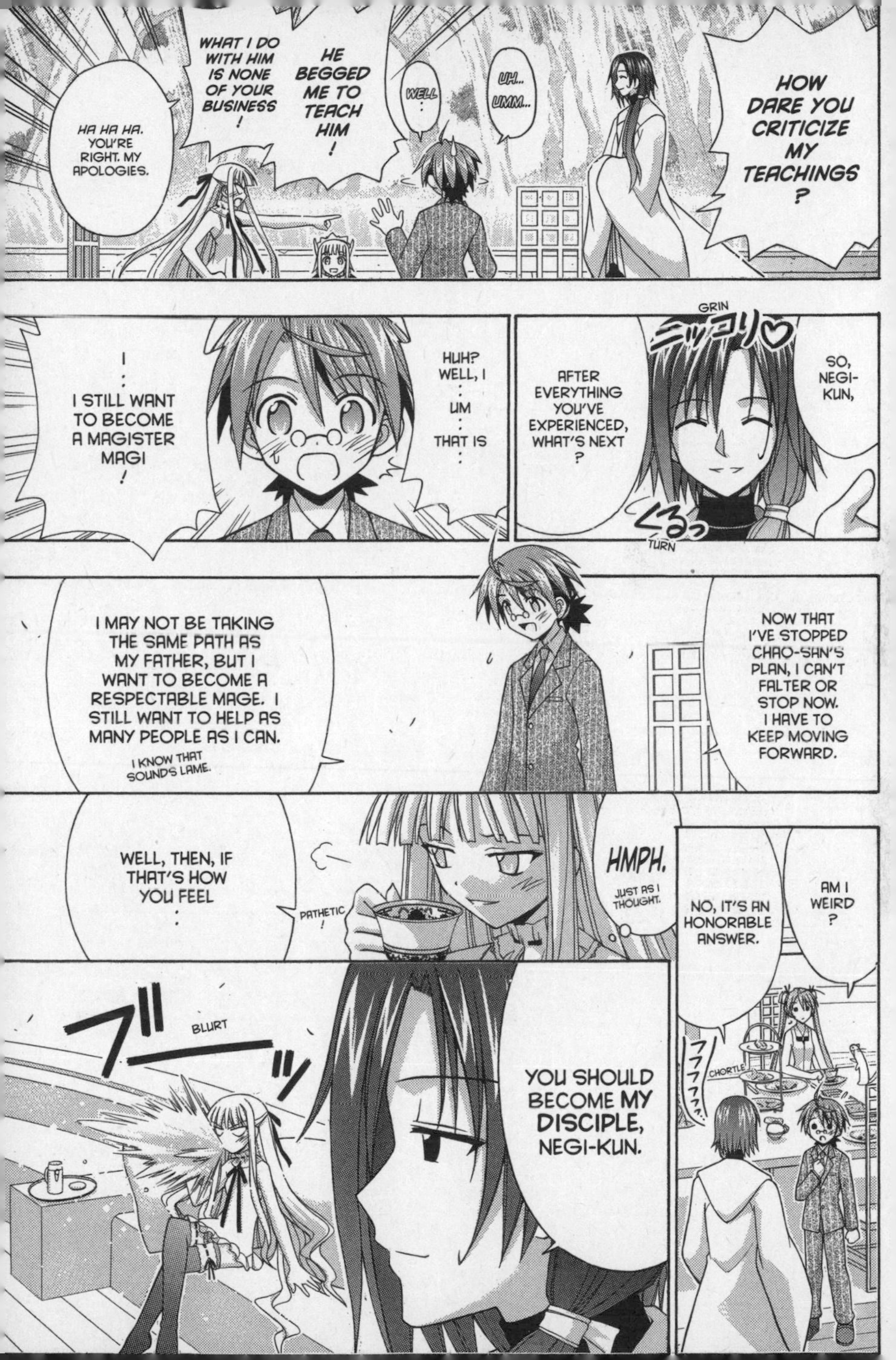
HOW DARE YOU CRITICIZE MY TEACHINGS?
UH... UMM...
WELL...
HE BEGGED ME TO TEACH HIM!
WHAT I DO WITH HIM IS NONE OF YOUR BUSINESS!
HA HA HA. YOU'RE RIGHT. MY APOLOGIES.
ニッコリ♡
GRIN
SO, NEGI-KUN,
AFTER EVERYTHING YOU'VE EXPERIENCED, WHAT'S NEXT?
くるっ
TURN
HUH? WELL, I... UM... THAT IS...
I... I STILL WANT TO BECOME A MAGISTER MAGI!
NOW THAT I'VE STOPPED CHAO-SAN'S PLAN, I CAN'T FALTER OR STOP NOW. I HAVE TO KEEP MOVING FORWARD.
I MAY NOT BE TAKING THE SAME PATH AS MY FATHER, BUT I WANT TO BECOME A RESPECTABLE MAGE. I STILL WANT TO HELP AS MANY PEOPLE AS I CAN.
I KNOW THAT SOUNDS LAME.
AM I WEIRD?
NO, IT'S AN HONORABLE ANSWER.
HMPH.
JUST AS I THOUGHT.
PATHETIC!
WELL, THEN, IF THAT'S HOW YOU FEEL...
フフフフ...
CHORTLE
YOU SHOULD BECOME MY DISCIPLE, NEGI-KUN.
ブーーッ
BLURT

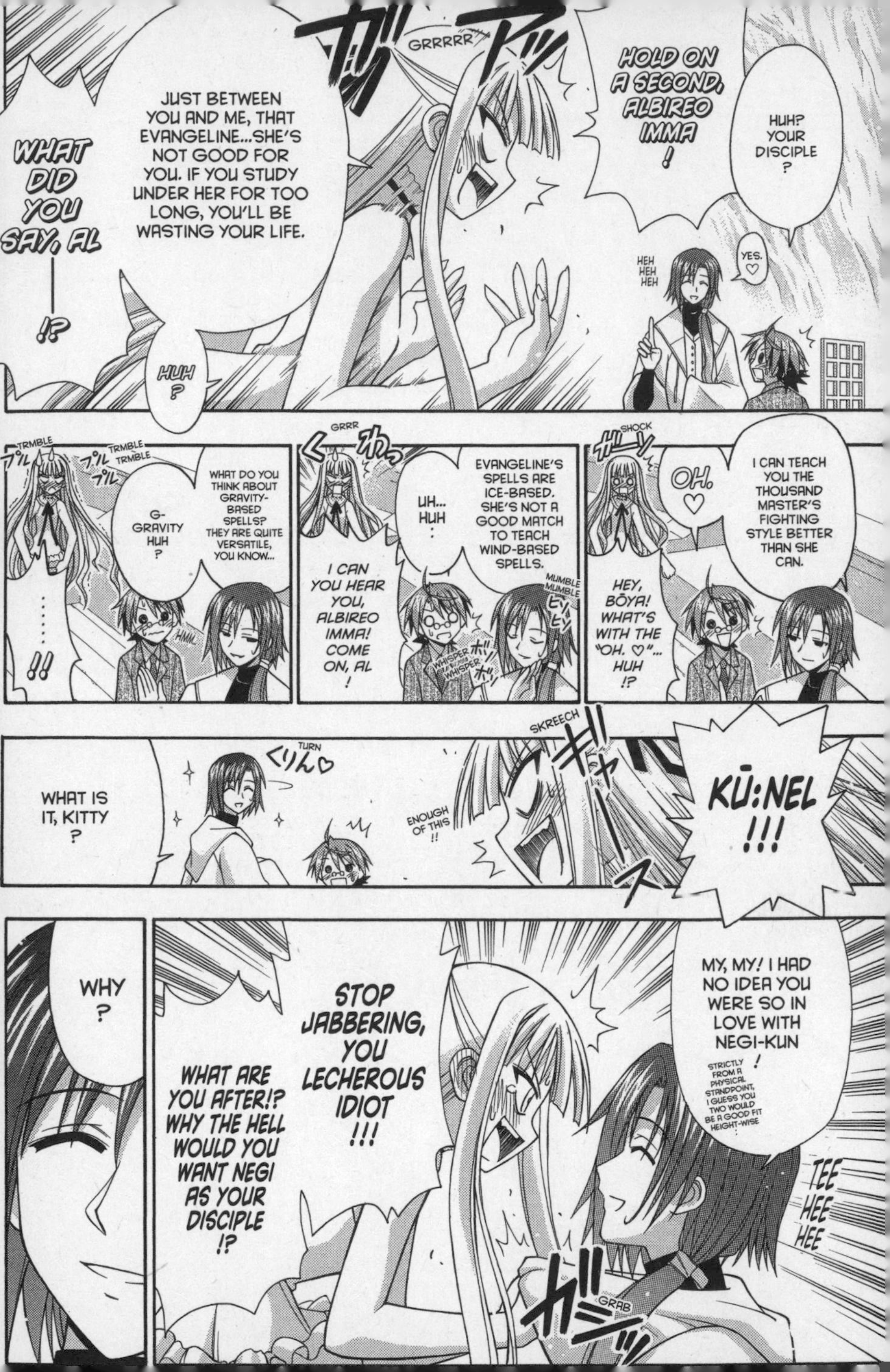
HUH? YOUR DISCIPLE?
HOLD ON A SECOND, ALBIREO IMMA!
YES. ♡
HEH HEH HEH
GRRRRR
JUST BETWEEN YOU AND ME, THAT EVANGELINE...SHE'S NOT GOOD FOR YOU. IF YOU STUDY UNDER HER FOR TOO LONG, YOU'LL BE WASTING YOUR LIFE.
WHAT DID YOU SAY, AL—!?
HUH?
SHOCK
I CAN TEACH YOU THE THOUSAND MASTER'S FIGHTING STYLE BETTER THAN SHE CAN.
OH. ♡
HEY, BŌYA! WHAT'S WITH THE "OH. ♡"... HUH!?
GRRR
EVANGELINE'S SPELLS ARE ICE-BASED. SHE'S NOT A GOOD MATCH TO TEACH WIND-BASED SPELLS.
UH... HUH...
MUMBLE MUMBLE
I CAN YOU HEAR YOU, ALBIREO IMMA! COME ON, AL!
WHISPER WHISPER
WHAT DO YOU THINK ABOUT GRAVITY-BASED SPELLS? THEY ARE QUITE VERSATILE, YOU KNOW...
G-GRAVITY HUH?
TRMBLE TRMBLE TRMBLE
HMM
......!!
KŪ:NEL!!!
SKREECH
ENOUGH OF THIS!!
TURN
WHAT IS IT, KITTY?
MY, MY! I HAD NO IDEA YOU WERE SO IN LOVE WITH NEGI-KUN!
STRICTLY FROM A PHYSICAL STANDPOINT, I GUESS YOU TWO WOULD BE A GOOD FIT HEIGHT-WISE...
TEE HEE HEE
STOP JABBERING, YOU LECHEROUS IDIOT!!!
WHAT ARE YOU AFTER!? WHY THE HELL WOULD YOU WANT NEGI AS YOUR DISCIPLE!?
GRAB
WHY?

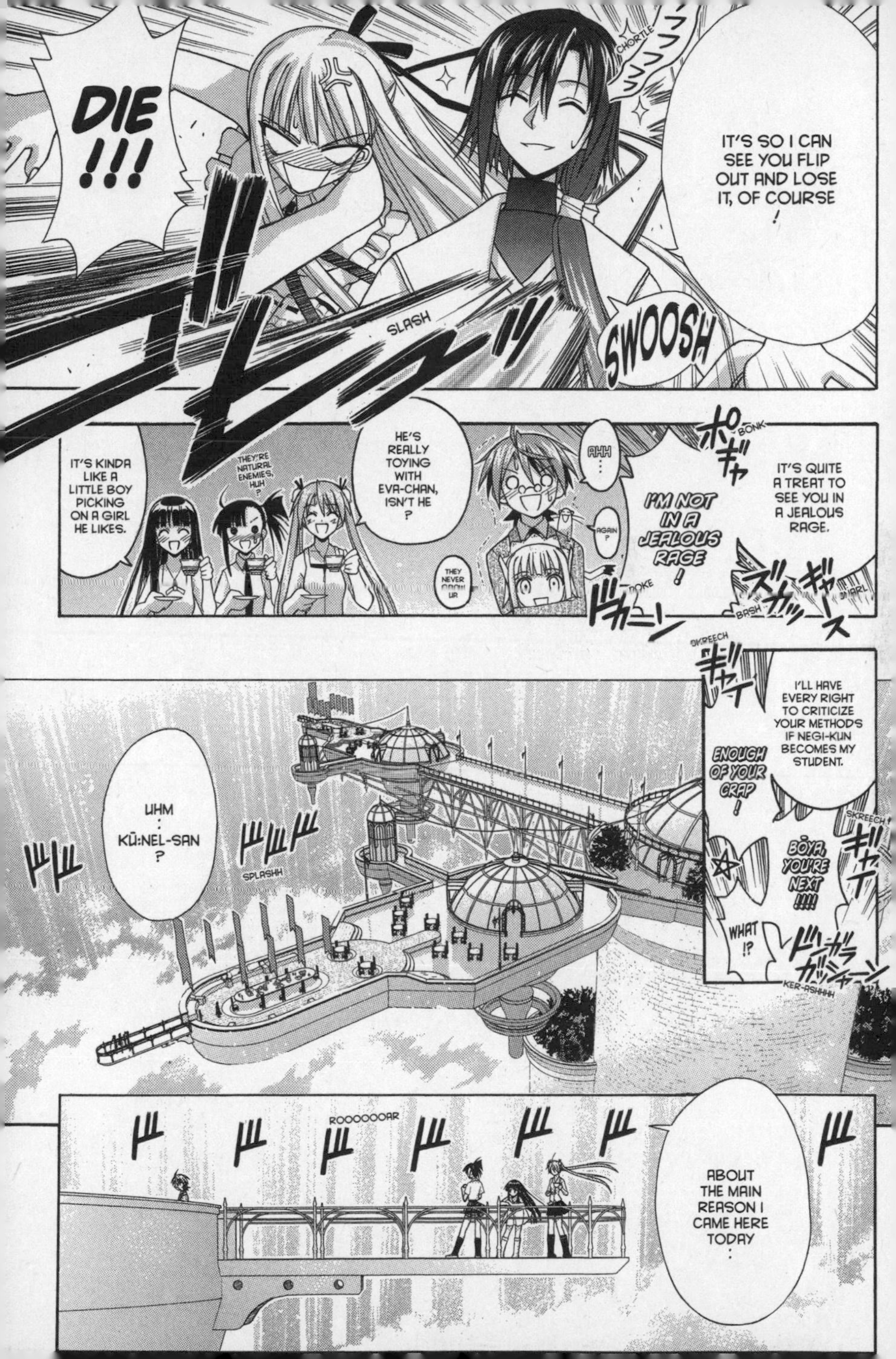
CHORTLE
IT'S SO I CAN SEE YOU FLIP OUT AND LOSE IT, OF COURSE!
SWOOSH
SLASH
DIE!!!
BONK
IT'S QUITE A TREAT TO SEE YOU IN A JEALOUS RAGE.
SNARL
BASH
I'M NOT IN A JEALOUS RAGE!
DOKE
AHH...
AGAIN?
THEY NEVER
HE'S REALLY TOYING WITH EVA-CHAN, ISN'T HE?
THEY'RE NATURAL ENEMIES, HUH?
IT'S KINDA LIKE A LITTLE BOY PICKING ON A GIRL HE LIKES.
SKREECH
I'LL HAVE EVERY RIGHT TO CRITICIZE YOUR METHODS IF NEGI-KUN BECOMES MY STUDENT.
ENOUGH OF YOUR CRAP!
SKREECH
BÔYA, YOU'RE NEXT!!!!
WHAT!?
KER-ASHHH
UHM... KŪ:NEL-SAN?
SPLASHH
ABOUT THE MAIN REASON I CAME HERE TODAY...
ROOOOOOAR

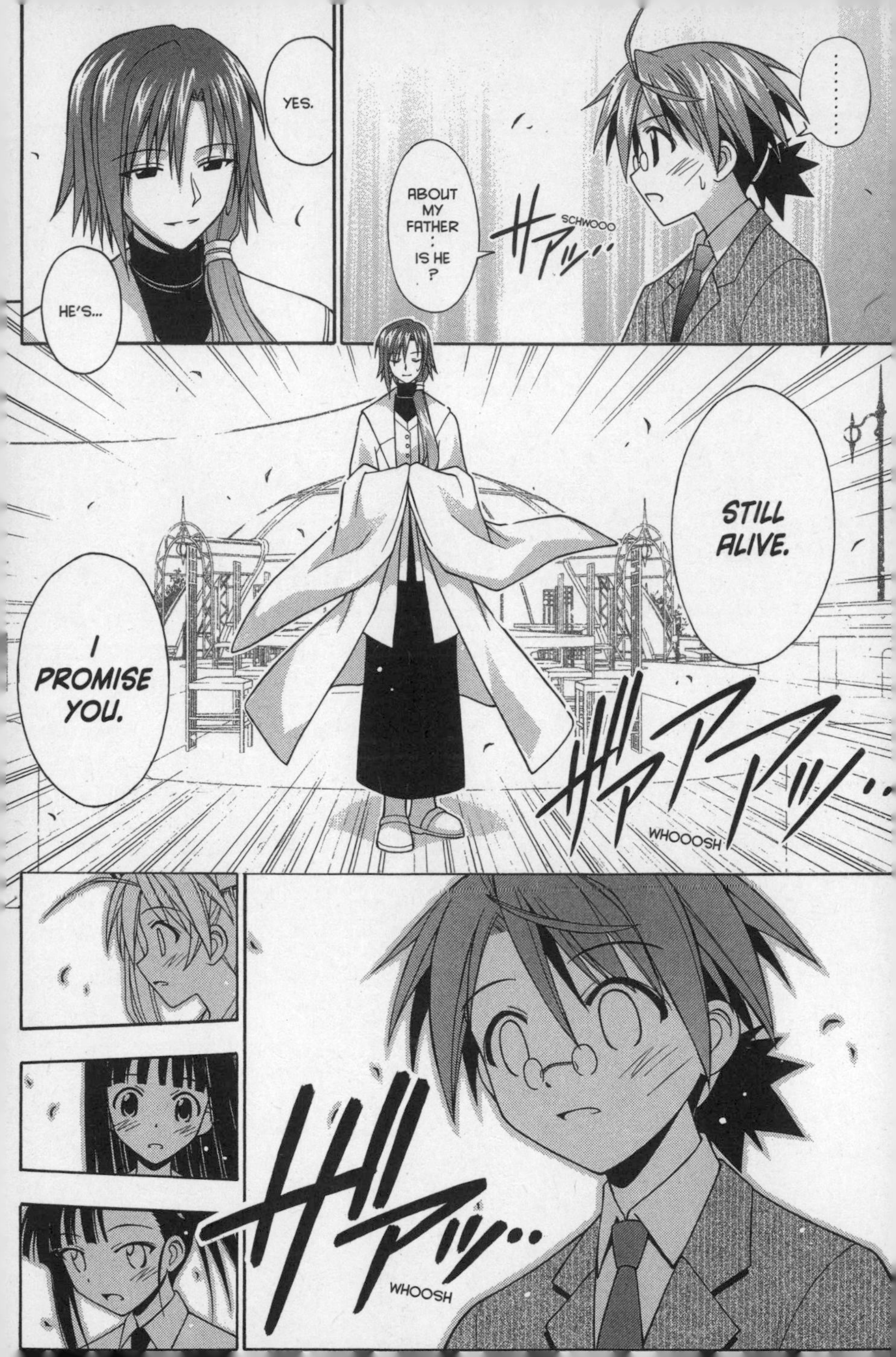
......
ABOUT MY FATHER : IS HE ?
SCHWOOO
YES.
HE'S...
STILL ALIVE.
I PROMISE YOU.
WHOOOSH
WHOOSH

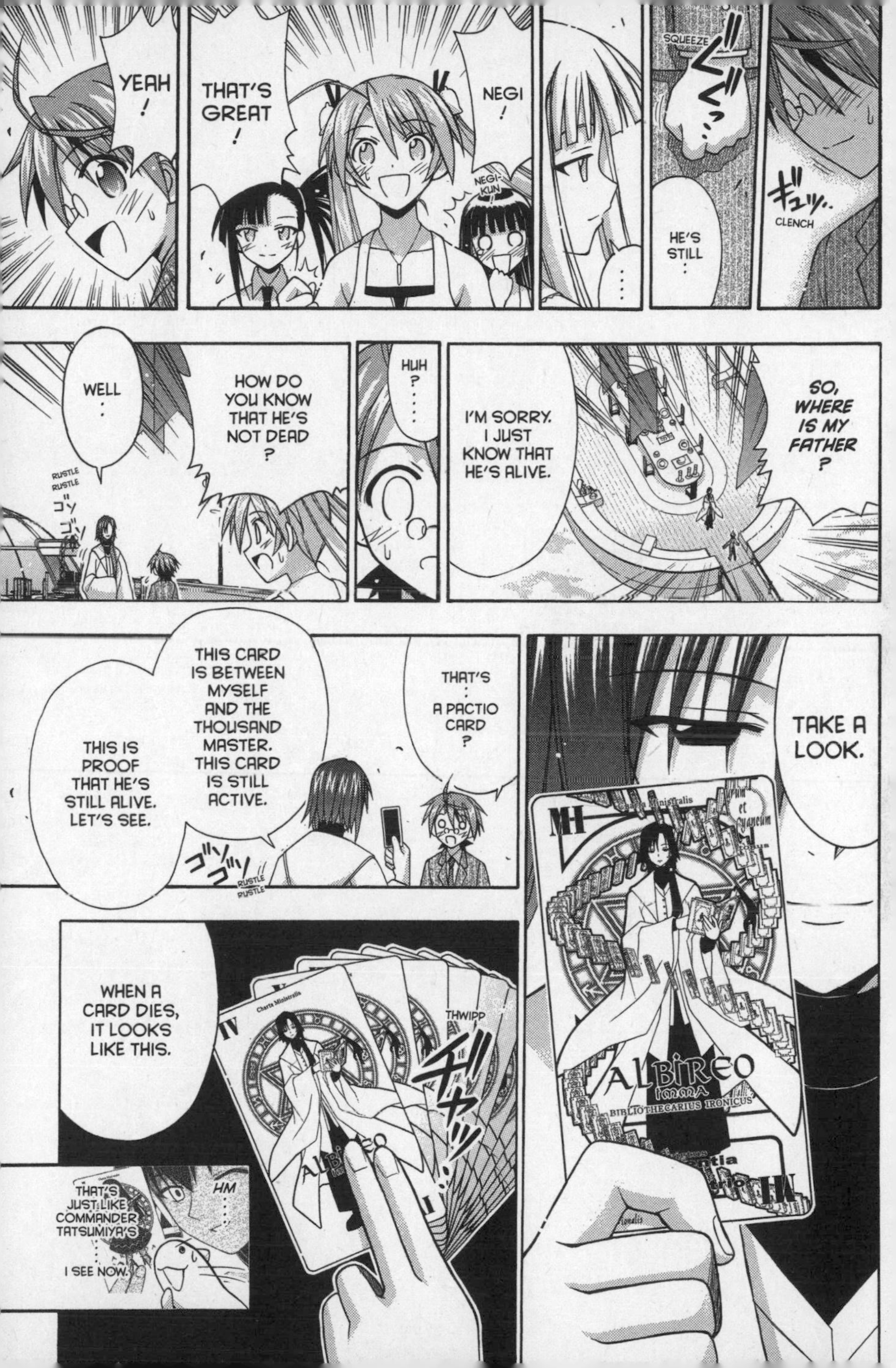
ギュッ..
CLENCH
SQUEEZE
ぐぐっ...
HE'S STILL...
.....
NEGI!
NEGI-KUN!
THAT'S GREAT!
YEAH!
SO, WHERE IS MY FATHER?
I'M SORRY. I JUST KNOW THAT HE'S ALIVE.
HUH?.....
HOW DO YOU KNOW THAT HE'S NOT DEAD?
WELL...
RUSTLE RUSTLE
ゴソゴソ
TAKE A LOOK.
Charta Ministralis
ALBIREO
IMMA
BIBLIOTHECARIUS IRONICUS
THAT'S... A PACTIO CARD?
THIS CARD IS BETWEEN MYSELF AND THE THOUSAND MASTER. THIS CARD IS STILL ACTIVE.
THIS IS PROOF THAT HE'S STILL ALIVE. LET'S SEE.
ゴソゴソ
RUSTLE RUSTLE
THWIPP
ヂャッ
WHEN A CARD DIES, IT LOOKS LIKE THIS.
HM...
THAT'S JUST LIKE COMMANDER TATSUMIYA'S...
I SEE NOW.

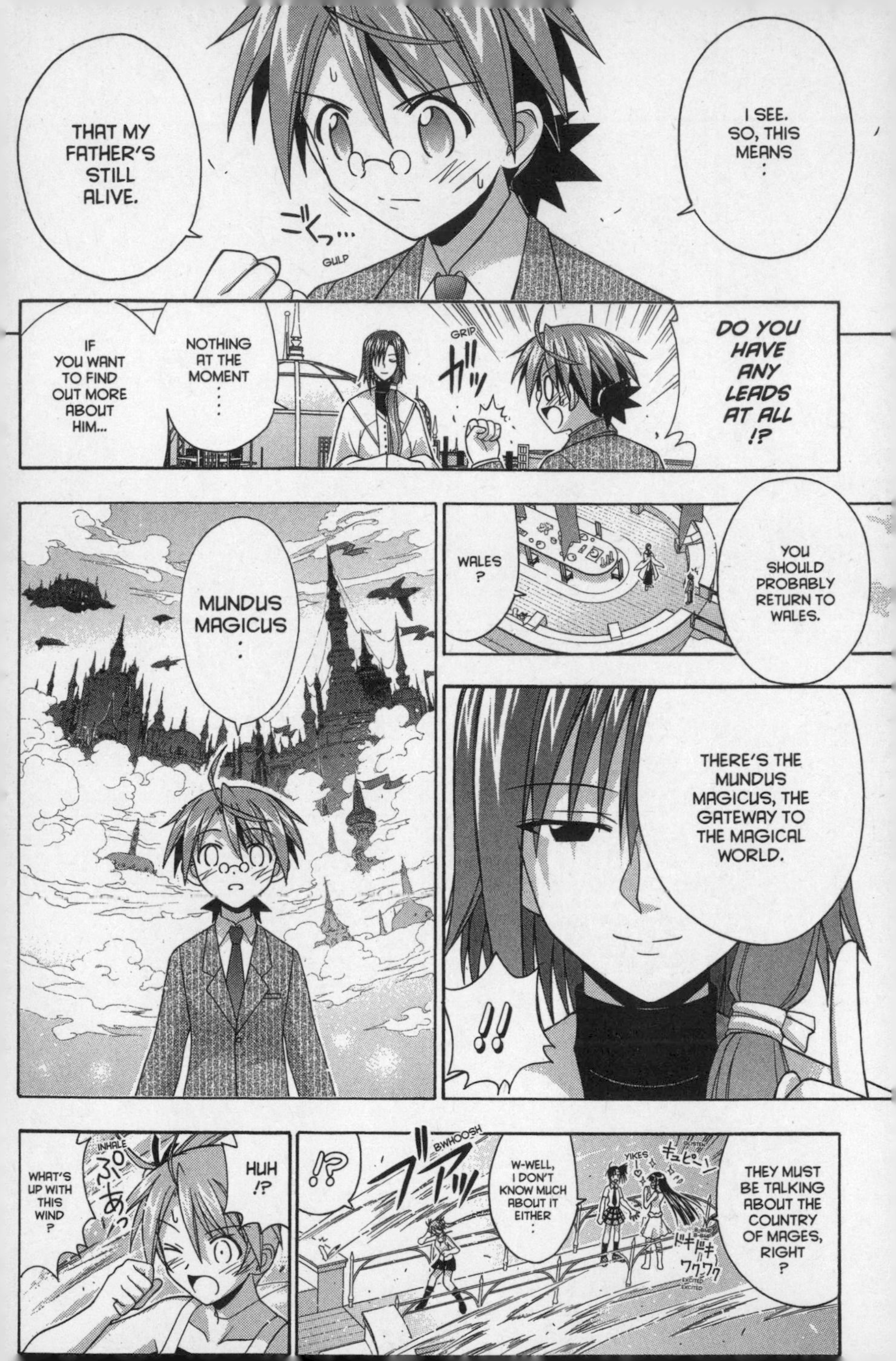
I SEE. SO, THIS MEANS :
THAT MY FATHER'S STILL ALIVE.
ごくっ…
GULP
DO YOU HAVE ANY LEADS AT ALL !?
ガッ
GRIP
NOTHING AT THE MOMENT ...
IF YOU WANT TO FIND OUT MORE ABOUT HIM...
YOU SHOULD PROBABLY RETURN TO WALES.
WALES ?
THERE'S THE MUNDUS MAGICUS, THE GATEWAY TO THE MAGICAL WORLD.
!!
MUNDUS MAGICUS :
THEY MUST BE TALKING ABOUT THE COUNTRY OF MAGES, RIGHT ?
キュピーン
YIKES
ドキドキ
ワクワク
EXCITED
EXCITED
W-WELL, I DON'T KNOW MUCH ABOUT IT EITHER :
ブアッ
BWHOOSH
!?
HUH !?
ぷあっ
INHALE
WHAT'S UP WITH THIS WIND ?

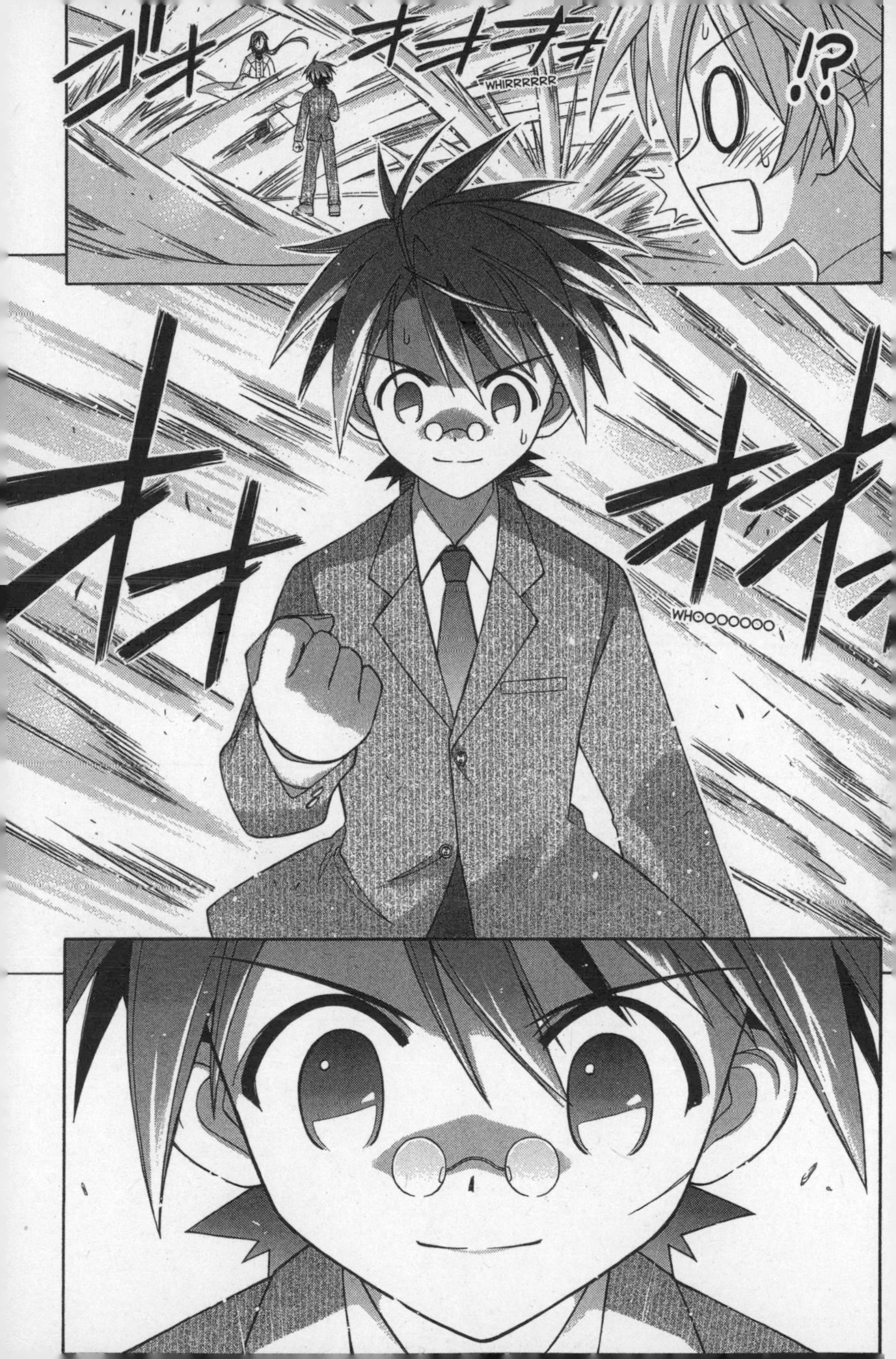
!?
WHIRRRRRR
WHOOOOOOO

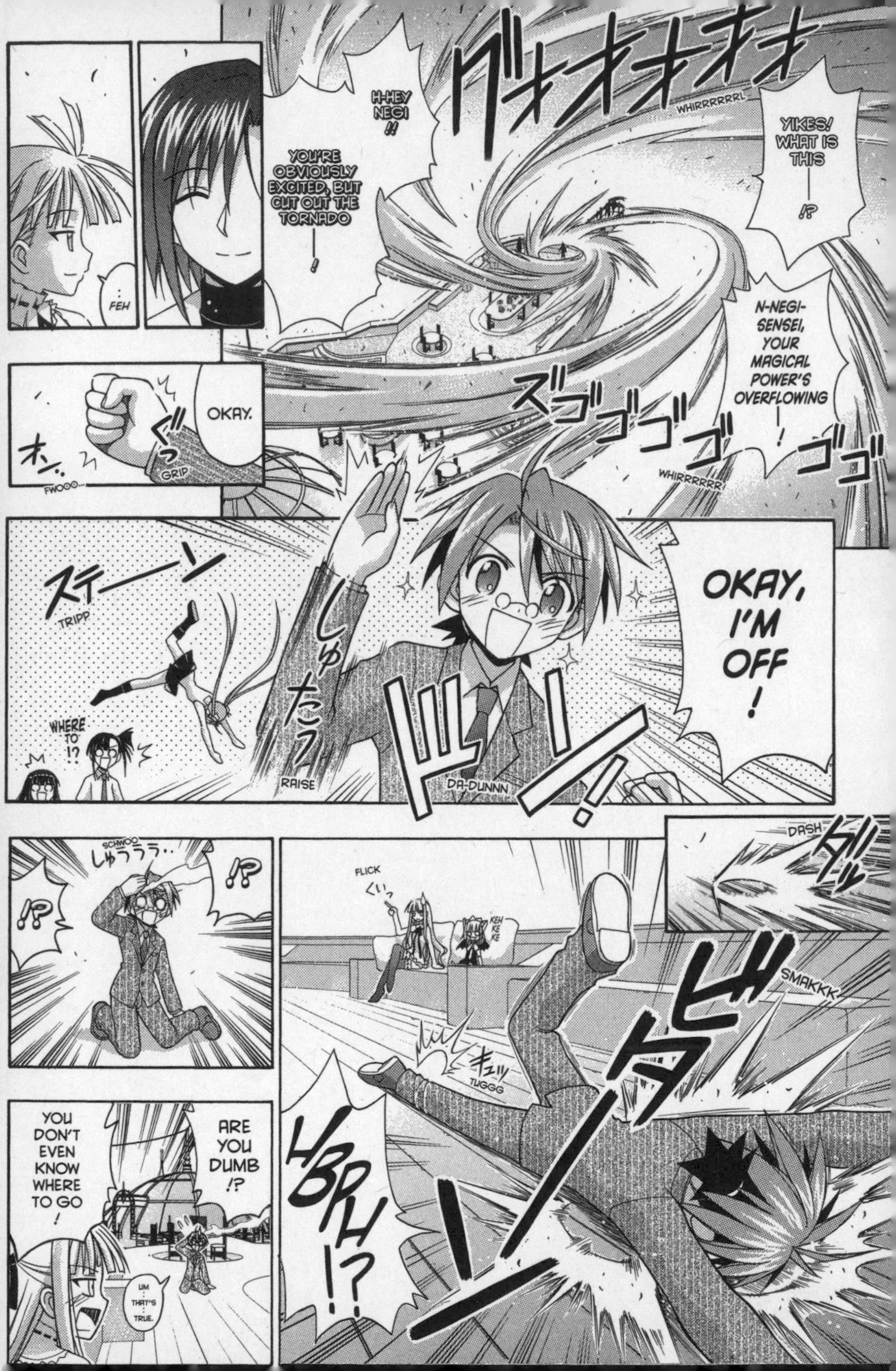
WHIRRRRRL
YIKES! WHAT IS THIS—!?
H-HEY NEGI!!
YOU'RE OBVIOUSLY EXCITED, BUT CUT OUT THE TORNADO—!
N-NEGI-SENSEI, YOUR MAGICAL POWER'S OVERFLOWING—!
WHIRRRRRR
... FEH
OKAY.
GRIP
FWOOO...
OKAY, I'M OFF!
DA-DUNNN
RAISE
TRIPP
WHERE TO!?
DASH
SMAKKK
FLICK
KEH KE KE
TUGGG
UBPH!?
SCHWOO
!?
!?
ARE YOU DUMB!?
YOU DON'T EVEN KNOW WHERE TO GO!
UM... THAT'S TRUE.

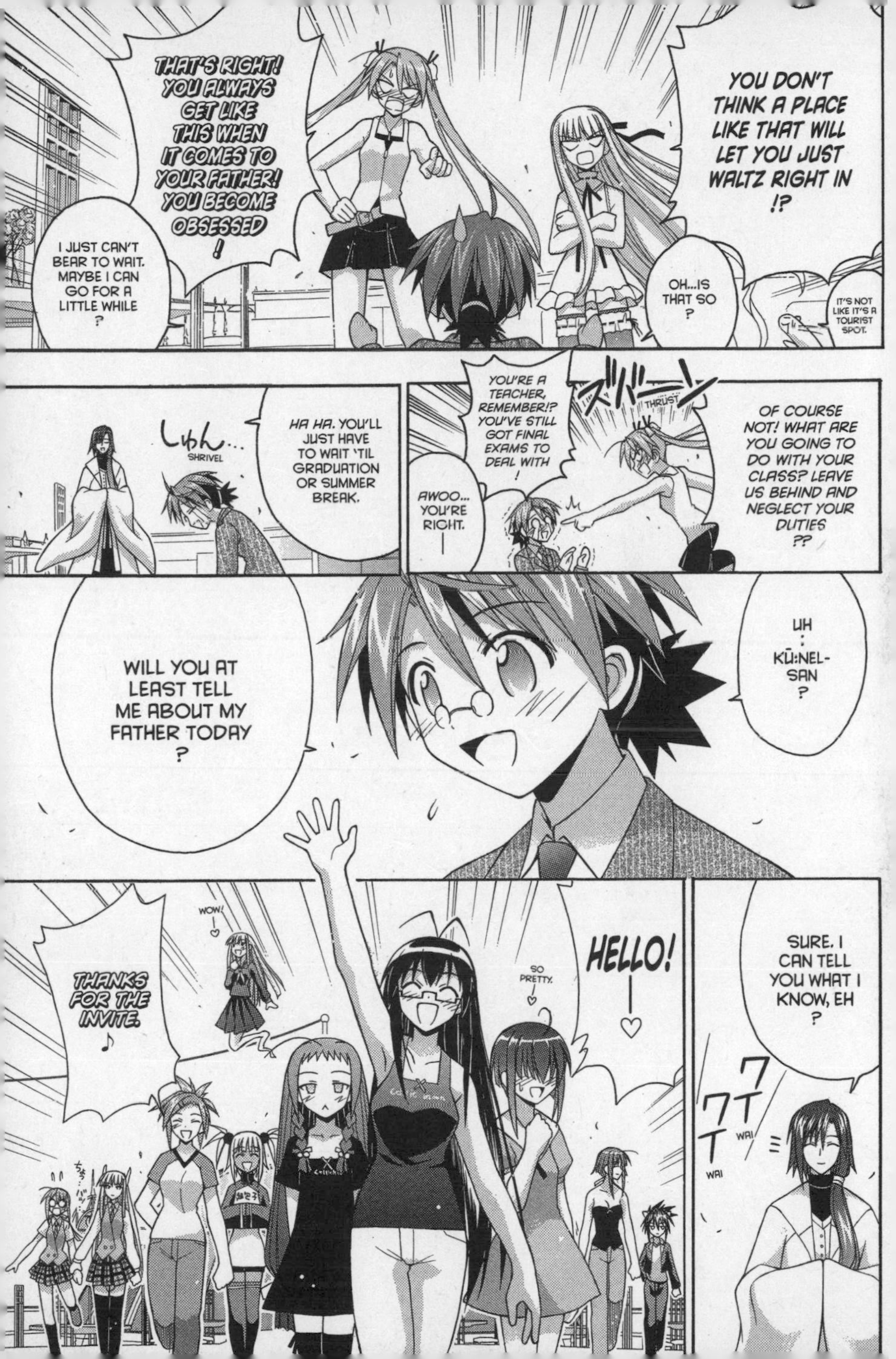
YOU DON'T THINK A PLACE LIKE THAT WILL LET YOU JUST WALTZ RIGHT IN!?
IT'S NOT LIKE IT'S A TOURIST SPOT.
OH...IS THAT SO?
THAT'S RIGHT! YOU ALWAYS GET LIKE THIS WHEN IT COMES TO YOUR FATHER! YOU BECOME OBSESSED!
I JUST CAN'T BEAR TO WAIT. MAYBE I CAN GO FOR A LITTLE WHILE?
ズバーン
THRUST
OF COURSE NOT! WHAT ARE YOU GOING TO DO WITH YOUR CLASS? LEAVE US BEHIND AND NEGLECT YOUR DUTIES??
YOU'RE A TEACHER, REMEMBER!? YOU'VE STILL GOT FINAL EXAMS TO DEAL WITH!
AWOO... YOU'RE RIGHT.
HA HA. YOU'LL JUST HAVE TO WAIT 'TIL GRADUATION OR SUMMER BREAK.
しゅん...
SHRIVEL
UH : KŪ:NEL-SAN?
WILL YOU AT LEAST TELL ME ABOUT MY FATHER TODAY?
SURE. I CAN TELL YOU WHAT I KNOW, EH?
ワイ
WAI
ワイ
WAI
HELLO!
SO PRETTY.
WOW!
THANKS FOR THE INVITE. ♪

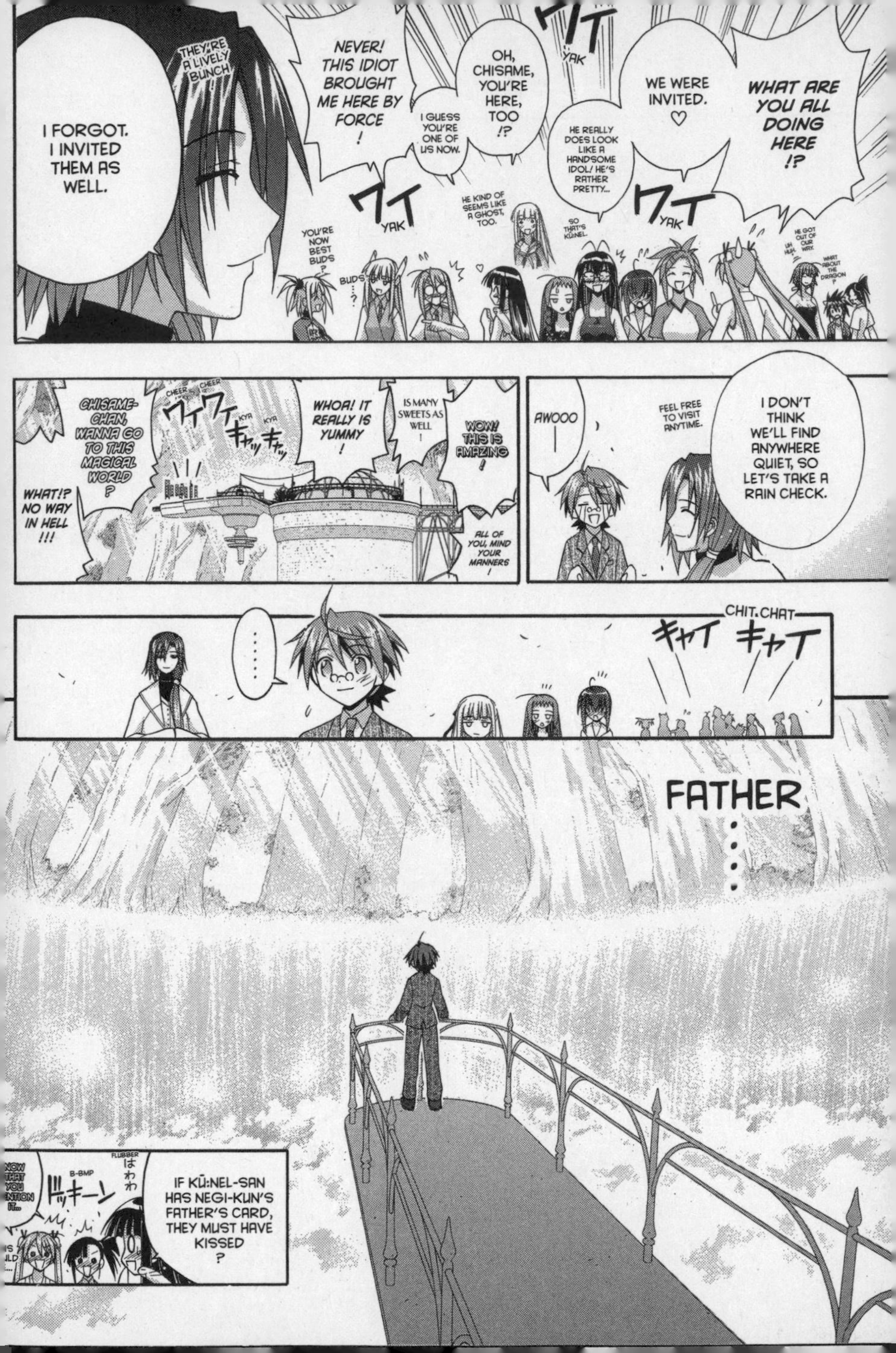

WHAT ARE YOU ALL DOING HERE!?
WE WERE INVITED. ♡
HE REALLY DOES LOOK LIKE A HANDSOME IDOL! HE'S RATHER PRETTY...
OH, CHISAME, YOU'RE HERE, TOO!?
I GUESS YOU'RE ONE OF US NOW.
NEVER! THIS IDIOT BROUGHT ME HERE BY FORCE!
THEY'RE A LIVELY BUNCH!
I FORGOT. I INVITED THEM AS WELL.
ワイ YAK
ワイ YAK
ワイ YAK
HE GOT OUT OF OUR WAY.
UH HUH.
WHAT ABOUT THE DRAGON?
SO THAT'S KŪ:NEL.
HE KIND OF SEEMS LIKE A GHOST, TOO.
YOU'RE NOW BEST BUDS?
BUDS...?
I DON'T THINK WE'LL FIND ANYWHERE QUIET, SO LET'S TAKE A RAIN CHECK.
FEEL FREE TO VISIT ANYTIME.
AWOOO—
WOW! THIS IS AMAZING!
ALL OF YOU, MIND YOUR MANNERS!
IS MANY SWEETS AS WELL!
WHOA! IT REALLY IS YUMMY!
CHEER CHEER
KYA KYA
CHISAME-CHAN, WANNA GO TO THIS MAGICAL WORLD?
WHAT!? NO WAY IN HELL!!!
CHIT CHAT
......
FATHER....
IF KŪ:NEL-SAN HAS NEGI-KUN'S FATHER'S CARD, THEY MUST HAVE KISSED?
FLUBBER
B-BMP
NOW THAT YOU MENTION IT...

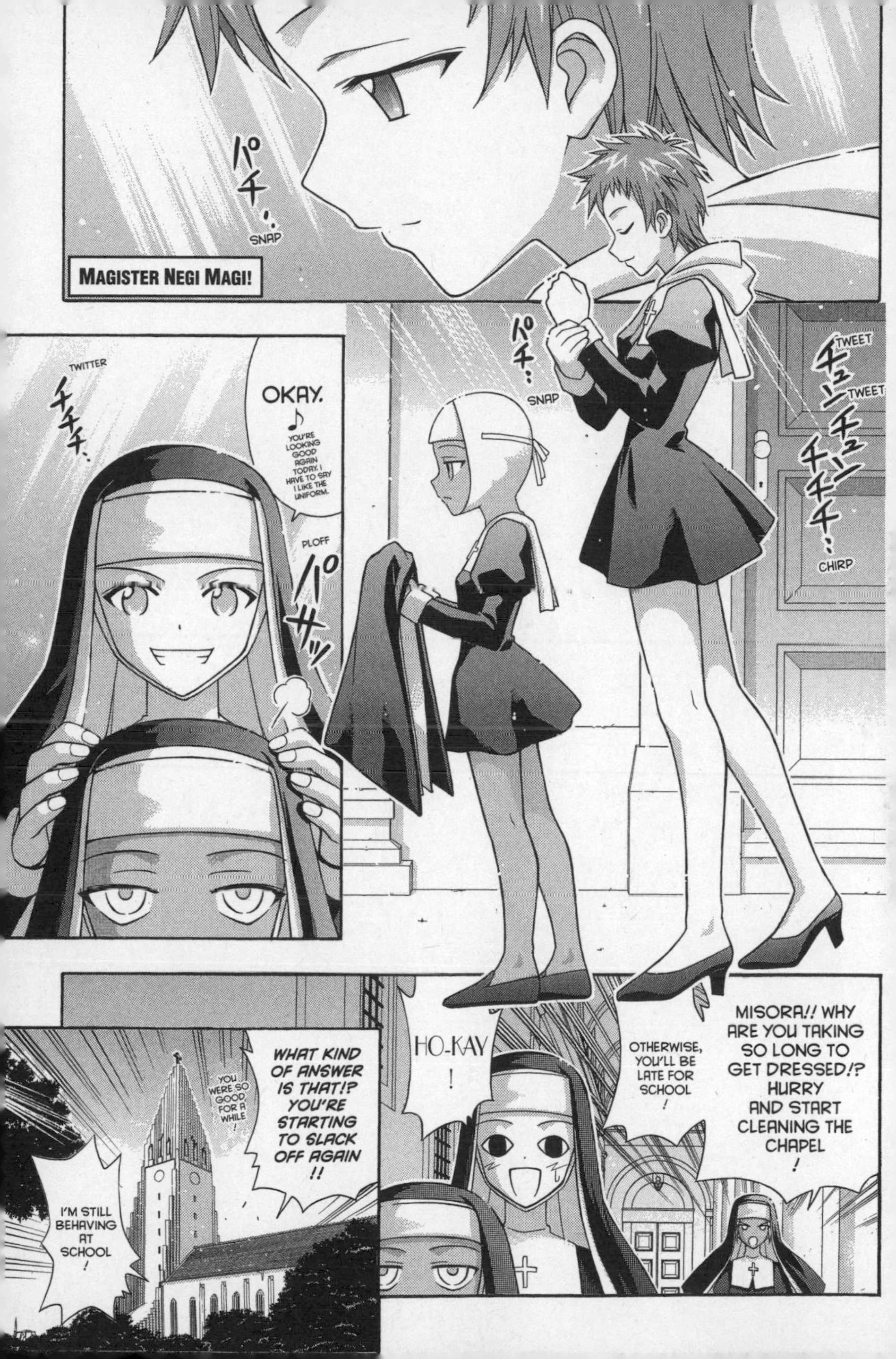
パチ、
SNAP
MAGISTER NEGI MAGI!
チュンチュンチチチ、
TWEET
TWEET
CHIRP
パチ、
SNAP
パサッ
PLOFF
OKAY. ♪
YOU'RE LOOKING GOOD AGAIN TODAY. I HAVE TO SAY I LIKE THE UNIFORM.
チチチ、
TWITTER
MISORA!! WHY ARE YOU TAKING SO LONG TO GET DRESSED!? HURRY AND START CLEANING THE CHAPEL!
OTHERWISE, YOU'LL BE LATE FOR SCHOOL!
HO-KAY!
WHAT KIND OF ANSWER IS THAT!? YOU'RE STARTING TO SLACK OFF AGAIN!!
YOU WERE SO GOOD FOR A WHILE!
I'M STILL BEHAVING AT SCHOOL!

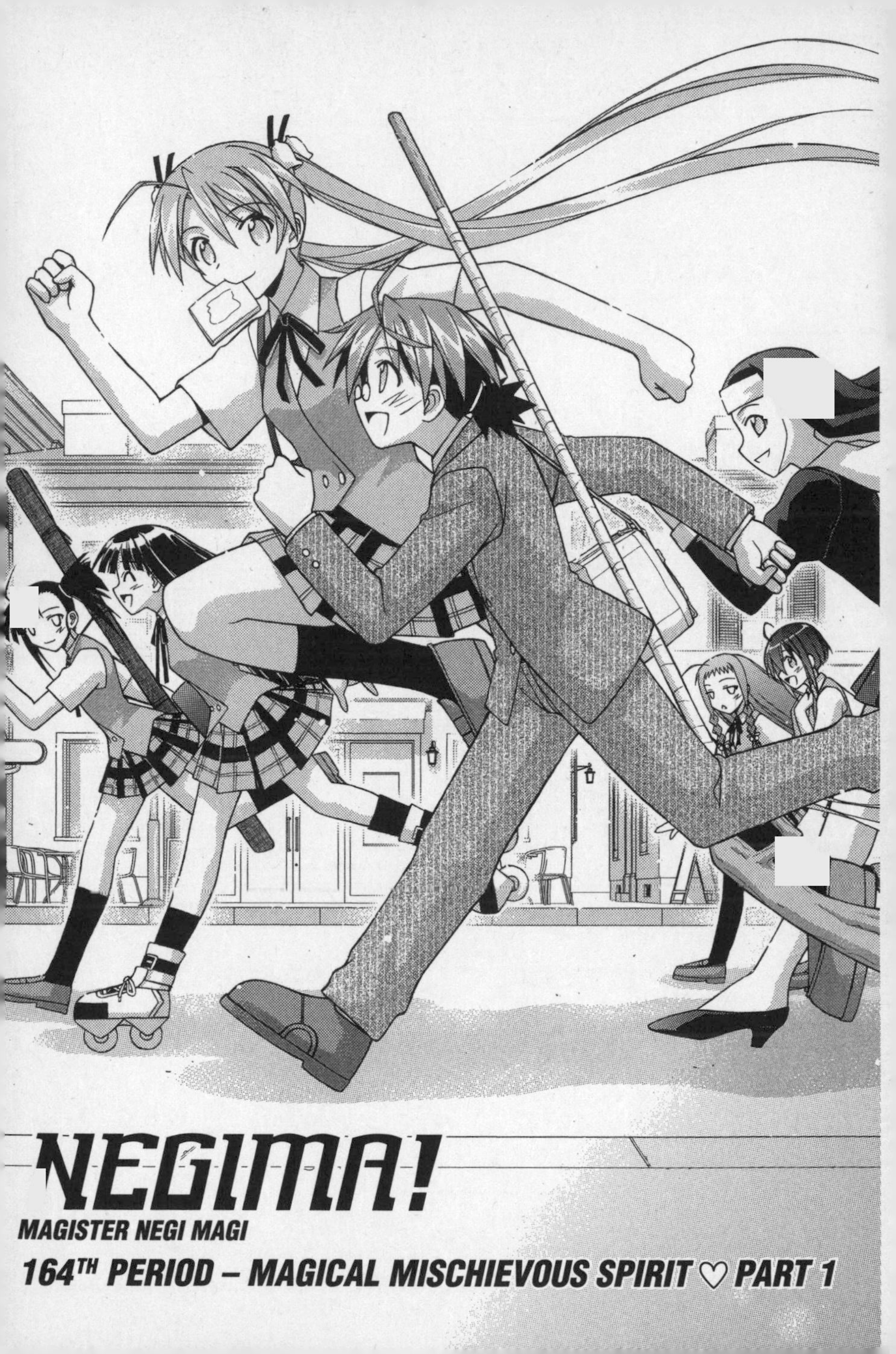

NEGIMA!

MAGISTER NEGI MAGI

164TH PERIOD – MAGICAL MISCHIEVOUS SPIRIT ♡ PART 1

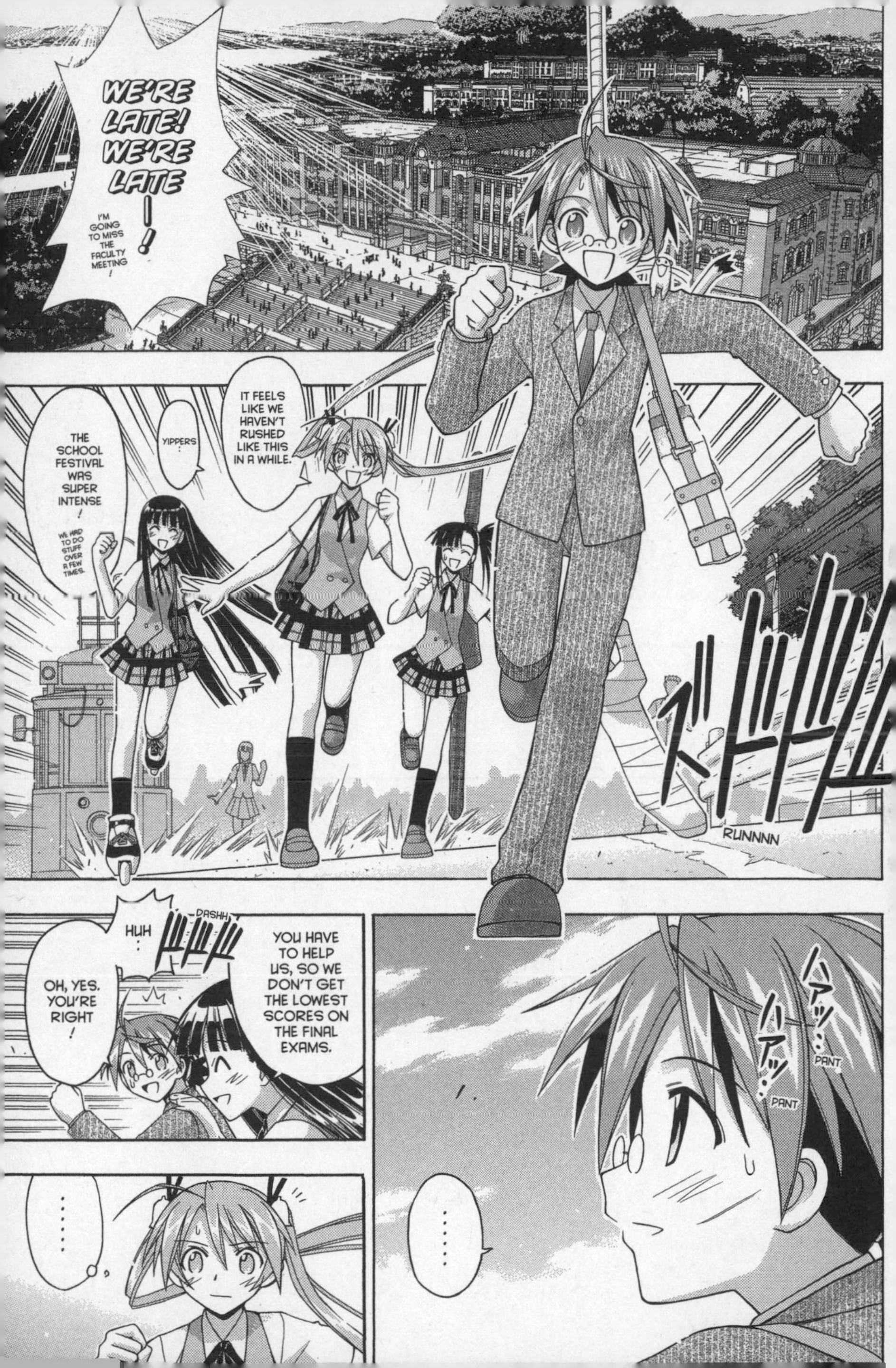
WE'RE LATE! WE'RE LATE —!
I'M GOING TO MISS THE FACULTY MEETING!
RUNNNN
IT FEELS LIKE WE HAVEN'T RUSHED LIKE THIS IN A WHILE.
YIPPERS...
THE SCHOOL FESTIVAL WAS SUPER INTENSE!
WE HAD TO DO STUFF OVER A FEW TIMES.
PANT
PANT
......
DASHH
YOU HAVE TO HELP US, SO WE DON'T GET THE LOWEST SCORES ON THE FINAL EXAMS.
HUH...
OH, YES. YOU'RE RIGHT!
......

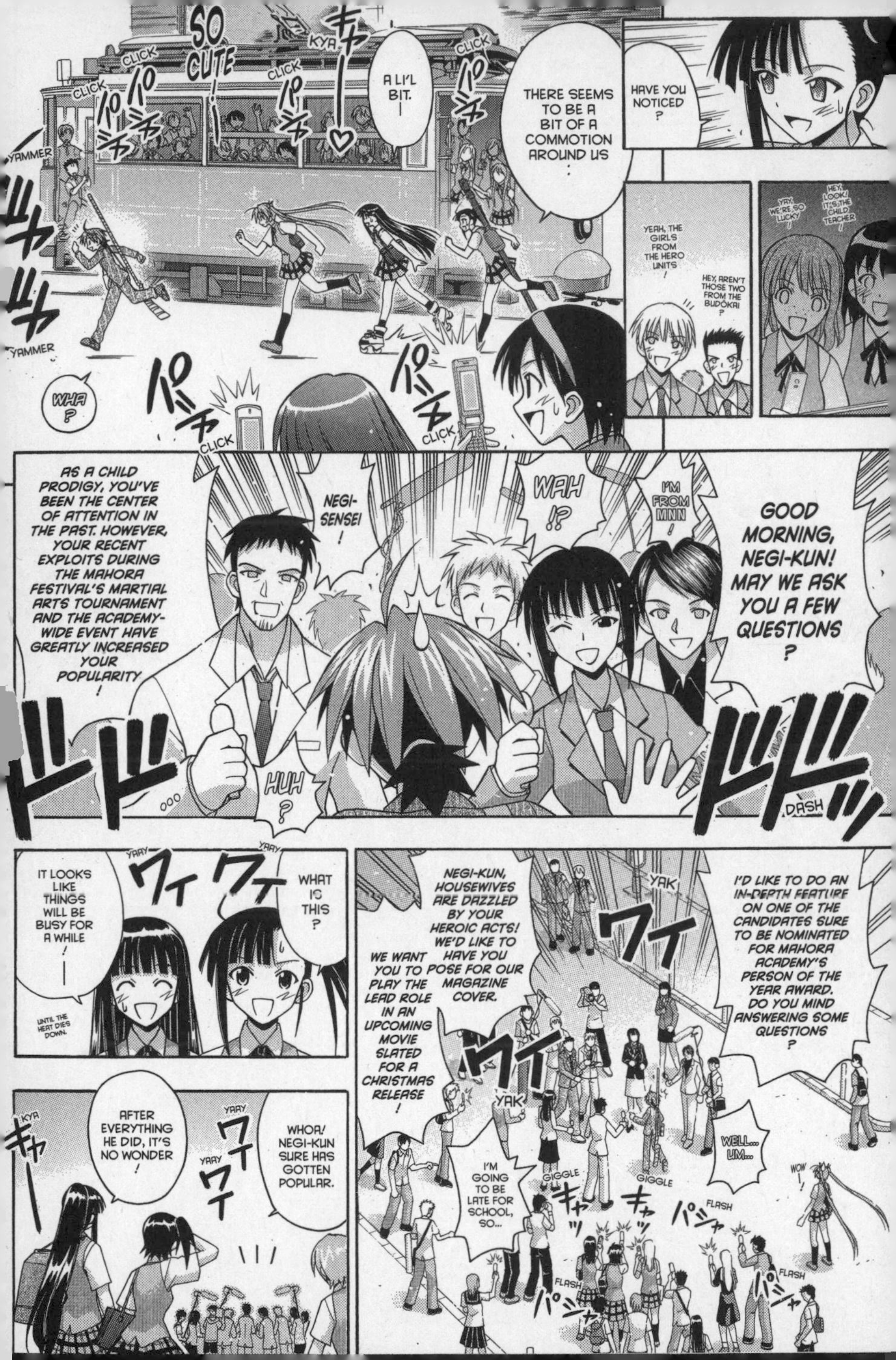
HAVE YOU NOTICED?
HEY, LOOK! IT'S THE CHILD TEACHER!
YAY, WE'RE SO LUCKY!
HEY, AREN'T THOSE TWO FROM THE BUDŌKAI?
YEAH, THE GIRLS FROM THE HERO UNITS!
THERE SEEMS TO BE A BIT OF A COMMOTION AROUND US:
CLICK
A LI'L BIT.
KYA
SO CUTE!
CLICK
CLICK
CLICK
YAMMER
YAMMER
WHA?
CLICK
CLICK
GOOD MORNING, NEGI-KUN! MAY WE ASK YOU A FEW QUESTIONS?
I'M FROM MNN!
WAH!?
NEGI-SENSEI!
AS A CHILD PRODIGY, YOU'VE BEEN THE CENTER OF ATTENTION IN THE PAST. HOWEVER, YOUR RECENT EXPLOITS DURING THE MAHORA FESTIVAL'S MARTIAL ARTS TOURNAMENT AND THE ACADEMY-WIDE EVENT HAVE GREATLY INCREASED YOUR POPULARITY!
HUH?
DASH
I'D LIKE TO DO AN IN-DEPTH FEATURE ON ONE OF THE CANDIDATES SURE TO BE NOMINATED FOR MAHORA ACADEMY'S PERSON OF THE YEAR AWARD. DO YOU MIND ANSWERING SOME QUESTIONS?
YAK
NEGI-KUN, HOUSEWIVES ARE DAZZLED BY YOUR HEROIC ACTS! WE'D LIKE TO HAVE YOU POSE FOR OUR MAGAZINE COVER.
WE WANT YOU TO PLAY THE LEAD ROLE IN AN UPCOMING MOVIE SLATED FOR A CHRISTMAS RELEASE!
YAK
WELL... UM...
I'M GOING TO BE LATE FOR SCHOOL, SO...
WOW!
GIGGLE
GIGGLE
FLASH
FLASH
FLASH
YAAY
WHAT IS THIS?
YAAY
IT LOOKS LIKE THINGS WILL BE BUSY FOR A WHILE!
UNTIL THE HEAT DIES DOWN.
WHOA! NEGI-KUN SURE HAS GOTTEN POPULAR.
YAAY
YAAY
AFTER EVERYTHING HE DID, IT'S NO WONDER!
KYA

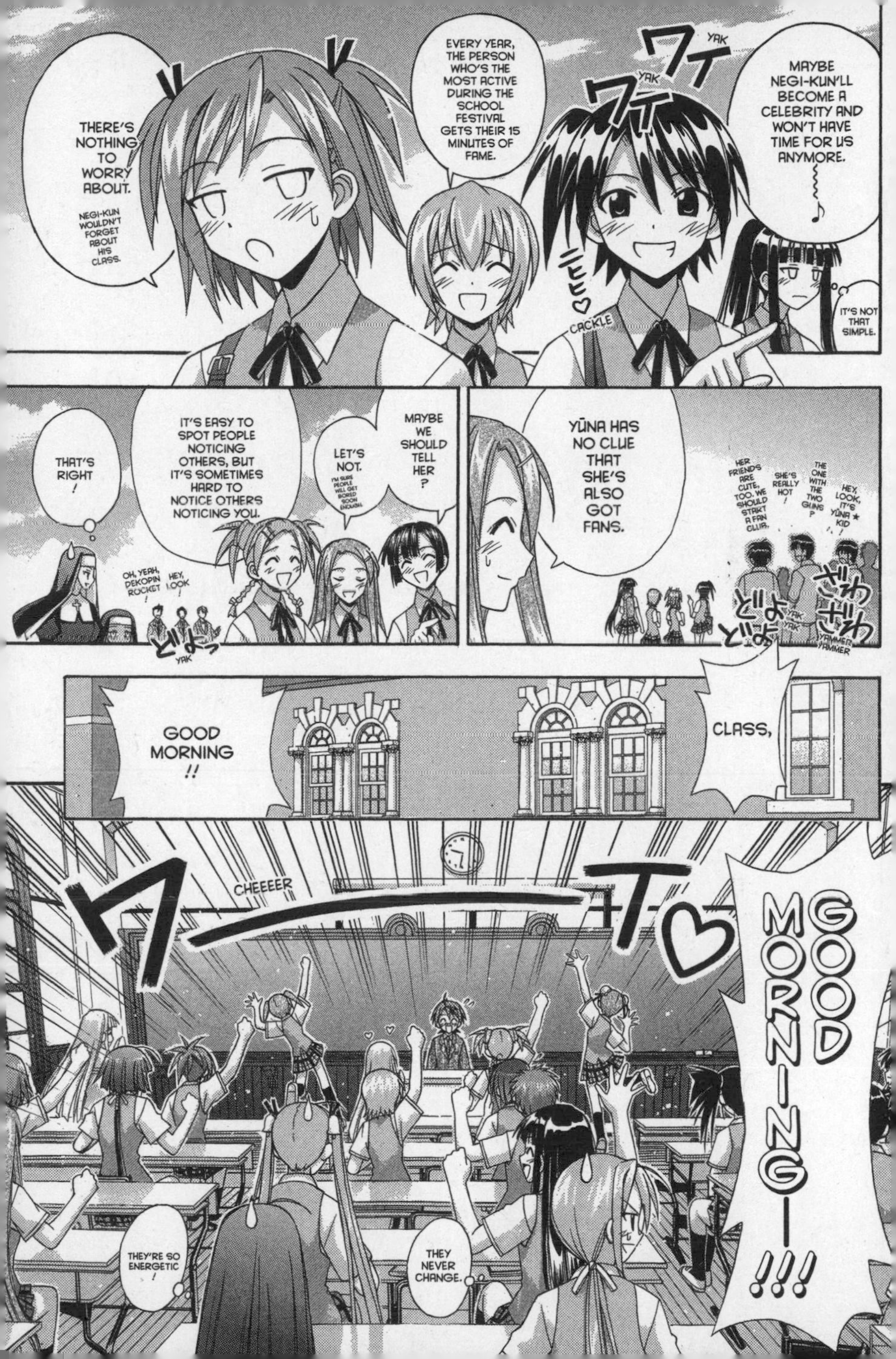
MAYBE NEGI-KUN'LL BECOME A CELEBRITY AND WON'T HAVE TIME FOR US ANYMORE.
YAK YAK
EVERY YEAR, THE PERSON WHO'S THE MOST ACTIVE DURING THE SCHOOL FESTIVAL GETS THEIR 15 MINUTES OF FAME.
THERE'S NOTHING TO WORRY ABOUT.
NEGI-KUN WOULDN'T FORGET ABOUT HIS CLASS.
IT'S NOT THAT SIMPLE.
CACKLE
YŪNA HAS NO CLUE THAT SHE'S ALSO GOT FANS.
HEY, LOOK, IT'S YŪNA ★ KID!
THE ONE WITH THE TWO GUNS?
SHE'S REALLY HOT!
HER FRIENDS ARE CUTE, TOO. WE SHOULD START A FAN CLUB.
YAMMER YAMMER
YAK YAK
MAYBE WE SHOULD TELL HER?
LET'S NOT.
I'M SURE PEOPLE WILL GET BORED SOON ENOUGH.
IT'S EASY TO SPOT PEOPLE NOTICING OTHERS, BUT IT'S SOMETIMES HARD TO NOTICE OTHERS NOTICING YOU.
THAT'S RIGHT!
HEY, LOOK
OH, YEAH, DEKOPIN ROCKET!
YAK
CLASS,
GOOD MORNING!!
GOOD MORNING—!!!
CHEEEER
THEY NEVER CHANGE.
THEY'RE SO ENERGETIC!

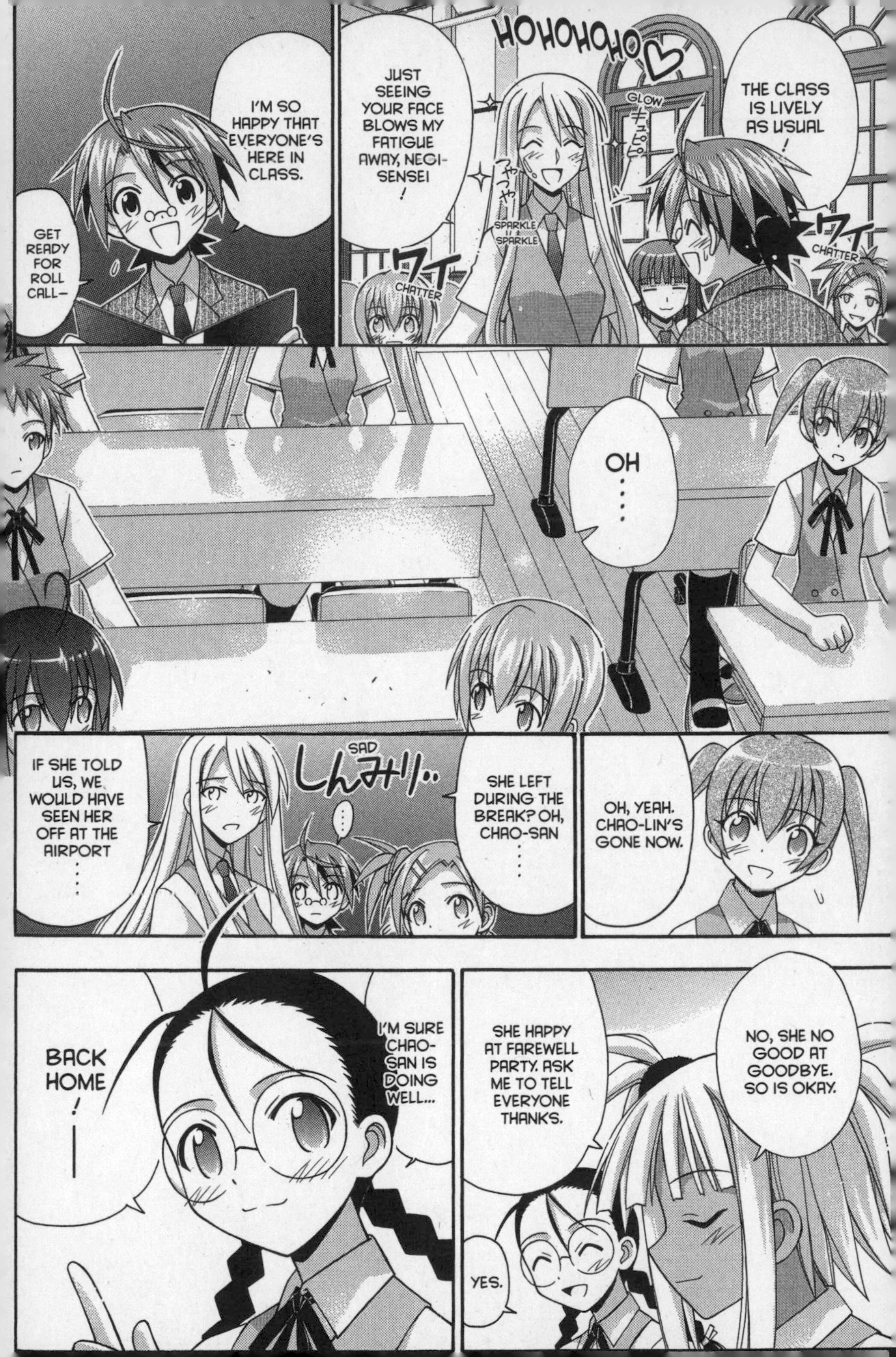
HOHOHOHO♥
THE CLASS IS LIVELY AS USUAL!
GLOW
JUST SEEING YOUR FACE BLOWS MY FATIGUE AWAY, NEGI-SENSEI!
SPARKLE SPARKLE
ワイ CHATTER
ワイ CHATTER
I'M SO HAPPY THAT EVERYONE'S HERE IN CLASS.
GET READY FOR ROLL CALL—
OH...
OH, YEAH. CHAO-LIN'S GONE NOW.
SHE LEFT DURING THE BREAK? OH, CHAO-SAN...
しんみり.. SAD
...
IF SHE TOLD US, WE WOULD HAVE SEEN HER OFF AT THE AIRPORT...
NO, SHE NO GOOD AT GOODBYE. SO IS OKAY.
SHE HAPPY AT FAREWELL PARTY. ASK ME TO TELL EVERYONE THANKS.
YES.
I'M SURE CHAO-SAN IS DOING WELL...
BACK HOME!

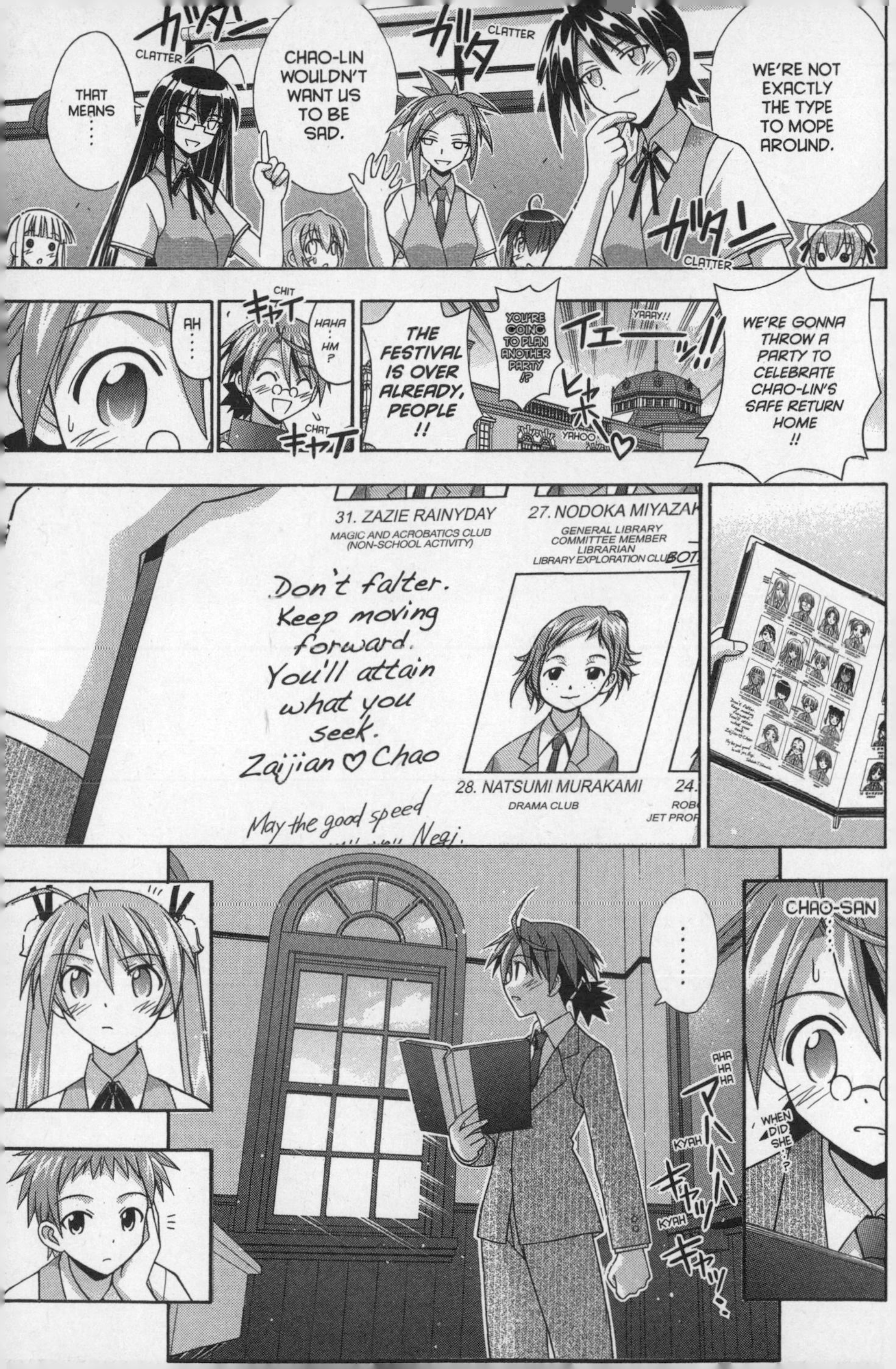

WE'RE NOT EXACTLY THE TYPE TO MOPE AROUND.
ガタン
CLATTER
CHAO-LIN WOULDN'T WANT US TO BE SAD.
ガタ
CLATTER
THAT MEANS ....
CLATTER
WE'RE GONNA THROW A PARTY TO CELEBRATE CHAO-LIN'S SAFE RETURN HOME !!
YOU'RE GOING TO PLAN ANOTHER PARTY !?
イェーーッ!!
YAAAY!!
YAHOO
THE FESTIVAL IS OVER ALREADY, PEOPLE !!
CHIT
HAHA ... HM ?
CHAT
AH ....
27. NODOKA MIYAZAKI
GENERAL LIBRARY COMMITTEE MEMBER LIBRARIAN LIBRARY EXPLORATION CLUB
31. ZAZIE RAINYDAY
MAGIC AND ACROBATICS CLUB (NON-SCHOOL ACTIVITY)
Don't falter. Keep moving forward. You'll attain what you seek. Zaijian ♡ Chao
28. NATSUMI MURAKAMI
DRAMA CLUB
May the good speed
CHAO-SAN ....
WHEN DID SHE ...?
......
AHA HA HA
KYAH
KYAH

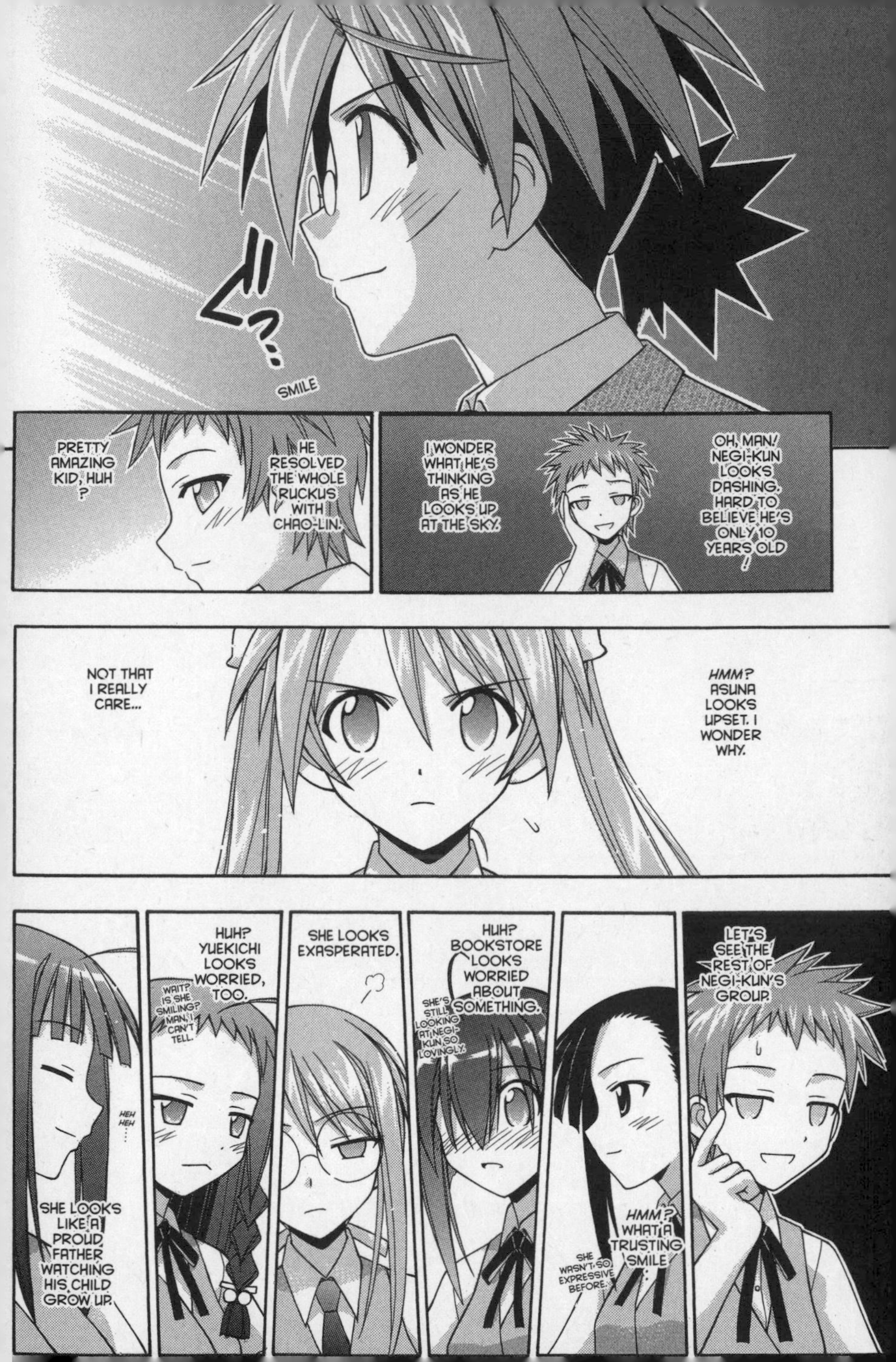
SMILE
OH, MAN! NEGI-KUN LOOKS DASHING. HARD TO BELIEVE HE'S ONLY 10 YEARS OLD!
I WONDER WHAT HE'S THINKING AS HE LOOKS UP AT THE SKY.
HE RESOLVED THE WHOLE RUCKUS WITH CHAO-LIN.
PRETTY AMAZING KID, HUH?
HMM? ASUNA LOOKS UPSET. I WONDER WHY.
NOT THAT I REALLY CARE...
LET'S SEE THE REST OF NEGI-KUN'S GROUP.
HMM? WHAT A TRUSTING SMILE.
SHE WASN'T SO EXPRESSIVE BEFORE.
HUH? BOOKSTORE LOOKS WORRIED ABOUT SOMETHING.
SHE'S STILL LOOKING AT NEGI-KUN SO LOVINGLY.
SHE LOOKS EXASPERATED.
HUH? YUEKICHI LOOKS WORRIED, TOO.
WAIT? IS SHE SMILING? MAN, I CAN'T TELL.
HEH HEH...
SHE LOOKS LIKE A PROUD FATHER WATCHING HIS CHILD GROW UP.

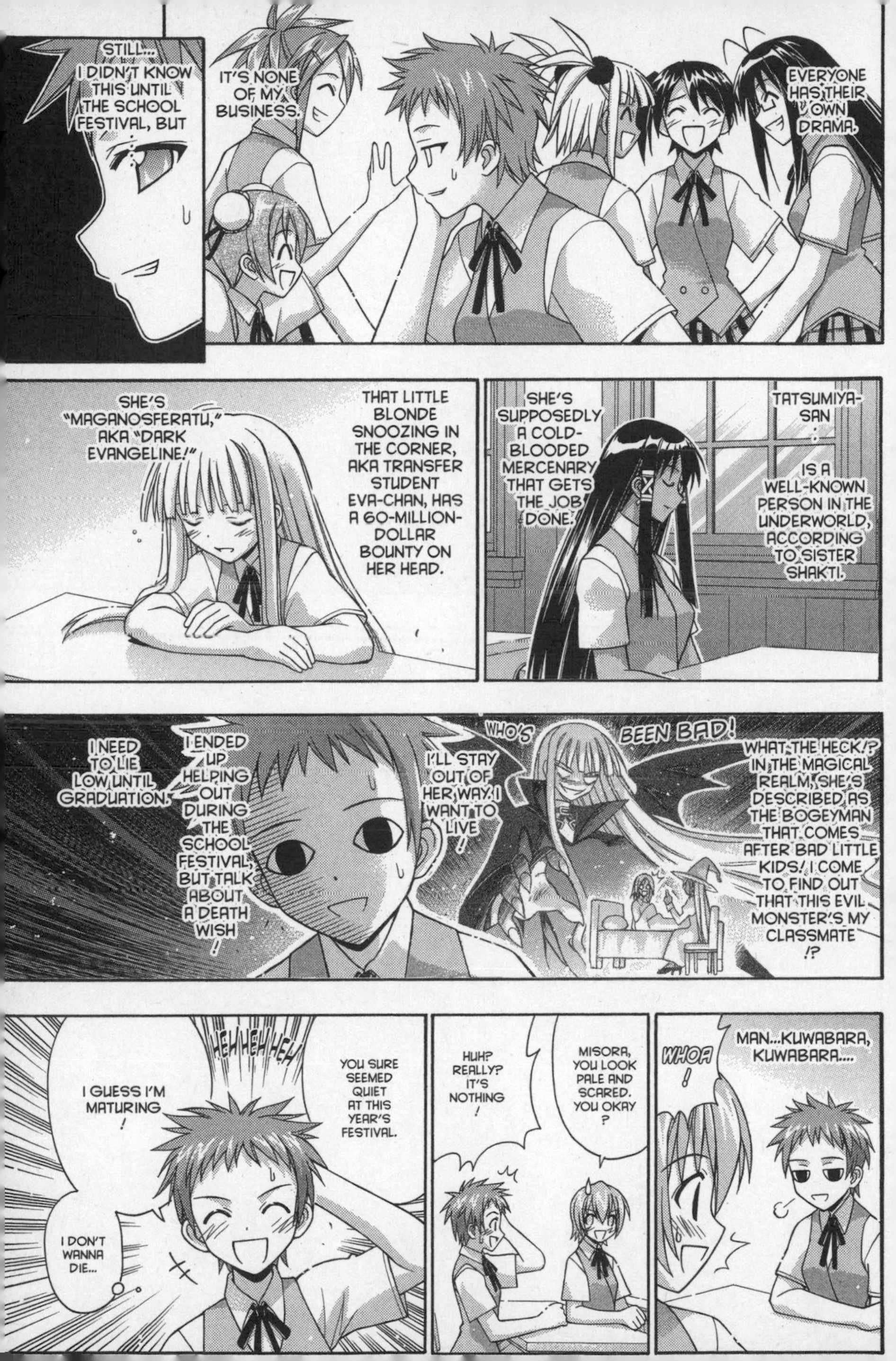
EVERYONE HAS THEIR OWN DRAMA.
IT'S NONE OF MY BUSINESS.
STILL... I DIDN'T KNOW THIS UNTIL THE SCHOOL FESTIVAL, BUT
TATSUMIYA-SAN:
IS A WELL-KNOWN PERSON IN THE UNDERWORLD, ACCORDING TO SISTER SHAKTI.
SHE'S SUPPOSEDLY A COLD-BLOODED MERCENARY THAT GETS THE JOB DONE.
THAT LITTLE BLONDE SNOOZING IN THE CORNER, AKA TRANSFER STUDENT EVA-CHAN, HAS A 60-MILLION-DOLLAR BOUNTY ON HER HEAD.
SHE'S "MAGANOSFERATU," AKA "DARK EVANGELINE!"
WHAT THE HECK!? IN THE MAGICAL REALM, SHE'S DESCRIBED AS THE BOGEYMAN THAT COMES AFTER BAD LITTLE KIDS! I COME TO FIND OUT THAT THIS EVIL MONSTER'S MY CLASSMATE!?
WHO'S BEEN BAD!
I'LL STAY OUT OF HER WAY. I WANT TO LIVE!
I ENDED UP HELPING OUT DURING THE SCHOOL FESTIVAL, BUT TALK ABOUT A DEATH WISH!
I NEED TO LIE LOW UNTIL GRADUATION.
MAN...KUWABARA, KUWABARA....
WHOA!
MISORA, YOU LOOK PALE AND SCARED. YOU OKAY?
HUH? REALLY? IT'S NOTHING!
YOU SURE SEEMED QUIET AT THIS YEAR'S FESTIVAL.
HEH HEH HEH
I GUESS I'M MATURING!
I DON'T WANNA DIE...

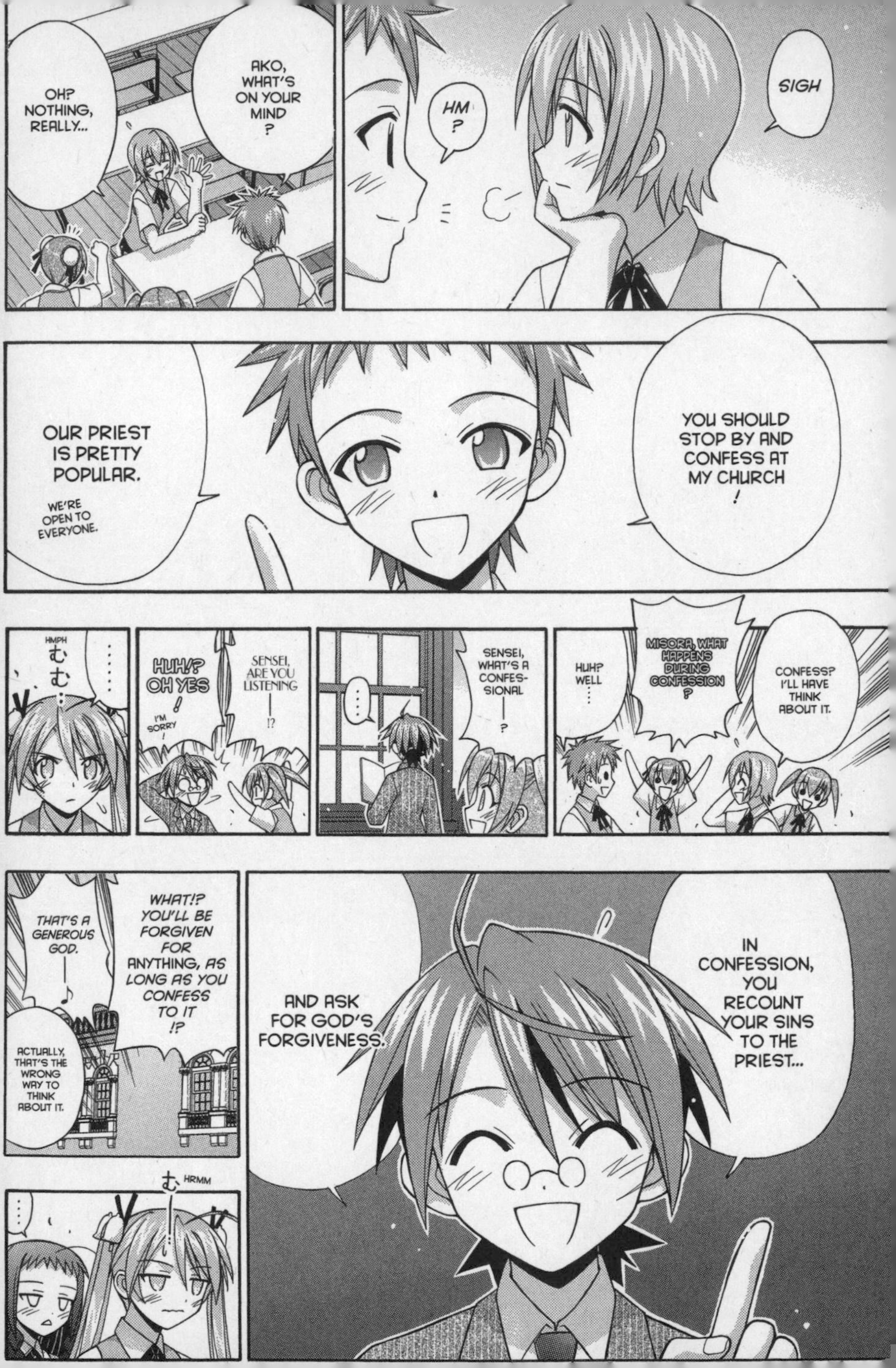

SIGH
HM?
AKO, WHAT'S ON YOUR MIND?
OH? NOTHING, REALLY...
YOU SHOULD STOP BY AND CONFESS AT MY CHURCH!
OUR PRIEST IS PRETTY POPULAR.
WE'RE OPEN TO EVERYONE.
CONFESS? I'LL HAVE THINK ABOUT IT.
MISORA, WHAT HAPPENS DURING CONFESSION?
HUH? WELL....
SENSEI, WHAT'S A CONFES-SIONAL—?
......
SENSEI, ARE YOU LISTENING—!?
HUH!? OH YES!
I'M SORRY!
......
むむ...
HMPH
IN CONFESSION, YOU RECOUNT YOUR SINS TO THE PRIEST...
AND ASK FOR GOD'S FORGIVENESS.
WHAT!? YOU'LL BE FORGIVEN FOR ANYTHING, AS LONG AS YOU CONFESS TO IT!?
THAT'S A GENEROUS GOD—♪
ACTUALLY, THAT'S THE WRONG WAY TO THINK ABOUT IT.
む
HRMM
......

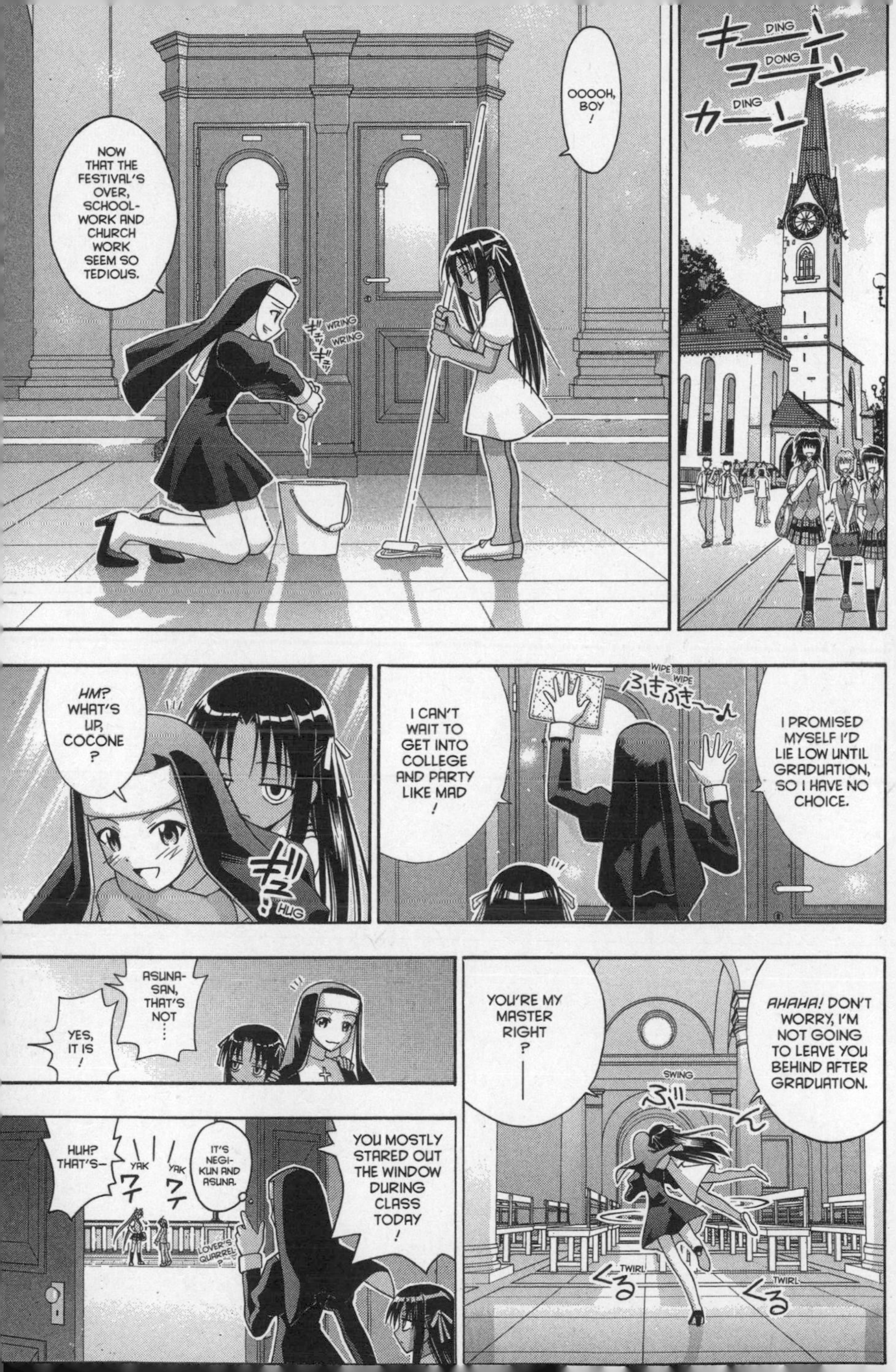

DING
DONG
DING
OOOOH, BOY!
NOW THAT THE FESTIVAL'S OVER, SCHOOLWORK AND CHURCH WORK SEEM SO TEDIOUS.
WRING WRING
I PROMISED MYSELF I'D LIE LOW UNTIL GRADUATION, SO I HAVE NO CHOICE.
WIPE WIPE
I CAN'T WAIT TO GET INTO COLLEGE AND PARTY LIKE MAD!
HM? WHAT'S UP, COCONE?
HUG
AHAHA! DON'T WORRY, I'M NOT GOING TO LEAVE YOU BEHIND AFTER GRADUATION.
YOU'RE MY MASTER RIGHT?
SWING
TWIRL
TWIRL
ASUNA-SAN, THAT'S NOT...
YES, IT IS!
YOU MOSTLY STARED OUT THE WINDOW DURING CLASS TODAY!
IT'S NEGI-KUN AND ASUNA.
YAK
YAK
HUH? THAT'S—
LOVER'S QUARREL?

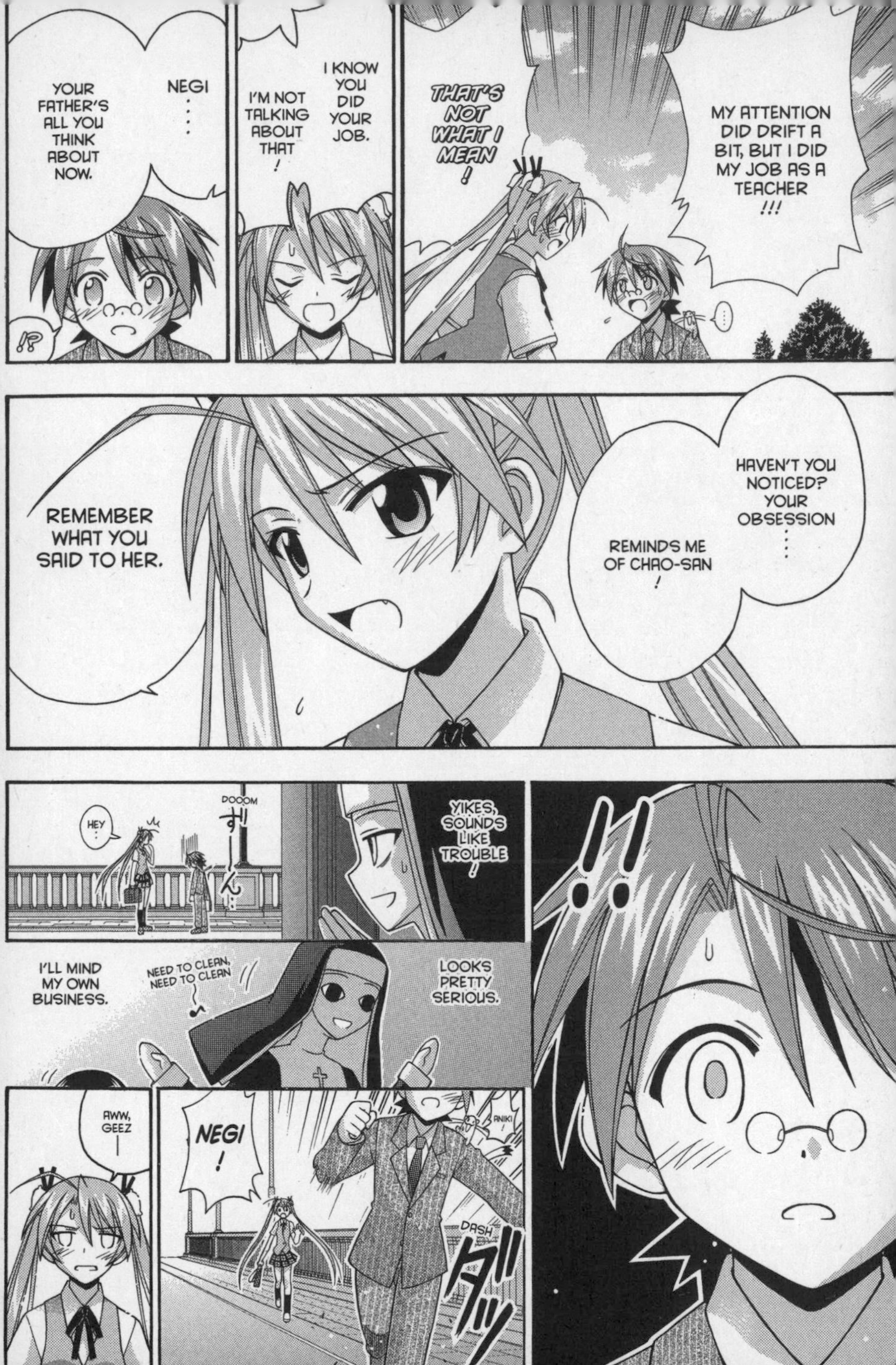

MY ATTENTION DID DRIFT A BIT, BUT I DID MY JOB AS A TEACHER!!!
THAT'S NOT WHAT I MEAN!
…
I KNOW YOU DID YOUR JOB.
I'M NOT TALKING ABOUT THAT!
NEGI…
YOUR FATHER'S ALL YOU THINK ABOUT NOW.
!?
HAVEN'T YOU NOTICED? YOUR OBSESSION…
REMINDS ME OF CHAO-SAN!
REMEMBER WHAT YOU SAID TO HER.
YIKES, SOUNDS LIKE TROUBLE!
DOOOM
すーん…
HEY…
LOOKS PRETTY SERIOUS.
NEED TO CLEAN, NEED TO CLEAN
I'LL MIND MY OWN BUSINESS.
ANIKI!
NEGI!
DASH
AWW, GEEZ—

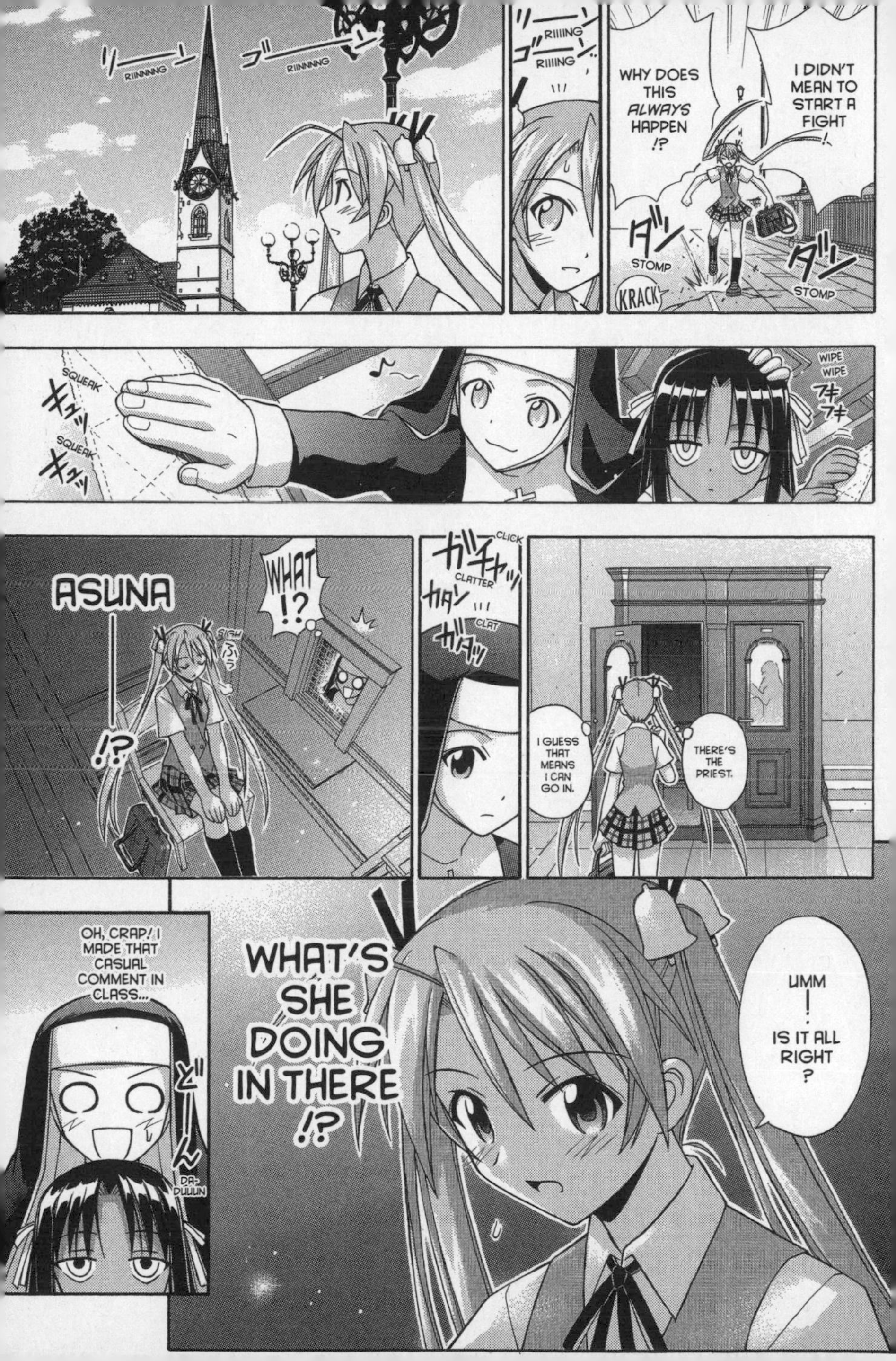
I DIDN'T MEAN TO START A FIGHT!
WHY DOES THIS ALWAYS HAPPEN!?
STOMP
KRACK
STOMP
RIIIING
RIIIING
RIINNNG
RIINNNG
WIPE WIPE
SQUEAK
SQUEAK
THERE'S THE PRIEST.
I GUESS THAT MEANS I CAN GO IN.
CLICK
CLATTER
CLAT
WHAT!?
SIGH
ASUNA—!?
UMM! IS IT ALL RIGHT?
WHAT'S SHE DOING IN THERE!?
OH, CRAP! I MADE THAT CASUAL COMMENT IN CLASS...
DA-DUUUN

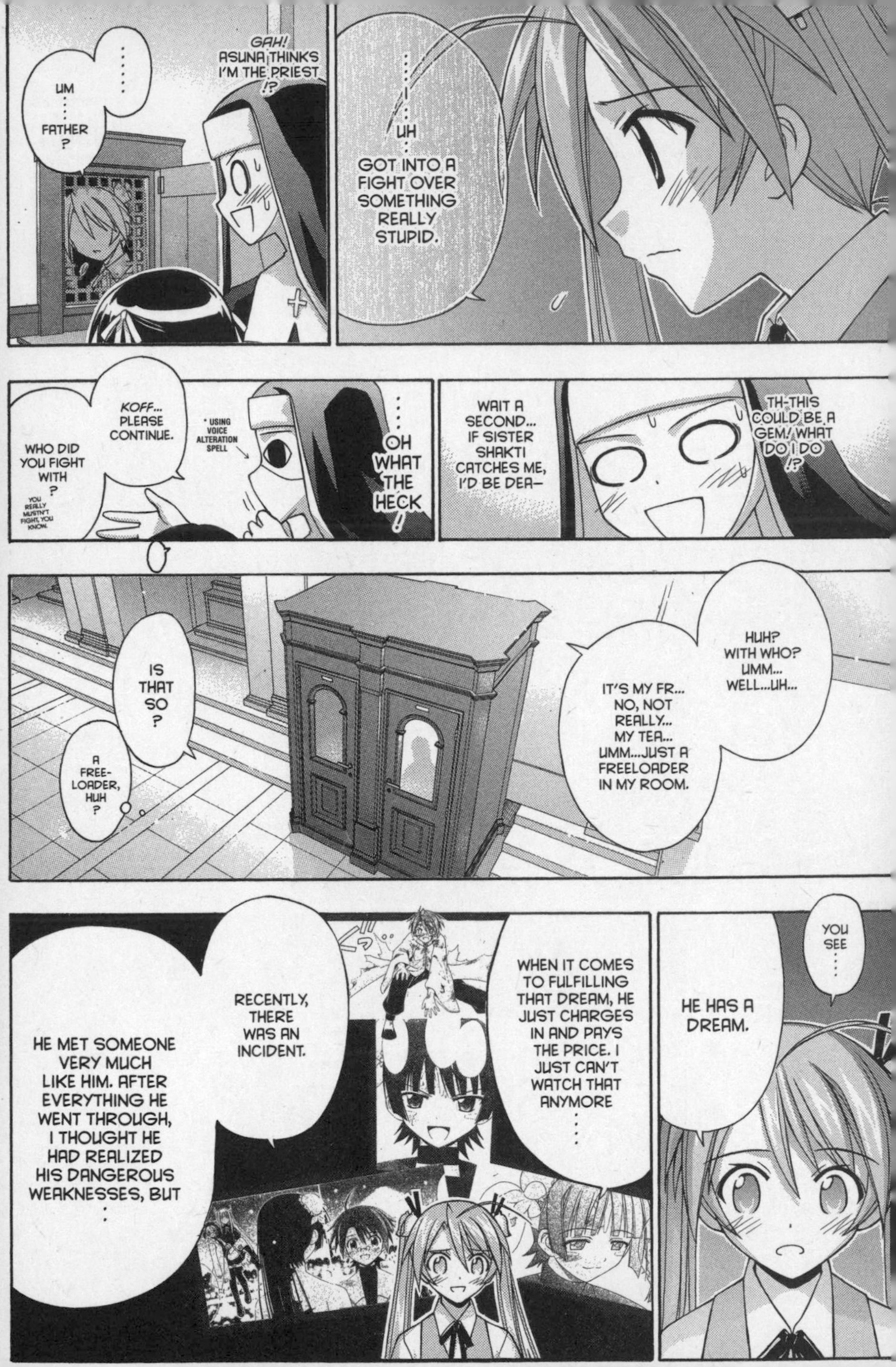
......I......UH......
GOT INTO A FIGHT OVER SOMETHING REALLY STUPID.
GAH! ASUNA THINKS I'M THE PRIEST!?
......
UM... FATHER?
TH-THIS COULD BE A GEM! WHAT DO I DO!?
WAIT A SECOND... IF SISTER SHAKTI CATCHES ME, I'D BE DEA—
...OH WHAT THE HECK!
* USING VOICE ALTERATION SPELL
KOFF... PLEASE CONTINUE.
WHO DID YOU FIGHT WITH?
YOU REALLY MUSTN'T FIGHT, YOU KNOW.
HUH? WITH WHO? UMM... WELL...UH...
IT'S MY FR... NO, NOT REALLY... MY TEA... UMM...JUST A FREELOADER IN MY ROOM.
IS THAT SO?
A FREE-LOADER, HUH?
YOU SEE...
HE HAS A DREAM.
WHEN IT COMES TO FULFILLING THAT DREAM, HE JUST CHARGES IN AND PAYS THE PRICE. I JUST CAN'T WATCH THAT ANYMORE...
RECENTLY, THERE WAS AN INCIDENT.
HE MET SOMEONE VERY MUCH LIKE HIM. AFTER EVERYTHING HE WENT THROUGH, I THOUGHT HE HAD REALIZED HIS DANGEROUS WEAKNESSES, BUT...

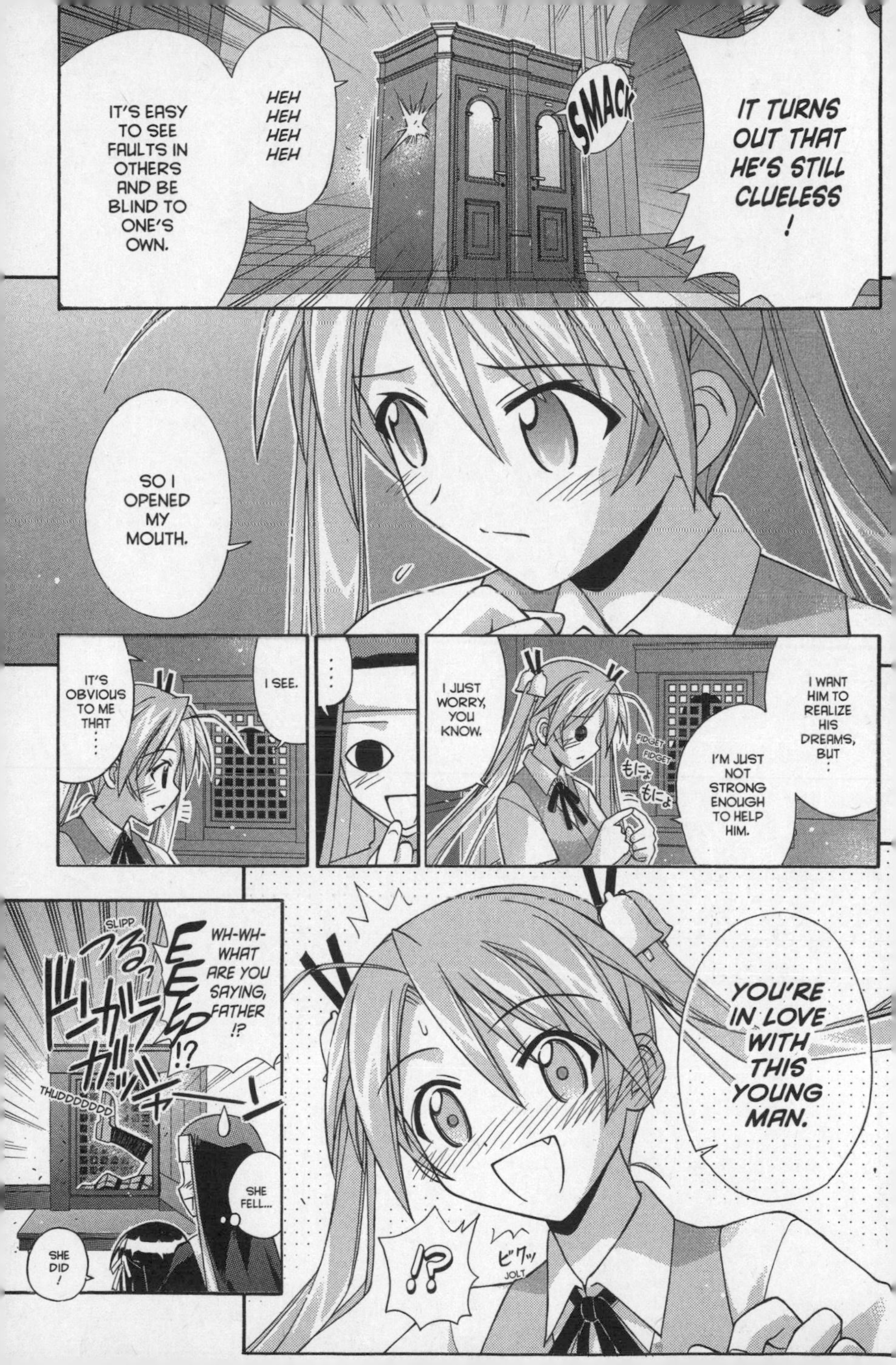
IT TURNS OUT THAT HE'S STILL CLUELESS!
SMACK
HEH HEH HEH HEH
IT'S EASY TO SEE FAULTS IN OTHERS AND BE BLIND TO ONE'S OWN.
SO I OPENED MY MOUTH.
I WANT HIM TO REALIZE HIS DREAMS, BUT...
I'M JUST NOT STRONG ENOUGH TO HELP HIM.
FIDGET FIDGET
もにょ もにょ
I JUST WORRY, YOU KNOW.
...
I SEE.
IT'S OBVIOUS TO ME THAT...
YOU'RE IN LOVE WITH THIS YOUNG MAN.
ビクッ
JOLT
!?
WH-WH-WHAT ARE YOU SAYING, FATHER!?
EEEP!?
SLIPP
つるっ
THUDDDDDDD
SHE FELL...
SHE DID!

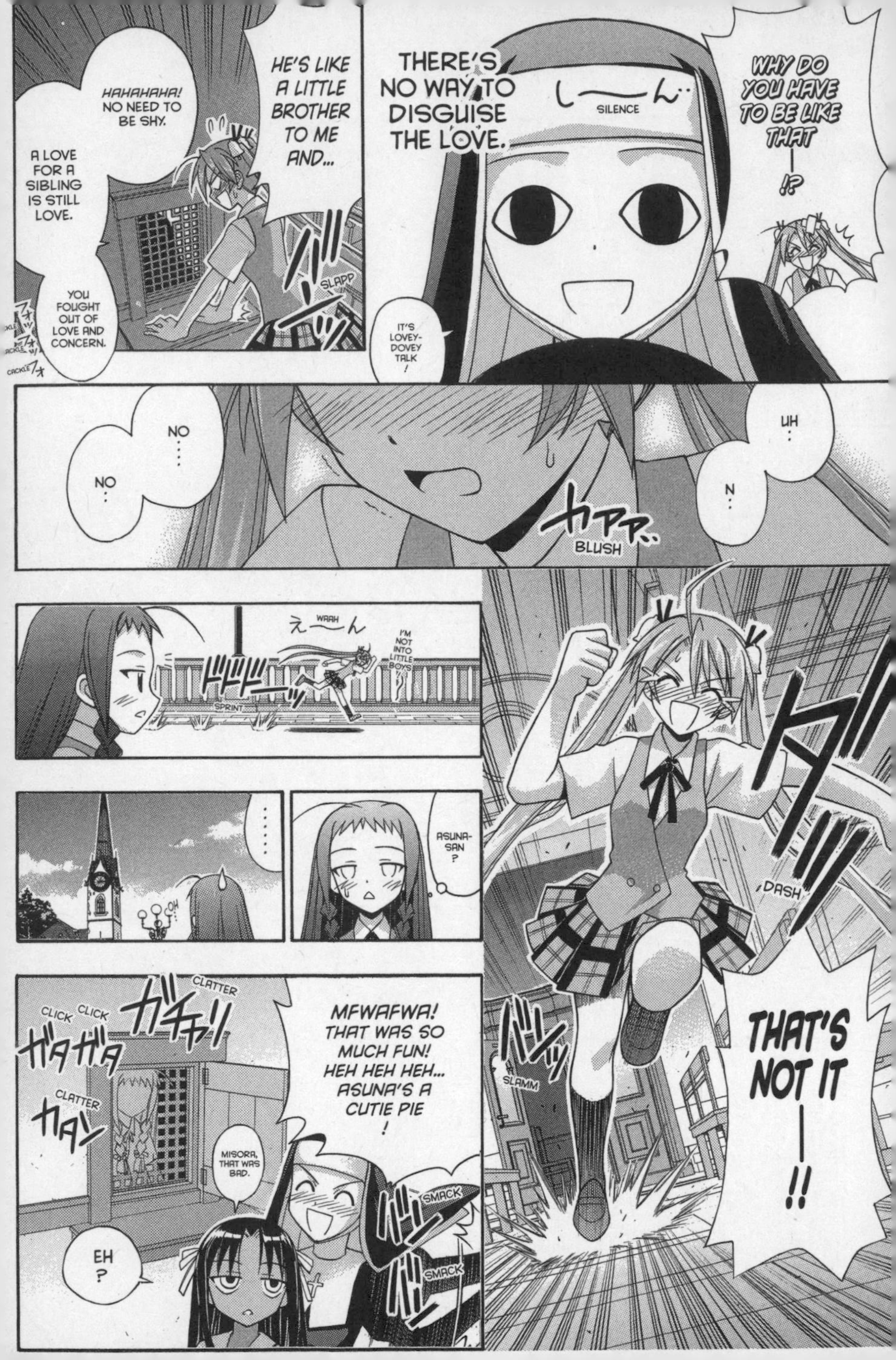

WHY DO YOU HAVE TO BE LIKE THAT—!?
THERE'S NO WAY TO DISGUISE THE LOVE.
SILENCE
IT'S LOVEY-DOVEY TALK!
HE'S LIKE A LITTLE BROTHER TO ME AND...
HAHAHAHA! NO NEED TO BE SHY.
A LOVE FOR A SIBLING IS STILL LOVE.
SLAPP
YOU FOUGHT OUT OF LOVE AND CONCERN.
CACKLE
CACKLE
CACKLE
UH... N...
BLUSH
NO.... NO...
DASH
THAT'S NOT IT—!!
SLAMM
I'M NOT INTO LITTLE BOYS
WAAH
SPRINT
ASUNA-SAN?
......
OH
MFWAFWA! THAT WAS SO MUCH FUN! HEH HEH HEH... ASUNA'S A CUTIE PIE!
SMACK
SMACK
MISORA, THAT WAS BAD.
CLATTER
CLICK CLICK
CLATTER
EH?

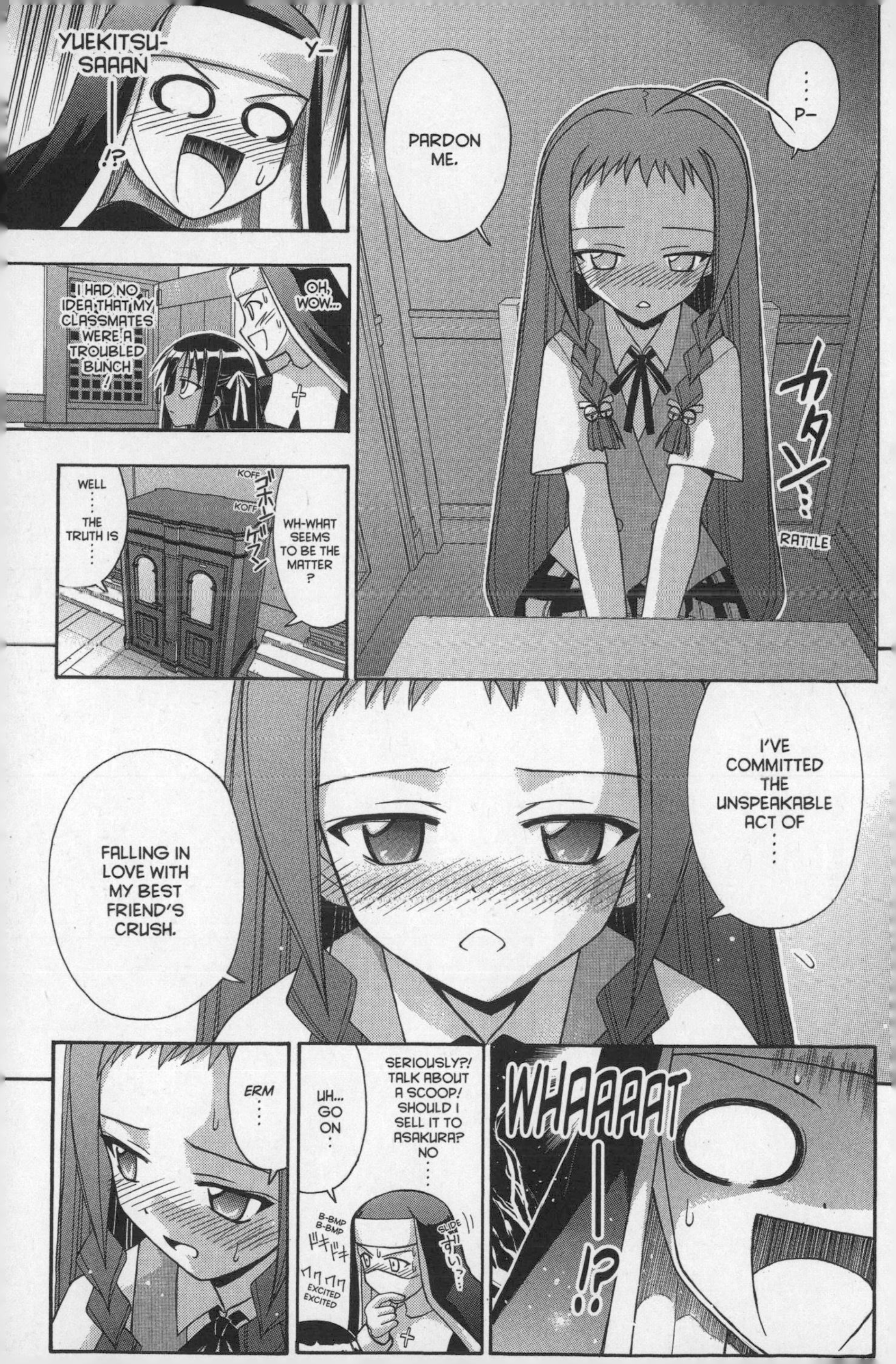

...P–
カタン...
RATTLE
PARDON ME.
Y–
YUEKITSU-SAAAN!?
OH, WOW...
I HAD NO IDEA THAT MY CLASSMATES WERE A TROUBLED BUNCH!
WH-WHAT SEEMS TO BE THE MATTER?
ゴホンゲフン
KOFF KOFF
WELL... THE TRUTH IS...
I'VE COMMITTED THE UNSPEAKABLE ACT OF...
FALLING IN LOVE WITH MY BEST FRIEND'S CRUSH.
WHAAAAT!!?
SERIOUSLY?! TALK ABOUT A SCOOP! SHOULD I SELL IT TO ASAKURA? NO...
UH... GO ON...
すいっ...
SLIDE
ドキドキ
B-BMP B-BMP
ワクワク
EXCITED EXCITED
ERM...

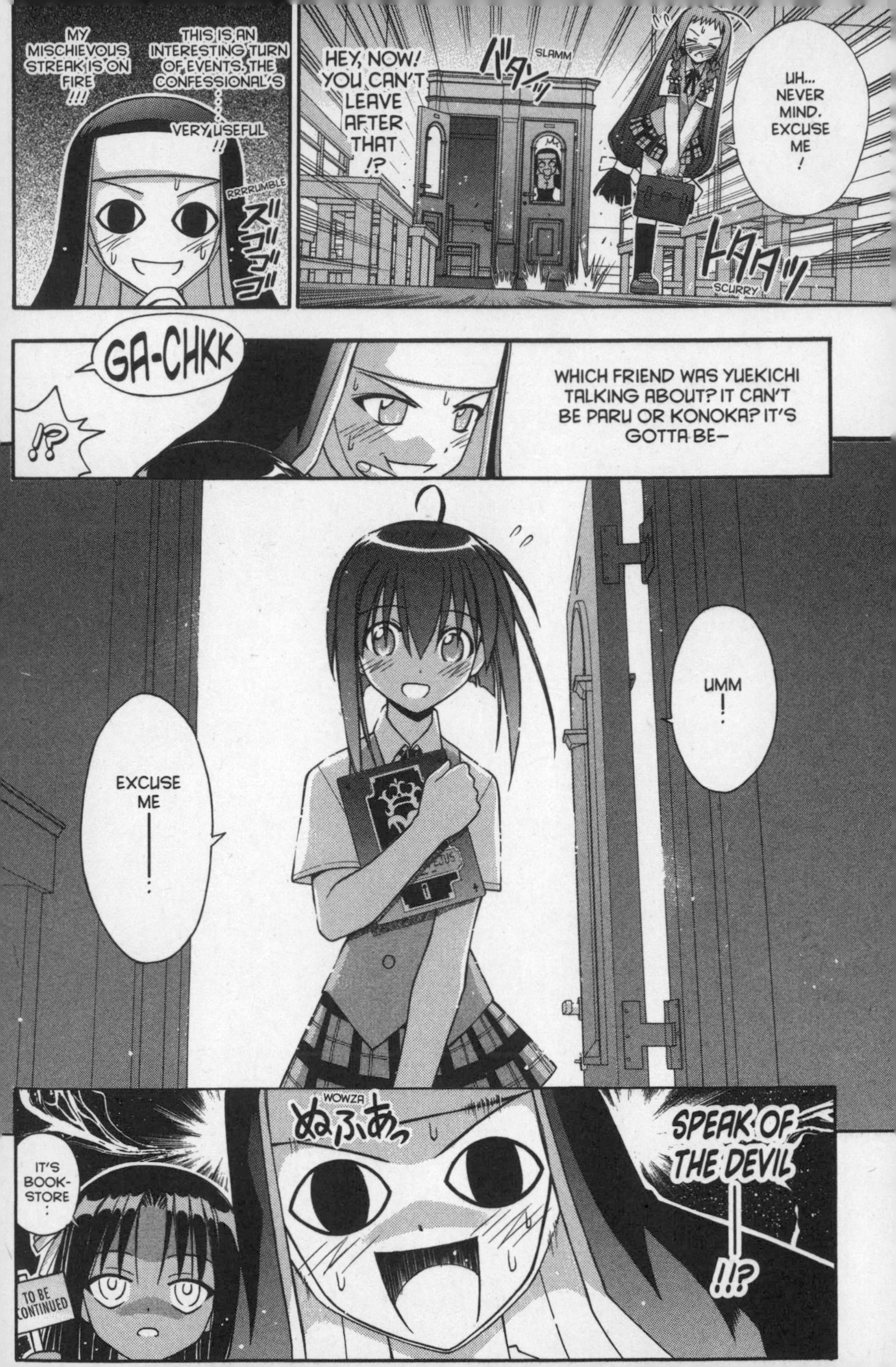

UH... NEVER MIND. EXCUSE ME!
バタンッ
SLAMM
HEY, NOW! YOU CAN'T LEAVE AFTER THAT!?
トタタッ
SCURRY
THIS IS AN INTERESTING TURN OF EVENTS. THE CONFESSIONAL'S... VERY USEFUL!!
MY MISCHIEVOUS STREAK IS ON FIRE!!!
RRRRUMBLE
ズゴゴゴ
WHICH FRIEND WAS YUEKICHI TALKING ABOUT? IT CAN'T BE PARU OR KONOKA? IT'S GOTTA BE—
GA-CHKK
!?
UMM!
EXCUSE ME—!
SPEAK OF THE DEVIL—!!?
WOWZA
ぬふあっ
IT'S BOOK-STORE:
TO BE CONTINUED

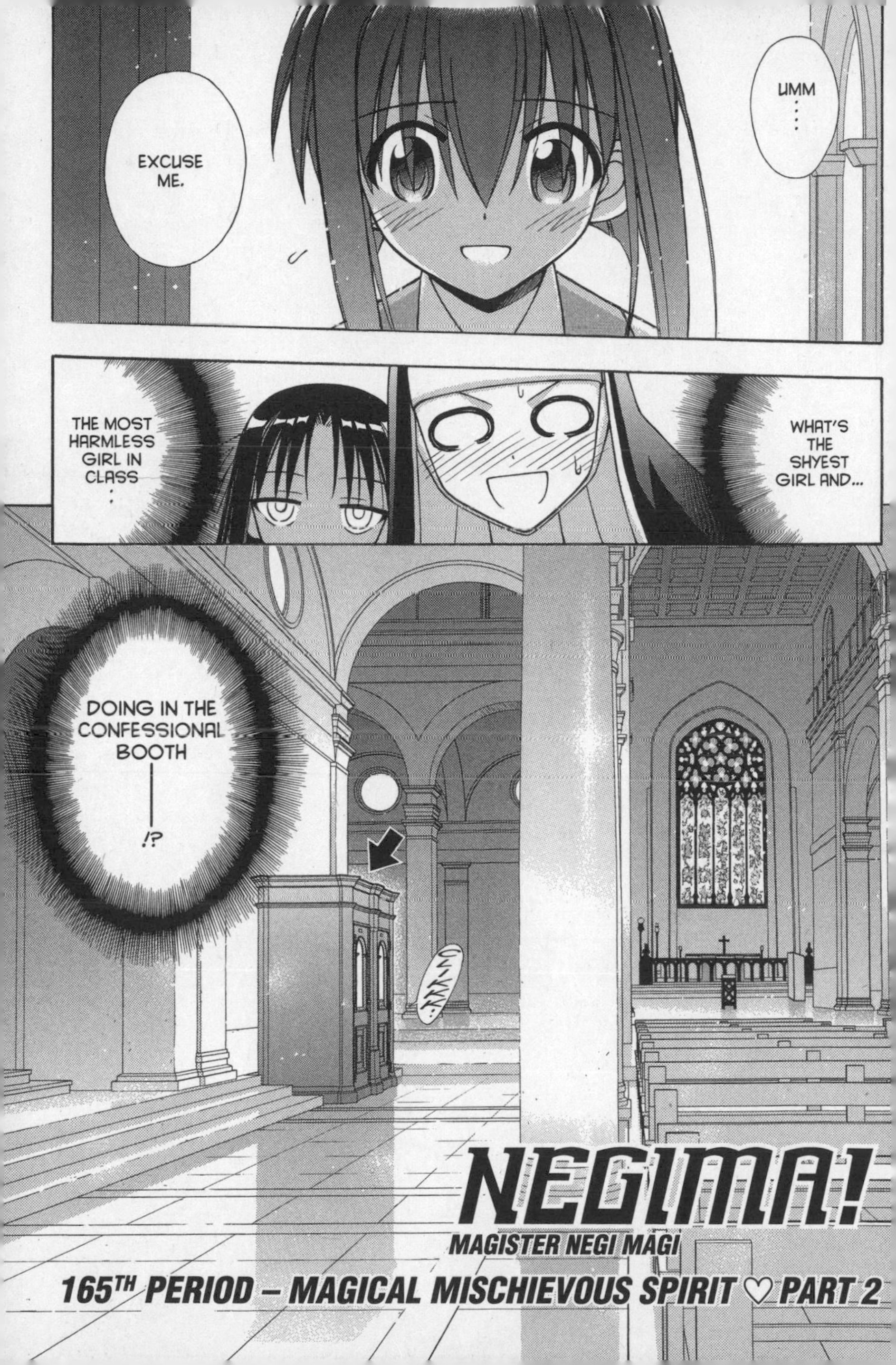
UMM ....
EXCUSE ME.
WHAT'S THE SHYEST GIRL AND...
THE MOST HARMLESS GIRL IN CLASS
DOING IN THE CONFESSIONAL BOOTH —!?
NEGIMA!
MAGISTER NEGI MAGI
165TH PERIOD – MAGICAL MISCHIEVOUS SPIRIT ♡ PART 2

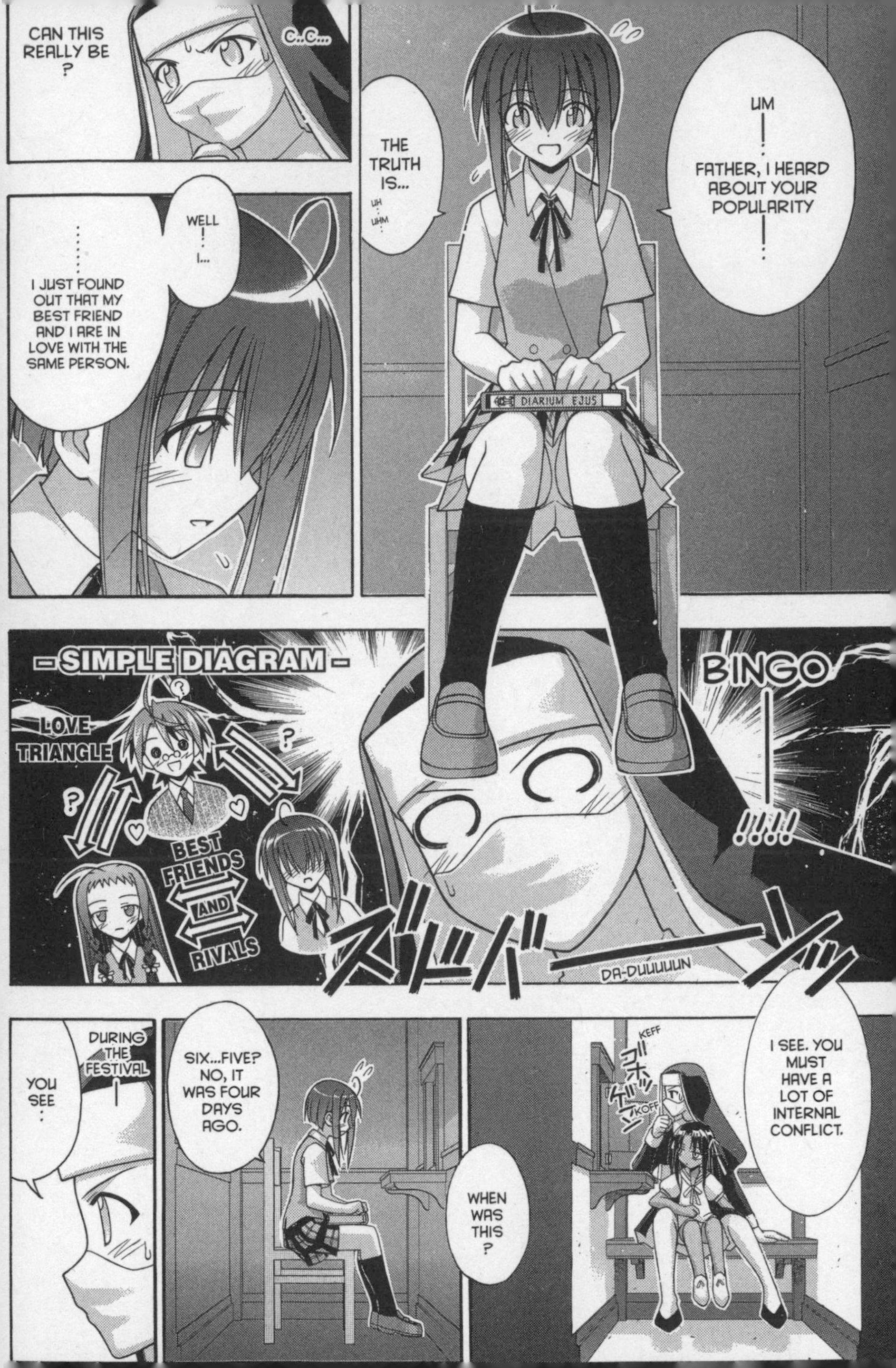
UM —! FATHER, I HEARD ABOUT YOUR POPULARITY —!
THE TRUTH IS...
UH... UHM...
C...C...
CAN THIS REALLY BE?
WELL! I...
...... I JUST FOUND OUT THAT MY BEST FRIEND AND I ARE IN LOVE WITH THE SAME PERSON.
BINGO —!!!!
DA-DUUUUUN
- SIMPLE DIAGRAM -
LOVE TRIANGLE
BEST FRIENDS AND RIVALS
I SEE. YOU MUST HAVE A LOT OF INTERNAL CONFLICT.
KEFF
KOFF
WHEN WAS THIS?
SIX...FIVE? NO, IT WAS FOUR DAYS AGO.
DURING THE FESTIVAL —
YOU SEE...

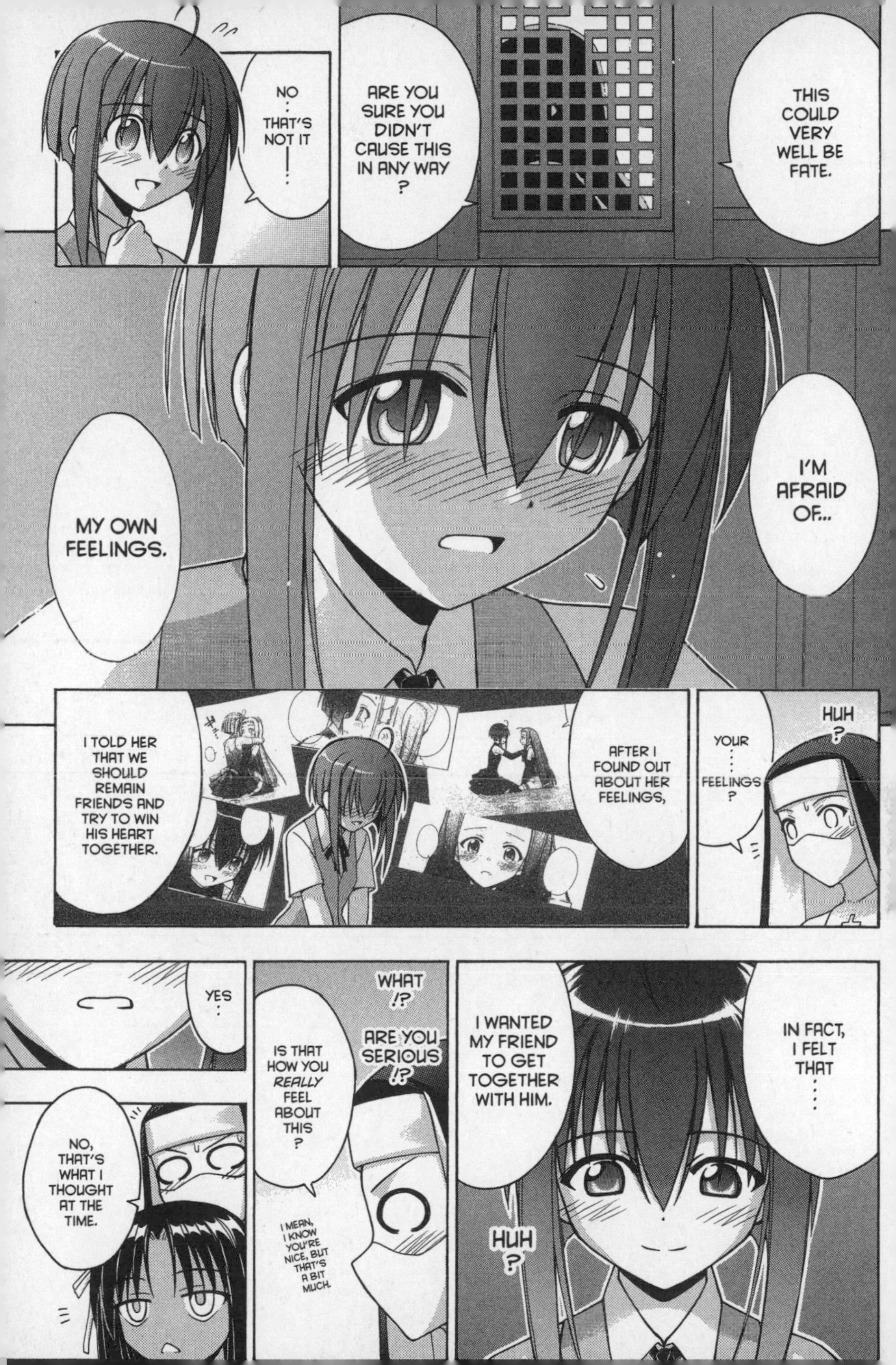
THIS COULD VERY WELL BE FATE.
ARE YOU SURE YOU DIDN'T CAUSE THIS IN ANY WAY?
NO... THAT'S NOT IT...!
I'M AFRAID OF...
MY OWN FEELINGS.
HUH?
YOUR... FEELINGS?
AFTER I FOUND OUT ABOUT HER FEELINGS,
I TOLD HER THAT WE SHOULD REMAIN FRIENDS AND TRY TO WIN HIS HEART TOGETHER.
IN FACT, I FELT THAT...
I WANTED MY FRIEND TO GET TOGETHER WITH HIM.
HUH?
WHAT!?
ARE YOU SERIOUS!?
IS THAT HOW YOU *REALLY* FEEL ABOUT THIS?
I MEAN, I KNOW YOU'RE NICE, BUT THAT'S A BIT MUCH.
YES...
NO, THAT'S WHAT I THOUGHT AT THE TIME.

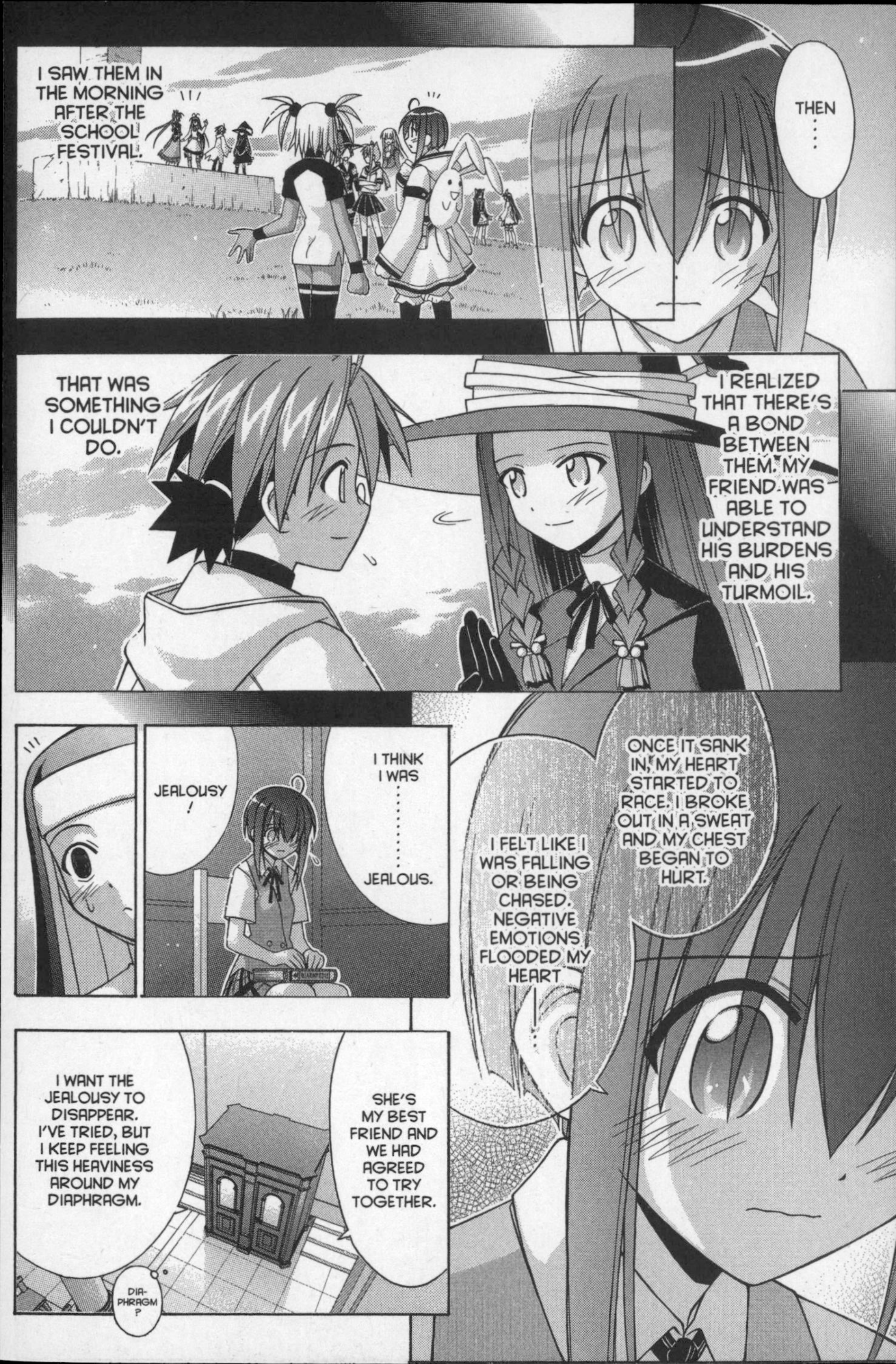
THEN ......
I SAW THEM IN THE MORNING AFTER THE SCHOOL FESTIVAL.
I REALIZED THAT THERE'S A BOND BETWEEN THEM. MY FRIEND WAS ABLE TO UNDERSTAND HIS BURDENS AND HIS TURMOIL.
THAT WAS SOMETHING I COULDN'T DO.
ONCE IT SANK IN, MY HEART STARTED TO RACE. I BROKE OUT IN A SWEAT AND MY CHEST BEGAN TO HURT.
I FELT LIKE I WAS FALLING OR BEING CHASED. NEGATIVE EMOTIONS FLOODED MY HEART ......
I THINK I WAS ...... JEALOUS.
JEALOUSY!
SHE'S MY BEST FRIEND AND WE HAD AGREED TO TRY TOGETHER.
I WANT THE JEALOUSY TO DISAPPEAR. I'VE TRIED, BUT I KEEP FEELING THIS HEAVINESS AROUND MY DIAPHRAGM.
DIA-PHRAGM?

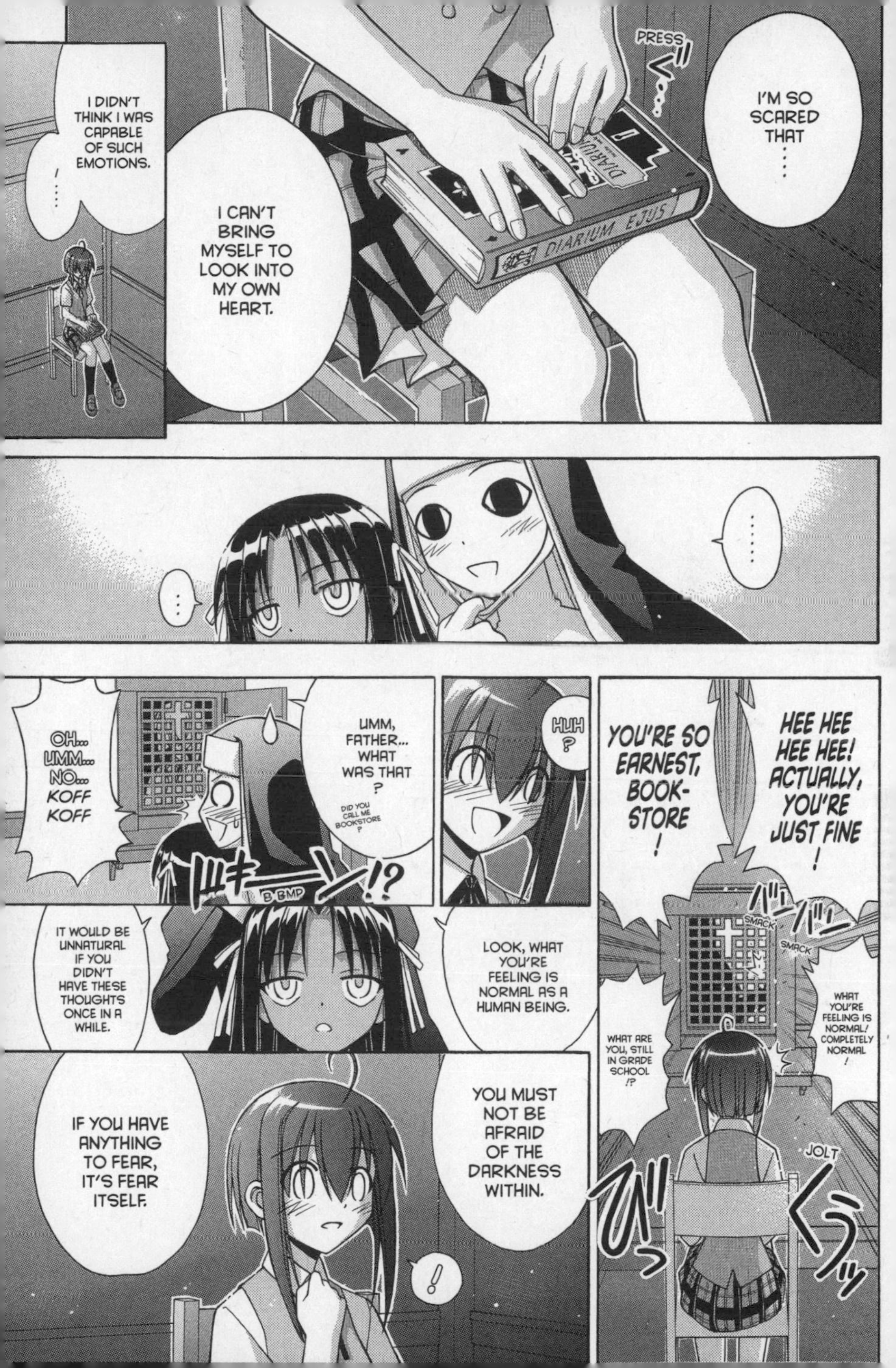

I'M SO SCARED THAT ......
PRESS
I CAN'T BRING MYSELF TO LOOK INTO MY OWN HEART.
I DIDN'T THINK I WAS CAPABLE OF SUCH EMOTIONS. ......
......
...
HEE HEE HEE HEE! ACTUALLY, YOU'RE JUST FINE!
YOU'RE SO EARNEST, BOOK-STORE!
SMACK
SMACK
WHAT YOU'RE FEELING IS NORMAL! COMPLETELY NORMAL!
WHAT ARE YOU, STILL IN GRADE SCHOOL!?
JOLT
HUH?
UMM, FATHER... WHAT WAS THAT?
DID YOU CALL ME BOOKSTORE?
OH... UMM... NO... KOFF KOFF
B-BMP
LOOK, WHAT YOU'RE FEELING IS NORMAL AS A HUMAN BEING.
IT WOULD BE UNNATURAL IF YOU DIDN'T HAVE THESE THOUGHTS ONCE IN A WHILE.
YOU MUST NOT BE AFRAID OF THE DARKNESS WITHIN.
IF YOU HAVE ANYTHING TO FEAR, IT'S FEAR ITSELF.
!

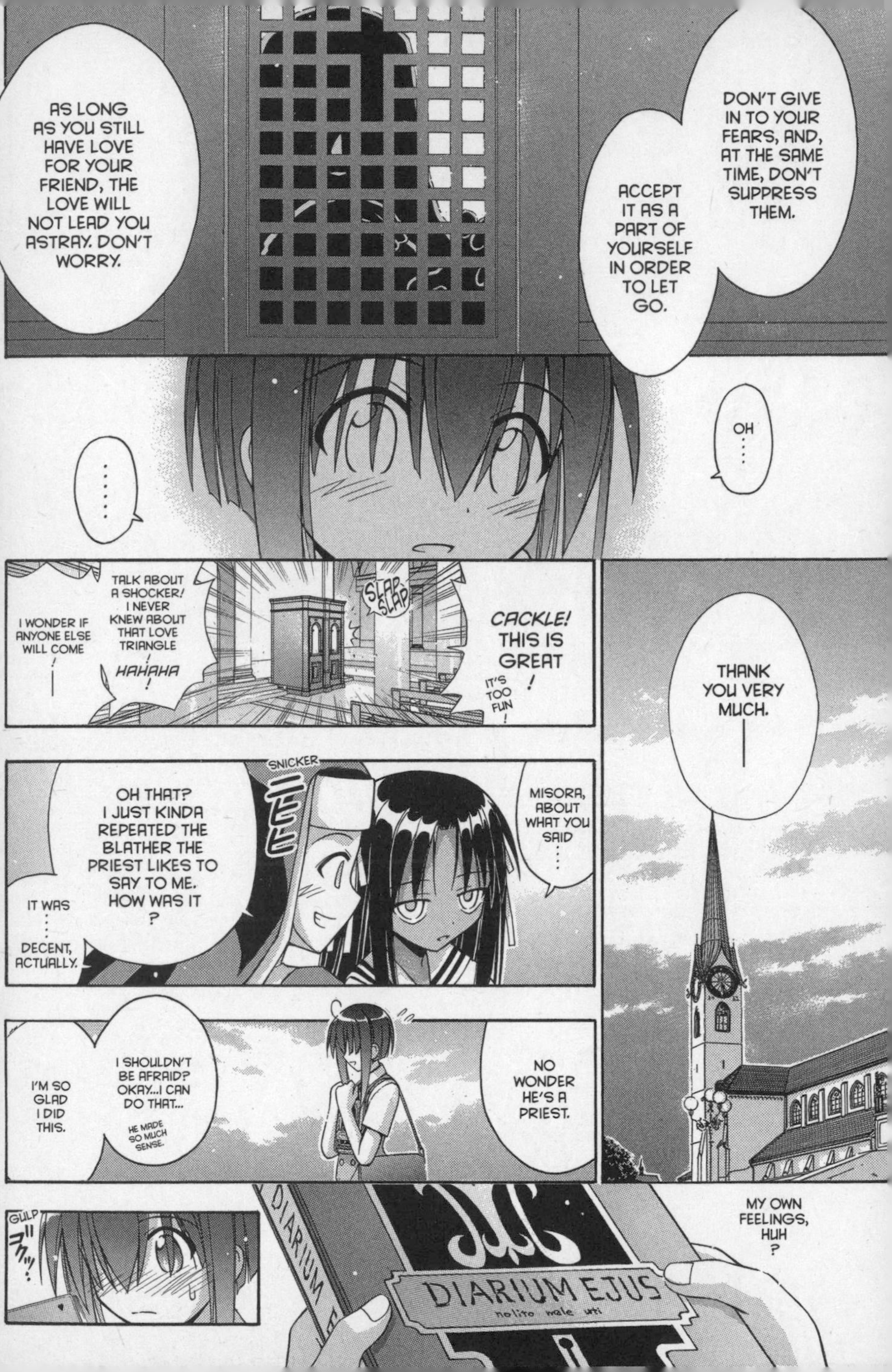
DON'T GIVE IN TO YOUR FEARS, AND, AT THE SAME TIME, DON'T SUPPRESS THEM.
ACCEPT IT AS A PART OF YOURSELF IN ORDER TO LET GO.
AS LONG AS YOU STILL HAVE LOVE FOR YOUR FRIEND, THE LOVE WILL NOT LEAD YOU ASTRAY. DON'T WORRY.
OH......
......
THANK YOU VERY MUCH.—
CACKLE! THIS IS GREAT!
IT'S TOO FUN!
SLAP SLAP
TALK ABOUT A SHOCKER! I NEVER KNEW ABOUT THAT LOVE TRIANGLE! HAHAHA!
I WONDER IF ANYONE ELSE WILL COME!—
MISORA, ABOUT WHAT YOU SAID......
SNICKER
OH THAT? I JUST KINDA REPEATED THE BLATHER THE PRIEST LIKES TO SAY TO ME. HOW WAS IT?
IT WAS......DECENT, ACTUALLY.
NO WONDER HE'S A PRIEST.
I SHOULDN'T BE AFRAID? OKAY...I CAN DO THAT...
HE MADE SO MUCH SENSE.
I'M SO GLAD I DID THIS.
MY OWN FEELINGS, HUH?
DIARIUM
DIARIUM EJUS
GULP

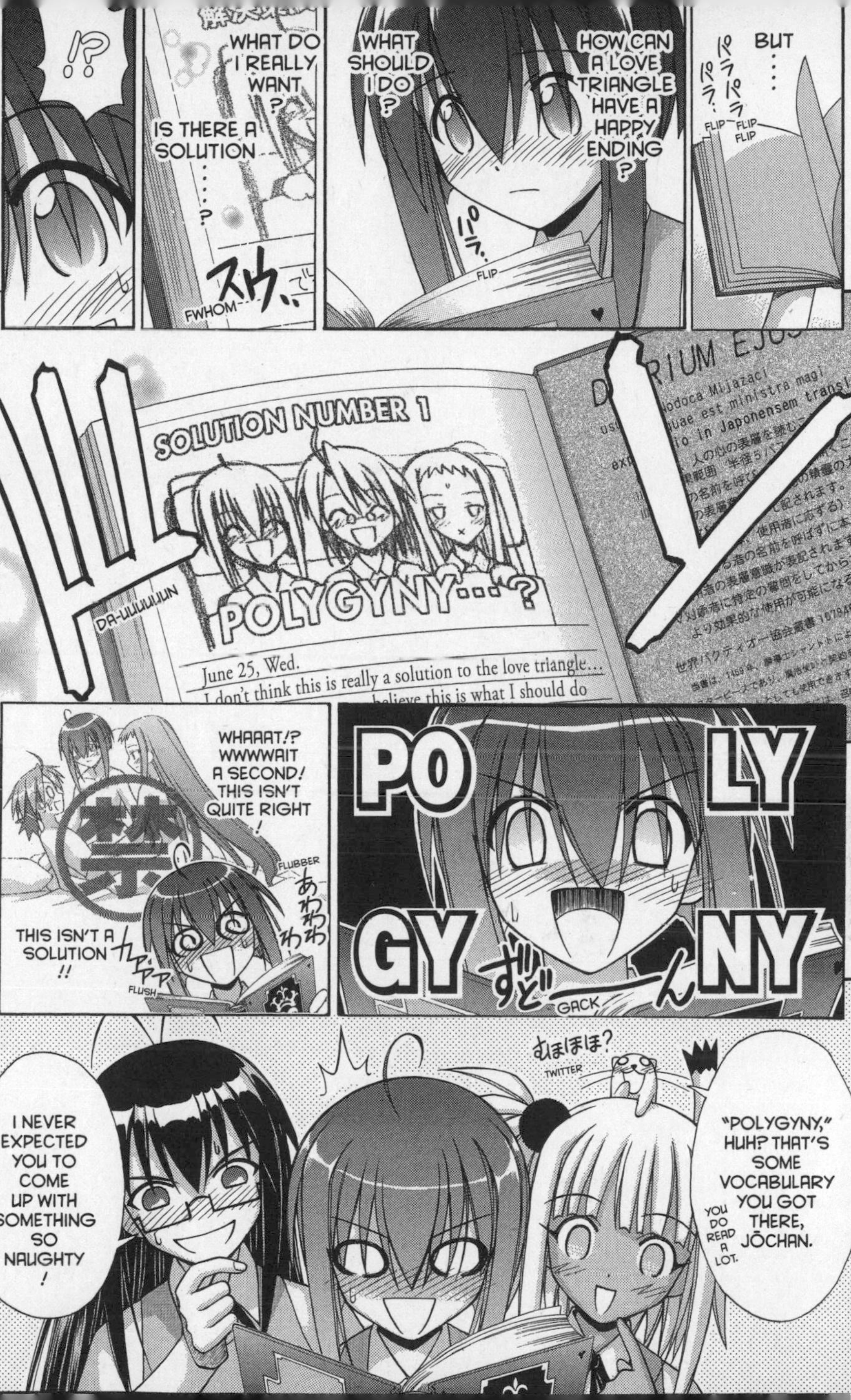

BUT......
パラパラパラ
FLIP FLIP FLIP
HOW CAN A LOVE TRIANGLE HAVE A HAPPY ENDING?
WHAT SHOULD I DO?
パラ...
FLIP
WHAT DO I REALLY WANT?
IS THERE A SOLUTION......?
スウ
FWHOM
!?
DA-UUUUUUN
SOLUTION NUMBER 1
POLYGYNY...?
June 25, Wed.
I don't think this is really a solution to the love triangle…
POLYGYNY
ずどーん
GACK
WHAAAT!? WWWWAIT A SECOND! THIS ISN'T QUITE RIGHT!
あわわわわ
FLUBBER
THIS ISN'T A SOLUTION!!
カアアア
FLUSH
"POLYGYNY," HUH? THAT'S SOME VOCABULARY YOU GOT THERE, JŌCHAN.
YOU DO READ A LOT.
むほほほ?
TWITTER
I NEVER EXPECTED YOU TO COME UP WITH SOMETHING SO NAUGHTY!

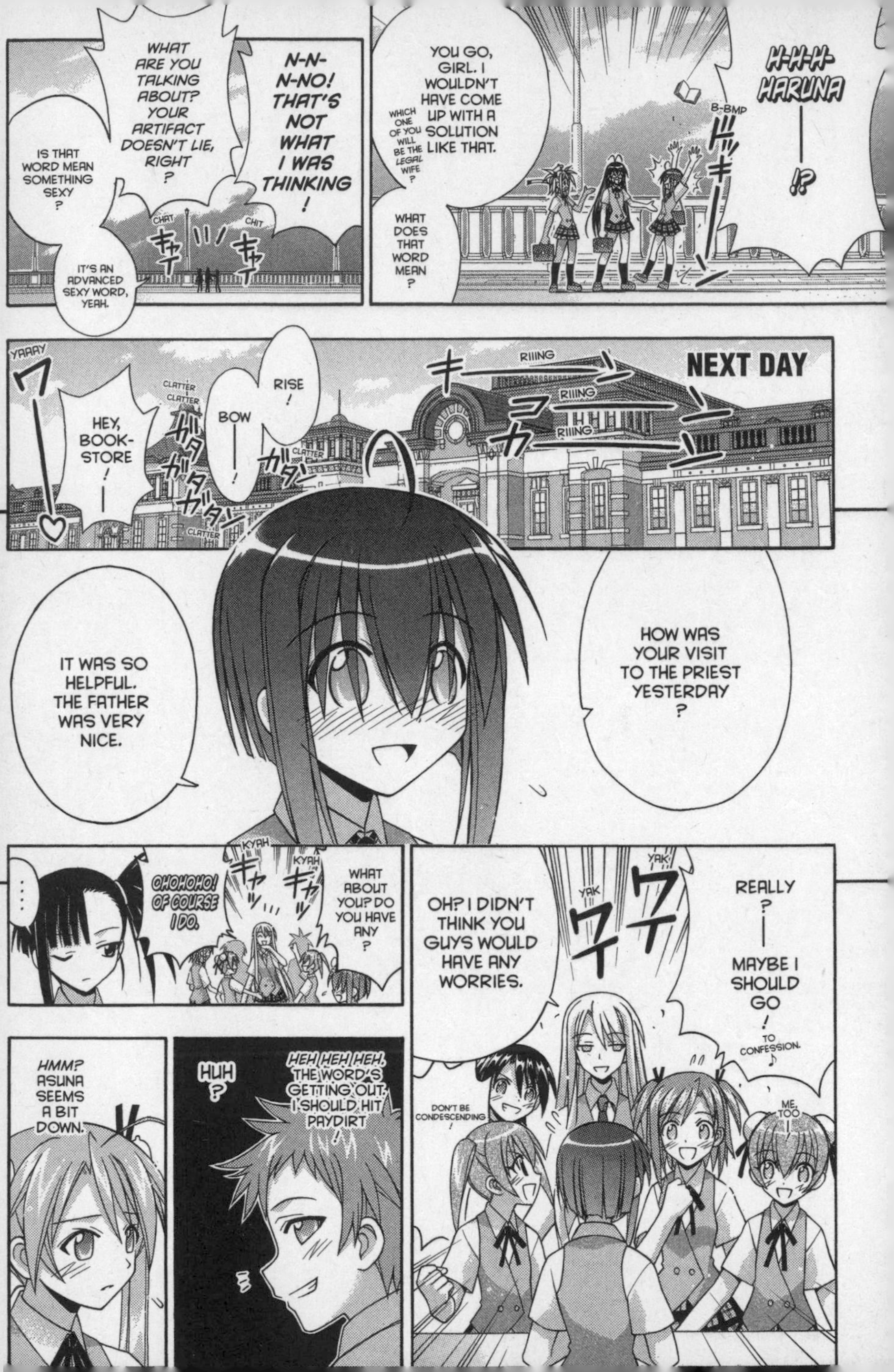
H-H-H-H-HARUNA—!?
B-BMP
YOU GO, GIRL. I WOULDN'T HAVE COME UP WITH A SOLUTION LIKE THAT.
WHICH ONE OF YOU WILL BE THE LEGAL WIFE?
WHAT DOES THAT WORD MEAN?
N-N-N-NO! THAT'S NOT WHAT I WAS THINKING!
WHAT ARE YOU TALKING ABOUT? YOUR ARTIFACT DOESN'T LIE, RIGHT?
CHIT
CHAT
IS THAT WORD MEAN SOMETHING SEXY?
IT'S AN ADVANCED SEXY WORD, YEAH.
NEXT DAY
RIIING
RIIING
RIIING
RISE!
BOW—!
CLATTER
HEY, BOOK-STORE!—
CLATTER CLATTER
YAAAY
CLATTER
HOW WAS YOUR VISIT TO THE PRIEST YESTERDAY?
IT WAS SO HELPFUL. THE FATHER WAS VERY NICE.
REALLY?— MAYBE I SHOULD GO!
TO CONFESSION.♪
YAK
YAK
OH? I DIDN'T THINK YOU GUYS WOULD HAVE ANY WORRIES.
ME, TOO!
DON'T BE CONDESCENDING!
WHAT ABOUT YOU? DO YOU HAVE ANY?
KYAH
KYAH
OHOHOHO! OF COURSE I DO.
....
HEH HEH HEH. THE WORD'S GETTING OUT. I SHOULD HIT PAYDIRT!
HUH?
HMM? ASUNA SEEMS A BIT DOWN.

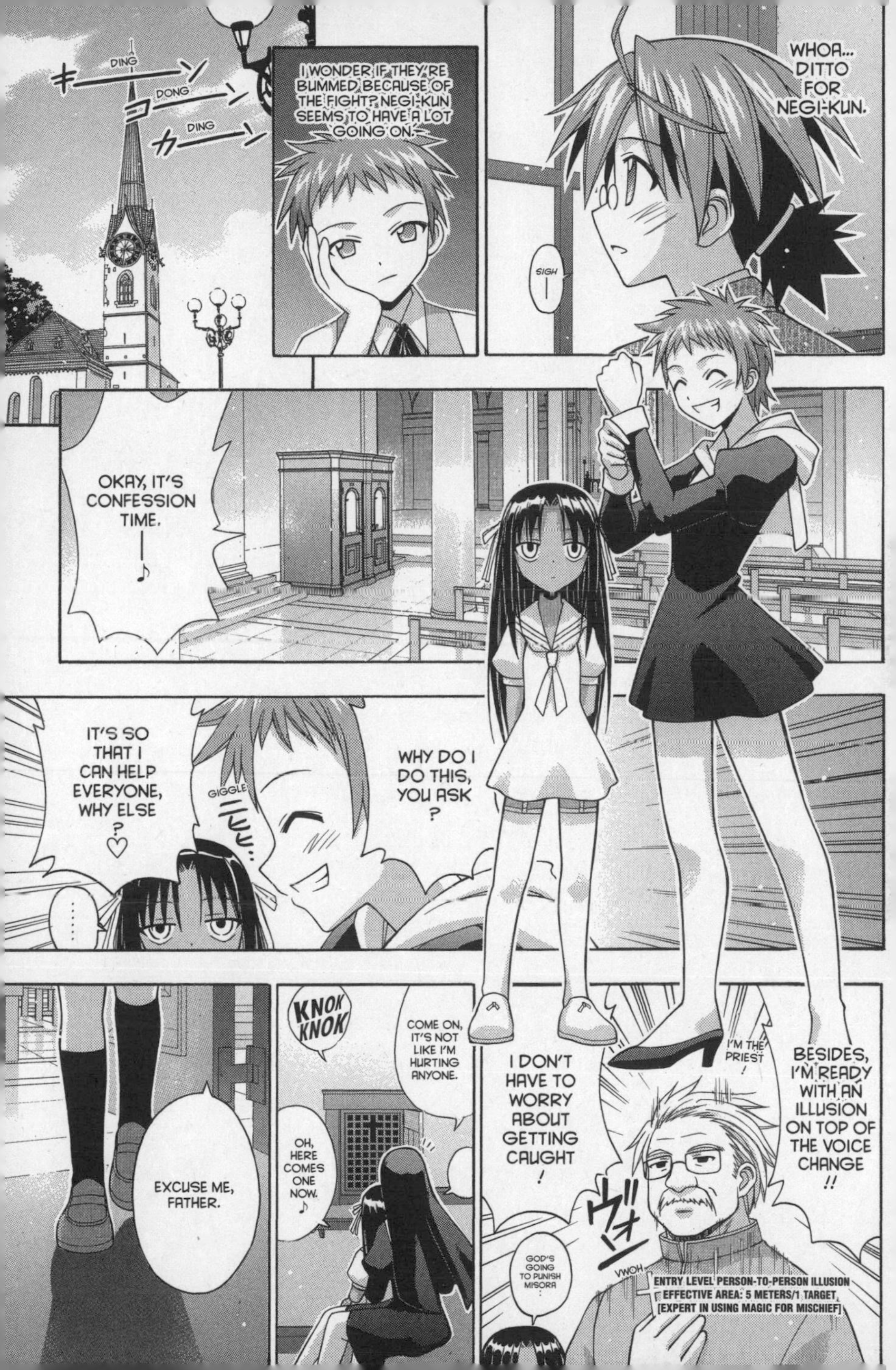
WHOA... DITTO FOR NEGI-KUN.
SIGH
I WONDER IF THEY'RE BUMMED BECAUSE OF THE FIGHT? NEGI-KUN SEEMS TO HAVE A LOT GOING ON.
キーン
DING
コーン
DONG
カーン
DING
OKAY, IT'S CONFESSION TIME. ♪
WHY DO I DO THIS, YOU ASK?
IT'S SO THAT I CAN HELP EVERYONE, WHY ELSE? ♡
GIGGLE
......
BESIDES, I'M READY WITH AN ILLUSION ON TOP OF THE VOICE CHANGE!!
I'M THE PRIEST!
I DON'T HAVE TO WORRY ABOUT GETTING CAUGHT!
ヴォン
VWOH
GOD'S GOING TO PUNISH MISORA:
ENTRY LEVEL PERSON-TO-PERSON ILLUSION
EFFECTIVE AREA: 5 METERS/1 TARGET
[EXPERT IN USING MAGIC FOR MISCHIEF]
KNOK KNOK
COME ON, IT'S NOT LIKE I'M HURTING ANYONE.
OH, HERE COMES ONE NOW. ♪
EXCUSE ME, FATHER.

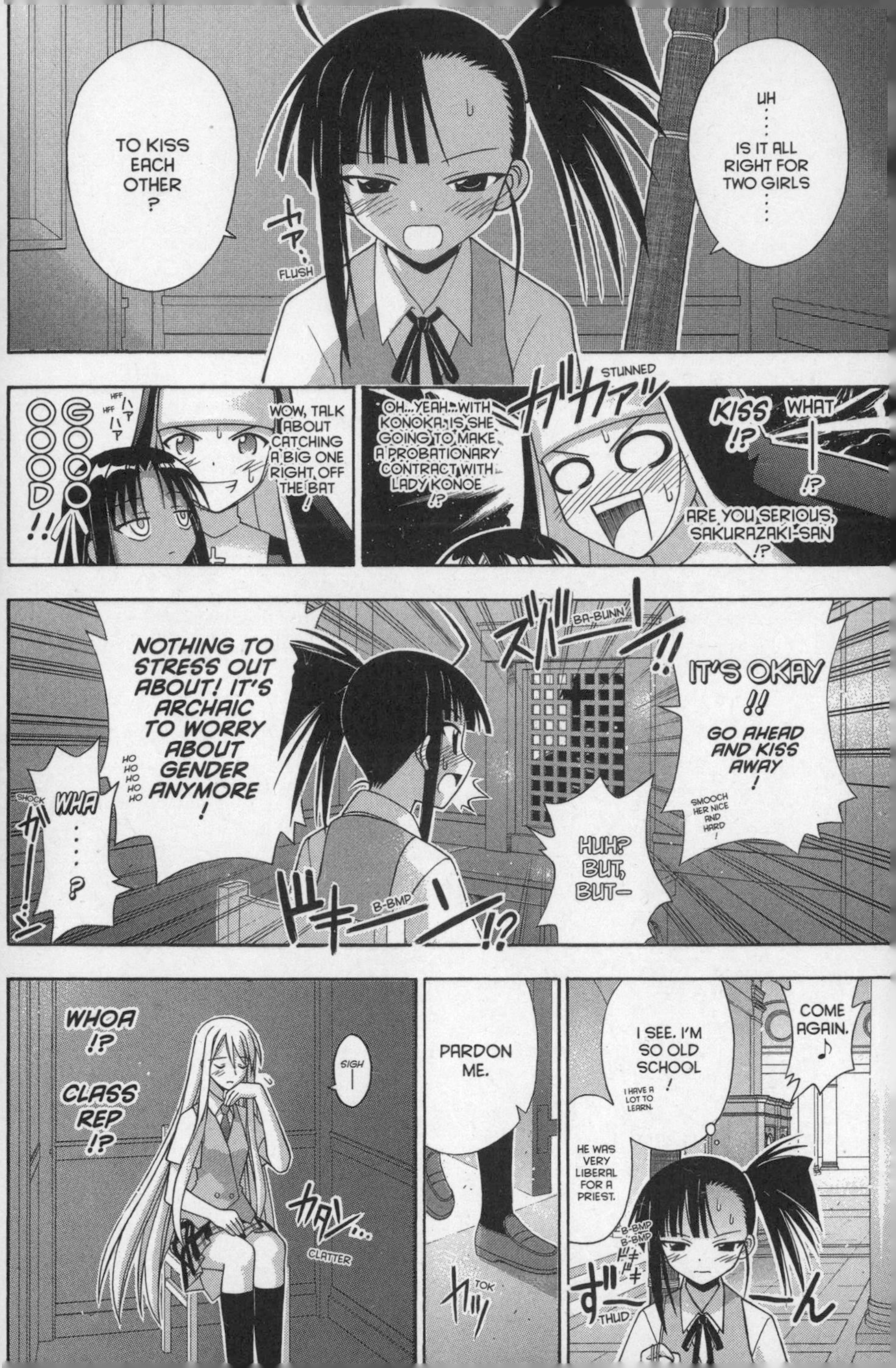
UH... IS IT ALL RIGHT FOR TWO GIRLS...
TO KISS EACH OTHER?
FLUSH
WHAT—!?
KISS!?
STUNNED
ARE YOU SERIOUS, SAKURAZAKI-SAN!?
OH...YEAH...WITH KONOKA, IS SHE GOING TO MAKE A PROBATIONARY CONTRACT WITH LADY KONOE!?
WOW, TALK ABOUT CATCHING A BIG ONE RIGHT OFF THE BAT!
HFF HFF
GOOOOD GOOOOD!!
BA-BUNN
IT'S OKAY!! GO AHEAD AND KISS AWAY!
SMOOCH HER NICE AND HARD!
HUH? BUT, BUT—
B-BMP
NOTHING TO STRESS OUT ABOUT! IT'S ARCHAIC TO WORRY ABOUT GENDER ANYMORE!
HO HO HO HO HO
WHA....?
SHOCK
COME AGAIN. ♪
I SEE. I'M SO OLD SCHOOL!
I HAVE A LOT TO LEARN.
HE WAS VERY LIBERAL FOR A PRIEST.
B-BMP B-BMP
THUD
PARDON ME.
TOK
SIGH
WHOA!? CLASS REP!?
CLATTER

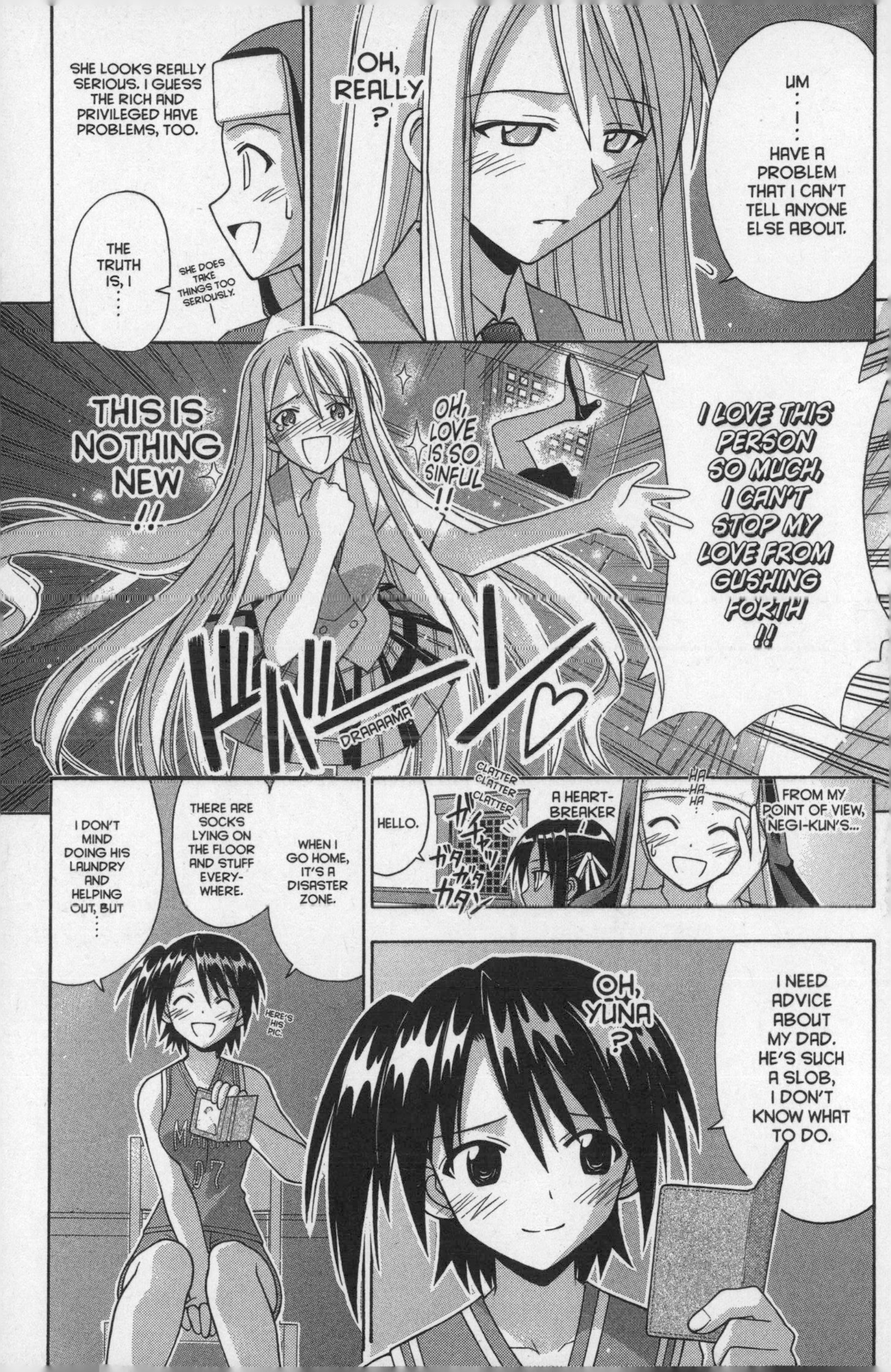
UM... I... HAVE A PROBLEM THAT I CAN'T TELL ANYONE ELSE ABOUT.
OH, REALLY?
SHE LOOKS REALLY SERIOUS. I GUESS THE RICH AND PRIVILEGED HAVE PROBLEMS, TOO.
THE TRUTH IS, I...
SHE DOES TAKE THINGS TOO SERIOUSLY.
I LOVE THIS PERSON SO MUCH, I CAN'T STOP MY LOVE FROM GUSHING FORTH!!
OH, LOVE IS SO SINFUL!!
THIS IS NOTHING NEW!!
DRAAAAMA
FROM MY POINT OF VIEW, NEGI-KUN'S...
HA HA HA
A HEART-BREAKER
CLATTER CLATTER CLATTER
HELLO.
I NEED ADVICE ABOUT MY DAD. HE'S SUCH A SLOB, I DON'T KNOW WHAT TO DO.
OH, YUNA?
WHEN I GO HOME, IT'S A DISASTER ZONE.
THERE ARE SOCKS LYING ON THE FLOOR AND STUFF EVERY-WHERE.
I DON'T MIND DOING HIS LAUNDRY AND HELPING OUT, BUT...
HERE'S HIS PIC.

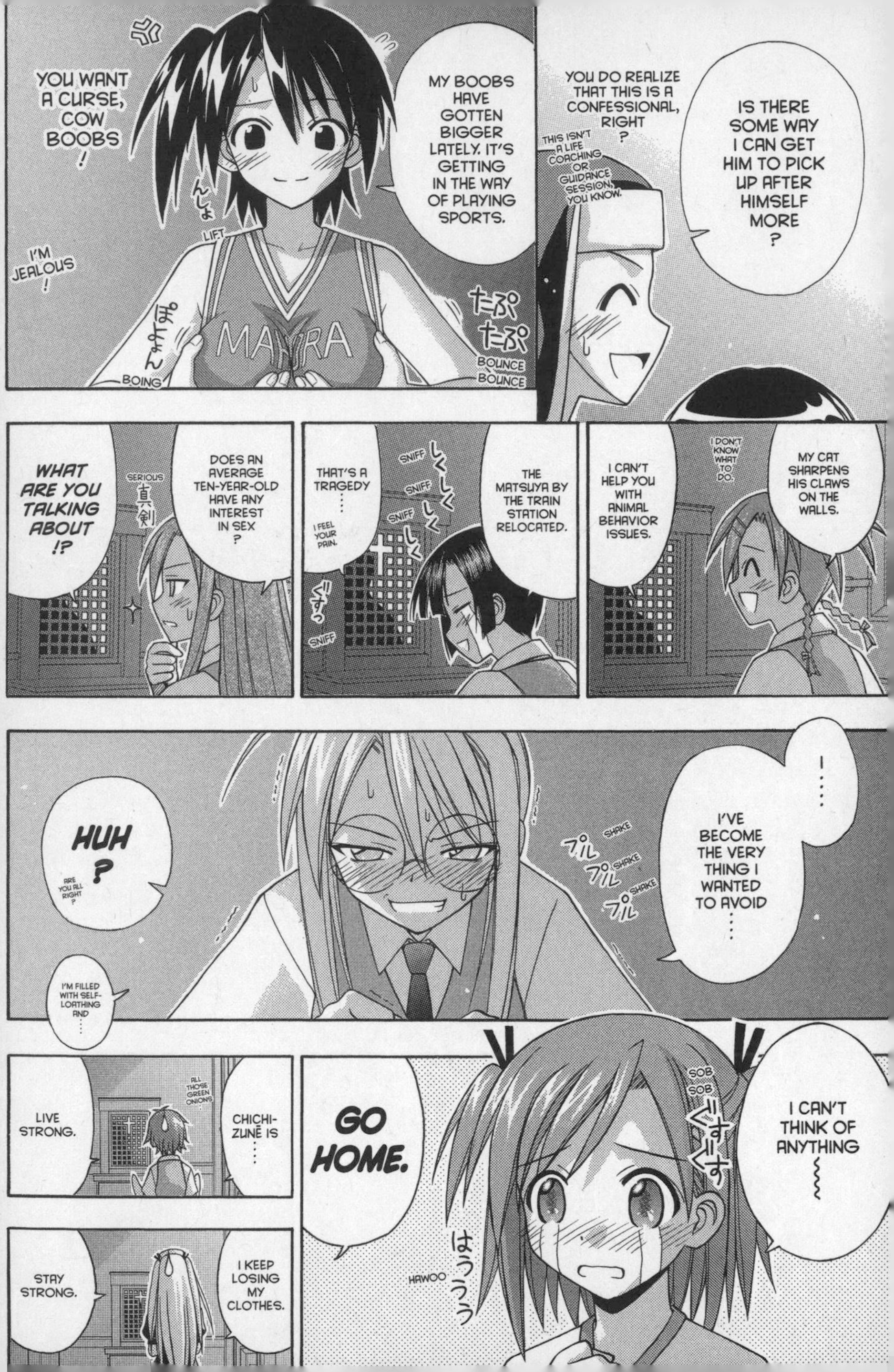
IS THERE SOME WAY I CAN GET HIM TO PICK UP AFTER HIMSELF MORE?
YOU DO REALIZE THAT THIS IS A CONFESSIONAL, RIGHT?
THIS ISN'T A LIFE COACHING OR GUIDANCE SESSION, YOU KNOW.
MY BOOBS HAVE GOTTEN BIGGER LATELY. IT'S GETTING IN THE WAY OF PLAYING SPORTS.
んしょ
LIFT
たぷ たぷ
BOUNCE BOUNCE
YOU WANT A CURSE, COW BOOBS!
I'M JEALOUS!
ぽよん
BOING
MAYURA
MY CAT SHARPENS HIS CLAWS ON THE WALLS.
I DON'T KNOW WHAT TO DO.
I CAN'T HELP YOU WITH ANIMAL BEHAVIOR ISSUES.
THE MATSUYA BY THE TRAIN STATION RELOCATED.
しく しく しく
SNIFF SNIFF SNIFF
THAT'S A TRAGEDY...
I FEEL YOUR PAIN.
ぐすっ
SNIFF
DOES AN AVERAGE TEN-YEAR-OLD HAVE ANY INTEREST IN SEX?
真剣
SERIOUS
WHAT ARE YOU TALKING ABOUT!?
I.... I'VE BECOME THE VERY THING I WANTED TO AVOID....
プル プル プル
SHAKE SHAKE SHAKE
HUH?
ARE YOU ALL RIGHT?
I'M FILLED WITH SELF-LOATHING AND....
I CAN'T THINK OF ANYTHING~~~
ぐすぐす
SOB SOB
はうう
HAWOO
GO HOME.
CHICHIZUNE IS....
ALL THOSE GREEN ONIONS....
LIVE STRONG.
I KEEP LOSING MY CLOTHES.
STAY STRONG.

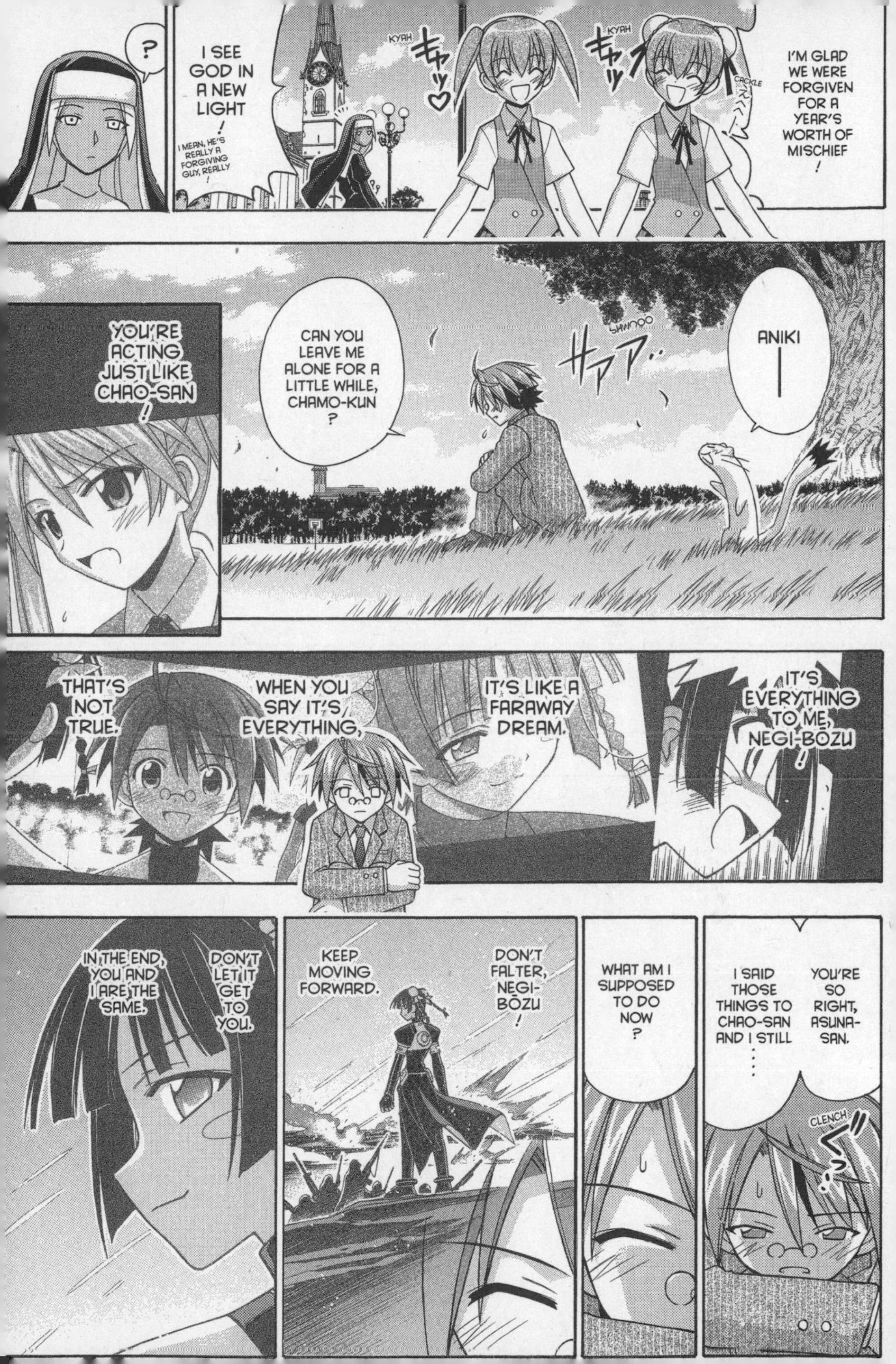
I'M GLAD WE WERE FORGIVEN FOR A YEAR'S WORTH OF MISCHIEF!
CACKLE
KYAH
KYAH
I SEE GOD IN A NEW LIGHT!
I MEAN, HE'S REALLY A FORGIVING GUY, REALLY!
?
ANIKI—
SHWOOO
CAN YOU LEAVE ME ALONE FOR A LITTLE WHILE, CHAMO-KUN?
YOU'RE ACTING JUST LIKE CHAO-SAN!
IT'S EVERYTHING TO ME, NEGI-BŌZU!
IT'S LIKE A FARAWAY DREAM.
WHEN YOU SAY IT'S EVERYTHING,
THAT'S NOT TRUE.
YOU'RE SO RIGHT, ASUNA-SAN.
I SAID THOSE THINGS TO CHAO-SAN AND I STILL ......
CLENCH
WHAT AM I SUPPOSED TO DO NOW?
DON'T FALTER, NEGI-BŌZU!
KEEP MOVING FORWARD.
DON'T LET IT GET TO YOU.
IN THE END, YOU AND I ARE THE SAME.

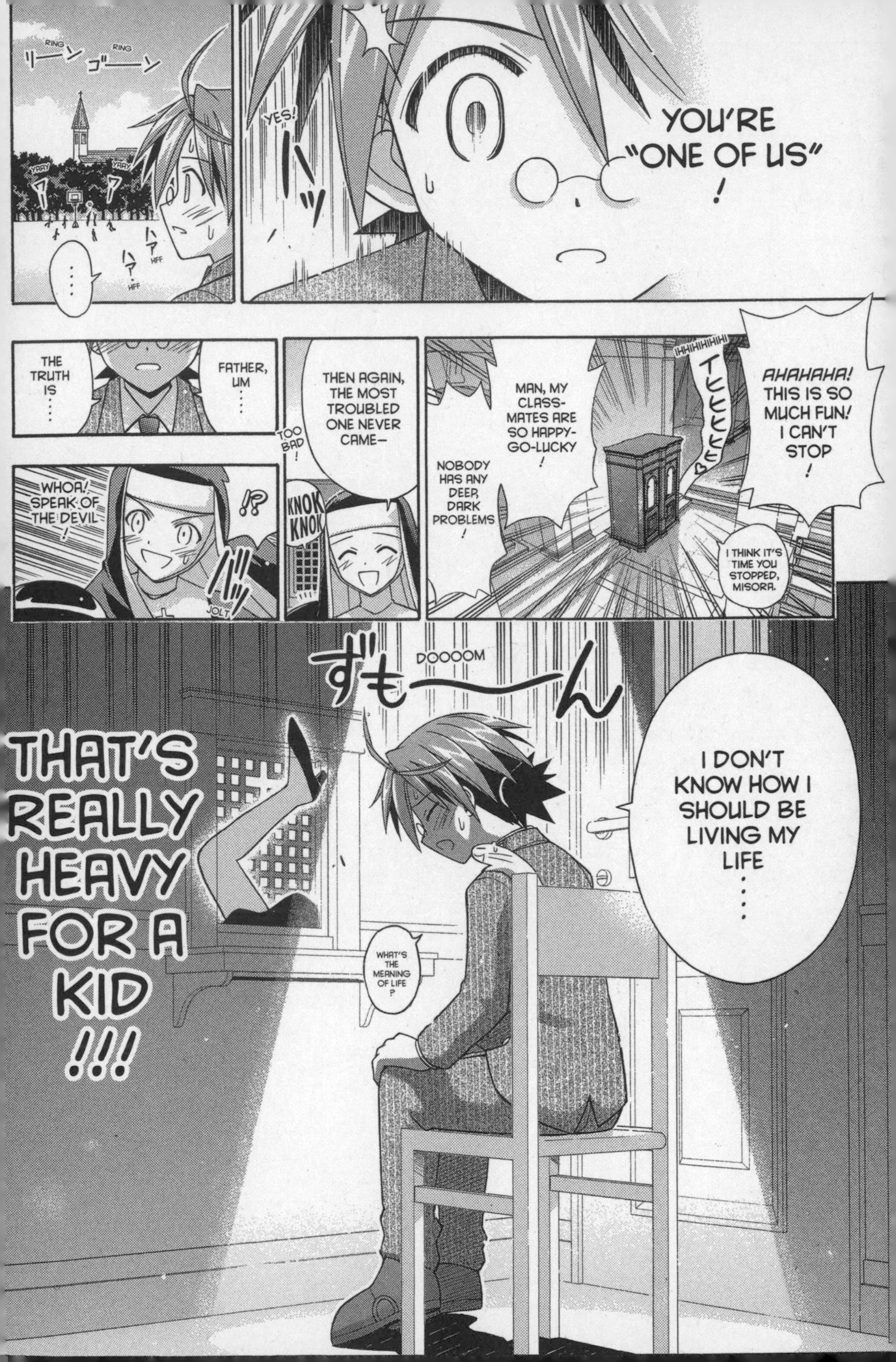
YES!
YOU'RE "ONE OF US"!
RING RING
YAAY YAAY
HFF HFF
....
AHAHAHA! THIS IS SO MUCH FUN! I CAN'T STOP!
IHIHIHIHIHI
I THINK IT'S TIME YOU STOPPED, MISORA.
MAN, MY CLASSMATES ARE SO HAPPY-GO-LUCKY!
NOBODY HAS ANY DEEP, DARK PROBLEMS!
THEN AGAIN, THE MOST TROUBLED ONE NEVER CAME—
TOO BAD!
KNOK KNOK
FATHER, UM....
THE TRUTH IS....
!?
WHOA! SPEAK OF THE DEVIL!
JOLT
DOOOOM
I DON'T KNOW HOW I SHOULD BE LIVING MY LIFE....
WHAT'S THE MEANING OF LIFE?
THAT'S REALLY HEAVY FOR A KID!!!

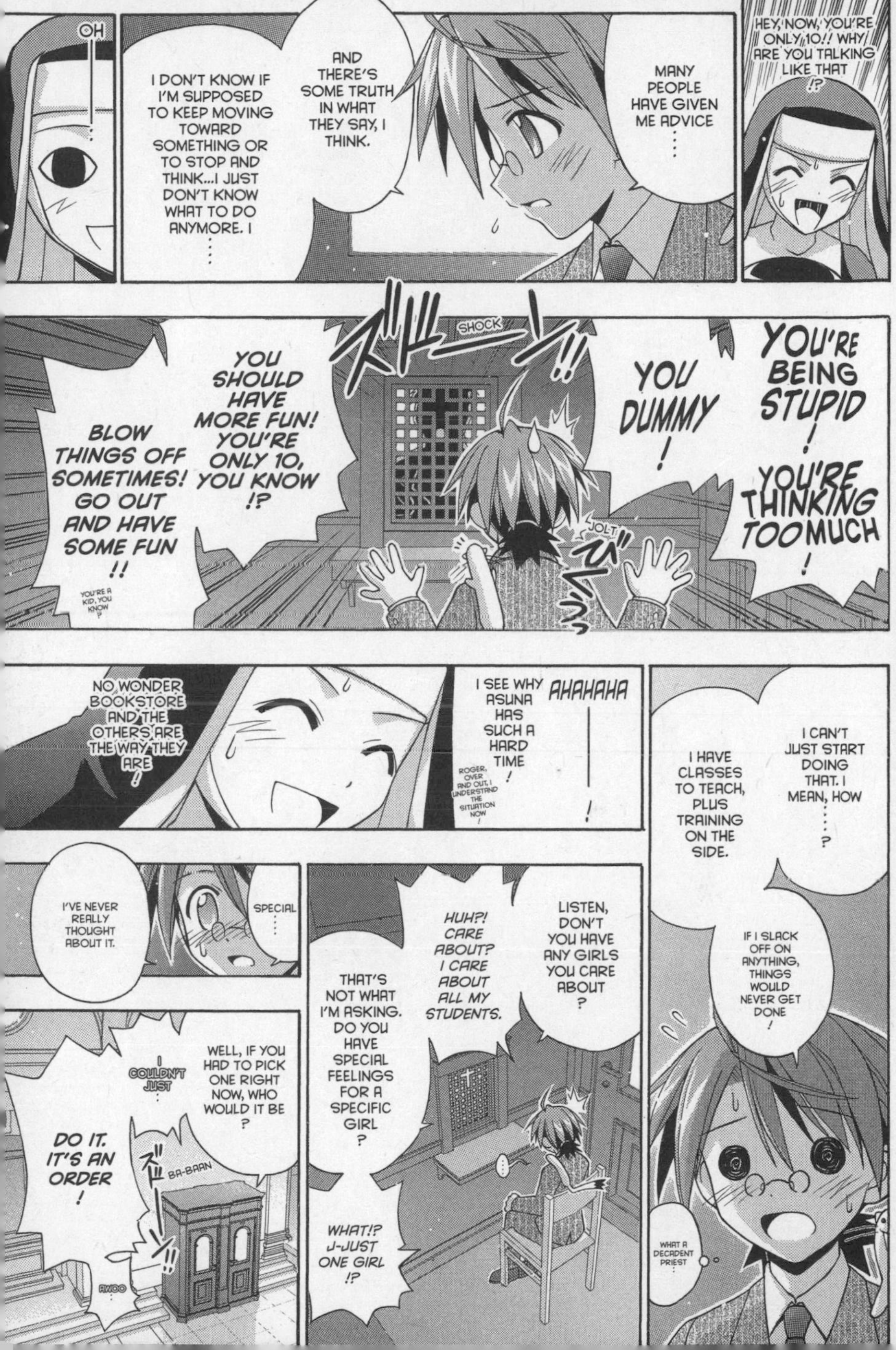

HEY, NOW, YOU'RE ONLY 10!! WHY ARE YOU TALKING LIKE THAT !?
MANY PEOPLE HAVE GIVEN ME ADVICE ...
AND THERE'S SOME TRUTH IN WHAT THEY SAY, I THINK.
I DON'T KNOW IF I'M SUPPOSED TO KEEP MOVING TOWARD SOMETHING OR TO STOP AND THINK...I JUST DON'T KNOW WHAT TO DO ANYMORE. I ...
OH ...
YOU'RE BEING STUPID !
YOU'RE THINKING TOO MUCH !
YOU DUMMY !
SHOCK
JOLT
YOU SHOULD HAVE MORE FUN! YOU'RE ONLY 10, YOU KNOW !?
BLOW THINGS OFF SOMETIMES! GO OUT AND HAVE SOME FUN !!
YOU'RE A KID, YOU KNOW !?
I CAN'T JUST START DOING THAT. I MEAN, HOW ... ?
I HAVE CLASSES TO TEACH, PLUS TRAINING ON THE SIDE.
IF I SLACK OFF ON ANYTHING, THINGS WOULD NEVER GET DONE !
WHAT A DECADENT PRIEST ...
AHAHAHA !
I SEE WHY ASUNA HAS SUCH A HARD TIME !
ROGER, OVER AND OUT, I UNDERSTAND THE SITUATION NOW !
NO WONDER BOOKSTORE AND THE OTHERS ARE THE WAY THEY ARE !
LISTEN, DON'T YOU HAVE ANY GIRLS YOU CARE ABOUT ?
HUH?! CARE ABOUT? I CARE ABOUT ALL MY STUDENTS.
THAT'S NOT WHAT I'M ASKING. DO YOU HAVE SPECIAL FEELINGS FOR A SPECIFIC GIRL ?
...
WHAT!? J-JUST ONE GIRL !?
SPECIAL ...
I'VE NEVER REALLY THOUGHT ABOUT IT.
WELL, IF YOU HAD TO PICK ONE RIGHT NOW, WHO WOULD IT BE ?
I COULDN'T JUST ...
DO IT. IT'S AN ORDER !
BA-BAAN
AWOO ...

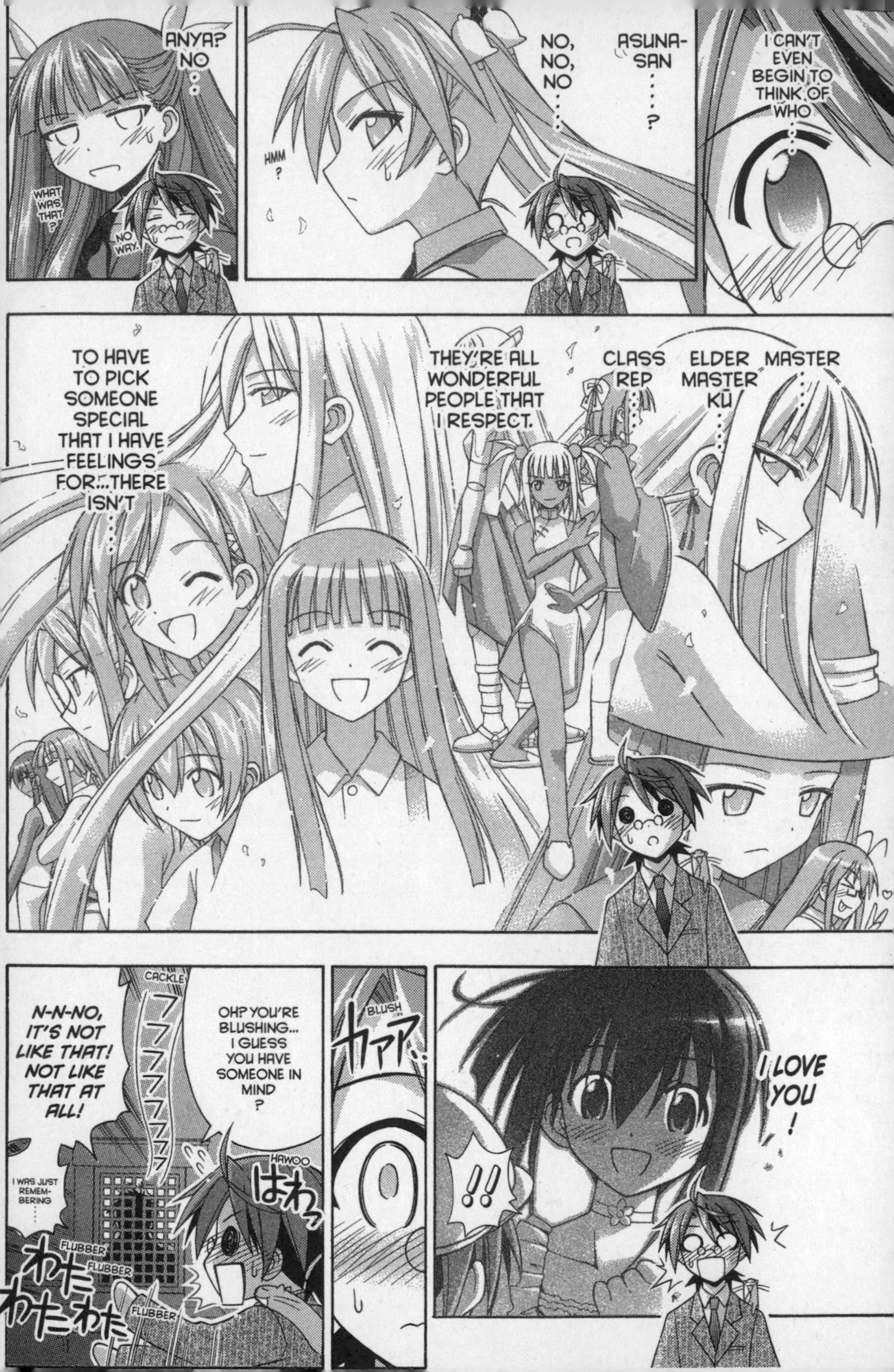
I CAN'T EVEN BEGIN TO THINK OF WHO...
ASUNA-SAN...?
NO, NO, NO...
HMM?
ANYA? NO...
WHAT WAS THAT?
NO WAY.
MASTER...
ELDER MASTER KŪ...
CLASS REP...
THEY'RE ALL WONDERFUL PEOPLE THAT I RESPECT.
TO HAVE TO PICK SOMEONE SPECIAL THAT I HAVE FEELINGS FOR...THERE ISN'T...
I LOVE YOU!
!!
BLUSH
カァア..
OH? YOU'RE BLUSHING... I GUESS YOU HAVE SOMEONE IN MIND?
CACKLE
N-N-NO, IT'S NOT LIKE THAT! NOT LIKE THAT AT ALL!
HAWOO
はわっ
I WAS JUST REMEMBERING...
FLUBBER
FLUBBER
FLUBBER
わたわたわたわた

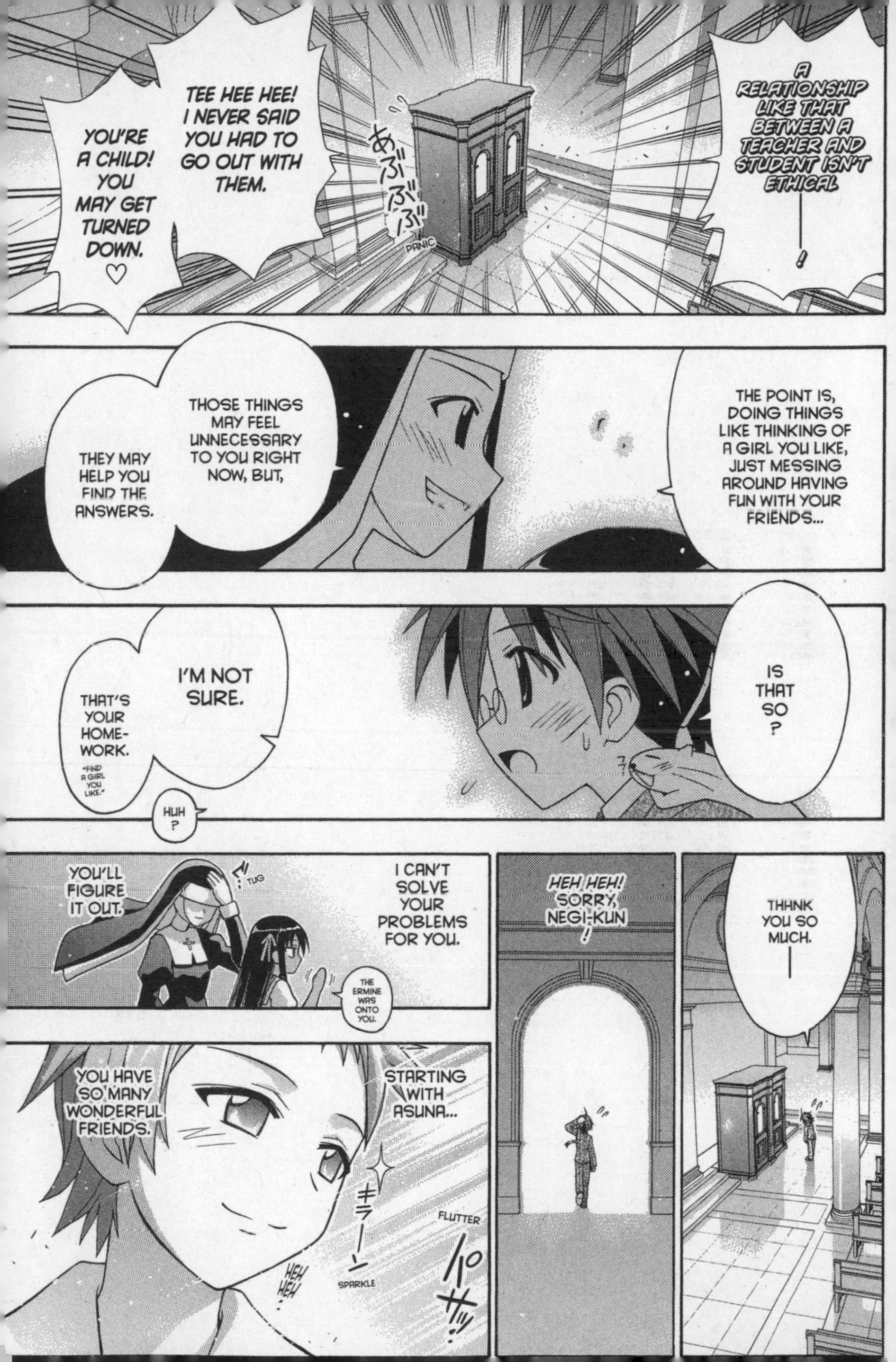
A RELATIONSHIP LIKE THAT BETWEEN A TEACHER AND STUDENT ISN'T ETHICAL!
あぶぶぶ
PANIC
TEE HEE HEE! I NEVER SAID YOU HAD TO GO OUT WITH THEM.
YOU'RE A CHILD! YOU MAY GET TURNED DOWN. ♡
THE POINT IS, DOING THINGS LIKE THINKING OF A GIRL YOU LIKE, JUST MESSING AROUND HAVING FUN WITH YOUR FRIENDS...
THOSE THINGS MAY FEEL UNNECESSARY TO YOU RIGHT NOW, BUT,
THEY MAY HELP YOU FIND THE ANSWERS.
IS THAT SO?
I'M NOT SURE.
THAT'S YOUR HOMEWORK.
*FIND A GIRL YOU LIKE.
HUH?
THANK YOU SO MUCH.—
HEH HEH! SORRY, NEGI-KUN!
I CAN'T SOLVE YOUR PROBLEMS FOR YOU.
YOU'LL FIGURE IT OUT.
TUG
THE ERMINE WAS ONTO YOU.
STARTING WITH ASUNA...
YOU HAVE SO MANY WONDERFUL FRIENDS.
SPARKLE
FLUTTER
HEH HEH!

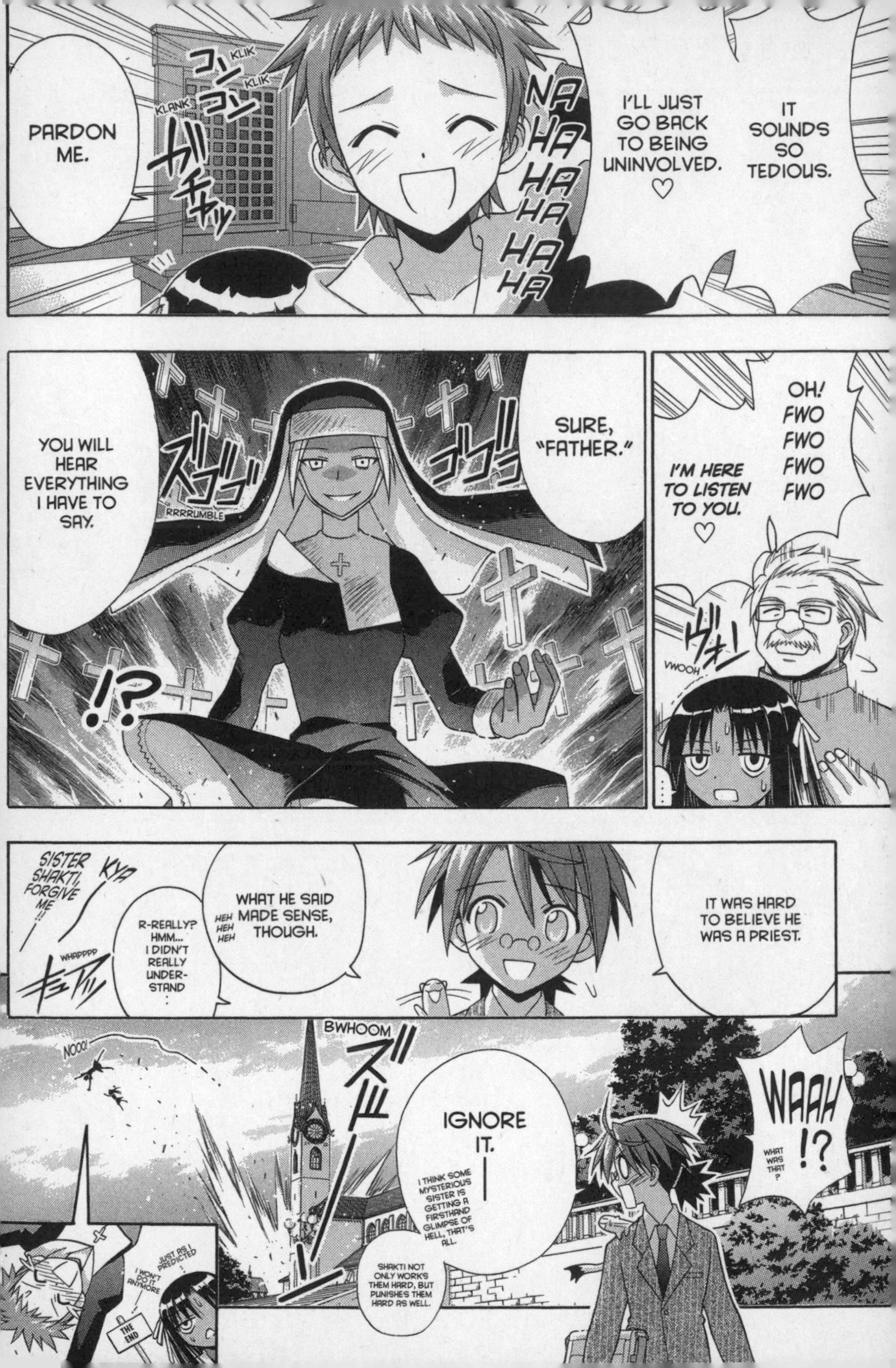
IT SOUNDS SO TEDIOUS.
I'LL JUST GO BACK TO BEING UNINVOLVED. ♡
NAHAHAHAHAHAHA
KLIK
KLIK
KLANK
PARDON ME.
OH! FWO FWO FWO FWO
I'M HERE TO LISTEN TO YOU. ♡
VWOOH
SURE, "FATHER."
RRRRUMBLE
YOU WILL HEAR EVERYTHING I HAVE TO SAY.
!?
IT WAS HARD TO BELIEVE HE WAS A PRIEST.
WHAT HE SAID MADE SENSE, THOUGH.
HEH HEH HEH
R-REALLY? HMM... I DIDN'T REALLY UNDER-STAND
KYA
SISTER SHAKTI, FORGIVE ME!!
WHAPPPP
WAAH!?
WHAT WAS THAT?
IGNORE IT.
I THINK SOME MYSTERIOUS SISTER IS GETTING A FIRSTHAND GLIMPSE OF HELL, THAT'S ALL.
SHAKTI NOT ONLY WORKS THEM HARD, BUT PUNISHES THEM HARD AS WELL.
BWHOOM
NOOO!
JUST AS I PREDICTED
I WON'T DO IT ANYMORE
THE END

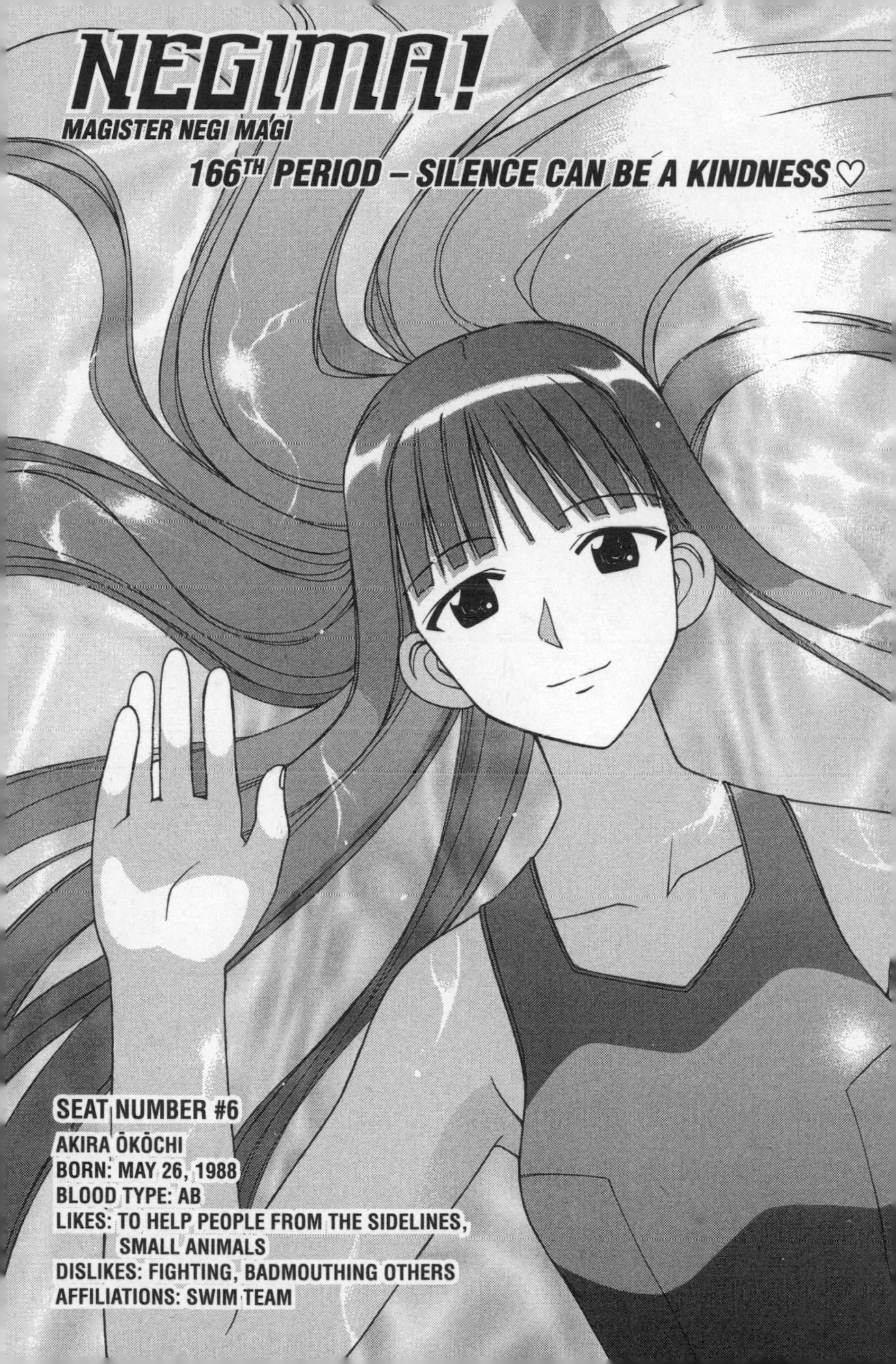
NEGIMA!
MAGISTER NEGI MAGI
166TH PERIOD – SILENCE CAN BE A KINDNESS ♡
SEAT NUMBER #6
AKIRA ŌKŌCHI
BORN: MAY 26, 1988
BLOOD TYPE: AB
LIKES: TO HELP PEOPLE FROM THE SIDELINES, SMALL ANIMALS
DISLIKES: FIGHTING, BADMOUTHING OTHERS
AFFILIATIONS: SWIM TEAM

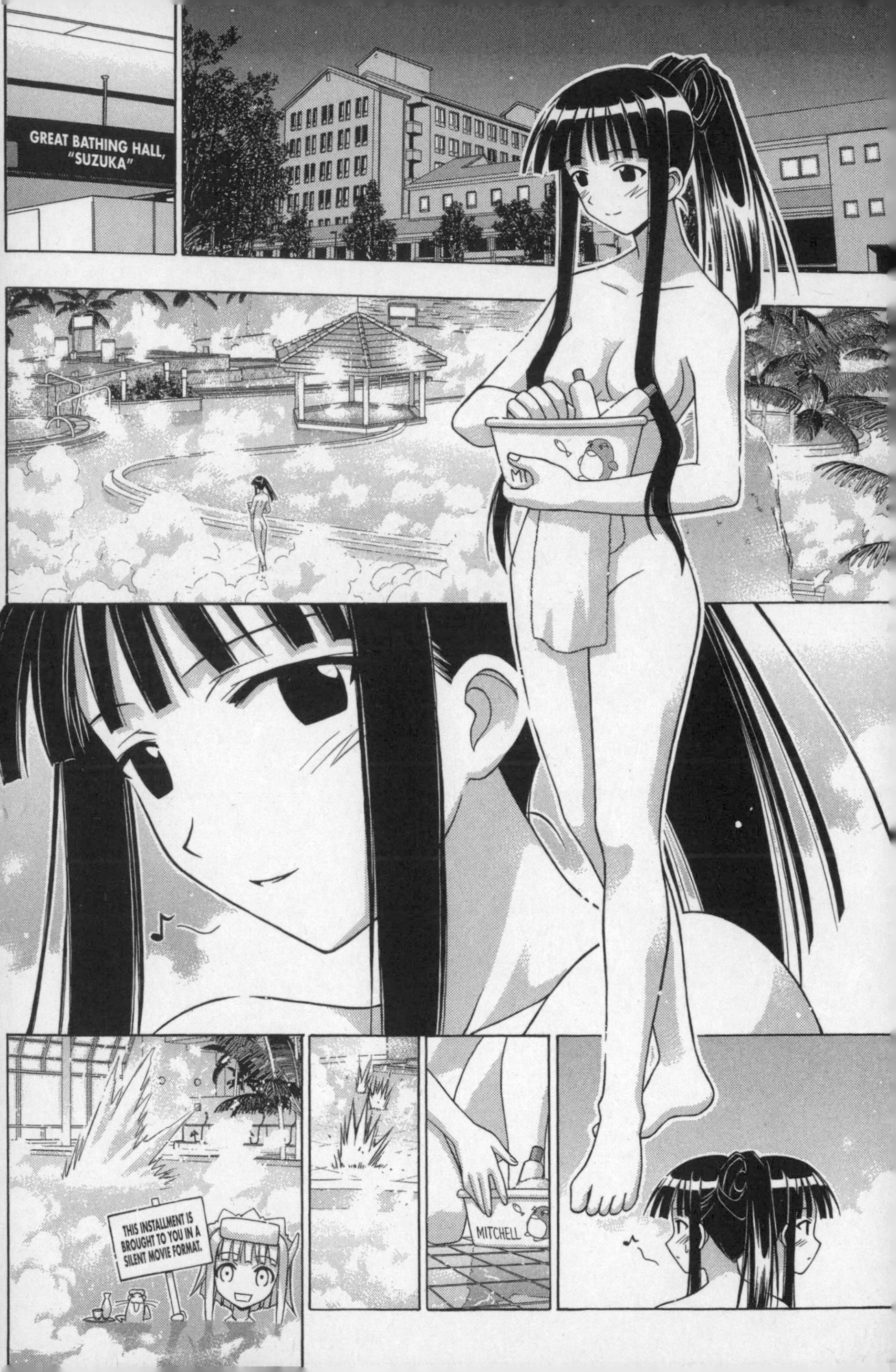
GREAT BATHING HALL, "SUZUKA"
MITCHELL
THIS INSTALLMENT IS BROUGHT TO YOU IN A SILENT MOVIE FORMAT.

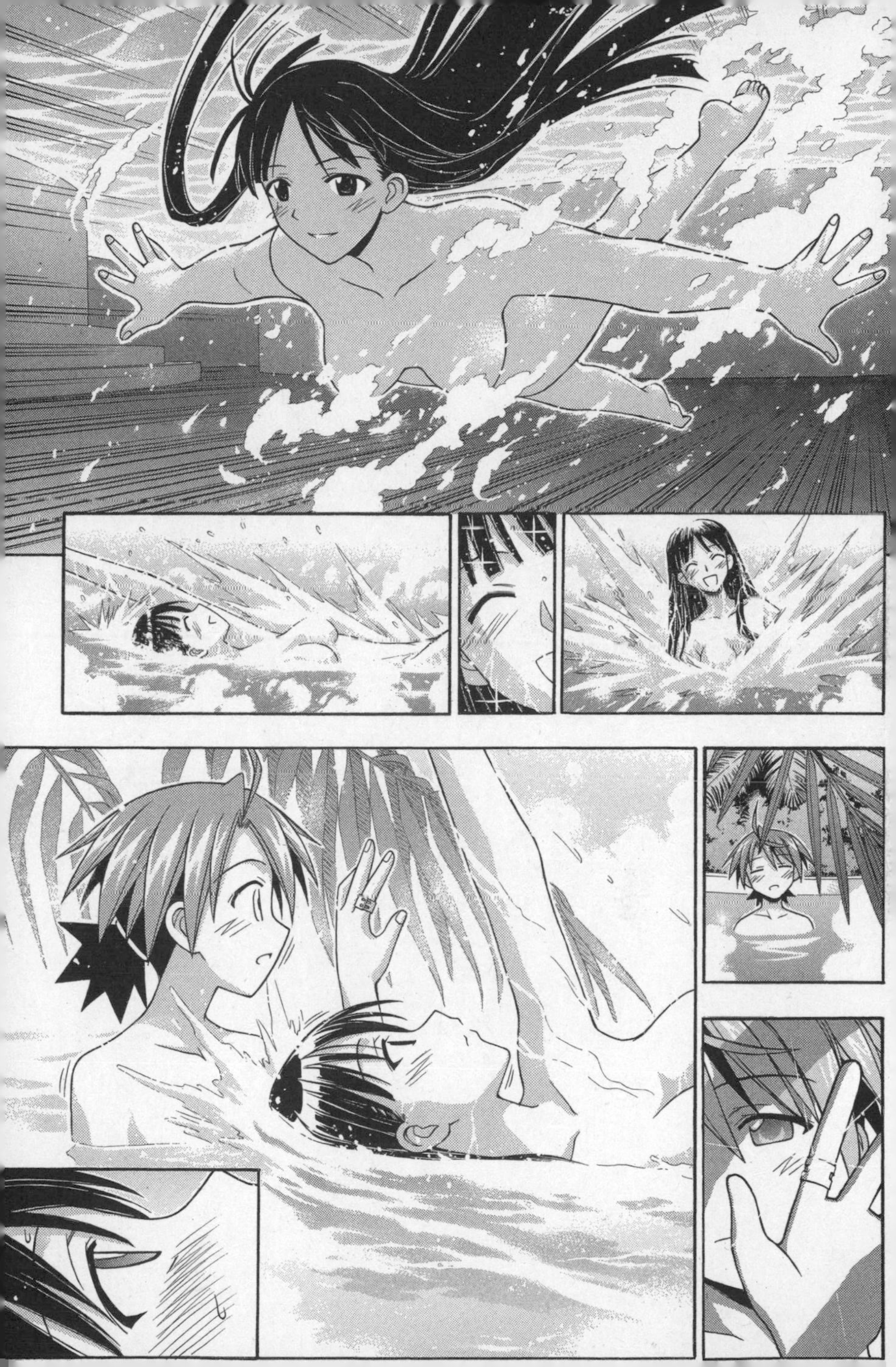

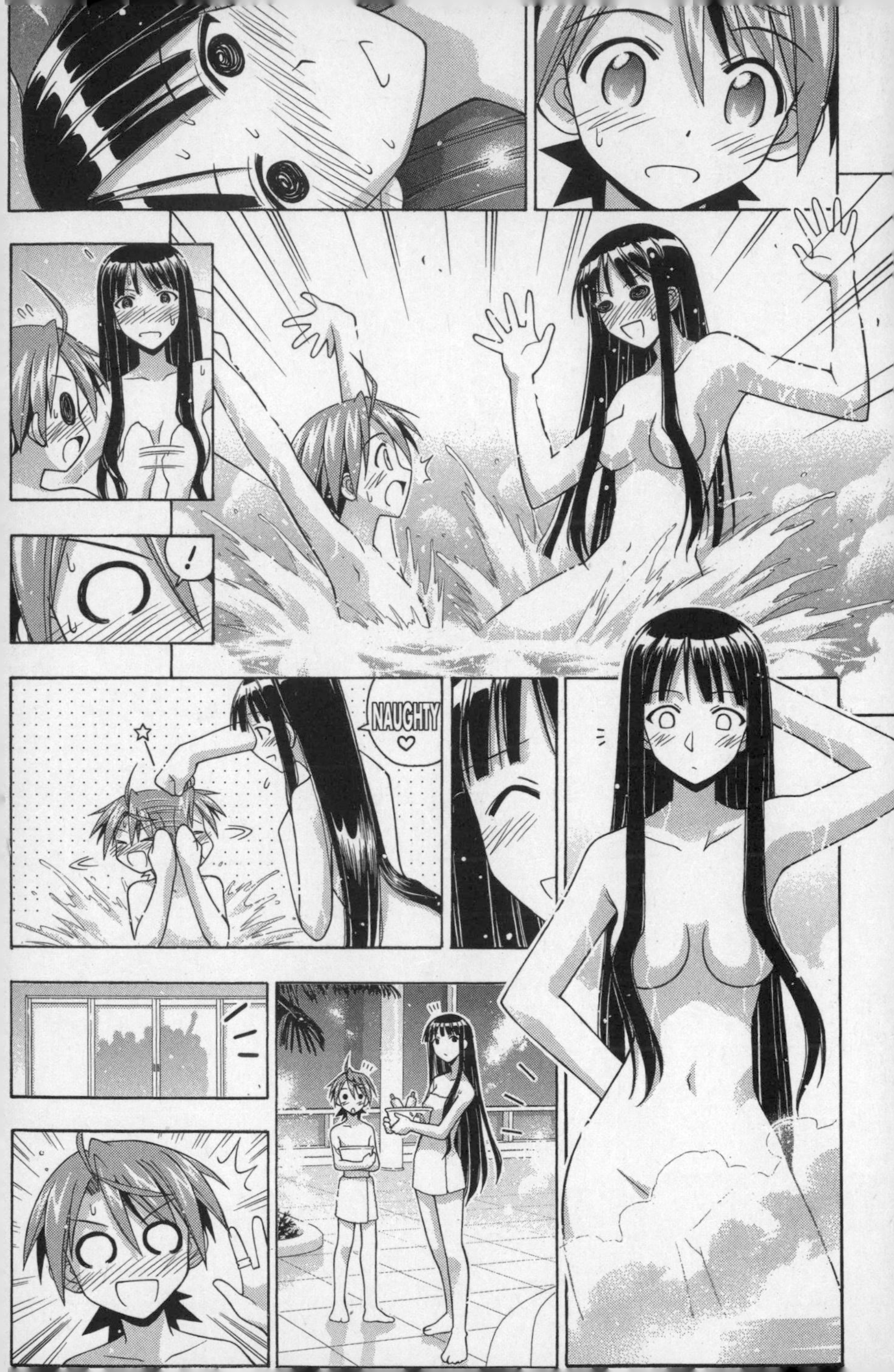
!
NAUGHTY ♥

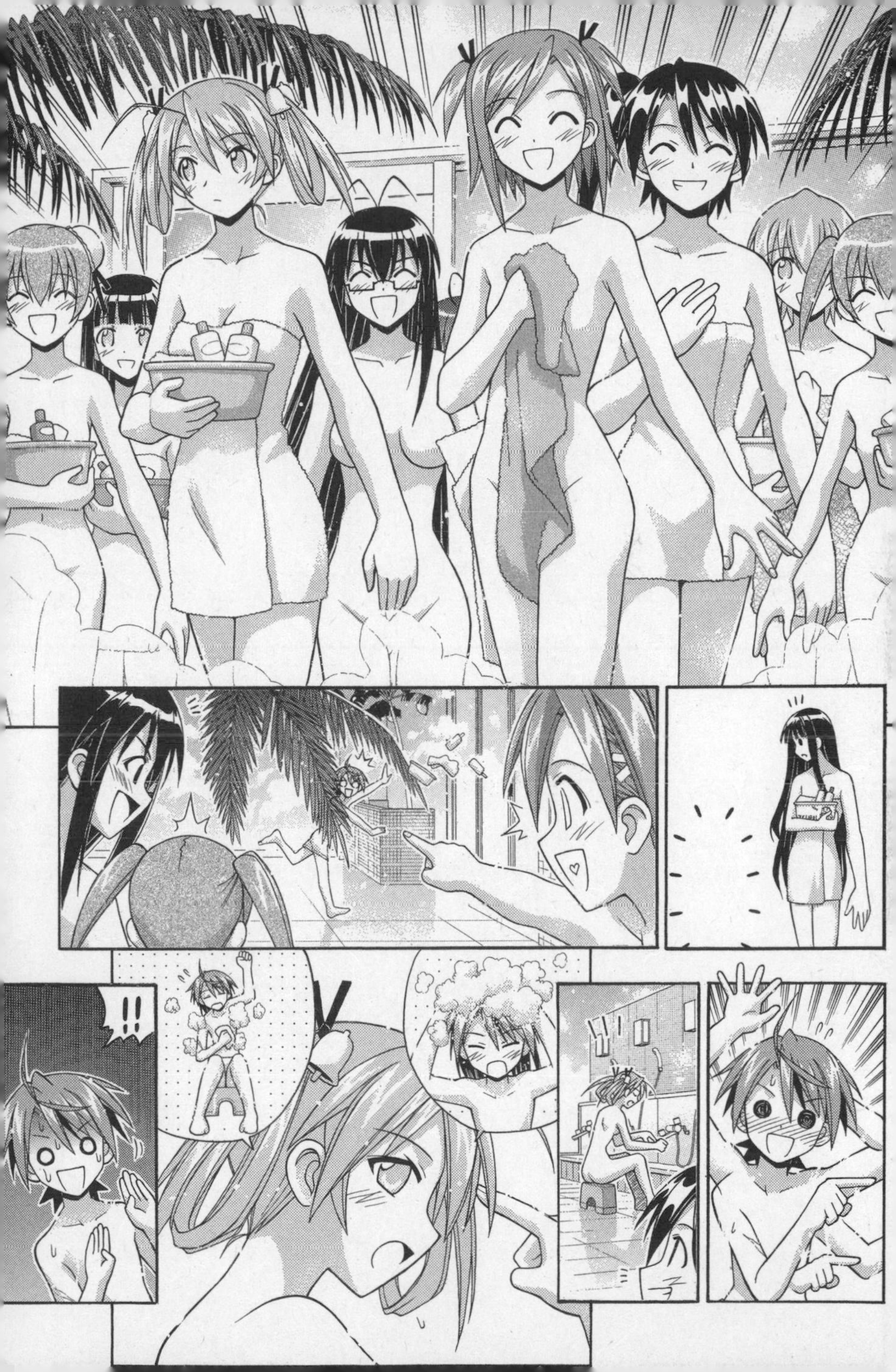
!!

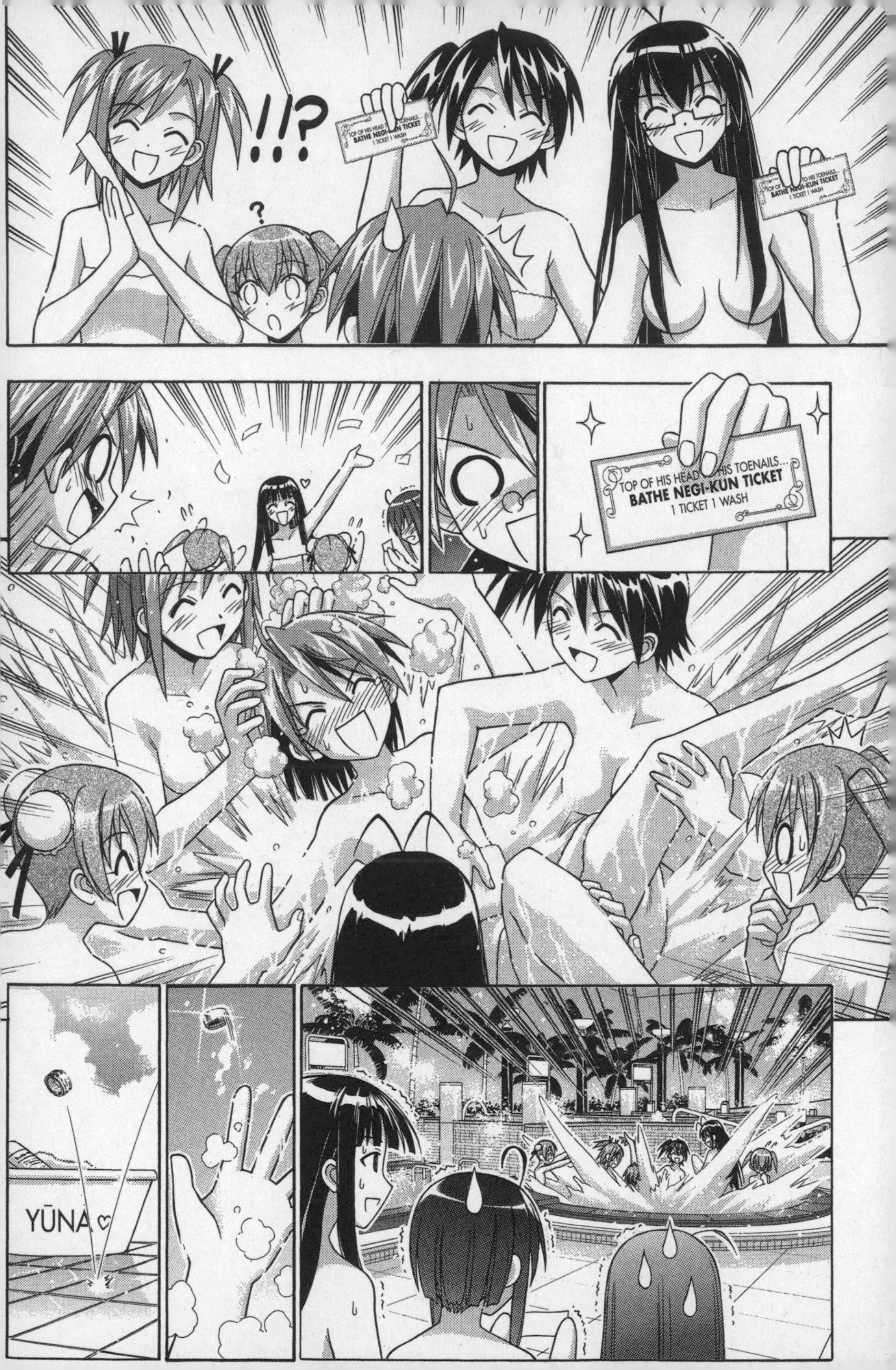
!!?
?
TOP OF HIS HEAD TO HIS TOENAILS...
BATHE NEGI-KUN TICKET
1 TICKET 1 WASH
TOP OF HIS HEAD HIS TOENAILS...
BATHE NEGI-KUN TICKET
1 TICKET 1 WASH
YŪNA ♡

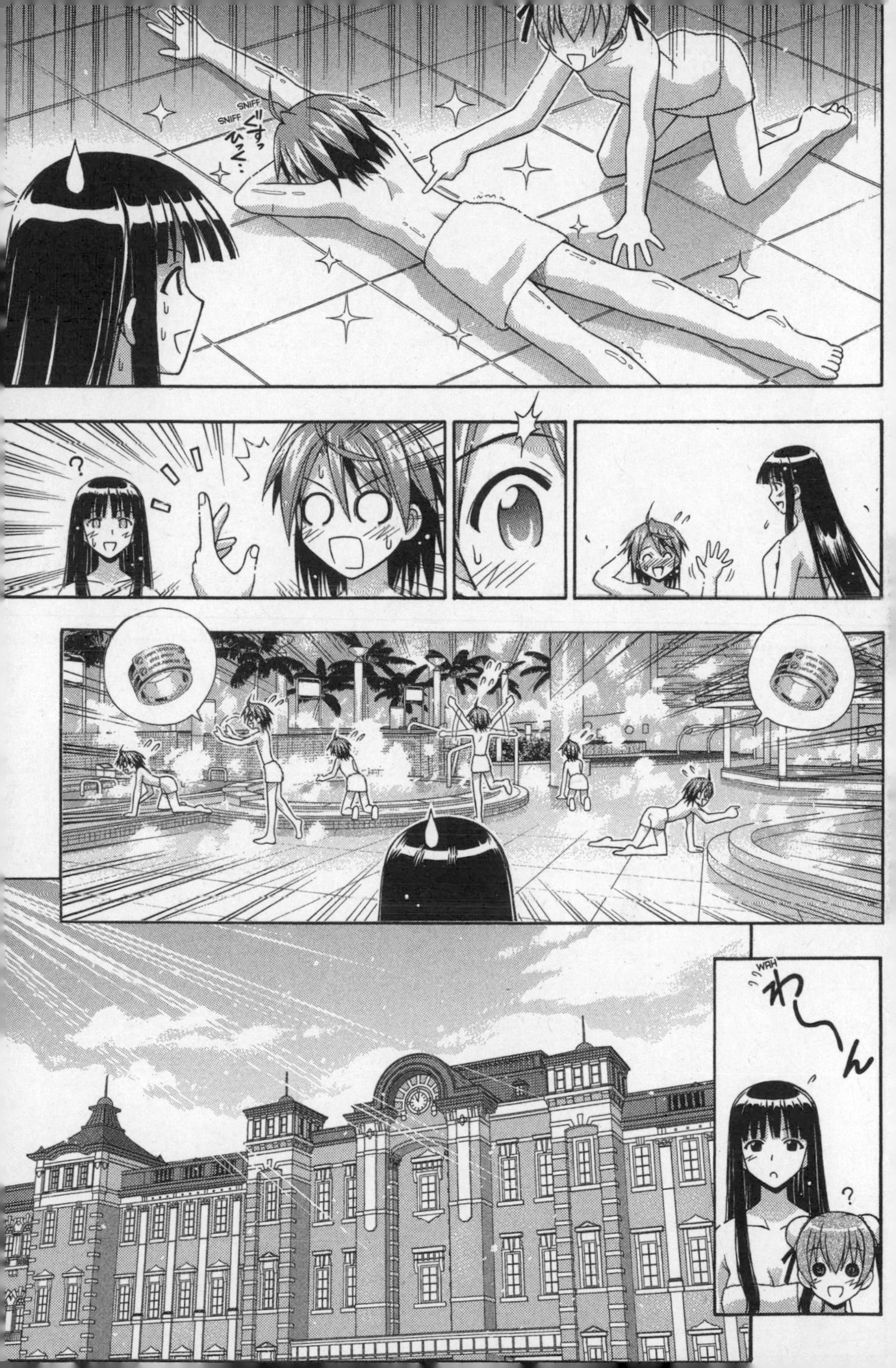
SNIFF
ぐすっ
SNIFF
ひっく…
WAH
わ〜〜ん

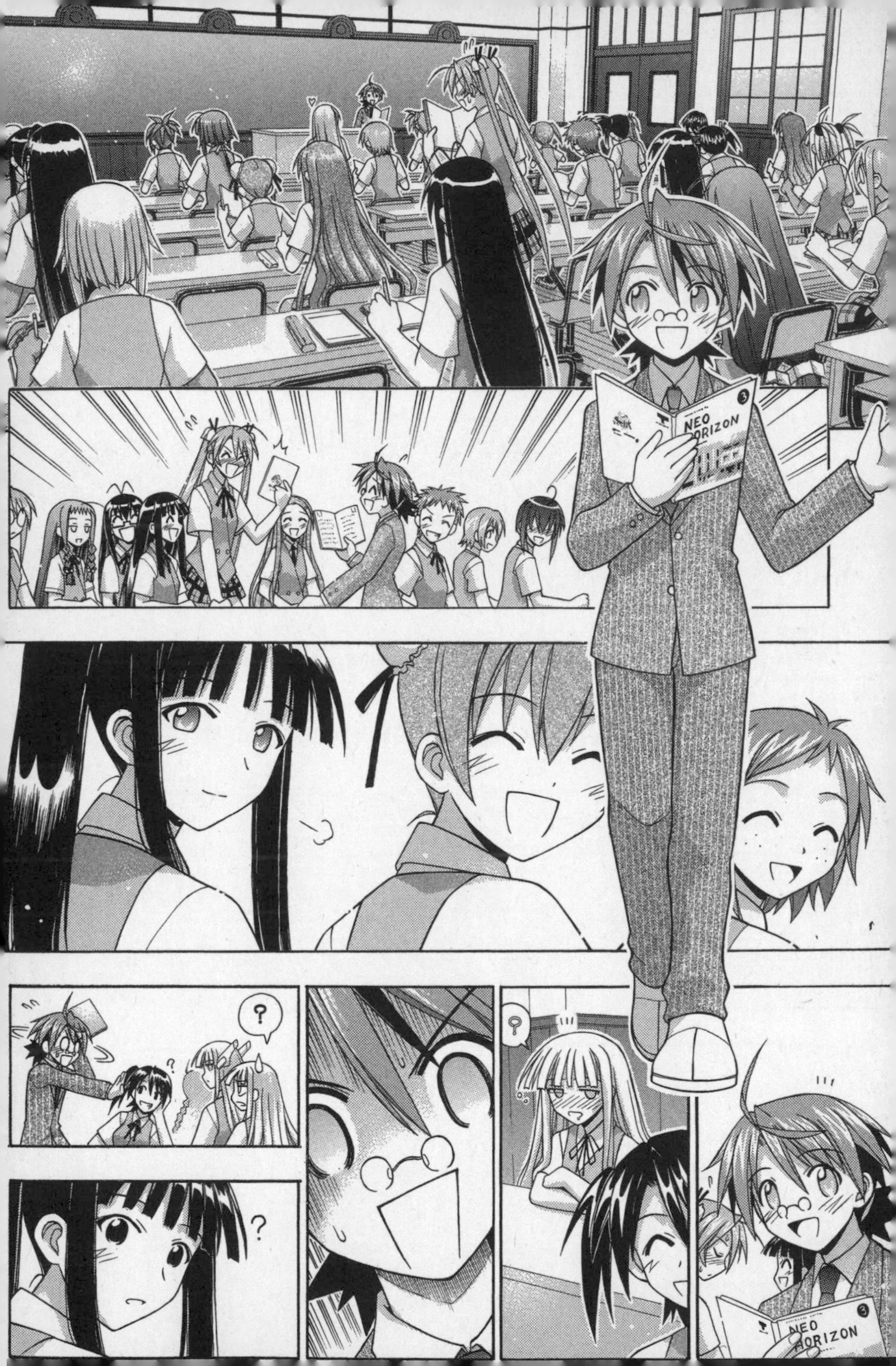
NEO HORIZON
NEO HORIZON
?
?
?
?

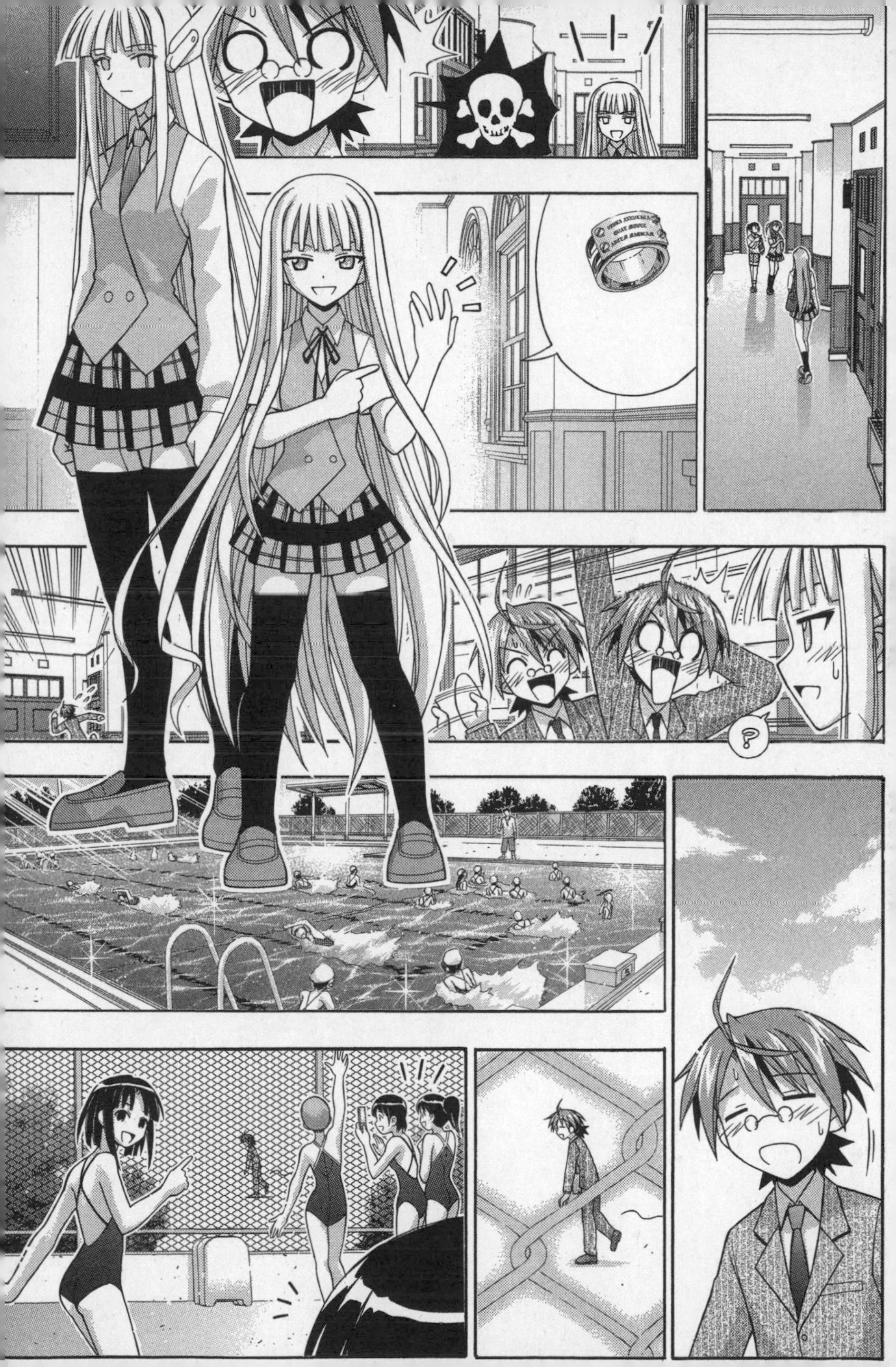
?

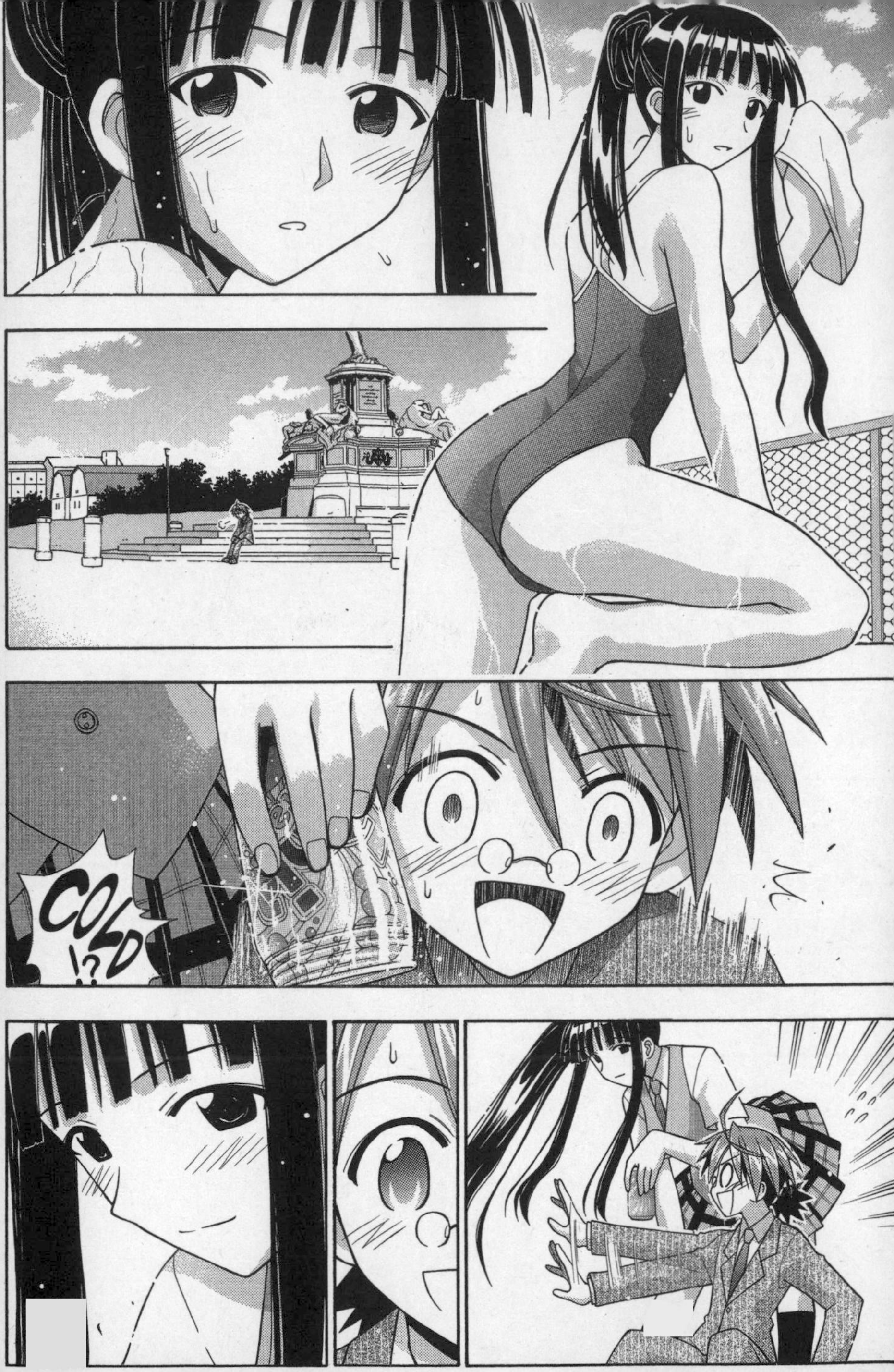
COLD!?

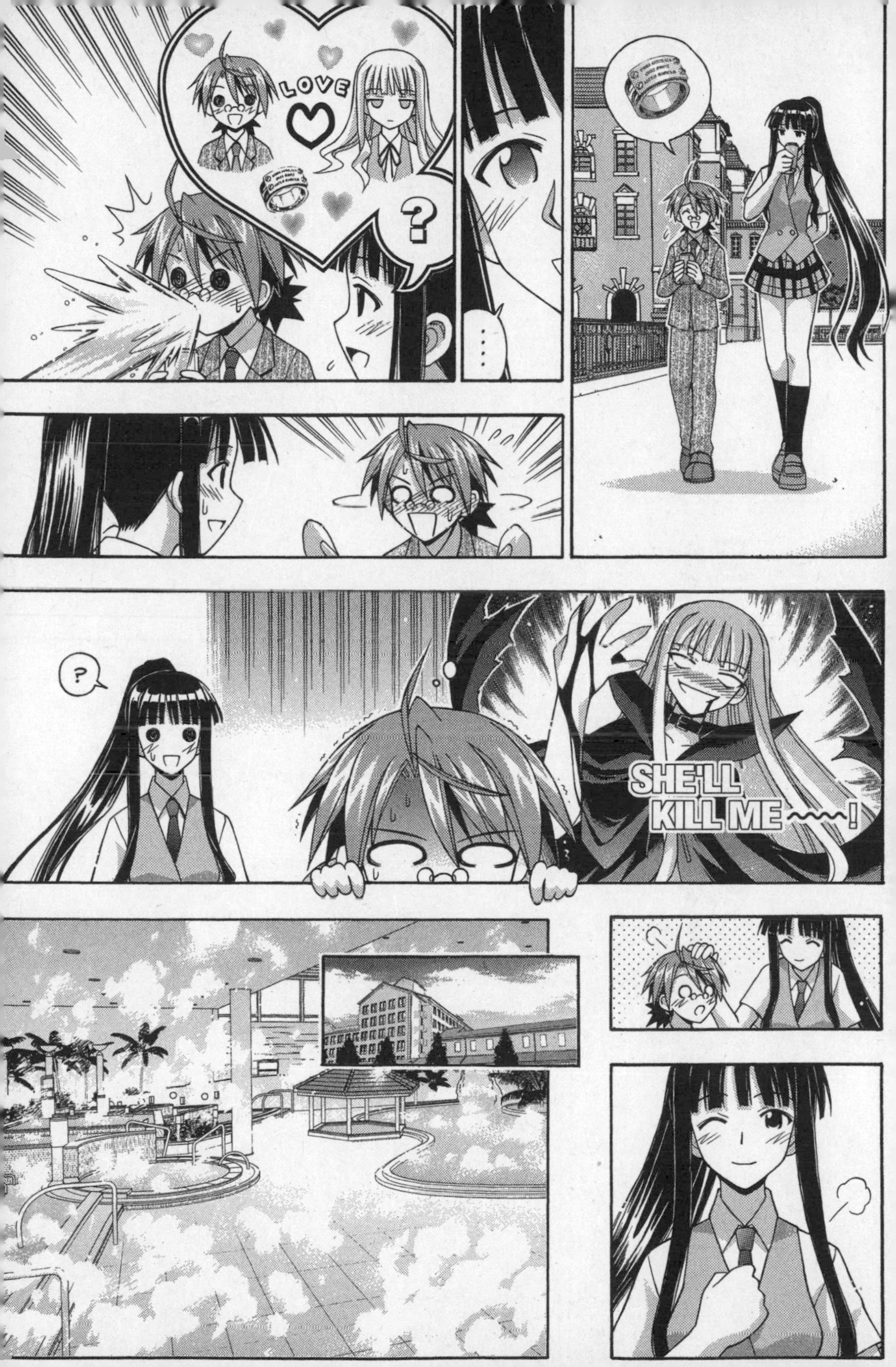
....
LOVE
?
?
SHE'LL KILL ME ~~~!

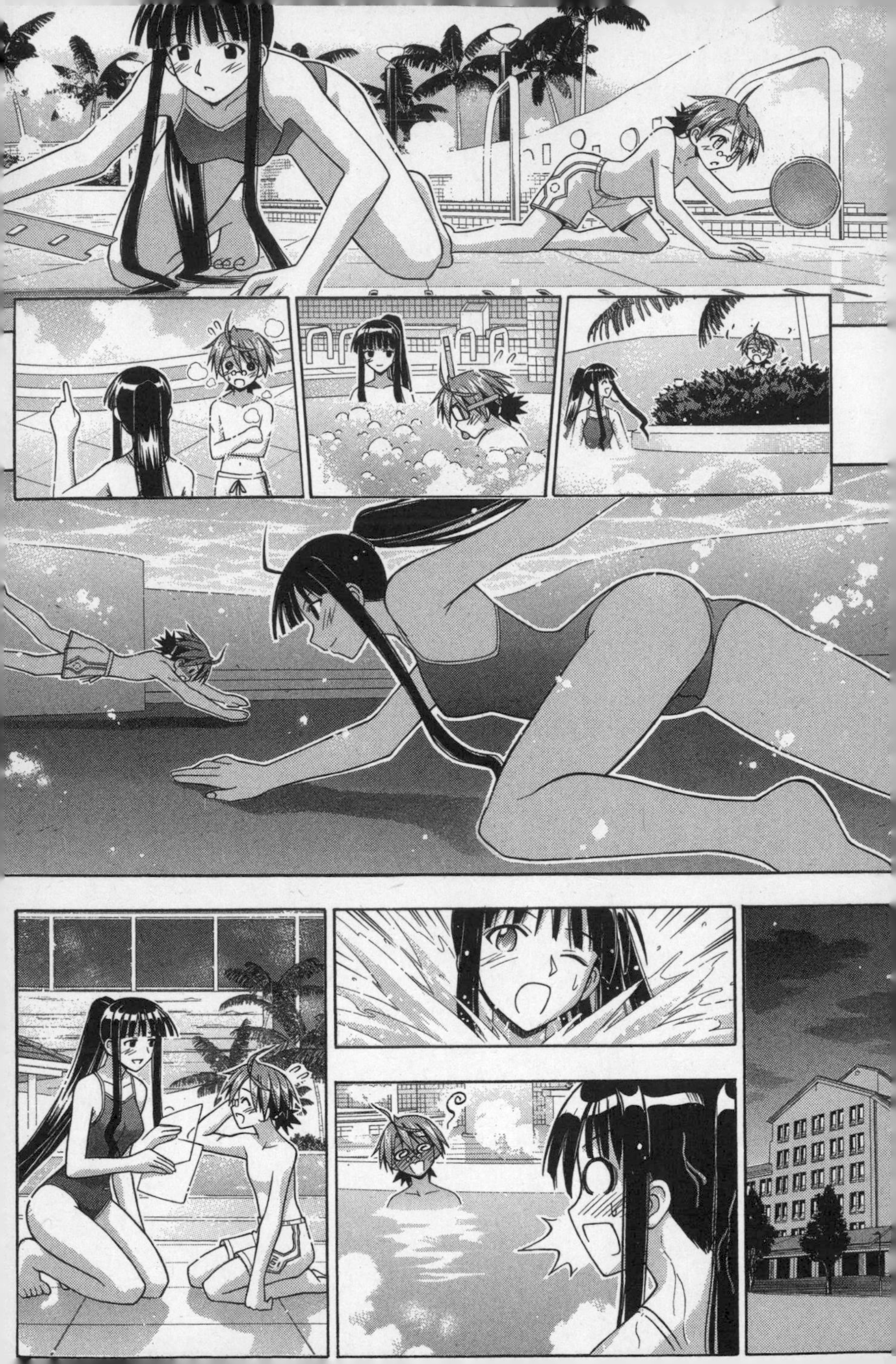

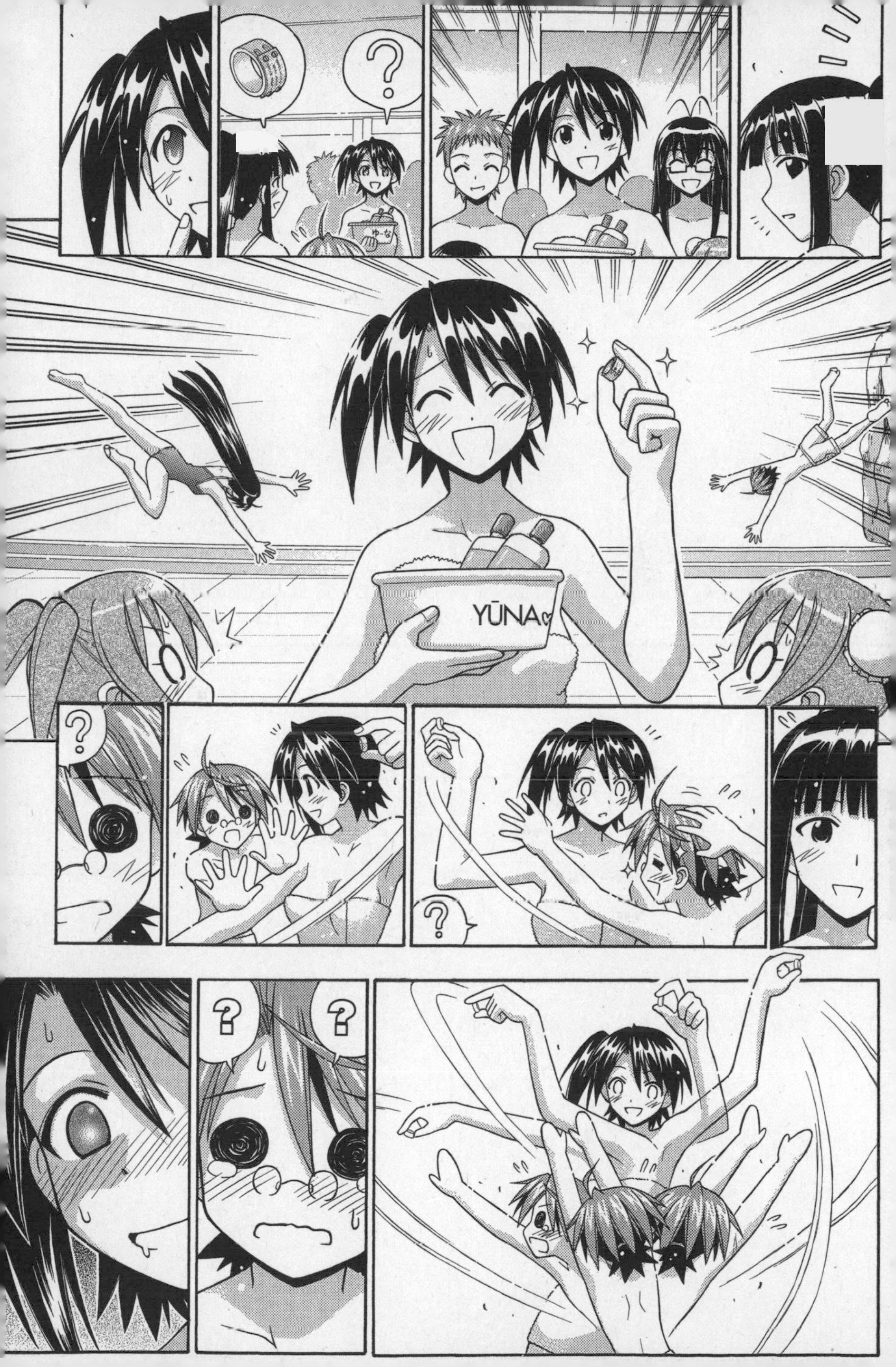

?
ゆーな
YŪNA♡
?
?
?
?

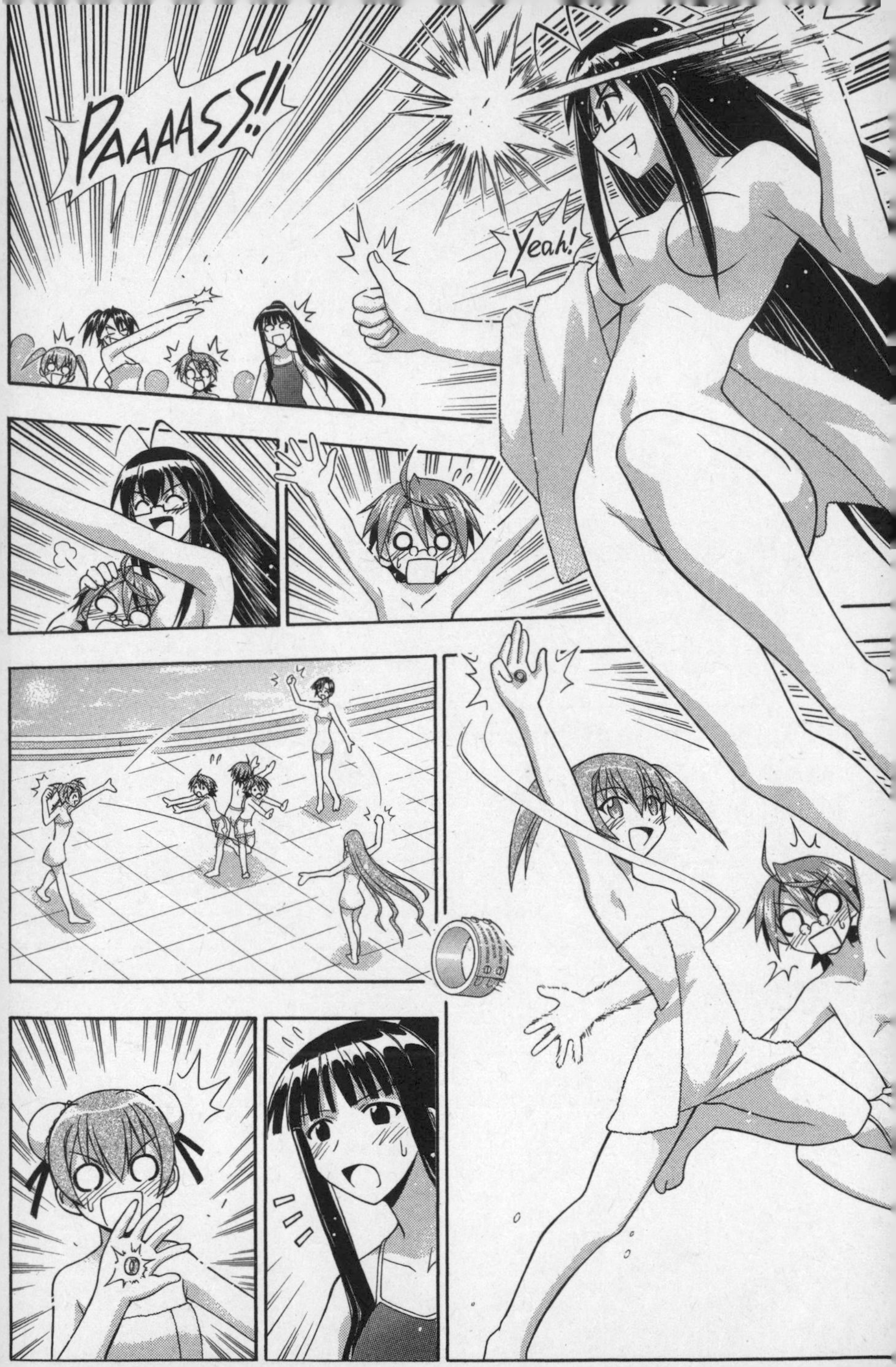
PAAAASS!!
Yeah!

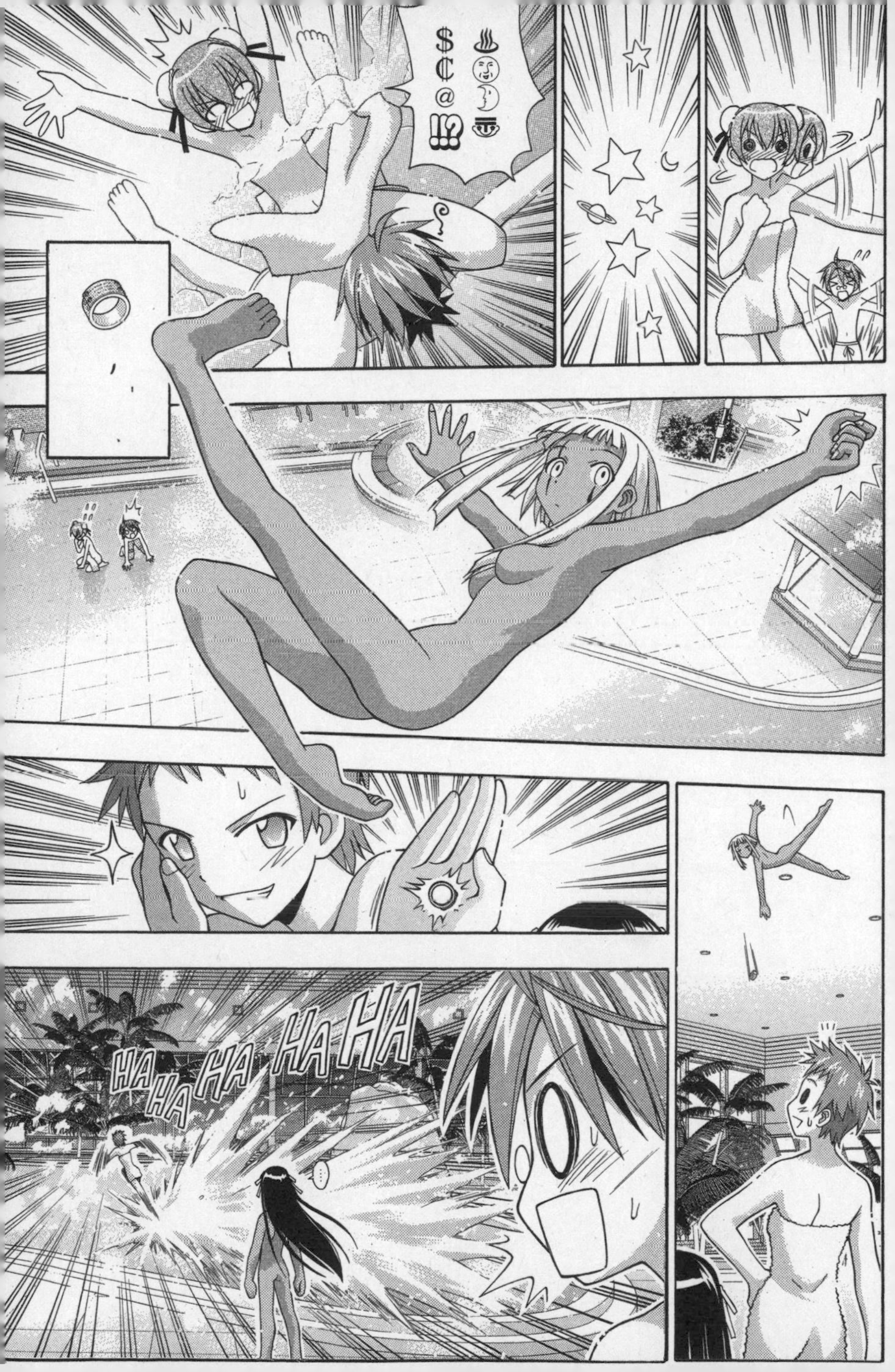
$
₵
@
!!?
HA HA HA HA HA

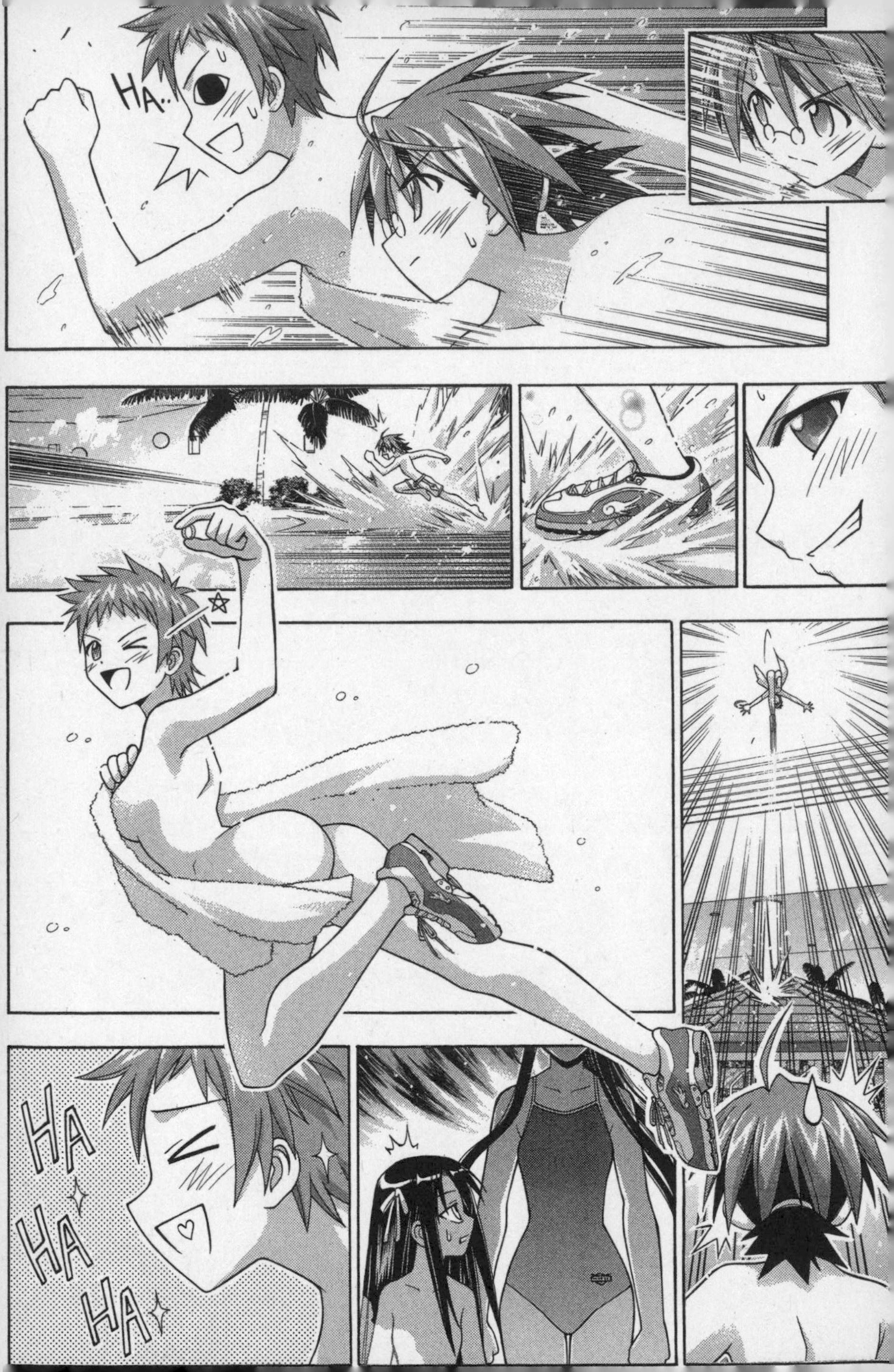
HA..
HA HA HA HA

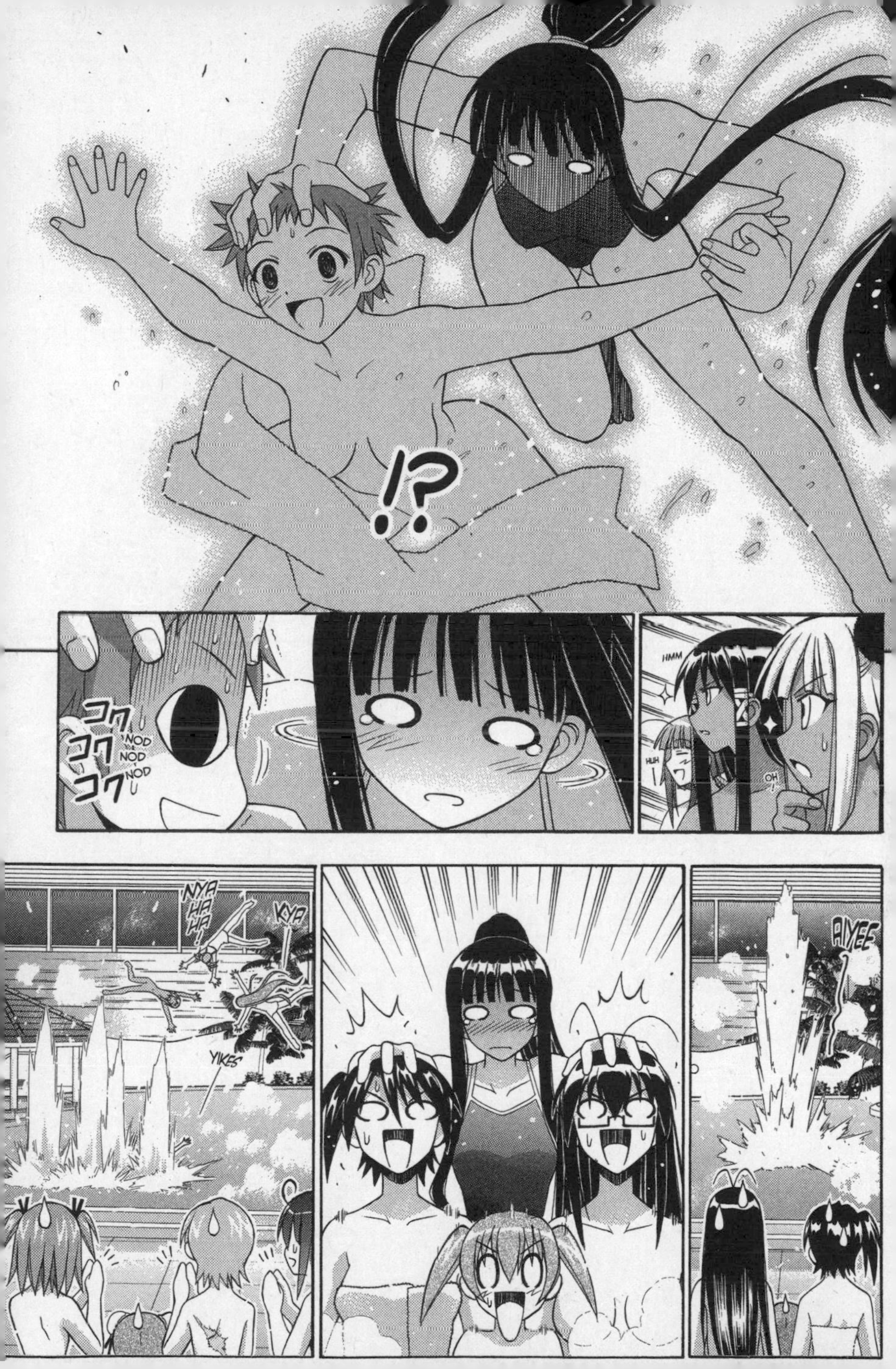
!?
HMM
HUH
OH
コク NOD
コク NOD
コク NOD
AIYEE
NYA HA HA
KYA
YIKES

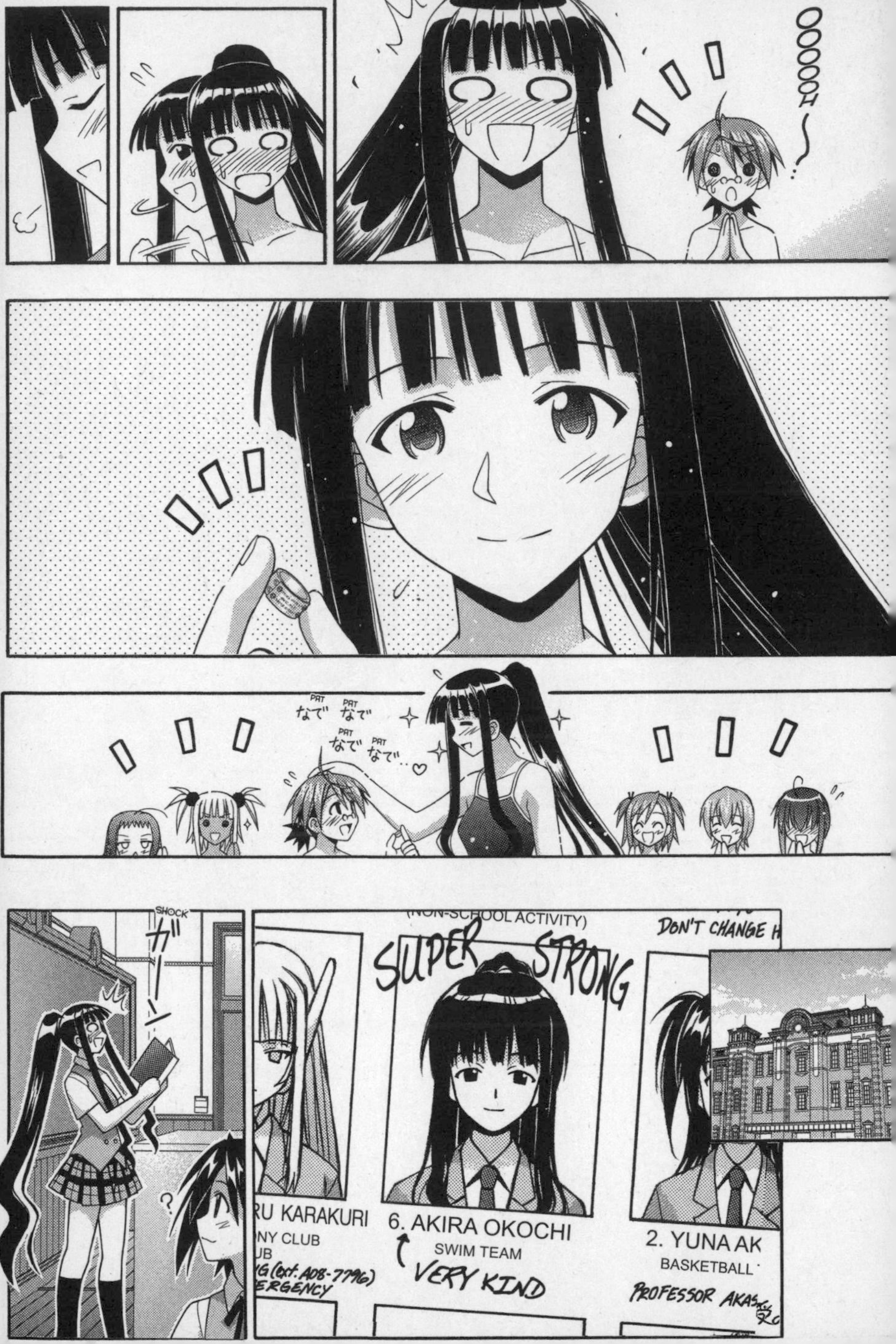
OOOOOH~...
PAT なで PAT なで
PAT なで PAT なで...♡
(NON-SCHOOL ACTIVITY)
DON'T CHANGE H
SUPER STRONG
6. AKIRA OKOCHI
SWIM TEAM
VERY KIND
2. YUNA AK
BASKETBALL
PROFESSOR AKAS
RU KARAKURI
NY CLUB
UB
G (ext. A08-7796)
ERGENCY
SHOCK
ガーン
?

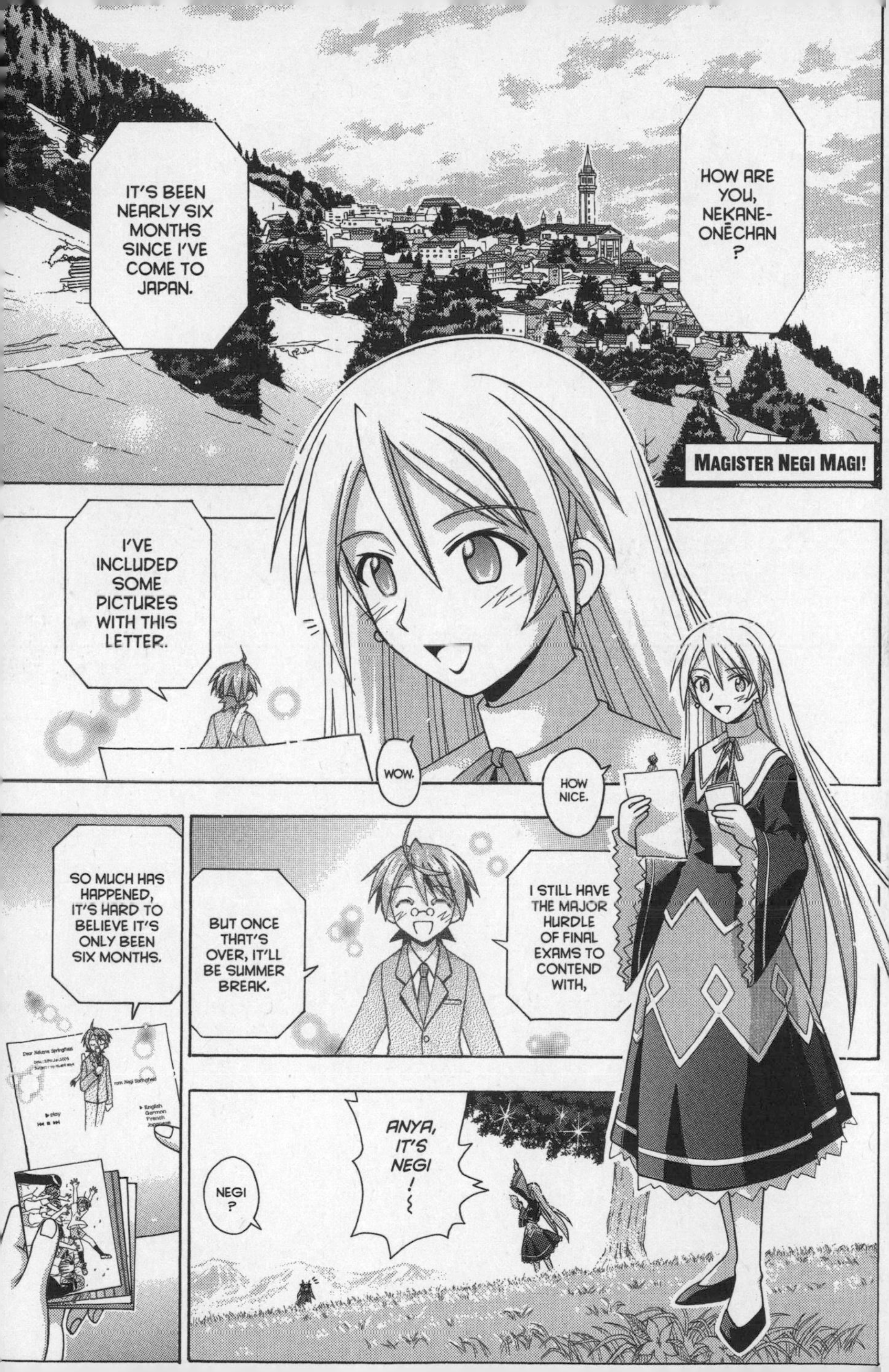

HOW ARE YOU, NEKANE-ONĒCHAN?
IT'S BEEN NEARLY SIX MONTHS SINCE I'VE COME TO JAPAN.
MAGISTER NEGI MAGI!
I'VE INCLUDED SOME PICTURES WITH THIS LETTER.
WOW.
HOW NICE.
I STILL HAVE THE MAJOR HURDLE OF FINAL EXAMS TO CONTEND WITH,
BUT ONCE THAT'S OVER, IT'LL BE SUMMER BREAK.
SO MUCH HAS HAPPENED, IT'S HARD TO BELIEVE IT'S ONLY BEEN SIX MONTHS.
ANYA, IT'S NEGI!
NEGI?

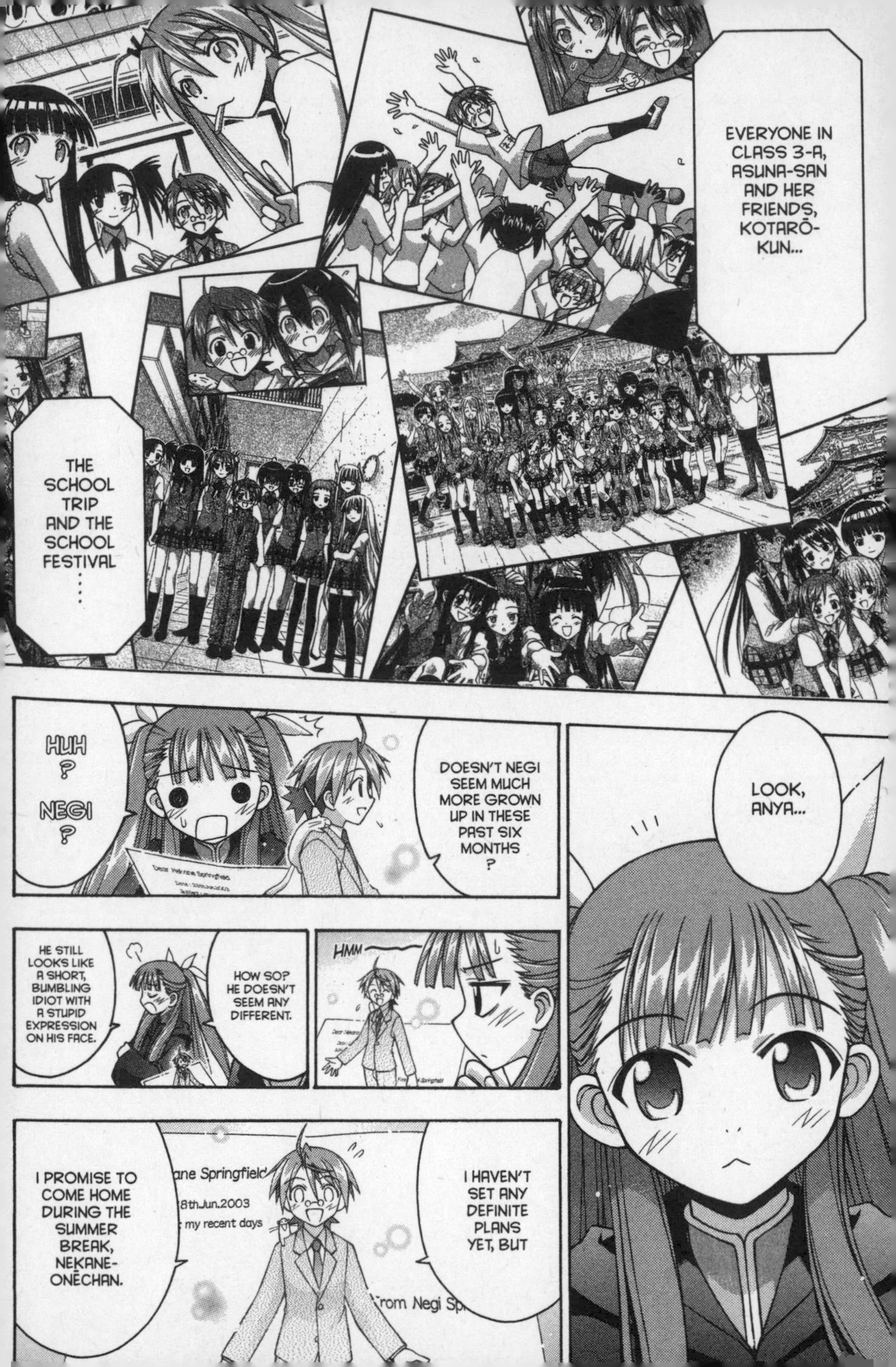
EVERYONE IN CLASS 3-A, ASUNA-SAN AND HER FRIENDS, KOTARŌ-KUN...
THE SCHOOL TRIP AND THE SCHOOL FESTIVAL .....
LOOK, ANYA...
DOESN'T NEGI SEEM MUCH MORE GROWN UP IN THESE PAST SIX MONTHS?
HUH? NEGI?
HMM
HOW SO? HE DOESN'T SEEM ANY DIFFERENT.
HE STILL LOOKS LIKE A SHORT, BUMBLING IDIOT WITH A STUPID EXPRESSION ON HIS FACE.
I HAVEN'T SET ANY DEFINITE PLANS YET, BUT
I PROMISE TO COME HOME DURING THE SUMMER BREAK, NEKANE-ONĒCHAN.

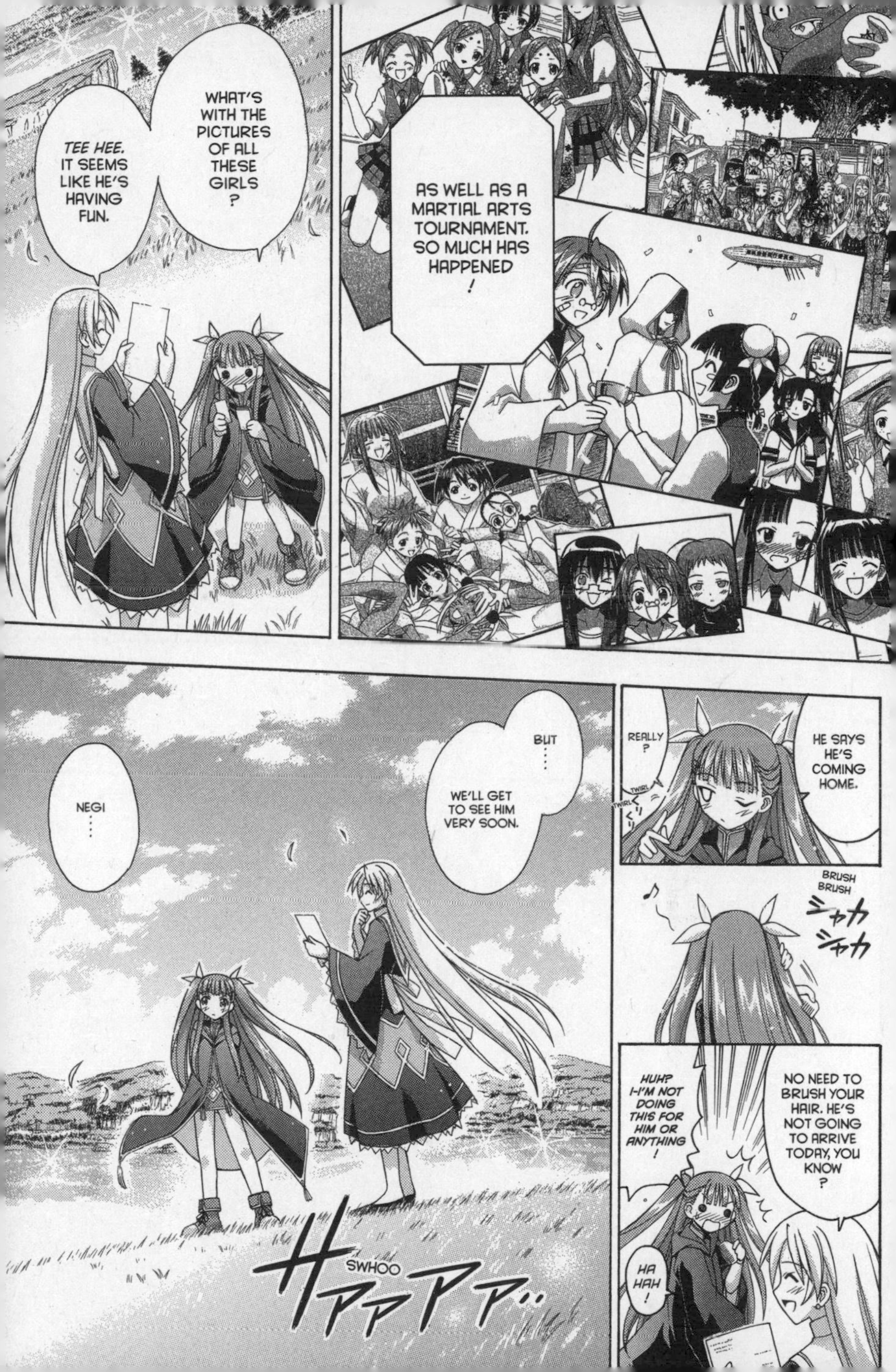
AS WELL AS A MARTIAL ARTS TOURNAMENT. SO MUCH HAS HAPPENED!
WHAT'S WITH THE PICTURES OF ALL THESE GIRLS?
TEE HEE. IT SEEMS LIKE HE'S HAVING FUN.
HE SAYS HE'S COMING HOME.
REALLY?
TWIRL TWIRL
BRUSH BRUSH
シャカ シャカ
NO NEED TO BRUSH YOUR HAIR. HE'S NOT GOING TO ARRIVE TODAY, YOU KNOW?
HUH? I-I'M NOT DOING THIS FOR HIM OR ANYTHING!
HA HAH!
BUT....
WE'LL GET TO SEE HIM VERY SOON.
NEGI....
SWHOO

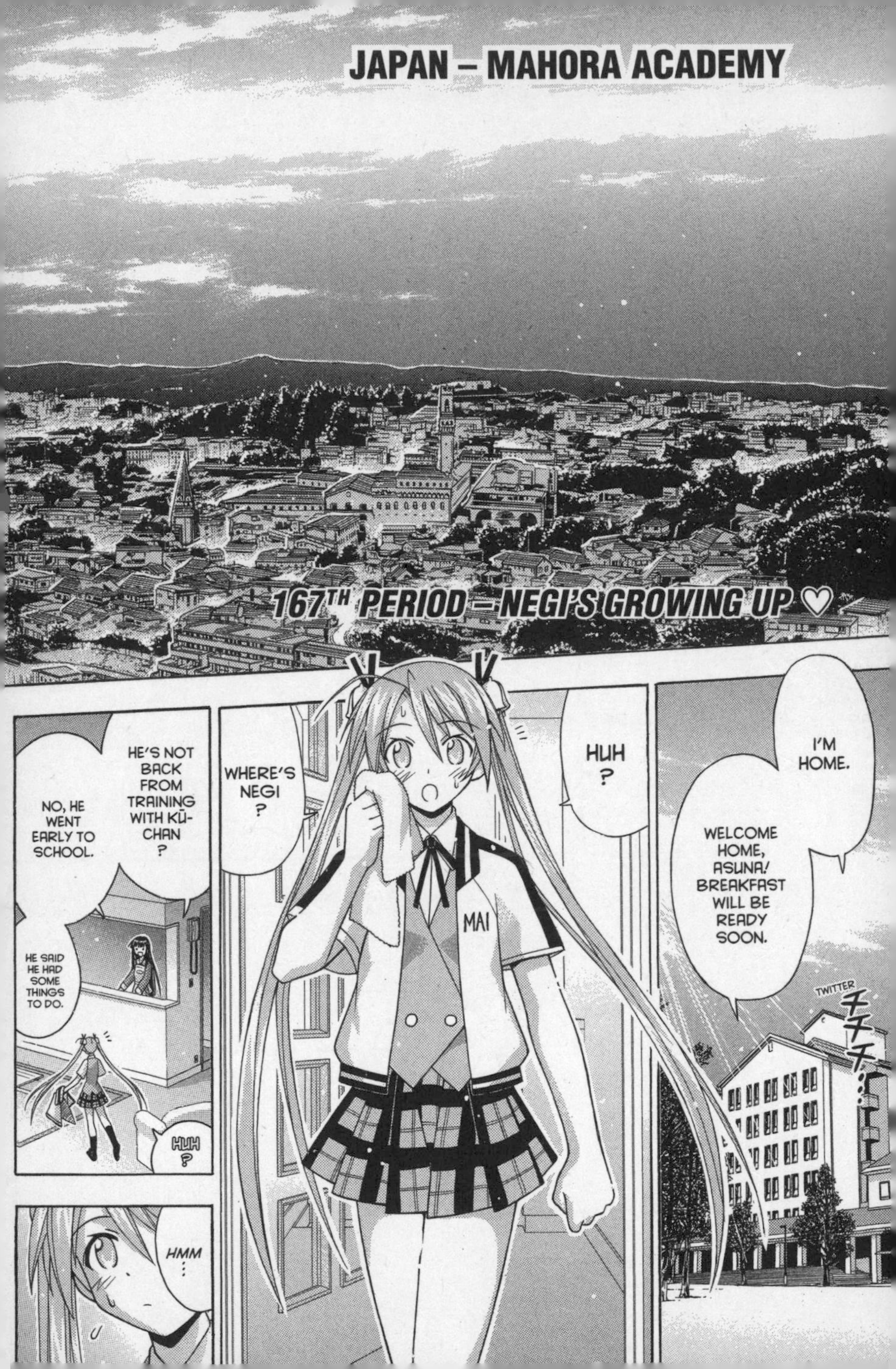
JAPAN – MAHORA ACADEMY
167TH PERIOD – NEGI'S GROWING UP ♡
I'M HOME.
WELCOME HOME, ASUNA! BREAKFAST WILL BE READY SOON.
TWITTER
チチチ…
HUH?
WHERE'S NEGI?
MAI
HE'S NOT BACK FROM TRAINING WITH KŪ-CHAN?
NO, HE WENT EARLY TO SCHOOL.
HE SAID HE HAD SOME THINGS TO DO.
HUH?
HMM…

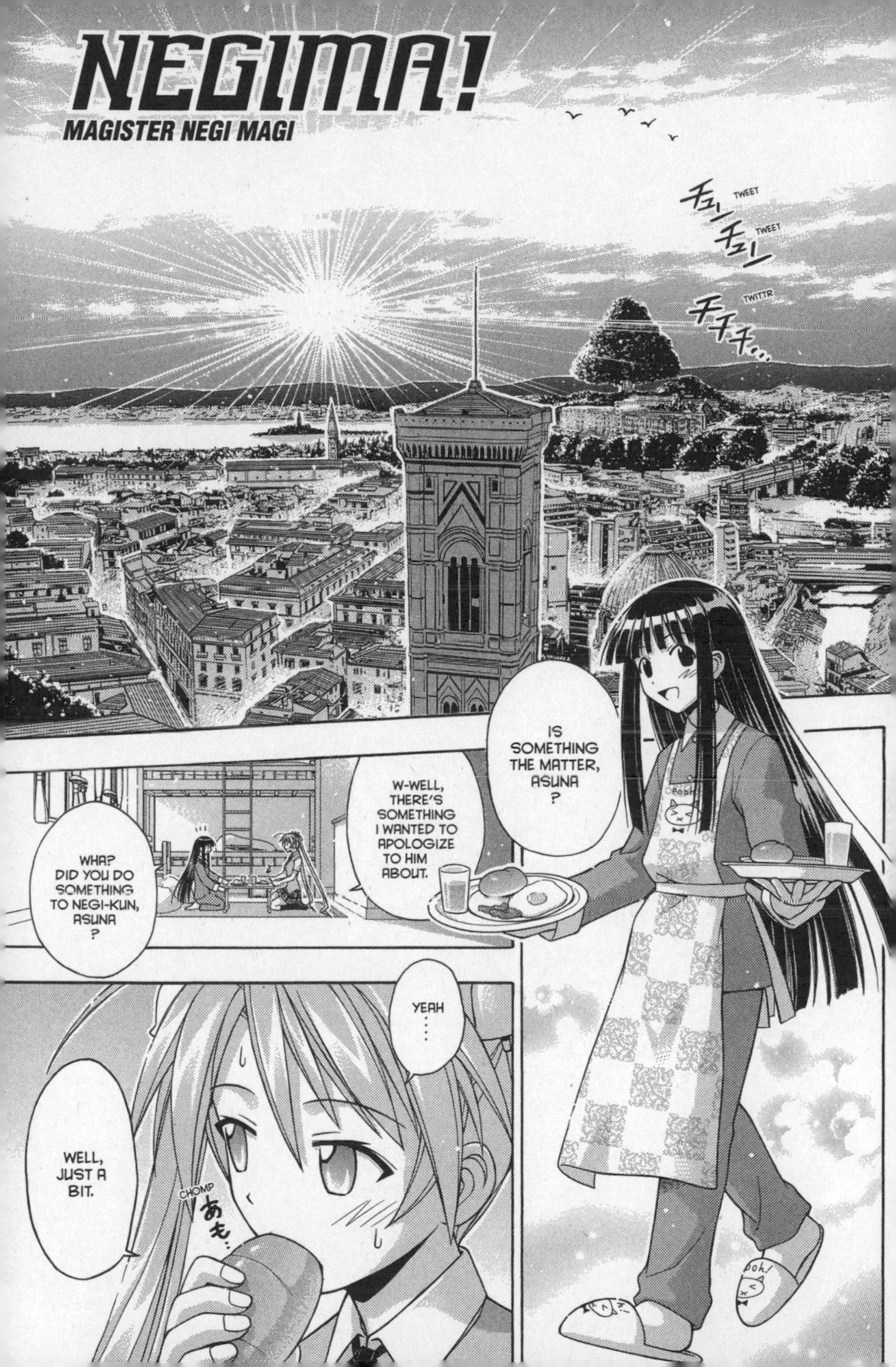
NEGIMA!
MAGISTER NEGI MAGI
チュンチュン TWEET TWEET
チチチ… TWITTR
IS SOMETHING THE MATTER, ASUNA?
W-WELL, THERE'S SOMETHING I WANTED TO APOLOGIZE TO HIM ABOUT.
WHA? DID YOU DO SOMETHING TO NEGI-KUN, ASUNA?
YEAH ....
WELL, JUST A BIT.
あむ… CHOMP

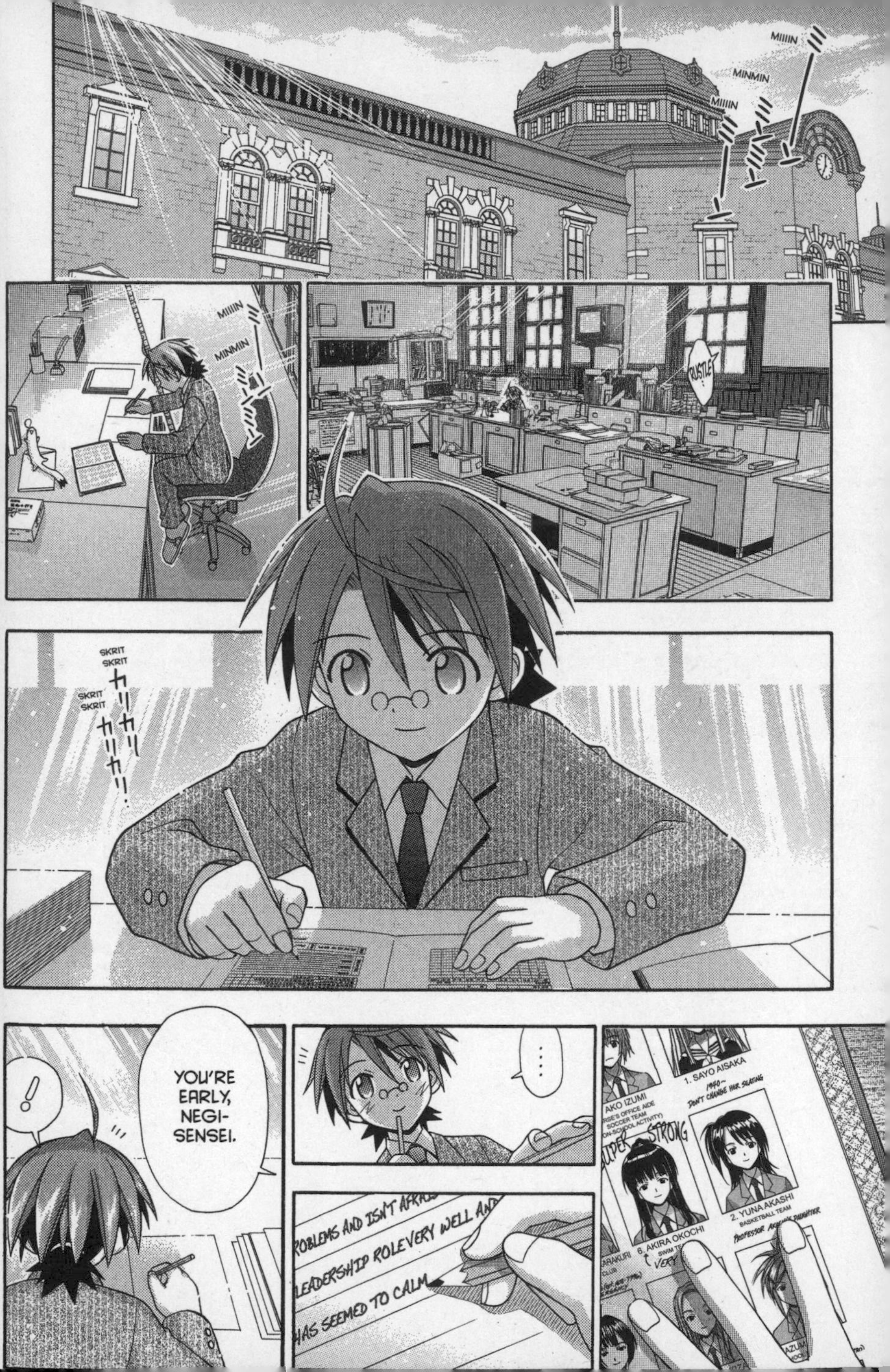
MIIIN
MINMIN
MIIIN
RUSTLE
MIIIN
MINMIN
SKRIT SKRIT
カリカリ
SKRIT SKRIT
カリカリ
1. SAYO AISAKA
1940~
DON'T CHANGE HER SEATING
AKO IZUMI
SOCCER TEAM
SUPER STRONG
2. YUNA AKASHI
BASKETBALL TEAM
6. AKIRA OKOCHI
SWIM TEAM
VERY
....
ROBLEMS AND ISN'T AFRAI
LEADERSHIP ROLE VERY WELL AND
HAS SEEMED TO CALM
YOU'RE EARLY, NEGI-SENSEI.
!

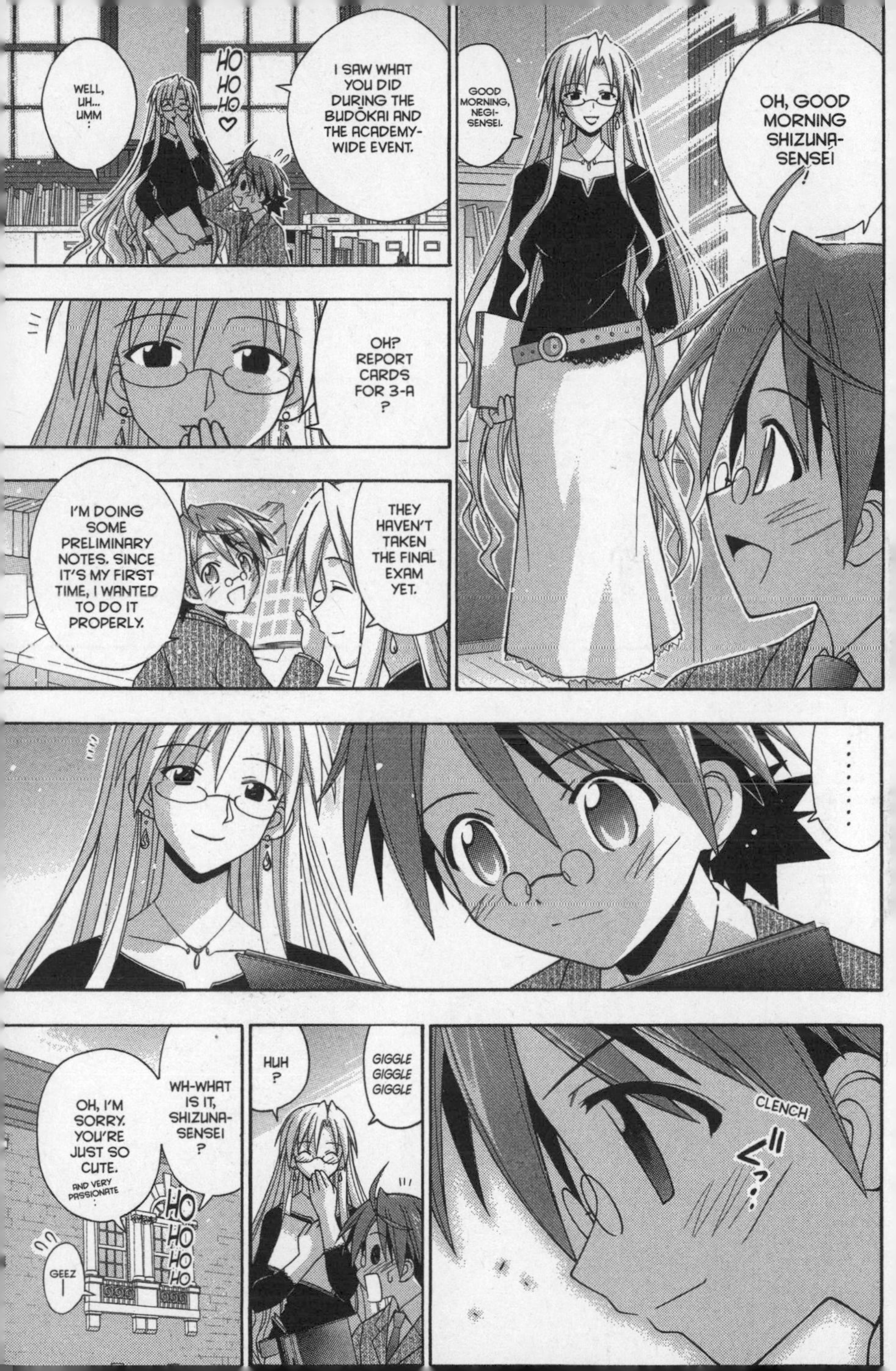

OH, GOOD MORNING SHIZUNA-SENSEI!
GOOD MORNING, NEGI-SENSEI.
I SAW WHAT YOU DID DURING THE BUDŌKAI AND THE ACADEMY-WIDE EVENT.
HO HO HO ♡
WELL, UH... UMM...
OH? REPORT CARDS FOR 3-A?
THEY HAVEN'T TAKEN THE FINAL EXAM YET.
I'M DOING SOME PRELIMINARY NOTES. SINCE IT'S MY FIRST TIME, I WANTED TO DO IT PROPERLY.
....
CLENCH
GIGGLE GIGGLE GIGGLE
HUH?
WH-WHAT IS IT, SHIZUNA-SENSEI?
OH, I'M SORRY. YOU'RE JUST SO CUTE.
AND VERY PASSIONATE...
HO HO HO HO
GEEZ!

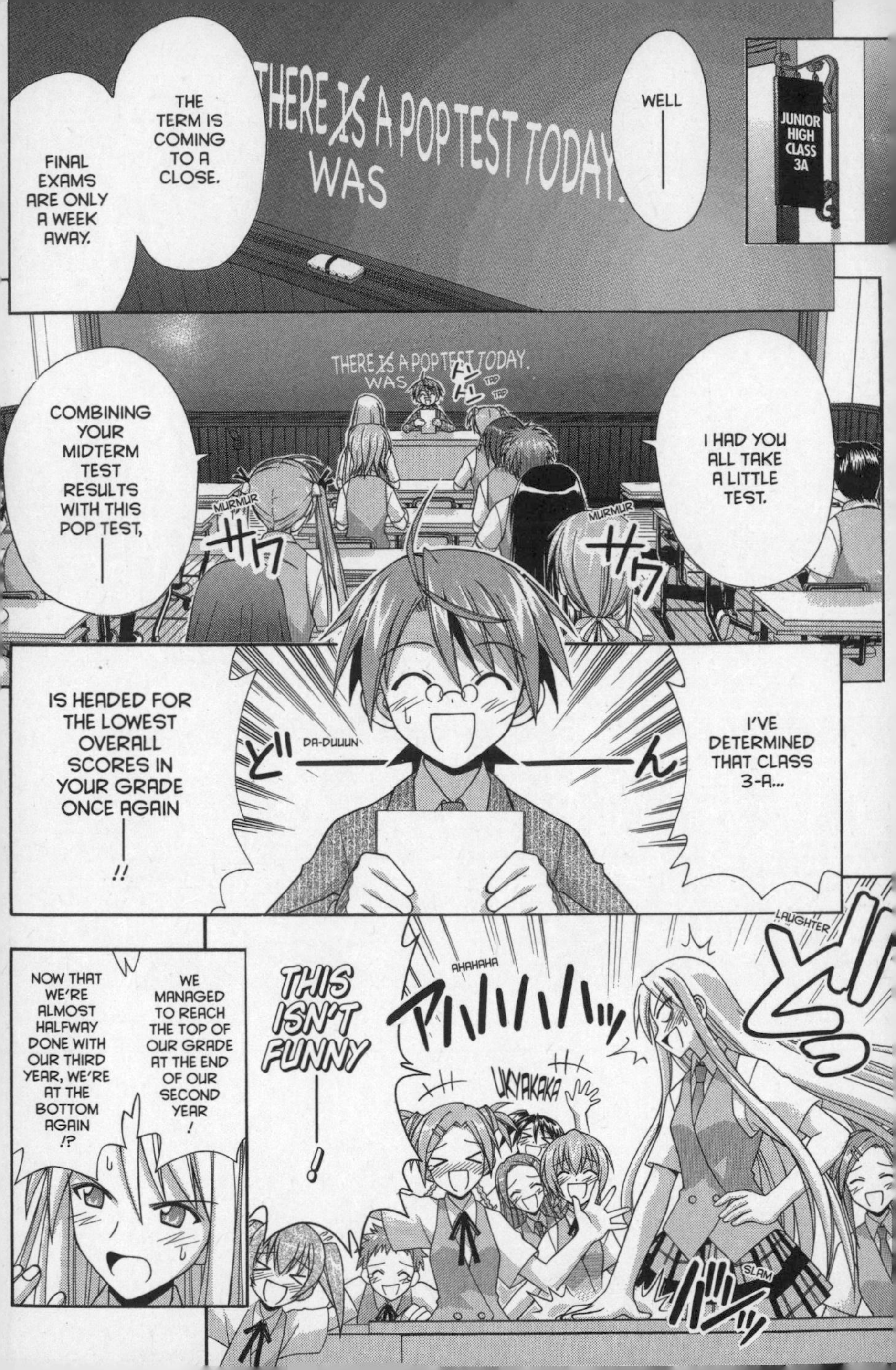

JUNIOR HIGH CLASS 3A
WELL—
THERE IS A POP TEST TODAY. WAS
THE TERM IS COMING TO A CLOSE.
FINAL EXAMS ARE ONLY A WEEK AWAY.
I HAD YOU ALL TAKE A LITTLE TEST.
THERE IS A POP TEST TODAY. WAS
TAP TAP
MURMUR
MURMUR
COMBINING YOUR MIDTERM TEST RESULTS WITH THIS POP TEST, —
I'VE DETERMINED THAT CLASS 3-A...
DA-DUUUN
IS HEADED FOR THE LOWEST OVERALL SCORES IN YOUR GRADE ONCE AGAIN — !!
LAUGHTER
AHAHAHA
UKYAKAKA
THIS ISN'T FUNNY — !
SLAM
WE MANAGED TO REACH THE TOP OF OUR GRADE AT THE END OF OUR SECOND YEAR !
NOW THAT WE'RE ALMOST HALFWAY DONE WITH OUR THIRD YEAR, WE'RE AT THE BOTTOM AGAIN !?

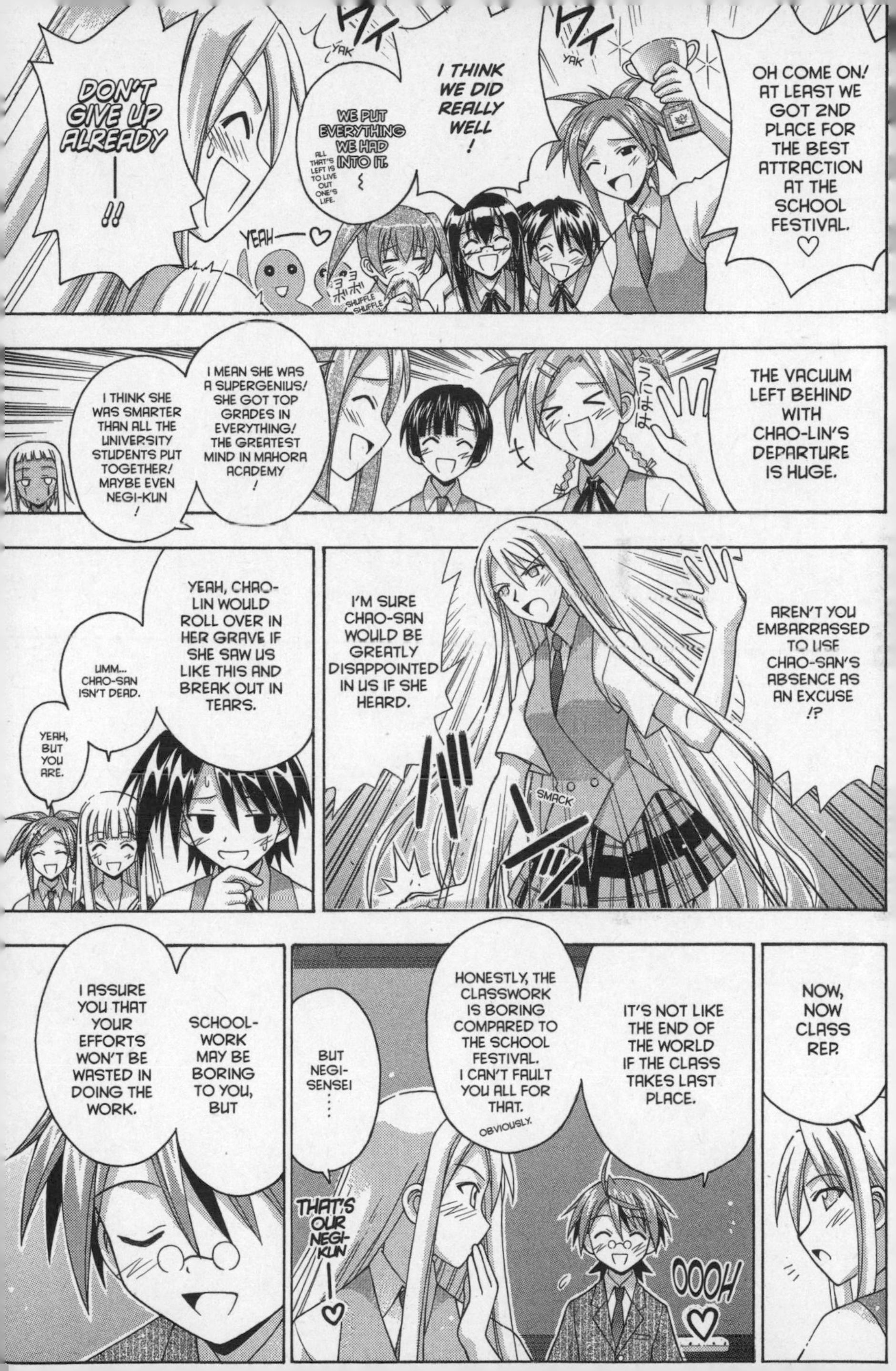
OH COME ON! AT LEAST WE GOT 2ND PLACE FOR THE BEST ATTRACTION AT THE SCHOOL FESTIVAL. ♡
YAK
I THINK WE DID REALLY WELL!
YAK
WE PUT EVERYTHING WE HAD INTO IT.
ALL THAT'S LEFT IS TO LIVE OUT ONE'S LIFE.
YEAH— ♡
SHUFFLE SHUFFLE
DON'T GIVE UP ALREADY—!!
THE VACUUM LEFT BEHIND WITH CHAO-LIN'S DEPARTURE IS HUGE.
GIGGLE
I MEAN SHE WAS A SUPERGENIUS! SHE GOT TOP GRADES IN EVERYTHING! THE GREATEST MIND IN MAHORA ACADEMY!
I THINK SHE WAS SMARTER THAN ALL THE UNIVERSITY STUDENTS PUT TOGETHER! MAYBE EVEN NEGI-KUN!
AREN'T YOU EMBARRASSED TO USE CHAO-SAN'S ABSENCE AS AN EXCUSE!?
I'M SURE CHAO-SAN WOULD BE GREATLY DISAPPOINTED IN US IF SHE HEARD.
SMACK
YEAH, CHAO-LIN WOULD ROLL OVER IN HER GRAVE IF SHE SAW US LIKE THIS AND BREAK OUT IN TEARS.
UMM... CHAO-SAN ISN'T DEAD.
YEAH, BUT YOU ARE.
NOW, NOW CLASS REP.
IT'S NOT LIKE THE END OF THE WORLD IF THE CLASS TAKES LAST PLACE.
HONESTLY, THE CLASSWORK IS BORING COMPARED TO THE SCHOOL FESTIVAL. I CAN'T FAULT YOU ALL FOR THAT.
OBVIOUSLY.
BUT NEGI-SENSEI......
THAT'S OUR NEGI-KUN—♡
OOOH ♡
SCHOOL-WORK MAY BE BORING TO YOU, BUT
I ASSURE YOU THAT YOUR EFFORTS WON'T BE WASTED IN DOING THE WORK.

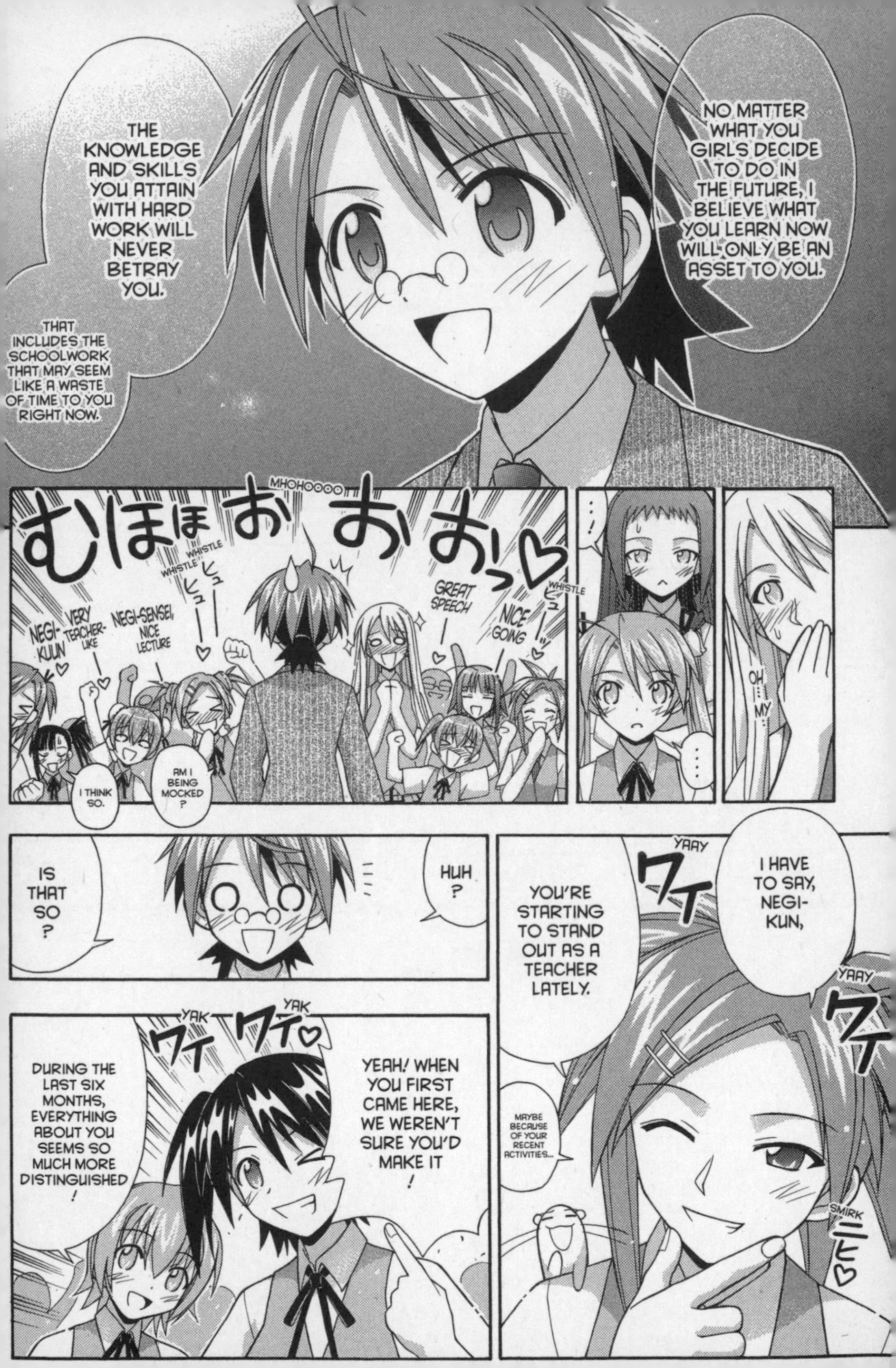
NO MATTER WHAT YOU GIRLS DECIDE TO DO IN THE FUTURE, I BELIEVE WHAT YOU LEARN NOW WILL ONLY BE AN ASSET TO YOU.
THE KNOWLEDGE AND SKILLS YOU ATTAIN WITH HARD WORK WILL NEVER BETRAY YOU.
THAT INCLUDES THE SCHOOLWORK THAT MAY SEEM LIKE A WASTE OF TIME TO YOU RIGHT NOW.
OH... MY...
...!
...
MHOHOOOO
むほほおおおっ♡
WHISTLE
ヒュー
NICE GOING
GREAT SPEECH
WHISTLE
WHISTLE
ヒュー
ヒュー
NEGI-SENSEI, NICE LECTURE
VERY TEACHER-LIKE
NEGI-KUUN ♡
AM I BEING MOCKED?
I THINK SO.
I HAVE TO SAY, NEGI-KUN,
YAAY
ワイ
YOU'RE STARTING TO STAND OUT AS A TEACHER LATELY.
YAAY
ワイ
MAYBE BECAUSE OF YOUR RECENT ACTIVITIES...
SMIRK
ニヒ♡
HUH?
IS THAT SO?
YAK
YAK
ワイワイ♡
YEAH! WHEN YOU FIRST CAME HERE, WE WEREN'T SURE YOU'D MAKE IT!
DURING THE LAST SIX MONTHS, EVERYTHING ABOUT YOU SEEMS SO MUCH MORE DISTINGUISHED!

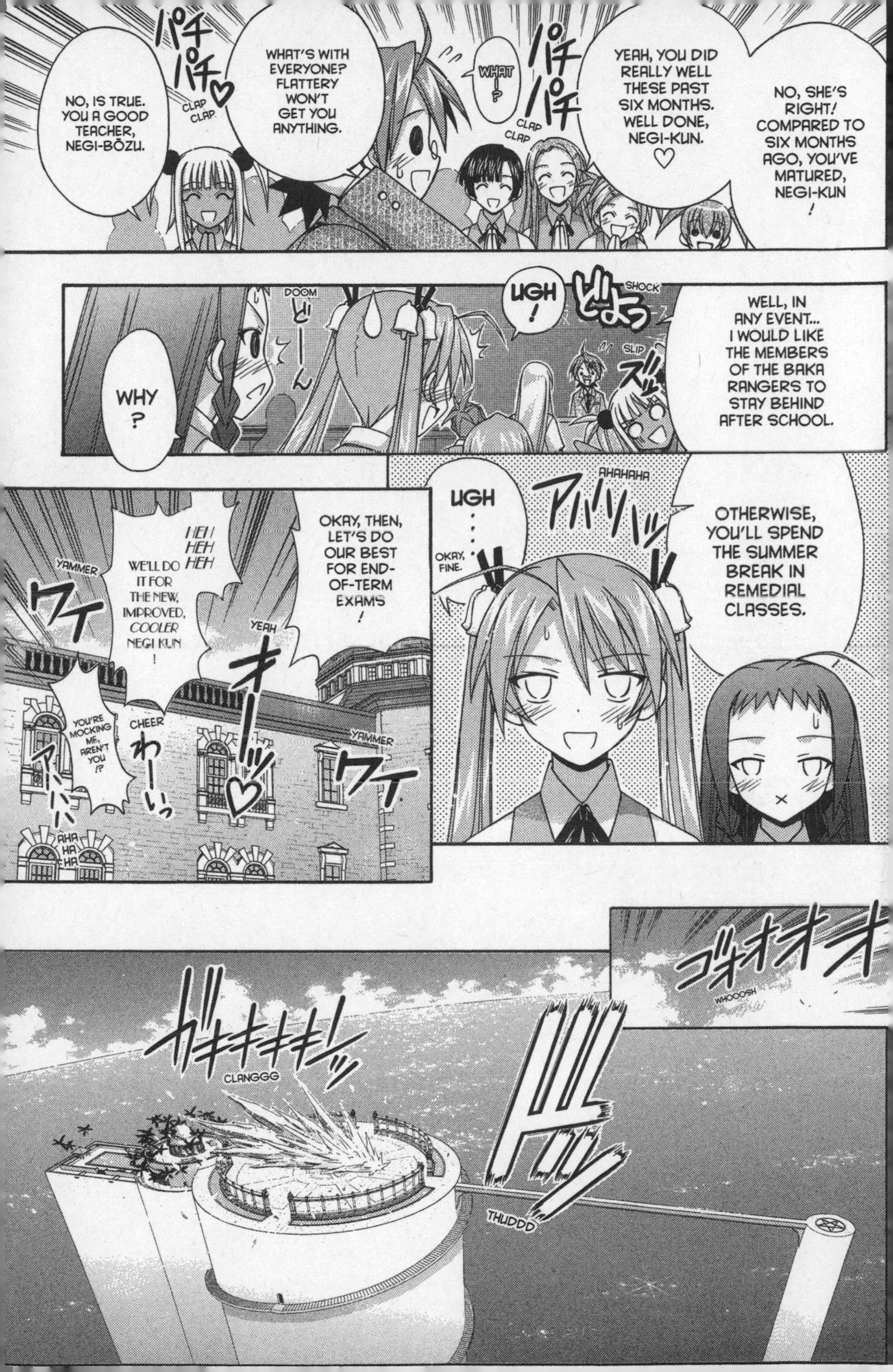
NO, SHE'S RIGHT! COMPARED TO SIX MONTHS AGO, YOU'VE MATURED, NEGI-KUN!
YEAH, YOU DID REALLY WELL THESE PAST SIX MONTHS. WELL DONE, NEGI-KUN. ♡
CLAP CLAP
WHAT!?
WHAT'S WITH EVERYONE? FLATTERY WON'T GET YOU ANYTHING.
CLAP CLAP
NO, IS TRUE. YOU A GOOD TEACHER, NEGI-BŌZU.
WELL, IN ANY EVENT... I WOULD LIKE THE MEMBERS OF THE BAKA RANGERS TO STAY BEHIND AFTER SCHOOL.
SHOCK
SLIP
UGH!
DOOM
WHY?
OTHERWISE, YOU'LL SPEND THE SUMMER BREAK IN REMEDIAL CLASSES.
AHAHAHA
UGH...
OKAY, FINE.
OKAY, THEN, LET'S DO OUR BEST FOR END-OF-TERM EXAMS!
HEH HEH HEH
WE'LL DO IT FOR THE NEW, IMPROVED, COOLER NEGI-KUN!
YEAH
YAMMER
YAMMER
CHEER
YOU'RE MOCKING ME, AREN'T YOU!?
AHA HA HA
WHOOOSH
THUDDD
CLANGGG

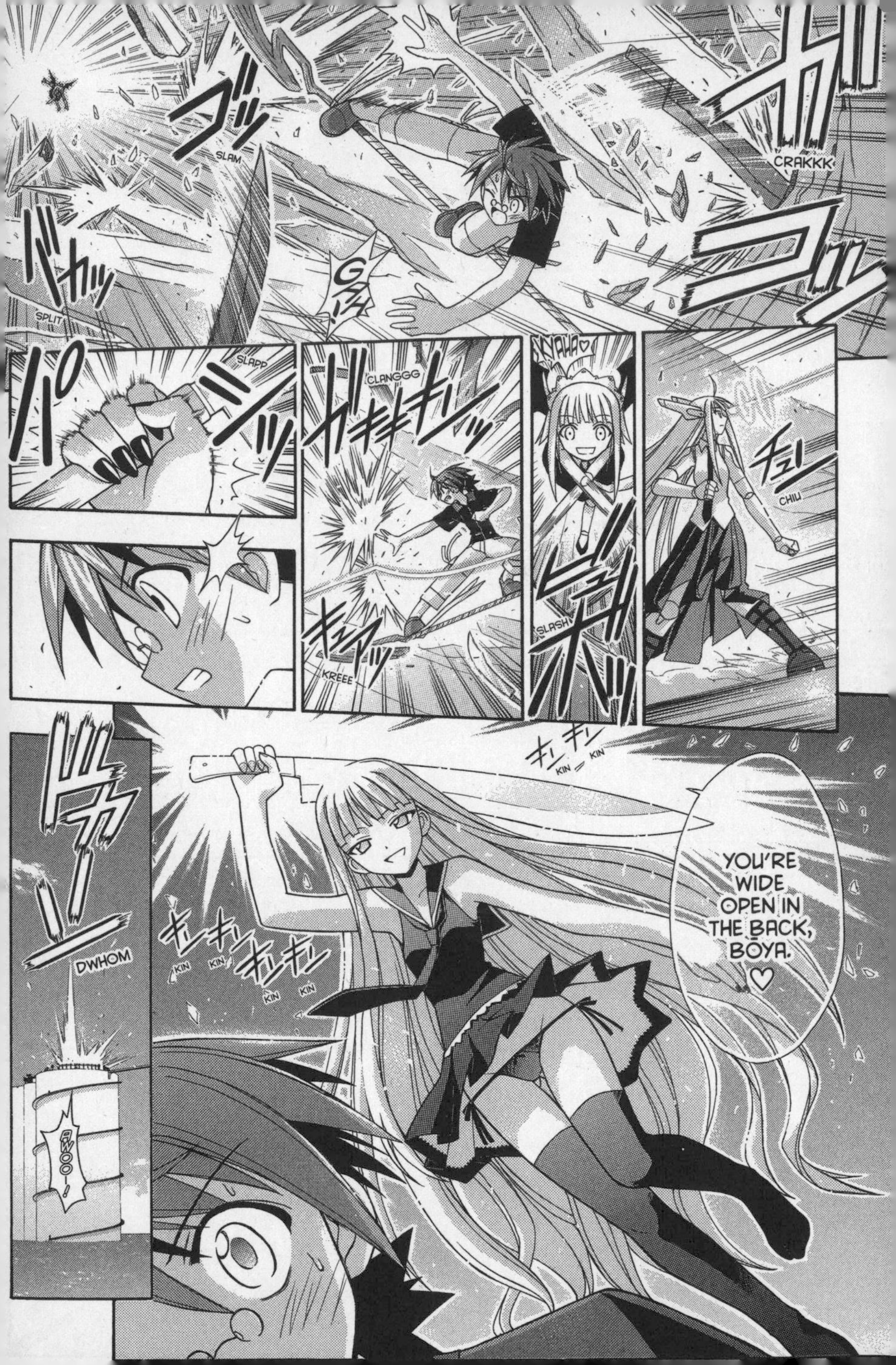
CRAKKK
SLAM
GAH!
SPLIT
CHIU
KYAHA♥
SLASH
CLANGGG
KREEE
SLAPP
KIN KIN
YOU'RE WIDE OPEN IN THE BACK, BŌYA. ♥
DWHOM
KIN KIN KIN KIN
AWOO!

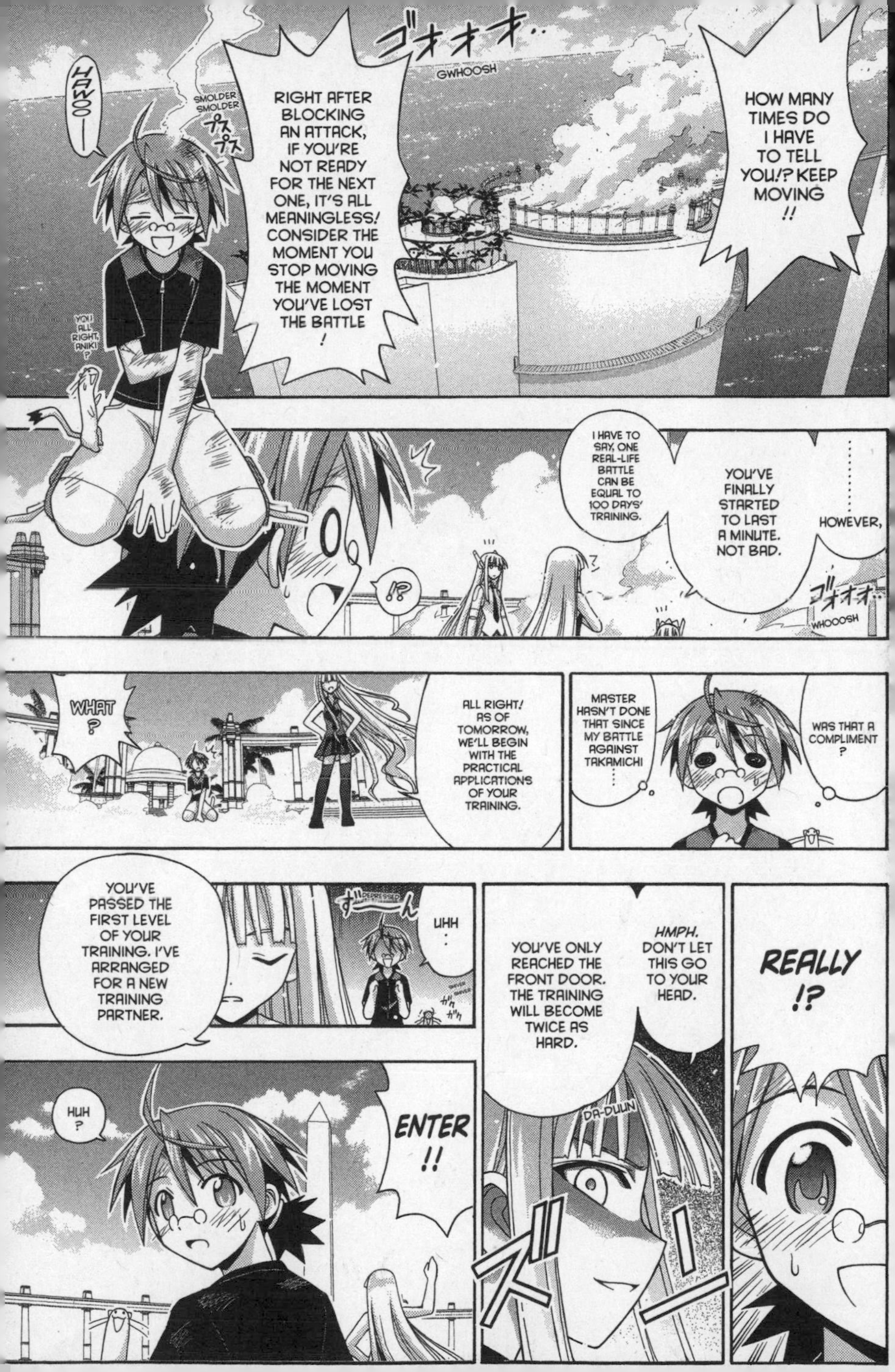
HOW MANY TIMES DO I HAVE TO TELL YOU!? KEEP MOVING !!
ゴオオオ..
GWHOOSH
RIGHT AFTER BLOCKING AN ATTACK, IF YOU'RE NOT READY FOR THE NEXT ONE, IT'S ALL MEANINGLESS! CONSIDER THE MOMENT YOU STOP MOVING THE MOMENT YOU'VE LOST THE BATTLE !
SMOLDER SMOLDER
プスプス
HAWOO—
YOU ALL RIGHT, ANIKI ?
......
HOWEVER,
YOU'VE FINALLY STARTED TO LAST A MINUTE. NOT BAD.
I HAVE TO SAY, ONE REAL-LIFE BATTLE CAN BE EQUAL TO 100 DAYS' TRAINING.
ゴオオオ..
WHOOOSH
!?
WAS THAT A COMPLIMENT ?
MASTER HASN'T DONE THAT SINCE MY BATTLE AGAINST TAKAMICHI ...
ALL RIGHT! AS OF TOMORROW, WE'LL BEGIN WITH THE PRACTICAL APPLICATIONS OF YOUR TRAINING.
WHAT ?
REALLY !?
HMPH. DON'T LET THIS GO TO YOUR HEAD.
YOU'VE ONLY REACHED THE FRONT DOOR. THE TRAINING WILL BECOME TWICE AS HARD.
ずーん
DEPRESSED
UHH ..
ガクガク
YOU'VE PASSED THE FIRST LEVEL OF YOUR TRAINING. I'VE ARRANGED FOR A NEW TRAINING PARTNER.
DA-DUUN
ズー
ENTER !!
HUH ?

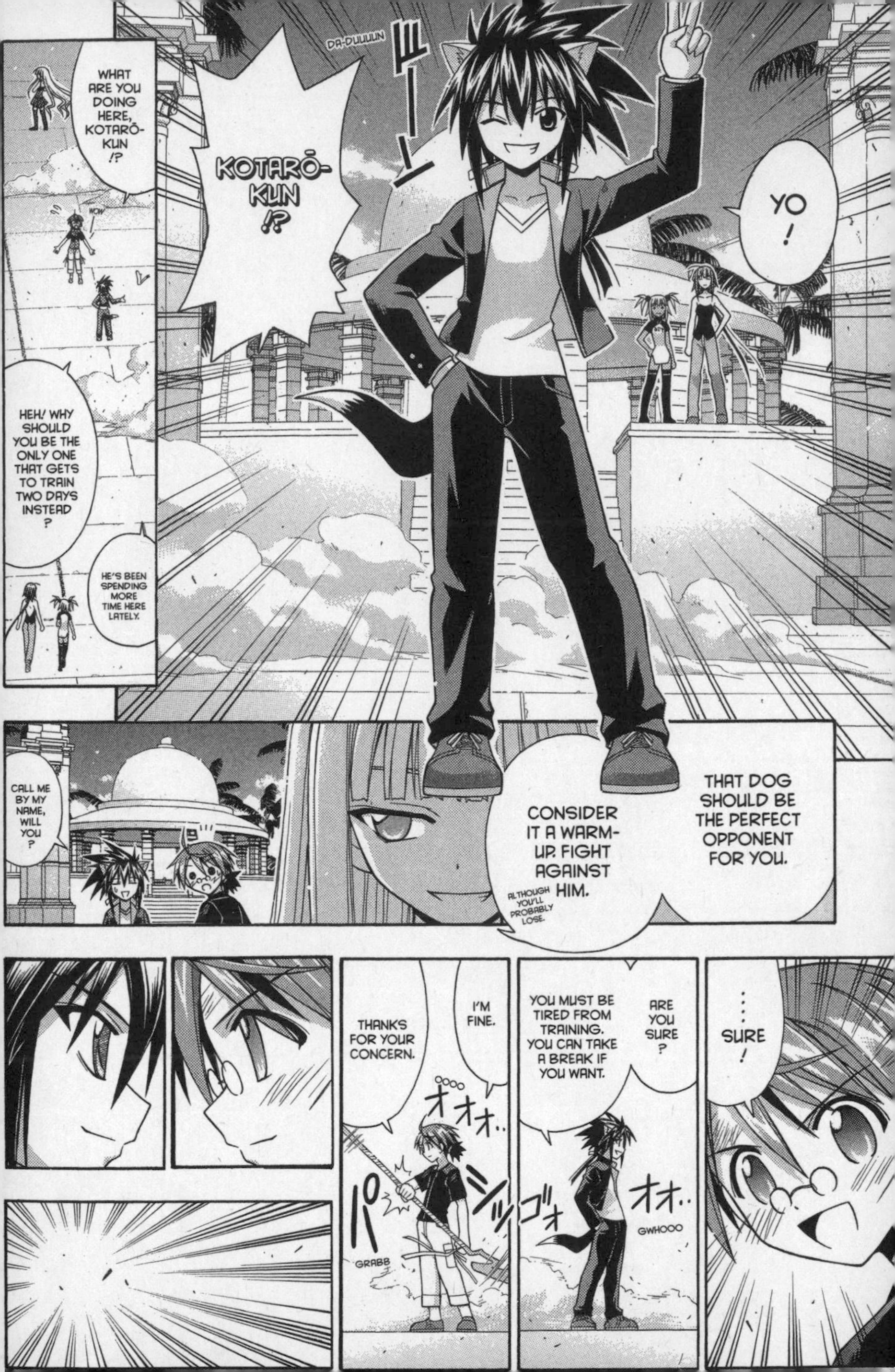
YO!
DA-DUUUUN
KOTARŌ-KUN!?
WHAT ARE YOU DOING HERE, KOTARŌ-KUN!?
WOW
HEH! WHY SHOULD YOU BE THE ONLY ONE THAT GETS TO TRAIN TWO DAYS INSTEAD?
HE'S BEEN SPENDING MORE TIME HERE LATELY.
THAT DOG SHOULD BE THE PERFECT OPPONENT FOR YOU.
CONSIDER IT A WARM-UP. FIGHT AGAINST HIM.
ALTHOUGH YOU'LL PROBABLY LOSE.
CALL ME BY MY NAME, WILL YOU?
...SURE!
ARE YOU SURE?
YOU MUST BE TIRED FROM TRAINING. YOU CAN TAKE A BREAK IF YOU WANT.
ゴォ オオ..
GWHOOO
I'M FINE.
THANKS FOR YOUR CONCERN.
オオオ..
OOOO
パシッ
GRABB

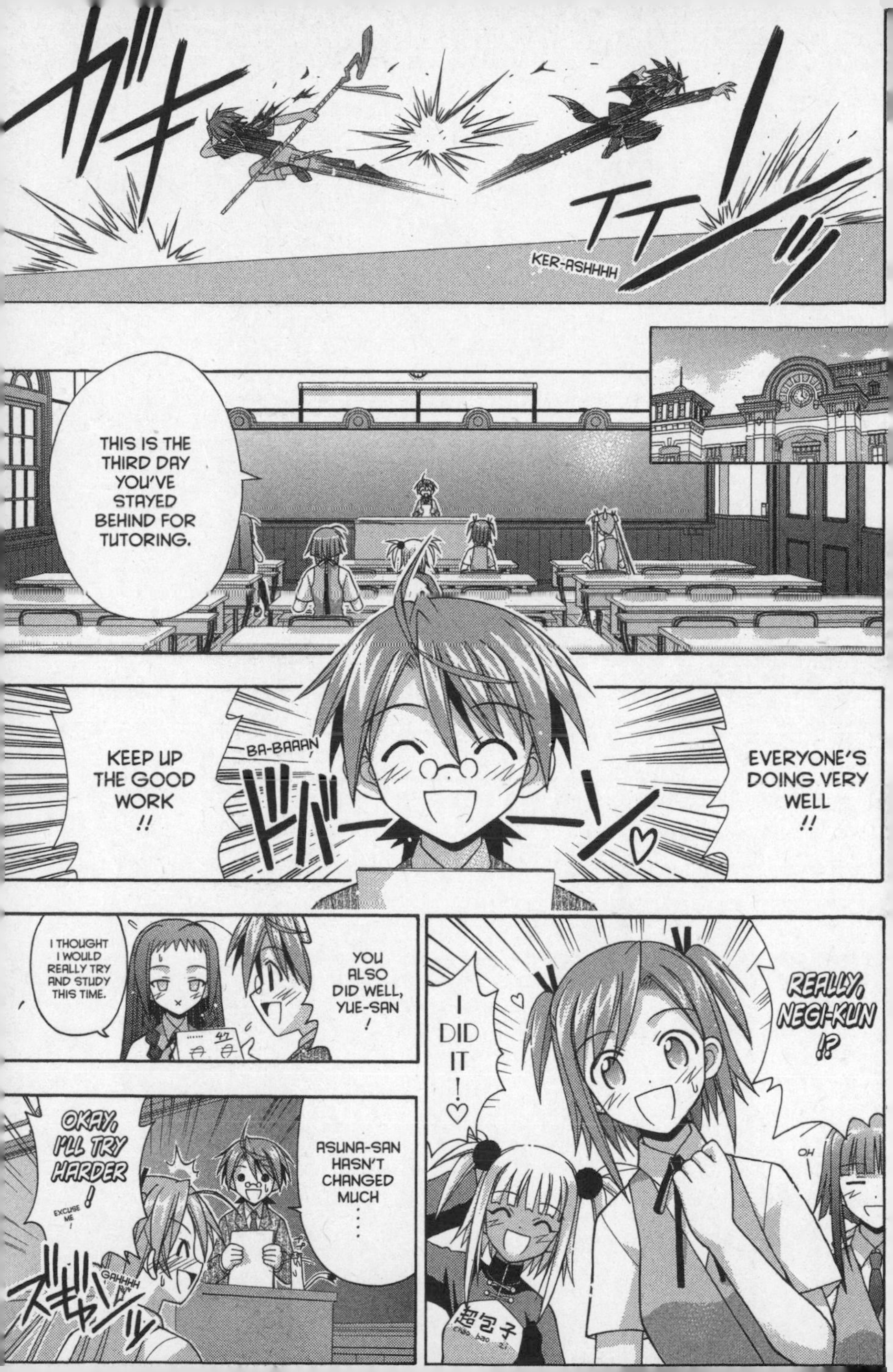
KER-ASHHHH
THIS IS THE THIRD DAY YOU'VE STAYED BEHIND FOR TUTORING.
EVERYONE'S DOING VERY WELL !!
BA-BAAAN
KEEP UP THE GOOD WORK !!
REALLY, NEGI-KUN !?
I DID IT !
OH
超包子
Chao bao zi
YOU ALSO DID WELL, YUE-SAN !
I THOUGHT I WOULD REALLY TRY AND STUDY THIS TIME.
ASUNA-SAN HASN'T CHANGED MUCH ....
OKAY, I'LL TRY HARDER !
EXCUSE ME !
GAHHHH

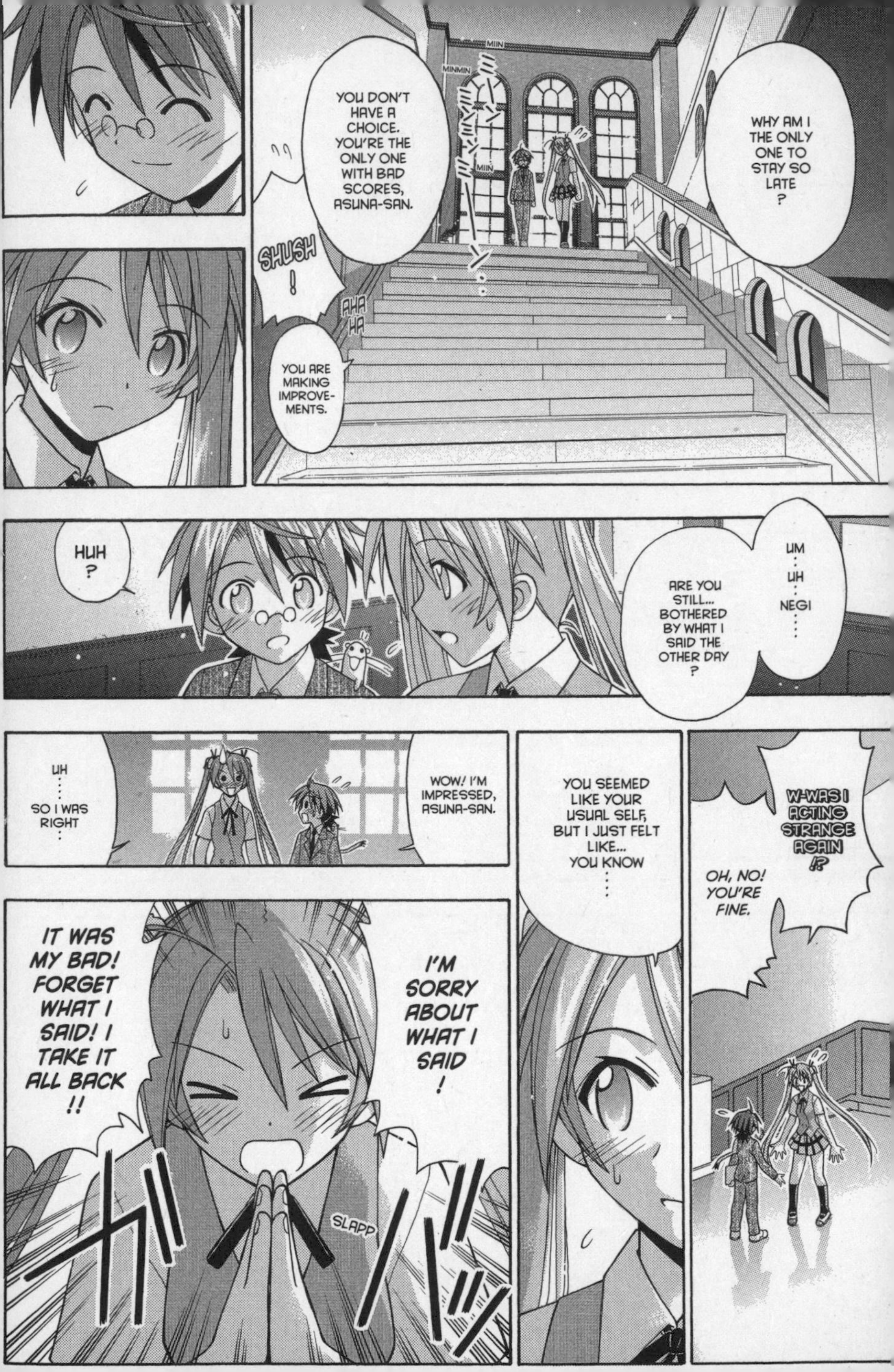
WHY AM I THE ONLY ONE TO STAY SO LATE?
MIIN
MINMIN
MIIN
YOU DON'T HAVE A CHOICE. YOU'RE THE ONLY ONE WITH BAD SCORES, ASUNA-SAN.
SHUSH!
AHA HA
YOU ARE MAKING IMPROVE-MENTS.
UM... UH... NEGI...
ARE YOU STILL... BOTHERED BY WHAT I SAID THE OTHER DAY?
HUH?
W-WAS I ACTING STRANGE AGAIN!?
OH, NO! YOU'RE FINE.
YOU SEEMED LIKE YOUR USUAL SELF, BUT I JUST FELT LIKE... YOU KNOW...
WOW! I'M IMPRESSED, ASUNA-SAN.
UH... SO I WAS RIGHT...
I'M SORRY ABOUT WHAT I SAID!
IT WAS MY BAD! FORGET WHAT I SAID! I TAKE IT ALL BACK!!
SLAPP

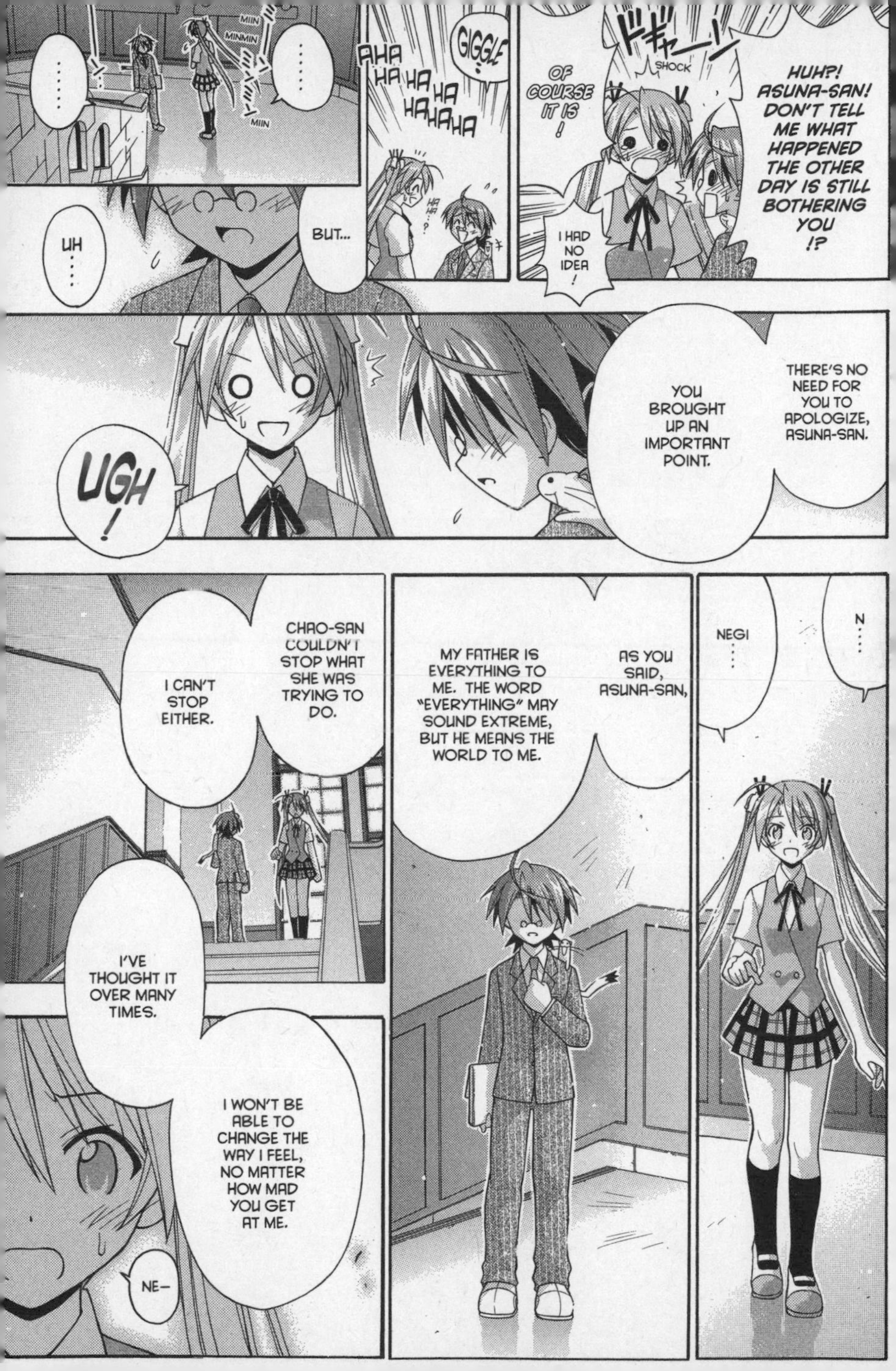
ドギャーン!
SHOCK
HUH?! ASUNA-SAN! DON'T TELL ME WHAT HAPPENED THE OTHER DAY IS STILL BOTHERING YOU !?
OF COURSE IT IS !
I HAD NO IDEA !
GIGGLE
AHA HA HA HA HAHAHA
HA HA...?
......
MIIN MINMIN
MIIN
......
BUT...
UH......
THERE'S NO NEED FOR YOU TO APOLOGIZE, ASUNA-SAN.
YOU BROUGHT UP AN IMPORTANT POINT.
UGH !
N......
NEGI......
AS YOU SAID, ASUNA-SAN,
MY FATHER IS EVERYTHING TO ME. THE WORD "EVERYTHING" MAY SOUND EXTREME, BUT HE MEANS THE WORLD TO ME.
CHAO-SAN COULDN'T STOP WHAT SHE WAS TRYING TO DO.
I CAN'T STOP EITHER.
I'VE THOUGHT IT OVER MANY TIMES.
I WON'T BE ABLE TO CHANGE THE WAY I FEEL, NO MATTER HOW MAD YOU GET AT ME.
NE–

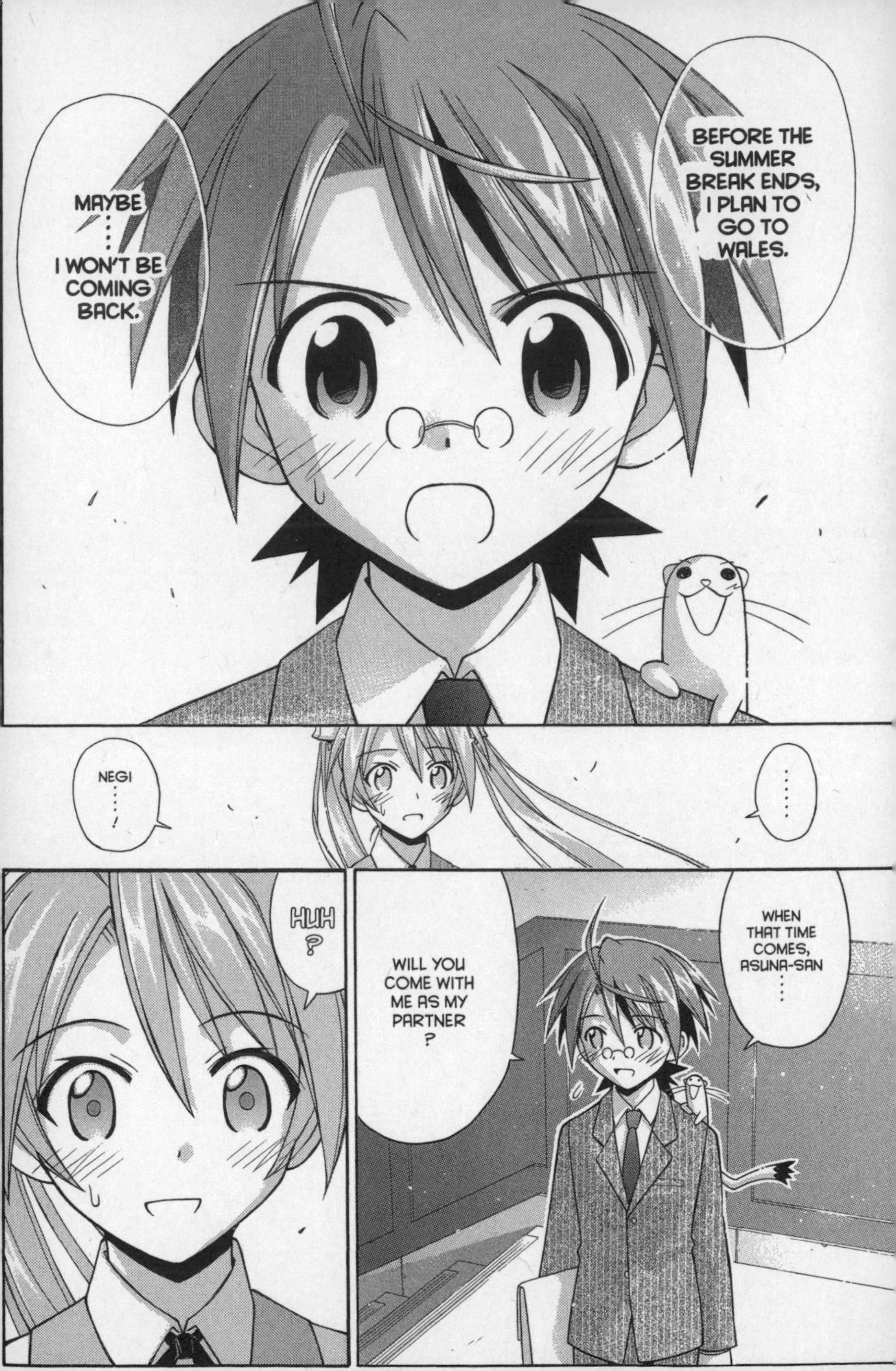
BEFORE THE SUMMER BREAK ENDS, I PLAN TO GO TO WALES.
MAYBE... I WON'T BE COMING BACK.
......
NEGI......!
WHEN THAT TIME COMES, ASUNA-SAN...
WILL YOU COME WITH ME AS MY PARTNER?
HUH?

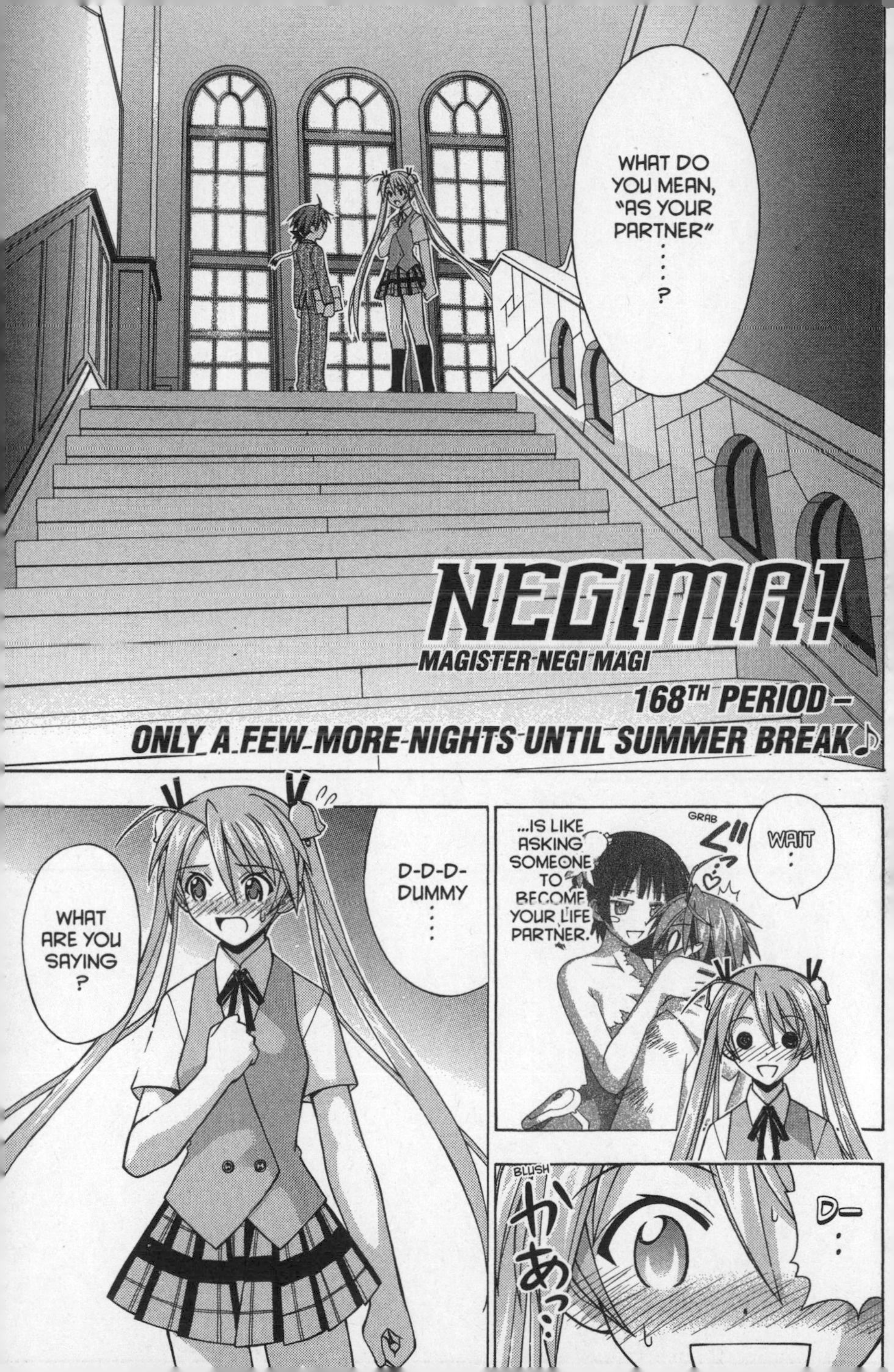
WHAT DO YOU MEAN, "AS YOUR PARTNER" ....?
NEGIMA!
MAGISTER NEGI MAGI
168TH PERIOD – ONLY A FEW MORE NIGHTS UNTIL SUMMER BREAK♪
WAIT ..
GRAB
...IS LIKE ASKING SOMEONE TO BECOME YOUR LIFE PARTNER.
BLUSH
D– ..
D-D-D-DUMMY ....
WHAT ARE YOU SAYING ?

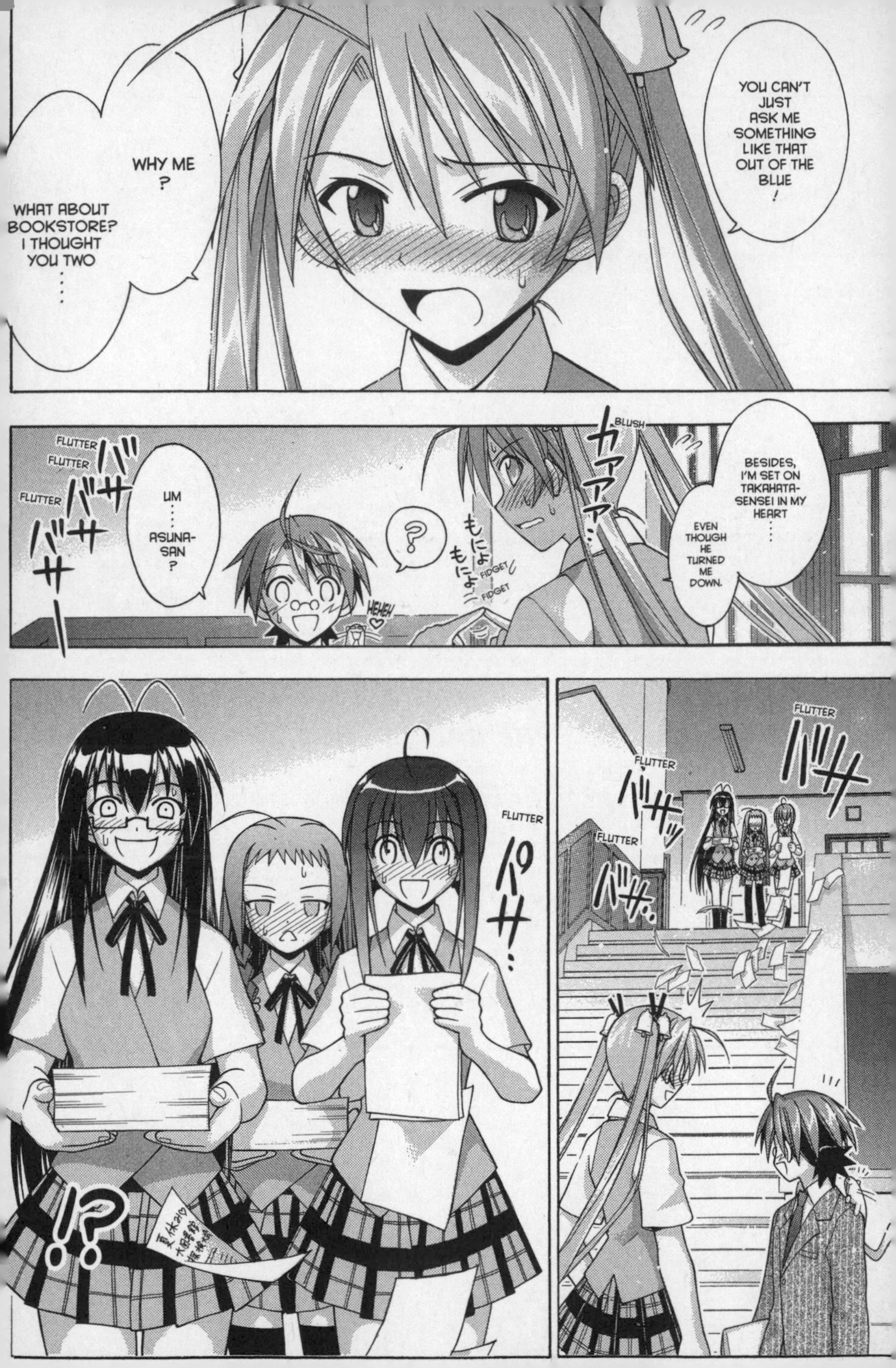
YOU CAN'T JUST ASK ME SOMETHING LIKE THAT OUT OF THE BLUE!
WHY ME?
WHAT ABOUT BOOKSTORE? I THOUGHT YOU TWO......
カァァァ...
BLUSH
BESIDES, I'M SET ON TAKAHATA-SENSEI IN MY HEART...
EVEN THOUGH HE TURNED ME DOWN.
もにょもにょ
FIDGET FIDGET
?
HEHEH
UM... ASUNA-SAN?
バサバサバサー
FLUTTER FLUTTER FLUTTER
バサ
FLUTTER
バサッ
FLUTTER
バサ。
FLUTTER
パサ!
FLUTTER
!?

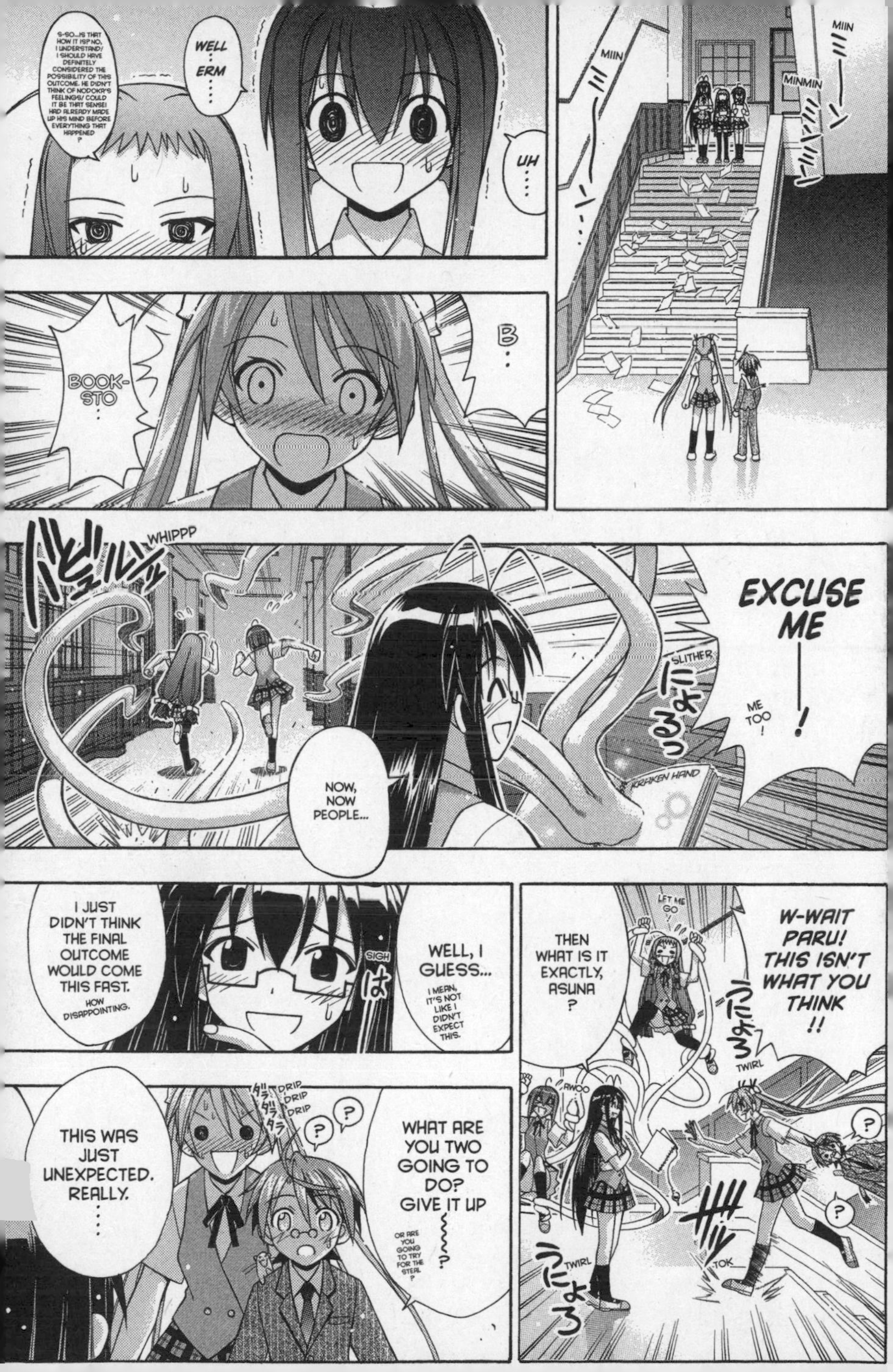
MIIN
MIIN
MINMIN
UH....
WELL...ERM.....
S-SO...IS THAT HOW IT IS? NO, I UNDERSTAND/ I SHOULD HAVE DEFINITELY CONSIDERED THE POSSIBILITY OF THIS OUTCOME. HE DIDN'T THINK OF NODOKA'S FEELINGS/ COULD IT BE THAT SENSEI HAD ALREADY MADE UP HIS MIND BEFORE EVERYTHING THAT HAPPENED ?
B..
BOOK-STO...
EXCUSE ME—!
ME TOO!
SLITHER
KRAKEN HAND
NOW, NOW PEOPLE...
WHIPPP
W-WAIT PARU! THIS ISN'T WHAT YOU THINK!!
TWIRL
LET ME GO!
THEN WHAT IS IT EXACTLY, ASUNA?
?
?
AWOO
TOK
TWIRL
WELL, I GUESS...
I MEAN, IT'S NOT LIKE I DIDN'T EXPECT THIS.
SIGH
I JUST DIDN'T THINK THE FINAL OUTCOME WOULD COME THIS FAST.
HOW DISAPPOINTING.
WHAT ARE YOU TWO GOING TO DO? GIVE IT UP~~?
OR ARE YOU GOING TO TRY FOR THE STEAL ?
? ?
DRIP DRIP DRIP
THIS WAS JUST UNEXPECTED. REALLY. ....

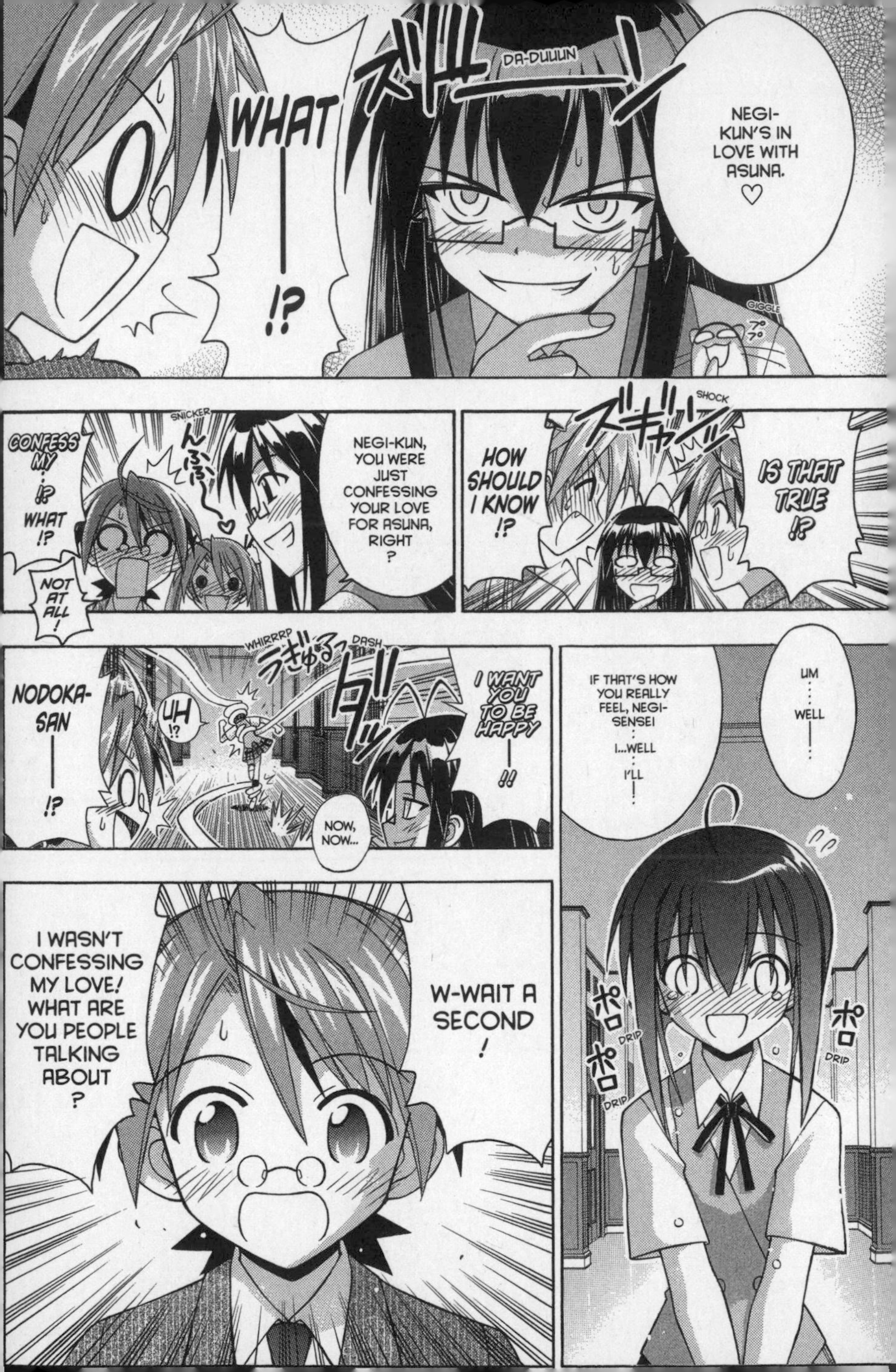
NEGI-KUN'S IN LOVE WITH ASUNA. ♡
DA-DUUUN
WHAT —!?
GIGGLE
SHOCK
IS THAT TRUE !?
HOW SHOULD I KNOW !?
NEGI-KUN, YOU WERE JUST CONFESSING YOUR LOVE FOR ASUNA, RIGHT ?
SNICKER
CONFESS MY ... !? WHAT !?
NOT AT ALL !
UM ... WELL — ...
IF THAT'S HOW YOU REALLY FEEL, NEGI-SENSEI ... I...WELL ... I'LL —
DRIP
DRIP
DRIP
I WANT YOU TO BE HAPPY — !!
DASH
WHIRRRP
UH !?
NODOKA-SAN — !?
NOW, NOW...
W-WAIT A SECOND !
I WASN'T CONFESSING MY LOVE! WHAT ARE YOU PEOPLE TALKING ABOUT ?

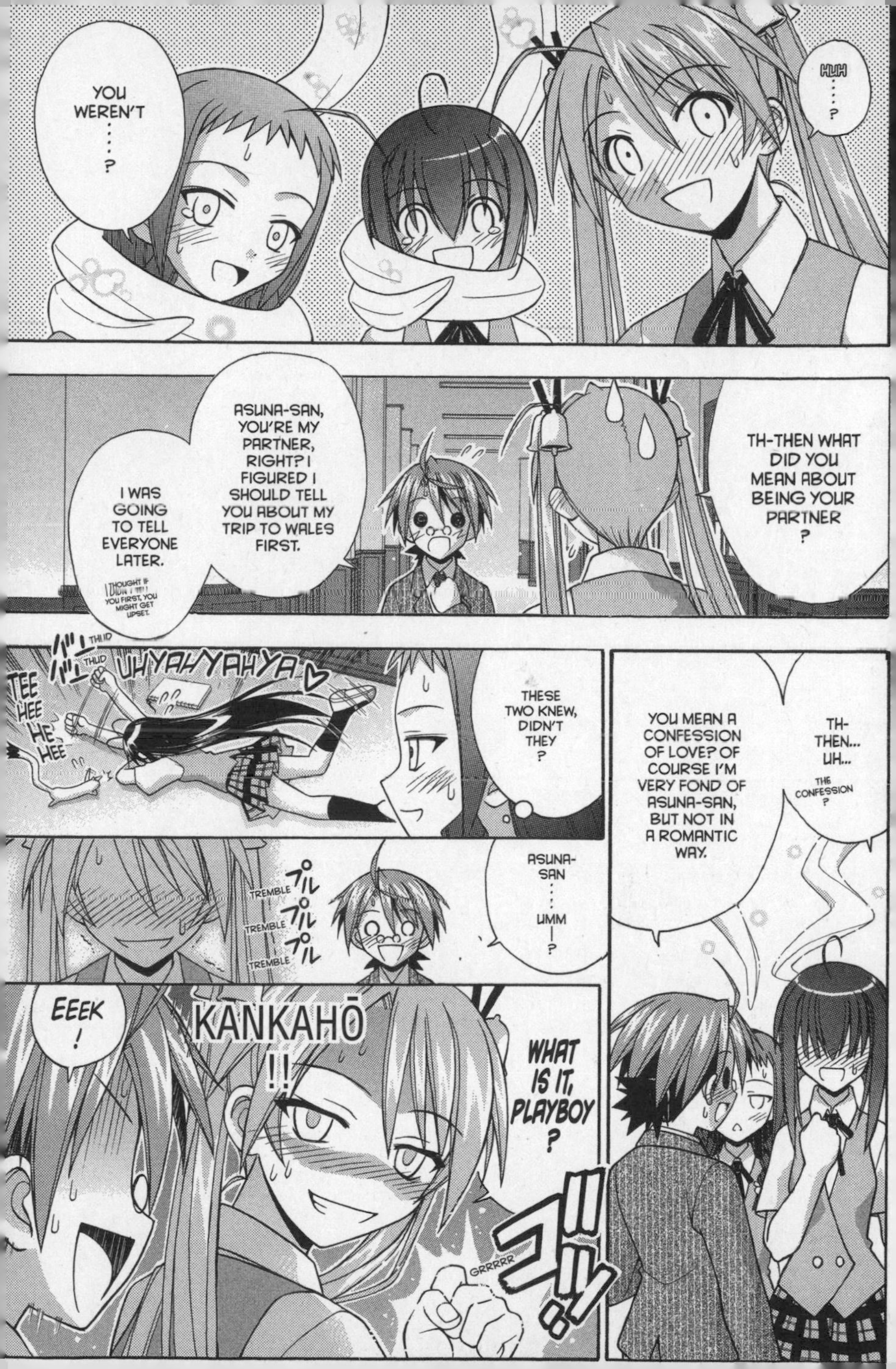
HUH . . . ?
YOU WEREN'T . . . ?
TH-THEN WHAT DID YOU MEAN ABOUT BEING YOUR PARTNER?
ASUNA-SAN, YOU'RE MY PARTNER, RIGHT? I FIGURED I SHOULD TELL YOU ABOUT MY TRIP TO WALES FIRST.
I WAS GOING TO TELL EVERYONE LATER.
I THOUGHT IF I DIDN'T YOU FIRST, YOU MIGHT GET UPSET.
TH- THEN... UH...
THE CONFESSION?
YOU MEAN A CONFESSION OF LOVE? OF COURSE I'M VERY FOND OF ASUNA-SAN, BUT NOT IN A ROMANTIC WAY.
THESE TWO KNEW, DIDN'T THEY?
UHYAHYAHYA♥
THUD
THUD
TEE HEE HEE HEE
ASUNA-SAN . . . UMM—?
TREMBLE
TREMBLE
TREMBLE
WHAT IS IT, PLAYBOY?
KANKAHŌ!!
EEEK!
GRRRRR

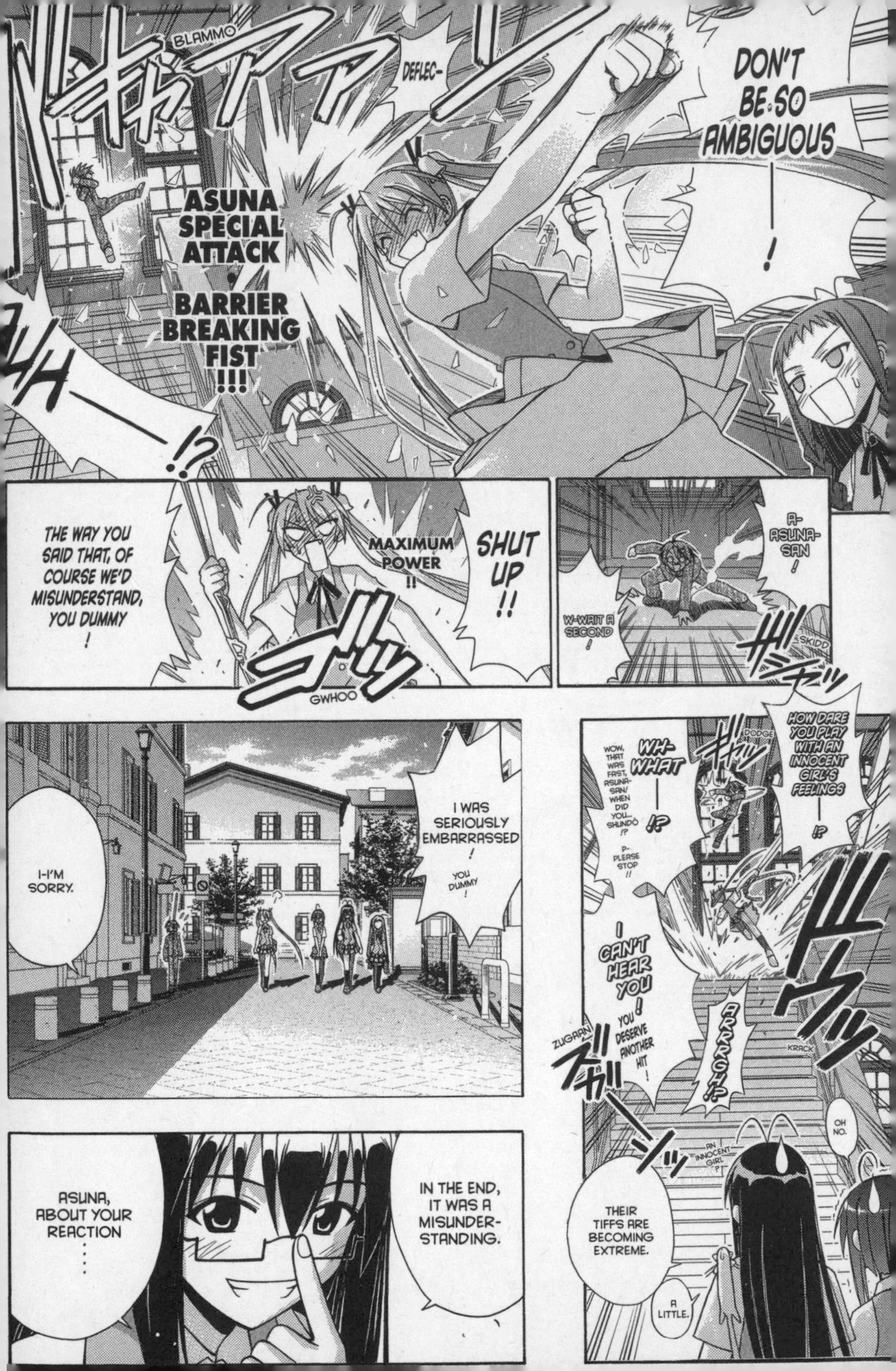
DON'T BE SO AMBIGUOUS —!
BLAMMO
DEFLEC-
ASUNA SPECIAL ATTACK • BARRIER BREAKING FIST!!!
!?
A-ASUNA-SAN!
W-WAIT A SECOND!
SKIDD
SHUT UP!!
MAXIMUM POWER!!
THE WAY YOU SAID THAT, OF COURSE WE'D MISUNDERSTAND, YOU DUMMY!
GWHOO
HOW DARE YOU PLAY WITH AN INNOCENT GIRL'S FEELINGS —!?
DODGE
WH-WHAT —!?
WOW, THAT WAS FAST, ASUNA-SAN! WHEN DID YOU... SHUNDŌ!?
P-PLEASE STOP!!
KRACK
I CAN'T HEAR YOU!
YOU DESERVE ANOTHER HIT!
ARRRGH!?
ZUGAAN
OH NO.
AN INNOCENT GIRL?
THEIR TIFFS ARE BECOMING EXTREME.
A LITTLE.
I WAS SERIOUSLY EMBARRASSED!
YOU DUMMY!
I-I'M SORRY.
IN THE END, IT WAS A MISUNDERSTANDING.
ASUNA, ABOUT YOUR REACTION....

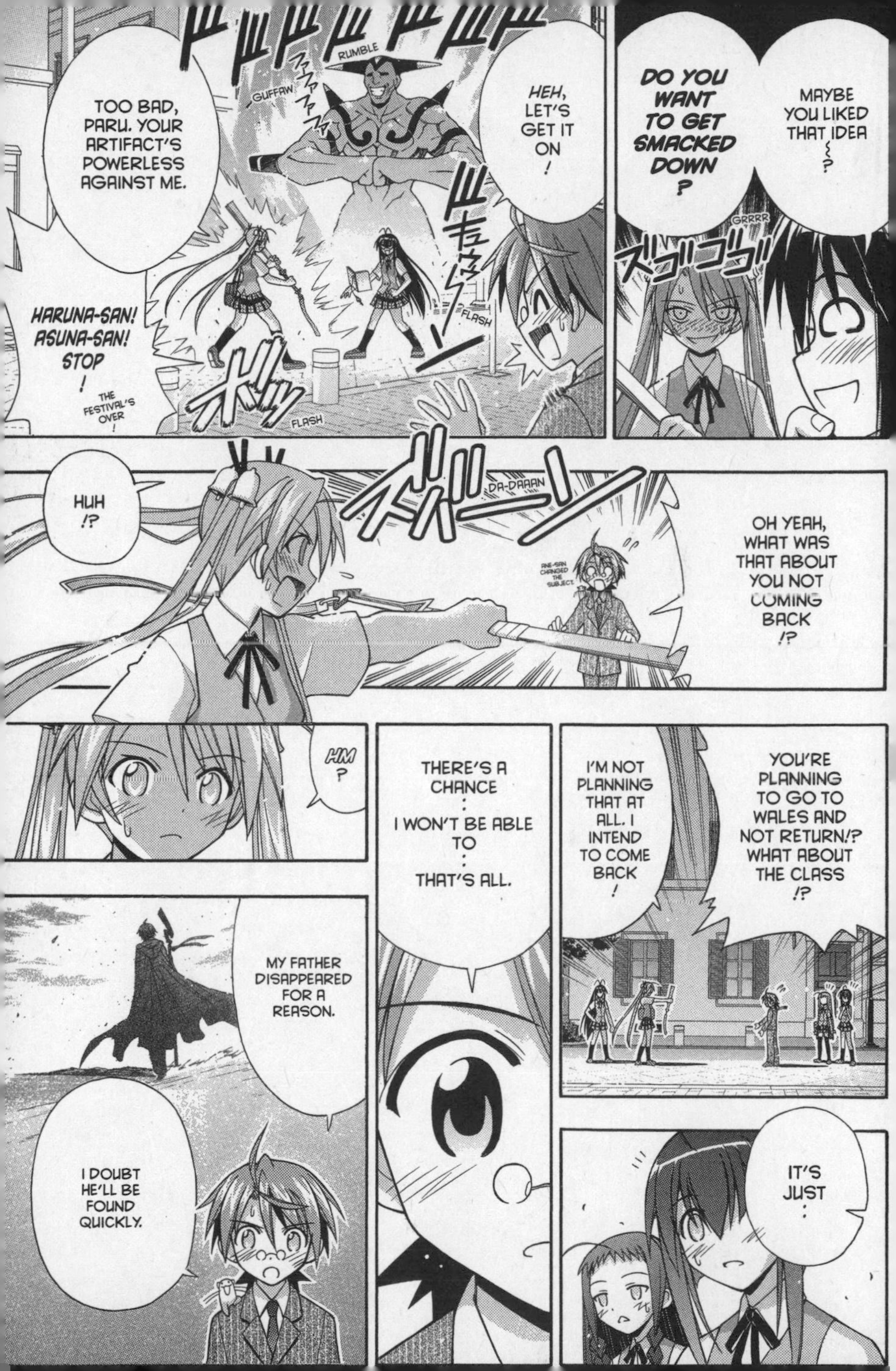
MAYBE YOU LIKED THAT IDEA ~?
DO YOU WANT TO GET SMACKED DOWN?
GRRRR
HEH, LET'S GET IT ON!
RUMBLE
GUFFAW
TOO BAD, PARU. YOUR ARTIFACT'S POWERLESS AGAINST ME.
FLASH
HARUNA-SAN! ASUNA-SAN! STOP!
THE FESTIVAL'S OVER!
FLASH
OH YEAH, WHAT WAS THAT ABOUT YOU NOT COMING BACK!?
DA-DAAAN
ANE-SAN CHANGED THE SUBJECT.
HUH!?
YOU'RE PLANNING TO GO TO WALES AND NOT RETURN!? WHAT ABOUT THE CLASS!?
I'M NOT PLANNING THAT AT ALL. I INTEND TO COME BACK!
IT'S JUST...
THERE'S A CHANCE... I WON'T BE ABLE TO... THAT'S ALL.
HM?
MY FATHER DISAPPEARED FOR A REASON.
I DOUBT HE'LL BE FOUND QUICKLY.

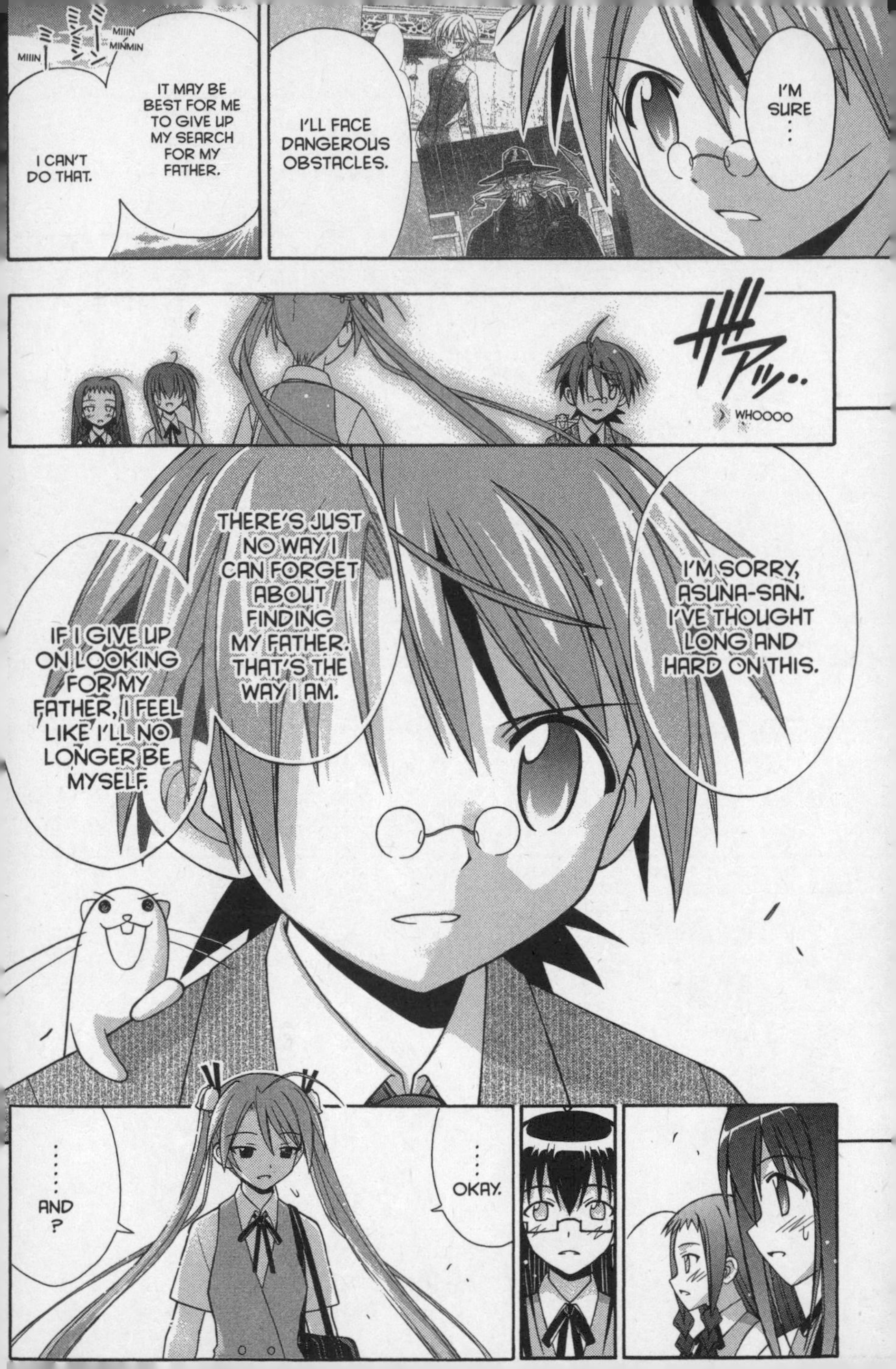

I'M SURE . . .
I'LL FACE DANGEROUS OBSTACLES.
IT MAY BE BEST FOR ME TO GIVE UP MY SEARCH FOR MY FATHER.
MIIIN MINMIN
MIIIN
I CAN'T DO THAT.
ザアッ..
WHOOOO
I'M SORRY, ASUNA-SAN. I'VE THOUGHT LONG AND HARD ON THIS.
THERE'S JUST NO WAY I CAN FORGET ABOUT FINDING MY FATHER. THAT'S THE WAY I AM.
IF I GIVE UP ON LOOKING FOR MY FATHER, I FEEL LIKE I'LL NO LONGER BE MYSELF.
. . . OKAY.
. . . . . . AND ?

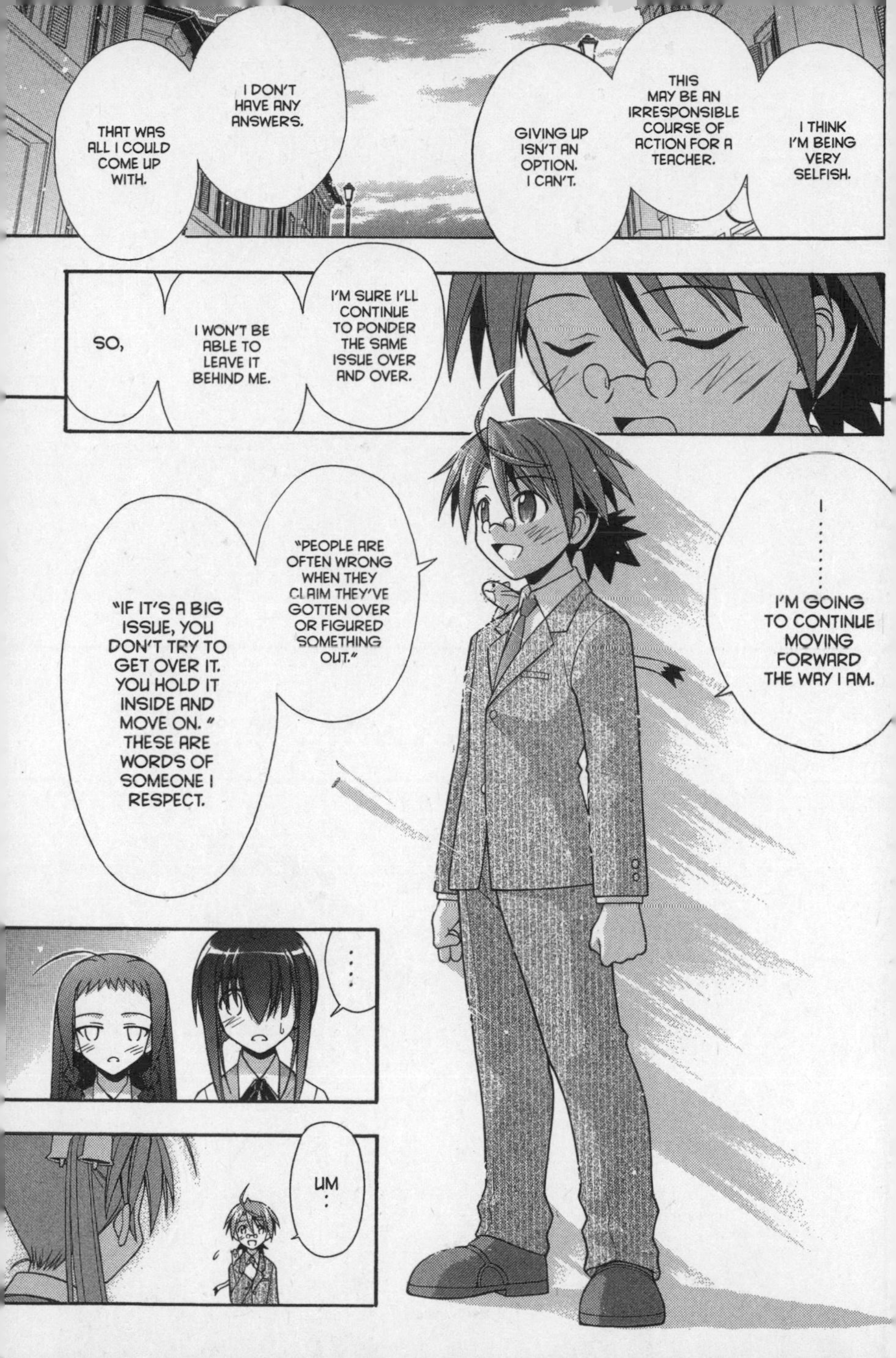
I THINK I'M BEING VERY SELFISH.
THIS MAY BE AN IRRESPONSIBLE COURSE OF ACTION FOR A TEACHER.
GIVING UP ISN'T AN OPTION. I CAN'T.
I DON'T HAVE ANY ANSWERS.
THAT WAS ALL I COULD COME UP WITH.
I'M SURE I'LL CONTINUE TO PONDER THE SAME ISSUE OVER AND OVER.
I WON'T BE ABLE TO LEAVE IT BEHIND ME.
SO,
I ...... I'M GOING TO CONTINUE MOVING FORWARD THE WAY I AM.
"PEOPLE ARE OFTEN WRONG WHEN THEY CLAIM THEY'VE GOTTEN OVER OR FIGURED SOMETHING OUT."
"IF IT'S A BIG ISSUE, YOU DON'T TRY TO GET OVER IT. YOU HOLD IT INSIDE AND MOVE ON." THESE ARE WORDS OF SOMEONE I RESPECT.
....
UM ..

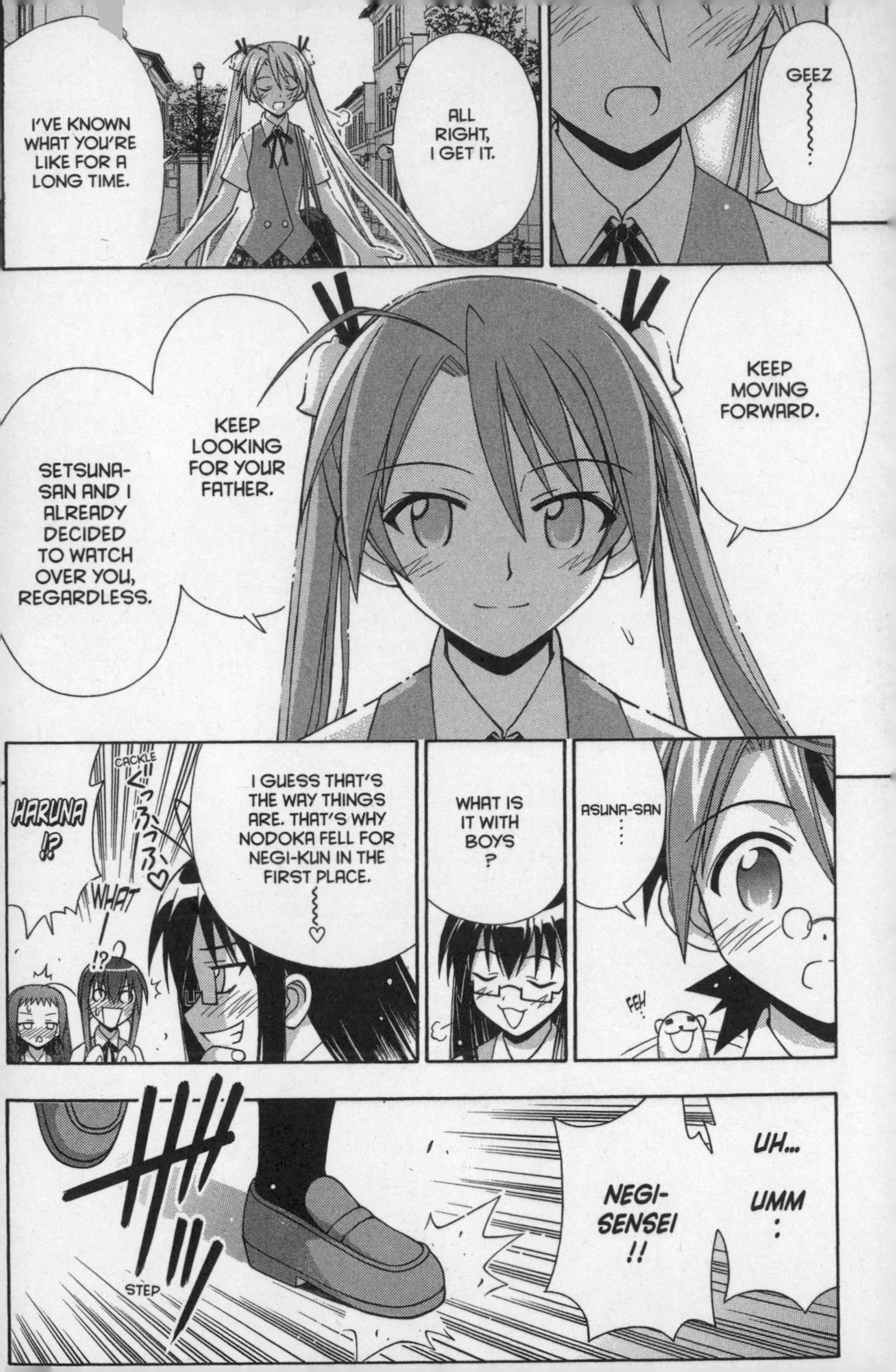
GEEZ ~~~…
ALL RIGHT, I GET IT.
I'VE KNOWN WHAT YOU'RE LIKE FOR A LONG TIME.
KEEP MOVING FORWARD.
KEEP LOOKING FOR YOUR FATHER.
SETSUNA-SAN AND I ALREADY DECIDED TO WATCH OVER YOU, REGARDLESS.
ASUNA-SAN …
FEH
WHAT IS IT WITH BOYS ?
I GUESS THAT'S THE WAY THINGS ARE. THAT'S WHY NODOKA FELL FOR NEGI-KUN IN THE FIRST PLACE. ~~♡
CACKLE
WHAT !!?
HARUNA !?
UH…
UMM :
NEGI-SENSEI !!
STEP

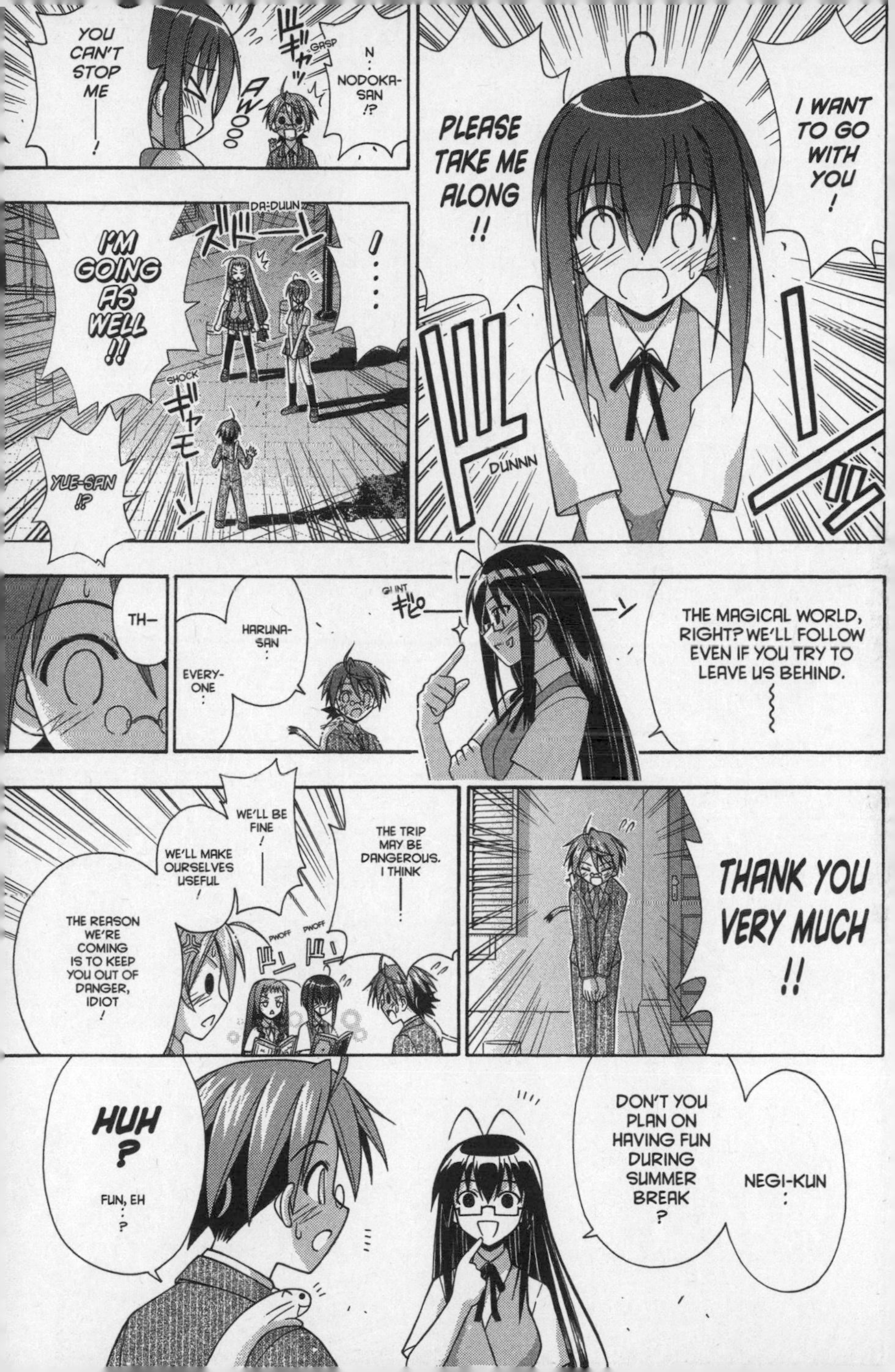
I WANT TO GO WITH YOU!
PLEASE TAKE ME ALONG!!
DUNNN
N... NODOKA-SAN!?
GASP
YOU CAN'T STOP ME—!
I'M GOING AS WELL!!
DA-DUUN
SHOCK
YUE-SAN!?
THE MAGICAL WORLD, RIGHT? WE'LL FOLLOW EVEN IF YOU TRY TO LEAVE US BEHIND.
GLINT
HARUNA-SAN... EVERYONE...
TH—
THANK YOU VERY MUCH!!
THE TRIP MAY BE DANGEROUS. I THINK—
WE'LL BE FINE!—
WE'LL MAKE OURSELVES USEFUL!
PWOFF PWOFF
THE REASON WE'RE COMING IS TO KEEP YOU OUT OF DANGER, IDIOT!
NEGI-KUN:
DON'T YOU PLAN ON HAVING FUN DURING SUMMER BREAK?
HUH?
FUN, EH...?

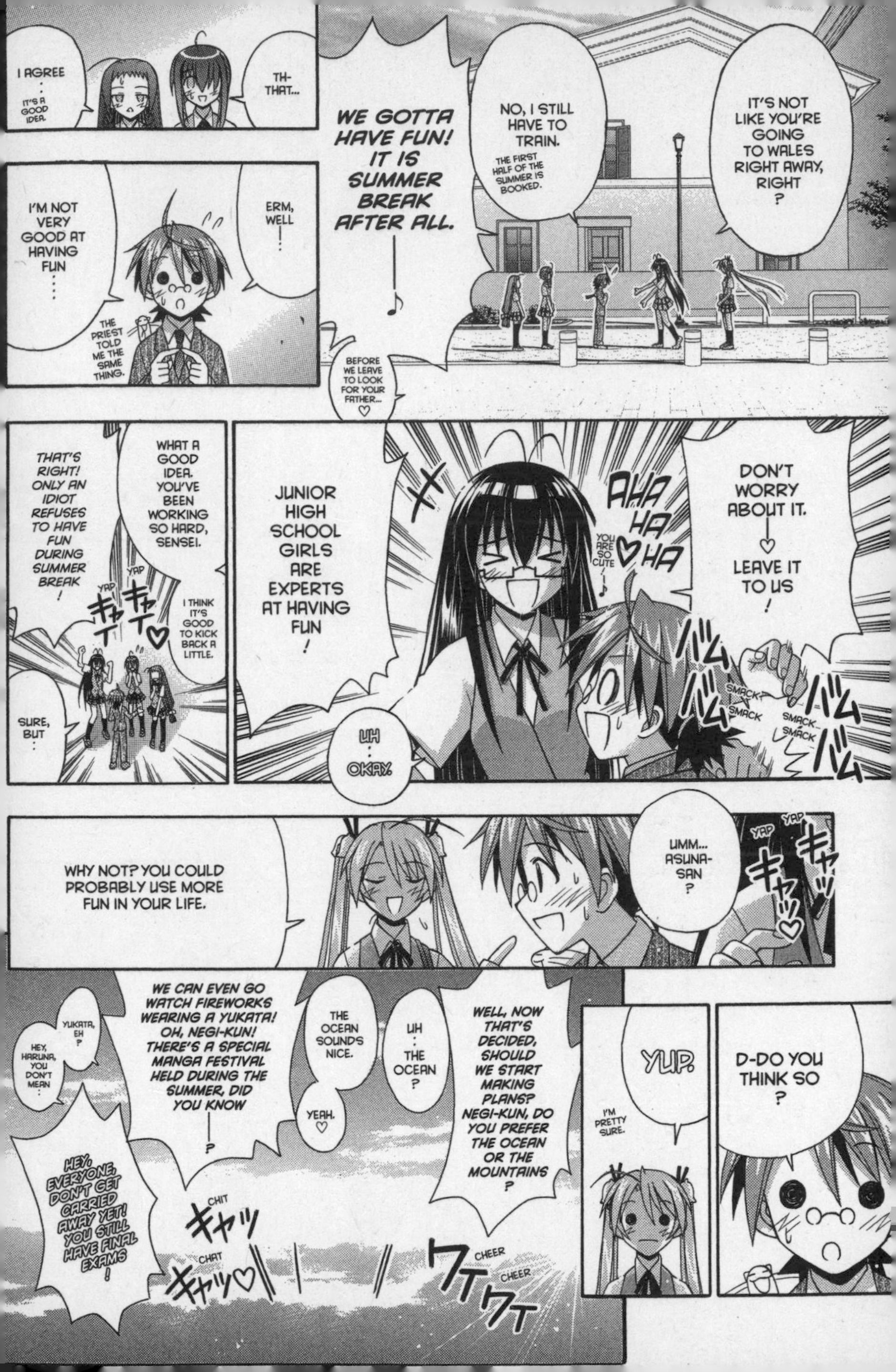
IT'S NOT LIKE YOU'RE GOING TO WALES RIGHT AWAY, RIGHT?
NO, I STILL HAVE TO TRAIN.
THE FIRST HALF OF THE SUMMER IS BOOKED.
WE GOTTA HAVE FUN! IT IS SUMMER BREAK AFTER ALL. ♪
BEFORE WE LEAVE TO LOOK FOR YOUR FATHER... ♡
TH-THAT...
I AGREE...
IT'S A GOOD IDEA.
ERM, WELL!...
I'M NOT VERY GOOD AT HAVING FUN...
THE PRIEST TOLD ME THE SAME THING.
DON'T WORRY ABOUT IT. ♡ LEAVE IT TO US!
AHA HA ♡ HA
YOU ARE SO CUTE! ♪
JUNIOR HIGH SCHOOL GIRLS ARE EXPERTS AT HAVING FUN!
バムバム
SMACK SMACK
バムバム
SMACK SMACK
UH... OKAY.
WHAT A GOOD IDEA. YOU'VE BEEN WORKING SO HARD, SENSEI.
THAT'S RIGHT! ONLY AN IDIOT REFUSES TO HAVE FUN DURING SUMMER BREAK!
I THINK IT'S GOOD TO KICK BACK A LITTLE.
キャ YAP キャ YAP ♡
SURE, BUT...
キャッ YAP キャッ YAP ♡
UMM... ASUNA-SAN?
WHY NOT? YOU COULD PROBABLY USE MORE FUN IN YOUR LIFE.
D-DO YOU THINK SO?
YUP.
I'M PRETTY SURE.
WELL, NOW THAT'S DECIDED, SHOULD WE START MAKING PLANS? NEGI-KUN, DO YOU PREFER THE OCEAN OR THE MOUNTAINS?
UH... THE OCEAN?
THE OCEAN SOUNDS NICE.
YEAH. ♡
WE CAN EVEN GO WATCH FIREWORKS WEARING A YUKATA! OH, NEGI-KUN! THERE'S A SPECIAL MANGA FESTIVAL HELD DURING THE SUMMER, DID YOU KNOW?
YUKATA, EH?
HEY, HARUNA, YOU DON'T MEAN
HEY, EVERYONE, DON'T GET CARRIED AWAY YET! YOU STILL HAVE FINAL EXAMS!
ワイワイ CHEER CHEER
キャッ CHIT キャッ♡ CHAT

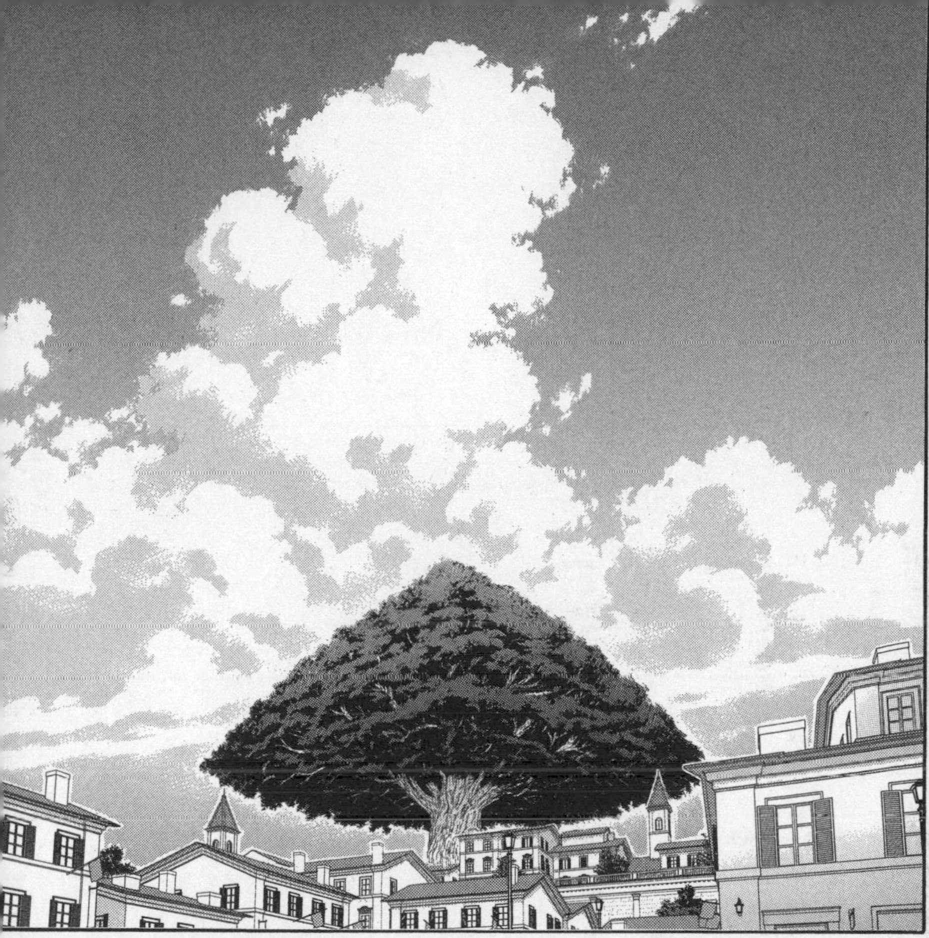

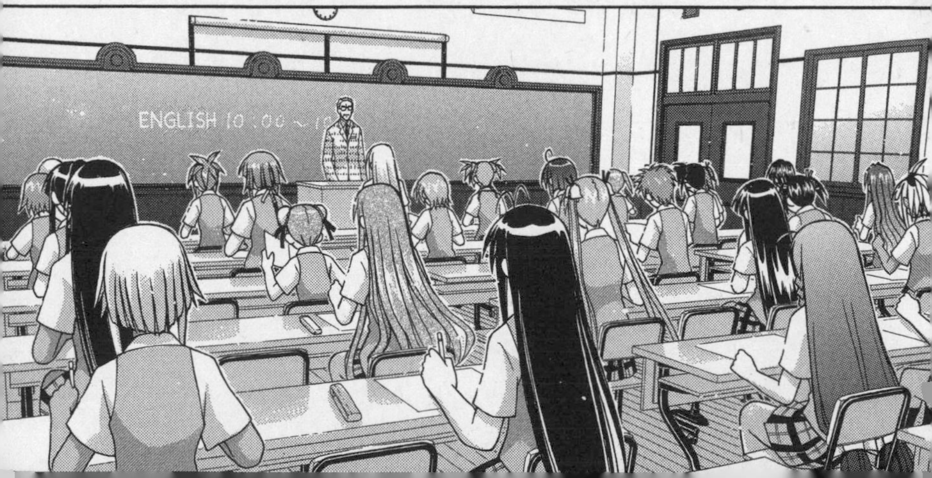
ENGLISH 10:00 ~

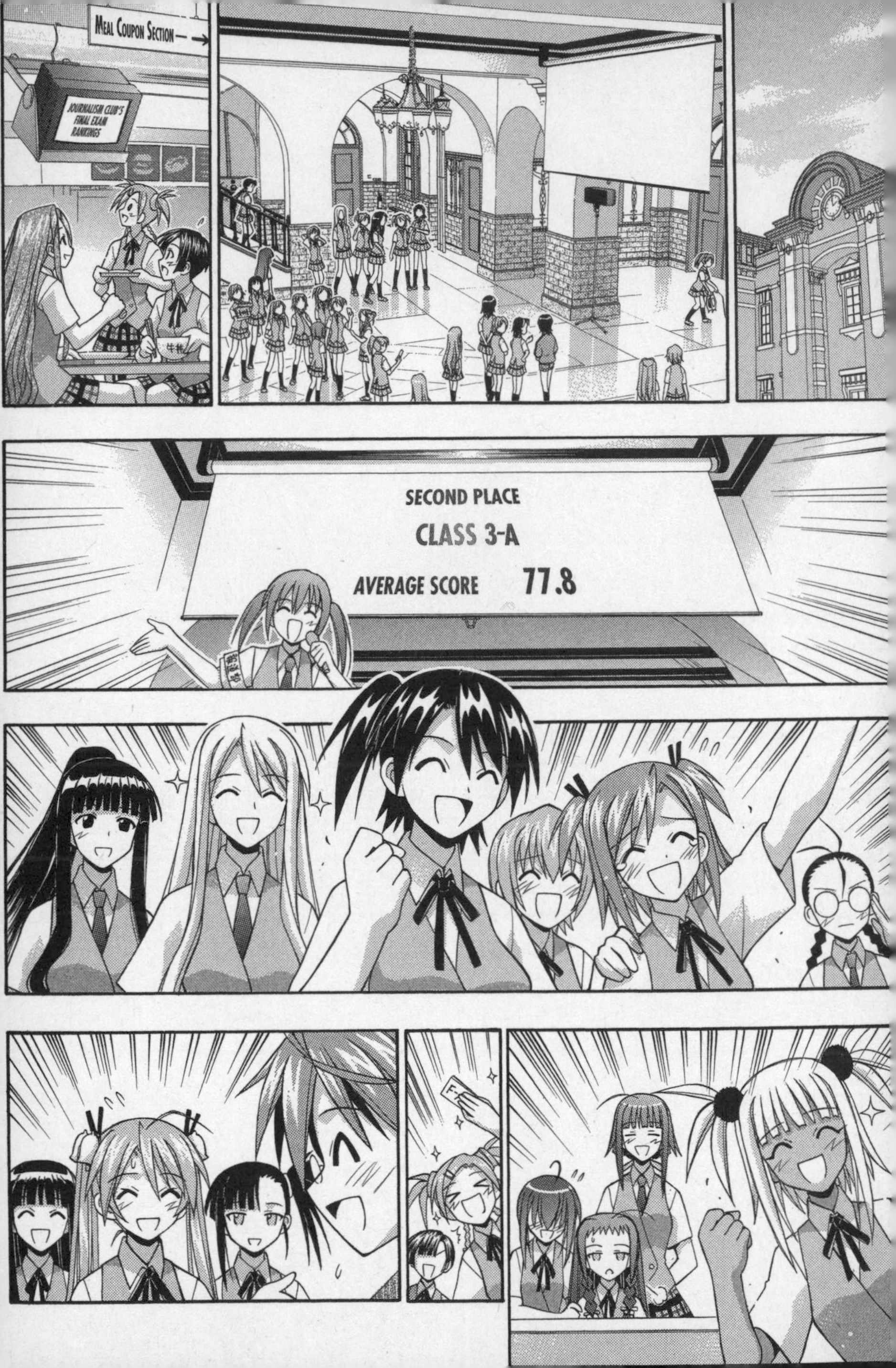
MEAL COUPON SECTION
JOURNALISM CLUB'S FINAL EXAM RANKINGS
SECOND PLACE
CLASS 3-A
AVERAGE SCORE 77.8

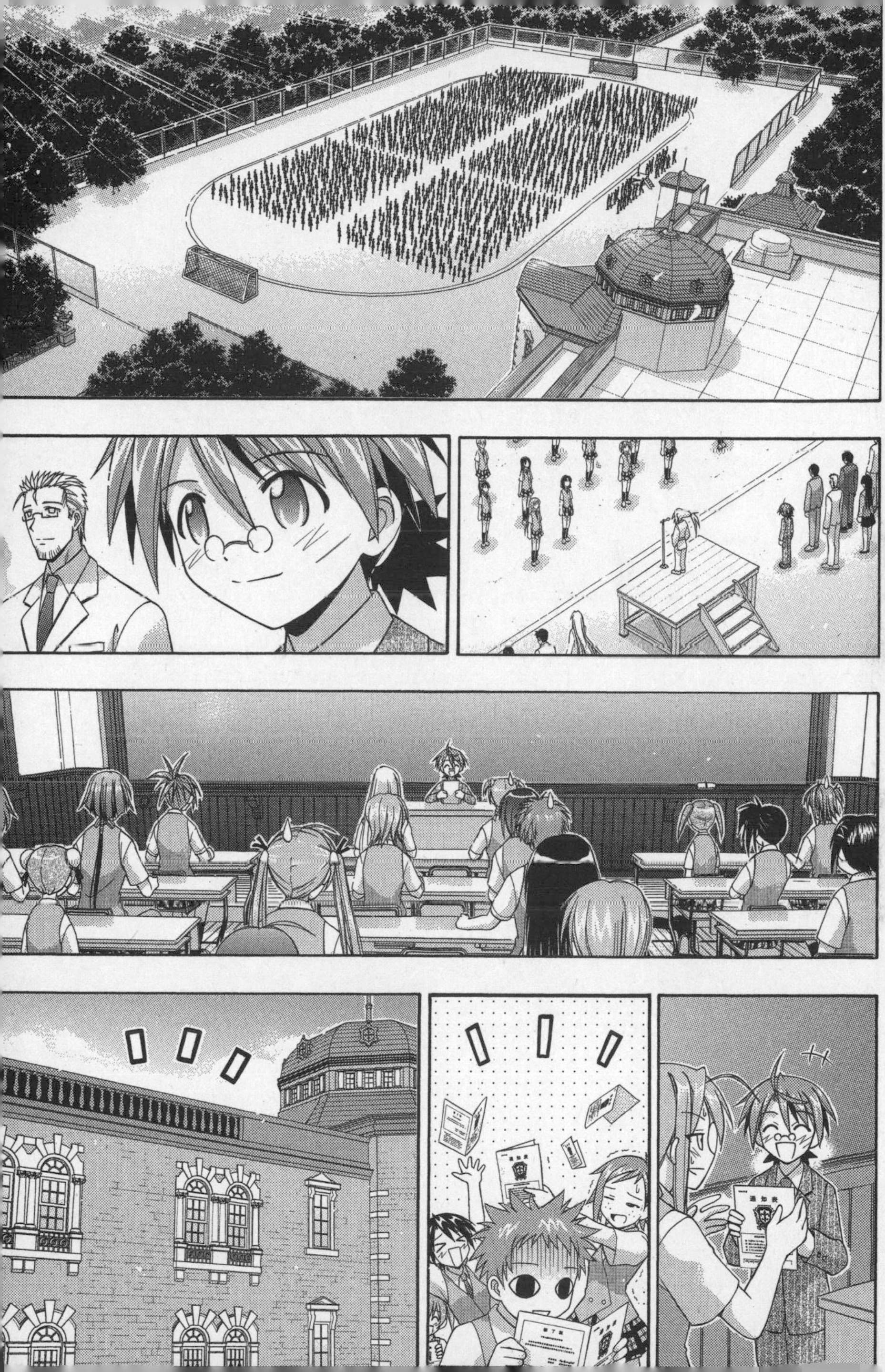

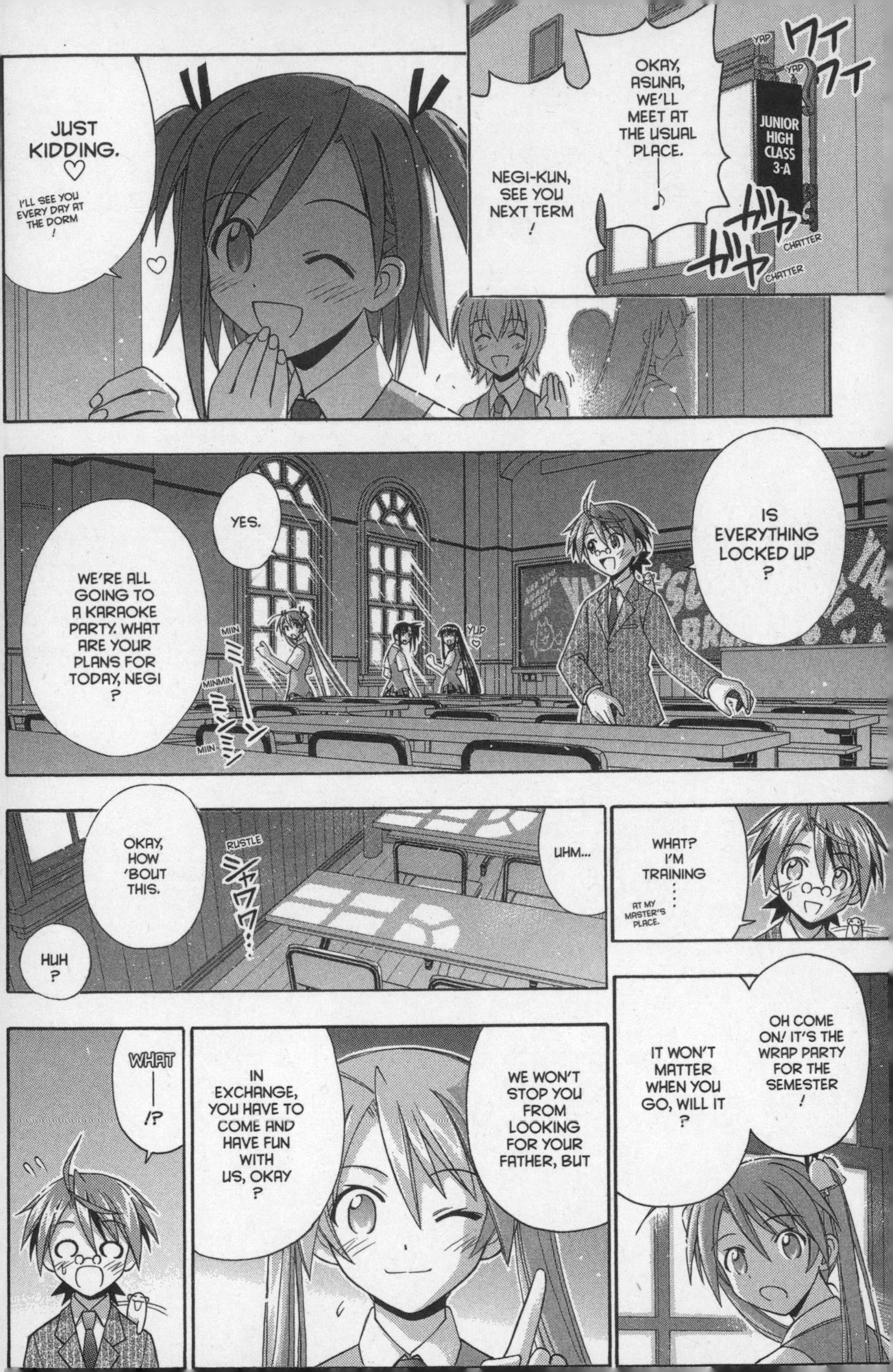

YAP
YAP
JUNIOR HIGH CLASS 3-A
OKAY, ASUNA, WE'LL MEET AT THE USUAL PLACE. ♪
NEGI-KUN, SEE YOU NEXT TERM!
CHATTER
CHATTER
JUST KIDDING. ♡
I'LL SEE YOU EVERY DAY AT THE DORM!
IS EVERYTHING LOCKED UP?
YES.
WE'RE ALL GOING TO A KARAOKE PARTY. WHAT ARE YOUR PLANS FOR TODAY, NEGI?
YUP ♡
MIIN
MINMIN
MIIN
WHAT? I'M TRAINING.... AT MY MASTER'S PLACE.
UHM...
RUSTLE
OKAY, HOW 'BOUT THIS.
HUH?
OH COME ON! IT'S THE WRAP PARTY FOR THE SEMESTER!
IT WON'T MATTER WHEN YOU GO, WILL IT?
WE WON'T STOP YOU FROM LOOKING FOR YOUR FATHER, BUT
IN EXCHANGE, YOU HAVE TO COME AND HAVE FUN WITH US, OKAY?
WHAT—!?

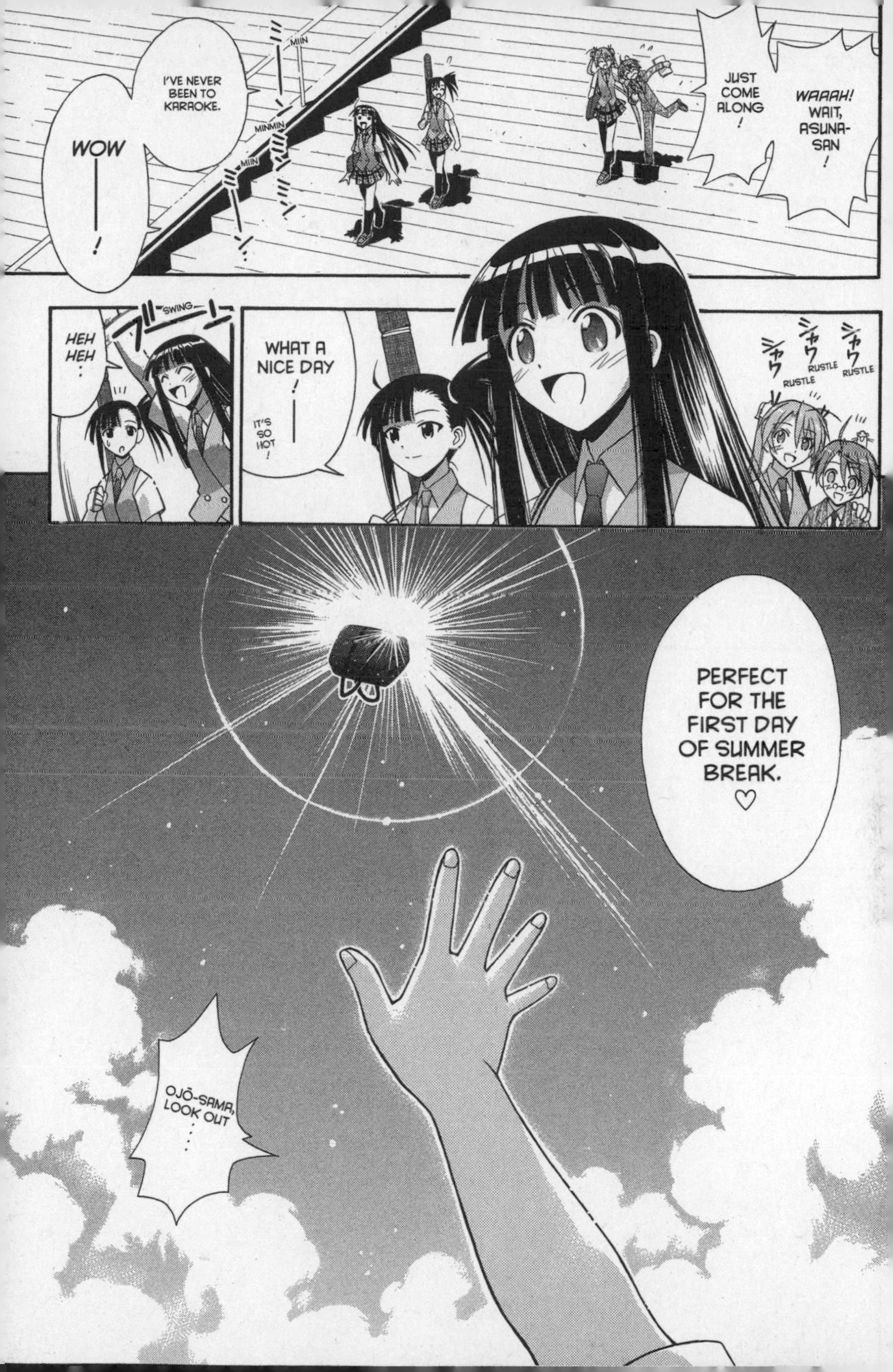
WAAAH! WAIT, ASUNA-SAN!
JUST COME ALONG!
MIIN
MINMIN
MIIN
I'VE NEVER BEEN TO KARAOKE.
WOW—!
RUSTLE
RUSTLE
RUSTLE
WHAT A NICE DAY!
IT'S SO HOT!
SWING
HEH HEH...
PERFECT FOR THE FIRST DAY OF SUMMER BREAK. ♡
OJŌ-SAMA, LOOK OUT...

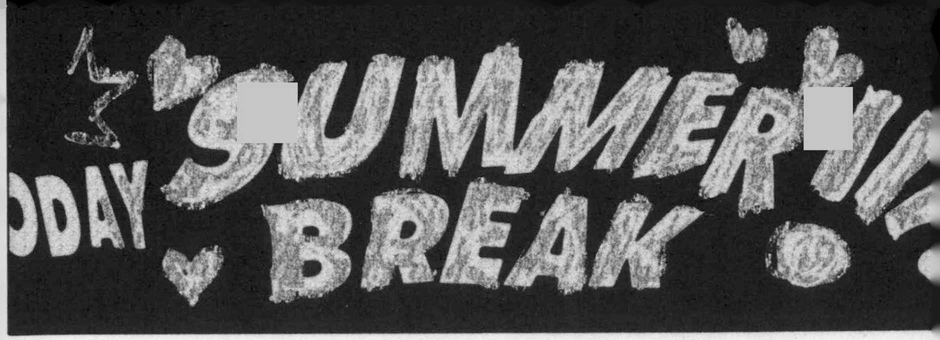
ODAY
SUMMER BREAK

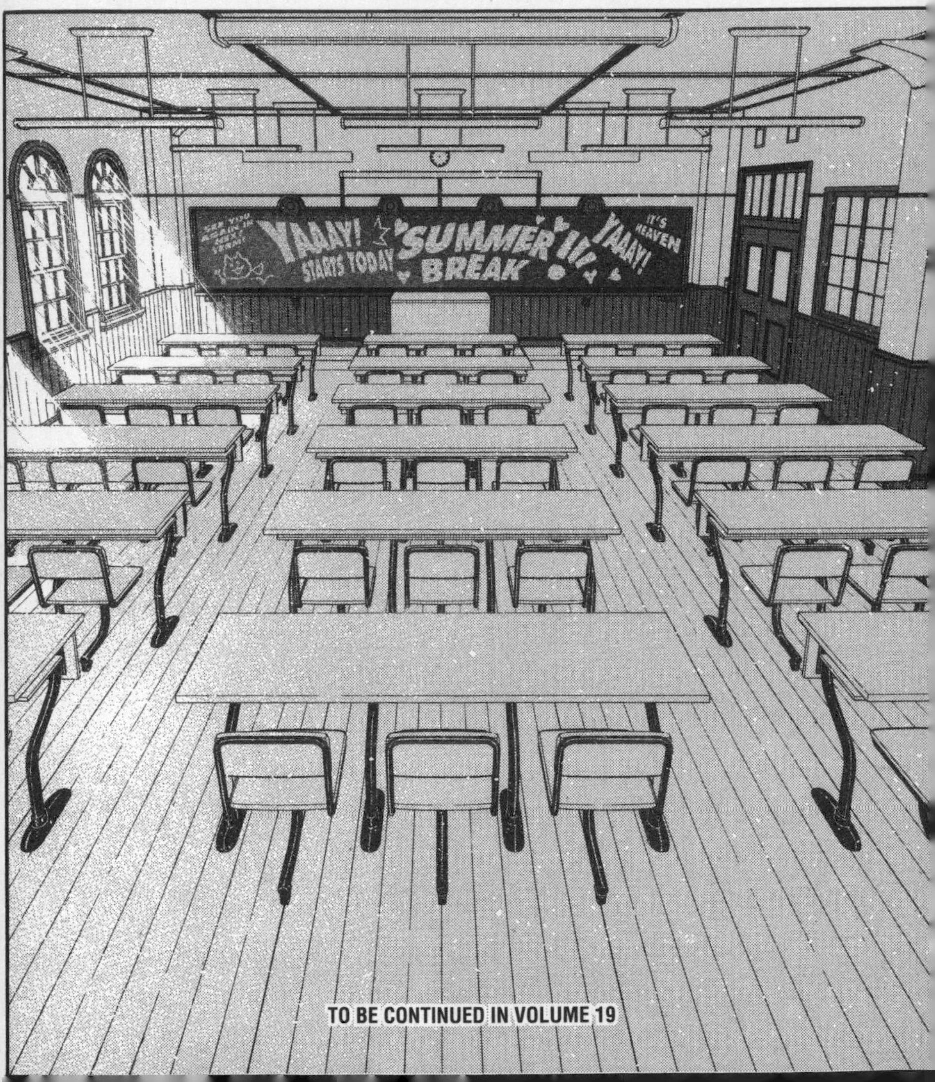
IT'S HEAVEN
YAAAY!
SUMMER BREAK
YAAAY!
STARTS TODAY
TO BE CONTINUED IN VOLUME 19

- STAFF -

Ken Akamatsu
Takashi Takemoto
Kenichi Nakamura
Masaki Ohyama
Keiichi Yamashita
Tadashi Maki
Tohru Mitsuhashi

Thanks To

Ran Ayanaga

LEXICON NEGIMARIUM
DE CANTU ET ARTIFACTO

[140th Period]

■ dig dir dilic Volholl

This magic activation key belongs to the Magical Teacher who looks like a Secret Service agent, with his dark sunglasses and black suit. In the casting of an unincanted spell, it is possible to start an incanted spell while the first is still in progress. However, casting an unincanted spell during the incantation of a spell is very difficult, as the caster needs to activate the spell in his heart/mind while speaking the incantation, unless it is one the caster can cast almost unconsciously.

■ vertatur tempestas aestiva, illis carcarem circumvertentem

(Let the Summer Storm Turn! Send a Tornado Prison upon Them! Blusterous Tornado Prison!)

A spell that creates a powerful tornado that surrounds the target in the middle of the tempest. Those trapped inside are safe from harm, unless they try to escape through the tornado.

[141st Period]

■ rap tjap la tjap ragpur

The magic activation key of Mahora Arts University, Junior High School second-year student Nutmeg (real name: Megumi Natsume).

■ Ex somno exsitat, exundans Undina, inimicum immergrat in alveum.VINCTUS AQUARIUS

(Let the Wave-Tossed Undine Appear from Sleep and Submerge the Enemy into the Riverbed! Water Binder!)

This spell creates a column of water and binds the target within it. The conjured column of water is very rich in oxygen and allows living things without gills to breathe. The oxygen can also be cut off to drown the target inside.

This spell utilizes alliteration in its incantation pattern: *Ex somno exsitat, exundans Undina, inimicum immergrat in alveum.*

■ Undina

These are water spirits or elementals from German mythology. The word *undina* (the English spelling is *undine*) comes from the Latin word *unda*, which means "an ocean wave." By adding the feminine ending *–ina* to it, the word comes to mean "virgin of the ocean waves." In T.P.A.B. Paracelsus's *Liber de Nymphis, Sylphis, Pygmaeis et Salamandris et de Caeteris Spiritibus* (sometimes called the *Book of Fairies*), he writes, "In water there are nymphs, in the wind there are sylphs, in the earth are *pygmae*, and in fire there are salamanders. Now, these beings do not have proper names. ... Truth be told, the water beings are the *undina*, the wind beings are *sylvester*, the mountain beings are *gnomus*, and the name of the fire beings are *vulcanos*." (Tractatus II)

According to Paracelsus, these four races are both *Geist* (spirits) and *Mensch* (human) but, at the same time, neither. These are special beings that have spirit bodies but are not immortal. However, unlike human beings, they lack a *Seele** (soul). But even so, they can talk like humans and even laugh. (Tractatus I Caput II) Of the four races, the *undina* look the most human, as seen in the passage: "Male and female water beings act and move about like normal humans." (Tractatus II)

The fact that *undina* and humans could marry was well-known, and Paracelsus wrote that "By marrying a human, an *undine* female can bear children. By having a child with the descendant of Adam, the child will resemble the father and the child will have a soul. And since it has a soul, the child will be truly human." (Tractatus III)

■ Ex somno exsitat, exurens Salamandra, inimicum involvat igne. CAPTUS FLAMMEUS

(Everything Burning with the Flame of Purification, Lord of Destruction and Sign of Rebirth, Residing in My Hand! Let It Eat the Enemy! Red Blaze!)

This spell creates a ring of fire and binds the target within it. As the column of fire is in a ring form, the target inside is not burned by the fire but does suffer saunalike conditions. The flames themselves are shielded, so in order to break out of the confinement, one must employ magic. Prolonged exposure to the spell can cause circulatory damage from the heat and heat stroke.

This spell also utilizes alliteration in its incantation pattern: *Ex somno exsitat, exurens Salamndara, inimicum involvat igne.*

■ Salamandra

An elemental of fire from the Greek/Roman mythology. Its form is that of a lizard. *Salamandra* means "lizard" in ancient Greek and in Latin. According to Paracelsus, "*Salamandra* are long, narrow

---

*This translation uses the ancient German spelling *Seele* rather than the modern *Seel*.

and very thin." (Tractatus II) The ending formation of the word *salamandra*, according to dictionaries such as Lewis & Short, is feminine, but Paracelsus uses it as a masculine noun.

In Aristotle's *History of Animals, salamandra* are described as animals that can live in fire. He goes on to say, "Now the *salamandra* is a clear case in point, to show us that animals do actually exist that fire cannot destroy; for this creature, so the story goes, not only walks through the fire but puts it out in doing so." (552b15–17)

■ favor purgandi

(*Osjōi Daisuki*—I love to clean/sweep)

By the power of the Pactio with a mage, Mei Sakura is awarded a magical broom. As touched upon in the story, this broom is standard issue to the Order of the Mage Knights in the Magical Realm. It is a superior magical item with many possible uses. How it is determined what artifact each *ministra* receives is unknown, but as with Negi's *ministra*, it is believed that the person's inner being and desires for their future play a role in the selection of the artifact.

■ Ad Summam Exarmatio

(Total Disarmament)

A spell that disarms everyone in its area of operation. It affects anyone in the area, including one's allies. However, that can aid in the laying down of arms for all parties involved.

■ Sagitta Magica Series Ignis

(Magic Arrow, Fire Series)

A magic arrow spell with the element of fire as its basis. A line of fire attacks the enemy. As it's a flaming arrow, it can set the target ablaze. Because of this, it is one of the most attack-oriented and damaging of the magic arrow spells.

Mei is able to launch three arrows unincanted, showing her level of skill with the spell. Should Mei have faced off with Negi when he first arrived at the academy, Negi would not have lasted long in that battle!

[142nd Period]

■ Cerberus

(Κέρβερος)

The three-headed canine guardian of Hades in Greek mythology. The description that Nodoka gives, with the mane of snakes, comes from Virgil's (70–19 BC) *Aeneid*, "Grim Cerberus, who soon began to rear/His crested snakes, and armed his bristling hair/The prudent Sibyl had before prepared a sop, in honey steeped, to charm the guard;/which,

mixed with powerful drugs, she cast before his greedy, grinning jaws."
(*Aeneid*, Book 6, 417–421)

On the other hand, in *Thogeny* by Hesiod (700? BC) it is written,
"and then again she bare a second, a monster not to be overcome and
that may not be described, Cerberus who eats raw flesh, the brazen-
voiced hound of Hades, fifty-headed, relentless and strong" (310–
312), which shows that in older legends it had fifty heads.

However, the common image of Cerberus having three heads with
a mane of snakes came from the tragedy *Hercules* written by Euripides
(485?–406? BC), "I passed through a herd of countless other toils
besides and came to the dead to fetch to the light at the bidding of
Eurystheus the three-headed hound, hell's porter." (1277–1278)
Furthermore, the Jar of Cairéa found in Etruria depicts Hercules with
a three-headed and snake-maned Cerberus.

[143rd Period]

■ se dissolvent circumstantial falsa
(Let the False World Dissolve Itself!)

A spell utilizing the power of the artifact being wielded by Asuna
Kagurazaka, a *ministra* of Negi. A spell is not a keyword that is uttered
to activate some supernatural power. As written by Virgil, "Songs can
even draw the moon down from heaven" (*Eclogue* VIII.69)—there
is power in words. So the power of a spell comes from the power
contained in its words. Even the words of an ordinary person can
have a certain level of magic contained within them. Yue, as she is
not yet well trained in the ways of magic, did not have the ability
to activate the spell. So by using her words along with the power of
Asuna's artifact, she was able to break the illusion. Using a tool to
amplify the power of words is a very popular manner in which to cast
spells. For example, words did not have much power until they were
inscribed on stone tablets. In the Middle Ages, the jongleur (minstrels)
gained recognition by adding words to their music. Even today,
unaccompanied singing is said to be a way of using tools to increase
the power of words.

[144th Period]

■ Hippogriff (or Hippogryph)
(ιππογυψ)

The word roots for Hippogriff come from the amalgamation of the
ancient Greek words for horse (ιππος) and griffin (γρυψ). Generally
speaking, a hippogriff is a monster with the body of a horse and
the head and wings of a hawk. It is said to be the hybrid offspring
of a mare and griffin. The Latin term *gryps* is most often translated

as griffin, but one theory says that the creature is closer to a dragon in appearance, so in reality, no one really knows what a hippogriff is supposed to look like.

[145th Period]

■ limes aerialis
(Boundary Wall of Air)

A spell that creates a mid-level magical barrier by using air currents. It's especially suited for protecting against fire, cold, poison gas, and other air-related attacks. Of the air-based spells, it is a fairly basic one compared to others that can block physical attacks, such as the *Deflectio* and *Flans Paries Aeriales*.

[147th Period]

■ jaculetur
(assail the enemy)

As said in a previous entry, even the words of a common person can hold magical power—a little or a lot. Makie and the others use the tools attained by the Headmaster to cast the spells, but as Kakizaki joked about pretending to be Magical Girls, it is undoubtedly the power within each person's words that exerts the magic for the spell.

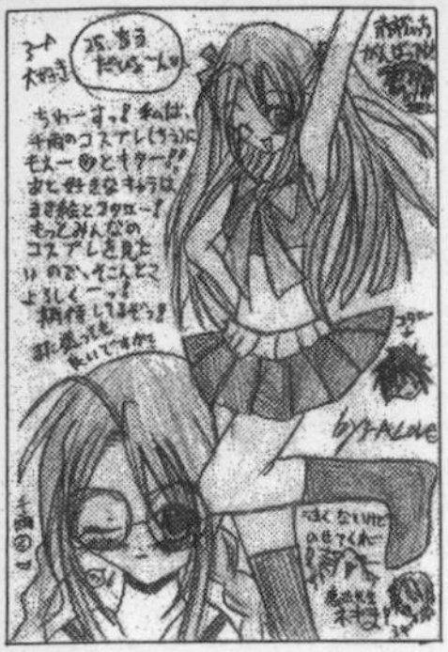

▲ WE LOVE THE COSTUME!

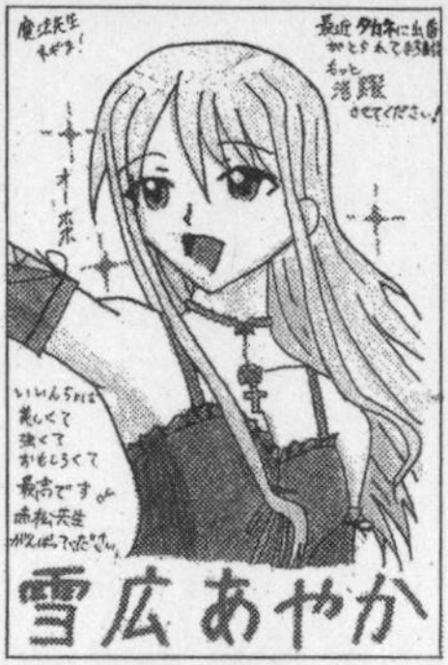
雪広あやか

▲ WE DON'T GET VERY MANY PICTURES OF AYAKA LATELY...

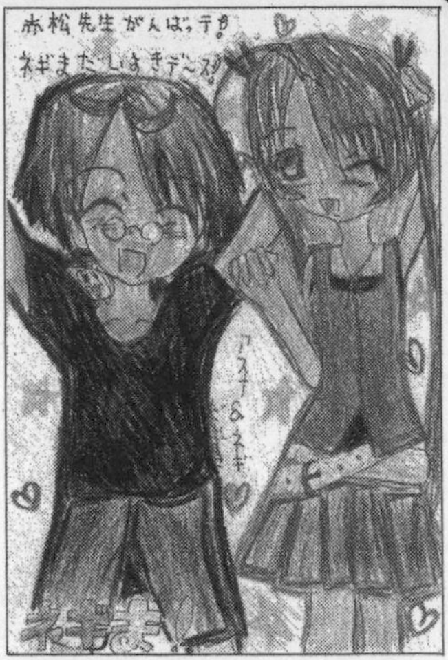
赤松先生がんばって!

▲ THESE TWO LOOK VERY HAPPY!

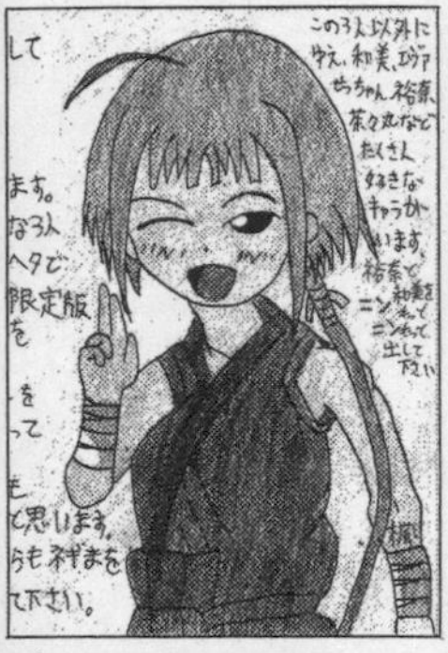

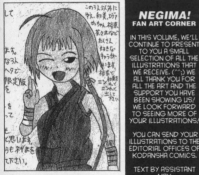

▲ HERE'S A NICE ONE OF KAEDE ★

NEGIMA!
FAN ART CORNER

IN THIS VOLUME, WE'LL CONTINUE TO PRESENT TO YOU A SMALL SELECTION OF ALL THE ILLUSTRATIONS THAT WE RECEIVE. (^^;) WE ALL THANK YOU FOR ALL THE ART AND THE SUPPORT YOU HAVE BEEN SHOWING US! WE LOOK FORWARD TO SEEING MORE OF YOUR ILLUSTRATIONS!

YOU CAN SEND YOUR ILLUSTRATIONS TO THE EDITORIAL OFFICES OF KODANSHA COMICS.

TEXT BY ASSISTANT MAX

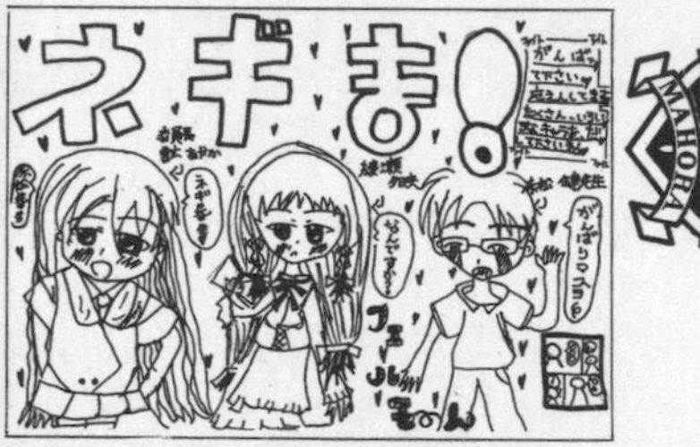
ネギま!

▲ AKAMATSU-SAN IS CRYING TEARS OF BLOOD! (LAUGHS)

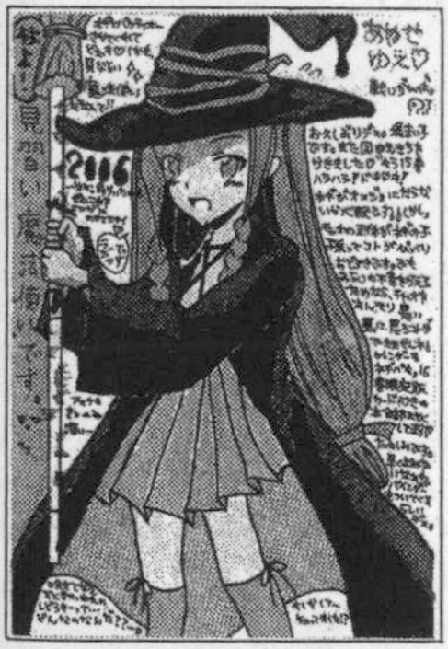

▲ WE CAN FEEL YOUR LOVE FOR YUE-KICHI.♪

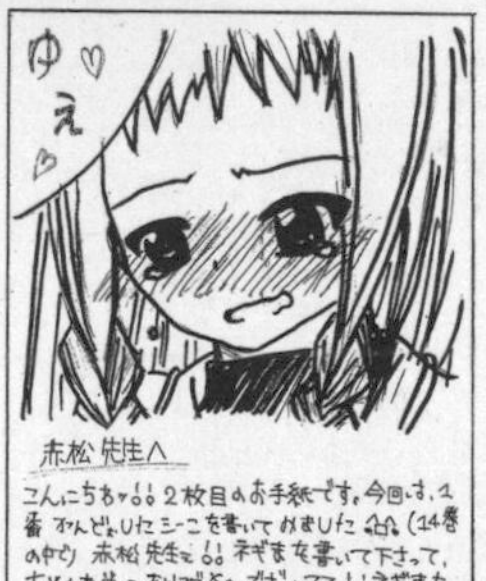
赤松先生へ

▲ A NICE YUE!

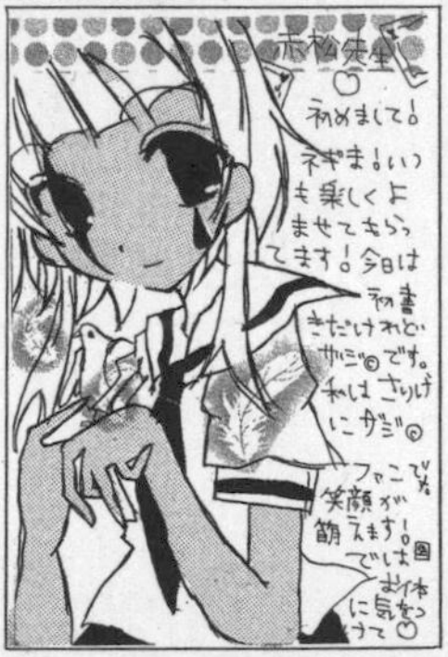
赤松先生

▲ THIS IS A VERY CUTE-LOOKING ZAZIE (^^)

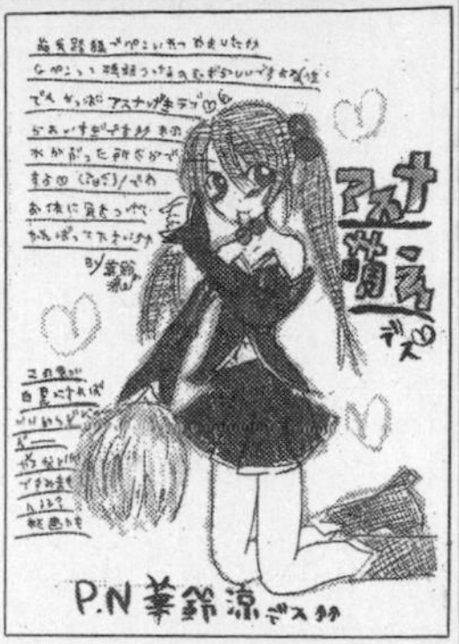
アスナ萌え
P.N 華鈴涼デス

▲ THIS ONE IS OVERFLOWING WITH CUTE.

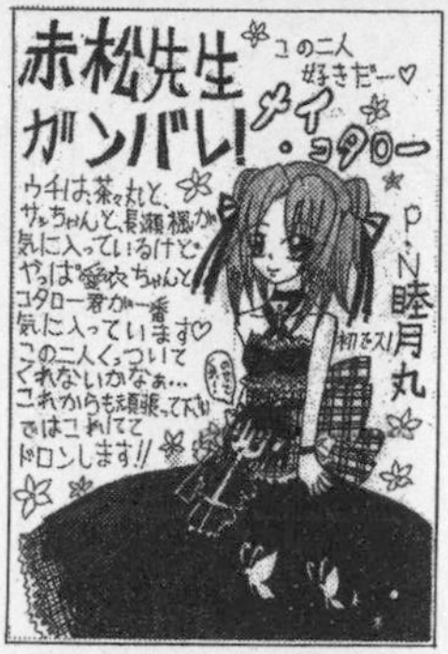
赤松先生ガンバレ!
この二人好きだー♡
メイ・コタロー
P.N睦月丸

▲ WE LOVE THE KŌTARO DOLL! (LAUGHS)

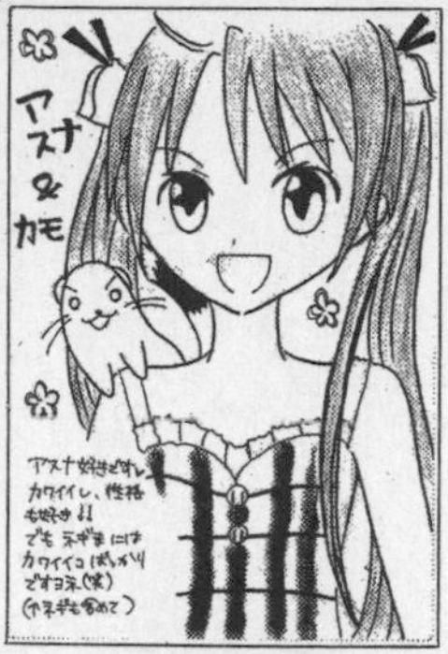
アスナ&カモ

▲ ASUNA LOOKS VERY FEMININE HERE.

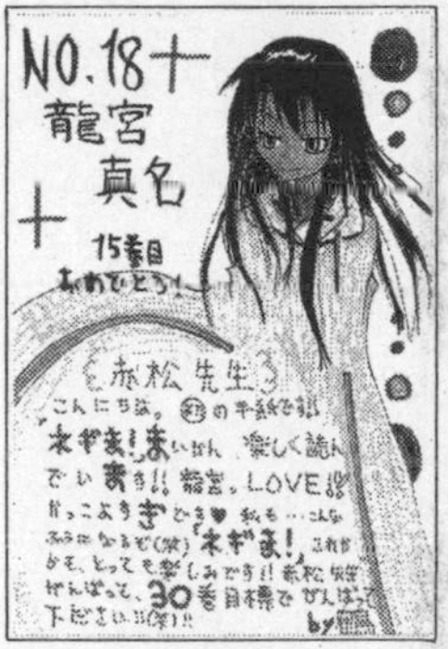
NO.18
龍宮真名
赤松先生

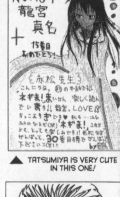

▲ TATSUMIYA IS VERY CUTE IN THIS ONE!

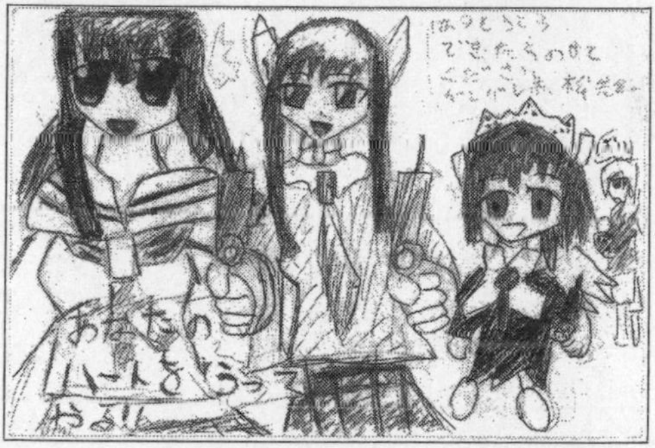

▲ EVERYONE SMILE!♪

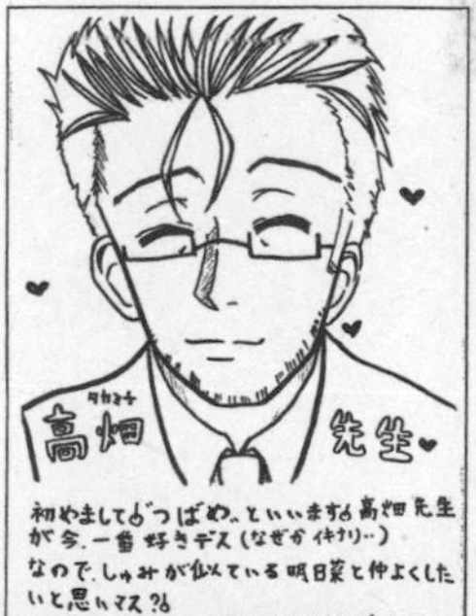
高畑先生

▲ TAKAMICHI FANS ARE VERY PRECIOUS!

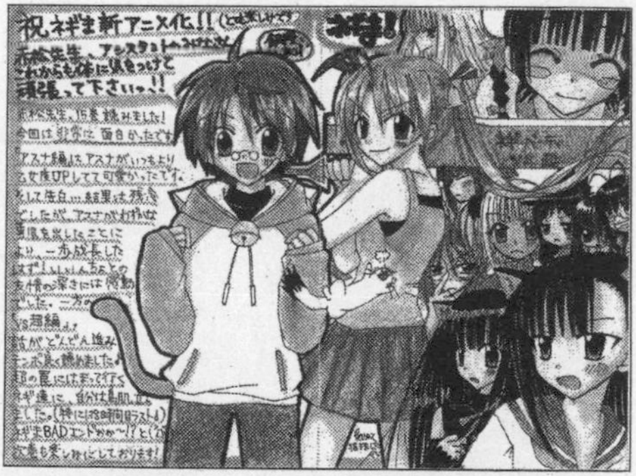
祝ネギま新アニメ化!!

▲ WE CAN FEEL YOUR DETERMINATION FROM THIS PICTURE!

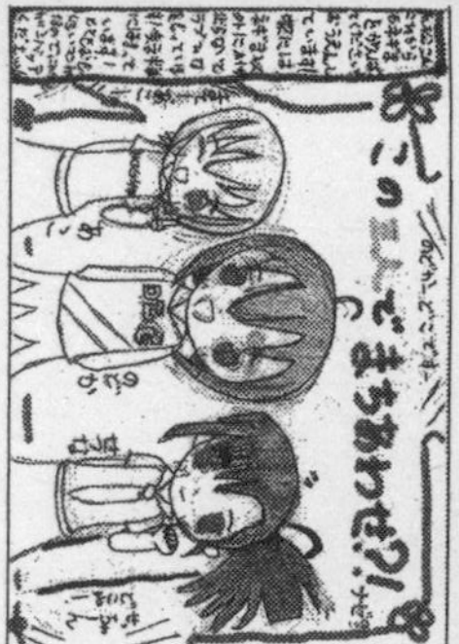
この3人でまちあわせ?!

ARE THESE THREE OUT SHOPPING?

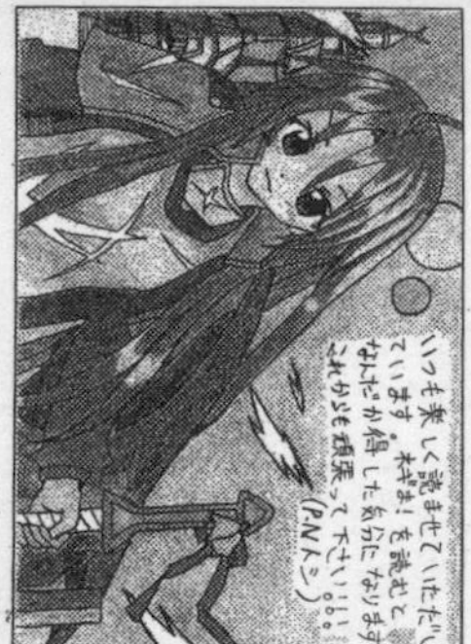
いつも楽しく読ませていただいています。ネギま!を読むとなんだか得した気分になります。これからも頑張って下さい!!!
(P.Nトシ)

ASUNA LOOKS REALLY TOUGH IN THIS ONE.

THE USE OF RED IN THIS PICTURE OF ASAKURA WAS NICE!

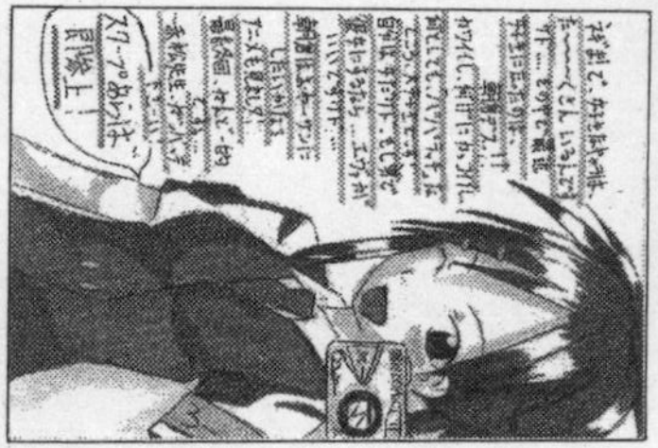
スクープあらば 見参上!

NEGI LOOKS VERY CALM AND COOL IN THIS PICTURE!

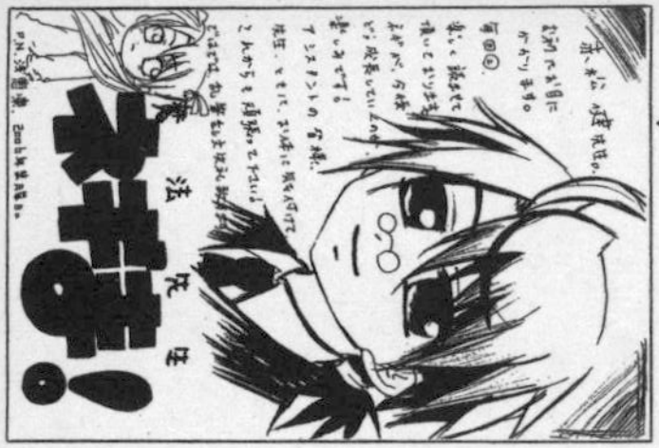
魔法先生
ネギま!

A VERY NICE WEDDING DRESS!

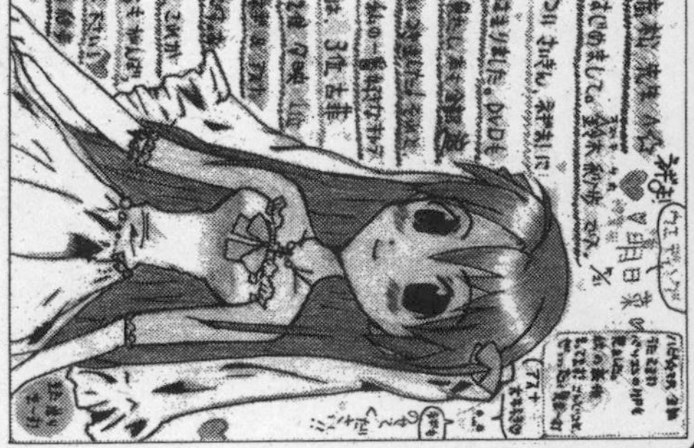

PARU MANAGES TO APPEAR A LOT LATELY!

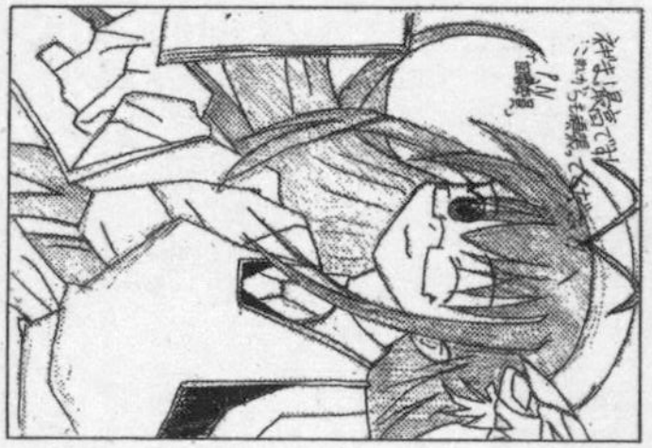

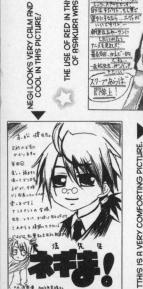

TTHIS IS A VERY COMFORTING PICTURE.

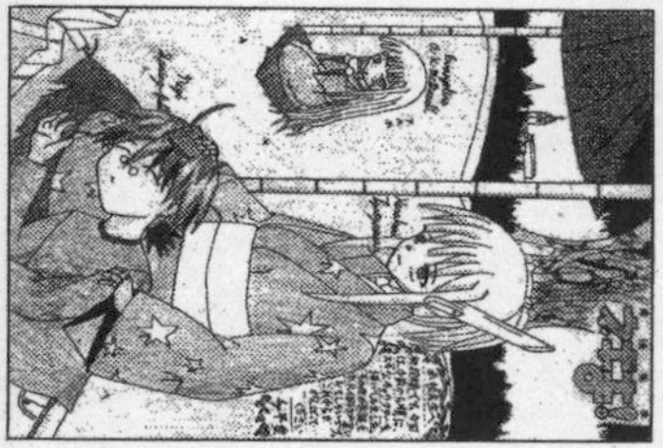

THE TWINS LOOK VERY CLOSE IN THIS PICTURE. ★

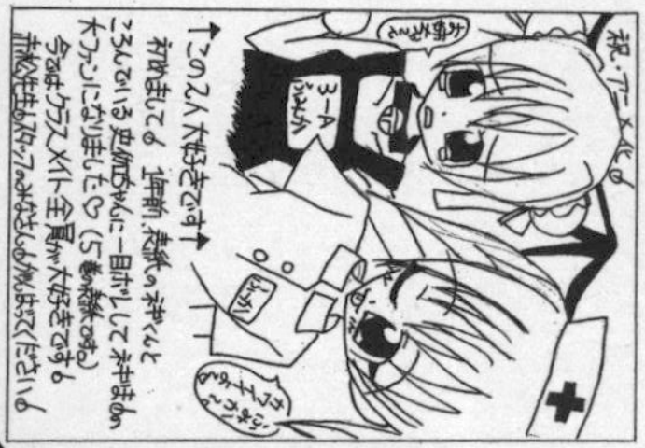
祝・アニメ化
3-A ふみか
↑この2人大好きです↑
初めまして 1年前、表紙のネギくんところんでいる史伽ちゃんに一目ボレしてネギまの大ファンになりました♡(5巻の表紙です)
今ではクラスメイト全員が大好きです
赤松先生&スタッフのみなさんがんばってください

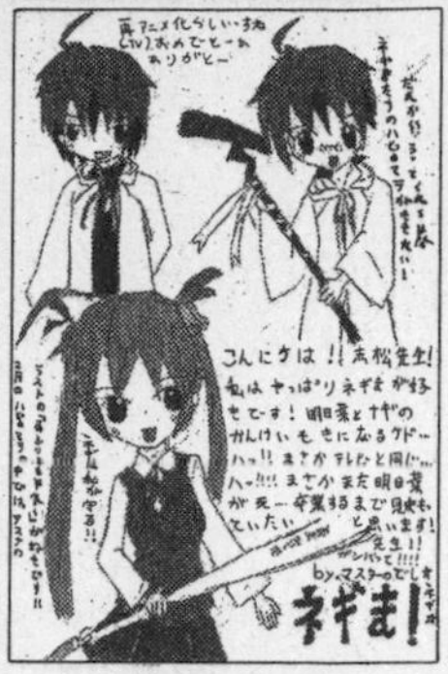
ネギま!
▲ NAGI LOOKS VERY CUTE!

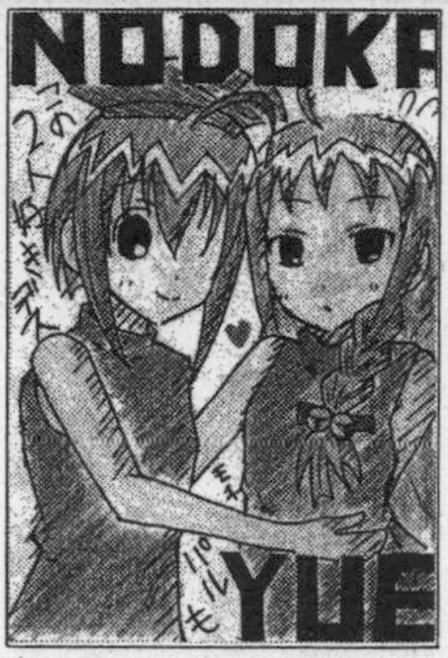
NODOKA
YUE
▲ YOU CAN ALMOST FEEL THE WARMTH COMING FROM THE PICTURE!

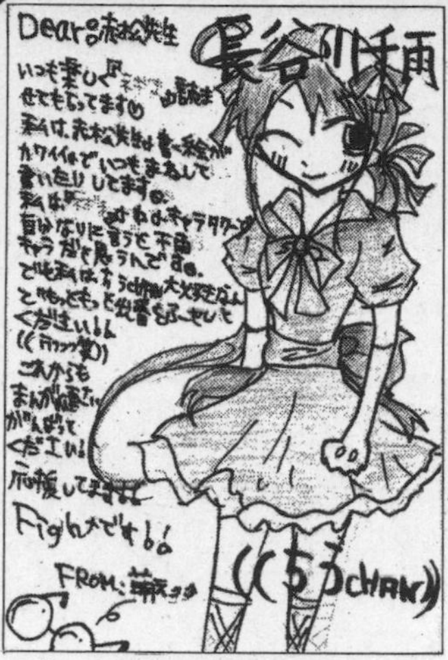
長谷川千雨
Fightです!!
▲ CHIU LOOKS KIND OF RAMBUNCTIOUS IN THIS ONE!

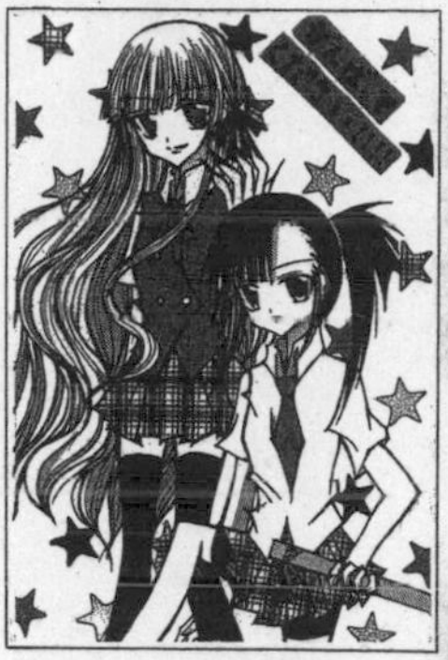
▶ IF EVA AND SETSUNA WERE TO TEAM UP, THEY'D BE UNSTOPPABLE! ★

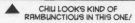

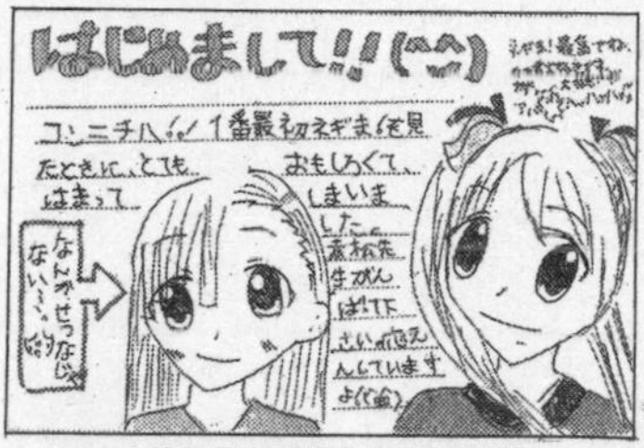
はじめまして!!
▲ BOTH ASUNA AND SETSUNA LOOK CUTE! ♪

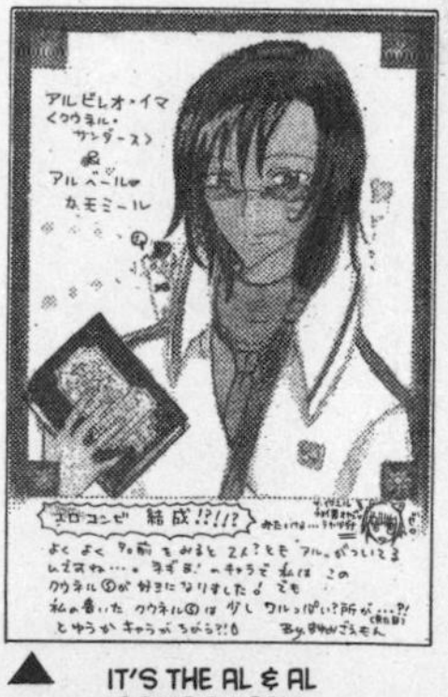
アルビレオ・イマ
アルベール・カモミール
▲ IT'S THE AL & AL COMBO TEAM.

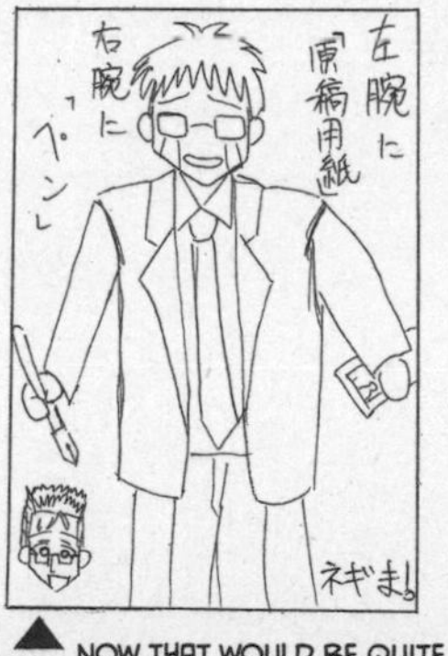
右腕に「ペン」
左腕に「原稿用紙」
ネギま!
▲ NOW THAT WOULD BE QUITE THE *KANKAHŌ* (LAUGHS)

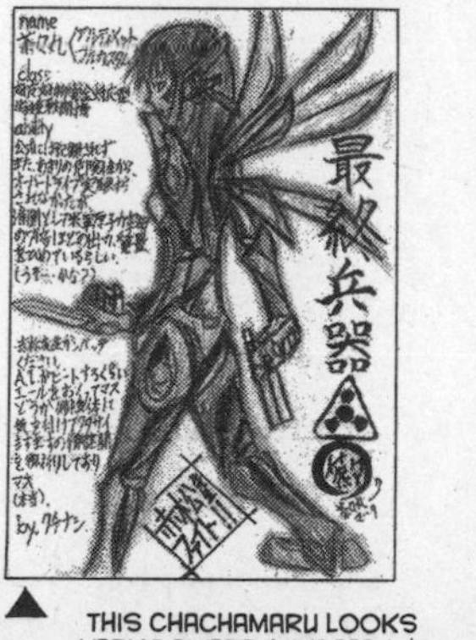
最終兵器
▲ THIS CHACHAMARU LOOKS VERY POWERFUL INDEED! ★

3-D BACKGROUNDS EXPLANATION CORNER

AS THE VOLUMES INCREASE IN NUMBER, SO DO THE NUMBER
OF 3-D BACKGROUNDS. WE'LL FEATURE THE 3-D BACKGROUNDS
FROM VOLUME 15 AS WELL AS ONES FROM THIS BOOK.

• EVANGELINE'S HOUSE
SCENE NAME: EVA'S HOUSE
POLYGON COUNT: 37,604

AT THE BEGINNING OF THIS VOLUME, IT WAS THE SCENE OF THE BATTLE WITH THE MAGICAL TEACHERS. A 3-D VERSION OF THE HOUSE WAS CREATED. IN AN ACTION SEQUENCE, IT'S VERY HELPFUL TO BE ABLE TO FREELY ADJUST THE ANGLES FROM PANEL TO PANEL. WE'RE REALLY HAPPY WITH THE FACT THAT IT STILL LOOKS HAND-DRAWN!

ALTHOUGH, AS I'M SURE A FEW EAGLE-EYED READERS HAVE ALREADY NOTICED, THE NUMBER AND SIZE OF THE WINDOWS ARE DIFFERENT FROM THE ONES YOU SEE ON THE INSIDE. (^^;)

A GOOD EXCUSE WOULD BE TO SAY THAT EVA USES MAGIC AND ILLUSIONS TO CAMOUFLAGE THE OUTSIDE OF HER HOUSE. YES, MAGIC IS A POWERFUL TOOL INDEED. (LAUGHS)

• EVANGELINE'S RESORT (INTERIOR)
SCENE NAME: DINNER ROOM
POLYGON COUNT: 106,487

EVA'S RESORT HAS BEEN FEATURED BEFORE, BUT THE INTERIOR OF THE RESORT MADE ITS FIRST APPEARANCE IN VOLUME 15. WE WANTED TO KEEP THE EXOTIC "ASIAN BEACH RESORT" FEEL BY CREATING THIS LARGE OPEN ROOM WITH A BEACH VIEW AND A BIG INDOOR SWIMMING POOL.

BUT AGAIN, IF YOU TRY TO FIND THIS LOCATION FROM THE OUTSIDE SHOTS OF THE RESORT, YOU WON'T BE ABLE TO. PERHAPS THIS TOO IS HIDDEN BY MAGIC. (LAUGHS) THEN AGAIN, IF WE START POINTING THESE THINGS OUT, THERE WOULD BE NO END TO IT! (^^;)

• STONE CASTLE
SCENE NAME: STONE CASTLE
POLYGON COUNT: 13,334

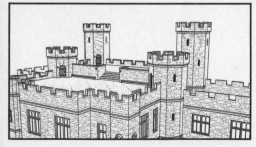

THIS IS THE CASTLELIKE BUILDING THAT ASUNA AND TAKAHATA VISITED DURING THEIR DATE IN VOL. 15. IT'S NORMALLY USED AS A MUSEUM AND A REGIONAL REFERENCE LIBRARY. THE UNADORNED ARCHITECTURE GIVES THE BUILDING A MEDIEVAL FEEL, BUT BECAUSE OF THE SPECTACULAR VIEWS FROM THE ROOF, IT'S BECOME A VERY POPULAR DATE SPOT.

PART OF THE DESIGN IS BASED ON WARWICK CASTLE IN THE UNITED KINGDOM.

• CITY HALL AND PLAZA
SCENE NAME: CITY HALL
POLYGON COUNT: 775,446

THIS IS THE BUILDING AND THE PLAZA WHERE NEGI FOUGHT CHAO IN VOL. 15. THE CITY HALL IS OFTEN USED FOR EVENTS AND AS A POPULAR MEETING PLACE AND IS THE CENTER OF THE CITY'S ECONOMIC ACTIVITY. THE DECORATIVE ARCHITECTURE IS AN EXAMPLE OF THE CITY'S ELEGANCE.

THE BUILDING IS PARTIALLY BASED ON THE CITY HALL IN BELFAST, IRELAND.

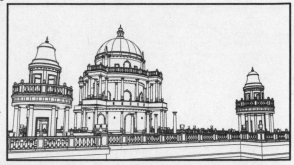

• UNDERGROUND WORLD TREE ALTAR
SCENE NAME: LARGE ALTAR
POLYGON COUNT: 97,485

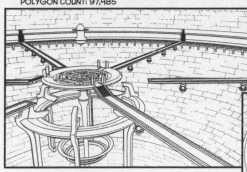

THE MYSTERIOUS RUINS FOUND AT THE DEEPEST DEPTHS BENEATH THE WORLD TREE. ONE THEORY SAYS THAT THE MAGES OF OLD HAD USED THIS PLACE TO COLLECT THE MAGIC OF THE WORLD TREE IN ORDER TO PERFORM SOME KIND OF GREAT RITUAL.

AT THE CENTER OF THE LARGE CAVERN IS A MAGIC CIRCLE THAT DEPICTS THE BEGINNINGS OF ALL LIVING AND NON-LIVING THINGS.

- BONUS -

• AIRSHIP

THIS WAS MADE INTO A 3-D OBJECT FOR VOL. 16. YOU'LL SEE IT FLYING AROUND EVERYWHERE.

• MYSTERIOUS STONE SCULPTURES

WHY THESE THINGS ARE AROUND IS AN EVEN BIGGER MYSTERY. (LAUGHS)

• POLY-MEN MAGE VERSION

THESE WERE A MUST AND A SAVING GRACE FOR MOB SCENES. SEEING THEM LIKE THIS, THEY LOOK MORE LIKE VIDEO-GAME CHARACTERS. (LAUGHS)

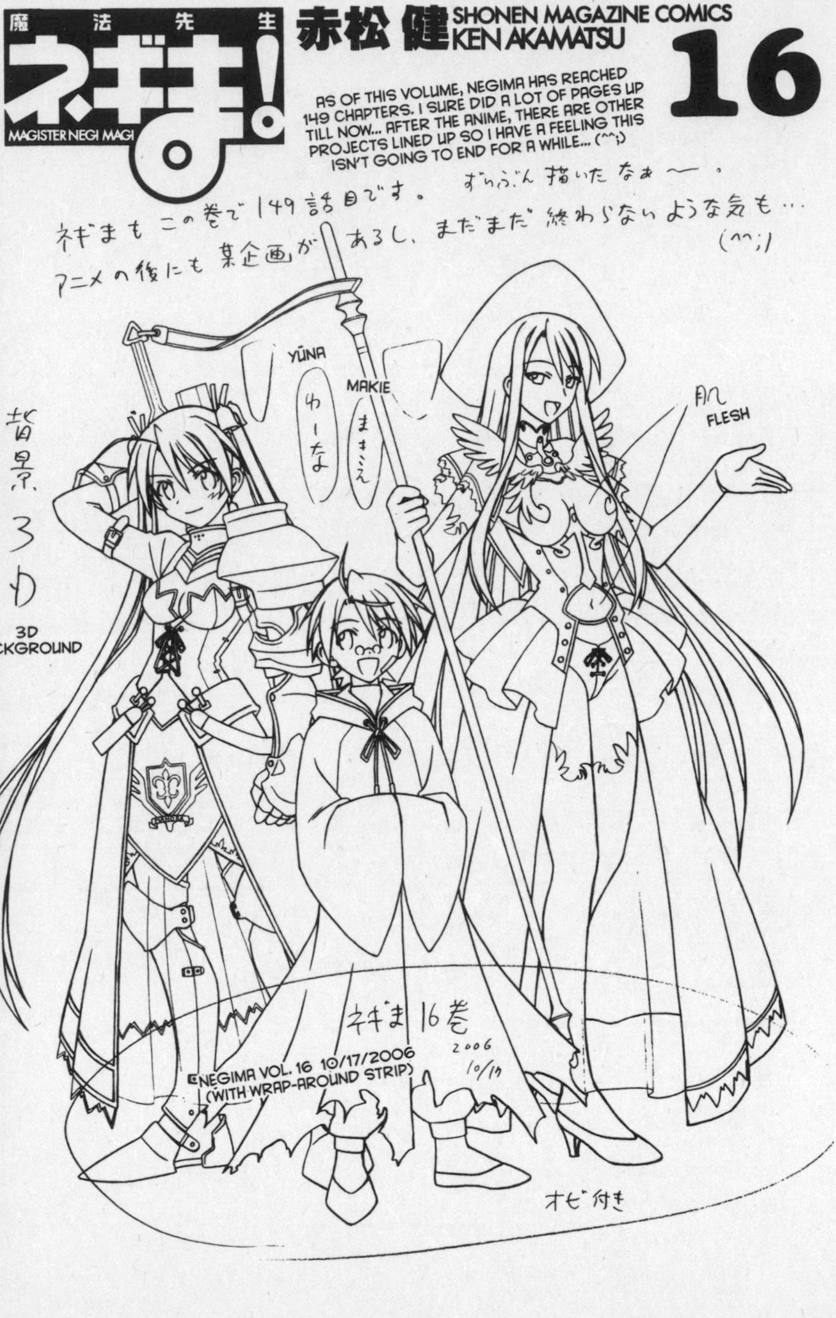

魔法先生
ネギま!
MAGISTER NEGI MAGI
赤松 健
SHONEN MAGAZINE COMICS
KEN AKAMATSU
16
AS OF THIS VOLUME, NEGIMA HAS REACHED 149 CHAPTERS. I SURE DID A LOT OF PAGES UP TILL NOW... AFTER THE ANIME, THERE ARE OTHER PROJECTS LINED UP SO I HAVE A FEELING THIS ISN'T GOING TO END FOR A WHILE... (^^;)
ネギまもこの巻で149話目です。 ずいぶん描いたなぁ〜。
アニメの後にも某企画があるし、まだまだ終わらないような気も…
(^^;)
YŪNA
ゆーな
MAKIE
まきえ
肌
FLESH
背景3D
3D BACKGROUND
ネギま16巻
2006 10/17
(NEGIMA VOL. 16 10/17/2006 (WITH WRAP-AROUND STRIP)
オビ付き

キャラ解説
CHARACTER
PROFILE

② 明石 裕奈 しんねが
② YUNA AKASHI

最近めっきり成長してきた裕奈
RECENTLY, YUNA HAS BEEN GROWING A LOT (<- IN
ですが. そんな彼女の好きなものは
BREAST SIZE). AND HER FAVORITE PERSON HAPPENS
「お父さん」。一体 今後. どんなドキドキ
TO BE HER FATHER. I WONDER WHAT KIND OF
エピソードが待っているのでしょうか?! (^^;)
EXCITING STORY LINES AWAIT HER IN THE FUTURE/? (^^;)

運動神経は良い方で. この 16 ～ 17 巻でも
SHE IS VERY ATHLETICALLY COORDINATED AND WILL BE
かなり活躍しています.
DOING A LOT IN VOL 16 & 17.

13話目で髪の結びを逆に
TO THIS DATE, I'M STILL HAUNTED BY THE FACT
描いてしまったのが. 今でも
THAT I PUT THE KNOT ON HER HAIR ON THE
心残りです。(笑)
WRONG SIDE IN 13TH PERIOD. (LAUGHS)

CVは. 今イチオシの
HER VOICE ACTOR IS THE UP-AND-
木村まどか さん。
COMING MADOKA KIMURA.

ショートの あわあわ 妹系
WITH HER SHORT HAIR AND FLUSTERED
キャラで. かわいいんですよ
LITTLE SISTER-LIKE PERSONALITY YUNA
IS REALLY CUTE. ♡

麻帆良祭も. 次巻でいよいよ クライマックスです。
THE MAHORA FESTIVAL WILL REACH ITS CLIMAX IN THE NEXT VOLUME.
もうしばらく おつきあい 下さいませ。
PLEASE BEAR WITH ME A LITTLE BIT LONGER.

赤松
AKAMATSU

LEXICON NEGIMARIUM

[Negima! 150th Period Lexicon Negimarium de Cantibus]

■ tui gratia jupiter gratia sit. CURA.
(Let the grace of Jupiter be for your sake. HEAL.)

• One of the most basic healing spells, this spell, along with ones for fortune-telling and telekinesis, is taught in the early stages of magical training. It can cure bruises, sprains, scratches, and minor cuts and, depending on the spell caster's skill, burns and frostbite. However, if the wound or disease is severe, this spell cannot keep up with the level of damage to the body. This is the spell that Negi used when he first met Chamo five years ago.

[Negima! 152nd Period Lexicon Negimarium de Cantibus]

■ nihil nullum, zephirum. Spiritus Magnus, unum. spiritus electronice! nantur super aquas. EGO ELECTRIUM REGNO.
(The Barren Nothingness, Zero. The Great Spirit, One. Electron Spirits, drift across the watery surface. I am the Electric Ruler.)

• By the power of the Pactio with Negi, Chisame Hasegawa is awarded the Sceptrum Virtuale for her use. By using the artifact and reciting the above incantation, Chisame is able to dive into cyberspace...but not really. What this spell actually does is organize the Electron Sprites (spiritus electronice) with the power of the Sceptrum Virtuale.

Since the latter half of the 1960s, computers have become faster and able to handle greater and greater amounts of data, which in turn has allowed programs to become more complex. For this reason, using software has become more difficult. This has created a new problem for many people—a great deal of time and energy now has to be spent learning to use new computer programs. Computers were created as labor-saving devices, but in some cases, they've actually created more work.

Since most mages follow an older way of life, one rooted in pre-modern culture, they've seldom had to face this problem. In fact, advanced technology played no significant role in the lives of mages until these human-world technologies began to affect the magical world. This was when computers became important to people who were not computer professionals. (For example, calculators and cellular phones are computers, and the important role they play in our daily lives should be obvious.) In order to deal with these new technologies, mages needed to make some revolutionary innovations of their own.

The Sceptrum Virtuale is a magical user interface for computers. At their lowest layers, the sprites have limited intelligence, but they are able to control electricity, magnetism, and electromagnetic fields by organizing themselves into basic commands that allow them to not only access devices and gather information from them but write new information into them as well. The Sceptrum can also create a virtual input peripheral for computers. (For example, it can move the cursor on a computer screen without using a mouse.) The information gathered by the lower-layer sprites is passed along to the higher layers, after having been analyzed and converted to analog form along the way. Eventually this data is passed on to the sprites in the highest layers, who are able to understand the psyche of the sprite leader and possess the ability to express emotion. They pass on the information to the user of the Sceptrum Virtuale. So this artifact, in short, can gather a tremendous amount of complex data from a computer and sift through it, sorting the useful information from the useless and therefore saving the human user some strain and tedious labor. The high-level sprites can also read the psychological condition of the Sceptrum Virtuale user through telepathy and act accordingly, making sure that only the information needed by the user is passed along. Even though not all data is passed along, it is stored and ready to be converted into analog for the user if it should be needed.

The communication between the user of the Sceptrum Virtuale and the higher-layer sprites is done by telepathy, so if visual data is sent, the user will see it as if it were literally before his or her own eyes. This can cause a problem should the user be awake, so to avoid such problems, when the user is on the computer, the physical body goes into a state of dormancy and appears to be asleep. (However, it is possible to receive audio data only while awake as the artifact can be used like a portable audio player.)

The Sceptrum controls a massive number of sprites, allowing more than just the mage and the partner to use them. If anything, having several people available allows for a more efficient use of its abilities.

The commands the user sends to the computer through the Sceptrum Virtuale work pretty much in reverse of what was described before. The commands are sent to the higher-layer sprites and then sent down the lower layers after being translated and converted into a digital signal. Once they reach the lowest layers, the commands can form a pseudocontrol signal of electronic, magnetic, or electromagnetic means to control various devices.

The Sceptrum Virtuale itself has calculation and recording abilities and can be used as a stand-alone computer if necessary. In order to do so, the higher-level sprites must download software from the Maho-net that they deem necessary or create programs of their own.

[Negima! 155th Period Lexicon Negimarium de Cantibus]

■ Shukuchi Mukyō

(suodiwujiang)

• *Shukuchi* is the Eastern technique of manipulating the *chimiyaku* (earth pulse) to achieve superhuman speed. (For more details, see the Lexicon in *Negima!* volume 11) *Mukyō* is a word that appears in the text of the *I-Ching* in the writings of the *K'un* hexagram: "The Receptive brings about sublime success, furthering through the perseverance of a mare." The hexagram symbolizes the earth, and the mare symbolizes having the potential to reach the ends of the earth.

[Negima! 156th Period Lexicon Negimarium de Cantibus]

■ rapide subsistat

(rapid stop)

• As the words clearly indicate, this spell causes a sudden deceleration. It is not often a spell is used while flying on a broom or staff, but these spells allow for the rapid acceleration and deceleration of flight. The *mobiliter* (high-speed maneuverability) spell from the 158th period is another example of such a spell.

■ [...] ό δὲ κόσμος κινεῖται έν τῷ αἰῶνι ό δὲ χρόνος περαιοῦται έν τῷ κοσμῷ ἡ δὲ γένεσις γίνεται έντῷ χρόνῷ.

(Aeon stands firm round God; Cosmos is moved in Aeon; Time hath its limits in the Cosmos; Becoming doth become in Time.)

• This is the last line of the second chapter of the *Hermetica*. This passage talks of the connection of the spiritual soul within nature and God. Nature is governed by God at the apex, along with Aeon (eternity), the World (or the laws within), Chronos (time), and Genesis. In the ancient world of the Mediterranean countries, Cosmos (κόσμος) was not all-encompassing as there existed a being of even greater power. But Cosmos occupied a prominent position as a symbol of the unchanging order of the world. Chronos (χρόνος) is one of the orders of Cosmos, and through it the natural end of Genesis becomes possible. Aeon, who stands atop the world, is similar to Chronos. Aeon is also a form of time, but Chronos is "change" whereas Aeon is "eternity," which is unchanging. Those who exist in the world are always in a state of change (as well as approaching extinction), which means that the X factor is ever changing, but at the same time X has to be self-identical, as without it it can't be said that something has changed. Such a self-identical X is called the nature of existence (ούδία).

[Negima! 157th Period Lexicon Negimarium de Cantibus]

■ **ἐιμογε χρηματίσαντων δῶδεκα ἱερειαι Πυό, Λοῦοιαν Ὕγγαν, Ἀνγκωρ [...] οὐ ζωὴ ὁρίζει δύνεδιν, ἀλλὰ δύνεδις ζωήν**

(Answer me, twelve sacred lands...Buyeo, Luoyang, Yungang, Angkor...Life does not stipulate consciousness. Consciousness stipulates life. Life exists because of the soul; the soul is consciousness.)

• This magic spell takes away one's initiative for consciousness and implants a suggestion to manipulate perception. Casting of this spell requires a long incantation. Buyeo (capital of the ancient Baekje Kingdom), Luoyang (capital of the Zhou dynasty), Yungang (ancient Buddhist temple grottos located in Shanxi Province), and Angkor Wat (in Cambodia) are sacred magical points (like the World Tree) around the globe. The spell connects all the points to amplify the spell's range. Most of the sacred lands are in the northern hemisphere as most of the modernized societies that left magic behind reside there.

[Negima! 158th–159th Period Lexicon Negimarium de Cantibus]

■ **Τὸ συμβόλαιον διακονήτω μοί, ὁ τύραννε φλογός. Ἐπιγενηθήτω, φλόξ κάταρσεως, φλογίνη ῥομφαία. Ῥευσάντων, τῦρ καὶ θεῖον. Ἃ ἐπεφλέγον Σοδομα, ἁμαρτωλούς εἰς χοῦν θανάτου. ΟΥΡΆΝΙΑ ΦΛΌΓΩΣΙΣ!**

(Fire and brimstone surged forth, Sodom was burning. They turned the sinners into the dust of death! Blazing heat in the sky!)

• An area-effect spell that causes an extremely high-temperature flame to engulf and incinerate the target area. This is a high-level spell that's nearly as difficult as Evangeline's ΚΟΣΜΙΚΗ` ΚΡΥΣΤΑΛΛΟΠΗΓΊΑ (Freezing World) and must be incanted in ancient Greek. However, increasing the temperature, as compared to reducing it to sub-zero levels, does not break the second law of thermodynamics, so this spell is slightly less advanced than Evangeline's.

■ EVOCATIO SPIRITUALIS DE UNDETRIGINTA SALAMANDRIS LANCIFERIS

(A Spiritual Evocation for Twenty-nine Lance-Wielding Salamanders)

• This spell summons forth the elemental of fire, the Salamandra of Greek and Roman cultures. For more information on the Salamandra, see the Lexicon in *Negima!* volume 16.

■ EVOCATIO SPIRITUALIS DE SEPTENDECIM VALCYRIIS MORTIFERIS

(A Spiritual Evocation for Seventeen Deadly Valkyries)

• A spell that summons forth the Valkyries, the female deities that serve Odin in Norse mythology. According to Snorri's *Edda* (Book One, Chapter 36), the Valkyries decided the victor of a battle and chose the most heroic soldiers who died in battle to reside forever in Valhalla.

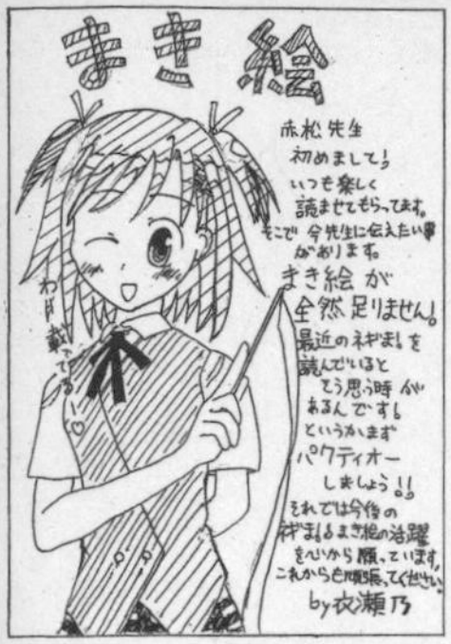
まき絵
赤松先生
初めましてっ
いつも楽しく
読ませてもらってます。
まき絵が
全然足りません!
by 衣瀬乃

▲ IT WOULD BE NICE TO SEE MORE OF MAKIE!

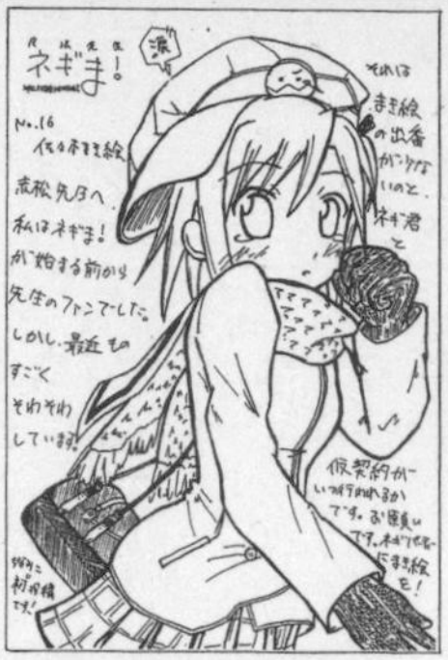
ネギま!
赤松先生へ
私はネギま!
が始まる前から
先生のファンでした。

▲ PLEASE FEEL FREE TO FIDGET. (LAUGHS)

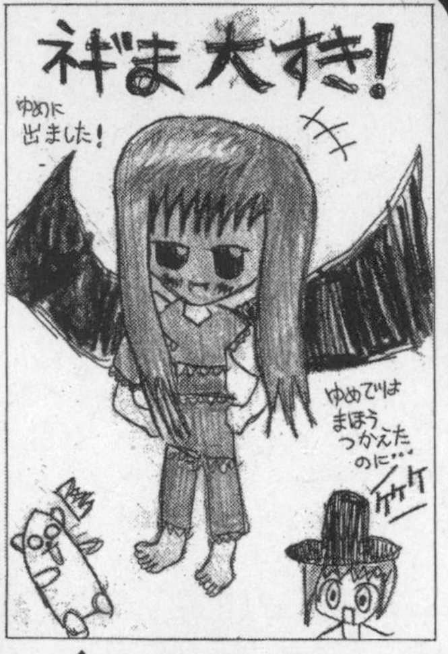
ネギま大すき!
ゆめに
出ました!
ゆめでは
まほうつかえた
のに…

▲ IT MUST HAVE BEEN NICE TO USE MAGIC, EVEN IN A DREAM. ★

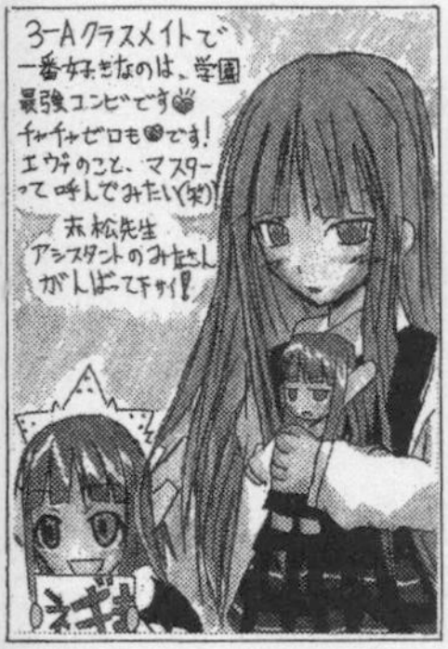
3-Aクラスメイトで
一番好きなのは、学園
最強コンビです
チャチャゼロも♡です!
赤松先生
アシスタントのみなさん
がんばって下さい!
ネギま

▲ SUPERCUTE EVA-SAN!

NEGIMA!
FAN ART CORNER

AS USUAL, WE'RE GOING TO BE FEATURING ILLUSTRATIONS FROM ALL YOU READERS OUT THERE. (^^) RECENTLY, WE'VE BEEN SEEING MORE AND MORE MAKIE AND KOTARŌ PICTURES. ☆ EVA AND SETSUNA REMAIN POPULAR, BUT CHISAME SEEMS TO BE CATCHING UP FAST. ASUNA CONTINUES TO HAVE A STRONG FAN BASE. ☆ WE'D LOVE TO SEE OTHER CHARACTERS TRICKLE IN AS WELL. ☆ EVERYONE, GET SCRIBBLING! ☆

TEXT BY ASSISTANT MAX

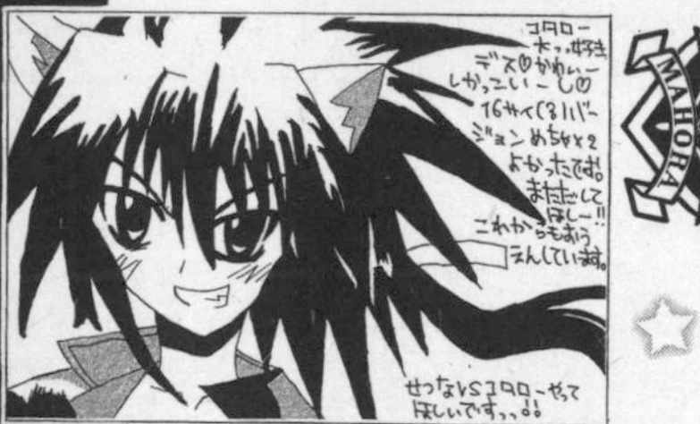
これからもおう
えんしています。

▲ HOT-BLOODED KOTARŌ ♪♪

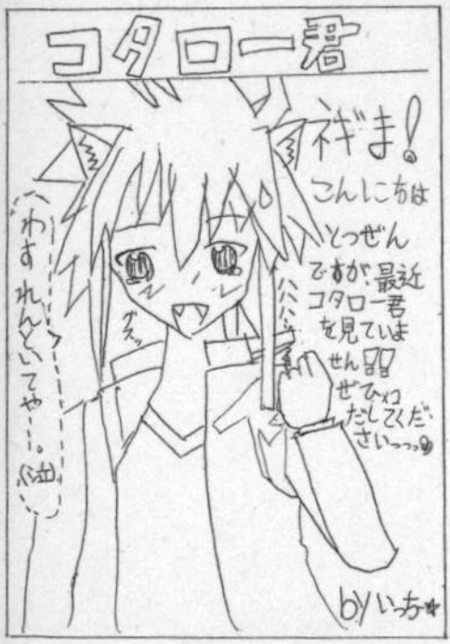
コタロー君
ネギま!
こんにちは
by いち

▲ WE HAVEN'T FORGOTTEN HIM. (LAUGHS)

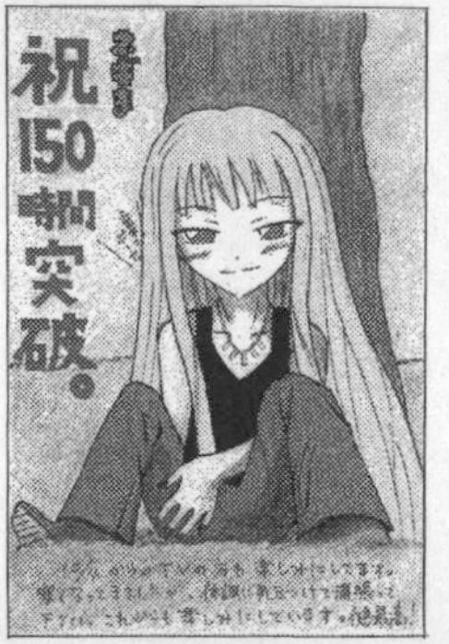
祝
150
時間
突破。

◀ THANK YOU. ★

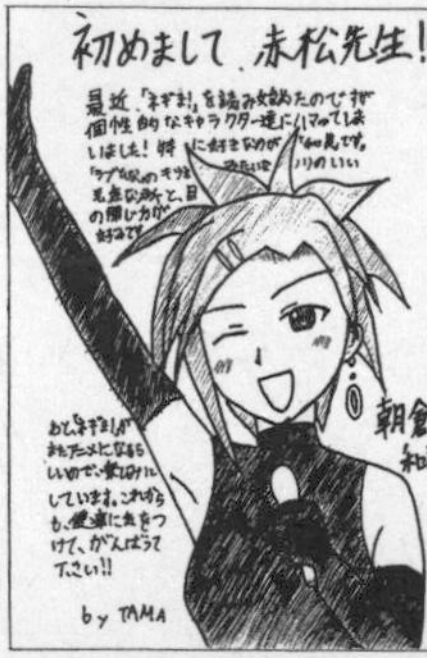
初めまして 赤松先生!!
朝倉
和美
by TAMA

▼ ASAKURA'S ALWAYS SO ENERGETIC!

NEGI MA!

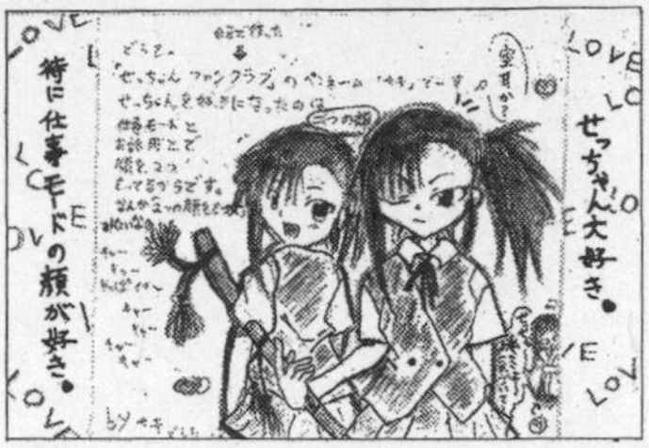
せっちゃん大好き。
特に仕事モードの顔が好き。

▲ WE CAN FEEL YOUR LOVE FOR SETSUNA.♪

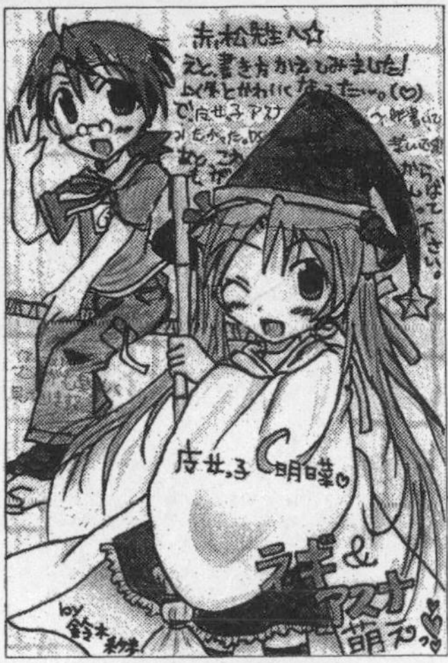

▲ SHE LOOKS VERY GIRLISH.♪

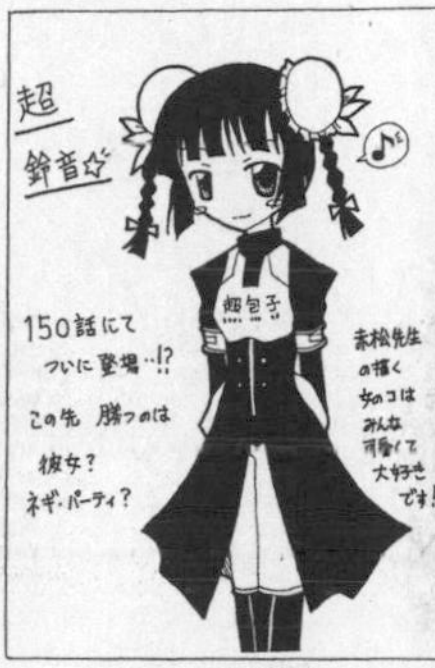
超
鈴音☆

▲ SUCH A PRECOCIOUS-LOOKING CHAO.

▼ ADORABLE CHAO

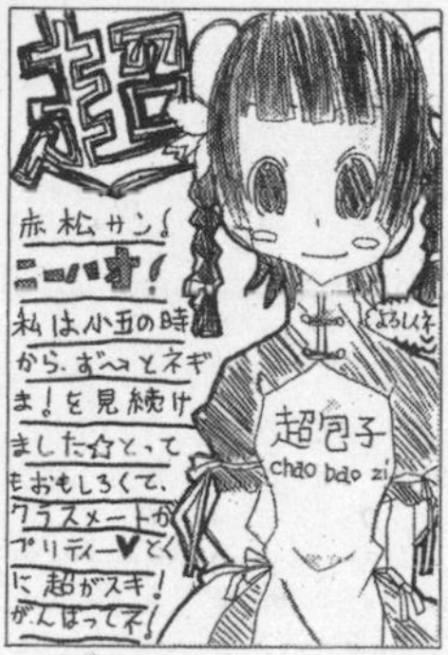
超包子
chao bao zi

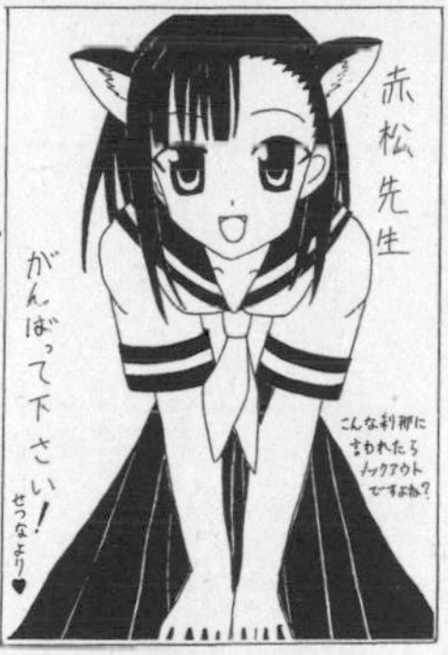
赤松先生
がんばって下さい!

▲ WE WERE KNOCKED OUT. (LAUGHS)

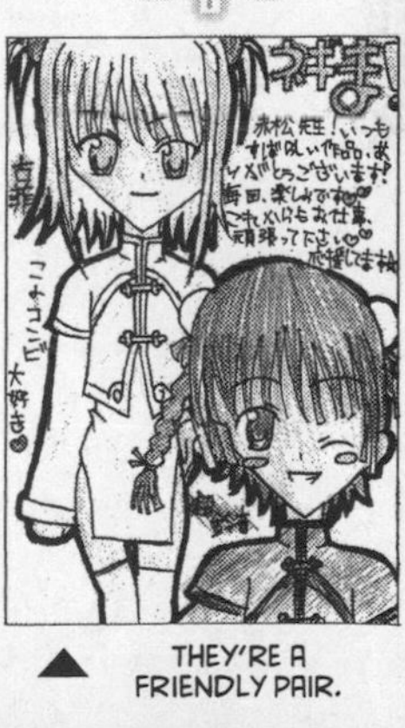

▲ THEY'RE A FRIENDLY PAIR.

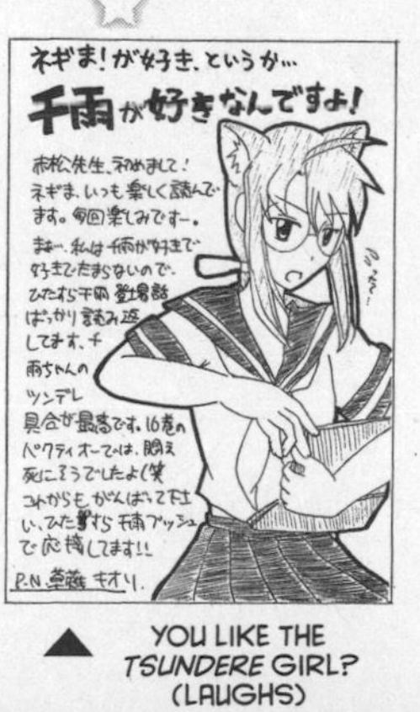
ネギま!が好き、というか…
千雨が好きなんですよ!

▲ YOU LIKE THE *TSUNDERE* GIRL? (LAUGHS)

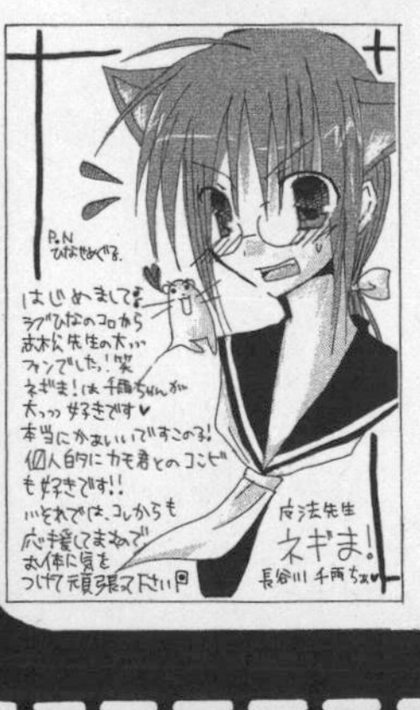

▲ CHISAME AND CHAMO ★

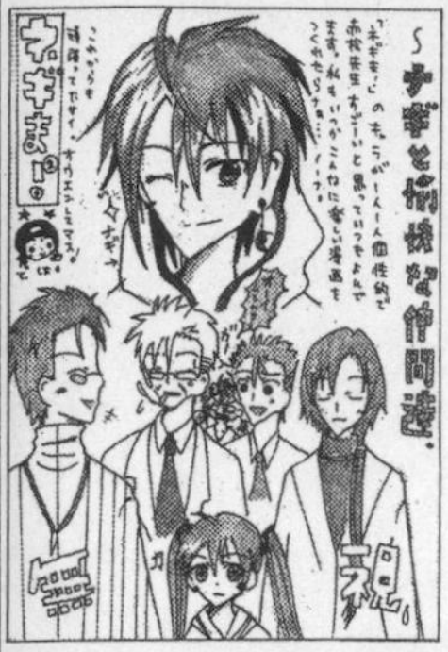
▲ LOOKS LIKE THEY'RE HAVING FUN...

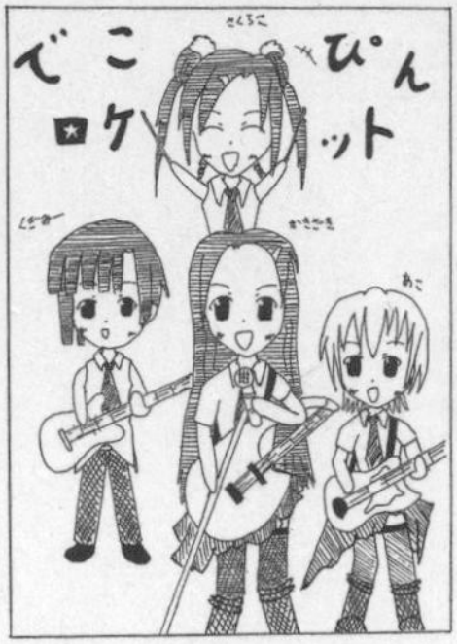
でこぴん
ロケット
▲ DEKOPIN DOKOPIN♪

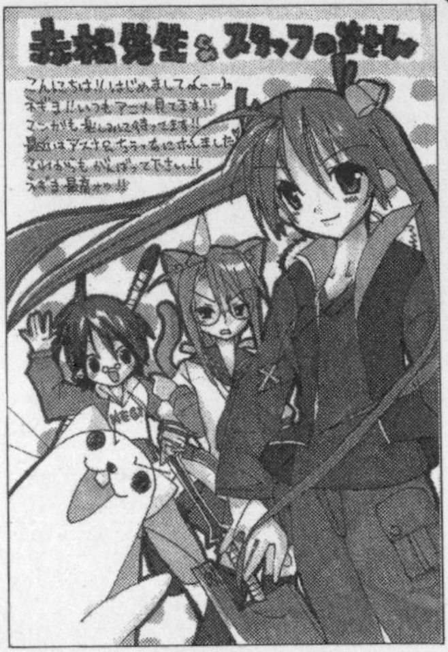
赤松先生&スタッフのみなさん
THEY LOOK VERY COOL.♪ ◥

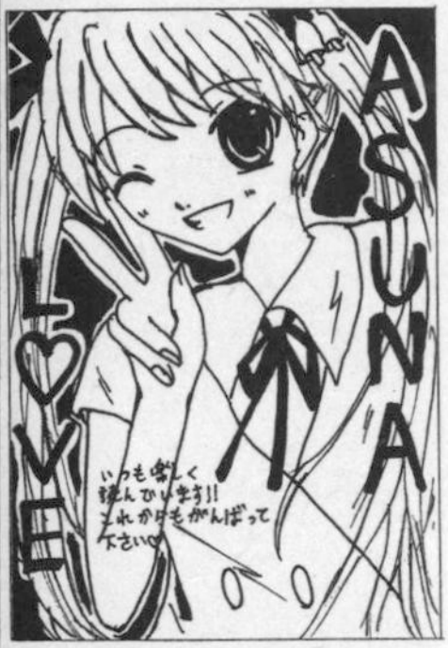
ASUNA
LOVE
▲ THE ALWAYS-ENERGETIC ASUNA ★

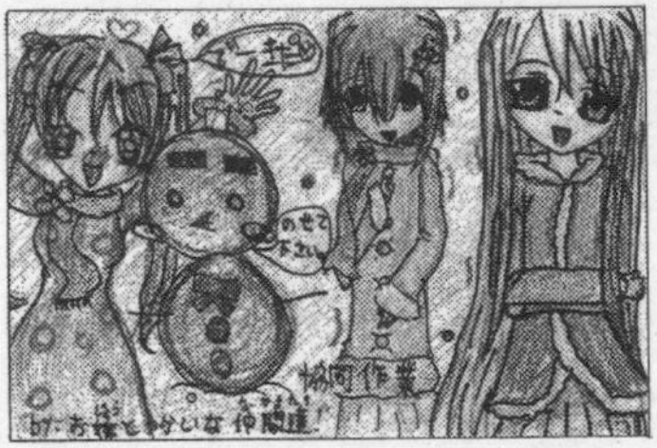
▲ IS NEGI THE SNOWMAN? (LAUGHS)

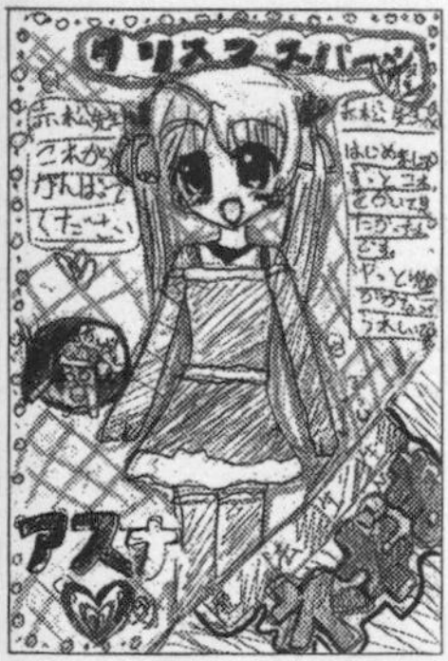
▲ ASUNA IN A SANTA COSTUME♪

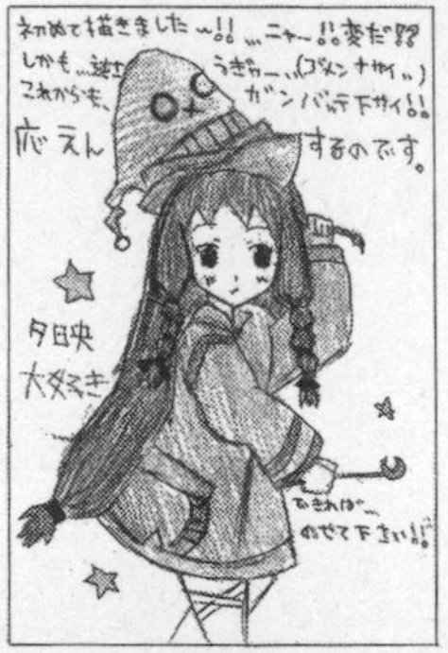
▲ WHAT A GREAT-LOOKING HAT! (LAUGHS)

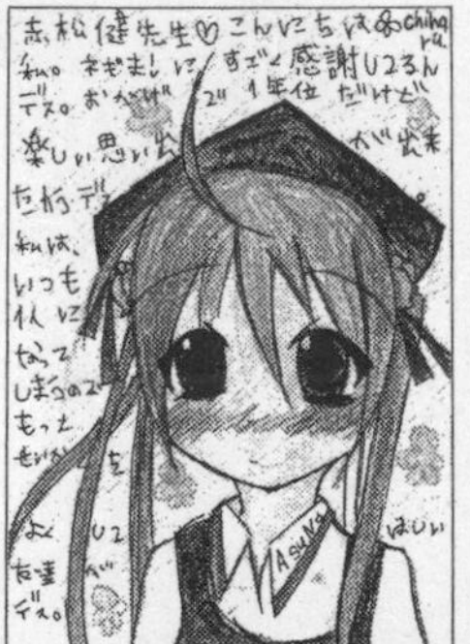
▲ THAT LOOK MAKES MY HEART SKIP A BEAT. (LAUGHS)

NEGI MA!

MAGISTER NEGI MAGI

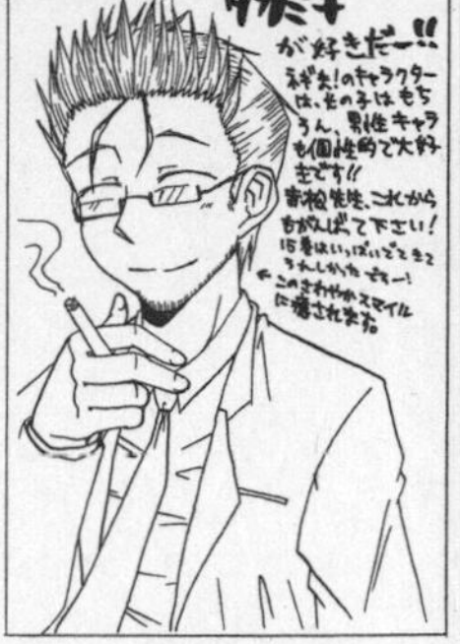
サカミチ
が好きだー!!

LOVE THAT REFRESHING SMILE.♪

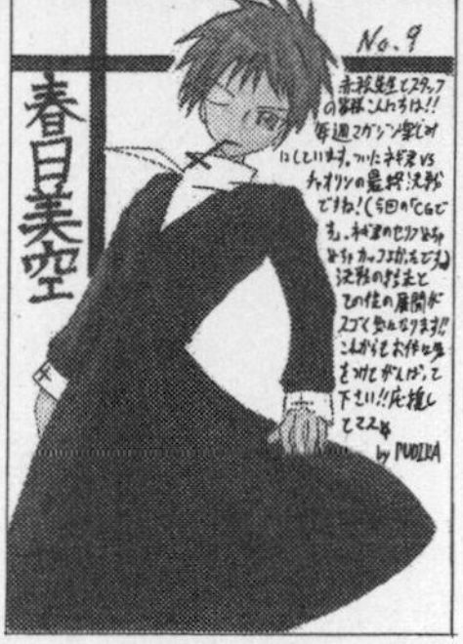
No.9
春日美空

VERY SHARP-LOOKING MISORA!

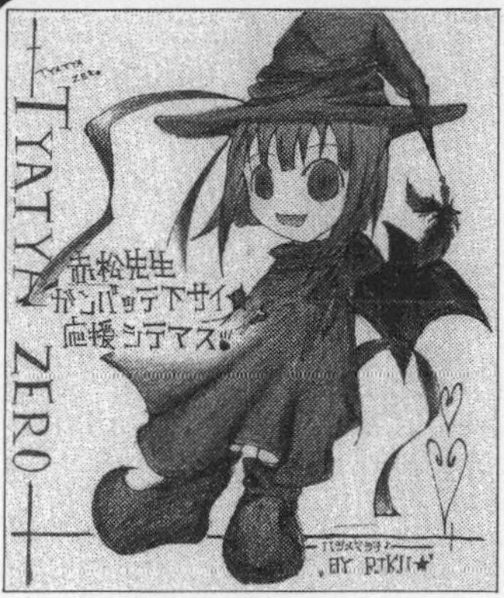
TYATYA ZERO
赤松先生
ガンバッテ下サイ★
応援シテマス!!

HOW CUTE!

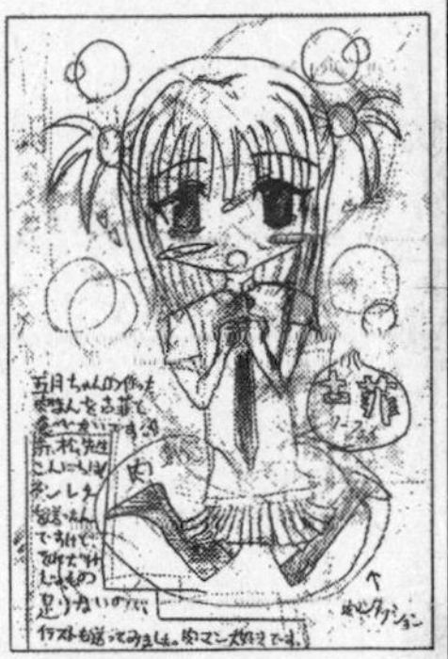

THE PORK BUNS LOOK TASTY!

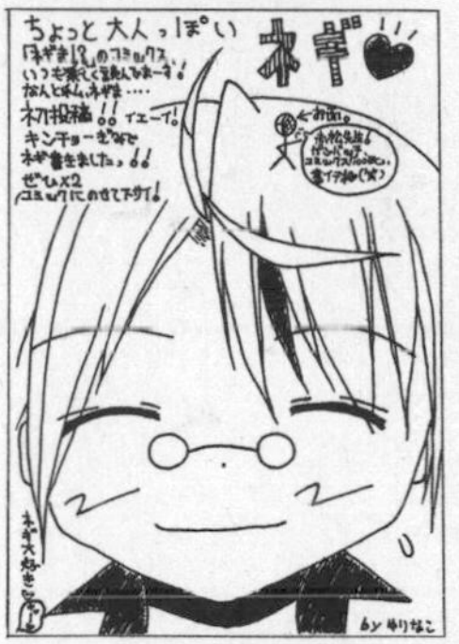
ちょっと大人っぽい

WHAT AN AMAZING SMILE. ★

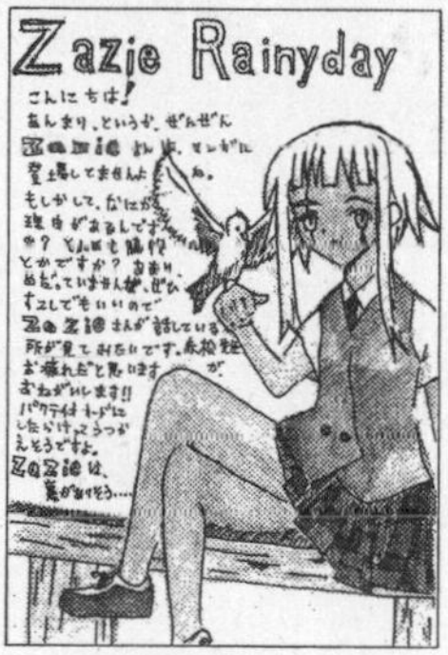
Zazie Rainyday
こんにちは!

A VERY CALM ZAZIE

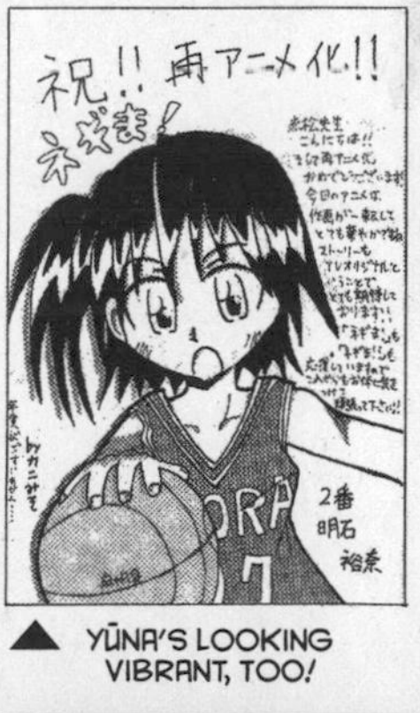
祝!! 再アニメ化!!
ネギま!
2番
明石
裕奈

YŪNA'S LOOKING VIBRANT, TOO!

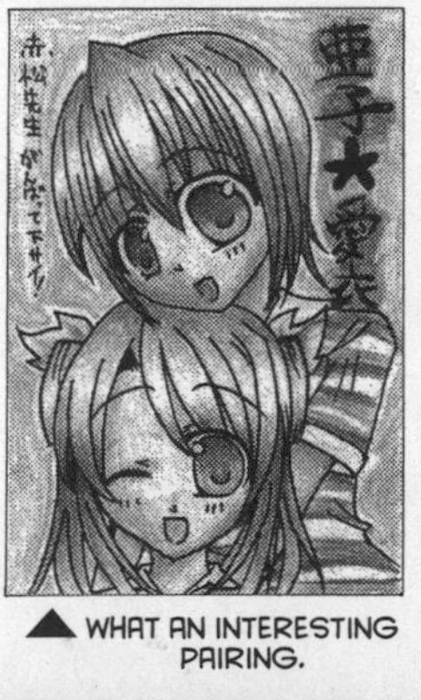
赤松先生がんばって下サイ!

WHAT AN INTERESTING PAIRING.

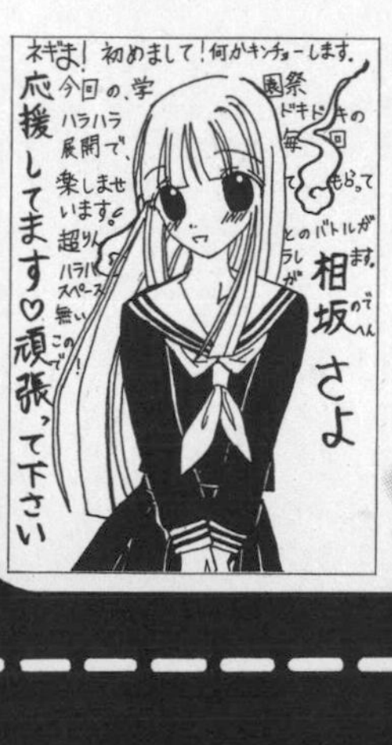
ネギま! 初めまして! 何かキンチョーします。
相坂
さよ
頑張って下さい

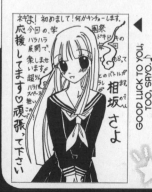

GOOD LUCK TO YOU, TOO, SAYO.♪

3-D BACKGROUNDS EXPLANATION CORNER

IN THIS VOLUME, THERE WERE A LOT OF 3-D SCENES INVOLVING MAHORA ACADEMY CITY AND VARIOUS OBJECTS.

• ROOFTOP CAFÉ (SMALL)

SCENE NAME: ROOFTOP CAFÉ
POLYGON COUNT: 163,180

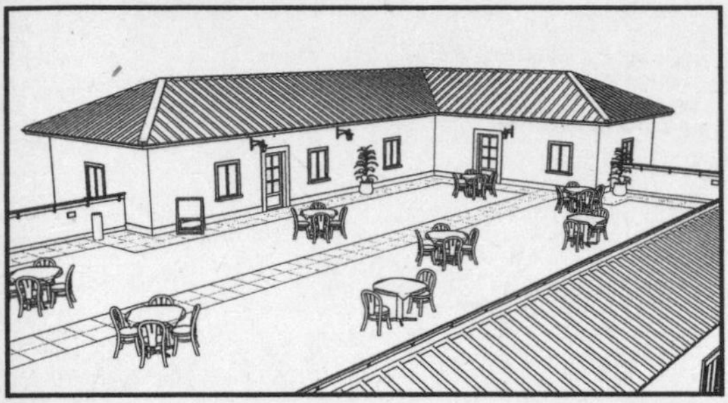

THIS IS A DIFFERENT ROOFTOP CAFÉ FROM THE ONE THAT APPEARED IN VOLUME 10. MAHORA ACADEMY CITY HAS MANY OUTDOOR ROOFTOP COFFEE SHOPS.

IT DOESN'T FACE THE STREET, SO ITS QUIET ATMOSPHERE IS VERY POPULAR WITH THE STUDENTS. IT'S A NICE, RELAXING PLACE TO GET A GREAT VIEW OF THE CITY WHILE ENJOYING THE COOL BREEZE.

• STREET WITH A TRAM

SCENE NAME: TRAM STREET
POLYGON COUNT: 609,203

ONE OF THE MORE NOTICEABLE CHARACTERISTICS OF MAHORA ACADEMY CITY ARE THE STREET TROLLEYS THAT RUN THROUGHOUT THE CITY. HERE, YOU CAN SEE A SECONDARY LINE CROSS THE MAIN LINE.

DURING THE ACADEMY-WIDE EVENT, THIS SECTION WAS CORDONED OFF AS PART OF THE GAME AREA, SO THE CHAO BAO ZI WAS CLOSED FOR BUSINESS. ON A NORMAL DAY (ALSO DURING NORMAL FESTIVAL HOURS), THIS IS A VERY POPULAR AND OFTEN CROWDED PLACE.

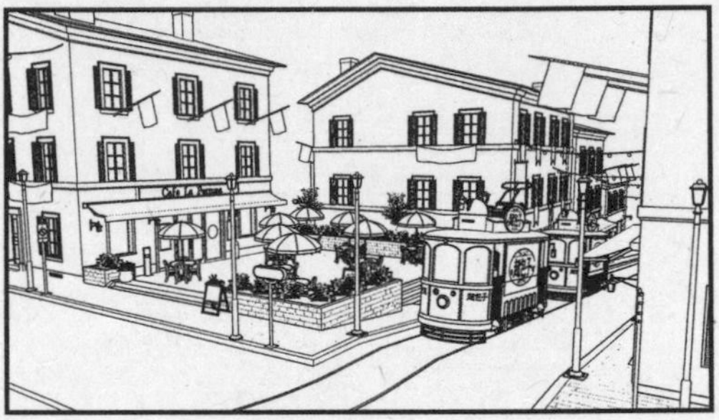

- BONUS -

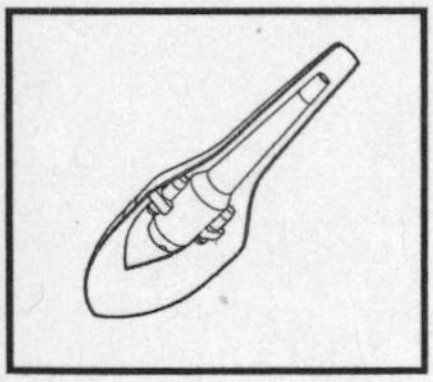

• CHAO'S SATELLITE WEAPON

IN THE ACTUAL STORY, THIS WAS NEVER NAMED, BUT IN AKAMATSU STUDIO, IT WAS CALLED THE FUN...S (LAUGHS)

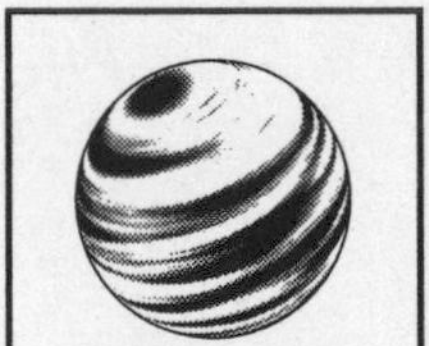

• BULLET OF COMPULSORY TIME TRAVEL

SIMILAR TO KŪ:NEL'S GRAVITY MAGIC, THIS WAS CREATED BY APPLYING A TEXTURE TO A SPHERE. WE WANTED TO DIFFERENTIATE IT A BIT BY MAKING THE TEXTURE LOOK AS IF THE SPHERE WAS SPINNING RAPIDLY.

• SCEPTRUM VIRTUALE

THIS IS CHISAME'S ARTIFACT. THIS ITEM IS RENDERED IN 3-D EXCEPT FOR THE RIBBONS, WHICH WOULD HAVE POSED A PROBLEM, SINCE THEY'RE FRILLY AND ALWAYS IN MOTION. SO THE RIBBONS WERE HAND DRAWN. AS A RESULT, WE FORGOT TO INCLUDE THE RIBBONS IN THE DIAGRAM DEPICTED HERE. (^^;)

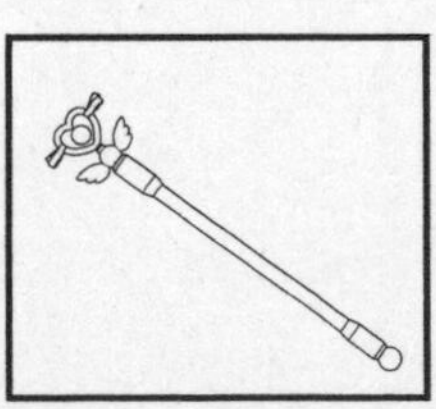

• JAPANESE SAKE, "BISHŌNEN"

EVANGELINE WAS DRINKING THIS SAKE. PLEASE NOTE THAT THE KANJI FOR "SHŌ" IS DIFFERENT FROM THAT IN THE ACTUAL SAKE BRAND BISHŌNEN. (LAUGHS) BY THE WAY, THIS IS A PURE RICE *GINJŌ* SAKE.

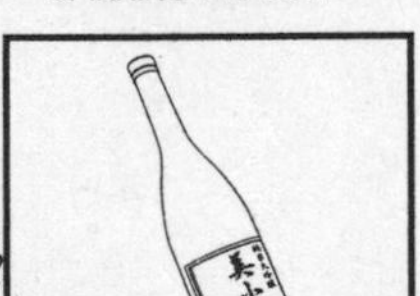
美小年

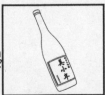

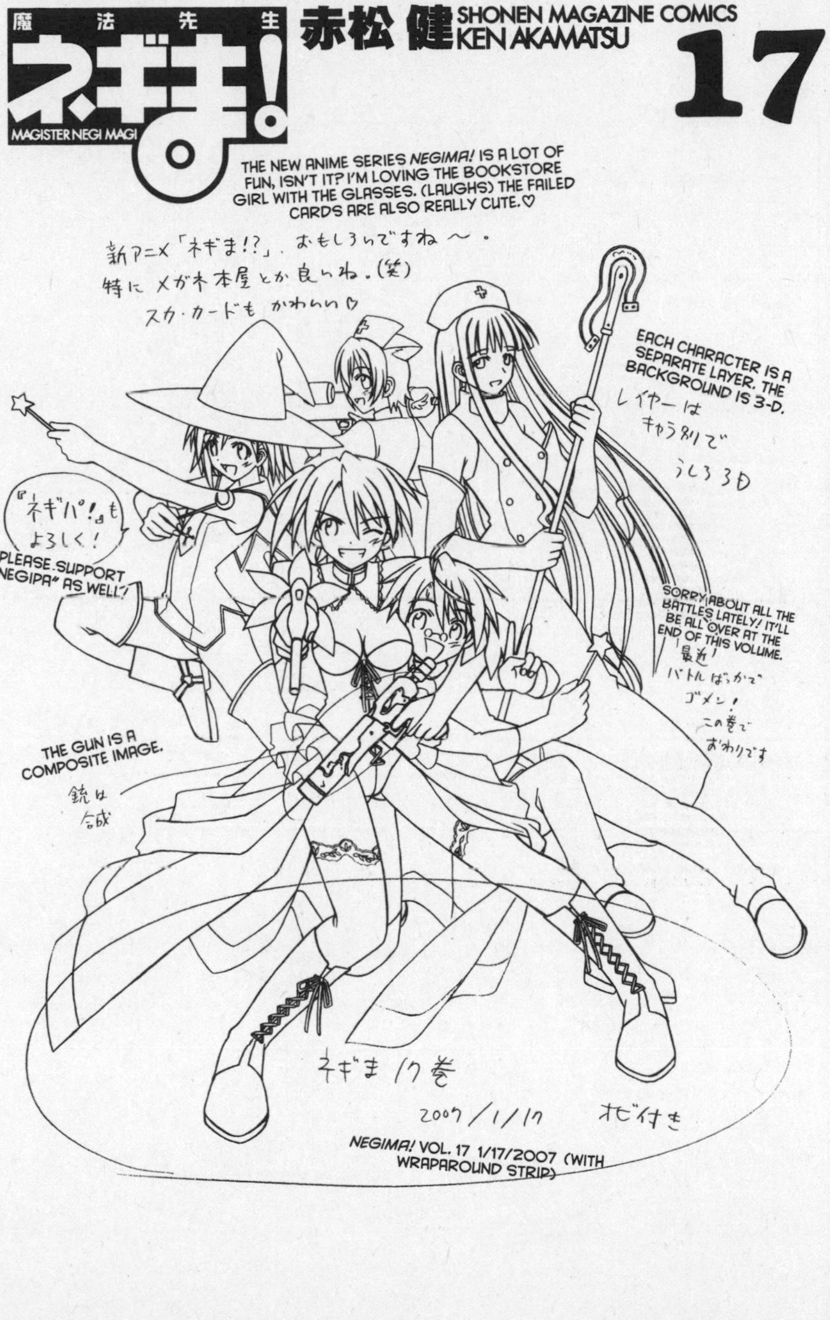

魔法先生
ネギま!
MAGISTER NEGI MAGI
赤松 健
SHONEN MAGAZINE COMICS
KEN AKAMATSU
17
THE NEW ANIME SERIES *NEGIMA!* IS A LOT OF FUN, ISN'T IT? I'M LOVING THE BOOKSTORE GIRL WITH THE GLASSES. (LAUGHS) THE FAILED CARDS ARE ALSO REALLY CUTE.♡
新アニメ「ネギま!?」、おもしろいですね〜。
特にメガネ本屋とか良いね。(笑)
スカ・カードもかわいい♡
EACH CHARACTER IS A SEPARATE LAYER. THE BACKGROUND IS 3-D.
レイヤーは
キャラ分りで
うしろ3D
『ネギパ!』も
よろしく!
PLEASE SUPPORT "NEGIPA" AS WELL!
SORRY ABOUT ALL THE BATTLES LATELY! IT'LL BE ALL OVER AT THE END OF THIS VOLUME.
「最近」
バトルばっかで
ゴメン!
この巻で
おわりです
THE GUN IS A COMPOSITE IMAGE.
銃は
合成
ネギま17巻
2007/1/17
オビ付き
NEGIMA! VOL. 17 1/17/2007 (WITH WRAPAROUND STRIP)

CHARACTER
PROFILE

⑥ 大河内アキラ
⑥ AKIRA ŌKŌCHI

普段は 物静かだけど、
AKIRA'S NORMALLY VERY QUIET, BUT SHE'S AN

スポーツ万能で 思いやりがあって、
EXCEPTIONAL ATHLETE. SHE'S VERY CONSIDERATE OF

クラス みんなに 好かれている のが
OTHERS, AND AS A RESULT, SHE'S POPULAR WITH HER

アキラ。
CLASSMATES.

ポニーテールを おろすと、ぶっちゃけ
IF SHE WEARS HER HAIR DOWN, I HAVE TO

素子との 描き分けが できなくなって
ADMIT THAT SHE LOOKS VERY MUCH LIKE

しまう のですが (^^;)、ちょっとだけ
MOTOKO. (^^;) THE ONE WITH

髪が ウェーブしてるのが アキラです。
SLIGHTLY WAVY HAIR IS AKIRA.

単独での ストーリーは まだ ありません
SHE HASN'T HAD A FEATURE STORY YET, BUT I

けど そのうち 必ずやります!
PROMISE TO DO ONE VERY SOON! TO ALL AKIRA

待っててね。> アキラ ファン
FANS OUT THERE, PLEASE BE PATIENT!

CVは、山本 改め 浅倉杏美ちゃん。
HER VOICE ACTOR IS AZUMI ASAKURA (FORMERLY YAMAMOTO). WHEN SHE WAS

決まった当時は まだ 高校生でした、け
FIRST CAST TO PLAY AKIRA, SHE WAS STILL IN HIGH SCHOOL. SHE'S LOOKING

最近 めっきり 大人っぽくなりました。
VERY GROWN-UP LATELY. SHE CAN ALSO PLAY LITTLE-BOY ROLES, SO I THINK WE

少年役も できちゃうので、今後に 期待です!
CAN LOOK FORWARD TO A LOT MORE FROM HER IN THE FUTURE!

AKAMATSU

NEGI MA!

NEGIMA! FAN ART CORNER

ONCE AGAIN, WE'RE GOING TO FEATURE ILLUSTRATIONS FROM THE READERS OUT THERE. ☆ WE'VE RECEIVED A LOT OF PASSIONATE ILLUSTRATIONS. ☆ I THINK I'M STARTING TO SEE A TREND TOWARD LESS FEATURED CHARACTERS LATELY. (LAUGHS) ANYHOW, LET'S GET STARTED. ☆ MAKE SURE THAT THE ART YOU SEND IN IS POSTCARD SIZE. ☆ YOU CAN SEND THEM TO THE ADDRESS LISTED IN THE BACK OF THE BOOK FOR THE KODANSHA EDITORIAL OFFICE. ☆

TEXT BY ASSISTANT MAX

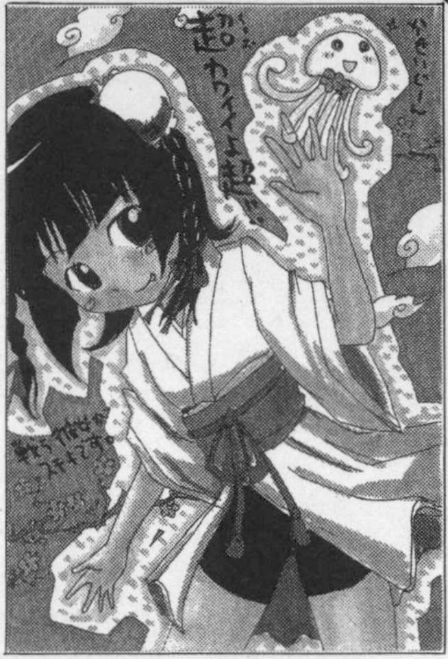

NICE AND CUTE♪ ▶

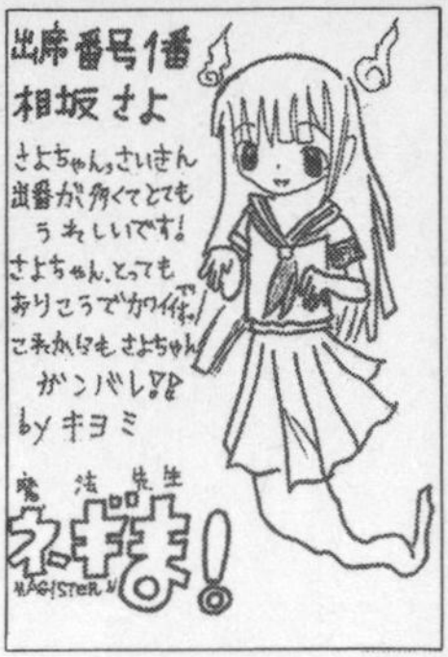

相坂さよ
ネギま！

▲ NOW THIS IS A VERY GHOSTLIKE POSE.

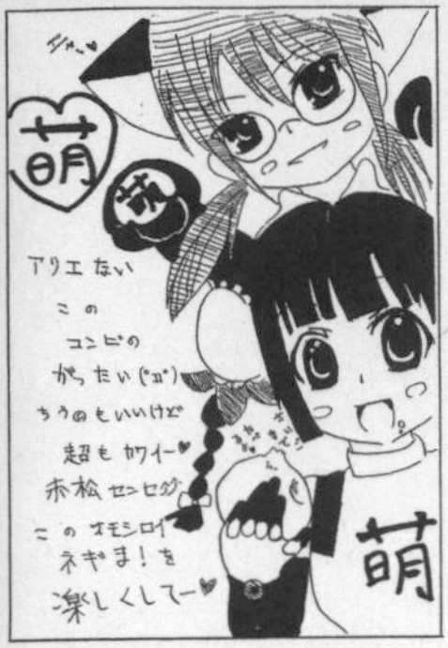

萌

▲ CHIU AND CHAO ★

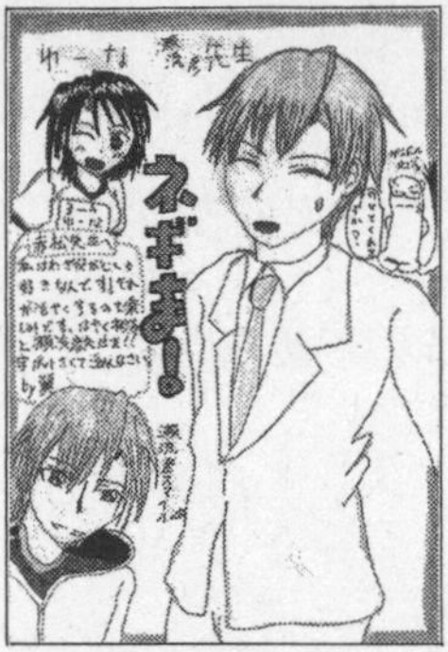

ネギま！

▶ AN AVID SERUHIKO FAN IS QUITE RARE!

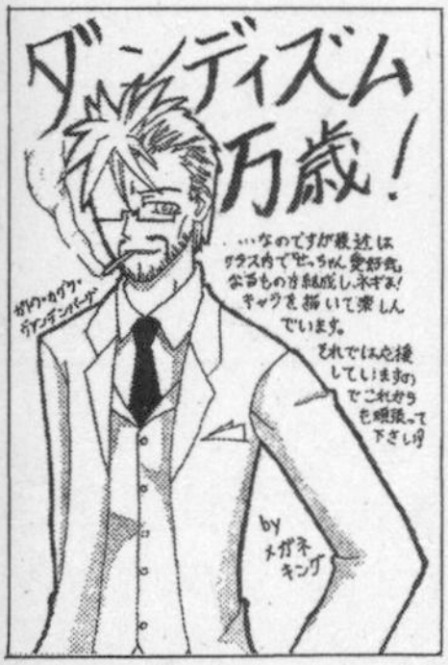

ダンディズム万歳！

▲ NOW THAT'S VERY DANDY LOOKING!

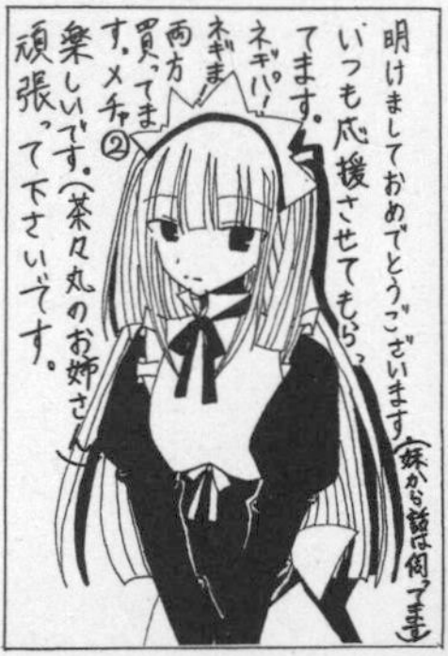

明けましておめでとうございます

▶ A FAN OF CHACHAMARU'S SISTER, HUH? (LAUGHS)

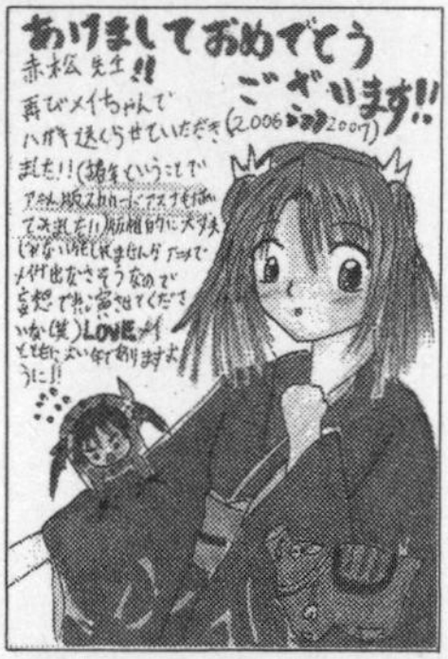

あけましておめでとう
ございます!!

▲ THE RED KIMONO LOOKS GOOD ON MEI.

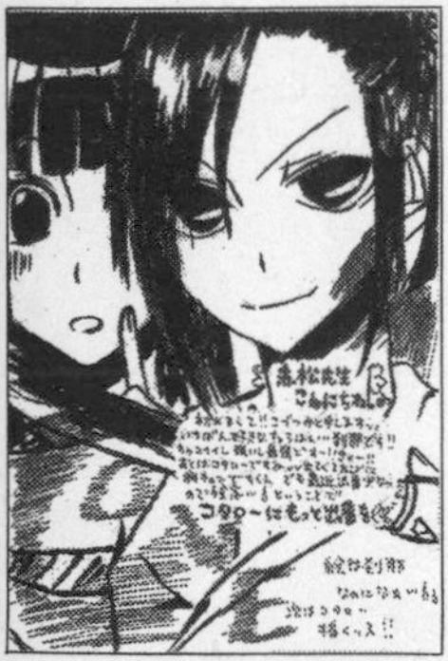

▲ WE LOVE THE EYES!

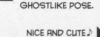

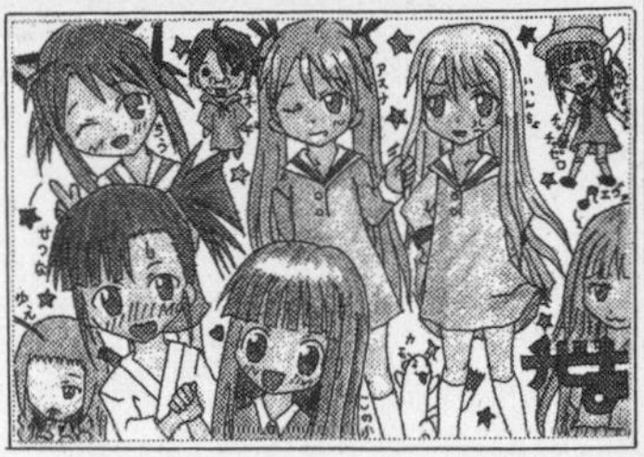

WE CAN FEEL THEIR FRIENDSHIP.★

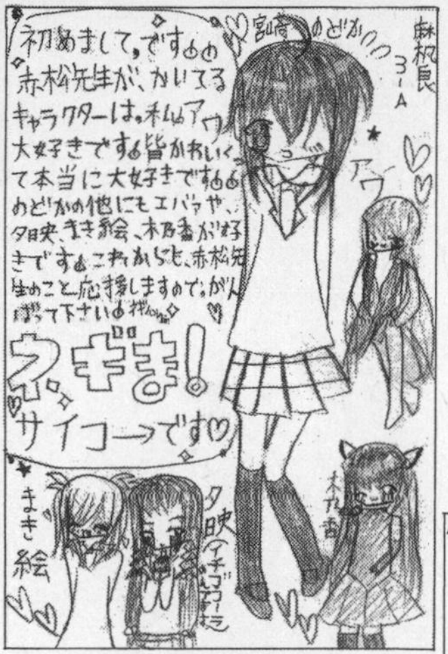

A NICE PANICKED LOOK ON NODOKA (LAUGHS)

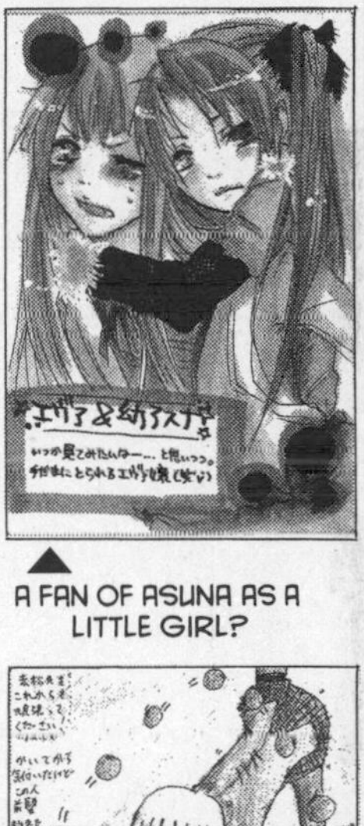

A FAN OF ASUNA AS A LITTLE GIRL?

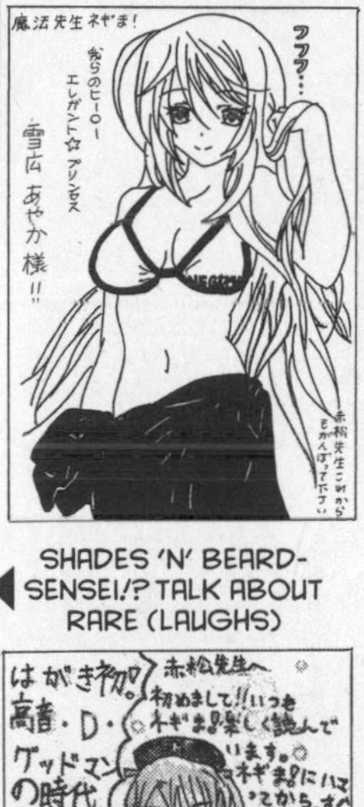

VERY SEXY★

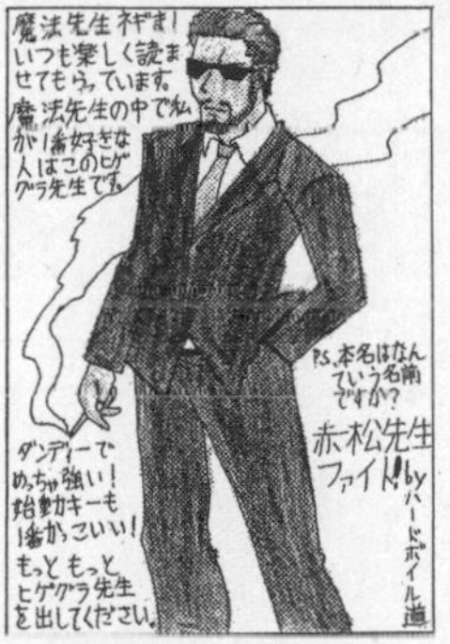

SHADES 'N' BEARD-SENSEI!? TALK ABOUT RARE (LAUGHS)

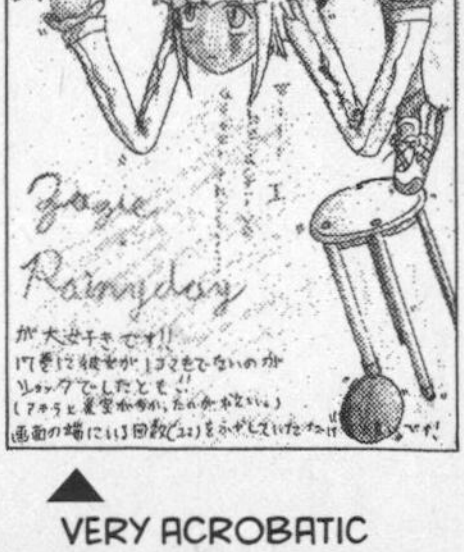

VERY ACROBATIC

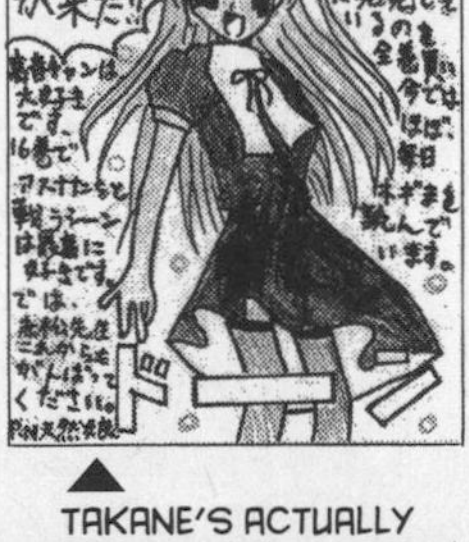

TAKANE'S ACTUALLY PRETTY RARE AS WELL.★

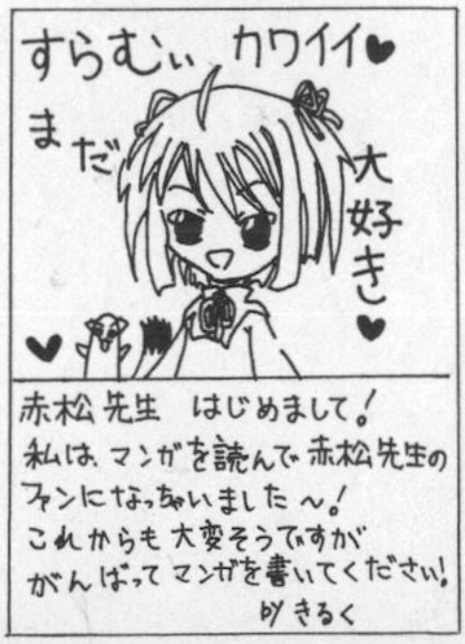
すらむぃ カワイイ♥
まだ
大好き
赤松先生　はじめまして！
私は、マンガを読んで 赤松先生の
ファンになっちゃいました～！
これからも大変そうですが
がんばって マンガを書いてください！
by きるく

SURAMUI!? ANOTHER RARE ONE ♪

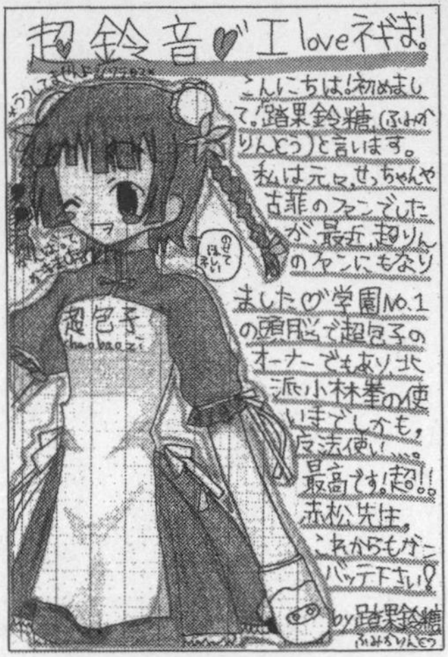
超鈴音♡工 love ネギま!
こんにちは!初めまして!踏果鈴糖(ふみかりんとう)と言います。私は元々、せっちゃんや古菲のファンでしたが、最近、超りんのファンにもなりました♡学園No.1の頭脳で超包子のオーナーでもあり、北派小林拳の使い手でしかも、魔法使い!…最高です!超!!赤松先生、これからもガンバッテ下さい!
超包子
by 踏果鈴糖
ふみかりんとう

CHAO HAS A LOT OF FANS NOW. ★

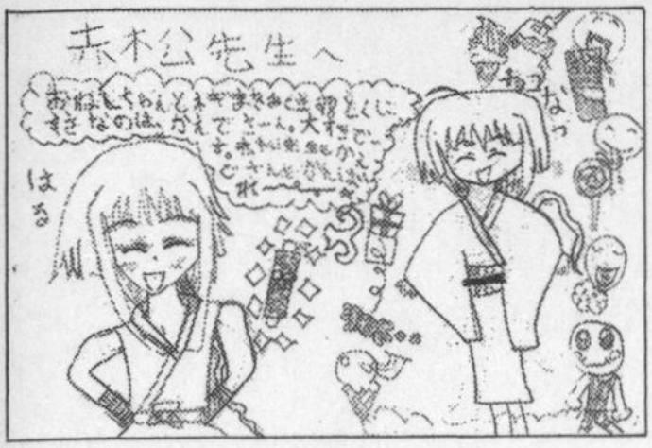

A VERY CUTE KAEDE

LOOKS LIKE A VERY POWERFUL PARTY ★

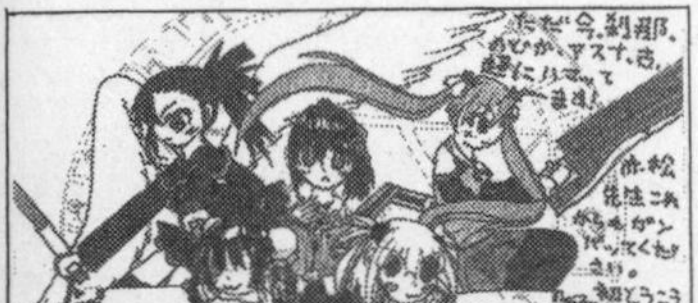
ネギま!

COSPLAY IS A LOT OF FUN, ISN'T IT?

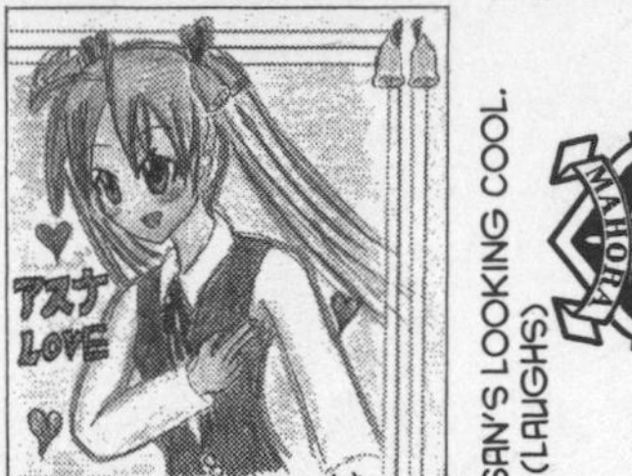
アスナ LOVE
あけましておめでとうございます。
赤松先生、これからも頑張ってくださいね。毎日本誌と一緒に過ごしています♡
アスナのコスプレ期待大です!

WHAT A REALLY NICE SMILE ★

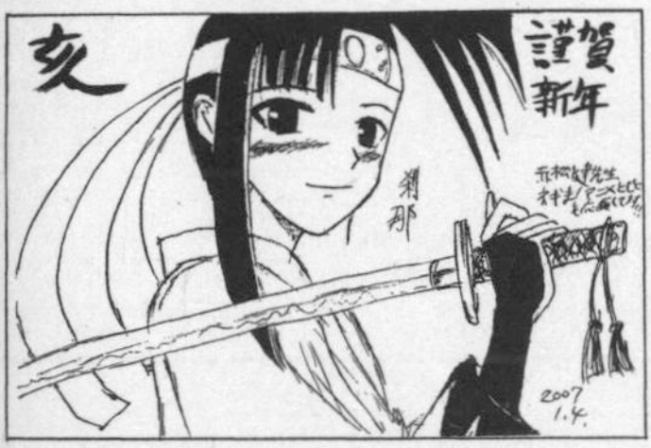
亥
謹賀新年
刹那
2007 1.4.

AKAMATSU-SAN'S LOOKING COOL. (LAUGHS)

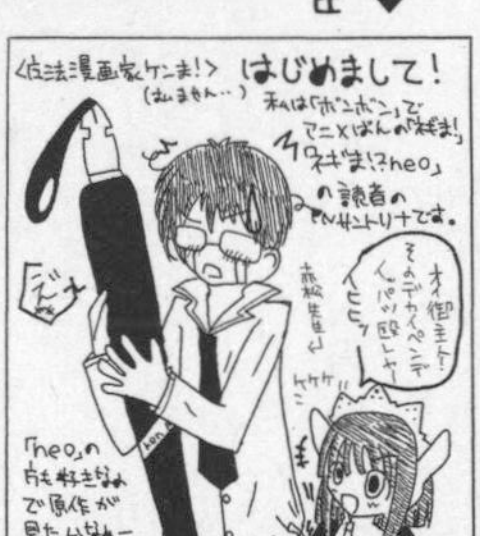
はじめまして!
by サントリナ

ASUNA'S ARMOR WAS FANTASTIC, WASN'T IT? (LAUGHS)

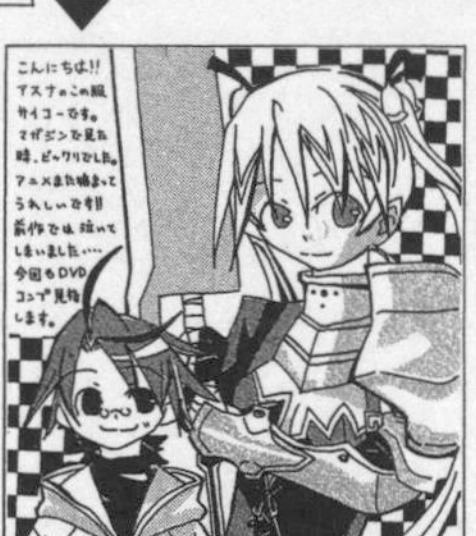
こんにちは!!

NICE DETAILS ON THE CLOTHING!

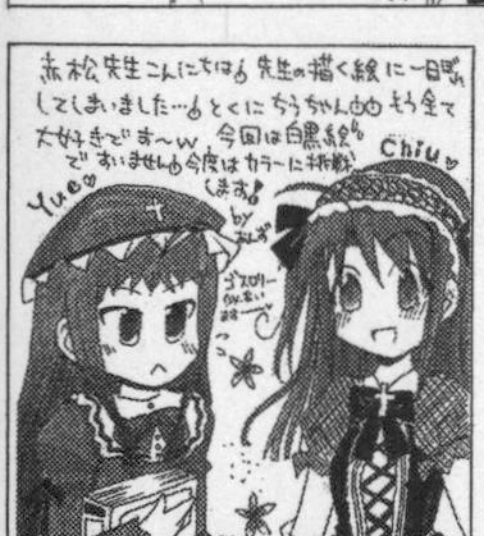
Chiu
Yue

NEGI MA!

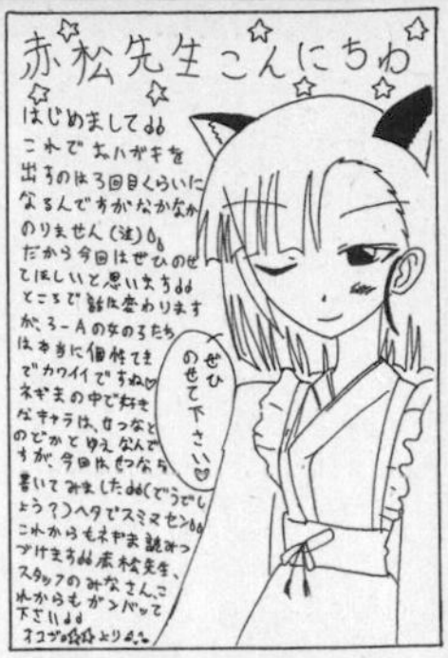
赤松先生こんにちわ
はじめまして
ぜひのせて下さい

▶ SETSUNA LOOKS VERY PLEASED.

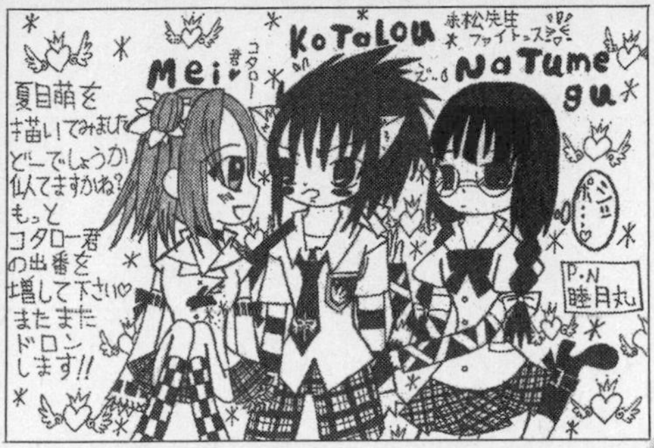
赤松先生ファイトッス
KoTaLou
Mei
NaTume gu
夏目萌を描いてみました
どーでしょうか
似てますかね?
もっとコタロー君の出番を増して下さい♡
またまたドロンします!!
P.N 睦月丸

▲ WE LIKE KOTARŌ'S PLAID PANTS.♪

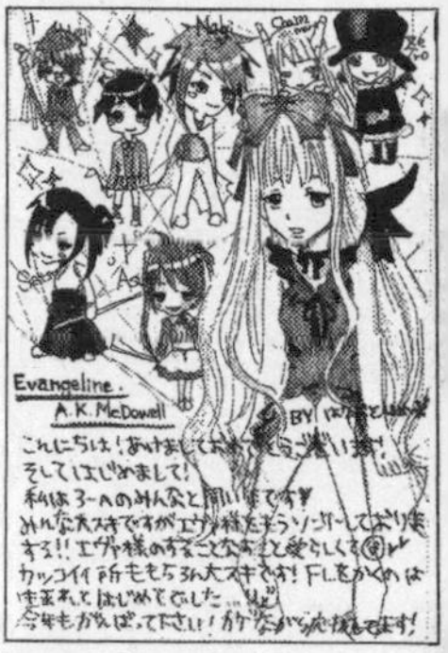
Evangeline.
A.K.McDowell

▲ EVA'S LOOKING BORED.★

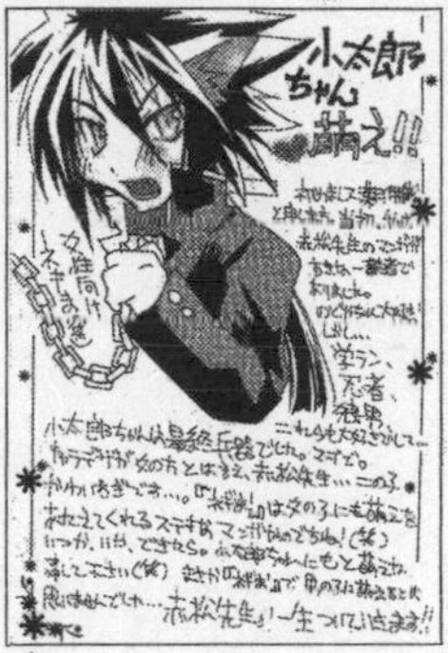
小太郎ちゃん萌え!!

▲ KEEP LOVING KOTARŌ!

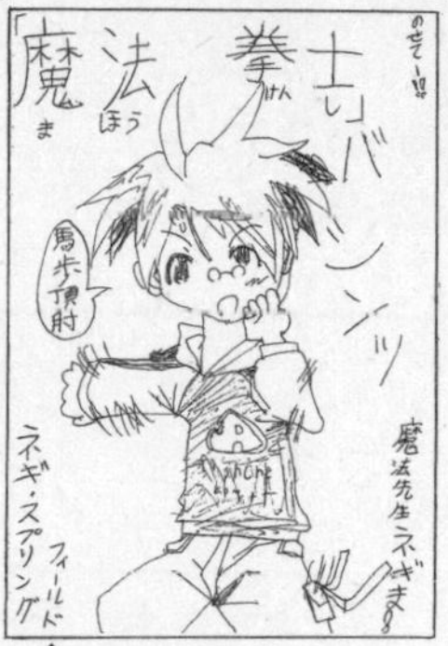
のせて～!!
「魔法拳士」バンッ
馬歩頂肘
魔法先生ネギま!
ネギ・スプリングフィールド

▲ NEGI LOOKS VERY DETERMINED.

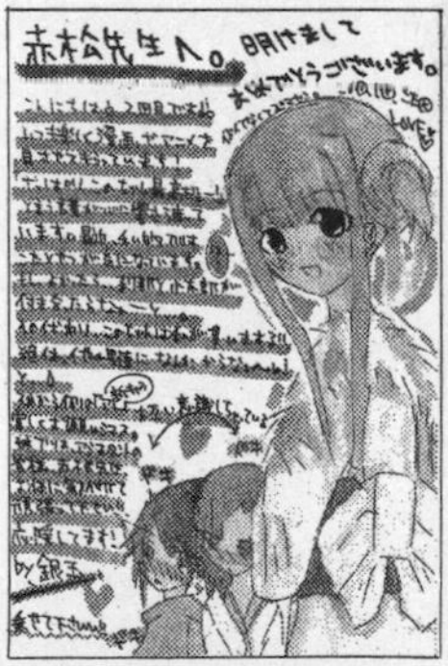
赤松先生へ。明けましておめでとうございます。
by 銀子

▲ KOTARŌ AND SETSUNA, HUH? (LAUGHS)

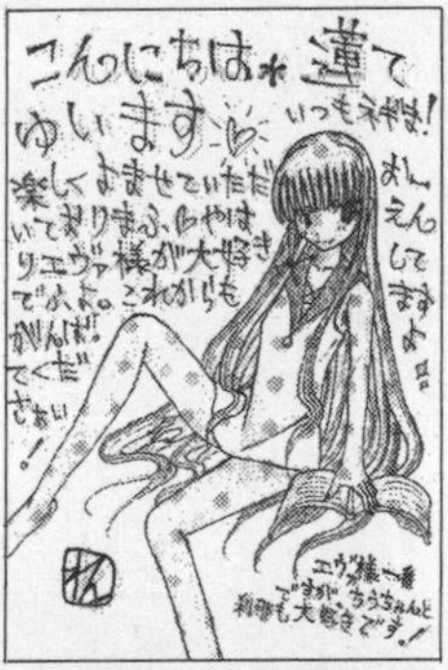
こんにちは* 蓮でゆいます
いつもネギま!
おうえんしてますよ!

▲ EVA'S STRIKING A NICE POSE.★

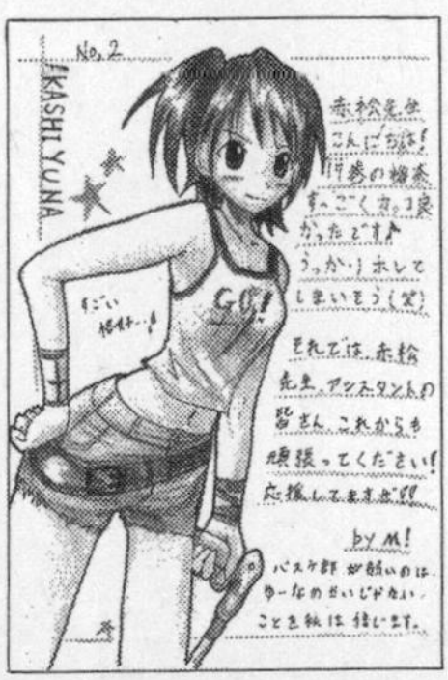
No.2
AKASHI YUNA
赤松先生こんにちは!
GO!
by M!

▲ THOSE HOT PANTS ARE...HOT! (LAUGHS)

3-D BACKGROUNDS EXPLANATION CORNER

IN THIS VOLUME, A NEW STORY LINE INCLUDED SEVERAL LARGE STRUCTURES. LET'S TAKE A LOOK AT THEM!

• KŪ:NEL'S RESIDENCE

SCENE NAME: AL'S CASTLE
POLYGON COUNT: 822,095

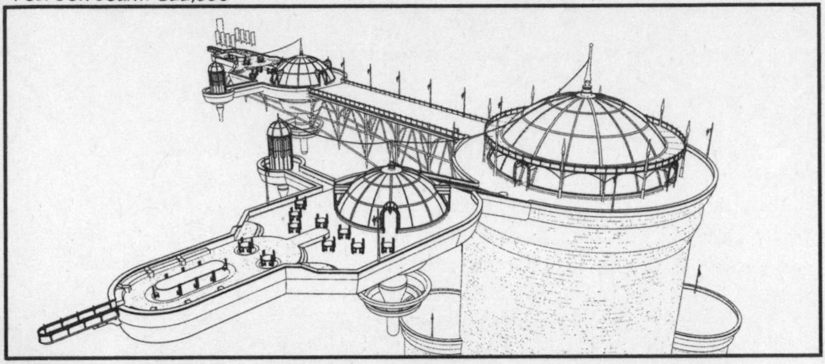

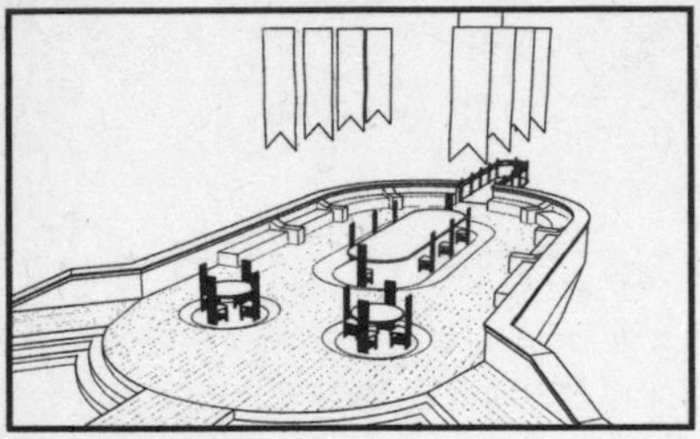

THIS IS KŪ:NEL'S RESIDENCE, HIDDEN DEEP UNDERGROUND BENEATH LIBRARY ISLAND. A LARGE GLASS DOME IS SURROUNDED BY THREE SMALLER ONES. MULTIPLE BRIDGES AND SUPPORTS ADD BEAUTY AND A WELCOMING ATMOSPHERE TO THIS STRUCTURE. HOWEVER, IT'S SURROUNDED BY WATERFALLS ON THREE SIDES AND A TALL CASTLE WALL, MAKING THIS PLACE VERY HARD FOR ANYONE TO INFILTRATE.

DURING THE PLANNING STAGE, THIS WAS SUPPOSED TO HAVE AN ART NOUVEAU FEEL TO IT, BUT I'M NOT SURE IT CAME THROUGH. (^_^;)

• THE CONFESSIONAL

SCENE NAME: CONFESSIONAL
POLYGON COUNT: 85,440

DEPENDING ON THE CHURCH, A CONFESSIONAL COMES IN VARIOUS FORMS AND STYLES. IT'S OFTEN A SMALL BOOTH PLACED IN THE CHURCH. FOR OUR STORY, IT'S ACTUALLY A STRUCTURE BUILT INTO THE CHURCH.

AS FOR THE CHURCH, WE TOOK THE COSPLAY STAGE FROM VOLUME 11 AND ALTERED IT TO FIT OUR NEEDS. WE SEEM TO DO A LOT OF RECYCLING. (LAUGHS)

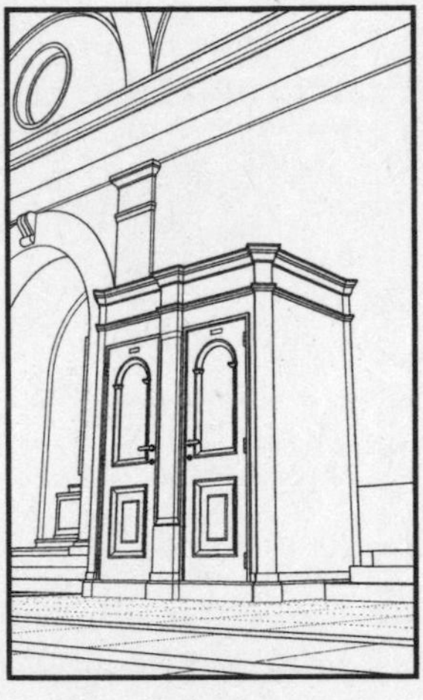

- BONUS -

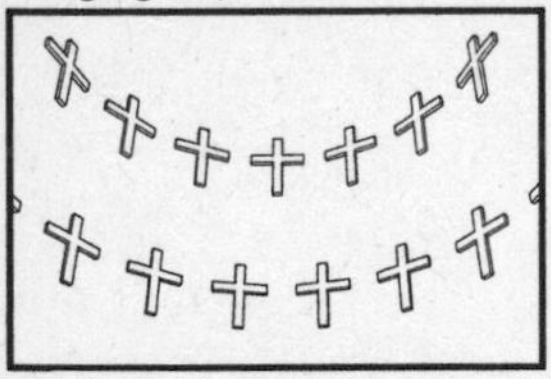

• SISTER SHAKTI'S CROSSES

WE CREATED THEM IN 3-D AS THEY NEEDED TO FLOAT AROUND HER IN A CIRCULAR PATTERN.

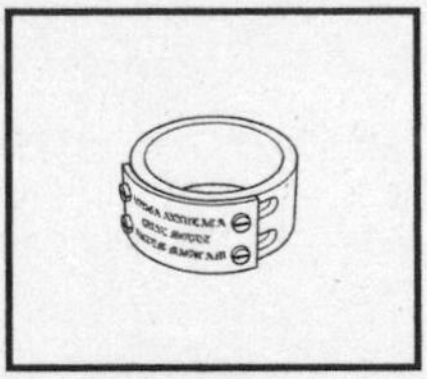

• NEGI'S RING

IT'S A FREQUENTLY APPEARING ITEM, SO WE CREATED IT AS A 3-D OBJECT FOR THIS VOLUME.

LEXICON NEGIMARIUM

[*Negima!* 163rd Period Lexicon Negimarium]

■ Mundus Magicus

• *Mundus Magicus* means "Magical World" in Latin. Mages live in this other world, which Chao, Takane, and Mei mentioned earlier (see *Negima!* vols. 12 & 14). It is a real, physical space, as compared to the purely conceptual space of the "Magianitas," which refers to the group or society of mages. In other societies based on the culture of the Middle Ages, the idea of "other worlds" was not a conceptualization of a physically real place but a way of describing things that could not be described by mythology. For example, in Greek mythology, the guardian of Hades's manor in the underworld was Cerberus. Cerberus would devour anyone who tried to leave (*Theogony* 767–773). The tale was not really about a man-eating monster who lived approximately 3,657,830,400 kilometers* underground but, rather, a way of explaining that no one can return to life after death.

This "other world" that Chao describes is a physical place, which a living person can enter and exit, unlike the example above. These types of worlds exist mainly in Celtic cultures and legends of the Chinese gods. *Mundus Magicus* is capitalized because it's the name of a particular place rather than a generic phrase used to refer to any magical world.

Tartarus is said to exist in a place that a brazen anvil would reach only after falling for ten days (ibid. 724–725). If distance is rate of change of velocity, as the second derivative of position, it is thus a vector quantity with dimension length/time^2, and then Tartarus is 9.8 x (60 x 60 x 24 x 10)^2/2. As a comparison, the radius of Earth at the equator is 6,378 kilometers.

[*Negima!* 164th Period Lexicon Negimarium]

■ Kuwabara Kuwabara

• This is an ancient Japanese spell to ward off lightning. For example, in the Kabuki Kyōgen "Narukami Fudo Kitayama-Zakura," during the third curtain, second act, there is a line that says, "The rain ... falls. The lightning ... sounds. Kuwabara Kuwabara." This comes from Japanese folklore, which is rich in spells to ward off disaster. However, the reason Misora chants this while looking at Tatsumiya and Evangeline is unknown and only enhances her image as "the mysterious sister."

---

*2,272,870,436 miles!

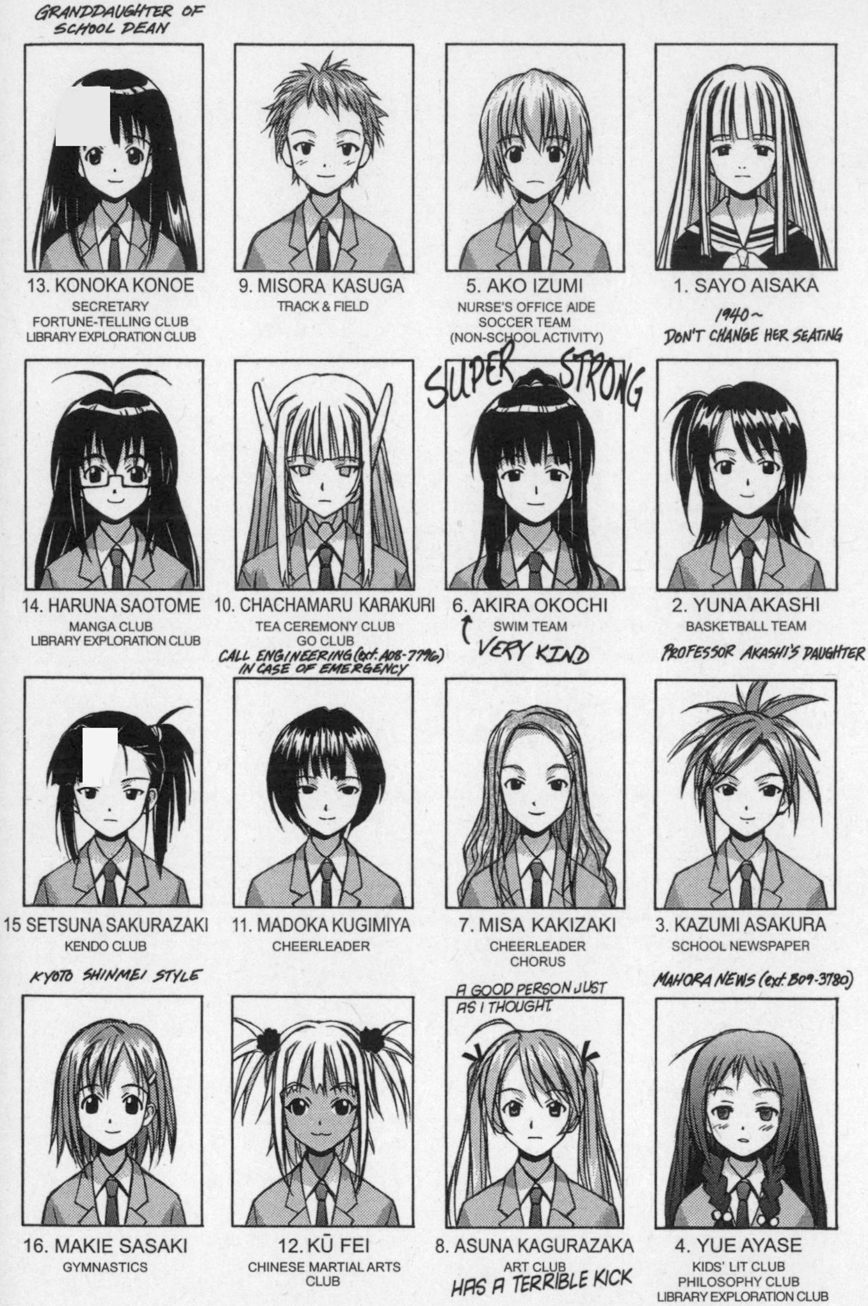

1. SAYO AISAKA
1940~
DON'T CHANGE HER SEATING
5. AKO IZUMI
NURSE'S OFFICE AIDE
SOCCER TEAM
(NON-SCHOOL ACTIVITY)
9. MISORA KASUGA
TRACK & FIELD
GRANDDAUGHTER OF SCHOOL DEAN
13. KONOKA KONOE
SECRETARY
FORTUNE-TELLING CLUB
LIBRARY EXPLORATION CLUB
2. YUNA AKASHI
BASKETBALL TEAM
PROFESSOR AKASHI'S DAUGHTER
SUPER STRONG
6. AKIRA OKOCHI
SWIM TEAM
VERY KIND
10. CHACHAMARU KARAKURI
TEA CEREMONY CLUB
GO CLUB
CALL ENGINEERING (ext. A08-7796) IN CASE OF EMERGENCY
14. HARUNA SAOTOME
MANGA CLUB
LIBRARY EXPLORATION CLUB
3. KAZUMI ASAKURA
SCHOOL NEWSPAPER
MAHORA NEWS (ext. B09-3780)
7. MISA KAKIZAKI
CHEERLEADER
CHORUS
11. MADOKA KUGIMIYA
CHEERLEADER
15 SETSUNA SAKURAZAKI
KENDO CLUB
KYOTO SHINMEI STYLE
4. YUE AYASE
KIDS' LIT CLUB
PHILOSOPHY CLUB
LIBRARY EXPLORATION CLUB
A GOOD PERSON JUST AS I THOUGHT.
8. ASUNA KAGURAZAKA
ART CLUB
HAS A TERRIBLE KICK
12. KŪ FEI
CHINESE MARTIAL ARTS CLUB
16. MAKIE SASAKI
GYMNASTICS

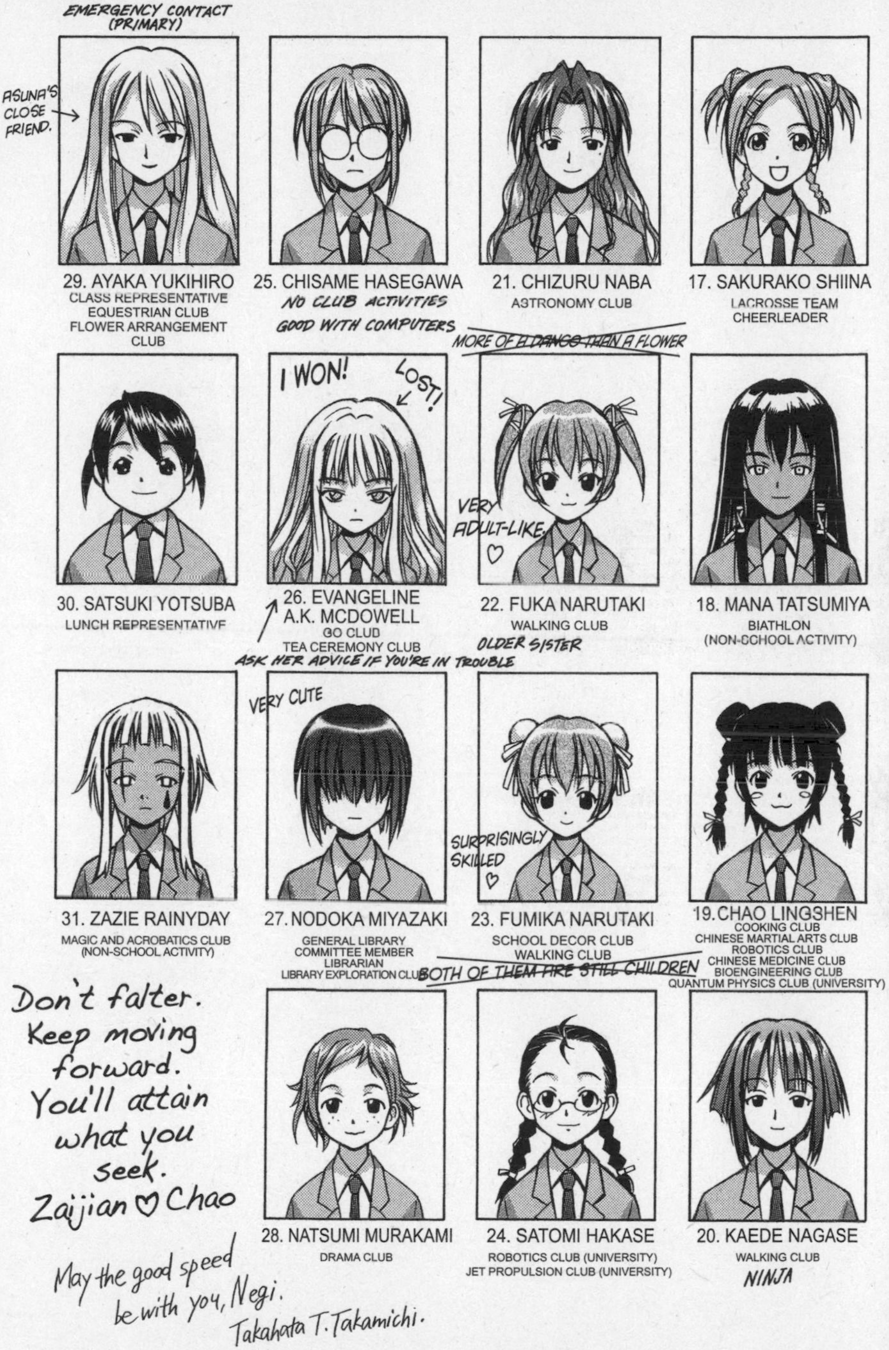

17. SAKURAKO SHIINA
LACROSSE TEAM
CHEERLEADER
21. CHIZURU NABA
ASTRONOMY CLUB
MORE OF A DANGO THAN A FLOWER
25. CHISAME HASEGAWA
NO CLUB ACTIVITIES
GOOD WITH COMPUTERS
EMERGENCY CONTACT (PRIMARY)
ASUNA'S CLOSE FRIEND.
29. AYAKA YUKIHIRO
CLASS REPRESENTATIVE
EQUESTRIAN CLUB
FLOWER ARRANGEMENT CLUB
18. MANA TATSUMIYA
BIATHLON
(NON-SCHOOL ACTIVITY)
VERY ADULT-LIKE.
22. FUKA NARUTAKI
WALKING CLUB
OLDER SISTER
LOST!
I WON!
26. EVANGELINE A.K. MCDOWELL
GO CLUB
TEA CEREMONY CLUB
ASK HER ADVICE IF YOU'RE IN TROUBLE
30. SATSUKI YOTSUBA
LUNCH REPRESENTATIVE
19. CHAO LINGSHEN
COOKING CLUB
CHINESE MARTIAL ARTS CLUB
ROBOTICS CLUB
CHINESE MEDICINE CLUB
BIOENGINEERING CLUB
QUANTUM PHYSICS CLUB (UNIVERSITY)
SURPRISINGLY SKILLED
23. FUMIKA NARUTAKI
SCHOOL DECOR CLUB
WALKING CLUB
BOTH OF THEM ARE STILL CHILDREN
VERY CUTE
27. NODOKA MIYAZAKI
GENERAL LIBRARY COMMITTEE MEMBER
LIBRARIAN
LIBRARY EXPLORATION CLUB
31. ZAZIE RAINYDAY
MAGIC AND ACROBATICS CLUB
(NON-SCHOOL ACTIVITY)
20. KAEDE NAGASE
WALKING CLUB
NINJA
24. SATOMI HAKASE
ROBOTICS CLUB (UNIVERSITY)
JET PROPULSION CLUB (UNIVERSITY)
28. NATSUMI MURAKAMI
DRAMA CLUB
Don't falter. Keep moving forward. You'll attain what you seek.
Zaijian ♡ Chao
May the good speed be with you, Negi.
Takahata T. Takamichi.

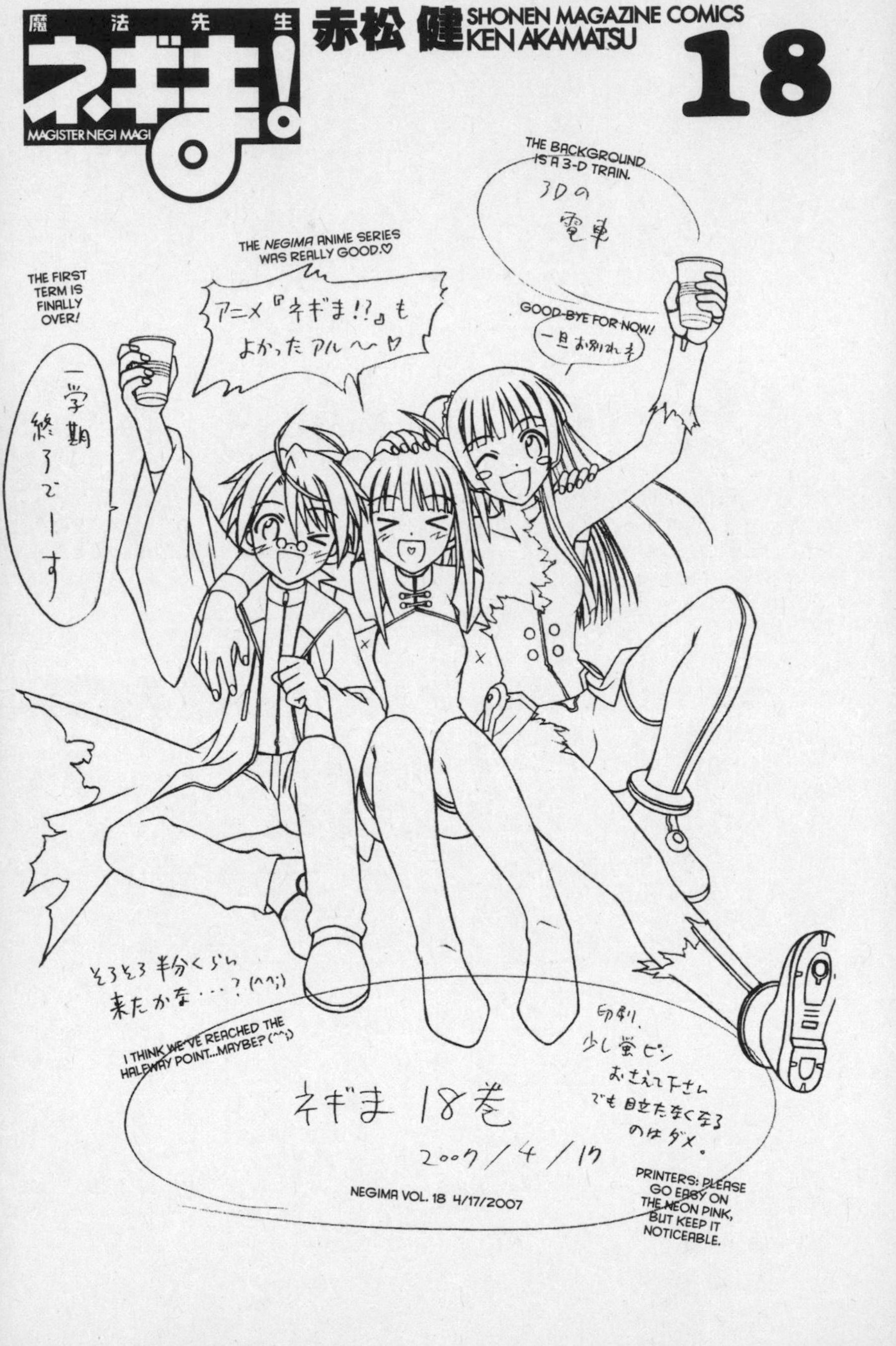

魔法先生
ネギま!
MAGISTER NEGI MAGI
赤松 健
SHONEN MAGAZINE COMICS
KEN AKAMATSU
18
THE BACKGROUND IS A 3-D TRAIN.
3Dの電車
THE NEGIMA ANIME SERIES WAS REALLY GOOD.♡
アニメ『ネギま!?』もよかったアル〜♡
THE FIRST TERM IS FINALLY OVER!
一学期終了でーす
GOOD-BYE FOR NOW!
一旦お別れネ
そろそろ半分くらい来たかな…?(^^;)
I THINK WE'VE REACHED THE HALFWAY POINT...MAYBE? (^^;)
ネギま 18巻
2007/4/17
NEGIMA VOL. 18 4/17/2007
印刷、少し蛍ピンおさえて下さい でも目立たなく至るのはダメ。
PRINTERS: PLEASE GO EASY ON THE NEON PINK, BUT KEEP IT NOTICEABLE.

キャラ解説

**CHARACTER
PROFILE**

㉔ 葉加瀬 聡美

㉔ SATOMI HAKASE

典型的な マッド サイエンティスト
I ORIGINALLY CREATED HAKASE TO BE A STEREOTYPICAL

キャラとして デザインされた ハカセですが、
EXAMPLE OF A MAD SCIENTIST. HOWEVER, SHE'S

実は おしゃれすると結構 かわいいですよね。
DARN CUTE ONCE SHE'S DRESSED IN TRENDY THREADS.

大学の工学部の男子学生の中にも、
I'M SURE THERE ARE GUYS IN THE UNIVERSITY ENGINEERING

狙ってるやつ, 意外と多いんじゃないかなぁ?(笑)
CLUB THINKING ABOUT GOING FOR HER...MAYBE? (LAUGHS)

(そんな話も おもしろいかも。)
(PERHAPS A STORY ABOUT THAT MIGHT BE FUN.)

CVは、見た目 そのまんまの 門脇舞以ちゃん。
HER VOICE ACTOR IS MAI KADOWAKI. I THINK SHE LOOKS JUST LIKE HAKASE.

初めて見たときから、も~彼女以外の人は
SINCE THE FIRST TIME I SAW HER, I COULDN'T THINK OF ANYONE ELSE TO

考えられない って感じです。(笑) 絵が上手なの。
VOICE THE ROLE. (LAUGHS) SHE'S ALSO A GOOD ILLUSTRATOR.
ライブとか 行ってみたい…
I'D LOVE TO GO SEE HER LIVE CONCERT!

次の 19巻から、「夏休み編」です。
AS OF VOLUME 19, WE'LL BE GOING INTO THE SUMMER

冒頭から とばしていきますので
VACATION CHAPTER. WE'RE GOING TO HIT THE GROUND

絶対 読んで下さいね~!!
RUNNING, SO MAKE SURE YOU READ IT!!

赤松
AKAMATSU

Translation Notes

Japanese is a tricky language for most westerners, and translation is often more an art than a science. For your edification and reading pleasure, here are notes on some of the places where we could have gone in a different direction, or where a Japanese cultural reference is used.

Volume 16

Bad ending, page 5

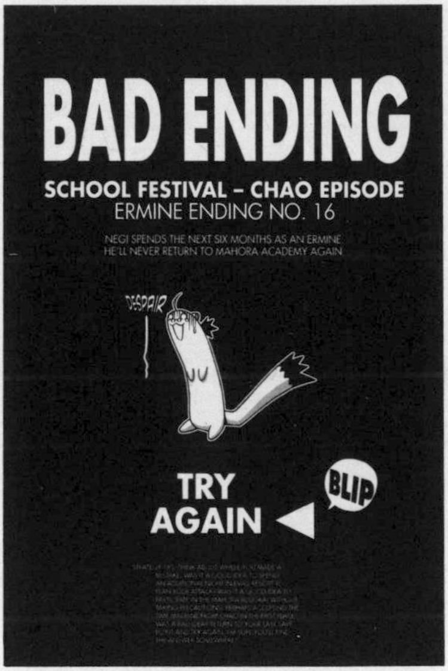
BAD ENDING
SCHOOL FESTIVAL – CHAO EPISODE
ERMINE ENDING NO. 16
NEGI SPENDS THE NEXT SIX MONTHS AS AN ERMINE
HE'LL NEVER RETURN TO MAHORA ACADEMY AGAIN
DESPAIR
TRY AGAIN
BLIP

One may come across this in some simulation video games when you make the wrong choices. Dating and mystery games typically have more than one outcome. A bad ending occurs when the main character didn't improve his parameters enough in a game (for example, getting to know a girl well enough in a dating game or missing important clues in a mystery game).

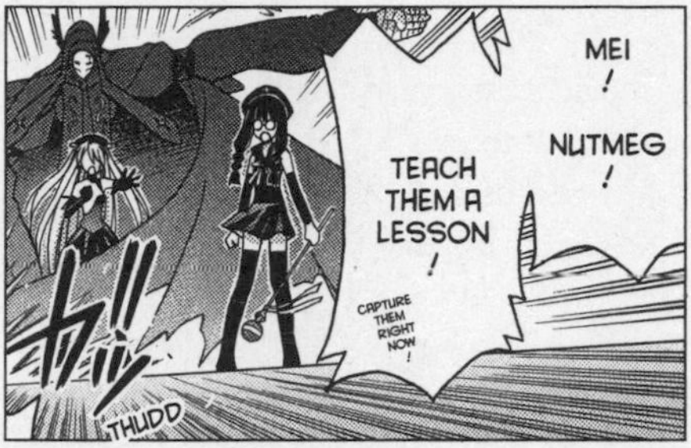
MEI!
NUTMEG!
TEACH THEM A LESSON!
CAPTURE THEM RIGHT NOW!
THUDD

Nutmeg, page 25

In the original Japanese text, Takane calls Megumi Natsume "Natsu Megu," a nickname that is not only a cute abbreviation of her full name but roughly translates to "nutmeg."

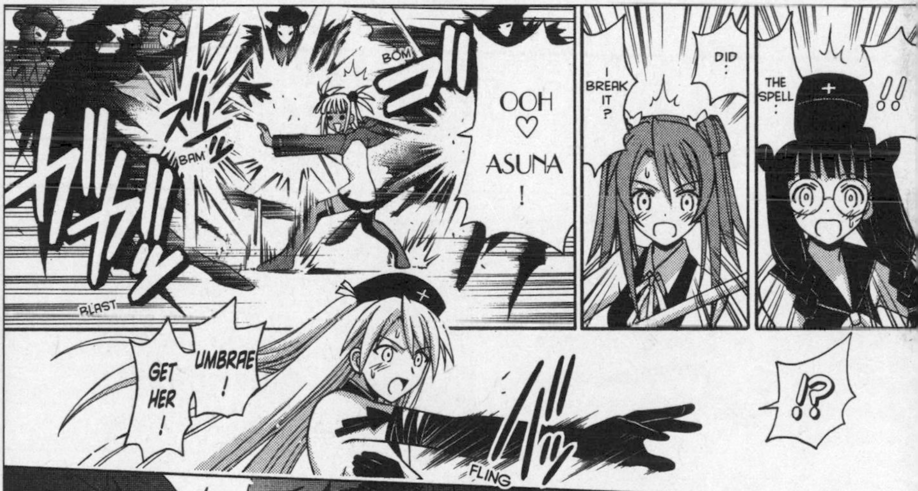
THE SPELL...
!!
DID...
I BREAK IT?
OOH ♡ ASUNA!
BOM
BAM
BLAST
!?
UMBRAE!
GET HER!
FLING
LEAP

Umbrae, page 27

Umbrae is Latin for "shadows."

Mei Sakura artifact, page 28

The Japanese name for this artifact is *Osoji Daisuki*, which means something like "I love to clean" or "I love to sweep."

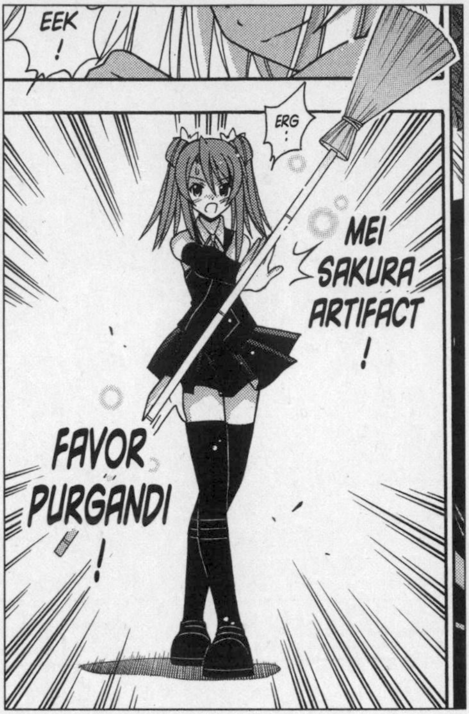
EEK!
ERG...
MEI SAKURA ARTIFACT!
FAVOR PURGANDI!

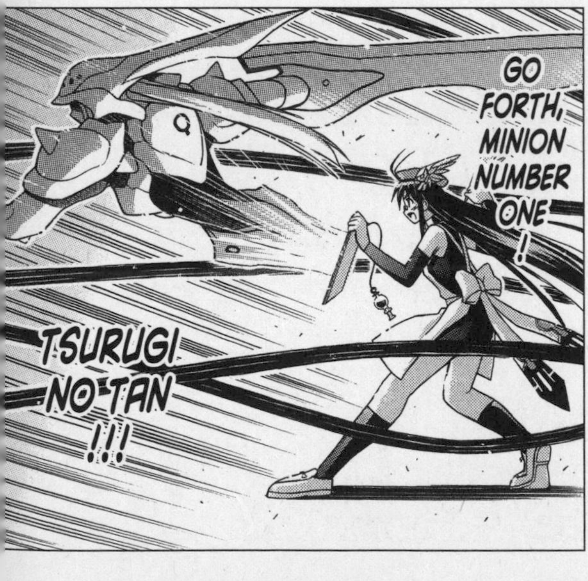
GO FORTH, MINION NUMBER ONE!
TSURUGI NO TAN!!!

Tsurugi no Tan, page 67

The name of this attack translates to "Goddess of the Sword" in English.

Vente Nos, page 112

Negi's spell literally means "Wind, protect us

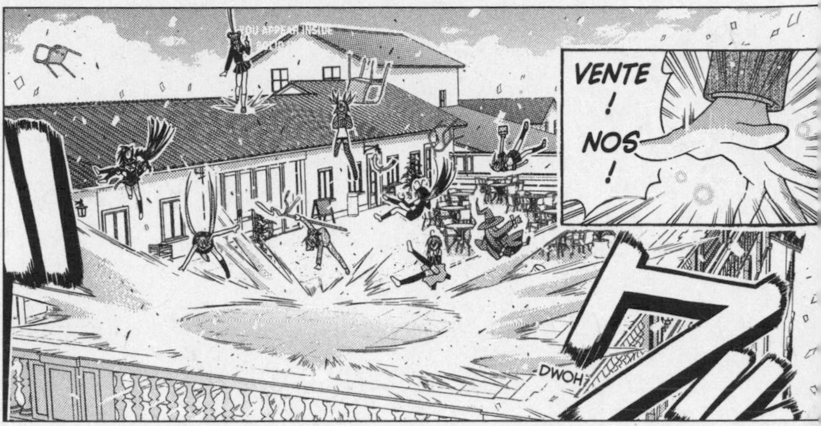
VENTE ! NOS !
DWOH

Appearing inside a rock, page 113

The original Japanese phrase was made famous by the Japanese version of the classic 1980s computer game series Wizardry, by Andrew C. Greenberg and Robert Woodhead (who later went on to found one of the first anime companies in the U.S., AnimEigo). It was a basic adventure game in which a group traveled through a multilevel dungeon. Along the way, the player would learn the Malor spell, which allowed the party to travel to any location simply by punching in its coordinates. However, if you put in the wrong coordinates, you could end up materializing inside a rock, instantly killing your entire party.

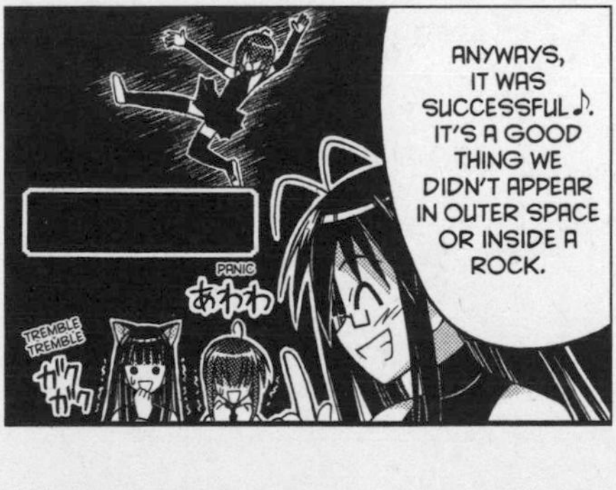
ANYWAYS, IT WAS SUCCESSFUL♪. IT'S A GOOD THING WE DIDN'T APPEAR IN OUTER SPACE OR INSIDE A ROCK.
PANIC
あわわ
TREMBLE TREMBLE
ガクガク

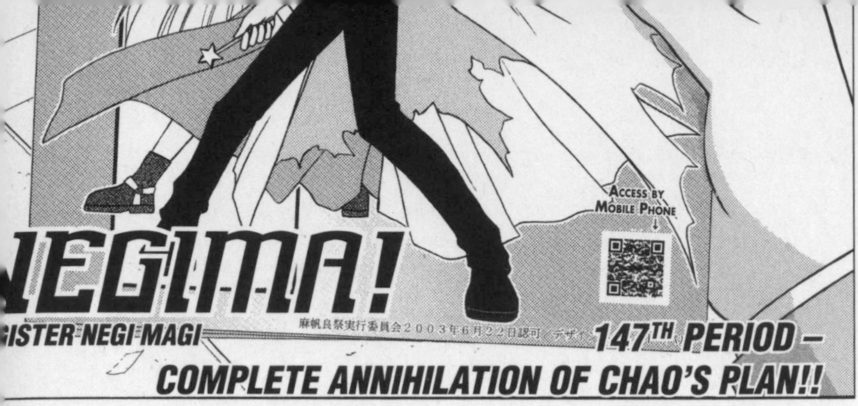
ACCESS BY
MOBILE PHONE
IEGIMA!
ISTER NEGI MAGI
麻帆良祭実行委員会２００３年６月２２日認可 デザイ
147TH PERIOD – COMPLETE ANNIHILATION OF CHAO'S PLAN!!

QR codes, page 128

The squares you see on the corners of Japanese ads are actually a matrix code (two-dimensional bar codes) that were created by the Denso Wave Corporation of Japan in 1994. QR stands for Quick Response, which was developed so that information could be decoded quickly. As cell phones gained popularity and technological advances took place, camera phones in Japan became equipped with a QR decoder. By pointing the camera at the QR code, one can go directly to a URL. These days, many Japanese business cards incorporate QR code technology so that information can quickly be entered into a PDA or cell phone.

Kyo●hei and Gun●am, pages 163 and 164

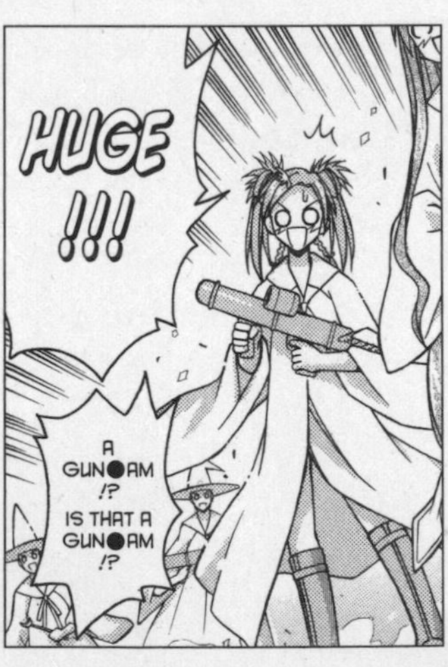
HUGE !!!
A GUN●AM !?
IS THAT A GUN●AM !?

The first word with the blacked-out character in the middle is probably Kyoshinhei, or God-Soldier, from Hayao Miyazaki's *Nausicäa of the Valley of the Wind*. On the next page, Sakurako name-checks the popular Gundam series of giant-robot anime and manga sagas.

Volume 17

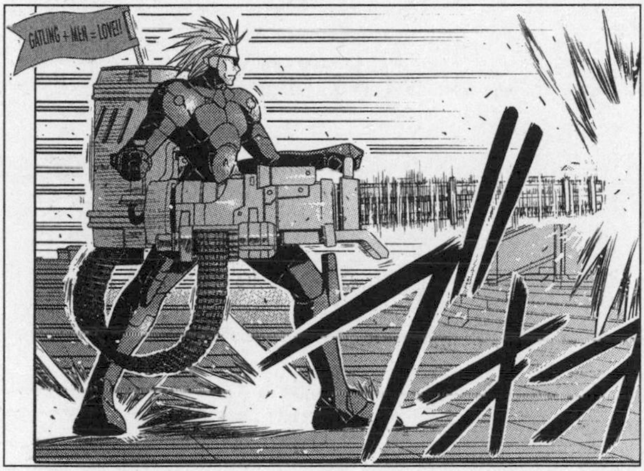
GATLING + MEN = LOVE!

Gatling + Men = Love!, page 194

In the original Japanese, the flag literally reads "Gatling Is the Romance of Men." The term *Otoko no Roman* (Men's Romance) is common in Japanese but often misunderstood in English. The dictionary defines "romance" in several ways: first as "a medieval tale based on legend, chivalric love, and adventure," and secondly as a love story or a love affair. In English, the second definition has become the most common. But in Japan, the word *roman* refers to stories of adventure and chivalry. So Japanese has a second word, *romansu*, that means "love story."

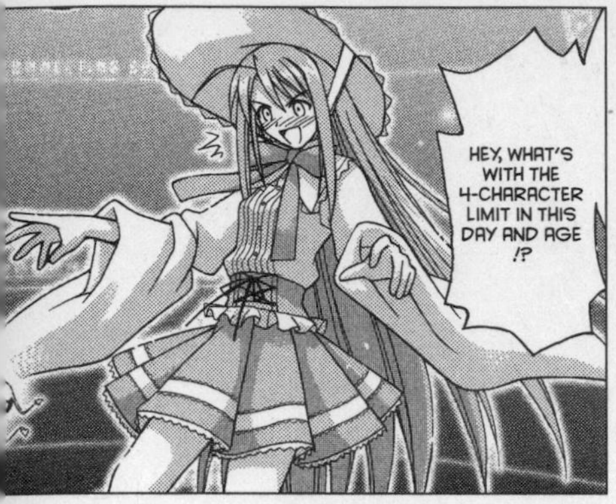
HEY, WHAT'S WITH THE 4-CHARACTER LIMIT IN THIS DAY AND AGE !?

Four-character limit, page 253

Chisame is upset that she cannot input a name that's more than four characters. In Japanese, each character in the alphabet stands for an entire syllable, so that, in the English transliterations, each sprite's name will be more than four letters.

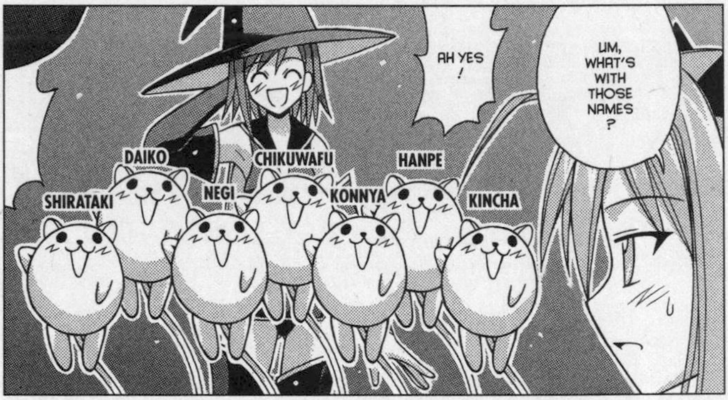
UM, WHAT'S WITH THOSE NAMES ?
AH YES !
HANPE
CHIKUWAFU
DAIKO
KINCHA
KONNYA
NEGI
SHIRATAKI

The sprites' names, page 254

The seven commanders of Chisame's *Spiritus Electronicus* were named by Makie as Kincha, Hanpe, Konnya, Chikuwafu, Negi, Daiko, and Shirataki. All of these are food names, although some have been cut short or the pronounciation altered a bit. Kincha is short for *kinchaku*, a rice cake wrapped in a deep-fried tofu pouch. Hanpe is short for *hanpen*, which is a puffy white fish cake made with yam. Konnya is short for *konnyaku*, which are translucent blocks made from starch. *Chikuwafu* are wheat-gluten cakes made in tube form. *Negi* is, of course, green onion. Daiko is short for *daikon*, a Japanese radish. *Shirataki* is as it sounds and are translucent noodles made from *konnyaku*. All of these foods are the ingredients in a well-known Japanese stew called *oden*.

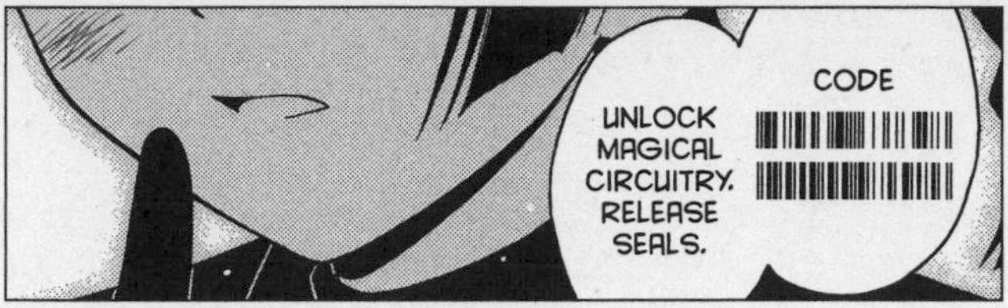
CODE
UNLOCK MAGICAL CIRCUITRY. RELEASE SEALS.

Secret of the Bar Code, page 339

The bar code 9784063637328 1929979004002 is actually the code used on the back of the Japanese edition (standard) of the *Negima!* volume 16 tankobon. The 9979 in the second set of numbers designate it as a comic.

Fun..., page 368

The blocked-out word is "funnels," which is the name of a satellite weapon that certain mobile suits use in the famous *Gundam* giant-robot saga. It's very common in manga for references to materials under copyright to be disguised in this manner.

Volume 18

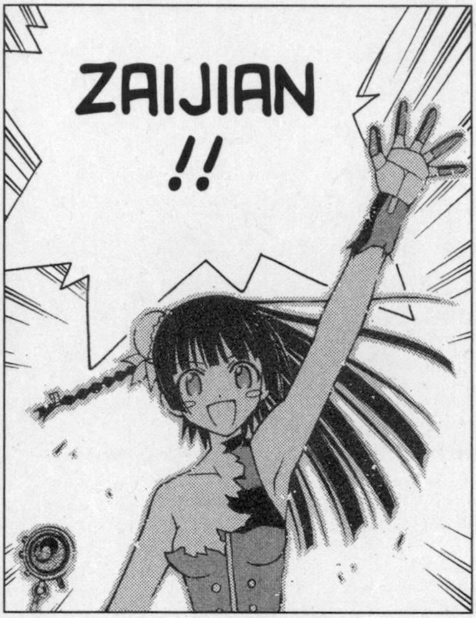
ZAIJIAN !!

Zaijian, page 410

This word means farewell in Chinese. It uses kanji characters for "again" and "see." The actual meaning is closer to "until we meet again" than "good-bye."

Evangeline's middle name, page 419

One of Eva's middle names is Athanasia. The dictionary defines this word as "the quality of being deathless; immortality." Did Eva give herself this name after she became a vampire, or was it given to her at birth?

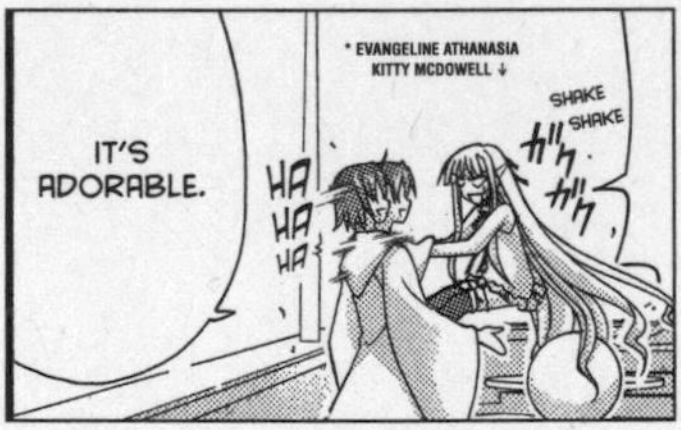
SHAKE SHAKE
* EVANGELINE ATHANASIA KITTY MCDOWELL ↓
HA HA HA
IT'S ADORABLE.

About the Creator

Negima! is only Ken Akamatsu's third manga, although he started working in the field in 1994 with *AI Ga Tomaranai* (released in the United States with the title *A.I. Love You*). Like all of Akamatsu's work to date, it was published in Kodansha's *Shonen Magazine*. *AI Ga Tomaranai* ran for five years before concluding in 1999. In 1998, however, Akamatsu began the work that would make him one of the most popular manga artists in Japan: *Love Hina*. *Love Hina* ran for four years, and before its conclusion in 2002, it would cause Akamatsu to be granted the prestigious Manga of the Year award from Kodansha, as well as going on to become one of the best-selling manga in the United States.

ANIMAL LAND

BY MAKOTO RAIKU

In a world of animals, where the strong eat the weak, Monoko the tanuki stumbles across a strange creature the likes of which has never been seen before–a human baby! While the newborn has no claws or teeth to protect itself, it does have the special ability to speak to and understand all different animals. Can the gift of speech between species change the balance of power in a land where the weak must always fear the strong?

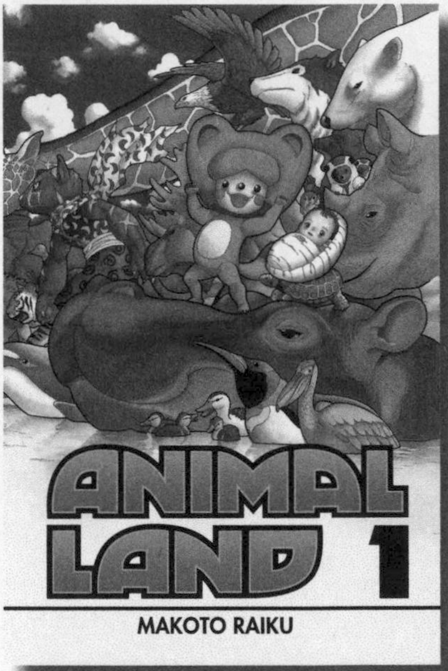
ANIMAL LAND 1
MAKOTO RAIKU

Ages 13+

VISIT KODANSHACOMICS.COM TO:

- View release date calendars for upcoming volumes
- Find out the latest about upcoming Kodansha Comics series